Canadian
HUMAN RESOURCE
MANAGEMENT
A Strategic Approach
Sixth Edition

Hermann Schwind

Professor Emeritus
Saint Mary's University

Hari Das

Saint Mary's University

Terry Wagar

Saint Mary's University

McGraw-Hill
Ryerson

Toronto   Montréal   Boston   Burr Ridge, IL   Dubuque, IA   Madison, WI
New York   San Francisco   St. Louis   Bangkok   Bogotá   Caracas
Kuala Lumpur   Lisbon   London   Madrid   Mexico City   Milan
New Delhi   Santiago   Seoul   Singapore   Sydney   Taipei

McGraw-Hill
Ryerson Limited

A Subsidiary of The McGraw·Hill Companies

CANADIAN HUMAN RESOURCE MANAGEMENT
A Strategic Approach
Sixth Edition
Schwind/Das/Wagar

ISBN: 0-07-088735-7

1 2 3 4 5 6 7 8 9 10 TCP 0 9 8 7 6 5 4 3 2

Printed and bound in Canada.

Care has been taken to trace ownership of copyright material contained in this text; however, the publisher will welcome any information that enables them to rectify any reference or credit for subsequent editions.

This text has been approved by the Human Resources Professionals Association of Ontario and is listed as a recommended text in HRPAO's "Curriculum Summary."

Vice President and Editorial Director: Pat Ferrier
Sponsoring Editor: Lenore Gray-Spence
Developmental Editor: Kim Brewster
Supervising Editor: Alissa Messner
Copyeditor: Dianne Broad
Permissions Editor: Alison Derry
Senior Marketing Manager: Jeff MacLean
Production Coordinator: Paula Lowes-Brown
Compositor: Bookman Typesetting Co. Inc.
Cover Design: Dianna Little
Interior Design: Yvonne Chung
Cover Image: © Terry Vine/Stone
Printer: Transcontinental Printing Group

National Library of Canada Cataloguing in Publication Data

Schwind, Hermann Franz, 1935-
    Canadian human resource management : a strategic approach

6th ed.
First and 2nd ed. published under the title: Canadian personnel management and human resources. 3rd ed.: Canadian human resources management / William B. Werther ... [et al.]. 4th ed.: Canadian human resource management / Hermann F. Schwind ... [et al].
Includes bibliographical references and index.
ISBN 0-07-088735-7

1. Personnel management.   2. Personnel management – Canada.
I. Das, Hari, 1948- .   II. Wagar, Terry H.   III. Title.

HF5549.C35 2001   658.3   C2001-930092-1

ABOUT THE AUTHORS

Dr. Hermann F. Schwind

Dr. Schwind is Professor Emeritus (Human Resource Management) at Saint Mary's University in Halifax. He received his Ph.D. from the University of British Columbia, BBA and MBA degrees from the University of Washington, and mechanical and industrial engineering degrees from German institutions. He has 15 years of industrial experience and has taught as Visiting Professor at the University of Ottawa, in Japan at Sophia University in Tokyo, and at the Institute for International Studies and Training in Fujinomiya, a Japanese management training centre.

Dr. Schwind was a founding member and Vice-President of the British Columbia Society for Training and Development, President of the Halifax and District Personnel Association (1984/86; now the Human Resource Association of Nova Scotia), and President of the Administrative Science Association of Canada (1989). In addition to co-authoring the present text on Canadian human resource management, now in its sixth edition, Dr. Schwind has published and presented over 80 articles and papers and contributed chapters to seven books. He also worked as a human resource consultant for 25 years.

Dr. Hari Das

Dr. Das received his M.Sc. and Ph.D. from the University of British Columbia. Currently, he is a Full Professor in the Department of Management at Saint Mary's University teaching human resource management, performance management, international management, and organizational design and change. Dr. Das has served as Director of the MBA Program and Chair of the Department of Management and has received a teaching excellence award for his work in the EMBA program.

Dr. Das, who began his career as an accountant, has written over 100 articles and papers in areas such as organizational control, performance appraisal, power and influence, training and development, motivation, and research methodology. He wrote *Organization Theory with Canadian Applications*, the first Canadian text in the area of organizational theory, and has contributed chapters to *Canadian Human Resource Management* and *Retail Environments in Developing Countries*. His latest book, *Strategic Organization Design: For Canadian Firms in a Global Economy*, examines the challenge of preparing Canadian firms to face today's global economy.

Dr. Das has served as a consultant to a number of organizations in both the private and public sector in Canada and abroad. In addition to being a member of the Academy of Management and the Administrative Sciences Association of Canada, he has served as academic reviewer for professional meetings, journals, and granting agencies.

Dr. Terry H. Wagar

Terry H. Wagar is a Professor of Human Resource Management and Industrial Relations at Saint Mary's University. He is also a Research Associate at the National Institute of Labour Studies, Flinders University of South Australia. In 1999, he was a Visiting Scholar at the University of Waikato in Hamilton, New Zealand. His degrees include an M.B.A. from the University of Toronto, a Master of Industrial Relations from Queen's University, an LL.B. from the University of Ottawa Law School, and a Ph.D. in labour relations, human resource management and statistics/research methods from Virginia Tech.

Dr. Wagar has also taught at Wilfrid Laurier University and the University of South Australia. He has been the recipient of teaching awards at both the MBA and EMBA level. He was recently named the Atlantic Canada winner of the National Post's Leaders in Management Education award and was also the Association of Atlantic Universities Distinguished Teacher Award recipient for the year 2000.

Dr. Wagar has published several articles in journals in Canada, the United States, Europe, Asia, Australia, and New Zealand, and his research has been presented at conferences in both North America and overseas. In addition, he has conducted training workshops and consulted with a number of organizations and unions. Dr. Wagar has received several awards for his research including the Saint Mary's University President's Award for Research Excellence. He is listed in the *Canadian Who's Who 2001*.

LETTER TO STUDENTS

Canadian Human Resource Management:
A Strategic Approach, Sixth Edition
H. Schwind, H. Das, T. Wagar

Dear Student,

This book was written with you, our customer, in mind. We have tried to make it readable and, wherever possible, we have included practical "how-to-do" steps.

Each chapter includes many common elements, such as learning objectives, terms for review, and case studies. We hope the following guide will help you make maximum use of the textbook so that you will be successful with your studies in human resource management.

At the beginning of each chapter, we offer a quotation from an expert on the subject matter to give you an insight into the concepts or issues discussed. Following the opening quotation, you will find the chapter objectives. These will give you an overview of the chapter content.

Within each chapter, you will find a "Spotlight on HRM" box. These timely articles from journals and magazines in the field illustrate a manager's or consultant's point of view on HRM or offer a sharing of practical HRM experiences relevant to the chapter.

We highlight important terms and concepts with boldface and italic type in the text. All terms appearing in boldface are also defined in the margin and referenced in the Terms for Review section at the end of each chapter and in the Subject Index, highlighted in a secondary colour. If you prefer to use a full list of glossary terms, please go to our online learning centre at www.mcgrawhill.ca/college/schwind6 to download the complete list. Wherever appropriate, we also provide World Wide Web addresses, where you will find additional information to research the topic under discussion.

An end-of-chapter summary offers you an abbreviated version of the chapter content for review. The Terms for Review, where all important terms (and buzzwords) are listed, is an excellent tool for conducting a self-test. Similarly, the Review and Discussion Questions will help you test your understanding of the most critical topics in the chapter.

For a higher level of self-testing, the Critical Thinking Questions help you to discover whether you are able to see the broader relationships and interactions of the concepts discussed.

The Web Research assignments offer you the opportunity to make use of a computer and the Internet to search for additional information. As a self-test, it assesses your ability to conduct on-line research.

The Incidents are short cases that usually do not require extensive analytical work, unlike the more comprehensive case studies later in the chapter, which test your thorough understanding of concepts and their impact on an organization.

Exercises are usually conducted under the supervision of your instructor; however, they can also be used as part of a group exercise, away from the classroom.

The Suggested Readings offer research articles and books that contain more detailed information than is possible to include in a textbook. A Suggested Reading list is included at the end of every chapter.

The References provide you with the sources for the information given in each chapter. They can also be used as a starting point for more detailed research.

If you have any feedback regarding the readability of the textbook or suggestions on how we could improve the next edition, please contact us via the e-mail addresses given below.

Good luck with your studies!

hermann.schwind@stmarys.ca
hari.das@stmarys.ca
terry.wagar@stmarys.ca

TABLE OF CONTENTS

Employee assistance plan [handwritten marginalia]

question why union

PREFACE

> We believe that human resource departments will play a critical role in determining the success of Canadian organizations in the twenty-first century.
>
> — The Authors

Teachers and students ultimately determine the value of any university textbook. *Canadian Human Resource Management: A Strategic Approach* is no exception. Its fifth edition passed the test of the marketplace by earning adoptions and re-adoptions in more than 60 colleges and universities in Canada and becoming the best-selling human resource management text in this country. The book's thrust on presenting key concepts, issues, and practices of this exciting field without being encyclopedic, its practical focus, and its emphasis on readability have endeared it to hundreds of instructors and thousands of students in Canada. Equally gratifying, many students retained this book for their professional libraries after course completion, suggesting they found real value in the book.

Balanced Coverage

We attribute the book's popularity to its balanced coverage of both theory and practice, and of traditional materials and emerging concerns. Regardless of their orientation, readers will sense our belief that people are the ultimate resource for any employer. How well an organization obtains, maintains, and retains its human resources determines its success or failure. And the success or failure of our organizations shapes the well-being of every individual on this planet. If the events of the late 1980s and 1990s are any indication, the human race is entering a totally new phase in its evolution. The breakup of protectionist trade barriers and ideological walls that separate countries of the world may mean that the manager of the twenty-first century must operate in a more complex and dynamic global setting that is also much more interdependent. Training in human resource management (HRM) will become even more critical in this new setting.

The sixth edition of *Canadian Human Resource Management* builds on the strengths of the fifth edition and further expands several key human resource functions. The book is divided into seven parts:

- **Part 1: The Strategic Human Resource Management Model** introduces the strategic model that will be used as a guide through all chapters.

- **Part 2: Planning Human Resources** describes the two pre-hiring processes, analyzing the jobs in question and planning for future staff needs.

- **Part 3: Attracting Human Resources** covers the legal aspects of any hiring decision and discusses recruitment and selection processes.

- **Part 4: Placing, Developing, and Evaluating Human Resources** discusses the importance of preparing employees for new challenges through training and development and providing timely performance feedback.

- **Part 5: Motivating Human Resources** reviews the many ways a human resource department can contribute to a more effective organization through a fair and equitable compensation system and proficient benefits administration. New job options must be integrated into the organization and it is one of the responsibilities of a human resource manager to create a motivating job environment.

- **Part 6: Maintaining High Performance** brings up the issues related to managing a diverse workforce, something Canadian managers have to become familiar with. Workplace safety is of concern to every manager and this concern must be conveyed to all employees through an effective communication system. Good interpersonal relations require appropriate and fair discipline procedures. This part also discusses in detail the union-management framework, union organizing, collective bargaining, and collective agreement administration.

- **Part 7: Strategy Evaluation**, the final part, reveals how human resource departments should evaluate their own effectiveness.

Updated in the Sixth Edition

The chapters in the new edition have been streamlined and organized for easier reading and retention of material by students. The focus of the text continues to be the strategic contribution of HR function in organizations; however, an explicit recognition of the relationship between HR strategies, tactics, and systems has been incorporated into the model and throughout the text material. Within this format, both present and emerging concerns of a significant nature are highlighted. This edition provides thorough coverage of Canadian human rights legislation and in-depth discussion of the Canadian Charter of Rights and Freedoms. A number of recent trends and potentially promising HRM strategies have been incorporated into appropriate chapters of the new edition. HRM has recently played a more important role in the overall strategy of companies. This trend is strongly reflected in the new edition. All chapters now include a discussion of how the topic dealt with in the chapter should be mirrored in the HRM strategy and how this strategy fits into the overall strategy of the organization. This edition also discusses the national Certified Human Resource Professional (CHRP) designation requirements and the competencies identified by the task force on this matter. All HR associations, including Ontario and Alberta, are referenced and all relevant weblinks are included.

All chapters have been updated. Information on legislative changes, especially in the area of employment equity (women, sexual orientation, people with disabilities, and First Nations people), statistics, and demographics, is the latest available. Diversity management, discussed in Chapter Fourteen, has become an important topic. Canada's immigration policy now brings into the country mostly immigrants from Asia, people with very different cultural values and behaviours, and Canadian managers must learn to cope with these new challenges. Similarly, growing international trade dictates that Canadians may be required to go abroad to manage subsidiaries or to work in joint ventures. A thorough pre-departure training is a must. New work options provide organizations not only with opportunities to be more effective but also offer employees more flexible work opportunities, better suited to their needs. The text provides over 100 examples and anecdotes of Canadian and global firms—private and public, large and small.

Some reviewers suggested that more emphasis be placed on the "how to do it" discussions. This suggestion has been followed in almost all chapters and, whenever possible, a step-by-step approach has been used. The topic of motivation has been brought back from the first edition (it had been eliminated because it was viewed as a repetition of OB concepts). We feel strongly that HR managers are able to significantly influence the creation of a motivating work environment. The topic, presented as part of Chapter Twelve, is discussed in a much more hands-on fashion than is usually presented in an OB text. It should be mentioned that human resource auditing is still a concept that is practised only by progressive organizations (Chapter Seventeen).

Key Features

In addition to new features, important key features from previous editions have been retained.

Running Cases—This is the only Canadian HR text to have *two* cases anchored to material in *every chapter*. The issues in these cases reflect the latest challenges facing human resource managers, including evaluating the effectiveness of selection tools and introducing diversity management in the workplace. *Maple Leaf Shoes Limited* symbolizes traditional HR practices—mostly responding to problems in a reactive fashion. In contrast, *Canadian Pacific and International Bank Limited* symbolizes the progressive, proactive, and strategic role of HR in today's organizations. By comparing the practices of the two firms, students should be able to learn how HR can make a significant contribution to organizational success and growth.

Spotlights—Each chapter provides a "*Spotlight on HRM*" focusing on an emerging practice, issue, or HR opportunity. Some Spotlights from previous editions have been retained at the request of reviewers but most are new to this edition and represent current trends and practices.

Web Research—To assist students to make optimal use of the Internet for more information on HR topics, *extensive listings of HR Web sites* are provided in the margins throughout the text. To facilitate class discussion, a *Web research question* has been added to the end material in every chapter. We have also included a *handy reference list of Important Homepages Related to Human Resource Management* in the preliminary section of the text.

In-Margin Glossary—Important terms and concepts are *highlighted with boldface and italic type* in the text. Allowing students to find critical definitions at a glance, all terms appearing in boldface are also *defined in the margin* and *referenced in the Terms for Review* section at the end of each chapter and in the *Subject Index*, highlighted in a secondary colour. If you prefer to reference a *full list of glossary terms*, please go to our online learning centre at www.mcgrawhill.ca/college/schwind6 to download the complete glossary.

Learning and Pedagogical Devices—Also retained from previous editions are the following features:

- **Figures**—Charts and diagrams are included to illustrate relevant ideas and concepts.

- **Terms for Review**—All important terms and buzzwords are included. It is an excellent tool for self-testing.

- **Chapter Objectives**—This useful tool enables students to gauge their progress and understanding while working through each chapter.

- **End-of-Chapter Summaries**—The authors provide an abbreviated version of the main ideas, theories, and strategies of each chapter.

- **Review and Discussion Questions**—Review and Discussion Questions test students' understanding of the chapter material and suggest topics for class or group discussions.

- **Critical Thinking Questions**—These questions challenge students to expand on what they have just learned, discussing broader relationships and interactions of the concepts in the chapter.

- **Incidents**—These short cases test students' understanding of concepts and their impact on the organization.

- **Exercises**—These offer students the opportunity to apply strategies to specific situations and arrive at their own conclusions or discuss with the instructor and fellow students.

- **Suggested Readings**—The authors offer research articles and books on related topics for students or instructors who wish to pursue chapter topics further.

- **Subject Index**—All chapter topics are indexed by subject. Glossary terms and page references are included in a secondary colour.

- **Reference Notes**—Specific cases and other source references are gathered at the end of the text for more detailed research purposes.

Full Colour—This edition has moved to a *four-colour print*, which is designed to make the text visually attractive and stimulating to read. Over *70 colour photographs* have been added to illustrate concepts and to make the text more student-friendly.

For the Instructor

Canadian Human Resource Management, Sixth Edition, includes a variety of supplemental materials to help instructors prepare and present the material in the textbook. Please contact your local McGraw-Hill Ryerson representative for details concerning policies, prices, and availability.

Instructor Online Learning Centre—www.mcgrawhill.ca/college/schwind6

Along with the Student OLC (see below), *Canadian Human Resource Management,* Sixth Edition includes a password-protected Web site for instructors. The site offers downloadable supplements, relevant legislation, and other resources.

Instructor's Manual—The Instructor's Manual includes a wealth of information to assist instructors in presenting this text and their course to its best advantage. It includes lecture notes, answers to end-of-chapter questions, and other valuable aids.

Computerized Test Bank—The computerized test bank has been developed to provide a variety of testing methods for instructors. The software allows instructors to design their own examinations from over 1200 test bank questions. Included in the test bank are multiple-choice questions, true/false questions, fill in the blank questions, and essay questions.

Microsoft ® PowerPoint ® Powernotes—This supplement includes a complete set of PowerPoint ® slides for each chapter.

CBC Video Package—A video package containing segments from various CBC shows such as *The National, Venture,* and *Undercurrents* is available to supplement lectures and in-class discussions. Each video case corresponds to specific topics covered in the text.

Create a custom course Website with **PageOut,** free with every McGraw-Hill Ryerson textbook.

To learn more, contact your McGraw-Hill Ryerson publisher's representative or visit www.mhhe.com/solutions

PageOut—PageOut is the McGraw-Hill Ryerson Web site development centre. This Web page generation software is free to adopters and is designed to help faculty create online courses, complete with assignments, quizzing, links to relevant sites, lecture notes, and more in a matter of minutes.

For The Student

Student Online Learning Centre—www.mcgrawhill.ca/ college/schwind6

The student centre is organized by chapter and provides a Chapter Summary, Learning Objectives, hotlinks to all Web resources provided in the text, a searchable Glossary, Web Research Questions, and other valuable resources.

Acknowledgements

The writing of a textbook requires the cooperation and support of many people. *Canadian Human Resource Management* is no exception. We are deeply indebted to the following persons for reviewing and commenting on the third edition, fourth edition, fifth edition, and sixth edition manuscripts: Tim DeGroot, McMaster University; Raymond Lee, University of Manitoba; Cliff Barrett, Kwantlen University; Maureen Nummelin, Conestoga College; Shirley Richards, Humber College; Dave McPherson, Humber College; Laurie Kondo. Sheridan College; Nelson LaCroix, Niagara College; Pierre Vallee, Dalhousie University; Judith Hunter, Sheridan College; Monica Belcourt, Atkinson College, York University; Brian Bemmels, University of British Columbia; Jim Burns, Okanagan College; Virginia Clare, Sheridan College, Brampton; Hugh Cowley, Grant MacEwan Community College; Gary Docherty, St. Clair College; Armin Gebauer, Northern Alberta Institute of Technology; Susan Gribbon, Mount Royal College; John Hardisty, Sheridan College; Anne Harper, Humber College; Kristi Harrison, Centennial College, John Hart, Humber College; Leeann Henry, Sheridan College; Brad Hill, St. Lawrence College; David Hunter, Humber College; David Inkster, Red Deer College; John D. Kyle, Mount St. Vincent University; Robert Loo, University of Lethbridge; Jerry Mendek, Confederation College; Megan Mills, Medicine Hat College; Ron Munro, Durham College; John Redston, Red River Community College; Beth Rubin, University of Manitoba; Ed Rowney, Southern Alberta Institute of Technology; Ian Sakinofsky, Ryerson Polytechnic University; Eileen Stewart, British Columbia Institute of Technology; Ed Sutherland, William M. Mercer Limited; Virginia Sutherland, Sir Sandford Fleming College; Gerald Swartz, Sheridan College; Andrew Templar, University of Windsor; Christine Tomchak, Humber College; Anil Verma, University of Toronto; Diane White, Seneca College; and Ann Wylie, Niagara College.

We are deeply indebted to the many students, instructors, researchers, and practitioners who have used and commented on our last edition. Ultimately, it is the users of a book who can tell us about what we did right in the past and what we should do in the future. We hope the readers will find this sixth edition even more useful in teaching and learning about human resource management.

A very special thank you goes to the editorial staff of McGraw-Hill Ryerson, Lenore Gray-Spence, Sponsoring Editor; Kim Brewster, Developmental Editor; Alissa Messner, Supervising Editor; Dianne Broad, Copy Editor; and Alison Derry, Permissions Editor, who, with their special expertise, guided us toward a better product.

And finally, we would like to express our deeply felt thanks to those who assisted us in many tangible and intangible ways: Ruth, Mallika, and Leslie.

Hermann F. Schwind
Hari Das
Terry H. Wagar

McGraw-Hill Ryerson
Online Learning Centre

McGraw-Hill Ryerson offers you an online resource that combines the best content with the flexibility and power of the Internet. Organized by chapter, the SCHWIND Online Learning Centre (OLC) offers the following features to enhance your learning and understanding of Human Resource Management:

- Online Quizzing
- Web Resources and Research
- Microsoft® PowerPoint® Presentations
- Online Glossary

By connecting to the "real world" through the OLC, you will enjoy a dynamic and rich source of current information that will help you get more from your course and improve your chances for success, both in the course and in the future.

For the Instructor

Downloadable Supplements

All key supplements, including Instructor's Manual and Microsoft® PowerPoint® Powernotes are available, password-protected for instant access!

PageOut PageOut

Create your own course Web page for free, quickly and easily. Your professionally designed Web site links directly to OLC material, allows you to post a class syllabus, offers an online gradebook, and much more! Visit www.pageout.net

Online Resources

McGraw-Hill Ryerson offers various online resource tools such as CBC video streaming and links to federal and provincial legislation to help you get the latest information for immediate use in class.

Higher Learning. Forward Thinking.™  **McGraw-Hill Ryerson**

ning Centre

For the Student

Online Quizzing

Do you understand the material? You'll know after taking an Online Quiz! Try the Key Term questions, and the Multiple Choice, True/False and Fill in the Blank questions for each chapter. They're auto-graded with feedback and the option to send results directly to faculty.

Web Resources

This section links you to various Web sites, including all company Web sites linked from the text.

Microsoft® PowerPoint® Presentations

View and download presentations created for each text. Great for pre-class preparation and post-class review.

Web Research

Go online to learn how companies use the Internet in their day-to-day activities. Test your Internet savvy: answer questions based on current organization Web sites and strategies.

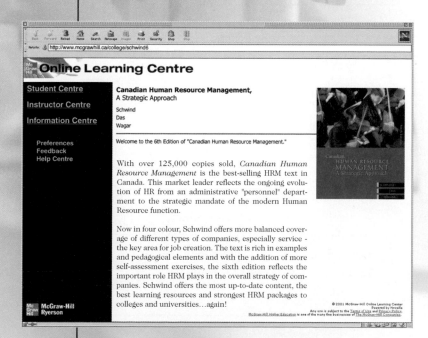

Your Internet companion to the most exciting educational tools on the Web!

The Online Learning Centre can be found at:
www.mcgrawhill.ca/college/schwind6

HOMEPAGES

Important Homepages Related to Human Resource Management

For more relevant and interesting homepages, publications, and links please go to the homepage of the book; www.mcgrawhill.ca/college/schwind6. The book's homepage contains also the active links below.

Government-related

Canada Customs and Revenue Agency (formerly Revenue Canada) Test of Self-Employment	www.ccra-adrc.gc.ca/E/pub/tg/rc4110ed/rc4110ed.html
Canada Labour Code	www.cirb-ccri.gc.ca/eng/clc.html
Canada Pension Plan	www.hrdc-drhc.gc.ca/isp/common/cpptoc_e.shtml
Canadian Human Rights Commission	www.chrc-ccdp.ca
Employment Insurance	www.hrdc-drhc.gc.ca/ae-ei/employmentinsurance.shtml
Federal Gov. Report on the Changing Workplace	www.reflection.gc.ca/report_e.html
Federal Workers Compensation	http://info.load-otea.hrdc-drhc.gc.ca/fwcs/home.htm
Government of Canada	http://canada.gc.ca
Human Resource Development Canada	www.hrdc-drhc.gc.ca
Minimum Wage Tables	http://labour-travail.hrdc-drhc.gc.ca/policy/leg/e/stanf5-e2.html
Ontario Government Workplace Safety and Insurance Act	www.gov.on.ca/lab/leg/bill99e.pdf
Ontario Ministry of Labour	www.gov.on.ca/lab/main.htm
Ontario Pay Equity Commission	www.gov.on.ca/lab/pec/acte.htm
Provincial and Territorial Governments	http://canada.gc.ca/othergov/prove.html
Revenue Canada: see Canadian Customs and Revenue Agency	
Statistics Canada	www.statcan.ca/start.html
WorkSearch	http://worksearch.gc.ca/english/index.pl?tid=19

HRM Publications

Canadian Human Rights Reporter	http://cdn-hr-reporter.ca
Content of Management Journals (McMaster U)	http://mint.mcmaster.ca/mint/journals/journals.htm
Employment Review (online)	www.employmentreview.com
Free Management Library	www.managementhelp.org
HR Journals (list)	www.anbar.co.uk/awards/hum-res.html
HR Magazine	www.shrm.org/hrmagazine/archive
HRProfessional	www.hrprofessional.org
Human Resource Management Journals (list)	www.anbar.co.uk/awards/hum-res.html
International Labour Review	www.ilo.org/public/english/support/publ/revue/index.htm
International Personnel Mgt. Association	www.ipma-hr.org/pubs/publications.html
Links to International HR Publications (with description)	www.mtsu.edu/~rlhannah/ier.html#A

HRM Publications—Continued

Managing Human Resources (online)	http://erc.msh.org/hr
Personnel Psychology	www.personnelpsychology.com/Default.htm
Relations industrielles/Industrial Relations	www.rlt.ulaval.ca/ri-ir/journal.html
Society of Human Resource Management Magazine	www.shrm.org/hrmagazine
Training & Development Magazine	www.astd.org/virtual_community/td_magazine
Workforce Online	www.hronline.com/lib/workforce
Workforce Magazine	www.workforce.com

Private Organizations and HR-Related Sites

AFL-CIO	www.aflcio.org/home.htm
American Society for Training and Development:	www.astd.org
Bank of Montreal Career Centre	www.bmo.com/careers/index_studentcareer.html
Big Dog's HR Development Page	www.nwlink.com/~donclark/hrd.html
Canadian Association for Flexible Staffing	www.acsess.org/english/acsess.php?id=01
Canadian Benefit Resource Homepage	www.benefits.org
Canadian Centre on Substance Abuse	www.ccsa.ca
Canadian Compensation Association: see WorldofWork	
Canadian Council of Human Resource Associations	www.chrpcanada.com
Canadian Health Network (AIDS)	http://canadian-health-network.ca/1aids_hiv.html
Canadian HIV/AIDS Legal Network	http://aidslaw.ca/home.htm
Canadian Labour Congress (CLC)	www.clc-ctc.ca
Canadian Race Relations Foundation	www.crr.ca/en
Canadian Telecommuting Centre	www.ivc.ca
Conference Board of Canada	www.conferenceboard.ca
Chart Your Course International (HR Info Net)	www.chartcourse.com/default.htm
Cross-Cultural and Diversity Training I	www.globalworkshop.com/canada.html
Cross-Cultural and Diversity Training II	www.diversityupdate.com
Disability News Service	www.disabilitynews.com
Encarta Encyclopedia	http://encarta.msn.com
Fast Company Magazine (HR/Management Topics)	www.fastcompany.com/online/resources
HR Articles	www.pmihrm.com/articles.htm
HR Guide (Info Net)	www.hr-guide.com
HR Information (Info Net)	www.hr-esource.com
HR Links	http://students.uww.edu/stdorgs/shrm/hrlinks.htm
HR Online (Info Net)	www.hr2000.com
HR Topics	www.opm.gov/html/topics.htm
Human Resource Net (Info Net)	www.hr.com
Human Resources (Info Net)	http://humanresources.about.com
Human Resource Professionals Association of Ontario	www.hrpao.org/

Private Organizations and HR-Related Sites—Continued

Independent Contractor Test	www.bcarter.com/tip073.htm
International Association for Flexible Staffing	www.ciett.org/main.htm
International Federation of Employee Benefit Plans	www.ifebp.org/pbbengen.html
International Labour Organization (ILO)	www.ilo.org
International Lesbian and Gay Association	www.ilga.org
International Personnel Management Association	www.ipma-hr.org
JRC Consulting (Training Topics)	www.jrctrainingsolutions.com
National Center For Employee Ownership	www.nceo.org
Online Dictionaries	www.yourdictionary.com
Ontario Network for Human Rights	www.geocities.com/capitolhill/6174/index.html
Profit Sharing Council of America	www.psca.org
Society for Human Resource Management (US)	http://shrm.org
Statistics	www.statsoftinc.com/textbook/stathome.html
Training & Development Community Center	www.tcm.com/trdev
University of Alberta HR Services Website	www.hrs.ualberta.ca
Virtual Organization Research Center	http://isds.bus.lsu.edu/cvoc
Web-based Training Information Center	www.filename.com/wbt
William M. Mercer Ltd. (Benefits Consultant)	www.wmmercer.com
Workplace Diversity Web site (Cornell U)	www.ilr.cornell.edu/depts/wdn
World of Work (formerly American and Canadian Compensation Associations)	www.cca-acr.org

Fun Pages

www.humor.com
www.netfunny.com
www.humorspace.com/admin/hlist.htm
http://humor.neopages.com
http://humor.ncy.com
www.jokes.com
www.jokeaddicts.com/jokes.html
www.pcgameworld.com
www.allfunnypictures.com/bmw.htm
www.funnyrealpictures.com/people.html
www.gotlaughs.com
www.laughpost.com
http://sport.all-humor.com

Part One

1

The Strategic Human Resource Management Model

A human resource department helps people and organizations reach their goals. But it faces many challenges along the way. This chapter explores some of these challenges and outlines a strategic human resource management model upon which the rest of this book builds.

The Strategic Human Resource Management Model

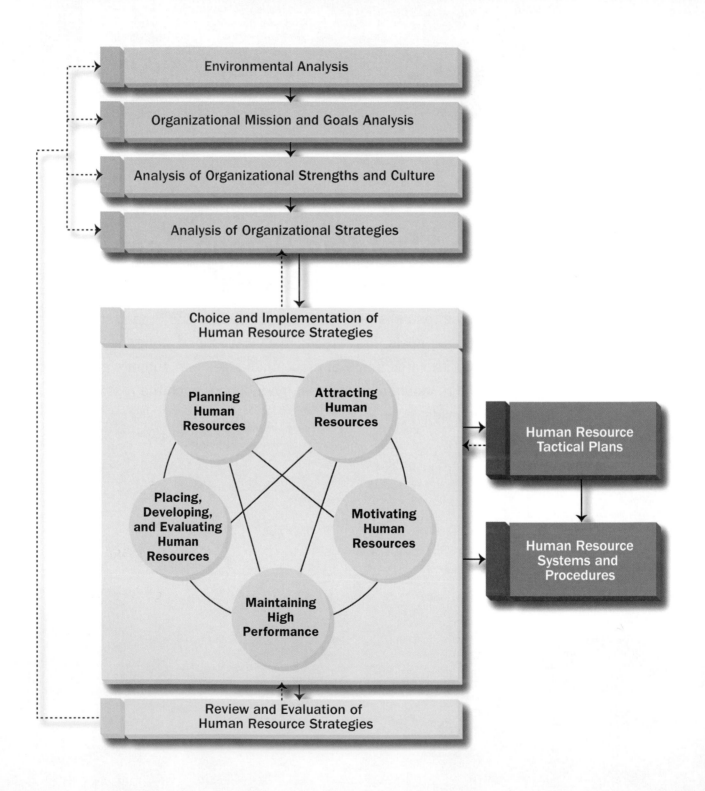

Chapter 1

Strategic Importance of Human Resource Management

"The successful 21st-century organization will not take the loyalty of talented people for granted. It will constantly try to recruit and keep them... The mutual commitment of an employer and an employee will be one of the most important factors for a 21st-century organization."

Subhir Chowdhury[1]

CHAPTER OBJECTIVES

After studying this chapter, you should be able to:

- *List* challenges facing Canadian organizations in the context of managing their workforce.

- *Discuss* the objectives of human resource management.

- *Discuss* the meaning of strategic human resource management and steps in implementing the same.

- *Discuss* how human resource departments are organized and function.

- *Discuss* future roles of the human resource profession in this country.

NAME THE GREATEST accomplishment of the last century. Landing on the moon? Computers? Biogenic engineering? Cloning of life forms?[2] And what awaits us in the new millennium? Routine travel to distant planets? Human longevity unimaginable in the past? Working and shopping without ever stepping out of our homes? Flying to any destination of our choice in automatically piloted flying cars? Living in undersea settlements? The possibilities are immense. Indeed, our future achievements may be limited only by our imagination. All major achievements and technological advances share a common feature: organizations.

> The large part of today's Canada that was originally known as Rupert's Land was opened up to settlers by the Hudson's Bay Company. Canada is the world's largest producer of newsprint, nickel, and asbestos, thanks to the efforts of several companies and small organizations in those industries. Canadian cities such as Vancouver, Toronto, and Montreal are rated as some of the best cities in the world on various criteria including health care, education, and crime rates. The Canadian Broadcasting Corporation, which owns and operates several radio and television stations and networks, brings you the news, music, and entertainment. In each case, it is organizations that have marshalled the resources needed to achieve these results.

> Even on a more day-to-day basis, organizations play a central role in our lives. The water we drink, the food we eat, the clothes we wear, and the vehicles we drive are products of organizations. When future historians view our era, they may see organizations as one of our greatest accomplishments. It is nothing but a marvel to have tens of thousands of people with highly individualized backgrounds, skills, and interests coordinated in various enterprises to pursue common institutionalized goals.[3]

People are the common element in all social organizations. They create the objectives, the innovations, and the accomplishments for which organizations are praised. When looked at from the perspective of the organization, people are resources. They are not inanimate resources, such as land and capital; instead, they are human resources. Without them, organizations would not exist. The following incident shows how important human resources can be:

> TransCanada Minerals was a small company that owned several nickel and zinc leases. In exchange for several million dollars, it sold all its mineral claims. Total balance-sheet assets consisted of some office furniture, miscellaneous prospecting equipment of little value, and nearly $15 million on deposit with the Royal Bank of Canada. While the president of the company looked for investments in the brewing industry, one of the firm's few remaining geologists discovered a large deposit of zinc. Within a short period the company's stock doubled.

It can be seen that although TransCanada Minerals' balance sheet did not list the human "assets," these resources were at work. Before the zinc discovery, a casual observer would have considered the $15-million deposit as the company's most important asset; afterward, the mineral claim would have been considered the major asset. However, a keen observer would note that neither the bank account nor the mineral claim could be of great value without capable people to manage them.

More and more top managers are beginning to recognize that organizational success depends upon careful attention to human resources. Some of the best-managed and most successful Canadian organizations are those that effectively make employees meet organizational challenges creatively:

> In a high-tech organization such as Nortel, this often means getting the best out of engineers, who must be creative problem-solvers to meet the ever-present challenges. In research organizations, fostering creativity by encouraging a free flow of ideas among researchers may be the key to success. In some manufacturing organizations, cost control spells success. In retail and other service industries, the difference between success and failure and between growth and extinction is marked by the quality of service.

Organizational responses such as the above can be planned only after a clear identification of the challenges facing a firm. This means that the human resource practices are intricately intertwined with the organizational challenges. Before proceeding any further, it is necessary to discuss the key challenges facing Canadian organizations and what implications they hold for managing the workforce.

CHALLENGES FACING CANADIAN ORGANIZATIONS

IN THE CONTEXT of managing their workforce, Canadian organizations face a number of challenges today. Some of the more important ones are listed in Figure 1-1. These challenges may be economic (e.g., competition), technological (e.g., computerization), political (e.g., new government policies), social (e.g., concern for our environment), demographic (e.g., changing composition of our workforce), legal (e.g., changes in minimum wage laws), cultural (e.g., ethnic diversity), or otherwise in nature. For discussion purposes, the major challenges facing a Canadian organization (especially those affecting human resource management) can be grouped under five heads: *economic, technological, demographic, cultural,* and *legal.* The first four challenges will be discussed in this chapter. The critical importance of legal compliance for the human resource function warrants a more elaborate review of the subject matter. Hence, this topic is detailed in Chapter Four.

Economic challenges
Economic factors facing Canadian business today, including global trade challenges and increases in competitiveness and productivity levels.

Economic Challenges

Today, Canadian business faces two critical *economic challenges*: *the global trade challenge* and *the challenge of productivity improvement*. Although these are interrelated challenges, for the purpose of discussion, they are considered separately below.

FIGURE 1-1

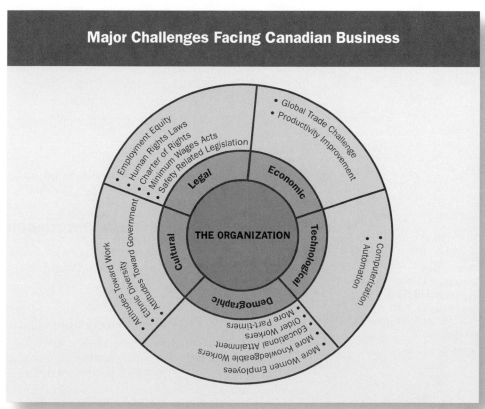

Global Trade Challenge

International trade has always been critical to Canada's prosperity and growth. Canada ranks high among exporting nations: on a per-capita basis, we export much more than either the United States or Japan. The combination of a relatively small population and a large natural resource base gives Canada a trade advantage internationally.

> Consider these facts: In the first 35 years after the Second World War, Canada's total trade—exports and imports—amounted to 35 per cent of GDP. In the 1980s, it climbed to 44 per cent; and in the 1990s, to 61 per cent. By 1999, it had reached 72 per cent.[4]

More than ever before, Canadian jobs and economic prosperity depend upon our international trade. Currently, Canada has approximately 200 international trading partners and Canadian exports are valued at over $370 billion a year. By 2005, this is expected to rise to over $500 billion.[5]

To capture the growing market opportunities abroad, Canadian organizations are opening new plants and expanding activities in foreign countries that are closer to their customers or where labour is cheaper. While the United States continues to be our largest trading partner, Canada today exports to varying locations.

> In the recent past, Nortel was actively involved in upgrading Mexico's and China's telephone systems; Bombardier Inc., in the past, purchased a railcar company near Mexico City and was involved in refurbishing the country's transportation system. Today, several Canadian firms have major involvement in countries such as India, Thailand, and Chile.

What are the implications for managing human resources in Canadian organizations? The emergence of several low-cost trading nations (which have vast resources of highly skilled, cheap labour) such as Thailand, China, and India have caused us to lose our market shares in traditional strongholds such as pulp and paper, cotton yarn, and steel manufacturing. Unless we are able to add value to our products or reduce the costs of production, many firms may be unable to survive in the new market place.

> For example, the North American Free Trade Agreement (NAFTA) meant considerable initial pain to the Canadian economy causing as many as 8000 Canadian factories to shut down in the early 1990s.[6]

In recent years, Canada has also become an important global player in high-tech industries. To attract and maintain skilled, innovative employees, these firms must embrace progressive human resource practices.

In summary, the arrival of the global village has necessitated major rethinking in the way we look at and manage our employees. Progressive human resource practices have been found to be the key to add value to our products and services and maintain high productivity levels. The challenge of productivity improvement is so critical today that it deserves separate discussion below.

Challenge of Productivity Improvement

Productivity
The ratio of a firm's outputs (goods and services) divided by its inputs (people, capital, materials, energy).

Productivity refers to the ratio of an organization's outputs (goods and services) to its inputs (people, capital, materials, and energy), as seen in Figure 1-2. Productivity increases as an organization finds new ways to use fewer resources to produce its output.

In a business environment, productivity improvement is essential for long-run success. Through gains in productivity, managers can reduce costs, save scarce resources, and enhance profits. In turn, improved profits allow an organization to provide better pay, benefits, and working conditions. The result can be a higher quality of work life for employees, who are more likely to be motivated toward further

FIGURE 1-2

Productivity Defined as a Ratio

$$\text{Productivity} = \frac{\text{outputs (goods and services)}}{\text{inputs (people, capital, materials, energy)}}$$

improvements in productivity. Human resource managers contribute to improved productivity directly by finding better, more efficient ways to meet their objectives and indirectly by improving the quality of work life for employees.

How do we measure productivity? The index that relates all *inputs* (e.g., capital, raw materials, labour, etc.) to *outputs* (shown in Figure 1-2), while theoretically meaningful, may not help decision-makers to identify potential areas of improvement. For practical use, productivity measures of each of the major components of production may be more useful. For example, one can think of labour productivity, productivity of machinery, and so on. Employee productivity can be measured using output per worker or output per work hour, while productivity of equipment and machinery may be measured by sales or production per dollar of investment in equipment, and so on.

A major challenge facing Canadian managers is productivity improvement while maintaining a high quality of work life for the employees. Cost pressures are not new to most organizations. What is new, however, is the strength and relative permanence of these competitive pressures:

> The competitors of a Canadian manufacturer of computer software typically live not next door, but abroad. They may be operating in some remote part of the world such as a small town in South Korea, Singapore, India, or Mexico. Often, Canadian organizations must compete for investment capital not with other Canadian or U.S. organizations, but with a firm in Hungary, the Czech Republic, Chile, or China.

Workplace innovation and redesign of jobs to achieve high productivity levels are two popular means used to attain these objectives.[7] However, Canada's recent record raises some concerns.

> Canada is steadily losing its ability to innovate and create wealth compared with other rich countries, according to a study done by Massachusetts Institute of Technology in 1999. In this study, which ranked the 16 leading members of the Organization for Economic Cooperation and Development, Canada had slipped to ninth spot from sixth over the past decade. What is even more troublesome is the study's forecast that unless Canada changes its course soon, the country will lose more ground early in this millennium (the report projects that Canada's rank is likely to remain at the tenth position in the immediate future).[8]

Innovation on two fronts, namely people management and technology, will be the major challenge of the immediate future. Since a large percentage of Canadian production is currently geared for highly competitive export markets, updating technology to increase our productivity levels becomes a high-priority task facing managers in this country. While Canada has improved its overall global competitiveness in the past, we still have scope for improvement. Indeed, our high standard of living may depend on our ability to maintain and improve our world competitiveness.

> In early 2000, Canada ranked eleventh in overall world competitiveness. The most competitive nation was the United States (with a score of 100), followed by Singapore (75.22), as seen in Figure 1-3. While Canada's overall score of 63.42 was higher than

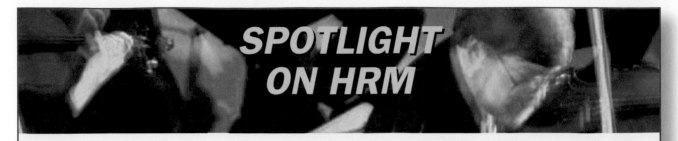

SPOTLIGHT ON HRM

WILL THE 21ST CENTURY BELONG TO CANADA?

The ingredients are all there, but human capital is the key.

Today it is recognized that natural, financial, and technical resources no longer provide a sufficient basis for improving productivity at a rate equal to or better than other developed countries. These traditional foundations for productivity improvement are widely available globally through international trade and electronic commerce. In addition, we now understand that more money and technology do not by themselves increase productivity. It is the ability of people to effectively use these resources, through their knowledge and skills, that creates value and enhances results. (The) capability of people is seen as key to sustaining continuous improvement in productivity. This improvement depends on our ability to keep enhancing the knowledge and skills of people, using their knowledge and skills, and creating and disseminating new knowledge.

The challenge is that the productive capacity of people does not improve quickly. Developing expertise in any field takes years of development and experience. In addition, it takes time to adapt the organizational and cultural context in order to apply an individual's capability to the fullest. An added complexity is that people don't work in isolation—group or team dynamics are powerful forces impacting both behavior and productivity in the workplace. In short, how well we develop and manage people is critical to sustaining significant improvements in productivity.

Productivity depends on investment

Increasing productivity must be viewed as a long-term investment in developing and using human capital. Investments need to take a wide range of forms with sustained effort over significant periods of time. They require continuing efforts by government, individuals, and organizations.

The most obvious form of investment is through education and training. To continue to improve productivity and living standards, Canada needs a well-educated workforce that is knowledgeable and skilled to fill jobs in the growing occupations.

Formal education programs need to focus on providing a liberal science education that prepares people entering the workforce for the 21st century. Employment rates and salaries are higher in the business, science and technology fields, yet enrolment in these educational areas remains stagnant.

Training is everyone's responsibility

As a society, we need to promote furthering the minimum education of everyone. Completing a quality secondary education must be the minimum education for every person in this country.

Organizations must also invest in the continuing development and specialized training of their employees. Organization-funded training must be seen as a long-term rather than a variable operating cost that is cut or reduced during poor economic times.

Individuals must also invest in improving their capabilities. We live in an age where continual change is the norm and lifelong learning is no longer a vague concept or jargon from training professionals.

To sustain increasing levels of productivity, Canada must invest heavily in the research and developing of new knowledge in a broad range of disciplines.

Investment in developing new knowledge is really an investment in Canada's people and their future well-being. This not only keeps Canada's best and brightest at home, but it also keeps the innovation and subsequent jobs within Canada.

To survive, all organizations invest in innovation, particularly around their products, services and core operating processes. Most organizations are also increasingly investing in new technology, especially information technology. Far fewer organizations have recognized the need for significant investment in the development of the human resource management systems, processes and capabilities. . . .

In summary, to maintain our standard of living relative to other countries, Canada must reverse the current trend by making substantial, sustained investments in developing its human resources. Improving our standard of living in the 21st century will require world-class human resource management capability.

Source: Brian Orr, "Will the 21st Century Belong to Canada?" *Canadian HR Reporter*, December 29, 1997, pp. 18–19. Courtesy of *Canadian HR Reporter* published by Carswell, Thomson Professional Publishing.

that of the United Kingdom (59.36) or Japan (57.36), it was still behind a number of other countries including Germany (64.49) and Sweden (63.86). A major reason for this difference was the lower Canadian productivity. Compared with countries such as the United States, Belgium, Italy, Ireland, France, Germany, and Norway, the overall productivity of Canadian workers was lower.[9]

A recent report estimates that if the gap in overall productivity growth between the United States and Canada were to persist, this factor alone would reduce Canadian living standards from 61 per cent of U.S. levels in 1999 to 52 per cent in 2010.[10] In recent years, Canadian managers and policy makers have recognized the urgency of improving Canadian productivity. As a consequence, the Canadian economy has undergone a dramatic transformation—we have learned to produce more outputs with fewer workers:

> Improvements in technology and automation have helped the British Columbia lumber industry to increase its production by 25 per cent in the past decade with 6000 fewer workers. In the pulp and paper industry, the production has increased by a quarter in the past decade; however, we have nine per cent fewer jobs now (having lost 12 000 jobs in the change process).[11]

These are not jobs lost temporarily to adjust to a business cycle or to make short-term adjustments to competition—the new ways of working mean that these positions are lost forever. Productivity improvement has also left a painful scar on Canadian society; in the last two decades, more than 350 000 manufacturing jobs (many of them blue-collar) have disappeared—never to return.[12]

Outsourcing
Contracting tasks to outside agencies or persons.

One strategy that is getting increasingly popular to cut costs (thus indirectly raising the productivity figures) is **outsourcing**. Outsourcing enables organizations to reduce the number of workers on permanent payroll and contract out tasks to outside agencies as and when needs arise, thus reducing the total wage bill. A survey of 303 multinational companies in North America and Europe found that over 90 per cent plan to do so by end of year 2000.[13]

> The most commonly outsourced function is legal work, followed by transportation and information systems management. Kodak, which in the past employed 1400 persons

FIGURE 1-3

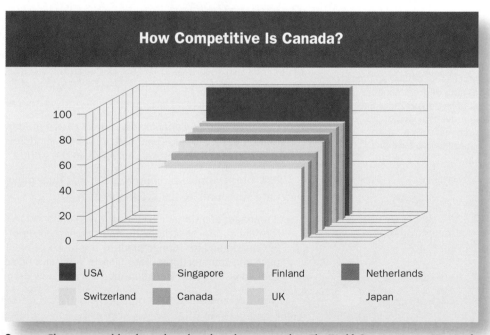

Source: Chart prepared by the authors based on data reported in *The World Competitiveness Year Book*, 2000, IMO, www.imd.ch/wcy

in its data processing and information system sections, began outsourcing its information system needs. Air Canada began outsourcing the maintenance of its Boeing 747s in 1996.[14] Other common outsourcing areas include printing, payroll, security, and accounting.

Outsourcing has major implications for the human resource manager. Reduced employee morale caused by job insecurity is a major issue. During contract negotiations with unions, this may pose a major hurdle for the human resource manager. Further, to meet employee goals, a human resource department may have to initiate retraining for displaced workers (to take up other jobs) or help them find jobs elsewhere (referred to as **outplacement**).

Outplacement
Assisting employees to find jobs with other employers.

In summary, the current emphasis on productivity improvement has necessitated a renewed emphasis on strategic thinking and creative responses. It also involves using new technology to improve productivity and create value. This will be discussed in the next section.

Technological Challenges

Technology influences organizations and the way people work. Often it can affect an entire industry, as the following example illustrates:

> The technology of cars and airplanes modified the transportation industry—often to the detriment of railway companies. Automobile and aviation companies grew and created demand for more employees and training. The career opportunities for employees improved substantially. On the other hand, in railway companies, reduced revenues and limited growth opportunities reduced the advancement opportunities for employees. HR departments in several of these companies had to reduce the workforce and create early retirement systems.

In the foreseeable future, technological innovations may cause fundamental shifts in our lifestyles, how and where we work, and what we do. Generally, two major technological changes have revolutionized Canadian businesses: computerization and automation. Each of these is discussed below.

Computerization

Computerization
A major technological change allowing the processing of vast amounts of data at great speeds, enabling organizations to improve efficiency, responsiveness, and flexibility in operations.

Since the early 1980s, Canada has witnessed the rapid growth of **computerization** and access to high-speed information transmission systems affecting almost all walks of life. An unprecedented degree of computerization has changed the way we work, play, study, and even entertain ourselves, while access to the information highway has affected the way several organizations conduct their business:

> Currently, half of Canadian households have at least one person with regular access to the Internet. Over 40 per cent of Canadian adults have access to the Internet, making us one of the most wired nations in the world.[15]

Part of the appeal of computers is that they make it possible to process and provide large amounts of data to managers:

> A manager of a Canadian company with multinational operations can compare the performance, pay, absenteeism, and safety records of its hourly and salaried workforce in Canada and its foreign plant by the touch of a computer keyboard. The same manager can transfer large data files to Australia or southern Africa in seconds. Often, decisions that took weeks in the past can now be made in hours or even minutes.

Another advantage of computers is that they make information available with great speed. Soon after events occur, the computer can list them in summary fashion—giving the information the important property of *timeliness*. Given the turbulence in today's business environments, this is a very useful attribute as it enables managers to take timely corrective actions.

Mai's Chicken, which sold fried chicken for over 15 years in Saint John, was popular for its quality, fresh taste, and price. The firm had always monitored customer satisfaction levels informally and made changes whenever necessary. Recently, it purchased a personal computer, which permitted it to do detailed data analysis. By doing a thorough analysis of data it collected in a recent questionnaire survey, the firm found that its younger customers preferred low-fat, low-cholesterol food. Among teens, crispy chicken was found to be popular. Older customers were satisfied with the chicken as served and did not want any changes. Based on the findings, Mai's Chicken introduced two new products: low-fat baked chicken and crispy chicken fingers. Both items proved to be instantly successful on the market.

Telecommuting
Paid labour performed at the employee's home, full-time or part-time, with assistance of PCs, modems, fax machines, etc.

Computers bring considerable flexibility into when and where the work is carried out. In several instances, computers permit employees to work without ever leaving their homes. Workers communicate with other employees through telephone, facsimile (fax) machines, and computerized information systems. Such *telecommuting* has been found to cut employee stress and boost worker productivity in several instances, while also reducing the costs of operations.[16]

AT&T in the United States in a project that introduced telecommuting in selected departments, found that in 80 per cent of the cases, the change led to improved worker productivity. Two-thirds of the supervisors also indicated that it increased the overall efficiency of their departments.[17]

Not all jobs lend themselves to at-home work; but with the advances in computer technology, virtually any job—or any part of a job—that involves work that is independent of other people and special equipment may, one day, be performed away from the workplace. Currently, jobs such as word processing, copy editing, routine accounting, and data entry are increasingly carried out by telecommuters. The major obstacle to telecommuting appears to be "conservative management with industrial revolution mind-sets"[18] who fear that they might lose control over employees who are not physically near them. When making a decision on telecommuting, organizations should focus on jobs that do not require day-to-day interaction with others and prepare their managers to supervise employees who are not physically present. Several Canadian organizations such as Bell Canada and Royal Bank have developed policies on telecommuting.

Finally, computers also enable organizations to manage their operations innovatively, often reducing costs or capitalizing on new opportunities.

McCarthy Tetrault, Canada's biggest law firm, saw technology as an area of opportunity and began recruiting lawyers with high-tech expertise. This, in turn, enabled the firm to take advantage of the opportunities in intellectual capital management.[19]

Many organizations today have *intranets* or private information networks that are accessible to all or selected organizational members, thus increasing the speed of decision making and the speed of response to customers, employees, and other stakeholders.

At Mackenzie Financial, a Toronto-based mutual fund company, intranet technology is now used to remotely administer computer systems at the company's branch offices in Vancouver, Calgary, and Montreal and prepare portfolio management reports that are used by individual fund managers when making investment decisions.[20]

The exact effects of computerization on organizations will vary (depending on size, management practices, culture, and so on). In general, computerization results in a faster, multi-way of communication, non-traditional marketing strategies, improved quality control, and more online inventory control. This in turn requires newer human resource practices in the areas of hiring, compensation, training, performance evaluation, and employee relations. For example, the new competencies needed on the part of employees in a highly computerized firm makes it necessary to continually upgrade employee skills.

Automation

Automation
The automatically controlled operation of a process, system, or equipment by mechanical or electronic devices.

Automation is the other major technological change that has affected Canadian organizations and their human resource management practices:

> Before the introduction of automatic banking machines, human resource departments of major Canadian banks used to recruit large numbers of semiskilled clerks. Not anymore. Computers have eliminated several of these routine jobs; further, automation means that highly skilled programmers who can process data and program computers are needed. The recruiting and training programs in these banks had to be changed dramatically to meet the needs of new technology.

Why do organizations automate various activities?

The first reason is the push for *speed*. Competition from other countries has made it imperative that we improve our manufacturing practices if we want to stay competitive.

> For instance, capital equipment items that on average take six to twelve months to make in Canada take six to twelve weeks to make in Japan. The desire to control labour cost and increase productivity continues to drive automation.

A second reason for automation is to provide *better service* to the customer, to increase predictability in operations, and to achieve higher standards of quality in production. Machines do not go on strike, nor do they ask for raises.

Automation also allows *flexibility* in operations. In several automated production facilities, even small production batches become economically viable since the time, cost, and effort involved in changing set-ups are minimal. The ability to produce

Robots, such as this robotic welder, are increasingly becoming a key factor of Canada's factory production. Machines do not go on strike, nor do they ask for raises.

CP Photo Archive (Bernd Franke)

small batches, in turn, enables a firm to focus on the needs of different customers and market segments and speed up delivery schedules.

Automation is not the sole answer to a firm's productivity problems. Experienced human resource managers recognize this fact. Automation, to be beneficial, should permit elegant meshing of existing and new technologies. Further, the lack of availability of capital for buying expensive robots puts such purchases beyond the reach of most small- and medium-sized organizations. Negative union attitudes towards mechanization is another barrier to the introduction of robots in the workplace. Automation may result in a smaller workforce together with fewer opportunities for socialization on the job. Lastly, to use expensive robots effectively (during an automation), more and more factories may find it necessary to work two or three shifts a day.

Despite these issues, it is a reasonable prediction that in the future most hazardous and boring jobs will be taken over by robots.

Dangerous jobs—such as working with toxic chemicals and paints—will be changed by substituting robots for people. Likewise, highly repetitive assembly tasks will continue to be taken over by robots in the future. Already, in several automobile plants like those of General Motors, there are thousands of robot painters and robot welders.

In summary, human resource managers, today, must be conversant with the emerging technologies and their implications for organizational strategies, processes, and employee behaviours. New procedures for employee recruitment, training, communication, appraisal, and compensation may have to be designed to meet the challenges posed by computerization and automation while negotiations with the unions may prove more challenging for at least some organizations.

Demographic Challenges

The demographics of the labour force describe the composition of the workforce: the education levels, the age levels, the percentage of the population participating in the workforce, and other population characteristics.

Demographic changes
Changes in the demographics of the labour force (e.g., education levels, age levels, participation rates) that occur slowly and are usually known in advance.

While *demographic changes* occur slowly and can be predicted in most instances, they still exert considerable influence on organizational decisions. A close look at the labour market indicates several trends.

Trend 1: The Increasing Number of Women in the Workforce

As Figure 1-4 shows, the labour-force participation rates for females has been steadily increasing. It is estimated that by 2005, 85 per cent of Canadian women aged 25 to 54 will enter the labour force. It is interesting to note that compared to several other industrialized nations, the participation rate of Canadian women is high. More women have also left traditional, nonprofessional occupations (such as clerical and sales) and now work in management, law, engineering, and medical fields. The fact that women accounted for 70 per cent of the total employment growth in Canada in the last two decades has raised new issues of child care, counselling for two-career families, and employment equity.[21]

Trend 2: Shift toward Knowledge Workers

Currently, there is a shift from employment in primary and extractive industries (such as mining, fishing) to service, technical, and professional jobs. The relative contribution of different industries to national wealth is shown in Figure 1-5. Service industries make the largest contribution to Gross Domestic Product (GDP) today—

www.hrdc-drhc.gc.ca

FIGURE 1-4

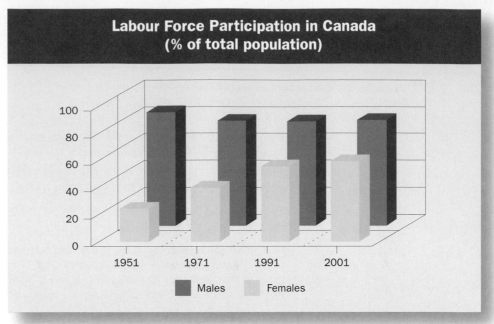

Source: Chart prepared by authors on the basis of data reported in Statistics Canada, *The Labour Force*, Bulletin No. 71-001, 1966-81; Pradeep Kumar, Mary Lou Coates, and David Arrowsmith, *The Current Industrial Relations Scene in Canada*, 1986, Kingston, Ont., Industrial Relations Centre, Queen's University, 1986; Woods Gordon and Clarkson Gordon, *Tomorrow's Customers*, 20th ed., Toronto, 1986; Projections are by the authors based on data from Statistics Canada Web site, June 2000. www.statcan.ca

exceeding 66 per cent in mid-2000.[22] Within the service industry, the demand for workers in information industry has been consistently growing.

Today's workforce can be divided into two main categories: information and non-information workers. Information workers can be further divided into two groups: *data* and **knowledge workers**. Data occupations involve the manipulation of symbolic information, whereas knowledge occupations involve the development of ideas or expert opinions. Thus, data workers (e.g., most clerical occupations) use, transmit, or manipulate knowledge, while knowledge workers such as scientists, engineers, management consultants, and so on, produce it.[23] The non-information category is composed of persons working in the manufacturing and service sectors (e.g., machine operators and assemblers, security guards, babysitters).

Knowledge workers have been the fastest-growing type of workers in the Canadian labour force over the last quarter century or so.[24] While total employment grew at an average rate of 2.1 per cent per year in the past two decades, the employment of knowledge workers grew at a rate of 5.2 per cent per year. This is twice the pace of service workers, the second fastest-growing group of workers over that period. Today, information workers constitute over 54 per cent of the workforce. The proportion of the labour force employed in blue-collar and unskilled jobs simultaneously reflects a decrease. In the foreseeable future, the demand for knowledge workers is likely to grow even faster than ever before.[25] The ability of organizations to find, keep, and continually retrain these workers might spell success in the coming years.

Trend 3: Educational Attainment of Workers

As mentioned above, today's Canadian economy needs highly skilled, well-educated workers. A look at the *educational attainment* of Canadian workers, however, presents an intriguing picture. On the one hand, the educational attainment of Canadians

Knowledge workers
Members of occupations generating, processing, analyzing, or synthesizing ideas and information (like scientists and mangement consultants).

Educational attainment
The highest educational level attained by an individual worker, employee group, or population.

www.statcan.ca

FIGURE 1-5

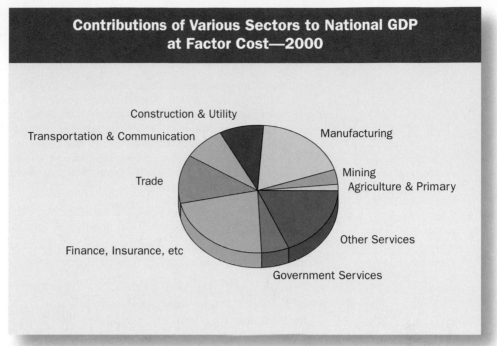

Contributions of Various Sectors to National GDP at Factor Cost—2000

Source: Chart prepared by the authors based on data in Statistics Canada, *Gross Domestic Product at Factor Cost March 2000*.www.statcan.ca.

has increased dramatically over the past several years and is expected to maintain its upward trend (see Figure 1-6). According to the latest census data available, over 13 per cent of the total Canadian population (aged 15 years or over) had a university degree or better (the corresponding figure a decade ago was 9.5 per cent).[26]

www.nald.ca

The disturbing news, however, is that about 22 per cent of Canadians aged 16 or over (or approximately five million Canadians) fall in the lowest level of literacy.[27] They have difficulty understanding printed materials and most likely experience problems reading any written words. Another 24 to 26 per cent of Canadians fall in

FIGURE 1-6

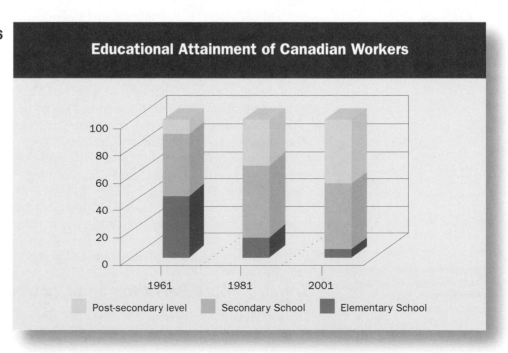

Educational Attainment of Canadian Workers

Post-secondary level   Secondary School   Elementary School

the second lowest level of literacy and can deal only with material that is simple and clearly laid out, and where tasks involved are not overly complex. Not only do such low literacy rates reduce the overall productivity levels in our industries, but they may also be a major contributor to safety violations and accidents.

> In an international survey of educational standards in 15 countries, Canadian performance was, at best, average. In this survey of 13-year-old students, 3000 students were randomly chosen in each country and asked more than 100 questions about science and mathematics. In both categories, students in South Korea achieved the top scores (78 per cent in science and 73 per cent in mathematics). Canada ranked ninth (with an average science score of 69 percent and mathematics score of 62 per cent); several countries, including Taiwan, Hungary, Switzerland, and Italy, were ahead of Canada in both categories.[28]

About 30 per cent of young Canadians drop out of school before they graduate. It is estimated that currently more than eight million Canadians lack a basic school certificate or diploma.[29] What is worse, our education system still frequently produces persons who do not have basic literary and numerical skills.

Faced with this daunting prospect, the Corporate Council on Education identified a set of "employability skills" consisting of basic academic skills (e.g., communication, thinking, learning), personal management skills (e.g., positive attitudes and behaviours, ability to accept responsibility, adaptability to new challenges), and teamwork skills (e.g., ability to work with others, ability to lead a team). These skills were considered to be the foundation skills for employability in the future.[30] Some of the more progressive employers have recognized workplace literacy as a serious issue and have taken proactive action to minimize its adverse consequences.

> Durabelt Inc., a company based in Prince Edward Island that manufactures conveyor belts for vegetable harvesters, was nominated for a national award for excellence in workplace literacy. The "Duraschool project," which has been in operation since 1997, converts the lunch room and offices into classrooms for two evenings each week where several employees and family members routinely gather to update their math, reading, and writing skills.[31]

Trend 4: Employment of Older Workers

One of the impending issues for human resource managers is what *Maclean's* termed our *"old age crisis."*[32] In 1996, about 28 per cent of the population (or almost 7.6 million Canadians) were more than 50 years old. By 2011, the age group comprising those age 65 and over will form over 14 per cent of the population (see Figure 1-7).

Old age crisis
Refers to the social (health care) and organizational (new workplace ergonomics) challenges caused by aging of population.

The exact consequences of this trend for the human resource management function are hard to predict. An increasingly hectic scramble for jobs (especially the traditional sectors) may be one consequence. This is because the fear of post-retirement poverty (fuelled by uncertainty about government-sponsored pension plans) may motivate employees to hold on to their current jobs. This may create unprecedented bottlenecks in professional and unionized industries. Pressures for expanded retirement benefits, variable work schedules, coordination of government benefits (e.g., Canada/Quebec Pension Plan benefits) with company benefits, and retraining programs are just a few of the challenges that await human resource specialists in the future. Whatever the precise consequences, an aging population has major implications for the human resource function, especially in the areas of recruitment and selection, job design, training, appraisal, and compensation and benefits administration.

Trend 5: More Part-time and Contract Workers

Part-time workers
Persons working fewer than required hours for categorization as full-time workers (so ineligible for many benefits).

The structure of employment in Canada has also changed in recent years. There are more **part-time workers** now than ever before. Indeed, the growth rate of part-time

FIGURE 1-7

Population Projections for Canada (Fertility Rate of 1.5 is Assumed) % Distribution of Population by Age Group

	0-14	15-64	65+	Mean Age
1991	20.5	68.1	11.4	35.5
1996	19.0	68.9	12.1	36.8
2001	17.2	70.2	12.6	38.2
2011	15.2	70.5	14.3	40.8
2021	14.3	66.7	19.0	43.2
2051	13.0	61.2	25.8	46.2

Source: Statistics Canada, *Fertility in Canada—From Baby Boom to Baby Bust*, Ottawa, Catalogue 91-524E.

www.statcan.ca

Contract (or contingent) workers
Freelancers (self-employed, temporary, or leased employees) who are not part of regular work force and are paid on a project completion basis.

employment has been higher than in the case of full-time jobs during the last decade. More than 15 per cent of all employment now is represented by part-time workers (numbering about 1.8 million). Further, many full-time jobs were converted into part-time jobs during the recessions in the early 1980s and 1990s to reduce labour costs. The increasing proportion of part-time workers has raised new concerns about pay inequity and has provided momentum to the "equal pay for work of equal value" concept. Part-timers (typically, women aged 25 or older in lower-paying sales or service jobs) are far less likely to reap the benefits of increased demand and pay for highly skilled jobs.[33]

There is also an increasing trend to use *contract (or contingent) workers* in the workplace. By using contingent workers, organizations can benefit from the services of trained personnel without increasing their payroll costs in a permanent fashion. The use of contractors is not restricted to lower-level, clerical, or secretarial jobs; today, many lawyers, accountants, bankers, executives, and even scientists provide freelance services. Information systems, finance, and engineering were functions that were most likely to be contracted out. Contractors have often been found to be more productive and efficient than in-house employees because freelancers do not spend a lot of time in complying with company bureaucracy and attending meetings. They can also provide an outsider's fresh perspective on things. However, the contractor's loyalty to the firm may be limited, especially if the contractor is working for several different clients concurrently.

Cultural Challenges

Cultural challenges
Challenges facing a firm's decision makers because of changes in core cultural or social values.

As cultural values change, human resource departments discover new challenges. While several *cultural challenges* face Canadian managers, three more important ones are discussed below: attitude toward work, ethnic diversity, and attitudes toward government and those in power.

Attitudes Toward Work

Attitudes toward work
Variety of work-related assumptions and values including the role of work in a person's life and the role of women and diverse groups in organizations.

The increasing entry of women and educated young persons into the labour force has resulted in some changes in employee expectations. The old cultural value that "men work and women stay home" underwent radical modification during the last two decades.

This shift carries implications for human resource managers. For example, child-care facilities provided by the employer will become a more common demand confronting human resource departments. Sick days—paid days off for illness—have become "personal leave days" and "maternity leave" has been renamed "parental leave" to reflect the reality of working men leaving the workforce to take care of their young children.

Due to changing attitudes toward work and leisure, human resource departments have been confronted with requests for longer vacations, more holidays, and varied workweeks. Supervisors increasingly turn to human resource professionals for help with employee motivation.

Ethnic Diversity

The co-existence of anglophones and francophones along with dozens of other national, racial, and ethnic groups, each with its unique cultural and social background, makes Canadian society a *cultural mosaic*.[34] "Business immigrants" have often acted as engines of economic growth in this country, while immigrants from nontraditional sources such as Hong Kong, Vietnam, India, Sri Lanka, and the Philippines have added to the cultural diversity and richness of this country. Indeed, in recent years, the entire face of the Canadian population has undergone a major change.

Cultural mosaic
Canadian ideal of encouraging each ethnic, racial, and social group to maintain own cultural heritage, forming a national mosaic of different cultures.

> According to the latest census results, for the first time in history, less than half of Canada's immigrants came from European countries. Currently, only 47 per cent of the total immigrants originate from Britain or other European countries.[35]

Unlike the American notion of the "melting pot," Canada has encouraged each ethnic minority to maintain its unique cultural heritage to form part of the Canadian

Canada's workplaces become more and more diverse as each ethnic minority is encouraged to maintain its unique cultural heritage.

Digital Imagery © 2000 Photo Disc Inc. Photo by Ryan McVay

cultural mosaic. Canada is no longer a two-language nation; millions of Canadians have neither English nor French as their language of origin.

> Today, almost five million Canadians are referred to as allophones, which literally means "other speaking." That is a 15 per cent increase over 1991, with Chinese surpassing Italian for the first time as the most common non-official language.[36]

For the practising manager, this cultural diversity simultaneously brings additional opportunities and challenges, some of which will be discussed in Chapter Thirteen. Often, it is the human resource department's responsibility to maximize the beneficial outcomes and minimize the challenges posed by a diverse workforce.

Attitudes Toward Governments

Historically, Canadians have always been far more positive than Americans to government participation in economic activities (even in the earliest days of Confederation, private and public capital was combined to create the Canadian Pacific Railway). In the past, issues such as government-funded health care and education were of higher importance to Canadians than for Americans.[37] However, in recent years, government has slowly fallen out of favour with many Canadians. "The notion that governments have the ability and wisdom to steer the economy is being dispelled. The growing view is that the government is just an economic facilitator that provides the appropriate infrastructure for prosperity."[38] This sentiment has already been reflected in basic attitudinal shifts in how the government and the public view unemployment insurance, family allowances, welfare payments, and the overall focus of regional development plans.

In the past, the Canadian national character was called a "conservative syndrome,"[39] to reflect Canadians' tendency to be guided by tradition and focus on maintenance of order and predictability. Canadians were said to be a hybrid product of several nationalities and ethnic groups "not quite as American as the Americans, not quite as British as the British ... and not quite as French as the French."[40] However, more recently, Canada's national self-image has changed somewhat (symbolized in the Charter of Rights and Freedoms, aggressive entry into foreign markets, reduced dependence on governmental programs). As a result, individuality and a kind of do-it-yourself attitude seem to be supplanting faith in government in the minds of many.

In summary, a fundamental shift is under way in how and where the world's work gets done, with potentially serious consequences for Canada. Today's "global village" requires major changes in the way managers—especially human resource managers—think and operate. Those Canadian firms that will succeed in the future will be the ones that can survive amid fierce global competition and successfully meet challenges posed by incessant and rapid changes in technology, changing social expectations, and the emergence of a diverse workforce. How critical human resource management is to face the new realities is discussed in the following pages.

www.ilr.cornell.edu

Attitudes toward governments
Basic assumptions on the role of government in business and society, including desirability of a welfare state with a key interventionist role for the government.

OBJECTIVES OF HUMAN RESOURCE MANAGEMENT

HUMAN RESOURCE MANAGEMENT *aims to improve the productive contribution of individuals while simultaneously attempting to attain other societal and individual employee objectives.* The field of human resource management thus focuses on what managers—especially human resource specialists—do and what they should do.

Improving the contribution of human resources is so ambitious and important that all but the smallest firms create specialized human resource departments to enhance the contributions of people.[41] It is ambitious because human resource departments do not control many of the factors that shape the employee's contribution, such as capital, materials, and technology. The department decides neither strategy nor the supervisor's treatment of employees, although it strongly influences both. Nevertheless, the role of human resource management is critical to the success—indeed, even the very survival—of the organization. Without a motivated and skilled workforce, and devoid of gains in employee productivity, organizations eventually stagnate and fail.

While the role of human resource departments (HRD) shows considerable variation across organizations, almost all HRDs carry out several common activities, including the following:

- assist the organization to attract the right quality and number of employees;

- orient new employees to the organization and place them in their job positions;

- develop, disseminate and use job descriptions, performance standards and evaluation criteria;

- help establish adequate compensation systems and administer them in an efficient and timely manner;

- foster a safe, healthy and productive work environment;

- ensure compliance with all legal requirements in so far as they relate to management of workforce;

- help maintain a harmonious working relationship with employees and unions where present;

- foster a work environment that facilitates high employee performance; and

- establish disciplinary and counselling procedures.

To guide its many activities, a human resource department must have objectives. Objectives are benchmarks against which actions are evaluated. These must be formulated after a detailed analysis of the organization and its environments. Human resource management in most organizations attempts to achieve three key objectives—organizational, societal, and employee.

Organizational Objectives

Organizational objectives
An organization's short- and long-term goals that the HR department aims to achieve.

The major aim of the human resource department is to contribute to organizational effectiveness. Human resource management is not an end in itself; it is a means of helping the organization to achieve its primary objectives. It should help an organization to identify the right quality, type, and number of employees. The importance of this function is illustrated by the following example where a change in employee selection procedure contributed to improved organizational effectiveness:

> The Atlantic Brewery always sought the best workers it could find. "Best" meant, among other things, the brightest and most reliable individuals. Usually, the company recruited students from surrounding schools and universities. With one job, however, this strategy created problems. The job required the worker to stand in the bottling plant eight hours a day inspecting beer bottles for damage. The work floor was damp, noisy, and full of fumes coming from the beer tanks. Employees usually quit within four months. Bright, ambitious persons found this simple, repetitive job boring. A possible solution was to assign this job to individuals with lower ambitions and career expectations, or to rotate the job assignment among several people in shorter shifts.

It should be emphasized that the contribution of a human resource department should be kept at a level appropriate to the organization's needs. Resources are wasted when the human resource department is more or less sophisticated than the organization demands. The department's level of service must be appropriate for the organization it serves. Cost-benefit analyses and systematic program reviews are vital to achieve this goal. This text provides sample measures for evaluating several HR activities such as recruitment, selection, training, and orientation in the following chapters.

Societal Objectives

Societal objectives
Societal priorities (e.g., lower pollution levels) that HR department targets while setting own objectives and strategies.

Human resource management should be responsive to the needs and challenges of society while minimizing the negative impact of such demands upon the organization. The failure of organizations to use their resources for society's benefit may result in restrictions being imposed on the organizations. In effect, society may pass laws that limit human resource decisions.

> For example, employees of many organizations are environmentally conscious. They demand that their employer recycle and reduce waste wherever possible. Everything from paper clips to large cardboard cartons or metal containers is routinely recycled in many organizations today. In some instances, employees' concern for their environment surpasses their concern for other tangible rewards.

Human resource strategies in such organizations will need to reflect society's ecological concerns.

Employee Objectives

Employee objectives
Goal set by HR department to assist employees to achieve personal goals that will enhance their contribution to the organization.

Human resource strategies should assist employees in achieving their personal goals, at least insofar as these goals enhance the individual's contributions to the organization. If employees' personal objectives are ignored, then worker performance may decline, or employees may even leave the organization.

The above three objectives are beacons that guide the strategies and day-to-day activities of human resource departments. However, not every human resource decision meets the above three objectives every time or in equal degree. Trade-offs do occur. The relative importance of the three objectives in any single situation is decided after a careful analysis of all relevant variables involved in the particular situation. But these objectives serve as a check on decisions. The more these objectives are met by the human resource department's actions, the better will be its contribution to the organization, its people, and the larger society.

STRATEGIC HUMAN RESOURCE MANAGEMENT

A STRATEGY IS similar to a game plan. In its earlier military sense a strategy involved the planning and directing of battles or campaigns on a broad scale. In an organizational setting, it involves large-scale, future-oriented, integrated plans to achieve organizational objectives and respond to uncertain and competitive environments facing the organization.

Strategies are typically formulated at three levels: *corporate,* involving the entire organization; *business,* involving a major activity, business, or division in a large multi-business organization; and *functional,* involving managers of different activities, services (e.g., finance, marketing), or geographical areas. Depending on organizational conditions, strategies may be developed at any or all of these three levels.

Strategies can vary significantly.

Thus, one organization's strategy may be to be a low-cost producer of a product, while another in the same industry may aim to produce a high-quality, higher-priced product that aims to satisfy a particular customer market. A firm may invest considerable resources in research and development to come out with new products while another may decide to focus on aggressive marketing of existing products.

Strategic human resource management

Integrating human resource management strategies and systems to achieve overall mission, strategies, and success of the firm while meeting needs of employees and other stakeholders.

Strategic human resource management is *systematically linked to the strategic needs of an organization and aims to provide it with an effective workforce while meeting the needs of its members and other constituents in the society.* In contrast to strategies, human resource departments also employ varying tactics periodically. *Tactics* are methods, procedures, or systems employed by human resource professionals to achieve specific strategies.

It is important that human resource strategies and tactics are mutually consistent. Even the best-laid strategies may fail if they are not accompanied by sound programs or procedures.

For example, a strategy of attracting and maintaining a technically qualified and innovative workforce is unlikely to be successful unless accompanied by sound hiring and training and development procedures.

Further, a human resource strategy should almost always reflect the larger organizational mission and strategy. When the human resource strategy and tactics accurately reflect organizational priorities, the results can be very positive. Consider Camco's experience:

The experience of Camco Inc., the country's largest appliance manufacturer, illustrates the importance of sound human resource management in raising employee productivity and organizational profits. After eight years of operation, Camco management decided to break its organizational chain of command and listen to its workers. The organization's structure became "flat" when every worker was encouraged to talk to everyone else. The results went beyond the most optimistic expectations. Employees made several recommendations that at first seemed not workable, but because of the commitment of employees, they became realities. For example, in the production of glass microwave shelves, the employees made a suggestion that was originally considered to be impractical, but when implemented it saved Camco $25 000 annually. Productivity improvement in just one year after the change was 25 per cent, and absenteeism was reduced by 30 per cent.[42]

Steps in Strategic Human Resource Management

Human resource management as a specialist function evolved from very small beginnings. (See Appendix A to this chapter for an outline of the growth of human resource functions over time.) What began as a role to assist employees to deal with their personal problems, such as housing and medical help, grew over a period of time to arrive at today's role where it is an integral part of the strategic position that an organization assumes—inseparable from key organizational goals, product-market plans, technology and innovation, and last but not least, an organization's strategy to respond to governmental and other pressures. Figure 1-8 outlines a strategic human resource management model that is used in this book.

To be effective, a human resource management strategy should be formulated after considering an organization's environment, mission and objectives, strategies, and internal strengths and weaknesses including its culture. Typically, the strategy formulation and implementation process consists of the six steps outlined below.

Step 1: Environmental Analysis

By careful and continuous monitoring of economic, social and labour market trends and noting changes in governmental policies, legislation, and public policy

FIGURE 1-8

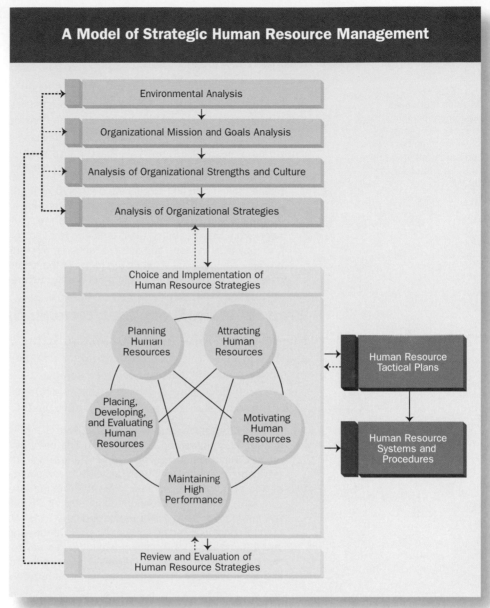

A Model of Strategic Human Resource Management

Note: Bold lines indicate primary effect or sequence. Dotted lines indicate secondary and feedback loop.

statements, a human resource manager will be able to identify environmental threats and opportunities that in turn help formulate new action guidelines:

> A large electric utility, sensing society's increasing concern about air pollution, decided to reduce coal burning and shift to hydro power. This in turn necessitated replacement of its plant and equipment as well as making major changes in its human resource strategy. Not only were new skills required, but the changeover from existing procedures and systems (e.g., compensation, appraisal, training) also had to be smooth and cause as little disruption to the work as possible. A strategy based on considerable in-house and external training was drawn up and implemented. By the time the utility switched to hydro power, it had the necessary supply of skilled labour.

www.hrdc-drhc.gc.ca/
maps/national/canada.shtml

Step 2: Organizational Mission and Goals Analysis

An organizational analysis, involving a close look at the organization's overall mission and goals, is a second integral aspect of identifying human resource strategies.

Even similar organizations often pursue different goals; however, some goals such as profitability (or revenue surplus), organizational growth, employee satisfaction, efficiency, adaptiveness to environmental changes, and so on are common across most Canadian organizations.

The way in which an organization defines its mission also significantly influences human resource strategies. A *mission statement* specifies what activities the organization intends to pursue and what course is charted for the future. It is a concise statement of "who we are, what we do, and where we are headed" and gives an organization its own special identity, character, and path of development.

Mission statement
Statement outlining the purpose, long-term objectives, and activities the organization will pursue and the course for the future.

> For example, two similar electronic manufacturers may have varying missions. One may define the mission as " to become a successful organization in the entertainment business," while the other may define it as "to occupy a technological leadership position in the industry." The associated strategies are likely to show significant differences. Apart from manufacturing electronic goods used for home entertainment, the former firm may acquire video and film production firms and get into the music industry (e.g., produce compact discs); while the focus of the second firm may be more committed to developing innovative electronic products through research and development.

Step 3: Analysis of Organizational Strengths and Culture

Human resource strategies should be formed only after a careful look at the strengths and weaknesses of the organization concerned and its culture. In the same way, organizational strategies that cannot be built on existing human resource capabilities should be avoided (unless it is possible to remove these deficiencies immediately either through training or selection of employees). Consider this example:

> Calgary Electronics, which employs 12 salespeople and seven service and repair personnel, was concerned about the growing competition in the electronics equipment market. Historically, the firm had sold and repaired all makes of electronic and electrical equipment (ranging from blenders to large-screen TV and complex security alarm systems). To meet the competition, the firm initially decided to implement an aggressive advertising and personal selling strategy. However, a detailed investigation into the company's past performance indicated that the strength of the firm lay in its prompt and cheap repair service. A review of the employee skills and training also indicated that several of the salespeople lacked any formal training in selling. Based on the results of the internal analysis, Calgary Electronics decided to focus on repairs and after-sales service in its advertising campaigns.

Organization character
The product of all the organization's features—people, objectives, technology, size, age, unions, policies, successes, and failures.

Every organization is unique. Similarities between organizations can be found among their parts, but each whole organization has a unique character. *Organization character* is the product of all the organization's features: its employees, its objectives, its technology, its size, its age, its unions, its policies, its successes, and its failures. Organization character reflects the past and shapes the future.[43] Human resource specialists should be clearly familiar with and adjust to the character of the organization. For example, it is sometimes overlooked that objectives can be achieved in several acceptable ways. This idea, called *equifinality*, means there are usually many paths to any given objective. The key to success is choosing the path that best fits the organization's character:

> Human resource manager Aaron Chu feared that his request to hire a training assistant would be turned down. So instead of asking for funds to hire someone, Aaron expressed concern that poor supervisory skills were contributing to employee complaints and some resignations. He observed at the weekly management meeting that unskilled replacements could lead to rising labour costs. Knowing that top management was concerned that the company remain a low-cost producer, Aaron was not surprised when the plant manager suggested hiring "someone to do training around here." Aaron received a budget increase for training. By adjusting to the organization's character, he achieved his objective.

The understanding of organization character is so critical for the success of a HR manager that this will be discussed in some greater depth later in this chapter.

Step 4: Analysis of Organizational Strategies

Even organizations with similar goals show remarkable differences in their strategies to achieve those goals. There are at least three major generic strategies that a firm may pursue: cost leadership, differentiation, or focus.[44]

Cost leadership strategy
Strategy to gain competitive advantage through lower costs of operations and lower prices for products.

Firms that pursue a *cost leadership strategy* aim to gain a competitive advantage through lower costs. They aggressively seek efficiencies in production and use tight controls (especially in managing costs) to gain an advantage over their competitors.

> The Bic Pen Company is a good example of a firm that attempts to compete successfully by producing pens as cheaply as possible. Similar cost leadership strategy is seen in the case of Timex (watches) and Federal Express (overnight package delivery).

Differentiation strategy
Strategy to gain competitive advantage by creating a distinct product or offering a unique service.

Product *differentiation strategy* focuses on creating a distinctive or even unique product that is unsurpassed in quality, innovative design, or other feature. This may be accomplished through product design, unique technology, or even through carefully planned advertising and promotion. Firms that use this strategy may even be able to charge higher-than-average prices for their products.

> Nikon (cameras) and Calvin Klein (fashion apparel) are firms that employ a differentiation strategy.

Focus strategy
Strategy to gain a competitive advantage by focusing on needs of a specific segment(s) of the total market.

Under the *focus strategy*, a firm concentrates on a segment of the market and attempts to satisfy it with a low-priced or a highly distinctive product. Within this specific market or target customer group, a focused firm may compete on the basis of either differentiation or cost leadership. The target market in this instance is usually set apart either by geography or by specialized needs.

> Honda sells Accord station wagons only in North America since Americans and Canadians seem to like station wagons more than people in other countries. The same firm sells its Civic in less developed countries because consumers there have lower disposable income.

Depending on the overall strategy employed by the firm, the human resource strategies will show substantial variation. (See Figure 1-9 for some variations in organizational priorities under the three strategies.)

Step 5: Choice and Implementation of Human Resource Strategies

Given the firm's objectives, strategies, and constraints, the human resource manager should examine each strategic option for its viability. Unsuitable strategic options must be dropped from consideration. The ones that appear viable should be scrutinized in detail for their advantages and weaknesses before being accepted for implementation. Some of the questions to ask at this time include:

- Are our assumptions realistic?
- Do we really have the skills and resources to make this strategy viable?
- Is this strategy consistent internally? Do the various elements of the strategy "hang together"?
- What are the risks? Can we afford them?
- What new actions must be taken to make the strategy viable?

FIGURE 1-9

Variations in HR Priorities and Practices under Different Competitive Strategies[45]

	Cost Leadership	Focus	Differentiation
Desired employee behaviours	Predictable, repetitive	Predictable, repetitive	Creative, innovative
Skill application by employees	Narrow	Moderate	Broad
Employee flexibility to change emphasized	Low	Moderate	High
Concern for quantity of production	High	Moderate	Moderate
Emphasis on training	Lower	Higher	Higher
Focus of employee performance appraisal procedures	Control	Mostly control; Some development	Employee development

Strategic choice and implementation involves identifying, securing, organizing, and directing the use of resources both within and outside the organization. Consider the following example:

> Maple Leaf Grocers Ltd., which operated grocery stores in six residential districts in a large metropolitan city, had followed a strategy of high volume, low margin, limited selection, and limited service in the past. Recently, a new grocery chain, Trans Canada Superstores, made a major breakthrough in several other cities by operating large warehouse-style stores with rock-bottom prices. The typical "superstore" was about three times as large as a Maple Leaf store, offered little service, but had considerably more variety of produce at prices that were 10 to 15 per cent lower. The superstore was planning to start a new unit close to where one of the Maple Leaf stores was situated. Unable to match the competitor's low prices and wider selection and not inclined to move to a new, more spacious location, the management at Maple Leaf decided to follow a new strategy based on superior customer service and "a family atmosphere." This required all cashiers and store personnel (including the store manager) to receive additional training in listening to and serving customers. Greater emphasis was placed on each employee knowing about all major products in at least three different store departments; special assistance was provided to the elderly and single parents who shopped there (the shop also allocated a portion of its floor space for a mini playpen). Store management and staff were actively encouraged to participate in community activities and to donate to neighbourhood parties and sports activities. When the superstore began operations in the area about a year later, Maple Leaf Grocers was able to retain over 80 per cent of its customers.

As the above example shows, the human resource strategy must reflect every change in the organizational strategy. In formulating strategies, the human resource department must continuously focus on the following five major groups of activities:

1. **Planning Human Resources.** A *job analysis* enables the human resource manager to collect important information about the various jobs, including required job behaviours and performance standards. *Human resource planning* enables the determination of demand and supply of various types of human resources within the firm. The results of job analysis and human resource plans shape the overall human resource strategies in the short run and facilitate employment and training planning.

www.hronline.com

2. **Attracting Human Resources.** In recruitment and selection of workers, a human resource manager should *meet all legal requirements* (e.g., equal employment opportunity laws, affirmative action policies). *Recruitment* is the process of finding and attracting capable job applicants and results in a pool of high-quality candidates. The *selection* process is a series of specific steps used to decide which recruits should be hired and aims to match job requirements with an applicant's capabilities.

3. **Placing, Developing, and Evaluating Human Resources.** Once hired, new employees need to be *oriented* to the organization's policies and procedures and placed in their new job positions. Since new workers seldom fit the organization's needs exactly, they must be *trained* to perform effectively. Employees must also be *developed* to prepare them for future responsibilities through systematic *career planning*.

   Performance appraisals give employees feedback on their performance and can help the human resource department identify future training needs. This activity also indicates how well human resource activities have been carried out since poor performance might often mean that selection or training activities need to be redesigned.

4. **Motivating Employees.** When employees perform acceptably, they must receive *compensation*. Some of the *employee benefits* are required (for example, Canada/Quebec Pension Plan), while several others are voluntary (for example, dental plans). Since *employee motivation* is also partially determined by internal work procedures, climate, and schedules, these must be continually modified to maximize performance.

5. **Maintaining High Performance.** The human resource strategy should ensure that the productive contribution from every member is at the maximum possible level. Most effective organizations have well-established *employee relations* practices including good communication between managers and employees, standardized disciplinary procedures, and counselling systems. In today's work setting, internal work procedures and organizational policies must be continuously monitored to ensure that they meet the needs of a *diverse workforce* and ensure *safety* to every individual. In many organizations, employees may decide to join together and form self-help groups called unions. When this occurs, management is confronted with a new situation, *union-management relations*. To respond to the collective demands by employees, human resource specialists may have to negotiate a collective agreement and administer it.

Strategic choice and implementation involves an examination of the entire management philosophy, the formal and informal organizational structures, and the climate of the organization. It should also pay close attention to the organization's history, culture, and overall character. To be effective, a strategy should also have clearly defined action plans with target achievement dates (see Figure 1-10). Otherwise, it will simply end up being an exercise on paper.

Step 6: Review and Evaluation of Human Resource Strategies

Human resource strategies, however effective they prove to be, must be examined periodically. An organization's contextual factors, such as technology, environments, government policies, and so on, change continuously; so do several of its internal factors, such as membership characteristics, role definitions, and internal procedures. All these changes necessitate periodic strategy evaluation to ensure their continued appropriateness.

This evaluation process produces *feedback*, which is information that helps evaluate success or failure. Consider the situation faced by Natalie Marchand, human resources manager at Municipal General Hospital:

FIGURE 1-10

Metro Hospital's Strategic Approach to Human Resource Management

Background Information

Metro Hospital, a large hospital in a major Canadian city, currently faces an 18 per cent turnover among its nursing staff. In fact, the turnover among nurses has been on the increase in the last two years. Kim Cameron, the hospital's newly appointed human resource manager, would like to reverse this trend and bring down the turnover rate to under 5 per cent in the near future. As a first step, she looked through all available company records to find out more about the background of nurses who left the organization. She interviewed 14 nurses who had left the hospital recently and another 10 nurses who are currently employed in the hospital. Here are some of Cameron's findings:

- 40 per cent of the nurses who left the hospital commented that their supervisors did not "treat them well"; only about 25 per cent of the nurses who are with the hospital currently made the same comment;

- six of the nurses who left and five of the present staff complained that the heating and air-conditioning systems in the hospital do not work well so that it is very hot inside the hospital in the summer months and too cold in the winter;

- 55 per cent of those whom she talked to said that the fringe benefits in the hospital were not as good as elsewhere, while the salary level was found to be similar to those available elsewhere; and

- research of hospital records indicated that only about 10 per cent of the nursing supervisors had undergone any type of supervisory leadership skills training in the past.

Kim Cameron's Objective

After her initial research, Kim Cameron identified the following as one of her major objectives for the immediate future: "To reduce the turnover among nursing staff from the present 18 per cent to 4 per cent by July 1, 2002, by incurring costs not exceeding $—— (at current dollars)."

Kim Cameron's Overall Strategy

To achieve the above goal, Kim Cameron realized that it was critical that the overall job satisfaction of nurses (especially their satisfaction with supervisors, working conditions, and rewards) be monitored and improved (if necessary). She set out the following action plans for the immediate future for herself and others in her department.

Kim Cameron's Action Plans

Action Number	Action Description	Person Responsible for Action	Date by which Action to be Completed	Budget Allocated
1.	Conduct an attitude survey among all nurses; collect information on their attitudes toward their job, supervisor, pay, benefits, working conditions, and colleagues	Asst. HRM	31–3–2001	$5000
2.	Identify steps for improving morale among nurses	Self (in consultation with others)	30–5–2001	——
3.	Ask physical plant to check condition of A/C and heating systems	Self	25–1–2001	——
4.	Complete training program for 50 percent of nursing supervisors	Training Manager	15–2–2002	$9000
5.	(Depending on the survey findings, other actions that have to be initiated			
6.	will be listed here.)			

A predicted shortage of medical technologists caused Natalie to start an in-house development program to prepare six lab assistants to become licensed medical technologists. After 15 months, they finished the program and passed the provincial certification test. Since the program was a success and the shortage had grown worse, eight more lab assistants were recruited for the second program.

The objective here was to achieve the organizational objective of finding qualified medical technologists. The strategy employed by the human resource manager was an in-house development program. When all six technologists passed the provincial certification test, those results provided feedback that the strategy was a success.

Proactive Human Resource Management Strategies

Strategic human resource management often enables an organization to anticipate a problem and respond to it before it can cause serious damage to the organization. For example, reconsider Natalie Marchand's situation when she learned of the impending shortage of technologists:

> Natalie Marchand: My department budget must be increased by $20 000 so we can train more technologists.
>
> Anna Newman: Hold on! The municipality has put a freeze on the hospital budget for six months and as director of administrative services my hands are tied. Why not wait until we can show the Municipal Council complaints from the doctors? Then the shortage will be real and we can get the board to react to it now.
>
> Natalie Marchand: But then we will probably have to spend $25 000 for training. We will probably have to pay another $30 000 for overtime to the technologists we now have while we train new ones. Besides, with all that overtime, error rates will jump and so will lawsuits for faulty lab work. All I need is $20 000, but I need it now.

Anna was suggesting that Natalie's department wait until an actual problem occurred and then react. Natalie wanted to take action in anticipation of the problem without waiting for the feedback of doctors' complaints or lawsuits. Anna's approach to this human resource challenge was *reactive*, while Natalie's was proactive.

Reactive human resource management occurs when decision-makers respond to human resource problems. *Proactive* human resource management occurs when human resource problems are anticipated and corrective action begins before the problem exists. For example:

> A large electronics firm uses contract labour to staff its human resource needs during periods of peak business activity. During peak demand, some of the workers it uses will be contracted from a temporary help agency. Not only can the agency provide extra staff more quickly, but these agency workers also do not become the firm's employees. The result is that the human resource department is able to meet the staffing needs of its divisions while providing high levels of employment security to its own employees.

The policy of using contract labour is another example of how proactive strategies can better meet the needs of organizations. In the example of the electronics firm, the human resource department did not wait for the economy to go up or down and then react. Rather, it developed strategies that allowed the organization to adjust smoothly to changes caused by technology, the economy, and other factors beyond its control.

Reactive
A management approach wherein decision-makers *respond* to problems rather than anticipate them.

Proactive
A management approach wherein decision-makers anticipate problems and likely challenges and take action before a problem occurs.

THE ORGANIZATION OF HUMAN RESOURCE MANAGEMENT

THE RESPONSIBILITY for human resource management (HRM) activities rests with each manager. If a manager does not accept this responsibility, then human resource activities may be done only partially or not at all. When a manager finds that HRM work seriously disrupts other responsibilities, this work may be reassigned. The assignment might be to a worker or a specialized department that handles human resource matters. This process of getting others to share the work is called *delegation*. But delegation requires the manager to assign duties, grant authority, and create a sense of responsibility; if these three elements are not explained clearly to the delegate, delegation often fails. And even though others may have been asked to handle human resource activities, the manager still remains responsible. Delegation does not reduce a manager's responsibility; it only allows the sharing of that responsibility with others.

> For example, many managers ask a senior worker to train new employees. However, if the senior worker errs and the new employee makes a costly mistake, the manager will appropriately be held responsible by superiors.

A separate department usually emerges only when human resource activities would otherwise become a burden to other departments in the organization—that is, when the expected benefits of a human resource department usually exceed its costs. Until then, managers handle human resource activities themselves or delegate them to subordinates. When a human resource department emerges, it is typically small and reports to some middle-level manager. Figure 1-11 illustrates a common placement of a human resource department at the time it is first formed. The activities of such a department are usually limited to maintaining employee records and helping managers find new recruits. Whether the department performs other activities depends upon the needs of other managers in the firm.

As demands on the department grow, it increases in importance and complexity. Figure 1-12 demonstrates the increased importance by showing the head of human resources reporting directly to the chief operating officer, who is the company president in this figure. The greater importance of the head of human resources may be signified by a change in title to vice-president. In practice, increased complexity also

FIGURE 1-11

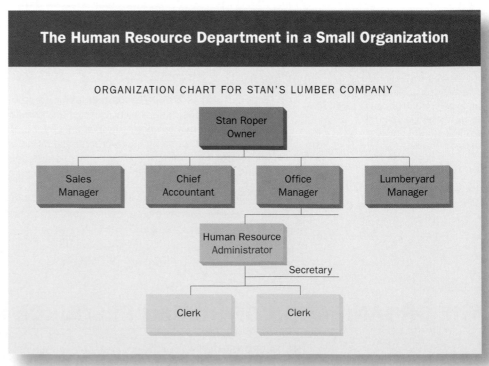

The Human Resource Department in a Small Organization

ORGANIZATION CHART FOR STAN'S LUMBER COMPANY

Stan Roper
Owner

Sales Manager

Chief Accountant

Office Manager

Lumberyard Manager

Human Resource Administrator

Secretary

Clerk

Clerk

FIGURE 1-12

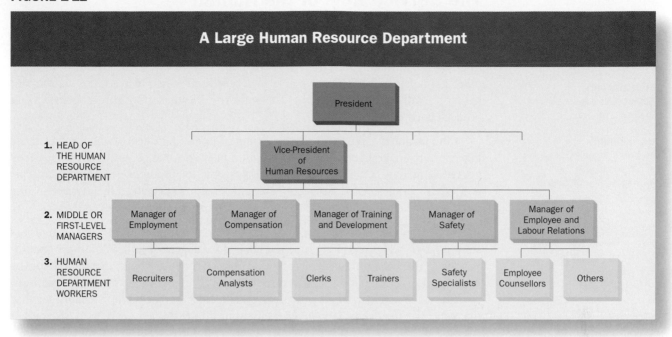

A Large Human Resource Department

1. HEAD OF THE HUMAN RESOURCE DEPARTMENT

2. MIDDLE OR FIRST-LEVEL MANAGERS

3. HUMAN RESOURCE DEPARTMENT WORKERS

President

Vice-President of Human Resources

Manager of Employment
Manager of Compensation
Manager of Training and Development
Manager of Safety
Manager of Employee and Labour Relations

Recruiters
Compensation Analysts
Clerks
Trainers
Safety Specialists
Employee Counsellors
Others

results as the organization grows and new demands are placed on the department, or jobs in the department become more specialized. As the department expands and specializes, it may become organized into highly specialized subdepartments.

The size of the human resource department varies widely, depending largely on the size of the organization being supported. One study reported a high ratio of workers to human resource employees of 277 to 1. The low ratio in that study was 29:1.[46] Another study reported an average of 36 human resource professionals per 1000 employees for a ratio of 28:1.[47] By and large, a ratio of 1:100 (i.e., 1 human resource staff to 100 employees) may be adequate in most settings.

Departmental Components

The subdepartments of a large human resource department approximately correspond with the activities already mentioned. For each major activity, a subdepartment may be established to provide the specialized service, as shown in Figure 1-12. The employment department assists other managers with recruiting and selection. The compensation manager establishes fair pay systems. The training and development manager provides guidance and programs for those managers who want to improve their human resources. Other activity managers contribute their expertise and usually report directly to the head of human resources. This specialization allows members of the department to become extremely knowledgeable in a limited number of activities.

Activities not shown in Figure 1-12 are shared among the different sections. For example, employment, training, and development managers may share in human resource planning and placement. Performance appraisals are used to determine pay, and so the compensation division may assist managers in appraising performance. Required services fall to the benefits and safety sections. Control activities (communications and counselling) are divided among all subdepartments, with employee and labour relations doing much of the work. Employee and labour relations sections also provide the official union-management coordination.

The Service Role of the Human Resource Department

Staff authority
Authority to advise, but not to direct, others.

Line authority
Authority to make decisions about production, performance, and people.

Functional authority
Authority that allows staff experts to make decisions and take actions normally reserved for line managers.

Human resource departments are service departments. They exist to assist employees, managers, and the organization. Their managers do not have the authority to order other managers in other departments to accept their ideas. Instead, the department has only *staff authority*, which is the authority to advise, not direct, managers in other departments.

Line authority, possessed by managers of operating departments, allows these managers to make decisions about production, performance, and people. It is the operating managers who normally are responsible for promotions, job assignments, and other people-related decisions. Human resource specialists merely advise line managers, who alone are ultimately responsible for employee performance.

Sample job responsibilities of line and human resource managers in key areas are summarized in Figure 1-13. While the list is not exhaustive and will require modifications to meet the unique needs of an individual organization, it does highlight the importance of human resource responsibilities of all managers. In most organizations, human resource departments provide the technical expertise while line managers use this expertise to effectively manage their subordinates.

In highly technical or extremely routine situations, the human resource department may be given *functional authority*. Functional authority gives the department the right to make decisions usually made by line managers or top management. For example, decisions about fringe benefits are technically complex, so the top manager may give the human resource department the functional authority to decide the type of benefits offered employees. If each department manager made separate decisions about benefits, there might be excessive costs and inequities. To provide control, uniformity, and the use of expertise, functional authority allows human resource specialists to make crucial decisions effectively.

The size of the department affects the type of service provided to employees, managers, and the organization. In small departments, the human resource manager handles many of the day-to-day activities related to the organization's human resource needs. Other managers bring their problems directly to the head of human resources, and these meetings constantly remind the human resource manager of the contribution expected.

When the human resource function grows larger, more problems are handled by subordinates. Not only do human resource managers have less contact with lower-level managers, but others in the department become increasingly specialized. At this point, human resource managers and their subordinates may lose sight of the overall contributions expected of them or the limits on their authority. Experts sometimes become more interested in perfecting their specialty than in asking how they may serve others. While improving their expertise, they may fail to uncover new ways of serving the organization and its employees. Consider what happened at a fast-growing maker of minicomputers:

> For the past five years, Imaxum Computers Ltd. had grown at an average rate of 25 per cent a year. To keep up with this growth, the HR department manager, Earl Bates, used budget increases to hire new recruits. His strategy meant that the human resource department was well prepared to find new employees. But recruiting specialists paid little attention to other human resource problems. In one month, three of the company's best computer design engineers quit to go to work for a competitor. Before they left, they were interviewed. They complained that they saw desirable job openings being filled by people recruited from outside the organization. No design

FIGURE 1-13

Sample Job Responsibilities of Line and Human Resource Managers

Sample Activity	Line Manager	Human Resource Manager
Human Resource Planning	Provide details of all job positions and associated skills needed to human resource manager. Identify training needs of employees and communicate to the human resource department.	All activities associated with human resource planning. More specifically: • Translate organization needs into forecast of people required (both type and number). • Forecast potential supply of qualified workers from internal and external sources. • Plan strategies to match supply with demand.
Job Analysis	Provide all necessary data to conduct job analysis. Identify performance standards and communicate to human resource department. Collaborate with the human resource manager in preparation of job description and specifications.	Conduct job analysis. Prepare job description and specification in collaboration with the line manager.
Recruitment and Selection	Provide details of performance standards and job success and skill factors. Interview job applicants. Integrate the information collected by HR department and make a final decision on hires.	Ensure compliance with human rights laws and organization's policy on employment equity. Plan and actual conduct of all activities related to hiring, interviewing, and communication with job applicants.
Development and Evaluation	Provide on-the-job training. Provide orientation to the job and co-workers. Implement job enrichment and enlargement programs. Offer timely and valid appraisal of subordinates and communication to the human resource department. Promote and transfer employees using agreed-upon criteria. Coach subordinates.	Facilitate accurate and timely appraisal. Provide orientation to the organization and its policies. Arrange for technical and management development programs. Offer organizational development activities. Develop valid appraisal programs in collaboration with line managers. Keep accurate records of each employee's skills, past training, and work accomplishments and make these available to line managers. Offer career counselling to employees.
Compensation and Safety	Decide on pay raises to employees on the basis of merit or other agreed-upon criteria. Provide technical safety training. Enforce all safety regulations. Ensure fair treatment of employees. Provide all necessary data for accurate job evaluation.	Oversee compensation policy and administration. Provide safety training and ensure compliance with safety rules. Provide job evaluation. Offer retirement counselling. Oversee benefit planning and administration.
Employee and Labour Relations	Ensure noise-free communication to employees. Discipline and discharge from own unit after due warnings. Implement motivational strategies. Implement organizational change. Coach employees. Provide conflict resolution. Promote teamwork.	Conduct employee surveys to assess satisfaction with organizational policies and initiate corrective actions. Provide outplacement service. Offer career counselling. Establish grievance handling procedures. Negotiate with unions. Initiate organizational change efforts.

engineer had been promoted to supervisor in three years. So each of these engineers found jobs where the promotion possibilities looked better.

When Earl reminded these engineers that they lacked experience or training as supervisors, one of them commented that the company should have provided such training. As a result, when the HR department received its next budget increase, Earl hired a specialist in employee training and development.

The human resource manager and the recruiting specialists at Imaxum Computers overlooked the variety of activities that their department is supposed to perform. And they failed to identify the services that the organization needs from the human resource department. They also did not recognize the connection between different human resource management activities.

To be effective, human resource specialists must determine the areas of concern of different levels of management and different departments of the organization. Otherwise, their advisory authority will be less effective and more likely ignored.

Human Resource Function and the Organization Character

Every organization has a unique history and way of doing business. As already pointed out, organization character refers to the sum of an organization's history, culture, philosophy and unique ways of doing things. To be effective, a human resource manager must recognize the organizational character and the constraints imposed by it on its own function. Three factors that are related to an organization's character are particularly noteworthy here:

Technology

The technology employed by different firms shows considerable variation. In organizations such as a large steel factory or lumber mill, the production processes are fairly routine. In several such organizations, improving predictability of operations assumes great importance. This often requires human resource managers to focus more on predictability of employee performance (e.g., by providing explicit job descriptions, job specific training and focusing on performance monitoring). In contrast, in firms with nonroutine production processes (such as advertising firms, software developers), flexible human resource practices that foster creativity, innovation, and entrepreneurship may add more value.

Managerial Philosophy

Often, several key managerial decisions and values are a "given" for the human resource manager. There are several organizations where the top management may follow an autocratic decision-making style and foster a strong organizational hierarchy. In contrast, there are other organizations that consciously make an effort to create an egalitarian, participative, and entrepreneurial work climate. HR practices such as seniority and rank-based pay and top-down communication channels are likely to work best in the former situation while result-oriented (and competency based) pay and up-and-down communication channels are likely to work best in the latter instance. The managerial philosophy also influences the type of organization structure and HR department's role within the firm. For instance, in a highly formal bureaucracy that is structured along functional lines (e.g., marketing, finance, production, etc.), HR's role is often to preserve the existing division of work through clear job descriptions, hiring of specialists for each division, and introducing training systems that foster functional expertise. In contrast, in organizations that have flexible structures, socialization of employees to create an organization-wide perspective, creation of broad job classes, etc. may assume greater importance.

Organization's Strategic Posturing

In the preceding pages, we looked at the impact of strategic differences on the role of human resource function. Organizations differ on other strategic dimensions as well. For example, some organizations are *defenders*[48]—or conservative business units that prefer to maintain a secure position in relatively stable product or service areas instead of attempting to expand into unchartered territories. In contrast, some other organizations are *prospectors* that emphasize growth, entrepreneurship, and an eagerness to be the first players in a new market or selling a new product, even if some of these efforts fail. Human resource managers in a defender organization are more likely to be asked to support control systems, emphasize reliability and predictability in operations, and foster employee policies that encourage long-term employee attachment to the firm. In contrast, human resource managers in prospector organizations are more likely to be asked to foster a flexible, decentralized organization structure, emphasize creativity and adaptability, and support systems that reward risk taking and performance.

Before concluding this section it should be emphasized that human resource management is the management of people. Thus, human resource management should be done professionally—in fact, humanely! The importance and dignity of human beings should not be ignored for the sake of expediency. Only through careful attention to the needs of employees do organizations grow and prosper.

THE HUMAN RESOURCE MANAGEMENT PROFESSION OF THE FUTURE

IN THE LAST decade or so, there has been an enormous growth in the number of human resource managers. In 1971, there were only 4055 human resource managers in this country; in 1999, the corresponding number was estimated to be over 43 000.[49] However, the status of human resource professionals within organizations historically has not been high. In a national survey of chief human resources officers, it was found that only 60 per cent of respondents report directly to the chief executive officers and only 62 per cent were members of their organization's executive committee.[50]

Thus, despite its enormous growth, human resource management has been slow to evolve into a full-fledged profession. Until recently in many Canadian provinces, there were no minimum qualifications for practising as a human resource professional. Since the actual capability of practising human resource experts varies widely, it became increasingly evident that professionalism of the human resource management field was needed. To meet these ever-increasing challenges, human resource managers were expected to possess a number of competencies, including the following:[51]

- **Business Mastery**: HR professionals must know the business of their organization thoroughly and recognize and incorporate financial and economic realities into their analyses and decisions. They should understand and foster customer orientation and be familiar with external realities and challenges facing the organization and the larger industry.

- **Mastery of Human Resource Management Tools**: As professionals, they should be familiar with state-of-the-art tools in areas such as staffing, training, compensation planning, performance appraisal and planning, employee relations and communication, and organizational change interventions.

- **Change Mastery**: Not only should HR professionals possess an abundance of problem solving, critical thinking, negotiation and interpersonal skills, but they should also be well versed in using these to bring about changes in the organization and its various subsystems.

- **Personal Credibility**: The HR professional should project an image of a trustworthy, ethical, socially responsive, courageous leader who can build relationships and inspire others to work for larger causes.

www.hrpao.org

www.chrpcanada.com

Certified Human Resources Professional (CHRP)
Human resource practitioner, formally accredited to practise, who reflects a threshold professional level of practice.

To achieve this goal, accreditation and/or certification of the HR professional was considered as an imperative. At present, several provincial human resource associations including those in British Columbia, Alberta, Saskatchewan, Manitoba, Ontario, Quebec, and Nova Scotia offer certification programs. The *Certified Human Resources Professional (CHRP)* designation is currently available in these provinces. However, "there is considerable lack of uniformity across Canada in the designation granting process in key areas such as certification, membership criteria, skills and competencies required, renewal/recertification procedures and fee structures."[52] For example, in Ontario, the certification is based on a candidate successfully completing specific academic requirements, passing a comprehensive examination, and having three years' managerial experience. In British Columbia, a greater number of years of work experience is typically expected, especially for candidates with lower levels of formal education. The requirements in other provinces also show variations. The result has been that "the CHRP designation lacks the market designation that a number of other professional designations enjoy."[53]

This disparity has resulted in a move towards a set of uniform national standards for HR practitioners. The Canadian Council of Human Resource Associations (CCHRA) is a collaborative effort of Human Resource Associations across Canada that currently represent the interests of all HR practitioners in this country. Apart from establishing national core standards, CCHRA also fosters communication among participating associations and provides a national and international collective voice on human resource issues.

In the recent past, CCHRA has undergone a series of national consultations with employers, human resource professionals, and researchers in the human resource field to arrive at a set of "required professional capabilities" (RPCs) in key HR areas such as compensation, staffing, and employee relations apart from possessing skills in fundamental business areas, such as accounting (see Figure 1-14). The viability of a comprehensive assessment process was successfully tested in Nova Scotia in 1999. When completed, CCHRA aims to have an economically viable, nationally recognized assessment process that supports regional (or provincial) CHRP granting and renewal processes. These standards will be applicable to the HR profession all over the country and will recognize the knowledge and skill requirements needed for different settings.

For human resource staff in the civil service and government organizations, the *Certified Canadian Human Resource Professional (CCHRP)* designation is granted on the basis of academic and/or professional work experience in the HRM area. In this case the accreditation body is the Canadian Public Personnel Management Association, which is based in Ottawa.

Certification alone does not make human resource management a profession or improve its status in the eyes of organizations. One approach to improving the human resource manager's status within the organization may be to strengthen the position's contribution to the enhancement of organizational performance and effectiveness. This is already beginning to take place. The higher status given to human resource

FIGURE 1-14

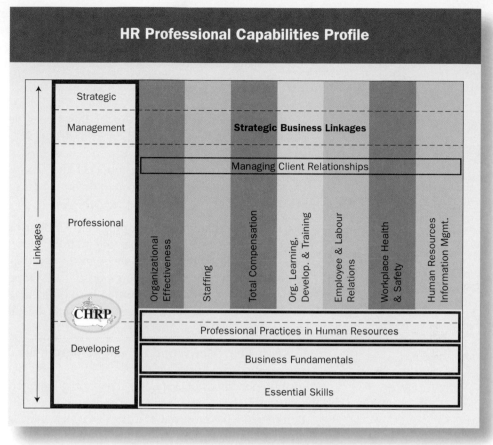

HR Professional Capabilities Profile

experts in want ads and organizational charts indicates that the importance of human resource management activity is being recognized.

The typical business of tomorrow may bear little resemblance to that of 30 or 40 years ago. "It will be knowledge based, an organization composed largely of specialists who direct and discipline their own performance through organized feedback from colleagues, customers and headquarters."[54] The typical organization will be information based where the intellectual capital (that is, the knowledge and expertise possessed by the employees) will spell success or failure. Already, jobs today demand a level of expertise unimagined 30 years ago. For managers, the challenge of managing intellectual capital lies in the fact that today's knowledge workers must be managed differently than in the past. New HR strategies, systems, and procedures are a must to succeed in this context. Continuous upgrading of own skills and fostering an attitude of continuous learning may separate the superior HR manager from the mediocre one in future.

THE FRAMEWORK USED IN THIS BOOK

THIS TEXT IS divided into seven parts.

Part One: The Strategic Human Resource Management Model offers a strategic model of managing human resources in Chapter One. The key objectives of the human resource function are outlined here along with the steps in implementing a strategic HR approach in practice.

Part Two: Planning Human Resources is contained in two chapters. Chapter Two deals with the important topic of job analysis—detailing the various methods of collecting data about jobs, the steps involved in writing job descriptions and job specifications and setting performance standards. Chapter Three discusses the various factors that need to be considered when planning the supply and demand for human resources in organizations.

Part Three: Attracting Human Resources deals with the various steps in acquiring human resources. Chapter Four details key provisions of human rights legislation and the Canadian Constitution along with their implications for hiring employees. Chapters Five (Recruitment) and Six (Selection) deal with the various tools, options, and strategies open to the human resource manager in attracting and selecting qualified applicants for the job.

Part Four: Placing, Developing, and Evaluating Human Resources deals with all key activities involved in orienting, training, developing, and evaluating employees. Chapter Seven outlines the key steps involved in the orientation and training of employees; Chapter Eight focuses on the development of employees to take on greater responsibilities in the future including career counselling to staff. Chapter Nine deals with various appraisal techniques that help an organization to monitor and improve employee performance.

Part Five: Motivating Human Resources discusses the critical tasks of motivating and rewarding employees. Chapter Ten deals with direct compensation, including methods of evaluating the worth of each job and the incentive schemes currently available. Chapter Eleven discusses how careful planning enables an organization to make the most out of its benefits package. Chapter Twelve deals with various work options and other arrangements that have implications for employee motivation.

Part Six: Maintaining High Performance focuses on the various human resource actions to ensure high performance. Chapter Thirteen details the methods of improving communication and enforcing discipline when employees violate organizational policies. Chapter Fourteen deals with the special challenges of managing a diverse workforce. Chapter Fifteen discusses two types of security offered by modern human resource departments: financial and physical. Chapter Sixteen discusses strategies for dealing with unions and outlines the human resource manager's role during negotiations with unions.

Part Seven: Strategy Evaluation deals with the various approaches to assess the effectiveness of human resource strategy. The final chapter in this book discusses how a human resource department's contribution—and the effectiveness of its strategy—can be evaluated. Indices that measure an organization's success in human resource management are listed along with strategies for collecting data in each case.

SUMMARY

The central challenge for organizations today is to survive and prosper in a very turbulent world. To do this, most organizations find it necessary to maintain high productivity and effectiveness levels and have a global focus. Strategic management of organizations is suggested as one method for coping with this environmental turbulence. **Human resource management** *aims to improve the productive contribution of individuals while simultaneously attempting to attain other societal and individual* *employee objectives.* The field of human resource management thus focuses on what managers—especially human resource specialists—do and what they should do. While the role of human resource departments (HRD) shows considerable variation across organizations, almost all HRDs carry out several common activities. These include:

- assist the organization to attract the right quality and number of employees;

- orient new employees to the organization and place them in their job positions;

- develop, disseminate and use job descriptions, performance standards and evaluation criteria;

- help establish adequate compensation systems and administer them in an efficient and timely manner;

- foster a safe, healthy and productive work environment;

- ensure compliance with all legal requirements insofar as they relate to management of workforce;

- help maintain a harmonious working relationship with employees and unions where present;

- foster a work environment that facilitates high employee performance; and

- establish disciplinary and counselling procedures.

Human resource departments in most organizations have three major objectives: to contribute to organizational effectiveness, to be responsive to larger societal concerns, and to meet the personal needs of its employees. It was pointed out that human resource management is the responsibility of every manager. The human resource department provides a service to other departments in the organization. In the final analysis, however, the performance and well-being of each worker is the dual responsibility of that worker's immediate supervisor and the human resource department.

Strategic human resource management is *systematically linked to the strategic needs of an organization and aims to provide it with an effective workforce while meeting the needs of its members and other constituents in the society.* In contrast to strategies, human resource departments also employ varying tactics periodically. *Tactics* are methods, procedures, or systems employed by human resource professionals to achieve specific strategies. It is important that human resource strategies and tactics are mutually consistent. Even the best-laid strategies may fail if they are not accompanied by sound programs or procedures.

Strategic human resource management necessitates an exhaustive evaluation of an organization's internal and external environments. Factors that should be reviewed before formulating human resource strategies were discussed. These include economic, technological, demographic, and cultural challenges. Continuous evaluation of strategy and proactive management were pointed out as critical to ensure successful management of human resources.

The profession of human resource management has undergone rapid changes in recent years as well. In some provinces, an accreditation process now exists that ensures all human resource professionals possess minimum standards of expertise. While this will certainly elevate the status of the profession in the long term, the status of the function within an organization is likely to be determined by its contribution to the organization's overall success. Strategic management of human resources may be one key to this success.

TERMS FOR REVIEW

Visit the Web site at www.mcgrawhill.ca/college/schwind6 for a full glossary.

REVIEW AND DISCUSSION QUESTIONS

1. What are the goals of a human resource department? Choose an organization that you are familiar with and indicate which of these goals will be more important in this organization and discuss why.

2. Draw a diagram of a human resource department in a firm that employs over 5000 persons and name the likely components of such a department. Which of these functions are likely to be eliminated in a small firm employing 50 persons?

3. Identify and briefly describe three major external challenges (choosing one each from economic, technological, and demographic categories) facing human resource managers in Canada, and their implications.

4. Outline the three major strategies pursued by Canadian businesses. What implications do they have for the human resource function within the firms? Illustrate your answer with suitable examples.

5. What are four trends (or attributes) in the Canadian labour market that have implications for a human resource manager? Explain your answer, citing which of the human resource functions will be affected and how.

CRITICAL THINKING QUESTIONS

1. Suppose your employer is planning a chain of high-quality restaurants to sell food products that it already produces. Outline what areas of human resource management will be affected.

2. If a bank is planning to open a new branch in a distant city, with what inputs will the human resource department be concerned? What activities will the department need to undertake in the transition to a fully staffed and operating branch? What type of feedback do you think the department should seek after the branch has been operating for six months?

3. Find two recent news items and explain how these developments might affect the demands made on the human resource department of an organization.

4. Suppose the birthrate during the early 2000s was to double from the low rates of the 1990s. What implications would this growth have in the years 2020 and 2030 for (a) grocery stores, (b) fast-food restaurants, (c) Canadian Armed Forces, (d) large metropolitan universities?

5. Assume you were hired as the human resource manager in a firm that historically gave low importance to the function. Most of the human resource management systems and procedures in the firm are outdated. Historically, this function was given a low-status, "record-keeping" role within the firm. Armed with sophisticated HR training, you recently entered the firm and want to upgrade the HR systems and status of the department. In other words, you want to make the management recognize the true importance of sound HR practices for strategic success. What actions will you take in the short and long term to achieve your goal? Be specific in your action plans and illustrate your steps where relevant.

WEB RESEARCH

Select three jobs: one knowledge-based, one manufacturing, and one in the service sector. Based on your search of Web sites of Human Resource Development Canada (www.hrdc-drhc.ca), Statistics Canada (www.statcan.ca), and other relevant Web sources, what patterns in employment and job vacancies do you see? What are the implications for large human resource departments in these industries?

INCIDENT 1-1

Human Resource Decision Making at Calgary Importers Ltd.

Calgary Importers Ltd. is a large importer of linens, china, and crystal. It has branch offices in six provinces and has long been plagued by problems in its human resource practices. These problems led to the following discussion between the vice-president of human resources and the vice-president of distribution:

Rob Whittier: You may not agree with me, but if we are going to have consistency in our human resource policies, then key decisions about those policies must be centralized in the human resource department. Otherwise, branch managers will continue to make their own decisions focusing on different aspects. Besides, the department has the experts. If you needed financial advice, you would not ask your doctor; you would go to a banker or other financial expert. When it comes to deciding compensation packages or hiring new employees, those decisions should be left to experts in salary administration or selection. To ask a branch manager or supervisor to make those decisions deprives our firm of all of the expertise we have in the department.

Henri DeLahn: I have never questioned your department's expertise. Sure, the people in human resources are more knowledgeable than the line managers. But if we want those managers to be responsible for the performance of their branches, then we must not deprive those managers of their authority to make human resource decisions. Those operating managers must be able to decide whom to hire and whom to reward with raises. If they cannot make those decisions, then their effectiveness as managers will suffer.

1. If you were the president of Calgary Importers Ltd. and were asked to resolve this dispute, whose argument would you agree with? Why?

2. Can you suggest a compromise that would allow line managers to make these decisions consistently?

INCIDENT 1-2

Canadian Bio-Medical Instruments Ltd.

Canadian Bio-Medical Instruments Ltd., founded 10 years ago, manufactures a variety of bio-medical instruments used by physicians and surgeons both in their clinics as well as in hospitals. The high quality of its products led to quick market success, especially for products such as artificial heart valves, operating-room pumps, and respiratory modules. The company, which had sales of less than $900 000 in the first year, today enjoys an annual turnover of $150 million. However, the industry is competitive and the research development and promotional budgets of some of the key players in the industry are several times that of the firm.

Given the successful track record for its existing products and the competitiveness of the North American market, the management of the firm believed that gaining new market shares in Europe was easier than expanding against well-entrenched domestic producers. Preliminary market studies supported management's thinking.

A decision was made to open a small sales office in Europe, probably in Frankfurt, Germany, given the nonstop flight facilities that currently exist from Toronto where the firm's head office is located. Three persons were sent to Germany to identify possible office sites and to learn about European testing procedures and what documentation would be legally required to prove the safety and effectiveness of the company's medical instruments. All three persons were fluent in German. If the reports on Germany are favourable, the firm expects to have about 20 persons working in Europe within the next year.

1. Assume you are the vice-president in charge of human resources. What additional information would you want these three employees to find out?

2. What human resource issues or policies are you likely to confront in the foreseeable future?

CASE STUDY

Maple Leaf Shoe Company Ltd.: A Strategic Management Exercise[1]

Maple Leaf Shoe Company Ltd. is a medium-sized manufacturer of leather and vinyl shoes located near Wilmington, Ontario. It began operations in 1969 and currently employs about 400 persons in its Ontario plant and 380 others in offices and warehouses across Canada and internationally.

[1] *Case Prepared by Professor Hari Das of Department of Management, Saint Mary's University, Halifax, Canada. All rights retained by the author. Das © 2000.*

HISTORY

Maple Leaf was the brainchild of Mario Mansini, an Italian immigrant who left his native country to begin a new life in Canada in the late 1950s. After a couple of unsuccessful ventures (a stage show and a sail boat business), Mansini hit upon the idea of starting a shoe factory. "As long as people walk, they need shoes," he is said to have told the bank, which asked for a financial guarantee, given his past failures. Though not well educated (he dropped out of grade 8), Mansini was an extrovert and a flamboyant man who could impress and inspire others around him. In the end, his personality and optimism swayed the bank manager to extend a small loan for the new venture.

With the bank loan and financial assistance from some friends and relatives, Mansini built a small plant near Wilmington—two floors of shoes and about a dozen temporary sheds where employees lived and slept. In 1969, the firm formally opened for business.

What began as a small operation quickly grew into a regional and national operation. Despite his lack of education, Mansini was an astute businessman and he was also able to successfully recruit skilled workers. The folklore is that many of his erstwhile artist friends worked for practically no wages in his factory during the day and played music and rehearsed plays in the evenings. He had very close friendships with his employees and many were willing to pitch in whenever he needed help. The firm quickly developed a reputation for quality footwear, especially shoes used for outdoor and sports purposes. Apart from a couple of major footwear firms in the United States, competition was virtually absent and the firm thrived.

Mansini worked long hours to make Maple Leaf a success. He was a loyal citizen (the firm's original name was Quality Footware; Mansini changed it to Maple Leaf Shoes when the new Canadian flag was introduced). He also employed a paternalistic management style. He knew most workers by name and always took the time to inquire about their welfare. No one but Maple Leaf workers lived in the area where the factory was located. Over time, the location where Maple Leaf operated became unofficially known as "Leaf Town," although the closest town was Wilmington. For most workers, their houses were close enough to work to enable them to walk home for lunch. There was a Maple Leaf Grocery Store, Maple Leaf Recreation Hall, Maple Leaf teams, Maple Leaf Drug Store and Dispensary, and Maple Leaf Club for the higher echelon of the workforce. There was even a Leaf Cinema and Leaf Pub. Virtually everything was available in Leaf Town; residents only had to travel to nearby Wilmington for schools and medical assistance.

Consistent with his management style, Mansini had few organized procedures or systems in place. He noted: "If you lose touch with your men, you lose them. Systems come and go; people are more important." There were few formal procedures—each event

was looked at for its unique features and responded accordingly. Mansini often worked 15 to 18 hours—he was involved in most decisions including hiring of personnel, product planning, financing strategy, shoe design, and handling employee grievances. During his time, efforts were made by local and international unions to organize the workers; however, they were unsuccessful (in the most recent attempt, the union was able to get less than 10 per cent of the workers to sign up).

But Mansini's first love was music and arts. So, when a national conglomerate approached him with an offer to purchase a controlling share of Maple Leaf in the mid-1980s, he was only too willing to sell it. "I don't have any children to take over the firm," he said. (He died a bachelor soon after the sale of the company; a part of his estate was donated to Leaf Art Guild and Sports Team and the remainder was divided among his relatives and the Canadian Cancer Society.) "In any case, how long can a man spend his life looking at what is under the feet than above?" he mused.

SINCE THE TAKEOVER

The group that took over the firm modernized the manufacturing operations and attempted to extend its operations both nationally and internationally. During these efforts, it found that many of the company's past practices were archaic and inefficient. There was an attempt to improve efficiency and gross margin. New equipment was installed and several routine activities were automated or otherwise mechanized to reduce costs. While attempts were also made to update management practices, the firm was slow in this regard. Unfortunately, there was also above-average turnover in the top management team in the company in the initial years. Robert Clark, who was hired as the CEO of the firm, has now been with the firm for eight years and holds a significant share of the company stock apart from holding options.

While Maple Leaf Shoe makes shoes of all kinds, descriptions, and sizes today, it specializes in the manufacture of women's and youth athletic shoes. The company's designers were successful in producing a product that was both stylish and yet comfortable to wear and durable. The firm's shoes, marketed under the brand names of Fluffy Puppy, Cariboo, and Madonna, were very popular among ladies in the 19-40 age group. Its Young Athlete brand, aimed at boys and girls in the 9-14 age group, was a market leader in the children's sports shoes market in British Columbia. Historically, the shoes produced by the

Recent Financial Information on Maple Leaf Shoe Company Limited

	Current Year	Last Year	Year before	Three-year growth rate
Total Revenue ($000)	1 512 904	1 461 604	1 488 840	1.45%
Earnings before interest & tax ($000)	65 645	65 772	59 200	8.06%
Profit/Loss ($000)	26 258	29 597	29 008	–10.53%
Earnings per share	1.33	1.47	1.35	–7.85%
Dividends per share	.30	.33	.35	
Total assets ($000)	617 814	622 469	660 241	
Number of employees	783	843	897	

firm were cheaper than those of its competitors. This price advantage was a critical aspect of the company's marketing strategy in the past.

EMERGING CHALLENGES

Recently, the company has faced a number of issues that require immediate attention by its management. First, the cost of production at Maple Leaf Shoes has been rising slowly but steadily. Labour costs currently account for over 45 per cent of manufacturing costs and have been increasing rapidly. The productivity levels of the employees have not shown any increase in the last three years. If the present trend continues, the firm is likely to lose its price advantage over its competitors. Already, for two out of six popular brands sold by Maple Leaf Shoes, the prices for the firm's products are equal to or higher than its competition. This has stalled the firm's growth and profitability. Some financial details of the firm are shown in Table 1. Figure 1 shows the firm's stock price in the last five years. The market reaction to the firm's potential has not been very positive, as indicated by the overall decline of its share price from a high of $25 about five years back to close to $11 today.

FIGURE 1

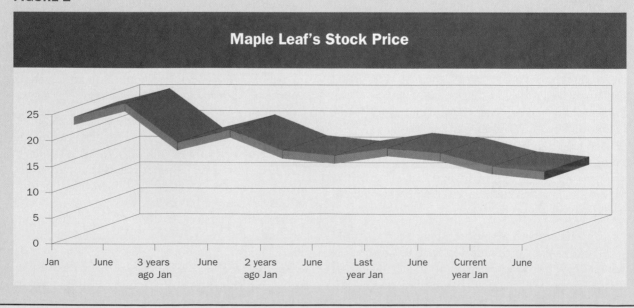

Maple Leaf's Stock Price

Second, over 60 per cent of the company's staff are unionized. There are indications that remaining nonmanagerial staff are also about to be unionized. Management believes that this will reduce the already limited autonomy it possesses in hiring, terminating, and managing employees.

Third, in the recent past, competition in the shoe industry has been intense. Over the years, trade barriers across countries have disappeared, which has meant that cheaper, high-quality shoes made in countries such as Korea, Taiwan, Singapore, India, and Mexico pose serious competition to the firm within and outside Canadian markets. Despite this, Maple Leaf Shoes has been able to perform fairly well in the export markets. Currently, over 15 per cent of its production is exported—mainly to western parts of the United States and Europe (the corresponding figure five years back was a tiny two per cent). While the company increased its U.S. sales after the Canada–U.S. Free Trade Agreement, it is somewhat apprehensive about the future. Robert Clark, president of Maple Leaf Shoes, commented:

> The market has changed dramatically in the last five years. The Asians and the Chinese are fast conquering the world footwear market. How can we compete with the Malaysians, Thais, and the Indians who pay a fraction of the wages we pay here? In China, from where most of the shoes sold in North America originate, the labour is cheap and employment standards are low. And mind you, those Asian workers are good. It will be a totally new game now with a new set of rules. ... we simply would not be able to compete with them on labour costs ... but what we have on our side is technology. We will constantly need to think of new products and newer strategies if we are to survive.

The firm's past strategy of responding to these challenges has been one of downsizing and automation of manufacturing functions. It has also sold off some of its non-performing assets and facilities and contracted out some of the services in a bid to cut costs. This strategy, while it has resulted in some improvements in the financial picture, has also brought with it negative union reaction and a decline in employee morale.

Maple Leaf recently signed an agreement with the producers of *Bumpy Bears*, a popular TV series aimed at young children. Under this agreement, the firm will have exclusive rights to reproduce the vari-

ous animal characters seen in the show on its footwear. Ticky, the black bear, Rumpy the arctic bear, and Moosy the white bear are beloved characters in the show. This is expected to increase the sales of children's shoes; however, the embossing technology is expensive and may require initial heavy capital investments and additional training for some members of the workforce.

Finally, the need for managerial training is felt now more than ever. The firm expects its activities to grow; however, given market conditions, it is not keen on expanding the size of its managerial cadre significantly. Instead, it would like to provide managerial and team-management skills to more of its employees and empower them to make decisions.

In a recent interview, Robert Clark identified a number of issues that require immediate attention:

1. Contracts with two of the four unions in the company will expire in another eight months. The remaining two unions will not start their contract negotiations for another 18 months; however, what happens in the negotiations with these two unions could have a significant impact on all future contract negotiations. One of the unions with which negotiations are to begin soon, the Leather Workers' Association, recently elected a leader who is rumoured to be militant and highly focused on results. A strike in the immediate future could paralyze the firm, and it is doubtful whether the firm would recover from its debilitating results for quite some time.

2. Recently, there were two complaints of sex discrimination from women employees. One complaint was settled internally in consultation with the concerned union, while the other had to go before the provincial Human Rights Commission. The decision of the commission was in favour of the employee who had filed the grievance.

3. The management of Maple Leaf Shoes believes that growth through expanded activities is critical now, especially given the competitive challenge. Growth is possible only by expanding its operations within and outside Canada. The management would like to expand its operations to Atlantic Canada and Quebec in the next three years—a new plant in Quebec is being considered for entry into that market since the product styling must be somewhat modified to meet the demands of the French market. It is felt that the

same plant can produce footwear that can be exported to France and other parts of Europe. Currently, Maple Leaf shoes are sold (although in small numbers) in Belgium and Luxembourg. These markets were developed almost accidentally: a few years back, a cousin of Robert Clark, the president, took samples of "Young Athlete" shoes for display in his sports equipment shops in Belgium and Luxembourg; the shoes became popular locally. Maple Leaf Shoes also sells its shoes through a home-building and hardware store in England. About 80 per cent of its foreign sales are, however, in Oregon and California where the shoes are displayed and sold through fashion boutiques and a chain of Canadian hardware stores.

4. Production levels in Maple Leaf Shoes have been continuously increasing; however, management has fought hard not to increase its workforce. The company currently uses a large number of part-time and contract workers for various services. While this strategy has resulted in some reduction in costs, it has also been accompanied by negative reactions from workers, supervisors, and unions. This is expected to be a major issue during the next bargaining session.

5. As far as possible, the company attempts to fill managerial positions through internal promotions and transfers; however, this has meant that management training is more critical today than ever before.

6. In an effort to take advantage of the cheap labour abroad, the firm, in the recent past, has attempted to enter into joint-venture partnerships with firms in Indonesia, Mexico, and India. However, this has also resulted in exposing the firm to additional risks characteristic of international operations. While its negotiations with the Mexican and Indian partners have been proceeding according to schedule, its experience in Indonesia was less than satisfactory. The firm's Indonesian partner fell victim to the "Asian crisis" of 1997-98 when the Indonesian currency, the rupiah, fell by more than 33 per cent in a matter of days. Its partner was on the verge of declaring insolvency. Maple Leaf is currently looking for another Indonesian partner.

Added to the above is the void created by the resignation of John McAllister, the personnel manager who left the firm to take up a similar position in the west. Currently, the position of personnel manager in the firm is vacant. Pat Lim, general manager (marketing) is currently in charge of the human resource function, although all routine decisions and procedures are handled by Jane Reynolds, special assistant to the personnel manager. (Indeed, because of increased national and international marketing activities, Lim is often away from the office.) Robert Clark recently decided to rename the function as "human resource manager" to reflect the increasing importance of the activity. The management recognizes that a number of human resource procedures and systems within the firm are antiquated and must be replaced; however, cost pressures and day-to-day priorities have prevented the firm from systematizing various HR functions such as hiring, orientation, training, appraisal, and compensation. The firm hopes to hire a new human resource manager (HRM as the position is now called) in the near future who will bring about the needed changes.

McAllister was with the company for only about three years. While he was credited with having "run a tight ship," several of his colleagues complained about his dominating and centralized leadership style. One of the managers went as far as saying that "Maple Leaf Shoes would not have been unionized this fast and to this extent but for John." McAllister's predecessor, Tim Donovan, was not a popular personnel manager either. Donovan, who resigned his position after a mere 10-month stay at Maple Leaf Shoes, did not have positive things to say about the company and its management. On the eve of his departure, he is reported to have confided in an associate: "The management system here is primitive. It's as if you are surrounded by forces of darkness. Of course, I could stay here and fight it out—maybe I would win in the end. But then I'm not masochistic!"

Discussion Questions

1. What are some changes within Maple Leaf Shoes and in its environments that have caused a shift in its strategy? List the challenges facing the company using the classification provided in your text.

2. Assume you are hired as a consultant to help the firm hire a new human resource manager. What immediate and long-term job responsibilities will you identify for the new job incumbent?

3. Identify three sample objectives of the human resource department at Maple Leaf Shoes and list associated strategy and action plans to be implemented by the department.

CASE STUDY

Canadian Pacific and International Bank

Canadian Pacific and International Bank (CPIB) is one of Canada's premier financial institutions with assets over $150 billion. CPIB, which began as a "western" bank in the early 1950s with its head office in Vancouver, British Columbia, spread its operations all over Canada and the United States by the mid-1960s. Originally called "Pacific and Western Bank," the bank changed its name about 15 years ago to reflect its international character. Today, more than 25 000 employees provide personal, commercial, corporate, and investment banking services to individuals and businesses in 33 countries. Some recent financial and employee statistics for CPIB are shown in Figure 1.

CPIB, through its strategic initiatives, was successful in building long-term value for its shareholders while providing regular return on their investments. The market price of CPIB's share increased by over 40 per cent in the last two years, bringing the bank's total market capitalization to nearly $18 billion, up from $10 billion just a few years back. In the current year, the share price has remained more or less static largely due to investor preferences for Internet stocks over "conservative" bank stocks.

Globally, CPIB serves more than six million customers in three key areas: personal and commercial banking, wealth management, and wholesale and corporate banking—marketed under the name "CPIB Securities" (Figure 2).

Personal and Commercial Banking: Through its 673 retail outlets, CPIB offers a wide variety of products and services. In addition, *"CP Anytime,"* CPIB's electronic banking service, offers customers access to retail products, services and accounts via telephone banking. The 1781 automated banking machines that form the Purple Touch network, CP Web Banking and CP Day-Night Investor provide service around the clock. In a recent independent survey, the bank was cited as number two in four out of seven dimensions of customer service including friendliness and customer responsiveness. The bank aims to further enhance customer service levels and flexibility (e.g., a single-number dial or a single Web site to meet all retailing and investment needs of small volume customers). Through such efforts, it aims to build market share in small and medium-sized businesses.

Wealth Management: CPIB's wealth management business includes its discount brokerage and mutual

---

[2] Case written by Professor Hari Das of Department of Management, Saint Mary's University, Halifax, Canada. All rights retained by the author. Das©2000.

FIGURE 1

Summary Financial and Employee Statistics				
	This year	**Last Year**	**Year before last**	**3 year growth**
Total revenue ($000)	13 442 571	11 309 142	8 979 429	20.02%
Earnings before interest and taxes ($000)	3 980 571	2 806 286	2 435 143	26.16%
Profit/Loss ($000)	2 555 143	960 857	932 571	48.12%
Earnings per share	4.20	1.55	1.52	49.17%
Total assets ($000)	183 786 000	155 855 140	140 444 570	18.18%
Dividends per share	0.62	0.57	0.48	
Return on equity	27.39	12.77	14.05	
Employees	25 059	26 594	24 500	

FIGURE 2

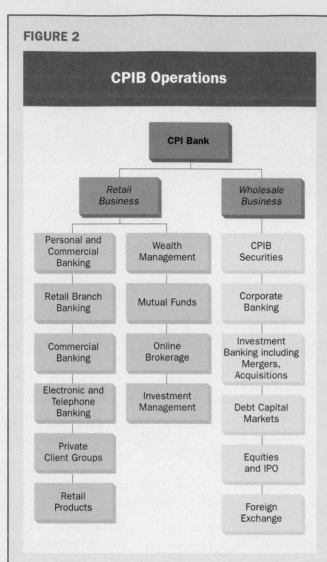

CPIB Securities: CPIB offers a full range of services to its clients in all key areas of finance and specialized solutions for corporate and government clients. Included here are investment banking (which include merchant banking, corporate banking and syndications), foreign exchange, loans, debt-capital markets (including initial public offerings and underwritings), mergers and acquisitions, and derivatives. In a recent ranking by a business magazine of North American firms offering integrated corporate services, CPIB was rated eighth in North America. The bank's priorities continue to be developing stronger client relationships, expanding industry specialty groups, and achieving maximum operating efficiency.

ORGANIZATION OF THE BANK

Since CPIB is an extremely large organization with operations in over 30 countries, the overall structure of the bank is very complex and not easily depicted. It also varies somewhat from one country to another to better respond to the local realities and challenges.

The chair and chief executive officer of the Bank is Michael Bennett, who is also chair of the board of directors to which he is accountable. The 18-member Board (17 men, one woman) represents a cross-section of top leaders in manufacturing and service industries and academic and professional institutions in Canada. The board has several committees entrusted with special tasks. Examples: *audit and risk management committee*, which among other duties, reviews the audited financial statements and approves policies related to risk and liquidity management and internal control; *management resources committee*, which reviews and approves senior office appointments and executive compensation plans; and *corporate governance committee*, which, among other activities, deliberates on the board composition and functioning. CPIB's hybrid organizational structure attempts to maximize the advantages of functional, product-based, and geographic structures (Figure 3). The Bank has a 472-page manual that describes in detail the position descriptions and required competencies of various managerial positions.

The chair, assisted by a deputy chair and five vice-chairs, approves all critical decisions affecting the bank's future. Three of the vice-chairs are in charge of personal and commercial banking, wealth management, and CPIB Securities; the fourth is in charge of global operations and the last one in charge

fund operations. CPIB Investment is one of Canada's leading discount brokerages, currently with over one million customer accounts in the United States and Canada and a growing clientele in Australia, the United Kingdom, and Japan. Although smaller than Toronto Dominion Bank's TD Waterhouse Group or Royal Bank's Action Direct, CPIB is attempting to make fast inroads into this highly competitive but lucrative sector of banking. Historically, CPIB had charged lower commissions ($25 for most transactions compared to $29 charged by TD Waterhouse and Action Direct). In the near future, the firm plans to increase its market penetration ratio. Currently, CPIB manages nearly $24 billion in mutual funds, pension funds, trusts, and endowments. In the near future, the bank wants to reorganize and integrate wealth management activities to improve customer service and sales support for all products.

FIGURE 3

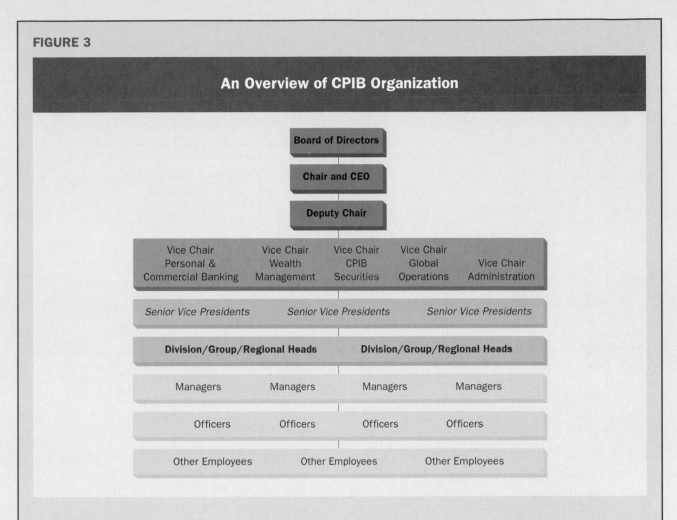

An Overview of CPIB Organization

of overall administration. The seven senior vice presidents are in charge of retail banking, commercial banking, mutual funds and brokerage, investment management, corporate and investment banking, human resources, and global operations. Below the senior vice presidents are heads of various divisions including human resources, economic analysis, securities and foreign exchange, retail banking, real estate operations, and risk management. There are 36 heads of divisions or groups or regions currently. With the Bank's expansion into electronic banking and foreign markets, more group heads and even vice presidents may have to be hired in the near future. The three foreign division heads are located outside Canada: Asian Division in Singapore, European Division in London, and Middle East and African Division in Istanbul.

For ease of administration and to better respond to customer requirements, the domestic banking is divided into five regions (head offices in parentheses): Atlantic (Halifax), Quebec (Montreal), Ontario (Toronto), Prairie (Winnipeg), and Pacific (Vancouver). The corporate head office is also located in Vancouver.

Several other functions are centralized at the head office to reap economies of scale and facilitate communication. Example: CP Economics Division that monitors Canadian and world economic trends and prepares routine and special reports for use by the Bank in its various investment and client divisions. Some of the other functions (e.g., CP Ombudsperson) are located at the head office but with strong regional presence and frequent meetings with staff at various regions and branches to better respond to their queries and proactively deal with emerging issues or likely problems.

CORPORATE STRATEGIES

CPIB, which is known for its ability to capitalize on opportunities, was one of the first Canadian banks to enter Asian and Latin American markets, introduce automated tellers throughout Canada, begin a web-based brokerage and offer integrated wealth management and financial counselling services. Its extensive online delivery of wealth management and banking services has made CPIB a key player in the development of e-commerce and places it in the top dozen financial services firms in the world as measured by the number of online customer accounts. In a bid to dominate the market, CPIB recently acquired Maple Leaf Trust, a large trust firm with its head office in Toronto. CPIB is currently concluding negotiations for the acquisition of International Investors Inc., a large stock exchange brokerage firm located in New York. When completed (it is expected that the deal will be finalized in less than two months), the new investment arm of CPIB, namely Canadian and International Investors, will be among the top dozen financial services firms in the world. Reflecting its strategy of investing in the future of financial services, CPIB is entering the new millennium as a leader in online delivery.

CPIB has always prided itself on its record of enhancing shareholder value. Its consistently high net incomes (in some years, reflecting record growth for the entire banking industry in this country) and its focus on running a lean operation have resulted in considerable increase in shareholder value over the years. To finance its newer acquisitions, the firm plans to make initial public offerings (IPO) soon. Already, a number of large investors and brokerage firms have expressed considerable interest in the IPOs.

CPIB has a solid reputation as a good corporate citizen, having increased its charitable donations by 9.2 per cent to $7.3 million last year. Two years ago, the bank created a slogan "Bank for Your Community" and began contributing one per cent of pre-tax domestic income to improve the community. Its donations have primarily focused on children's health and education, university scholarships (its Canadian University Scholarship is a coveted award), and donations for art and sports events (over 100 children attend minor league sports or the Canadian Conservatory of Music each year). The bank is a major sponsor of Save the Children Network, a network of hospitals serving over a million children across Canada. In the future, the bank wants to expand its community service to include foreign countries as well.

IMMEDIATE CHALLENGES

CPIB recognizes that it has no time to rest on its laurels. To maintain and improve its competitive position, it must innovate and grow. Big competitors such as Royal Bank, Toronto Dominion Bank, Canadian Imperial Bank of Commerce, Bank of Nova Scotia, and Bank of Montreal have been making fast inroads into electronic banking and foreign markets while smaller banks and credit unions, because of their small volumes, are able to provide more personal service compared to the large banks. Standardization and automation brought in considerable predictability and efficiency in operations, but it was also fraught with the risk of impersonal service and bureaucratic red tape. How to improve efficiency and predictability while offering personal and custom service? How to reap the advantages of smaller organizations such as flexibility without losing the economies of scale? There seem to be no simple answers.

More recently, a large number of "virtual banks" have appeared on the scene. These banks pay four to five per cent interest even on small balances irrespective of the type of accounts (most Canadian banks do not pay any significant interest on chequing accounts). Because of the absence of any overhead costs, these virtual banks have been able to offer premium interest rates on other types of accounts as well as offer loans at cheaper rates. How can the bank compete with the virtual banks without losing the advantages of traditional banking and sacrificing the security and reputation?

Some have predicted that future societies may be "money free"—in an Internet age, where most commodities can be virtually traded (including air miles, bonus points issued by gas stations, Canadian Tire coupons, and gift certificates), there is no reason why people should continue to use only currency notes or bank cheques as medium of transaction.[55] If this scenario occurs, what will be the fate of traditional banks? No one quite knows.

While computerization and Internet trading have brought substantial benefits, they have also exposed banks and their systems to hackers and computer viruses that paralyze trading and in some instances wipe out entire computer memory. For instance, in early 2000, the "love bug" infected more than two million computer files around the world—over 90 per cent of the sites being in North America—causing damage exceeding US$ 1 billion.[56] In future years, when banks increase their reliance on computerized trading, the risk element is only likely to grow.

In recent years, "shareholder democracy" has been gaining momentum. Organizations such as the Association for the Protection of Quebec Savers and Investors (APQSI) have been demanding a greater voice in bank decisions. In a recent Bank of Montreal shareholders' meeting[57] APQSI proposed a course of action that was accepted by majority shareholders—even when the bank management recommended voting against it. The banks have been the focus of activist efforts because they are all widely held national institutions with a great deal of power. In the near future, there may be greater accountability of directors and senior bank executives to shareholders who are asking tough questions on all aspects of their operations. How can the bank respond to shareholder concerns without losing managerial authority and decision-making power? That is the question many bank managers ask themselves today.

Canada's banks operate in a highly regulated environment. Among the various restrictions they face is the complicated approval process needed for any merger (In 1999, when Royal Bank and Bank of Montreal wanted to merge, the necessary approval was not granted.) In early 2001, the federal government was drafting legislation that could impose an even more complicated approval process on any merger among the big banks.[58] When the legislation is complete, any banking merger would require extensive public hearings on practically every aspect of the deal—a factor causing considerable frustration for Canadian banks, which find that their global status is coming down (the U.S. and Japanese banks have considerable resources and opportunity for cross-ownership of banks). In Royal Bank's CEO John Cleghorn's words, "We are in a highly competitive game and we are hamstrung in our ability to deal with it."[59] Canadian bankers have also been complaining about intrusive consumer regulations that risk placing them at a disadvantage to their U.S. competitors. The existing and proposed regulations will restrict the banks from using their customer databases to sell products to a targeted audience, including selling insurance through the branches. This is especially worrisome since large credit card companies have no similar restrictions imposed on them in this regard. "I worry a bit about the propensity to put consumer-type safeguards on banks only," Peter Godsoe, Chairman of Bank of Nova Scotia, pointed out. " I think it has some dangers in it because database marketers can sit in the United States and sell the databases and all sorts of products."[60]

As an international organization, the Bank is susceptible to all political and economic uncertainties in foreign countries. In the recent past, there was a significant slowdown in several Asian economies, resulting in, at times, massive losses to all major banks including CPIB. There were also instances where for-

eign governments suddenly changed their investment policies, prohibiting repatriation of capital and profits. How can the bank expand without overexposing itself to risk? Clearly, there are no easy answers.

HUMAN RESOURCE FUNCTION

While its financial goals have been the driving force behind CPIB's externally focused strategies, management always recognized that it could not have achieved any of these results but for its highly competent and motivated employees—whether they are senior executives or clerks in remote branches. From its inception, the Bank was committed to progressive human resource management practices in all its operations. It was one of the first banks to institute standardized selection and performance appraisal procedures, a well-designed human resource planning system, a detailed counselling system for employees, and financial assistance for university education for its employees. While occasional layoffs and staff reduction have been inevitable to cut costs, this has been done as humanely as possible. Mary Keddy, senior vice president—human resources, an MBA from Saint Mary's specializing in human resources with an outstanding performance record in the steel industry, joined the firm six years ago. Since her arrival, she has tried to introduce state-of-the-art techniques and systems to the management of human resources. Compared to other banks, the staff turnover rate in CPIB was two per cent lower. Past employee surveys have indicated that staff morale is high and rising. In Keddy's words,

> I know it is a cliche to say that 'human resources are our most important assets'. Many organizations proclaim this as their policy, but then it is business as usual. Honestly, I do believe in the maxim and what is fortunate for me, CPIB also believes in it. My predecessor, John Galsworthy, was a progressive human resource manager. He was one of those visionaries—he realized the potential of humans and was determined to tap that to the fullest extent. What is more, he genuinely cared for the employees. I am told that he knew several tellers in distant branches by their first names. Even a year before his retirement from the bank, he was found to spend long hours—often 12 to 13 hours—in his office to refine our HR practices. Fitting into his shoes, naturally, was a daunting task initially. But he also left a good system to build on. And, that is

what I have been doing: building on our strengths.

Keddy's views on the importance of human resources are echoed by several senior executives, including the CEO. At a time when several Canadian banks had their HR function represented only at the divisional or group level, CPIB raised its status to a vice-president level. In the foreseeable future, especially if the present expansion and merger plans proceed according to plans, HR may be elevated to vice-chair level, adding organizational change to the function.

Most of the specialized HR functions are located at the Vancouver head office. The regional offices do have their own HR managers and staff, but all major policy decisions are made at the head office—of course, after extensive consultations with all concerned (see Figure 4).

According to Keddy, some areas that HR is currently investigating are:

While the Bank has been a progressive employer, the number of female senior managers in its ranks continues to be low. At the junior levels of management, the ratio between male and female managers is currently 65:35; however, as one goes up the hierarchy, the ratio changes drastically in favour of the males. Of the eight vice presidents, only one is a woman; of the remaining senior managers, less than five per cent are women. While the Bank has been aware of the situation and would like to correct it, it has not been easy. There is also a larger turnover among female managers, making the task even more difficult. An examination of the employee records does not show any significant differences between males and females either in terms of educational qualifications or prior work experience. Also, at lower levels, in many branches, female employees seem to score higher on tenure and overall productivity. The situation, thus, is somewhat perplexing.

In many large cities such as Toronto and Vancouver, the percentage of visible minorities in the general population and labour market has been significant—often totalling 40 per cent of the workforce. CPIB has also a number of clerks and lower-level staff who belong to this group. However, even at the supervisory and junior managerial level, the percentage of minorities has been insignificant (often less than one-tenth of one percent). The Bank would like to encourage more minorities and people with physical disabilities to reach middle-level and senior managerial levels.

After the merger with Investors, all duplication in services needs to be eliminated, which is likely to result in some job losses. How can the bank

FIGURE 4

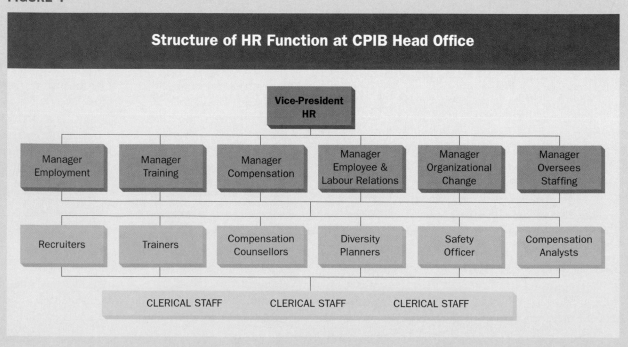

Structure of HR Function at CPIB Head Office

Vice-President HR

Manager Employment

Manager Training

Manager Compensation

Manager Employee & Labour Relations

Manager Organizational Change

Manager Oversees Staffing

Recruiters

Trainers

Compensation Counsellors

Diversity Planners

Safety Officer

Compensation Analysts

CLERICAL STAFF   CLERICAL STAFF   CLERICAL STAFF

minimize job losses and employee anxiety? Keddy is currently heading a human resource steering committee that is looking into this matter and deliberating on staff reductions. She also wants to regularize communication flow to the employees on the matter to minimize rumours. The new employees from Investors also need to be socialized into CPIB's culture.

In recent months, Keddy and some of her senior colleagues have been seriously debating an ethical issue. Several manufacturers in developing economies employ young children (often aged seven or eight years) at very low wages (some times as low as less than a dollar per day) for long hours[61] (12 hours and more in some cases) to produce cheap products such as soccer and volley balls, jeans, and shoes. These manufacturers are important customers of the bank—often accounting for 25 per cent or more of its loans in some regions. Keddy believes that the bank has a moral responsibility to do what is ethically right, but is not sure how it can influence the events in other countries.

Finally, how to reduce labour costs while minimizing the adverse impact on employee morale and customer satisfaction? Automation and computerization can reduce labour costs significantly, but could also result in layoffs, lower employee morale, and longer waiting lines for customers in some cases. What is the optimal tradeoff between efficiency and morale?

IMMEDIATE GOALS

For the next year, the bank has the following financial objectives:

Efficiency Ratio: This ratio (also called "productivity" ratio) measures non-interest expenses as a percentage of revenue; the lower the percentage, the greater the efficiency. The bank aims to maintain an efficiency ratio of 58 per cent (the six other major Canadian banks have productivity ratios ranging from 63 to 68 per cent) compared to 61.6 per cent last year and 63.8 per cent two years ago.

Earnings on Share: The bank aims to generate growth in earnings per common share from the present $4.20 to $4.62, or a 10 per cent increase.

Return on Equity. The bank wants to maintain its earning premium over risk-free Government of Canada Bonds, which presently translates into a return on equity (on cash basis) to about 17 per cent. The bank wants to improve its overall return by one percentage point.

Provision for credit losses. Most Canadian banks have average 0.37 per cent (some banks with as high a rate as 0.5 per cent) of net average loans as provision for credit losses. CPIB would like to keep it at 0.30 per cent.

Market ratings for debt. The bank's credit ratings from Moody's and Standard Poor are strong at Aa3 and AAMinus respectively. The bank would like to maintain or improve these.

Discussion Questions

1.   What are some major challenges facing CPIB?

2.   What are the specific implications for the human resource function?

3.   What suggestions do you have for the current challenges faced by the HR function?

SUGGESTED READINGS

Chowdhury, Subir. *Management 21C*, London: Pearson Education Limited, 2000.

Hagan, Christine, "The Core Competence Organization: Implications for Human Resource Practices," *Human Resource Management Review*, Vol. 6, No. 2, 1996, pp. 147–164.

Schuler, Randall, "Repositioning the Human Resource Function: Transformation or Demise?" *Academy of Management Executive*, 1990, pp. 49–60.

Tapscott, Don, *Creating Value in the Network Economy*, Boston: Harvard Business School Press, 1999.

Ulrich, Dave, *Human Resource Champions*, Boston: Harvard Business School Press, 1997.

APPENDIX A

Origins of Human Resource Management

The origins of human resource management are unknown. Probably the first cave dwellers struggled with problems of utilizing human resources. Even the Bible records selection and training problems faced by Moses. Moses was confronted with one of the earliest recorded personnel challenges when Jethro, his father-in-law, advised: "And thou shalt teach them ordinances and laws, and shalt shew them the way wherein they must walk, and the work they must do. Moreover, thou shalt provide out of all the people able men ... to be rulers" (Exod. 18: 20–21).

During the thousands of years between Moses and the Industrial Revolution, there were few large organizations. Except for religious orders (the Roman Catholic Church, for example) or governments (particularly the military), small groups did most of the work. Whether on the farm, in small shops, or in the home, the primary work unit was the family. There was little need for formal study of human resource management.

The Industrial Revolution changed the nature of work. Mechanical power and economies of scale required large numbers of people to work together. Big textile mills, foundries, and mines sprung up in England and then in North America. Collectively, people were still an important resource, but the Industrial Revolution meant greater mechanization and unpleasant working conditions for many workers.

By the late 1800s, a few employers reacted to the human problems caused by industrialization and created the post of welfare secretary. Welfare secretaries existed to meet worker needs and to prevent workers from forming unions. Social secretaries, as they were sometimes called, helped employees with personal problems such as education, housing, and medical needs. These early forerunners of human resource specialists sought to improve working conditions for workers. The emergence of welfare secretaries prior to 1900 demonstrates that the personnel activities in large organizations had already become more extensive than some top operating managers alone could handle. Thus, social secretaries marked the birth of specialized human resource management, as distinct from the day-to-day supervision of personnel by operating managers.

Scientific Management and Human Needs

The next noteworthy development was scientific management. The scientific management proponents showed the world that the systematic, scientific study of work could lead to improved efficiency. Their arguments for specialization and improved training furthered the need for HR management. The first decades of this century saw primitive "personnel departments" replace welfare secretaries. These new departments contributed to organizational effectiveness by maintaining wages at proper levels, screening job applicants, and handling grievances. They also assumed the welfare secretary's role of improving working conditions, dealing with unions, and meeting other employee needs.

By the First World War, personnel departments were becoming common among very large industrial employers. But these early departments were not important parts of the organizations they served. They were record depositories with advisory authority only. At that time, production, finance, and marketing problems overshadowed the role of personnel management. The importance of personnel departments grew slowly as their contribution and responsibilities increased.

From the end of the First World War until the Great Depression of the 1930s, personnel departments assumed growing roles in handling compensation, testing, unions, and employee needs. More and more attention was paid to employee needs. The importance of individual needs became even more pronounced as a result of the research studies in the United States at Western Electric's Hawthorne plant during this period. These studies showed that the efficiency goals of scientific management had to be balanced by considerations of human needs. These observations eventually had a profound impact on personnel management. But the Depression and the Second World War diverted attention to more urgent matters of organizational and national survival.

Modern Influences

The Depression of the 1930s led citizens to lose faith in the ability of business to meet society's needs. They turned to government. Government intervened to give workers minimum wages and the right to join labour unions. In 1940, Canada started an unemployment insurance program to help alleviate financial problems during the transition from one job to another. In general, the government's emphasis was on improving employee security and working conditions.

This drafting of legislation during the 1930s helped to shape the present role of personnel departments by adding legal obligations. Organizations now had to consider societal objectives and the need for legal compliance, which elevated the importance of personnel departments. In practice, personnel departments were made responsible for discouraging unionization among employees. But with newfound legal protection, unions grew dramatically. These organizing successes startled many organizations into rethinking their use of paternalism, their "management knows best" approach to employee welfare. Personnel departments began replacing a paternalistic approach with more proactive approaches that considered employee desires. When workers did organize, responsibility for dealing with unions also fell to the personnel department, sometimes renamed the industrial relations department to reflect these new duties.

Personnel departments continued to increase in importance during the 1940s and 1950s. The recruiting and training demands of the Second World War added to the credibility of the personnel departments that successfully met these challenges. After the war, personnel departments grew in importance as they contended with unions and an expanding need for professionals such as engineers and accountants. The increasing attention given to behavioural findings led to concern for improved human relations. These findings helped underscore the importance of sound personnel management practices.

In the 1960s and 1970s, the central influence on personnel was again legislation. Several laws were passed that affected the working conditions, wage levels, safety, and health and other benefits of employees. These acts began to provide personnel department managers with a still larger voice—a voice that began to equal that of production, finance, and marketing executives in major corporations.

Human resource management—as the personnel function is known today—did not emerge until recently. It is only very recently that human resource specialists have started to exert great influence on organizational strategy or have been chosen as chief executives. But today, in many organizations, there is a genuine recognition that human resources spell the difference between strategic success and organizational decline. The emphasis placed on strategic human resource management and formal certification of HR specialists are evidence of this growing role of human resource management.

Part Two

2

Planning Human Resources

This part introduces you to the important task of planning for human resources. Chapter Two discusses the various approaches to conduct a job analysis. Steps to derive valid job descriptions, specifications, and performance standards are outlined in this chapter. Chapter Three discusses the various factors that need to be considered when forecasting the demand for and supply of human resources. It also outlines several popular techniques for making such forecasts. Together, these two chapters help you to identify the type, number, and degree of sophistication of human resources needed by your firm.

Planning Human Resources

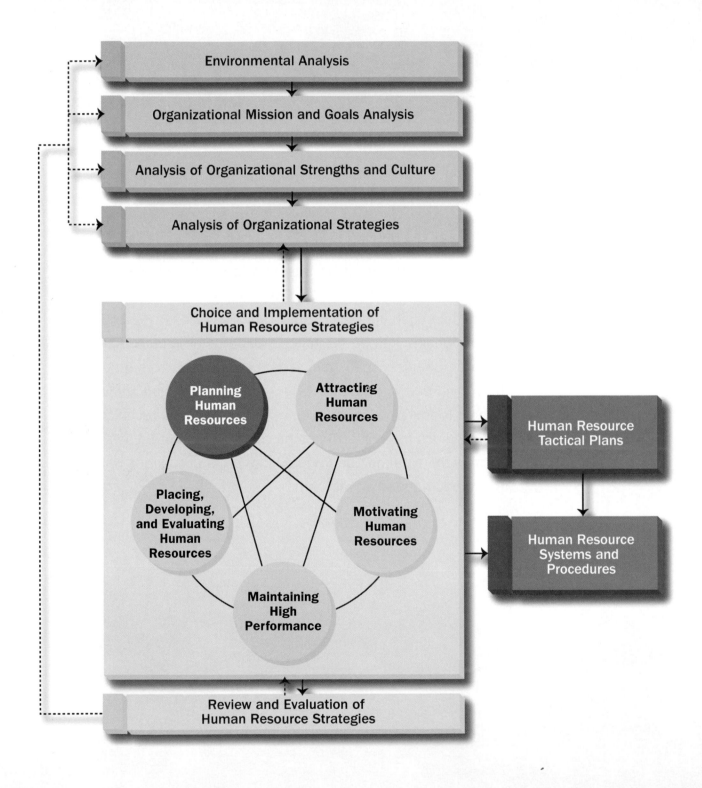

Environmental Analysis

Organizational Mission and Goals Analysis

Analysis of Organizational Strengths and Culture

Analysis of Organizational Strategies

Choice and Implementation of Human Resource Strategies

Planning Human Resources

Attracting Human Resources

Placing, Developing, and Evaluating Human Resources

Motivating Human Resources

Maintaining High Performance

Human Resource Tactical Plans

Human Resource Systems and Procedures

Review and Evaluation of Human Resource Strategies

Chapter 2

Job Analysis and Design

The data generated by job analyses have significant use in nearly every phase of human resource administration: designing jobs and reward systems; staffing and training; performance control and more. Few other processes executed by organizations have the potential for being such a powerful aid to management decision making.

Philip C. Grant[1]

CHAPTER OBJECTIVES

After studying this chapter, you should be able to:

- *Explain* the importance of job analysis information for human resource managers.

- *Discuss* the various steps in conducting job analysis and methods of job data collection.

- *Describe* the contents of a job description and a job specification.

- *Discuss* the various approaches to setting performance standards.

- *Outline* the key considerations in job design.

For a human resource department to be proactive, it needs information about various external challenges facing the organization (e.g., changes in technology, government regulations) and factors internal to the firm. This chapter explains how human resource specialists discover the actual characteristics that presently exist in each job.

Where there is no human resource department, all employee-related matters are handled by individual managers who already should know the characteristics, standards, and human abilities required for each job and who probably do not feel the need for any formal record of this knowledge. After a human resource department is created, however, knowledge about jobs and their requirements must be collected through *job analysis*. This is done by specialists called job analysts. This knowledge is vital to the effective functioning of a HR department as exemplified in the following dialogue:

Job analysis
Systematic study of a job to discover its specifications, skill requirements, etc. for wage-setting, recruitment, training, or job-simplification purposes.

> **Service Manager:** Before we had a human resource department, we took care of people matters pretty well. Now there is too much paperwork on each job. I wonder if it's a help or a hindrance.
>
> **HR Manager:** I can sympathize. Before the department was set up, you probably had complete authority for people matters. Right?
>
> **Service Manager:** I sure did! And I did it without a lot of paperwork.
>
> **HR Manager:** Sure you did. You know every job in your department, in and out. You had all the information you needed stored in your experiences.
>
> **Service Manager:** That's my point. If I got along without all this paperwork, why can't you?
>
> **HR Manager:** Why? Because you deal with those jobs every day. You've probably done most of them yourself. But my department is also responsible for jobs in sales, production, warehouse, supervision, and others. Without the paperwork describing these jobs, we would have no idea of their requirements.

Jobs are at the core of every organization's productivity. If they are not well designed and done right, productivity suffers, profits fall, and the organization is less able to meet the demands of society, customers, employees, and other stakeholders. The importance of well-designed jobs is perhaps best illustrated by an example:

> Rapid growth in a Calgary construction company led to an increase in the number of invoices and a decrease in the quality and timeliness of its departments' performance. Consultants who were hired to investigate the problems faced by the company conducted workshops and taught employees to apply job diagnostic tools to their activities. The result of all these activities was a 12.3 per cent increase in the number of invoices processed, a saving of $127 200 in salaries, overtime, and overheads, and a better understanding among the workers of the importance of their work roles.

Not all attempts to restructure jobs succeed as well as this example. However, improvements in productivity, quality, and cost often begin with the jobs employees do. For a human resource department to be effective, its members must have a clear understanding of the jobs found throughout organizations. Without this information base, the human resource department would be less able to redesign jobs, recruit new employees, train present employees, determine appropriate compensation, and perform many other human resource functions.

Job
Group of related activities and duties.

Position
Collection of tasks and responsibilities performed by an individual.

A job consists of a group of related activities and duties. A *job* may be held by a single employee or several persons. The collection of tasks and responsibilities performed by an individual employee is called a *position*.

> In a department with one supervisor, three clerks, and twelve service personnel, there are sixteen positions but only three jobs.

With hundreds—or even thousands—of jobs, it is nearly impossible for the human resource professionals in large companies to know the details of every job. It is, however, unnecessary to collect information on identical jobs separately. Consider this example:

One insurance company has 90 clerical employees who process incoming premium payments. Each job is the same. Therefore, job analysis requires only a random sample of these positions. Data collection on a few of these jobs generates an accurate information base for all 90 positions.

www.hrzone.com/topics/joba.html

Large organizations store information on various jobs using a *Human Resource Information System (HRIS)*. A sophisticated HRIS permits easy retrieval of relevant job details; it also provides a variety of information about the job, job holders, and past performance standards. Further details about designing a HRIS will be discussed in the next chapter.

Even small businesses can benefit from a proper job analysis. Consider the example of this small furniture manufacturing unit in Ontario:

Quality Furniture is a small furniture manufacturing unit that, until recently, employed three full-time and three to four part-time employees. In the last year, however, the demand for the firm's furniture had grown, resulting in the firm hiring four more full-time and eight part-time workers. The growth was also accompanied by some new challenges. In the last eight months, Steve Smith, the owner-manager of the firm, has received a number of complaints about the reliability and quality of the firm's products. On inquiry, Smith found that different assemblers had differing ideas about how best to assemble the various components. The assembly-line type production format also required some workers to speed up their work in case the next person in the assembly chain waited for work. Steve called a meeting of all the workers and everyone eventually agreed on the production process. Work was also rearranged: all the employees now worked on initial product manufacturing in the mornings, while the afternoons were spent on final assembly and finishing. In less than three months, customer complaints were reduced by 45 per cent while production volume increased by 33 per cent.

In the case of Quality Furniture, an improvement in the task definition resulted in fewer customer complaints. Further, even an unsophisticated job analysis helped improve the performance standards.

Figure 2-1 lists major human resource actions that rely on job analysis information. For example, without job analysis information, human resource specialists would find it difficult to evaluate how environmental challenges or specific job

FIGURE 2-1

Major Human Resource Management Activities that Rely on Job Analysis Information

1. Efforts to improve employee productivity levels necessitate careful study of jobs.

2. Elimination of unnecessary job requirements that can cause discrimination in employment.

3. Matching of job applicants to job requirements.

4. Planning of future human resource requirements.

5. Determination of employee training needs.

6. Fair and equitable compensation of employees.

7. Efforts to improve quality of work life.

8. Identification of realistic and challenging performance standards.

9. Redesign of jobs to improve performance and/or employee morale.

10. Fair and accurate appraisal of employee performance.

requirements affect workers' quality of work life. To match job applicants to openings, human resource specialists must understand what each job requires. Similarly, compensation analysts could not be expected to determine a fair salary without detailed knowledge of each job. Even before a human resource department exists, successful managers consider the informal job information they have acquired. Human resource departments formalize the collection, evaluation, and organization of this information.

This chapter describes the specific information sought by job analysis and the techniques used to collect it. The chapter also describes how the data collected are converted into a useful human resource information system.

STEPS IN JOB ANALYSIS PROCESS

JOB ANALYSIS has three phases: preparation, collection of job information, and use of job information for improving organizational effectiveness (see Figure 2-2). Each phase consists of several actions, which are discussed below:

Phase 1: Preparation for Job Analysis

Three key activities are performed in this phase:

1. Familiarization with the Organization and Its Jobs

Before studying jobs, it is important to have an awareness of an organization's objectives, strategies, structure, inputs (people, materials, and procedures), and desired outcomes. Job analysts may also study industry and government reports about the

see other big picture

FIGURE 2-2

The Job Analysis Process

Phase 1

Preparation for Job Analysis

| Familiarization with the Organization and the Jobs | Determination of Uses of Job Analysis | Identification of Jobs to be Analyzed |

Phase 2

Collection of Job Analysis Information

| Determine Sources of Job Data | Data Collection Instrument Design | Choice of Method for Data Collection |

Phase 3

Use of Job Analysis Information

- Job Description
- Job Specification
- Job Performance Standards
- Job Design
- Formulation of HR strategies

jobs to be analyzed. In all instances, the intent is to collect relevant and accurate information about jobs and factors determining job success.

2. Determination of Uses of Job Analysis Information

As shown in Figure 2-1, job analysis plays a critical role for many HR functions. While the most common uses of job analysis are in human resource selection, and training and designing performance appraisal and compensation systems,[2] job analysis may also be done to eliminate discrimination against specific employee groups or job redesign. In some cases, job analysis also aids the accomplishment of other objectives such as identifying "non-traditional career" paths for employees as the following example shows:

> One job analysis study[3] found that the skills, knowledge, and abilities essential for performance in secretarial and clerical positions are very similar to those needed in entry-level management positions. If female or minority employees are concentrated in secretarial or clerical positions, this information can be used to move them into managerial positions. Such employees can also utilize this information to make the best use of their work experience and training and plot future career paths.

The specific details collected during a job analysis are influenced by the objectives of the study; hence, it is critical to crystallize the objectives early on.

3. Identification of Jobs to be Analyzed

While almost all job positions could benefit from an in-depth analysis, resource and time constraints often preclude organizations from this. Likely targets of job analysis are jobs that are critical to the success of an organization; jobs that are difficult to learn or perform (since this determines the extent of training); jobs where the firm continuously hires new employees (since identification of clear job requirements assumes great importance); or jobs that preclude members of the protected classes described in Chapter Four. Jobs should also be analyzed if new technology or altered work environments affect the way the job is performed. If inappropriate job requirements are used, the organization may even be in violation of laws as the following example illustrates:

> In the past, the Vancouver Fire Department required that all successful job applicants to the Department be at least five foot nine inches (175 cm) tall. When one of the applicants complained, the Human Rights Board looked into the Department's selection practices. It could not find any correlation between the height of a fire fighter and injuries or productivity of the employees. The Department was found to be in violation of the Human Rights Act.[4]

In general, senior management and all key supervisors of the firm should be consulted before selecting jobs for in-depth analysis since the jobs selected for analysis can affect the strategic success and overall human resource policies (e.g., hiring, training) of the firm. The type, number, and the geographical dispersion of the jobs selected for analysis also influence the choice of data collection method.

Phase 2: Collection of Job Analysis Information

This phase contains three interrelated activities: determining the source of job data, data collection instrument design, and choosing the method of data collection.

1. Determination of the Source of Job Data

Although the most direct source of information about a job is the job incumbent, various other sources—both human and non-human—may be used for this purpose. Figure 2-3 lists alternate sources of job information.

As long as a person can demonstrate that he or she can do the job, discriminatory practices such as a height restriction for fire fighters are illegal in Canada.

CP PHOTO ARCHIVE (Ryan Remiorz)

If job analysis has been done before, previous records may be used. Moreover, existing job descriptions, process specifications, and reports relating to individual and work group performance may also help in establishing the nature of the various jobs. Other sources such as equipment design blueprints, maintenance manuals and records, safety manuals, and videos and films from suppliers of machinery also provide valid insights into the manner in which jobs are performed. Several company records including organizational charts and reporting relationships often provide clues on the job outcomes, responsibilities, and interdependencies among jobs.

FIGURE 2-3

Sources of Job Data

Non-Human Sources	Human Sources
Existing job descriptions and specifications	Job incumbents
Equipment design blueprints	Supervisors
Equipment maintenance manuals and records	Job experts
Training and safety manuals	Work colleagues
Organization charts and other company records	Subordinates
National Occupational Classification	Customers
Videos/films supplied by appliance/machine manufacturers	
Professional journals/magazines/publications	
Internet research	

www.ihrim.org

www.hrpao.org

www.entrenet.com

www.hr2000.com

On several occasions, material published in professional journals and magazines provide information about how jobs are performed in other organizations and settings. This information can be valuable when establishing performance standards and benchmarks for quality. Other publications such as *National Occupational Classification* (NOC) in Canada and the U.S. Department of Labor's *Handbook for Analyzing Jobs* provide information on various jobs. The NOC will be discussed in greater detail later in this chapter.

More recently, the Internet is a valuable source for information for various jobs and occupational groups. Web sites of several professional associations and private consulting firms offer a wealth of information relevant in the context of job analysis and design of job descriptions.

The Web sites of professional human resource associations list the job duties of several job categories, while the Internet "want ads" provide clues about the way in which jobs are defined and performed in other similar organizations.

The current job incumbents, their supervisors, and colleagues provide the most valid information about the way jobs are performed in the firm. However, other parties can also provide important information about jobs:

> In the case of a salesperson, added insights about job behaviours can be obtained by contacting past customers. In the case of college or university faculty, students may be able to provide important information on in-class behaviours related to effective job performance.

2. Data Collection Instrument Design

Job analysis schedules
Checklist that seeks to collect information about jobs in a uniform manner.

To study jobs, analysts most often develop questionnaires that are sometimes called checklists or **job analysis schedules**. These questionnaires seek to collect job information uniformly. They uncover the duties, responsibilities, human abilities, and performance standards of the jobs investigated.

The questionnaires are particularly important when collecting information from human sources; although, even in the case of non-human sources, the quality and comparability of information collected can be enhanced by the use of common checklists. It is important to use the same questionnaire on similar jobs. Analysts want differences in job information to reflect differences in the jobs, not differences in the questions asked. Uniformity is especially hard to maintain in large organizations; where analysts study similar jobs in different departments, only a uniform questionnaire is likely to result in usable data:

> After two appliance producers merged, each initially retained its own human resource department and job analysis schedules. As a result, all the production supervisors evaluated by one form had their jobs and pay substantially upgraded. Even though the supervisors in the other plant had identical jobs, they received only modest pay raises.

As this example points out, similar jobs, if not studied with identical lists of questions, can result in confusion and inequity. This does not mean that the human resource department is limited to one questionnaire. Job analysts often find that technical, clerical, and managerial jobs require different checklists. Figure 2-4 shows an abbreviated sample form for conducting job analysis that can be modified to suit the needs of specific situations. Most standardized forms, however, attempt to measure the following items:

Status and Identification. *Status* refers to whether the job is exempt from overtime laws. Other *identification* information includes job title, division, and title of supervisor(s) (and sometimes a unique job identification number). Without these entries, users of job analysis data may rely on outdated information or apply it to the wrong job. Since most jobs change over time, outdated information may misdirect other human resource activities:

> At Maple Leaf Department Stores, new job analysis information had not been collected for two years for the job of billing clerk. The outdated information indicated that bookkeeping experience was the major skill needed by clerks. However, in the last two years, the store's entire billing system had been computerized, thereby making bookkeeping skills unimportant; instead, billing clerks now needed keying skills to process billing information into the computer.

Duties and Responsibilities. Many job analysis schedules briefly explain the purpose of the job, what the job accomplishes, and how the job is performed. This summary provides a quick overview. The specific duties and responsibilities are also listed to give more detailed insight into the position. Questions on responsibility are expanded significantly when the checklist is applied to management jobs. Additional questions map areas of responsibility for decision-making, controlling, organizing, planning, and other management functions.

http://mime1.marc.gatech
.edu/mm_tools/JCAT.html

Human Characteristics and Working Conditions. Besides information about the job, analysts need to uncover the particular skills, abilities, training, education, experience, and other characteristics that jobholders need. This information is invaluable when filling job openings or advising workers about new job assignments. Information about the job environment improves understanding of the job. Working conditions may explain the need for particular skills, training, knowledge, or even a particular job design. Likewise, jobs must be free from recognizable health and safety hazards. Knowledge of hazards allows the human resource department to redesign the job or protect workers through training and safety equipment. Unique working conditions also influence hiring, placement, and compensation decisions:

> During the Second World War, one airplane manufacturer had problems installing fuel tanks inside the wings of the bombers, which had extremely narrow and cramped crawl space. These tight conditions caused considerable production delays. When the human resource department learned about this situation, it recruited welders who were less than five feet (152 cm) tall and weighed less than 100 pounds (45.5 kg).

Performance Standards. The job analysis questionnaire also seeks information about job standards, which are used to evaluate performance. This information is collected on jobs with obvious and objective standards of performance. When standards are not readily apparent, job analysts may ask supervisors or industrial engineers to develop reasonable standards of performance.

Various standardized forms are currently available for job analysis. Two of the more popular ones are Functional Job Analysis and Position Analysis Questionnaire.

Functional Job Analysis (FJA). The FJA classifies tasks using three functional scales related to data, people, and things.[5] Each functional scale lists behaviours hierarchically. For example, the lowest level in "people" dimension is "taking instruction" while the highest is "mentoring others." Similarly, "comparing data" is the simplest of the behaviours in dealing with data ("synthesizing" is the most complex). The job analyst, when studying a job, indicates the level at which the employee is operating for each of the three categories. For example, the job might involve "50 per cent copying." This is done for each of the three areas. The result is a quantitatively evaluated job.

FIGURE 2-4

Job Analysis Questionnaire

Maple Leaf Department Stores
Job Analysis Questionnaire
(Form 18-JAQ)

A. Job Analysis Status

1. Job analysis form revised on _____
2. Previous revisions on _____
3. Date of job analysis for specified job _____
4. Previous analysis on _____
5. Job analysis is conducted by _____
6. Verified by _____

B. Job Identification

1. Job title _____
2. Other titles _____
3. Division(s) _____
4. Department(s) _____
5. Title of supervisor(s) _____

C. Job Summary

Briefly describe purpose of job, what is done, and how. _____
_____

D. Duties

1. The primary duties of this job are best classified as:

Managerial _____   Technical _____
Professional _____   Clerical _____
2. List **major** duties and the proportion of time each involves:
a. _____   _____ %
b. _____   _____ %
c. _____   _____ %
3. List other duties and the proportion of time each involves:
a. _____   _____ %
b. _____   _____ %
c. _____   _____ %
4. What constitutes successful performance of these duties? _____
5. How much training is needed for normal performance of these duties? ____

E. Responsibility

1. What are the responsibilities involved in this job and how great are these responsibilities?
Extent of Responsibility

Responsibility for:	Minor	Major
a. Equipment operation		
b. Use of tools		
c. Materials usage		
d. Protection of equipment		
e. Protection of tools		
f. Protection of materials		
g. Personal safety		
h. Safety of others		
i. Others' work performance		
j. Other (Specify _____)		

F. Human Characteristics
1. What physical attributes are necessary to perform the job? _____
_____

FIGURE 2-4 CONTINUED

2. Of the following characteristics, which ones are needed and how important are they?

Characteristic	Unneeded	Helpful	Essential
1. Vision			
2. Hearing			
3. Talking			
4. Sense of smell			
5. Sense of touch			
6. Sense of taste			
7. Eye-hand coordination			
8. Overall coordination			
9. Strength			
10. Height			
11. Health			
12. Initiative			
13. Ingenuity			
14. Judgment			
15. Attention			
16. Reading			
17. Arithmetic			
18. Writing			
19. Education (Level ___)			
20. Other (Specify _____)			

3. Experience for this job:
_____ a. Unimportant
_____ b. Includes _____ (months) as (job title)_____

4. Can training be substituted for experience?
_____ Yes How: _____
_____ No Why: _____

G. Working Conditions
1. Describe the physical conditions under which this job is performed.
2. Are there unusual psychological demands connected with this job?
3. Describe any unusual conditions under which the job is performed.

H. Health or Safety Features
1. Describe fully any health or safety hazards associated with this job.
2. Is any safety training or equipment required?

I. Performance Standards
1. How is the performance of this job measured?
2. What identifiable factors contribute most to the successful performance of this job?

J. Miscellaneous Comments
Are there any aspects of this job that should be especially noted? _____

_____

_____

_____   _____
Job Analyst's Signature   Date Completed

http://harvey.psyc.vt.edu/

Position Analysis Questionnaire (PAQ). The PAQ[6], designed to apply to all types of jobs, offers an even more quantitative and finely tuned description of jobs than FJA. Using a five-point scale, the PAQ aims to determine the degree to which 194 different task elements are involved in performing a particular job (the five-point scale measures a continuum of "nominal or very infrequent" at the lowest level to "very substantial" at the highest). The PAQ allows grouping of job elements in a logical and quantitative manner and the number of job elements covered under various categories are large (e.g., there are 36 different elements that measure "relationships with other people"). This, in turn, is claimed to make job comparison easy. Past research, however, has indicated PAQ to be more useful for lower-level jobs.[7]

3. Choice of Data Collection Method

There is no one best way to collect job analysis information. Analysts must evaluate the trade-offs between time, cost, and accuracy associated with each method.[8] Once they decide which trade-offs are most important, they use interviews, questionnaires, employee logbooks, observations, or some combination of these techniques.

Interview
Approach to collecting job and performance-related information by face-to-face meeting with job holder, typically using a standardized questionnaire.

Interviews. Face-to-face *interviews* are an effective way to collect job information. The analyst has the questionnaire as a guide, but can add other questions where needed. Although the process is slow and expensive, it allows the interviewer to explain unclear questions and probe into uncertain answers. Both jobholders and supervisors typically are interviewed. The analyst usually talks with a limited number of workers first and then interviews supervisors to verify the information. This pattern ensures a high level of accuracy. The validity of the information received depends on the representativeness of the sample of the respondents and the type of questions used.

Mailed questionnaires
Surveying employees using standardized questionnaires to collect information about jobs, working conditions, and other performance-related information.

Mailed Questionnaires. A fast and less costly option is to survey employees using a *mailed questionnaire*. This can be done using internal (or interoffice) mail or Canada Post (or by fax). This approach allows many jobs to be studied at once and at little cost. However, there is less accuracy because of misunderstood questions, incomplete responses, and unreturned questionnaires. Supervisors can also be given questionnaires to verify employee responses. Given today's technology, electronic surveys are also a viable option.

Employee log
Approach to collecting job and performance-related information by asking the jobholder to summarize tasks, activities, and challenges in a diary format.

Employee Log. An *employee log* or diary is a third option. Workers periodically summarize their tasks and activities in the log. If entries are made over the entire job cycle, the diary can prove quite accurate. It may even be the only feasible way to collect job information:

> The 35 account executives at New Brunswick Brokers each handled a bewildering array of activities for clients. Since interviews and questionnaires often overlooked major parts of the job, the human resource department suggested a logbook. Most account executives initially resisted the idea, but eventually agreed to a one-month trial. The human resource department obtained the information it wanted, and account executives learned how they actually spent their days.

Logs are not a popular technique. They are time-consuming for jobholders and human resource specialists. This makes them costly. Managers and workers often see them as a nuisance and resist their introduction. Moreover, after the novelty wears off, accuracy tends to decline as entries become less frequent.

Observation
An approach to collecting job and performance-related information by direct observation of job holder by a specialist.

Observation. Another approach is direct *observation*. It is slow, costly, and potentially less accurate than other methods. Accuracy may be low because the analysts may miss irregularly occurring activities. But observation is the preferred method in some situations. When analysts question data from other techniques, observation may confirm or remove doubts. The existence of language barriers may also necessitate the observation approach, especially in cases involving foreign-language workers.

Combinations. Since each method has its faults, analysts often use two or more techniques concurrently:

> A lumber company had six facilities scattered across Canada and the United States. To interview a few workers and supervisors at each facility was considered prohibitively expensive; to rely only on questionnaire data was thought to be too inaccurate. Therefore, the human resource department interviewed selected employees at the home office and sent questionnaires to other facilities.

Combinations can ensure high accuracy at minimum cost, as the example implies. Human resource departments may even use combined methods when all employees are at the same location. Regardless of the technique used, the job analysis information is of little value until analysts convert it into more usable forms.

Past research studies indicate that different job analysis methods better suit varying human resource management purposes.[9] Figure 2-5 provides a scheme for using job analysis information. It should be noted that the figure highlights only the relative strength of each method for each purpose. For example, information collected through observation is most useful for selection and appraisal of employees. Key considerations in the choice of job analysis method should include method-purpose fit, practical feasibility, cost, and reliability of the data collected for making valid decisions. Job analysis information enables an organization to take the proactive actions discussed.

Combinations
Concurrent use of two or more job analysis techniques (e.g., interviews and observation).

Phase 3: Use of Job Analysis Information

The information collected about various jobs is put into such usable forms as job descriptions, job specifications, and job standards. Together, these applications of job analysis information provide a minimum human resource information system and data necessary for formulating various HR strategies. The remainder of this chapter discusses these applications.

FIGURE 2-5

Different Job Analysis Methods Best Suit Different HR Goals

Method of Data Collection	Job Description and Design	Selection	Training	Compensation	Counselling
Interviews	*	*	*	*	*
Questionnaires	*	*	*	*	
Employee log	*				*
Observation	*	*	*		

Source: Based on several past writings including: E.L. Levine, R.A. Ash, and N. Bennett. "Explorative Comparative Study of Four Job Analysis Methods." *Journal of Applied Psychology*, Vol. 65, 1980. pp. 524–35 Copyright © 1980 by the American Psychological Association, adapted with permission, and E.L. Levine, R.A. Ash, H. Hall, and F. Sistrunk, "Evaluation of Job Analysis Methods by Experienced Job Analysts," *Academy of Management Journal*, Vol. 26, No. 2, 1983, pp. 339–48.

JOB DESCRIPTION

Job description
A recognized list of functions, tasks, accountabilities, working conditions, and competencies for a particular occupation or job.

www.salarysource.com/
description.cfm

A **JOB DESCRIPTION** is a written statement that explains the duties, working conditions, and other aspects of a specified job.

Contents of a Typical Job Description

Within a firm, all the job descriptions follow the same style, although between organizations, form and content may vary. One approach is to write a narrative description that covers the job in a few paragraphs. Another typical style breaks the description down into several subparts, as shown in Figure 2-6. This figure shows a job description that parallels the job analysis checklist that originally generated the data.

FIGURE 2-6

A Job Description

Maple Leaf Department Stores
Job Description

Job Title: _____   Job Code: _____

Date: _____   Author: _____

Job Location: _____   Job Grade: _____

Report to: _____   Status: _____

Job Summary:	Interacts with customers on a daily basis, promptly responding to all inquiries in a courteous and efficient manner. Encourages the sale of company products at every opportunity and applies exemplary customer relation skills that promote a superior company image. Provides information to customers about product features and substitutes when asked.
Responsibilities:	Responds to customer inquiries on product features, prices, services, and delivery terms.
	Takes customer orders for products and communicates these accurately to supply and servicing personnel in the company.
	Accepts returns of merchandise by customers and gives them credit for the same.
	Displays and stocks merchandise on shelves.
	Appropriately prices items based on instructions received from the supervisor.
	Prepares necessary documents and transmits/files copies to relevant offices within the company.
	Responds to other miscellaneous inquiries especially those related to warranties, delivery terms, servicing frequencies (in the case of equipment).
	Undertakes other tasks assigned by the supervisor.
	Operates cash register and balances accounts at the end of the shift.
Working Conditions:	Works in a well-ventilated office. Must be able to work shifts.

The above information is correct as approved by:

(Signed) _____   (Signed) _____

Customer Service Representative   Customer Service Supervisor

www.spb.ca.gov/
wwwcp1rd.cfm

Job identity
Key part of a job description, including job title, location, and status.

Job code
A code that uses numbers, letters, or both to provide a quick summary of the job and its content.

National Occupational Classification (NOC)
An occupational classification by federal government, using skill level and skill type of jobs.

The key parts of a job description are: job identity, job summary, job duties, and working conditions. Most job descriptions also identify the author, the work supervisor, and the date on which it was prepared.

Job Identity

The section on *job identity* typically includes job title, job location, job code, job grade, and its status (whether or not exempted from overtime laws). *Job codes* use numbers, letters, or both to provide a quick summary of the job. These codes are useful for comparing jobs. Figures 2-7 and 2-8 explain the coding used in the *National Occupational Classification (NOC)*. The two major attributes of jobs that were used as classification criteria in developing the NOC were *skill level* (amount and type of education and training) and *skill type* (type of work performed). Other factors, such as industry and occupational mobility, were also taken into consideration.[10]

Skill Level. Four skill level categories are identified in the NOC, describing the educational and training requirements of occupations (see Figure 2-7).

Skill Type. Skill type is defined generally as the type of work performed. Ten broad occupational categories (0 to 9) are identified in the NOC. Figure 2-8 describes these in detail.

FIGURE 2-7

NOC Skill Level Criteria

	Education/Training	Other
Skill Level A	University degree (Bachelor's, Master's, or postgraduate)	
Skill Level B	Two to three years of post-secondary education at community college, institute of technology, or CEGEP *or* Two to four years of apprenticeship training *or* Three to four years of secondary school and more than two years of on-the-job training, training courses or specific work experience	Occupations with supervisory responsibilities are assigned to skill level B. Occupations with significant health and safety responsibilities (e.g., firefighters, police officers, and registered nursing assistants) are assigned to skill level B.
Skill Level C	One to four years of secondary school education Up to two years of on-the-job training, training courses or specific work experience	
Skill Level D	Up to two years of secondary school and short work demonstration or on-the-job training	

Source: Human Resources Development Canada, National Occupation Classification. Reproduced with permission of the Minister of Public Works and Government Services Canada, 2001.

FIGURE 2-8

NOC Skill Type Categories

When the first digit is ... the Skill Type Category is

1   Business, Finance, and Administrative Occupations

2   Natural and Applied Sciences and Related Occupations

3   Health Occupations

4   Occupations in Social Science, Education, Government Service, and Religion

5   Occupations in Art, Culture, Recreation, and Sport

6   Sales and Service Occupations

7   Trades, Transport and Equipment Operators, and Related Occupations

8   Occupations Unique to Primary Industry

9   Occupations Unique to Processing, Manufacturing, and Utilities

When the second digit is ... the Skill Level Category is

1   Skill Level A (Professional Occupations)

2 or 3   Skill Level B (Technical, Paraprofessional, and Skilled Occupations)

4 or 5   Skill Level C (Intermediate Occupations)

6   Skill Level D (Labouring and Elemental Occupations)

Important Note: This applies to all occupations except management occupations. For management, the first digit is "0" and the second digit represents the skill type categories, from 1 to 9, as above.
Source: Human Resources Development Canada, National Occupation Classification. Reproduced with permission of the Minister of Public Works and Government Services Canada, 2001.

www.cthrb.ca

An even more refined job classification for certain jobs is provided by Canadian Technology Human Resources Board. It is particularly useful for applied science and engineering disciplines.

Job Summary and Duties

After the job identification section (in Figure 2-6), the next part of the description is the job summary. It is a written narrative that concisely summarizes the job in a few sentences. It tells what the job is, how it is done, and why. Most authorities recommend that job summaries specify the primary actions involved. Then, in a simple, action-oriented style, the job description lists the job duties.

This section is important to human resource specialists. A well-developed job description helps an organization to define clearly the required duties and responsibilities associated with a position.[11] In essence, it explains what the job requires. The effectiveness of other human resource actions depends upon this understanding because each major duty is described in terms of the actions expected. Tasks and activities are identified. Performance is emphasized. Even responsibilities are implied or stated within the job duties. If employees are members of a union, the union may want to narrow the duties associated with specific jobs:

> Before the union organized, the employee job descriptions contained the phrase "or other work as assigned." The union believed supervisors abused this clause by assigning idle workers to do unrelated jobs. With the threat of a strike, management removed the phrase, and supervisors lost much of their flexibility in assigning work.

Working Conditions

Working conditions
Includes physical environment, hours, hazards, travel requirements, etc. associated with a job.

A job description also explains *working conditions*. It may go beyond descriptions of the physical environment. Hours of work, safety and health hazards, travel requirements, and other features of the job expand the meaning of this section.

Approvals

Since job descriptions affect most human resource decisions, their accuracy should be reviewed by selected jobholders and their supervisors. Then supervisors are asked to approve the description. This approval serves as a further test of the job

FIGURE 2-9

Examples of NOC Unit Groups

NOC Coding System. A two-digit code is assigned at the major group level. A third digit is added at the minor group level, and a fourth digit is added at the unit group level. For example:

- Major Group 31 — Professional Occupations in Health
- Minor Group 314 —Professional Occupations in Therapy and Assessment
- Unit Group 3142 — Physiotherapists

Using the above coding system, the following codes are identified:

0211	Engineering Managers
0212	Architecture and Science Managers
0721	Facility Operation Managers
0722	Maintenance Managers
2231	Civil Engineering Technologists and Technicians
2234	Construction Estimators
3223	Dental Technicians
3412	Dental Laboratory Bench Workers
4164	Social Policy Researchers, Consultants, and Program Officers
4165	Health Policy Researchers, Consultants, and Program Officers
4214	Early Childhood Educators
6473	Early Childhood Educator Assistants
6443	Amusement Attraction Operators and Other Amusement Occupations
6671	Attendants in Recreation and Sport
7265	Welders
9515	Welding, Brazing, and Soldering Machine Operators

Source: Human Resources Development Canada, National Occupation Classification. Reproduced with permission of the Minister of Public Works and Government Services Canada, 2001.

description and a further check on the collection of job analysis information. Neither human resource specialists nor managers should consider approval lightly. If the description is incorrect, the human resource department will become a source of problems, not assistance:

> In explaining the job of foundry attendant to new employees, human resource specialists at one firm relied on an inaccurate job description. Many new employees quit the job during the first two weeks. When asked why, most said the duties were less challenging than they were led to believe. When analysts checked, it was found that the job description had never been verified by the supervisors.

JOB SPECIFICATIONS

Job specification
A written statement that explains what a job demands of job holders and the human skills and factors required.

THE DIFFERENCE between a job description and a job specification is one of perspective. A job description defines what the job does; it is a profile of the job. A *job specification* describes what the job demands of employees who do it and the human factors that are required. It is a profile of the human characteristics needed by the job. These requirements include experience, training, education, physical demands, and mental demands.

Since the job description and job specification both focus on the job, they are often combined into one document. The combination is simply called a job description. Whether part of a job description or a separate document, job specifications include the information illustrated in Figure 2-10. The data to compile specifications also come from the job analysis checklist.

Job specifications contain a job identification section if they are a separate document. The subheadings and purpose are the same as those found in the job identification section of the job description.

A job specification should include specific tools, actions, experiences, education, and training (i.e., the individual requirements of the job). For example, it should describe "physical effort" in terms of the special actions demanded by the job. "Lifts 40-kilogram bags" is better than "Lifts heavy weights." Clear behaviour statements give a better picture than vague generalities.[12] Specifications of mental effort help human resource experts to determine the intellectual abilities that are needed to perform the job. Figure 2-10 contains several examples of the kind of information about physical and mental efforts needed by customer service representatives working for a department store.

The job specification for these Hydro workers should clearly state that working outdoors under extreme conditions is a regular part of the job.

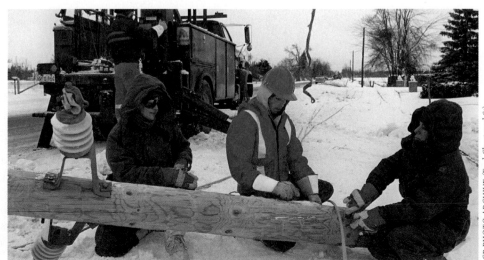

CP PHOTO ARCHIVE (Fred Chartrand St)

FIGURE 2-10

A Job Specification Sheet

Maple Leaf Department Stores
Job Specification

Job Title: _____   Job Code: _____

Date: _____   Author: _____

Job Location: _____   Job Grade: _____

Report to: _____   Status: _____

SKILL FACTORS

Education: Ten years of general education or equivalent.

Experience: Prior selling experience in a consumer-goods industry is desirable.

Communication: Strong interpersonal skills a must.

Ability to empathize with customer needs when communicating.
Knowledge of French highly desirable.
Should have strong oral communication skills.

EFFORT FACTORS

Physical Demands: Normally limited to those associated with clerical jobs although long periods of standing may be required in some instances.

Should be able to lift products weighing 10 kilograms or less.

Finger dexterity to operate a computer keyboard and cash register is essential.

Mental Demands: Ability to respond to customer inquiries regarding prices, service terms, etc. a must. This requires good short term memory.

Ability to learn and remember product codes of popular items.

Working Conditions: Works in a well-ventilated office.

May have to work outdoors in the case of lawn/gardening-related equipment.

The above information is correct as approved by:

(Signed)_____   (Signed) _____

    Customer Service Representative   Customer Service Supervisor

Do the working conditions make any unusual demands on jobholders? The working conditions found in job descriptions may be translated by job specifications into demands faced by workers. Figure 2-11 provides examples for the job of hospital orderly. It shows that a simple statement of working conditions found in the job description can hold significant implications for jobholders. For example, compare points 2 and 3 under the job description column with points 2 and 3 under job specifications.

FIGURE 2-11

Translation of Working Conditions for Job Description to Job Specification

Calgary General Hospital
Hospital Orderly

Job Description Statement of Working Conditions	Job Specifications Interpretation of Working Conditions
1. Works in physically comfortable surroundings.	1. (Omitted. This item on the job description makes no demands on jobholders.)
2. Deals with physically ill and diseased patients.	2. Exposed to unpleasant situations and communicable diseases.
3. Deals with mentally ill patients.	3. May be exposed to verbal and physical abuse.

When preparing specifications, it is critical not to include needless job requirements, as the following example illustrates:

> In one instance, an employer required a high-school diploma for nearly all jobs within the company except those in the labour pool. When the need for a diploma was challenged, the employer could not show that it was absolutely necessary to perform many of the jobs for which it was officially required, and although this requirement was applied equally to all applicants, it had an unequal impact on applicants from minority groups. As a result, many persons belonging to such groups were offered labour-pool jobs only.

Further, needless job requirements exclude potentially qualified individuals from consideration, which may reduce the effectiveness not only of hiring, but also of other human resource activities.

Competency
A knowledge, skill, ability, or characteristic associated with superior job performance.

More recently, competency-based job descriptions and specifications have become increasingly popular. A *competency* is a knowledge, skill, ability, or characteristic associated with high performance on a job, such as problem solving, analytical thinking, or leadership.[13] Others have defined the concept "an attribute bundle," consisting of task competencies, results competencies, and knowledge, skills, behaviours, and attitude competencies.[14] Whatever the precise definition, the objective in most cases is to identify characteristics that are associated with superior job performance.

www.wiso.uni-augsburg.de/
sozio/hartmann/psycho/
journals.html

Competencies are identified after a careful analysis of the work of high performers. This may be done through observation, listings of critical behaviours or incidents at work, interviews, employee logs, or otherwise. Some organizations have used competencies as the foundation for job design, new performance management systems, selection and career pathing, compensation, training and development, and in a few cases, a highly integrated human resource management system called "competency-based management."

> A survey of 219 Canadian organizations by The Conference Board of Canada found that 45 per cent of the responding firms used a competency framework for training and development activities. A large number of the respondents had also used it for hiring, compensation, and performance management. According to 85 per cent of the respondents, the adoption of a competency framework had enabled their training programs to become more strategic, while facilitating decision making. This was because a competency framework allowed employees to quickly identify the success factors in their organizational and personal work.[15]

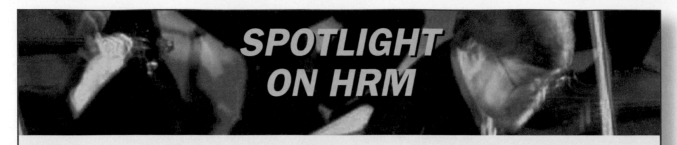

SPOTLIGHT ON HRM

EVERYTHING YOU WANTED TO KNOW ABOUT COMPETENCY MODELLING

A current hot topic in HRD is competency modelling. For the record, the idea of testing for competence rather than intelligence was first proposed in the early 1970s by David McClelland, a former Harvard psychologist. McClelland was asked by the U.S. Foreign Service to find new research methods that could predict human performance and reduce the bias of traditional intelligence and aptitude testing. Thus, the notion of competence measurement was born. . . .

Let's start with a glossary of terms used by most proponents of competency modelling.

Ability. This refers to a talent, such as manual dexterity, visual or spatial acuity, or conceptual thinking. The premise is that though abilities may be taught, learned, or enhanced, there's a natural predisposition to them.

Behaviour. This is the observable demonstration of some competency, skill, ability, or characteristic. It is a set of actions that, presumably, can be observed, taught, learned, and measured.

Behavioural anchors. These are more specific than behaviours, which are descriptive but independent of each other. Anchors are built in levels; each level of description is more complex than the previous one.

Cluster. This is a group of competencies, skills, or behaviours, organized for the purpose of simplification. An example might be a technical cluster under which various behaviours describe the cluster for a job or group of jobs. Cluster can also refer to a group of jobs connected by a common knowledge base or by organizational structure.

Competency. This is a knowledge, skill, ability, or characteristic associated with high performance on a job, such as problem solving, analytical thinking, leadership. Some definitions of a competency include motives, beliefs, and values.

Competency model. This term describes the output from analyses that differentiate high performers from average and low performers. Competency models are represented in different formats, depending on the methods used to collect the data, customers' requirements, and the particular biases of the people creating the model.

Core competency. This term refers to organizational capabilities or strengths—what an organization does best. A core competency might be product development or customer service.

Criticality. This is a measure of how important a particular competency is for a job or group of jobs.

Constructing the Model

Here are some tools for building a competency model.

Job-analysis interviews. Job-analysis interviews can be conducted in person or on the phone, and one-on-one or in focus groups. Interviews are probably the best method of data collection because the interviewer can probe and ask follow-up questions. It is, however, time-consuming.

Focus groups. Focus groups are useful for collecting information ... when it's not practical to conduct one-on-one interviews. Focus groups also stimulate dialogue, though the information can be biased in favour of dominant participants.

Questionnaires. These are useful when it's necessary to interview many.. experts.. and when there are time constraints. It's imperative to have appropriate questions, a sufficient sample returned, and the results analyzed and interpreted accurately.

Job descriptions. These can be useful sources of information, assuming that they are up-to-date and supplemented with some data from interviews or questionnaires.

Competency-model formats. The best way to explain the different formats for building a competency model is to give examples. Some models use statistical data to describe the competency requirements in specific detail and use less detail in the competency descriptions. Others reverse the balance.

In a competency model for a district sales manager, the approach might be to identify success factors (competencies), provide a behavioural description of each one, rank-order the factors by criticality, and establish a proficiency level for each factor. Success factors might include "leadership," "integrity," "self-motivation," and "tenacity."

Such models are useful for identifying job or role requirements at the competency level and for matching jobs with people.

A cluster-type model of leadership success factors for manufacturing managers might list behavioural descriptors under broad categories or themes, such as "developing oneself" and "working with others." For example, under the category "taking initiative," the behavioural descriptions might include "finds innovative paths to effective results" and "takes risks." No criticality or proficiency is established for the clusters or descriptors. These types of models are useful for capturing information in groups and for grouping jobs in such horizontal categories as "managers" or "executives.". . .

The most important point about competency models is that the formats be governed by the collective wisdom of the people that need and build them. Still, if those people have only one way of producing output, a second opinion might be desirable. The decision to use a particular type of competency model should be determined by the desired applications.

For example, if the model's intended purpose is performance management, it's best to have more detail or specificity in the model.

If the applications are to be succession planning, staffing, or 360 feedback, it might not be necessary to have a high level of detail, depending on how the competencies or success factors are defined.

Remember: Applications that seem unnecessary at first may prove useful down the road. . . .

Competency models provide potentially valuable information, but they're useless if there's no coherent and systemic implementation strategy for leveraging the information....

Content. Process. Structure. Those make up the foundation for successful change. No matter what anyone tells you, implementing a competency model is a change effort. For instance, new information will be used to modify HRD efforts or introduce new ones. The model will also affect the way people do their jobs, and it will affect decisions on employees' careers, their perceptions of their competence, their potential for advancement, and other job and career issues.

On an administrative level, a competency model requires someone to manage the new information to ensure confidentiality, accuracy, and relevance to current circumstances. Therefore, it's crucial that the "drivers" of the model implementation maintain an appropriate perspective. Without that, the changes and the organization's complexities can become obstacles to success.

Source: Richard J. Mirabile, "Everything You Wanted to Know About Competency Modeling," *Training & Development*, August 1997, pp. 73-77. Copyright August 1997, The American Society for Training and Development. Reprinted with permission. All rights reserved.

JOB PERFORMANCE STANDARDS

Job performance standards
The work performance expected from an employee on a particular job.

JOB ANALYSIS has a third application, *job performance standards*. These standards serve two functions. First, they become objectives or targets for employee efforts. The challenge or pride of meeting objectives may serve to motivate employees. Once standards are met, workers may feel accomplishment and achievement. This outcome contributes to employee satisfaction. Without standards, employee performance may suffer.

Second, standards are criteria against which job success is measured. They are indispensable to managers or human resource specialists who attempt to control work performance. Without standards, no control system can evaluate job performance.

All control systems have four features: standards, measures, correction, and feedback. The relationship among these four factors is illustrated in Figure 2-12. Job performance standards are developed from job analysis information, and then actual employee performance is measured. When measured performance strays from the job standard, corrective action is taken. The corrective action, in turn, may result in changes in either the standards (if they were inappropriate) or actual job performance:

In the Calgary Trust Company, current standards dictated that each loan supervisor review 350 mortgage-loan applications per month. Yet the actual output averaged 290. When more recent job information was collected, analysts discovered that since

FIGURE 2-12

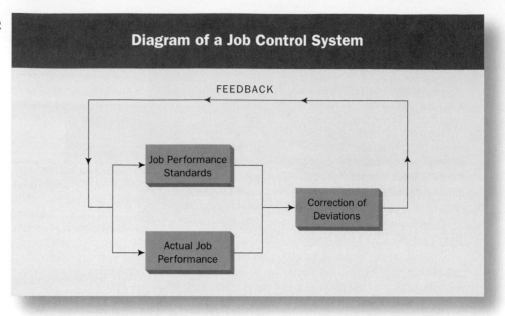

the standards had been first set, several new duties had been added for each supervisor. Corrective action resulted in new job designs, revised job descriptions, and more realistic standards.

When the standards are wrong, as in the trust company example, they alert managers and human resource specialists to problems that need correction. The example also underscores the need for keeping job analysis information current.

Job standards are obtained either from job analysis information or from alternative sources. For example, industry standards may be used as benchmarks for performance in certain jobs (especially service functions such as human resource management function).[16] Job analysis information is usually sufficient for jobs that have the following features:

- performance is quantified;

- performance is easily measurable;

- performance standards are understood by workers and supervisors; and

- performance requires little interpretation.

Jobs with short work cycles often exhibit these features. An example is an assembly-line job. For these jobs, questions on the job analysis checklist may generate specific, quantitative answers. When confirmed by supervisors, this information becomes the job performance standard. In the case of some service jobs, quantifiable "outputs" may not be readily available; but even here, performance can be appraised by looking at the behaviours of the job holders. More details of behaviourally oriented performance appraisals will be discussed in Chapter Nine.

Alternative Sources of Standards

Although job analysis information does not always provide a source of job standards, it is necessary even if analysts use other means to develop reasonable standards. The most common alternative sources of job standards are work measurement and participative goal setting.

Work Measurement

Work measurement side definition:

Work measurement techniques estimate the normal performance of average workers; the results dictate the job performance standard. Such techniques are applied to non-managerial jobs and are created from historical data, time study, and work sampling. They may be used by the human resource department, line management, or industrial engineering. Regardless of who applies work measurement techniques, however, job analysis information is also needed.

Work measurement
Methods for evaluating what a job's performance standards should be.

Historical data
Use of past production records to understand jobs and their performance standards.

Historical Data. **Historical data** can be obtained from past records if job analysis does not supply performance standards. For example, the number of shirts produced per month by a clothing manufacturer indicates how many sleeves, collars, and buttons should be sewn on by each worker. One weakness of this approach is that it assumes past performance is average performance. Another weakness is that historical data are useless on new jobs. However, if production records are reviewed for longstanding jobs, historically based standards may be more accurate than standards drawn from a job analysis checklist.

Time studies
Identification and timing of each element in a job to find out how long the entire job takes to be performed.

Time Study. **Time studies** produce standards when jobs can be observed and timed. Time studies identify each element within a job. Then each element is timed while being repeated by an average worker using the standard method of doing the job. The average times for each element of the job are summed up to yield the *rated job time*. Allowances for rest breaks, fatigue, or equipment delays are added to produce a *standard time*. The standard time allows human resource specialists to compute performance standards:

> Assume an administrative assistant can key a page of straight copy in an average of four minutes, based on several direct observations. To this rated job time of four minutes, allowances for changing disks, replacing printer paper, taking rest breaks, and so on, are added. The total is a standard time of five minutes. This means that the administrative assistant's standard of performance should be an average of one page of keying per five minutes, or 12 pages an hour.

Work sampling
Process by which a particular job and its elements are observed on many occasions to identify the rated and standard time needed to carry out various job elements.

Work Sampling. How does the analyst know the number of minutes to add for allowances? Allowances are usually set through **work sampling**.

> By making 300 observations of clerks at different times during the day over a two-week period, for example, analysts might discover that the clerks were actually keying two-thirds of the time. If eight minutes of uninterrupted keying are required to key a page, then the standard time can be computed by dividing the rated time of eight minutes by the fraction of time spent working, or two-thirds in this example. The result is a standard time of twelve minutes. Mathematically, the computation is:

> Rated time ÷ observed proportion of work time used = standard time
> OR 8 minutes ÷ 2/3 = 12 minutes

Standards for some jobs cannot be determined by either job analysis information or work measurement. In service or managerial jobs, output may reflect changing trade-offs. For example, the number of customers handled by a grocery checkout clerk depends on how busy the store is and on the size of each customer's purchases. But standards are still useful, even though they are difficult to set. In some cases, mutual agreement between the worker and the manager—participative goal setting—is more likely to be effective.

Participative goal setting
A process of goal setting where managers develop performance standards through discussions with subordinates.

Participative Goal Setting

When a job lacks obvious standards, managers may develop them participatively through discussions with subordinates. These conversations discuss the purpose of the job, its role in relation to other jobs, the organization's requirements, and the employee's needs. The employee gains insight into what is expected. Implicit or explicit promises of future rewards may also result. From these discussions, the manager and the employee reach some jointly shared objectives and standards. The process may even lead to greater employee commitment, morale, satisfaction, and motivation. Since objectives are usually for individual positions (instead of jobs), they are seldom included in job descriptions.

Performance standards sometimes are set participatively with union leaders. Labour leaders understand the important role of job analysis information, and they may insist on negotiating performance standards for jobs. These negotiated agreements are written into legally enforceable contracts:

> In one paper products company, management decided to increase production rates by five per cent to meet customer demand. After this was done, the union threatened legal action because the new standards conflicted with those in the labour contract. Management was forced to retain the old standard.

Today, several organizations identify competencies associated with specific job positions, which are then used for hiring, training, and other human resource functions. While alternate approaches to designing performance standards under a competency approach exist, an example of one approach is shown in Figure 2-13. In this type of model, the key clusters and competencies are first identified. A *cluster* is a group of competencies, skills, or behaviours organized for the purpose of simplification, while competencies themselves (as defined earlier in this chapter) refer to the knowledge, skill, ability, and other characteristics associated with high performance on a job. The clusters and competencies are typically listed with the definitions on the left side and the possible performance behaviours for establishing a level of proficiency for each competency on the right side.

Other competency formats for describing performance exist. Some formats identify competencies, provide a behavioural description of each one, rank-order the competencies by criticality, and establish a proficiency level for each factor. Success competencies might include "leadership," "integrity," "tenacity," and so on. Such competency models are useful for identifying job or role requirements at the competency level and for matching jobs with people. Competency models in the context of job training will be discussed in Chapter Eight.

Cluster
A group of job competencies, skills, or behaviours organized for ease of description.

JOB DESIGN

WORLDWIDE competition, complex technology, and increasing worker expectations have necessitated redesign of many jobs. Computerization, which barely existed 50 years ago, has brought about a revolution changing millions of jobs—if not every job today. While some jobs have grown more challenging, others are increasingly being automated or eliminated altogether. And yet, despite this vast increase in automation and computerization, human resources have become more, not less, important in today's organizations:

> For example, the cost of a human error in a nuclear plant or in flying a supersonic jet can be enormous. Whether it is the high-speed computers or the traditional auto assembly plant now run by robots, the contribution of the human beings continues to be critical. Indeed, new technologies may be dangerous or unforgiving when operated by uncommitted or poorly skilled persons.

Job design
Identification of job duties, characteristics, competencies, and sequences taking into consideration technology, work force, organization's character, and environment.

How well people perform is shaped, at least in part, by the characteristics designed into their jobs.[17] Not only is productivity affected, but quality of work life is also tied to *job design*. Jobs are the central link between employees and the organization. Poorly designed jobs not only lead to low productivity, but they can also

FIGURE 2-13

Competency Model for a University or College Instructor

The key clusters for a university or college instructor include course design, use of appropriate teaching methods and aids, choice of pedagogy, evaluation of learning, knowledge of material, student counseling, and maintenance of learning climate. Competencies in each of these clusters will have to be defined clearly and different levels of proficiency indicated to assess the instructor's performance. The above clusters reflect only the "teaching" dimension of an instructor's job. Other performance dimensions such as research, administrative activities, and community service will have to be detailed in a similar manner. Below is a sample cluster for course design.

Cluster: Course Design

Course Objectives
Ability to provide clear course objectives and expectations to the students in simple and easy to understand language.

Proficiency Rating
0 Is unable to perform basic task.
1 Can adapt an existing course outline, making slight changes.
2 Can make major adaptations to an existing course outline, including new objectives.
3 Can make up own course outline without any help from outside or without referring to any existing outlines.
4 Is considered an expert in this area; can advise junior instructors on how to develop outlines that clearly communicate course objectives to the students.

Responsiveness to Students
Ability to incorporate student needs and desires into the course design.

Proficiency Rating
0 Does not include any student needs or desires when designing the course; uses the same outline irrespective of the audience (e.g., inexperienced students, mature students).
1 Can make minimal adaptations to the course to meet student needs.
2 Can survey student needs and incorporate some of their needs or desires if consistent with own objectives.
3 Can survey students and modify own course in light of suggestions emerging from them.
4 Considered an expert in designing student-responsive courses and can advise and train others.

Course Structure
Ability to provide detailed guidelines for various course requirements, including datelines for these.

Proficiency Rating
0 Does not provide any date or guidelines for various course requirements; no well-thought out course sequencing.
1 Can design outlines that provide datelines for key assignments and some guidance for major course requirements. The course is fairly well sequenced.
2 Can design outlines that provide clear guidelines for all course requirements. The course material is well sequenced.
3 Can design course outlines clearly explaining requirements and course sequencing; communicates these to the students and ensures that there are no misunderstandings.
4 Considered an expert instructor who can design comprehensive and clear course outlines with all necessary guidelines; can train or coach others in this area.

cause employee turnover, absenteeism, complaints, sabotage, unionization, resignations, and other problems and require job redesign at a later time, which can be a time-consuming and often unnecessary exercise. One insurance firm's experience of redesigning jobs is noteworthy in this context:

> In General Life and Home Insurance Company, each clerk had narrowly defined responsibilities. Each clerk performed a specific function and moved the "paperwork" on to someone else. The result was that no one was responsible for handling an application for a policy conversion. In fact, no one department had responsibility since activities were spread over three departments. In a job redesign effort, clerks were grouped into teams of five to seven employees and each team was trained to do the functions of all three departments. Members learned new skills, job satisfaction went up, and pay improved since each team member now had greater skills and responsibilities.

In this case, the company had to consider the various environmental, organizational, and employee-related factors before redesigning the jobs. Typically, job redesign results in some trade-offs. Under the new structure in General Life and Home Insurance Company, each clerk needs to have knowledge of several activities. Therefore, more training for these clerks is necessary. And, as they become more qualified, the company will need to pay them higher salaries.

Figure 2-14 illustrates four critical elements that deserve consideration when designing jobs: organizational considerations, ergonomic considerations, employee considerations, and environmental considerations. Each element will be discussed below.

Organizational Considerations of Job Design

Simply put, each job should contribute to the overall organizational objectives effectively and efficiently. The overall organizational mission is accomplished through a series of interrelated tasks or activities. If the organization is to remain successful and grow, these tasks and activities should be performed in a timely, effective, and efficient manner. This involves focus on two interrelated concepts: efficiency and work flow.

Efficiency

Concern for high task efficiency or achieving maximum output with minimum expenditure of time, effort or other resources was first underscored by *scientific management* (see Appendix to Chapter One) around the turn of the century. *Industrial engineering*, which evolved from this movement, focuses on analyzing work methods and establishing optimal time standards by finding the best ways to do jobs.[18] As discussed earlier, time standards are established by recording the time needed (typically

FIGURE 2-14

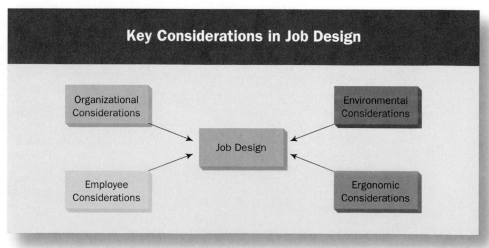

using a stop-watch or more recently video monitors) to complete each element in a work cycle. These industrial engineers study work cycles to determine which, if any, job elements can be combined, modified, or eliminated to reduce the overall time needed to perform the task. *Task specialization* was suggested as a key strategy to improve efficiency. According to these engineers, when workers are limited to a few repetitive tasks, output is usually higher. This is because specialized jobs lead to short *job cycles*. The automotive industry is a good example of such industrial engineering practices:[19]

> For example, an assembly-line worker in Windsor, Ontario, might pick up a headlight, plug it in, twist the adjustment screws, and pick up the next headlight within 30 seconds. Completing these tasks in 30 seconds means this worker's job cycle takes one-half a minute. The job cycle begins when the next headlight is picked up.

Headlight installation is a specialized job. It is so specialized that training takes only a few minutes. And the short job cycle means that the assembler gains much experience in a short time. Said another way, short job cycles require small investments in training and allow the worker to learn the job quickly. Training costs remain low because the worker needs to master only one job.

The above approach stresses efficiency in effort, time, labour costs, training, and employee learning time. Today, this technique is still widely used in assembly operations. It is especially effective when dealing with poorly educated workers or workers who have little industrial experience. But the efficient design of jobs also considers such organizational elements as work flow, ergonomics, and work practices.

Work Flow

Work flow
The sequence of and balance between jobs in an organization needed to produce the firm's goods or services.

The flow of work in an organization is strongly influenced by the nature of the product or service. The product or service usually suggests the sequence of, and balance between, jobs if the work is to be done efficiently. For example, the frame of a car must be built before the fenders and doors can be added. Once the sequence of jobs is determined, then the balance between jobs is established:

> Suppose it takes one person 30 seconds to install each headlight. In two minutes, an assembler can put on four headlights. If, however, it takes four minutes to install the necessary headlight receptacles, then the job designer must balance these two interrelated jobs by assigning two people to install the receptacles. Otherwise, a production bottleneck results. Since the work flow demands two receptacle installers for each headlight installer, one worker specializes on the right-side receptacle and another specializes on the left side.

These car frames are constructed on a suspended assembly line so employees work in ergonomically correct positions and do not become fatigued.

CP PHOTO ARCHIVE (Associated Press YONHAP)

Ergonomic Considerations

Ergonomics
The study of relationships between physical attributes of workers and their work environment to reduce physical and mental strain and increase productivity and quality of work life.

Optimal productivity requires that the physical relationship between the worker and the work be considered in designing jobs. Derived from the Greek words "ergo" meaning work and "nomos" meaning laws, *ergonomics* in a general sense means the "laws of work" and focuses on how human beings physically interface with their work.[20] The study of ergonomics is multi-disciplinary, using principles drawn from biology (especially anatomy and physiology), the behavioural sciences (psychology and sociology), as well as physics and engineering. Although the nature of job tasks may not vary when ergonomic factors are considered, the locations of tools, switches, and the work product itself are evaluated and placed in a position for ease of use. In other words, ergonomics focuses on fitting the task to the worker in many instances rather than simply forcing employees to adapt to the task.[21]

> On an automobile assembly line, for example, a car frame may actually be elevated at a work station so the worker does not become fatigued from stooping. Similarly, the location of dashboard instruments in a car is ergonomically engineered to make driving easier.

Attention to details of work settings can lead to significant improvements in efficiency and productivity as exemplified in the case of Saturn Corporation, a General Motors subsidiary that produces Saturn cars:

> Saturn uses state-of-the art manufacturing and job design techniques—including industrial engineering, ergonomics, and behavioural considerations. Cars pass through the assembly line on hydraulic lifts that allow employees to raise or lower the cars to suit their own height. Employees are allowed to ride the platform and take up to six minutes to finish the tasks correctly (traditional assembly lines allot less than one minute). Industrial engineers videotape employee actions and simplify operations to minimize motion. In one instance, employees saved one-third of the steps walking to and from cars, thereby conserving energy.[22]

Ergonomic considerations are also important to maintain safety at the workplace. Ignoring a proper fit between workstation and worker can be catastrophic.[23]

> Workplace accidents cost Canadian firms about $31 billion annually. A significant percentage of these accidents stem from poor workplace or task design.[24]

Ergonomics will become more important in the future when the Canadian workforce gets older:

> By 2015, the 45- to 54-year-old segment of the Canadian population will grow by 155 per cent (compared to the figures in the mid-1990s). Those of pre-retirement age (55 to 64 years) will grow by 194 per cent. Since aging results in a decrease in several hand functions (e.g., grip strength, precision), lowered muscular strength, and reduced vision and hearing loss, the need for ergonomic-based work improvements to reduce physical demands will be higher than ever before. Items such as mechanical assists for lifting (e.g., tilters, vacuum lifts) and for assembly (e.g., screwguns, adjustable tables) will be essential. Such improvements will also be needed for lighting arrangements and size of character displays in terminals to respond to older workers' diminished visual capabilities.[25]

Employee Considerations

Jobs cannot be designed by using only those elements that aid efficiency. To do so overlooks the human needs of the people who are to perform the work. Instead, job designers draw heavily on behavioural research to provide a work environment that helps satisfy individual needs. Later chapters on employee motivation (Chapter Twelve) and employee relations (Chapter Thirteen) deal with specific task arrangements that maximize challenge and autonomy for employees. This section briefly discusses the importance of high autonomy, variety, task identity, feedback, and task significance in job design context.[26]

Autonomy

Autonomy
Independence; in a job context, having control over one's work and one's response to the work environment.

Autonomy refers to assuming responsibility for what one does. It is the freedom to control one's response to the environment. While employee personality influences the relationship between autonomy and specific task performance,[27] in most instances, jobs that give workers the authority to make decisions tend to increase employees' sense of recognition, self-esteem, job satisfaction, and performance. The absence of autonomy, on the other hand, can cause employee apathy or poor performance:

> A common problem in many production operations is that employees develop an indifferent attitude because they believe they have no control over their jobs. On the bottling line of a small brewery, however, teams of workers were allowed to speed up or slow down the rate of the bottling line as long as they met daily production goals. Although total output per shift did not change, there were fewer cases of capping machines jamming or breaking down for other reasons. When asked about this unexpected development, the supervisor concluded, "Employees pride themselves on meeting the shift quota. So they are more careful to check for defective bottle caps before they load the machine."

Variety

Variety
An attribute of jobs wherein the worker has the opportunity to use different skills and abilities, or perform different activities.

A lack of *variety* may cause boredom. Boredom in turn leads to fatigue, and fatigue causes errors. By injecting variety into jobs, human resource specialists can reduce fatigue-caused errors.

> Being able to control the speed of the bottling line in the brewery example added variety to the pace of work and probably reduced both boredom and fatigue.

Past research studies have found that variety in work may be related to effective performance and can be a major contributor to employee satisfaction.

Task Identity

Task identity
The feeling of responsibility and pride that results from doing an entire piece of work, not just a small part of it.

One problem with some jobs is that they lack any **task identity**. Workers cannot point to some complete piece of work. They have little sense of responsibility and may lack pride in the results. After completing their job, they may have little sense of accomplishment. When tasks are grouped so that employees feel they are making an identifiable contribution, job satisfaction may be increased significantly.

> In the earlier General Life and Home Insurance Company example, we saw that productivity and satisfaction increased when employees became responsible for an identifiable and sensible group of tasks.

Feedback

Feedback
Information that helps evaluate the success or failure of an action or system.

When jobs do not give the workers any *feedback* on how well they are doing, there is little guidance or motivation to perform better.

> For example, by letting employees know how they are doing relative to the daily production quota, the brewery gives workers feedback that allows them to adjust their efforts. Providing feedback leads to improved motivation.

Task Significance

Task significance
Knowing that the work one does is important to others in the organization or to outsiders.

Closely related to the above dimensions is **task significance**. Doing an identifiable piece of work makes the job more satisfying for employees. Task significance, knowing that the work is important to others in the organization or outside it, makes the job even more meaningful for incumbents. Their personal sense of self-importance is enhanced because they know that others depend on what they do. Pride, commitment, motivation, satisfaction, and better performance are likely to result.

How Much Job Specialization Is Optimal?

In general, as jobs are made more specialized, productivity climbs until behavioural elements such as boredom offset the advantages of further specialization. Additional specialization beyond this point causes productivity to drop. It should be pointed out that jobs without any specialization take longer to learn; frustration is decreased and feedback is increased by adding some specialization. However, when specialization is extreme, employee satisfaction drops because of a lack of autonomy, variety, and task identification. This raises an important question: how much specialization is optimal? What level of specialization reduces employee satisfaction and productivity?

There is no simple answer to this question. Instead, human resource experts often make trade-offs between efficiency and behavioural elements. Using their expertise, they match degree of job specialization to the situational needs. When human resource specialists believe jobs are not specialized enough, they engage in work simplification. That is, the job is further simplified by assigning tasks of one job to two or more jobs. Unneeded tasks are identified and eliminated. What is left are jobs that contain fewer tasks:

> When the Yukon Weekly Newspaper operated with its old press, Guy Parsons could catch the newspapers as they came off the press, stack them, and wrap them. But when a new high-speed press was added, he could not keep up with the output. So the circulation manager simplified Guy's job by making him responsible for stacking the newspapers. Two part-time high-school students took turns catching and wrapping.

The risk with *work simplification* is that jobs may be so specialized that boredom causes errors or resignations. This potential problem is more common in advanced industrial countries that have a highly educated workforce. In less developed countries, highly specialized factory jobs may be acceptable and even appealing because they provide jobs for workers with limited skills.

As workers become more educated and affluent, routine jobs that are very specialized, such as assembly-line positions, hold less and less appeal for many people. These jobs seldom offer opportunities for accomplishment, recognition, psychological growth, or other sources of satisfaction. To increase the quality of work life for those who hold such jobs, human resource departments often use a variety of methods, the more popular among them being job rotation, job enlargement, and job enrichment.

Job Rotation

Job rotation
Moving employees from one job to another to allow them more variety and to learn new skills.

Job rotation moves employees from job to job. Jobs themselves are not actually changed; only the workers are rotated. Rotation breaks the monotony of highly specialized work by calling on different skills and abilities. The organization benefits because workers become competent in several jobs rather than only one. Knowing a variety of jobs helps the worker's self-image, provides personal growth, and makes the worker more valuable to the organization.

Human resource experts should caution those who desire to use job rotation. It does not improve the jobs themselves; the relationships between tasks, activities, and objectives remain unchanged. It may even postpone the use of more effective techniques while adding to training costs. Implementation should occur only after other techniques have been considered.

Job Enlargement

Job enlargement
Adding more tasks to a job to increase the job cycle and draw on a wider range of employee skills.

Job enlargement expands the number of related tasks in the job. It adds similar duties to provide greater variety. Enlargement reduces monotony by expanding the job cycle and drawing on a wider range of employee skills.

> IBM reported job enlargement led to higher wages and more inspection equipment, but improved quality and worker satisfaction offset these costs. Maytag Company claimed that production quality was improved, labour costs declined, worker satisfaction and overall efficiency were increased, and management production schedules became more flexible.[28]

Job Enrichment

Job enrichment
Adding more responsibilities and autonomy to a job, giving the worker greater powers to plan, do, and evaluate job performance.

Job enrichment adds new sources of needs satisfaction to jobs. It increases responsibility, autonomy, and control. Adding these elements to jobs is sometimes called *vertical loading*. (*Horizontal loading* occurs when the job is expanded by simply adding related tasks, as with job enlargement). Job enrichment views jobs as consisting of three elements: plan, do, and control. Job enlargement (or horizontal loading) adds more things to do. Enrichment (or vertical loading) attempts to add more *planning* and *control* responsibilities. These additions to the job coupled with rethinking the job itself often lead to increased motivation and other improvements:

> In a pilot project with one unit of the data capture section of Statistics Canada, job enrichment and other changes resulted in increased employee satisfaction, lower absentee rates, increases in the quality and quantity of work done, and improved relationships between the union and management. One employee recalled that prior to the changes, "We were watched every second. We weren't able to talk. We had no responsibility or variety in our work. We'd just go to the basket and take the job that was on top." The changes implemented included more variety and more worker responsibility, both for completing the work and for attendance, hiring, training, appraisals, and discipline. Aside from the success indicators already mentioned, when the rest of the section was asked whether they were interested in being involved in similar changes for their units, 171 of the remaining 177 employees were in favour.[29]

Job enrichment, however, is not a cure-all; if it were, this book could end here. Job enrichment techniques are merely tools, and they are not applicable universally. When the diagnosis indicates jobs are unchallenging and limit employee motivation and satisfaction, human resource departments may find job enrichment to be the most appropriate strategy. Even then, however, job enrichment faces problems.

Several potential challenges face the manager who is attempting to introduce job enrichment. The most compelling points are the existence of union resistance, the cost of design and implementation, and the scarcity of research on long-term effects. Another criticism of job enrichment is that it often does not go far enough. To enrich the job and ignore other variables that contribute to the quality of work life may simply increase dissatisfaction with the unimproved aspects of the job environment. The cultural values and social expectations surrounding the organization also have to be carefully considered before any job enrichment attempts are made.

Employee Involvement and Work Teams

More recently, other approaches such as employee involvement groups, quality circles, employee teams, and so on, have been introduced to increase employee involvement at the workplace. Work itself is increasingly being organized around teams and processes rather than activities or functions. Over 40 per cent of the respondents in a national survey by Conference Board of Canada reported use of teams in their workplaces.[30] Self-managed and autonomous work teams and quality circles have become a normal part of several organizations. These and other employee involvement approaches are discussed in detail in Chapter Twelve. The intent of all such approaches, however, is to provide more autonomy, feedback, and task significance to workers.

> At Compaq Computers, nearly a quarter of its 16 000 employees work in teams. A cross-section of other organizations, including CIBC, Xerox Canada, and Vancouver City Savings, have found that employee teams result in better quality, lower turnover and absenteeism and a sense of accomplishment for their workforce.[31]

As in the case of job enrichment, employee involvement and teams may not be appropriate for all organizations or all situations. The complexity of the task involved, the prevalence of shift system and the skill levels of employees involved may moderate the applicability of such systems in a particular situation.[32] Introduction of team management, if not accompanied by changes in other systems (e.g., performance appraisal, compensation), may cause frustration in some cases. To be successful, the management should also be truly committed to the notion of employee empowerment, that is, granting employees the power to initiate change and take charge of what they do.

Use of Job Families in HR Decisions

Job families
Groups of different jobs that are closely related by similar duties, responsibilities, skills, or job elements.

Often, in the context of job design, the human resource manager looks at job families rather than single jobs. *Job families* are groups of jobs that are closely related by similar duties, responsibilities, skills, or job elements.

> The jobs of clerk, word processor, clerk-typist, and secretary constitute a job family, for example.

Job families can be constructed in several ways. One way is by careful study of existing job analysis information. Matching of the data in job descriptions can identify jobs with similar requirements. A second method is to use the codes in the *National Occupational Classification* discussed earlier. Similarities in the job codes indicate similarities in the jobs. A third approach is to use the *Position Analysis Questionnaire* discussed earlier in this chapter and statistically analyze information on tasks and worker traits to identify clusters of similar jobs.

Job families allow human resource managers to plan job rotation programs and make employee transfer decisions. The compensation levels of jobs that form a family should also be comparable; this means that equitable compensation strategies cannot be formed without considering the entire job family. In some instances, it may also be economical to use similar recruitment methods and sources to hire individuals who belong to the same job family.

Environmental Considerations in Job Design

Environmental considerations in job design
Concerned with influence of the external environment on job design. Include employee ability, availability, and social expectations.

The environments within which the firm and job exist also need to be considered when redesigning jobs. As with most human resource activities, job designers cannot ignore the influence of the external environment, which affects workforce availability, values, and practices.

Workforce Availability

Efficiency considerations must be balanced against the abilities and availability of the people who are to do the work. Thought must be given as to who will actually do the work. An extreme example underlines this point:

> Governments of less developed countries often think they can "buy" progress. To be "up-to-date," they seek the most advanced equipment they can find. Leaders of one country ordered a computerized oil refinery. This decision dictated a level of technology

that exceeded the abilities of the country's available workforce. As a result, these government leaders have now hired Europeans to operate the refinery.

In less developed nations, the major risk is jobs that are too complex. Jobs that are too simple can produce equally disturbing problems in industrialized nations with highly educated workers.

For example, even when unemployment rates are high, many simple and overly specialized jobs are sometimes hard to fill, as longstanding newspaper want ads for janitors attest.

Social Expectations

Social expectations
The larger society's expectations from employees regarding job challenge, working conditions, and quality of work life.

The acceptability of a job's design is also influenced by the expectations of society. For example, working conditions that would have been acceptable to some early Canadian immigrants are no longer suitable to our present generation.

At the time when rail lines were being laid across Canada, many persons had to work long hours of hard labour. Often, they had fled countries where jobs were unavailable. This made a job—any job—acceptable to them. Today, industrial workers are much better educated and have higher expectations about the quality of work life.

Even where work flow may suggest a particular job design, the job must meet the expectations of workers. Failure to consider these social expectations can create dissatisfaction, poor motivation, and low quality of work life.

Work Practices

Work practices
The set ways of performing work in an organization.

Work practices are set ways of performing work. These methods may arise from tradition or the collective wishes of employees. Either way, the human resource department's flexibility to design jobs is limited, especially when such practices are part of a union-management relationship. Failure to consider work practices can have undesired outcomes:

General Motors decided to increase productivity at one of its American plants by eliminating some jobs and adding new tasks to others. These design changes caused workers to stage a strike for several weeks because traditional practices at the plant had required a slower rate of production and less work by the employees. The additional demands on their jobs by management were seen as an attempt by the company to disregard past work practices.

JOB ANALYSIS IN TOMORROW'S "JOBLESS" WORLD

GLOBAL COMPETITION, fast technological obsolescence, changing worker profile, and rapid increases in knowledge requirements for various jobs have made accurate and timely job descriptions difficult. Indeed, some writers have gone as far as to say that jobs as we see them today may not exist in the future.[33] Today's global village has resulted in "boundary-less" and "de-jobbed" organizations where traditional boundaries between a firm, its suppliers, customers, and even competitors have disappeared and where "jobs" as we knew them in the past have begun to disappear.[34] Many employees no longer are responsible for producing specific outcomes; rather they are members of teams that are entrusted with many responsibilities. In tomorrow's world, a firm may be valued by its ideas rather than its assets or products.[35] How do organizations that operate in such fast-changing environments conduct valid job analysis? How can the task and person requirements identified today be relevant for an unknown tomorrow?

www.siop.org/tip/backissues/
tipapr96/may.htm

Of course, there are no simple solutions. A few attempts have been made to meet the new-found challenges. A first strategy is to adopt a future-oriented style when describing job activities and specifications. Rather than asking what the current job incumbent *does*, the focus now will be on what the job incumbent *must do* to effectively carry out and further organizational strategies and the new competencies required of the job holder. Thus present and future requirements rather than past actions guide job descriptions and the hiring and training of employees. A second strategy utilizes the competency approach discussed earlier in the chapter. The focus, once again, is on the tasks and competencies that are needed to match an organization's strategy, structure, and culture. Rather than simply looking at the purely functional skills of today, this approach focuses on the many competencies (e.g., decision making, conflict resolution, adaptiveness) that are required of employees if the firm is to prosper in the future. Figure 2-15 shows an example of this approach in a civil engineering firm. In this organization, each of the six competencies are measured at seven levels (Level 1 being the lowest and 7 being the highest). For successfully executing the corporate strategies, all employees may be expected to possess all competencies, though to varying degrees. Thus an engineer may be expected to possess high technical expertise and medium-problem solving abilities while a manager is expected to possess higher problem-solving and lower technical expertise. Both are expected to have adequate communication abilities. Use of a competency matrix shifts the focus from performing specific duties to developing broader skills that are necessary to successfully execute corporate strategies. It also empowers employees to assume new responsibilities. To be effective, such a system must be supported by effective training and development strategy and a competency-based compensation system. These will be discussed in detail in later chapters.

Further, job analysis will continue to be relevant for legal compliance and defensibility in the event of a court action.[36] Traditional sources of information (such as job incumbents, supervisors), may, however, need to be supplemented by data emerging from customers, peers, and technical experts to incorporate the ever-changing job demands.

FIGURE 2-15

An Example of Competency Matrix in an Engineering Firm

Engineer: T=6; P=4; C1=3; C2=5; O=3; L=2
Manager: T=3; P=6; C1=5; C2=5; O=6; L=6

Levels

Levels	Technical Expertise (T)	Problem Solving (P)	Creativity (C1)	Communication Skills (C2)	Organizational Ability (O)	Leadership (L)
High	7	7	7	7	7	7
	6	6	6	6	6	6
	5	5	5	5	5	5
	4	4	4	4	4	4
	3	3	3	3	3	3
	2	2	2	2	2	2
Low	1	1	1	1	1	1

Competency:

SUMMARY

Job analysis information provides the foundations of an organization's human resource information system. Analysts seek to gain a general understanding of the organization and the work it performs. Then they design job analysis questionnaires to collect specific data about jobs, jobholder characteristics, and job performance standards. Job analysis information can be collected through interviews, mailed questionnaires, employee logs, direct observation, or some combination of these techniques. Once collected, the data are converted into such useful applications as job descriptions, job specifications, and job standards.

Job analysis information is important because it tells human resource specialists what duties and responsibilities are associated with each job. This information is then used when human resource specialists undertake other human resource management activities such as job design, recruiting, and selection. Jobs are the link between organizations and their human resources. The combined accomplishment of every job allows the organization to meet its objectives. Similarly, jobs represent not only a source of income to workers, but also a means of fulfilling their needs. However, for the organization and its employees to receive these mutual benefits, jobs must provide a high quality of work life. This means that when designing jobs, organizational priorities (e.g., efficiency) alone should not play the decisive role. The needs of employees as well as environmental realities also play critical roles in job design efforts. This is especially true with the emergence of a "de-jobbed" and boundary-less work world where employees are expected to take initiative and solve problems creatively.

TERMS FOR REVIEW

Visit the Web site at www.mcgrawhill.ca/college/schwind6 for a full glossary.

REVIEW AND DISCUSSION QUESTIONS

1. Suppose you work for an organization that does not conduct job analysis. What arguments will you make to introduce it? What method(s) of collecting job analysis information will you recommend and why?

2. Define job descriptions and job specifications, illustrating how the two are related yet different.

3. Why are clear job specifications important? What are the costs of imprecise specifications?

4. How can performance standards be set for production jobs when job analysis information is insufficient? How would you set standards of performance for a research scientist if you were chief scientist?

5. What factors need to be considered when redesigning jobs? Of these, which is (are) most important?

CRITICAL THINKING QUESTIONS

1. Suppose that you were assigned to write the job descriptions for a shirt factory in British Columbia employing mostly Chinese immigrants who spoke little English. What methods would you use to collect job analysis data?

2. You work in the human resource department of a large brewery in Atlantic Canada. You are in the process of writing job descriptions for all managerial and supervisory staff. One manager who is in the production division of the brewery refuses to complete a job analysis questionnaire.

   (a) What reasons would you use to persuade that individual to complete it?

   (b) If, after your best efforts at persuasion failed, you still wanted job analysis information on the manager's job, how would you get it?

3. Suppose you have been assigned to design the job of ticket clerk for a regional airline in Ontario. How would you handle the following trade-offs?

   (a) Would you recommend highly specialized job designs to minimize training or very broad jobs with all clerks cross-trained to handle multiple tasks? Why?

   (b) Would you change your answer if you knew that employees tended to quit the job of ticket clerk within the first six months? Why or why not?

4. Assume you are told to evaluate a group of jobs in a boat-building business. After studying each job for a considerable amount of time, you identify the

following activities associated with each job. What job redesign techniques would you recommend for these jobs, if any?

(a) Sailmaker. Cuts and sews materials with very little variety in the type of work from day to day. Job is highly skilled and takes years to learn.

(b) Sander. Sands rough wood and fibreglass edges almost continuously. Little skill is required in this job.

(c) Sales representative. Talks to customers, answers phone inquiries, suggests customized additions to special-order boats.

(d) Boat preparer. Cleans up completed boats, waxes fittings, and generally makes the boat ready for customer delivery. Few skills are required for this job.

5. What are the key performance dimensions of the instructor who is teaching this course? How will you go about setting performance standards for the individual? Establish performance standards and associated time-bound, specific objectives in any two areas of your choice.

WEB RESEARCH

Select any job position (e.g., a financial accountant) of your choice. Consider various recruiters on the Web (the chapter on recruitment provides some Web site addresses for you to begin your search). Are there any differences in the job specifications listed by different recruiters? Are any patterns visible across industry groups?

INCIDENT 2-1

Hillary Home Appliances Corporation

Hillary Home Appliances and Furnishings Corporation (HHAC) is a medium-sized manufacturer of home appliances. Historically, the firm had followed a low-cost strategy to successfully operate in a highly competitive industry. In the recent past, increasing global competition had made it necessary for the firm to revise its strategy in favour of improved customer service. Historically, the organization had paid virtually no attention to the human resource function. While there was a human resource department (called "personnel and staffing department"), it focused primarily on compensation administration and staffing. Currently, the top management of the firm is convinced of the need for strategic use of its human resources. An indication of this new thrust is the hiring of Leslie Wong, who has a reputation as a results-oriented HR manager (in two previous organizations) and the renaming of the department to "Human Resources." However, progressive HR practices have been slow to find acceptance at lower levels. In a recent meeting with two work supervisors, Jeff Gidoe and Mike Tarson, Leslie Wong, the newly hired human resource manager faced these arguments:

Jeff Gidoe: I agree that good employee relations are important. But, I simply cannot afford to let the HR staff interrupt our daily work with job analysis. Already, with the arrival of two new competitors, we have lost most of our cost advantage. Spending time on activities such as this further reduces our production and increases our costs.

Mike Tarson: Your plan to invite ideas from employees for product improvement is good; however, I should warn you that many of the workers in my section are school dropouts. They simply cannot accept responsibility. They care only for the wages they get and are constantly looking at the clock for quitting time.

Jeff Gidoe: At least a few of my employees will object to the time spent on job analysis. As you know, we have a production bonus plan in this plant. Every minute they spend on activities such as this costs them money. Already, several of them feel that the production standards are too high.

Mike Tarson: Your new idea of employee involvement teams is also likely to create problems. Already, they waste a fair bit of time each day jesting and horse-playing. If you put them into groups, things will only get worse; not better.

Leslie Wong: I value your comments. As supervisors, you know your employees best. I recognize that you are experts in your production areas. However, I can tell you this: the facts you have provided have simply reconfirmed the need for job analysis. Even more, it tells me that HR has a key role to play in this firm. I'll tell you why....

1. What prompted the HR manager to make the statement?

2. If you were the HR manager, what arguments will you provide to convince the two supervisors of the desirability of job analysis and employee involvement teams?

INCIDENT 2-2

Job Design at Marketing Newsletters Inc.

Marketing Newsletters Inc. is a small Montreal company that produces several different types of newsletters that are sold to companies and individual salespeople. Although each series of letters has a different market, they all provide readers with useful tips on how to be more effective at selling.

Pierre Martel, president of Marketing Newsletters, discovered he could sell these letters by carefully tailoring them to the concerns of different types of specialized salespeople. For example, one letter was directed at sellers of new cars. Another was directed at sellers of industrial supplies. Although the sales of each letter were modest, Pierre succeeded in developing a new newsletter market about every three months.

In Pierre's firm there were two developmental editors, two copy editors, and two marketing editors. The developmental editors sought out likely authors to write and develop newsletters. The copy editors were responsible for editing each newsletter before it was printed and mailed. The marketing editors were responsible for advertising and for building the circulation of each newsletter.

Whenever a newsletter did not meet its sales goal, the marketing editors blamed the copy editors for not producing a quality product. In turn, the copy editors would complain that they could only improve so much on the quality of the contributions, and they blamed the developmental editors for not finding better writers.

Suppose Pierre asked you to help him solve the problem of identifying responsibility for the success or failure of each newsletter.

1. What suggestions would you make to Pierre about the way editors' jobs are designed?

2. If each editor were made responsible for developing, editing, and selling selected newsletters, what advantages would result for the firm? For the editors?

3. If each editor were completely responsible for several newsletters, what kinds of favourable trade-offs might be encountered in the newly designed jobs?

EXERCISE 2-1

A Good Work Environment

Think of some work-related situation that you have found enjoyable. Think of the job and identify the features that made it more enjoyable than other jobs that you have held. The job need not have been a formal, full-time job. It may simply have been some temporary job or even some chore you have had to perform. Make a list of those characteristics of the job that made it so enjoyable.

1. In reviewing your answers with others, do you find any similarities between your list and the lists of others who did different jobs?

2. Do these characteristics indicate what job features provide a good work situation?

EXERCISE 2-2

Preparation of a Job Description

As discussed in this chapter, there are several ways to collect job analysis information. One way is through observation. Using the form in Figure 2-4, complete parts C through J for the job of an instructor in this institution. After you have completed those sections of the job analysis questionnaire, use the format in Figure 2-6 and write a job description for the job of an instructor. When you are finished, look up the definition of professor provided in the National Occupational Classification in your library.

1. How does the description in the NOC vary in format and content from the one you wrote?

2. What parts of the instructor's job are most important, in your opinion?

CASE STUDY

Maple Leaf Shoes Ltd.

An Exercise in Job Analysis[1]

Maple Leaf Shoes Ltd. is a medium-sized manufacturer of leather and vinyl shoes located near Wilmington, Ontario. It began operations in 1969 and currently employs about 400 persons in its Ontario plant and some 380 more in offices and warehouses throughout Canada and internationally. In recent months, the company has experienced a number of challenges and problems (see the Case Study in Chapter One for further background). Added to these problems was the departure of John

McAllister, the company's human resource manager. McAllister had been with the company for a little over three years and was reputed to have "run a tight ship."

Robert Clark, president and a major shareholder of Maple Leaf Shoes, decided to re-evaluate the role of the company's human resource manager before hiring a new person. Tim Lance, a graduate of the University of Manitoba and now the chief executive and owner of Productivity Systems, a management consulting operation located in Saskatoon, was hired to "look into the present and future role of Maple Leaf's human resource department and suggest

---

[1] *Case written by Professor Hari Das of Department of Management, Saint Mary's University. All rights reserved by the author © 2000.*

appropriate action plans to improve its contribution to the organization and help the company meet its future challenges."

VIEWS OF THE SENIOR MANAGERS

Lance began his assignment by interviewing the senior managers of Maple Leaf Shoes. He made a short checklist of questions to prepare for his interview with the managers (see Figure 1). He was, however, determined not to restrict his interview to these questions. By keeping an informal and free-flowing format, he felt that he could gain a better understanding of the structure, processes, and culture of the organization. His intent, therefore, was to use these questions as a springboard for letting the interviewee speak out and pursue any point that he or she might consider relevant. Lance was able to meet three of the five "key" managers in the company. Figure 2 shows an approximate chain of command in the company. At the time Lance conducted his study, André Cardin, manager (Design & Research), was away on holidays. Lance was also unable to have an interview with the production manager since he was away on trips to Montreal and Winnipeg investigating the potential of expanding the company's operations to those cities.

FIGURE 1

Checklist Prepared by Lance for Interviewing the Senior Managers

- *What do you expect from the human resource department in this company?*
- *What is your evaluation of the human resource department's contributions in the past?*
- *What activities should the human resource department of this company carry out?*
- *Which of these are done now? How well are you satisfied with the performance of the department in those fields?*
- *Overall, are you happy with the human resource staff? Why?*
- *What are the major challenges facing Maple Leaf Shoes in the next five years?*
- *What are the unique needs of your department?*
- *What new services or information should the human resource department provide you?*

Lance felt that the half-hour interview with Robert Clark (interrupted by three or four phone calls "on urgent matters that unexpectedly arose") was totally inadequate for his purpose. However, Clark was due to leave town the next day and Lance could not wait until Clark's return to proceed with his study.

After going through his notes, Lance realized that the human resource function was viewed very differently by the three senior managers to whom he spoke. Clark had told him:

I believe that we need a mover and shaker here. McAllister was all right, but he did not have the time or inclination to have a good system in place. He made most of the human resource decisions himself. I'm not saying that they weren't the correct decisions for those occasions; but he wasn't a popular man with either the employees or several managers. And as you know, this is one job where you need a lot of rapport with people at all levels.

Some of the excerpts from Lance's interview with Clark are given below:

I believe that the new person should be able to work with the people. In fact, not simply working with the people, but leading them. He or she should be able to look beyond today's needs ... into the technological and other challenges that face this company and our managers in the new millennium....

The future of Maple Leaf Shoes? I have mixed feelings on this. On the one hand, shoes are something that everyone needs—every day, every week, and throughout their lives. Also, most persons don't mind buying an extra pair if the price is right. But there's the catch. It's a pretty competitive market and what we do here and how well we do it depends quite a bit on how good our competitors are. To succeed, we need to have a clear market segment, control our costs, and meet our customers' needs. Two of our brands, which were leaders in the western Canada shoe market, are facing intense competition from products manufactured in China, Indonesia, and Korea....The currency crisis in Asia (especially in Korea and Indonesia) can both hurt and help us. On the one hand, the prices of the imported shoes are getting lower by the day, thus cutting into our markets. The other side is that western investments in these countries may

FIGURE 2

An Approximate Chain of Command in Maple Leaf Shoes Limited

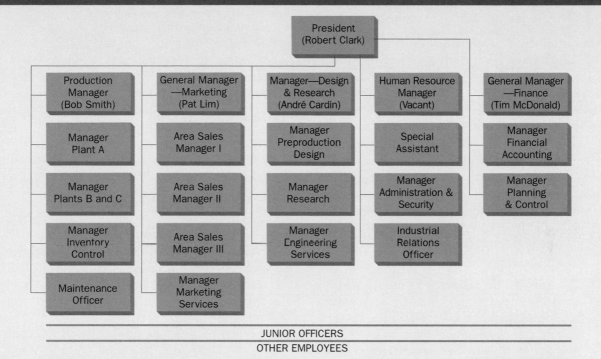

President
(Robert Clark)

Production Manager (Bob Smith)	General Manager —Marketing (Pat Lim)	Manager—Design & Research (André Cardin)	Human Resource Manager (Vacant)	General Manager —Finance (Tim McDonald)
Manager Plant A	Area Sales Manager I	Manager Preproduction Design	Special Assistant	Manager Financial Accounting
Manager Plants B and C	Area Sales Manager II	Manager Research	Manager Administration & Security	Manager Planning & Control
Manager Inventory Control	Area Sales Manager III	Manager Engineering Services	Industrial Relations Officer	
Maintenance Officer	Manager Marketing Services			

JUNIOR OFFICERS

OTHER EMPLOYEES

slow down—at least in the short run. This means that we have a breathing time to cope with this onslaught.. So, all in all.... who knows?

The most immediate problem? I should say we have two pressing issues: first, we must upgrade our production processes if we are to improve our efficiency and competitiveness. I personally believe that we have more employees than we need. If we could automate many of the production processes, we could improve the efficiency and reduce costs. But that is easier said than done. We have strong unions, and firing someone is going to be awfully hard in the future. At the same time, the reality is that no customer is going to pay 15 or 20 per cent extra for our shoes if we cannot give a damn good reason for that. With the free trade worldwide, the market is flooded with Asian and South American products. We simply cannot compete with the Chinese and the Mexicans on the labour costs... Our survival may very well depend on technological upgrading and improving worker productivity.

A second and related issue is dealing with unions. We have four major unions and I would term two of them as militant. Actually, our workers are pretty good—many of them have been with us for several years now—it's the union leadership that's causing much of the problem. The new human resource manager hired must be tough with the unions, yet caring and understanding. In the last three or four years, union-management relations have gone from bad to worse. We have to turn a new leaf now or else all of us will sink.

The responses to Lance's questions from the other two senior managers at Maple Leaf Shoes were varied. Excerpts from his interview with Tim McDonald, general manager, finance, are provided below:

I don't think human resource management is the most critical activity in the management of a shoe company. True, we have to pay the employees adequately and there must be a system for keeping employee records. But, beyond that, I don't think that the human resource department has anything major to offer that has a significant impact on an organization's working. What we really should focus on now is how to control our costs and come out with a sound marketing program. We especially need a good advertising campaign; we need to hire competent sales staff and upgrade the skills of the present sales force....

The human resource department here hasn't done much, if you ask me. They haven't had any input into job design or organizational planning. Part of the problem stems from the fact that there has been little continuity in that department. A typical manager in the human resource department stays for about three years before he moves out. Neither McAllister nor his predecessor stayed in the company for five years. Tony Rezkov, the manager in charge of administration and security, is new; so are several of the other junior officers and staff in the department.... I do believe that there is a problem there....

Oh, don't get me wrong. The human resource department staff are very friendly and cooperative. McAllister had a few rough edges, but overall, he was someone whom I grew to like. He was one of those tough guys—straight out of an old John Wayne movie. He made fast decisions and was sort of a trouble-shooter here....

The big challenge? Global competition, of course. We'd better be prepared to meet the Koreans, the Chinese, and the Mexicans. Unless we maintain our competitiveness, we are just not going to survive. It's as simple as that....

Of course, global free trade also brings with it a great opportunity. NAFTA gave us access to a market now that is several times the size of our local market. Freer trade in Asia and Eastern Europe will do the same... But can we make use of this opportunity? That's the big question.

Pat Lim, general manager, marketing, had a somewhat different vision of the role of the human resource department:

It's probably one of the most important functions in this company. In my university days, I was taught that human resources are the single most important asset of any organization. After working for nearly 25 years in the management area, I've grown to realize how true that statement is. In my mind, people make all the difference. You can have all the resources you want, but in the absence of good employees, all those resources

are worthless. The human resource department is the backbone of our employee relations....

What do I expect from the human resource department? Quite a lot, I should say. I believe that the department can play a leadership and developmental role. Until now, it has played a somewhat low-key, record-keeping, staff role. It's time that the department becomes involved seriously in employee planning, job redesign, career planning, organizational design, and other development activities. Gone are the times when it could simply play a support role. Look at all the successful companies in this country and the United States, especially those that are listed in books such as *In Search of Excellence*. It's the people and people management that differentiate them from the common crop....

The new human resource manager should be an expert—an expert on systems and people. We need new ideas here, and with a growing workforce we need more formal procedures and systems, whether it's orientation or performance appraisal. Right now, many of the human resource activities are done on an ad-hoc basis.

Above everything else, I believe that the new human resource manager needs to bring a new philosophy to deal with the unions. In the last several months, there has been an increasing degree of hostility between the unions and management. I'm not blaming anyone for this. But I do believe that we, as part of the management team, have the responsibility to solve some of these problems. It's up to us to take the initiative to improve the situation. Isn't that the essence of good management?

VIEW FROM THE HUMAN RESOURCE DEPARTMENT

As part of the study, Lance met with the three key staff members in the human resources department: Jane Reynolds, special assistant to the human resource manager; Tony Rezkov, manager of administration and security; and Joseph McDonald, the industrial relations officer (no relation to Tim McDonald). Rezkov, being new on the job, was unable to tell Lance much about his position or the human resources function. In Lance's opinion, his two meetings (lasting approximately an hour each) with Jane Reynolds were more productive.

Lance studied the various comments made by Reynolds:

The possibilities here are simply enormous. With a little determination and the right type of resources, we can make this one of the best human resource departments in this country. To be really effective, I believe that human resources management must be well integrated with the strategic and operational planning in a firm. That has not occurred here yet....

When I joined this company two years ago, it didn't have any system—at least, not anything that is worth mentioning. My job since I arrived has been to introduce new procedures and decision support systems. For example, recently, we started a formal orientation program for all plant workers. We are also in the process of developing two performance appraisal instruments—one for the plant employees and the other for administrative staff. We are beginning to provide absenteeism and turnover data to various department and section managers. But I want to emphasize that these are just the beginnings. With the right support, we can do wonders here....

Why do I sound pessimistic? Well, look at our department's staff strength compared to human resource departments in similar-sized organizations in this part of the country. We probably employ less than 50 per cent of the number you would see elsewhere. As a cost-cutting strategy, when we downsized the organization, we lost two positions in our department. We also do not have the computer hardware or software support and the necessary number of PCs to do an adequate job....

Sure, despite everything, we could have still done better if we had the will to do it. I will be totally frank with you—you will keep my observations confidential, won't you? Not that I mind too much if someone comes to know about it. It's as if we are a poor cousin here. Being in human resources is just not considered to be important or very useful. We're looked at by many others as an unnecessary appendage.

Lance found that Joseph McDonald ("*Call me Joe, everyone does*"), the industrial relations officer, was the toughest to handle. McDonald was very friendly and supportive, but did not give a direct or coherent answer to any of Lance's questions. Lance felt that McDonald was one of those people who talked to you for hours at a time nonstop without giving any useful information. Lance realized that he got only two points of information out of his 45-minute meeting with McDonald. First, one of the unions in the company was very militant and might go on strike when its contract expired in the next few months, and second, McDonald's son was planning to go to medical school—Lance knew the former fact already and didn't care to know about the latter.

In less than 10 days, Lance was scheduled to meet Robert Clark to give a summary of his findings and recommendations. Already, Lance had received a call from his office in Saskatoon informing him that one of his consultants had been injured in an automobile accident and would not be returning to work for the next several weeks. This meant that Lance had to return to his office soon to complete that project himself. Given the time constraints, Lance was wondering how he should proceed from here.

Discussion Questions

1. What is your evaluation of Lance's approach to the project?

2. What would you do if you were in Lance's position right now?

CASE STUDY

Canadian Pacific and International Bank
Redefining Jobs for Future[2]

Canadian Pacific and International Bank (CPIB) is a premier Canadian financial institution with assets over $150 billion and operations across Canada and internationally. Today, its over 25 000 employees provide personal, commercial, corporate, and investment banking services to individuals and businesses in 33 countries. More details of the bank are given at the end of Chapter One (see page 47).

[2] *Case written by Professor Hari Das of Department of Management, Saint Mary's University, Halifax, N.S. All rights reserved by the author © 2000*

CPIB, through its strategic initiatives, was successful in building long-term value for its shareholders while providing regular returns on their investments. A vital component of its recent strategy is growth through acquisition of smaller banks and other financial institutions in this country and internationally. The passage of the bill relating to bank mergers in June 2000 in Parliament is expected to accelerate this process for CPIB.

Last month, the bank acquired Central Canadian Trust Company (CCTC), a trust company located in Ontario employing over 3000 employees. While the trust company was a very successful player in the financial industry in Ontario and Quebec, CPIB management felt that the human resource practices in the firm were inferior to those of the bank.

Initially, the identity of CCTC will be maintained; however, over the next year or so, all branches will be converted into CPIB branches. This means that, with immediate effect, CCTC staff must be trained to offer the highest quality of customer service that CPIB customers have come to expect. Compared to CPIB, CCTC is also far behind in electronic and telephone banking. CPIB expects all its managers to be able to offer extensive counselling (including in areas such as portfolio management, margin trading, and the establishment of Internet banking accounts) to their customers; in contrast, CCTC being a trust company, historically had underplayed this role and concentrated on pension fund management and loan/mortgage services. CPIB also has a culture of transferring its employees to help them gain international experience whereas CCTC is primarily a regional institution where staff transfers are less common.

During the pre-acquisition survey, Mary Keddy, senior vice president—human resources of CPIB, observed that CCTC did not have any regular job analysis procedure built into its HR systems. Since CPIB was contemplating the installation of a bank-wide electronic job data system (called "Job Bank") in the next six months, Keddy decided to use the present opportunity to test the new system. Given the relatively small number of employees involved in CCTC (compared to CPIB), it was easier to fix all the "bugs" there before implementing it in its entirety in CPIB.

Under the proposed system, through their personal computers and other consoles, all managers will be able to store and retrieve human resource data from the company's mainframe computer. This means that when managers or human resource specialists needed a job description, they could simply obtain one from the computer.

After computerizing all human resource information in CCTC, HR staff began to notice that job descriptions, job specifications, and job standards were constantly being changed by jobholders. It seemed that whenever a manager or worker reviewed a job description or job specification that seemed outdated, he or she would "write in" a correction on the computer's memory.

Thus, although in the beginning human resource specialists were pleased that workers were showing an interest by updating the computerized job analysis information, they eventually became worried because workers with the same job titles had different views of their jobs. Changes would come from almost anyone, and there was no consistency in style or content.

The HR staff at CPIB were bewildered. On the one hand, they did not want to introduce too many restrictions on employees updating their job descriptions. This was also contrary to the "open" culture that existed in CPIB. On the other hand, if not controlled, the problem could get out of hand, especially when it is implemented within such a large and diverse multilingual workforce.

Discussion Questions

1. Assume that you are invited as a consultant by CPIB. What procedures would you introduce that would ensure that the restudied job information was correct?

2. Given the ability of most managers to "communicate" directly with the computer, can CPIB use this to its advantage in collecting job analysis information? Explain.

3. What additional skills and competencies would you focus on while planning a training program for CCTC staff? How should CPIB establish performance and skill standards for CCTC staff?

SUGGESTED READINGS

Coy, Peter, "The 21st Century Organization: the Creative Economy," *Business Week*, August 28, 2000.

Gael, Sydney, *Job Analysis*, San Francisco, CA: Jossey-Bass, 1983.

Grantham, Charles, *The Future of Work*, N.Y.: McGraw-Hill, 2000.

Sparrow, Paul, "New Employee Behaviours, Work Designs and Forms of Work Organization: What Is in Store for Future of Work?" *Journal of Managerial Psychology*, Vol. 15, No. 3, 2000, pp. 202–218.

Spencer, L. and S. Spencer, *Competence at Work: Models for Superior Performance*, N.Y.: John Wiley & Sons, 1993.

Chapter 3

Human Resource Planning

Human resource planning is ... designed to translate strategic objectives into targeted quantitative and qualitative skill requirements, identify the human resource strategies and objectives necessary to fulfil those requirements...and...to assess progress.

Abdul Rahman bin Idris and Derek Eldridge[1]

CHAPTER OBJECTIVES

After studying this chapter, you should be able to:

- *Explain* why an organization's human resource plan should be consistent with its strategic plan.

- *Discuss* methods for estimating an organization's demand for human resources

- *Explain* the various methods of estimating a firm's supply of human resources

- *Identify* solutions to shortages or surpluses of human resources.

- *List* the major items to be included in a Human Resources Information System (HRIS).

- *List* the major approaches to accounting for human resources.

Perhaps, more than any other human resource activity, planning allows the human resource department to be proactive. This, in turn, improves the department's contribution to the organization's objectives. Through human resource planning, management prepares to have the right people at the right places at the right times to fulfill both organizational and individual objectives. Human resource planning can make or break an organization, particularly over the long term since without planning an organization may find itself with a plant or an office without the employees to run it productively. The plans themselves may range from simple projections based on past trends to sophisticated computer models. However, it is important that some form of planning exists. Consider this dialogue:

> **Sy Wolfe**: All I ever seem to do is "put out fires." Every day different department heads tell me they need new employees. Well, we are a service department, so we rush around and try to find someone. And I thought being a city human resource manager would be a snap.
>
> **Jean-Marie Gasse**: Why don't you do like we do in the police department and develop plans?
>
> **Sy Wolfe**: Plans? How am I supposed to know who is going to quit?
>
> **Jean-Marie Gasse**: You don't need to know exactly. Try estimating job vacancies. No one tells us when crimes or accidents are going to happen. We try to anticipate the need for traffic and crime squads for each shift based on past experience.
>
> **Sy Wolfe**: Hey! Now that looks like a good idea. I could look at the various departments in our office and compare the employee turnover rates. I could then project these for next year. Thanks for the idea. I'll buy your coffee for that.

RELATIONSHIP OF HUMAN RESOURCE PLANNING TO STRATEGIC PLANNING

HUMAN RESOURCE PLANNING *systematically forecasts an organization's future demand for and supply of employees and matches supply with demand.* By estimating the number and types of employees that will be needed, the human resource department contributes to the success of an organization's strategic plan in a number of ways:

1. The Effectiveness of Human Resource Planning Determines the Very Survival of an Organization in the Long Run.

Organizations need short-range and long-range plans for success and coping with change. Long-range strategic plans involve fundamental decisions about the very nature of business. Among other things, they may result in new organizational goals, new business acquisitions, divestiture of current product lines or subsidiaries, new management approaches, and different ways of structuring internal activities. If an organization is not properly staffed with the right numbers and types of people, the long-term success and viability of the organization are endangered.[2]

> For example, the decision of high-technology firms such as Nortel, IBM, Cisco, and others to develop new products and enter new markets often depends on the availability of qualified technical and support staff. Without sufficient engineering talent, market opportunities can be lost to more appropriately staffed competitors.

2. Different Organizational Strategies Require Varying Human Resource Plans.

An organization's rapid growth is often associated with an increasing need for human resources. A growth or expansion strategy is, hence, usually accompanied by aggressive hiring, training, and/or promotions of employees. In contrast, a retrenchment or cost reduction strategy often necessitates layoff and early retirement of surplus employees. As seen in Chapter One, a shift from a cost leadership to a focus or differentiation strategy requires changes in the number and skill levels of employees.

3. Human Resource Planning Facilitates Proactive Response to Environmental and Legal Challenges.

Human resource planning—or *employment planning*, as it is also called—by facilitating better recruitment, selection, and training strategies not only helps companies meet their equal employment commitments, but also allows them to face environmental challenges more effectively and proactively.

www.hrps.org

> An anticipated change in the demographic composition of the local labour market can help an organization to take proactive corrective actions. Thus, several organizations that in the past depended on young school students for their temporary workforce now target the growing pool of seniors in their recruitment efforts.

4. Tactical Plans, to Be Successful, Require Matching Human Resource Plans.

A firm's strategic plan is often executed through a number of short-range, tactical (or operational) plans. These deal with current operations and are ways of meeting current challenges and using existing opportunities. Purchasing a new personal computing system to improve efficiency, recalling a defective product, and managing inventory more effectively are some examples of tactical planning. Whatever the plan, it is made and carried out by people. If an organization is not properly staffed with the right numbers and types of employees, tactics and in turn, long-range corporate plans may fail. Just as human resources act as a constraint in determining the success of operational plans, they are also affected by an organization's operational plans:

> A combination of a unique baking formula and good customer service has made Country Farm Do-Nuts extremely successful throughout Saskatchewan. Since the firm began operations in 1985, it has grown rapidly, now operating 12 stores across the province. Under the guidance of Cheryl Simkin, an MBA from the University of Alberta, the firm has embarked on an aggressive market development strategy. Initially, it plans to expand to the Alberta and B.C. markets by buying six existing doughnut shops in Vancouver, Calgary, and Edmonton. This means that the existing employees of these newly acquired doughnut shops have to be retrained in baking and customer service to retain the firm's strengths in product quality and customer service.

Figure 3-1 shows the relationship between strategic plans of an organization and its human resource plans. As can be seen, the overall organizational strategy defines the human resource objectives:

In summary, successful organizations—both large and small, and public as well as private—recognize the importance of "intellectual" or "human" capital. An effective human resource plan is a critical tool to take advantage of this valuable asset.

> In one large electronics firm, strategic business planning begins with "top down" revenue and profit targets established by the company's policy committee. Then executives of the different business areas develop the strategies and sales volumes needed to achieve these goals. From here, various divisions create functional

FIGURE 3-1

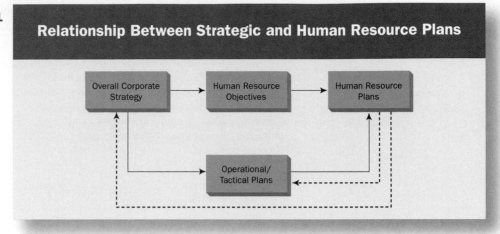

Relationship Between Strategic and Human Resource Plans

strategies for development, manufacturing, marketing, and service. Line managers are responsible for folding the functional plans into divisional ones. The human resource department's role is to review all divisional plans before they are sent to the top management. Although line managers have wide latitude in addressing human resource issues, human resource concerns are injected into the business plans by proactive human resource specialists who work closely with divisional managers. These managers are encouraged to involve human resource staff in decision making because the business plans will be reviewed for human resource considerations before they are finalized. Through their involvement in the strategic business planning process, the human resource planners in this firm are better able to develop their corporate and functional human resource plans.

In the case of large organizations, the human resource department is actively involved in formulating the basic strategy of the organization. Several large organizations develop three- and five-year strategic plans followed by shorter, tactical plans. Through such planning, these organizations are better able to develop their corporate and functional plans and integrate these with their human resource plans as well. It also means a better fit between short-term and long-term plans in such organizations. It should be noted that the human resource plans of an organization have an impact on the attainment of corporate strategy and tactical plans (this fact is recognized by the presence of dotted arrows in Figure 3-1).

Employment planning is more common in large organizations because it allows them to:

- *improve* the utilization of human resources;

- *match* human resource related activities and future organization objectives efficiently;

- *achieve* economies in hiring new workers;

- *expand* the human resource management information base to assist other human resource activities and other organizational units;

- *make* major demands on local labour markets successfully; and

- *coordinate* different human resource management programs such as employment equity plans and hiring needs.

Large Canadian employers such as Bell Canada, Imasco Ltd., George Weston, and Canada Post, employ several thousands of people. The importance of employment planning to these organizations cannot be overemphasized.

A small organization can expect similar advantages, but the gains in effectiveness are often considerably less because its situation is less complex. In fact, the benefits of human resource planning for small firms may not justify the time and costs. Consider the different situations faced by a small- and large-city government:

> Rural City employs 20 workers and is growing at a rate of 10 per cent a year. Metropolis has 8000 employees, and Sy Wolfe estimates it is growing by five per cent annually. That means 400 new employees every year plus replacement for those who leave. If it costs $400 to find and hire a typical employee, Rural City will spend $800 to hire two more workers. Metropolis will spend $160 000 just to add new employees. If employment planning saves 25 per cent, Rural City's manager cannot justify detailed planning efforts for $200. But for $40 000, Metropolis can afford a specialist and still save thousands of dollars after planning expenses are deducted.

Knowledge of human resource planning, thus, is useful to human resource specialists in both small and large organizations. It shows small employers the human resource considerations they will face should they expand rapidly. (For example, if Rural City attracted several large factories to its area, expansion of city services would depend partly on the city's human resource planning.) Large organizations can benefit from knowledge of employment planning because it reveals ways to make the human resource function more effective.

Figure 3-2 provides an overview of the material that will be discussed in this chapter. The figure identifies the major causes of human resource demand, which are external, organizational, and workforce factors. These causes of demand are forecast by experts, trend data, or other methods to determine the short- and long-range demand for human resources. This demand is fulfilled either internally by present employees or externally by newcomers. The internal supply is shown in replacement charts, which are based on audits of the organization's human resources. Sources of external candidates are identified by analysis of the labour market. The results

FIGURE 3-2

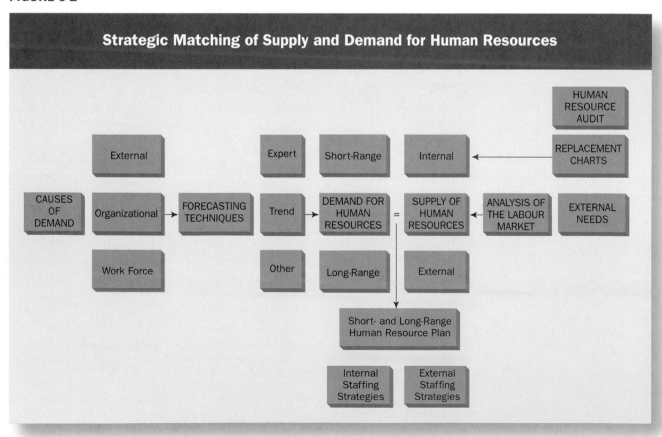

include both short- and long-range human resource plans. Strategies must be formulated to match supply and demand for human resources.

Each component in the figure will be discussed below. The discussion begins with a look at factors causing human resource demand, followed by strategies to estimate demand and supply and match current and future supply with demand.

THE DEMAND FOR HUMAN RESOURCES

AN ORGANIZATION'S FUTURE demand for people is central to employment planning. Most firms try to predict their future employment needs (at least informally), but they may not estimate their sources of supply. For example, one study found that employers are two times more likely to estimate demand than supply. The challenges that determine this demand and the methods of forecasting it merit brief review.

Causes of Demand

Although countless challenges influence the demand for human resources, changes in the environment, the organization, and the work force are usually involved. These factors are common to both short-range and long-range employment plans. The causes of these changes are summarized in Figure 3-3. Some of these causes are within the organization's control, and others are not.

External Challenges

Economic Developments. Developments in the organization's environment are difficult for human resource specialists to predict in the short run and sometimes impossible to estimate in the long run. Reconsider the example of the small-city government. City planners seldom know of major factory relocations until shortly before construction begins. Other economic developments have a noticeable effect, but are difficult to estimate.

> Examples include inflation, unemployment, and interest rates. High interest rates, for example, often curtail construction and the need for construction workers.

Social-Political-Legal Challenges. These challenges are easier to predict, but their implications are seldom clear. The impact on human resource planning of the Canadian Human Rights Act, passed more than 20 years ago, is still somewhat unclear. Major judicial verdicts, changes in employment laws such as minimum

FIGURE 3-3

Causes of Demand for Human Resources in the Future

External	Organizational	Workforce
• Economic developments	• Strategic plans	• Retirement
• Social-political-legal challenges	• Budgets	• Resignations
• Technologic changes	• Sales and production forecasts	• Terminations
• Competitors	• New ventures	• Deaths
	• Organization and job designs	• Leaves of absence

wages, federal and provincial government regulations, and so on all have great implications for the human resource planner. Although many large firms have established employment equity programs, the results of a change from the notion of "equal pay for equal work" to that of "equal pay for work of equal value" (see Chapter Four) will have profound implications.

> In September 2000, an independent committee recommended to the Department of Justice in Nova Scotia to make it mandatory for law firms in the province to hire a certain percentage (some members recommending 20 per cent) of lawyers from visible minorities in the future. If implemented, this can have profound implications for law firms operating in the province.[3]

Technological Changes. Technological challenges are difficult to predict and to assess. Further, technological changes can affect both demand for and supply of human resources.[4] Many thought the computer would mean mass unemployment, for example. While it is true that computerization has eliminated certain types of jobs, the computer industry today employs hundreds of thousands directly or indirectly and is a high-growth industry. Very often, human resource planning is complicated by technology because it tends to reduce employment in one department while increasing it in another.

> The increasing popularity of robots in the workplace impacts on future employment planning.[5] The rapid computerization and automation of many work activities may necessitate new skills on the part of employees which may be hard to accurately predict.

Competitors. Competitors are another external challenge that affects an organization's demand for human resources.

> Employment in some of the traditional manufacturing sectors (such as steel) barely grows, partially because of foreign competition and push for productivity improvement. But in the electronics industry, competition causes lower prices, larger markets, and additional employment.

Organizational Decisions

Major organizational decisions affect the demand for human resources. Five of these are discussed below:

Strategic plan
An identification of a firm's mission and objectives and its proposals for achieving those objectives.

Strategic Plan. The organization's *strategic plan* is the most influential decision. It commits the firm to long-range objectives such as growth rates and new products, markets, or services. These objectives determine the numbers and types of employees needed in the future. Growth is primarily responsible for the number of entry-level job openings. Obviously, a fast-growing firm has more beginning-level vacancies. The number of higher-level openings also depends on how well the human resource department assists employees to develop their capabilities. If workers are not encouraged to expand their capabilities, they may not be ready to fill future vacancies. A lack of promotable replacements creates job openings that need to be filled externally.

The firm's strategic plan to achieve objectives has a decisive influence on human resource plans. In Chapter One of this text, three alternate competitive strategies (focus, cost leadership, and differentiation) were identified. A firm making a fundamental change in its strategy should recognize the implications for its human resource management systems and priorities.

> An electronics manufacturer employing a cost leadership strategy may thus have to encourage high task specialization resulting in lower production costs, while another firm operating in the same field using a differentiation strategy may find it necessary

to encourage broad, innovative skill application on the part of the employees. The career progression paths in a firm that embraces a cost leadership strategy may also be narrower in scope than in a firm that follows a differentiation strategy.

Budgets. In the short run, planners find that strategic plans become operational in the form of budgets. Budget increases or cuts are the most significant short-run influence on human resource needs.

Sales and Production Forecasts. The sales and production forecasts are less exact than budgets, but may provide even quicker notice of short-run changes in human resource demand:

> The human resource manager for a nationwide chain of furniture outlets observed a sharp decline in sales, brought on by a recession. The manager quickly discarded the short-run human resource plan and imposed an employment freeze on all outlets' hiring plans.

New Ventures. New ventures mean new human resource demands. When begun internally, the lead time may allow planners to develop short-run and long-run employment plans. But new ventures begun by acquisitions and mergers cause an immediate revision of human resource demands.

> A reorganization, especially after a merger or an acquisition, can radically alter human resource needs. Several positions or jobs may have to be eliminated to avoid duplication while new integrating roles may have to created for smooth operating of merged units.

Organizational and Job Design. Changes in the structure have major implications for human resource needs.

> Gennum Corporation, a Canadian high-tech company that designs and manufactures silicon integrated circuits announced a new organizational structure in 2000. It was changing from its existing function-based structure (employing specialist functional departments like marketing and production) to a product-based structure. Under the new structure, there will be separate divisions for video products and for hearing instrument products. Already, this decision has resulted in the creation of new positions. The competencies required of several employees—especially at supervisory and managerial levels—will also be different in the future with implications for several HR functions, especially hiring and training.[6]

Automation, computerization, and job redesign also necessitate major revisions in human resource need estimates.

Workforce Factors

The demand for human resources is modified by employee actions. Retirements, resignations, terminations, deaths, and leaves of absence all increase the need for human resources. When large numbers of employees are involved, past experience usually serves as a reasonably accurate guide. However, reliance on past experiences means that human resource specialists must be sensitive to changes that upset past trends:

> Presently, Jim Stitz keeps close track of employees nearing retirement so that his human resource plan remains accurate. Currently, the establishment of a mandatory retirement age is not considered discriminatory; however, considering the fact that a large number of Canadians will be of retirement age in the next five to ten years, the law could change (especially in view of a shortage of young workers expected in the foreseeable future). In such a case, Jim could no longer use his past experience as a guide to predictions when older workers would retire. It is also possible that with the achievement of financial security, workers may opt for earlier retirement.

Forecasting Human Resource Needs

Forecasts
Estimates of future resource needs and changes.

Human resource *forecasts* are attempts to predict an organization's future demand for employees. As Figure 3-4 shows, forecasting techniques range from the informal to the sophisticated. Even the most sophisticated methods are not perfectly accurate; instead, they are best viewed as approximations. Most firms make only casual estimates about the immediate future. As they gain experience with forecasting human resource needs, they may use more sophisticated techniques (especially if they can afford specialized staff). Each of the forecasting methods in Figure 3-4 is explained below.

Expert Forecasts

Expert forecasts rely on those who are knowledgeable to estimate future human resource needs. At the first level of complexity, the manager may simply be convinced that the workload justifies another employee:

> **Manager:** How come the credit card balance statements haven't gone out yet?
>
> **Billing Clerk:** I know they should have, but we're short-handed. The new computer system has some bugs that haven't been fixed yet. Right now, the two computer systems are not mutually compatible. We've been working overtime on this; but nothing helps.
>
> **Manager:** Yes, I talked to Janet about it. It seems it will take at least another six months for the new system to be fully operational. Meanwhile, I'll ask the HR department to get us a temporary employee. The salary will be more than recovered by the cost of overtime and lost interest in unpaid accounts.

The example above illustrates an informal and instant forecast. But it is not part of a systematic planning effort. A better method is for planners to *survey* managers, who are the experts, about their department's future employment needs. The centralization of this information permits formal plans that identify the organization's future demand.

Nominal group technique
Structured meeting that identifies and ranks problems or issues affecting a group.

The survey may be an informal poll, a written questionnaire, or a focused discussion using the **nominal group technique** (NGT). The NGT presents a group of managers with a problem statement, such as, "What will cause our staffing needs to change over the next year?" Then each of the five to fifteen participants writes down as many answers as he or she can imagine. After about five to ten minutes, these ideas are shared in round-table fashion until all written ideas and any new ones they stimulated have been recorded. The group's ideas are then discussed and ranked by having each member of the group vote for the three to five most important ones.[7]

Delphi technique
The soliciting of predictions about specified future events from a panel of experts, using repeated surveys until convergence in opinions occurs.

If the experts cannot be brought together, sophistication can be added to the survey approach with the Delphi technique. The **Delphi technique** solicits estimates from a group of experts, usually managers. Then human resource department planners act

FIGURE 3-4

Forecasting Techniques for Estimating Future Human Resource Needs

Expert	Trend	Other
• Informal and instant decisions	• Extrapolation	• Budget and planning analysis
• Formal expert survey	• Indexation	• New-venture analysis
• Delphi technique	• Statistical analysis	• Computer models

as intermediaries, summarizing the various responses and reporting the findings to the experts. The experts are surveyed again after they get this feedback. Summaries and surveys are repeated until the experts' opinions begin to agree on future developments. (Usually four or five surveys are enough.) For example, the human resource department may survey all production supervisors and managers until an agreement is reached on the number of replacements needed during the next year.

Trend Projection Forecasts

Extrapolation
Extending past rates of change into the future.

Perhaps the quickest forecasting technique is to project past trends. The two simplest methods are extrapolation and indexation. *Extrapolation* involves extending past rates of change into the future. For example, if an average of 20 production workers were hired each month for the past two years, extrapolation indicates that 240 production workers will probably be added during the upcoming year.

Indexation
A method of estimating future employment needs by matching employment growth with some index, such as the ratio of production employees to sales.

Indexation is a method of estimating future employment needs by matching employment growth with some index. A common example is the ratio of production employees to sales. For example, planners may discover that for each million-dollar increase in sales, the production department requires 10 new assemblers. Figure 3-5 shows an example of the indexation method in the case of a direct marketing firm. The relevant business factor here is sales figures in dollars. An overall index productivity for all relevant sales personnel is computed. This ratio, with appropriate modifications, enables the firm to estimate its demand for personnel for the next period.

Extrapolation and indexation are crude, short-run approximations because they assume that the causes of demand—external, organizational, and workforce factors—remain constant, which is seldom the case. They are very inaccurate for long-range human resource projections. The more sophisticated *statistical analyses* make allowances for changes in the underlying causes of demand.

Other Forecasting Methods

There are several other ways planners can estimate the future demand for human resources. One approach is through *budget and planning analysis*. Organizations that need human resource planning generally have detailed budgets and long-range plans.

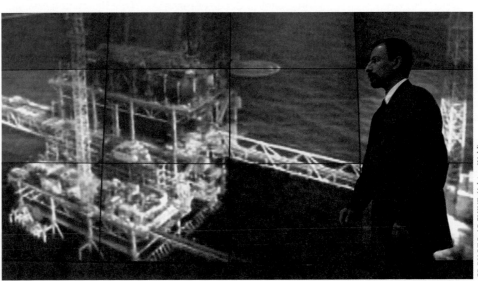

By analyzing staffing needs of existing oilrigs, planners of a new rig can forecast their human resource needs until changes in technology occur.

CP PHOTO ARCHIVE (Adrian Wyld)

FIGURE 3-5

An Illustration of the Indexation Method

Plastics, mugs and housewares (PMH), a direct marketer of household plastics products with its head office in Calgary, began operations in 1992. PMH, which began as a very small firm operating in Calgary, soon grew rapidly and employed 530 persons in 2000. The firm hopes to have even higher growth rates in the next two years. The dollar sales value and the staff strength for the last seven years (for which company information is readily available) are shown below. The firm forecasts it will have a 20 per cent increase in sales in 2001 and another 15 per cent (over 2001 figures) in year 2002. Because of technological improvements and improved training, the sales productivity is expected to show a 15 per cent improvement in 2001. (No substantial improvement is expected for the year after.) PMH is currently attempting to forecast its human resource needs for 2001 and 2002.

One possible approach here is:

Year	Number of employees	Dollar Sales (000s)	Sales Productivity Index (Dollar Sales divided by number of employees)
1994	300	150	0.5000
1995	310	160	0.5161
1996	400	210	0.5250
1997	430	222	0.5163
1998	430	228	0.5302
1999	520	273	0.5250
2000	530	280	0.5283

Sales targets for the next two years are:

2001	?	336	0.6075
2002	?	386.4	0.6075

Since the target sales are expected to rise by 20 per cent in 2001 and 15 per cent in 2002, the figures for the two years will be: 336 in 2001 (280 $\times$ 1.2) and 386.4 (336 $\times$ 1.15). The labour productivity is expected to increase by 15 per cent in 2001 (or reach 0.6075). The human resource needs for the next two years will, hence, be:

  2001 = 336   divided by 0.6075 = 553.09, and
  2002 = 386.4 divided by 0.6075 = 636.05

This means that the firm will need to hire approximately 23 (or 553 – 530) persons for 2001 and 83 persons (636 – 553) a year later. Of course, the exact numbers can be arrived at only after a detailed look at the various types of job positions within the organization, their interdependencies, and differences in productivity levels across job positions. These figures also do not include hiring needed to replace employees who retire or otherwise leave the organization.

A study of department budgets reveals the financial authorizations for more employees. These data plus extrapolations of workforce changes (resignations, terminations, and the like) can provide short-run estimates of human resource needs. Long-term estimates can be made from each department or division's long-range plans.

When new ventures complicate employment planning, planners can use new-venture analysis. *New-venture analysis* requires planners to estimate human resource needs by comparison with firms that already perform similar operations.

> For example, a petroleum company that plans to open a coal mine can estimate its future employment needs by determining them from employment levels of other coal mines.

The most sophisticated forecasting approaches involve computers. *Computer models* are a series of mathematical formulas that simultaneously use extrapolation, indexation, survey results, and estimates of workforce changes to compute future human resource needs. Over time, actual changes in human resource demand are used to refine the computer's formulas.

Across firms, human resource forecasting shows wide variations in their complexity (Figure 3-6). At the lowest level, it is portrayed in informal discussions and instant decisions. Computerized forecasting systems with online predictive capabilities reflect the highest level of complexity. Naturally, the more sophisticated techniques are found among large organizations that have had years of experience in human resource planning. Small firms or those just beginning to forecast human resource needs are more likely to employ Level 1 and progress to other levels as planners seek greater accuracy.

Listing Human Resource Requirements

Forecasts translate the causes of demand into short-range and long-range statements of need. The resulting long-range plans are, of necessity, general statements of *probable* needs. Specific numbers are either omitted or estimated.

Staffing table
A list of anticipated employment openings for each type of job.

Short-term plans are more specific and may be reported as a **staffing table**, as in Figure 3-7. A staffing table lists the future employment needs for each type of job. The listing may be a specific number or an approximate range of needs, depending on the accuracy of the underlying forecast. Staffing tables (also called manning tables) are neither complete nor wholly accurate. They are only approximations. But these

FIGURE 3-6

Increasing Levels of Complexity in Human Resource Planning

Low	← Complexity →		High
Level 1	**Level 2**	**Level 3**	**Level 4**
Highly informal and subjective.	Annual planning for human resources is present. There is a general recognition of potential human resource challenges.	Computers are increasingly used to systematically track demand and supply of human resources.	Existence of a sophisticated human resource information system permits modelling and simulation of talent needs, flows, and costs to project needs and take corrective actions.
Managers discuss goals and numbers of people needed in the short term.			
No long-term orientation.		Records of continuous employee turnover and absenteeism are used to predict future scenarios.	

FIGURE 3-7

A Partial Staffing Table for a City Government

Metropolis City Government Staffing Table

Date Compiled: _____

Budget Code Number	Job Title (As Found) on Job Description	Using Department(s)	Anticipated Openings by Months of the Year											
			Total	1	2	3	4	5	6	7	8	9	10	11	12
100-32	Police Recruit	Police	128	32			32			32			32		
100-33	Police Dispatcher	Police	3	2					1						
100-84	Meter Reader	Police	24	2	2	2	2	2	2	2	2	2	2	2	2
100-85	Traffic Supervisor	Police	5	2			1			1			1		
100-86	Team Supervisor —Police (Sergeant)	Police	5	2			1			1			1		
100-97	Duty Supervisor — Police (Staff Sergeant)	Police	2	1					1						
100-99	Shift Officer — Police (Inspector)	Police	1	1											
200-01	Car Washer	Motor Pool	4	1			1			1			1		
200-12	Mechanic's Assistant	Motor Pool	3				1			1			1		
200-13	Mechanic III	Motor Pool	2	1									1		
200-14	Mechanic II	Motor Pool	1						1						
200-15	Mechanic I (Working Supervisor)	Motor Pool	1	1											
300-01	Clerk IV	Administration	27	10			5			6			6		

estimates allow human resource specialists to match short-run demand and supply. They help operating departments run more smoothly and can enhance the image of the human resource department:

Sy Wolfe: You know, your suggestion worked! My employment projections helped me to start looking for people even before vacancies emerged.

Jean-Marie Gasse: The advantage of doing it this way is that it reduces the disruptions managers experience while waiting for replacements to be found, assigned, and taught their jobs.

Sy Wolfe: Yes. And their usual gripes about how long it takes the human resource department to fill jobs have diminished greatly. I owe you one!

With specific estimates of future human resource needs, personnel specialists can become more proactive and systematic. For example, a review of Figure 3-7 shows that the city's personnel department must hire 32 police academy recruits every three months. This knowledge allows recruiters in the human resource department to plan their recruiting campaign so that it peaks about six weeks before the beginning of the next police academy class. The advanced planning allows the department to screen applicants and notify them at least three weeks before the class begins. For those still in school or otherwise unable to be ready that quickly, recruiters can inform them when the following class begins. If the human resource department waited for the police department to notify them, notification might come too late to allow a systematic recruiting and screening process. Staffing tables enable recruiters to be proactive and to better plan their activities.

THE SUPPLY OF HUMAN RESOURCES

ONCE THE HUMAN resource department makes projections about future human resource demands, the next major concern is filling projected openings. There are two sources of supply: internal and external. The internal supply consists of present employees who can be promoted, transferred, or demoted to meet anticipated needs.

> For example, Jean-Marie Gasse (in the previous dialogue) works in the police department of Metropolis, but is applying for a transfer into the human resource department. She is part of the internal supply of human resources to the city government. The external supply consists of people in the labour market who do not work for the city. These include employees of other organizations and those who are unemployed.

Internal Supply Estimates

Estimating the internal supply involves more than merely counting the number of employees. Planners audit the present workforce to learn about the capabilities of present workers. This information allows planners to estimate tentatively which openings can be filled by present employees. These tentative assignments usually are recorded on a replacement chart. Considering present employees for future job openings is important if workers are to have lifelong careers with their employer rather than just dead-end jobs. The patterns of employee transition among jobs, hence, must be carefully assessed and taken into consideration. Audits, replacement charts, and employee transition matrices (more popularly called Markov analysis) also are important additions to the personnel department's information base. With greater knowledge of employees, the department can more effectively plan recruiting, training, and career-planning activities. A human resource department can also help meet its employment equity goals by identifying internal minority candidates for job openings. Since audits, replacement charts, and transition matrices are important to proactive human resource work, they are explained more fully below.

Human Resource Audits

Skills inventories
Summaries of each non-managerial worker's skills and abilities.

Human resource audits summarize the employee's skills and abilities. When referring to nonmanagers, the audits result in **skills inventories**. Audits of managers are called *management inventories*. Whatever name is used, an inventory catalogues each comprehensive understanding of the capabilities found in the organization's work force.

An example of a skills inventory is found in Figure 3-8. It is divided into four parts. Part I can be completed by the human resource department from employee records. It identifies the employee's job title, experience, age, and previous jobs. Part II seeks information about skills, duties, responsibilities, and education of the worker. From these questions, planners learn about the mix of employee abilities. The human resource department may collect these data by phone or in face-to-face interviews. Or the questions may be sent to the employee through the company mail.

The employee's potential is briefly summarized by the immediate supervisor in Part III. Performance, readiness for promotion, and any deficiencies are noted here.

The supervisor's signature helps ensure that the form's accuracy is reviewed by someone who knows the employee better than the human resource specialists. Part IV is added as a final check for completeness and for the addition of recent employee evaluations, which give more insight into past performance.

FIGURE 3-8

Skills Inventory Form for Metropolis City Government

Part 1 (To be completed by human resource department)

1. Name _____ 2. Employee Number_____
3. Job Title _____ 4. Experience_____ years
5. Age_____ 6. Years with City_____

7. Other Jobs Held:

         With City: Title_____ From _____ to _____
                       Title_____ From _____ to _____
      Elsewhere: Title_____ From _____ to _____
                       Title_____ From _____ to _____

Part II (To be completed by employee)

8. **Special Skills**. List below any skills you possess, even if they are not used in your present job. Include types and names of machines or tools with which you are experienced.

            Skills _____
      Machines _____
            Tools _____

9. **Duties**. Briefly describe your present duties_____
_____

10. **Responsibilities**. Briefly describe your responsibilities for:
          City Equipment:_____
               City Funds:_____
       Employee Safety:_____
Employee Supervision:_____

11. **Education.** Briefly describe your education and training background:

	Years Completed	Year of Graduation	Degree and Major
High School:	_____	_____	_____
University:	_____	_____	_____
Job Training:	_____	_____	_____
Special Courses:	_____	_____	_____

Part III (To be completed by human resource department with supervisory inputs)

12. Overall Evaluation of Performance_____
13. Overall Readiness for Promotion _____
       To What Job(s): _____
         Comments: _____
14. Current Deficiencies:
_____

15. Supervisor's Signature _____ Date:_____

Part IV (To be completed by human resource department representative)
16. Are the two most recent performance evaluations attached? _____ Yes ___ No
17. Prepared by _____ Date: _____

To be useful, inventories of human resources must be updated periodically. Updating every two years is sufficient for most organizations if employees are encouraged to report major changes to the human resource department when they occur. Major changes include new skills, degree completions, changed job duties, and the like. Failure to update skills inventories can lead to present employees being overlooked for job openings within the organization.

Management inventories should be updated periodically, since they also are used for key human resource related decisions. In fact, some employers use the same form for managers and nonmanagers. When the forms differ, the management inventory requests information about management activities. Common topics include:

- number of employees supervised;
- types of employees supervised;
- total budget managed;
- management training received;
- duties of subordinates;
- previous management duties.

Replacement Charts

Replacement charts
Visual representations of who will replace whom when a job opening occurs

Replacement charts are a visual representation of who will replace whom in the event of a job opening. The information for constructing the chart comes from the human resource audit. Figure 3-9 illustrates a typical replacement chart. It shows the replacement status of only a few jobs in the administration of a large city.

Although different firms may seek to summarize different information in their replacement charts, the figure indicates the minimum information usually included. The chart, which is much like an organization chart, depicts the various jobs in the organization and shows the status of likely candidates. Replacement status consists of two variables: present performance and promotability. Present performance is determined largely from supervisory evaluations. Opinions of other managers, peers, and subordinates may contribute to the appraisal of present performance. Future promotability is based primarily on present performance and the estimates by immediate superiors of future success in a new job. The human resource department may contribute to these estimates through the use of psychological tests, interviews, and other methods of assessment. Replacement charts often show the candidates' ages.

Replacement summaries
Lists of likely replacements for each job and their relative strengths and weaknesses.

Human resource and management decision-makers find these charts provide a quick reference. Their shortcoming is that they contain little information.[8] To supplement the chart—and, increasingly, to supplant it—human resource specialists develop *replacement summaries*. Replacement summaries list likely replacements and their relative strengths and weaknesses for each job. As Figure 3-10 shows, the summaries provide considerably more data than the replacement chart. This additional information allows decision-makers to make more informed decisions.

Most companies that are sophisticated enough to engage in detailed human resource planning computerize their human resource records, including job analysis information and human resource inventories. Then, through a simple computer program, planners can compile replacement summaries each time a job opening occurs. These summaries also show which positions lack human resource backups:

> Canada Grocers Ltd., which has a chain of grocery stores in five Canadian provinces, has computerized its search for fast trackers in the organization. Every six months, the organization's managers submit performance appraisals to the human resource department indicating the promotability of their subordinates. By consolidating these

FIGURE 3-9

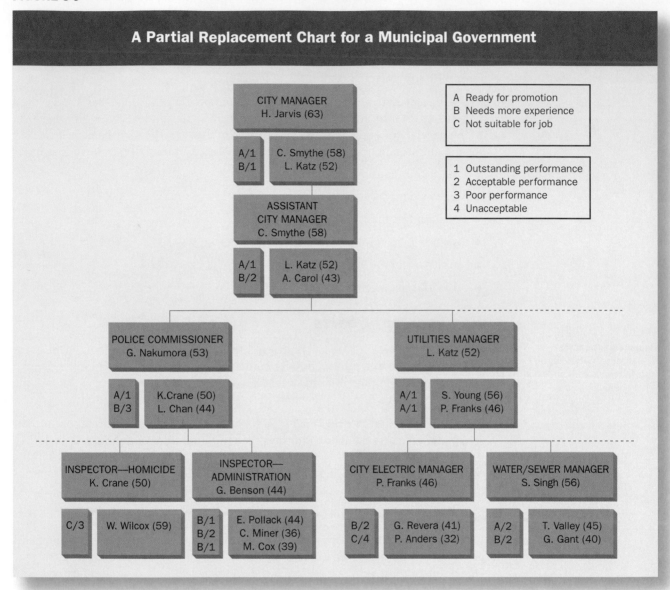

A Partial Replacement Chart for a Municipal Government

reports on a computer, the company has been able to identify the "outstanding" workers. A separate program helps produce career-development plans, pinpointing weaknesses and suggesting solutions—university courses, in-house training, or a different job assignment.

In the long run, the human resource department can encourage employees to upgrade their capabilities and prepare for future vacancies. In the short run, an opening without a suitable replacement requires that someone be hired from the external labour market.

Whether replacement charts or summaries are used, this information is normally kept confidential. Confidentiality not only guards the privacy of employees, but also prevents dissatisfaction among those who are not immediately promotable.

Markov Analysis

Markov analysis
Forecast of a firm's future human resource supplies, using transitional probability matrices reflecting historical or expected movements of employees across jobs.

Markov analysis is a fairly simple method of predicting the internal supply of human resources in the future. This is particularly useful in organizations where

FIGURE 3-10

A Replacement Summary for the Position of City Manager

Replacement Summary for the Position of City Manager

Present Office Holder	Harold Jarvis	**Age**	63
Probable Opening	In two years	**Reason**	Retirement
Salary Grade	99 ($86,000)	**Experience**	8 years

Candidate 1 Clyde Smythe

Current Position Assistant City Manager

Current Performance Outstanding   **Explanation** Clyde's performance evaluations by the City Manager are always the highest possible.

Promotability Ready now for promotion   **Explanation** During an extended illness of the City Manager, Clyde assumed all duties successfully, including major policy decisions and negotiations with city unions.

Training Needs None

Age 58

Experience 4 years

Candidate 2 Larry Katz

Current Position Utilities Manager

Current Performance Outstanding   **Explanation** Larry's performance has kept costs of utilities to citizens 10 to 15 percent below that of comparable city utilities through careful planning.

Promotability Needs more experience   **Explanation** Larry's experience is limited to utilities management. Although successful, he needs more broad administrative experience in other areas. (He is ready for promotion to Assistant City Manager at this time.)

Training Needs Training in budget preparation and public relations would be desirable before promotion to City Manager.

Age 52

Experience 5 years

employees move from one job (or rank) to another on a regular basis. Markov analysis reflects the patterns in these human resource movements. It is particularly useful in organizations where jobs or human resource movements do not fluctuate rapidly due to external (e.g., technological) or internal (e.g., strategic) changes.

For the purpose of predicting human resources, Markov analysis uses a transition probability matrix, which describes the probabilities of an incumbent staying in his or her present job for the forecast time period (usually one year), moving to another job position in the organization, or leaving the organization. When this matrix is multiplied by the number of employees in each job at the beginning of a year, the forecaster is easily able to identify the number of persons who will remain in the job at the end of the year.

Figure 3-11 shows a sample transition matrix. The table shows that 80 per cent (or 0.8) of the incumbents in Job A remain in their present position at the end of the year, 10 per cent (or 0.1) move to Job B, 5 per cent (or 0.05) more to Job C, none to Job D, and 5 per cent (or 0.05) leave the organization (through resignations or otherwise). When these probabilities are multiplied by the number of persons in Job A at the beginning of the year (namely, 200), we see that 160 of them remain in their present position, 20 of them move to Job B, 10 of them move to Job C, and the remaining 10 leave the organization. When similar calculations are performed for all the jobs (in the case of this firm, for Jobs A, B, C, and D), we are able to predict the approximate number of employees who will remain in each job position.

Many firms use the previous year's transition rates for predicting next year's movements. However, if the previous year was atypical, the predictions may be erroneous.[9] Markov analysis is popular because of the ease of its use. However, it is only as good as the transition probabilities used. The probabilities are not very reliable if there are only a few job incumbents in each job. Generally, Markov analysis works best if there are at least 50 employees in each job position.[10] This makes it more appropriate only for medium and large organizations.

Markov analysis can also be used speculatively to assess the impact of possible changes in transition analysis. Thus, "what if" analyses can be undertaken to understand the impact of possible future scenarios (e.g., "What if the quit rate for Job A doubles from its present 6 per cent per year?"). This makes it a useful tool for human resource forecasting, especially in the context of strategic planning.

> In the past, a leading lumber firm used a sophisticated Markov-type model to plan its human resources. The model analyzed the flow of human resources from the supply point (whether internal or external) to the point of demand (requirements for specific jobs). The model also allowed the company's planners to identify transition rates (rates at which staff moved from one level to the next in the hierarchy) and to use them as constraints in balancing supply and demand for human resources. For instance, under the assumptions of varying transition rates, the company could forecast the workforce supply and demand for different levels and different time periods. The Markov-type model enabled the policy-makers of the company to analyze the impact of different policies on human resource supply and demand.[11]

Most Markov models are closed systems. They do not interact with the environment or show dynamics that occur in their environment. Today's sophisticated computers permit the incorporation of these interactions with environments through complex modelling techniques. *Holonic modelling* is a technique that can be used today even by non-mathematical managers to portray interactions with environments and reflect the impact of strategic decisions on supply of human resources at different organizational levels.[12] The benefits associated with holonic modelling include improved formulation ability, greater flexibility, and greater insights to the decision maker.

External Supply Estimates

Not every future opening can be met with present employees. Some jobs lack replacements to fill an opening when it occurs. Other jobs are entry-level positions; that is, they are beginning jobs that are filled by people who do not presently work for the

FIGURE 3-11

An Example of Markov Analysis

(a) Transition Probability Matrix

Year Beginning			Year End		
	Job A	Job B	Job C	Job D	Exit
Job A	0.80	0.10	0.05	0.00	0.05
Job B	0.10	0.70	0.00	0.10	0.10
Job C	0.00	0.00	0.90	0.05	0.05
Job D	0.00	0.00	0.00	0.90	0.10

(b) Expected Movements of Employees

	Initial Staffing Level	Job A	Job B	Job C	Job D	Exit
Job A	200	160	20	10	0	10
Job B	70	7	49	0	7	7
Job C	60	0	0	54	3	3
Job D	100	0	0	0	90	10
Predicted End-of-the Year Staffing Level		167	69	64	100	30

organization. When there are no replacements or when the opening is for an entry-level job, there is a need for external supplies of human resources.

When estimating external supplies, three major factors must be examined: trends in the labour market, community attitudes, and demographic trends. These are briefly outlined below.

Labour Market Analysis

Labour market analysis
The study of the firm's labour market to evaluate the present or future availability of different types of workers.

The human resource department's success in finding new employees depends on an accurate *labour market analysis*. Even when unemployment rates are high, many needed skills are difficult to find:

> In August 2000, the unemployment rate in Canada was 7.1 per cent. However, human resource departments that sought software programmers had to compete for these personnel in a very tight market since the demand for programmers far exceeded supply in several regions in the country.[13]

In the short run, the national unemployment rate serves as an approximate measure of how difficult it is to acquire new employees. Human resource specialists realize that this rate varies for different groups, as well as from province to province and city to city:

> In August 2000, there were some wide variations in Canadian labour markets. The unemployment rate in Ontario was only six per cent, while in Quebec it exceeded eight per cent. Most parts of Atlantic Canada also had unemployment rates that were higher than the national average.[14]

Regardless of the unemployment rate, external needs may be met by attracting employees who work for others. In the long run, local developments and demographic trends have the most significant impact on labour markets. Local developments include community growth rates and attitudes. For example, many farm towns find their population declining. When they attempt to attract new business, employers fear a declining population may mean future shortages in the local labour market. So the new businesses often locate elsewhere. The lack of jobs results in still more people leaving the local labour market. Conversely, growing cities are attractive to employers because they promise even larger labour markets in the future.

Community Attitudes

Community attitudes also affect the nature of the labour market. Anti-business or nongrowth attitudes may cause present employers to move elsewhere. The loss of jobs forces middle-class workers to relocate, and the shrinking workforce discourages new businesses from becoming established.

Demographics

Demographic trends are another long-term development that affects the availability of external supply. Fortunately for planners, these trends are known years in advance of their impact:

> The low birthrates of the 1930s and early 1940s were followed by a baby boom during the late 1940s and 1950s. When the post-Second World War babies started to go to university in the 1960s, the low birthrates of the 1930s led to a shortage of university teachers. These demographic trends were already in motion by 1950. Long-range human resource planning, which was sensitive to demographic developments, could have predicted the shortage soon enough for proactive universities to take corrective action.

COPS
Canadian Occupational Projection System provides up to ten year projection of Canadian economy and human resource needs.

Human Resources Development Canada (HRDC) publishes both short- and long-term labour force projections. The ***Canadian Occupational Projection System (COPS)*** provides a highly detailed projection of the Canadian economy up to 10 years in the future.[15] This projection is a synthesis of the consensus among major private sector forecasters, the judgment of the Occupational Projections and Macroeconomic Studies Unit of HRDC and the judgment of COPS partners in HRDC's regional offices. COPS projects expected imbalances (between supply and demand of human resources) by occupation and type of education.

> For example, HRDC predicts that the largest growth in employment requirements until 2004 will be in personal services, followed by construction and business services industries. Employment requirements in fishing, forestry, and communication industries are expected to decline during the same period.[16]

The *COPS Macroeconomic Projections*, which provide long-range demographic and labour market supply forecasts, are supplied at both national and provincial levels.[17] It is done at a high level of industry detail for each province including major indicators for each province.

Job Futures 2000 is a group of products available from HRDC that identifies trends in the world of work. It outlines job outlooks by occupation as well as by field of study and estimates the prospect of finding jobs in a specific occupation or field. Job Futures provides Canadians with the latest information available about work—information that is important for anyone in the process of making decisions or advising others in the area of career planning.

> For example, HRDC's Job Futures forecasts that the chance of finding work as a financial auditor and accountant is fair (the scale used is 'limited', 'fair' and 'good'). The number of job openings is expected to be matched by the number of qualified job seekers. Concern about corporate fraud may create opportunities in forensic accounting. Payroll experts are also likely to be in high demand. The increasing use of computers will necessitate new skill requirements for these professionals.[18]

For the human resource manager as well as the job seeker, such information is invaluable. In the past, the Economic Council of Canada had developed another model useful in predicting the Canadian economy. The model called CANDIDE— Canadian Disaggregated Interdepartmental Econometric Model—which uses over 1500 regression equations to forecast unemployment, real domestic product, and so on, is yet another tool for the human resource planner on the future shape of the Canadian economy. The Microelectronics Simulation Model, which incorporates the impact of technological change on the occupational composition in this country, may also be found useful by human resource planners when forecasting occupational composition in Canada.

National human resource plans assume that the skill needs of a country can be validly assessed for a five- or ten-year period in order to take timely and effective corrective actions (such as retraining). In practice, many countries have found this to be a daunting task.[19] Indeed, Canada is one of the few (if not the first) western industrialized countries to adopt industrial human resource planning.

> In a cross-country comparison of national human resource forecasting methods, Canada's tools and methods rated well. The study, which looked at forecasting methods in the United States, the U.K., Germany, Netherlands, Sweden, and Canada, found that Canada's system was strong in many areas relative to other countries. Our strengths lay in our ability to analytically assess skill shortages through such tools as occupational forecasting models and sector studies. Our most serious shortcoming lay in our lack of processing of the administrative data that is collected as part of our normal operations. The Netherlands' system was found to be the best equipped overall.[20]

The Northern Pipelines Act and the Canada Oil and Gas Act, which contain clauses requiring the partner companies to develop comprehensive human resource plans, are indicative of this country's commitment to human resource planning at the national level:

> To build the 3360 kilometres of pipeline in Canada, the Alaska Highway Gas Pipeline would require 17 000 person-years. This would necessitate close cooperation among the managements of the firms involved, their labour unions, and the governments (municipal, provincial, and federal) involved. Clearly, a sophisticated human resource plan would be absolutely necessary in this instance.

Statistics Canada also publishes reports on labour force conditions on a monthly, quarterly, annual, and occasional basis. Information is available on total labour force projections by geographic, demographic, and occupational variables; labour income; census data; and population projections by sex and province over various years. (For an example of population projections by age group see Figure 1-7 in Chapter One). Data such as these have implications for many businesses:

> Fast-food restaurants depend on 16- to 24-year-olds for many jobs. By 2016, there will be a decline of 495 500 in this age category. At the same time, the trend toward eating more meals away from home will cause an increased demand for fast-food employees.

STRATEGIES TO MATCH SUPPLY AND DEMAND FOR HUMAN RESOURCES

TYPICALLY, human resource planners face two decision situations: they either find that the available supply of human resources is less or greater than their future needs. It is only the rare fortunate planner who finds that the supply and demand are equal. Each of the above two situations requires somewhat different corrective actions that are discussed below.

Strategies in the Wake of Oversupply of Human Resources

When the internal supply of workers exceeds the firm's demand, a human resource surplus exists. This is handled in a variety of ways.

Hiring Freeze

Most employers respond to a surplus with a hiring freeze. This freeze stops the human resource department from filling openings with external applications. Instead, present employees are reassigned. Voluntary departures, called *attrition*, slowly reduce the surplus. Attrition is the normal separation of employees from an organization as a result of *resignation*, *retirement*, or *death*. It is initiated by the individual worker and not by the company. In most organizations, the key component of attrition is resignation, which is a voluntary separation. Although attrition is a slow way to reduce the employment base in an organization, it presents the fewest problems. Voluntary departures simply create a vacancy that is not filled, and the staffing level declines without anyone being forced out of a job:

> Faced with a surplus of employees and a slow-growing economy, a major department store resorted to an employment freeze in the mid-1990s. On average, its attrition rate was five per cent; within 18 months, it had reduced its staff level from 30 000 to about 27 750.

Attrition
Loss of employees due to their voluntary departures from the firm through resignation, retirement, or death.

Early Retirement Offers

A special form of attrition is early retirement. It is one form of separation that the human resource department can actively control. It is used to reduce staffing levels and to create internal job openings. Early retirement plans are designed to encourage long-service workers to retire before the normal retirement age in the organization (say, 65 years). Since employees who retire before age 65 will draw benefits longer, their monthly retirement benefits may be reduced proportionately.

Job Sharing

Reducing the number of total work hours through *job sharing* is yet another strategy used by firms to cope with a temporary surplus of workers. Job sharing involves dividing duties of a single position between two or more employees. The employees benefit by having more free time at their disposal. From the employer's perspective, this eliminates the need to lay off one employee completely.

Job sharing
A plan whereby available work is spread among all workers in a group to reduce the extent of layoffs when production requirements cause substantial decline in available work.

Use of Part-time Workers

Eliminating full-time positions and replacing them with part-time positions, thus reducing the total work hours, is another popular strategy found in many Canadian organizations. The use of part-time and contract workers also increases the employer's flexibility to meet peak demands without having to increase the total number of workers on the permanent full-time payroll.

> Part-time work is growing so much in popularity in Canada that in this millennium it is expected to account for almost one-quarter of all employment in this country.

Internal Transfers

Organizations with progressive human resource policies attempt to find new internal jobs for surplus and displaced employees:

A financial services company with over 10 800 employees found itself forced to reduce staff in some areas to meet twin pressures of increased competition and a recessionary economy. Rather than simply letting the employees go, the firm retrained the employees to take up new positions in areas where the firm was expanding. In the first two months since the program began, 75 per cent of the over 130 displaced employees were retained by the firm in other positions. In almost every case, those employees not retained by the firm had had unsatisfactory performance records or had maintained a very narrow job focus or location requirements.[21]

Layoffs

Layoffs, the temporary withdrawal of employment to workers, are also used in cases of a short-run surplus. Layoffs are the separation of employees from the organization for economic or business reasons. The separation may last only a few weeks if its purpose is to adjust inventory levels or to allow the factory to retool for a new product. When caused by a business cycle, the layoffs may last many months or even years. However, if the layoff is the result of restructuring or rescaling of an industry, the "temporary" layoffs may be permanent.

As unpleasant as layoffs are for both workers and management, they may be required when attrition is insufficient to reduce employment to acceptable levels. In some organizations, each employee who is laid off may receive a supplemental employment benefit over and above government EI benefits. However, during severe economic downturns, the employer's ability to provide these benefits may be seriously jeopardized.

When the layoffs are expected to be of a short duration—as when an automobile plant temporarily closes to change its tooling for a new model—layoffs may not follow the normal pattern of forcing the most recently hired employees to accept unemployment. Rather than following seniority, some contracts have "juniority" clauses. Juniority provisions require that layoffs be offered first to senior workers. If the senior worker wants to accept the layoff, that person collects employment insurance and the other organizational benefits and the juniors keep their jobs. Senior workers are likely to accept layoffs of short duration because they receive almost the same take-home pay without working. When the layoff is of an unknown duration, the seniors usually decline to exercise their juniority rights and fewer senior employees are put on layoff.

Of course, employees may be separated by termination of the employment relationship.

Leave without Pay

One way to temporarily reduce the number of employees on the payroll is to give them an opportunity to take leave of absence without pay either for attending college or university or pursue other personal interests. Employees who are offered this leave are usually those who are financially able to leave the organization for a little while and whose jobs may be eliminated in the future. Thus, this strategy might help some employees to prepare for oncoming changes.

Loaning

The loaning of employees to other organizations is a way of keeping "loaned" employees on the firm's payroll and bringing them back at a later point. Typically, higher-paid employees are loaned for special projects with government, to civic bodies, or for work at charitable organizations. The firm pays these employees a reduced salary and the difference is made up by the agency.

Termination

Termination is a broad term that encompasses the permanent separation from the organization for any reason. Usually this term implies that the employee was fired as a form of discipline. When employees are discharged for business or economic reasons, it is commonly, although not always, called a layoff. Sometimes, however, the employer needs to separate some employees for business reasons and has no plans to rehire them. Rather than being laid off, those workers are simply terminated. In these cases, the employees may receive severance pay and outplacement assistance.

Severance pay is money—often equal to one or more week's salary—that is given to employees who are being permanently separated. Many organizations give severance pay only for involuntary separations and only to employees who have been performing satisfactorily. For example, if a factory is going to close and move operations to another province, employees who are terminated may be given an extra week's salary for each year they have worked for the organization. Some organizations have developed innovative severance pay policies to achieve their human resource objectives, as the following example illustrates:

> Herman Miller Inc., a major manufacturer of office furniture employing over 7000 persons in 40 countries, instituted a novel approach to severance pay, called a "silver parachute." Unlike the "golden parachutes" offered only to senior executives at firms likely to be targets of a takeover, the "silver parachutes" extend to all employees who have been with the company for two or more years. "The parachute would be activated in the event of a hostile takeover, and the rip cord would be pulled if a worker's job were eliminated, salary reduced, or working conditions or benefits altered." Those employees with between three and five years' tenure with the company would receive one full year's compensation. Longer-service employees receive 2.5 times their previous 12 months' salary. Besides assuring employees of severance pay should they lose their job in a hostile takeover, this benefit makes the company a less attractive takeover target.[22]

Outplacement

Outplacement
Assisting employees to find jobs with other employers.

The blow of discharge may be softened through formal ***outplacement*** procedures, which help present employees find new jobs with other firms. These efforts may include the provision of office space, secretarial services, photocopying machines, long-distance phone calls, counselling, instructions on how to look for work, and even invitations to competitors to meet with employees. Not only do such efforts help the former employee, but they also give evidence to the remaining employees of management's commitment to their welfare.

Strategies to Overcome Shortage of Employees

If the internal supply of human resources cannot fulfil the organization's needs, a human resource *shortage* exists. In the short and long runs, somewhat different strategies are employed. Planners have very few options in the short run, while a long-term shortage can be handled through carefully crafted human resource strategies.

Overtime

A popular strategy is to ask existing employees to work beyond the normal hours. Indeed, even during a non-shortage situation, regular overtime has become a fact of life in many firms that do not want to incur additional fixed expenses of hiring permanent employees.

> Statistics Canada reports that approximately two million Canadians regularly work an average of nine hours of overtime per week, most of it unpaid.[23]

Higher employee fatigue, stress levels, accident and wastage rates, and so on, are some of the unwanted consequences of using overtime on a recurring basis. Recognizing this fact, some of the progressive employers have gone against the mainstream—namely reducing the number of work hours—and ended up improving their productivity levels and competitiveness in the labour market. One U.S. manufacturer's experience is noteworthy:

> Metro Plastics Technologies Inc. in Columbus, Indiana, could not fill eight vacancies in its plant as the unemployment rate in the area hovered between one and three per cent. To get a recruiting advantage, it adopted an innovative "30-hour work week for 40-hour pay" strategy under which an employee had to put in only 30 hours a week instead of the traditional 40 hours. A single newspaper ad brought hundreds of qualified applicants to the firm and the firm was able to fill the vacancies immediately. The benefits did not stop there. Within two years, customer returns had fallen by 72 per cent and many internal costs had dropped dramatically. The same results have been reported in a number of other plants, in a variety of industries.[24]

Part-time Workers

An increasingly popular strategy for meeting human resource needs is to use part-time employees. Part-time employees are an attractive option to the employer since it adds flexibility in scheduling and reduces overall payroll costs since part-timers are, typically, not eligible for several of the expensive benefits offered to the full-time workforce. Traditionally, part-timers have been employed by service businesses such as restaurants and retail stores that experience considerable fluctuation in demand during peak and off-peak times. However, more recently, many firms, after a downsizing or restructuring, employ part-timers to provide services that had previously been offered by full timers.

> For example, in recent years, United Parcel Service has created 25-hour-per-week part-time jobs for shipping clerks and supervisors who sort packages at its distribution centres. Until the change, the same jobs were carried out by full-time staff.

Temporary Employment Agencies

Temporary employees, or "temps" as they are called, are provided by a number of private agencies. Temps work for a temporary employment agency and are assigned to different employers that contact the agency for the temporary filling of positions. This is particularly suitable for the supply-demand imbalance caused by short-term leaves of absence of permanent employees. Such employment can also be used to

Unionized workers at Canadian Airlines Corp. consulted lawyers in a bitter clash over seniority with their counterparts at Air Canada.

CP PHOTO ARCHIVE (Marcos Townsend)

increase output when there is a sudden spurt in demand for the firm's products or services and some of the activities performed by "core" employees can be contracted out to someone else. Temps usually receive lower salaries or wages than core workers and are not eligible for several health, insurance, and retirement benefits. Traditionally, temps have been popular in clerical and secretarial jobs; however, more recently, even highly skilled scientific and professional jobs have been contracted out to temporary workers.

Transfers

Transfer
Movement of an employee from one job to another that is relatively equal in pay, responsibility, and organizational level.

A typical internal action used is the *transfer* of employees within the organization. Transfers occur when an employee is moved from one job to another that is relatively equal in pay, responsibility, and/or organizational level. Besides improving the utilization of their human resources, organizations can also make transfers beneficial to jobholders. The broadening experience of a transfer may provide a person with new skills and a different perspective that makes him or her a better candidate for future promotions. Transfers may even improve an individual's motivation and satisfaction, especially when a person finds little challenge in the old job. The new position, although not a promotion, may offer new technical and interpersonal challenges. In turn, these challenges may prove to be a growth opportunity for the transferee. Even when the challenges are minimal, the transfer at least offers some variety, which may enhance feelings of job satisfaction.

It should be noted that transfers result in the creation of a vacancy in another part of the same organization. Further, as Pinder and Das[25] observed, there may be hidden costs associated with transfers, such as the psychological stress and social uprooting of the transferee and his or her family. In the case of two-career families (where both spouses pursue careers), it may be difficult to persuade an employee to move to a place where his or her spouse cannot attain career progress.

Contract Workers

Contract workers (also sometimes called consultants and freelancers) are employees who have a direct contractual working relationship with the firm employing them. Many professionals with specialized skills are hired as contract workers.

> Universities use adjunct and part-time instructors; hospitals use emergency-room physicians on a contract basis; publishers use editors on a project basis; several civil engineering and construction firms use architects and other skilled persons on a contract basis. Underlying all these is the objective of meeting human resource needs without incurring permanent payroll costs to the firm.

Contract workers are likely to be more productive and efficient since they are not constrained by the firm's routines and policies except in a broad sense. They do not have to attend meetings or go through channels to get approvals or the right information. However, they are not part of the organization and may not feel loyalty to any one client. Their focus is also likely to be on getting the present job done rather than what is good for the organization in the long term.

Promotions

A promotion occurs when an employee is moved from one job to another that is higher in pay, responsibility, and/or organizational level. It is one of the more pleasant events that happens to people in an organization. Generally, a promotion is given as a recognition of a person's past performance and future promise. Promotions usually are based on merit and/or seniority. Merit-based promotions occur when an employee is promoted because of superior performance in the present job. However, promotion as "reward" for past efforts and successes may raise two major problems. One problem is whether decision-makers can objectively distinguish the strong performers from the weak ones. When merit-based promotions are being used, it is important that the decision reflect the individual's performance and not the biases of the decision-maker.[26]

> An example would be when the best performer is a member of a protected class and the decision-maker is prejudiced.

The decision-maker should not allow personal prejudices to affect promotions. Decisions that are swayed by personal feelings are more common when job performance is not measured objectively. When promotion decisions result from personal biases, the organization ends up with a less competent person in a higher, more important position. The resulting resentment among those not promoted is likely to harm their motivation and satisfaction.

A second problem with merit-based promotions is put forth in the *Peter Principle*.[27] It states that, in a hierarchy, people tend to rise to their level of *incompetence*. Although not universally true, the "principle" suggests that good performance in one job is no guarantee of good performance in another.

> If one of the new engineers hired at a telephone company consistently made major cost-saving design changes, that would be an example of superior performance. However, suppose the engineer were promoted to supervisor. The skills needed to be an effective supervisor are very different from those needed to be a top engineer. As a result of such a promotion, the firm might gain an ineffective supervisor and lose a superior engineer.

In some situations, the most *senior employee* receives the promotion. "Senior" in this case means the employee who has the longest service with the employer. The advantage of this approach is that it is objective. All one needs to do is compare the seniority records of the candidates to determine who should be promoted.

Part of the rationale for this approach is to eliminate biased promotions and to require management to develop its senior employees since they will eventually be promoted. Seniority-based promotions usually are limited to hourly employees.

> For example, a promotion from mechanic second class to mechanic first class may occur automatically by seniority whenever an opening for mechanic first class occurs. Labour organizations often seek this type of promotion to prevent employers from discriminating among union members.

Most human resource experts express concern about the competency of those promoted solely because of seniority since not all workers are equally capable. Sometimes the person who is the best mechanic, for example, is not the most senior one. Under seniority-based promotions, the best person is denied the job unless the individual happens to be the most senior worker as well. This approach to promotion causes human resource departments to focus their efforts on training senior workers to ensure that they are prepared to handle future promotions. In addition, the human resource department must be concerned with maintaining an accurate seniority list. When promotions are not based solely on seniority, both merit and seniority are guiding factors.

Full-time Employees

For several positions where internal transfer or promotion may not be feasible, hiring full-time employees is the only alternative. As mentioned already, many organizations are averse to this strategy since it incurs additional fixed costs. Hiring full-time staff also requires a more detailed look at their competencies in terms of the organization's long-term strategies. The steps involved in hiring employees are discussed in Chapters Five and Six.

Using the Information System to Formulate Proactive Strategies

www.workopolis.com

As already mentioned, human resource planning becomes increasingly sophisticated, it is able to provide an organization with valuable information that can be critical in strategic planning. Many successful organizations now have sophisticated human resource information systems (HRISs) for this purpose. The more enlightened human resource departments periodically assess the value of their human resources and account for the same. Human resource accounting (HRA) provides these organizations with valuable information about one of the most (if not the most) important ingredients of organizational success—namely human resources. HRIS and HRA are discussed in greater detail below.

HUMAN RESOURCE INFORMATION SYSTEMS

Human Resource Information System
Gathers, analyzes, summarizes, and reports important data for formulating and implementing strategies by HR specialists and line managers.

A *Human Resource Information System* (HRIS) is a *system used to collect, record, store, analyze, and retrieve data concerning an organization's human resources*. All good human resource decisions require timely and accurate information. A good HRIS is, hence, critical for the effective functioning of the HR department and the larger organization. The larger the organization and the more dynamic an organization's environments, the greater the need for a sophisticated HRIS. Consider Chevron:

> Chevron Corporation, a large, international oil company with several thousands of employees working in over 50 countries, in the past initiated a sophisticated information system called "CHRIS" (Chevron Human Resource Information System). CHRIS can provide all necessary information on the firm's human resources to the managers of this conglomerate (containing thirteen distinct companies) widely separated geographically.[28]

A HRIS can be as large or as small as is necessary.[29] The information contained in a HRIS varies from one organization to the next. Figure 3-12 lists some key elements seen in HRISs of several large organizations. The following provides another example:

> A major investment firm has a computerized human resources inventory that enables a manager to find out all relevant information on the firm's employees using a series of questions that require only a "yes" or "no" decision. For example, to find an appropriate person for a higher position, the manager can use this inventory; he or she should first specify the requirements such as education, years of experience, number of languages in which the job incumbent should be fluent, and so on. The computer will automatically identify appropriate candidate(s) and flash their brief résumés on the screen.

When designing a HRIS, the organization must pay careful attention to several factors. Some of these are discussed below:

Relational versus Non-relational Systems. Sophisticated HRI systems use relational databases. That is to say, information about an employee needs to be entered only once into the system to make it available for all HR purposes.

www.hronline.com

> For instance, if an employee has completed a new university program, in an advanced HRIS, it will need to be entered into the files only once; this information will appear in all appropriate tables (or computer screens and files). The computer program behind the HRIS will know how to use this new information for all relevant decisions

FIGURE 3-12

Information Typically Contained in a HRIS in a Large Organization

- Wage and salary data (pay structure, raises received by employees, wage histories of employees).
- Benefits (types, choices, used/accumulated by employees, choices by employee group).
- Staff profile (minorities, women, people with physical disabilities, managerial versus nonmanagerial).
- Grievances (types, frequency, decisions by adjudicator).
- Training and development (types, dates offered, training records of employees, training needs of personnel, training costs).
- Health and safety (accidents, costs, tolerance limits for various dangerous substances).
- Succession plans (skills, specialties, work experience, performance record, promotion capabilities of employees).
- Job families (jobs, number, training needs, salary).
- Employee information (all relevant data including those for tax and pension plan purposes).
- Organizational data (structure, levels, reporting pattern, major policies).
- Demographics (staff profiles including education, age, etc.).
- Environmental and census data (population trends, economic indices).
- Productivity data.

affecting this employee—for example, compensation, skills listing, performance competencies, benefits, and so on.

In the older, non-relational systems, information on employee name, age, home address, job title, pay rate, and so on will have to be separately entered into the payroll file, the benefits file, performance appraisal records, and several other places. Any change in employee information will have to be updated separately in each file. The probability of an error in inputting information was very high in the non-relational systems. Probability of delays and inconsistencies in information updating was also higher in the non-relational systems. Figure 3-13 shows how a relational database would help an organization in its strategic and operational plans.

2. Referential Integrity. Some relational databases have built-in systems to prevent errors and catch inconsistencies. This feature, called referential integrity, ensures that an organization's policies are operationalized or implemented consistently throughout the organization.

> For example, in a sophisticated HRIS, a new employee cannot be hired until a vacancy has been approved or established (through retirement or departure). There are also built-in checks against out-of-range values (e.g., employees whose age is shown as below 15 or above 70) and automatic red flags for violation of laws (e.g., when wage rate is shown as less than $3.00).

3. Breadth and Size of HRIS. Based on the organization's needs, a decision must be made on the type, size, and breadth of coverage of HRIS. Will the HRIS reside on a microcomputer? Several computers? Mainframe computer? If the organization is not too large, the entire system could be maintained on one computer or a few networked

FIGURE 3-13

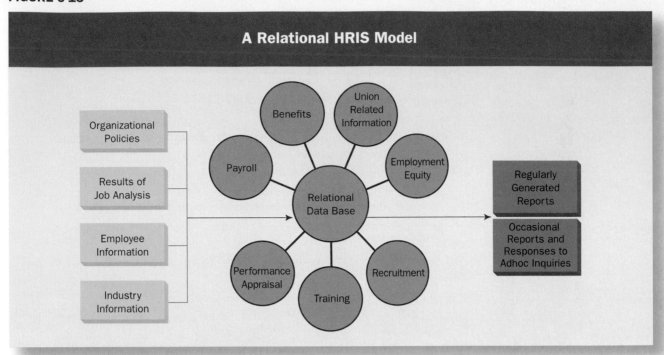

A Relational HRIS Model

computers. On the other hand, if the organization is very large and operating in several countries, several networked computers that continuously transmit data to each other may be essential. Often, the firm may begin with a simple HRIS and expand to cover several areas and meet various HR and organizational needs as illustrated by the experience of Federal Express:

> Federal Express, which has a very sophisticated HRIS, began its system with only basic employee records consisting of ten screens of data. In a few years, it had grown into a multi-function system with over 600 different screens. More than 25 000 paperless transactions are processed each day covering transfers, promotions, merit raises, and internal job placements of its more than 90 000 employees.[30]

4. Type of Outputs. All HRISs produce some regular reports such as employee records, salary and benefit details, retirement benefits, and so on. However, as a firm's HRISs increase in sophistication, they go beyond these regular reports and are able to produce special reports, answer questions interactively, and play an important role in decision support.

> For example, suppose an organization is considering a new dental benefit program. In a sophisticated HRIS, it will be able to generate predictions of not only how many employees are likely to qualify for and probably accept the new program, but also how much it will cost the firm over a specific period of time, how it will affect recruitment success and employee turnover, and so on.

Today, even moderately sophisticated HRISs have a number of modules that perform specific functions such as applicant tracking, recruitment source evaluation and costing, performance appraisal recording, compensation and payroll, training records maintenance, and human resource forecasts. The decision on the proposed HRIS's sophistication should be made only after a careful analysis of the firm's objectives and strategy, managerial decision needs, organizational size, and current technical capabilities and resources. Since the addition or upgrading of an HRIS requires careful analysis and planning (and is usually expensive, complex, and time-consuming), the desired outcomes from the HRIS should be clearly identified before proceeding with system installation. Figure 3-14 shows the more popular applications of HRIS in organizations.

5. Developing Internal Softwares versus Buying. Another decision is whether to develop the software using internal experts or to buy and use off-the-shelf softwares. This, of course, is related to type and size of HRIS planned by the firm. Building an HRIS within an organization requires a great deal of time, expertise, and money. Custom purchased software is quicker than building from scratch, but still requires extensive in-house documentation and substantial development time. In the early days of HRISs, it was necessary to extensively modify or customize off-the-shelf softwares to meet a firm's requirements. However, this is no longer the case. In the recent past, many programs have become commercially available. Except in the case of a few large organizations with very unique HR needs, it is seldom necessary or cost effective today to design your own system from scratch. Purchased systems also have the advantage of regular updates.

6. Access to HRIS Information. Who should have access to the information contained in HRIS? Needless to say, HR staff and key managers should have access to all information that enables them to make informed decisions; however, this should be weighed against the need for confidentiality and the need to respect employees' privacy. Most HRISs collect and retain only the employee information needed for business or legal reasons and establish controls for internal use and external release of this information. Sensitive information—such as security and medical reports, investigative and grievance files, insurance and benefit records, information related to performance

FIGURE 3-14

Selected HRIS Outcomes in Organizations

- Absenteeism figures for employees, job categories, and departments
- Applicant tracking
- Benefits utilization categorized by employee and employee groups; cost summaries and projections of benefits programs
- Employee records and employment histories
- Employment equity related reports, especially concentration and underutilization patterns across jobs and job families
- Health and safety records
- Human resource plans
- Job descriptions, specifications, and standards
- Job evaluation information
- Job postings
- Safety and health figures and trends
- Payroll
- Pension and retirement plans
- Skills inventories
- Short- and long-term disability records
- Succession plans
- Performance records
- Time and attendance
- Turnover indices
- Union contract details

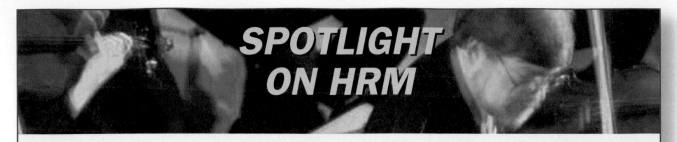

SPOTLIGHT ON HRM

BRAIN POWER: WHO OWNS IT... HOW THEY PROFIT FROM IT

The logic of capitalism was simple. Mr. Moneybags got an idea for a business. He turned his money, plus some from a bank, into fixed assets—a factory, machines, offices. He hired a Man in a Gray Flannel Suit to manage the assets. The manager, in turn, hired workers to operate the machines. Moneybags paid them—hourly wages to the easily replaceable workers; annual salaries to the managers, a reflection of their longer-term value. Moneybags kept all the profits; he was also responsible for paying the bank, maintaining the machines, and buying new ones. He might offer the public a chance to share ownership with him; occasionally he gave managers the option to buy a piece too. He almost never let the workers in on the action, though in good years he gave them a goose for Christmas........

Intellectual capitalism is different. In knowledge-intensive companies, it's not clear who owns the company, its tools, or its products. Moneybag's modern-day descendant starts with seed money from a Silicon Valley venture capitalist. He leases office space in some Edge City corporate village and doesn't own a factory; a company in Taiwan manufactures his products. The only plant and equipment the company owns are computers, desks, and a 1950s Coke machine someone picked up at auction. Whereas Moneybags bought the assets of his company, it is unclear who makes the investments on which intellectual capitalism depends, the investments in people. The manager—the Man in the Ralph Lauren Polo Shirt—paid his own way through business school. The worker is shelling out for an electronics course she takes at night, though the company will reimburse her for half the cost when she completes it. Every manager and worker receives stock options—as a group they may own as much stock as the capitalists.

Many jobs still and always will require big, expensive machines bought by someone else. But in the age of intellectual capital, the most valuable parts of those jobs are the human tasks: sensing, judging, creating, building relationships. Far from being alienated from the tools of his trade and the fruit of his labour, the knowledge worker carries them between his ears. If I write a story, fortune owns the copyright, but I still own whatever knowledge is in it; if you buy the magazine,

you don't get sole possession of the knowledge. I have it; fortune has it; and hundreds of thousands of others have it too. Employees, companies, and customers share joint and several ownership of the assets and output of knowledge work.

This change upsets the nature and governance of corporations. Look at Cordiant, the advertising agency that used to be known as Saatchi & Saatchi. In 1994 institutional investors, unhappy at what they viewed as the arrogance and fecklessness of CEO Maurice Saatchi, forced the board of directors to dismiss him. Protesting, several other executives left too, and some large accounts—first Mars, the candymaker, and later British Airways—defected. As far as the balance sheet was concerned, Saatchi's dismissal was a non-event. Nevertheless the stock, which had been trading on the New York Stock Exchange at 8 5/8, immediately fell to 4. The moral of the story: The shareholders thought they owned Saatchi & Saatchi; in fact they owned less than half of it. Most of the value of the company was human capital, embodied in Saatchi.

There's lots of evidence of the value of human capital. Why, then, do companies manage it so haphazardly? One reason is that they have a hard time distinguishing between the cost of paying people and the value of investing in them. At the same time, compensation systems and governance structures fail to recognize who owns intellectual assets.

Human capital is, to quote Yeats out of context, the place where all the ladders start: the wellspring of innovation, the home page of insight. Money talks, but it does not think; machines perform, often better than any human being can, but they do not invent. Thinking and invention, however, are the assets upon which knowledge work and knowledge companies depend.

The point bears emphasizing: Routine, low-skill work, even if it's done manually, does not generate or employ human capital for the organization. Often the work involved in such jobs can be automated, which is why these are the jobs most at risk nowadays; when it cannot be automated, the worker, contributing and picking up little in the way of skill, can easily be replaced if he leaves—he is a hired hand, not a hired mind....

Our point of view must be organizational, not individual: The question for companies is how to acquire as much human capital as they can use profitably. Human capital grows two ways: when the organization uses more of what people know and when more people know more stuff that is useful to the organization.

The first, unleashing the human capital already in the organization, requires minimizing mindless tasks, meaningless paperwork, unproductive infighting. The Taylorized workplace squandered human assets in such activities. Frank Ostroff, a fellow at Perot Systems, realized the extent of the waste when as a college student he took a summer job at a tiremaking factory in Ohio: "We'd spend eight hours a day doing something completely mindless like applying glue to rubber to tire after tire, all day long. And then these same people would go home and spend their evenings and weekends rebuilding entire cars from scratch or running volunteer organizations." The company got eight hours' work from those people but no benefit from their minds.

In the Information Age no one can use human capital so inefficiently. With competition fierce, says GE's Chairman Jack Welch, "the only ideas that count are the A ideas. There is no second place. That means we have to get everybody in the organization involved. If you do that right, the best ideas will rise to the top." To use more of what people know, companies need to create opportunities for private knowledge to be made public and tacit knowledge to be made explicit. GE's Work-Out program—a never-ending series of town meetings in which employees propose changes in work processes and bosses are required to approve or reject them on the spot—is one proven way to begin the process of getting at the ideas of more people. Some companies are setting up electronic networks and other knowledge-sharing systems. But every company already has informal networks and forums where tips are exchanged and ideas are generated, and which at their best become powerful learning forums.

Second, to get more people to know more useful stuff, leaders need to focus and amass talent where it is needed. The link to strategy is essential. Kodak, for example, a great company built on the silver-halide chemistry that underlies the photography business, is struggling to build the human capital it needs as digital photography threatens to erode the chemistry-based business. As the 1990s began, task forces all over Kodak were busy trying to find ways to use digital imaging in its product line. The effort led nowhere, though the company in a decade had invested $5 billion in digital-photography R&D.

Kodak's problem was one of scale and focus: The small groups were imprisoned in the divisional boxes that created them; the boundaries made it difficult for them to collaborate or share their knowledge—at one point there were 23 different groups working to develop digital scanners. Kodak had a few teams of snipers; it needed a corps.

Recognizing the problem when he became CEO in 1993, Kodak's George Fisher dismantled the department task forces, putting most of them into a new digital and applied imaging division. Its sales (of such products as "smart" film, which stores shutter speed and other data to allow better photo-processing, and a CopyPrint station, now set up in many photo stores, which uses digital technology to make on-the-spot enlargements of ordinary prints) totalled $500 million in 1994 and an estimated $1 billion in 1996. There's a lesson in Kodak's early experience with digital imaging: Human capital is easily dissipated. It needs to be massed and concentrated. Intelligence, like any assets, needs to be cultivated in the context of action: Random hiring of Ph.D.s won't cut it....

A fundamental paradox lies at the heart of the Information Age organization: At the same time that employers have weakened the ties of job security and loyalty, they more than ever depend on human capital. For their part, knowledge workers, because they bring to their work not only their bodies but their minds—even their souls—are far more loyal to their work (though not to their employer) than those tiremakers whose first love was for the hobbies that waited for them at home. Compounding the problem is the fact that the most valuable knowledge workers are also best able to leave their employers, taking their talent and their work with them.

The implicit way is to foster intellectual communities in areas that are central to competitive advantage— that is, in hard-to-replace, high-value activities like marketing if you're Nike or engine design if you're Ford. To create human capital, a company needs to foster teamwork, communities of practice, and other social forms of learning. Individual talent is great, but it walks out the door. Interdisciplinary teams capture, formalize, and capitalize talent; it becomes less dependent on any individual. A vibrant learning community gives the company an ownership stake; if Sally leaves, three other people know what she knows—and though Sally has left, she will probably remain unofficially part of the group.

and disciplinary actions, and so on—should be tightly protected and offered to persons only on a need-to-know basis.

The decision about who should have the right to change input data is also critical. On the one hand, restricting data entry to a few persons can improve consistency and prevent errors; on the other hand, it can also result in delays. The system should also have built-in checks against errors and system malfunction, yet be easily accessible by all concerned.

> At Federal Express, managers and employees do much of their own data entry. For instance, managers wanted to reduce the time it took to get a new employee on the payroll; now they can do it themselves in a few minutes rather than submitting a form to the HR department and waiting several days. All employees can also access the system to enter their change of address or other personal particulars.[31]

7. Security. Closely related to the above is the issue of security of HRIS data. In a survey of more than 1320 Chief Information Officers and senior systems professionals, more than 80 per cent of respondents said employees posed the greatest danger to unauthorized disclosure of confidential information. Next on the list were computer terrorists, feared by about another 80 per cent. Nearly eight out of ten firms surveyed reported financial losses in the immediate past due to breaches of security.[32]

> As one manager noted, "The difficulty in this day and age for management is that employees are not looking at long-term employment. So, if they've been downsized or not handled well or harassed the attitude is 'I'm going to fix my employer. I'll take the data with me or I'll destroy it.' " An employee who suspects he or she might be let go from the organization puts a virus in the computer system set to go off in six months. If not let go at that time, (s)he will eliminate it. But if the employee is terminated two months after planting the virus, when four months later the virus completely wipes out the database, there are no obvious suspects.[33]

It is not only evil-intentioned workers who pose a threat to valuable information, but also those who do not protect their passwords or download virus-infected games or other files off the Internet. Sometimes even simple passage of time can corrupt disks where important data are stored.

Intranet
Organization-specific internal computer network.

In recent years, several organizations, especially large ones, use internal Web sites—referred to as *intranets*—for a variety of purposes including dissemination of corporate policy information to employees and the general public, informing current employees and potential recruits about personnel benefits and employee services, and conveying information related to marketing. Indeed, the growth of intranets in the recent past has been incredible.[34]

> Disney placed its corporate HRIS on the Disney Corporate Web to provide support and share information among departments. The site has become an important communications tool for corporate HRIS. It includes status information on corporate and business unit projects, a calendar of HR related events, links to other Disney Web sites, company-wide meeting notes and downloadable power-point presentations and HR related tables.[35]

> Royal Bank's intranet called Leonet is designed to be used for training its 48 000 employees, allowing them to share best practices and exchange information electronically via chat groups. The $2-million cyber-classroom that is part of its intranet uses video, graphics, sound, text and animation. Royal employees can use it to access a range of training materials on demand.[36]

Intranets are the logical extension of HRIS. There will be enterprise-wide business management systems of which information pertaining to human resources will be only one component. Such an Integrated Information System (IIS) may cross all boundaries—often going even beyond the organizational database.[37] Future organizations may also be able to outsource several components of HRIS and obtain information needed directly via the Internet and corporate intranet.[38]

HUMAN RESOURCE ACCOUNTING

Human resource accounting
A process designed to measure the present cost and value of human resources as well as their future worth to the organization.

HUMAN RESOURCE ACCOUNTING (HRA) has been gaining in popularity in recent years. HRA is the process of identifying, measuring, accounting, and forecasting the value of human resources in order to facilitate effective management of an organization.[39] HRA attempts to put a dollar figure on the human assets of an organization. In Chapter One of this book, it was pointed out that human resources constitute the single most important asset of any organization (see Spotlight on HRM on page 136 for the importance of human capital today). However, unless this asset is valued, an organization will not have any idea of the changes in the value and composition of human resources. Besides, HRA enables an organization to receive complete information on the costs of staff turnover; valid estimates of the usefulness of organizational training programs on a regular basis are also available in organizations that implement HRA. It is also suggested by some writers that the ratio of investments in human resources to total assets acts as an indicator of an organization's potential to generate future revenues and profits. Measures of human resources are, thus, likely to be relevant and useful in several phases of human resource planning, development, and compensation decisions.

The various models of HRA currently in vogue can be broadly classified into two groups:[40] cost models and value models. The cost models attempt to place a dollar value on human assets based on some kind of cost calculation—acquisition, replacement, or opportunity costs. The value-based models, on the other hand, attempt to evaluate human resources on the basis of their economic value to the organization.

Whatever the approach used, most HRA models involve some degree of subjective assignment of a dollar figure to an employee's services and contribution to the organization. Some writers and practitioners feel that the nature of human assets is such that any attempt to quantify them may be unrealistic and fruitless. Investments in people also have been considered more tenuous than investments in physical assets, and accountants have chosen to ignore their investment character. Despite these criticisms, HRA might be a blessing to salary administrators, trainers, human resource planners, and union-management negotiators if it provides them with the kind of objective and reliable information they have long needed to plan these functions.

SUMMARY

HUMAN RESOURCE planning requires considerable time, staff, and financial resources. The return on this investment may not justify the expenditure for small firms. Increasingly, however, large organizations use human resource planning as a means of achieving greater effectiveness. Human resource planning is an attempt by companies to estimate their future needs and supplies of human resources. Through an understanding of the factors that influence the demand for workers, planners can forecast specific short-term and long-term needs.

Given some anticipated level of demand, planners try to estimate the availability of present workers to meet that demand. Such estimates begin with an audit of present employees. Possible replacements are then identified. Internal shortages are resolved by seeking new employees in the external labour markets. Surpluses are reduced by normal attrition, leaves of absence, layoffs, or terminations.

Both external and internal staffing strategies can be used to meet human resource needs. The figure also summarizes other key points discussed in this chapter. Finally, the usefulness of a human resource information system and human resource accounting was also outlined.

Chapters Five and Six elaborate on the external staffing strategy. Material in later chapters will examine various issues involved in the management of human resources with a focus on internal strategies. But before that, it is important to study the impact of governmental policies on a firm's human resource policies and practices. This will be attempted in the next chapter.

TERMS FOR REVIEW

Visit the Web site at www.mcgrawhill.ca/college/schwind6 for a full glossary.

REVIEW AND DISCUSSION QUESTIONS

1. What are the key steps in human resource planning in organizations? Which of your actions, if any, will be different if you were planning human resources for a smaller firm (that employs fewer than 50 persons in all) than a larger firm (which has 500 employees)?

2. Briefly describe the factors that affect an organization's demand and supply of human resources.

3. What are staffing tables and replacement charts? Of what use are they to a human resource manager?

4. Discuss any three techniques for estimating the demand for human resources. Provide examples where relevant.

5. What are some factors you have to consider when you are about to implement a Human Resource Information System?

6. Why is accounting for "human capital" increasingly becoming important? What is the nature of "human capital" that a rapidly growing high-tech firm possesses currently? What human resource accounting system would you suggest for the organization?

CRITICAL THINKING QUESTIONS

1. Suppose human resource planners estimated that due to several technological innovations your firm will need 25 per cent fewer employees in three years. What actions would you take today?

2. Suppose you managed a restaurant in a winter resort area. During the summer it was profitable to keep the business open, but you needed only one-half the cooks, table servers, and bartenders. What actions would you take in April when the peak tourist season ended?

3. If your company locates its research and development offices in downtown Windsor, Ontario, the city is willing to forego city property taxes on the building for 10 years. The city is willing to make this concession to help reduce its high unemployment rate. Calgary, Alberta, your company's other choice, has a low unemployment rate and is not offering any tax breaks. Based on just these considerations, which city would you recommend and why?

4. Assume you are the human resource manager in a Canadian university employing approximately 300 faculty members. Since these faculty members constitute a "valuable" resource of your organization, you decide to install an accounting procedure for changes in the value of this asset. How will you go about it? What problems do you anticipate in the process?

5. For a high-tech organization where the job specifications and customer needs continually change, which of the forecasting techniques discussed in the text are likely to be relevant? Why?

6. Assume you work for a firm that employs 30 managerial and 70 clerical/sales employees. As a cost-cutting strategy, your firm is forced to terminate the services of 10 per cent of your managers and five per cent of your clerical staff. What specific actions will you take to help the departing employees?

WEB RESEARCH

Visit the sites of agencies such as Statistics Canada (www.statcan.ca) and Human Resource Development Canada (www.hrdc-drhc.gc.ca). Identify trends in employment and occupational demand patterns for two job positions in two industries (each) for two provinces. Compare your findings and present your summary findings to the class.

INCIDENT 3-1

Eastern University's Human Resource Needs

For years, Eastern University operated at a deficit. This loss was made up from the provincial budget, since Eastern was provincially supported. Because of the government cutbacks in the 1990s, the deficits had continued to increase forcing the university to raise its tuition fees every year after 1995. The university's total budget in 2000 was approximately $100 million.

Several members of the provincial cabinet heard that university enrolments were to decline from 2000 to 2010. A decline in enrolment would lead to overstaffing and even larger deficits. The president of the university hired Bill Barker to develop a long-range human resource plan for the university. An excerpt from his report stated:

> The declining birthrates of this country in the past will cause a decline in university-age students at least to the year 2010. The healthy Canadian economy also keeps away a large number of high school graduates from higher studies. If the university is to avoid soaring deficits, it must institute an employment freeze now. Furthermore, a committee should be formed to develop new curricula that appeal to those segments of the work force that are going to experience rapid growth between now and 2010.

Zach Taylor, president of Eastern University Faculty Union, argued,

"An employment freeze would cut the university off from hiring new faculty members who have the latest training in new areas. Besides, our enrolments have grown by two to four per cent every year since 1993. I see no reason to doubt that trend will continue. Even if our past birth rates are low, there are other creative options to this university rather than opting for an employment freeze."

1. Assuming you are a member of the provincial cabinet, would you recommend that the university implement an employment freeze or not?

2. If Bill Barker had used national birthrate information, what other population information could the president of the faculty union use to support his argument that the university will probably keep growing?

3. Are there any strategies you would recommend that would allow the university to hire newly trained faculty and avoid serious budget deficits in the early 2000s if enrolments do drop?

INCIDENT 3-2

Human Resource Consultants

In 2000, Human Resource Consultants of Hamilton, Ontario, employed 10 consultants (including two trainees), five secretaries, two clerical assistants, an office manager-cum-accountant, and a marketing representative. Consulting work and secretarial work are both expected to increase by 20 per in 2001. However, a new computer system, which will be operational by January 1, 2001, will do the equivalent of 80 hours of secretarial work per week and 40 hours of clerical work per week (but will require maintenance of 40 hours per week). As of January 1, 2001, a number of employees are leaving the firm. Bill, a 64-year-old consultant, is planning to retire; John, a Queen's MBA and first-year consultant trainee, has accepted a position with CUSO; Clara, the senior secretary (and supervisor of the secretarial/clerical staff), has agreed to join Ontario Consultants and is taking two other secretaries with her; and Herman, the office manager/accountant, is planning to move to western Canada.

1. Determine the human resource needs at Human Resource Consultants for 2001.

EXERCISE 3-1:

Your Career Choice

Consider the job you plan to search for after graduation. (If you are already working and do not plan to leave your present job, you can look at the job rank (or grade) you want to be in five years after graduation.)

1. What kind of changes in technology are affecting the way the job is done? Are your chances of achieving your objectives higher or lower because of these changes?

2. What kind of demographic changes are affecting the probability of your success in achieving the career goal?

3. Are the community attitudes related to your career changing? In what way? What are the implications?

4. What are the supply and demand figures for this career currently? What are the forecasts for the foreseeable future? (Hint: You can get these estimates from Human Resource Development Canada and Statistics Canada.)

Considering the above factors, are there any specific actions needed right now on your part? What?

CASE STUDY

Maple Leaf Shoes Ltd., A Human Resource Planning Exercise[1]

Maple Leaf Shoes Ltd. is a medium-sized manufacturer of leather and vinyl shoes located near Wilmington, Ontario. It began operations in 1969 and currently employs about 400 persons in its Ontario plant and some 380 more in offices and warehouses throughout Canada and internationally. More information on the firm and its operations is provided at the end of Chapter One.

The cost of production at Maple Leaf Shoes has been rising slowly but steadily. Labour costs currently account for over 53 per cent of manufacturing costs and have been increasing rapidly. The productivity levels of the employees have not shown any significant increase in recent years. Concerned with the situation, Maple Leaf Shoes' management has been attempting to introduce more sophisticated technology in its various plants. More capital-intensive, automated production processes are being considered by the management as part of the solution to the productivity challenge facing the firm.

The company is now in the midst of a strategic reorientation. As part of the exercise, Robert Clark, the president, has asked Jane Reynolds, personnel assistant in the firm, to prepare a human resources forecast for the company.

Reynolds examined the company records that were likely to help her in her task. To her dismay, she found that very few plans or systematic procedures existed that will assist her in human resource planning. She decided to begin her analysis with the division in charge of shoes for children and youths (commonly—and half humorously—referred to as the "juvenile division" in the company). It currently employed fewer than 150 persons in total and seemed to have the most complete records related to employee hiring, transfers, exits, and training. But even here, production and labour statistics for several years were incomplete or inaccurate.

Her survey of company records resulted in the information given below. Reynolds also met with key managers in the firm (including Clark) several times to find out more about their goals and action plans for the immediate future. Her findings are also summarized below. Briefly, her findings were:

[1] Case prepared by Professor Hari Das of Saint Mary's University. All rights retained by the author. Das © 2000

1. All of the juvenile division's manufacturing operations were located in Ontario. Reynolds considered that there were four distinct manufacturing stages: cutting, shaping, assembling, and finishing. [Of course, each of these stages contained several tasks; for example, "shaping" involved several sub-tasks such as bending the leather (or vinyl or plastic, as the case may be), making lace holes, attaching reinforcers, padding, and so on.] Reynolds also found that the operations progressively became more complex from "cutting" to "finishing." Workers were normally hired as cutters and then progressively moved up to do shaping, assembling, and then finishing as they gained experience.

2. Cutting and shaping were more repetitive and boring, while assembling and finishing required greater attention and expertise and therefore were more challenging. Despite this, a few workers who were doing assembling chose to do shaping since the latter almost always fetched them more overtime work (and significantly higher earnings). No one doing final finishing had so far asked for reassignment to shaping or cutting. Employee movements during 1998–99 among the four operations are shown in Table 1.

3. The firm's labour productivity has not shown any significant improvement in the recent past. This has also been true of the juvenile division. Table 2 shows the production and staffing records of the entire division.

4. Through the introduction of computer-integrated technology and automated work systems, the firm expects to increase the division's productivity level by 25 per cent in 2001 over its 2000 record. Much of this will be achieved by automating much of the cutting operations. It is expected that automation will reduce the need for 33 per cent of cutters. The productivity of other operations (namely, shaping, assembling and finishing) is also expected to increase, but at lower levels than in the case of cutting. The productivity improvement in these operations is expected to be equal. Workers who lose their jobs as a result of automation and computerization will receive severance pay.

TABLE 1

Movements of Workers Across the Four Operations (1998-1999)

From	Cutting	Shaping	To Assembling	Finishing	Exits	Total
Cutting	21	3	1	0	1	26
Shaping	0	32	4	2	2	40
Assembling	0	2	26	5	0	33
Finishing	0	0	0	37	0	37
Total at the end (after accounting for Exits)						133

5. Compared to other divisions, the juvenile division has an aging workforce. (On average, three to eight per cent of the division's workforce retire each year.) For calculation purposes, Reynolds is planning to use a flat five per cent retirement figure. Table 1 figures do not include exits through retirement.

6. There are 10 persons in sales and order processing associated with the Juvenile Division products. Another 15 clerical staff are involved in a variety of related activities (such as billing, product movement, and so on) in the division. There are four managerial persons in the division.

7. As a cost-cutting measure, two of the above managerial positions will be eliminated in the next year. Because of the computerized billing initiated recently, the productivity of the clerical staff is expected to increase by 50 per cent, making some of the clerical positions redundant. Where possible, the displaced workers will be transferred to other divisions or trained to do other activities in the firm.

8. The firm plans to open two new sales outlets in the next year. It is estimated that each outlet will require one supervisor and two sales assistants initially.

9. The percentage of women workers in the four operations were as follows: Cutting, 72 per cent; Shaping, 70 per cent; Assembling, 63 per cent, and Finishing, 61 per cent. Women account for 68 per cent of the sales assistants and 55 per cent of the clerical staff. No woman occupies a managerial position in the juvenile division.

10. A number of women in the past have requested job sharing and flextime work arrangements. The firm currently has no provision for nontraditional work arrangements.

11. Estimated production (based on projected market demand for shoes) for 2001 is 98 000 pairs of shoes. As is the case with several shoe manufacturers in this country (and the U.S.), footwear production has declined each year due to international competition.

Discussion Questions

1. Prepare a human resources plan for the juvenile division for 2001.

2. What other suggestions and comments would you make to the management if you were in Reynolds' position?

TABLE 2

Production and Workforce Statistics in the Juvenile Division

Year	Production (000s of pairs)	Number of Employees
1978	50	65
—	—	—
1988	75	91
—	—	—
1991	90	110
1992	92	120
1993	93	122
1994	98	125
1995	102	127
1996	110	140
1997	109	140
1998	106	136
1999	105	133
2000	93	125

(Projected figures based on first eight months' production)

CASE STUDY

Canadian Pacific and International Bank
Planning Human Resources at HBI[2]

Canadian Pacific and International Bank (CPIB) is a premier Canadian financial institution with assets over $150 billion and operations across Canada and in 33 countries. Today, its over 25 000 employees provide personal, commercial, corporate, and investment banking services to individuals and businesses around the world. More details of the bank are given at the end of Chapter One.

CPIB, through its strategic initiatives, was successful in building long-term value for its shareholders while providing regular return on their investments. A vital component of its recent strategy is growth through acquisition of smaller banks and other financial institutions in this country and internationally. The passage of the bill relating to bank mergers in June 2000 in Parliament accelerated this process for CPIB.

Recently, the bank acquired Hudson Bay Investors (HBI), a medium-sized investment banking firm located in Central Canada with 38 branches operating in five Canadian provinces. For now, CPIB intends to maintain the separate identity of HBI; however, the internal systems and procedures of the firm will be rationalized to bring them in line with those at CPIB. In the long term, HBI branches are likely to be replaced by CPIB branches.

HBI's major sources of income are trade processing and brokerage commissions, revenues from mutual funds sales, securitization and underwriting fees, fund transfer fees, portfolio and estate management fees, and custody and safekeeping fees. Like most other investment and asset management firms, HBI uses the services of not only in-house financial advisors and counsellors but also hundreds of independent financial advisors in other dealer firms actively distributing HBI's products and services. In recent years, this strategy has been particularly important to reduce salary and overhead expenses. Hiring outside advisors on a commission basis not only reduces fixed salary expenses but also reduces investments in overheads such as office space, electricity, and computer systems. In future years, this strategy is likely to be used even further to maintain a lean operation.

Compared to CPIB, HBI is somewhat behind in electronic services. This is expected to change in the next two years. CPIB expects all HBI advisors to be able to offer extensive counselling (including in areas such as portfolio management, margin trading, and setting up of Internet banking accounts) to their customers using multiple tools including the Internet. CPIB plans to install counselling booths in various locations where customers can sit in front of a TV monitor and receive assistance from advisors located thousands of kilometres away and print out recommendations at the end of the session.

During the pre-acquisition survey, Mary Keddy, senior vice president—human resources, observed that HBI's human resources practices were somewhat inferior compared to those of CPIB. She is determined to improve this situation. CPIB has a culture of transferring its employees to provide them with cross-cultural and international experience while HBI has been primarily a regional institution where staff transfers are less common.

ORGANIZATIONAL STRUCTURE

Currently, HBI's 155 managers and officers are organized functionally (see Figure 1) into three major divisions: operations, marketing, and administration. Each of the three divisions is headed by a vice president. Human resources, public relations, legal and liaison work, and transportation were grouped under administration. The 43 regional and branch offices of HBI fell under operations, while the vice president in charge of marketing controlled all marketing initiatives including advertising and new product development. While the branch managers reported to VP Operations, they had extensive communication lines with members of marketing and administration departments. While HBI had clear reporting relationships within each function, it always encouraged the free flow of communication and continuous evolvement of jobs.

Recently, HBI has been considering a possible shift to a product structure, under which a product manager would be responsible for the success or failure of one or more products/services rather than that

[2] Case prepared by Professor Hari Das of Department of Management, Saint Mary's University, Halifax. All rights retained by the author ©2000.

FIGURE 1

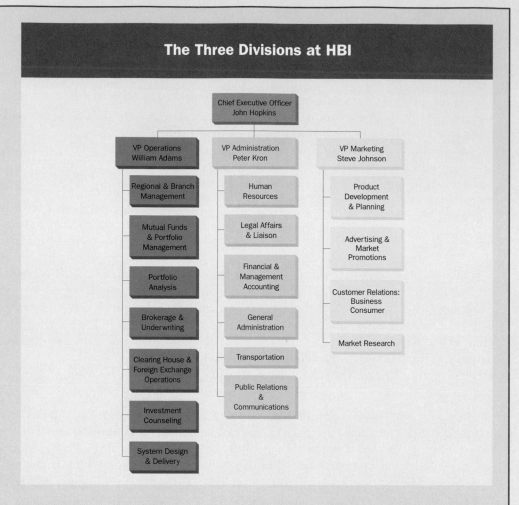

of a region, branch, or function. CPIB encouraged this proposal, given its own corporate philosophy of delegation and employee empowerment. Steve Johnson, VP (Marketing) indicated the scope of the responsibilities of a manager under the proposed system:

> I am sure HBI can significantly benefit from a product-type of organization structure. Most of the large consumer products companies, General Foods, Kellogg, and Procter & Gamble to mention just three, are built on the product manager idea. There is no reason why financial institutions cannot also follow this pattern. In fact, CPIB itself is a good example of a bank whose structure is focused on products and customers. The product manager will be held responsible for the product planning and for constant monitoring of the products' success. Here at HBI we don't believe in lines and arrows to show relationships among people. If problems at the branch are holding up sales of specific types of investments, we expect the sales staff to go to the branch or call the branch manager to iron out the

problems. That is already the way we work here. What we are trying to do is to make it more systematic so that our reward system recognizes responsibility and individual achievement."

Details on the number of managerial employees in HBI are given in Figure 2.

Compared to other investment firms of its size, HBI has done remarkably well. Its earnings for the recent past and future projection are shown in Figure 3.

HBI was in the midst of planning a major expansion of its activities when CPIB acquired the firm. Some of the details are given below:

1. By 2002, HBI plans to expand its operations to two more provinces and open 20 more branches. This will involve the creation of two new regional offices as well.

2. As Figure 3 indicates, the mutual funds and underwriting activities are expected to grow rapidly in the next two years. By and large the number of managers or officers associated with

FIGURE 2

HBI Managers and Officers Classified by Function or Activity

	Years		
	2000	**1999**	**1995**
Operations			
Regional & Branch Management	43	30	19
Mutual Funds & Portfolio Management	13	9	4
Portfolio Analysis	6	4	2
Brokerage & Underwriting	6	4	2
Clearing House & Foreign Exchange Operations	8	6	2
Investment Counselling	35	23	16
System Design & Delivery	8	4	2
Administration			
Human Resources	4	3	2
Legal Affairs & Liaison	3	3	2
Financial & Management Accounting	5	3	2
General Administration	4	2	2
Transportation	3	1	1
Public Relations & Communication	3	2	1
Marketing			
Product Development & Planning	4	3	2
Advertising & Market Promotions	2	2	1
Customer Relations:			
Business	2	1	1
Consumer	3	2	1
Market Research	3	2	1
Total	**155**	**104**	**63**

each business has shown a steady relationship with volume of business; however, improved efficiency and computerization is expected to bring in a 33 per cent improvement in efficiency, resulting in lower need for managerial staff.

3. To take advantage of the aging Canadian population, HBI is planning to give special focus on estate planning. It is expected that the number of customers of HBI aged 60 and over will increase by 25 per cent in the next five years. To meet the needs of growth, the firm estimates that it will need to hire three new middle-level managers and seven junior officers.

4. By the end of next year, HBI will complete its reorganization into a product structure. Under the new structure, the firm will have four divisions: investments, mutual funds, estate management, and underwriting. Each division will have its own associated accounting, HR, administration, and marketing services, with these functions centrally coordinated at the vice president level. The reorganization is expected to result in a 10 per cent reduction in most services except product development and human resource management where the change will necessitate a 10 per cent increase in staff size including managerial staff.

Many of the managers realized that the promise of continued rapid growth of the company would mean changes in the structure and processes of the company. As one manager in the operations division pointed out:

Growth for HBI means something quite different from what it is for most other firms. For a

FIGURE 3

HBI's Earnings
(Note: Only major headings are reported below)

	2002	2000	1999	1995
	(Estimate) (In millions of dollars)			
EARNINGS				
Investment Counselling & Estate Management	73	49	33	21
Mutual Funds Operations	47	24	16	8
Interest on Loans & Advances	9	8	4	2
Other Interest and Dividends	18	12	6	2
Gains on Marketable Securities	12	8	4	2
Underwriting and Brokerage Fees	16	12	8	4
Foreign Exchange & Clearing Operations	6	4	3	1
EXPENSES				
General Administrative Expenses	27	18	12	8
Commissions, Fees, Salaries	23	15	10	5
Interest Expenses	7	5	3	1
Depreciation and Amortization	15	10	7	5

conglomerate, growth may often mean new acquisitions or new diversified units that will be operating independently. For a company like HBI, however, it means entering new product-market situations and finding new ways of delivering our services. The competition in the industry is fierce, to put it mildly. But, if you have a reputation for the quality of your service, there is a growing market out there for you to grab. The proposed product structure may be a good idea to take advantage of this opportunity; however, it will also necessitate massive changes in our present style of operating.

Note: The following inventory lists top and senior middle-level managers in the firm. The firm is in the process of preparing a more exhaustive inventory that includes all managerial and supervisory personnel. Almost every one listed below has undergone corporate-sponsored training programs in specific subject areas.

HUMAN RESOURCE POLICIES

HBI has a policy of promoting qualified personnel from within the company before seeking outside candidates. The policy further implies consideration of the best-qualified people from all departments within HBI, rather than simply promoting only from within the department in which the opening occurs (unless the skill needed is very specific or legal requirements prevent someone without specific qualifications to be considered for the position, as in the case of legal or brokerage positions) Typically, the human resource department provides assistance in locating qualified candidates and takes pride in its "managerial inventory" used for this purpose. This inventory consists of names, certain characteristics (e.g., age, education), and skills of the managers working for HBI. Figure 4 shows relevant portions of the managerial inventory in the company. Currently, this inventory only lists senior officers of the firm, although plans are under way to include all supervisory and managerial personnel in the inventory in the near future. The company uses the services of an assessment centre located in Toronto. Periodically, managers were sent to this centre where, for periods ranging from two to four days, they were given tests and interviews. During their stay, participants also took part in management games, group discussions, in-basket exercises, and other role-plays. These managers were later rated by the centre for their leadership potential. Frequent performance or client ratings (in the case of advisors and brokers) are also carried out to improve quality of service provided by HBI. This information is also used in designing training programs for staff.

The salaries offered by HBI are competitive compared to industry standards. Despite this, the firm had problems in attracting qualified managers. This

FIGURE 4

Managerial Inventory For Senior Officers (excluding CEO) at HBI Ltd.

Manager	Division	Current Performance Level (1=Lowest 5=Highest)	Gender (M=male F=female)	Education	Age	Current Management Level (1=Lowest 5=Highest)	Assessment Centre Rating of Leadership Skill	Time in present job in months
W.C. Adams	Opers.	5	M	CFA	58	6	10	90
S.R. Allen	Admn.	4	F	CGA	56	5	9	62
P.T. Anderson	Opers.	5	M	MA,CFA	63	6	8	92
R. Bensoff	Admn.	5	M	HS	58	6	7	105
R.K. Bloom	Opers.	4	M	BSc,CFA	37	5	7	26
T.P. Buyer	Opers.	4	M	MBA CMA	39	5	9	16
N.T. Cayon	Opers.	4	M	CFA CMA	38	3	4	17
E.S. Conway	Opers.	3	M	CA	39	4	7	36
R.T. Dickoff	Admn.	5	F	MBA, CHRP	47	6	8	60
P. Frost	Mktg.	5	M	HS	48	5	7	30
W.K. Goodwin	Mktg.	4	F	MBA	48	5	7	50
K.N. Griggs	Admn.	4	M	MBA, LL.B	49	5	7	16
P. Hack	Mktg.	5	M	BComm	40	6	8	42
K. Heneman	Opers.	4	M	MS	44	6	8	43
S. Hickory	Opers.	5	M	BSc LL.B	64	6	10	108
P. Jackson	Opers.	3	M	HS	47	5	5	60
S.P. Johnson	Mktg.	5	M	BA	51	6	9	64
S. Kiefel	Mktg.	4	M	HS	61	5	7	59
P.Q. Kimble	Opers.	5	F	BSc CFA CMA	31	4	9	11
T. Knoll	Opers.	5	M	MSc	29	4	7	19
P. Kron	Admn.	5	M	HS	61	6	8	31
E.F. Pederson	Opers.	4	M	BComm CFA	47	5	6	19
N.T. Potler	Opers.	5	M	BTech	31	5	7	20
A. Ranallo	Admn.	4	M	BA LL.B	39	5	5	29
H.C. Reeves	Opers.	5	M	BSc	60	6	8	63
T. Reitman	Mktg.	4	F	BCom MBA	39	5	9	39
J. Sorenson	Admn.	5	M	BComm	32	6	7	11
H. Walden	Admn.	4	M	HS	59	5	8	69

BA= Bachelor of Arts, BComm= Bachelor of Commerce, BSc= Bachelor of Science, CA= Chartered Accountant, CFA=Certified Financial Advisor, CMA=Certified Management Accountant, HS= High School, LL.B=Bachelor degree in Law, MBA= Master of Business Administration, MSc=Master of Science,

is likely to become even worse in terms of attracting software managers and financial counsellors in the foreseeable future. The mandatory retirement age at HBI is 65. The company is committed to the development of its employees and in the past has sent many of its employees for training to local universities and colleges, apart from refunding tuition paid by its employees for training program done elsewhere.

Discussion Questions

1. Assume you are R.T. Dickoff, the human resource manager of HBI. You have been asked to prepare a staffing forecast for 2002.

2. What challenges face the HR manager in the firm?

3. What improvements, if any, would you recommend to its HR policies and practices?

SUGGESTED READINGS

1.   Abdul Rahman bin Idris and Derek Eldridge, "Reconceptualising Human Resource Planning in Response to Institutional Change," *International Journal of Manpower*, Vol. 19, No. 5, 1998, p. 346.

2.   Charles Grantham, *The Future of Work*, N.Y.: McGraw Hill, 2000.

3.   Dave Ulrich, *Human Resource Champions*, Boston: Harvard Business School Press, 1997.

Part Three 3

Attracting Human Resources

A company hires employees to meet its objectives. First, it must identify the target groups and find ways and means to get the necessary information to them, taking into account the requirements of human rights legislation regarding discrimination. Then it must select those candidates who best meet its needs.

Attracting Human Resources

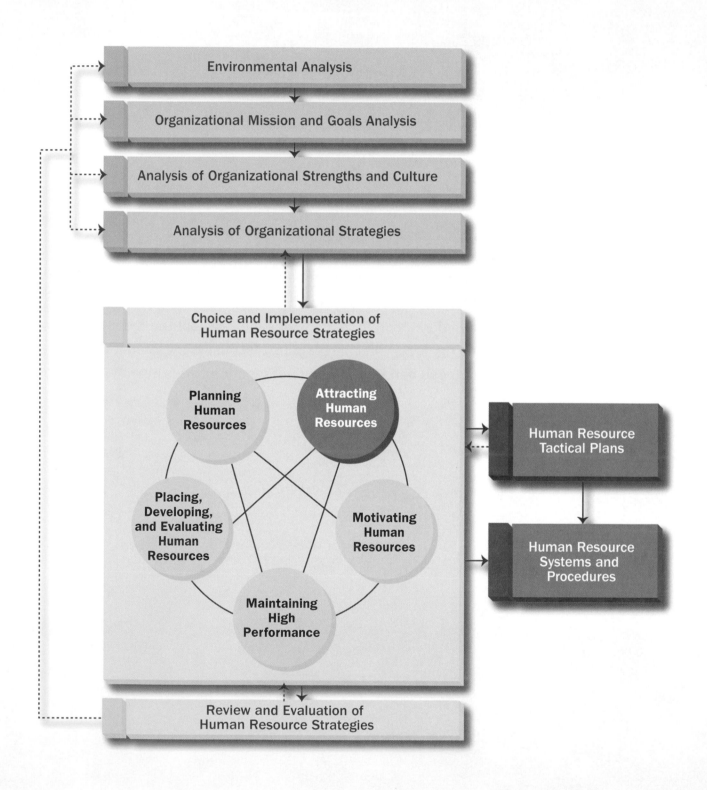

Environmental Analysis

Organizational Mission and Goals Analysis

Analysis of Organizational Strengths and Culture

Analysis of Organizational Strategies

Choice and Implementation of Human Resource Strategies

Planning Human Resources

Attracting Human Resources

Placing, Developing, and Evaluating Human Resources

Motivating Human Resources

Maintaining High Performance

Human Resource Tactical Plans

Human Resource Systems and Procedures

Review and Evaluation of Human Resource Strategies

Chapter 4

Meeting Legal Requirements

All human beings are born free and equal in dignity and rights.

—Article 1, the Universal Declaration of Human Rights, December 1948, United Nations

All individuals should have an equal opportunity to make for themselves the lives that they are able and wish to have, consistent with their duties and obligations as members of society, without being hindered in or prevented from doing so by discriminatory practices based on race, national or ethnic origin, colour, religion, age, sex, sexual orientation, marital status, family status, disability or conviction for an offence for which a pardon has been granted.

—Section 2, the Canadian Human Rights Act

CHAPTER OBJECTIVES

After studying this chapter, you should be able to:

■ *Explain* the impact of government on human resource management.

■ *Identify* the jurisdictions of Canadian human rights legislation.

■ *List* the major provisions of the Canadian Human Rights Act.

■ *Explain* the effect of human rights legislation on the role of human resource specialists.

■ *Define* harassment and explain what is meant by the term sexual harassment.

■ *Outline* an Employment Equity Program.

GOVERNMENT IMPACT

http://canada.gc.ca

FEW CHALLENGES encountered by human resource departments are as overwhelming as those presented by government. Government—through the enforcement of laws—has a direct and immediate impact on the human resource function. The federal and provincial laws that regulate the employee-employer relationship challenge the methods human resource departments use. Some laws, such as the Canada Labour Safety Code of 1968, make major demands on human resource departments. The impact of these laws has helped elevate the importance of human resource decisions.

Many aspects of human resource management are affected by human rights legislation. To human resource specialists, government involvement requires compliance and proactive efforts to minimize the organizational consequences. At appropriate points throughout this book, employee-related laws are explained to illustrate the challenges modern human resource departments encounter and the actions they must take.

To avoid flooding the courts with complaints and the prosecution of relatively minor infractions, federal and provincial governments often create special regulatory bodies, such as commissions and boards, to enforce compliance with the law and to aid in its interpretation. Examples are the various human rights commissions and labour relations boards, which evaluate complaints and develop legally binding rules, called **regulations**. Human resource specialists become involved because legislation and regulations affect the employment relationship. The involvement creates three important responsibilities. First, human resource experts must stay abreast of the laws, their interpretation by regulatory bodies, and court rulings. Otherwise, they will soon find their knowledge outdated and useless to the organization. Second, they must develop and administer programs that ensure company compliance. Failure to do so may lead to the loss of government contracts, poor public relations, and suits by regulatory bodies or affected individuals. Third, they must pursue their traditional roles of obtaining, maintaining, and retaining an optimal work force. No organization benefits from compliance with government constraints at the expense of a well-qualified workforce.

Regulations
Legally enforceable rules developed by governmental agencies to ensure compliance with laws that the agency administers.

THE CHARTER OF RIGHTS AND FREEDOMS

http://dsp-psd.pwgsc.gc.ca

Charter of Rights and Freedoms
Federal law enacted in 1982, guaranteeing individuals equal rights before the law.

AN EXAMPLE of government legislation that has profound implications for employers is the Constitution Act of 1982, which contains the **Canadian Charter of Rights and Freedoms**.[1] The Charter provides some fundamental rights to every Canadian. These are:

1.   freedom of conscience and religion;

2.   freedom of thought, belief, opinion, and expression, including freedom of the press and other media of communication;

3.   freedom of peaceful assembly; and

4.   freedom of association.

The Charter provides protection to every Canadian in the following specific areas:[2]

1.   fundamental freedoms;

2.   democratic rights;

3.   the right to live and seek employment anywhere in Canada;

4. legal rights: the right to life, liberty, and personal security;

5. equality rights for all individuals;

6. officially recognized languages of Canada;

7. minority language education rights;

8. Canada's multicultural heritage; and

9. Aboriginal people's rights.

The Canadian Charter of Rights and Freedoms is probably the most far-reaching legal challenge for human resource managers. When it came into effect in 1982, it created high expectations among collective bargaining partners, unions, and management. All parties hoped that the Charter would strengthen their positions vis-a-vis each other. A review of the application of the Charter to human resource and industrial relations issues after the intervening years reveals that the impact has been modest so far. One reason is that it takes considerable time for cases to reach the Supreme Court of Canada, the ultimate interpreter of the Charter. In the following sections, we will examine the effects that the Charter has had on human resource management and industrial relations in Canada.

Content and Applicability of the Charter

Section 1 of the Charter guarantees rights and freedoms "subject only to such reasonable limits prescribed by law as can be demonstrably justified in a free and democratic society." Of course, such adjectives as "reasonable" and "demonstrably justified" will lead to different interpretations by different judges. This is one of the reasons why many cases wind their way through the judicial system up to the Supreme Court, just to get a final opinion. Every time a court invokes one of the rights or freedoms, it must determine whether the infringement is justified.

Section 2 of the Charter guarantees freedom of association, an important aspect in industrial relations, especially for unions. A key question in this context is whether the freedom to associate carries with it the right to bargain collectively and the right to strike, the main reasons for the existence of unions. As will be shown, these rights cannot be taken for granted anymore. Section 15—the equality rights part—came into effect on April 17, 1985, delayed for two years in its enactment to allow the federal government and the provinces to create or change laws to ensure compliance with the Charter. It states in its first paragraph:

> Every individual is equal before the law and under the law and has the right to the equal protection and benefit of the law without discrimination and, in particular, without discrimination based on race, national or ethnic origin, colour, religion, sex, age, or mental or physical disability.

This section of the Charter was expected to—and has—caused a flood of litigation that will take many years to resolve.

The Charter of Rights and Freedoms applies only to individuals dealing with federal and provincial governments and agencies under their jurisdiction, but its impact is far-reaching since potentially every law can be challenged. Courts have the delicate task of balancing individual and collective rights.

Areas of Application

Some of the more prominent issues that have been before the courts relate to the use of closed-shop union security provisions whereby workers must be members of a union in order to be hired; the imposition of first collective agreements designed to help weak unions; the use of union-shop arrangements whereby workers must become union members within specified time periods after they are hired; the right to picket; the right to strike; the right to bargain collectively; Employment Equity Programs; and mandatory retirement. Some of the latest issues relate to sexual orientation and benefits to same-sex partners.

The Right to Bargain Collectively and to Strike

On April 9, 1987, the Supreme Court of Canada rendered a long-awaited judgment on the impact of the Charter on federal and provincial collective bargaining laws. The three cases in question arose from challenges of the federal public sector laws imposing compulsory arbitration for the right to strike, back-to-work legislation, and wage-restraint legislation.

In a 4-2 split decision, the Supreme Court held that Section 2 of the Charter does not include the right to bargain collectively and to strike. The judgment was a real blow to Canadian unions, since workers have taken these rights for granted. The court affirmed that Section 2 protects the freedom to work for the establishment of an association, to belong to an association, to maintain it, and to participate in its lawful activities without penalty or reprisal. However, it also held that the rights to bargain collectively and to strike are not fundamental freedoms, but are statutory rights created and regulated by the legislature. Under this ruling, governments can curtail the collective bargaining process by limiting salary increases, legislating strikers back to work, and imposing compulsory arbitration.

The Right to Picket

In another decision, the Supreme Court ruled that the right to picket is not protected under the Charter since it applies only to situations involving government action. It follows that this right is not available to employees in the private sector, where the vast majority of workers are employed. Employers can ask for injunctions to restrict the number of pickets or any other reasonable limitation of picketing activity.

From the rulings of the Supreme Court it can be seen that the effect of the Charter of Rights and Freedoms on human resource management and industrial relations so far has been significant to a certain degree, but not drastic. It appears that the court takes a conservative approach in interpreting the Charter with respect to union activities, meaning that it appears to associate more with employers' interests and the public's interests rather than with unions' and workers' interests. As one law professor put it:

> Anglo-Canadian courts have been dealing with issues of individual and collective labour law for at least 200 years. During that entire period, the courts virtually never, not on any given occasion, created a right which might be asserted by or on behalf of working people. Nor have they since the enactment of the Charter. Nor, I conclude, is it likely that they ever will.[3]

The Right to Work

The Supreme Court of Canada has upheld in two decisions Section 15(c) of the Canadian Human Rights Act, which excludes mandatory retirement at the normal age from its prohibition on age discrimination. The court concluded that the objectives of mandatory retirement were of sufficient significance to justify the limitation of a constitutional right to equality if a province chose to impose one, with the limitation that this discriminatory practice be reasonable and justifiable.

In 1985, Professor Olive Dickason, who taught history at the University of Alberta, was asked to retire at the age of 65. Dr. Dickason claimed that mandatory retirement at age 65 violated her constitutional rights. The Supreme Court, which rendered its decision in September 1992, ruled that mandatory retirement at age 65 is permissible.

HUMAN RIGHTS LEGISLATION

www.chrc-ccdp.ca/
Legis&Poli/Index.asp?l=e

WHILE THE CHARTER of Rights guarantees equality before the law for every Canadian, the Human Rights Act seeks to provide equal employment opportunities without regard to a person's age, race, religion, sex, marital status, handicap, sexual preference, or national origin. Common sense dictates such a policy, but the human rights legislation requires every employer to ensure that equal opportunities are, in fact, reality and that there is no discrimination either intentional or unintentional. No other laws—perhaps no other single development—rival the impact that human rights legislation has on human resource management.[4]

Scope

Usually, employment-related laws and regulations are limited in scope; their impact on the human resource management process is confined to a single human resource activity. For example, minimum-wage laws specify the lowest amount an employer can pay for each hour worked; in spite of their importance, these laws affect only the compensation management function. Other human resource activities—selection, training, and labour relations—are largely unaffected.

Human rights legislation, however, is an exception. Its role is not limited to a single human resource activity. Instead, human rights legislation affects nearly every human resource function: human resource planning, recruiting, selection, training, compensation, and labour relations.

Overview

Human rights legislation is a family of federal and provincial acts that have as a common objective the provision of equal employment opportunity for members of protected groups. These acts outlaw discrimination based on race, colour, religion, national origin, marital status, sex, or age. Under special circumstances, they also outlaw discrimination against people with disabilities. Figure 4-1 summarizes these two layers of

Women occupy more and more jobs that were traditionally considered "male" jobs. The Armed Forces began a campaign to attract more women into the military.

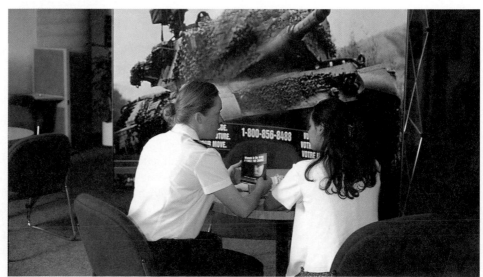

CP PHOTO ARCHIVE (Peter Bregg)

FIGURE 4-1

Types, Sources, Objectives, and Jurisdiction of Canadian Human Rights Legislation

Type	Source	Objectives and Jurisdiction
Federal Law	Passed by Parliament and enforced by federal Human Rights Commission	To ensure equal employment opportunities with employers under federal jurisdiction
Provincial Law	Enacted by provincial governments and enforced by provincial human rights commissions	To ensure equal employment opportunities with employers under provincial jurisdiction

employment laws. Discrimination between workers on the basis of their effort, performance, or other work-related criteria remains both permissible and advisable:

> Shelly Rossie complained to her provincial Human Rights Commission and charged her former employer with discrimination. When questioned, she insisted to the commission that the real reason for her discharge as a welder was that the company discriminated against women in traditionally male jobs. Shelly's case was dismissed when the company showed the commission records of her excessive absenteeism and poor productivity. (Undoubtedly, the company's case was strengthened when, later, a woman was hired to replace Shelly.)

Human rights legislation does permit employers to reward outstanding performers and penalize insufficient productivity. Its only requirement is that the basis for rewards and punishments be work-related, not based on a person's race, sex, age, or other prohibited criteria.

The following discussion will focus on federal human rights legislation, because *provincial human rights laws* tend to differ only slightly, mainly in terminology (e.g., some provinces use "national origin," others use "ethnic origin"). The examples used in the discussion of federal legislation are also quite typical of provincial situations. By and large, provincial laws mirror the federal law.

The Canadian Human Rights Act

Provincial human rights laws
All provinces and the two territories have their own human rights laws and human rights commissions, with discrimination criteria, regulations, and procedures.

Canadian Human Rights Act
A federal law prohibiting discrimination.

The *Canadian Human Rights Act* was passed by Parliament on July 14, 1977, and took effect in March 1978. The Act proclaims that:

> Every individual should have an equal opportunity with other individuals to make for himself or herself the life that he or she is able and wishes to have, consistent with his or her duties and obligations as a member of society, without being hindered in or prevented from doing so by discriminatory practices based on race, national or ethnic origin, colour, religion, age, sex or marital status, or conviction for an offence for which a pardon has been granted or by discriminatory employment practices based on physical handicap.[5]

The Act applies to all federal government departments and agencies, and Crown corporations, and to business and industry under federal jurisdiction—such as banks, airlines, and railway companies—in their dealings with the public and in their employment policies.

In areas not under federal jurisdiction, protection is given by provincial human rights laws. Each of the 10 Canadian provinces has its own antidiscrimination laws, which are broadly similar to the federal law. Figure 4-2 compares federal and

FIGURE 4-2

Prohibited Grounds of Discrimination in Employment*

Prohibited Grounds	Federal	British Columbia	Alberta	Saskatchewan	Manitoba	Ontario	Quebec	New Brunswick	Prince Edward Island	Nova Scotia	Newfoundland	Northwest Territories	Yukon
Race or colour	●	●	●	●	●	●	●	●	●	●	●	●	●
Religion or creed	●	●	●	●	●	●	●	●	●	●	●	●	●
Age	●	● (19-65)	● (18+)	● (18-64)	● (18-65)	●	●	●	●	●	● (19-65)	●	●
Sex (incl. pregnancy or childbirth)	●	●	●	●	●[1]	●[2]	●	●	●	●[3]	●[3]	●	●
Marital status	●	●	●	●	●	●	●[4]	●	●	●	●	●	●
Physical/Mental handicap or disability	●	●	●	●	●	●	●	●	●	●	●	●	●
Sexual orientation	●	●		●	●	●	●	●	●	●	●[3]		●
National or ethnic origin (incl. linguistic background)	●			●[5]	●	●[6]	●	●	●	●	●	●[5]	
Family status	●	●	●	●[7]	●	●	●[4]			●			
Dependence on alcohol or drug	●	●[3]	●[3]	●[3]	●[3]	●[3]		●[3,8]	●[3]	●[8]			
Ancestry or place of origin	●	●	●	●	●	●	●	●					
Political belief	●			●			●	●	●		●		●
Based on association				●			●	●	●	●	●		●
Pardoned conviction	●					●	●					●	
Record of criminal conviction		●					●						●
Source of income				●	●[9]	●					●		
Assignment, attachment or seizure of pay												●	
Social condition/origin							●					●	
Language						●[3]	●						

Harassment on any of the prohibited grounds is considered a form of discrimination.

* Any limitations, exclusion, denial or preference may be permitted if a bona fide occupational requirement can be demonstrated.

1) includes gender-determined characteristics
2) Ontario accepts complaints based on a policy related to female genital mutilation in all social areas on the grounds of sex, place of origin and/or handicap
3) complaints accepted based on policy
4) Quebec uses the term "civil status"
5) defined as nationality
6) Ontario's Code includes only "citizenship"
7) defined as being in a parent-child relationship
8) previous dependence only
9) defined as "receipt of public assistance"

This document is also available on computer diskette and as a recording to ensure it is accessible to people who are blind or vision impaired.

Threatening, intimidating or discriminating against someone who has filed a complaint, or hampering a complaint investigation, is a violation of provincial human rights codes, and at the federal level is a criminal offence.

Source: Reproduced with the permission of the Minister of Public Works and Government Services Canada and The Canadian Human Rights Commission.

individual provincial human rights legislation as to different grounds of discrimination prohibited.

Discrimination Defined

Webster's New World Dictionary of the American Language defines discrimination as: "a showing of partiality or prejudice in treatment; specific action or policies directed against the welfare of minority groups."

Discrimination is not defined in the Charter of Rights and Freedoms, nor in any federal or provincial human rights legislation with the exception of Quebec. Section 10 of the Quebec Charter states:

> Every person has a right to full and equal recognition and exercise of his human rights and freedoms without distinction, exclusion, or preference based on race, colour, sex, sexual orientation, civil status, religion, political convictions, language, ethnic or national origin, social condition, or the fact that he is a handicapped person, or that he uses any means to palliate his handicap. Discrimination exists where such a distinction, exclusion, or preference has the effect of nullifying or impairing such a right.

www.chrc-ccdp.ca/
publications/prohibit-motifs.asp

Bona fide occupational qualification (BFOQ)
A justified business reason for discriminating against a member of a protected class.

Systemic discrimination
Any company policy, practice, or action that is not openly or intentionally discriminatory, but that has an indirectly discriminatory impact or effect.

Direct versus Indirect (Systemic) Discrimination

Normally, intentional direct discrimination on grounds specified in the human rights legislation is illegal. However, under certain circumstances intentional direct discrimination is acceptable. A fashion store catering to women will be allowed to advertise for female models, and schools controlled by religious groups are permitted to limit their hiring to members of the specific faith. This legal discrimination is called *bona fide occupational qualification (BFOQ)*.

Indirect, unintentional, or *systemic discrimination* takes place if there is no intention to discriminate, but the system, arrangements, or policies allow it to happen. Such employment practices may appear to be neutral and may be implemented impartially, but they exclude specific groups of people for reasons that are not job-related or required for safe or efficient business operations. As a chief commissioner of the Ontario Human Rights Commission put it:

> The traditional flight of stairs leading into a building was not put there specifically to keep people with mobility impairments out. There's nothing intentional about it; it simply was the way that buildings were designed. But it operates as a very real and substantial and inappropriate barrier to access and entry by people with mobility impairment. That's systemic discrimination.[6]

Examples include:

- minimum height and weight requirements for employment with police forces, which make it more difficult for women and Canadians of Asian origin to be hired;

- minimum scores on employment tests, which discriminate against distinct groups (e.g., the use of culturally biased intelligence tests, which tend to screen out a disproportionate number of minorities);

- internal hiring policies, word-of-mouth hiring, or the requirement to submit a photograph with the application form;

- limited accessibility of buildings and facilities, which often makes it impossible for persons with disabilities to be employed with organizations using such places;

- psychological inability of people to deal with persons with disabilities;

- unavailability of alternative formats or forms of tools (e.g., publications in Braille for the blind or telephone devices for the deaf);

- job evaluation systems that tend to undervalue jobs traditionally held by women (e.g., give more points to compensable factors that favour men, such as physical strength, and fewer points to such factors as dexterity);

- promotion criteria that favour factors such as seniority and experience in traditionally male-dominated organizations where women did not have the chance to acquire either;

- organizational culture where minority groups feel not welcome and uneasy, resulting in a disproportionate turnover rate for such groups; and

- lack of explicit anti-harassment guidelines, which allows an atmosphere of abuse to develop in the workplace.

Indirect or systemic discrimination is more difficult to detect and to fight because it often is hidden and it requires a special effort to deal with it effectively. The *Canadian Human Rights Commission* has taken specific steps to define and detect the causes and sources of indirect or systemic discrimination. It initiated a number of surveys to assess the accessibility of federal government offices, and the availability of facilities, tools, and services for persons with disabilities. The commission believes that the Charter of Rights and Freedoms gives it the legal basis to combat such discrimination.[7]

www.chrc-ccdp.ca

Canadian Human Rights Commission
The CHRC supervises the implementation and adjudication of the Canadian Human Rights Act.

Race and Colour

It is sometimes difficult to see which of these two characteristics is the actual basis of discrimination; often both are involved. The discrimination can be intentional or unintentional, subtle or very open, as two examples will show:

www.gov.nb.ca/
hrc-cdp/e/sayno.htm

www.crr.ca/en/

The Western Guard Party of Toronto was operating a tape-recorded message that could be heard by telephone. The message proclaimed the supremacy of the white race and attacked Jews for being determined to destroy the white race by means of communism. The party refused to withdraw or change the message. The Human Rights Commission therefore held a tribunal, which found the messages to be discriminatory and ordered the respondents to refrain from using this subject matter in any future messages.

A bank in a small town advertised a position specifying that the applicant should have a pleasing appearance and requested that a recent photograph be submitted. The bank personnel were all Caucasian. A black community leader filed a discrimination complaint, which was settled when the bank agreed to include human rights training in its courses on interviewing, human resource selection, and counselling.

Of course, not all cases end in favour of the employee.

Daljit Dhanjal, a Sikh, was employed in the Engineering Branch of Air Canada. He claimed that he was harassed and subjected to racial slurs by his supervisor, who at one point hit him. Shortly after this latter incident, he was offered an early retirement package. Dhanjal contended that he was forced to accept this offer because of the atmosphere of discrimination prevailing in this workplace. A human rights tribunal found the complaint to be unsubstantiated: Dhanjal was not a victim of racial harassment, race, or religion. The tribunal accepted the employer's evidence that Dhanjal was a poor employee who had trouble getting along with his fellow workers.

There is an interesting side issue in this case. In the tribunal's words, "the poor performance reviews received by the complainant [were] due to the fact that Dhanjal refused to accept the overbearing and authoritarian management style of his supervisor and that he interpreted this management style subjectively as colonialist and racist behaviour toward him while, in fact, the supervisor was behaving in the same manner toward all of his subordinates." In other words, the supervisor did not discriminate in his abusive behaviour.[8]

National or Ethnic Origins

It is also illegal for human resource decisions to be influenced by the national or ethnic origins of applicants or of their forebears. Hence the discrimination process can be either direct or indirect. The refusal to hire or promote people because of their national or ethnic origins is a direct and obvious violation:

> A Canadian citizen originally from Haiti was refused entrance into the Armed Forces because he was not eligible for security clearance until he had lived in Canada for at least 10 years. He had been in this country for six years and was unusually highly qualified in every other respect. During investigations of his complaint, the Armed Forces agreed to invoke a rule already in place that allowed for the 10-year residency requirement to be waived for exceptional candidates. He was cleared and offered enrollment as an officer cadet.

An example of an indirect (systemic) violation based on ethnic origin can be briefly summarized. In one case (which will be detailed later) the hiring requirements for a certain job specified that the candidate had to be 5′ 8″ (173 cm). But reflection reveals that such a standard disproportionately discriminates against Asian Canadians, who tend to be shorter than descendants of immigrants from European countries. So, although the height rule may not intend to discriminate, the result is discriminatory.

Religion

A person's religious beliefs and practices should not affect employment decisions. An employer must accommodate an employee's religious practices, unless those practices present undue hardship to the employer:

> A Moslem employee of a communications company lost his job over the question of having time off each week to attend prayers at his mosque. After conciliation, a settlement was reached, which did not impose undue hardships on the employer and by which the employee was allowed to take one and a half hours per week of leave without pay. He was reinstated with retroactive pay and benefits.

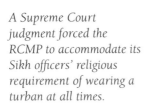

A Supreme Court judgment forced the RCMP to accommodate its Sikh officers' religious requirement of wearing a turban at all times.

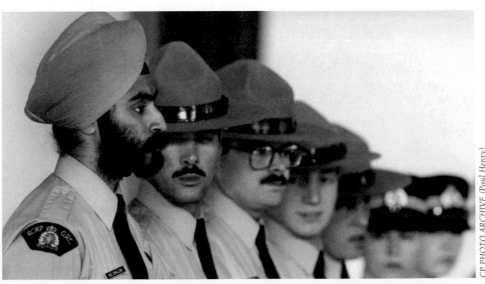

CP PHOTO ARCHIVE (Paul Henry)

If an employer does not make a reasonable attempt to accommodate workers' religious practices, he or she can be found guilty of violating the Human Rights Act.

Duty to accommodate
Requirement that an employer must accommodate the employee to the point of "undue hardship."

The terms "undue hardship" and *"duty to accommodate"* have been extended in another important decision by the Supreme Court of Canada in a ruling against Central Alberta Dairy Pool (1990). The complainant worked at a milk processing plant. After becoming a member of the Worldwide Church of God, he requested unpaid leave for a particular Monday in order to observe a holy day of his church. The request was refused because Mondays were especially busy days at the plant. When the employee did not report for work, he was fired.

The court ruled that Dairy Pool had discriminated on the basis of religion. Although the company had not done so directly, it had an adverse effect on the complainant due to his religion. It is of importance to note that the court stated that the employer must meet the "duty to accommodate." It means that the employer must accommodate the employee up to the point of "undue hardship."

The court did not define "undue hardship." However, it stated that relevant considerations would include financial cost, disruption of a collective agreement, problems of morale of other employees, and interchangeability of work force and facilities. It found that Dairy Pool could cope with employee absences on Mondays because of illnesses. Therefore, it could also accommodate a single instance for absence due to religious reasons, particularly where the employee had tried to accommodate the employer.[9]

A question receiving considerable attention these days is whether the practice of structuring employees' general paid-leave provisions around the traditional Christian calendar discriminates against employees whose religious beliefs require them to observe other holy days. The outcome of several cases indicates that it is an employer's duty to accommodate such observances.

In 1995, 27 employees of the Public Service Commission, the Department of National Defence, and the Canada Customs and Revenue Agency filed grievances against the federal government, alleging that its refusal to grant them discretionary leave to observe Rosh Hashana and Yom Kippur constituted discrimination based on religion. The employer had offered the applicants various options to accommodate their religious obligations, among them the opportunity to work extra hours to make up the related time-off without loss of pay and without using accumulated leave credits. The grievors were not satisfied with this arrangement.

A Public Service Staff Relations Board Adjudicator dismissed their grievances, citing a Supreme Court decision. The employees asked a Federal Court for a judicial review, but the Court found the Adjudicator's conclusion to be correct: a reasonable offer had been made by the employer and there was no need to resort to other leave-with-pay provisions to accommodate those affected.[10]

Age

The use of age as an employment criterion has also received considerable attention in the past. Many employers consider that the laying down of minimum or maximum ages for certain jobs is justified, although evidence is rarely available that age is an accurate indication of one's ability to perform a given type of work:

> The General Pilotage Regulations require that a pilot be removed from the eligibility list after reaching the age of 50. A special human rights tribunal found that such a regulation was invalid and ordered that pilots affected by this rule be restored to their former positions. An appeal court set aside the tribunal's decision on the basis that the removal of the pilots from the eligibility list because of age was not a discriminatory

practice. The Canadian Human Rights Commission appealed to the Supreme Court of Canada, but the appeal was denied.

Age consideration also has important implications for collective bargaining, where seniority rights are often based on the age of an employee (as opposed to seniority based on length of service):

> In the collective agreement between an employer and the Brotherhood of Railway, Airline, and Steamship Clerks, age was the determining factor for ranking of employees on the seniority list when hired on the same day. In her complaint against the union, Susan Tanel alleged that the policy resulted in her being denied upgrading from a part-time to a full-time position because of her age. The union and the employer have since recognized that age is not an appropriate measure of seniority between two employees with equal service; they no longer apply this policy or any other age-based seniority policy. Ms. Tanel received compensation in settlement of the complaint.

As mentioned earlier, the law makes an exception when it comes to retirement age. It is not considered a discriminatory practice if a person's employment is terminated because that person has reached the normal age of retirement for employees working in similar positions.

Sex

The Canadian Human Rights Act also prevents discrimination on the basis of an individual's sex. Not only is it illegal to recruit, hire, and promote employees because of their sex, it is unlawful to have separate policies for men and women. For example, it is discriminatory to reserve some jobs for men only or women only. It is even illegal to apply similar standards to men and women when such standards arbitrarily discriminate more against one sex than against the other. When standards discriminate against one sex (or race, national or ethnic origin, religion, age, or marital status), the burden is on the employer to prove that the standards are necessary:

> A woman complained that she had been refused an interview for a job as a bus driver because she was under the minimum height requirement of 5'8" (173 cm). She claimed that this height requirement discriminated against women. After conciliation, the case was settled with the company discontinuing the practice of requiring applicants to be 5'8" for drivers' jobs. Two women under 5'8" have since been hired. As part of the settlement, the company agreed that the Canadian Human Rights Commission would monitor the company's driver application records for one year. The complainant was paid $3500 for lost wages and general damages.

Although the standard did not discriminate against women per se, the arbitrary height requirement tended to exclude most female applicants. To keep the height rule, since it discriminates against women, the employer must show that it is necessary given the nature of the job. If this cannot be shown, the employer can be compelled to drop the requirement.

The most recent (handed down in 1999) and far-reaching Supreme Court decision relating to sex discrimination concerns the earlier mentioned bona fide occupational qualification (BFOQ). The case involved a woman who had been employed by the province of British Columbia in an elite firefighting unit for more than two years. In 1994, Ms. Meiorin failed one of several new fitness tests, a 2.5-km run to be completed in 11 minutes, and lost her employment. A subsequent grievance launched by her union was appealed to the Supreme Court. The Court decided in favour of Ms. Meiorin, agreeing with an earlier arbitrator's ruling that the government had failed to justify the test as a bona fide occupational qualification by providing credible evidence that her inability to meet the standard created a safety risk.[11]

The Court established three new criteria to assess the appropriateness of a BFOQ:

1. Is the standard rationally connected to the performance of the job?

2. Was the standard established in an honest belief that it was necessary to accomplish the purpose identified in stage one?

3. Is the standard reasonably necessary to accomplish its purpose?

The new and stricter rules will make it more difficult for human resource managers to establish and defend BFOQs.

Until 1989, it was acceptable practice that insurance programs defined pregnancies and related illnesses as not job-related events and excluded pregnant women from coverage. The Supreme Court, in a decision against Canada Safeway Ltd., ruled that although pregnancy was not a sickness or an accident, it was a valid health-related reason for absence from work. The result is that pregnancy discrimination is now recognized as sex discrimination. This is an important decision. Health benefit plans and office policies must be examined to ensure that this new understanding of sex discrimination is applied.[12]

In another related—and for human resource managers important—decision, a human rights tribunal ruled that women are not entitled to accumulate annual sick leave or sick leave credits when they are on maternity leave. The reason given was that since pregnancy was not an "illness," maternity leave could not be understood as a form of sick or disability leave. The tribunal found that the denial of these benefits did not discriminate against pregnant women because their collective agreement treated pregnancy leave in the same manner as all other unpaid leaves of absence under the agreement.[13]

Marital Status

The idea of what constitutes a family has undergone considerable changes in Canadian society in recent years. Nontraditional families, such as those resulting from common-law marriages, or single-parent families, are now far more numerous than in the past. But there is still a strong feeling that the traditional family is a unique institution deserving special consideration.

The Canadian Human Rights Act spells out quite clearly that any discrimination based on marital status is illegal:

> A woman was denied a job with the CBC because her husband was already employed by the corporation at the same station. After a complaint and hearing, the CBC changed its employment practices, which formerly discriminated on the basis of marital status, and placed the woman in a position in the same station in which her husband was employed.

Family Status

In a widely cited case regarding family status, the Canadian Human Rights Commission initiated action against the Canada Employment and Immigration Commission (CEIC). Ina Lang alleged that the CEIC denied her application for funding under the Challenge 86 program because she wished to hire her daughter to help in her family child-care business. A tribunal held that the CEIC had discriminated against Lang on the basis of her family status when it denied her the funding she sought, and awarded her $1000 for hurt feelings. The CEIC appealed the decision to the Federal Court of Appeal, but the court upheld the decision.

Marital and family status are often linked, as in the case of Diane Richer's complaint against the Canadian Armed Forces. Richer alleged that the CAF discriminated against her on the basis of marital and family status when she was refused admittance as a guest to the Junior Ranks Mess because she was married to an officer. The complaint was settled when the CAF agreed to admit such visitors into messes regardless of the rank of their military spouses. Richer received $500 for hurt feelings and a letter of apology.

In 1996, a human rights review tribunal upheld Paul Lagace's marital status complaint against the CAF. Lagace claimed that he had been excluded from an officer training program and denied a promotion because he was living in a common-law relationship. The CAF policy denied common-law couples access to married quarters. The tribunal's decision was upheld by a Federal Court of Appeal. Although Lagace was not entitled to reinstatement or lost wages or benefits, he was awarded $3500 damages.

That *nepotism* is a form of discrimination based on family status is something a Canadian airline discovered. It had a policy of hiring the children of its employees for summer jobs. The CHRC ruled that this amounted to discrimination. A federal court rejected an appeal.

Pardoned Convicts

The Canadian Human Rights Act prohibits discrimination against a convicted person if a pardon has been issued for the offence. Pardon may be granted by a parole board after five years following release, parole, or the completion of a sentence:

> A person convicted and paroled on a drug offence applied for a job with a government agency dealing with drug abuse. He was denied employment because of his conviction. Subsequently, the National Parole Board granted his request for a full pardon. The government agency maintained, however, that, pardoned or not, he remained a security risk and that being without a criminal record was a bona fide occupational qualification of a correctional service's staff. He appealed to the Canadian Human Rights Commission, and after the commission's investigation, the government agency decided that a criminal record would not, in fact, inhibit the applicant's ability to meet the requirements of the job, and, satisfied that he was suitable, offered him the position.[14]

The Canadian Human Rights Commission has also been approached by several persons who claim to have been refused employment on the basis of their arrest record, even when the arrest did not lead to a conviction. These persons are without legal protection since the Canadian Human Rights Act does not address this type of discrimination. For the human resource manager, this does not mean that all applicants can be asked for their arrest record. It must still be shown that it is relevant to the job. For this reason, the commission has advised employers under federal jurisdiction that applicants should not be asked, "Have you ever been convicted of an offence?" It is recommended—if such information is legitimately needed for employment purposes—that the question be phrased: "Have you ever been convicted of an offence for which you have not received a pardon?" (see "A Guide to Screening and Selection in Employment" in Appendix A to this chapter).

It should be noted, however, that Quebec and Yukon include records of criminal conviction in their list of prohibited discrimination criteria.

Disability

No person should be denied employment solely for the reason of his or her being disabled. Of course, there are exceptions. A blind person cannot be a truck driver, or a deaf person a telephone operator. However, the principle of "reasonable accommodation" has been established. It means that an employer can be expected to take reasonable measures to make available a suitable job to a person with a physical disability if it does not impose undue hardships on the organization:

www.disabilitynews.com/

A man was refused a technician's job because he failed a hearing test. However, he had been tested without his hearing aid; he asserted that he could perform the job using a hearing device. Medical advisers for the company claimed that the job required perfectly normal hearing. After conciliation, the company agreed that with a hearing aid the man would be able to do the job. The complaint was settled with the complainant being hired as a technician and paid damages of $750.

Many organizations have established rigid physical standards for certain jobs without being able to show that these standards are truly relevant to the requirements of the job. Some complainants have been refused jobs when their disability might be a problem in a speculative situation; for example, the firm might argue that a deaf person would be unable to hear a fire alarm. Other complainants have been disqualified for jobs not because they are physically handicapped now, but because they may become so in the future:

A machinist who had suffered an injury to his leg was refused a position on the hypothesis that at some time in the future he might develop complications that might affect his ability to work, which might in turn lead to a finding against the employer for compensation. After an investigation by the Canadian Human Rights Commission, the company had to agree that its assumptions were highly speculative. In the settlement, the complainant was paid the additional wages, approximately $2000, that he would have earned if he had not been denied the position, as well as compensation in respect of his feelings and self-respect.

www.cpha.ca/
english/index.htm

www.aidslaw.ca/
home.htm

Being drug-dependent can also be interpreted as a disability. In 1991, the Toronto Dominion Bank introduced a mandatory drug test for new and returning employees. A Federal Court ruled that this policy was discriminatory, reversing an earlier human rights tribunal's decision. Although the policy in question appeared to be applied in a neutral manner, the Court confirmed that it clearly affected the protected group of drug-dependent persons and therefore constituted "adverse impact" discrimination.[15]

Another case also has interesting consequences for human resource managers. In *Fortin v. CP Rail*, a Federal Court ruled that a company's obligation to accommodate an alcoholic employee may be quite far-reaching and is not influenced by that employee's misconduct.

Louis Fortin, a 30-year employee of CP Rail, was caught taking office funds, making unauthorized use of company expenses, and misappropriating company money for his own use. While the Canadian Human Rights Commission rejected his complaint of unfair dismissal based on his disability, a Federal Court found that the medical evidence indicated that the employee's conduct was recognizable as the behaviour of an alcoholic.[16]

The settlement of two human rights complaints has helped Canada's largest bank make its services more accessible to visually impaired and functionally illiterate people across Canada.

Chris and Marie Stark, who are blind, discovered that they could have been paying down their mortgage faster by making weekly rather than monthly payments. However, this information, which was contained in brochures available at any branch of the Royal Bank, was not accessible to them. As a result of the Starks' complaint, the Bank announced a policy to improve service to people with visual impairments. It has made 18 of its most popular publications available in Braille, large print, audio cassette, and on computer disk. The Bank will also study a new type of voice-activated automated banking machine in a pilot project to take place in London, Ontario.

Acquired Immune Deficiency Syndrome (AIDS) continues to draw the attention of the Canadian Human Rights Commission. It holds that discrimination on grounds of HIV infection or AIDS, whether factual or in suspicion, is a violation of the Canadian Human Rights Act. The Commission recommends that employers develop and publicize corporate AIDS policies to provide information and offer reassurance.

It states: "Discrimination and AIDS both thrive on ignorance and concealment. Education not only removes unnecessary fears, it may encourage both fairness and compassion."[17]

Sexual Orientation

As stated in the 1999 Canadian Human Rights Commission Annual Report, that year may come to be regarded as a watershed year for gay and lesbian Canadians. The issue of discrimination against same-sex relationships was effectively addressed by the Supreme Court of Canada when it decided that same-sex couples must be treated in the same way as heterosexual couples. Polls show that the majority of Canadians not only favour legislation to eliminate discrimination against lesbians and gay men, but also increasingly approve of measures to protect and support their families.

It began in 1996, when a human rights tribunal ordered the federal government to extend medical and dental benefits to the same-sex partners of its employees. The same year, the government amended the Canadian Human Rights Act to add sexual orientation as a prohibited ground of discrimination. Since then several Supreme Court decisions have forced provinces to amend their benefit and tax laws to include same-sex couples into their considerations.

The significance in change in attitude is reflected in the introduction of a bill by the federal Minister of Justice to create the Modernization of Benefits and Obligations Act, which would amend 68 federal statutes to extend benefits and obligations to same-sex couples. These obligations would include taxation, pension benefits, access to employment insurance, conflict of interest requirements, conjugal visits in prison, and immigration regulations.

Harassment

The Canadian Human Rights Act contains the following prohibition against harassment:

> It is a discriminatory practice,
>
> a) in the provision of goods, services, facilities, or accommodation customarily available to the general public,
> b) in the provision of commercial premises or residential accommodation, or
> c) in matters related to employment to harass an individual on a prohibited ground of discrimination.

Such behaviour may be verbal, physical, deliberate, unsolicited, or unwelcome; it may be one incident or a series of incidents. Protection against harassment extends to incidents occurring at or away from the workplace, during or outside normal working hours, provided such incidents are employment-related.

Harassment may include:

- verbal abuse or threats;

- unwelcome remarks, jokes, innuendo, or taunting about a person's body, attire, age, marital status, ethnic or national origin, religion, and so on.

- displaying of pornographic, racist, or other offensive or derogatory pictures;

- practical jokes that cause awkwardness or embarrassment;

- unwelcome invitations or requests, whether indirect or explicit, or intimidation;

- leering or other gestures;

- condescension or paternalism that undermines self-respect;

Harassment
Occurs when a member of an organization treats an employee in a disparate manner because of that person's sex, race, religion, age, or other protective classification.

- unnecessary physical contact such as touching, patting, pinching, punching; and

- physical assault.

It will be assumed that harassing behaviour has taken place if a "reasonable person ought to have known that such behaviour was unwelcome."[18]

Sexual harassment has become an important topic in human resource management, evidenced by the increased number of complaints lodged. A Canadian Human Rights Tribunal identified three characteristics of sexual harassment:

- the encounters must be unsolicited by the complainant, unwelcome to the complainant, and expressly or implicitly known by the respondent to be unwelcome;

- the conduct must either continue despite the complainant's protests or, if the conduct stops, the complainant's protests must have led to negative employment consequences; and

- the complainant's cooperation must be due to employment-related threats or promises.

The most consequential case undoubtedly was that of *Robichaud v. Department of National Defence (DND)*, since it made its way up to the Supreme Court. The court ruled that the employer shared the responsibility for the actions of one of its supervisors who had sexually harassed Ms. Robichaud. It added that "only an employer can remedy undesirable effects [of discrimination]; only an employer can provide the most important remedy—a healthy work environment." The DND was ordered to pay Ms. Robichaud $5000 for pain and suffering, to issue a written apology, and to post the written apology in all DND facilities.

Not only women are subjected to sexual harassment:

Rodney R., a deck-hand on a tugboat owned by Sea-West Holdings Ltd., was sexually harassed by the tug's skipper. Rodney complained to the owner of Sea-West, but nothing was done. He was eventually fired. A tribunal held that the sexual harassment had created a poisoned work situation where the individual is given a work environment that is intimidating, hostile, and offensive. The tribunal also felt that there is a duty upon the owner so informed [of harassment] to put an immediate stop to such practices. Rodney R. was awarded $2000 for hurt feelings and $1760 for lost wages.

How far the definition of sexual harassment can go is best illustrated in the following case:

A job applicant was asked by the person interviewing her if she liked the poster of a nude woman hanging on his wall. She felt she had to reply. She did not express her true reaction, however, because she believed her answer would affect her chances of getting the position. A settlement was reached during an investigation by the Canadian Human Rights Commission. The complainant received a letter of apology from the interviewer. A letter of reprimand was placed in his personnel file, and he attended a training session on sexual harassment. The employer also destroyed the poster and revised its office policy on harassment to make it consistent with the provisions of the act.

Employer Retaliation

It is a criminal act to retaliate in any way against those who exercise their rights according to the Human Rights Act. Those who file charges, testify, or otherwise participate in any human rights action are protected by law. If a supervisor tries to get even with an employee who filed charges, he or she violates the Act.

Enforcement

The responsibility for the enforcement of the Canadian Human Rights Act lies in the hands of a specially created Canadian Human Rights Commission (CHRC).

Sexual harassment
Unsolicited or unwelcome sex- or gender-based conduct that has adverse employment consequences for the complainant.

www.chrc-ccdp.ca

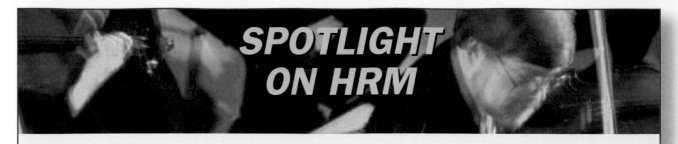

SPOTLIGHT ON HRM

WHEN A MANAGER IS ACCUSED OF SEXUAL HARASSMENT

How you first respond to a complaint of sexual harassment filed against you is extremely critical. Knowing what to do and what not to do can have a big impact on the results of the investigation that follows.

Employers have an obligation to conduct an inquiry into the allegations when a complaint of sexual harassment has been lodged.

Although every case is different and the nature and extent of the investigation will depend on the circumstances, here are a few suggestions on how you should react if a complaint is filed against you:

Avoid any emotional reaction when first confronted with the complaint. It is not unusual for an accused person to become defensive, angry, threatening or incoherent after being advised of a complaint. Restrain yourself from any overt behaviour that can later be categorized one way or the other. Try to keep the first meeting brief so you can leave to collect your thoughts and seek appropriate advice.

Never provide any response when first advised of the complaint. It will be hard to stay rational when you are first told about the complaint. You are at a disadvantage at this point, therefore avoid any knee-jerk response that you may regret later.

It is important to understand the nature of the complaint. As an accused, you are entitled to know every allegation that has been made by both the complainant and any witnesses. Ask to be provided with a copy of the written complaint and any statement by witnesses.

If the complaint has not been recorded in writing, ask that the employer go back to the complainant and obtain a signed copy. This also applies to witnesses. The reason is that you want to confine the complaint and avoid any subsequent changes. And ask what the complainant is seeking by filing it.

Does the employer have a sexual or workplace harassment policy? Whether the conduct that you are accused of will be characterized as sexual harassment may depend on the definition in the company policy. It should outline how the investigation will be conducted and what types of corrective action could be taken by the employer if you are found guilty.

Retain an employment lawyer who has experience in sexual harassment cases. You are entitled to retain a lawyer, usually at your cost. An experienced counsel will provide you with a clear understanding of the law of sexual harassment and will assist you throughout the investigation. Your lawyer may not be permitted to accompany you during your interview with investigators. Still, you should press your employer for the right to have counsel present.

You have a right to respond to all allegations made against you. This will normally occur during your interview with investigators and it is usually done orally. However, circumstances may require that you provide a written response along with your oral interview. Be prepared to explain the context in which any behaviour occurred and to provide the names of any witnesses that you want the investigators to talk to.

You should avoid being unco-operative or engaging in any retaliatory behaviour. There could be serious consequences for you if you engage in this type of conduct. Co-operation does not mean waiving any of your rights, but you should always be respectful of the process and be honest in your approach.

Avoid any conduct that could be characterized as interfering with the investigation. This usually means trying to contact the complainant or any of the witnesses. Do not engage in any kind of retaliation against either of these parties.

For example, changing the terms of employment or threatening to discipline or terminate the complainant or any witnesses could qualify as retaliation. Threatening to sue the complainant for defamation during the course of the investigation may also be considered a form of retaliation. Such conduct will usually be treated as a violation of company policy.

Avoid making denials where the truth is required. You may be surprised to know that just because you deny something occurred and there are no witnesses does not mean you can't be found guilty of sexual harassment. In many cases there are no witnesses and investigators must make a decision based on conflicting evidence and credibility.

If there is no reasonable explanation for your conduct, be honest in your response and acknowledge any shortcomings in your behaviour. Misleading or lying to investigators can only make things worse for you.

When a complaint of sexual harassment is filed against you, it is a very serious matter. It could result in discipline or even termination and, in most cases, would undermine your relationship with your co-workers and your reputation. The manner in which you respond may well determine your fate.

Source: Courtesy of Malcolm MacKillop.

It consists of a chief commissioner, a deputy chief commissioner, and from three to six other members all appointed by the governor-in-council. The chief commissioner and his or her deputy are full-time members. Full-time members are appointed for a term of not more than seven years, and part-time members for a term of not more than three years.

The commission deals with complaints it receives concerning discriminatory practices covered by the Act. The commission may also act on its own when it perceives a possible infraction. It also has the power to issue guidelines interpreting the act. If warranted, the commission can ask the president of the Human Rights Tribunal Panel to appoint a tribunal, which may order cessation of the discriminatory practice and the adoption of measures to ensure that it will not recur, as well as compensation.

Figure 4-3 summarizes the CHRC enforcement procedures. Any individual or group may file a complaint with the commission, given that they have reasonable

FIGURE 4-3

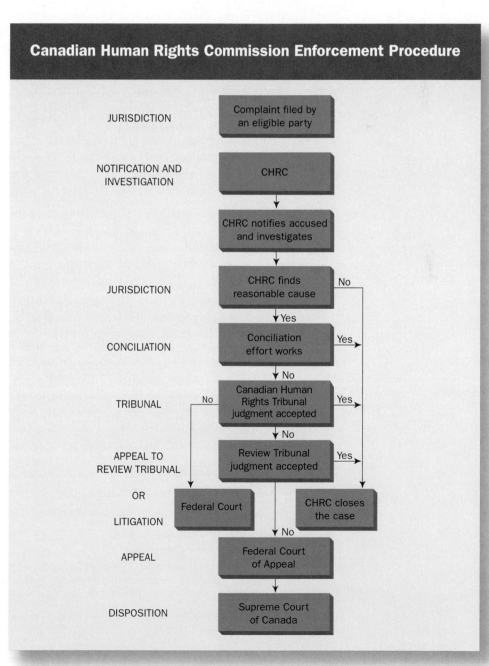

Canadian Human Rights Commission Enforcement Procedure

grounds to believe they have been discriminated against. The commission may refuse to accept the complaint if it is submitted by someone other than the person who allegedly has been discriminated against, unless the alleged victim permits investigation of the claim. It is also possible for the commission itself to initiate a complaint, if it has reasonable grounds to assume that a party is engaging in a discriminatory practice.

The commission must deal with any complaint filed with it if it involves a federal government department or agency or any business or industry under federal jurisdiction. The commission, however, may refuse to deal with complaints if other procedures seem more appropriate, if the complaint seems trivial or made in bad faith, or if too much time (one year) has elapsed since the alleged discrimination took place.

After a complaint has been accepted by the commission, an investigator is appointed to gather facts about the case. The investigator submits a report to the commission recommending a finding of either substantiation or nonsubstantiation of the allegation. If the allegation is substantiated, a settlement may be arranged in the course of the investigation, or the commission may, after adoption of the investigator's report, appoint a conciliator.

Should the parties involved be unable to reach a conciliation agreement, a Human Rights Tribunal consisting of up to three members—most consist of one—may be appointed to investigate the complaint. Figure 4-4 describes the discretion of the tribunal in settling a complaint. Should the tribunal find that the discriminatory practice was maintained purposely or recklessly, or that the victim's feelings or self-respect have suffered as a result of the practice, it may order the person or organization responsible to compensate the victim appropriately.

A person who obstructs an investigation or a tribunal, or fails to comply with the terms of a settlement, or reduces wages in order to eliminate a discriminatory practice, can be found guilty of an offence punishable by a fine and/or jail sentence. If the guilty party is an employer or an employee organization, the fine might be up to $50 000. For individuals, the penalty might be up to $5000:[19]

> In the Western Guard Party case mentioned earlier (see page 161 under "Race and Colour") the tribunal had ordered that the party cease preparing recorded telephone messages that expose persons to hatred or contempt because of their religion or race. When the respondents persisted with their messages, the Canadian Human Rights Commission successfully moved in the court that the respondents be found

FIGURE 4-4

Remedies for Violations

A Canadian Human Rights Tribunal can order a violator to:

- Stop the discriminatory practice.
- Restore the rights, opportunities, and privileges denied the victim.
- Compensate the victim for wages lost and any expenses incurred as a result of the discriminatory practice.
- Compensate the victim for any additional cost of obtaining alternative goods, services, facilities, or accommodation as a result of the discriminatory practice.
- Develop and implement employment equity programs to equalize opportunity for certain groups that have suffered from discriminatory practices in the past.

guilty of contempt. The party's leader, John Ross Taylor, was sentenced to one year in jail and the Western Guard Party was sentenced to a $5000 fine. The respondents appealed their conviction and sentence to the Federal Court of Appeal and the Supreme Court of Canada, but both let the conviction stand.

Provincial Human Rights Laws and Human Rights Commissions

All provinces and two territories (NWT and Yukon) have their own human rights laws and human rights commissions, with similar discrimination criteria, regulations, and procedures. The new territory of Nunavut is still under federal jurisdiction until legislators enact their own laws and create a human rights commission. If a person feels discriminated against, he or she will contact a provincial human rights officer who will investigate the complaint and attempt to reach a settlement that will satisfy all parties. Experience has shown that most cases are settled at this stage. Should there be no agreement, then the case will be presented to the Human Rights Commission. The members of the commission will study the evidence and then submit a report to the minister in charge of administration of the Human Rights Act. The minister may appoint a Board of Inquiry, which has powers similar to those of a tribunal at the federal level. Noncompliance with the course of action prescribed by the Board of Inquiry may result in prosecution in a provincial court of law. Individuals can be fined between $500 and $1000 and organizations or groups between $1000 and $10 000, depending on the province. If an issue at hand has nationwide implications, any provincial court decision may ultimately be appealed to the Supreme Court of Canada.

The major differences in the activities of the federal and provincial human rights commissions seem to be in the sophistication of cases. While the federal commission deals mainly with government agencies and Crown corporations, which tend to have well-developed human resource policies and experienced human resource professionals, provincial commissions deal mostly with small- and medium-sized businesses, whose employees and human resource staff often have little experience in discrimination cases.

Employment Equity

The Abella Commission on Equality in Employment (chaired by Judge Rosalie Abella) was appointed in 1983 to inquire into the most effective, efficient, and equitable methods of promoting employment opportunities for four designated groups: women, people with disabilities, native people, and visible minorities. The commission recommended that all organizations set mandatory equality programs and urged the provincial and federal governments to pass equity legislation—a recommendation that has since been implemented by the federal and all provincial governments. The commission also recommended the use of the term "employment equity" in Canada to distinguish it from the U.S. term "affirmative action" because, in the opinion of the commission, the latter carried too many negative associations with it.

As a result of the Abella Commission's report, the federal government proclaimed the ***Employment Equity Act*** in August 1987. Its intent is to remove employment barriers and promote equality of the four designated group members. The act requires employers with 100 and more employees under federal jurisdiction to develop annual plans setting out goals and timetables and to maintain these plans for three years. The act requires further that each employer submit annual reports describing the progress in attaining the goals set out in the above-mentioned plans.

www.chrc-ccdp.ca/
publications/index.asp?l=e

Employment Equity Act
Federal law to remove employment barriers and to promote equality.

The Canada Employment and Immigration Commission forwards employer reports to the Human Rights Commission. Employers who do not comply may be investigated by the Human Rights Commission and, if necessary, prosecuted under the Canadian Human Rights Act.

The Employment Equity Act was amended in 1996. It now contains two specific provisions regarding "reasonable accommodation." Section 5 of the act provides that:

> "Every employer shall implement employment equity" by, among other measures, "making such reasonable accommodations as will ensure that persons in a designated group achieve a degree of representation commensurate with their representation in the Canadian workforce and their availability to meet reasonable occupational requirements."

Section 10 of the act specifies that an employer shall prepare an "employment equity plan" that provides for "reasonable accommodation... to correct... under-representation."

Examples of "reasonable accommodation" would be the provision of a sign language interpreter for a job interview with a deaf applicant; the provision of telephone or computer equipment to accommodate persons who are hard of hearing or blind; a barrier-free work site for wheelchair-bound employees; allowing religious minorities to alter their work schedules to accommodate religious obligations; or altering dress or grooming codes to allow aboriginal people to wear braids.

The amended act also established the Canadian Human Rights Commission as the monitoring agency that would carry out compliance audits for federally regulated public- and private-sector employers.

Functional Impact

Virtually every human resource function is affected by employment equity plans:

- *Human resource plans* must reflect the organization's employment equity goals.
- *Job descriptions* must not contain unneeded requirements that exclude members of protected classes.
- *Recruiting* must ensure that all types of applicants are sought without discriminating.
- *Selection* of applicants must use screening devices that are job-relevant and nondiscriminatory.
- *Training and developmental* opportunities must be made available for workers without discrimination.
- *Performance appraisal* must be free of biases that discriminate.
- *Compensation programs* must be based on skills, performance, and/or seniority and cannot discriminate against jobholders in other respects.

Even when human resource specialists know their intent is not to discriminate, they must carefully review the results of these human resource functions to ensure that the results are not discriminatory. Otherwise, lawsuits may arise and the current employment equity plan may need to be revised or scrapped.

Employment Equity Programs

The Canadian Human Rights Act gives the Canadian Human Rights Commission great latitude in pursuing the enforcement of the act. One way for the Commission

Employment equity programs
Developed by employers to undo past employment discrimination or to ensure equal employment opportunity in the future. Called Affirmative Action Programs in the U.S.

to comply with the intent of the act to improve equal employment opportunities for special groups is for it to encourage *Employment Equity Programs*, also known as *Affirmative Action Programs* (a U.S. term).

Section 15(1) of the act specifies special programs as a legitimate mechanism for improving the opportunities of a group through the elimination, reduction, or prevention of discrimination:

> It is not a discriminatory practice for a person to adopt or carry out a special program, plan, or arrangement designed to prevent disadvantages that are likely to be suffered by, or to eliminate or reduce disadvantages that are suffered by, any group or individuals when those disadvantages would be or are based on or related to the race, national or ethnic origin, colour, religion, age, sex, marital status, or physical handicap of members of that group, by improving opportunities respecting goods, services, facilities, accommodation, or employment in relation to that group.

Such programs are developed by employers to remedy past discrimination or to prevent discrimination in the future. It usually implies on the part of the organization a self-evaluation with respect to hiring, promotion, and compensation policies. If discrepancies are found, it would be good human resource practice to check the criteria used for different decisions, adjust them if necessary, and ensure that they are consistently applied.

Employment Equity Programs exist for several reasons. From a practical standpoint, employers seldom benefit by excluding people who belong to some particular group. To exclude an entire class of workers, such as women or minorities, limits the labour pool available to the human resource department. Open discrimination can also lead to negative public relations, boycotts by consumers, and government intervention. To ensure that such discrimination does not occur, employers often develop Employment Equity Programs voluntarily.

It should be noted that mandated Employment Equity Programs occur mainly at the federal level, i.e., in organizations and industries under federal jurisdiction. At the provincial level such programs are implemented almost exclusively on a voluntary basis, when organizations see an advantage in it. An example would be Saint Mary's University in Halifax, where an Employee Equity Program, approved by the Nova Scotia Human Rights Commission, was implemented to balance a perceived employment inequity between male and female faculty.

Regardless of the reasons or goals of such programs, human resource departments should adhere to the guidelines discussed below and summarized in Figure 4-5.

FIGURE 4-5

Major Steps in Employment Equity Programs

1. Exhibit strong employer commitment.
2. Appoint a high-ranking director.
3. Publicize commitment internally and externally.
4. Survey the workforce for underutilization and concentration.
5. Develop goals and timetables.
6. Design remedial, active, and preventive programs.
7. Establish control systems and reporting procedures.

Exhibit Commitment

No matter how favourably the human resource department is viewed by others in the organization, the president of the company should support the Employment Equity Program in writing. Anything less than total backing from top officials raises questions about the sincerity of the organization's commitment in the eyes of government agencies, courts, and employees. To exhibit this commitment forcefully, company officials may make raises, bonuses, and promotions dependent upon each manager's compliance.

Appoint a Director

Some member of the organization should be responsible for equity issues. Commonly, the vice-president of human resources is appointed director, although day-to-day implementation may be delegated to a compliance specialist in the human resource department.

Publicize Commitment

Equal employment is meaningless unless it is publicized both externally and internally. Outside the company, sources of potential recruits must be made aware of the new policy. School guidance counsellors, employment agencies, and officers of Canada Employment Centres are likely candidates for notification. The phrase "an equal opportunity employer" is frequently used on company stationery and in classified ads to further publicize the policy. That it is also important that first-line supervisors who make hiring decisions are informed is demonstrated in the following case:

> The president of a large company in Halifax boasted during an annual meeting about the successful Employment Equity Program his company had started. He was challenged from the floor. The speaker told the story of an obvious discriminatory hiring practice that had recently occurred in one of the company's branches. The embarrassed president promised to investigate. It turned out that top management had made a commitment to an Employment Equity Program, but this commitment had not been communicated to those who made first-line hiring decisions.

Survey the Workforce

Underutilization
A condition that exists when a department or employer has a lesser proportion of members of a protected class than are found in the employer's labour market.

Concentration
A condition that exists when a department or employer has a greater proportion of members of a protected class than are found in the employer's labour market.

The human resource department needs to know how the composition of the employer's workforce compares with the composition of the workforce in the labour market. For example, if the employer's mix of male and female employees differs significantly from the labour market from which the employer attracts workers, then it is possible that discrimination has occurred. When a survey of the employer's workforce indicates such differences, the employer may find examples of *underutilization* or *concentration*. Underutilization exists when a company or department has a smaller proportion of protected class members than is found in the labour market. For example, when a company has no female managers even though the labour market is 37 per cent female, underutilization exists. Concentration is just the opposite. It occurs when protected class members are concentrated in a few departments out of proportion with their presence in the labour market.

Develop Goals and Timetables

When, through surveys, underutilization and concentration are found (possibly consequences of past discrimination), human resource specialists should set up goals and timetables to eliminate them.

Design Specific Programs

To reach goals, human resource specialists must design remedial, active, and preventive programs. Remedial programs correct problems that already existed. Active programs imply that management goes beyond instructing supervisors about new hiring policies and waiting for things to happen. It means going to high schools in areas dominated by minorities, approaching community leaders in such areas for assistance, inviting residents to attend information sessions, and advertising in newspapers or other media outlets accessible to minorities and special target groups:

> The Law School at Dalhousie University in Halifax developed an Indigenous Black and Mi'kmaq Program to train more black and Mi'kmaq lawyers. It appointed a director and began a publication campaign aimed at these groups by advertising in local newspapers and association publications. The program director visits high schools and universities and holds information sessions at reserves and community centres. An advisory board made up of Law School representatives, community leaders, and the two student groups assists in identifying ways to reach the target groups. The program has graduated 63 lawyers from these minority groups so far.[20]

Preventive programs are more proactive. They involve an assessment of human resource management policies and practices. Policies that discriminate (such as height rules) or practices that continue past discrimination (such as hiring exclusively from employee referrals) must be eliminated.

Establish Controls

An Employment Equity Program is likely to fail unless controls are established. Human resource specialists and line managers must perceive their rewards as depending upon the success of the employment equity plan. To evaluate that success, monthly, quarterly, and yearly benchmarks should be reported directly to the director of the program and to the president or another senior official.

Contract Compliance Policy

In addition to the Employment Equity Act, the federal government issued a new policy that requires compliance with the Employment Equity Act for any company doing business with the federal government. Companies with 100 or more employees bidding on contracts for goods and services of $200 000 or more will be subject to the employment equity criteria listed in the act. Under this policy, companies will be required to certify in writing at the tendering stage of a contract their commitment to implement employment equity. Employers will be subject to random reviews to ensure their compliance with the act.

Pay Equity

www.gov.on.ca/
lab/pec/acte.htm

In 1997, according to Statistics Canada, women earned on average 80 cents for every $1 earned by men. There are many reasons for this pay gap, including differences in work experience, education, major field of study, occupation and industry of employment, as well as reasons that are still not understood. Pay equity legislation attempts to remedy these inequities. At the federal level, the Canadian Human Rights Act prohibits discrimination based on sex. It is therefore illegal to pay women less than men if their jobs are of equal value, a principle known as "equal pay for work of equal value," which is discussed in more detail in Chapter Ten. All provinces have their own pay equity legislation, but they differ in coverage. Quebec and Ontario have legislation covering the public and private sector, while other provinces restrict the application to the public sector.

That the "equal pay for work of equal value" concept can be very costly was shown in the case of 390 federal library science employees—mostly women—who earned less than historical researchers—mostly men—though the library science work was claimed to be of equal value. The settlement, requiring individual salary increases of up to $2500 a year, cost the federal government $2.4 million.

On October 19, 1999, the longest and largest pay equity case was resolved when Mr. Justice John Evans upheld a human rights tribunal's ruling that the federal government owed about 230 000 mostly female workers 13 years of back pay. The final settlement is estimated to cost the Treasury Board $3.5 billion. The federal government decided not to appeal this decision.

In the private sector the largest case involves Bell Canada and about 20 000 employees, mostly women. The Supreme Court of Canada decided not to hear an appeal by Bell Canada against a judgment by a human rights tribunal that it paid female-dominated jobs between $1.50 and $5.00 per hour less than male-dominated jobs of equal value. The Supreme Court held that it was up to the tribunal to decide on a settlement for Bell employees. Estimates of a final settlement range from $400 million to $500 million. At the time of this writing in late 2000, no decision had been made.

The implication for human resource people is that they must ensure that their wage and salary system does not subtly discriminate on the basis of sex.

Reverse Discrimination

The use of employment equity plans can lead to charges of reverse discrimination against employers. These charges usually arise when an employer seeks to hire or promote a member of a protected group over an equally (or better) qualified candidate who is not a member of the protected group. For example, if an employer has an Employment Equity Program that gives preference to women over men when promotions occur, a qualified male may sue the employer and claim that he was discriminated against because of his sex.

Charges of reverse discrimination may place human resource departments in a difficult position. On the one hand, the human resource manager is responsible for eliminating concentration and underutilization. On the other hand, to give preference to members of a protected class (such as women, for example) raises questions about whether the human resource department is being fair:

> In a landmark decision in 1984, the Canadian Human Rights Commission imposed a mandatory Employment Equity Program on CN. It was ordered to hire women for one in four nontraditional or blue-collar jobs in its St. Lawrence region until they held 13 per cent of such jobs. CN appealed the decision to the Supreme Court of Canada, which let stand the order for quotas. This ruling is important since it allows Employment Equity Programs as acceptable measures, even if they result in potential reverse discrimination.

Although preferential treatment will always raise questions of fairness, the Canadian Human Rights Act declares employment equity programs nondiscriminatory if they fulfill the spirit of the law.

Line Management

The implementation of an employment equity program may cause line managers to feel a loss of authority.[21] Operating managers may lose the right to make final hiring and promotion decisions. To achieve the objectives of the plan, the human resource department may even have to overrule line managers. In time, supervisors may believe that members of protected classes are getting different treatment. If workers also sense an element of reverse discrimination, conflicts may arise that lessen the effectiveness of the work group.

To overcome potentially damaging side effects of employment equity plans, human resource specialists must educate line managers—particularly first-line supervisors. Training programs, seminars, and explanations of human resource decisions affecting protected groups must be given to managers. Otherwise, their support and understanding of the employment equity program is likely to be low and, in turn, the perceived quality of the work environment may decline.[22]

Other Legal Challenges

www.cirb-ccri.gc.ca/
eng/clc.html

This chapter has dealt mainly with legal discrimination and harassment issues. Of course, there are many other potential legal challenges, not all of which can be detailed here. The following list outlines some of these relevant issues, most of which will be discussed in later chapters:

- *Canada Labour Code.* Originally the Industrial Disputes Investigation Act of 1907, it was modified and re-enacted in 1971 as the Canada Labour Code. It regulates union certification, right to organize, union prosecution, and mediation and arbitration procedures, all of which are discussed in more detail in Chapter Sixteen. Provincial equivalents to the Code are the Employment (or Labour) Standards Acts.

- *Dismissal.* According to common law, every employee has a contract with his or her employer, even if there is nothing in writing. An employee or employer can terminate an employment relationship by giving reasonable notice. An immediate dismissal is possible if an employee is compensated through appropriate severance pay. See Chapter Fifteen.

- *Hours of Work and Overtime Regulations.* The Canada Labour Code sets the standard workday at eight hours and the standard workweek at 40 hours, and overtime pay at one and one-half times the regular pay.

- *Minimum Wages.* These are set by provincial and federal boards and discussed in Chapter Ten.

- *Occupational Health and Safety.* The Labour Standards Code also regulates occupational health and safety issues, discussed in Chapter Fourteen.

- *Weekly Rest Day.* The Canada Labour Code specifies that employees must be given at least one full day of rest during the week, preferably on Sunday.

- *Workplace Hazardous Material Information System (WHMIS).* WHMIS regulates the handling of dangerous material, discussed in Chapter Fourteen.

These are some of the federal laws that have an impact on human resource managers. Most of these laws have their provincial equivalent. The human resource manager is ultimately responsible for knowing and enforcing the law.

Strategic Implications of Legal Challenges

If there is a basic rule in human resource management, it has to be: "Obey the law." The human resource manager is responsible for ensuring that all policies and rules take legal aspects into account (for example, hiring and termination procedures, pay equity regulations, health and safety rules, the handling of dangerous products, and so on). Given the current priority accorded employment equity, human resource managers also have to ensure that all long-range strategic plans that have an impact on staff and staffing follow employment equity requirements. Not doing so can be costly, as some of the examples given in this chapter have shown.

It is also desirable for the corporate image to be perceived by the public as being a "good corporate citizen." One of the objectives of an organization is to project external equity, which determines its attractiveness as perceived by job applicants (discussed in Chapters Five, Six, and Ten).

Following legal requirements also has implications for training. Managers and supervisors must be familiar with the laws as they apply to human resource management. Sexual harassment is an issue that has cost business and government organizations large amounts of money in fines, court costs, and compensation to the victims. Unjust dismissal is another prominent issue. More and more employees dismissed for unsatisfactory performance or other reasons have challenged their dismissal, and management has had to prove that the decision was valid.

Finally, if a company plans to do business with the federal government, it must make sure that all the requirements of the Employment Equity Act are fulfilled. This chapter has made clear that the legal aspects of human resource management play a significant role in strategic planning and decision making.

SUMMARY

www.geocities.com/
CapitolHill/6174/index.html

Government is a significant variable that strongly shapes the role of human management. It influences human resources through laws governing the employment relationship. The application of the Charter of Rights and Freedoms was awaited with high expectations from both labour and management. However, its impact on the human resource management field has been modest so far. Decisions of the Supreme Court of Canada affirmed the right to associate, but found that the right to bargain collectively and to strike is not a fundamental one, but rather is subject to government regulations. The Charter does not apply to picketing, which means that employers can ask for injunctions to restrict the number of pickets. The court upheld the right of governments to impose mandatory retirement, subject to limitations that are reasonable and justifiable.

The two sources of equal employment laws are the federal and provincial human rights statutes. The Canadian Human Rights Act of 1978 applies to federal government departments and agencies, Crown corporations, and businesses and industries under federal jurisdiction, such as banks, airlines, and railway companies. Areas that are not under federal jurisdiction are protected by provincial human rights laws. Each of the 10 Canadian provinces has its own antidiscrimination laws that are broadly similar to the federal law.

To eliminate past discrimination and ensure future compliance, many organizations have developed employment equity plans. The plans are designed to identify areas of past and present discrimination, develop affirmative goals, and design remedial, active, and preventive programs.

To actively promote the employment of women, aboriginal peoples, persons with disabilities, and visible minorities, the federal government introduced the Employment Equity Act, which requires employers with 100 employees or more under federal jurisdiction to develop plans and timetables for the employment of these groups. It also requires annual reports that must be submitted to the Canadian Employment and Immigration Commission. Also, a new policy requires employers with 100 employees or more bidding for government contracts worth $200 000 or more to comply with the above-mentioned guidelines.

Appendix A to this chapter contains "A Guide to Screening and Selection in Employment," which describes acceptable and unacceptable questions to ask during job interviews and on application forms.

TERMS FOR REVIEW

Visit the Web site at www.mcgrawhill.ca/college/schwind6 for a full glossary.

REVIEW AND DISCUSSION QUESTIONS

1. Suppose during your first job interview after graduation you are asked, "Why should a company have an employment equity plan?" How would you respond?

2. List the major prohibitions of the Canadian Human Rights Act.

3. Since a human resource department is not a legal department, what role does it play in the area of equal employment law?

4. Suppose you are told that your first duty as a human resource specialist is to construct an employment equity plan. What would you do? What types of information would you seek?

5. What conditions would have to be met before you could bring suit against an employer who discriminated against you because of your sex?

6. A job applicant for a teller's job tells you that he has been convicted of cash theft, which he committed on his previous job, but that he received a full pardon. The applicant appears to be the most qualified, but you are afraid that he might steal again. Is there a legal way to deny him the job?

7. Under the Charter of Rights and Freedoms, the Supreme Court of Canada has made a number of important decisions pertaining to union rights. What impact do these decisions have on management and unions?

8. A job candidate answers "yes" to the question of whether she is a smoker. She is well qualified, but you decide not to hire her. Does she have a legal recourse?

CRITICAL THINKING QUESTIONS

1. If you are a supervisor in a bank and an employee demands to be allowed to miss work on Fridays for religious reasons, what would you do? Under what circumstances would you have to let the employee have time off? Under what circumstances could you prohibit it?

2. You have a job opening for a warehouse helper, a position that requires sometimes heavy lifting, up to 50 kg. A woman applies for the job and claims that she is able to do the work. She looks rather petite and you are afraid that she may hurt herself. When you deny her the job, she threatens to complain to the Human Rights Commission. What do you do?

3. You are the human resource manager in a hospital. A nurse informs you, in confidence, that he has been diagnosed HIV positive. Are you required to take action? What legal options do you have in dealing with this case?

4. Do you think more groups will receive special legislation to protect them from discrimination? Which groups might receive additional protection?

WEB RESEARCH

1. Government of Canada

   http://canada.gc.ca

   (a) Find the Canadian Human Rights Commission's view on the national AIDS policy and action taken. Provide a summary of your findings.

   (b) How many agencies and government services, which relate to human resources in a broad sense, are you able to identify?

2. Canadian Human Rights Commission

   www.chrc.ca

   (a) Find and summarize three cases decided last year in favour of employers and three cases decided in favour of employees.

   (b) Based on the latest case decisions on gay rights, what are the implications for human resource managers?

3. Ontario Network for Human Rights

   www.geocities.com/capitolhill/6174/index.html

   (a) Find a case that offers an example of a discrimination situation. Can we generalize from this case to other organizations?

   (b) Find an article on racism in companies and give a summary. What action would management have to take to combat racism in its organization?

4. Canadian Public Health Association

   www.cpha.ca

   (a) Give some examples of organizational success stories in fighting AIDS.

   (b) List and discuss programs and resources available to Canadian organizations to assist employees who are HIV-positive.

5.   Pay Equity Commission of Ontario

www.gov.on.ca/lab/pec/contacte.htm

(a)   How is progress in the pay equity process monitored?

Web Site Addresses for Human Rights Commissions

Canadian Human Rights Commission

   www.chrc.ca

Prince Edward Island Human Rights Commission

   www.gov.pe.ca/caag/human/index.asp

Nova Scotia Human Rights Commission

   www.gov.ns.ca/just/hr.htm

New Brunswick Human Rights Commission

   www.gov.nb.ca/ael/human/english

Ontario Human Rights Commission

   www.gov.ohrc.on.ca

Saskatchewan Human Rights Commission

   www.gov.sk.ca/shrc

Alberta and Northwest Territories Human Rights and Citizenship Commission

   www.gov.ab.ca/~med/med.htm

British Columbia Human Rights Commission

   www.bchrc.gov.bc.ca/

Yukon Human Rights Commission

   www.yhrc.yk.ca/

INCIDENT 4-1

Metropolitan Hospital's Employment Equity Needs

A large metropolitan hospital in Ontario recently developed an employment equity plan. Under the program the hospital agreed to promote two women into supervisory ranks for each man promoted. This practice was to continue until 40 to 45 per cent of all supervisory jobs in the hospital were held by women.

The need for the first supervisory promotion occurred in the medical records department. The manager of medical records was one of the few female managers in the hospital. Nevertheless, she argued that Roy Biggs should become a medical records supervisor since he was best qualified. Roy had two years of medical school and was a graduate of a medical records program at the local community college. The assistant director of hospital operations agreed that Roy should receive the promotion. The equal employment compliance specialist in the human resource department argued that Kate VanDam should get the promotion because of the employment equity plan and because she had more seniority and experience in the department than Roy. The records manager, assistant administrator, and compliance specialist decided that the human resource manager should make the final decision.

1. What weight would you give to (a) Kate's seniority and experience, (b) Roy's superior training, (c) the recommendation of the records manager, (d) the new employment equity plan?

2. What are the implications for the employment equity plan if Roy gets the job? What are the implications for the employees presently taking job-related courses if Kate gets the promotion?

3. What decision would you make if you were the human resource manager?

EXERCISE 4-1

Carver Jewellery Company

Carver Jewellery Company Ltd. has the following workforce composition:

Job Classes	Male	Female	White	Black	Asian	Native Peoples
Executive	9	1	10	0	0	0
Management	71	9	79	0	1	0
Salaried/Commission	43	31	74	0	0	0
Hourly Paid	24	164	168	10	8	2

An analysis of the local labour force from which Carver draws its employees is as follows:

Male	Female	White	Black	Asian	Native Peoples
53%	47%	84%	8%	3%	5%

On the basis of this information:

1. Identify which job classes at Carver exhibit underutilization.

2. Identify which job classes at Carver exhibit concentration.

CASE STUDY

Maple Leaf Shoes Ltd., Legal Challenges

Maple Leaf Shoes Ltd. is a medium-sized manufacturer of leather and vinyl shoes located in Wilmington, Ontario. It was started in 1969 and currently employs about 400 persons in its Wilmington plant and some 380 more in offices and warehouses throughout Canada.

Eva White was the operator of a leather-cutting machine. When Eva heard the bell ring, indicating the end of the workday, she shut down her cutting machine and headed toward the women's locker room. It had been a long day and standing for eight hours on the machine didn't do her back any good.

When she approached her locker she saw that Rosetta Maurizio, who used the locker next to hers, was already there, changing into her street clothing. Eva and Rosetta had been hired together 10 months earlier. They had not known each other before and although they worked in different parts of the building, they kept each other company in the cafeteria during their lunch breaks. Rosetta was of Italian descent and, although she had immigrated to Canada from Italy with her parents several years earlier, her Italian accent was still quite noticeable.

Eva noticed that Rosetta had red eyes, as if she had been crying. She asked Rosetta whether she had problems and whether she could be of any help. Rosetta seemed reluctant to talk, but when she finally responded she sounded quite agitated. The following dialogue developed:

Rosetta: As you know, I am one of the two women in the finishing section working with about 20 guys. They seem to enjoy making fun of me. It starts in the morning when I arrive. They call me risotto, which means rice with gravy in Italian, and give me some mock Italian greetings. They sometimes ask me whether I had a good time with my Italian boyfriend the night before and what we had done together. They also tell each other their own experiences with their girlfriends, one more bragging than the other, but always so that I can hear it. I think they do it intentionally to embarrass me. I tend to blush and that seems to amuse them. When they tell a dirty joke they ask me whether I understood it or whether I could tell one myself. Some of them have centrefolds pinned to the wall behind their machines. Today one guy asked me whether I prefer Italian men over Canadian men and when I told him to let me alone and to mind his own business he said that Italians are just braggarts, only good with their mouths. I was so angry that I had to go to the washroom to hide my tears. I am thinking of quitting this job, it is just getting too much.

Eva: Have you talked to Al, the supervisor, about that?

Rosetta: I don't want to talk to him about this. He's very friendly with the guys, and when they tell jokes when he's around he laughs with them, which seems to encourage them. But they never tell the type of jokes they tell me. I mentioned to him that I would like to find another job in the company. When he asked why I told him that I had trouble breathing the vapour of the polish in the air. He said that he would see whether there were other jobs open, but that was over a month ago. I do not dare to bring it up again.

Eva: You have to talk to him. Don't let it go on, otherwise you will suffer too much.

Rosetta: But when I complain to him and he talks to the guys they probably make it worse for me. No, I'd rather not.

Eva: Should I talk to him?

Rosetta: No, no, please don't. I will think about it.

Next morning, when they met in the change room again, Eva encouraged Rosetta once more to talk to her supervisor. She even offered to come with her if she wanted some support. Rosetta promised to do something, but declined Eva's offer.

In the evening Eva noticed that Rosetta's locker was empty. The next day she asked the personnel department about what had happened to Rosetta and was told that Rosetta had quit, citing family reasons.

Eva was upset. She felt that Rosetta had been treated unfairly and that she should not be forced to quit her job because some rogues made her life miserable.

She decided to do something. She asked her own supervisor for a break and went over to the finishing workroom to talk to Al.

Al was sitting in his office when Eva walked in. He looked surprised when he saw her. He knew that she worked in the company, but had never talked to her. He offered her a seat and asked what he could do for her, but added quickly that if she was looking for a job in his division he had one opening, due to a recent vacancy.

Eva: That's not the reason I want to talk to you, although it is related to that vacant job. What happened to Rosetta?

He seemed to be taken aback by her aggressive tone, but kept his cool and answered: "Rosetta quit. She didn't like the job anymore."

Eva: Was that all she said?

Al: Well, she said that she didn't like to work in a place that made her feel uncomfortable. She mentioned that the guys in the finishing room were telling dirty jokes she didn't like and that they made fun of her. Well, I told her that I have been supervisor for 10 years in this division, and that I never heard an outright dirty joke, just some good old fashioned fun jokes, nothing to be shocked by. I think she was just too sensitive. The guys just want to have a good time. The job is boring and they need something to distract them. They are not mean guys.

Eva: But there was more to this than just telling jokes. Rosetta told me that the guys also made fun of her Italian background.

Al: I think it's ridiculous to make that an issue. We have Ukrainians, Germans, British, Chinese, Indians, and some others. There has never been a problem. And as far as making fun of her: we all make fun of each other, but that's good natured. I think she takes herself too seriously. My philosophy is that we have to be able to laugh at ourselves now and then. Life is tough enough.

Eva: But she did feel uncomfortable. She even cried because of what she went through. Don't you think that you have to accept some responsibility for that? I think that she has been treated unfairly and that you should have made an attempt to help her.

Al: I resent being called unfair. I think that I'm a very fair supervisor. We have the lowest number of grievances in our division, so I think that such a complaint is totally unjustified. She left of her own will and I will not run after her.

Eva, angrily: Well, I don't think that you have heard the last of that," and she left, determined to take some action on behalf of Rosetta and her own female coworkers.

Discussion Questions

1. Is there a case of sexual harassment in this situation or is it only fun?

2. If you were Eva, what would—and could—you do? What are the options? What is the probability of success of each option?

3. What are Al's responsibilities in this instance? Did he carry them out well? Why or why not?

CASE STUDY

Canadian Pacific and International Bank

Mary Keddy, senior vice president—human resources, had a problem on her hands, literally, in form of a letter from the Canadian Human Rights Commission. In 2000 the Commission had audited the bank and this was the report. While the Commission lauded the bank's employment equity program for women as exemplary, the audit report pointed out that the bank was deficient in its objectives in employing aboriginal peoples and people with disabilities. Ideally, an organization's employee composition reflects the make-up of the community at large, but Mary had to admit that the employee composition of the CPIB did not even come close to the Canadian population mix. While aboriginal peoples made up 10.3 per cent of Canada's citizens, based on the 1996 census, CPIB's employee mix showed only 3.2 per cent representation. People with disabilities made up 6.5 per cent of the population; CPIB's mix, however, had only 0.7 per cent. The report asked specifically for the bank to establish an employment equity program with the objective of reaching 50 per cent of the benchmark consensus data within two years and a 90 per cent compliance after five years.

Mary felt somewhat frustrated. In previous years the bank had been criticized for its apparent "glass ceiling" and Mary had focused her efforts on correcting this problem and had been successful at resolving it, regrettably at the expense of the objectives to increase the representation of aboriginal peoples and people with disabilities. Now this had to be the new priority. She knew that it was quite a challenge, especially with the hiring of aboriginal peoples. In every hiring advertisement the bank encouraged aboriginal peoples and people with disabilities to apply, but very few actually did, particularly aboriginals. She wondered what the bank had to do to change this problem. She had to come up with more effective measures, that was obvious, but with what? The turnover rate was another issue. While people with disabilities had the lowest turnover of all groups, aboriginal peoples had triple the turnover rate of the average CPIB employee. What was the explanation of that, Mary wondered?

Discussion Question

1. You are a human resource consultant. What advice will you give Mary? What measures should the bank take to increase a) the applications of aboriginal peoples and people with disabilities, b) the actual hiring of such candidates, and c) their survival in the organization?

SUGGESTED READINGS

Canadian Human Rights Commission, *Anti-Harassment: Policies for the Workplace; Employers' Guide,* December 1998, 77 pages.

Canadian Human Rights Commission, *Human Rights and the Internet,* Forum (A publication of the CHRC), Summer/Fall 1997, Vol. 7, Issue 1.

Canadian Human Rights Commission, *The Duty to Accommodate: An Interpretive Commentary,* June 17, 1997.

Canadian Human Rights Commission, *Employment Equity, Framework for Compliance Audits Under the Employment Equity Act,* March 1998, Catalogue Number 8R21-51/1998.

Canadian Human Rights Commission, *Human Rights and the Canadian Human Rights Commission,* 1999, Catalogue Number H21-35/1999.

APPENDIX A

A Guide to Screening and Selection in Employment

Subject	Avoid Asking	Preferred	Comment
Name	about name change: whether it was changed by court order, marriage or other reason maiden name		ask after selection if needed to check on previously held jobs or educational credentials
Address	for addresses outside Canada	ask place and duration of current or recent address	
Age	for birth certificates, baptismal records, or about age in general	ask applicants if they are eligible to work under Canadian laws regarding age restrictions	if precise age required for benefits plans or other legitimate purposes, it can be determined after selection
Sex	males or females to fill in different applications about pregnancy, child bearing plans, or child care arrangements	can ask applicant if the attendance requirements can be met	during the interview or after selection, the applicant, for purposes of courtesy, may be asked which of Mr/Mrs/Miss/Ms is preferred
Marital Status	whether applicant is single, married, divorced, engaged, separated, widowed, or living common-law	if transfer or travel is part of the job, the applicant can be asked if he or she can meet these requirements	information on dependents can be determined after selection if necessary

Continued

APPENDIX A—*Continued*

A Guide to Screening and Selection in Employment—*Continued*

Subject	Avoid Asking	Preferred	Comment
Marital Status —*Continued*	whether an applicant's spouse is subject to transfer about spouse's employment	ask whether there are any circumstances that might prevent completion of a minimum service commitment	
Family Status	number of children or dependants about child care arrangements	ask whether the applicant would be able to work the required hours, and, where applicable, overtime	contacts for emergencies and/or details on dependants can be determined after selection
National or Ethnic Origin	about birth-place, nationality of ancestors, spouse, or other relatives whether born in Canada for proof of Citizenship	since those who are entitled to work in Canada must be citizens, permanent residents, or holders of valid work permits, applicants can be asked if they are legally entitled to work in Canada	documentation of eligibility to work (papers, visas, etc.) can be requested after selection

Source: A Guide to Screening and Selection in Employment © Minister of Supply and Services Canada ISBN 0-662-59731-1.

)

Chapter 5

Recruitment

"In this ever-changing, global, technologically demanding business environment, sourcing and retaining talent becomes the competitive battleground. Just as sports teams recruit aggressively for best athletes, business organizations in the future will compete aggressively for the best talent...Successful firms will be those most adept at attracting, developing and retaining individuals with the skills, perspective and experience sufficient to drive a global business.."

Dave Ulrich[1]

CHAPTER OBJECTIVES

After studying this chapter, you should be able to:

- *Explain* the strategic importance of the recruitment function.
- *Discuss* the constraints facing a typical recruiter.
- *Identify* the appropriate recruiting methods for different types of jobs.
- *Design* a job application form.
- *List* key measures for evaluating the effectiveness of the recruitment function.

Finding new employees for the organization is a continuing challenge for most human resource departments. Sometimes the need for new workers is known well in advance because of detailed human resource plans. At other times, the human resource department is faced with urgent requests for replacements that must be filled as quickly as possible. In either case, finding qualified applicants is a key activity:

> Shirley Dodd was a junior mechanical engineer for Ontario Electronics when she quit to work for a competitor. Her resignation created a problem for the head of the mechanical engineering department, Sid Benson. As he expressed it, "She was doing an important job of developing the mechanical tolerances for our new electronic scale. It was all theoretical work, but it was going to save three months worth of product development time. We must have a bright junior engineer to complete her work. I hope someone can be recruited."

Recruitment
The process of finding and attracting capable applicants to apply for employment.

Recruitment is the process of finding and attracting capable individuals to apply for employment. The process begins when new recruits are sought and ends when their applications are submitted. The result is a pool of job seekers from which new employees are selected.

Responsibility for recruitment usually belongs to the human resource department. This responsibility is important because the quality of an organization's human resources depends on the quality of its recruits. Since large organizations recruit almost continuously, their human resource departments use specialists for the activity. These specialists are called *recruiters*.

As Figure 5-1 illustrates, recruitment can be done only after the identification of job openings through human resource planning or requests by managers. As mentioned in Chapter Three, advance knowledge of job openings allows the recruiter to be proactive.

FIGURE 5-1

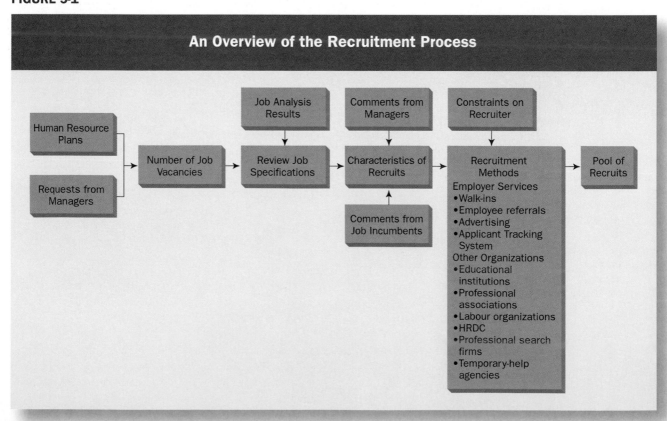

An Overview of the Recruitment Process

After identifying openings, the recruiter learns what each job requires by reviewing job analysis information, particularly the job descriptions and specifications. This information tells the recruiter the characteristics of both the jobs and the future job incumbents. When the job analysis information appears outdated or superficial, recruiters can learn more about a job's requirements from the requesting manager. The job's requirements influence the recruiter's methods of finding satisfactory applicants.

Almost all recruiters face a variety of constraints. Some of these constraints may be imposed by the employer while others may be environmental such as a shortage of highly skilled employees in the local labour market.

Typically, most recruiters use more than one recruitment method to find suitable candidates for vacant job positions. Recruitment methods included school, college and university campus visits, recruitment advertisements, contacts with professional and labour associations, and use of government agencies such as Human Resources Development Canada. Sometimes, to attract high-quality applicants, a recruiter may have to use unconventional procedures, as the following example shows:

> A large insurance firm routinely had to fill approximately 1000 full-time, part-time, and temporary jobs in its head office each year. While many of the jobs were temporary or part-time, they required specific skills on the part of potential job incumbents. To attract high-quality recruits, the human resource director encouraged the recruiters to "sell" the company to graduates of local schools, community colleges, and training agencies for minorities and the physically challenged. In addition, she also joined forces with other local groups to lobby for increased governmental aid to local schools to enhance business education. Further, the human resource director extensively used the company's in-house training program to train marginally qualified applicants and make them competent to handle various responsibilities.

Recruitment is far more than just getting people to apply for jobs, and success in recruitment is not simply measured by the number of applications received. The right type of applicants is far more important than the number of applicants. Many successful organizations have realized the strategic importance of recruitment and made it an integral part of their overall human resource management strategy. The following section discusses the strategic importance of the recruitment function.

STRATEGIC IMPORTANCE OF RECRUITMENT FUNCTION

THE HUMAN resource manager must often make a number of important decisions in the context of recruitment. Each of these decisions has profound implications for the organization and its strategic success. The more important decisions in the context of HR strategic planning are examined below:

Competitive advantage
Creating an environment in which people are open to new ideas, responsive to change, and eager to develop new skills and capabilities.

Gaining Competitive Advantage from Human Capital

Successful firms recognize that today, more than ever before, human capital spells the difference between success and failure (see Spotlight on pages 136–137 for a discussion on the importance of human capital). Despite the existence of state-of-the-art human resource systems and procedures, poorly qualified and motivated recruits often prove extremely costly to firms. In contrast, in today's global knowledge economy, the presence of highly skilled and motivated workers can be a real competitive advantage. Further, if applicants lack the necessary skills and/or aptitudes, considerable additional resources may have to be invested into selection, training and development, employee communication systems, and employee relations practices. A small pool of recruits also poses a major challenge to the selection procedure (which will be discussed in the next chapter).

Reaping the Benefits of Diversity Management

Diversity management
Recognition of differences among employees belonging to heterogeneous groups and creating a work environment where members of diverse groups feel comfortable.

Today, many Canadian firms recognize the vitality and competitive advantage that often accompanies a diverse workforce (see Chapter Fourteen for a discussion on leveraging diversity). Further, as discussed in Chapter Four, if the firm's workforce does not reflect the larger labour market composition, the firm may be asked to pursue an employment equity program to correct imbalances. Progressive employers monitor their environments continuously and adjust their recruitment strategies to deal with the emerging trends in a proactive manner:

> Maple Leaf Electronics, a software manufacturer, has 50 computer programmers on its payroll, of which 45 are men. Recently, the Statistics Canada figures on the local labour market indicated that, in the larger labour market, about 35 per cent of the programmers were women. The company's human resource manager realized that the current 10 per cent utilization rate of women was far below the societal figure and decided to actively seek out women when recruiting.

Hiring from a larger, diverse pool of candidates offers greater choice of job applicants to the firm. A diverse workforce also offers greater flexibility and additional capabilities in some instances. It reflects an organization's commitment to broader social goals and projects a better image of the firm to clients and other constituents.

Focusing on Employee Development

When recruiting (especially for middle- and upper-level jobs), a firm has a choice: it can either develop and promote internal candidates or hire from outside. The strategic choice of internal versus external recruitment has profound implications for an organization. The advantage of hiring skilled employees from outside is that they already possess the necessary skills to begin work immediately and little training may be needed. However, this must be weighed against the fact that current employees, especially in smaller organizations, know a lot more about the organization, its strategy, and its culture. This means that in the latter instance employees do not have to go through the learning process. A conscious effort to train and develop employees to assume higher job positions in the future also acts as a strong motivator for many employees. The amount of money it might take to attract high-calibre employees from outside is usually higher. Figure 5-2 lists some of the advantages and weaknesses of each strategy. Needless to say, the specific strategy chosen by the firm has major implications for recruitment and salary costs, employee morale, and organizational innovation and change.

Investing Resources into Recruitment

The decision on the total recruitment budget affects the quality of recruits and the overall effectiveness of recruitment activity. It is important to note that the costs of recruitment are not simply the hiring costs (such as the costs of advertisement, recruiter's travel, and so on). Often the costs of a bad hire may not be translatable into monetary terms as there is no accurate way of measuring the number of lost customers or resources lost due to delays and inefficient handling of a situation.[2] Further, inappropriate recruits often leave the organization, causing significant additional costs to hire and train replacements. Often such costs are not apparent. However, some organizations such as the National Cash Register Company (NCR)

FIGURE 5-2

Internal versus External Recruiting

Internal Recruiting

Advantages

- Employee is familiar with the organization and its culture.

- Lower recruitment costs.

- Employee is "known" to the firm; this improves the organization's ability to predict the person's success in the new job.

- Improves workforce morale and motivation.

Weaknesses

- Internal rivalry and competition for higher positions; can reduce interpersonal and interdepartmental cooperation.

- No "new blood" is brought into the system, which can prevent creative solutions from emerging.

- Poor morale (leading to possible turnover) of employees who were not promoted.

External Recruiting

Advantages

- Organization is able to acquire skills or knowledge that may not be currently available within.

- Newer ideas and novel ways of solving problems may emerge.

Weaknesses

- Newcomers may not fit in with the organization and into its present culture.

- Newcomers take a longer time to learn about the organization's culture, policies, and practices.

- Usually, hiring from the outside is more expensive.

- Lowered morale and motivation levels of current employees who don't see any career growth possibilities within the firm.

have recognized the importance of the recruitment function and have found innovative ways to recruit qualified persons and reduce recruitment costs:

> NCR, which operates in a highly turbulent industry, maintains its competitive edge by hiring employees at the entry level, retraining them, and promoting from within. Its recruitment program called "Project 6K" uses standardized procedures to recruit the best university students for entry-level positions. Universities and colleges are rated on a four-point scale ("1" being the best). In the number 1 category, students with a GPA of 3.2 or higher will be contacted; at a school rated in the number 4 category, only students with a GPA of 3.4 or better would be considered by the recruiter. The company believes that such a focused recruitment effort helps it to secure high-quality recruits while minimizing the recruitment costs. In the words of the vice-president (Human Resources), "Having top people and productive people working for NCR is an advantage.... We have to seek a competitive advantage in the people we hire."

Key issues in the context of evaluating the effectiveness of the recruitment function and its contribution to organizational success will be discussed in a later section in this chapter. But first, it is important to recognize the several constraints a recruiter faces.

CONSTRAINTS ON RECRUITMENT

A SUCCESSFUL recruiter must be sensitive to the *constraints on* the *recruitment* process. These limits arise from the organization, the recruiter, and the external environment. Although the emphasis may vary from situation to situation, the following list includes the most common constraints:

- organizational policies;

- human resource plans;

- employment equity programs;

- recruiter habits;

- environmental conditions;

- job requirements;

- costs;

- inducements.

Organizational Policies

Organizational policies
Internal policies that affect recruitment, such as "promote-from-within" policies.

Organizational policies can constrain the recruiter. Policies seek to achieve uniformity, economies, public relations benefits, and other objectives unrelated to recruiting. Four policies that have implications for recruitment are highlighted below.

1. Promote-from-Within Policies. As already pointed out, promote-from-within policies are formulated to give present employees the first opportunity for job openings and facilitate their career growth. These policies are widespread. Promote-from-within policies aid employee morale, attract recruits looking for jobs with a future, and help retain present employees. Although these policies reduce the flow of new people and ideas into different levels of the organization, the alternative is to pass over employees in favour of outsiders.

> Sid Benson, head of mechanical engineering at Ontario Electronics, requested that the human resource department find two new junior engineers. Charles Shaw, a recruiter, reviewed the job's requirements and discovered that applicants should have a basic understanding of mechanical engineering concepts. No experience was required. Charles decided to seek applicants from among the graduating class of a small engineer-oriented university in the area. Two technicians in the firm who were studying engineering at night school were disheartened to hear about the external search. They expressed their unhappiness to the HR manager. Charles was instructed to search for internal talents before going outside.

Bypassing current employees can lead to employee dissatisfaction and turnover. On the other hand, promoting a positive organizational culture encourages people to join and stay with a firm.[3] Employees are likely to be loyal to their employer only if they believe the organization values them:

> A recent survey of 2000 Canadian workers indicated that almost three-quarters of all respondents intend to stay with their organization for "several years." However, the same survey found that there is an underlying mood of ambivalence in the workforce. Less than 50 per cent were willing to recommend their organizations as one of the best places to work. Almost 30 per cent would leave for a pay hike of 10 per cent or less.[4]

The "employee goal" discussed in Chapter One also necessitates the human resource manager to recognize and foster employee aspirations at the workplace.

2. Compensation Policies. A common constraint faced by recruiters is pay policies. Organizations with human resource departments usually establish pay ranges for different jobs. Recruiters seldom have the authority to exceed stated pay ranges:

> If Charles Shaw in Ontario Electronics decides to recruit externally, the pay range will influence the job seeker's desire to become a serious applicant. For example, when the market rate for junior engineers is $3500 to $3800 per month, satisfactory applicants will be few if Charles can offer only $3000 to $3200 per month.

3. Employment Status Policies. Some companies have policies restricting the hiring of part-time and temporary employees. Although there is growing interest in hiring these types of workers, several unionized settings have limitations against hiring part-time, temporary, and contract workers, which can cause recruiters to reject all but those seeking full-time work. Likewise, policies against hiring employees who "moonlight" by having second jobs also inhibit recruiters. Prohibitions against holding extra jobs are intended to ensure a rested workforce.

4. International Hiring Policies. Policies in some countries, including Canada, may also require foreign job openings to be staffed with local citizens. The use of foreign nationals, however, does reduce relocation expenses, lessen the likelihood of nationalization, and if top jobs are held by local citizens, minimize charges of economic exploitation. Moreover, unlike relocated employees, foreign nationals are more apt to be involved in the local community and understand local customs and business practices.

Human Resource Plans

Human resource plan
A firm's overall plan to fill existing and future vacancies, including decisions on whether to fill internally or by recruiting from outside.

The *human resource plan* is another factor recruiters consider. Through skills inventories and promotion ladders, the plan outlines which jobs should be filled by recruiting and which ones should be filled internally. The plan helps recruiters because it summarizes future recruiting needs. This foresight can lead to economies in recruiting:

> At Ontario Electronics, Charles Shaw checked the human resource plan before recruiting junior mechanical engineers. The plan indicated a projected need for three junior electrical engineers and one more mechanical engineer (in addition to the two current vacancies) during the next four months. The two internal candidates were hired for two of the junior positions. For the other positions, there were no internal candidates available. Charles decided to recruit electrical engineering candidates at the same time he was looking for the remaining junior mechanical engineer. If advertisements were to be placed in the university newspaper, there would be no additional cost for seeking both types of engineers. Travel costs, advertising costs, and the time devoted to a second recruiting trip would be saved.

Diversity Management Programs

Where diversity management and employment equity programs exist, recruitment must also take these programs into account.

> Ontario Electronics never pursued policies that intentionally discriminated against any group. But over the years, its sources of engineering recruits had been mostly white males who attended the small local university. In the recent past, the firm had initiated a voluntary diversity management program that focused on bringing more women and minorities into its technical and managerial cadres. To fulfil the intent of the diversity management program, Charles decided to recruit engineering technicians at a large metropolitan university, where female recruits were more likely to be found.

As we saw in Chapter Four, employers can't discriminate against people with physical disabilities unless the disability would prevent the person from doing the job after reasonable accommodation by the employer. Proactive employers such as Pizza Hut use innovative recruitment programs to tap the skills of a diverse workforce:

> Realizing that there are thousands of physically challenged individuals who want to work but are without jobs, Pizza Hut actively started to seek entry-level personnel among this group, even among those with mental disabilities.[5]

Recruiter Habits

Recruiter habits
The propensity of a recruiter to rely on methods, systems, or behaviours that led to past recruitment success.

A recruiter's past success can lead to habits. Admittedly, habits can eliminate time-consuming deliberations that reach the same answers. However, *recruiter habits* may also perpetuate past mistakes or obscure more effective alternatives. So although recruiters need positive and negative feedback, they must guard against self-imposed constraints.

> Consider again the recruitment of the junior engineer at Ontario Electronics. Suppose that the engineering department expresses satisfaction with recruits from the nearby university. Such positive feedback encourages recruiters to make a habit of using this source for beginning engineers. Since all these engineers have a similar curriculum, they may also share strengths and weaknesses. As a result, the engineering department may suffer because of the educational uniformity of new recruits.

Environmental Conditions

External conditions strongly influence recruitment. Changes in the labour market and the challenges mentioned in Chapter Two affect recruiting. The unemployment rate, the pace of the economy, spot shortages in specific skills, projections of the labour force by Statistics Canada, labour laws, and the recruiting activities of other employers—all of these affect the recruiter's efforts. Although these factors are considered in human resource planning, the economic environment can change quickly after the plan is finalized. To be sure that the plan's economic assumptions remain valid, recruiters can check three fast-changing measures:

1. **Leading Economic Indicators.** Statistics Canada routinely publishes the direction of the leading indicators. The economic indices suggest the future course of the national economy. If these indices signal a sudden downturn in the economy, recruiting plans may have to be modified. Other agencies such as Human Resources Development Canada, Industry Canada, the World Bank, and International Monetary Fund also publish information that is of great interest to national and international organizations.

2. **Predicted versus Actual Sales.** Since human resource plans are partially based upon the firm's predicted sales, variations between actual and predicted sales may indicate that these plans also are inaccurate. Thus, recruiting efforts may need to be changed accordingly.

3. **Want-Ads Index.** Statistics Canada routinely reports the volume of want ads in major metropolitan newspapers. An upward trend in this index indicates increased competition for engineers and managers who are recruited on a nationwide basis. For clerical and production workers, who are usually recruited on a local basis, the human resource department may want to create its own index to monitor local changes in want ads.

As the economy, sales, and want ads change, recruiters also must adjust their efforts accordingly. Tighter competition for applicants may require more vigorous recruiting. When business conditions decline, an opposite approach is called for—as the following example illustrates:

As a major recreation centre was opening in Quebec, the leading economic indicators dropped. Although the human resource plan called for recruiting 100 workers a week for the first month, the employment manager set a revised target of 75. Lower recruiting and employment levels helped establish a profitable operation even though first-year admissions fell below the projections used in the human resource plan.

Job Requirements

Of course, the requirements of each job are a constraint. Highly specialized workers, for example, are more difficult to find than unskilled ones. Recruiters learn of a job's demands from the requesting manager's comments and job analysis information. Job analysis information is especially useful because it reveals the important characteristics of the job and applicants. Knowledge of a job's requirements allows the recruiter to choose the best way to find recruits, given the constraints under which the recruiter must operate.

"Find the best and most experienced applicant you can" is often a constraint that is imposed on recruiters as though it were a job requirement. At first, this demand seems reasonable: all managers want to have the best and most experienced people working for them. But several potential problems exist with this innocent-sounding request. One problem in seeking out the "best and most experienced" applicant is cost. People with greater experience usually command higher salaries than less experienced people. If a high level of experience is not truly necessary, the recruit may become bored soon after being hired. Moreover, if the human resource department cannot show that a high degree of experience is needed, then experience may be an artificial requirement that discriminates against some applicants. Another point about experience is worth remembering: for some people in some jobs, 10 years of experience is another way of saying one year of experience repeated 10 times. Someone with 10 years of experience may not be any better qualified than an applicant with only one year.

Costs

Costs
Expenses related to attracting recruits.

Like all other members of an organization, recruiters must also operate within budgets. The *cost* of identifying and attracting recruits is an ever-present limitation:

> Manitoba Engineering Company Ltd. found that the average cost of recruiting engineers in the company was more than $3300 per hire. To hire senior engineers and managers, the cost was even higher. To fill a $70 000-a-year position, the company often had to pay $5000 to $6000 to search firms. To monitor and control costs, the human resource manager of the company was asked to assess the effectiveness of the company's recruitment programs and costs of recruitment under alternative recruitment methods.

Careful human resource planning and forethought by recruiters can minimize these expenses. For example, recruiting for several job openings simultaneously may reduce the cost per recruit. Of course, a better solution would be to take actions to reduce employee turnover, thus minimizing the need for recruiting. Proactive human resource management actions go far in achieving this objective.

Inducements

Inducements
Monetary, nonmonetary, or even intangible incentives used by a firm to attract recruits.

The recruiter is very much like a marketer—he or she is selling the company as a potential place of work to all eligible recruits. As with any marketing effort, *inducements* may be necessary to stimulate a potential recruit's interest. The growing global marketplace means that workers are also mobile and attracting them may require unconventional incentives or inducements:

KFC in Japan developed a unique strategy for attracting qualified employees by offering them a trip to Hawaii. This enabled the company to meet local competition and competition from other international organizations for Japanese workers effectively.[6]

Not all inducements are monetary or even tangible.

A department of an Atlantic Canadian university takes all its potential faculty recruits to the scenic areas for a day's car tour in an effort to "sell" the location (and through that the institution). Faced with severe constraints on the compensation package it can offer, the department decided to use its "intangible" assets to assist in its recruitment and selection process.

Flextime, high quality of life, etc., can be potential selling points for a firm; in some instances, certain items (such as flextime) can also be a constraint if all major employers are using them. In such an instance, a firm needs to meet the prevailing standards. Inducements may be a response to overcoming other limitations faced by the recruiter:

The fast-food industry, which employs a large percentage of young workers, typically experiences high employee turnover. To reduce turnover and thereby its recruiting costs, one fast-food chain introduced an educational assistance program. Under the program, an employee could accrue up to $2000 worth of tuition credits over a two-year period. Result? Turnover among participants in the program is a mere 22 per cent compared to a 97 per cent turnover of those who were not part of the plan. It significantly reduced the firm's recruitment efforts and costs.

More recently, several employers have been using non-traditional benefits to attract and retain their employees:

Some of the benefits offered today include fitness centre subsidies, reimbursement of professional membership fees and course fees, on-site vaccination programs, employee mental health insurance, retiree health care benefits, financial planning assistance, and on-site parking.[7]

The key in all cases is to understand the needs and motivations of the target recruits and offer a set of inducements that appeal to them.

RECRUITMENT METHODS

TRADITIONALLY, recruiters and applicants have contacted each other using a few popular methods. In the past, applying directly (by sending a *résumé*) to the employer was the most popular job search method in this country. However, today, applicants tend to use several methods in their search for employment. Research evidence also indicates that persons with higher educational qualifications tend to use more methods to find a job than those with lower educational levels.[8]

Walk-ins and Write-ins

Walk-ins/Write-ins
Job seekers who arrive at or write to the human resource department in search of a job without prior referrals and not in response to a specific ad.

Walk-ins are job seekers who arrive at the human resource department in search of a job. **Write-ins** are those who send a written inquiry. With the emergence of the Internet, it is common for applicants today to record the information at the Web sites of employers. Indeed, today, a significant percentage of human resource managers prefer to receive résumés via email because of the ease of storage and retrieval.[9] Whatever the format used, in most cases, the applicant is asked to complete an application form describing his or her training, experience, interests, and skills. Suitable applications are kept in an active file until an appropriate opening occurs or until the application is too old to be considered valid—usually six months. Larger firms relate information collected like this into their overall human resource information systems.

Using scanners, recruiters can store résumés on databases for fast, easy access using a few key words:

> Organizations such as MCI Telecommunications and Disneyland Resorts use computer scanning to take advantage of the large number of applications they receive (apart from Internet queries). When résumés arrive at either MCI or Disneyland Resorts, clerks scan the résumés into a computer database. Later, recruiters can search the database for candidates with specific qualifications. When the hiring manager needs to fill a position, he or she tells the recruiter the job requirements and applicant profile. The recruiter then searches the database using key words. The computer displays the number of résumés that meet the required criteria. If the number is too large or too small, the recruiter can change the required qualifications (for example, if a search for candidates who have had 10 years of work experience yields only five résumés, the recruiter can change the search criterion to seven years of experience). Once the program finds a manageable number of applicants, the recruiter can view the résumés or résumé summaries on-line and eliminate any that are not appropriate. Then, the recruiter can print selected résumés.[10]

Employee Referrals

Present employees may refer job seekers to the human resource department. *Employee referrals* have several unique advantages. First, employees with hard-to-find job skills may know others who do the same work.

> For example, faced with an acute shortage of software programmers and information technologists in some geographical areas in early 2000, several high-tech firms requested their present employees to recommend professional colleagues and classmates for job openings in the firm. Organizations such as Nortel offered a "finder's fee" to employees who recommended someone who is eventually hired.

Employee referrals
Recommendations by present employees to the recruiter about possible job applicants for a position.

Second, new recruits already know something about the organization from those employees who referred them. Thus, referred applicants may be more strongly attracted to the organization than are walk-ins. Third, employees tend to refer friends whom they identified through personal networking. These persons are likely to have similar work habits and work attitudes. Even if work values are different, these candidates may have a strong desire to work hard so that they do not let down the person who recommended them:

> In the past, at some locations, McDonald's paid a referral bonus to current employees who recommend qualified candidates.[11]

Employee referrals are an excellent and legal recruitment technique. However, recruiters must be careful that this method does not intentionally or unintentionally discriminate. The major problem with this recruiting method is that it tends to maintain the racial, religious, sex, and other features of the employer's workforce. Such results can be viewed as discriminatory.

Advertising

Advertising is another effective method of seeking recruits. Since it can reach a wider audience than employee referrals or unsolicited walk-ins, many recruiters use it as a key part of their efforts.

Want ads
Advertisements in a newspaper, magazine, etc. that solicit job applicants and describe duties, compensation, and reply address.

Want ads describe the job and the benefits, identify the employer, and tell those who are interested how to apply. They are the most familiar form of employment advertising. For highly specialized recruits, ads may be placed in professional journals or out-of-town newspapers located in areas with high concentrations of the desired skills.

> For example, recruiters in finance often advertise in Vancouver, Toronto, Montreal, and Halifax newspapers because these cities are major banking centres.

Want ads have some severe drawbacks. They may lead to thousands of job seekers for one popular job opening. Often the ideal recruits are already employed and not reading want ads. Finally, secretly advertising for a recruit to replace a current employee cannot easily be done with traditional want ads.

These problems are avoided with blind ads. A **blind ad** is a want ad that does not identify the employer. Interested applicants are told to send their résumé to a box number at the post office or to the newspaper. The *résumé* (or curriculum vitae), which is a brief summary of the applicant's background, is then forwarded to the employer. These ads allow the opening to remain confidential, prevent countless telephone inquiries, and avoid the public relations problem of disappointed recruits.

As far as possible, recruitment advertisements should be written from the viewpoint of the applicant and his or her motivations rather than exclusively from the point of view of the company. Since the cost of most classified advertising is determined by the size of the advertisement, short blurbs are the norm. These ads usually describe the job duties, outline minimum job qualifications, and tell interested readers how to apply. Figure 5-3 provides an example of an ad that appeared in *The Globe and Mail* on October 13, 2000.

Blind ads
Want ads that do not identify the employer.

Résumé
A brief listing of an applicant's work experience, education, personal data, and other information relevant for the job.

FIGURE 5-3

Sample Want Ads

Why work for one of the best banks in the country, when you can work for one of the best in the world?

Recipient of BCAMA Marketer of the Year Award

HSBC is the leading international bank in Canada with over 150 offices across the country. We're part of the HSBC Group, one of the world's largest financial services companies with over 6,000 offices in 81 countries and territories. Providing our employees with the best possible work environment has ranked us among the country's top 35 companies to work for (The Globe and Mail, Feb. 2000). If you're looking for a career in a dynamic environment and feel that your qualifications meet the requirements below, we'd like to hear from you.

**SENIOR MANAGER
ADVERTISING AND PROMOTIONS**
(VANCOUVER)

This exciting opportunity will appeal to a strong marketing professional who is ready to develop advertising and communication strategies that support marketing objectives. This position will see you manage, plan, execute and track expenditures of advertising and promotions programs while ensuring that all materials produced support the brand positioning and corporate image. In addition, you will assist in managing marketing communications activities and integrate marketing plans to ensure consistency of global brand image and positioning.

You possess a degree in Marketing and a minimum of 7 years of experience in advertising or product/brand management. You have a history of developing successful marketing strategies and programs, including direct-response marketing, direct mail, advertising research and creative development. As a result, you have a sound knowledge of advertising and promotions practices, and are able to set priorities and build relationships with internal and external clients. Proficiency with PCs and excellent management, organization and presentation skills will reinforce your success.

*If you see this opportunity as an exciting path to a financial career with a promising future and room for growth, send your resume, in confidence to: **Laura Suter, Manager, Human Resources, HSBC Bank Canada, 3rd Floor, 885 West Georgia Street, Vancouver, B.C., V6E 3E9.** HSBC recognizes the value of diversity in our workforce and encourages all qualified applicants to apply. We appreciate all qualified responses and advise that follow-up phone calls are not necessary as all applicants will be acknowledged.*

YOUR WORLD OF FINANCIAL SERVICES   *Issued by HSBC Bank Canada*   **www.hsbc.ca**

Source: Courtesy of HSBC.

CP PHOTO ARCHIVE (Christina Strong)

Frustrated by U.S. software giants nabbing the best and brightest IT (Information Technology) students, CIBC recently consulted new hires and co-op students in creating a recruiting campaign that would be more attractive to future prospective job-seekers.

Traditional recruitment advertisements may be insufficient, particularly when recruiting people with hard-to-find skills or when labour markets are tight. Want ads must contain not only information about the job but also information presented in a way that effectively portrays a message about the job, the work environments, management style, organizational climate, and future growth potential. This can't be done if the ad contains information that explains only what responsibilities the job includes, who can be qualified, where it is located, and how and when to apply. Figure 5-4 lists some of the information contained in good want ads along with other desirable attributes.

Advertisements for recruits through other media—billboards, television, and radio, for example— are seldom used because the results rarely justify the expense. However, these approaches may be useful when unemployment is low and the target recruits are not likely reading want ads.

Because most readers will be travelling in an automobile, the amount of information that can be conveyed on a billboard is limited. Another limitation of this approach is that it generally requires considerable lead time to prepare a sign. In deciding whether to use a billboard, the recruiter should consider the type of job to be advertised. If it is a job for which the firm is continuously recruiting, it may be worthwhile to have a billboard in visible locations.[12]

Transit advertising involves placing posters in buses, commuter trains, and subway stations. By and large these are only used by employers who have difficulty filling positions using traditional methods.

In the past, one major U.S. airline placed ads along mass transit routes in immigrant neighbourhoods and significantly enhanced its recruitment success rate.[13]

FIGURE 5-4

Attributes of Good Want Ad

Good want-ads, in general, seem to have several common characteristics such as:

1. They address the audience and use a language that the applicant finds comfortable.

2. They use short sentences and familiar words that are action oriented.

3. They contain all relevant information about the job and the firm. Some major items here are:

   - job title
   - working conditions
   - a clear description of the job
   - training offered
   - organizational and work culture
   - major skills, competencies and educational requirements
   - career and personal development possibilities
   - location of the job
   - salary, benefits, and other incentives
   - travel and other requirements
   - company selling points

4. They sequence the content logically and in an engaging manner.

5. They respect provisions of human rights and other laws and the dignity of the readers.

6. They do not use sexist, racist, or otherwise unacceptable language. Even the use of adjectives that are normally associated with males or whites may be unacceptable to other groups (e.g., use of adjectives such as "assertive," "dominant," "aggressive," etc., usually connote male sex roles; while terms such as "compassionate," "gentle," and "sympathetic" signify female sex roles[14]).

7. They stand out from other advertisements with good copy lay-out, visual balance, visual tension, and colour contrast.

8. Their size and presentation should be cost effective compared to other recruitment methods and considering size and location of target audience

9. They should make a favorable projection of corporate image and activities without boasting or making unsupported claims

Transit job advertising is relatively inexpensive. If it is placed in a specific geographic location (such as a particular bus stop), it allows an organization to target its advertising to a specific demographic or even ethnic group. If placed in a bus or train, a job advertisement can be seen by thousands of persons each week (or even day). In order to make it easy to respond, the organization should attach coupons that can be torn off, completed, and mailed.

Whatever media are used, the layout, design, and copy of an advertisement should reflect the image and character of the company and departments that are being represented. This includes dimensions such as the size of the organization, the degree of decentralization seen in the firm, the degree of dynamism and progressive policies typical of the unit, and so on. This, in turn, means that an ad should emphasize the nature of the organization and the benefits of the package that it offers to attract the applications of qualified people, but at the same time be specific enough to screen out the wrong persons.

Human Resources Development Canada

Human Resources Development Canada (HRDC), employing more than 20 000 people and with hundreds of service outlets, offers a variety of programs and services for both employers and prospective employees. HRDC has three fundamental and complementary objectives:

1. To help Canadians prepare for, find, and keep work;

2. To assist workers in this country in their efforts to provide financial security for themselves and their families; and

3. To promote a fair, safe, healthy, stable, cooperative, and productive work environment for Canadians.

HRDC attempts to achieve these objectives through programs and activities such as a job bank, electronic labour exchange, employment insurance, human resource investment, income security, and labour program. HRDC's activities related to the recruiting function are discussed below. The other functions will be elaborated in later chapters (e.g., Chapters Fifteen and Sixteen). (At the time this text is going to print, there is a proposal to reorganize HRDC to divest the organization of some of its activities related mainly to the last two objectives listed above. Even when this happens, it is unlikely that it will significantly reduce HRDC's contributions in the area of employee recruiting).

www.hrdc-drhc.gc.ca
http://jb-ge.hrdc.drhc.gc.ca/
owa-job/owa/provRes?cLang=E
www.ele-spe.org/

The National Job Bank. The Job Bank provides a comprehensive database of thousands of jobs and work opportunities available across Canada.

When an employer has a job opening, the human resource department voluntarily notifies HRDC of the job and its requirements. Typically, the job opening information is then posted at HRDC's regional office(s) and Human Resource Centres. Human Resource Centres provide information on employment programs, including special services for youths and persons with disabilities. Here prospective employees can scan the job openings and discuss any vacancy with one of the counsellors available. When an applicant expresses interest in some particular job, counsellors interview that person. The potential applicant can also look for jobs posted in the last 48 hours. There is also a separate section for jobs for students. In early 2000, over 40 000 employers used the HRDC Internet site to advertise full-time, part-time, and summer job opportunities.[15]

Electronic Labour Exchange. The Electronic Labour Exchange (ELE) is a computer-based recruitment tool that can match employer profiles with job seeker profiles.

Thousands of people lined up to apply for a job in response to a General Motors advertisement. People even slept outside in freezing temperatures to be among the first in line.

CP PHOTO ARCHIVE (Frank Gunn)

It relies on standard occupation checklists, with categories such as education, experience, and skills. The ELE uses information entered in the profile to automatically match job seekers to employers who are looking for candidates with the suitable skills for the job.

Canada WorkInfoNet. This bilingual directory provides fast and efficient links to information on jobs and recruiting, self-employment, workplace issues and supports, employment trends, and various occupations and careers. It covers everything from résumé writing to interview techniques and from potential employment opportunities to starting one's own business.

www.workinfonet.ca

www.pch.gc.ca/YCW-JCT

www.jobs.gc.ca

Federal Government Employment Opportunities. Job opportunities in all major government departments and services are listed in the HRDC offices and Web site. Included here are: Public Service Commission of Canada, Department of Foreign Affairs and International Trade, Canadian Space Agency Recruitment, Correctional Services of Canada recruitment, and Health Canada.

Young Canada Works. This provides young persons the opportunity to work at heritage institutions, national parks, and national historic sites as well as in other locations in Canada and abroad.

HRDC provides a virtually no-cost and effective recruitment source for employers. Many of the job vacancies posted in the HRDC are still for white-collar, blue-collar, or technical employees rather than managerial and professional persons. In the future, HRDC's role in recruiting other types of employees is likely to increase significantly.

Private Employment Agencies

Private employment agencies—which now exist in every major metropolitan area—arose to help employers find capable applicants. Placement firms take an employer's request for recruits and then solicit job seekers, usually through advertising or from walk-ins. Candidates are matched with employer requests and then told to report to the employer's human resource department. The matching process conducted by private agencies varies widely.

Some placement services carefully screen applicants for their client. Others simply provide a stream of applicants and let the client's human resource department do most of the screening. Some of the private employment firms match their strategies to the emerging environmental trends, as the following illustration shows:

> A metropolitan placement agency marketed its services on the basis of skill, dedication, and ready availability of its temporary workers. When faced with a shortage of school students who worked part-time, the agency began looking at other population segments. One group met all the three requirements of the agency—the recently retired and about-to-retire persons were skilled, dedicated, and prepared to accept temporary assignments. In a short while, the firm began to rely solely on this group for all its temporary staff needs.

Use of a private employment agency may be necessary when the employer needs only a few persons and on a temporary or irregular basis. Also, when the employer has a critical need to fill a position quickly, this method can be very useful. In times of tight labour markets, it may be necessary to attract individuals who are already employed on a part-time basis. Private employment agencies can achieve this more cost-effectively, especially if the employer has limited experience in the local labour market.

In many provinces it is either illegal for private employment agencies to charge applicants a fee for placement, or the fees charged are regulated. Most fees are paid by the agencies' clients, that is, the prospective employers. The fees commonly equal either 10 per cent of the first year's salary or one month's wages, but the amount may vary with the volume of business provided by the client and the type of employee sought.

Professional Search Firms

Professional search firms
Agencies who, for a fee, recruit specialized personnel by telephone and, at times, recruit from a competitor.

Professional search firms are much more specialized than placement agencies. Search firms usually recruit only specific types of human resources for a fee paid by the employer. For example, some search firms specialize in executive talent, while others use their expertise to find technical and scientific personnel. Perhaps the most significant difference between search firms and placement agencies is their approach. Placement agencies hope to attract applicants through advertising, but search firms actively seek out recruits from among the employees of other companies. Although they may advertise, the telephone is their primary tool for locating and attracting prospective recruits:

> B.C. Radar Company needed a quality control manager for its assembly line. After several weeks of unsuccessful recruiting efforts, the human resource manager hired a search firm. The search firm reviewed the in-house phone directories of competing firms and telephoned the assistant quality control manager at one of B.C. Radar's competitors. The phone call was used to encourage this assistant manager to apply for the position at B.C. Radar.

This brief example illustrates several important points. First, search firms have an in-depth experience that most human resource departments lack. Second, search firms are often willing to undertake actions that an employer would not do, such as calling a competitor. Third, it can be seen that some human resource professionals would consider search firms unethical because these firms engage in "stealing" or "raiding" among their clients' competitors. This last example shows why search firms are sometimes called "headhunters."[16]

www.recruitersonline.com

In the past few years, the number of executive recruiting firms in Canada has been growing rapidly. While most of them are located in large metropolitan cities such as Toronto, Montreal, or Vancouver, an increasing number of these firms are making an appearance in smaller cities and towns.

Many human resource departments view executive search firms as a regular part of their operations. As one writer wrote, "The enlightened human resource executive...views executive search as corporate management does its accounting firm, law firm or other consultants."[17] Retainer search firms—those that work on fee-paid assignments—are more popular among HR managers than contingency search firms—those that receive a fee only if an employer hires the candidate suggested by the search firm. The latter are considered to be more aggressive and, given their reward structure, at times tempted to fill a position at any cost—even if the fit between the job and applicant is less than optimal.[18]

What is the reason for the growing popularity of executive search firms? According to one writer, the use of a search firm leads to more objectivity, less cost per recruit, and an overall higher success rate in recruiting the right quality personnel.[19]

> In one survey of 107 Canadian organizations, over 75 per cent of the responding human resource departments indicated that executive search firms could reach applicants who were unreachable through other means. However, the same survey found that a majority of respondents felt search firms were more appropriate for larger firms. Over 60 per cent also indicated that their own recruiters and departments had a better understanding of the firm's employment needs than search firms.[20]

Many physically challenged people are very able and quite willing to work. Employers cannot discriminate against the physically challenged unless the disability would prevent the person from doing the job after reasonable accommodation by the employer.

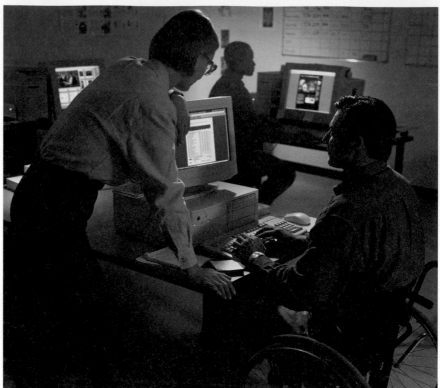

Digital Imagery © 2001 Photo Disc Inc. Photo by Keith Brofsky

When choosing a search firm, care must be taken to test the "fit" between the firm and the client organization. Some of the search firms, especially the smaller ones, are often highly specialized and may not be able to meet the general needs of a client. Checking the recruiting record of the firm and its reputation is, consequently, very important. The larger firms can be quite expensive, often charging 30 per cent of the candidate's gross starting salary as fees (not inclusive of other expenses).[21] Some of the factors that should be considered in evaluating a recruiting firm include: size of the firm, staff qualifications, ability to meet time requirements, financial soundness of the firm, proven validity of the testing/selection instruments and practices, and provision of measurable results from previous contracts (track record and acceptable references).

Educational Institutions

Educational institutions
High schools, technical schools, community colleges, and universities where applicants for job positions are sought.

For entry-level openings, *educational institutions* are another common source of recruits. Counsellors and teachers often provide recruiters with leads to desirable candidates in high schools. Many universities, community colleges, and technical schools offer their current students and alumni placement assistance. This assistance helps employers and graduates to meet and discuss employment opportunities and the applicant's interest.

Past research studies indicate that students desire campus recruiters to be well informed, honest, and skilled. The title and age of the recruiter may also be important factors in creating a favourable impression on recruits.[22] Some other characteristics of successful campus recruiters are shown in Figure 5-5. However, not many recruiters are successful in getting the best talents during their campus visits. Wasted staff time to interview unqualified applicants, difficulties with assessing applicants who possess no relevant experience, applicants who provides standardized answers to interview questions, can all lead to selection of wrong candidates. Focus on the actual job duties and performance requirements can significantly overcome these problems.[23]

Increasingly, several organizations find that summer internships significantly facilitate college and university recruitment efforts. These summer internships are

FIGURE 5-5

A Profile of the Ideal Recruiter

A good campus recruiter:

- hires for specific positions rather than looking for future recruits without any clear idea about job vacancies.

- possesses considerable knowledge about the firm and the job position.

- discusses strengths and limitations of the firms knowledgeably.

- never exaggerates or oversells the employers.

- studies the student's résumé carefully before the interview and asks specific questions.

- validly assesses the student's awareness of and interest in the job and the company.

- asks thought-provoking questions to measure student's knowledge on relevant job matters.

- expresses interest in the student as an individual.

- is upbeat about the company and own role in the firm.

- displays good interpersonal skills and appears polite and sincere.

- follows up promptly with feedback and evaluation.

- is professional and ethical in demeanour.

Source: Based partially on and expanded from: John E. Steele, "A Profile of the Ideal Recruit," *Personnel Journal*, February 1997, pp. 58-59.

more popular in large companies such as Procter & Gamble and Aetna Life Insurance; however, even smaller organizations find that hiring students to complete summer projects helps them to identify qualified, motivated, and informed recruits. Students can be evaluated on the basis of their success in completing their special projects in summer months. These interns are also exposed to the organization so that they have a clear idea of what to expect from the firm when they later join as full-time employees. Such "informed" recruits are less likely to leave the firm soon after they are hired.

In recent years, cooperative education has become increasingly popular in Canada. Under the "co-op education" program, students alternate study and work terms. Their work terms expose them to the realities of the work world. This also provides an excellent opportunity for the employer to assess the potential employee's ability and attitudes without incurring any significant costs.[24] Universities that provide business administration programs aimed at senior- and middle-level managers (such as Executive MBA programs) are also a valuable source for recruiting managers.

www.cecs.uwaterloo.ca
www.coop.uvic.ca
www.sfu.ca/coop/

Professional Associations

Recruiters find that professional associations also can be a source of job seekers. Many associations conduct placement activities to help new and experienced professionals get jobs; some have publications that accept classified advertisements. Professionals who belong to the appropriate associations are considered more likely to remain informed of the latest developments in their field, and so this channel of recruitment may lead to higher-quality applicants. Another advantage of this source of applicants is that it helps recruiters zero in on specific specialties, particularly in hard-to-fill technical areas.

www.ama.org

www.cica.ca

www.cga-canada.org

www.cmc-consult.org

www.campusworklink.com

www.youth.gc.ca

Labour Organizations

When recruiters want people with trade skills, local labour organizations have rosters of those people who are looking for employment. The local union of plumbers, for example, keeps a list of plumbers who are seeking jobs. In the construction industry, many contractors often hire on a per-project basis. A union hiring hall is a convenient channel for attracting large numbers of pretrained recruits for new projects.

Armed Forces

Trained personnel leave the armed forces every day. Some veterans, such as those who have been trained as mechanics, welders, or pilots, have hard-to-find skills. Human resource departments that need skills similar to those found in the military often find nearby military installations a valuable source of recruits.

> Many of the technicians who maintain commercial jet airliners were first trained in the military, for example.

Government of Canada Youth Programs

For firms that desire to hire young persons, several sources of information currently exist. *Campus Worklink* is a comprehensive career database and employment source especially designed for university and college students, recent graduates, and the employers seeking to hire them. *The Youth Resource Network of Canada* lists work opportunities and opportunities in starting a business. For work opportunities in remote and isolated communities in Northern Canada, *Junior Canadian Rangers* provides valuable information.

Temporary-Help Agencies

Temporary-help agencies
Agencies that provide supplemental workers for temporary vacancies caused by employee leave, sickness, etc.

Most large cities have ***temporary-help agencies*** that can respond quickly to an employer's need for help. These agencies do not provide recruits. Instead, they are a source of supplemental workers. The temporary help actually work for the agency and are "on loan" to the requesting employer. For temporary jobs—during vacations, peak seasons, illnesses, and so on—these agencies can be a better alternative than recruiting new workers for short periods of employment. Besides handling the recruiting and bookkeeping tasks caused by new employees, these agencies can often provide clerical and secretarial talent on short notice—sometimes less than a day. And when the temporary shortage is over, there is no need to lay off surplus workers, because "temporaries" work for the agency, not the company.[25] Occasionally, temporary help are recruited to become permanent employees.

Departing Employees

Buy-back
A method of convincing an employee who is about to resign to stay in the employ of the organization, typically by offering increased wage or salary.

An often overlooked source of recruits is among departing employees. These workers might gladly stay if they could rearrange their schedules or change the number of hours worked. Family responsibilities, health conditions, or other circumstances may lead a worker to quit when a transfer to a part-time job could retain valuable skills and training. Even if part-time work is not a solution, a temporary leave of absence may satisfy the employee and some future recruiting need of the employer.

Buy-backs are a channel worthy of mention, although human resource specialists and workers tend to avoid them. A ***buy-back*** occurs when an employee resigns to take another job and the original employer outbids the new job offer. The following dialogue provides an example:

Employee: I quit. I'm going to work as a computer programmer for International Plastics.

Manager: You're too valuable for us just to let you walk out the door. How much is International offering?

Employee: They're offering me $5000 a year more!

Manager: Stay and I'll make it $5500.

Employee: No. I'm going.

Manager: How about $6000?

Employee: Well, okay.

Even when the authority to enter into a bidding war exists, the manager may discover that other workers expect similar raises. Employees may reject a buy-back attempt because of the ethical issue raised by not reporting to a job that has already been accepted. Besides, what is to prevent the manager from using a blind ad to find a replacement?

Open House

A relatively new technique of recruiting involves holding an open house. People in the adjacent community are invited to see the company facilities, have refreshments, and maybe view a film about the company. This method has proved successful for recruiting clerical workers when people with office skills are in tight supply.

Job Fairs

Attending job fairs can pay rich dividends to recruiters who are looking for specialized talents or a number of personnel. Over years, budgetary constraints and the emergence of Internet recruitment have resulted in a decline in the popularity of job fairs. However, even today, there are examples of striking successes:

> The Job Fair organized by the University of Waterloo, Wilfrid Laurier University, Conestoga College, and University of Guelph has tripled in size of attendees since 1994. In 1999, the event attracted some 200 companies and 2500 to 3000 students, making it the largest job fair in Canada. Over 10 000 visitors were estimated to have attended the event.[26]

The Internet

The Internet is increasingly becoming one of the most important tools to match jobs with candidates—whether one is a recruiting firm or a job applicant. There are four major reasons for this. First, the Internet is accessible all the time—without the limitations of a public library, an employment office, or even a newspaper ad. This means that a person can access the Internet 24 hours a day, seven days a week, without even leaving the house. Second, it broadens the recruitment area significantly. The Internet offers a cost-effective distribution of information to over 100 countries and millions of users. Third, by specifying the exact qualifications and job skills needed, the time needed to weed out unsuitable job candidates is minimized. Indeed, the applicants themselves may, on the basis of information supplied, decide not to apply for unsuitable positions. This also adds to the recruiting process the important attribute of timeliness. Fourth, it is relatively inexpensive. Compared to the commissions to be paid to an executive search firm or the travel expenses of a campus recruiter, the cost of putting an ad on the Internet is minimal, making it an attractive alternative to many organizations.

> One company reported savings of $70 000 a day in paper costs related to recruiting apart from $73 000 in annual savings in employee forms.[27]

Internet recruiting
Job recruitment using the Internet.

No wonder then that there has been great interest in *Internet recruiting* in recent months (see "Spotlight on HRM" on page 212). The emergence of new softwares permit the recruiter to store, classify, and share resumes and other information in digital format, thus increasing the speed and overall value of information.[28] Despite this, much of the recruiting on the Internet (or "*the Net*" as it is popularly referred to) to date has focused on technical and information technology-related jobs and has been used by firms operating in that industry or other large organizations. A large majority of Canadians—in some regions as high as 95 per cent—still do not use the Net,[29] thus limiting its recruitment effectiveness currently. However, this is expected to change considerably in the near future as job seekers and employers recognize the power of this medium.

Non-traditional Recruitment Methods

Several other approaches, not very popular in the past, are becoming increasingly popular. These are briefly discussed below:

Applicant Tracking Systems. Advances in computer technology and information transmission have made it possible to use newer methods in recruiting employees. Several employers and placement agencies now rely on videos and disks to convey information about job positions to potential recruits. In high-tech professions, electronic mail is also sometimes used to reach recruits. Some organizations have installed *applicant tracking systems* (ATS) to identify ideal candidates for each vacant job position. Under this system, the recruiter keeps a large file (or is electronically connected to other master files) of potential candidates, which not only broadens the recruitment pool but also enables a good match between the job requirements and applicant skills.[30]

Applicant tracking systems
Databases of potential candidates that enable a good match between job requirements and applicant characteristics and also enlarge recruitment pool.

> When a manager submits a requisition for an opening, the recruiter simply matches the key requirements of the job with applicant characteristics. Thus, job requirements such as "needs significant selling experience" and "should know French" can immediately be matched with applicant characteristics. Such computerized systems not only lead to a better match between jobs and candidates, but also significantly reduce recruitment time and costs.[31]

Contingent/Contract/Leased Workers. A very large segment of our labour market is composed of *contract workers*. They include the self-employed, temporary or leased employees (those who work for an agency that has trained them and supplies these employees on a need basis), and independent contractors.[32] *Contingent workers* are useful when the work is of limited duration, so the firm can avoid fixed salary commitments. *Employee leasing* is a term used to reflect the hiring of employees for longer periods of time. One reason for leasing's popularity is cost. The employer pays a flat fee for the employees (and is not responsible for benefits). Contract and self-employed workers, often, are compensated on the basis of task completion and hence need less supervision. Often, they also require lower training costs. making this an attractive proposition.

Contingent/contract workers
Freelancers (self-employed, temporary, or leased employees) who are not part of regular work force and are paid on a project completion basis.

> More organizations today employ contract workers now than ever before. In many organizations, the proportion of the staff who were on contract is seven to ten per cent. Information systems personnel were most likely to be on contract. Administration, finance, engineering, legal, and technical positions also use contract staff to an extent.[33]

It should be noted that contract and leased employees may not always be committed to the goals and philosophy of the organization. Because the contingent employees are not part of an organization's regular workforce, they do not benefit from the statutory protections offered by various provincial employment laws. The contracting firm is also not responsible for remitting Canada Pension Plan premiums or withholding income tax. However, determining whether an individual is an independent contractor or an employee is not as easy as it appears. Courts and arbitrators have been increasingly monitoring contractual agreements to ensure that the employer is not using the independent contractor relationship to avoid its statutory and common law obligations.[34] Accordingly it is important for the contracting parties to know where they stand in order to understand their rights and obligations. (For a more detailed discussion of this issue, see Chapter Twelve.)

Alumni Associations. Another source for experienced employees are *alumni associations* of schools, colleges, and institutes.[35] These are particularly useful for hiring technical and managerial staff.

Direct Mail Solicitations. Drawing upon marketing strategies, some firms have attempted *direct mail recruiting* with some success. This enables an organization to target a specific segment of the population or a geographical area (using postal codes). Some firms use door hangers, bargain shopper price lists, welcome wagons, and point-of-sale messages as their recruiting media as well.[36]

Recruitment abroad. More recently, several Canadian employers are looking abroad for securing skilled, hard-to-find employees.

> Many high-tech and software companies today look at India as a major source of highly skilled programmers. Some of the software manufacturers have gone as far as locating their operations in Indian cities such as Bangalore and Hyderabad while others have formed partnerships with Indian firms that periodically send their own staff to North America on a contract basis.

Foreign workers, especially from developing countries, may be less expensive in some instances (at least initially). Relocation expenses may have to be paid in some instances, which can significantly add to the total cost. Firms hiring from abroad will need to train new recruits to adapt to local and organizational culture. The process of getting employment visas may also be time-consuming in some instances.

Alumni associations
Associations of alumni of schools, colleges, or other training institutions.

Direct mail recruiting
Recruitment targeted at specified poulation segments or regions using a variety of means.

JOB APPLICATION FORMS

THE JOB application form collects information about recruits in a uniform manner and hence is an important part of all recruitment efforts. Even when recruits volunteer detailed information about themselves, applications are often required so that the information gathered is comparable. Each human resource department generally designs its own form. Nevertheless, certain common features exist. Figure 5-6 provides a typical example of an application form and its major divisions.

Computer software writers work on a program in their Bangalore, India, office. Many high-tech companies are taking advantage of India's low labour costs and highly skilled programmers.

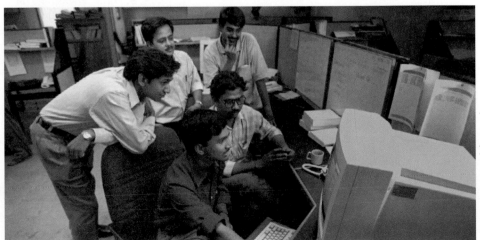

CP PHOTO ARCHIVE (John Moore)

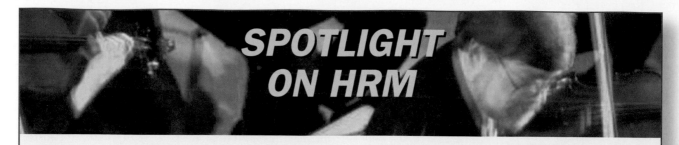

SPOTLIGHT ON HRM

RECRUITING ON THE NET

Recruiting on the Internet is one of the hottest topics in human resource management currently; however, its effectiveness is dependent on the care and planning behind the strategy. Recruiting is often among the first functions developed on a corporate Web page.[37] This means that the message and tone you convey on the Web page can affect not only your recruitment effectiveness but also the general public image of the company. Some of the suggestions for improving a firm's recruitment success on the Internet are:

1. **Publish your Web address on everything** — your traditional want ads in the newspapers, marketing information, public relations notices, and all other corporate communication devices.

2. **Continue to look for unconventional recruitment outlets** (e.g., a minority language newspaper), but publish your Web site address in your message.[38]

3. **When publishing material for college, university, or trade school markets, always include your Internet address.** This group, of all population segments, accesses the Internet most often. Research evidence indicates that Internet surfers are younger, well educated, technologically oriented, and male.

4. **Make sure that you register your site with all popular search engines** such as Yahoo, AltaVista, Excite, and HotBot.

5. **Use specialized recruitment Web sites.** Today, there is a plethora of recruitment sites specializing in different kinds of personnel. By advertising in specialized Web sites, you are likely to target specific markets. Examples include:

   For teachers: www.recruitingteachers.org

   For fire and police personnel: www.ifpra.com

   For engineers: www.engineeringjobs.org

   For information technology personnel: www.jobserve.com

6. **Target the Web sites in the province or territory where the job is.** HRDC can give you a breakdown of applicants in each province for a specific job.

There are also specialized Web sites for each province. (e.g., for Government of B.C. recruitment: http://rao.gov.bc.ca)

7. **When national recruitment efforts fail, you might want to consider attracting foreign nationals.** Once again, there are many choices in terms of recruitment Web sites. Samples:

   For New Zealand: www.iconrec.co.nz

   For UK: www.topjobs.co.uk

   For E-countries: www.ecountries.com

8. **Post the recruitment ad in Internet newsgroups.** They are free (at least most of them are). Since the newsgroups continuously update materials, you will need to periodically insert your ad. This also gives you an opportunity to revise your ad. Some of the popular newsgroups are "can.jobs", "ont.jobs", and "tor.jobs". Some of the other interesting Web sites (most of them originating in the U.S).[39] are:

   Headhunter.net
      www.headhunter.net
   Career Magazine
      www.careermag.com
   JobTrak
      www.jobtrak.com
      www.occ.com

   Irrespective of where the ad is listed, it should contain all key words likely to be used by a firm's recruits when accessing the information using search engines.[40]

9. **Take advantage of special "net" advertisement offers** given by popular newspapers and magazines since their Web sites are well surfed.

10. **List your ad with all major Web-based job banks** (including HRDC's). Use the various career sites to send applicants to you.[41] Included here are:

    www.workopolis.com
    www.monsterboard.com
    www.recruitersonline.com
    www.brassring.ca

FIGURE 5-6

A Typical Application Form

Kanata Electronics, Inc.
"An Equal-Opportunity Employer"
Application for Employment

Personal Data

1. Name_____

2. Address _____ 3. Phone Number _____

Employment Status

4. Type of employment sought _____ Full-time _____ Part-time
   _____ Permanent _____ Temporary

5. Job or position sought _____

6. Date of availability, if hired _____

7. Are you willing to accept other employment if the position you seek is unavailable?
   _____ Yes _____ No

8. Approximate wages/salary desired $ _____ per month

Education and Skills

9. Circle the highest grade or years completed.

   9 10 11 12 13   1 2 3 4   1 2 3 4
   High School   University   Graduate School

10. Please provide the following information about your education.

(Include only vocational schools and colleges.)

a. School name _____ Degree(s) or diploma _____

School address _____

Date of admission_____ Date of completion _____

b. School name _____ Degree(s) or diploma _____

School address _____

Date of admission_____ Date of completion _____

11. Please describe your work skills. (Include machines, tools, equipment, and other abilities you possess.)

Work History

Beginning with your most recent or current employer, please provide the following information about each employer. (If additional space is needed, please use an additional sheet.)

12. a. Employer _____ Dates of employment _____

Employer's address_____

Job title _____ Supervisor's name _____

Job duties _____

Starting pay_____ Ending pay _____

b. Employer _____ Dates of employment _____

Employer's address_____

Job title _____ Supervisor's name _____

Job duties _____

Starting pay_____ Ending pay _____

FIGURE 5-6 (CONTINUED)

Military Background

If you were ever a member of the Canadian Armed Forces, please complete the following:

13. Branch of service_____ Rank at discharge _____

Dates of service _____ to _____

Responsibilities _____

Type of discharge_____

Memberships, Awards, and Hobbies

14. What are your hobbies? _____

15. List civic/professional/social organizations to which you have belonged. _____

_____

16. List any awards you have received. _____

References

In the space provided, list three references who are not members of your family.

17. a. Name _____ Address _____

b. Name _____ Address _____

c. Name _____ Address _____

18. Please feel free to add any other information you think should be considered in evaluating your application.

By my signature on this application, I:

a. Authorize the verification of the above information and any other necessary inquiries that may be needed to determine my suitability for employment.

b. Affirm that the above information is true to the best of my knowledge.

Applicant's Signature _____ Date _____

Name and Address

Most application forms begin with a request for personal data. Name, address, and telephone number are nearly universal. But requests for some personal data such as place of birth, marital status, number of dependants, sex, race, religion, or national origin may lead to charges of discrimination. Since it is illegal to discriminate against applicants, an unsuccessful applicant may conclude that rejection was motivated by discrimination when discriminatory questions are asked. The human resource department must be able to show that these questions are job-related if it asks them.

Applications may solicit information about health, height, weight, disabilities that relate to the job, major illnesses, and claims for injuries. Here again, there may be legal problems. Discriminating against people with disabilities is prohibited under the Canadian Human Rights Act. The burden of proof that such questions are job-related falls on the employer.

Employment Status

Some questions on the application form concern the applicant's employment objective and availability. Included here are questions about the position sought, willingness to accept other positions, date available for work, salary or wages desired, and acceptability of part-time and full-time work schedules. This information helps a recruiter match the applicant's objective and the organization's needs. Broad or uncertain responses can prevent the application from being considered. An example follows:

> **Inexperienced Recruiter**: Under "position sought," this applicant put "any available job." Also, under "wages desired" the applicant wrote "minimum wage or better." What should I do with this application?

> **Employment Manager**: You are not a career counsellor. You are a recruiter. Put that application in the inactive file and forget about it.

Education and Skills

The education and skills section of the application form is designed to uncover the job seeker's abilities. An understanding of the applicant's personality may be gained from this section too. Traditionally, education has been a major criterion in evaluating job seekers. Educational attainment does imply certain abilities and is therefore a common request on virtually all applications. Questions about specific skills are also used to judge prospective employees. More than any other part of the application form, the skills section reveals the suitability of a candidate for a particular job.

Work History

Job seekers must frequently list their past jobs. From this information, a recruiter can tell whether the applicant is one who hops from job to job or is likely to be a long-service employee. A quick review of the stated job title, duties, responsibilities, and ending pay also shows whether the candidate is a potentially capable applicant. If this information does not coincide with what an experienced recruiter expects to see, the candidate may have exaggerated job title, duties, responsibilities, or pay.

Military Background

Some applications request information on military experience. Questions usually include date of discharge, area of service, rank at discharge, and type of discharge. Such information clarifies the applicant's background and ability to function in a structured environment.

Memberships, Awards, and Hobbies

Recruits are more than potential workers. They are also representatives of the employer in the community. For managerial and professional positions, off-the-job activities may make one candidate preferable over another. Memberships in civic, social, and professional organizations indicate the recruit's concern about community and career. Awards show recognition for noteworthy achievements. Hobbies may reinforce important job skills and indicate outlets for stress and frustrations, or opportunities for further service to the company:

> When handed a pile of completed applications for manager of the car- and truck-leasing department, Frank Simmons (the human resource manager for a Toronto Ford dealership) sorted the completed applications into two piles. When asked what criteria were being used to sort the applications, he said, "I'm looking for golfers. Many of our largest car and truck accounts are sold on Saturday afternoons at the golf course."

References

Besides the traditional references from friends or previous employers, applications may ask for other "reference-like" information. Questions may explore the job seeker's criminal record, credit history, friends and relatives who work for the employer, or previous employment with the organization. Criminal record, credit history, and friends or relatives who work for the company may be important considerations if the job involves sensitive information, cash, or other valuables. Job-relatedness must be substantiated if these criteria disproportionately discriminate against some protected group. Previous employment with the organization means there are records of the applicant's performance.

Signature Line

Candidates are usually required to sign and date their applications. Adjacent to the signature line, a blanket authorization commonly appears. This authorization allows the employer to check references, verify medical, criminal, or financial records, and undertake any other necessary investigations. Another common provision of the signature line is a statement that the applicant affirms the information in the application to be true and accurate as far as is known. Although many people give this clause little thought, falsification of an application form is grounds for discharge in most organizations:

> Jim LaVera lied about his age to get into the police officers' training program. As he neared retirement age, Jim was notified that he would have to retire in six months, instead of 30 months as he had planned. When Jim protested, the lie he made years before came to the surface. Jim was given the option of being terminated or taking early retirement at substantially reduced benefits.

When the application is completed and signed, the recruitment process is finished. Its unanswered questions and implications continue to affect human resource management, as the Jim LaVera example illustrates. In fact, the end of the recruitment process marks the beginning of the selection process, discussed in the next chapter.

EVALUATING THE RECRUITMENT FUNCTION

LIKE MOST OTHER important functions, the recruiting activity in an organization should also be subjected to periodic evaluation. Sweeping changes continue to reshape the workplace; this means that today, more than ever before, knowledgeable employees constitute a key component of a firm's competitive strategy.[42] Typically, the recruitment process is expensive. Unless efforts are made to identify and control these costs, the potential benefits from the activity may end up being lower than the costs. Like all other corporate HR functions, recruiters will not be able to justify their own efforts unless these contribute to "bottom line" financial performance.[43] Recruitment costs can run as high as 50 per cent of the yearly salary for professionals and managers; what is even more important, recruitment can reflect a firm's overall human resource strategy.[44] This means that the effectiveness of the recruiting function should be evaluated on an ongoing basis. Several indices have been suggested in the past. The more popular ones are discussed below

1. Cost per Hire. The dollar cost per person recruited is one possible measure of the effectiveness of the recruiting function. The costs should include not only the direct costs (e.g., recruiters' salaries, costs of advertisement, consultants' fees, and so on), but also apportioned costs and overheads (e.g., time of operating personnel, stationery, rent). However, often cost data are either not collected at all or are not interpreted so as to facilitate the evaluation of recruiting. Cost data collected from previous recruiting activities could serve as useful benchmarks for comparison.

2. Quality of Hires and Cost. A major criticism of using a simple dollar cost per hire as a measure of effectiveness is that it ignores the quality of the people hired. The

performance, absenteeism, and motivation levels of employees recruited from one source (or using one media) may differ from those of other sources.

> Recruits selected through advertisements in professional journals and professional conventions may be qualitatively superior on performance than those who were selected through campus recruitment efforts.

The number and quality of résumés received gives an indication of the overall effectiveness of a recruitment method or source.

3. Offers: Applicants Ratio. A somewhat better index is the ratio between the number of job offers extended and the total number of applicants calculated for each recruitment method or media. Even if a recruiting source brings in better-quality résumés, this may not be translated finally to job offers; an offers:applicants ratio gives a better picture of the overall quality of the applicant pool. The ratio of number of offers accepted to total number of job offers extended to applicants gives an indication of the overall effectiveness of the recruiting. Caution is, however, in order. The acceptance of a job offer is dependent on a number of extraneous variables, including the labour market situation, the compensation package offered by the organization and its competitors, the firm's location, and so on. However, when used judiciously, this measure can point up weaknesses such as lack of professionalism and long delays in the recruiting process that could encourage a prospective employee to go elsewhere. This is particularly true for good candidates, who may receive multiple job offers from employers.

4. Time Lapsed per Hire. The number of days, weeks, or months taken to fill a position provides yet another measure of the effectiveness of the recruitment system. Clearly, a firm that takes a week to fill a position when the industry average is 10 days or two weeks is, in comparison, more efficient. Once again, several external and uncontrollable factors (including the nature of the job, labour market conditions, location, and so on) affect the time for recruiting; consequently, this index should be used in conjunction with other information.

Figure 5-7 shows some of the more popular measures used to evaluate the recruiting function. Naturally, many of these measures are influenced by a firm's selection, training, and compensation systems. Indeed, an evaluation system that explicitly considers various factors related to the selection process and that contains job performance information (including tenure and value of job to the organization) may be very useful in several organizational settings. The next chapter will look at the various steps involved in the selection of personnel from the pool of applicants identified during recruiting.

FIGURE 5-7

Popular Measures Used for Evaluating Effectiveness of Recruitment Function

1. Total number of applications received.
2. Time required to get applications.
3. Time elapsed before filling positions.
4. Costs per hire.
5. Offers extended:Number of applicants.
6. Offers accepted:Number of offers extended.
7. Number of qualified applicants:Total number of applicants.
8. Performance rating of hires.
9. Turnover of hires.

SUMMARY

Recruitment is the process of finding and attracting capable applicants for employment. This responsibility normally is associated with specialists in the human resource department called recruiters. Before recruiters can solicit applicants, they should be aware of the constraints under which they operate. Of particular importance are such limitations as organizational policies, human resource plans, employment equity plans, recruiter habits, environmental conditions, and the requirements of the job.

At the recruiter's disposal are a variety of methods to find and attract job seekers. Employer sources include walk-ins, write-ins, employee referrals, and direct solicitations through want ads and other forms of advertisement. Applicants can be found through the referrals of offices of Human Resources Development Canada, private placement agencies, or search firms. Of course, recruits can be found through a variety of institutions, such as educational, professional, and labour organizations, the military, and government training programs. Some firms have reported success in converting temporary employees into permanent ones, on a full- or part-time basis, and in inducing departing employees to remain. An open house may bring people into the facility and prompt them to submit applications.

The end of the recruiting process is a completed application form from ready, willing, and able candidates. Application forms seek a variety of answers from recruits, including personal, employment, educational, and work history information. Questions may be asked about hobbies, memberships, awards, and personal interests. References are usually solicited on the application form as well.

Like all other human resource functions, the recruitment activity also needs to be evaluated for its degree of effectiveness and efficiency. This is to ensure that the recruitment function achieves both organizational and individual objectives. A number of indices for evaluating the recruitment activity were suggested in this chapter. Bear in mind that all these indices are affected by a firm's selection, training, compensation, and general human resource related policies. With a pool of recruits and the information contained in completed application forms, the human resource department is now ready to assist line managers in the process of selecting new employees.

TERMS FOR REVIEW

Visit the Web site at www.mcgrawhill.ca/college/schwind6 for a full glossary.

REVIEW AND DISCUSSION QUESTIONS

1. What background information should a recruiter have before beginning to recruit job seekers?

2. Give three examples of how organizational policies affect the recruitment process. Explain how these influence a recruiter's actions.

3. Under what circumstances would a blind ad be a useful recruiting technique?

4. "If a job application form omits important questions, needed information about recruits will not be available. But if a needless question is asked, the information can be ignored by the recruiter without any other complications." Do you agree or disagree with this statement? Why?

5. Suppose your employer asks you, the human resource manager, to justify the relatively large recruiting budget that you have been historically assigned. What arguments would you provide? What indices or measures will you provide to show that your recruitment is cost effective?

CRITICAL THINKING QUESTIONS

1. After months of insufficient recognition (and two years without a raise), you accept an offer from another firm that involves a $2000-a-year raise. When you tell your boss that you are resigning, you are told how crucial you are to the business and are offered a raise of $2500 per year. What do you do? Why? What problems might exist if you accept the buy-back?

2. Suppose you are a manager who has just accepted the resignation of a crucial employee. After you send your request for a replacement to the human resource department, how could you help the recruiter do a more effective job?

3. If at your company the regular university recruiter became ill and you were assigned to recruit at six universities in two weeks, what information would you need before leaving on the trip?

4. In small businesses, managers usually handle their own recruiting. What methods would you use in the following situations? Why?

    (a) The regular janitor is going on vacation for three weeks.

    (b) Your secretary has the flu.

    (c) Two more salespeople are needed: one for local customers and one to open a sales office in Victoria, British Columbia.

    (d) Your only chemist is retiring and must be replaced with a highly skilled person.

5. You are the human resource manager in a large auto-assembly unit employing 2000 blue-collar and white-collar workers. Each year, you recruit dozens of full-time and part-time workers. Recently, the vice-president, Finance, pointed out that recruitment costs in your firm are increasing steadily. She was proposing a freeze in the recruitment budget. What kind of information will you provide in an effort to change her mind on the matter?

WEB RESEARCH

Choose any two Internet recruiting sites. Select advertisements for two different job positions in each site (that is, four in all). Compare their features and strengths. Do you expect different types of recruits to respond to these advertisements and sites? Why? Which of the four advertisements that you chose is the best? Which is the worst? Why? What suggestions do you have to enhance the effectiveness of poor ads? Report your findings to the class.

INCIDENT 5-1

Ontario Electronics Expansion

Ontario Electronics developed a revolutionary method of storing data electronically. The head of research and development, Guy Swensen, estimated that Ontario Electronics could become a supplier to every computer manufacturer in the world. The future success of the company seemed to hang on securing the broadest possible patents to cover the still-secret process.

The human resource director, Carol Kane, recommended that Swensen become a project leader in charge of developing and filing the necessary patent information. Swensen and Kane developed a list of specialists who would be needed to rush the patent applications through the final stages of development and the patent application process. Most of the needed skills were found among Ontario Electronics' present employees. However, after a preliminary review of skills inventories and staffing levels, a list of priority recruits was developed. It required the following:

- An experienced patent lawyer with a strong background in electronics technology.
- A patent lawyer who was familiar with the ins and outs of the patent process and the patent office in Hull, Quebec.
- Twelve engineers. Three had to be senior engineers with experience in the latest computer technology and design. Four had to be senior engineers with experience in photographic etching reduction. Five junior engineers were also requested in the belief that they could handle the routine computations for the senior engineers.
- An office manager, 10 keyboard operators, and four secretaries to transcribe the engineering notebooks and prepare the patent applications.

Swensen wanted these 29 people recruited as promptly as possible.

1. Assuming you are given the responsibility of recruiting these needed employees, what channels would you use to find and attract each type of recruit sought?

2. What other actions should the human resource department take now that there is the possibility of very rapid expansion?

INCIDENT 5-2

The Ethics of "Headhunting"

Darrow Thomas worked as a professional placement specialist for L.A. and D. Inc., an executive search firm. For the last three months Darrow had not been very successful in finding high-level executives to fill the openings of L.A. and D.'s clients. Not only did his poor record affect his commissions, but the office manager at L.A. and

D. was not very pleased with Darrow's performance. Since Darrow desperately needed to make a placement, he resolved that he would do everything he could to fill the new opening he had received that morning.

The opening was for a director of research and development at a major food processor. Darrow began by unsuccessfully reviewing the in-house telephone directories of most of the large companies in this industry. Finally, he stumbled across the directory of a small food processor in the West. In the directory he found a listing for Suzanne Derby, assistant director of product development. He called her, and the following conversation took place:

Suzanne: Hello. P.D. Department, Suzanne Derby speaking.

Darrow: Hello. My name is Darrow Thomas, and I am with L.A. and D. One of my clients has an opening for a director of research and development at a well-known food processor. In discussions with people in the industry, your name was recommended as a likely candidate. I was ...

Suzanne: Who recommended that you call me?

Darrow: I'm awfully sorry, but we treat references and candidates with the utmost confidentiality. I cannot reveal that name. But rest assured, he thought you were ready for a more challenging job.

Suzanne: What company is it? What does the job involve?

Darrow: Again, confidentiality requires that the company name go unmentioned for now. Before we go any further, would you mind answering a few questions? Once I feel confident you are the right candidate, I can reveal my client.

Suzanne: Well, okay.

Darrow: Good. How many people do you supervise?

Suzanne: Three professionals, seven technicians, and two clerks.

Darrow: Approximately how large a budget are you responsible for?

Suzanne: Oh, it's about half a million dollars a year.

Darrow: What degree do you hold, and how many years have you been assistant director?

Suzanne: My undergraduate degree and Master's are in nutrition science. After I graduated in 1985, I came to work here as an applications researcher. In 1993, I was promoted to chief applications researcher. In 1996, I was appointed assistant director of product development.

Darrow: Good career progress, two degrees, and managerial experience. Your background sounds great! This is a little personal, but would you tell me your salary?

Suzanne: I make $79 500 a year.

Darrow: Oh, that is disappointing. The opening I have to fill is for $96 000. That would be such a substantial jump that my client would probably assume your past experience and responsibility are too limited to be considered.

Suzanne: What do you mean?

Darrow: Well, the ideal candidate would be making about $90 000 a year. That figure would indicate a higher level of responsibility than your lower salary. We could get around that problem.

Suzanne: How?

Darrow: On the data sheet I have filled out I could put down that you are making, oh, say $88 000. That sure would increase my client's interest. Besides, then they would know a salary of $96 000 was needed to attract you.

Suzanne: Wow! But when they checked on my salary history, they'd know that $88 000 was an inflated figure.

Darrow: No, they wouldn't. They wouldn't check. And even if they did, companies never reveal the salary information of past employees. Besides, my client is anxious to fill the job. I'll tell you what, let me send them the data sheet; I'm sure they'll be interested. Then we can talk about more of this. Okay?

Suzanne: Well, if you think it would mean a raise to $96 000, and they really need someone with my background, I guess I'd be interested.

1. Although "headhunters" do not necessarily engage in the practice of "inflating" an applicant's wage, it does happen occasionally. What would you do in Suzanne's place? Would you allow your name to be used?

2. Since most "headhunters" receive a commission that is a percentage of the successful applicant's starting salary, what safeguards would you suggest to prevent "headhunters" from inflating salaries?

3. If Suzanne goes along with Darrow's inflated salary figure and she is hired, what problems may she face?

EXERCISE 5-1

What Do Employers Want?

Consider your ideal job after graduation from this program.

1. Look up want advertisements for this position in at least one national newspaper and one regional or local newspaper. Collect two advertisements from each source. What job specifications are listed in the advertisements? What kind of competencies should the job incumbent have?

2. Go to the Web sites of two firms (that provide recruitment information) in the industry in which you would ideally like to work in the future. What attributes do they require of potential job applicants?

3. Look up the description of your ideal job in the National Occupational Classification (NOC). (See Chapter Two of this text or visit HRDC Web site for more information on NOC.)

Based on the information you collected from the above three sources, what characteristics seem to be valued by employers? What gaps do you need to fill before you will qualify for this position? What action should you take today? Next month?

CASE STUDY

Maple Leaf Shoes Ltd., A Case Study in Recruitment[1]

Robert Clark was a worried man.

He looked at the letter from Sam Polanyi, president of the Leather Workers' Union's local unit in Maple Leaf Shoes again. Polanyi had warned him of

[1] Case prepared by Professor Hari Das of Department of Management, Saint Mary's University, Halifax. All rights reserved by the author ©2000.

"dire consequences" if the firm did not proceed slowly on automation in its local plant. The union had urged its members to adopt a "work slow" tactic beginning next month. In three months' time, the contract negotiations with the same union had to be concluded. Automation and the newly proposed work-week would surely be important bargaining items.

But what option did the firm have now? The competition from China, Korea, Indonesia, and Malaysia was devastating. Just in the last six months, the firm had lost two major retail suppliers in the United States, which had pointed out that Maple Leaf's shoes were too high-priced for its customers. Meanwhile, there are industry rumours that a major Indian footwear firm is planning to enter the North American Market. When that materializes, Maple Leaf Shoes is likely to face even greater competition at home. India has had a long history of producing quality footwear and can also take advantage of its cheap labour and emerging high-tech industries in producing high fashion, cheap dress shoes, and high-endurance "cross-trainer" footwear.

The recent warning from the local Human Rights Commission (HRC) did not help matters either. Apparently two female employees, who were denied promotion in the past, had complained to the Commission. They had argued that the promotion criteria employed by the firm for supervisory positions worked against women. When the HRC looked at the complaint, it did not consider their cases to be strong enough to proceed further. However, it had warned the company about the concentration of women in low-paid jobs and lack of clear job specifications for supervisory positions. The Commission had urged immediate remedial actions, including an in-depth look at supervisory competencies and job specifications. The firm was expected to come out with a remedial plan in the next 12 months.

To top it all, neither Pat Lim nor Jane Reynolds was there in Wilmington to help him. John McAllister, the firm's previous human resource manager, had resigned to take up a similar position in Western Canada. Maple Leaf Shoes had not hired a new manager in his place. Until now, Pat Lim, General Manager (Marketing) was overall in charge of the human resource function although most of the routine decisions were made by Jane Reynolds, who in the past had served as special assistant to John McAllister. But, recently, Reynolds was admitted to a local hospital for a surgical procedure. Clark has now been informed that Reynolds will not be returning for some time.

Given all the pressures, Clark decided to immediately fill the human resource manager's position. Clark retrieved the want ad the company had used

when hiring John McAllister. He made some minor changes to it and decided to place it in local newspapers as soon as possible. A copy of the final advertisement that Clark prepared is shown in Exhibit 1.

It was after making arrangements for the newspaper ad that Clark remembered his childhood friend, Joy Flemming, who ran a temporary help agency in Toronto. Clark and Flemming were schoolmates and had kept in touch with each other over the years. Flemming had built up a successful agency that supplied clerical and office staff on a temporary basis. While Clark knew that Flemming's agency primarily supplied clerical workers (and some technical/supervisory personnel), he was convinced that Flemming's years of experience in the local industry would have exposed her to successful human resource professionals elsewhere. He decided to hire Joy to also conduct a search.

Joy was certain to ask him what kind of a person he was looking for. In Clark's mind, he needed a tough individual—someone like John McAllister who could stand up to the unions and take charge. Clark personally disliked handling employee-related matters; he would like to hire someone who would consult him on major issues but who was capable of making decisions on his or her own. There was no formal job description for the HR manager's position in Maple Leaf Shoes, although a consultant was currently working on writing a detailed job description. However, Clark did not value such a document. He was a great believer that these documents meant little except adding to the paperwork. A good person was what he needed now—a well-rounded, tough, experienced person like John who would run a tight ship.

Oh, how much he misses John, Clark reflected sadly.

Discussion Questions

1. What is your evaluation of the recruitment strategy used by Maple Leaf Shoes?

2. Evaluate the recruitment advertisement.

3. Design a new recruitment advertisement for the position of the human resource manager.

4. Design an application form to be used for hiring a human resource manager in the firm.

Maple Leaf Shoes Limited

requires

A HUMAN RESOURCE MANAGER

Maple Leaf Shoes Limited, the maker of *Fluffy Puppy*, *Cariboo*, *Madonna*, and other brands of high-quality footwear, which currently employs over 700 persons, requires a Human Resource Manager for its head office in Wilmington, Ontario. We are a fast-growing company with plans to expand operations to several provinces and countries in the near future. Currently, we export to the United States and a number of European countries.

As the Human Resource Manager, you will be responsible for overseeing all human resource functions for this large, expanding organization. You will be directly reporting to the President and be part of the top management team.

We are looking for an aggressive, results-oriented individual who can meet the organization's challenges and facilitate our growth plans in the 21st century. This is a senior position and the typical recruit for this position will have at least 15 years' experience in a senior management capacity. The salary and benefits will be commensurate with qualifications and experience.

We are an Equal Employment Opportunity Employer and welcome applications from qualified women and minority candidates.

Apply in confidence to:
Office of the President
Maple Leaf Shoes Limited
1, Crown Royal Lane, Maple Leaf Town
Wilmington, Ontario.

We help you put your best foot forward!

CASE STUDY

Canadian Pacific and International Bank: Evaluating Recruitment Function[2]

Canadian Pacific and International Bank (CPIB) had achieved significant expansion in its operations in the recent past and is currently a major global financial institution (see end of Chapter One for more details on the bank). One key component of its growth strategy was the acquisition of other financial institutions. While in most instances CPIB has been able to achieve a seamless merger of operations, there were times when the systems and culture of the newly acquired organization were at variance with CPIB's. This had necessitated routine internal audits of all major systems in newly acquired institutions.

Mary Keddy, vice president—human resources, is currently looking through the results of an audit of the recruitment function in Ontario Financial Planners (OFP), a investment firm CPIB had acquired in the past. Table 1 shows a summary of relevant data for two major groups of employees: investment managers and analysts, and sales staff. The other categories of staff (such as administrative and clerical) remained more or less stable across time. Several other activities in the firm were also contracted out to agencies or carried out by part-time employees. Other details of the workforce are given below:

Discussion Questions

1. Make your recommendation on the best recruitment method(s) for each type of workforce.

2. What other conclusions can you arrive at when looking at the figures provided in the case?

[2] Case prepared by Professor Hari Das of Department of Management, Saint Mary's University, Halifax, N.S. as a basis for class discussion. All rights reserved by the author. Das ©2000.

TABLE 1

Recruiting Method Used

	Investment Managers And Analysts	Sales Staff
Gender:		
Males	85%	60%
Females	15%	40%
Age:		
Less than 30 years	60%	30%
30-45 years	20%	45%
46-65 years	20%	25%
Education:		
High school or less	10%	60%
University degree or higher	90%	40%

Recruiting Method Used

	Unsolicited Applications	HRDC	Campus Recruitment	Adverti- sements	Internet recruitment	Referrals from employees
Total number of applications						
Investment managers	50	70	60	200	250	30
Sales staff	40	60	40	300	100	10
Number of candidates who were offered Jobs						
Investment managers	1	7	9	12	13	9
Sales staff	2	3	2	30	10	2
Number of candidates who accepted job offers						
Investment managers	1	3	6	6	10	6
Sales staff	1	2	2	21	4	1
Cost per recruit in dollars (includes all overheads)						
Investment managers	15	12	22	20	12	12
Sales staff	14	10	21	16	17	14
Number of new hires who left the firm within two years						
Investment managers	0	1	1	3	6	1
Sales staff	1	1	0	2	1	1

SUGGESTED READINGS

Bolles, R.N., *Job-Hunting on the Internet*, Berkeley, CA: Ten Speed Press, 1997.

Catano, V., Cronshaw, S., Wiesner, W., Hackett, R., and Methot, L. *Recruitment and Selection in Canada*, Toronto, ON: ITP Nelson, 1997

Ulrich, Dave *Human Resource Champions*, Boston, MA: Harvard Business School Press, 1997.

Chapter 6

Selection

"The notion of trying to find "good employees" is not very helpful– organizations need to be as specific as possible about the precise attributes they are seeking... the skills and abilities hired need to be carefully considered and consistent with particular job requirements and the organization's approach to its market. Simply hiring the "best and the brightest" may not make sense in all circumstances.."

Jeffrey Pfeffer[1]

CHAPTER OBJECTIVES

After studying this chapter, you should be able to:

- ■ *Explain* the strategic significance of the selection function.
- ■ *Describe* the various steps in the selection process.
- ■ *Discuss* the types and usefulness of application blanks in selecting employees.
- ■ *Explain* the role of employment tests in the selection process.
- ■ *Discuss* the major approaches to test validation, and.
- ■ *Outline* the various steps in conducting an employment interview.

Once a pool of suitable applicants is created through recruiting, the process of selecting applicants begins. This process involves a series of steps that add time and complexity to the hiring decision. Consider the hiring process at Merrill Lynch:

> Merrill Lynch, a premier global investment company with 900 offices in 43 countries with more than $1.5 trillion in client assets in 2000, considers its selection function as critical to organizational success. Applicants for the position of account executive at Merrill Lynch complete an application, take a written test, and undergo an interview. In addition to this, the firm's account-executive simulation exercise tests how applicants perform under stressful conditions similar to those that a real stockbroker faces. The test works by telling each applicant that he or she is replacing a stockbroker who has gone to another office. The stockbroker left the client book, which describes the accounts of each client. In addition, the applicants are given a variety of unanswered memos, letters, and telephone messages that they must sort through and decide how to treat. In the background, recorded sounds of a brokerage office are played to add an air of confusing noises, shouts, telephone rings, and other unexpected distractions. During the three hours, fictitious clients call and other messages and reports are dropped on the applicant's "desk."[2]

www.ml.com

The simulation exercise is only one part of Merrill Lynch's selection process. Other steps precede and follow it. In the past, all aspiring recruits were encouraged to take a self-test available at the Merrill Lynch Web site. Only those who can truthfully answer "yes" to at least 15 of the 17 questions in the quiz were considered to "have what it takes to become a Merrill Lynch Financial Consultant" and encouraged to proceed.[3]

Selection process
A series of specific steps used by an employer to decide which recruits should be hired.

Although most employers do not use such elaborate screening devices, all but the smallest employers put applicants through a variety of steps called the *selection process*. The selection process is a series of specific steps used to decide which recruits should be hired. The process begins when recruits apply for employment and ends with the hiring decision. The steps in between match the employment needs of the applicant and the organization. When these steps are not understood, selection seems like a stressful time and a bureaucratic process rather than the important function it is.

STRATEGIC SIGNIFICANCE OF THE SELECTION FUNCTION

IN MANY human resource departments, recruiting and selection are combined and called the employment function. In very small firms, the owner-manager typically does the hiring.[4] In large human resource departments, the employment function is the responsibility of the employment manager. In smaller departments, human resource managers handle these duties. Whatever the title, in most firms, employment is associated closely with the human resource department.

A proper selection process is integral to the strategic success of firms. Below we discuss the more critical dimensions of an organization's strategy affected by this function.

1. Successful execution of an organization's strategy depends on the calibre of its employees.

An organization's overall effectiveness and success depends on the quality and calibre of the employees it hires. Poor selection practices also result in the HR department not meeting the three objectives specified in Chapter One. In turn, an organization's mission and overall strategy affects the selection process and places major constraints on the human resource manager when selecting employees. This is because the skills and qualifications of the new hires need to closely match the organization's culture and strategic requirements, as the following example of Apple Computer illustrates:

> In the past, Apple Computer Inc. wanted to hire a line manager to take over a business unit in which (s)he would, in addition to daily administrative duties, also "sell" new ideas and strategies to the firm's top management. The person hired had to be very comfortable dealing with ambiguity because no aspect of the job was totally defined. The newly hired manager was expected to take charge and define the job and then sell to others why this approach was better. The company interviewed a woman candidate whose past experience and qualifications (as detailed in her résumé) would have indicated hiring on the spot. However, during the interview it became clear that the person wanted a well-defined, predictable task. This led to a closer look at the applicant's past job. When past job duties were examined, it became clear that the person's past job duties focused mostly on implementation of ideas mapped out by someone else. Clearly, this was not the type of individual that Apple Computer wanted.[5]

It should be noted that selection practices not only affect the strategic success of the organization, but also often shape internal and external realities of the organization.

2. An organization's selection decisions must reflect job requirements.

As we saw in Chapter Two, the results of job analysis help an organization to identify job duties, specifications, and performance standards. A mismatch between these and the selection criteria will result not only in poor hires, but will also expose the organization to possible lawsuits from job applicants who believe that they have been discriminated against. On the other hand, performance-based job descriptions may provide clearer guidelines while selecting employees for various positions.[6]

3. Selection strategy should be linked to an organization's stage in its life cycle.

Organizational characteristics which, in turn, are related to its stage in its life cycle, largely decide its selection strategy. These characteristics—such as product lines, market share, and organizational priorities—change over time. As a firm grows and reaches a different stage in its life cycle, different priorities start emerging:

> A start-up business (or an organization in its infancy) faces a few product lines, heavy emphasis on entrepreneurship and innovation, and little customer loyalty. In contrast, a mature organization emphasizes the maintenance of market share, cost reductions through economies of scale, and greater systems and controls to manage the operations. An aging or declining organization struggles to hold market share; economic survival assumes paramount importance in this case. Given such differing priorities, an infant organization attempts to hire entrepreneurial employees, while a mature organization needs managers who can continually search for economies of scale, control repetitive operations efficiently, and implement efficient systems and procedures. In contrast, a declining organization may seek managers who can cut costs, generate revenues, and turn the firm around.

The specific needs of an organization are determined by a variety of factors (and not merely by its stage in the life cycle); however, an organization's stage in the life cycle provides a starting point in linking an organization's overall needs and its selection strategy.

4. Selection strategy should recognize organizational constraints.

All organizations have finite resources. This means that the systems employed for selection of human resources should be cost-effective. The selection process is not an end; it is a means through which the organization achieves its objectives. Most organizations impose some limits, such as budgets and policies, that may hinder the selection process. Without budget limitations, selection procedures could be refined. But without limits, employment expenses could be so high that organizational effectiveness would suffer.

> The firm's policies may expand existing challenges or simply add more constraints. Policies against discrimination reinforce external prohibitions, for example. Internal decrees may exceed legal demands from outside. For example, policies to hire ex-convicts further societal objectives (discussed in Chapter One), but are not legally required. Such internal policies add still another challenge for employment specialists.

5. Selection strategy should recognize labour market realities.

It is important to have a large, qualified pool of recruits from which to select applicants. But some jobs are so hard to fill that there are few applicants per opening.

> For example, Canada currently has a shortage of qualified information technology personnel. Thus, firms looking for these employees will face small selection ratios.

Selection ratio
The ratio of the number of applicants hired to the total number of applicants.

A *selection ratio* is the relationship between the number of applicants hired and the total number of applicants available. A large selection ratio is 1:25; a small selection ratio is 1:2. A small selection ratio means there are few applicants from which to select. In many instances a small selection ratio also means a low quality of recruits. The ratio is computed as follows:

$$\frac{\text{Number of applicants hired}}{\text{Total number of applicants}} = \text{Selection Ratio}$$

> Wes Klugh, an employment manager for a chain of motels, faced a low selection ratio for the third-shift desk clerk's job. Although it paid 50 cents an hour more than the day or evening clerk jobs, few people applied for it. Wes decided to redesign the job by enriching it. The job was expanded to include responsibility for completing the daily financial report and other bookkeeping tasks. The additional duties justified the substantial raise and new title—night auditor. The result was more applicants.

The number of applicants for a position is also partially dependent on a firm's salary and benefit package compared to others in the industry. Industry information can be secured from Statistics Canada, Human Resources Development Canada, or other associations.

6. Selection strategy should be ethical.

Since employment specialists strongly influence the hiring decision, that decision is shaped by their ethics. Hiring a neighbour's relative, accepting gifts from a placement agency, and taking bribes all challenge the employment specialist's *ethical standards*. If those standards are low, new employees may not be properly selected:

Ethical dimensions in selection
Ethical standards mployed by the manager during hiring of personnel.

> Every summer, Athena Klemmer was told to find jobs for some of the executives' children. To disobey would affect her career. On the other hand, hiring some of them would be an admission that she selected people on criteria other than merit. Although many of her peers in the local human resource association thought employing the

bosses' children was merely a benefit of the executive suite, Athena felt it was improper. Accordingly, she found summer jobs for them in other companies.

Figure 6-1 summarizes the key factors that influence and are affected by a firm's selection strategy. As can be seen, selection affects virtually all major human resource functions within the organization. It should be noted that an organization's policies on other matters (e.g., compensation levels, training) have an impact on selection strategy at least in the long term. This fact is indicated by the dotted arrow in Figure 6-1.

This chapter introduces you to various tools at the disposal of human resource managers in formulating an effective selection strategy. The next section begins the discussion by outlining major steps in the selection of human resources.

STEPS IN THE SELECTION OF HUMAN RESOURCES

THE SELECTION process is a series of steps through which applicants pass. Sometimes the process can be made simple and effective; however, simplicity should not be achieved at the cost of lower effectiveness. Consider this:

At a large bank, the selection process was simplified and computerized in order to match present employees with internal openings. The specific tasks required of various jobs were programmed into the computer along with the specific abilities of employees. Whenever clerical or routine job openings emerged, employee profiles were computer-matched with task requirements. Those employees with the highest match for a given opening are then considered for the job. A major shortcoming of this computerized approach is that the matching process largely ignored other factors such as attitudes, personality, and the like.

To ensure that both task and non-task factors are considered, human resource departments commonly use a more involved sequence of steps, as shown in Figure 6-2. Note that these steps reflect considerable variation from one organization to the next. An applicant may also be rejected at any step in the process.

For example, for internal applicants, there is seldom a need to verify references from outsiders, or do a medical evaluation. But with external applicants, the steps in Figure

Can't deal w/ factors not easily quantifiable. Or complex.

FIGURE 6-1

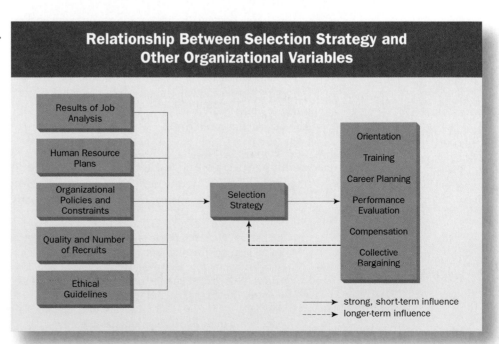

Relationship Between Selection Strategy and Other Organizational Variables

FIGURE 6-2

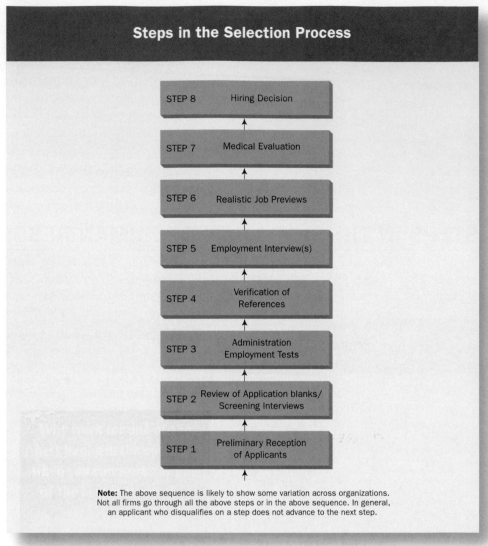

Steps in the Selection Process

STEP 8 — Hiring Decision

STEP 7 — Medical Evaluation

STEP 6 — Realistic Job Previews

STEP 5 — Employment Interview(s)

STEP 4 — Verification of References

STEP 3 — Administration Employment Tests

STEP 2 — Review of Application blanks/ Screening Interviews

STEP 1 — Preliminary Reception of Applicants

Note: The above sequence is likely to show some variation across organizations. Not all firms go through all the above steps or in the above sequence. In general, an applicant who disqualifies on a step does not advance to the next step.

6-2 are common. In most organizations, medical evaluation, if done at all, is carried out only after a hiring decision is made. In such cases, the job offer is conditional on the applicant satisfactorily completing the medical evaluation.

Also, it should be noted that in small organizations the hiring decision is based on a single interview by the owner or manager concerned. Further, depending on the unique constraints facing an organization, some of the stages may be combined or their sequence altered

Whatever the exact steps employed and their sequence, an organization's selection system should be integrally related to the job descriptions and specifications. The job specifications should form the basis of all selection decisions. Continuous job analysis should also ensure that these specifications reflect changes in tasks, technology, and job demands.

A cashier in a grocery store in the 1960s needed to have mathematical skills (such as adding, subtracting, and multiplying) since cash registers with calculators were relatively uncommon. However, in the 1970s and 1980s, with the abundance of calculators, this skill became relatively less important. Today, with the availability of electronic scanners, mathematical skills have become even less important for cashiers. Continuous job analysis and monitoring of technological trends would be necessary to develop valid job specifications.

The type of selection procedure used by an organization depends on a variety of factors including the size of the organization, the stage of its growth (e.g., new versus established for some time), and the jobs involved. There are also variations across industries. For example, use of honesty tests and checks for bondability are seen in the Canadian retail industry, but not in the education sector.

> Canadian retailers lose billions of dollars each year due to employee and customer thefts. It is estimated that employee thefts alone cost employers $3 million each day. To overcome the problem, Canadian retailers have been doing more personal reference checks, paper and honesty tests, credit and bondability assessments, and multiple interviews to screen out undesirable employees. Over 80 per cent of employers verify past performance through reference checks while 10 per cent conduct honesty tests. Multiple tools are often used to check honesty levels (for example, over 20 per cent test for bondability and past criminal behaviours, and 17 per cent verify past educational attainment).[7]

Past surveys of employers indicate that letters of reference and weighted application blanks are most popular for the selection of white-collar professional workers while biographical information blanks are more frequently used for white-collar nonprofessional jobs.[8] Personality tests are popular for selecting middle-management employees, and aptitude tests are most common for white-collar nonprofessional jobs. Nearly 50 per cent of employers use at least one paper-and-pencil test. A summary of the selection practices in Canadian organizations is shown in Figure 6-3. Figure 6-4 shows the major predictors used by the same organizations in selecting persons for different positions.

FIGURE 6-3

Selection Practices in Canadian Organizations

% of Respondents Who Use This Selection
Code:

✖ indicates 75% or more
◆ indicates 50% to 74%
❏ indicates 10% to 49%
▲ indicates less than 10%

Selection Tool	SIZE OF THE ORGANIZATION		
	Small	Medium	Large
Application blanks	✖	✖	✖
Letters of reference	✖	◆	◆
Weighted application blanks	▲	▲	▲
Biographical information blanks	❏	❏	❏
Personality tests	❏	❏	❏
Aptitude tests	❏	❏	◆
Honesty tests	▲	▲	▲
Interests inventories	❏	❏	❏

Source: Adapted from J.W. Thacker and R.J. Cattaneo, "Survey of Personnel Practices in Canadian Organizations," Working Paper, Faculty of Business Administration, University of Windsor, February 1987. Courtesy of J.W. Thacker and R.J. Cattaneo of the Faculty of Business Administration, University of Windsor.

FIGURE 6-4

Major Predictors Used in Selecting Employees for Different Positions

Code:
- ✖ indicates 75% or more
- ◆ indicates 50% to 74%
- ❑ indicates 10% to 49%
- ▲ indicates less than 10%

	% of Respondents Using this Selection Tool for This Class of Employees			
	Managerial	**Professional**	**White collar**	**Blue collar**
Letters of reference	✖	✖	✖	❑
Weighted application blanks	◆	✖	✖	◆
Biographical blanks	◆	✖	✖	◆
Tests (personality)	◆	◆	◆	❑
Assessment centre reports	◆	❑	❑	▲

Source: Adapted from J.W. Thacker and R.J. Cattaneo, "Survey of Personnel Practices in Canadian Organizations," Working Paper, Faculty of Business Administration, University of Windsor, February 1987. (Some of original figures have been rounded off.) Courtesy of J.W. Thacker and R.J. Cattaneo of the Faculty of Business Administration, University of Windsor.

Step 1: Preliminary Reception of Applicants

Job applicants may make initial contact either in person, in writing, or more recently through e-mail. Sometimes applicants may "walk in," inquiring about possible job vacancies—often, the receptionist providing them with basic information on jobs available, pay rates, and hours of work. When the applicant is a "walk-in," a preliminary interview—typically with a representative of the human resource department or the store manager in the case of a very small firm—is often granted as a courtesy. This "*courtesy interview*," as it is sometimes called, is unlikely to be as rigorous as otherwise, but it does attempt to screen out obvious "misfits" (e.g., someone who is not willing to travel but is interested in a salesperson's job with the firm requiring considerable travel). Such courtesy interviews are also an important part of good public relations by the firm as information conveyed during these meetings and the professionalism displayed by the HR manager during this early encounter may have lasting implications for its future recruitment and marketing success. Candidates applying in writing are often sent a polite letter of acknowledgment. If the applicant looks promising (either on the basis of their initial letter or the courtesy interview), he or she is typically asked to complete a formal application form. With the increasing use of the Internet for providing general information about the company and responding to preliminary inquiries from applicants, this particular step in selection has disappeared in several organizations, especially larger ones.

Step 2: Review of Application Blanks/Screening Interviews

Application blank
A job application form.

Undoubtedly, one of the most popular selection tools is an *application blank*. Most Canadian organizations require a job applicant to complete an application form, especially for lower-level jobs. However, an application form, if not carefully developed, can serve little purpose and may even be illegal.

An Ontario security firm that required applicants to fill out a form that asked information regarding place of birth, eye and hair colour, and complexion was found to be discriminatory.[9]

Application forms, hence, should be developed with great care.[10] A good application form can provide valuable information on a number of job-relevant dimensions (see Figure 6-5). A typical job application form was presented in Chapter Five.

One might suspect that some aspects of a person's background (e.g., years of education, previous experience in similar positions) would have a greater relationship to job success than some other factors (e.g., number of part-time jobs held while in school). A *weighted application blank* (WAB) technique provides a means of identifying which of these aspects reliably distinguish groups of satisfactory and unsatisfactory job incumbents.[11] Weights are assigned in accordance with the predictive power of each item so that a total "success score" can be calculated for each job applicant. A cut-off score can be established that, when used in selection, will eliminate the maximum number of potentially unsuccessful candidates. WABs have been found to be particularly valuable for job positions that require long and expensive training, where a large number of applicants apply for a few positions, and where employee turnover or attrition is abnormally high.[12]

In some instances, *biographical information blanks* (BIBs) have been developed. The BIB is similar to WAB and is a self-report instrument. However, it is exclusively in a multiple-choice format and typically includes items that are not usually covered in a WAB. Thus, questions pertaining to a job candidate's early life experiences, hobbies, opinions, attitudes, and interests are common in a BIB. Although primary emphasis is on past behaviours as a predictor of future behaviour, BIBs frequently also look at present behaviours and attitudes.

Properly developed WABs and BIBs have been found to be useful in several occupations including life insurance agents, sales clerks, engineers, research scientists, and architects. A review of 58 studies that used biographical information as a predictor of

Weighted application blank
A job application form in which various items are given differential weights to reflect their relationship to criterion measure.

Biographical information blank
A type of application blank that uses a multiple-choice format to measure a job candidate's education, experiences, opinions, attitudes, and interests.

FIGURE 6-5

Usefulness of Application Forms

A well-designed application form, among other things, will:

- collect specific information about applicant's past work experience in similar and related jobs
- collect information on applicant's educational background summarizing key competencies and job relevant skills
- collect information on applicant's special training or unique skills/competencies
- help identify gaps and unaccounted-for-time in the record
- help summarize the overall direction and consistency in the applicant's career progression
- provide insights into applicant's motivation indicating whether the energies are all focused in one direction or diffused in several directions
- avoid illegal, unethical, and personally intrusive questions
- assess the applicant's overall leadership qualities and outside interests
- reveal potential problem areas such as language deficiency, inability to travel, and ethical concerns (e.g., if the applicant is currently working for a competitor in a sensitive area)
- indicate how the applicant introduce innovative practices on the job

www.medhunters.com

www.world.hire.com

www.microsoft.com/jobs/

job success showed that over various occupations, the average validity was 0.35.[13] A subsequent analysis of 44 such studies showed the average validity to be 0.37.[14] Given this, carefully designed application blanks (especially in WAB and BIB format) seem to hold considerable potential as a selection tool.

Today, more progressive employers have applicant tracking systems that store key information from each applicant and retrieve them as job vacancies emerge (see Chapter Five for details). It is expected that in the near future, interactive résumé-building will become the norm for several employers.[15]

> Many firms today are developing Web applications that build a résumé for the applicant by asking a series of questions. Applicants must answer the questions to get through the application, and in so doing supply the information the firm needs to decide whether to interview the applicant.

Step 3: Administration of Employment Tests

Employment tests
Devices that assess the probable match etween applicants and job requirements.

Employment tests are useful for obtaining relatively objective information, which can be compared with that pertaining to other applicants and present workers. Employment tests are devices that assess the match between applicants and job requirements. Some are paper-and-pencil tests; others are exercises that simulate work conditions. A math test for a bookkeeper is an example of a paper-and-pencil test, and a manual-dexterity test for an assembly worker is an example of a simulation exercise. These tests are used more frequently for jobs that pay an hourly wage than for salaried positions because hourly jobs usually call for a limited number of skills or activities that can be tested easily. Management and professional jobs are often too complex to be tested fairly and economically in this manner.

www.sales.org

In general, tests are popular for selecting white-collar and managerial positions in Canada, but not for blue-collar jobs. Personality tests are popular for selecting managers. The use of personality and aptitude tests become more popular as the firm size increases. In contrast, honesty tests are not very popular. One past study found that they were restricted mostly to small firms (see Figure 6-3).[16]

Test Validation

Biographical information blanks (BIBs) have been found to be useful in several occupations, including research scientists, architects, life insurance agents, and engineers.

Testing became popular on a large scale during the First World War when intelligence tests were given to army recruits. During the following 60 years, tests were developed

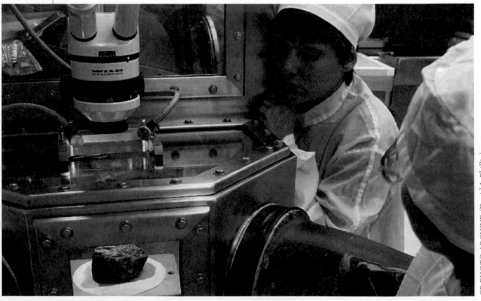

CP PHOTO ARCHIVE *(David J. Phillip)*

for a wide range of employment uses, but many of these tests were assumed to be valid without sufficient proof.

For a test to be relied upon, it must be valid. *Validity* requires that the test scores significantly relate to job performance or some other relevant criterion. The stronger the relationship between test results and performance, the more effective the test is as a selection tool. When scores and performance are unrelated, the test is invalid and should not be used for selection:

> An Ontario trucking company once gave all its applicants an extensive reading test. However, because the drivers received their instructions orally and were shown on a map where to go, the reading test had no relationship to job performance; it did not distinguish good drivers from bad ones. It only distinguished between those who could read English well and those who could not.

When an invalid test rejects people of a particular race, sex, religion, or national origin, it violates the Canadian Human Rights Act or related provincial legislation. However, test validity as it is related to discrimination has not received a great deal of attention in Canada. Given that many of the tests we use were developed in the United States, one wonders whether they are particularly valid, since they were developed for a different group of workers. Too often, tests fail to predict job performance.[17] A Toronto-based industrial psychologist has estimated that "only three per cent of firms use properly validated selection tests."[18] If this estimate is correct, then an increased scrutiny of testing and its relationship to discrimination may well be a future trend in the human resource area.

To assure that its tests are valid, human resource departments should conduct *validation studies*. These studies compare test results with performance of traits needed to perform the job. Figure 6-6 summarizes the most common approaches to validation.

Empirical approaches rely on predictive or *concurrent validity*. Both methods attempt to relate test scores to some criterion, usually performance. The higher the correlation between test scores and the criterion, the more effective the test is. Empirical approaches are generally preferred because they are less subjective than rational methods.

Rational approaches include *content* and *construct validity*. These techniques are used when empirical validity is not feasible because the small number of subjects does not permit a reasonable sample upon which to conduct the validation study.

Regardless of which approach is used, testing experts advise separate validation studies for different subgroups, such as women and minorities. These separate studies for different subgroups are called *differential validity*. Without differential validity, a test may be valid for a large group (white male applicants), but not for subgroups of minorities or women. Yet even when tests have been validated, the type of validation used is still important. Faulty procedures, no matter how well intentioned, cannot be relied on to prove a test's validity. An example of this point follows:

> The Albemarle Paper Company, a U.S. firm, gave several black workers a battery of tests that had not been validated. The workers sued Albemarle, so the company then implemented a validation study. But the study had several weaknesses, and the court ruled the tests as invalid and discriminatory.
>
> The problem was that Albemarle:
>
> - Used the tests that had been validated for advanced jobs, not the entry-level positions to which tests were being applied. Such validation does not prove tests are valid for entry-level jobs. Tests must be validated on those jobs to which tests are being applied.
> - Validated the test on one group (white workers) and then applied the test to another group (black workers). Tests must be validated for all the groups to whom the test applies.[19]

Validity
A key attribute of a selection device that indicates its accuracy and relationship to job relevant criteria.

Concurrent validity
An empirical approach to validation that measures the predictor and criterion scores concurrently.

Content validity
A rational approach to validation that examines the extent to which the selection device includes elements of the job domain.

Construct validity
A rational approach to validation that seeks to establish a relationship to a construct, attribute, or quality related to job performance.

Differential validity
Test validation involving different subgroups, e.g., males, females, minorities.

FIGURE 6-6

An Explanation of Common Approaches to Test Validation

Empirical Approaches

Empirical approaches to test validation attempt to relate test scores with a job–related criterion, usually performance. If the test actually measures a job-related criterion, the test and the criterion exhibit a positive correlation between 0 and 1.0. The higher the correlation, the better the match.

- *Predictive validity* is determined by giving a test to a group of applicants. After these applicants have been hired and have mastered the job reasonably well, their performance is measured. This measurement and the test score are then correlated.

- *Concurrent validity* allows the human resource department to test present employees and correlate these scores with measures of their performance. This approach does not require the delay between hiring and mastery of the job.

Rational Approaches

When the number of subjects is too low to have a reasonable sample of people to test, rational approaches are used. These approaches are considered inferior to empirical techniques, but are acceptable validation strategies when empirical approaches are not feasible.

- *Content validity* is assumed to exist when the test includes reasonable samples of the skills needed to successfully perform the job. A keyboarding test for an applicant that is being hired simply to do keying is an example of a test with content validity.

- *Construct validity* seeks to establish a relationship between performance and other characteristics that are assumed to be necessary for successful job performance. Tests of intelligence and scientific terms would be considered to have construct validity if they were used to hire researchers for a chemical company.

Reliability
A selection device's ability to yield consistent results over repeated measures. Also, the internal consistency of a device or measure.

Besides being valid, a test should also be reliable. *Reliability* means that the test yields consistent results.

For example, a test of manual dexterity for assembly workers should give a similar score each time the same person takes the test. If the results vary widely with each retest because good scores depend on luck, the test is not reliable.

When tests are not reliable, they are also, in almost all instances, invalid since they are not measuring the trait or competency with any degree of consistency.

It is also important to test for systemic differences in reliability and validity for different employee groups (on the basis of their gender, race, or other criteria).[20] Otherwise, the test may, over time, result in the systemic discrimination against specific, protected groups.

Testing Tools and Cautions

There are a wide variety of employment tests. But each type of test has only limited usefulness. The exact purpose of a test, its design, the directions for its administration, and its applications are recorded in the test manual, which should be reviewed before a test is used. The manual also reports the test's reliability and the results of validation efforts by the test designer. Today, many tests have been validated on large

www.apa.org/science/test.html

www.fmarion.edu/~personality/
corr/big5/traits.htm

pmc.psych.nwu.edu/perproj/
theory/Big5.table.html

www.queendom.com/
tests.html

www.2h.com

www.state.mi.us/census2000/
sampletestqs.htm

Psychological tests
Tests that measure a person's personality or temperament.

Knowledge tests
Tests that measure a person's information or knowledge.

Performance tests
Tests that measure ability of job applicants to perform the job for which they are to be hired.

Assessment centre
A standardized form of employee appraisal that relies on several types of evaluation and multiple assessors.

populations. But human resource specialists should conduct their own studies to make sure a particular test is valid for its planned use. The HR specialist should be also aware of the confounding effects of situational variables on a job applicant's performance in a specific test.

> For example, test-taking anxiety levels may vary across applicant groups. Some past studies indicate that females exhibit higher levels of emotionality and worry than do males.[21]

Each type of test has a different purpose. Figure 6-7 lists examples and a brief explanation of several different types of tests.

Psychological Tests: These tests measure personality or temperament. They are among the least reliable. Validity suffers because the exact relationship between personality and performance is unknown and perhaps nonexistent. More recently, some personality dimensions such as conscientiousness (e.g., achievement oriented, organized), openness to experience (e.g., imaginative, intellectually curious), and agreeableness (e.g., cooperative, eagerness to help) have shown some promise as predictors of job performance.[22] For example, measures of conscientiousness have been shown to be inversely related to absenteeism.[23] "Big Five Personality Factors," such as neuroticism, extraversion, openness to experience, agreeableness, and conscientiousness, have been found to have some relationship with performance, but, even here, the average correlation has been modest (typically, 0.20 to 0.30).[24] Some measures of personality and cognitive abilities may, thus, be a useful part of a HR manager's arsenal of selection tools.[25]

Knowledge Tests: These tests are more reliable because they determine information or knowledge.

> Arithmetic tests for an accountant, knowledge of tax laws for a tax specialist, and a weather test for a pilot are examples of knowledge tests.

Human resource specialists must be able to demonstrate that the knowledge is needed to perform the job. The Ontario trucking company example is a case wherein the tested knowledge (reading at an advanced level) was not needed. Figure 6-8 shows an example of a knowledge test.

Performance Tests: These tests measure the ability of applicants to do some parts of the work for which they are to be hired.

> A keying test for keyboard operators or a driving test for cab or truck drivers are obvious examples of performance tests.

Validity is often assumed when the test includes a representative sample of the work the applicant is to do when hired. However, if the test discriminates against some minority group, human resources department's assumption must be supported by detailed validation studies.

Assessment Centres: A popular procedure used for identifying managerial potential is the assessment centre (AC).[26] Currently, ACs are popular at Alcan, Nortel, and Steinberg Ltd., to mention a few organizations in the private sector. Assessment centres are increasing in popularity in several municipal, provincial, and federal government units as well. Assessment centres use several methods of assessment, including paper-and-pencil tests, job simulations, in-basket exercises, projective tests, interviews, personality inventories, and/or leaderless group discussions. Typically, the tests are used to measure intellectual ability, work orientation, and career orientation. Leaderless group discussions, role-playing, and in-basket exercises measure an applicant's administrative skill. However, assessment centres do more than simply test applicants. Through the use of multiple assessment techniques and multiple assessors (or panel judges), ACs are able to predict a candidate's future job

FIGURE 6-7

Explanations of Application of Employment-Related Tests

Psychological Tests

NAME	APPLICATION (SUBJECTS)
Minnesota Multiphasic Personality Inventory	Measures personality or temperament (executives, nuclear power security)
California Psychological Inventory	Measures personality or temperament (executives, managers, supervisors)
Guilford-Zimmerman Temperament Survey	Measures personality or temperament (sales personnel)
Watson-Glaser Critical Thinking Appraisal	Measures logic and reasoning ability (executives, managers, supervisors)
Owens Creativity Test	Measures creativity and judgment ability (engineers)

Knowledge Tests

How to Supervise?	Measures knowledge of supervisory practices (managers and supervisors)
Leadership Opinion Questionnaire	Measures knowledge of leadership practices (managers and supervisors)
General Aptitude Test Battery	Measures verbal, spatial, numeric, and other aptitudes and dexterity (job seekers at unemployment offices)

Performance Tests

Stromberg Dexterity Test	Measures physical coordination (shop workers)
Revised Minnesota Paper Form Board Test	Measures spatial visualization (draftsmen and draftswomen)
Minnesota Clerical Test	Measures ability to work with numbers and names (clerks)
Job Simulation Tests, Assessment Centres	Measures a sample of "on-the-job" demands (managers, professionals, supervisory, and nonsupervisory employees)

Integrity Tests

Lie Detector	Honesty and truthfulness (police, retail store workers)
Honesty Test	Measures attitudes about theft and related subjects (retail workers, securities employees, banks)

Attitude Tests

Work Opinion Questionnaire	Measures attitudes about work and values (entry-level, low-income workers)

Medical Tests

Drug Tests	Measures the presence of illegal or performance-affecting drugs (athletes, government employees, equipment operators)
Genetic Screening	Identifies genetic predispositions to specific medical problems
Medical Screening	Measures and monitors exposure to hazardous (miners, factory workers, researchers), as well as applicant's ability to perform the job at required level

FIGURE 6-8

A Segment of a Verbal Ability Test

Directions: Each of the following questions consists of a word printed in capital letters followed by four words or phrases, lettered (a) through (d). Choose the word that is most nearly IDENTICAL in meaning to the word in capital letters.

1. AFFECT: (a) to insult (b) to move, stir, or have influence upon (c) to imitate or pretend (d) the impression or result produced
2. INANE: (a) humorous (b) careless (c) dejected (d) silly
3. SOPORIFIC: (a) soapy (b) sleep inducing (c) unsophisticated (d) saturated
4. LATENT: (a) backward (b) dormant (c) extreme (d) obvious

Source: Adapted from Hari Das and Nathan Kling, Verbal Ability and Composition Test, Faculty of Commerce, Saint Mary's University, Halifax, 1981.

behaviour and managerial potential. The assessment process itself may vary in length from a few hours to several days, depending on an organization's needs and objectives. A typical AC evaluation for a first-level supervisory job lasts one to two days. In recent years, the AC technique has become increasingly popular for nonsupervisory and skilled labour as well.

> A major automobile manufacturer uses an 18-hour assessment-centre procedure for all its production staff.

Research studies evaluating the validity of the assessment centre technique have reported positive conclusions, by and large, indicating a median 0.40 correlation coefficient between AC ratings and such criteria as career progress, salary advances, supervisor ratings, and evaluations of potential progress. This has led to a phenomenal growth in the number of organizations using the AC technique. Currently, over 20 000 organizations on this continent are estimated to use the AC technique; and more are doing so each year. More details on AC procedures will be given in Chapter Nine.

Computer-interactive performance tests
Performance tests using computer simulations that can measure skills, comprehension, spatial visualization, judgment, etc.

Computer-interactive Tests: A more recent development is the use of computer-interactive performance tests. The advent of microprocessors and minicomputers has opened up new possibilities for measuring perceptual-motor skills (e.g., reaction time, control precision), perceptual speed, and spatial visualization. Computers can also measure human capabilities not measurable by printed tests:

> For instance, through simulation, an applicant's abilities such as time sharing, ability to concentrate, ability to work under different time pressures, and so on, can be measured using computer-interactive performance tests. In one life insurance company, fact-based scenarios are presented to job applicants on the computer. The candidates' reactions to the scenarios, both mental (e.g., comprehension, coding, calculation) and motor (e.g., keying speed, accuracy) are assessed as the job candidate processes "claims" presented on the computer screen.[27]

The computer can also be used to capture the complex and dynamic dimensions of managerial work. By utilizing video, it is possible to show movement and depict richer and more detailed behavioural incidents. By presenting a more detailed and accurate portrayal of the situation, the fidelity with which judgment is measured is presumably increased.

> A program called AccuVision shows the job applicant actual job situations likely to be encountered on the job on videotape. In turn, the applicant selects a behavioural

option in response to that situation. The response is entered in the computer and scored according to predetermined criteria.[28]

Watching a video-based test also exposes the candidate to the types of activities encountered on the job, which in turn provide a realistic job preview (discussed later in this chapter). Finally, video-based tests can be administered to groups of candidates at the same time, thus reducing the costs. Available research evidence seems to indicate high reliability for such interactive tests.[29]

Relying on the old adage that "behaviour predicts behaviour," developers of these interactive tests assume that behaviour in situations similar to those encountered on the job will provide a good indication of the actual behaviour on the job.[30] An example of an interactive test is shown in Figure 6-9.

Integrity Tests: Tests that measure an applicant's honesty and trustworthiness are of great interest to employers for two reasons: first, if the candidate is not honest in filling out the job application form and in his or her answers during the job interview, much of the information collected to assess the applicant's suitability for the position is useless; second, all employers desire employees whom they can trust.

> One U.S. study places the amount of workplace theft at $40 billion annually in that country.[31] Over six per cent of job applicants may be involved in thefts in previous jobs; many others commit felonies or minor crimes. It is estimated that crime increases retail prices by approximately 15 per cent. While comparable Canadian data are not available, statistics such as these have prompted several employers to use tests and other devices to measure the integrity of job applicants.

A number of methods have been developed to help employers assess the integrity level of new hires. All methods are controversial. The various methods currently in vogue include graphic response tests, paper-and-pencil tests, credit report checks, and voice stress analyzers. The first two, which are also the more popular methods, will be discussed here.

Integrity tests
An employment test that measures an applicant's honesty and trustworthiness.

FIGURE 6-9

An Example of a Computer-Interactive Performance Test

You are the human resource manager in our firm. At 8 a.m. when you walk into your office, you find the following e-mail messages on your computer:

Sharon (your colleague): Can we start our meeting at 10? It should take two hours to get the Job Evaluation briefing sharpened up. As planned, we should be able to do the presentation in 90 minutes leaving 30 minutes for questions.

Chan (a manager): Can we meet for, say, one hour - NO, make that one and a half hours - today? It is urgent. I am free any time between 9:30 to 12 and after 3 p.m.

Andre (your boss): Can you interview a job candidate this morning. She is in town only this morning; so you will have to meet her between 9 and 10.30 a.m. She looks really good for the position we advertised. So, I would not want to miss this opportunity.

Jim (your secretary): Just to let you know that the Job Evaluation briefing to the staff is now moved up. It is going to be at 1 p.m. and not at 2 p.m. The message came in only as I was leaving the office at 6 p.m. Didn't want to call you at home and inform.

What is the earliest time you can meet with Chan?

a. 9:30   **b.** 3*   **c.** 4:30   **d.** 12:30   **e.** not possible today

* correct answer

Graphic response tests
Tests that attempt to measure an applicant's honesty by measuring body responses.

Polygraph
Machine that attempts to measure a person's honesty by assessing body reactions. Often called a lie detector.

Paper-and-pencil integrity tests
Measures of honesty that rely on written responses rather than observations.

www.bsgcorp.com/
journal/journal.html

Graphic response tests seek information about applicants in ways that cannot be distorted easily. The *polygraph* (or lie detector) is the most common. It measures physiological changes as a person responds to questions. When a person tells a lie, the conscience usually causes involuntary physiological reactions that are detected by the polygraph. At $30 to $60 per test, it is more economical than a detailed background check on applicants. In addition to ethical and public relations considerations, there are serious questions about the ability of most lie detector operators to administer and interpret the results validly.[32] Despite this, Canadian companies continue to use them. In the United States, almost one-half of all retail firms are reported to use polygraph tests.

> In Ontario, the use of lie-detector tests for the purpose of employment is prohibited under the Employment Standards Act. Employers desiring to use this test should check its legality in other provinces.[33]

Employers have turned to *paper-and-pencil integrity tests* because of their ease of use and inexpensiveness (typically available at less than $20 per administration). Unlike the use of polygraphs, there is also less organized opposition to these tests. Most paper-and-pencil integrity tests (also called "*honesty tests*") fall into one of two categories: overt tests that ask direct questions about past thefts or attitudes toward dishonest behaviours, or *covert* measures of the same.

> Stanton Survey, an honesty test developed by Pinkerton Services Group, was tested for its validity using 4665 applicants. Fifty per cent of the applicants were given the Stanton Survey, the other 50 per cent were not. Of the applicants, 37 per cent of those not tested were later dismissed for theft while only 22.6 per cent of those tested with Stanton Survey were dismissed for the same reason. The number of policy violators in the untested group was 10.4 per cent compared to 1.5 per cent in the tested group. The average loss from the untested group was approximately $208 higher compared to the tested group.[34]

When confronted by direct questions, many individuals are likely to openly admit theft. *Personality-oriented integrity tests*, on the other hand, do not ask direct questions about theft or other dishonest behaviours, but measure the reliability and social conformity of employees and make inferences about their honesty from these scores. A review of a dozen paper-and-pencil integrity tests found potential validity for some of the tests.[35] Other comprehensive analyses of honesty and integrity tests also reveal that they have some degree of validity in predicting a wide range of disruptive behaviours such as theft, disciplinary problems, and absenteeism.[36]

> For example, the London House Personnel Selection Inventory (PSI) significantly predicted employees who were caught stealing. The PSI, which resulted from over 15 years of research by psychologists, criminologists, and legal experts, is reported to have a reliability of over 0.9 and convergent validity with polygraph scores, anonymous admissions of theft by the applicants, and results of quasi-experiments using the same respondents.[37]

Graphic response and honesty tests present human resource specialists with an inherent dilemma. On the one hand, these methods offer some additional screening tools to better ensure an optimal workforce. On the other hand, such tests are subject to errors. When they are inaccurate, needless discrimination results. Similarly, when tests discriminate against members of a protected class disproportionately, human rights violations may occur. In the United States, in some jurisdictions, for example, carriers of the HIV virus are protected by new laws or ordinances or by coverage under laws intended to protect people with disabilities. In Canada, a clear national policy on this issue has been slow to emerge, so that each province has its own policies and standards on these tests. Also, to many applicants and employees these tests are an invasion of their privacy.

Attitude tests: Attitude tests are being used in some circumstances to learn about the attitudes of applicants and employees on a variety of job-related subjects. As polygraph tests draw criticisms about their accuracy and appropriateness, attitude tests are being used to assess attitudes about honesty and, presumably, on-the-job behaviours.[38] For example, a paper-and-pencil test on honesty has been developed to measure cheating, deceiving, and stealing.[39] Attitude tests also reveal employee attitudes and values about work. The Work Opinion Questionnaire, for example, has been effectively used in predicting job performance of entry-level, low-income workers.[40]

Besides specific cautions associated with individual tests, human resource specialists should realize that testing is not always feasible. Even when tests can be developed or bought, their cost may not be justified for jobs that have low selection ratios or that are seldom filled. Examples include technical, professional, and managerial jobs. Even when feasible, the use of tests must be flexible. They need not always be the first or last step in the selection process. Instead, human resource experts use tests during the selection process at the point they deem appropriate. Consider the comments of an experienced human resource manager of a large chain of grocery stores:

> "Many human resource managers in other industries use testing only after other steps in the selection process. In the grocery business you must test first. Why waste time interviewing a grocery clerk who doesn't know that three for 88 cents is 30 cents apiece? Besides, when we take applications on Tuesdays, we may have 300 of them. Interviews would take 75 hours a week, and my staff consists of a clerk and myself. But through testing, we can test the entire group in an hour. Then we interview only those who score well."

Lastly, employment tests are only one of several techniques used in the selection process because they are limited to factors that can be tested and validated easily. Other items, not measurable through testing, may be equally important.

Step 4: Verification of References

What type of person is the applicant? Is the applicant a good, reliable worker? To answer these questions, employment specialists use references. Many professionals have a very skeptical attitude toward references. *Personal references*—those that attest to the applicant's sound character—are usually provided by friends or family. Their objectivity and candor are certainly questionable. When a reference is in writing, the author usually emphasizes only positive points. Thus, personal references are not commonly used.

Employment references
Evaluations of an employee's past work performance and job-relevant behaviours provided by past employers.

Employment references differ from personal references because they discuss the applicant's work history. Many human resource specialists doubt the usefulness of these references because former supervisors or teachers may not be completely candid, especially with negative information. Further, many managers do not seek the right information or ask the right questions while checking references.

> A survey conducted in 1999 shows that 84 per cent of companies have had to fire people for reasons that could have been discovered by proper reference checks. More than 93 per cent of the respondents said they had found exaggerations on résumés and 86 per cent had found outright misrepresentations.[41]

Often, many employment references are little more than confirmation of prior employment. Many employers are concerned about the risk of possible legal action by past employees who were not given positive references. In some cases, employers provide only basic information to protect themselves (e.g., simply stating that a person worked for them in the past in a certain capacity during specific dates). This lack of candour has caused some human resource specialists to omit this step entirely from the selection process. Other specialists have substituted telephone inquiries for written references. Besides getting a faster response, often at lower cost, telephone inquiries have the advantage of directness: voice inflections or hesitation over blunt questions may tip off the interviewer to underlying problems. In practice, however, only a small proportion of all reference checks seek negative information. Most reference checks are used to verify application information and gather additional data:

> John Adams impressed his interviewers a few minutes after the interview began. The position was that of a store manager in a large building supplies chain. His ready wit, ability to think on the spot, and keen mind appealed to the interviewers. Equally attractive was what his previous employers had to say about him. One of the references called him a young dynamo because of his drive and enthusiasm; another commented on John's ability to "come out with totally creative ideas" and his "methodical approach to problems." John Adams, who was hired for the position by the firm, did perform true to these statements for the first three months. It was by sheer accident that one day a colleague noted a shortfall in the cash register. On investigation, it was found that Adams had been systematically stealing money from his employer. Even worse, he had a history of embezzling accounts with his three previous employers. One of the previous employers admitted being aware of a couple of incidents where Adams had received kickbacks from vendors. None of the references, however, made any mention of these facts in their letters.[42]

Reference letters
Written evaluations of a person's job-relevant skills, past experience, and work relevant attitudes.

Lack of candour in *reference letters* may be due to a variety of reasons, including fear of legal reprisal, legal requirements (as in the United States) to show reference letters to an applicant, desire to get rid of an employee, and reluctance to pass judgment on a fellow human being. Given this state of affairs, an employer can get to the truth about a potential employee's character and work performance in a number of ways. Some of the possible strategies are shown in Figure 6-10. In all cases, the references should be combined with information from other predictors such as biographical data, tests, and interviews. Questions such as "what are your general impressions about the applicant's suitability for this position?" or "does the applicant have initiative, integrity, a positive attitude, and willingness to learn?" should be avoided since they are too subjective and susceptible to personal bias. They also do not provide quantifiable information or measurable results.[43]

More recently, several firms have begun to include a background investigation as part of their selection process. Some applicants exaggerate their skills, education and/or past work experience. While virtually every qualification listed in an application form or resume can be verified, the cost of doing it may be prohibitive, especially for smaller employers. Some large organizations today use the services of specialized agencies to conduct background checks:

Employment references discuss the applicant's work history. They are often checked by phone which is direct and elicits a quick response.

FIGURE 6-10

How to Get the Truth Out of References

Use the phone: Most references are more likely to be honest over the phone or in person rather than in a formal letter.

Seek information on job-related behaviour: Ask for details on job behaviours, such as tardiness and absenteeism, rather than on personality traits, such as ambition and intelligence, which are hard to evaluate reliably.

Ask direct questions: Questions such as "Would you rehire this employee now?" or "How is this person's behaviour in a group setting?" would result in more honest answers than when a person is asked to write a paragraph on the strengths and weaknesses of the employee.

Combine references with other predictors: Reference letters are no substitute for application blanks, tests, and interviews.

Use credible sources only: Former work supervisors are, typically, the most useful reference sources. Letters from acquaintances and friends are usually worthless for predicting future job success.

Note frequency of job changes: A person who has not stayed in any organization for more than a few months may be either an extremely successful employee or a problem employee. Persons who have been moving laterally across organizations without any apparent change in job challenge, rewards, or working conditions should be carefully watched.

Watch out for phrases with hidden meanings: Most references do not blatantly lie; they simply don't tell the whole truth. A person who is described as "deeply committed to family and friends" may be someone who will not work beyond five o'clock; an "individualist" may be a person who cannot work with others.

Source: Adapted and summarized from Hari Das and Mallika Das, "But He Had Excellent References: Refining the Reference Letter," *The Human Resource*, June-July 1988, pp. 15-16.

It is reported that Pinkerton Security and Investigation Services screens more than one million job applicants each year.[44]

Step 5: Employment Interview(s)

The immediate supervisor is ultimately responsible for newly hired workers. Since that responsibility is ever-present, supervisors should have input into the final hiring decision. The supervisor is often better able to evaluate the applicant's technical abilities than is the human resource department. Likewise, the immediate supervisor can often answer the interviewee's specific job-related questions with greater precision. As a result, one study reported that in more than three-quarters of the organizations surveyed, the supervisor had the authority to make the final hiring decision.

When supervisors make the final decision, the role of the human resource department is to provide the supervisor with the best applicants available. From these two or three applicants, the supervisor decides whom to hire. Some organizations leave the final hiring decision to the human resource department, especially when applicants are hired into a training program instead of for a specific job. If supervisors constantly reject particular groups of applicants, such as minorities or women, the human resource department may be given final hiring authority to avoid future charges of discrimination.

In larger organizations, it is also common for the applicant to be interviewed by several persons (especially for supervisory and managerial positions). The immediate work supervisor will, still, have considerable influence on the final decision; however, the "satisfactory" candidate also will have to satisfy larger organizational requirements and fit well with the culture of the organization.

Regardless of who has the final hiring authority, the personal commitment of supervisors is generally higher when they participate in the selection process. Their participation is best obtained through the supervisory interview. Through a variety of structured and nonstructured questions, the supervisor attempts to assess the technical competency, potential, and overall suitability of the applicant. The supervisory interview also allows the recruit to have technical, work-related questions answered. Often, the supervisory interview is supplemented with a realistic job preview that better enables the employee to comprehend the job before being hired and stay on the job longer.

When the supervisor recommends hiring an individual, he or she has made a psychological commitment to assist the new employee. If the candidate turns out to be unsatisfactory, the supervisor is then more likely to accept some of the responsibility for failure.

Since interviewing is a critical step in the selection process, this will be discussed in some detail at a later section in this chapter.

Step 6: Realistic Job Previews

Realistic job preview (RJP) Involves showing the candidate the type of work, equipment, and working conditions involved in the job before the hiring decision is finalized.

Often, the supervisory interview is supplemented with a realistic job preview. A *realistic job preview (RJP)* allows the potential employee to understand the job setting before the hiring decision is made—often by showing him or her the type of work, equipment, and working conditions involved.

Unmet expectations about a job probably contribute to initial job dissatisfaction. The realistic job preview attempts to prevent job dissatisfaction by giving the newcomer an insight into the job. Recently hired employees who have had a realistic job preview are less likely to be shocked by the job or the job setting on the first day they report to work.[45] Two writers concluded the following:

> The RJP functions very much like a medical vaccination.... The typical medical vaccination injects one with a small, weakened dose of germs, so that one's body can develop a natural resistance to that disease. The RJP functions similarly by presenting job candidates with a small dose of "organizational reality." And, like the medical vaccination, the RJP is probably much less effective after a person has already entered a new organization.[46]

Past experience has shown that in nine out of ten cases, employee turnover was higher when job previews were not used.

> In one organization, a film was used to "warn" potential employees about the unpleasant aspects of a job. The job was that of a telephone operator. The film made it clear that the work was repetitive and closely supervised and sometimes required dealing with rude or unpleasant customers. Use of realistic job preview (RJP) was found to be related to decreased turnover rates, but RJP had no effect on job performance.

The adverse effect of RJP may be more candidates refusing to accept job offers when the working conditions do not appear appealing. Many of the RJPs may also be focusing unduly on extrinsic and job-context factors rather than on job content (or intrinsic) factors. Also, RJPs are no substitute for continuous monitoring of working conditions and in-depth job analysis. Informing job applicants about unpleasant working conditions may improve the probability that they will remain on the job once hired; however, they are unlikely to be any more satisfied with the job than those who were not told and did not leave. This means that only a conscious and continuous effort at improving "irritants" at the workplace is the real, long-term solution.

Step 7: Medical Evaluation

Medical evaluation
Assessment of health and accident information of job applicant through self-reports or physical exam by company medical personnel.

The selection process may include a *medical evaluation*. Normally, the evaluation is a health checklist that asks the applicant to indicate health and accident information. The questionnaire is sometimes supplemented with a physical examination by a company nurse or physician. The medical evaluation may:

- entitle the employer to lower health or life insurance rates for company-paid insurance;

- be required by provincial or local health officials—particularly in food-handling operations where communicable diseases are a danger;

- be useful to evaluate whether the applicant can handle the physical or mental stress of a job.

Many employers have done away with this step because of the costs involved. Also, if an applicant is rejected, charges of discrimination under the Canadian Human Rights Act or related provincial legislation may be brought. A congenital health condition may be considered a disability, and failure to hire may be seen as discrimination against the qualified applicant. If the employer wants a medical evaluation, it may be scheduled *after* the hiring decision. Medical examinations are usually conducted only if the job requires a clearly determined level of physical effort or other abilities (e.g., ability to climb poles). Even here, an applicant can be rejected only if reasonable accommodations cannot be made to allow the person to perform the job.

> For example, imposing a height restriction for telephone installers on the grounds that short persons cannot get ladders from the truck would be deemed discriminatory. Provision of stools for workers to stand on while removing the ladders permit even short persons to perform the job.

Drug tests
Tests that indicate whether job applicant uses marijuana, cocaine, or other drugs.

One noteworthy exception to the trend of fewer medical evaluations is *drug testing*. Since the use of drugs such as marijuana and cocaine by employees on the job as well as outside the workplace has been on the increase, a growing number of employers in Canada have begun to include drug testing as part of the selection process.

> In the United States, the U.S. Department of Labor estimates that drug use in the workplace costs employers $75 to $100 billion annually in lost time, accidents, health care, and workers' compensation costs. Sixty-five per cent of all accidents on the job are directly related to drugs or alcohol.[47]

In the United States, more than two-thirds of large employers test job applicants for drugs. The drug tests continue even after hire—on a periodic or random basis and of all persons involved in accidents or suspected of drug use.

> Concern about employee drug use has spurred IBM, American Airlines, and many other organizations to require all job applicants to pass a urinalysis test for marijuana and cocaine. Typically, drug screening is done either before or immediately after the hiring decision. These organizations seek to avoid the economic and legal risks associated with drug users.

Increases in mortality rates, accidents, theft, and poor performance affect the employer's economic performance. Moreover, if the drug user's performance carries negative consequences for customers or fellow employees, lawsuits are likely. Through the analysis of urine or blood samples, laboratories are able to screen for the presence of drugs. While professional and amateur intercollegiate athletes have been

A growing number of employers have instituted drug testing as part of the selection process. Substance abuse in the workplace costs employers billions of dollars each year.

Digital Imagery © 2001 Photo Disc Inc. Photo by Tomi/Photolink

tested for many years to assure the absence of steroids and stimulants, their popularity in work organizations has been more recent.

> Workplace substance abuse is estimated to cost Canadian employers $2.6 billion annually.[48] Although drug abuse among workers in Canada is still quite moderate when compared to the state of affairs in the United States, it warrants serious attention in major centres such as Toronto, Vancouver, and Montreal. The Toronto Dominion Bank, Imperial Oil Limited, and the Federal Transport Department are among organizations that use drug testing in Canada.

A large majority (86 per cent) of CEOs of Canadian organizations who responded to a survey considered substance abuse as a serious or a very serious problem. A similar survey in the United States resulted in a figure of US$26 billion annually in higher health-care costs and lost productivity.[49] Given these figures, it is not surprising that some companies are advocating the use of drug tests.

> CN Rail introduced this measure in the mid-1980s as a screening test for its blue-collar workers.[50] Toronto Dominion Bank and Imperial Oil followed suit in the private sector, as did the Winnipeg police force and transportation industry (under federal jurisdiction) in the public sector.[51]

Executives of Toronto Dominion Bank argued that drug users are more likely to associate with criminal elements and are therefore more susceptible to criminal influence that might lead to blackmail and perhaps theft.

> TD Bank's policies required all new and returning employees to undergo urinalysis within 48 hours of accepting an offer of employment. TD's aim was to address the potential impact of drugs on health and work performance of the employees and preserve the safety of funds and employees. If habitual substance abusers refused to participate in rehabilitation services (funded by the bank or under government health plans) or those services were of no avail, the abuser faced dismissal. The same fate awaited casual users if they tested positive on three or more occasions and persisted in drug use. The bank paid full wages and benefits to employees in rehabilitation programs.[52]

The Canadian Civil Liberties Association called for an outright ban on employee drug tests, saying no person should "be required to share urine with a stranger" as a condition of employment.[53] It pointed out that there was no evidence to suggest that Canadian society has a serious drug problem or such a problem among those with full- or part-time employment. Nor "are drug tests totally reliable indicators of safe performance in the here-and-now—at best they show only that an employee may have used a particular drug at some point in the past, perhaps several weeks before."[54] The Association launched a complaint against the mandatory drug test imposed by the Toronto Dominion Bank but lost it.[55] However, the court did find the mandatory urinalysis intrusive. In 1998, the Federal Court of Appeal in a 2-1 decision found the bank's anti-drug program discriminatory. Justice F. Joseph Macdonald held that the bank's policy resulted in indirect discrimination against drug-dependent employees. While the bank's rule of three positive tests leading to dismissal applied to both new and returning employees, "the rule directly impacts more negatively on a protected class of individuals under the Canadian Human Rights Act—drug dependent users."[56]

This means that, today, an employer must delicately balance individual right of the employee against risk of liability and lack of safety at the workplace. Because most drug tests do not yield accurate data on current impairment or usage level and may be unreliable, even the pursuit of a productive, safe workplace may not justify universal, mandatory drug testing. More recently, simple tests that measure impairment of manual dexterity and eye-hand coordination have been developed with considerable promise for identifying impaired employees.[57] Hopefully, the arrival of more such tests would help firms achieve their objectives while maintaining employee dignity and privacy.

As technology has improved, genetic and other forms of testing have become technically and financially feasible. Genetic screening may alert employers to those with higher chances of developing specific diseases. Likewise, medical monitoring of diseases such as Acquired Immune Deficiency Syndrome (AIDS) or the build-up of toxic chemicals such as lead or mercury poisoning among workers may alert employers to high-risk employees or shortcomings in health standards at the workplace. Note that employers in Ontario are prohibited from subjecting job applicants to any medical tests for the HIV virus that is associated with AIDS.

Step 8: Hiring Decision

Whether made by the supervisor or the human resource department, the final hiring decision marks the end of the selection process. From a public relations standpoint, other applicants should be notified that they were not selected. Employment specialists may want to consider rejected applicants for other openings since these recruits have already gone through various stages of the selection process. Even if no openings are available, applications of candidates not hired should be kept on file for future openings. Retaining these applications can be useful if the employer is charged with employment discrimination.

The job applications of those hired should be carefully preserved as well. This not only enables the HR department to update its HR information system (HRIS), but also helps to learn about the source of its applicants, their age, sex, race, or other work-related characteristics. Information on sex, race, and age of employees helps the human resource department to assess the extent of *underutilization* and *concentration* (referred to in Chapter Four) and to take necessary corrective action proactively. If some recruits prove unsatisfactory after they are hired, for example, human resource specialists may be able to reconstruct the selection process beginning with the application. In their reconstruction, they may uncover invalid tests, improperly conducted interviews, or other flaws in the selection process.

The newly hired employee should be treated with respect and consideration. An employer does not get a second chance to make a first good impression with the new hire. The new hire's supervisor or coworker should call the person a few days before the start date. Sending a welcome note to the entire family may be appropriate in some instances, especially if the employee's family is moving from another location. The time and place the new hire should report on arrival should be clearly communicated.[58] Some of the unwritten rules (such as dress code) should also be communicated so that the new hire does not arrive formally dressed on casual Friday. A detailed orientation should follow on arrival. More on orientation and job placement will be discussed in the next chapter.

EMPLOYMENT INTERVIEW

THE EMPLOYMENT interview is a formal, in-depth conversation conducted to evaluate the applicant's acceptability. The interviewer seeks to answer two broad questions: Can the applicant do the job? How does the applicant compare with others who are applying for the job?

Employment interviews, or in-depth interviews as they are also known, are the most widely used selection technique. Their popularity stems from their flexibility. They can be adapted to unskilled, skilled managerial, and staff employees. They also allow a two-way exchange of information: interviewers learn about the applicant and the applicant learns about the employer.

Interviews do have shortcomings. The most noticeable flaw is their varying reliability and validity. Some early studies reported an average validity coefficient (i.e., the correlation between the interview assessment of candidates and their actual performance) of 0.10, or virtually nil.[59] More recently, validity coefficients of 0.24 or above have been reported—still not high enough to allow a supervisor to make accurate predictions as far as job performance is concerned. Why then are they still so widely used? There are several reasons:

- An interview allows a personal impression. Besides assessing a candidate's ability to perform well on the job, an interviewer also wants to make sure that there is a match between the person's personality and the team he or she has to work with. An interview provides an opportunity to do this.

- An interview offers the firm an opportunity to sell a job to a candidate. In high-demand areas such as engineering, electronics, and business administration, "selling" the company to top candidates assumes great importance. Typically, the employment policies, compensation, flexible work arrangements, career opportunities and overall quality of worklife are highlighted in an effort to convince top applicants to choose the firm.

- An interview offers the organization an opportunity to answer the candidate's questions regarding the job, career opportunities, and company policies.

- An interview is an effective public relations tool. Interviewees are potential consumers, clients, or voters; their perception of fair treatment could have important consequences.

High reliability means that the interpretation of the interview results should not vary from interviewer to interviewer. In reality, it is common for different interviewers to form different opinions. Reliability is improved when identical questions are asked, especially if interviewers are trained to record responses systematically. Validity is questionable because few human resource departments conduct validation studies on their interview results. However, proactive human resource departments are beginning to realize this problem and are comparing interview results with actual performance or other criteria, such as stability of employment. More validation of interviews is needed because they may relate more to personal features of candidates than to the candidates' potential performance. Human rights tribunals also look for explicit links of job descriptions to interview questions when making decisions on discrimination cases.[60]

> For example, one study reported that two of the most important variables that influence an interview are fluency of speech and composure.[61] If these findings are applicable to most employment interviews, the results of the interviews may correlate with fluency and composure, instead of potential performance.

Validity coefficients such as 0.24 make interviews a weak predictor of future performance. (A validity coefficient of 0.24 means that less than six per cent of future performance can be predicted by an interview alone.) This suggests that human resource practitioners should always combine interviews with other predictors while selecting human resources. Carefully structured interviews based on a thorough job analysis may be more useful and valid than unstructured interviews that dwell on applicant opinions about topics not directly related to the job. Also, interviews that probe what the applicant has actually done in the past in situations similar to those described in the job analysis may be better predictors of future performance.

Types of Interviews

Interviews are commonly conducted between the interviewer and the applicant on a one-to-one basis. Panel and group interviews, however, are sometimes used. Variations of group interviews appear in Figure 6-11.

In a panel interview, the applicant(s) meet with two or more interviewers. This allows all interviewers to evaluate the individual(s) on the same questions and answers. Since the interviewers are more apt to reach the same conclusion, reliability is improved. A variation is a group interview where two or more applicants are interviewed together by one interviewer. This saves time, especially for busy executives. It also permits the answers of different applicants to be compared immediately.

Whether a one-to-one, panel, or group interview, there are different interview formats that depend on the type of questions that are asked. Questions can be unstructured, structured, mixed, behavioural description, or stress-producing. Figure 6-12 compares these different formats. Although the mixed format is most common in practice, each of the others has an appropriate role to play.

FIGURE 6-11

Different Combinations of Interviewers and Applicants

Number of Applicants Interviewed	Number of Interviewers	
	1	2 or More
1	One-to-One Interview	Panel Interview of One Candidate
2	Group Interview	Panel Interview of Group of Candidates

FIGURE 6-12

Different Question Formats in Interviews

Interview Format	Types of Questions	Useful Applications
Unstructured	Few if any planned questions. Questions are made up during the interview.	Useful when trying to help interviewees solve personal problems or understand why they are not right for a job.
Structured	A predetermined checklist of questions, usually asked of all applicants.	Useful for valid results, especially when dealing with large numbers of applicants.
Mixed	A combination of structured and unstructured questions, which resembles what is usually done in practice.	Realistic approach that yields comparable answers plus in-depth insights.
Behavioural Description	Questions are limited to actual behaviours. Evaluation is on the solution and the approach of the applicant.	Useful to understand applicant's past work behaviour and abilities under specific work situations.
Stress-Producing	A series of harsh, rapid-fire questions intended to upset the applicant.	Useful for stressful jobs, such as handling complaints.

Unstructured Interviews

Unstructured interviews
Interviews using few if any planned questions to enable the interviewer to pursue, in depth, the applicant's responses.

As the summary in Figure 6-12 indicates, ***unstructured interviews*** allow human resource specialists to develop questions as the interview proceeds. The interviewer goes into topic areas as they arise, and the end result is more like a friendly conversation. Unfortunately, this unstructured method lacks the reliability of a structured interview because each applicant is asked a different series of questions. Even worse, this approach may overlook key areas of the applicant's skills or background.

Structured Interviews

Structured interviews
Interviews wherein a predetermined checklist of questions usually asked of all applicants is used.

Structured interviews rely on a predetermined set of questions. The questions are developed before the interview begins and are asked of every applicant. This approach improves the reliability of the interview process, but it does not allow the interviewer to follow up interesting or unusual responses. Here, the end result is an interview that seems quite mechanical to all concerned. The rigid format may even convey lack of interest to applicants who are used to more flexible interviews.

Mixed Interviews

Mixed interviews
This interview format is a combination of structured and unstructured interviews.

In *mixed interviews*, interviewers typically use a blend of structured and unstructured questions. The structured questions provide a base of information that allows comparisons between candidates. But the unstructured questions make the interview more conversational and permit greater insights into the unique differences between applicants. Community college and university recruiters, for example, use mixed interviews most of the time.

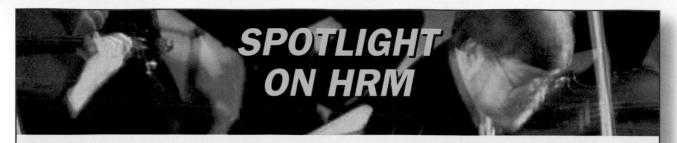

SPOTLIGHT ON HRM

LONG-DISTANCE INTERVIEWS

Interviews, while they provide rich, face-to-face information, are expensive to conduct. This is especially so if the interviewer(s) has to travel from one location to the next. Apart from the more obvious travel and lodging costs, there are also other invisible costs such as time lost in travel and lost candidates because of delays in reaching sites (especially in the case of campus-interviews where top graduates are whisked away by early arriving recruiters).

To overcome this, some employers are increasingly resorting to what is called **long-distance interviews**. Some of the options currently available include audio or videotaping an interview and then having the decision-makers listen to or watch the playback. "Real time" interviews conducted through teleconferencing and videoconferencing represent more innovative approaches. Issues that have contributed to increasing interest in this technology are the expansion of national and international markets, satellite or off-site offices for many organizations, increasing frequency of employees and contractors working from home, and increased competitiveness and reduced budgets.

While most employers still prefer the traditional face-to-face interviews, videoconferencing interviews may be the only option available in some instances (e.g., when several college campuses open their recruiting fairs on the same day). Most employers who have used the technique seem to believe that they are able to gather all relevant information on the basis of video-conference interviews and screen out less qualified candidates. They did not, however, feel ready to make a job offer at the conclusion of the videoconference interview. Both employers and candidates indicate that this enables them to access a wider pool of candidates and prospective employers while reducing the overall time commitment.

Public videoconference room rentals range from about $60 to $200 per hour. The cost of videoconferencing itself is charged on a per minute basis with the costs based on a combination of long-distance telephone rates and the speed of transmission. Currently, three speeds of transmission of images are available: the slower the speed, the cheaper the transmission, but the more blurred the images. One telecommunications company advertises a one-hour videoconferencing between Toronto and Montreal for as little as $272. This compares very favourably to the cost of bringing one or two persons to an interview from Toronto to Montreal plus the time that they would lose from their work.

Long-distance interviews are still very new for most organizations and most managers may not feel comfortable with the process and equipment. Interviewer training is a must if this process is to be effective. Test the equipment and process beforehand; the smoother the technology works, the smoother the interview will go. The limited research evidence available on the process indicates that rating errors (e.g., halo or leniency) and rating patterns (e.g., the spread of ratings) were comparable to traditional interviews. Criterion-related validity studies on long-distance interviews have not emerged to any great extent until now.

Video-conference interviews may become more popular in the future as aggressive marketing and improved technology reduce its costs. At the same time, increasing competition and growing value of managerial time may also raise the demand for this selection tool.

Source: Copyright, 1998 by MPL Communications Inc. Excerpted from the *Canadian HR Reporter*, October 20, 1997. Courtesy of *Canadian HR Reporter* published by Carswell, Thomson Professional Publishing.

Behavioural description/ situational interviews
An interviewing technique of identifying important behavioural dimensions of a job and assessing the applicants against those dimensions.

Behavioural Description Interviews

In recent years, there has been an increasing interest in understanding actual job behaviours during interviews. *Behavioural description interviews* and *situational interviews* are based on the principle that the best predictor of people's future behaviour is their past behaviour in a similar circumstance. This is especially so if the behaviour being considered occurred most recently and, in addition, is of a long-enduring nature:

Thus, a job applicant who, in the last job, handled conflict with a co-worker by walking away and refusing to discuss the matter and who has had that pattern in all his or her work life is likely to handle conflict in a new job in a similar manner.

Behaviours in specific "problem situations" are assessed. These problem situations are common across job families:

Thus, practically everyone who has worked in retail sales for any considerable length of time has had to deal with an angry customer. Everyone who has worked in an office would have faced a situation where they had to do something outside of their regular job duties.

Behavioural description interviews attempt to find out how job applicants responded to such situations in the past. The question posed to the candidate could be along these lines:

"When a group of people work closely together, it is almost inevitable that conflict will arise. Tell me about the most serious disagreement that you have had with a co-worker."

> or

"All of us, from time to time, are asked to take on new duties and responsibilities, even if they don't appear formally in our job description. Tell me about a time in your last job (or in your present job) where you were asked to do so and how you dealt with it."

For the purpose of interview questions, real events that describe either effective or ineffective work behaviour (called "critical incidents") are identified. These are situations faced or actions taken by actual workers on the job and may be gathered from past or present employees themselves, supervisors, clients, and others who come into contact with the persons doing the job. When it is not practical to collect such incidents, the interviewer may do a comparative analysis by considering the most effective and most ineffective employees in the same position. Whatever the approach, the focus is on getting information on relevant job behaviour during the employment interview:

For example, an organization that attempts to hire managers who must maintain tight cost controls may ask the applicant to describe a past work situation where he or she faced escalating costs. The applicant's behaviour in that situation (e.g., cooperating with others to reduce costs, initiating own action plans to reduce costs, or seeking boss's advice on the matter) is noted during the interview and its appropriateness evaluated.

Situational interviews such as the above are claimed to be highly job related because they reflect behavioural intentions of the job applicant and the critical behaviours needed for successful job performance.[62] Some past research studies have indicated improved reliability and validity for the situational and behavioural description interviews over traditional, unstructured interviews.[63] For example, one study reported interrater reliability estimates ranging from 0.76 to 0.87.[64] A past research study that looked at several situational interview validity coefficients (with a sample exceeding 900) reported an average validity of 0.50 in predicting later job performance.[65] Some other studies have also produced encouraging validity coefficients in the range of 0.50 to 0.57.[66] In addition to the absolute level of predictive validity, the situational interview has also been shown to be relatively superior to other interview forms. One study that examined 143 validity coefficients found that the average validity for situational interviews was 0.50 and higher than all other job-related interviews (0.39).[67] In the aggregate, the available evidence indicates that this form of interview may currently offer the best hope among interview techniques.

In summary, past studies recommend the following steps to improve the overall validity of interview method:

1. conduct a job analysis and develop critical incidents;

2. select criteria for job success based on results of job analysis;

3. select one or more incidents that indicate a specific performance criterion (for example, cost-consciousness in the previous illustration);

4. turn each critical incident into a "What did you do when ..." question;

5. develop a scoring guide to facilitate agreement among interviewers on what constitutes a good, acceptable, or unacceptable response to each question;

6. evaluate the validity of the instrument and implement.

Stress-Producing Interviews

Stress-producing interviews
Job interviews that use a series of harsh, rapid-fire questions to upset the applicant and learn how he or she handles stress.

When the job involves much stress, a *stress-producing interview* attempts to learn how the applicant will respond. Originally developed during the Second World War to see how selected recruits might react under stress behind enemy lines, these interviews have useful application in civilian employment.

For example, applicants for police work are sometimes put through a stress interview to see how they might react to problems they encounter on the job. The interview itself consists of a series of harsh questions asked in rapid succession and in an unfriendly manner.

Since stressful situations are usually only part of the job, this technique should be used in connection with other interview formats. Even then, negative public relations are likely to result among those who are not hired.

Computer-Assisted Interviewing

Technology is changing how organizations recruit and select in ways that could not have been imagined a few years ago. While automated hiring technologies are still in their infancy, one can envision a future where hiring cycle time is reduced by over 90 per cent and recruiters can call up information about a potential hire on their computer screens.

Nike is one example of a company that has begun to use computer-assisted interviewing. When 6000 persons responded to ads for workers needed to fill 250 positions, Nike used Interactive Voice Response Technology (IVR) to interview the candidates. Applicants responded to eight questions over the telephone; 3500 applicants were screened out because they were not available when needed or did not have the retail experience. The rest had a computer-assisted interview at the store, followed by a personal interview. Using computer-assisted interviews has helped Nike not only to fill positions fast but also to reduce turnover in their retail division by 21 per cent in two years.[68]

Computer-assisted interviews
Use of computers to electronically profile job candidates and screen new hires.

Some controversy surrounds the use of computers in screening new hires. While *computer-assisted interviews* may make the interviews uniform (thus potentially increasing their reliability), a number of human resource managers feel uncomfortable with the in-depth electronic profiling typical of these interviews. Such an approach may exclude persons who do not fall within the desired response range, even though the person might have skills the firm really needs. Thus, human interviewers may pick up valuable information that computers do not and may be able to factor in information the computer does not anticipate. Finally, if profiling selects persons who have the same personality traits, diversity, which can be a company's strength, may be lost.

The Interview Process

The five *stages of* a typical employment *interview* are listed in Figure 6-13. These stages are interviewer preparation, creation of rapport, information exchange, termination, and evaluation. Regardless of the type of interview used, each of these steps must occur for a successful interview to result. They are discussed briefly to illustrate how the actual interview process develops.

Interviewer Preparation

Obviously, before the interview begins, the interviewer needs to prepare. This preparation requires that specific questions be developed by the interviewer. It is the answers to these questions that the interviewer will use in deciding the applicant's suitability. At the same time, the interviewer must consider what questions the applicant is likely to ask. Since the interview is used to persuade top applicants to accept subsequent job offers, the interviewer needs to be able to explain job duties, performance standards, pay, benefits, and other areas of interest. A list of typical questions asked by recruiters and other interviewers appears in Figure 6-14. Note that several of these questions, while popular, are of questionable predictive power in assessing the future work performance of the applicant. As can be seen from the list, these questions are intended to give the interviewer some insight into the applicant's interests, attitudes, and background. The same figure provides modified versions of the same questions that provide greater insights into an applicant's strengths and attitudes. Specific or technical questions are added to the list according to the type of job opening. Note that in all instances, the questions should not be discriminatory (see Appendix to Chapter Four for specific recommendations in this context).

Another action the interviewer should undertake before the interview is to review the application form. Research shows that the quality of the interviewer's decision is significantly better when the application form is present.[69] With or without the application form, interviewers seem to take about the same length of time to reach a conclusion—from four to ten minutes.[70] The longer the interview is scheduled to last and the better the quality of the applicants, the longer it takes the interviewers to reach a decision.

With the average cost of hiring new employees often exceeding $5000 for managerial and professional employees, the interviewer's preparation should be aimed at making the interview process efficient and comfortable for the applicant. Often the

www.hrs.ualberta.ca

FIGURE 6-13

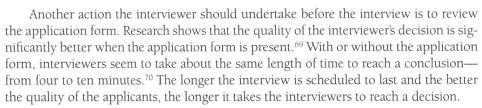
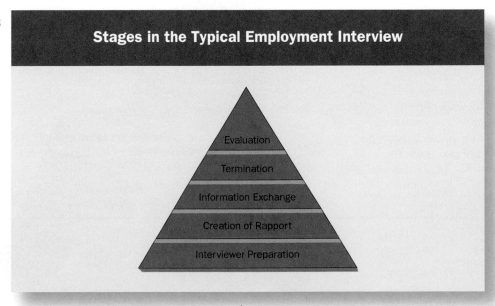

interviewer is one of the first representatives of the company with whom the applicant has an opportunity to talk. A strong and lasting impression of the company is likely to be formed at this stage. If the interviewer does not show courtesy to the applicant, that impression is certain to be negative. If the applicant is a promising candidate for the job, he or she likely has other job prospects.

Given the importance of interviewer preparation and skills in determining the overall effectiveness of the interview (as a selection tool), several organizations have begun to train their managers in interview techniques. Large companies often train their interviewers in matters such as human rights legislation and techniques to get more information from job candidates.[71] However, such training sessions may not be effective if the interviewers are not made aware of their own stereotypes and biases and behaviours that cause the job candidates discomfort during the interview. Interviewers should also be trained to link interview questions tightly to job analysis results, use a variety of questions, ask the same questions of each candidate, and anchor the rating scales for scoring answers with examples and illustrations.[72]

Creation of Rapport

Once the interview begins, the burden is on the interviewer to establish a relaxed rapport with the recruit. Without a relaxed rapport, the interviewer may not get a clear picture of the applicant's potential. Rapport is aided by beginning the interview on time and starting with nonthreatening questions such as, "Did you have any parking problems?" At the same time, the interviewer may use body language to help relax the applicant. A smile, a handshake, relaxed posture, and moving paperwork aside all communicate without words; such nonverbal communications maintain rapport throughout the interview session. The interviewer has to act the perfect host or hostess, greet the candidate with a warm smile showing him or her into the office, make small talk, and reduce the nervousness of the applicant by friendly conversation. Only in a relationship of mutual trust and comfort will a candidate talk freely. By projecting an image of confidence, competence, and concern, especially in the early stages of the interview, an interviewer can create trust.

Information Exchange

The heart of the interview process is the exchange of information. To help establish rapport, some interviewers may begin by asking the applicant if there are any

The purpose of a selection interview is to answer two questions: Can the applicant do the job? How does this applicant compare with other applicants?

questions. This establishes two-way communication and lets the interviewer begin to judge the recruit by the type of questions asked. Consider the following dialogue. Which response creates the most favourable impression?

Interviewer: Well, let's start with any questions you may have.

Applicant 1: I don't have any questions.

Applicant 2: I have several questions. How much does the job pay? Will I get two weeks' vacation at the end of the first year?

Applicant 3: What will the responsibilities be? I am hoping to find a job that offers me challenges now and career potential down the road.

Each response creates a different impression on the interviewer. But only Applicant 3 appears concerned about the job. The other two applicants appear to be either unconcerned or interested only in what benefits they will receive.

www.cnr.berkeley.edu/ucce50/
ag-labor/7labor/b003.htm

www.ipmaac.org/acn/
jun00/pracexch.html

In general, an interviewer will ask questions worded to learn as much as possible. Questions that begin with how, what, why, compare, describe, expand, or "Could you tell me more about ..." are likely to solicit an open response, while questions that can be answered with a simple "yes" or "no" do not give the interviewer much insight.[73] Specific questions and areas of interest to an interviewer are suggested in Figure 6-14. Besides those questions, the interviewer may want more specific information about the applicant's background, skills, and interests (Other popular interview questions relate to expected salary levels, career goals, own strengths and weaknesses, description of ideal boss, and so on). As already noted, asking specific behavioural description questions that assess an applicant's knowledge, skill, ability, and other characteristics (such as work-shift availability, personality characteristics) significantly add to the validity of the information collected. The above four factors, popularly referred to as KSAO, define the essential job requirements.

Termination

As the list of questions dwindles or available time ends, the interviewer must draw the session to a close. Here again, nonverbal communication is useful. Sitting erect, turning toward the door, or glancing at a watch or clock all clue the applicant that the end is near. Some interviewers terminate the interview by asking, "Do you have any final questions?" At this point, the interviewer informs the applicant of the next step in the interview process, which may be to wait for a call or letter.

Evaluation

Immediately after the interview ends, the interviewer should record specific answers and general questions. Figure 6-15 shows a typical checklist used to record these impressions of the interviewee. Use of a checklist like the one in the figure can improve the reliability of the interview as a selection technique. As the checklist shows, the interviewer is able to obtain a large amount of information even from a short interview.

Interviewer errors
Mistakes like biases and domination that reduce the validity and usefulness of job interviews.

Halo effect
Use of limited information about candidate to bias interviewer's evaluation.

Interviewer Errors

Caution must be exercised to avoid some common pitfalls of the interviewer, summarized in Figure 6-16, that lower the effectiveness of the interview. When the applicant is judged according to the *halo effect* or other personal biases, the results of the interview are misinterpreted. Applicants are accepted or rejected for reasons that may bear no relation to their potential performance. Likewise, leading questions and domination do not allow the interviewer to learn of the applicant's potential either. The evaluation of the applicant then becomes based on a guess, with little or no substantiation. No matter which pitfall is involved, it reduces the validity and reliability of

FIGURE 6-14

Popular Employment Interview Questions and Suggested Modifications

Popular Interview Questions	Suggested modifications
1. Why do you want to work for our organization?	1. How do your skills and career goals match with our organizational activities?
2. What are your hobbies?	2. How do your hobbies/spare-time activities add to your value as an employee in this organization?
3. Describe your last job.	3. What were your duties in the last job? What measures of success or failure were employed? How did you fare on those criteria?
4. Tell me about a project you did recently.	4. Tell me about a project you were involved in the recent past. What was your role in the project? Do you think that it helped you acquire any skills or competencies that can be used in the present position?
5. What was your favourite subject in school/college/university?	5. What was your favourite subject in school/college/university? Can you relate the subject matter to this job or other jobs that you might hold here?
6. Do you have any geographical preferences?	6. This job requires approximately two days of travel each month and periodic (typically, once in three years) relocations. Are there any factors that will prevent you from meeting this requirement?
7. What was your favourite sport at school/college/university?	7. Were you involved in any extracurricular activities at school/college/university? Do you think that the activity provided you with specific competencies that might be relevant for the present job?
8. Have you played any team sports?	8. Your ability to work in a team is critical for success in this position. Can you describe your work in a team that faced a conflict? How was the conflict resolved? What role did you play in the resolution of the conflict?

the interview. All the interview does when biases are present is waste organizational resources and the applicant's time. Figure 6-17 summarizes some major do's and don'ts in the employment interview.

Interviewee errors
Interviewee mistakes like boasting, not listening, or lack of preparation that reduce validity and usefulness of interview.

Interviewee Errors

Interviewees make errors too. Some may be to cover job-related weaknesses. Others may emerge from simple nervousness. Although interviewers—especially those in the human resource department—may conduct hundreds of job interviews in a year, most applicants never experience that many in a lifetime. Common interview mistakes made by job candidates are:

FIGURE 6-15

A Post-Interview Checklist

Canadian Home Appliances Limited
Post Interview Checklist

Job Position: Sales Representative   **Date interviewed:** _____ **Time:** _____

Applicant: _____   **Interviewer:** _____

Selection Criteria	Poor	Fair	Good	Very Good	Excellent	Comments
1. Knowledge of product line	☐	☐	☐	☐	☐	_____
2. Customer service skills	☐	☐	☐	☐	☐	_____
3. Prior selling experience	☐	☐	☐	☐	☐	_____
4. Job related training/education	☐	☐	☐	☐	☐	_____
5. Interpersonal and persuasion skills	☐	☐	☐	☐	☐	_____
6. Match between candidate's career expectations and company opportunities	☐	☐	☐	☐	☐	_____
7. Potential for future development into supervisory/other positions	☐	☐	☐	☐	☐	_____
8. Availability	☐	☐	☐	☐	☐	_____
9. Knowledge of the firm and industry in general	☐	☐	☐	☐	☐	_____

Follow-up action:

None	☐	_____
Further testing	☐	_____
Further interview	☐	_____
Reject for this job; reconsider for other jobs	☐	_____
Reject–Notify applicant of rejection	☐	_____
Other (specify)	☐	_____

- playing games;
- talking too much;
- boasting;
- not listening; and
- being unprepared.

Playing games—for example, acting nonchalant—is often taken at face value: the candidate is not interested. The candidate may be excited or nervous and talk too much, especially about irrelevant topics such as sports or the weather. Instead, applicants should stick to the subject at hand.

Likewise, boasting also is a common mistake. Applicants need to "sell themselves," but credential distortion—even if just "embellishment"— about responsibilities and accomplishments or simply bragging too much can turn off the interviewer's interest. Failure to listen may result from anxiety about the interview. Unfortunately, it usually means missing the interviewer's questions and failing to maintain rapport. And, of course, being unprepared means asking poorly thought-out questions and even conveying disinterest, neither of which are likely to land the job being sought.

EVALUATING THE SELECTION

HOW DO YOU KNOW whether the selection procedures in your organization are effective? How can you evaluate whether they achieved your organization's goals? Even if the procedures are effective (namely, they achieve the objective of hiring the right candidates), are they efficient and worth the costs and trouble? In Chapter One, it was pointed out that all human resource activities should be cost effective. The department's contribution in various areas should also be at levels appropriate to an organization's needs. If the selection system is more or less sophisticated than the

FIGURE 6-16

A Summary of Typical Interviewer Errors

Halo Effect

Interviewers who use limited information about an applicant to bias their evaluation of that person's other characteristics are subject to the halo effect. In other words, some information about the candidate erroneously plays a disproportionate part in the final evaluation of the candidate.

Examples:

- *An applicant who has a pleasant smile and firm handshake is considered a leading candidate before the interview begins.*
- *An applicant who wears blue jeans to the interview is rejected mentally.*

Leading Questions

Interviewers who "telegraph" the desired answer by the way they frame their questions are using leading questions.

Examples:

- *"Do you think you'll like this work?"*
- *"Do you agree that profits are necessary?"*

Stereotypes

Interviewers who harbour prejudice against specific groups are exhibiting a personal bias based on stereotypical thinking.

Examples

- *"I prefer sales persons who are tall."*
- *"Accountants are not outgoing people."*

Interviewer Domination

Interviewers who use the interview to oversell the applicant, brag about their successes, or carry on a social conversation instead of an interview are guilty of interviewer domination.

Examples:

- *Spending the entire interview telling the applicant about the company plans or benefits.*
- *Using the interview to tell the applicant how important the interviewer's job is.*

FIGURE 6-17

Some Do's and Don'ts of Conducting Employment Interviews

Do:

1. Collect only job-related information and not information on general personality traits.

2. Concentrate on securing information about the applicant's past job behaviour.

3. Use several interviewers (to interview each candidate) to increase the reliability of the interview process.

4. Treat all interviewees equally and impartially.

5. Have a checklist of questions to ask each job applicant.

6. Attempt to create a relaxed setting by asking easy, nonthreatening questions first and showing support to the applicant.

7. Provide job-related information to the candidate.

8. Compare your evaluation of each candidate with other interviewers and find out why discrepancies exist.

Do Not:

1. Attempt to predict personality traits from a single interview.

2. Be guided by initial impressions (or nonverbal cues) and generalize them to all relevant work and nonwork behaviour of the applicant.

3. Allow your evaluation of the candidate's job performance to be influenced by a single characteristic (such as how well the applicant dresses).

4. Be tempted to make "snap" judgments of the candidate early in the interview, thus locking out further information.

5. Ask leading questions that communicate the correct or desired answer to the applicant (e.g., "Do you believe that women workers should be treated equally with males?").

6. Exhibit personal biases ("In my experience, good sales managers are all talkative").

7. Dominate the interview; rather, use the interview to collect relevant information about the candidate.

www.shrm.org/
hrmagazine/archive/

organization requires, then resources are wasted. This necessitates continuous monitoring of the effectiveness and efficiency of selection procedures.

The final outcome of the selection process is the people who are hired. As one writer pointed out, the goal of HR is "to get more productive workers who show up for work, who use better judgement, who don't harass anyone, who don't cost the company money, and who can inspire people."[74] If the preselection inputs are considered carefully and the major steps of the selection process have been followed correctly, then new employees are likely to be productive. And productive employees are the best evidence of an effective selection process. Some of the questions to ask in this context include:

1. Are the superiors and peers of new hires indicating dissatisfaction with them?

2. Is the selection process too expensive?

3. Are the hiring criteria and practices showing too much variation across even similar jobs and regions?

4. Are the training costs of newer employees increasing?

5. Do managers spend too much time managing new hires?

6. Is the grievance, absenteeism and turnover inordinately high?[75]

To evaluate both new employees and the selection process requires feedback. Feedback on successful employees is sometimes hard to find for employment managers, since supervisors often claim responsibility for their successes. Feedback on failures is ample. It can include displeased supervisors, growing employee turnover and absenteeism, poor performance, low employee satisfaction, union activity, and legal suits.

More constructive feedback is obtained through specific questions. How well does the new employee adapt to the organization? To the job? To the career of which the job is a part? And lastly, how well does the employee perform? Answers to each of these questions provide feedback about the employee and the selection process.

In the ultimate sense, the utility of a selection procedure is decided by looking at the quality and productivity of the workforce hired and the costs incurred in the process. An elaborate human resource audit is sometimes attempted[76] (see Chapter Seventeen for more details on audit). The costs include not only the out-of-pocket costs (such as costs of testing, interviewing, postage, and stationery), but also the costs associated with errors in the decisions made. If the wrong candidate is hired or promoted, the costs are particularly high. However, an exhaustive look at all costs (actual and potential) associated with a selection system may be very difficult in real life. Appendix A to this chapter describes a procedure to assess the utility of the selection system.

SUMMARY

The selection process depends heavily upon inputs such as job analysis, human resource plans, and recruits. These inputs are used within the challenges of the external environment, ethics, and guidelines established by the organization.

With these inputs and challenges, the selection process takes recruits and puts them through a series of steps to evaluate their potential. These steps vary from organization to organization and from one job opening to another. In general, the selection procedure relies on interviews for virtually every opening that is to be filled. References and application blanks are also other steps commonly found in the selection process of most employers. It was pointed out that weighted and biographical application blanks and situational interviews offer great promise as reliable and valid instruments. The increasing popularity of drug tests in several organizations was also noted here. It was also pointed out that the use of any tests that are not empirically justifiable by performance criteria is vulnerable to human rights violation charges.

The supervisor's role should include participation in the selection process, usually through provision of valid job-relevant information and an interview with job candidates. Through participation, the supervisor is more likely to be committed to the new worker's success.

Growing research evidence supports the use of a realistic job preview (RJP). After considerable expense and effort to recruit and select employees, the use of realistic job previews seems well advised as a means of reducing turnover among new employees.

Like all other human resource functions, the costs and benefits of the selection process also have to be compared periodically to evaluate the utility of various predictors. However, this is a very complex activity, often requiring fairly advanced mathematical skills. Notwithstanding, all human resource management systems have to implement evaluation studies to maintain their effectiveness and efficiency.

TERMS FOR REVIEW

Visit the Web site at www.mcgrawhill.ca/college/schwind6 for a full glossary.

REVIEW AND DISCUSSION QUESTIONS

1. What is the strategic importance of the selection function for an organization?

2. List and briefly discuss the various steps in the selection process.

3. What are the five stages of the employment interview? What specific actions should you, as an interviewer, take to conduct a proper interview?

4. What are the different types of validity? If you want to validate a new dexterity test (which measures physical coordination) for workers in an assembly plant, how will you go about it?

5. What attributes of behavioural description and situational interviews make them appear more promising than traditional interview formats?

6. What is a weighted application blank? How is it different from a traditional application form?

CRITICAL THINKING QUESTIONS

1. Suppose you are an employment specialist. Would you expect to have a large or small selection ratio for each of the following job openings?

   (a) Janitors.

   (b) Nuclear engineers with five years' experience designing nuclear reactors.

   (c) Pharmacists.

   (d) Software programmers.

   (e) Elementary-school teachers in the Yukon.

   (f) Elementary-school teachers in Ontario.

   What are the implications for human resource managers?

2. If a human resource manager asked you to streamline the firm's selection process for hourly paid workers, which steps described in this chapter would you eliminate? Why?

3. A Canadian university has been experiencing high student dropout rates in recent years. One calculation showed that although the first-year enrolment in commerce courses increased from 650 to 980 students in the last four years, the dropout rate for first-year students has worsened from 9 per cent to 15 per cent. The university has been using uniform admission standards during the years and has not made any significant changes in the grading or instructional procedures. Based on what you learned in this course until this point, what recommendations would you make to the university to improve its retention rates? Why?

4. If you are hired as a consultant to evaluate the selection process for salespersons in a large car dealership in the Toronto area, what kind of information will you collect?

5. Assume you are hired to improve the interview process employed by a large real estate organization when it hires sales and customer service representatives. When suggesting improvements, what factors will you focus on? What steps will you recommend to check whether your suggestions indeed resulted in better hires in the future?

6. Suppose you are approached by the human resource department in a large insurance firm that routinely hires dozens of clerical workers. Of the various types of tests discussed in the text, which would you recommend? What are the steps you will suggest to validate the test(s) you recommended?

WEB RESEARCH

Using the Human Resources Development Canada and other Web sites, estimate the demand (and supply where available) of pharmacists, software programmers, accountants, salespersons and financial analysts in Canada. What selection ratios do they indicate? What are the implications for human resource managers employed in the relevant sectors?

INCIDENT 6-1

A Selection Decision at Empire Inc.

At Empire Inc., the turnover rate is very high among assembly workers. Supervisors in the production department have told the human resource department that they do not have time to conduct a supervisory interview with the large number of applicants who are processed to fill assembly-line openings. As a result, the human resource department's employment specialists make the final hiring decisions. The profiles of three typical applicants are presented below.

	Applicant A	Applicant B	Applicant C
Years of Experience	4	8	1
Education	1 year of university	Finished eighth grade	High-school diploma
Age	24	43	32
Test Score	77/100	74/100	82/100
Medical Evaluation	OK	OK	OK
Performance Evaluation (last job)	Very good	Excellent	Fair/good
Work History	Limited data	Stable	Stable
Ranking by:			
Interviewer 1	1	2	3
Interviewer 2	3	2	1
Apparent Eagerness	Moderate	Strong	Weak
Availability	4 weeks	2 weeks	Immediately

The nature of the assembly jobs is rather simple. Training seldom takes more than an hour or two. Most people master the job and achieve an acceptable level of production during the second full day on the job. The tasks involve very little physical or mental effort. The employment test is valid, but has only a weak relationship between scores and actual performance.

1. What information would you consider irrelevant in the preceding selection profiles?

2. Are there any changes you would recommend in the selection process?

3. Which of the three candidates would you select, given the limited knowledge you possess? Why?

INCIDENT 6-2

National Food Brokers Selection Process

National Food Brokers buys carload orders of nonperishable food products for resale to food wholesalers. Phone-sales personnel take orders from major food wholesalers, write up the orders, and send them to the appropriate food producers. Nearly 90 of National's 130 employees work in the phone-sales department. Since the job requires long hours on the phone to different accounts, the work is not very pleasant and turnover is high.

The manager of the phone-sales department, Carol Decinni, made the following observations in the presence of the human resource manager, Craig Reems:

"Most of the people who work in the department fall into two groups. There are those who have been here for two or more years. They seem reasonably content and are the top sellers we have. The other group consists of people who have been here for less than two years. Most of our turnover comes from this group. In fact, we lose one of every three new employees during the first two months. When I talk with the people who are quitting, most of them tell me that they had no idea how much time they had to spend on the phone. I am generally pleased with the quality of recruits the human resource department provides. But we cannot continue with this high turnover. My supervisors are spending most of their time training new workers. Is there anything the human resource department can do to hire more stable workers?"

1.   Suppose you are asked by the human resource manager to suggest some strategies for improving the selection process in order to hire more stable workers, what suggestions would you make?

2.   What role should the supervisory interview play in the selection process? What information conveyed to the applicants can help reduce the future worker turnover rates?

EXERCISE 6-1

How Do You Select Your Friends?

Consider your closest friend. What are this person's attributes? (List as many items as you can think of including this person's education, age, race, family background, economic situation, interests, behaviours, attitudes, biases, and so on.)

Now consider another close friend you have. Do the same as above for this person.

Consider a person whom you like least at this point in time. Do the same as above in the case of this person.

Choose another person whom you dislike. What are this person's attributes?

Now list the attributes of the persons whom you like and those you dislike. Are they different?

Now rate each attribute on a five-point scale (5 = extremely important from your point of view; 1 = least important).

Do the ratings give you an idea of your own values? Do you think your friends would value the same attributes?

CASE STUDY

Maple Leaf Shoes Limited, Selection of a Human Resource Manager[1]

Robert Clark, president and key shareholder of Maple Leaf Shoes, knew that he had a tough situation on his hands. In less than a month, Maple Leaf Shoes will have to negotiate a contract with a newly formed union in its plant covering approximately 23 per cent of the nonmanagerial workforce. A second and a more militant union is due for contract negotiations a few months later. Recently, the firm's human resource manager, John McAllister, left the firm for a better position in Toronto. Despite its best recruitment efforts, Maple Leaf Shoes has not been able to fill the vacancy. The firm had run want ads in *The Globe and Mail*, *National Post*, *Vancouver Sun*, and *Halifax Herald*. The ads yielded only 34 potential candidates, out of which a preliminary screening had reduced the number to nine (including a current employee of Maple Leaf Shoes). All nine were interviewed by Clark and five were eliminated from further consideration after this preliminary interview. The remaining four were interviewed a second time by Clark and three senior officers. Summaries of the résumés submitted by the four candidates are given in Exhibits 1 through 4.

Based on their résumés and on his impressions of the interviews with the four candidates, Robert Clark made the following mental evaluations of the applicants: Michael Anderson, Arthur Dougherty, Jane Reynolds, and Steven Robinson. Clark felt that each applicant had several strong points, but also possessed weaknesses.

Michael Anderson: Anderson was the oldest of the lot (observed Clark). A widower with two grown-up children, he had the most diverse background. Anderson impressed Clark as a very interesting, if somewhat reserved, person. He had seven years' experience in the Canadian Armed Forces (with an outstanding record there) and knew several trades ("Jack of all trades"?). During the interview, Anderson came across as a results-oriented individual. As a previous employer noted, Corner Brook Arts and Crafts where Anderson worked in the past, was about to be declared bankrupt when Anderson entered the company ("for peanuts money") and turned it around to

become a successful firm by refining its planning and control systems. In Clark's mind, Anderson was someone who could take charge, but one of the references had warned about Anderson's "need for autonomy in his workplace." Clark felt that personally he would

EXHIBIT 1

Michael Anderson

Personal:	Age 53 years; widower, two children, Ken (25 years) and Maggie (23 years)
Education:	Grade 12, Belvedere High School, Vancouver
	Two years in B.Com., University of B.C.
	Over 10 Extension courses in Human Resource Management in B.C. and Ontario. Subjects include: Negotiation Skills, Human Resource Information Systems, Safety and Health, Employee Involvement and Organizational Change.
Experience:	7 years in Canadian Armed Forces; honorary discharge; outstanding record
	4 years, Production Scheduler, Corner Brook Arts & Crafts Ltd., Newfoundland
	6 years, Production Supervisor, Hamilton Steel Limited, Ontario
	12 years, Administrative Manager, De-Brook Safety Glasses Ltd., Mississauga, Ontario
	5 years, Assistant Human Resource Manager, U-Save Groceries Limited, Ontario
Other Activities:	Member, Council for Free Trade, Corner Brook (3 years)
	Initiated Young Entrepreneurs Program in association with a local bank, Mississauga
	Coach for the Town Soccer Team (during the three years he coached, the team won all local games)

EXHIBIT 2

Arthur Dougherty

Personal:	Age 48 years; married for the last 23 years, three children, Jack (22), John (20), and Martha (17)
Education:	Grade 12 from St. John's High School, Mississauga, Ontario
	2 years in Bachelor of Arts Program, University of Toronto.
	Dale Carnegie course
	Public Speaking workshop
	4 Human Resource Management courses (non-credit) at McMaster University, Hamilton, Ontario. Topics include: Employee Relations, Diversity Management, Safety and Information systems
Experience:	2 years, Clerical (accounting), Great West Insurance Company, Toronto
	4 years, Sales Assistant, Classic Leather Shoes Ltd., Vancouver
	6 years, Sales Supervisor, Metro Auto Lines, Vancouver
	6 years, Senior Sales Supervisor, Fashion Foot Wear Ltd., Ontario
	4 years, Human Resource Supervisor, Ontario EngineeringWorks, Hamilton, Ontario
	4 years, Assistant Human Resource Manager, Madman McIsaac's Carpets and Home Furnishings Ltd., Hamilton, Ontario
Other Activities:	Member, Parish Council Executive (5 years)
	Member, Executive Committee for Trade, Vancouver Chamber of commerce (3 years)
	Founding member of Local Animal Shelter, Wanderbury, Ontario

EXHIBIT 3

Jane Reynolds

Personal:	Age 33 years; single, one child, John (8 years)
Education:	B.A. Sociology, University of New Brunswick (Dean's Honour List)
	6 Credit courses in Human Resource Management, Saint Mary's University, Halifax, Nova Scotia. The courses were Human Resource Management, Industrial Relations, Wage and Salary Administration, Staffing and Training, Interpersonal Communication, and Organizational Theory and Design
	3 courses (Stress Management, Negotiation Skills and Interpersonal Communication) offered by Ontario Human Resources Association
Experience:	1 year, Employment Recruiter, Atlantic Fishery Products, Saint John
	2 years, Recruiter, Nova Brewery, Halifax
	1 year, Human Resource Assistant, Nova Scotia Power Corporation, Halifax
	3 years, Senior Human Resource Assistant, Ontario Steel Limited, Hamilton
	4 years, Human Resource Supervisor, Maple Leaf Shoes Ltd., Leaf Town
Other Activities:	Volunteer, United Way, Saint John (2 years)
	Leader, Girl Guides, Halifax (4 years)
	Member, Lions Club, Hamilton (3 years) and Leaf Town (2 years)

get along better with someone else (for example, Dougherty) than with Anderson. But then, his personal feelings shouldn't play that important a role in the hiring decision. Or should they?

Arthur Dougherty: Dougherty impressed Clark as the most gregarious of the four he interviewed. He

was totally at ease with the interviewers and displayed the best interpersonal skills among the four. Not only was he comfortable in the presence of others, but he seemed to have the knack of making others feel comfortable as well. It was true that Dougherty's past experience was mostly in sales—he had moved to human resources after more than 15

EXHIBIT 4

Steven Robinson

Personal:	Age 35 years; divorced, one child under Robinson's custody, Melanie (7 years)
Education:	B.A. (Honors) (Political Science), University of Alberta
	Certified Human Resources Professional, Alberta
	Two extension courses on Human Resources Information Systems and the Internet
Experience:	2 years, Correspondent for *The Bugle*, Calgary
	2 Years, Human Resources Assistant, *The Bugle*, Calgary
	4 years, Assistant Human Resource Manager, St. Xavier High School, Calgary
	4 years, Assistant Human Resource Manager, Bedford Town, Nova Scotia
Other Activities:	Member, Basketball Team, University of Alberta
	Organized literacy program for African-Canadians in Edmonton for two years
	Founding member and treasurer, African-Canadian Association, Calgary
	Member, Organizational Transitions Committee, Human Resources Association, Nova Scotia

Jane Reynolds: The fact that struck Clark about Reynolds every time he saw her was the way she dressed. She was so meticulously dressed and had impeccable manners (she reminded him of his German aunt who was very formal and methodical). Reynolds was popular among her colleagues, except for the finance manager, Tim McDonald, who didn't like her at all ("I can't stand that female! She is always asking me do new things and she wants it yesterday!"). Considered a real "mover," Reynolds had been active at Maple Leaf Shoes, always working on some project or other. John McAllister, the previous human resources manager and Reynolds' boss, had, however, mixed evaluations of Reynolds' job performance ("She is very competent, I will say that; but her management style can alienate at least some folks here"). Reynolds was also probably quite junior for the position—after all, she had not held any senior administrative positions until this point. Will she be able to meet the challenges posed by Maple Leaf's growth and change? Clark did not know. Clark also had doubts about the wisdom of hiring a woman for the position. Can Reynolds really face up to Steven Mathews, the new leader of the Leather Workers' Association, who was known for his aggressive bargaining? Mathews has the reputation of being a tough, militant leader who is out to get results for his union. And while Clark didn't consider himself prudish, he still found it hard to accept having a child out of wedlock. Do other managers hold any prejudices against her? Will she fit into the team? The references from Reynolds' previous employers had given her consistently very high to outstanding ratings. There is a rumour that Reynolds has been offered a better position in another local firm and may move out soon. Reynolds impressed Clark as very career-minded.

Steven Robinson: The first thing that struck Clark about Robinson was what hiring him would do to the public's and employees' image of the company. Hiring an African-Canadian is just the thing to do right now—no one could criticize you any more about being insensitive to the multicultural mosaic of Canada. Just by hiring Robinson, you could create the impression of being a "progressive employer." Maple Leaf Shoes Limited has been facing a barrage of criticisms about human rights law violations; now, just by a single act of hiring Robinson, the firm could eliminate all those negative impressions. During the interview, Clark had received good "vibes" from Robinson. Robinson, who is divorced, has a small

years of a sales career ("I wanted bigger and more challenging things to do; You can only do so much selling shoes and steel"). He also had a good knowledge of the shoe industry. His references described Dougherty as "a very pleasant person to work with" and "always offering help to any one who need him." But Clark wondered whether Dougherty would be able to play the leader and catalyst role in HR at Maple Leaf. In favour of Dougherty was another fact: his children had all grown up, so he should be able to devote extra time to the new position. This job, with all these union contract negotiations ahead, was going to require a lot of 18-hour workdays!

child. Robinson's mother lives with him to take care of the child. Robinson's referees gave him satisfactory recommendations, although not outstanding. Robinson was the youngest of all the four applicants and seemed full of energy and enthusiasm. Robinson was also the only one with a CHRP certification and extension courses in new information technology and the Internet. If the firm is to embrace new technology soon, Robinson will be the person to hire, Clark concluded.

Clark knew that he had a difficult decision to make. To complicate matters, there was not much agreement among the three managers who interviewed the four job applicants. The rankings given by the finance, marketing, and production managers to the four candidates are shown below (1 = first, 4 = last).

INTERVIEWER	APPLICANT			
	Anderson	Dougherty	Reynolds	Robinson
Finance manager	2	1	4	3
Marketing manager	3	4	1	2
Production manager	1	3	2	4

Clark realized that he didn't approve of any one of the four applicants completely. Each also had specific strengths that others did not have. He also knew that he urgently needed an energetic, results-oriented person. The person selected should be able to deal with unions, redesign jobs to cut down costs, handle the growing number of employee complaints, and manage the challenges posed by the firm's growth. In the next three years, the firm was planning to expand its operations to other Canadian provinces and two other countries. The firm's management cadre is expected to grow by roughly three per cent each year for the next four to five years, and the need for management training exists now more than ever before. This meant that the new person who is hired should be a mover and shaker, but at the same time be able to work with people without offending them.

"A tough problem to resolve," murmured Clark to himself as he sipped the seventh cup of coffee of the day. His doctor had warned him against having too much caffeine in his system due to his heart condition; but this was going to be one of those long, dreary days. In less than an hour, Clark had a meeting with Sam Polanyi, shop steward of the Vinyl and Leather Workers' Union, who wanted to talk about a "serious problem that exists in Plant 1." How much he wished he had a manager who could do all these thankless jobs!

Discussion Questions

1. Based on the information given in the case, what education, experience, job skills, and other competencies would seem to be required for the future human resource manager of Maple Leaf Shoes?

2. How do the various candidates rate on these factors you identified?

3. What is your evaluation of the selection process employed by the firm (especially Robert Clark) in this instance? If you were in charge, would you have done anything differently? How?

4. Among the candidates, who (if any) would seem to be suitable for the position? What are the issues you should consider and trade-offs you should make when selecting one of these candidates for the position?

CASE STUDY

Canadian Pacific and International Bank– Evaluating a New Selection Test[1]

CPIB's rapid expansion into foreign markets had necessitated changes in its selection practices. Some of the factors considered by the bank when hiring

[2] Case prepared by Professor Hari Das of Department of Management, Saint Mary's University, Halifax. All rights retained by the author ©2000

employees (e.g., behaviour description interviews, assessment centre reports, reference checks over phone, and so on) were either not possible in some of the foreign countries (because of technical and infrastructural difficulties) or not valid due to cultural differences. In one Asian region, this challenge was particularly felt. In this region, in the past only 50 per cent of the new hires were considered "satisfactory" by their supervisors. Although the bank expanded its orientation and initial job training program (which now costs the organization approximately $300 per employee), this still has not improved the success rate.

Recently, R. Dennison, CPIB's regional human resource director, attended a HR conference where she came across a selection test that appeared to have considerable promise. The Financial Services Aptitude Test, designed by a large international consulting firm, had a good validation record for job positions similar to those found in the bank. Initial concurrent validation studies at CPIB using two groups of employees also indicated the test's potential usefulness to the organization. The cost of the test per applicant was $30, which included all costs associated with the administration, scoring, and interpretation of test results.

CPIB added the test as an additional predictor in its selection kit. Table 1 shows the scores received by 100 applicants on the test, with a breakdown of number of applicants who were deemed "successful" on the job by their supervisors. The firm will continue to use its orientation and training program for all its selected employees.

Assume that the distribution of the test scores and "success rates" for the next 100 applicants will follow similar patterns as indicated in Table 1. At present, the firm wants to use these test results to fill 40 existing vacancies in the region.

Discussion Questions

1. Calculate the cutoff test score that will minimize the overall cost of testing plus training.

2. To get 40 "successful" employees, how many persons will have to be hired who have:

   (a) a score of 70 or higher on the test?

   (b) a score of 60 or higher on the test?

3. What suggestions will you make to the bank in validating and using the above test?

TABLE 1:

Financial Services Aptitude Test: Scores of "Successful" and "Unsuccessful" Candidates (n = 100)

Score in the test	Number of persons who received this score	Number of persons deemed "successful"	Number of persons deemed "unsuccessful"
10	4	—	4
20	5	—	5
30	9	—	9
40	12	2	10
50	14	5	9
60	13	6	7
70	15	9	6
80	13	13	—
90	8	8	—
100	7	7	—
Total	**100**	**50**	**50**

APPENDIX A

Utility Analysis

The utility of a selection procedure should be assessed only after considering a number of factors. The more important ones among these are: (1) the validity of the predictor; (2) the variability in job performance; (3) the selection ratio; (4) the base rate of job success; and (5) selection costs.

1. *Validity of the Predictor.* Different predictors have differing validity coefficients. One study by Hunter and Hunter[1] showed that predictors such as tests and assessment centres had average validities in the range of 0.43 to 0.54, while others such as reference checks (0.26) and interviews (0.14) were much lower. Of course, when choosing between predictors with equal validity, the cost of the predictor becomes an important consideration; however, as one writer noted, the trade-off between the cost of a predictor and its validity should almost always be resolved in favour of validity.[2] This is because the potential cost of an error in the course of the test is extremely high.

2. *Variability in Job Performance.* A useful measure of a job's value to the organization is the variability of job performance for a job expressed in dollar terms. For some jobs, the differences in performance ranges (example: "outstanding" to "totally incompetent") have relatively little effect in terms of dollar value to the organization. For example, the variability of performance of a receptionist or window cleaner is relatively less significant to the organization than that of a production planner or marketing manager. Thus, a "good" receptionist may contribute, say, $6000 over his or her salary and benefits to the organization, while a "poor" one may cost the firm, say, $2000 in terms of lost sales because of disgruntled customers who had bad experiences when paying visits to the organization. In the case of a marketing manager, the effects of outcomes may be far more serious. A good marketing manager may contribute $500 000 above his or her salary and benefits, while a poor one may cost the firm $200 000 in lost sales or decreased market share. The variability in performance in dollar terms for the receptionist is about $8000; for the marketing manager's position, the corresponding figure may be $700 000. The statistical index used for computing this type of variability is the standard deviation of performance. Hunter and Schmidt's[3] research led them to conclude that a "40 per cent rule" prevails for most common job positions—namely, the variability in job performance is typically 40 per cent of the average annual salary of a position. Clearly, in the above example, an organization is more likely to spend $5000 on improving the selection procedures for its marketing manager than for the receptionist.

3. *Selection Ratio.* As already mentioned in this chapter, a large selection ratio (such as 1:25) means that the firm can afford to be choosy, while a small ratio of 1:2 does not give much freedom to the organization to make selection decisions. On the one hand, a ratio such as 1:25 means that a large number of applicants must be tested and screened (thus adding to the selection costs). On the other hand, it also means that only the "cream" of the applicant group will be selected, thus implying that even a predictor with relatively low validity can be employed.

4. *Base Rate of Job Success.* The base rate denotes the relative incidence of any given attribute or behaviour in the total population.[4] If 70 per cent of the people between 22 and 40 years old are married, then the base rate for marriage for that segment of the society is 70. A low base rate of job success in an organization indicates that few employees reach an acceptable level of job performance. Typically, base rates of success tend to be high for easy and simple jobs. For complex jobs requiring many skills and years of training, the base rates tend to be lower. Generally, the usefulness of a selection procedure increases when it is able to increase the base rate of success for a job. If the base rate is already high at 80 or 90, it is very difficult to find a predictor that will improve on it as the typical validity coefficients for various predictors currently in use range from 0.15 to 0.60.

5. *Selection Costs.* Selection costs may be actual or potential. Actual costs include costs of administering standardized tests, collecting and processing biographical blanks, conducting employment interviews, and offering money and other benefits to job candidates who are selected. The potential costs include cost of selection errors, as when the wrong person is hired for a job. The benefits of a selection process should also be defined broadly to include not only current benefits, but also likely future events (e.g., potential of an employee to hold additional responsibility).

Clearly, a thorough evaluation of all the above variables is a very complex and difficult task. In the past, several writers have offered somewhat different algorithms and formulas to assess the usefulness of the selection procedure.[5] One formula suggested to calculate the utility of the selection procedure is[6]:

$$P = (N) \times (T) \times (C) \times (S) \times (Z)$$

where

P = increase in productivity in dollars

N = number of persons hired

T = average job tenure in years of those hired

C = the correlation between a selection predictor and job performance (or validity coefficient)

S = variability in job performance (measured by standard deviation of job performance in dollars, roughly 40 per cent of annual wage)[7]

Z = the average predictor score of those selected (in standard score form)

As an illustration, consider the job position of marketing manager in a consumer goods organization. Let us assume that the organization used an assessment centre technique (which had an estimated validity of 0.6) to hire 10 managers who are paid a salary of $80 000 each year. Further, let us assume that each manager will stay with the organization for five years. Assuming an average predictor score (standardized) of 1.4, it can be shown that the assessment centre procedure would increase productivity by $1.344 million over five years or an average of $268 800 each year of their tenure.

Utility analysis such as the above has been successfully used in a number of organizations and different work settings.[8] It should be noted that utility analysis does not require reducing all selection-decision outcomes to a dollar figure; indeed, what is more important may be identifying all possible outcomes of a decision and weighing their relative importance systematically.[9] The factors identified earlier in this section (namely, selection ratio, base rate of success, and so on) interact; hence they must be considered together. For example, typically the utility is higher with a low base rate of job success or when the variability in job performance is high. However, given identical base rates of job success, different selection ratios can make a major difference in the context of selection. For example, it can be mathematically shown that with a base rate of 50 per cent and a validity coefficient of 0.40, a selection ratio of 70 per cent will yield 58 per cent successful employees. Keeping the other things the same, if the selection ratio is changed to 40 per cent, the proportion of successful employees climbs to 66 per cent, while for a 10 per cent selection ratio the corresponding figure is a whopping 78 per cent.[10] Such interdependence among the relevant selection variables makes utility analysis a very complex procedure indeed. Yet its contribution to an effective human resource management system should not be underestimated.

References (For Appendix Only)

1. Hunter and Hunter, "Validity and Utility of Alternative Predictors of Job Performance," pp. 72-98; see also Schwind, "How Well Do Interviews Predict Future Performance?"

2. Cascio, Managing Human Resources, p. 199.

3. J.E. Hunter and F.L. Schmidt, "Quantifying the Effects of Psychological Interventions on Employee Job Performance and Work Force Productivity," *American Psychologist*, 38, 1983, pp. 473-78; see also J.E. Hunter and F.L. Schmidt, "Fitting People to Jobs: The Impact of Personnel Selection on National Productivity," in Marvin D. Dunnette and E.A. Fleishman, eds., *Human Capability Assessment*, Hillsdale, N.J.: Lawrence Erlbaum Associates, 1982.

4 Dunnette, Personnel Selection and Placement.

5.Hunter and Schmidt, "Fitting People to Jobs"; F.L. Schmidt, J.E. Hunter, R.C. McKenzie, and T.W. Muldrow, "Impact of Valid Selection Procedures on Work Force Productivity," *Journal of Applied Psychology*, 64, 1979, pp. 609-26; Ralph B. Alexander and Murray R. Barrick, "Estimating the Standard Error of Projected Dollar Gains in Utility Analysis," *Journal of Applied Psychology*, 72, 1987, pp. 463-74; J.E. Hunter, *The Economic Benefits of Personnel Selection Using Ability Tests: A State of the Art Review Including a Detailed Analysis of the Dollar Benefit of U.S. Employment Service Placement and a Critique of the Low Cutoff Method of Test Use,* Washington, D.C.: U.S. Employment Service, U.S. Department of Labor, January 15, 1981; F.L. Schmidt, J.E. Hunter, and K. Pearlman, "Assessing the Economic Impact of Personnel Programs on Work Force Productivity," *Personnel Psychology*, Vol. 35, No. 3, 1982, pp. 333-43; Wayne F. Cascio, *Costing Human Resources: The Financial Impact of Behaviour in Organizations*, Boston: Kent Publishing, 1982; Cascio and Silbey, "Utility of the Assessment Centre"; Cascio and Philips, "Performance Testing."

6. Adapted from Cascio, *Managing Human Resources*, p. 199.

7. See Hunter and Schmidt, "Quantifying the Effects of Psychological Interventions," pp. 474-7.

8. See, for example, note 5 above: Schmidt, Hunter, McKenzie, and Muldrow; Cascio; Schmidt, Hunter, and Pearlman. See also Steven F. Cranshaw, "The Utility of Employment Testing for Clerical/Administrative Trades in the Canadian Military," *Canadian Journal of Administrative Sciences,* Vol. 3, No. 2, 1986, pp.376-85; Steven F. Cranshaw, Ralph A. Alexander, Willi H. Weisner, and Murray R. Barrick, "Incorporating Risk into Selection Utility: Two Models of Sensitivity Analysis and Risk Simulation," *Organizational Behaviour and Decision Processes*, Vol. 40, 987, pp. 270-86.

9. Dunnette, Personnel Selection and Placement, p.174.

10 H.C. Taylor and J.T. Russell, "The Relationship of Validity Coefficients to the Practical Effectiveness of Tests in Selection: Discussion and Tables," *Journal of Applied Psychology*, 23, 1939, pp. 565-78.

SUGGESTED READINGS

Diane Arthur, *Recruiting, Interviewing, Selecting and Orienting New Employees,* N.Y.: Amacom, 1998.

S.D. Maurer, "The Potential of the Situational Interview: Existing Research and Unresolved Issues," *Human Resource Management Review*, Vol. 7, No. 2, 1997, pp.185-201.

Robert Wood and Tim Payne, *Competency Based Recruitment and Selection*, Chichester, England: Wiley, 1998.

Weekley, J. and C. Jones, "Video-based Situational Testing," *Personnel Psychology*, Vol. 50, 1997, pp. 25-49.

Part Four

4

Placing, Developing, and Evaluating Human Resources

New employees need to know what is expected of them and what their responsibilities are, and they have to be trained properly to carry out these responsibilities effectively. A concerned employer will provide a career path for each employee and will provide the opportunities to develop all employees to their fullest potential. Also, employees need feedback on their performance to experience job satisfaction or to find out where they can improve. The next three chapters address the topics of employee development and evaluation. As a student, you need to understand the human resource department's role in these activities. They affect you whether you work in a human resource department or elsewhere in an organization. Knowledge of these activities will assist you to be a better employee or manager.

Placing, Developing, and Evaluating Human Resources

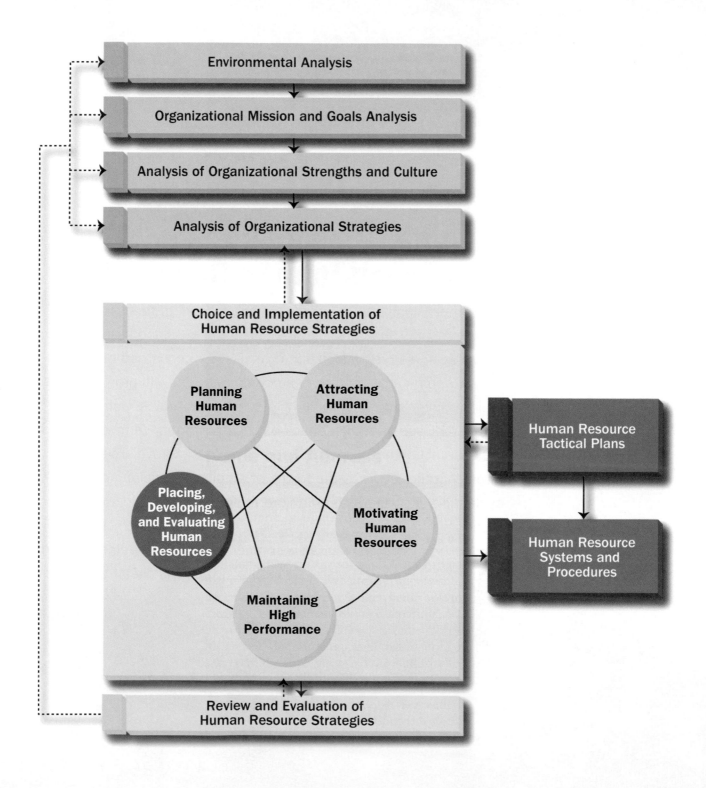

Chapter 7

Orientation and Training

Sound employee orientation program boosts productivity and safety.

—**Bill Pomfret**[1]

In today's marketplace, a well-trained workforce is no longer a competitive advantage, it's a competitive necessity.

—**John Thomas Howe**[2]

CHAPTER OBJECTIVES

After studying this chapter, you should be able to:

- *Describe* the content and scope of a two-tier orientation program.

- *Explain* the impact of a new employee orientation program on turnover and learning.

- *Identify* the human resource department's and the supervisor's responsibilities in employee orientation.

- *Describe* the importance of training as part of the long-range strategy of an organization.

- *Describe* the characteristics of a learning organization.

- *Explain* different approaches to needs analysis in designing training and development programs.

- *Describe* the major learning principles associated with each training technique.

- *Develop* an evaluation procedure to assess the results of a training and development program.

Human resource management is much more than simply hiring people. Once employee selection is completed, a proactive human resource department should still help the new employees to become productive and satisfied. The process of becoming a productive and satisfied employee is important to the organization and to the employee. As the last two chapters on recruitment and selection have shown, organizations devote considerable time and resources to hiring people. By the first day of work, the employer already has an investment in the new worker. And there is a job—or at least a potential job—that the organization needs to have done. At the same time, the newcomer has needs that may hinder the transition from recruit to worker. Anxieties leading to questions such as "Will I be able to do the job?" or "Will I fit in around here?" or "Will the boss like me?" are common among new employees. These "first-day jitters" may be natural, but they reduce both the employee's ability to learn and the employee's satisfaction with the organization. Psychologists tell us that initial impressions are strong and lasting because newcomers have little else by which to judge the organization and its people. As a first step to helping the employee become a satisfied and productive member of the organization, the human resource department must make those initial impressions favourable.

The gap between a new employee's abilities and the job's demands may be substantial. As Figure 7-1 suggests, orientation and training supplement the new worker's abilities. The hoped-for result is a balance between what the new employee can do and what the job demands. Although these efforts are time-consuming and expensive, they reduce employee turnover and help new employees to be productive sooner. This part of the chapter will discuss the key steps involved in the orientation process, and the next part will discuss the training and development of an organization's workforce.

PURPOSE OF ORIENTATION

Socialization
The process by which people adapt to an organization.

SUCCESSFUL organizational entry and maintenance is the objective of employee socialization. *Socialization* is the continuing process by which an employee begins to understand and accept the values, norms, and beliefs held by others in the organization. New employees need to know, accept, and demonstrate behaviours that the organization views as desirable, in other words, "learning the ropes and how to skip them." The overall process involves turning outsiders into insiders.

FIGURE 7-1

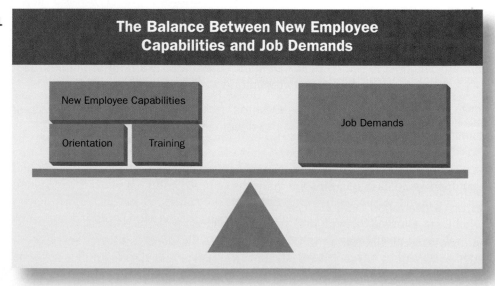

The Balance Between New Employee Capabilities and Job Demands

New Employee Capabilities

Orientation Training

Job Demands

http://bristoltn.org/newhr.html

http://members.tripod.com/
~cooperate/orient.htm

www.escape.ca/~rbacal/
orient.htm

http://groups.yahoo.com/group/
orientation/

Stages of Socialization

Anticipatory Socialization

Even before employees join organizations, socialization may have taken place: a formal education will prepare, to a degree, a candidate for specific jobs, such as accounting or engineering; a summer job may give a candidate an informal experience relating to a position; even watching television shows or movies will create certain expectations relating to jobs, such as police officers, paramedics, or archaeologists. The candidate's and the organization's expectations about each other will form a psychological contract. Some of these expectations may be explicitly stated, while others may be implicit assumptions about each other. For example, a company policy may state that an employee is expected to follow the company's ethics guidelines; the employee, on the other hand, may assume that he or she will be treated fairly by the supervisor.

Encounter

During this stage, a recruit, having some expectations about organizational life, will encounter the realities of the job, the daily routines and challenges, the positive and negative characteristic of a job. Formal methods at this stage may include orientation programs, training, and job rotation. Informal approaches may include getting to know and understand the style and personality of one's boss and co-workers.

Change and Acquisition

After the above day-to-day interactions, with their conditioning and reinforcement properties, recruits will have acquired new values and will solidify new attitudes and behaviours. At this point, the individual has been transformed from an outsider into a full-fledged member of the organization.

Orientation Programs

http://rcmp-learning.org/civilian/
civorpa.htm#w&i5

Formal orientation programs familiarize new employees with their roles, with the organization, and with other employees. Orientation, if properly done, can serve several purposes; it can:

1. reduce employee turnover;
2. reduce errors and save time;
3. develop clear job and organizational expectations;
4. improve job performance;
5. attain acceptable job performance levels faster;
6. increase organizational stability;
7. reduce employee anxiety;
8. reduce grievances;
9. result in fewer instances of corrective discipline measures.

1. Reduce Employee Turnover

Employees are more likely to quit during their first few months than at any other time in their employment. The difference between what a person expects to find at the workplace and what one actually finds is referred to as cognitive dissonance. If the

Effective orientation should cover such topics as the company's history, policies, rules and procedures, as well as a tour of the company's facilities.

dissonance is too high, employees take action. For new employees, that action may mean quitting:

> At the Royal Bank of Canada, the annual turnover averages five per cent of its workforce. While this at first glance looks reasonable and almost insignificant, the size of the bank's workforce warrants action to reduce it. The bank's annual report shows its domestic workforce to be about 50 000, which means that approximately 2500 employees leave the bank annually.[3]

To a large firm, a few thousand dollars may seem inconsequential. But if thousands of employees leave each year, the costs of turnover can quickly escalate into the millions of dollars. Moreover, when experienced, long-service employees quit, the loss may be incalculable because of the training, knowledge, and skills that these workers take with them.[4] In general, the human resource department can reduce turnover by meeting the personal objectives of employees. When that happens, both the employee and the organization can benefit.

2. Reduce Errors and Save Time

A well-oriented employee knows exactly what is expected of him or her and, hence, is likely to make fewer mistakes. Typically, a new employee is less efficient than an experienced employee. This factor combined with other additional costs involved in getting a new employee started (e.g., supervisor's time and attention) makes the **start-up costs** of new employees very significant.[5] Effective orientation can reduce these start-up costs as well as the number of mistakes committed by the inexperienced employees.

Start-up costs
The additional costs associated with a new employee because the new employee is typically less efficient than an experienced worker and also requires additional supervisory time.

3. Develop Clear Job and Organizational Expectations

For some jobs, the duties and job expectations are clear. However, for a majority of other jobs, this is simply not the case. There are no clear-cut lists of "desirable" behaviours, outcomes, and job attitudes. Most new employees would like to know "what it takes to survive and get ahead in this organization." In the absence of clear guidelines from their employer, they may have to find answers to their questions informally through the grapevine and by gossiping with others. Unfortunately, in the latter instance, there is no guarantee that they will find the right answers. To tell employees what the organization expects of them and what they can expect in return, effective orientation is absolutely necessary. Orientation is thus a part of the larger socialization of the employee.[6]

www.hc-sc.gc.ca/future
org/english/resources/
learning/untit02.htm

www.fws.gov/R3PAO/
ADMIN/employee/orientat/
index.html

http://hr.sc.edu/hr/
orientat.htm

www.doi.gov/hrm/
pmanager/ed6e.html

www.attcanada.com/
English/fAbout_Career_Over
view.html?SubPages/About/
Career/eop.html~Content

4. Improve Job Performance

Employees who establish a good relationship with the organization, their colleagues, and supervisors tend to be more productive. An orientation program greatly improves the probability that the new employee will feel a stronger commitment to the organization and with that a stronger obligation to live up to performance expectations.

5. Attain Acceptable Job Performance Levels Faster

Spelling out expected job performance standards at the beginning eliminates uncertainty about what is expected on the job:

> The Queen Elizabeth II Health Sciences Centre in Halifax uses critical incidents as part of its job descriptions to illustrate to new employees effective and ineffective job behaviours. Many new employees comment on how useful such job descriptions are in explaining what is expected of them on the job.

6. Increase Organizational Stability

Communicating policies and regulations to new employees early clearly reduces undesirable behaviour and friction points.

7. Reduce Employee Anxiety

New employees will experience less stress if an organization communicates with new employees openly, clarifies their roles, and familiarizes them with organizational objectives.

8. Reduce Grievances

Grievances often result from ambiguous job expectations and unclear responsibilities. An orientation program specifies both.

9. Result in Fewer Instances of Corrective Discipline Measures

An effective orientation program clarifies the rights and duties of employees, outlines disciplinary requirements, and spells out the consequences of deviating from the prescribed path.

In summary, the orientation program helps the individual understand the social, technical, and cultural aspects of the workplace. As new employees are accepted, they become part of the social fabric of the organization. Orientation programs help speed up the socialization process and benefit both the employee and the organization.

CONTENT OF ORIENTATION PROGRAMS

Orientation programs
Programs that familiarize new employees with their roles, the organization, its policies, and other employees.

THERE ARE various approaches to orienting new employees, although all are not popular to the same extent. Most organizations conduct orientation on an individual basis, although group orientation programs are also used in large organizations where several employees are hired at the same time.

Most *orientation programs* introduce new employees to their jobs, colleagues, and the organization's policies. Figure 7-2 lists the topics typically covered during orientation. The program usually explains the organizational issues that new employees need to know. Often a film or slide show describes the history, products, services, and

Employee handbook
A handbook explaining key benefits, policies, and general information about the employer.

Buddy systems
Exist when an experienced employee is asked to show a new employee around the job site, conduct introductions, and answer the newcomer's questions.

policies of the organization. Commonly, workers are given an *employee handbook* that explains key benefits, policies, and general information about the company. Human resource experts may also discuss pay rates as part of the program. The human resource department's role in the program often ends when the employees meet their future supervisors or trainers.

Trainers or supervisors continue the orientation program by introducing the new employee to the other trainees and co-workers. Introductions are usually followed by a tour of the facilities and an explanation of the job, its objectives, and related information.

In organizations that hire large numbers of employees, the orientation program may take a half or even a whole day to discuss the topics in Figure 7-2. For employers that hire workers only occasionally and in small numbers, there may be no formal orientation program. Instead, the employee is introduced to a senior worker who shows the new person around. These highly informal *buddy systems* are also used in large companies to help orient the new employee.

Formal programs explain orientation topics systematically. These programs are also more likely to create a favourable impression on new employees, which may explain why in a U.S. survey 92 per cent of firms had formal programs.[7] A Canadian study showed that roughly 10 per cent of orientations lasted one hour, but 51 per cent took a day or longer. The same study reported that more than two-thirds of the firms conducted the orientation immediately after the employee reported to work.[8] Of course, the experiences of employees during orientation can differ greatly. Here is an example of how an orientation can affect new employees:

Caroline Mathau: I reported to the human resource department 10 minutes early. I was told to have a seat and that someone would "show me around." An hour later I

FIGURE 7-2

Topics Often Covered in Employee Orientation Programs

Organizational Issues

History of employer	Product line or services provided
Organization of employer	Overview of production process
Names and titles of key executives	Company policies and rules
Employee's title and department	Disciplinary regulations
Layout of physical facilities	Employee handbook
Probationary period	Safety procedures and enforcement

Employee Benefits

Pay scales and paydays	Insurance benefits
Vacations and holidays	Retirement program
Rest breaks	Employer-provided services to employees
Training and education benefits	Rehabilitation programs
Counselling	

Introductions

To supervisor	To co-workers
To trainers	To employee counsellor

Job Duties

Job location	Overview of job
Job tasks	Job objectives
Job safety requirements	Relationship to other jobs

was led to an interview room. After a few minutes the interviewer realized that I was not an applicant, but a new employee. After apologies, I was taken to meet my supervisor. The supervisor screamed for a claims processor to show me around. While I was being introduced to other people, the claims processor, Irv Porter, complained about what a grouch the supervisor was all the time. At lunch, I asked if I could get a transfer to another claims department. They told me that transfers were not permitted until after the three-month probation period. I am thinking about finding another job.

Harvey Jackson: My orientation was really super! When I arrived, I was shown to the auditorium. After coffee and pastry, we were given an employee handbook that explained most of the company's benefits and policies. We also received some forms to complete and a brief lecture about company policies. The lecture was followed by a really interesting film that explained the company's history, facilities, and how different jobs related to one another. The following hour was spent on questions and answers. We had a tour of the plant and then we were treated to lunch by the company. At lunch, our supervisors joined us to answer questions and tell us about their departments. Afterward, the supervisors introduced us to the people in my department and training began.

If Caroline's experience is a typical one in her company, employees probably begin work with low motivation, poor morale, and a lot of anxiety. The company is "saving" the cost of orientation, but it is paying a high cost in employee attitudes and performance.

Responsibility for Orientation

Responsibility for orientation is shared between the human resource department and the immediate supervisor.[9] Human resource departments usually explain to employees the broad organizational concerns and benefits. Supervisors handle introductions and on-the-job training and help employees "fit in" with the work group.

A research study carried out by McShane and Baal in Western Canada indicates that human resource departments play the key role in conducting formal orientations, typically followed by the new employee's supervisor.[10] Other senior executives seem to play a minor role. Other persons who participate in the orientation process include heads of various departments, representatives of the firm's public relations department, safety officers, and union officials. In recent years, some organizations have also been using the services of experienced workers who have already retired to orient new employees. These social interactions and the "buddy system" of orientation give the newcomers an introduction to the organization and its people in a more relaxed setting.[11]

It should be emphasized that the buddy system is a supplement to the supervisor's orientation efforts. If the buddy system is substituted for the supervisory orientation, the supervisor loses an excellent opportunity to establish open communications with new employees. Very soon, newcomers may find it more comfortable to ask co-workers, rather than the supervisor, about job-related issues. Supervisors who pass up the opportunity to spend some time with new employees miss a chance to create a favourable relationship before the employee becomes influenced by what other people think about the supervisor and the organization.

Professor John Wanous suggests using an orientation approach he calls ROPES—"Realistic Orientation Programs for new Employees' Stress.[12] A ROPES program offers the following advantages:

- *Provides realistic information.* Orientation should provide realistic information about the job environment and the organization.

- *Gives general support and reassurance.* It means telling new employees that the stress they experience during the first days or weeks is normal.

- *Demonstrates coping skills.* The orientation program should include stress training.

- *Identifies specific potential stressors.* The program should identify specific stressors, explain their impact, and explain an appropriate coping behaviour.

Orientation Follow-up

Successful orientation programs include a built-in follow-up procedure. Follow-up is needed because new employees are often reluctant to admit that they do not recall everything they were told in the initial orientation. As one writer pointed out, "The worst mistake a company can make is to ignore the new employee after orientation."[13] Even if the organization has an "open-door" policy, very rarely are new employees assertive enough to seek out new information by meeting their supervisors or the human resource staff. Systematic **orientation follow-up** after a week, a month, and probably a quarter of a year helps to assess the information needs of the new employee. It also tells the employee that the organization cares. The follow-up can be a prescheduled meeting or a simple checklist that asks the employee to assess the weaknesses of the orientation program. Weak areas, presumably, are topics about which an employee needs more information. The checklist also serves as feedback to the human resource department so that it can identify parts of the program that are good or bad. Poor orientation efforts by supervisors will also become apparent through feedback. A research study indicates that Canadian organizations typically follow up orientation within three months—one-third of the organizations studied having such follow-up sessions within one month and another third doing it between one and three months.[14]

Orientation follow-up
Procedures used after the orientation program to assess the information needs of new employees.

Evaluating the Effectiveness of Orientation

Orientation programs, however systematically done, can be ineffective in some instances. The human resource manager and the immediate supervisor should recognize several common **orientation pitfalls** that detract from successful programs.[15] Both are responsible for seeing that the employee is not:

Orientation pitfalls
Problems in the orientation program that detract from its effectiveness.

- overwhelmed with too much information to absorb in a short time;

- given only menial tasks that discourage job interest and company loyalty;

- overloaded with forms to fill out and manuals to read;

- pushed into the job with a sketchy orientation under the mistaken philosophy that "trial by fire" is the best orientation;

- forced to fill in the gaps between a broad orientation by the human resource department and a narrow orientation at the department level.

A good employee orientation program focuses on various aspects of an employee's life in the organization, both on the job and off the job.[16] On the job, the new recruits should be sponsored and guided by an experienced supervisor or colleague who can respond to questions and keep in close touch. The orientation program should introduce new employees to their colleagues and co-workers *gradually* rather than give a superficial introduction to all of them on the first day itself.[17] Also, a good orientation program will ensure that employees have sufficient time to get their feet on the ground before job demands on them are increased. *Off the job*, an effective orientation program will provide the most relevant and immediate information on the company first. Above all, it will emphasize the human side—it will tell the employees what supervisors and co-workers are like and encourage them to seek help and advice when needed. Orientation is also an occasion to communicate the culture of the organization. Indeed, the available research evidence indicates a growing emphasis on corporate culture during orientation in Canadian companies:[18]

> Organizational stories and folklore are important for the newcomer to an organization in understanding the prevailing culture. At a large Canadian telecommunications company, there is a story about prospective employees being asked to come for a job interview at 9 a.m. on a Sunday. The intent is to weed out undedicated employees who do not want long hours and are not prepared to make sacrifices when necessary. At Digital Equipment of Canada Ltd., new employees often hear stories that highlight the first rule in the company, namely, "When dealing with a customer or an employee, do what is 'right.' " "Doing right" often may mean turning down business that is profitable for the company, but not right for the customer.[19]

How does one evaluate the effectiveness of orientation programs? A few of the approaches are discussed below.

1. *Reactions from New Employees.* Probably the single most useful method of evaluating the effectiveness of orientation is getting the reactions of new employees who went through the process. The feedback itself can be obtained through in-depth interviews with randomly selected employees and through questionnaire surveys. Questionnaires are particularly useful if the organization wants responses from a large number of recently hired employees. They also allow the identity of the respondent to be kept anonymous, thus increasing the overall truthfulness and validity of responses. Whether an interview or survey format is used, the questions included should measure the appropriateness and effectiveness of the orientation procedures used. Questions on the readability of the literature supplied to employees during orientation, the appropriateness of the lectures and other presentations, the degree of structure visible in the program, the ease of understanding various ideas and organizational policies, etc., should form part of the feedback checklist used.

2. *Effects of Socialization on Job Attitudes and Roles.* The socialization process may be an effective method to change employee values and beliefs to make them conform with an organization's requirements. It is through socialization that major shifts in a new employee's values take place. On entering an organization, a new recruit encounters the reality of the organization—he or she sees what the organization is really like. Some initial shifting of values, attitudes, and skills occurs soon, along with a definition of his or her role in the organization, the work group, and the task. If the newcomers survive the initial change process, relatively long-lasting changes take place within the new employees: they master the job skills, successfully perform their new roles, and make adjustments to their work group's and organization's values and culture. The progress in a person's socialization can be measured attitudinally (e.g., overall satisfaction with the organization and the job, work motivation, and so on) and behaviourally (e.g., labour turnover, ability to carry out roles effectively, spontaneity visible in job performance, and so on). Ideally, an orientation program should hasten this socialization process by enabling a recruit to interact with new colleagues extensively. Measures of job satisfaction, work motivation, and job performance may be some useful indications of the effectiveness of the program to achieve this end.

3. *Degree to Which the Program Is Economical.* All human resource activities should be at a level appropriate to the organization's needs. If the orientation program in an organization is more or less sophisticated than the firm's needs, then resources are wasted. Cost-benefit studies on orientation activities should be carried out continually. The costs of an orientation program typically include cost of materials, salaries of instructors and human resource department staff,

rent, lost work time of other employees and supervisors, and the cost of tools such as films, slides, tours, and so on. The monetary benefits emerging from an orientation program include lower labour turnover, shorter time to learn a job, lower scrap rates and wastage, reduced rework, and so on. Obviously, the cost-benefit analysis should take into consideration the unique needs of a business and an organization.

That well-prepared orientation programs are effective has been proven in a recent research study. Klein and Weaver examined the impact of attending a new employee orientation program. Results revealed that employees attending the program were significantly more socialized on three of six socialization measures than employees who did not attend the orientation. Employees attending the program also had significantly higher levels of organizational commitment than nonattendees.[20]

EMPLOYEE TRAINING

http://canada.gc.ca/publications
/publication_e.html

www.hrreporter.com/

www.ipma-hr.org/pubs/
publications.html

www.tcm.com/trdev

www.filename.com/wbt

Purpose of Training

Canadian companies must compete in a global economy and in a fast-changing business environment. This requires a workforce that has the capability to respond quickly and reliably to new challenges. In turn, this makes training an important part of an organization's long-range strategy. Examples of the new requirements for survival include:

1. Competing globally against companies from countries with low wage levels has forced many Canadian companies to flatten their organization and to reduce the number of employees. A flatter organization—with fewer managers and supervisors—needs employees who are able to schedule their work, manage their team, and do their own quality control. Greater flexibility requires multi-skilled (or cross-trained) employees who perform diverse tasks. This has significant implications for the training function.

2. Multi-skilled employees prefer to be paid according to their competencies, not jobs performed. This, in turn, requires that a company's compensation and performance appraisal system be changed, again with important consequences for training. Multi-skilled employees have to keep up-to-date with their skills, implying the ability—and motivation—for lifelong learning. The organizational environment must foster and support this new concept.

3. Recent changes in immigration policies bring approximately 200 000 new immigrants to Canada annually, mostly from Asian countries. This makes it essential that Canadian managers learn to work with colleagues who often have very different cultural values. Diversity training alerts supervisors and employees against the use of stereotypes and prejudices.

4. Changing information technology, recent developments in computer applications, innovative multi-media training methods, pioneering use of the Internet and intranet, high-tech videoconferencing—these new uses of technology in management and the business environment require the mastering of fresh skills, necessitating novel training programs and training strategies.

As mentioned above, training is an essential part of an organization's long-term strategy. As we will discuss in the following paragraphs, training is an investment in human capital, and human capital is really "the most important asset a company has," as so many CEOs claim during annual meetings and year-end parties.

www.trainingsupersite.com/

www.astd.org/

www.astd.org/virtual_
community/infoline/

www.astd.org/virtual_
community/td_magazine

Relationship Between Training and Development

Training refers to a planned effort by an organization to facilitate the learning of job-related behaviour of its employees. The term *behaviour* is used broadly to include any knowledge and skill acquired by an employee through practice. When management wants to prepare employees for future job responsibilities, this activity is called human resource development, which is discussed in the following chapter. This distinction between *training* and development is primarily one of intent. Training prepares people to do their *present* job. *Development* prepares them for *future* jobs. These activities are usually the responsibility of the human resource department and the immediate supervisor. The rest of this chapter explains the major types of training programs, along with the underlying learning principles involved.

New employees seldom perform satisfactorily. They must be trained in the duties they are expected to perform. Even experienced employees may need training to reduce poor work habits or to learn new skills that improve their performance. Although *training* seeks to help employees do their present job, the *benefits of training* may extend throughout a person's entire career and help develop that person for future responsibilities.[21] To illustrate the developmental impact of training, consider one human resource director's observations:

> When I was first promoted to head all the job analysts a few years ago, I did not know the first thing about supervising. So I was sent to a training program for new supervisors. In that seminar I learned a lot of things. But the section on delegation really impressed me. I have relied on that knowledge ever since. Probably the reason I head the human resource department today is because that training helped to develop me into a manager.

Consider the description of one company's training policy. The HSBC Bank Canada makes training count. Its training program is closely linked with the bank's career advancement policy. Simply taking the bank's training courses is not enough to assure promotion. The bank's assistant general manager of HRD explains that the main criterion for promotion is performance, so the training must develop skills that give a competitive edge. The competitive-edge aspect ties in with training profitability. The "virtuous circle" (as opposed to the "vicious circle") denotes increased training leading to increased profits, which pays for further training, and so forth. The bank developed the following guidelines:

1. Analyze the strategic context of your training. Identify closely with the mission, strategy, goals, and objectives of our organization.

2. Define the role of human resource development broadly. Integrate your training into other HR functions, such as career development.

3. Measure the profitability of training.

4. Focus on "critical skills," the ones that impact heavily on the bottom line of our organization. Avoid getting on the bandwagon with the latest training fads.

5. Concentrate your efforts on achieving excellence in program design. Make it entertaining as well as instructive.

6. Involve line management in the implementation of training programs. The design and coordination is more difficult, but the payoff is much greater in terms of speed, cost-benefit, and skills transfer.

7. Dedicate time and effort to the evaluation of our programs and link it back to the training needs analysis.

The HSBC Bank Canada obviously has a well-integrated strategy for the training of its employees and their career development. Both are tied in with the strategic vision of the organization: training must lead to improved profits and greater effectiveness of the company, which in turn makes it easier to pay for better training and development of the bank's employees. Management of the bank demands that its trainers make employees aware of how training relates to the bottom line, which requires creating an awareness among bank employees of how training fits into their career development and how it helps the organization as a whole to move ahead. Making employees aware of this demands dealing with strategy and structure and the part training plays; in short, it requires the services of a training and development professional.[22]

The Training System

An effective training programs benefits employees and the organization. Some of the benefits for the employees are: skill improvement, self-development and stronger self-confidence, more effective handling of stress and conflicts, providing a sense of growth. For the organization the benefits may include improved profitability through higher productivity, improved morale, better corporate image, lower costs, and stronger identification with corporate goals.

To develop an effective training program human resource specialists and managers must assess the needs, objectives, content, and learning principles associated with training. Figure 7-3 shows a training systems approach that plots the sequence of events to be followed before training begins. First, the person who is responsible for the training (usually a trainer) must assess the needs of the employee and the organization in order to learn what objectives should be sought. Once objectives are set, the specific content and learning principles are considered. Whether the learning process is to be guided by trainers in the human resource department or by first-level supervisors, these preliminary steps should be undertaken to create an effective program.

Needs Assessment

www.perc.net/Needs
Anal.html

www.decpoint.com/tna.html

Although precise figures are not available, it is estimated that the cost of industrial training in Canada is around $4 billion annually, while federal and provincial governments spend over $40 billion on training and education.[23] If organizations are to get maximum benefit from this staggering expenditure, then efforts must concentrate

FIGURE 7-3

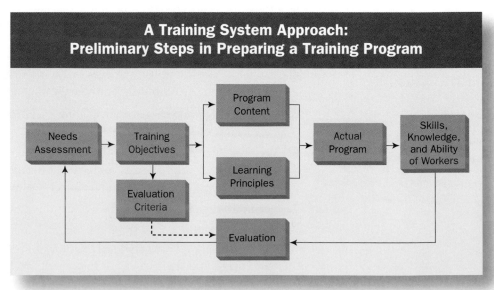

A Training System Approach:
Preliminary Steps in Preparing a Training Program

Needs assessment
A diagnosis that presents problems and future challenges that can be met through training or development.

on people and situations that can benefit most. To decide what approach to use, the trainer assesses the needs for training and development. ***Needs assessment*** diagnoses present problems and environmental challenges that can be met through training, or the future challenges to be met through long-term development. For example, changes in the external environment may present an organization with new challenges. To respond effectively, employees may need training to deal with the change. The comments of one training director illustrate the impact of the external environment:

> After enactment of the human rights legislation, we had to train every interviewer in the human resource department. This training was needed to ensure that our interviewers would not ask questions that might violate federal or provincial laws. When managers in other departments heard of the training, they, too, wanted to sign up. What was to be a one-time seminar became a monthly session for nearly three years. We evaluated the requests of these other managers and decided that they interviewed recruits and that they should be trained also.

Sometimes a change in the organization's strategy can create a need for training. For example, new products or services usually require employees to learn new procedures. Xerox encountered this challenge when it decided to produce computers. Sales personnel, programmers, and production workers had to be trained to produce, sell, and service this new product line. Training can also be used when high accident rates, low morale and motivation, or other problems are diagnosed. Although training is not an organizational cure-all, undesirable trends may be evidence of a poorly prepared workforce.

Regardless of these challenges, needs assessment must consider each person. Needs may be determined by the human resource department, supervisors, or self-nomination. The human resource department may find weaknesses among those who are hired or promoted. Supervisors see employee performance daily, and so they are another source of recommendations for training. But their suggestions may be made to banish troublemakers, "hide" surplus employees who are temporarily expendable, or reward good workers. Since these are not valid reasons, the human resource department often reviews supervisory recommendations to verify the need for training. Likewise, the department also reviews self-nominations to determine whether the training is actually needed.

Even when employees are allowed to nominate themselves for available training programs, training directors have little assurance that they are offering the correct mix of courses or that the courses have the right content. To better narrow the range of courses and define their content, more refined approaches to needs assessment are used. One approach is through task identification. Trainers begin by evaluating the job description to identify the salient tasks that the job requires. Then with an understanding of these tasks, specific plans are developed to provide the necessary training so that jobholders can perform the tasks.[24]

Another approach is to survey potential trainees to identify specific topical areas that they want to learn more about. The advantage of this method is that trainees are more likely to see the subsequent training programs as relevant, and thus they are more likely to be receptive to them. Of course, this approach to assessing training needs presumes that those surveyed know what training they need. For new employees needing specific individual or departmental training, this method is unlikely to be successful. In the case of more general training needs, however, group recommendations may be the best way to identify training needs. The group's expertise may be tapped through a group discussion, questionnaire, a Delphi procedure, or through a nominal group meeting (see Chapter Three for a discussion of the latter two procedures).

Besides being aware of possible language barriers when training foreign workers, it is important to realize that seemingly equivalent educational levels of employees in industrial and developing nations are not equivalent. Twelve years of education may have different meanings in different societies.

Trainers are alert to other sources of information that may indicate a need for training. Production records, quality control reports, grievances, safety reports, absenteeism and turnover statistics, and exit interviews among departing employees may indicate problems that should be addressed through training and development efforts. Training needs may also become apparent from career planning and development discussions or performance appraisal reviews—both of which are discussed in subsequent chapters. Regardless of how needs assessment takes place, it is important because the success of the remaining steps in Figure 7-3 depends on an accurate assessment. If the trainer's assessment of needs is not correct, training objectives and program content will be inappropriate.

Training Objectives

An evaluation of training needs results in training objectives. These objectives should state:

1. the desired behaviour;
2. the conditions under which it is to occur;
3. the acceptable performance criteria.

These statements serve as the standard against which individual performance and the program can be measured. For example, the objectives for an airline reservation agent might be stated as follows:

1. Provide flight information to call-in customers within 30 seconds.
2. Complete a one-city, round-trip reservation in 120 seconds after all information is obtained from the customer.

Objectives such as these give the trainer and the trainee specific goals that can be used by both to evaluate their success. If these objectives are not met, failure gives the human resource department feedback on the program and the participants.

Soldiers in the armed forces go through intensive and vigorous training exercises with clear training objectives.

CP PHOTO ARCHIVE (Associated Press)

Program Content

The program's content is shaped by the needs assessment and the learning objectives. This content may seek to teach specific skills, provide needed knowledge, or try to influence attitudes. Whatever the content, the program must meet the needs of the organization and the participants. If company goals are not furthered, resources are wasted. Similarly, participants must view the content as relevant to their needs, or their motivation to learn may be low.

Learning Principles

Although it is widely studied, little is known about the learning process. Part of the problem is that learning cannot be observed; only its results can be measured. From studies of learning, however, researchers have sketched a broad picture of the learning process and have developed some tentative principles of learning.

Learning curve
A visual representation of the rate at which one learns given material through time.

Perhaps the best way to understand learning is through the use of a ***learning curve***, pictured in Figure 7-4. As the curve illustrates, learning takes place in bursts (from points A to B) and in plateaus (from points B to C). Trainers have two goals related to the shape of each employee's learning curve. First, they want the learning curve to reach a satisfactory level of performance. This level is shown as a dashed line in the figure. Second, they want the learning curve to get to the satisfactory level as quickly as possible.

Although the rate at which an individual learns depends upon the person, the use of various learning principles speeds up the learning process.

Learning principles
Guidelines to the ways in which people learn most effectively.

Learning principles are guidelines to the ways in which people learn most effectively. The more they are included in training, the more effective training is likely to be. The principles are participation, repetition, relevance, transference, and feedback.

Participation

Participation
Being active in a learning process, e.g., using a computer instead of just listening to a lecture about its use.

Learning is usually quicker and more long-lasting when the learner can participate actively. *Participation* improves motivation and apparently engages more senses that help reinforce the learning process. As a result of participation, we learn more quickly and retain that learning longer. For example, once they have learned, most people never forget how to ride a bicycle or drive a car.

FIGURE 7-4

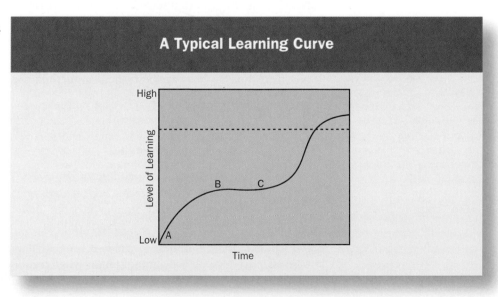

A Typical Learning Curve

Repetition

Repetition
Facilitates learning through repeated review of the material to be learned.

Although it is seldom fun, **repetition** apparently etches a pattern into our memory. Studying for an examination, for example, involves memorization of key ideas to be recalled during the test. Likewise, most people learned the alphabet and the multiplication tables by repetition.

Relevance

Relevance
Relating to the matter in hand.

Learning is helped when the material to be learned is meaningful. For example, trainers usually explain the overall purpose of a job to trainees before explaining specific tasks. This explanation allows the worker to see the **relevance** of each task and the importance of following the given procedures.

Transference

Transference
Applicability of training to job situations; evaluated by how readily the trainee can transfer the learning to his or her job.

Transference is the application of training to actual job situations. The closer the demands of the training program match the demands of the job, the faster a person learns to master the job. For example, pilots are usually trained in flight simulators because the simulators very closely resemble the actual cockpit and flight characteristics of the plane. The close match between the simulator and the plane allows the trainee to transfer quickly the learning in the simulator to actual flight conditions.

Feedback

Feedback
Information that helps evaluate the success or failure of an action or system.

Feedback gives learners information on their progress. With feedback, motivated learners can adjust their behaviour to achieve the quickest possible learning curve. Without feedback, learners cannot gauge their progress and may become discouraged. Test grades are feedback on the study habits of test takers, for example.

TRAINING TECHNIQUES

BEFORE REVIEWING the various training techniques, it is important to remember that any method may be applied to both training and development. For example, a class on management techniques may be attended by supervisors and workers who are likely to be promoted to those positions. For supervisors, the class covers how to do their present job better. In the case of workers who have no management responsibilities, the classes are intended to develop them into supervisors. The classroom instruction would be identical for both groups, but it has two different purposes: training for supervisors and development for workers.

In selecting a particular training technique, there are several trade-offs. That is, no one technique is always best; the best method depends upon:

- cost-effectiveness;
- desired program content;
- appropriateness of the facilities;
- trainee preferences and capabilities;
- trainer preferences and capabilities;
- learning principles.

The importance of these six trade-offs depends upon the situation. For example, cost-effectiveness may be a minor factor when training an airline pilot in emergency manoeuvres. But whatever method is selected, it has certain learning principles associated with it. Figure 7-5 lists the most common training techniques and the learning principles each includes. As the figure reveals, some techniques make more effective use of learning principles than others. Even those approaches that use few learning principles, such as the lecture, are valuable tools because they may satisfy one of the other five trade-offs listed above. For example, lectures may be the best way to communicate some academic content in the most cost-effective manner, especially if the classroom is large and the room does not lend itself to other approaches. Although these six trade-offs affect the methods used, human resource specialists must be familiar with all the techniques and learning principles found in Figure 7-5.

On-the-Job Training

On-the-job-training (OJT)
A method whereby a person learns a job by actually performing it.

On-the-job training is received directly on the job and is used primarily to teach workers how to do their present job. A trainer, supervisor, or co-worker serves as the instructor. This method includes each of the five learning principles (participation, repetition, relevance, transference, and feedback) in a series of carefully planned steps.

First, the trainee receives an overview of the job, its purpose, and the desired outcomes, which emphasizes the relevance of the training. Then the trainer demonstrates the job to provide the employee with a model to copy. Since the employee is

FIGURE 7-5

Learning Principles in Different Training Techniques

	Participation	Repetition	Relevance	Transference	Feedback
On-the-Job Techniques					
Job instruction training	Yes	Yes	Yes	Yes	Sometimes
Job rotation	Yes	Sometimes	Yes	Sometimes	No
Apprenticeships	Yes	Sometimes	Yes	Sometimes	Sometimes
Coaching	Yes	Sometimes	Yes	Sometimes	Yes
Off-the-Job Techniques					
Lecture	No	No	No	Sometimes	No
Video presentation	No	No	No	Yes	No
Vestibule training	Yes	Yes	Sometimes	Yes	Sometimes
Role-playing	Yes	Sometimes	Sometimes	No	Sometimes
Case study	Yes	Sometimes	Sometimes	Sometimes	Sometimes
Simulation	Yes	Sometimes	Sometimes	Sometimes	Sometimes
Self-study	Yes	Yes	Sometimes	Sometimes	No
Programmed learning	Yes	Yes	No	Yes	Yes
Laboratory training	Yes	Yes	Sometimes	No	Yes
Computer- based training	Yes	Yes	Sometimes	Yes	Yes
Virtual Reality	Yes	Yes	Yes	Yes	Yes

Source: Adapted from and amended: *From Training in Industry: The Management of Learning*, by B.M. Bass and J.M. Vaughan. Copyright © 1966 Brooks/Cole Publishing Company, an imprint of the Wadsworth Group, Pacific Grove, CA 93950, a division of International Thomson Publishing Inc. By permission of the publisher.

being shown the actions that the job actually requires, the training is transferable to the job. Next, the employee is allowed to mimic the trainer's example. Demonstrations by the trainer and practice by the trainee are repeated until the job is mastered by the trainee. Repeated demonstrations and practice provide the advantage of repetition and feedback. Finally, the employee performs the job without supervision, although the trainer may visit the employee periodically to see if there are any lingering questions.

Job Rotation

Cross-training
Training employees to perform operations in areas other than their assigned jobs.

To cross-train employees in a variety of jobs, some trainers will move the trainee from job to job. Each move is normally preceded by job instruction training. Besides giving workers variety in their jobs, *cross-training* helps the organization when vacations, absences, and resignations occur. Learner participation and high job transferability are the learning advantages to job rotation.

Godfather system
Widely used in Japanese companies, senior employees guide new employees through a job rotation program that puts the new employees into all of the organization's functional units.

Job rotation is also widely used in Japanese companies, and in some firms it is used together with the *godfather system*.[25] Godfathers are usually senior employees who are asked to play this role to four or six new employees. Their task is to guide the new employees through a two-year job rotation program that puts new employees into all the organization's functional units, for example, accounting, engineering, finance, human resource management, manufacturing, marketing, sales, and so on.

The godfather will keep in touch with all the supervisors the trainees will encounter during their training rotation. The godfather is available at all times for consultation, counselling, and coaching. After the two-year rotation, the godfather, the trainee, and the supervisors will sit down to decide which career the trainee should pursue.

Apprenticeships and Coaching

Apprenticeships involve learning from a more experienced employee or employees. This approach to training may be supplemented with off-the-job classroom training. Most tradespeople, such as plumbers and carpenters, are trained through formal apprenticeship programs. Assistantships and internships are similar to apprenticeships. These approaches use high levels of participation by the trainee and have high transferability to the job.

Coaching is similar to apprenticeship in that the coach attempts to provide a model for the trainee to copy. Most companies use some coaching. It tends to be less formal than an apprenticeship program because there are few formal classroom sessions, and the coaching is provided when needed rather than being part of a carefully planned program. Coaching is almost always handled by the supervisor or manager and not the human resource department. Participation, feedback, and job transference are likely to be high in this form of learning.

Someone who receives coaching by another person to assume that person's specific job is called an *understudy*. A senior executive may designate a replacement well before retirement so that that person can serve as an understudy.

Assignments to task forces or committees can also help to develop people in much the same way that apprenticeships and coaching do. Through periodic staff meetings or work with task forces and committees, a manager develops interpersonal skills, learns to evaluate information, and gains experience in observing other potential models.

www.presentations.com/
#_open

Off-the-Job Training

Lecture and Video Presentations

Lecture and other off-the-job techniques tend to rely more heavily on communications rather than modelling, which is used in on-the-job programs. These approaches are applied in both training and development. Lecture is a popular approach because it offers relative economy and a meaningful organization of materials. However, participation, feedback, transference, and repetition are often low. Feedback and participation can be improved when discussion is permitted after the lecture.

Television, films, slides, and filmstrip presentations are comparable to lectures. A meaningful organization of materials and initial audience interest are potential strengths of these approaches.

Vestibule Training

So that training does not disrupt normal operations, some organizations use *vestibule training*. Separate areas or vestibules are set up with the same kind of equipment that will be used on the job. This arrangement allows transference, repetition, and participation. The meaningful organization of materials and feedback are also possible:

> At the corporate training facilities of Best Western motels and hotels, vestibules exist that duplicate a typical motel room, a typical front counter, and a typical restaurant kitchen. This allows trainees to practise housekeeping, front-counter service, and kitchen skills without disrupting the operations of any one property.

Role-Playing

Role-playing
A training technique that requires trainees to assume different identities in order to learn how others feel under different circumstances.

Role-playing is a device that forces trainees to assume different identities. For example, a male worker and a female supervisor may trade roles. The result? Usually participants exaggerate each other's behaviour. Ideally, they both get to see themselves as others see them. The experience may create greater empathy and tolerance of individual differences. This technique seeks to change attitudes of trainees, such as to improve racial understanding. It also helps to develop interpersonal skills. Although participation and feedback are present, the inclusion of other learning principles depends on the situation.

Many companies employ role-playing to train supervisors to give performance feedback, a crucial managerial skill in motivating employees. Supervisors often avoid giving negative feedback, because they feel uneasy about it. However, since it is normal for an employee to exhibit ineffective job behaviour, managers must learn to provide their employees with constructive criticism. During the role-play exercise, two supervisors assume the roles of a rater, who gives feedback, and of a ratee, who is at the receiving end. Once the role-play is over, observers (usually trainers) give both comments about their effectiveness as feedback provider and receiver. Then the roles are reversed. Through the exercises and subsequent discussions, supervisors can learn about their attitudes toward negative feedback and how to change it into constructive criticism:

> The RCMP in British Columbia uses role-playing exercises to reduce tensions between members of the force who are of Caucasian and Indian (mainly Sikh) origin. Friction between members of the different cultures on the force caused breakdowns in communications between officers on extended patrol duties, especially when they were in the confinement of a patrol car.
>
> The role-playing exercises required a small number of members of the two groups to assume the role of the other race. The role-playing leader gave each group an assignment and then directed them to carry it out as they thought members of the other race

would do it. With the other group watching, each group in turn acted out the behaviour of the other. Through these exercises and the subsequent discussions, members of the different cultural groups were able to learn how their behaviour and attitudes affected each other. These role-playing exercises were an important step in reducing racial tensions.

Closely related to this form of role-playing is *behaviour modelling*. Behaviour modelling was described by two writers as follows:

> Modelling is one of the fundamental psychological processes by which new patterns of behavior can be acquired, and existing patterns can be altered. The fundamental characteristic of modelling is that learning takes place, not through actual experience, but through observation or imagination of another individual's experience. Modelling is a "vicarious process," which implies sharing in the experience of another person through imagination or sympathetic participation.[26]

Whether behaviour modelling is referred to as "matching" or "copying," "observational learning" or "imitation," "all of these terms imply that a behavior is learned or modified through the observation of some other individual."[27] Employees may learn a new behaviour through modelling by observing a new or novel behaviour and then imitating it. The re-creation of the behaviour may be videotaped so that the trainer and trainee can review and criticize the behaviour. Often, when watching the ideal behaviour, the trainee also gets to see the negative consequences of not behaving in the ideal way. Observing both the positive and negative consequences of the taped behaviour gives the employee vicarious reinforcement to adopt the right behaviour.

Case Study

By studying a case, trainees learn about real or hypothetical circumstances and the actions others took under those circumstances. Besides learning from the content of the case, trainees can develop decision-making skills. When cases are meaningful and similar to work-related situations, there is some transference. There also is the advantage of participation through discussion of the case. Feedback and repetition are usually lacking. This technique is most effective for developing problem-solving skills.

Simulation

Simulation exercises are in two forms. One form involves a mechanical simulator that replicates the major features of the work situation. Driving simulators used in driver's education programs are an example. This training method is similar to vestibule training, except that the simulator more often provides instantaneous feedback on performance.

Computer simulation is another technique. For training and development purposes, this method is often employed in the form of games. Players make a decision and the computer determines the outcome of the decision, given the conditions under which it was programmed. This technique is used most commonly to train managers, who otherwise might have to use trial and error in decision making.

Self-Study and Programmed Learning

Carefully planned instructional materials can be used to train and develop employees. These are particularly useful when employees are dispersed geographically or when learning requires little interaction. Self-study techniques range from manuals to prerecorded cassettes or videotapes. Unfortunately, few learning principles are included in this type of training:

www.phppo.cdc.gov/dls/nltn/

Pepsi Cola Management Institute is responsible for training bottlers all over the world. To contend with this dispersion, it created a network of videotape recorders and supplied bottlers with videotaped materials. The institute also uses other techniques.

Programmed learning materials are another form of self-study. Commonly, these are printed booklets that contain a series of questions and answers. After a question is read, the answer can be uncovered immediately. If the reader was right, he or she proceeds. If wrong, the reader is directed to review accompanying materials. Of course, computer programs with visual displays may be used instead of printed booklets. Programmed materials do provide learning participation, repetition, relevance, and feedback. The major advantage appears to be the savings in training time.[28]

Laboratory Training

Laboratory training is a form of group training used primarily to enhance interpersonal skills. It too can be used to develop desired behaviours for future job responsibilities. Participants seek to improve their human relations skills by better understanding themselves and others. It involves sharing their experiences and examining the feelings, behaviour, perceptions, and reactions that result. Usually a trained professional serves as a facilitator. The process relies on participation, feedback, and repetition. One popular form of laboratory training is sensitivity training—also known as T-group, encounter group, or team building—which seeks to improve a person's sensitivity to the feelings of others.

Laboratory training
A form of group training primarily used to enhance interpersonal skills.

In a typical sensitivity training meeting, the facilitator explains his or her role as a resource person, then lapses into silence, leaving participants to grapple with establishing a purpose for their meeting. The trainer will intervene only to help participants understand the dynamics of their relations during the meeting, such as their own feelings and behaviours and the impact of their behaviour on themselves and others. In this respect, learning results from the "here-and-now" experiences of the participants through one's own disclosures and the immediate feedback from others during the session.[29]

Computer-Based Training

Computer-based training (CBT), also known as computer-assisted learning, has been gaining prominence in Canada in recent years. CBT offers the student control over the pace of learning and even other training contents in modular-type training programs. It offers the benefits of interactive learning, participation, and positive reinforcement during training.

Computer-based training (CBT)
The use of computers to facilitate the training process.

www.cybernetic-learning.com/multimediacbtweb.htm

www.comlearn.com/

www.clat.psu.edu/homes/bxb11/CBTGuide/CBTGuide.htm

www8.zdnet.com/eweek/reviews/0818/18ibt.html

Current available CBT courses fall into three main categories: off-the-shelf courses on generic topics, support courses with software packages, and custom courseware.

Off-the-Shelf Courses. Courses available in this category are typically in the areas of personal or professional skills. A number of topics currently exist, ranging from business writing and time management on the one end to complex statistical techniques on the other end.

Support Courses. Increasingly, courses on a number of topics are making their appearance on diskettes with supplementary tutorial packages. Many of these courses are on simple skills development (e.g., learning how to use a spreadsheet), but training on more complex skills and management topics can be found in complete tutorial packages (e.g., strategic planning).

Custom Courseware. Here the focus is on producing customized courses for a particular type of employee or organization. An increasing number of Canadian organizations are using customized CBT techniques for their staffs. One of the most successful CBT programs is used by the Edmonton Police Department (EPD). Called DIIT (Decentralized, Individualized, Inservice Training), the program uses modern forms of training delivery: a powerful combination of video-based training, for realism and accuracy, plus computer-based training for efficiency, cost-effectiveness, and record-keeping.

The traditional method of instruction consisted of a two-week classroom course offered every five years and lasting 80 hours. DIIT training now requires only 60 hours and provides training on a monthly basis. The net training cost to the EPD has been reduced by $70 000 per year for five years due to a reduction in student hours devoted to training and reduced delivery costs; improved job performance; a decrease in the number of failures on promotional exams of upgrades; and an increase in the average score of participants. In addition to its record-keeping abilities, the EPD considers CBT to be an effective means of increasing retention, improving motivation, and providing standardized information.[30]

CBT is unlikely to be very beneficial unless:

1. it meets the specific needs of the individual;

2. it is supported by other material that facilitates or reinforces learning;

3. the skill learned is usable in the organization's context; and

4. students do not have a mental block against the use of computers.

Some employees may need to change their attitude toward computers and their relevance for the workplace. Unless the human resource manager understands the "fear" or "awe" of some employees toward computers and works to eliminate it, gaining wide acceptance for computer-based training may be impossible. Also, there are some skills that can never be effectively communicated through computers.[31]

Subcategories of CBT are *computer-assisted instruction (CAI)* and *computer-managed instruction (CMI)*. CAI is an educational medium in which instructional content or activities are delivered by a computer. Students learn by interacting with the computer and are provided with immediate feedback. CMI, on the other hand, uses the computer's branching, storage, and retrieval capabilities to organize instruction and track student records and progress.[32]

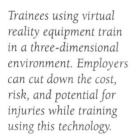

Trainees using virtual reality equipment train in a three-dimensional environment. Employers can cut down the cost, risk, and potential for injuries while training using this technology.

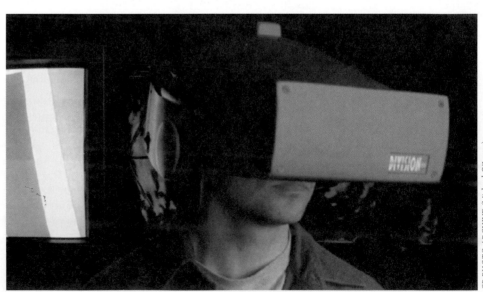

CP PHOTO ARCHIVE (Michael O'Leary)

www.activeworlds.com/
www.vrs.org.uk/
www.itl.nist.gov/iaui/ovrt/hotvr.html
www.cms.dmu.ac.uk/~cph/
vrstuff.html
www.sandia.gov/media/NewsRel/NR
1999/biosim.htm

Virtual Reality
The use of a number of technologies to replicate the entire real-life working environment.

Virtual Reality (VR)

Virtual reality uses modern computer technology to create a realistic visual impression of an actual work environment. It allows trainees to respond to job requirements as if they worked on the job, like in a simulation. However, while simulation deals with certain aspects of the job, virtual reality combines "all" aspects of the job. The trainee works in a three-dimensional environment and is able to interact with and manipulate objects in real time.

It allows companies to prepare trainees for job experiences that normally would involve high costs (e.g, flying an airplane); have the risk of costly damage to equipment (e.g., landing a plane on an aircraft carrier); or have the potential for injuries to the trainee (e.g., training in a race car).[33]

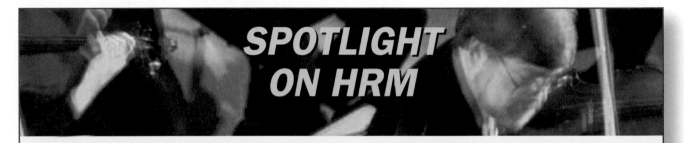

VIRTUAL REALITY TRAINING TAKES OFF

Virtual reality (VR) is a computer-based technology that gives learners a realistic, three-dimensional, interactive experience. Unlike animation or video, in which images are played and replayed in preset sequences, VR can be viewed, interacted with, and examined from any number of perspectives in any sequence. . . .

Currently, VR is used in such fields as architecture, medicine, and engineering as a highly interactive training tool. Many PC-based VR training applications exist for teaching technical skills. For instance, when the National Guard wanted to improve the skills of maintenance mechanics, it sent a virtual tank, via a PC, to local armories rather than sending real tanks at great cost. Now, even in rural locations, new recruits can practice critical troubleshooting skills rather than just reading the manuals.

VR and Training

VR technology makes it possible for trainees to work in realistic settings with real equipment, any time and any place.

VR is particularly beneficial

- when such hazards as radiation or toxic chemicals are involved
- when trainees cannot access new products or expensive equipment
- when trainees cannot travel to a training site.

Some speculate that VR may improve a trainee's ability to learn and retain information and skills. While most of this evidence is anecdotal, studies are underway to examine the effectiveness of VR-based learning.

At Research Triangle Institute in North Carolina, for example, we are conducting VR effectiveness studies in a controlled setting. The studies are looking at how much realism is required to improve learning and skill performance, what types of learning benefit most from using VR, and whether VR can increase a trainee's motivation and retention. . . .

VR can build on other training systems. It can be incorporated into existing CBT modules and is compatible with many authoring software programs. VR is also useful in conjunction with traditional classroom and laboratory instruction.

VR requires special computer hardware and software. Many types of computers and VR software development tools are capable of displaying VR, so determining what it takes to do VR requires careful analysis. . . .

A VR experience gets better with increases in a computer's speed, memory, graphics-handling, and screen resolution, and by adding 3-D devices and sound, realism, and interaction. . . .

A program developer should first collect visual and performance data. Then, based on that data, three-dimensional objects can be created and placed together in virtual environments. Those objects are given behaviors and rules for how to perform. For example, when a key turns, an engine starts, which in turn causes movement and sound.

VR development requires a complex set of skills. Most VR projects are best accomplished by a team in which instructional designers work closely with 3-D modelers and software application programmers.

The cost of VR depends on the features you need tempered by your budget. The factors affecting the cost of VR include:

● the amount and complexity of visual and other data it will include

● the amount of realism or detail in visual images

● how users will access VR materials.

To better understand the costs involved, compare standard multimedia with VR development. While the cost of multimedia courseware varies widely, average costs of $40 000 per hour of finished instruction have been reported in the *Multimedia Training Newsletter* and in *New Media* magazine. . . .

VR Outlook

We take for granted how easily computers handle number-and word-processing. In the future, though, VR may be in nearly every computer program, providing a rich source of interactive, visual experiences.

Experts predict that VR over the Internet using VRML (virtual reality modeling language), soon will be more robust and will allow many users to share and manipulate a common virtual environment. Even though increased bandwidth will give access to high-quality video images, VR will be critical for accessing things that don't yet exist physically, are too dangerous or difficult to access, or require interaction in three dimensions.

While today's VR training programs concentrate on the development of technical skills, tomorrow's VR may help trainees develop interpersonal skills. For example, negotiation skills could be practiced in a virtual environment that looks like a room full of people.

The virtual "opponents" in such a negotiation would be modeled on a variety of people's speech patterns, gestures, and experiences. These simulated people (intelligent robots, often referred to as agents) would use both predictable and unpredictable responses in the negotiation session. . . .

VR is an emerging technology that today is bringing new forms of interactivity to training programs. In the next few years, as VR technology advances, it promises to take training into a whole new dimension wherever learning takes place.

Source: Carol Gunther-Mohr, "Virtual Reality Training Takes Off," *Training & Development*, June 1997, pp. 47-48. Courtesy of The American Society for Training and Development.

Internet or Web-based Training, Virtual Education, and e-Learning

www.learnativity.com/#_open

www.linezine.com/index.htm

www.internettime.com/e.htm

www.filename.com/wbt/
index.html

http://eec.edshop.com/

Internet or Web-based training, virtual education, and e-learning are three terms that share similar meanings: training or education delivered via the Internet. These new approaches allow highly specific training to be delivered at any time and any place in the world. Advances in computer network technology and improvements in bandwidth allow the use of three-dimensional virtual reality, animation, interactions, chat and conferencing, and real-time audio and video. These approaches offer several benefits:

● the provision of "just-in-time" training or information;

● the ability for the learner to learn when it is convenient;

● the ability to target the instruction to what the learner needs to know, not what a traditional class must cover; and

● a reduction in travel and instruction costs.

Although these methods can be expensive and time consuming to develop, the costs are usually recovered quickly through savings in instructor time, reduced travel, less or no time-off-the-job, better retention, and general higher effectiveness.[34]

TRAINING EVALUATION

TRAINING SERVES as a transformation process. Untrained employees are transformed into capable workers, and present workers may be trained to assume new responsibilities. To verify the program's success, human resource managers increasingly demand that training activities be evaluated systematically.

www.trainingevaluation.org/

www.itrain.org/itinfo/1999/
it991007.html

www.enquirewithin.co.nz/
howtraining.htm

The lack of evaluation may be the most serious flaw in most training efforts. Simply stated, human resource professionals too seldom ask, "Did the program achieve the objectives established for it?" They often assume it had value because the content seemed important. Or trainers may rely on the evaluation of trainees who comment on how enjoyable the experience was for them, but who cannot yet determine how valuable it is.

Evaluation of training should follow the steps in Figure 7-6. First, evaluation criteria should be established before the training program begins. There are five types of criteria (see footnote):[35]

1. reaction;
2. knowledge;
3. attitudes;
4. behaviour;
5. organizational results.

Training objectives determine which of the criteria is the best suited for evaluation purposes. If the objective is to increase the knowledge of the participants, the obvious choice would be the knowledge criterion; if it is behaviour change, then the behaviour criterion would be the most appropriate measure. Each criterion has its advantages and disadvantages as described below.

1. *Reaction.* Also known as the happiness or smile sheet, reaction is the most widely used criterion in training evaluation. The usual question asked is: "How satisfied are you with the program?" or "Would you recommend it to a colleague?" This measure evaluates the set-up of the program, but not its effectiveness. However, it can provide valuable information for the organizers of programs as to the proper training environment, seating arrangement, satisfaction with training facilities, food, and accommodation.

2. *Knowledge.* Very popular in learning institutions in exams, it is legitimate if increase in knowledge is the intended objective of a training program (e.g., improved product knowledge). However, it can be reliably assessed only if before and after tests are used. Otherwise, it is uncertain whether a high score means the program was effective or whether the students knew the material beforehand.

3. *Attitudes.* Changes in attitudes are often the objectives of supervisor and leadership training programs. Attitudes are feelings toward something and are not visible. They have to be assessed through self-reports, a very unreliable measure. Respondents often give a "social desirability response," that is, they answer the way they think they should answer to save face. The validity of self-reports can be increased by assuring the respondent's anonymity.

FIGURE 7-6

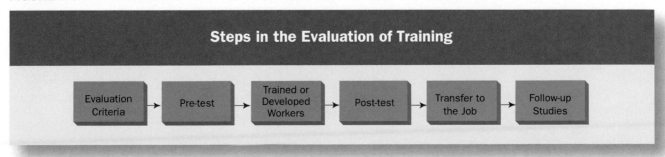

Steps in the Evaluation of Training: Evaluation Criteria → Pre-test → Trained or Developed Workers → Post-test → Transfer to the Job → Follow-up Studies

Most publications discussing training evaluation criteria use Kirkpatrick's four criteria: reaction, knowledge, behaviour, and organizational results. However, it is the first author's contention that, since changes of attitudes are important training objectives, e.g., a part of leadership or supervisory training, they should be included in evaluation discussions.

4. *Behaviour.* For the measurement of behaviour change, self-reports and observations by others are used (e.g., neutral observers, superiors, peers, subordinates, or customers). With self-reports, the same response problems discussed above under attitude measurements are encountered. Supervisor observation of behaviour change is more effective, but this approach has an inherent weakness. It is usually the supervisor who sent the employee to the training program and, because of this, is less likely to admit that he or she made an error in judgment.

5. *Organizational Results.* Organizational results would be ideal measurements were it not for the difficulty in determining the cause-effect relationship between training programs and organizational results. The time difference between a training program and the availability of reports on organizational results can be many months. Who is then to say whether it was the training program or some other event that caused the results?

Evaluation Methodology

According to *Webster's*, a method is an orderly and logical procedure, and methodology is the science of method. An example of a nonscientific method to assess the effectiveness of a training program is the popular post-test design; one test is applied at the end of a training program to test its effectiveness:

T   O

(training)   (observation/test)

There are inherent problems with this method. Do we know it was the training that caused a high score? We cannot be sure. Perhaps the participants were already experienced and did not need the training in the first place.

A more effective approach is the pre-test post-test design where the instructor applies tests at the beginning and at the end of the training program to measure first the precondition (baseline characteristic) of the participants and then the outcome:

O   T   O

(observation/test)   (training)   (repeat observation/test)

which allows a more realistic assessment of the outcomes of a training program. Examples of the two approaches are given below:

> One of the authors conducted a human resource management seminar in Slovakia. At the end of the 10-day seminar, the organizers used a reaction sheet to assess the outcome of the program. Although it was obvious that participants enjoyed it very much, nobody could say how effective the program really was and whether it had achieved its objectives.

> A similar seminar was offered the following year. This time the author suggested to the organizers that a pre-test post-test method be used. At the beginning, a knowledge test and an application test (case) were given to the participants, and equivalent tests were given at the end of the program. The average score at the beginning was 23 out of 100 points; the average score at the end was 66, an almost 200 per cent improvement. It was concluded that the training had been effective.

The pre-test and post-test is not a scientific method since it does not control for other influences on the training outcome, but it should suffice as a practical measurement. If trainers want to test the outcome of training programs scientifically, more appropriate methods can be found in relevant research literature.[36]

Cost-Benefit Analysis

www.michaelgreer.com/
cost-ben.htm

A training investment should be treated like any other investment decision. No manager worth his or her salt would invest a significant amount of money without an

Cost-benefit analysis
Analysis undertaken to assess the cost-effectiveness of a project or program.

appropriate *cost-benefit analysis*. Such an analysis assesses the cost-effectiveness of a project or program. It also assists a trainer or human resource manager in demonstrating the contribution the training or human resource management department makes to the organization's profit.

Contributions to profit can be made through increasing revenues or by decreasing expenditures according to the formula:

$$\text{revenue} - \text{costs} = \text{profit}$$

Training can contribute to increased revenue by improving the performance of revenue-producing employees, either by increasing output or by reducing production costs, or by both. If training is used to increase productivity, then training costs have to be included in the pricing of the product. Figure 7-7 presents factors associated with different training activities.

An example of a realistic cost/benefit analysis of a training program is described in Appendix A.

TRAINING AS A STRATEGIC TOOL

TRAINING IS AN INVESTMENT in human capital.[37] Managers must understand that large investments in physical plant, modern machinery, and new technology cannot be fully realized if there is no equivalent investment in human capital.[38] The acquisition of new skills is not only vital to improving quality and productivity, but is also essential if companies want to meet global competition. See Figure 7-8 for an overview of what companies spend on training.

Especially for quality-oriented companies, training objectives become part of the overall long-range strategy. As one of the world's leading suppliers of digital

FIGURE 7-7

Contributing Factors to Training Costs

Activities	Costs
Needs analysis	Labour: consultant, clerical staff
Program development	Labour: consultant, clerical staff
	Material: office material; video films
	Equipment rental
	Other potential costs: travel; accommodation; per diem expenses
Course delivery	Equipment
	Room rental
	Food
	Trainers' salaries
	Trainees' salaries
	Lost production
Program evaluation	Evaluator's fee
	Travel and accommodation
	(assuming external evaluator)
	Overhead costs: staff and clerical support, office space, utilities

FIGURE 7-8

Percentage of Payroll Spent on Training

Percentage of Payroll Spent on Training	Frequency	Comment
.5 to 1.5	common	most Canadian/U.S. companies
1.6	average	average of Canadian/U.S. companies
2–3	above average	not many companies
4–5	outstanding	very few companies
5–6	exceptional	very rare

Sources: Jean-Pascal Souque: "Focus on Competencies: Training and Development Practices, Expenditures, and Trends," Report 177-96; Ottawa: Conference Board of Canada, 1996; David McIntyre, "Getting the Most from Your Training Dollar," Report 163-96; Ottawa: Conference Board of Canada, 1996. The Conference Board of Canada is a membership based, not-for-profit, independent applied research organization.

telecommunications systems, Nortel has been aggressively restructuring and realigning its operations for global competition. At its Bramalea plant outside of Toronto, the company began to organize all employees into teams of eight to ten persons. Training is provided in a variety of new and traditional skills, such as problem-solving, statistical processes, and quality control. On average, each employee participating in teamwork receives 23 days of full-time training. As a result, quality has improved 10 to 30 per cent in a number of areas; improvements have also reduced downtime and waste. Workers took pride in these accomplishments. As one put it:

> I am doing it not only because that is my job, but I am doing it for me. The company is becoming flatter and there is not that much room at the top for all of us to be promoted. I have got to rely on making my own job more interesting and rewarding. I am learning so much and acquiring the confidence that comes with getting a chance to do several things. With each new training, each new project, I feel that I am securing my job—maybe not in this company forever—but in the job market out there.[39]

SUMMARY

www.jrctrainingsolutions
.com

After workers are selected, they are seldom ready to perform successfully. They must be integrated into the social and work environment of the organization. Orientation programs help a worker begin this socialization process. The organization benefits because training time and costs are lowered, employee satisfaction is higher, and initial turnover is lower.

A variety of orientation programs are currently available, although all are not popular to the same degree. Typically, orientation is done on an individual basis and consists of introductions to a person's job, colleagues, and the organization's policies. The responsibility for orientation is usually shared between the human resource department and the recruit's immediate boss. Whatever the method used, to be successful an orientation program should include a built-in follow-up procedure. The criteria employed in evaluating the orientation function may vary from one organization to another depending on unique needs; however, measures of employee satisfaction with the job and the orientation program, the turnover among new recruits, and measures of job-related attitudes should be included in the evaluation. All successful orientation programs enhance and strengthen the socialization process by which the new employee and the organization are bonded, resulting in mutual acceptance and trust.

Training is an essential part of an organization's long-range strategy. If a company wants to survive in a competitive global environment, it requires an efficient and flexible workforce that is adaptable to fast-changing technologies and new approaches to doing business. Canadian managers also have to learn to manage a diverse workforce, made up of new immigrants from very different cultures. Flatter organizations necessitate new skills for employees, who have to shoulder more responsibilities. This, in turn, leads to greater emphasis on employees' competencies, resulting in the need for lifelong learning.

Training begins with an assessment of training needs. Specific training objectives can then be set. These objectives give direction to the training program and serve to evaluate the training program at its completion. The content of the program depends on the training objectives. The design of the training should consider such learning principles as participation, repetition, relevance, transference, and feedback.

Once training is completed, it is essential that it is evaluated. Without evaluation a company does not know what it gets in return for its training investment. Evaluations include a pre-test and post-test measurement of how well the training content has been transferred to the actual job, and some form of follow-up studies to ensure that the learning has been retained. A cost-benefit analysis should be conducted whenever possible to assess the contribution that any training program makes to the profits of the company.

TERMS FOR REVIEW

Visit the Web site at www.mcgrawhill.ca/college/schwind6 for a full glossary.

REVIEW AND DISCUSSION QUESTIONS

1. "If employees are properly selected, there should be no need for an orientation program or training." Do you agree or disagree? Why?

2. What are the employee benefits from orientation programs? The organizational benefits?

3. What are the common pitfalls of an informal orientation program?

4. Suppose your organization hired six new clerical workers. What type of orientation program would you design to help these workers become productive and satisfied?

5. If the student services office of your college or university asked you to evaluate the effectiveness of the orientation program, what measures would you use? Why?

6. For each of the following occupations, which training techniques do you recommend? Why?

    (a) A cashier in a grocery store.

    (b) A welder.

    (c) An assembly-line worker.

    (d) An inexperienced supervisor.

7. If you were directed to design a program for managers that made use of all five learning principles, which two training techniques would you combine? Why?

8. Suppose you were a supervisor in an accounting department and the training manager wanted to implement a new training program to teach bookkeepers how to complete some new accounting forms. What steps would you recommend to evaluate the effectiveness of the training program?

9. Assume you were hired to manage a research department. After a few weeks you noticed that some researchers were more effective than others, and that the less effective ones received little recognition from their more productive counterparts. What forms of training would you consider for both groups?

10. What is the purpose of a cost-benefit analysis?

11. What factors do you take into account for a cost-benefit analysis?

CRITICAL THINKING QUESTIONS

1. Before you entered your college or university, you had certain ideas about what your values and expectations would be as a student. How did the institution's socialization process change those values and expectations?

2. Training is an investment in human capital, but some companies prefer to save training money and use it to "raid" other companies for skilled employees by offering higher salaries. Is raiding cheaper than training? Is it ethical?

3. Developed countries tend to have better skilled workers, resulting in higher productivity and economic wealth. Should governments subsidize company training? Why or why not?

WEB RESEARCH

On Employee Orientation

1. Robert Bacal of Bacal & Associates

www.escape.ca/~rbacal/orient.htm

A quick guide to employee orientation

  a) What does Bacal have to say about the outcomes of an effective orientation program?

  b) What different types of orientation programs does he describe? How do they differ?

On Training

1. The TrainingSuperSite

www.trainingsupersite.com/

  a) list the names of training publications available;

  b) identify five common popular topics;

  c) give a summary of the relevant articles (you can use the abstracts, if available).

2. HR.com

http://hr.com/HRcom/index.cfm

- go to the "Training" part and choose a "Feature". Summarize it (then enjoy the cartoon part)

3. Information Technology and Training

www.itworldcanada.com/it

- go to "Skills Management", then to "Related News"; choose any training related article and summarize it. How does it related to information technology? What are the major recommendations?
  Enjoy the "Break Zone" (humour)

4. Human Resource Development Canada (HRDC)

www.hrdc-drhc.gc.ca/common/home.shtml

- go to "Learning Opportunities", then "Learning and Training Resources";

  a) What type of training resources are available across Canada? Give a brief description of at least five programs.

  b) What financial assistance is available from the federal government?

5. Public Service Commission of Canada

http://learnet.gc.ca/eng/

- go to "The Learning Resource Network", then to "Continuous Learning: An Investment in You. Take the self-test to determine your learning style.

6. Canada Work-InfoNet

www.workinfonet.ca/cwn/english/main.html

- go to "Learning, Education and Training", then to "Specialized Training"; choose five special training programs and describe what they offer in terms of training objectives.

INCIDENT 7-1

The Follow-up Orientation at Chever's Carpets

During the first six months with Chever's Carpets, Oliver Talbot was promoted from supervisor to assistant warehouse manager. He also received two pay increases during that time. Thus, Leslie Coulter expected the follow-up orientation session with Oliver to be a short and pleasant experience. But when she asked Oliver what questions he had about Chever's operations, he replied: "For a business employing nearly 200 people, I am dumbfounded by the orientation and training new employees are provided with or, more correctly, the lack of orientation and training. My orientation program consisted of being shuffled in to see Mr. Chever for 15 minutes, over 10 of which he spent on the phone. My encounters with other managers around here were equally unimpressive. Most spent the few minutes I had with them complaining about all of their problems. If the warehouse manager had not taken a couple of hours with me after work the first day to explain procedures and my job, I would have failed as a supervisor or quit.

"The training I received was essentially nonexistent. I was thrown in with drivers, forklift operators, and sales clerks and shown how to complete the necessary ordering and shipping forms. Three-quarters of that training applied to office procedures the salespeople are supposed to follow, not I.

"I do not let new warehouse supervisors go to the training or orientation sessions. I may be new and have a narrow perspective, but I know they get a better orientation and better training from me than I was given when I came here. This follow-up orientation is a nice idea, but it is six months too late. I hope my criticisms have been useful to you. I sure do not have any compliments about orientation and training around here."

1. On the basis of what Oliver Talbot said, what changes would you suggest in the orientation program? In the training program?

2. If you were Leslie Coulter, what specific questions would you want to ask Oliver Talbot?

3. What problems do you see in Oliver Talbot's conducting his own orientation and training programs?

CASE STUDY

Maple Leaf Shoes Ltd.: Developing a Training Program

"How can we develop a training program that will have a significant impact on our manufacturing staff?"

Jane Reynolds, special assistant in the personnel department, faced that challenge from a vice-president of the largest division of Maple Leaf Shoes, manufacturing. Training had never been a high priority at Maple Leaf Shoes, having always been viewed as an expense item, not an investment. If skilled workers were needed, Maple Leaf Shoes preferred to raid other companies to save training costs. If raiding was not successful, a quick on-the-job training was provided by more experienced employees, limited to essential skills since there was little incentive for the employees to be more involved.

However, when the vice-president attended a convention of shoe manufacturers, he was surprised to learn how cost efficient some other shoe producers were, especially in Italy and France. Although wages there were similar to the wages paid in Canada, the productivity of the Italian and French workers was significantly higher. The VP found that the Italian and French companies invested heavily in training, allowing them to use cross-trained, flexible staff.

The VP asked Reynolds to develop a training plan, suitable to improve the overall skill level of Maple Leaf Shoes' employees. Reynolds vaguely remembered something about training from her few courses in human resource management quite some time ago, but she felt that it was not sufficient to develop a training program on her own. Besides, she knew nothing about the skill requirements in the manufacturing division.

She decided to ask Russ Summers, manager of the cutting operation, to chair a committee of first-line supervisors to assist her in the program development.

Discussion Questions

1. You are Russ. Describe the steps you would recommend to Reynolds to go through before actually designing the content of the training.

2. What training methods would you suggest to be used to train production workers? (First you may ask: What determines the methods?)

3. How would you evaluate the training program to determine how effective it was? (What criteria would you use?)

4. Do you think the first-line supervisors are the appropriate people to design the training program? Whom else would you add, if anyone, to this group?

CASE STUDY

Canadian Pacific and International Bank

Mary Keddy, senior vice-president—human resources, felt somewhat embarrassed. She had just received a call from Michael Bennett, the CEO of the bank. He had asked a blunt question: "Mary, how much bang do we get for our training bucks?" First she had not understood what he meant, but he explained that the board of directors had discussed her proposal to increase the training budget to four per cent of payroll and that one Board member had asked whether the Bank really knew how effective its training programs were and whether the money was well spent. She had to admit that she did not know. Bennett then had asked her to come up with an answer in time for the board meeting next month.

Mary had expected that sooner or later this question would arise, but she had hoped it would not happen that soon. She had been occupied with breaking the glass ceiling in the bank hierarchy and had been quite successful with it—so much so that even the Canadian Human Rights Commission had praised the bank for its employment equity program, which targeted women and minorities. Training had a high priority in the Bank's strategy as evidenced by its training budget, which exceeded three per cent of payroll, much more than the average Canadian company and even its bank competitors spent (see Figure 7–8).

The evaluation of its training programs had not been a high priority. So far training sessions had been assessed mainly by using reaction measurements and the occasional feedback requested from supervisors some time after sessions. Mary remembered from her HR courses that in order to assess the effectiveness of training programs, somewhat more sophisticated instruments and methods had to be used. Now she had to come up with some good ideas.

Discussion Questions

a) You are Mary Keddy. Please develop a proposal that Mr. Bennett could present to the board. Consider also the practicality of the plan.

b) As a rule of thumb, five to ten per cent of the cost of a training program should be used for the evaluation part of a program, depending on the complexity of the assessment.* Please develop a "cheap" and an "expensive" proposal. A brief description of your approach and reasons will suffice (why would one method be cheaper or more expensive than the other?)

Advanced Question, requiring extra readings:

c) If you wanted to recommend a "foolproof" evaluation, e.g., rule out other causes of success than the training program itself, what approach would you suggest?

*This is an experience-based figure. The first author worked for five years as the training director for a German company with 2000 employees and an instructor/consultant for Canadian government programs.

SUGGESTED READING

On Orientation:

Ashforth, B.E., and A.M. Saks, "Socialization Tactics: Longitudinal Effects on Newcomer Adjustment," *Academy of Management Journal* Vol. 39, pp. 149-178, 1996.

Hicks, Sabrina, "Successful Orientation Programs," Info-line, American Society for Training and Development, www.ASTD.com, April 2000.

Wanous, John. P., *Organizational Entry* (second edition); Reading, Mass.: Addison-Wesley, 1992.

Wanous, John P., T.D. Poland, S.L. Premark, and K.S. Davis, "The Effects of Met Expectations on Newcomer Attitudes and Behavior: A Review and Meta-analysis," *Journal of Applied Psychology*, Vol. 77, pp. 288-297, 1992.

Van Maanen, J., and E.H. Schein, "Toward a Theory of Organizational Socialization," in B.M Staw (editor), *Research in organizational behavior*, Vol. 12, pp. 209-264; Greenwich, CT: JAI Press, 1991.

Young, C.A., and C.C. Lundberg, "Creating a Good First Day on the Job," *Cornell Hotel and Restaurant Administration Quarterly,* Vol. 37, pp. 26-33, December 1996.

On Training:

Belcourt, Monica, Phillip C. Wright, and Alan M. Saks, *Managing Performance through Training and Development*, Toronto: Nelson Canada, 2000.

Chute, A.G., M.M. Thopson, and B.W. Hancock, *The McGraw-Hill Handbook of Distance Learning*, New York: McGraw-Hill, 1999.

Davenport, Thomas O., *Human Capital: What It Is and Why People Invest in It*, San Francisco: Jossey-Bass, 1999.

Driscoll, Margaret, *Web-based Training: Using Technology to Design Adult Learning Experiences*, San Francisco: Jossey-Bass, 1999.

Fitz-enz, Jac, *How to Measure Human Resources Management*, (second edition), New York: McGraw-Hill, Inc., 1995.

Goldstein, Irwin L, *Training in Organizations*, (third edition), Pacific Grove, CA: Brooks-Cole, 1993.

Harris, David M. and Randy L. DeSimone, Human Resource Development, Fort Worth: Harcourt Brace College Publishers, 1994.

Marquardt, M.J. and Kearsley, G. *Technology-Based Learning: Maximizing Human Performance and Corporate Success*. Boca Raton: CRC Press LLC, 1999.

McCormack, C. and Jones, D., *Building a Web-Based Education System*. New York: John Wiley, 1998.

Schank, Roger, (1997) *Virtual Learning: A Revolutionary Approach to Building a Highly Skilled Workforce*. New York: McGraw-Hill,1997.

Wexley, Kenneth N. and Gary P. Latham, *Developing and Training Human Resources in Organizations* (second edition), New York: HarperCollins Publishers, 1991.

APPENDIX A

A Cost-Benefit Analysis of a Training Program

Calculation of Costs

Let's assume that an auto-repair shop employs 20 mechanics who earn $15 per hour. Benefits are calculated at $5 per hour, producing a total cost of $20 per hour. There is one master mechanic who is not involved in repair work. The average mechanic repairs three cars a day, generating a potential profit of $50 a car. However, because of faulty workmanship, one in three cars comes back for warranty work, which takes an additional two hours to perform on the average, resulting in only two profitable repairs per mechanic a day. It is assumed that the workshop is open 250 days a year and that each mechanic works eight hours a day.

The owner learned that another repair shop implemented a training program that reduced the cost of faulty repairs by 30 per cent. Further inquiries revealed that such savings through training were actually quite common. He asked his master mechanic to develop an appropriate training program.

To assess the potential return on the training investment, it is necessary to determine the additional income resulting from training. We must calculate the increase in profit due to the reduction in faulty repairs. First we calculate the potential profit:

$$3 \text{ repairs} \times 20 \text{ mechanics} \times 250 \text{ days} = 15\ 000 \text{ repairs/year}$$

$$15\ 000 \text{ repairs} \times \$50 \text{ profit} = \$750\ 000 \text{ profit}$$

If all repairs were without fault, the auto-repair shop would generate $750 000 in profit. Actually, one-third of a mechanic's time was used for rework, which did not allow the mechanic to generate profitable repairs; in other words, a mechanic performed one repair work per day for free. These costs must be subtracted from the profit. In addition, the profit that could have been generated if the mechanics had used their time fully for repairs must also be subtracted. These costs are calculated as follows (assuming two hours of repair time and that no new material is used and neglecting depreciation):

$$1 \text{ faulty repair} \times 20 \text{ mechanics} \times (2 \text{ hours repair time @ } \$20 + \$50 \text{ lost profit})$$

$$\times 250 \text{ days} = \$450\ 000$$

Close to 60 per cent of the potential annual profit is lost due to faulty repairs.

To calculate the possible annual savings through training, subtract the post-training costs from the pre-training costs. The pre-training costs are calculated by multiplying the costs of bad repairs by the potential 30 per cent savings due to less rework:

$$\$450\ 000 \times 30\% = \$135\ 000$$

Subtracting the post-training costs from the pre-training costs provides the additional gross income resulting from training:

$$\$450\ 000 - \$135\ 000 = \$315\ 000$$

If we assume a 50 per cent tax on this additional income, the net income is $157 500 that could be generated through training.Of course, the cost of the training program has to be taken into account also:

Cost of developing the program:

30 days of the master mechanic's time

at $60 000/year $7 200

Training material

   (handouts, manuals, films)   <u>$5 000</u>

                                Subtotal <u>$12 200</u>

Actual training (assuming 2 days for groups of 4 mechanics = 10 days):

   10 days of master mechanic's time $2 400

   Materials and equipment $4 200

   20 mechanics for 16 hours at $20/hour $6 400

   Lost profit (potential profit − cost

   of faulty repairs for two days)

   (20 mechanics $\times$ 2 $\times$ 3 repairs $\times$ $50 profit)

   − (20 mechanics $\times$ 2 $\times$ $50 in lost profits)*

   = $6000 − $2000 $4 000

   Meals, coffee, juice, muffins   <u>$1 000</u>

                                Subtotal <u>$18 000</u>

Overhead:

   Using company formula   <u>$5 500</u>

Total Training Costs   <u>$35 700</u>

*20 mechanics would have generated at least one faulty repair each day.

Looking at these figures, it appears that the owner of the auto-repair shop has invested $35 700 and received a $157 500 return. This amounts to a 341 per cent return on a one-year investment. This figure is not as unrealistic as it sounds. Improvements in performance or reductions in costs of 10 or 20 per cent through training are not unusual, depending on the complexity of the job. A training department worth its money should have no problem in accomplishing performance improvements of this magnitude.

Chapter 8

Career Planning and Development

In a recent survey the competency of senior Canadian managers ranked 11th out of 22 countries.

—World Competitiveness Report[1]

"Some of the most successful corporations in the world are the ones that invest the most in their people."

—Ron Muns, President Help Desk Institute[2]

CHAPTER OBJECTIVES

After studying this chapter, you should be able to:

- *Explain* the difference between training and development.
- *Define* strategic human resource development.
- *List* the components of developmental strategies.
- *Describe* different methods for developing managerial personnel.
- *Advise* someone about the major points in career planning.
- *Describe* how human resource departments encourage and assist career planning.
- *Identify* the major advantages of career planning.
- *Explain* the relationship between career planning and career development.
- *List* the major actions that aid career development.

EMPLOYEE DEVELOPMENT

www2.
conferenceboard.ca/cfld/

www.canlearn.ca

In the previous chapter the focus was on orientation and skill training. In this chapter the focus is on the development of human resources as part of a long-range strategic human resource plan that goes beyond skill training. When employees join an organization, they typically have career aspirations. It makes good business sense to provide incentives to employees to remain with the organization, especially when management makes considerable investments in training and developing its human resources.

To be successful, employees must acquire technical, human, and conceptual skills. The objective of employee development activities is to instill a sound analytical and reasoning capability in managers to solve problems and at the same time enhance their ability to acquire, comprehend, interpret, and utilize relevant knowledge. Employee development is more future oriented and, consequently, is predominantly an education process rather than a training process.

As an orientation document for employees, employers, and schools on skills required for current jobs, The Conference Board of Canada developed an "Employability Skills Profile," listing critical abilities in three different areas: Academic Skills, Personal Management Skills, and Teamwork Skills (see Figure 8-1).

It is interesting to note that the Board document puts great emphasis on interpersonal skills, such as communication and working with others, but also on the ability to think and learn, two crucial requirements for the future more complex jobs Canadians can expect.

As has been described in Chapters One and Four, external and internal pressures have changed the skill and attitude requirements for managers and employees. Economic changes force organizations to do more with less, downsizing requires managers to delegate responsibilities further down the line, and changes in technology demand greater willingness and preparedness of managers and employees to accept change and to learn continuously. Constant change, a contradiction in terms, is an organizational reality. Effective organizations cope with this by including employee development in their strategic human resource development plan.

STRATEGIC HUMAN RESOURCE DEVELOPMENT

Strategic human resource development
The identification of needed skills and active management of employees learning in relation to corporate strategies.

Benchmarking
Comparing one's own standards against those of a competitor.

www.iiib.org/

STRATEGIC *human resource development* can be defined as "the identification of essential job skills and the management of employees' learning for the long-range future in relation to explicit corporate and business strategies." The last part is the most critical in this sentence, namely the linkage between development needs and activities to the organization's mission and strategy:

> In 1979 Xerox Corporation in the United States and its Canadian subsidiary launched a study that compared their manufacturing costs with those of domestic and foreign competitors. The findings revealed that competitors were selling products at a price equal to Xerox's cost of producing them. As a result, the company shifted to adopt externally set benchmark targets to drive its business plans. The results were so dramatic that today benchmarking is a key component in Xerox's human resource strategic development plans.

The idea to compare one's own quality and production standards with those of industry leaders has become a movement. In 1991, Xerox's success in **benchmarking** resulted in the creation of the Benchmarking Forum of the American Society for Training and Development, which by 1996 included 60 of the top U.S. organizations and leaders in training and development. These companies provide data for

FIGURE 8-1

Employability Skills Profile: The Critical Skills Required of the Canadian Workforce

Employability Skills 2000+

The skills you need to enter, stay in, and progress in the world of work—whether you work on your own or as a part of a team.

These skills can also be applied and used beyond the workplace in a range of daily activities.

Fundamental Skills	**Personal Management Skills**	**Teamwork Skills**
The skills needed as a base for further development	The personal skills, attitudes, and behaviours that drive one's potential for growth	The skills and attributes needed to contribute productively

You will be better prepared to progress in the world of work when you can:

You will be able to offer yourself greater possibilities for achievement when you can:

You will be better prepared to add value to the outcomes of a task, project, or team when you can:

Communicate
- read and understand information presented in a variety of forms (e.g., words, graphs, charts, diagrams)
- write and speak so others pay attention and understand
- listen and ask questions to understand and appreciate the points of view of others
- share information using a range of information and communications technologies (e.g., voice, e-mail, computers)
- use relevant scientific, technological, and mathematical knowledge and skills to explain or clarify ideas

Manage Information
- locate, gather, and organize information using appropriate technology and information systems
- access, analyze, and apply knowledge and skills from various disciplines (e.g., the arts, languages, science, technology, mathematics, social sciences, and the humanities)

Use Numbers
- decide what needs to be measured or calculated
- observe and record data using appropriate methods, tools, and technology
- make estimates and verify calculations

Think & Solve Problems
- assess situations and identify problems
- seek different points of view and evaluate them based on facts
- recognize the human, interpersonal, technical, scientific, and mathematical dimensions of a problem
- identify the root cause of a problem
- be creative and innovative in exploring possible solutions
- readily use science, technology, and mathematics as ways to think, gain, and share knowledge, solve problems, and make decisions
- evaluate solutions to make recommendations or decisions
- implement solutions
- check to see if a solution works, and act on opportunities for improvement

Demonstrate Positive Attitudes & Behaviours
- feel good about yourself and be confident
- deal with people, problems, and situations with honesty, integrity, and personal ethics
- recognize your own and other people's good efforts
- take care of your personal health
- show interest, initiative, and effort

Be Responsible
- set goals and priorities balancing work and personal life
- plan and manage time, money, and other resources to achieve goals
- assess, weigh and manage risk
- be accountable for your actions and the actions of your group
- be socially responsible and contribute to your community

Be Adaptable
- work independently or as a part of a team
- carry out multiple tasks or projects
- be innovative and resourceful: identify and suggest alternative ways to achieve goals and get the job done
- be open and respond constructively to change
- learn from your mistakes and accept feedback
- cope with uncertainty

Learn Continuously
- be willing to continuously learn and grow
- assess personal strengths and areas for development
- set your own learning goals
- identify and access learning sources and opportunities
- plan for and achieve your learning goals

Work Safely
- be aware of personal and group health and safety practices and procedures, and act in accordance with these

Work with Others
- understand and work within the dynamics of a group
- ensure that a team's purpose and objectives are clear
- be flexible: respect, be open to, and supportive of the thoughts, opinions, and contributions of others in a group
- recognize and respect people's diversity, individual differences, and perspectives
- accept and provide feedback in a constructive and considerate manner
- contribute to a team by sharing information and expertise
- lead or support when appropriate, motivating a group for high performance
- understand the role of conflict in a group to reach solutions
- manage and resolve conflict when appropriate

Participate in Projects & Tasks
- plan, design, or carry out a project or task from start to finish with well-defined objectives and outcomes
- develop a plan, seek feedback, test, revise and implement
- work to agreed quality standards and specifications
- select and use appropriate tools and technology for a task or project
- adapt to changing requirements and information
- continuously monitor the success of a project or task and identify ways to improve

The Conference Board of Canada

255 Smyth Road, Ottawa
ON K1H 8M7 Canada
Tel: (613) 526-3280
Fac (613) 526-4857
Internet: www.conferenceboard.ca/nbec

Source: *Employability Skills 2000+* Brochure 2000 E/F (Ottawa: The Conference Board of Canada, 2000).

**www.benchmarking
reports.com/**

Management development
The process of enhancing an employee's future value to the organization through careful career planning.

comparative analyses for training professionals and identify the most successful training and performance improvement practices.[3]

   Employee development can be defined as the process of enhancing an employee's future value to the enterprise through careful career planning. In plain English, it means that human resource management must plan for the future now. It also means that management must be willing to commit the financial resources to employee development programs, even if there is no short-term payoff. Employee development is a long-term process that requires the same attention and concern as capital investment, because it is an investment in human capital:

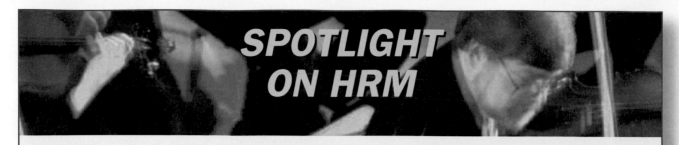

SPOTLIGHT ON HRM

HUMAN CAPITAL: HARD TO GROW, VITAL TO SOW

. . . Although the term human capital has come into vogue recently, the concept dates back to work at the University of Chicago around 1957. To date it has been largely developed from an economic perspective, and only recently has the subject been looked at from an organizational perspective.

The fundamental idea is that the long-term success of an organization depends on its ability to attract, retain, enhance and effectively use the human capital of its employees. Optimizing the competitiveness, growth rate, and cost-effectiveness of any organization depends on its ability to apply its human capital to all aspects of its operations.

Human capital is the most difficult resource for an organization to develop quickly. As organizations become more dependent on highly skilled and knowledgeable employees, enhancing human capital becomes an increasingly critical HR function. A U.S. study by Peter Cappelli, released in 1995, found that increasing the education level of employees by 10 per cent generated about three times the return in productivity as a 10 per cent investment in capital stock.

Pay versus Investment

In his 1997 book *Intellectual Capital*, Thomas Stewart notes that companies do not manage human capital well because "they have a hard time distinguishing between the cost of paying people and the value of investing in them." It is becoming increasingly important that HR professionals understand the difference.

It is key to note that the human capital of employees is independent of their current job or employer. Rather, it is a reflection of the depth and breadth of their talents, education, experience, knowledge, and skills.

The potential value of a person to an organization depends on the degree of match between the person's human capital and the needs of the organization, as well as the productive value of their capability. The employment cost of a person also depends on the scarcity of his or her human capital and the competition for that person's services from other employers.

Increasing human capital-the personal view

The decision by people to increase their employability depends on their belief that investing in developing their human capital makes sense. The value of human capital to a person depends on the expected increase in their income and employment security throughout their working career.

From an economic perspective, the expected personal gains must be greater than the cost of more education, the foregone income, and the risk that the targeted job opportunities will not exist in the future. (Another interesting implication is that maintaining good health becomes increasingly important in order for people to maximize the return on their investment in developing their human capital.)

Increasing an organization's human capital

Every organization also benefits from investing in developing the human capital of its employees. In today's rapidly changing environment, an organization must invest in developing the specialized knowledge, skills and experiences that enhance the value of its employees and equip them to be highly productive.

A long-term investment

Governments and employers must view employee training and development as a long-term capital investment, not an operating expense or short-term expedient program. Investing in human capital is a symbiotic relationship; both the employee and employer must contribute in order for both to reap the benefits.

It is ironic that organizational success is increasingly dependent on assets that do not show up on the balance sheet—namely, the human capital of employees. Increasingly, human resource professionals must view themselves as human capital managers. We need to begin to understand how we best invest in and make use of the productive capacity of employees.

We must always remember that employees own the critical productivity capability of our organizations. What we purchase, through our total compensation package, is their time, talents, knowledge, and skills. We need to ask ourselves two questions. What are we doing to enhance the human capital of our organization? And what are we doing to make more productive use of the human capital of our employees?

Ford Motor Company has recognized the strategic importance of employee development as a way to provide flexibility of the work force so that it can respond to external market conditions faster. Not only are the line workers continually trained, but managers are also prepared to meet the competitive challenges. As William Clayford, Chairman of Ford Motor Company, put it: "Training of our employees is an investment in the future of our company."[4]

Wexley and Latham propose three basic developmental strategies for organizations:

- cognitive: being concerned with altering thoughts and ideas (knowledge, new processes);

- behavioural: attempts to change behaviour (e.g., management style);

- environmental: strategies to change attitudes and values.[5]

Figure 8-2 describes examples of instruments and programs that are used in the above employee development strategies.

Employee development is the responsibility of top management and has to be part of the overall strategic plan. Figure 8-2 provides the basis for such a plan.

The cognitive component is part of the ongoing information-sharing process necessary in an "organic" organization, the adaptable type needed in a fast-changing business environment. Cognitive development implies constant learning and upgrading, principles so strongly advocated in the learning organization concept discussed later in this chapter.

The cognitive strategy is probably the least effective in employee development. The methods used are relatively passive: lectures, seminars, and academic education. While this approach tends to increase the knowledge and expertise of individuals, it does little to change a person's behaviour, attitudes, and values, important elements of an employee's career development. This approach fulfills at least part of the definition of employee development: it adds to the value of the person. However, increased knowledge and expertise are necessary, but not sufficient, attributes of an effective employee. Unfortunately, this seems to be the dominant strategy in employee development.

The ideal organizational setting continuously reinforces desirable behaviour, the second of the development strategies. Desirable behaviour includes the appropriate

FIGURE 8-2

Training and Development Strategies

Strategies	Instruments/Programs
Cognitive	articles, lectures, videos, university courses, management seminars
Behavioural	role-playing, behaviour modelling, Managerial Grid, sensitivity training, outdoors, team building, mentoring
Environmental	job rotation, organizational development, the learning organization concept, temporary assignments, employee exchange programs, matrix management, project team, internal consulting, cross-cultural management training

management style (modelled after top management and being part of the corporate culture), proper leadership style (strongly influenced by the Chief Executive Officer, or CEO), type of communication, conflict resolution, and interaction with customers.

It should, however, be emphasized that employee development goes beyond the change in behaviour or skills, since it requires changes in attitudes and values, as the following example demonstrates:

> When in 1989 the Bank of Montreal's balance sheet showed dangerous signs of distress, the bank's board of directors decided that it was time to look for a new CEO with a different vision. For the last 15 years William Mulholland had been at the helm. His style of management was very authoritarian. King Billy, as he was called, was notorious for his capricious temperament, caustic wit, and public putdowns of colleagues.
>
> His successor was Matthew Barrett, whose management style was the opposite: he favoured a consultative approach, flattened the organization, delegated more authority to branch managers, and tied pay to performance. He visited all major branches in Canada and encouraged his managers to seek direct contact with customers; that is, to get out of their offices and to visit corporate clients. Within two years the Bank of Montreal had become one of the most aggressive and profitable banks in Canada.[6]

Behavioural strategies aim at making individuals more competent in interacting with their environment—for example, with colleagues, subordinates, or customers. Common instruments or programs used in this strategy are outlined below:

- *Role-playing* is a well-known and effective method to familiarize an employee with how to apply concepts learned in the classroom in a practical setting.

- *Behaviour modelling* teaches a desired behaviour effectively by providing the trainee with a vivid and detailed display of desirable behaviour by a manager (the model), often with strong social reinforcement (see also the discussion in Chapter Seven).[7]

- *The Managerial Grid* approach is an example of attempting to change the dominant management style in an organization—for example, to make managers more person or task oriented to increase their effectiveness.[8]

- *Sensitivity training* is considered to be a very effective method for making managers more aware of the impact of their own behaviour on others or to prepare them for more effective interactions with staff in foreign subsidiaries or joint ventures.[9]

- *Outdoors* has become a fashionable development method, involving team-oriented tasks that take place in the wilderness (e.g., mountain climbing, white-water paddling, or even in a jungle environment). The objective is to develop a strong team spirit and to help people learn how to maximize their strengths and stretch their potential.[10]

- *Team building* helps team members to diagnose group processes and to devise solutions to problems.[11]

- *Mentoring* involves establishing a close relationship with a boss or someone more experienced who takes a personal interest in the employee's career and who guides and sponsors it.[12]

The behavioural strategy has undoubtedly a greater impact on the development of employees than the cognitive approach.

The environmental part is concerned with providing the organizational setting in which employees can thrive and develop (a more detailed discussion on how to develop such an environment is offered in Chapter Twelve under the topic of "motivation.") Here is an example of how effective it can be.

www.aia.ab.ca/
newsletter/9610/people.html

Jean Crepin, founder and CEO of Norwest Soil Research Ltd. in Edmonton, after experiencing a loss of one-quarter of his sales, decided to get his employees more involved in managing the company. He had read something about "Open-Book Management." It means that management shares financial goals, budgets, income statements, and forecasts with everyone in the organization.

Of course, it means that employees have to learn to read and understand monthly financial reports, so that they can gauge how their own actions affect the bottom line. They also have to learn to use this information to be able to contribute meaningfully to management decisions.

Diane Smathers, who worked for Norwest for more than eight years, mentioned that most of the staff had never seen a balance sheet and were intimidated. After thorough training, employees became very much interested in the goals and objectives of the company. According to Smathers: "It gives them a better understanding of where the company comes from. Morale is better. Employees feel they have more input because they have more information."

Besides becoming "managers" themselves, strong incentives for the employees' involvement were the implementation of a gain sharing and a stock ownership plan. At Christmas in 1997, Norwest awarded its 140 employees the first gain-sharing pay-out of $2000 each. After that, it expects to issue quarterly amounts of $1000. Mr. Crepin owns about 60 per cent. The employees now hold the rest.[13]

The *environmental approach* seems to be the most promising developmental strategy but, unfortunately, it is also the most difficult to implement. It involves a variety of methods, such as job rotation, organizational development, the learning organization concept, temporary assignments, employee exchange programs, matrix management, project teams, internal consulting, lateral transfer, and cross-cultural management training:

- *Job rotation* is extremely useful in developing managers with a systems concept in their decision-making style (e.g., the Japanese system of rotating management trainees for two years through all departments of an organization).[14]

- *Organizational development* is a system-wide effort applying behavioural science knowledge to the planned creation and reinforcement of organizational strategies, structures, and processes for improving an organization's effectiveness.[15]

- *The learning organization*, a concept created by Peter Senge, describes an organization where employees continually strive to expand their horizon, try new ideas, and where members of a team support each other in a collective attempt to make the organization more efficient and a better place to work.[16] (This concept is discussed in more detail below.)

Many companies are sending their employees on outdoor exercises to build teamwork and trust. Trust is an essential part of teamwork because team members must be able to rely on each other.

CP PHOTO ARCHIVE (Fred Chartrand)

- *Temporary assignments* allow management trainees to gain valuable special experiences they could not have had in one job (e.g., a salesperson assigned for a period of time to the engineering department to assist in the development of a "salable" product).

- *Employee exchange programs* have been implemented by companies such as Bell Canada, IBM, and Xerox, and the federal government of Canada. Usually, a manager takes a one-year leave (either paid or unpaid, depending on the arrangement with the host organization; the stipulation is that the exchange manager does not lose money) and joins another organization. The manager, the host, and the parent organization all tend to gain from this experience.

- *Matrix management* combines the use of different specialists while maintaining functional units. This approach is best suited for project management with fluctuating workloads. For example, a company may work on several projects. A project manager will "borrow" from different functional units the staff necessary to complete the project. These specialists will report for the duration of the project to the project manager, but will maintain their allegiance to their respective functional departments.[17]

- *Project teams* differ from matrix management in that the functional manager has no involvement with the team for the duration of the project. For example, when IBM developed the personal computer it put together a project team whose members were independent from their functional units. This strategy allows for a highly concentrated effort.[18]

- *Internal consulting* (or troubleshooting assignments) allows organizational needs and individual development needs to be combined simultaneously. For example, an expert in management information systems may assist the human resource department in developing a human resource information system, thereby enhancing the effectiveness of the department, but also gaining valuable personal experience.

- *Lateral transfer* is the movement of an employee from one position to another in the same class, but under another supervisor or in another department, or movement of an employee to a position in a different class that has substantially the same level of duties, responsibility, and salary.

- *Job redefinition/reclassification*—with the consent of the job incumbent—allows management to change an employee's job responsibilities, often to avoid a lay-off.

- *Cross-cultural management training* prepares employees to work in a different cultural environment (a more detailed discussion is given later in Chapter Fourteen).

- *Diversity training* deals specifically with preparing supervisors to manage employees from different cultures. It also sensitizes managers and employees in gender-dominated industries to work with colleagues from the opposite sex, e.g., in engineering or nursing (also discussed in Chapter Fourteen).

The Learning Organization

Learning organization
An organization that has an enhanced capacity to learn, adapt, and change.

Much has been written lately about the learning organization, a concept put forward first by Chris Argyris, then popularized by Peter Senge. According to Senge, a **learning organization** is where "people continually expand their capacity to create the results they truly desire, where new and expansive patterns of thinking are nurtured, where collective aspiration is set free, and where people are continually learning how to learn together."[19] Senge contrasts what is done in North American organizations with the Japanese approach:

In North America, the people who spend the most time learning about quality are those on the shop floor. They get the five-day course on statistical process control. Their bosses get the three-day course, and the CEO gets the two-hour briefing. In Japan, by contrast, it is exactly the opposite. This is very significant symbolically. There the leaders are the learners.[20]

Here is a description of the characteristics of a learning organization:

www.mislan.com/
books/thefifthdiscipline.htm

- *Systems thinking* is the ability to see things as a whole, perceive interrelationships, recognize patterns of change, infer associations and connections.

- *Personal mastery* is the ability to continually clarify and deepen personal visions, focusing energies, and seeing reality objectively. It combines personal learning and organizational learning.

- *Mental models* are deeply ingrained assumptions, generalizations, or images that influence how we understand the world and how we take action. In organizations, such mental models control what people perceive can or cannot be done. Change rarely takes place until management teams change their shared mental models.

- *Shared vision* binds people together around a common identity and a sense of destiny. A genuine vision causes people to do things because they want to, not because they have to.

- *Team learning* is a tool for raising the collective intelligence of a group above that of anyone in it. It includes talking and thinking together and the ability to recognize and overcome patterns of defensiveness that undermine group learning:

> Molson Breweries seems to be a model of a learning organization. In 1997, it opened the Molson Personal Learning and Development Centre in Etobicoke, Ontario. The objective was to help employees sharpen and broaden the skill sets needed for their jobs and beyond. As Lloyd Livingstone, brewing training specialist and co-ordinator for the development of the Learning Centre put it: "It really is a fun place; to look around and see these guys excited about learning, it really makes you feel excited too."
>
> Employees are offered a combination of mandatory training and personal career development. By the end of 1998, it was scheduled to be open 24 hours a day so that even employees on the third shift can use it.
>
> Training methods include Personal Learning Maps (a competency-based learning plan for each employee), a database of courses sorted by skills, a platform for launching multimedia training, and an administration program that allows managers to track employee progress and add new skills and courses to the system. The system encourages interaction between employees and managers, and even senior executives participate.[21]

According to Senge, teams are vital because they, not individuals, are the fundamental learning unit in modern organizations. Unless the team can learn, the organization cannot learn.[22] For human resource managers, this approach means delegating a higher responsibility for acquiring new expertise and skills to the managers and employees and, perhaps, providing guidance and counselling.

Knowledge Management

Knowledge management
Management's ability to utilize people's knowledge.

www.cio.com/
forums/knowledge/

The term "knowledge worker" was first used by Peter Drucker to describe an employee who "has the ability to use information to solve organizational problems."[23] Knowledge workers are the fastest-growing type of workers in Canada, according to research conducted by Human Resources Canada. Over the last 25 years the number of scientists, engineers, and others involved in the development of ideas increased at an annual average rate of 5.3 per cent, about two-and-a-half times the rate of growth of total employment. Today one in every eight workers in Canada is a knowledge worker.[24]

members.aol.com/
iqduru/knowledge.htm

www.city.grande-prairie.ab.ca/
ccy_km-htm

www.business
innovation.ey.com/mko/grdwk/
html/nonaka1297.html

www.conferenceboard.
ca/cben/pdf/case%2025.pdf

Today this concept has been expanded to the idea of "knowledge management," which can be defined as the ability to utilize people's knowledge, i.e., information stored in employees' heads.[25]*

It is a broader concept than "information management," which tends to focus on making information available to managers who need it for their decision-making. Knowledge management attempts to survey and assess the knowledge and expertise that exists in an organization, to increase it systematically, and apply it profitably. Not many managers are in a position to do this effectively, and for this reason many companies have created the position of a knowledge manager, whose role has been described by Williams and Bukowitz as:

- *Technology Expert.* Ensures members of the organization understand the available technology and use it to its fullest potential. A technology trainer and cheerleader.

- *Cataloguer/Archivist.* Organizes information to meet the professional needs of the decision makers.

- *Guide.* Directs information users to outside information when appropriate. Maintains high-level information about sources outside the organization.

- *Scout.* Screens information useful to the organization and brings it into the knowledge base.

- *Research Librarian.* Prioritizes highly relevant information from a pool of interesting information according to user preferences.

- *Analyst.* Adds value to information by creating a context for understanding.

- *Debriefer.* Elicits understanding so participants understand what they have learned.[26]

Competency Framework

Competencies
Skill. knowledge, and behaviours that distinguish high performance in a broad role, function, or level of the organization.

A *competency framework* is a list of *competencies* (abilities or skills) that provide a competitive advantage to an organization. As one survey indicates, competency-based performance management is becoming the HR model of choice in the Canadian industry. More than half of all organizations that participated in the 1995 survey reported that they have such a model in place, while others have it under development.[27] A competency approach allows management and employees to pinpoint unique personal and organizational characteristics that make the company successful in its struggle against competitors. As a result, trainers are able to offer training programs that focus on the very specific strengths of employees or, as one author put it "... to invest T & D effort where it increases value for the business and, in the process, to become more strategic."[28] Figure 8-3 illustrates the different meanings of a competency.

One advantage of using the competency framework is the opportunity for employees to manage their own development. The author of the survey, Jean-Pascal Souque, describes it as follows: "As everyone in the organization knows which competencies are needed to get to the next level or to perform in a way that adds value to the business, decision making relative to training and development can be pushed to lower levels—to the employees themselves."[29]

This is precisely what happened in the example described below.

MTT in Nova Scotia uses a competency model in its training programs. Job analysis interviews, focus groups, and questionnaires identify special skills and expertise

---

The University of Berkeley is the first university to have established a Chair of Knowledge, sponsored by a $1 million grant from Xerox Corporation in 1996. Renowned author and Japanese management expert Ikujiro Nonaka has been appointed the first Distinguished Professor of Knowledge.

FIGURE 8-3

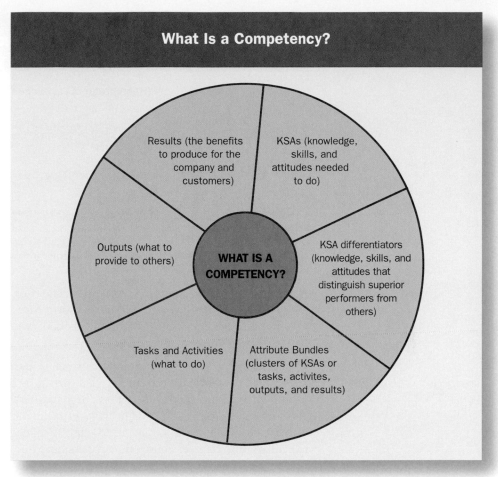

What Is a Competency?

Results (the benefits to produce for the company and customers)

KSAs (knowledge, skills, and attitudes needed to do)

Outputs (what to provide to others)

WHAT IS A COMPETENCY?

KSA differentiators (knowledge, skills, and attitudes that distinguish superior performers from others)

Tasks and Activities (what to do)

Attribute Bundles (clusters of KSAs or tasks, activites, outputs, and results)

needed to perform specific tasks. This information allows the training department to develop individual programs to increase the skill levels of, say, supervisors in dealing with their employees, e.g., more effective communication skills, team-building abilities, and greater know-how in dealing with people problems or, in the case of a customer service representative, to be more effective in dealing with customer complaints.

By focusing on competencies where they are needed most and are most beneficial to the organization, the training department was able to abandon its traditional approach of offering cafeteria-type programs, where managers and employees chose courses they liked, regardless of organizational needs. This resulted in more effective training programs and, since all employees were involved in developing the new approach, in improved employee morale.[30]

Figure 8-4 shows in what areas of the organization the competency model is applied in the companies that responded to the survey mentioned above.

Company and University/College Partnerships

Traditionally, achievers were employees who would work by day for their employer and study at night at the local university or college to enhance their career. This type of career development is still popular, but will be more and more replaced by in-house education, sometimes even by company business schools. The development of executives is now often tied into the strategies and competitive objectives of the organization.[31]

Four of Canada's retail giants, Hudson's Bay, Loblaws Supermarkets, Sears Canada, and Wal-Mart Canada, have put their support behind a $10-million

www2.conferenceboard.ca nbec/pdf/summary.pdf

FIGURE 8-4

What Is the Competency Framework Used For?

(Percentage of respondents)	
	Percentage
Training and development	45
Performance management	43
Hiring	36
Compensation	17
Other	6

Source: Jean-Paul Souque: "Focus on Competencies: Training and Development Practices, Expenditures, and Trends," Report 177–96; Ottawa. The Conference Board of Canada, 1996, p. 18. The Conference Board of Canada is a membership based, not-for-profit, independent research organization.

fundraising effort for Ryerson University's School of Retail Management, to make it the premier school for retail education in North America. Each company contributed $1 million to the endowment fund of the school, which offers Canada's only university-level program in retail management.[32]

Dalhousie University in Halifax formed a partnership with the Institute of Canadian Bankers (ICB). It counts credits earned by bank managers in ICB programs toward an MBA in Financial Services. These partnerships extend even into the international sphere: Saint Mary's University in Halifax has formed an alliance with the Chinese corporate giant Minmetals to offer its managers a special one-year full-time Executive MBA degree. Fourteen managers have already completed their degrees.

Such partnerships have several advantages. They offer companies the opportunity to have educational programs tailor-made to their needs; the university benefits financially; the university's faculty gains valuable practical experiences; the students earn a university/college degree; and they are able to use much of their acquired knowledge directly on the job. Of course, the university must be careful not to relinquish its control over course qualities and standards.

Trends Toward the Use of the Internet, Intranet, or Video-Conferencing Development Programs

www.filename.com/
wbt/index.html

canadiancareers.com/
disted.html

Opportunities for long-distance education abound. Athabasca University in Alberta specializes in long-distance degree programs up to the MBA level, using the Internet for delivery (it offers no in-class programs). Queen's University offers an Executive MBA Program through "multi-point interactive video-conferencing Boardroom Learning Centres" across Canada, allowing students to continue their career while earning a degree; or it offers the same degree in a distance education partnership—named National Electronic Campus—with individual companies, allowing students to earn their degree where they work.

Two Canadian banks use the concept of the Intranet, an intra-organizational computer network, to deliver their corporate training. The Canadian Imperial Bank of Commerce abolished its $30 million training and development department and delegated the acquisition of relevant professional knowledge to its employees. It uses as a guide a competency model that describes approximately 50 skills employees need to "provide value to customers." Employees have access to books and software in training rooms, learn from co-workers, and can take courses as needed. They even track their own progress.[33]

Similarly, the Royal Bank has put its training programs on its internal "Personal Learning Network." The bank invested $2 million in its PC-based system that uses video, graphics, sound, text, and animation. The program is now available at 400 sites and by the end of 1998 is expected to reach more than 1000 Royal Bank retail and business banking centres.[34]

The opportunities to use new technology to deliver development and training programs are growing exponentially. Moore's Law says that the capacity of computers is doubling every 18 months at one-half the price. (Gordon Moore was President and CEO of Intel Corporation. He retired in 1987.) The higher capacity allows new combinations of media to be used in training programs, making them more effective and, undoubtedly, more interesting. The virtual classroom is not a dream anymore.[35]

Cross-Cultural Management and Diversity Training

www.globalworkshop
.com/canada.html

www.ilr.cornell.
edu/depts/wdn/

www.diversity
update.com

www.training
supersite.com/tss_link/
trainset.htm

The growing importance of global competition forces companies to expand their business abroad, either through 100 per cent owned subsidiaries, joint ventures, or licensing. All three approaches require that managers communicate and negotiate with foreign managers and business people; but having subsidiaries or a joint venture necessitates managing foreign employees—quite a challenge for an expatriate manager who has no experience in doing it or does not have preparatory training before assuming the job abroad.

Given the demographic development of the Canadian population, i.e., immigration patterns, with the prospect that in the new millennium more than half of the Canadian workforce will be neither male nor white, it will be necessary for Canadian managers to manage very diverse employees.[36] Unfortunately, most managers lack this ability.[37]

Diversity management is important enough to be discussed in a separate chapter (Chapter Fourteen). Both of the above topics, cross-cultural management training and diversity training, will be discussed there.

Top Management Involvement

It is essential that top management takes its commitment to human resource development seriously and makes it part of the company's strategy. As Hall puts it: "Perhaps the most important factor in ensuring that development is done strategically is the participation of top management in the process. Because top management is the strategic level of the organization, and because top management represents the strategic business planners of the organization, they should also be the human resource planners. Top management should plan and execute employee development activities."[38]

CAREER PLANNING

INSEPARABLY LINKED with employee development is career planning and career management:

Joe: I didn't make it to executive vice-president of a major bank by chance. I wanted to be a banking executive since I was a customer service clerk trainee. Sure I worked hard, but I also tried to plan my career.

Joan: Career planning is a waste of time. There are too many variables. Who knows which openings will occur? Besides, promotions are largely a matter of luck, a matter of being in the right place at the right time.

Joe: I agree, luck plays a part. But you would not be an assistant branch manager if you didn't have some university education.

Joan: Well, sure, that's true. But whether I make branch manager is mostly luck.

Joe: Is it? Don't you think you can control your future to some extent? Don't you believe that a promotion is more likely if you develop the background needed to function as a branch manager? If your performance as a branch manager is superior to other branch managers, don't you think that your chances of promotion will be better? There are many things you can do to increase your chances of career success.

www.youth.gc.ca/

Merely planning a career does not guarantee success. Superior performance, experience, education, and some occasional luck play an important part. But when people like Joan rely almost wholly on luck, they seldom are prepared for opportunities that arise. To be ready for career opportunities, successful people develop career plans and then take action to achieve their plans. Simply stated, a successful career needs to be managed through careful planning. If it is not, employees are seldom ready for career opportunities, and human resource departments find it extremely difficult to meet their internal staffing needs.[39] Figure 8-5 illustrates an overview of the career planning and development framework.

Some people fail to manage their careers because they are unaware of the basic concept of career planning described in Figure 8-6. They do not realize that goals can shape their career and yield greater success. As a result, their planning is left to fate and their development rests in the hands of others. Awareness of the concepts in the figure is no guarantee of action. But when awareness leads to goal setting, career planning is more likely to occur. For example, if Joan set a goal of becoming a branch bank manager in two years, that goal would lead her to the next question: "How do I achieve the goal?" If Joan answers that question by taking a special bank management course, she becomes better prepared to be a branch manager and her chances for promotion increase.

Although every person's career is unique, a review of Joe's career in the banking industry shows how career planning works in practice. Joe's progress is summarized in Figure 8-7 and explained below:

- Four years after graduating from high school, Joe joined the Bank of New Brunswick as a customer service clerk trainee. At that point in his career his goal was to become a banking executive. He had no idea of the career path he would follow. But Joe realized that his first step would be to become a supervisor. This career planning caused him to enroll in the evening degree program of a nearby

FIGURE 8-5

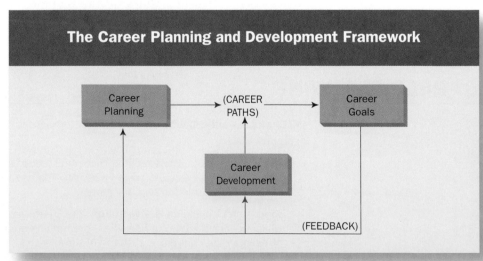

The Career Planning and Development Framework

FIGURE 8-6

Selected Career Planning Terms

- **Career.** A career is all the jobs that are held during one's working life.

- **Career path.** A career path is the sequential pattern of jobs that forms one's career.

- **Career goals.** Career goals are the future positions one strives to reach as part of a career. These goals serve as benchmarks along one's career path.

- **Career planning.** Career planning is the process by which one selects career goals and the path to those goals.

- **Career development.** Career development is the process by which one undertakes personal improvements to achieve a personal career plan.

university. During the next nine years he also entered some training programs organized by the local board of trade. These career development actions were the first of many that Joe undertook. He received two promotions and then at the age of 30 was made a loan officer.

- After he completed his degree, Joe was promoted to accounts manager and was transferred. Although the new job did not give him much of a salary raise in real terms (since the cost of living in the new city was comparatively very high), Joe knew that some diversification in his background would increase his chances of becoming a senior manager someday.

- Two years after he became accounts manager, Joe was promoted to branch manager and transferred to a small branch in a suburban area. After two years, he was again transferred to a major city branch as its manager.

- Joe realized that without further qualifications his future career progress was likely to be quite slow. He therefore enrolled in the Certified General Accountant's Program. At the same time, he began attending executive development seminars conducted by a nearby university. Three years later he was promoted to district manager, and five years later he was again transferred to a larger district.

- At the end of his fifth year in the new district, he had completed his Certified General Accountant's diploma. Since no promotion was forthcoming immediately, Joe left the Bank of New Brunswick a year later and joined the Ontario Dominion Bank as its vice-president of finance. Six years later he was promoted to senior vice-president (finance), in which position he remained for 10 years.

As a review of Figure 8-7 indicates, Joe's career plan involved well-timed transfers and an educational leave. Figure 8-8 superimposes Joe's career changes on the organization charts of the two banks for which he worked. As the organization chart shows, career progress is seldom straight up in an organization. Lateral transfers, leaves, and even resignations are used. When Joe started as a customer service clerk trainee at age 21, there was no way he could have predicted the career path he would follow. But through periodic career planning, he reassessed his career progress and then undertook development activities to achieve intermediate career goals, such as becoming a supervisor. As a result of career planning and development, Joe's career consisted of a path that led him to his goal of becoming an executive in the banking industry.

FIGURE 8-7

Career Path for a Retired Senior Vice-President in the Banking Industry

Job Number	Job Level	Job Title	Type of Change	Years on Job	Ending Age
1	Worker	Customer Service Clerk Trainee		1/2	22
2	Worker	Customer Service Clerk	Promotion	5	27
3	Supervising	Supervisor Customer Service	Promotion	2	29
4	Supervising	Loan Officer	Change in duties only	2	31
5	Management	Accounts Manager	Promotion and transfer	2	33
6	Management	Branch Manager	Promotion and transfer	2	35
7	Management	Branch Manager	Transfer	3	38
8	Management	District Manager	Promotion	5	43
9	Management	District Manager	Transfer (CGA)	6	49
10	Executive	Vice-President (Finance)	Resignation and promotion	6	55
11	Executive	Senior V.P. (Finance)	Promotion	10	6

CAREER PLANNING AND DEVELOPMENT OVERVIEW

www.adm.
uwaterloo.ca/infocecs/
CRC/manual-home.html

DURING THE 40 years of Joe's career, human resource departments in banks and other large organizations gave relatively little support to career planning. When promotable talent was scarce, human resource departments usually reacted with crash training programs or additional recruitment. Human resource planning and career planning seldom occurred. Instead, organizations and employees reacted to new developments rather than seeking proactive solutions.

Viewed historically, this limited role for human resource departments was understandable, because career plans were seen largely as a personal matter. Even when managers wanted their departments to provide assistance in career planning, they often lacked the resources to become involved. As a result, only a few (mostly large) organizations encouraged career planning by employees.

Today, an increasing number of human resource departments see career planning as a way to meet their internal staffing needs.[40] When employers encourage career planning, employees are more likely to set goals. In turn, these goals may motivate employees to pursue further education, training, or other career development activities. These activities then improve the value of employees to the organization and give the human resource department a larger pool of qualified applicants from which to fill internal job openings.

But what do employees want? A study of one group of employees revealed five areas of concern. These include:

- *Career equity*: Employees want to perceive equity in the organization's performance/ promotion system with respect to career advancement opportunities.

- *Supervisory concern*: Employees want their supervisors to play an active role in career development and provide timely performance feedback.

- *Awareness of opportunities*: Employees want knowledge of the career advancement opportunities that exist in their organization.

- *Employee interest*: Employees need different amounts of information and have different degrees of interest in career advancement depending on a variety of factors.

- *Career satisfaction*: Employees have different levels of career satisfaction depending on their age and occupation.

Effective career planning and development programs must consider these different perceptions and wants of employees. What employees expect from the career programs developed by the human resource department will vary according to age, sex, occupation, and other variables. In short, whatever approach the human resource department takes toward career planning and development, it must be a flexible, proactive approach. As one human resource manager in a large corporation concluded:

> Flexibility in career development programs is paramount if the goals of improved productivity, increased personal satisfaction, growth, and ultimately increased organizational effectiveness are to be achieved. In many cases, this will require the modification of basic existing programs to address the specific needs of a particular group of employees.

HUMAN RESOURCE DEPARTMENTS AND CAREER PLANNING

HUMAN RESOURCE departments should, and increasingly do, take an active interest in employee career planning.[41] Planning and managing human resources are emerging as an increasingly important determinant of organizational effectiveness.[42]

Human resource departments often handle career planning because their human resource plans indicate the organization's future employment needs and related career opportunities. In addition, human resource experts are more likely to be aware of training or other developmental opportunities. Of course, individual managers also should encourage career planning, as Joe did in the opening dialogue. But if human resource specialists leave career planning to managers, it may not get done. Not all managers take as strong an interest in their employees' careers as Joe appears to.

The involvement of human resource managers in career planning has grown during recent years because of its benefits. Here is a partial list of those benefits:

- *Develops promotable employees*: Career planning helps to develop internal supplies of promotable talent.

- *Lowers turnover*: The increased attention to and concern for individual careers generates more organizational loyalty and therefore lower employee turnover.

- *Taps employee potential*: Career planning encourages employees to tap more of their potential abilities because they have specific career goals.

- *Furthers growth*: Career plans and goals motivate employees to grow and develop.

- *Reduces hoarding*: Without career planning, it is easier for managers to hoard key subordinates. Career planning causes employees, managers, and the human resource department to become aware of employee qualifications.

FIGURE 8-8

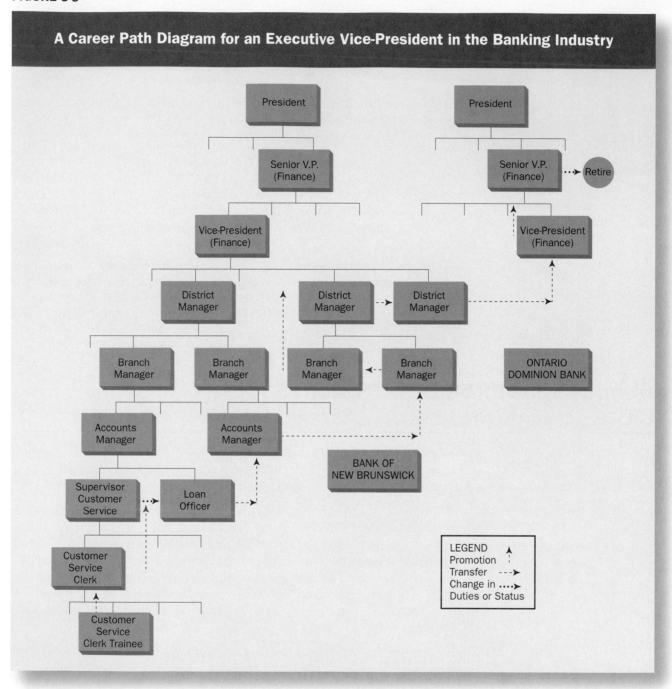

A Career Path Diagram for an Executive Vice-President in the Banking Industry

- *Satisfies employee needs*: With less hoarding and improved growth opportunities for employees, individual needs for recognition and accomplishment are more readily satisfied, and self-esteem is boosted.

- *Assists employment equity plans*: Career planning can help members of protected groups prepare for more important jobs.

To realize these benefits, more human resource departments are following the lead of a few pioneers and supporting career planning. In practice, human resource departments encourage career planning in three ways: through career education, information, and counselling.

Career Education

Surprisingly, many employees know very little about career planning. Often they are unaware of the need for and advantages of career planning. And once made aware, they often lack the necessary information to plan their careers successfully. Human resource departments are suited to solve both of these shortcomings.

Human resource departments can increase employee awareness through a variety of educational techniques. For example, speeches, memoranda, and position papers from senior executives stimulate employee interest at low cost to the employer. If executives communicate their belief in career planning, other managers are likely to do the same.

Workshops and seminars on career planning increase employee interest by pointing out the key concepts associated with career planning. Workshops help the employee set career goals, identify career paths, and uncover specific career development activities. These educational activities may be supplemented by printed or taped information on career planning.

When the human resource department lacks the necessary staff to design and conduct educational programs, public programs conducted by local institutions or consultants may help:

> One worldwide consulting firm, Towers Perrin, provides its clients with a four-step package. The package program develops (1) a strategy for the organization to solve its unique needs, (2) support systems based upon the present human resource management information systems to give employees the data they need to plan their careers, (3) workbooks that allow employees to engage in career planning, and (4) a career resource centre that offers employees assistance with their career planning.

www.towers.com/towers/

Information on Career Planning

Regardless of the educational strategy the human resource department selects, it should provide employees with other information they need to plan their careers. Much of this information is already a part of the human resource department's information system. For example, job descriptions and specifications can be quite valuable to someone who is trying to estimate reasonable career goals. Likewise, human resource departments can identify future job openings through the human resource plan. Human resource specialists can also share their knowledge of potential career paths. For example, they are often keenly aware of the similarities between unrelated jobs. If this information is given to employees, it may reveal previously unseen career paths:

> For example, consider the possible career paths faced by Leslie Stevens, who works at a newspaper. In this type of work, the jobs of advertising assistant, assistant account representative, and account manager call for similar characteristics. But Leslie, an advertising assistant, may not realize that her skills could be applied to a position that may earn her twice as much.

Job families
Groups of different jobs that require similar skills.

When different jobs require similar skills, they form *job families*. Career paths within a job family demand little additional training since the skills of each job are closely related. If human resource departments make information about job families available, employees can find feasible career paths. They can then assess these career paths by talking with those who already hold jobs along the path. Figure 8-8 showed the career path for an executive vice-president in the banking industry.

One problem with job families is that employees may want to skip over less pleasant jobs. To prevent employees from rejecting some jobs in a job family, the human resource department may establish a sequential progression of jobs.

Job progression ladder
A particular career path where some jobs have pre-requisites.

A *job progression ladder* is a partial career path where some jobs have prerequisites, as shown in Figure 8-9. The job progression ladder shown in the figure requires Leslie to become an account representative before moving to the better-paying job of account manager. This requirement assures the human resource department of an ample internal supply of account representatives because this job is a prerequisite for the well-paying position of account manager.

The human resource department can also encourage career planning by providing information about alternative career paths. Figure 8-10 shows that Leslie and other advertising assistants face several possible career paths. If a particular advertising assistant does not want to become an account representative, human resource specialists can provide information about alternative careers not considered by the advertising assistant. In the newspaper example, Leslie might prefer a career in editorial, secretarial, or advertising fields because those positions may offer more long-term potential.

Career Counselling

Career counselling
A process that assists employees to find appropriate career goals and paths.

To help employees establish career goals and find appropriate career paths, some human resource departments offer *career counselling* by counsellors who are a source of competent advice. The counsellor may simply be someone who has the employee's interests in mind and provides the specific job-related information. Or the counsellor may help employees discover their interests by administering and interpreting aptitude and skill tests. Two tests in particular—the Kuder Preference Record and the Strong Vocational Interest Blank—are useful for guiding people into occupations that are likely to be of interest. Other tests are also available to measure individual abilities and interests in specific types of work. But to be truly successful, career counsellors must get employees to assess themselves and their environment.

Employee Self-Assessment

Career counsellors realize that a career is not the entirety of one's life. It may be a large part or even a central part; but career planning is only a part of one's life plan. A life plan is that often ill-defined series of hopes, dreams, and personal goals each person carries through life. For example, broad objectives to be happy, healthy, and successful combine with specific goals to be a good spouse, parent, student, citizen, neighbour, or manager. Together, these roles form one's life plan. Ideally, a career plan

FIGURE 8-9

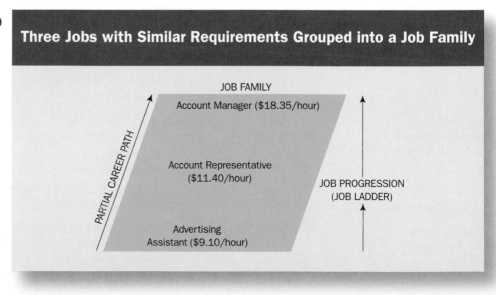

Three Jobs with Similar Requirements Grouped into a Job Family

JOB FAMILY
Account Manager ($18.35/hour)

Account Representative ($11.40/hour)

Advertising Assistant ($9.10/hour)

PARTIAL CAREER PATH

JOB PROGRESSION (JOB LADDER)

FIGURE 8-10

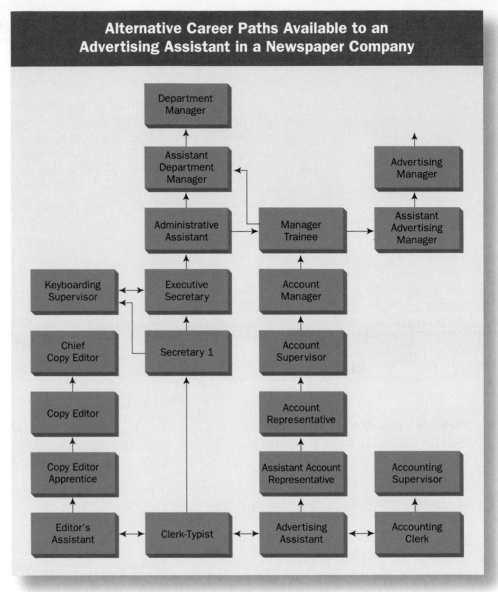

Alternative Career Paths Available to an Advertising Assistant in a Newspaper Company

is an integral part of a person's life plan. Otherwise, career goals become ends (sometimes dead ends!) rather than means toward fulfilling a life plan. A modern example would be:

> A husband and wife struggle for decades to achieve a degree of success in their respective careers. When the success is within reach, both realize that their personal life—friendships, parental relationships, perhaps even their marriage—is in a shambles. It is in this state because career plans were pursued to the exclusion of all else; there were no integral life plans for either one.

Why should people who are very successful in their careers develop feelings of personal failure? One research study[43] has suggested the following factors:

- *Contradictory life demands*: The realization that one has striven throughout one's life to attain goals that were irreconcilable.

- *Failure of expectations*: The realization that things one expected to happen will not ever happen and that one's beliefs about the work environment (e.g., the belief that rising in the organizational hierarchy will make one personally satisfied) are wrong.

- *Sense of external control*: The realization that one has been making too many of life's decisions in order to please others rather than oneself.

- *Loss of affiliative satisfaction*: A feeling of loneliness both at the workplace and at home.

To avoid this sense of personal failure, self-assessment coupled with life planning at the beginning of a career and at every major crossroads is crucial. Self-assessment includes a self-inventory. Components of a self-inventory are listed in Figure 8-11 (more self-assessment instruments are listed under "Web Research" at the end of the chapter). If a career counsellor can get employees to complete a detailed and honest self-evaluation, it helps to focus their thinking about themselves. Then employees can match their interests and abilities on the self-inventory with the career information available to them from the human resource department. Likewise, they can better match their attitudes and career paths with their personal life plan.

FIGURE 8-11

A Self-Inventory for Career Planning

Work Interests and Aptitudes — rated Low 1 to High 5:

Physical work (fixing, building, using hands)
Written work (writing, reading, using words)
Oral work (talking, giving speeches, using words)
Quantitative work (calculating, doing accounting, using numbers)
Visual work (watching, inspecting, using eyes)
Interpersonal work (counselling, interviewing)
Creative work (inventing, designing, ideas)
Analytical work (doing research, solving problems)
Managerial work (initiating, directing, coordinating)
Clerical (keeping records)
Outdoor work (farming, travelling, doing athletics)
Mechanical (repairing, fixing, tinkering)

Work Skills and Abilities

List below specialized skills, unique personal assets, enjoyable experiences, and major accomplishments. Then evaluate.

Columns: Physical, Written, Oral, Quantitative, Visual, Interpersonal, Creative, Analytical, Managerial, Clerical, Outdoor, Mechanical

Environmental Assessment

A career plan that matches employee interests with likely career paths may actually do a disservice to the employee if environmental factors are overlooked. Returning to the choices faced by Leslie Stevens at the newspaper provides an example:

> The job family of advertising assistant, account representative, and account manager may appear to be a reasonable career path for Leslie since she already has the basic skills needed for all three jobs. But changes in the newspaper industry have severely reduced the need for advertising assistants. If career counsellors in the human resource department do not point out this development to Leslie, she may find her career stalled in the job of advertising assistant.

Regardless of the match between one's skills and the organization's career paths, counsellors need to inform employees of likely changes that will affect their occupational choices. Occupational information is readily available from publications of Human Resources Development Canada (HRDC) and Statistics Canada. For example, HRCD periodically publishes information relating to the demand and supply of various jobs in its Job Future 2000 section. In another publication entitled *Canada Occupational Projection System* (COPS), HRDC provides forecasts on the demand for various types of jobs in the country. Some of the national daily newspapers and business magazines also provide useful information in this context. Figure 8-12 shows some of the trends in the Canadian job market up until 2004. Companies are increasingly looking for specific experience and skills in their employees (in contrast to general skills several years ago). Traditional occupations such as dentists, lawyers, doctors, and engineers have "flooded" the markets, which are fast becoming saturated. Fortunately for students in business administration, management positions show no signs of drying up.

Dual-Career Couples

http://nextwave.
sciencemag.org/fam.dtl

www.bc.edu/bc_org/
avp/csom/cwf/granteepages/
grantees.html

http://vifamily.ca/index.htm

http://careerjournal.com/
careers/resources/documents/
19990811-sandholtz.htm

Dual-career couple
A couple whose partners both have their own careers.

According to Statistics Canada in seven out of ten families both partners work, almost double the number from the 1980s.[44] The combination of each partner pursuing a career and carrying family responsibilities tends to create stress, especially on the woman's side, since she usually has to shoulder a higher burden of the family work, although men are increasingly willing to share household chores.[45] Still, a number of questions arise. Is each partner's career of equal importance? What if an advancement opportunity involves a relocation? Who has the stronger career commitment? Who will stay home if a child is sick? Many couples will work out these questions, but for others these issues may create problems or even crises, with potential negative consequences for personal relationships, e.g., break-up, divorce, or for the organization, e.g., low morale or even quitting.

A proactive HR department will have career counsellors, internal or outsourced, who are able to deal with the above issues. They will meet with the employees, individually and together, to map out career paths that are acceptable to both partners and the organization. Pro-active also means to offer dual-career couples options that will ease some of the problems they experience, such as flexible work arrangements, telecommuting, or job sharing (all discussed in Chapter Twelve) and child care and/or elder care (discussed in Chapter Eleven).

Career Plateauing

Career plateauing
Temporary flat point on the advancement continuum during the career of an individual.

We encountered the issue of *plateauing* in the previous chapter (see Figure 7-4), defined by Webster as "a relative absence of progress," especially in learning. However, we may see it also happening in a person's career, for a number of reasons. Many companies are removing management layers, downsizing, merging, or are pushing decisions closer to the actual work. Such measures, besides causing lay-offs,

FIGURE 8–12

	Skill Level					
Skill Type	**Managerial**	**Professional**	**Technical, Paraprofessional & Skilled**	**Intermediate**	**Labouring and Elemental**	**All**
	Current–2004	Current–2004	Current–2004	Current–2004	Current–2004	Current–2004
Business, Finance & Administration	good–good	good–good	good–good	fair–fair	—	good–good
Natural & Applied Sciences	good–good	good–good	good–good	—	—	good–good
Health	good–good	good–good	fair–fair	fair–fair	—	good–good
Social Sciences, Education, Government Services & Religion	good–good	fair–fair	fair–fair	—	—	fair–fair
Art, Culture, Recreation & Sport	good–good	fair–fair	fair–fair	—	—	fair–fair
Sales & Services	good–good	—	fair–good	fair–limited	limited–limited	fair–limited
Trades, Transport & Equipment Operators	fair–good	—	fair–fair	fair–fair	limited–limited	fair–fair
Primary Industry	good–fair	—	fair–fair	limited–limited	limited–limited	fair–fair
Processing, Manufacturing, & Utilities	good–good	—	good–good	fair–fair	limited–limited	fair–fair
All	good–good	good–good	fair–fair	fair–fair	limited–limited	fair–fair

Table title: **Trends in the Canadian Labour Market**

Source: Human Resource Development Canada. Summary Table of Labour Market Conditions—Current and 2001. www.hrdc-drhc.gc.ca/doc/ if/trends/trends.shtml. Reproduced with the permission of the Minister of Public Works and the Government Services Canada, 2001.

sometimes result in lowering the promotion opportunities for employees and middle managers. For ambitious employees it often means loss of their strongest motivator, the reward for long years of dedicated work. HR managers and career counsellors must anticipate such consequences and offer solutions. Examples include training for new skills, special assignments, job rotation, lateral moves, sabbaticals, skill-based compensation, or even a career change.

www.stmarys.ca/academic/
commerce/emba/hschwind
.html

> Hermann Schwind, the first author of this book, is a typical example. At the age of 35, having plateaued in a middle-management position, he realized that his education as a mechanical engineer was not sufficient to be promoted into an executive position in his organization. Taking an unpaid leave, he earned an MBA degree and, becoming hooked on academia, a Ph.D. He felt that his new career as a professor was an excellent choice and very rewarding.

CAREER DEVELOPMENT

THE IMPLEMENTATION of career plans requires career development. Career development comprises those personal improvements one undertakes to achieve a career plan. These actions may be sponsored by the human resource department or

CP PHOTO ARCHIVE (Keith Beaty/Toronto Star)

A mentor is someone who offers informal career advice. Suzanne Boyd, left, editor-in-chief of Flare, is mentor to Cassandra Leader, through Canada Association of Black Journalists program.

undertaken independently by the employee. This section reviews tactics that employees may use to achieve their career plans and then discusses the department's role in career development.

Individual Career Development

The starting point for career development is the individual. Each person must accept his or her responsibility for career development, or career progress is likely to suffer. Once this personal commitment is made, several career development actions may prove useful. These actions involve:

- job performance;
- exposure;
- resignations;
- organizational loyalty
- mentors and sponsors;
- key subordinates;
- growth opportunities.

Job Performance

The most important action an individual can undertake to further his or her career is good job performance. The assumption of good performance underlies all career development activities. When performance is substandard, regardless of other career development efforts, even modest career goals are usually unattainable. Individuals who perform poorly are excluded quickly by the human resource department and management decision-makers. *Career progress rests largely upon performance.*

Exposure

Career progress also is furthered by exposure.[46] Exposure means becoming known (and, it is hoped, held in high regard) by those who decide on promotions, transfers, and other career opportunities. Without exposure, otherwise good performers may not get a chance at the opportunities needed to achieve their career goals. Managers gain exposure primarily through their performance, written reports, oral presentations, committee work, community service, and even the hours they work. Simply put, exposure makes an individual stand out from the crowd—a necessary ingredient in career success, especially in large organizations. For example, consider how one management trainee gained some vital exposure early in her career:

> Paula Dorsey noticed that two executives worked on Saturday mornings. As one of 12 new management trainees, she decided that coming to work on Saturday mornings would give her additional exposure to these key decision-makers. Soon these two executives began greeting her by name whenever they passed in the halls. While still in the training program, she was assigned to the product introduction committee, which planned strategy for new products. At the end of the training program, Paula was made an assistant product manager for a new line of video recorders. The other 11 trainees received less important jobs.

In small organizations, exposure to decision-makers is more frequent and less dependent upon reports, presentations, and the like. In some situations—especially in other nations—social status, school ties, and seniority can be more important than exposure.

Resignations

When a person sees greater career opportunities elsewhere, a resignation may be the only way to meet one's career goals. Some employees—managers and professionals in particular—change employers as part of a conscious career strategy. If this is done effectively, they usually receive a promotion, pay increase, and new learning experience. Resigning in order to further one's career with another employer has been called "leveraging." Astute managers and professionals use this technique sparingly because too many moves can lead to the label of "job hopper," connoting lack of commitment.

Organizational Loyalty

In many organizations, people put career loyalty above organizational loyalty. Low levels of organizational loyalty are common among recent university graduates (whose high expectations often lead to disappointment with their first few employers) and professionals (whose first loyalty is often to their profession).[47] Career-long dedication to the same organization complements the human resource department's objective of reducing employee turnover.

Core employees
Those who are essential for the running of the organization.

Mentor
Someone who offers informed career guidance and support on a regular basis.

Sponsor
A person in an organization who can create career development opportunities for others.

There is another development that will work against organizational loyalty. According to some organizational experts, many companies will rely in the future mainly on *core employees*. Core employees will be those who are essential for the running of the organization. They will be highly trained and cross-functional, meaning that they can be used in different jobs if the necessity arises.[48] Contract workers will be hired to work on projects and disperse once the projects are completed.[49] Even the core employees may be forced to change their careers several times in their professional life because of changing technology. As a result, employees may have more loyalty toward their profession than to an organization.[50]

Mentors and Sponsors

Many employees quickly learn that a mentor can aid their career development. A *mentor* is someone who offers informal career advice. Neither the mentor nor the employee always recognizes that such a relationship exists; the junior worker simply knows that here is someone who gives good advice; the mentor sees the employee as simply someone who wants advice.[51]

If the mentor can nominate the employee for career development activities, such as training programs, transfers, or promotions, the mentor becomes a *sponsor*.

www.bestjobsusa.
com/employmentReview/
er_0699/0699011.asp

www.hrprofessional
.org/back/june_july99/
feature2.htm

A sponsor is someone in the organization who can create career development opportunities for others. Often an employee's sponsor is the immediate supervisor, although others may serve as nominators.

Key Subordinates

Key subordinates
Those employees who are crucial to a manager's success in a particular job.

A successful manager relies on subordinates who aid his or her development and performance. The subordinates may possess highly specialized knowledge or skills that the manager may learn from them. Or the employees may perform a crucial role in helping a manager achieve good performance. In either case, employees of this type are *key subordinates*. They exhibit loyalty and dedication to their boss. They gather and interpret information, offer skills that supplement their manager's, and work unselfishly to further their manager's career. They benefit when the manager is promoted by also moving up the career ladder. Key subordinates also benefit by receiving important delegations that serve to develop their careers. These people complement human resource department objectives through their teamwork, motivation, and dedication. But when a manager resigns and takes a string of key subordinates along, the results can be devastating:

> A small Ontario research firm had 10 months' lead in developing a new type of memory component for computers. A major electronics company hired away the project manager, the chief engineer, and their key subordinates. With this loss, the small firm was forced to recruit replacements at a higher salary and at a cost of several months' delay.

As a career strategy, perceptive subordinates are careful not to become attached to an immobile manager, also known as "shelf-sitters." Not only do shelf-sitters block promotion channels, but also their key subordinates can become unfairly labelled as shelf-sitters too. Although working for a shelf-sitter may develop an employee's skills, it can also arrest one's career progress.

Growth Opportunities

When employees expand their abilities, they complement the organization's objectives. For example, enrolling in a training program, taking noncredit courses, pursuing an additional degree, or seeking a new work assignment can contribute to employee growth. These growth opportunities aid both the human resource department's objective of developing internal replacements and the individual's personal career plan:

> Rachael Holmes was the chief recruiter in the employment department of Brem Paper Products. Her department manager was 60 years old and had indicated that he planned to retire at age 65. At 37 and with three years of experience as a recruiter, Rachael felt she was in a dead-end job. She obtained a transfer to the wage and salary department. Two years later the company planned a new facility and made Rachael the human resource manager for it. She was selected because of her broad experience in recruiting and compensation—two major concerns in starting the new operation.

Rachael initiated the transfer through self-nomination because she wanted to further her career development. But the real opportunity she obtained from the transfer was a chance to grow—a chance to develop new skills and knowledge.

Human-Resource-Supported Career Development

Career development should not rely solely on individual efforts, because they are not always in the organization's best interests. For example, employees may move to another employer, as in the example of the Ontario research firm. Or employees may simply be unaware of opportunities to further their careers and the organization's staffing needs. To guide career development so that it benefits the organization and employees, a human resource department often provides a variety of training and development programs for employees. In addition, departments should enlist the support of managers, provide feedback to employees, and create a cohesive work environment to improve the ability and desire of workers to undertake career development.

Management Support

Efforts by the human resource department to encourage career development have little impact unless supported by managers. Commitment by top management is crucial to gain the support of other managers. When support is lacking, managers are likely to ignore career development and devote their attention to their other responsibilities. Ideally, managers are also evaluated on their ability to develop their subordinates as part of their performance appraisal.

> The Ford Motor Company makes it explicit to its managers that they will be assessed, as part of their annual performance appraisal, on how well they have succeeded in developing a successor for themselves. The company is aware of the danger that if the "successors" have to wait too long for a promotion, they will look for opportunities elsewhere. However, the company has the experience that many of those who move return to Ford later with significantly more knowledge.[52]

Feedback

Without feedback about their career development efforts, it is difficult for employees to sustain the years of preparation sometimes needed to reach career goals. Human resource departments can provide this feedback in several ways. One way is to periodically tell employees, through their supervisor, how well they are performing in their present job. To do this, many human resource departments develop performance evaluation procedures. If performance is poor, this feedback allows workers to adjust their efforts or career development plans.

Another type of feedback concerns job placement. An employee who pursues career development activities and is passed over for promotion may conclude that career development is not worth the effort. Unsuccessful candidates for internal job openings should be told why they did not get the job they sought. This feedback has three purposes:

1. To assure bypassed employees that they are still valued and will be considered for further promotions, if they are qualified. Otherwise, valuable employees may resign because they think the organization does not appreciate their efforts.

2. To explain why they were not selected.

3. To indicate what specific career development actions should be undertaken. Care should be exercised not to imply that certain career development actions will automatically mean a promotion. Instead, the individual's "candidacy" for selection will be influenced by appropriate career development actions.

Cohesive Work Groups

Employees who want to pursue a career within an organization should feel that the organization is a satisfying environment. When they are a part of a cohesive work group, their career development efforts are more likely to be directed toward improving their opportunities within the organization.[53] To create such a satisfying environment, human resource departments must deal effectively with change and organizational development.

Succession Planning

Another responsibility of the HR department is to ensure that there are a sufficient number of candidates for key positions, ready to take over if an unexpected vacancy occurs, be it because of someone leaving the company, sickness, or death.

> A few years ago a small plane with seven executives of a Calgary-based oil company on a flight to New York crashed, killing all seven and the crew. It was a catastrophic event for the company, but it survived because it had a sufficient number of trained managers ready.

Succession planning
The process of making long-range management developmental plans to fill human resource needs.

www.criterioninc.com/
PWFSuccession.htm

www.workforce.com/
feature/00/05/25/

www.succession-planning.com/
succession-process.html

www.bmo.com/careers/
index_studentcareer.html

The technical aspect of *succession planning* has been addressed in Chapter Three under the topic Replacement Charts, but here we will discuss the topic in the context of career planning and development. As the example above has shown, having well-trained employees ready to take on critical responsibilities in case of an emergency can be crucial for the survival of a company.

An effective succession plan is based on the ability to recognize promising employees, identify their strengths and weaknesses, give them feedback on both, and allow them to gain the practical experiences necessary to take over whenever needed. A key element in this process is the participation of the employees in question in their career development program. HR managers or career counsellors must work with the employees to clarify the skill requirements for the advanced position and, very importantly, make sure that these competencies are maintained at the required level. This is a critical part of the performance appraisal process, called promotability forecast, discussed in the following chapter.

Recent Developments

Many organizations now use their intranet for career counselling purposes. The Bank of Montreal's virtual Career Possibilities Centre is a good example of this approach of shifting from employee direct counselling to letting them handle their own career management by providing the necessary tools on the intranet, such as self-testing and workshops on organizational change and how to cope with it. Professional career consultants are still available if employees need special advice.[54]

The Internet may play a significant role in career planning and career development. Richard Koonce sums it up nicely in a reply to the question: "What is the best way to use the Internet as part of a job search?"

> I don't think of the Internet as just a job search tool. I think of it as a professional development tool for educating yourself on job searches and career transitions, researching prospective employers, tracking trends, making contacts with other people and identifying and generating professional opportunities.[55]

Now not only are all major newspapers and journals available on the Net, but also job postings for national and international jobs, discussion groups that share career information, and listserves that provide a rich source of information on developments and trends in specific interest areas, such as training and development, human resource management, industrial relations, and many other relevant topic areas. At the end of the chapter, under "Web Research," are listings of Web sites providing the services mentioned.

A new concept is the *"360 degrees career development,"* describing a holistic approach to the various career development functions: attracting, finding, evaluating, developing, certifying, and promoting the employees in the organization. There can be little doubt that if these functions are well integrated, they will be more efficient and effective.[56] A similar concept, that of a 360-degree performance appraisal process, is discussed in Chapter Nine.

SUMMARY

External and internal pressures have changed the skill and attitude requirements for managers. Top management is expected to work with leaner organizations, requiring sharing of power and delegation of authority. This in turn necessitates that lower-level managers must assume greater responsibilities, for which they must be prepared. It is essential that top management makes strategic human resource development a key component in its long-range strategic business plan.

Similarly, if management wants to meet the global challenge and keep the organization competitive, if it wants its managers to be prepared for constant change, new skill requirements, and higher willingness to accept risks, it must make employee development plans part of its overall strategic business plan.

Different development strategies may be employed, at the cognitive, behavioural, and environmental level, with the cognitive method being the least promising and the environmental method the most promising approach.

Career planning and development are relatively new concepts to human resource specialists. In recent years, human resource departments have begun to recognize the need for more proactive efforts in this area. As a result, some (mostly large) departments provide career education, information, and counselling. But the primary responsibility for career planning and development rests with the individual employee. The planning process enables employees to identify career goals and the paths to those goals. Then, through developmental activities, the workers seek ways to improve themselves and further their career goals.

Even today, most developmental activities are individual and voluntary. Individual efforts include good job performance, favourable exposure, leveraging, building of alliances, and other actions. Human resource departments become involved by providing information and obtaining management support. The human resource department helps make career planning and development a success for both the employees and the organization.

Career planning does not guarantee success. But without it, employees are seldom ready for career opportunities that arise. As a result, their career progress may be slowed and the human resource department may be unable to fill openings internally.

TERMS FOR REVIEW

Visit the Web site at www.mcgrawhill.ca/college/schwind6 for a full glossary.

REVIEW AND DISCUSSION QUESTIONS

1. Discuss why it is so important that there is a linkage between an organization's human resource development needs and its mission and strategy.

2. Explain the differences between the cognitive, behavioural, and environmental approaches to strategic employee development.

3. Discuss the pros and cons of the policy adopted by Ford Motor Company to provide managers with an incentive to train their own successors.

4. In what way does a "learning" organization differ from a "traditional" organization?

5. Why should a human resource department be concerned about career planning, especially since employee plans may conflict with the organization's objectives? What advantages does a human resource department expect to receive from assisting career planning?

6. In what ways can a human resource department assist career planning?

7. Suppose you are in a management training position after completing university. Your career goal is not very clear, but you would like to become a top manager in your firm. What type of information would you seek from the human resource department to help you develop your career plan?

8. After you develop your first career plan while employed by a bank, what career development activities would you pursue? Why?

9. Why is employee feedback an important element of any organization's attempt to encourage career development?

10. Suppose a hard-working and loyal employee is passed over for promotion. What would you tell this person?

CRITICAL THINKING QUESTIONS

1. You are the training and development manager. Your president calls you in and tells you that the employee development budget must be cut because of the company's financial situation. What arguments can you use to persuade your boss that development money is well spent?

2. If you were interested in making a career out of your own ability to play a musical instrument, what types of career goals would you set for yourself? How would you find out about the career prospects for musicians before you took your first job?

3. Assume that you are the HR manager in a company that had downsized considerably, leaving a number of middle managers and some key employees with limited advancement opportunities. You heard through the grapevine that there were grumblings and that some key employees were looking for other jobs. What measures could you use to retain these employees and remotivate them?

WEB RESEARCH

Employee development

Adult Education Resources

http://adulted.about.com/education/adulted/mbody.htm

a)   Assume that you have a job a significant distance away from any university, but you are determined to earn a degree. What are the different options in distance education? Describe the advantages and disadvantages for these options.

Career

Career Planning

http://careerplanning.about.com/careers/careerplanning/mbody.htm

a)   Go to "Career Planning Process", then to "Planner's Notebook", and "Self-Assessment".

b)   Do a self-assessment. Do you agree with the results/recommendations?

c)   Assume that you want to pursue a career in accounting. What steps will you follow?

Other Self-assessment Instruments

www.keirsey.com/

www.teamtechnology.co.uk/

http://cbweb9p.collegeboard.org/career/html/searchQues.html

www.schoolfinder.com/career/carquiz.htm

Job Search

These sites tend to offer may types of career advice, e.g., self-assessment, resume writing, writing application letters, job requirements, job descriptions, and list job openings in different fields and countries.

http://worksearch.gc.ca/cgi-bin/start.pl

www.hrdc-drhc.gc.ca/hrdc/hrib/hrif/leis/career/index_e.html

http://youth.gc.ca/menue.shtml

http://globecareers.workopolis.com/

www.monster.ca/

www.jobdesk.com/

www.careers.org/

www.careerbuilder.com/

http://careers.wsj.com/

www.talentalliance.org/

INCIDENT 8-1

Career Planning and Development at Immobile Ltd.

Long-term employees at Saskatchewan Electric Company Ltd. nicknamed the company "Immobile Ltd." It seemed that the only time anyone received a promotion was when a manager retired or died. Even when job vacancies did occur, the human resource department frequently hired a replacement from some other electric utility, so that few employees received a promotion. Employee turnover was low, however, partially because the jobs paid very well, provided high job security, and offered outstanding fringe benefits.

Top management became concerned about the negative attitude reflected by the nickname "Immobile Ltd." and hired a large Toronto consulting firm to develop a career planning program. After several months, the consultants revealed a detailed plan, complete with a special office of career counselling in the human resource department. Initially, employees responded favourably and made extensive use of the counselling and career information services available to them. But by the fourth month, the chief career counsellor asked the human resource manager for a transfer into any other part of the human resource department. When asked why, the counsellor said that employees were not using the service and the job of counsellor had become lonely and boring. The human resource manager gave the counsellor an assignment to discover why the planning had failed and what might be done to revitalize it.

1. What explanations can you offer to explain the initial enthusiasm for career planning assistance followed by an almost total avoidance by employees?

2. Assuming part of the problem was a lack of support by middle and first-level management, what recommendations would you make? Could this company learn a lesson from the approach used by the Japanese?

INCIDENT 8-2

Continental Life Insurance

Ken Konopaski, a manager of a large branch of Continental Life in Toronto, was sitting in his office, looking through the glass partition to observe his employees at work.

The company had recently implemented an employment equity program and, as a result, had hired four members of a visible minority and two aboriginal persons. Each of the trainees was assigned to an experienced employee for an on-the-job training program.

To hire these trainees, the company had lowered its normal selection criteria, but had implemented the special on-the-job training program to bring them up to par with the rest of the employees.

Ken Konopaski felt frustrated. He had just had a heated discussion with Janet Lee, a longtime employee, who had one of the trainees under her supervision. Janet was quite upset. She had found out about the lower hiring standards for the trainees. What was galling her was that her sister had applied for an advertised position in the company, but had been turned down because "a more suitable person had been found."

Apparently, the sister was contemplating complaining to the Human Rights Commission about reverse discrimination. Ken felt quite safe on that issue, because the Human Rights Commission had approved the employment equity program. Continental Life had not had a good record of hiring minorities and, under some pressure, had agreed to the plan. But there was more trouble brewing.

Many employees apparently refused to work with the trainees, claiming that the latter got the job only because of the employment equity program, not because they were properly qualified. Some had complained privately to Ken about this, but nobody wanted to make a public issue out of it.

One of the trainees, Tom Robinson, an African Canadian, had also met with Ken and complained about the treatment he had received from the other employees. Tom felt that the employee responsible for his training treated him as if he were illiterate, explaining everything in great detail. On one occasion, when he had asked another employee for advice, she told him: "Look it up in the manual." Furthermore, during lunch hours in the cafeteria he felt that the other employees kept to themselves and would not sit at the same table with him. Tom had mentioned that he felt very uncomfortable in this environment and that he was looking for another job. Apparently he was not the only one among the trainees who was unhappy.

Ken felt that the atmosphere in the branch had been poisoned because of these developments, and he wondered what he could do to reduce the tension in the branch.

If you were Ken, what action(s) would you take?

CASE STUDY

Maple Leaf Shoes Ltd., Employee Development and Career Planning

Maple Leaf Shoes Ltd. is a medium-sized manufacturer of leather and vinyl shoes located in Wilmington, Ontario. It was started in 1969 and currently employs about 400 persons in its Ontario plant and some 380 more in offices and warehouses in Canada and abroad.

The company operates in a highly competitive market. Over the years, trade barriers across countries have been disappearing, resulting in increasing imports of cheaper, but still high-quality, shoes made in countries such as Korea, Taiwan, Singapore, India, and Mexico. Despite these threats, Maple Leaf Shoes has been able to perform well in the export markets. Currently, over 10 per cent of its production is exported—mainly to western parts of the United States and Europe (the corresponding figure five years back had been a tiny two per cent).

Management of Maple Leaf Shoes believes that growth through expanded activities is critical now, especially given the competitive challenge. Growth, however, is possible only by expanding its operations within and outside Canada. Management plans to expand its operations to the Maritimes and Quebec in the next three years and to the rest of Canada in the next five to six years. Currently, its shoes have found favour in Europe—especially in England, Belgium, and Luxembourg.

Jane Reynolds, special assistant in the personnel department, is sitting in her office, contemplating the future of the company. Robert Clark, the company's president and key shareholder, had met with her the day before to discuss his expansion plans and to inform her of his expectations to develop an employee development plan that would take care of the urgent need for Maple Leaf Shoes to improve its management staff. The need for managerial training at Maple Leaf Shoes was felt now more than ever. The firm expected its activities to grow; however, given current market conditions, it was not keen on expanding the size of its managerial cadre significantly. Instead, Janet saw the need to delegate more managerial responsibilities to employees and to provide them with managerial and team-management skills and empower them to make some decisions on their own.

Reynolds had no illusions about the quality of the management personnel at Maple Leaf Shoes. Most managers and supervisors had come through the ranks or, as they called it, the "school of hard knocks." Only a few had a college degree like her, and that was limited to those hired more recently. Tim Donovan, a manager who had recently left the company, had been overheard saying before his departure: "The management system here is primitive. It's as if forces of darkness surround you. Of course, I could stay here and fight it out—maybe I would win in the end. But then I'm not masochistic!"

Despite her reservations, Reynolds was optimistic about her assignment. She had come to Maple Leaf Shoes because she saw her position in personnel as a challenge. It was clear to her that the task before her was a difficult one, but Bob Clark had promised her his full backing for the employee development plan he expected her to come up with.

Discussion Questions

1. Robert Clark expects an employee development plan from Jane. Outline a framework for such a plan.
2. Which of the three development strategies described in Figure 8-2 do you think is most suitable for developing Maple Leaf Shoes' managers and employees? Why?
3. Would it be advisable to combine the employee development plan with a career plan? Why or why not?

CASE STUDY

Maple Leaf Shoes Ltd., Career Plan

Bernadine Halliday is an accounting clerk who has just joined Maple Leaf Shoes' accounting department. She grew up in Wilmington and has been living with her widowed mother, who works as a sales clerk. Her mother's moderate income is not enough to even think of a university education for Bernadine. She was proficient in math during her high school classes and excelled in an accounting course, which was offered during her last year.

Bernadine joined Maple Leaf Shoes for two reasons: the shoe plant was conveniently located near were she lived, which allowed her to stay with her mother and to save some money. Second, it offered her the opportunity to earn some money, which she planned to save for her university education at McMaster University, which was located nearby.

Bernadine liked her colleagues in the accounting office (there were only three of them besides the accounting supervisor). None of them had a university degree. The supervisor had a Certified General Accountant designation. He was 10 years away from retirement. If she planned it well, perhaps there was an advancement opportunity for her at Maple Leaf Shoes.

Discussion Question

1. Develop a career plan for Bernadine. What would she have to do to move up the ladder to the comptroller position, the chief financial officer of the company?

CASE STUDY

Canadian Pacific and International Bank

Any type of audit will cause apprehension in managers, and the audit by the Canadian Human Rights Commission (CHRC) regarding the Bank's compliance with the Employment Equity Act was no different. Although Mary Keddy, senior vice president—human resources, was convinced that the bank's overall employment equity policies were in line with the Act's requirements, she knew that not all objectives set out a few years earlier had been accomplished and, therefore, she expected to hear some criticism from the CHRC auditor.

The audit by the representative had progressed reasonably well. Sandra Fougere, a senior human rights officer with the commission, had been quite satisfied with the progress the bank had made regarding the promotion of women into higher positions, at least at the junior management level, where the ratio of males to females was 65 to 45—not quite the population ratio, but a significant improvement compared to the ratio of five years ago. However, Fougere had criticized the status of the promotion of females to senior management positions. For example, of the eight vice presidents, only one was female, and among the 36 district managers there were only 10 women. Keddy was aware of the shortcomings, but when she took over the vice presidency she had concentrated on changing the hiring, training, and promotion practices of the bank, especially with respect to females and minorities. The obstacles had been formidable. Although John Galsworthy, her predecessor, had been an excellent HR manager, he had had a hard time overcoming the old banking corporate culture, which was male dominated and which relied on the old-boys network for hiring and promotion. That was the past and the values and attitudes of top management had changed dramatically with the arrival of Michael Bennett, president and CEO who, right from the beginning, made it clear that effective human resource management was a high priority for him.

Fougere suggested that Keddy prepare and submit to her a memorandum of understanding, outlining a plan—complete with deadlines—to improve the promotion situation for females at the senior management level. Fougere mentioned that she understood that the bank could not just promote any female manager into senior positions, but she felt that it should be possible to develop a program that would improve the promotion chances of women without causing undue reverse discrimination.

Keddy knew that the bank was in a sensitive situation. The senior male managers had agreed with her that the bank had to do something about the male domination at the upper ranks, but it was understood that the best person would be promoted, regardless of racial, ethnic, and gender status. This policy had resulted in a few conflict situations where supervisors with promoting authority had disagreed on the suitability of candidates. Keddy had reserved the final decision in such cases for herself and all had been resolved more or less amicably.

The plan she had to develop had to satisfy several stakeholders:

- The Human Rights Commission
- Senior management
- All female and male candidates for higher positions

Discussion Questions

1. Outline a step-by-step plan to assist Mary Keddy in her objective to promote female candidates into senior positions.

2. Is it possible to avoid conflict situations described above regarding differing opinions about hiring and promotion decisions? If so, how? If not, can they be minimized?

3. Does the Canadian Human Rights Commission have the authority to set objectives or to punish the bank for non-compliance? (For more information log-on www.chrc.ca, click on "Employment Equity Division", and read the document "Framework for Compliance Audits").

SUGGESTED READINGS

Readings on Employee Development:

Belcourt, Monica, Phillip C. Wright, and Alan M. Saks, *Managing Performance Through Training & Development*, Toronto: Nelson Canada, 2000.

Brown, A.L., L. Brooks, and Associates, *Career Choice and Development*, (2nd ed.), San Francisco: Jossey-Bass, 1990.

Evered, R.D. and J.C. Selman, "Coaching and the Art of Management," *Organizational Dynamics*, Vol. 18, No. 2, pp. 16-32.

Fulmer, Robert M., Philip Gibbs, and J. Bernard Keys, "The Second Generation Learning Organizations: New Tools for Sustaining Competitive Advantage," *Organizational Dynamics*, Vol. 27, No. 2, 1998, pp. 7-20.

Harris, D.M. and R. L. DeSimone, *Human Resource Development*, Fort Worth, TX: The Dryden Press, 1994.

Kets De Vries, Manfred F.R., "High-performance Teams: Lessons from the Pygmies," *Organizational Dynamics*, Vol. 27, No. 3, 1999, pp. 66-77.

McIntyre, D., *Training and Development: Policies, Practices & Expenditures*, Toronto: Conference Board of Canada, 1994.

Readings on Careers:

Bendaly, Leslie, *Organization 2000: The Essential Guide for Companies and Teams in the New Economy*, Toronto: Harper-Collins, 1997.

Butler, John E., Gerald R. Ferris, and Nancy K. Napier, *Strategy and Human Resource Management*, Cincinnati, Ohio: South-Western Publishing, 1991.

Cianni, M., and D. Wnuck, "Individual Growth and Team Enhancement: Moving Toward a New Model of Career Development," *Academy of Management Executive*, February 1997, Vol. XI, No. 1, pp. 105-115.

Greenhaus, J.H., *Career Management*, Chicago, Ill.: Dryden Press, 1987.

Hall, D. T., Careers in Organizations, Santa Monica, Calif.: Goodyear Publishing, 1976.

Hall, Douglas T., and Jonathan E. Moss, "The New Protean Career Contract: Helping organizations and Employees Adapt," *Organizational Dynamics*, Vol. 26, No. 3, 1998, pp. 22-36.

Hall, Douglas T., and James Richter, "Career Gridlock: Baby Boomers Hit the Wall," *Academy of Management Executive*, Vol. 4, No. 3, 1990, pp. 7-22.

"Job Futures—A Two-Volume Reference Set for Career Planning," Human Resources Development Canada, Catalogue No. MP43-181/1996 E, 1996.

Hurley, Amy E., Ellen A. Fagenson-Eland, Jeffrey A. Sonnefeld, "Does Cream Always Rise To The Top? An Investigation of Career Attainment Determinants," *Organizational Dynamics*, Vol. 26, No. 2, 1997, pp. 65-71.

Leibowitz, Z., and D. Lea (Eds.) "Adult Career Development Concepts, Issues, and Practices," (National Career Development Association), 1986.

Moses, Barbara, *Career Intelligence*, Toronto: Stoddart, 1997.

Osberg, L., F. Wien and J. Grude, "Vanishing Jobs: Canada's Changing Workplaces," Toronto: Lorimer, 1995.

Schein, Edgar E., in J.W. Lorsch, ed., *Handbook of Organizational Behavior*, Englewood Cliffs, N.J.: Prentice-Hall, 1987, pp. 155-71.

"Special Issue: Careers of the 21st Century," *The Academy of Management Executive*, November 1996, Vol. X, No. 4.

Chapter 9

Performance Appraisal

The performance appraisal concept is central to effective management.

—Harry Levinson[1]

CHAPTER OBJECTIVES

After studying this chapter, you should be able to:

- *Identify* the issues that influence selection of a performance appraisal system.

- *Explain* the uses of performance appraisals.

- *Discuss* rater biases in performance appraisals.

- *Describe* commonly used appraisal methods.

- *Describe* how to improve the validity and reliability of performance appraisal systems

- *Discuss* how an effective appraisal leads to improved performance

- *Explain* how the results of performance appraisal affect human resource management.

Previous chapters discussed how employees are selected, developed, and formed into cohesive work groups. These are important activities. But the ultimate measure of a human resource department's success is employee performance. Both the human resource department and employees need feedback on their efforts. Unfortunately, managers in other departments may not understand the need for evaluating employee performance. Too often, they see performance appraisals as unnecessary conversation. The following discussion between Ellen, a line manager, and Sam, a human resource specialist, highlights these different views of performance appraisals:

Ellen: Don't you think I know who the good performers are in my department? I know the strengths and weaknesses of every employee who works for me. So why do we need to have a formal performance evaluation program?

Sam: No one in the human resource department is questioning whether you know who the good performers are. In fact, we in human resource management hope that all managers know who their best workers are. But we need a formal appraisal system to compare employees in different departments.

Ellen: Why is that so important?

Sam: We need that information for many reasons. We need to know who should receive additional training and development, who should be promoted, and who should get pay raises. Besides, employees need formal feedback on how they are doing their job.

Ellen: Well, I let my employees know how they are doing. And I do it without all the formality of a performance appraisal program.

Sam: Good managers, like yourself, always give employees feedback. The human resource department merely wants to formalize the process so that there is a written record of performance. Without such a record, we in the human resource department have no consistent way to compare employees when staff-related decisions are made. And one more point: employees appreciate written feedback, especially if it contains praise, because this becomes a permanent part of their personnel records.

Performance appraisal
The process by which organizations evaluate employee job performance.

Performance appraisal is the process by which organizations evaluate employee job performance. As the dialogue between Ellen and Sam indicates, appraisals expand the human resource department's information base. This knowledge can improve human resource decisions and the feedback employees receive about their performance.

www.zigonperf.com/PMNews/
Australian_PAS.html

The uses of performance appraisals are described in Figure 9-1. Accurate performance evaluations show employees where they are deficient. For the human resource department, appraisals make compensation, placement, training, development, and career guidance decisions more effective. At the same time, the department obtains feedback on its development activities, staffing process, job designs, and external challenges. In short, performance appraisals serve as a quality control check on employee and human resource department performance.

Without an effective appraisal system, promotions, transfers, and other employee-related decisions become subject to trial and error. Career planning and human resource development suffer because there is no systematic performance feedback. Moreover, the human resource department lacks adequate information to evaluate its performance objectively. This lack of feedback can cause the human resource department to miss its objectives. Sometimes the consequences of this failure are severe:

A large agricultural cooperative association in the western provinces rated employees twice a year. But employees were evaluated on personality characteristics, such as attitude, cooperation, and other factors that were related only indirectly to actual performance. Employees who were well liked by their managers received higher ratings than others. As a result, promotions, pay raises, and other employee-related decisions

FIGURE 9-1

Uses of Performance Appraisals

- *Performance improvement.* Performance feedback allows the employee, the manager, and human resource specialists to intervene with appropriate actions to improve performance.

- *Compensation adjustments.* Performance evaluations help decision-makers determine who should receive pay raises. Many firms grant part or all of their pay increases and bonuses on the basis of merit, which is determined mostly through performance appraisals.

- *Placement decisions.* Promotions, transfers, and demotions are usually based on past or anticipated performance. Often promotions are a reward for past performance.

- *Training and development needs.* Poor performance may indicate the need for retraining. Likewise, good performance may indicate untapped potential that should be developed.

- *Career planning and development.* Performance feedback guides career decisions about specific career paths one should investigate.

- *Deficiencies in staffing process.* Good or bad performance implies strengths or weaknesses in the human resource department's staffing procedures.

- *Informational inaccuracies.* Poor performance may indicate errors in job analysis information, human resource plans, or other parts of the human resource management information system. Reliance on inaccurate information may have led to inappropriate hiring, training, or counselling decisions.

- *Job design errors.* Poor performance may be a symptom of ill-conceived job designs. Appraisals help diagnose these errors.

- *Avoidance of discrimination.* Accurate performance appraisals that actually measure job-related performance ensure that internal placement decisions are not discriminatory.

- *External challenges.* Sometimes performance is influenced by factors outside the work environment, such as family, finances, health, or other personal matters. If such influences are uncovered through appraisals, the human resource department may be able to provide assistance.

www.zigonperf.com/PMNews/
acceptable_pas.html

www.zigonperf.com/PMNews/
Measure_What_Matters.htm

were biased by personalities. Eventually, several employees filed charges against the cooperative, alleging racial and sexual discrimination. When company lawyers defended past decisions as unbiased, they lost the case because they could not show how the ratings related to job performance.

As this example emphasizes, an organization cannot have just any appraisal system. It must be effective and accepted. If effective and accepted, it can identify developmental and career planning needs (see Chapter Eight). It also can help with replacement summaries (discussed in Chapter Three), along with the other uses illustrated in Figure 9-1.

ELEMENTS OF THE PERFORMANCE APPRAISAL SYSTEM

FIGURE 9-2 SHOWS the elements of an acceptable appraisal system. The approach must identify performance-related criteria, measure those criteria, and then give feedback to employees and the human resource department. If performance measures are

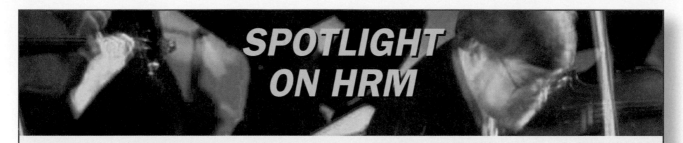

SPOTLIGHT ON HRM

PERFORMANCE APPRAISAL— A NECESSARY EVIL?

Performance appraisal is one of those difficult areas of business that seems to be a necessary evil—all the books say that a company should have a performance appraisal system, employees often express the desire for one, and (if my workload is any indication) businesspeople are keen to find out about them.

Why, then, is performance appraisal one of the areas of management most commonly complained about by employees and managers alike?

The major mistake made by companies is the failure to recognize what constitutes a performance appraisal system. It certainly is not just about a set of forms that must be completed by various individuals. Nor is it just an opportunity to have an annual chat with the boss to "get it all off your chest."

Seen in isolation, performance appraisal is simply a procedure, which involves the assessment of an individual's performance on a regular basis. That's fine, but it goes much deeper-performance appraisal lies at the heart of good business practice. A performance appraisal system can only function if the business has a clear idea of where it is heading, and has taken steps to ensure that it is taking the workforce along.

Of course, nothing is that simple. Or is it?

Try this—if you are a businessperson, ask the following questions of your own company. If you are an employee, copy this and give it to your manager, or ask the questions among your peers and pass the results up the chain of command. You never know what might result!

What follows are a series of questions that can be used to rate the performance appraisal mechanisms in organizations. You should be able to answer the questions and get a rating regardless of whether a formal performance appraisal system is in place, and you may be very surprised by the result—there is nothing that says a performance appraisal system must be written down or formalized!

The questions draw on my own experience in line management and consultancy, and from the UK Investors in People Initiative, which provides an excellent framework for business development.

For each of the questions, answer:

- 1 = strongly disagree
- 2 = disagree
- 3 = not sure
- 4 = agree
- 5 = strongly agree

Record your answers and total them up at the end.

1. Management have a clear idea of where they want the company to go
2. Every employee understands where the management are trying to take the company
3. All departments have clearly defined goals
4. The department goals fit together to help the company get to where it wants to go
5. Every employee understands how his or her job contributes to the overall department and company goals
6. Each employee and their supervisors/managers agree what is expected of the employee
7. Each employee, together with his/her supervisor/manager monitors whether he/she is achieving what he/she is expected to
8. Each employee's training and development needs are reviewed regularly to ensure that they continue to have the skills they need to achieve what is expected of them
9. Supervisors/managers ensure that employees understand why particular training and development actions are taking place
10. Supervisors/managers ensure that employees understand what they are expected to do better as a result of particular training and development actions
11. Employees are happy with the quality and frequency of feedback they receive from their supervisors/managers
12. Supervisors/managers and employees are trained for their roles in the appraisal process

How did you score?

Under 24—the company is like a sailing ship without a sail. Lack of a performance appraisal is the least of the worries. Management probably have little idea of where the company is heading, and the workforce almost certainly do not. I would not be surprised if you hit some rocks....soon. Get some help.

25 to 40—the Internal systems are poor and may be causing discontent and motivational difficulties in the workforce. It will be possible to improve matters, but firm action is needed. Management must decide on corporate goals, decide what they need to do to achieve them, and then tell the workforce not once, but every day. Communicate, communicate, communicate—that is the key.

41 to 50—I'm impressed. The company has all the basics in place and they are probably working well. There is obviously room for some improvement in specific areas, and I suggest looking in detail at the areas with the lowest scores.

Over 50—Wow—write a book on how you did it!

Source: Martin Finnigan, "Performance Appraisal—A Necessary Evil?", Marketing Magic, copyright 1998 Traynor Kitching & Associates, http://www.tka.co.uk/magic/feature7.html. Courtesy of Martin Finnigan of Finnigan Consulting.

not job-related, the evaluation can lead to inaccurate or biased results. Not only is performance feedback distorted, but errors in employee records can also lead to incorrect human resource decisions, as happened in the example of the agricultural cooperative.

Key Elements of Performance Appraisal Systems

The human resource department usually develops performance appraisals for employees in all departments. This centralization is meant to ensure uniformity. With uniformity in design and implementation, results are more likely to be comparable among similar groups of employees. Although the human resource department may develop different approaches for managers and workers, uniformity within each group is needed to ensure useful results.

Even though the human resource department usually designs the appraisal system, it seldom does the actual evaluation of performance. Instead, research shows

FIGURE 9-2

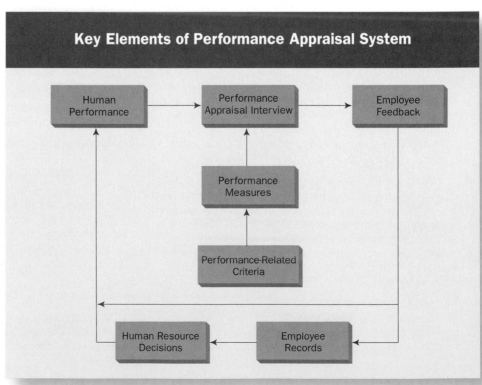

that the employee's immediate supervisor performs the evaluation 95 per cent of the time.[2] Although others could rate performance, the immediate supervisor is often in the best position to make the appraisal.

So important is the evaluation of performance that 85 per cent of all companies surveyed in one Canadian study used appraisals for clerical, professional, supervisory and management employees.[3] To explain the importance of this widely used tool of human resource management, the remainder of this chapter examines the preparation, methods, and implications of performance appraisals.

The appraisal should create an accurate picture of an individual's job performance. To achieve this goal, appraisal systems should be job-related, be practical, have standards, and use dependable measures. *Job-related* means that the system evaluates critical behaviours that constitute job success. If the evaluation is not job-related, it is invalid and probably unreliable. Without validity and reliability, the system may discriminate in violation of antidiscrimination laws. Even when discrimination does not occur, appraisals are inaccurate and useless if they are not job-related.

However, a job-related approach also must be *practical*. A practical system is one that, first of all, is understood by evaluators and employees; a complicated, impractical approach may cause resentment and nonuse. The confusion can lead to inaccuracies that reduce the effectiveness of the appraisal.

Performance evaluation requires **performance standards**. These are the benchmarks against which performance is measured. To be effective, they should relate to the desired results of each job. They cannot be set arbitrarily. Knowledge of these standards is collected through job analysis. As discussed in Chapter Two, job analysis uncovers specific performance criteria by analyzing the performance of existing employees. As one pair of writers has observed:

> It is important that management carefully examine the characteristics of effective performance. Job analysis coupled with a detailed performance analysis of existing employees should begin to identify what characteristics are required by a job and which of those are exhibited by "successful" employees. It is possible that such an investigation may reveal that what management has used in the past to define successful performance is inadequate or misleading. This should not deter management from the task of defining the criteria, but should reinforce management for the "house cleaning" which is being undertaken. This must be a careful scrutiny with an eye to what the performance criteria should be in the future, rather than what criteria have been used in the past.[4]

www.zigonperf.com/PMNews/
Empl_want_Appraisal.htm

Performance standards
The benchmarks against which performance is measured.

Performance feedback is crucial for the motivation of employees. It is also important that the feedback is given with tact and sensitivity.

Digital Imagery © 2001 Photo Disc Inc. Photo by Keith Brofsky

Performance measures
The ratings used to
evaluate employee
performance.

From the duties and standards listed in the job description, the analyst can decide which behaviours are critical and should be evaluated. If it should happen that this information is lacking or unclear, standards may be developed from observation of the job or discussion with the immediate supervisor.

Performance evaluation also requires dependable *performance measures*. These are the ratings used to evaluate performance. To be useful, they must be easy to use, be reliable, and report on the critical behaviours that determine performance. For example, a telephone company supervisor must observe each operator's:

- use of company procedures—staying calm, applying tariff rates for phone calls, and following company rules and regulations;

- pleasant phone manners—speaking clearly and courteously; and

- call-placement accuracy—placing operator-assisted calls accurately.

These observations can be made either directly or indirectly. *Direct observation* occurs when the rater actually sees the performance. Indirect observation occurs when the rater can evaluate only substitutes for actual performance. For example, a supervisor's monitoring of an operator's calls is direct observation; a written test on company procedures for handling emergency calls is *indirect* observation. Indirect observations are usually less accurate because they evaluate substitutes for actual performance. Substitutes for actual performance are called constructs. Since constructs are not exactly the same as actual performance, they may lead to errors:

> To test how well operators might respond to emergency calls, a provincial telephone company developed a paper-and-pencil test. The test was intended to determine if each operator knew exactly how to proceed when emergency calls were received for such requests as police, ambulance, or fire equipment. After several hundred operators were tested, it was noticed that fast readers scored better. The human resource department decided to scrap the test and use false emergency calls to evaluate the operators.

Another dimension of performance measures is whether they are objective or subjective. *Objective* performance measures are those indications of job performance that are verifiable by others. For example, if two supervisors monitor an operator's calls, they can count the number of misdialled ones. The results are objective and verifiable since each supervisor gets the same call-placement accuracy percentage. Usually, objective measures are quantitative. They typically include items such as gross units produced, net units approved by quality control, scrap rates, number of computational errors, number of customer complaints, or some other mathematically precise measure of performance.

www.zigonperf.com/PMNews/
appraise_appraisal.html.html

www.zigonperf.com/PMNews/
Train_mgrs_apprais.html

www.zigonperf.com/PMNews/
7_feedback_tips.html

Subjective performance measures are those ratings that are not verifiable by others. Usually, such measures are the rater's personal opinions. Figure 9-3 compares the accuracy of objective and subjective measures. It shows that subjective measures are low in accuracy. When subjective measures are also indirect, accuracy becomes even lower. For example, measurement of an operator's phone manners is done subjectively since supervisors must use their personal opinions of good or bad manners. Since the evaluation is subjective, accuracy is usually low even if the supervisor directly observes the operator. Accuracy is likely to be even lower when the rater uses an indirect measure, such as an essay test of phone manners. Whenever possible, human resource specialists prefer objective and direct measures of performance.

Rater Biases

The problem with subjective measures is the opportunity for bias. Bias is the (mostly unintentional) distortion of a measurement. Usually it is caused by raters who fail to

FIGURE 9-3

Types and Accuracy of Performance Measures

	Relative Degree of Accuracy	
Types of Performance Measures	**Direct**	**Indirect**
Objective	Very high	High
Subjective	Low	Very low

remain emotionally detached while they evaluate employee performance. The most common rater biases include:

- the halo effect;
- the error of central tendency;
- the leniency and strictness biases;
- personal prejudice; and
- the recency effect.

The Halo Effect

Halo effect
A bias that occurs when an evaluation allows some information to dispro-portionately affect the final evaluation.

The **halo effect** (discussed in Chapter Six) occurs when the rater's personal opinion of the employee sways the rater's measurement of performance. For example, if a supervisor likes an employee, that opinion may distort the supervisor's estimate of the employee's performance. The problem is most severe when raters must evaluate their friends.

> Sam was Jim's supervisor. They had been friends in school and were playing together in a minor league baseball team for years. Jim was a "happy-go-lucky" guy and his job performance was so-so, but he was very good with people. When Sam had to write a performance evaluation he praised Jim for his "excellent social" and "superior com-munication" skills, but overlooked his shortcomings in productivity aspects. Sam felt that he "could not let down" his friend.

The Error of Central Tendency

Error of central tendency
An error in rating employees that consists of evaluating employees as neither good nor poor performers even when some employees perform exceptionally well or poorly.

Some raters do not like to judge employees as "effective" or "ineffective," so they avoid checking extremes—very poor or excellent—and instead place their marks near the centre of the rating sheet so that employees appear to be "average." Thus, the term *error of central tendency* has been applied to this bias. Human resource departments sometimes unintentionally encourage this behaviour by requiring raters to justify extremely high or low ratings.

> The first author of this book did his Ph.D. dissertation on performance appraisals in Canadian banks. When he surveyed over 2000 appraisals, which used seven-point scales, he did not find a single evaluation that used one or seven.[5]

The Leniency and Strictness Biases

Leniency bias
A tendency to rate employees higher than their performance justifies.

Strictness bias
A tendency to rate employees lower than their performance justifies.

The **leniency bias** occurs when raters are too easy in evaluating employee perform-ance. The **strictness bias** is just the opposite; it results from raters being too harsh in their evaluation of performance. Both errors more commonly occur when perform-ance standards are vague. The leniency bias is much more common.

> The "average" performance assessment of officers in the Canadian Armed Forces is about 80 per cent.[6]

Personal Prejudice

A rater's dislike for a person or group may distort the ratings. For example, some human resource departments notice that male supervisors give undeservedly low ratings to women who hold "traditionally male jobs." Sometimes raters are unaware of their prejudice, which makes such biases even more difficult to overcome. Nevertheless, human resource specialists should pay close attention to prejudice in appraisals since it prevents effective evaluations and violates antidiscrimination laws.

> Ann was the only female welder in a maintenance team, and she was good. She had passed her welder's certification with flying colours and was chosen over a number of male applicants. Tom, the team's foreman, had opposed her hiring, saying that women would not fit into the team, but the HR manager insisted on "hiring the best person." Ann noticed that Tom scrutinized her work much more closely than that of other team members and publicly complained about her even minor mistakes. In her first annual performance assessment she was judged "average, with potential for improvement."

The Recency Effect

When using subjective performance measures, ratings are affected strongly by the employee's most recent actions. Recent actions—either good or bad—are more likely to be remembered by the rater. This is known as the ***recency effect***.

> John had been an average nurse, paying more attention to his female colleagues than his patients. However, a few weeks ago, by shear coincident, he had saved a patient's life. During the recent performance appraisal, Jennifer, the head nurse, concentrated on this one-time event and lavishly praised John's overall job performance.

Recency effect
A rater bias that occurs when the rater allows recent employee performance to sway unduly the overall evaluation of the employee's performance.

When subjective measures must be used, human resource specialists can reduce the distortion from biases through training, feedback, and the proper selection of performance appraisal techniques. Training for raters should involve three steps. First, biases and their causes should be discussed. Second, the role of performance appraisals in employee decisions should be explained to stress the need for impartiality and objectivity. Third, raters should be allowed to apply subjective performance measures as part of their training. For example, classroom exercises may require evaluation of the trainer or videotapes of various workers. Mistakes uncovered during simulated evaluations then can be corrected through additional training or counselling.

Once the use of subjective performance measures moves out of the classroom and into practice, raters should get feedback about their previous ratings. When ratings prove relatively accurate or inaccurate, feedback helps raters adjust their behaviour accordingly.

CHARACTERISTICS OF AN EFFECTIVE PERFORMANCE APPRAISAL SYSTEM

BEFORE DIFFERENT performance appraisal methods are discussed, it should be emphasized that it is important for managers to understand that the organization is better off if an effective appraisal system is used. An appraisal method typically consists of a special scale or a particular process; an appraisal system consists of interlocking, interdependent, and reinforcing methods and processes that make the results synergistic—that is, the system is larger than the sum of its parts. Figure 9-4 shows 12 characteristics of an effective appraisal system, put into a question format. These characteristics are outlined below.

Validity. Validity (relevance) is of utmost importance. Invalid (job-irrelevant) criteria lead to biased assessments. Results are the most valid criteria since they tend to be objective. It would be difficult, for example, to question the relevance of a 10 per cent increase in profits for a performance assessment of a manager in charge of a department. Job-related behaviours are also relevant. However, the still widely used personality traits, such as leadership or intelligence, are of questionable value for performance assessment. They are characteristics the employee brings to the job, not a job outcome. To paraphrase Kane and Lawler: even though traits may relate to performance—an intelligent employee will probably do better than a less intelligent one—this does not justify their use as performance measures any more than the use of intelligence scores as substitutes for school grades.[7]

Valid, or job-related, performance criteria must be based on a thorough job analysis (discussed in Chapter Two) and documented in the job description for each position. Validity is also crucial for the validation of any selection test (discussed in Chapter Six). And finally, validity is crucial for any court challenge of performance criteria, e.g., in case of a wrongful dismissal suit where an employee's performance is an issue.

Reliability. Reliability (consistency), although highly desirable, is difficult to achieve in an organizational setting because of different raters, different instruments, and changing work environments. As a consequence, reliability can be looked at only as a distant aim.[8] However, it is important to know that valid criteria tend to be reliable, but reliable criteria are not necessarily valid.[9]*

Input into System Development. Employee participation in the development of performance criteria, appraisal instruments, and the system increases significantly the probability of acceptance of the system by both supervisors and employees. It gives employees the feeling of ownership. It is true that employees hired after a system has

FIGURE 9-4

Characteristics of an Effective Performance Appraisal System

1. Is it valid?
2. Is it reliable?
3. Did employees have input into its development?
4. Are its standards acceptable to employees?
5. Are its goals acceptable to employees?
6. Are its standards under the control of employees?
7. How frequent is the feedback?
8. Have raters been trained?
9. Have ratees been trained?
10. Do employees have input into the appraisal interviews?
11. Do the appraisals have consequences?
12. Are different sources (raters) utilized?

Source: Hermann F. Schwind, "Performance Appraisal: The State of the Art," in Shimon L. Dolan and Randall S. Schuler, eds., *Personnel and Human Resources Management in Canada*, West Publishing, 1987.

A good example is the historical practice of craniology and phrenology, the study of skulls and their relationship to human characteristics. Early craniologists/phrenologists believed that the circumference of the human skull was a measure of intelligence (which is without foundation). It is an example of an absolutely reliable measure (every time one measures the circumference one gets the same results), but without any validity.

been installed will not have had input into it, but the knowledge that it was developed with the input of those who are rated by it will make it more acceptable.[9]

Acceptable Performance Standards. How often do supervisors make the mistake of using their own performance standards to assess an employee's performance? The temptation is high, but this approach mostly backfires. Performance standards are derived from a job analysis (discussed in Chapter Two). If standards are set unilaterally by management, they become "management's standards" and receive little or no commitment from the employees. This does not mean that employees should set their own performance standards, but rather that the standards should be set with the employees to gain their commitment. It may be necessary for a manager to start out with a lower standard for a new employee until he or she has developed some experience and more self-confidence. Here the skill of a manager to be a coach becomes crucial, as does open communication, trust, and support by colleagues.[10]

Acceptable Goals. Similar to performance standards, performance goals are often set unilaterally by managers, sometimes too high for an employee. Goals derive from the strategic business plans of the organization, operationalized at the department level by the manager. It is the responsibility of the manager, as a coach and counsellor, to set goals that are seen as achievable by the employee; otherwise the employee will be discouraged, often resulting in a self-fulfilling prophecy: "That's too high for me, I can't do it." Studies have consistently found that when supervisors set specific goals, performance improves twice as much as when they set general goals.[11]

Control of Standards. Current performance standards used in appraisals often seem to be based on the assumption that the job in question is independent of other jobs. However, several studies have shown that most jobs are highly interdependent, which means that job incumbents must rely on the contributions or cooperation of their colleagues. A standard of performance that is not fully under the control of the employee is not valid.[12]

www.zigonperf.com/PMNews
/quarterly_appr.html

Frequency of Feedback. Most appraisals take place once a year. Ideally, performance feedback would be given by the supervisor immediately after effective or ineffective job behaviour was observed. However, this is unrealistic in an organizational setting. A compromise may be feedback sessions on a monthly, quarterly, or at least biannual basis. These sessions should be seen by employees as opportunities to receive advice and support from their supervisor, not to be appraised or judged.

Rater Training. Raters need to be trained in observation techniques and categorization skills (e.g., the use of diaries or critical incidents and how to group job behaviours or apply organizational performance standards). Raters also must be familiar with the many potential rating errors (e.g., halo effect, leniency) and the ways to minimize them. Rater training has been shown to be very effective in reducing such errors.[13]

Ratee Training. If management wants to ensure that a performance appraisal system is well understood by employees and accepted, it should consider training the ratees in addition to the raters. The ratee training could be part of the process of developing the performance appraisal system, thereby serving two purposes.

Input into Interview Process. Allowing employees to have a high level of participation in the appraisal interview increases employee satisfaction and morale.[14]

Appraisal Consequences. Appraisals without consequences lose their effectiveness very quickly. Employees as well as supervisors must see that appraisal results are taken seriously by management and are followed up on. All too often evaluation results end up in the personnel file unread, leading to cynical employees and frustrated supervisors.[15] Of course, there is a crucial link to a merit pay system. Especially high-performing employees expect to be rewarded for their effort.[16]

Digital Imagery © 2001 Photo Disc Inc. Photo by Skip Nall

A maître-d', a waitress, and a wine steward all do restaurant-related work, but their performance evaluations will be based on different elements and standards.

Different Sources (Raters). Relying on the judgment of one person increases the risk of biases (rating errors). Using different sources either confirms an assessment if all or a majority point in the same direction, or it raises a caution flag if assessments are at variance. Appraisal information can be gathered from the direct supervisor, secondary supervisors, self, peers, subordinates, and clients or customers. Raters from different levels of the organization will have different but valid views of a job and the performance of the incumbent.[17]

A Nurturing Organizational Environment

www.zigonperf.com/PMNews
/best_practice_pas.html

The social climate in an organization has a significant impact on the effectiveness of a performance appraisal system. A trusting relationship between managers and employees tends to foster two-way communication processes and lead to mutually agreeable performance goals. In organizations with low trust levels, it is questionable whether a performance appraisal should be done at all. One study found that raters with low trust in the appraisal system process rated their subordinates significantly higher (with greater leniency) than raters with high trust in the process.[18]

The development of a performance appraisal system is also seen as an effective tool for organizational change. As one researcher put it: "Designing a successful performance appraisal system for use in an organization is as much an exercise in organizational development as it is a study of performance measurement."[19]

Legal Aspects of Performance Appraisal

A performance appraisal form is a legal document. The implication is that raters must be careful to use only performance criteria that are relevant to the job. In a court challenge—for example, where an employee lost a job as a result of inadequate job performance—the human resource manager must prove that the performance criteria used were *valid* and were used *consistently*. Nonrelevant criteria can be avoided if performance standards are established through a thorough job analysis and recorded in a job description.[20]

Other legal considerations that human resource managers should take into account include training the supervisors, who must give the feedback to their employees, to use the appraisal form properly; giving employees an appraisal sheet in advance and ensuring that they have access to their job descriptions, which contain the relevant performance criteria and standards; making sure that performance shortcomings are identified and clear instructions given for corrective actions; and, finally, having an appeals process in place to allow employees to grieve perceived unfair evaluations.

It is also a legal requirement that a *reasonable time frame* be set for agreed-upon performance improvement. The length of time would depend on the job. While it may be reasonable to expect an office clerk to improve his or her performance within a few weeks or months, it may take a manager a year or more to show improvement.[21]

Well-documented performance shortcomings can avoid serious embarrassments in courts or with arbitrators.

Performance appraisal systems can use different types of appraisal techniques. For ease of discussion, these techniques are grouped into those that focus on past performance and those that focus on future performance.

PAST-ORIENTED APPRAISAL METHODS

THE IMPORTANCE of performance evaluations has led academics and practitioners to create many methods to appraise past performance. Most of these techniques are a direct attempt to minimize some particular problem found in other approaches. None is perfect; each has advantages and disadvantages.

Past-oriented approaches have the advantage of dealing with performance that has already occurred and, to some degree, can be measured. The obvious disadvantage is that past performance cannot be changed. But by evaluating past performance, employees can get feedback about their efforts. This feedback may then lead to renewed efforts at improved performance. The most widely used appraisal techniques that have a past orientation include:

- rating scale;
- checklist;
- forced choice method;
- critical incident method;
- behaviourally anchored rating scales;
- field review method;
- performance tests and observations; and
- comparative evaluation methods.

Noncomparative Evaluation Methods

Rating Scale

Rating scale
A scale that requires the rater to provide a subjective evaluation of an individual's performance.

Perhaps the oldest and most widely used form of performance appraisal is the *rating scale*, which requires the rater to provide a subjective evaluation of an individual's performance along a scale from low to high. An example appears in Figure 9-5. As the figure indicates, the evaluation is based solely on the opinions of the rater. In many cases, the criteria are not directly related to job performance. Although subordinates or peers may use it, the immediate supervisor usually completes the form.

The form is completed by checking the most appropriate response for each performance factor. Responses may be given numerical values to enable an average score to be computed and compared for each employee. The advantages of this method are

FIGURE 9-5

A Sample of a Rating Scale for Performance Evaluation

Western Farm Cooperative Association
Rating Scale

Instructions: For the following performance factors, please indicate on the rating scale your evaluation of the named employee.

Employee's Name _____   Department _____

Rater's Name _____   Date _____

	Excellent	Good	Acceptable	Poor
	4	3	2	1
1. Dependability	_____	_____	_____	_____
2. Initiative	_____	_____	_____	_____
3. Overall Output	_____	_____	_____	_____
4. Attendance	_____	_____	_____	_____
5. Attitude	_____	_____	_____	_____
6. Cooperation	_____	_____	_____	_____
• •	•	•	•	•
• •	•	•	•	•
• •	•	•	•	•
20. Quality of Work				
Results	_____	_____	_____	_____
Totals	_____	+_____	+_____	+_____	=_____

Total Score

that it is inexpensive to develop and administer, raters need little training or time to complete the form, and it can be applied to a large number of employees.

Disadvantages are numerous. A rater's biases are likely to be reflected in a subjective instrument of this type. Specific performance criteria may be omitted to make the form applicable to a variety of jobs. For example, "maintenance of equipment" may be left off because it applies to only a few workers. But for some employees, that item may be the most important part of their job. These omissions tend to limit specific feedback. Also, descriptive evaluations are subject to individual interpretations that vary widely. And when specific performance criteria are hard to identify, the form may rely on irrelevant personality variables that dilute the meaning of the evaluation. The result is a standardized form and procedure that is not always job-related.

Checklist

Weighted checklist
Requires the rater to select statements or words to describe an employee's performance or characteristics. Different responses are given different values or weights in order that a quantified total score.

The checklist rating method requires the rater to select statements or words that describe the employee's performance and characteristics. Again, the rater is usually the immediate supervisor. But unknown to the rater, the human resource department may assign weights to different items on the checklist, according to each item's importance. The result is called a **weighted checklist**. The weights allow the rating to be quantified so that the total scores can be determined. Figure 9-6 shows a portion of a checklist. The weights for each item are in parentheses here, but are usually omitted from the actual form. If the list contains enough items, it may provide an accurate picture of employee performance. Although this method is practical and standardized, the use of general statements reduces its job-relatedness.

The advantages of a checklist are economy, ease of administration, limited training of raters, and standardization. The disadvantages include susceptibility to rater biases (especially the halo effect), use of personality criteria instead of performance criteria, misinterpretation of checklist items, and use of improper weights by the human resource department. Moreover, it does not allow the rater to give relative ratings. On item 1 in the figure, for example, employees who gladly work overtime get the same score as those who do so unwillingly.

Forced-Choice Method

Forced choice method
The rater chooses the most descriptive statement in each of several pairs of statements about the employee being rated.

The *forced-choice method* requires the rater to choose the most descriptive statement in each pair of statements about the employee being rated. Often both statements in the pair are positive or negative. For example:

1. Learns quickly ... Works hard.
2. Work is reliable and accurate ... Performance is a good example to others.
3. Absent too often ... Usually tardy.

Sometimes the rater must select the best statement (or even pair of statements) from four choices. However the form is constructed, human resource specialists usually group the items on the form into predetermined categories, such as learning ability, performance, interpersonal relations, and the like. Then effectiveness can be computed for each category by adding up the number of times each category is selected by the rater. The results in each category can be reported to show which areas need further improvement. Again, the supervisor is usually the rater, although peers or subordinates may make the evaluation.

FIGURE 9-6

An Example of a Weighted Performance Checklist

Hathaway Department Stores Ltd.
Performance Checklist

Instructions: Check each of the following items that apply to the named employee's performance.

Employee's Name _____ Department_____

Rater's Name _____ Date _____

Weights   Check here

(6.5) 1. Employee works overtime when asked.   _____

(4.0) 2. Employee keeps work station or desk well organized.   _____

(3.9) 3. Employee cooperatively assists others who need help.   _____

(4.3) 4. Employee plans actions before beginning job.   _____

(0.2) 30. Employee listens to others' advice, but seldom follows it. _____

100.0   Total of All Weights

The forced-choice method has the advantages of reducing rater bias, being easy to administer, and fitting a wide variety of jobs. Although practical and easily standardized, the general statements may not be specifically job-related. Thus, it may have limited usefulness in helping employees to improve their performance. Even worse, an employee may feel slighted when one statement is checked in preference to another. For example, if the rater checks "learns quickly" in number 1 above, the worker may feel that his or her hard work is overlooked. This method is seldom liked by either the rater or ratee because it provides little useful feedback.

Critical Incident Method

Critical incident method
The rater records statements that describe extremely effective or ineffective behaviour related to performance.

The *critical incident method* requires the rater to record statements that describe extremely effective or ineffective employee behaviour related to performance. The statements are called critical incidents. These incidents are usually recorded by the supervisor during the evaluation period for each subordinate. Recorded incidents include a brief explanation of what happened. Several typical entries for a laboratory assistant appear in Figure 9-7. As shown in the figure, both positive and negative incidents are recorded. Incidents are classified (either as they occur, or later by the human resource department) into categories such as control of safety hazards, control of material scrap, and employee development.

The critical incident method is extremely useful for giving employees job-related feedback. It can also reduce the recency bias. Of course, the practical drawback is the difficulty of getting supervisors to record incidents as they occur. Many supervisors start out recording incidents faithfully, but lose interest. Then, just before the evaluation period ends, they add new entries. When this happens, the recency bias is

FIGURE 9-7

Critical Incidents Record for a Lab Assistant

Hartford Chemicals Ltd.
Critical Incidents Worksheet

Instructions: In each category below, record specific incidents of employee behaviour that were either extremely good or extremely poor.

Employee's Name   Kay Watts (lab assistant)   Department   Chemistry Lab

Rater's Name   Nat Cordoba   Rating Period   of 10/1 to 12/31

Control of Safety Hazards

Date	Positive Employee Behaviour	Date	Negative Employee Behaviour
10/12	Reported broken rung on utility ladder and flagged ladder as unsafe	11/3	Left hose across storeroom aisle
10/15	Put out small trash fire promptly	11/27	Smoked in chemical storeroom

Control of Material Scrap

Date	Positive Employee Behaviour	Date	Negative Employee Behaviour
10/3	Sorted through damaged shipment of glassware to salvage usable beakers	11/7	Used glass containers for strong bases ruining glass
		11/19	Repeatedly used glass for storage of lye and other bases
			Poured acid into plastic container ruining counter top

exaggerated and employees may feel that supervisors are building a case to support their subjective opinions. Even when the form is filled out over the entire rating period, employees may feel that the supervisor is unwilling to forget negative incidents that occurred months before.

Behaviourally Anchored Rating Scales

Behaviourally anchored rating scales or BARS
Evaluation tools that rate employees along a rating scale by means of specific behaviour examples on the scale.

Behaviourally anchored rating scales (BARS) attempt to reduce the subjectivity and biases of subjective performance measures. From descriptions of effective and ineffective performance provided by incumbents, peers, and supervisors, job analysts or knowledgeable employees group these examples into performance-related categories such as employee knowledge, customer relations, and the like. Then specific examples of these behaviours are placed along a scale (usually from 1 to 7). Actual behaviours for a bank branch manager are illustrated on the rating scale shown in Figure 9-8. Since the positions on the scale are described in job-related behaviour, an objective evaluation along the scale is more likely. The form also cites specific behaviours that can be used to provide performance feedback to employees. The BARS are job-related, practical, and standardized for similar jobs. But the rater's personal biases may still cause ratings to be high or low, although the specific behaviours that

FIGURE 9-8

Behaviourally Anchored Rating Scale for Bank Branch Manager

Job Part:
Human Resource Management

Bank of Ontario

Outstanding Performance	7	Can be expected to praise publicly for tasks completed well, and constructively criticizes in private those individuals who have produced less than adequate results.
Good Performance	6	Can be expected to show great confidence in subordinates, and openly displays this with the result that they develop to meet expectations.
Fairly Good Performance	5	Can be expected to ensure that human resource management records are kept right up to date, that reports are written on time, and that salary reviews are not overlooked.
Acceptable Performance	4	Can be expected to admit a personal mistake, thus showing that he or she is human too.
Fairly Poor Performance	3	Can be expected to make "surprise" performance appraisals of subordinates.
Poor Performance	2	Can be expected not to support decisions made by a subordinate (makes exceptions to rules).
Extremely Poor Performance	1	Can be expected not to accept responsibility for errors and to pass blame to subordinates.

"anchor" the scale provide some criteria to guide the sincere rater.[22] If the rater collects specific incidents during the rating period, the evaluation is likely to be more accurate and more legally defensible, besides being a more effective counselling tool. One serious limitation of BARS is that they only look at a limited number of performance categories, such as customer relations or human resource management. Also, each of these categories has only a limited number of specific behaviours. Like the critical incident method, most supervisors are reluctant to maintain records of critical incidents during the rating period, which reduces the effectiveness of this approach when it comes time to counsel the employee.

Field Review Method

Field review method
Representatives of the human resource department go into the field and gather information about employee performance.

Whenever subjective performance measures are used, differences in rater perceptions cause bias. To provide greater standardization in reviews, some employers use the *field review method*. In this method, a skilled representative of the human resource department goes "into the field" and assists supervisors with their ratings. The human resource specialist solicits from the immediate supervisor specific information about the employee's performance. Then the expert prepares an evaluation based on this information. The evaluation is sent to the supervisor for review, changes, approval, and discussion with the employee who was rated. The human resource specialist records the rating on whatever specific type of rating form the employer uses. Since a skilled professional is completing the form, reliability and comparability are more likely. But the need for the services of skilled professionals may make this approach impractical for many firms.

Performance Tests and Observations

With a limited number of jobs, performance appraisal may be based on a test of knowledge or skills. The test may be of the paper-and-pencil variety or an actual demonstration of skills. The test must be reliable and valid to be useful. For the method to be job-related, observations should be made under circumstances likely to be encountered. Practicality may suffer when the cost of test development is high:

> Pilots of all major airlines are subject to evaluation by airline raters and Transport Canada. Evaluations of flying ability are usually made both in a flight simulator and while being observed during an actual flight. The evaluation is based on how well the pilot follows prescribed flight procedures and safety rules. Although this approach is expensive, public safety makes it practical, as well as job-related and standardized.

Comparative Evaluation Methods

Comparative evaluation methods
A collection of different methods that compare one person's performance with that of co-workers.

Comparative evaluation methods are a collection of different methods that compare one person's performance with that of co-workers. Usually, comparative evaluations are conducted by the supervisor. They are useful for deciding merit pay increases, promotions, and organizational rewards because they can result in a ranking of employees from best to worst. The most common forms of comparative evaluations are the ranking method, forced distributions, the point allocation method, and paired comparisons. Although these methods are practical and easily standardized, they too are subject to bias and offer little job-related feedback.

Many large companies use an elaborate group evaluation method. This method reduces biases because multiple raters are used, and some feedback results when managers and professionals learn how they compared with others on each critical factor. However, these comparative results are often not shared with the employee because the supervisor and the human resource department want to create an atmosphere of cooperation among employees. To share comparative rankings may lead to internal competition instead of cooperation. Nevertheless, two arguments in favour of comparative approaches merit mention before discussing specific methods:

> Arguments for a comparative approach are simple and powerful. The simple part of it is that organizations do it anyway, all the time. Whenever human resource decisions are made, the performance of the individuals being considered is ranked and compared. People are not promoted because they achieve their objectives, but rather because they achieve their objectives better than others.

> The second reason (the powerful one) for using comparative as opposed to noncomparative methods is that they are far more reliable. This is because reliability is controlled by the rating process itself, not by rules, policies, and other external constraints.[23]

Ranking Method

Ranking method
A method of evaluating employees that ranks them from best to worst on some trait.

The *ranking method* has the rater place each employee in order from best to worst. All the human resource department knows is that certain employees are better than others. It does not know by how much. The employee ranked second may be almost as good as the one who was first or considerably worse. This method is subject to the halo and recency effects, although rankings by two or more raters can be averaged to help reduce biases. Its advantages include ease of administration and explanation.

Forced Distributions

Ranked (: Best do (over) worst) ranked on a curve

Forced distributions require raters to sort employees into different classifications along the normal curve. Usually a certain proportion must be put in each category. Figure 9-9 shows how a rater might classify 10 subordinates. The criterion shown in the figure is for overall performance (but this method can be used for other performance criteria, such as reliability and control costs). As with the ranking method, relative differences among employees are unknown, but this method does overcome the biases of central tendency, leniency, and strictness. Some workers and supervisors strongly dislike this method because employees are often rated lower than they or their supervisor/rater think to be correct. However, the human resource department's forced distribution requires some employees to be rated low.

Paired Comparisons

Paired comparison method
Comparing each employee with all other employees who are being rated in the same group.

The *paired comparison method* requires raters to compare each employee with all other employees who are being rated in the same group. An example of paired

FIGURE 9-9

The Forced Distribution Method of Appraisal of Ten Subordinates

Captone Fisheries Ltd.
Forced Distribution Rating

Classification: Overall Performance

Best 10% of Subordinates	Next 20% of Subordinates	Middle 40% of Subordinates	Next 20% of Subordinates	Lowest 10% of Subordinates
A. Wilson	G. Carrs M. Lopez	B. Johnson E. Wilson C. Grant T. Valley	K. McDougal L. Ray	W. Smythe

comparisons appears in Figure 9-10. The basis for comparison is usually overall performance. The number of times each employee is rated superior to another can be summed up to develop an index. The employee who is preferred the most is the best employee on the criterion selected. In the figure, A. Wilson is selected nine times and is the top-ranked employee. Although subject to halo and recency effects, this method counteracts the leniency, strictness, and central tendency errors because some employees must be rated better than others.

FUTURE-ORIENTED APPRAISAL METHODS

THE USE OF past-oriented approaches is like driving a car by looking through the rearview mirror: you only know where you have been, not where you are going. Future-oriented appraisals focus on future performance by evaluating employee potential or setting future performance goals. Included here are three techniques used:

- self-appraisals;

- management-by-objectives approach; and

- assessment centre technique.

Self-Appraisals

Getting employees to conduct a self-appraisal can be a useful evaluation technique if the goal of evaluation is to further self-development. When employees evaluate themselves, defensive behaviour is less likely to occur. Thus, self-improvement is more likely. When self-appraisals are used to determine areas of needed improvement, they can help users set personal goals for future development.

Obviously, self-appraisals can be used with any evaluation approach, past- or future-oriented. But the important dimension of self-appraisals is the employee's involvement and commitment to the improvement process:

FIGURE 9-10

The Paired Comparison Method of Evaluating Employees

Captone Fisheries Ltd.
Paired Comparison Rating

Instructions: Compare each employee on overall performance with every other employee. For each comparison, write the number of the employee who is best in the intersecting box. Each time an employee is found superior to another employee, the better employee receives one point. Employees then can be ranked according to the number of times each is selected as best by the rater.

Employee	2	3	4	5	6	7	8	9	10
1 G. Carrs	1	1	4	1	1	1	1	9	1
2 C. Grant		3	4	2	2	2	2	9	2
3 B. Johnson			4	3	3	3	3	9	3
4 M. Lopez				4	4	4	4	9	4
5 K. McDougal					6	5	8	9	10
6 L. Ray						6	8	9	10
7 W. Smythe							8	9	10
8 T. Valley								9	10
9 A. Wilson									9
10 E. Wilson									

At the Bechtel Company, the largest privately held construction and engineering firm in the world, the performance planning system involves the employee in a process of self-appraisal. The process starts with the supervisor telling the employee what is expected. Then the employee gets a worksheet and writes down his or her understanding of the job. Then, 10 to 15 days before a performance evaluation is done, the employee completes the worksheet by filling in the portions that relate to job accomplishments, performance difficulties, and suggestions for improvement. Not only does it get the employee involved in forming a self-appraisal of improvement areas, but the completed sheet also indicates to the supervisor what he or she needs to do to "eliminate roadblocks to meeting or exceeding job standards."[24]

Management-by-Objectives Approach

Management-by-objectives approach (MBO)
Requires an employee and superior to jointly establish performance goals for the future. Employees are subsequently evaluated on how well they have obtained these objectives.

www.mapnp.org/library/ plan_dec/mbo/mbo.htm

www.webcom.com/duane/ mbo.html

The heart of the *management-by-objectives approach (MBO)* is that each employee and superior jointly establish performance goals for the future.[25] Ideally, these goals are mutually agreed upon and objectively measurable. If both conditions are met, employees are apt to be more motivated to achieve the goal since they have participated in setting it. Moreover, they can periodically adjust their behaviour to ensure attainment of an objective if they can measure their progress toward the objective. But to adjust their efforts, performance feedback must be available on a regular basis.

When future objectives are set, employees gain the motivational benefit of a specific target to organize and direct their efforts. Objectives also help the employee and supervisor discuss specific developmental needs of the employee. When done correctly, performance discussions focus on the job's objectives and not personality variables. Biases are reduced to the extent that goal attainment can be measured objectively.

In practice, MBO programs have encountered difficulties. Objectives are sometimes too ambitious or too narrow. The result is frustrated employees or overlooked areas of performance. For example, employees may set objectives that are measured by quantity rather than quality because quality, while it may be equally important, is often more difficult to measure. When employees and managers do focus on subjectively measured objectives, special care is needed to ensure that biases do not distort the manager's evaluation. Figure 9-11 shows the annual assessment of the performance of a salesperson, using an MBO approach.

Assessment Centre Technique

Assessment centres
A standardized form of employee appraisal that relies on several types of evaluation and several raters.

Assessment centres are rarely used for a current performance assessment, but are more commonly employed to evaluate future potential. Assessment centres are a standardized form of employee appraisal that relies on multiple types of evaluation and

FIGURE 9-11

MBO Evaluation Report for a Salesperson

Objectives Set	Period Objective	Accomplishments	Variance
1. Number of sales calls	85	98	+15%
2. Number of new customers	10	8	−20%
3. Sales of product xx	2,500	3,100	+24%
4. Sales of product yy	1,500	1,350	−10%
5. Customer complaints	10	22	+120%
6. Number of training courses taken	5	3	−40%
7. Number of monthly reports on time	12	11	−8%

multiple raters. The assessment centre technique is usually applied to groups of middle-level managers who appear to have potential to perform at more responsible levels in the organization. Often the members of the group first meet at the assessment centre. During a brief stay at the facility, candidates are individually evaluated. The process subjects selected employees to in-depth interviews, psychological tests, personal background histories, peer ratings by other attendees, leaderless group discussions, ratings by psychologists and managers, and simulated work exercises to evaluate future potential. The simulated work experiences usually include in-basket exercises, decision-making exercises, computer-based business games, and other job-like opportunities that test the employee in realistic ways.

These activities are usually conducted for a few days at a location physically removed from the job site. During this time, the psychologists and managers who perform the rating attempt to estimate the strengths, weaknesses, and potential of each attendee.[26] They then pool their estimates to arrive at some conclusion about each group member being assessed.

Some critics question whether the procedures used are objective and job-related, especially since rater biases are possible in forming the subjective opinions of attendees.[27] Nevertheless, assessment centres have gained widespread use, and human resource researchers are finding ways to validate the process.

Interestingly, research indicates that the results of assessment centres are a good prediction of actual on-the-job performance in 75 per cent of all cases.[28] Unfortunately, this accurate method is expensive since it usually requires a separate facility and the time of multiple raters.

Recent Developments

360-degree performance appraisal
Combination of self, peer, supervisor, and subordinate performance evaluation.

www.360-degree feedback.com/

www.mapnp.org/library/emp_perf/perf_rvw/360_rvws.htm

www.zigonperf.com/PMNews/think_twice_360.html

www.zigonperf.com/PMNews/360fb_amok.htm

www.shrm.org/hrmagazine/articles/0799soft.htm

The *360-degree performance appraisal*, or "all-around appraisal," is the most recent popular method of assessment, although the idea is not new (see Figure 9-4, characteristic 12). There can be little doubt that the combination of self, peer, supervisor, and subordinate evaluation will provide feedback on different aspects of the job, since every contributor probably has a different focus.[29] The trend toward the "three-sixty model" is also in line with the trend toward a flatter organization, which tends to result in a wider span of control. With fewer managers having to supervise more employees, it becomes more difficult to assess everybody's performance accurately. And there is the trend of today's managers towards teamwork and participative management, which makes the historic approach of one supervisor providing performance feedback appear obsolete.[30]

Not everybody is sharing the enthusiasm about the 360-degree approach. It certainly requires a suitable corporate culture.[31]

Performance appraisal software is a new tool many managers probably have been waiting for: developed by experts, adaptable to an organization's needs, easy to use, and with data easily analyzed, stored, and retrieved.[32] Ideally, such a program would be part of an enterprise-wide software system, and even that is already available.[33] It means that all human resources aspects, such as application data, interview guides for selection decisions, computer-based training, performance appraisal, payroll, job evaluation, as well as other organizational functions such as finance, purchasing, distribution, manufacturing, and more, are part of one software package. The development and application of such an integrated software system is often the result of "business process re-engineering," a radical rethinking of organizational functions to achieve higher efficiency, quality improvement, and better service.[34]

The advantage of such an integrated system is that everyone in the organization receives the same information. As Turnbull puts it:

The concept of entering data once, at source, saves time (there is no or very little duplication of data entry) and ensures that data can be treated as a corporate resource, used by any and all who have a need (and have authorized access). Through this horizontal integration of information, issues about whose/which data is correct are avoided, time is saved and the organization as a whole wins.[35]

The disadvantages are that the implementation of such a system is time-consuming, complex, and costly. However, it appears that the savings and higher efficiency offset the costs.[36]

Another development is the difficulties associated with the change of paying employees for—and accordingly assessing on—their *competencies* instead of job performance. Historically it was the performance standards set in job descriptions that guided supervisors in their assessment. Now the tendency is to focus more on skill levels than job performance (see discussion on compensation in Chapter Ten). As a consequence, employee assessment tends to involve tests rather then supervisor evaluations.

Balanced Scorecard
Integrated organizational performance measure, looking at organizational learning and innovation, financial management, internal operations, and customer management.

www.zigonperf.com/PMNews/
pas_hurts.html

www.zigonperf.com/PMNews/
making_bsc_payoff.html

www.zigonperf.com/PMNews/
Results_Government.htm

www.zigonperf.com/PMNews/
bsc_case_study.htm

The ***Balanced Scorecard*** concept has become a popular performance management approach, combining the performance measures of the total organization instead of relying on independent measures of its parts. The brainchild of Harvard Professor Robert Kaplan and David Norton of Renaissance Solutions (a consulting company), it provides an enterprise view of an organization's overall performance by integrating financial measures with other key performance indicators around customer satisfaction, internal organizational processes, and organizational growth, learning, and innovation.[37] A suitable illustration would be the cockpit of an airplane, with all its instruments and gauges. It would be foolish to rely only on one indicator. The pilot—the CEO—must take into account all measures to make sure that the plane—the organization—reaches its destination safely and efficiently.

Human resources play, of course, a critical part in an organization's performance. HR has direct links to innovation and learning, but will also influence customer satisfaction, quality improvement programs, and other internal processes. One survey found that "people management" made by far the greatest contribution to profitability and productivity compared with "other critical success factors." Factors highly associated with success were employee skills and job design, which promoted autonomy, flexibility, and problem solving.[38] Human resources will always play a major role in the Balanced Scorecard approach.

Finally, the problem of assessing the performance of contingency employees must be addressed (for a more detailed discussion on the use of contingency workers see Chapter Twelve). Since such employees are hired for the duration of a specific project, it makes little sense to sit down with them to develop long-range performance objectives. They also tend to have, by definition, little knowledge of the work culture of the organization, the supervisor's expectations, and their specific job responsibilities and performance standards. It is perhaps easiest to limit their performance assessment to highly specific tasks, which have been communicated to them, and to tie rewards to the satisfactory completion of these tasks.

IMPLICATIONS OF THE APPRAISAL PROCESS

THE APPRAISAL SYSTEM design and its procedures are usually handled by the human resource department. The specific approach is influenced by previous procedures and the purpose of the new appraisal. If the goal is to evaluate past performance to allocate rewards, comparative approaches may be preferred. Similarly, other past-oriented methods may be best if the appraisal system exists primarily to give employees counselling about their behaviour. Future-oriented appraisals may focus on specific goals, as is the case with MBO techniques. Self-appraisals or assessment centres may seek to uncover a specific weakness or help with internal placement. Regardless of the technique selected by the department, however, the approach must be converted into an ongoing practice among the line managers. Except in the field review method, raters are often unfamiliar with the procedures or the forms. And they may not be very interested in self-study to learn more, because the evaluation process may be seen as a project imposed by the human resource department and not something of immediate concern to those who supervise others.

Evaluation systems that involve others in their design may gain greater acceptance. Human rights legislation supports having employees involved in the design of the appraisal system. Involvement may increase interest and understanding of whatever performance appraisal system the human resource department eventually administers. However, to operate the performance appraisal system may require training for those who serve as raters.

Training Raters

Whether a simple comparative method or a sophisticated assessment centre is used, raters need knowledge of the system and its purpose. Just knowing whether the appraisal is to be used for compensation or placement recommendations may change the rater's evaluation of those being rated.

A major problem is rater understanding and consistency of evaluations. Some human resource departments provide raters with a rater's handbook that describes the employer's approach. Guidelines for conducting the evaluation or for providing ratees with feedback are often included in the handbook. Key terms—such as "shows initiative" or "provides leadership"—may also be defined in the handbook.

Companies such as the Royal Bank, Air Canada, and others solve this knowledge gap through training. Training workshops are usually intended to explain to raters the purpose of the procedure, the mechanics of it, likely pitfalls or biases they may encounter, and answers to their questions. The training may even include trial runs of evaluating other classmates just to gain some supervised experience. The Royal Bank and Air Canada use videotapes and role-playing evaluation sessions to give raters both experience and insight into the evaluation process. During the training, the timing and scheduling of evaluations are discussed. Typically, most companies perform formal evaluations annually, around the time of the individual's employment anniversary. For new employees or those having performance problems, evaluations may be performed more frequently as part of the human resource department's formal program or as the supervisor sees fit. Consider how one vice-president and manager of human resources viewed the implementation of his firm's program:

> With the new appraisal process and related forms in place, the next major step was educating managers and supervisors in the use of the program. Mandatory one-day training workshops were given, providing each manager an opportunity to review, discuss and understand the objectives of the program. The appraisal forms were reviewed in detail with an explanation of how to use the various sections in each form. A videotaped appraisal discussion was presented to demonstrate how performance appraisal worked. And finally, during the workshops, managers were given role-play situations using the new appraisal forms.

> Then on the bi-weekly payroll sheets that included everyone in the department or branch, the manager received a notification of who was due to be evaluated during the next month. If the review date was passed, a reminder would appear on the payroll sheets showing that the review date for the indicated employee was past due. As a result, managers know how to complete the forms and few delinquencies occur. The

human resource department also has valuable data that allow it to anticipate and respond to training needs and employee concerns.[39]

Although in the past rater training has focused on rating errors such as the halo effect, leniency bias, and central tendency, the emphasis has shifted now to the cognitive aspect of the rating process, that is, the ability of raters to make valid judgments based on relatively complex information. One model divides the performance appraisal process into four steps: attention, categorization, recall, and information integration.

Attention

The rater consciously or subconsciously records certain stimuli because they are relevant to a task performed (e.g., the rater is a supervisor and as part of her duty observes an employee performing his job). The more deviant the observed behaviour is from the expected norm, the more strongly the attention-arousing stimuli work. If, for example, the employee does something very wrong, the supervisor is much more likely to pay attention to the observed behaviour than if it were mildly off the mark.

Categorization

This is the process of classifying and storing data. Several studies have shown that humans have a limited capability of perceiving and processing information simultaneously, the upper limit being approximately seven items. Categorization helps us to make quick judgments with limited information about something. Stereotyping is one type of categorization that, as we all know, may result in biased conclusions.

Recall

When we have to make a judgment we try to remember all the relevant information we stored in our memory about the event or person in question. Depending on the strength of an impression we recorded, we will be able to recall some items more easily than others (see recency effect). When supervisors are asked to conduct a performance appraisal once a year, the probability is low that they recall all the important information about an employee's work. Only if a conscious effort to record such information is made, by writing down critical incidents, for example, will raters be able to perform an accurate evaluation.

Information Integration

Once a judgment is called for, such as the annual performance appraisal, the rater tries to recall as much information as possible and to generate an integrated picture of the employee. However, due to the attention-arousing process (only strong stimuli are recorded), the categorization process (limited information is stored), and the recall process (a limited number of events is remembered), the final picture that emerges will be understandably biased.

Several measures can be taken to improve the validity of supervisory ratings:

- use of behaviour-based scales, e.g., the use of critical incidents to categorize effective and ineffective job behaviour;
- training in the use of these scales;
- familiarization of raters with performance definitions, e.g., what constitutes outstanding performance (with practical examples);
- use of several raters (more eyes see more, and more eyes see different things, resulting in a more balanced judgment);

- use of quantitative criteria whenever possible (measurable results);

- use of job samples for important evaluation decisions, e.g., promotion and transfers;

- training of raters to make behaviour sampling a routine part of a supervisor's job to avoid memory-related biases;

- avoidance of trait ratings; and

- creation of positive consequences for both the rater and ratee.

One can easily see that the new focus of rater training makes the job of an instructor in performance appraisal much more difficult. On the other hand, it makes less likely such comments as this, offered by a human resource manager: "Of all the performance appraisal systems I have worked with in 15 years as a supervisor, not one really worked!"[40] Such experiences are as much the result of using invalid criteria as they are the outcome of inadequate rater training.[41]

Once raters are trained, the appraisal process can begin. But the results of the appraisal process do little to improve employee performance unless employees receive feedback on their appraisals. This feedback process is called the evaluation interview.

Evaluation Interviews

Evaluation interviews
Performance review sessions that give employees feedback about their past performance or future potential.

Evaluation interviews are performance review sessions that give employees feedback about their past performance or future potential. The evaluator may provide this feedback through several approaches: tell and sell, tell and listen, and problem-solving. The *tell-and-sell* approach reviews the employee's performance and tries to convince the employee to perform better. It is best used on new employees. The *tell-and-listen* approach allows the employee to explain reasons, excuses, and defensive feelings about performance. It attempts to overcome these reactions by counselling the employee on how to perform better. The *problem-solving* approach identifies problems that are interfering with employee performance. Then through training, coaching, or counselling, efforts are made to remove these deficiencies, often by setting goals for future performance.

Regardless of which approach is used to give employees feedback, the guidelines listed in Figure 9-12 can help make the performance review session more effective. The intent of these suggestions is to make the interview a positive, performance-improving dialogue. By stressing desirable aspects of employee performance, the evaluator can give the employee renewed confidence in his or her ability to perform satisfactorily. This positive approach also enables the employee to keep desirable and undesirable performance in perspective, because it prevents the individual from feeling that performance review sessions are entirely negative. When negative comments are made, they focus on work performance and not the individual's personality. Specific, rather than general and vague, examples of the employee's shortcomings are used, so that the individual knows exactly what behaviours need to be changed. The review session concludes by focusing on actions that the employee can take to improve areas of poor performance. In that concluding discussion, the evaluator usually offers to provide whatever assistance the employee needs to overcome the deficiencies discussed.

Human Resource Management Feedback

The performance appraisal process also provides insight into the effectiveness of the human resource management function. If the appraisal process indicates that poor performance is widespread, many employees are excluded from internal placement

FIGURE 9-12

Guidelines for Effective Performance Evaluation Interviews

1. *Emphasize* positive aspects of employee performance.

2. *Tell* each employee that the evaluation session is to improve performance, not to discipline.

3. *Conduct* the performance review session in private with minimum interruptions.

4. *Review* performance formally at least annually and more frequently for new employees or those who are performing poorly.

5. *Make* criticisms specific, not general and vague.

6. *Focus* criticisms on performance, not on personality characteristics.

7. *Stay* calm and do not argue with the person being evaluated.

8. *Identify* specific actions the employee can take to improve performance.

9. *Emphasize* the evaluator's willingness to assist the employee's efforts and to improve performance.

10. *End* the evaluation session by stressing the positive aspects of the employee's performance and reviewing plans to improve performance.

www.zigonperf.com/PMNews
/pas_research.html

www.zigonperf.com/PMNews
/PerfReviewWSJ.htm

www.zigonperf.com/PMNews
/Appr_And_Coaching.html

www.zigonperf.com/PMNews
/Brits_Irish_Appr_Sys.html

www.zigonperf.com/PMNews
/pas_case_study.html

decisions. They will not be promoted or transferred. In fact, they may be excluded from the organization through termination.

Unacceptably high numbers of poor performers may indicate errors elsewhere in the human resource management function. For example, human resource development may be failing to fulfill career plans because the people who are hired during the selection process are screened poorly. Or the human resource plan may be in error because the job analysis information is wrong or the employment equity plan seeks the wrong objectives. Likewise, the human resource department may be failing to respond to the challenges of the external environment or effective job design. Sometimes the human resource function is pursuing the wrong objectives. Or the appraisal system itself may be faulty because of management resistance, incorrect performance standards or measures, or a lack of constructive feedback.

Finally, a future-oriented performance appraisal allows the human resource department to provide feedback to employees as to the status of their career progression. If an employee's performance is inadequate, the cause must be investigated. If it is a lack of skill or experience, the necessary improvements have to be made part of the goals discussed with the employee. Ideally, a step-by-step plan will be the outcome of the interview process.

PERFORMANCE APPRAISAL AS A STRATEGIC TOOL

AN IMPORTANT PART of any strategic planning is the assessment of strengths and weaknesses of the human resources in the organization, often as part of a SWOT analysis (Strengths, Weaknesses, Opportunities, Threats). Thorough performance analyses offer management the necessary data to assess the current skill, experience, and performance level of every employee, and performance standards critical for future requirements. Such data may have a significant impact on human resource planning, training and development programs, career development, and compensation expense forecasts.

A performance appraisal system makes explicit what constitutes the effective and efficient behaviour on the part of an individual employee that is critical to implementing the strategic plan. Just as the engineering department is concerned with the design of equipment, the maintenance department is concerned with the running of equipment, and manufacturing is concerned with turning out a quality product at minimal cost, the human resource department should be concerned with the identification of what it is that the people in engineering, maintenance, and manufacturing must do (behaviour) to be proficient in their respective functions. Similarly, they should determine what top management must do to implement the strategic plan once it has been formulated.

The outcomes of these analyses are translated into a valid appraisal instrument. Validity refers to the fact that employees are being measured on areas that are truly important to the attainment of their departmental and/or organizational objectives. To the extent that valid appraisals are made, valid decisions can be made regarding who should be rewarded monetarily or with a promotion. To the extent that valid appraisals are not made, valid selection decisions and reward practices are impossible.

Valid performance appraisals are also critical to training departments because they identify people who lack the ability to perform the job effectively. Since a valid appraisal instrument defines what needs to be done, the appraisal process identifies not only who needs training, but also the type of training that is required.

SUMMARY

Performance appraisal is a critical activity of human resource management. Its goal is to provide an accurate picture of past and/or future employee performance. To do this, performance standards are established. Standards are based on job-related criteria that best determine successful job performance. Where possible, actual performance is then measured directly and objectively. From a wide variety of appraisal techniques, human resource specialists elect those methods that most effectively measure employee performance against the previously set standards. Techniques can be selected both to review past performance and to anticipate performance in the future.

The appraisal process is usually designed by the human resource department, often with little consultation from other parts of the organization. When it is time to implement a new appraisal approach, those who do the rating usually have little idea about the appraisal process or its objectives. To overcome this shortcoming, the department may design and deliver appraisal workshops to train managers.

A necessary requirement of the appraisal process is employee feedback through an evaluation interview. The interviewer tries to balance positive areas of performance and those areas where performance is deficient, so that the employee receives a realistic view of performance. Perhaps the most significant challenge raised by performance appraisals is the feedback they provide about human resource department performance. Human resource specialists need to be keenly aware that poor performance, especially when it is widespread, may reflect problems with previous human resource management activities that are malfunctioning.

TERMS FOR REVIEW

Visit the Web site at www.mcgrawhill.ca/college/schwind6 for a full glossary.

REVIEW AND DISCUSSION QUESTIONS

1. What are the uses of performance appraisals?

2. Suppose a company for which you work uses a rating scale. The items on the scale are generally personality characteristics. What criticisms would you have of this method?

3. If you were asked to recommend a replacement for the rating scale, what actions would you take before selecting another appraisal technique?

4. Why are direct and objective measures of performance usually considered superior to indirect and subjective measures?

5. If your organization were to use subjective measures to evaluate employee performance, what instructions would you give evaluators about the biases they might encounter?

6. Describe how you would conduct a typical performance evaluation interview.

7. How do the results of performance appraisals affect other human resource management activities?

8. Describe the characteristics of a 360-degree performance appraisal.

9. In what ways is the Balanced Scorecard approach a useful performance appraisal instrument?

10. What is the relationship between a performance appraisal system and a selection system?

11. Explain the legal aspects of a performance appraisal system. Under what circumstances could it become a crucial document?

CRITICAL THINKING QUESTIONS

1. If the dean of your faculty asked you to serve on a committee to develop a performance appraisal system for evaluating the faculty, what performance criteria would you identify? Of these criteria, which ones do you think are most likely to determine the faculty members' success at your school? What standards would you recommend to the dean, regardless of the specific evaluation instrument selected?

2. Your organization has dismissed an employee for not performing up to par. She sues the company for unjust dismissal, claiming that the company's performance appraisal instrument is not a valid assessment tool, since no woman had served on the committee responsible for developing it. Are you able to persuade a judge that, despite the fact that no woman served on the committee, your appraisal instrument is a valid one?

3. Can one performance appraisal instrument be used for all levels in an organization, i.e., executives, middle managers, white- and blue-collar employees? Why or why not?

WEB RESEARCH

Help Tips for Performance Appraisal

http://iso9k1.home.att.net/pa/performance_appraisal.html

Dexter Hansen describes two approaches to performance appraisal. How do they differ from the methods described in this book? He mentions the use of appraisal software, but he cautions against its use. Is this caution justified? Why?

Matthew Effect

www.performance-appraisal.com/bias.htm

What is the Matthew Effect in performance appraisals? Where does the name come from? Can it be avoided? How?

10 Stupid Things Managers Do to Screw-up Performance Appraisals

www.work911.com/performance/particles/stupman.htm

Are the 10 "stupid" things some managers do based on research or do they represent the personal opinion of the author? How valid are they? If they are valid, are there remedies?

7 Stupid Things HR Departments Do to Screw-up Performance Appraisals

www.work911.com/performance/particles/stuphr.htm

In what way are these seven "stupid" things different from the 10 "stupid" things managers do? (See above.) Who would initiate remedies?

Why should you think twice before introducing 360-degree feedback?

www.zigonperf.com/PMNews/think_twice_360.html

Discuss the potential problems with 360-degree feedback.

Other interesting and relevant homepages on performance appraisals:

Has 360 run amok?
www.zigonperf.com/PMNews/360fb_amok.htm

Five Paradoxes regarding 360 Feedback
www.zigonperf.com/PMNews/paradox_360.html

Developing 360 Leadership-Feedback Instruments
www.centerpointsystems.com/BSTframeset.htm

Best Practices—A Checklist
www.centerpointsystems.com/BSTframeset.htm

Need for Acceptance
www.zigonperf.com/PMNews/acceptable_pas.html

Best Practices, examples
www.zigonperf.com/PMNews/best_practice_pas.html

New approaches
www.zigonperf.com/PMNews/PerfReviewWSJ.htm

Predictors of Discomfort with Performance Appraisal
www.zigonperf.com/PMNews/discomfort_pas.html

Telecommuting and Performance Appraisal
www.zigonperf.com/PMNews/telecommute_pas.html

Performance Appraisal in the Public Sector
www.zigonperf.com/PMNews/public.html

Why Performance Appraisal doesn't work
www.work911.com/performance/permgt.htm

Stop Appraising and Start Coaching
www.zigonperf.com/PMNews/Appr_And_Coaching.html

Can we talk? Even supervisors are nervous
www.zigonperf.com/PMNews/Australian_PAS.html

Performance Appraisal and Pay
www.zigonperf.com/PMNews/Getting_Pay_Thing_Right.html
www.zigonperf.com/PMNews/Impact_Incentive_PFP.html

Balanced Scorecard Approach
www.zigonperf.com/PMNews/making_bsc_payoff.html

Quarterly Reviews
www.zigonperf.com/PMNews/quarterly_appr.html

Appraisal seldom pays
www.zigonperf.com/PMNews/Appraisal_seldom_pays.html

Train managers in appraising
www.zigonperf.com/PMNews/Train_mgrs_apprais.html

Ford: Using Performance Appraisal to weed out poor performers
www.zigonperf.com/PMNews/FordEmplPerf.htm

Employees want Performance Appraisal
www.zigonperf.com/PMNews/Empl_want_Appraisal.htm

INCIDENT 9-1

Multiple Appraisal Failures at Roget's Waterworks

For two years, the employees at Roget's Waterworks were evaluated with the same performance appraisal method as other employees of the Roget Municipal Services Corporation (a company-operated city utility). The human resource manager decided that the duties at the waterworks were sufficiently different that a specially designed appraisal should be developed. A weighted checklist was decided on and used for about one year. The human resource manager left, and the replacement disliked weighted checklists. Specialists then implemented behaviourally anchored rating scales. But no sooner was the method installed than top management decided to shift all evaluations at the Roget corporation to the critical incident method.

The critical incident method worked well in all phases of the corporation's operations except the waterworks. Supervisors in the waterworks would not keep a record of critical incidents until about a week before the incidents were due to be submitted to the human resource department. Training sessions were held for these supervisors, but little change in their behaviour resulted. To evaluate the supervisors, the company conducted a survey of employees at the waterworks. Most employees thought the supervision was fair to good in all dimensions except that supervisors showed too much favouritism. Thought was being given to other methods.

1. How would you suggest overcoming the resistance of the supervisors to using the critical incident method?

2. Should another evaluation method be tried?

3. What method would you recommend and why?

INCIDENT 9-2

The Malfunctioning Regional Human Resource Department

For one month the corporate human resource department of Universal Insurance Ltd. had two specialists review the operations of their regional human resource department in Vancouver. The review of the regional office centred on the department's human resource information base. A brief summary of their findings listed the following observations:

A. Each employee's performance appraisal showed little change from the previous year. Poor performers rated poor year in and year out.

B. Nearly 70 per cent of the appraisals were not initialled by the employee even though company policy required employees to do so after they had discussed their review with the rater.

C. Of those employees who initialled the evaluations, several commented that the work standards were irrelevant and unfair.

D. A survey of past employees conducted by corporate office specialists revealed that 35 per cent of them believed performance feedback was too infrequent.

E. Another 30 per cent complained about the lack of advancement opportunities because most openings were filled from outside, and no one ever told these workers they were unpromotable.

The corporate and regional human resource directors were dismayed by the findings. Each thought the problems facing the regional office were different.

1. What do you think is the major problem with the performance appraisal process in the regional office?

2. What problems do you think exist with the regional office's (a) job analysis information, (b) human resource planning, (c) training and development, (d) career planning?

EXERCISE 9-1

Match the most effective method(s) to reduce specific rater biases.

Biases	Appraisal Method(s)	Your Best Choices
1) Halo	_____	_____
2) Central Tendency	_____	_____
3) Leniency/Strictness	_____	_____
4) Prejudice	_____	_____
5) Recency	_____	_____

a) Rating Scale
b) Checklist
c) Forced Choice
d) Critical Incident
e) BARS
f) Field Review
g) Performance Test
h) Ranking
i) Forced Distribution
j) Paired Comparison
k) Self-appraisal
l) MBO
m) Assessment Centre
n) 360 Degree Appraisal

CASE STUDY

Maple Leaf Shoes Ltd., Performance Appraisal Issues

Maple Leaf Shoes Ltd. is a medium-sized manufacturer of leather and vinyl shoes located in Wilmington, Ontario. It was started in 1969 and currently employs about 400 persons in its Wilmington plant and some 380 more in offices and warehouses throughout Canada and abroad.

It was time for the annual performance appraisal—the "ritual" as some managers called it. They received the appraisal forms sent by the personnel department one week prior to the deadline. The current system was developed by John McAllister, the previous personnel manager, who had recently left the company for a similar job in Toronto. McAllister believed that performance appraisal forms should be simple to understand and easy to complete, so he made one up himself (see Table 1).

Supervisors had to assess each employee by August 31. The assessment was supposed to be dis-cussed with the employee and then returned to the personnel department for filing in the employee's personnel records. If promotions came up, the cumulative ratings were to be considered at that time. The ratings were also supposed to be used as a check when raises were given.

Jane Reynolds, special assistant in the personnel department at Maple Leaf Shoes, looked at the pile of completed rating forms in front of her and shook her head. She disliked the way performance evaluation in this company was conducted and would have preferred to develop a new approach. However, Bob Clark, the company president, had so far resisted any change and she felt hesitant to tell him what she thought of it.

A month ago she had conducted an informal survey to find out how managers and employees felt about the current system. The results confirmed

TABLE 1

Performance Evaluation Form of Maple Leaf Shoes Ltd.

Performance Evaluation

Supervisors: Please complete this form for each of your employees. Evaluate each performance aspect separately. Return this form by September 1.

	5	4	3	2	1	Score
Quantity of work	Excellent	Good	Average	Fair	Poor	
Quality of work	Excellent	Good	Average	Fair	Poor	
Dependability at work	Excellent	Good	Average	Fair	Poor	
Initiative at work	Excellent	Good	Average	Fair	Poor	
Cooperativeness	Excellent	Good	Average	Fair	Poor	
Communication	Excellent	Good	Average	Fair	Poor	
Energy and Enthusiasm	Excellent	Good	Average	Fair	Poor	
Getting along with co-workers	Excellent	Good	Average	Fair	Poor	
					Total	_____

Supervisor's signature _____

Employee name _____

Employee number _____

her hunch. Over 60 per cent of the managers and more than 75 per cent of the employees felt either indifferent or negative about the assessment system. Close to 50 per cent of the supervisors filled out the forms in three minutes or less and returned the form to personnel without discussing the results with their staff. Another 40 per cent spent some time with the employees for feedback, but without much discussion. Only 10 per cent tried to do an effective performance feedback job by giving each employee detailed feedback and setting new objectives.

Reynolds knew from her experience at the company that the forms had rarely been retrieved for promotion or pay-raise analyses by her previous boss, McAllister. Because of this, most supervisors may have felt the evaluation program was a useless ritual.

The company had never offered any training for its supervisors on how to conduct performance reviews.

Then she thought of Tim Lance, the consultant. Once Bob Clark had hired Tim to "look into the present and future role of Maple Leaf Shoes' personnel

department and suggest appropriate action plans to improve its contribution to the organization and help the company meet its future challenges." In his final report Tim had made several recommendations, but Clark had postponed any change until a new personnel manager was hired.

Reynolds remembered that, among other items, the consultant had recommended a new approach to appraising employee performance. She felt that this gave her a good reason to push for a revision of the current system. Time was a big issue. She had to prepare for contract negotiations with two separate unions next month. Two more would come up a month later. She felt confident that Bob Clark would accept her recommendation to hire Tim Lance again to develop a new performance appraisal system.

Discussion Questions

1. You are Tim Lance. Write an assessment of Maple Leaf Shoes' performance evaluation system.

2. What changes would you recommend to the company? Why?

CASE STUDY

Canadian Pacific and International Bank

Part I

The results were in and Mary Keddy, senior vice president—human resources, was quite pleased. She was looking at the data of the latest employee attitude survey. The vast majority of the bank's employees felt that the CPIB was a good place to work (which, of course, was borne out by a very low turnover rate, two per cent lower than that of other banks). Satisfaction with supervision, as measured by the JDI,* was also high, a score of 46 out of 54. The last survey two years ago had a score of 38, so it had been a significant improvement. She was also intrigued by the results of the measurement on the quality of communication between supervisors and employees, which was seen as close to excellent—4.6 on a five-point scale. That was really good news. Perhaps it was time to think of implementing a pet idea of hers: a 360-degree performance appraisal system. She had toyed with it for several years, but she had felt that the time had not come. But the current results of the survey were very encouraging. She knew that it was a somewhat daring undertaking, given the high risk of failure but, on the other hand, if it worked, the positive outcomes would be significant.

She remembered the attempt to introduce an "all around" feedback system by her previous employer, a large steel company in Ontario—an attempt that had failed miserably. It had been the idea of a quite progressive CEO, but only a handful of middle managers had supported the idea, while most of the managers feared that the approach would lead to backstabbing and would be seen by many employees as an opportunity to "get back" at their supervisors.

Given that experience, she wanted to ensure that her own attempt at the bank would succeed, since she knew that a failure would hurt her career. She felt confident that she had the full support of the CEO, and her VP colleagues. She was less con-

fident about the willingness of the bank's middle managers to embrace such a new approach. Being evaluated by subordinates, colleagues, and customers—in addition to the direct supervisor, of course—required a strong degree of self-confidence and significant trust in colleagues and subordinates. The result of the employee survey seemed to indicate that the trust was there. How about the self-confidence aspect? She was not so sure about that part. She certainly had to take this into account in her plan.

She thought that it was interesting that she had greater confidence in the employees' acceptance of the new approach. When she had taken her plan for greater diversity to the employees three years ago she was pleasantly surprised about the positive reception the plan had received. Of course, she had carefully planned the introduction through staff meetings and training sessions. She had to come up with something similar now.

Discussion Question

1. If you were in Mary Keddy's position, what would you do? Outline a step-by-step plan for the introduction and implementation of a 360-degree performance evaluation system. Include in your plan measures to overcome the anticipated resistance by middle managers.

Prepare some arguments you could use if a manager or employee challenges you on the advantages of a 360-degree appraisal system.

Part II

There was another issue relating to performance appraisal Mary Keddy had to deal with. In a recent decision an arbitrator had ruled to reinstate an employee who had been dismissed for inadequate performance. His ruling was somewhat of an embarrassment for the bank because the arbitrator had argued that the two performance evaluations given the employees over the two years of her employment had rated her performance as below standard, but promising. There was nothing in the written assessment, which indicated serious shortcomings. The supervisor had argued that she had given the employee several verbal warnings after some

---

*The Job Description Index (JDI) is undoubtedly the best validated measure of job satisfaction. It includes five measures of satisfaction with nature of work, supervision, peers, advancement opportunities, and pay. It is copyrighted by, and available from, the Psychology Department of Bowling Green University, Bowling Green, Ohio.

repeated mistakes, but had not recorded it since she did not want to put a blemish on the employee's personnel record. However, after another, and more serious mistake, she decided enough was enough and let her go. The union grieved on behalf of the employee and the case went to arbitration, with the above result. Michael Bennett, the CEO, had asked Mary to make sure that such a case would not happen again.

Discussion Question

1. How can the bank develop a system, which will be legally foolproof?

SUGGESTED READINGS

Edwards, Mark R., and Ann J. Ewen (Contributor), 360 Degree Feedback: The *Powerful New Model for Employee Assessment & Performance Improvement*, AMACOM, 1996

Grote, Dick, *The Secrets of Performance Appraisal: Best Practices from the Masters*, Across the Board, publication of the Conference Board, Inc. May 1., 2000, pp.14-20.

Harbour, Jerry L., *The Basics of Performance Measurement*, Productivity Inc., 1997.

Ilgen, Daniel R., (Introduction), Elaine Diane Pulakos (Editor), *The Changing Nature of Performance: Implications for Staffing, Motivation, and Development (Frontiers of Industrial and Organizational Psychology)*, Jossey-Bass, 1999.

Kaplan, Robert S., and David P. Norton, *The Balanced Scorecard: Translating Strategy into Action*, Harvard Business School Press, 1996.

Markle, Garold L., *Catalytic Coaching: The End of the Performance Review*, Quorum Books, 2000.

McKirchy, Karen, *Powerful Performance Appraisals: How to Set Expectations and Work Together to Improve Performance*, Career Press, 1998.

Neal, James E., *Effective Phrases for Performance Appraisals: A Guide to Successful Evaluations*, Neal Publishing, 2000.

Peters, Paula, "Seven Tips for Delivering Performance Feedback," *Supervision*, May 1, 2000, pp.12-14.

Rossett, Allison, *First Things Fast: A Handbook for Performance Analysis*, Pfeiffer & Co, 1998.

Smither, James W., *Performance Appraisal: State of the Art in Practice*. San Francisco: Jossey-Bass, 1998.

Whetzel, Deborah L., and George R. Wheaton (Editors), *Applied Measurement Methods in Industrial Psychology* , Davies-Black Publishing, 1997.

Part Five 5

Motivating Human Resources

Employees must be compensated for their performance fairly and equitably. The human resource department assists managers in assessing the value of a job and determining an appropriate salary, and it will administer the proper benefits. New job options must be integrated into the organization, and it is one of the responsibilities of a human resource manager to create a motivating job environment.

Each of these topics is discussed in Part Five. They are important management tools for human resource specialists and managers alike. Regardless of your job, you will find that these tools are helpful ways to ensure effective performance.

Motivating
Human Resources

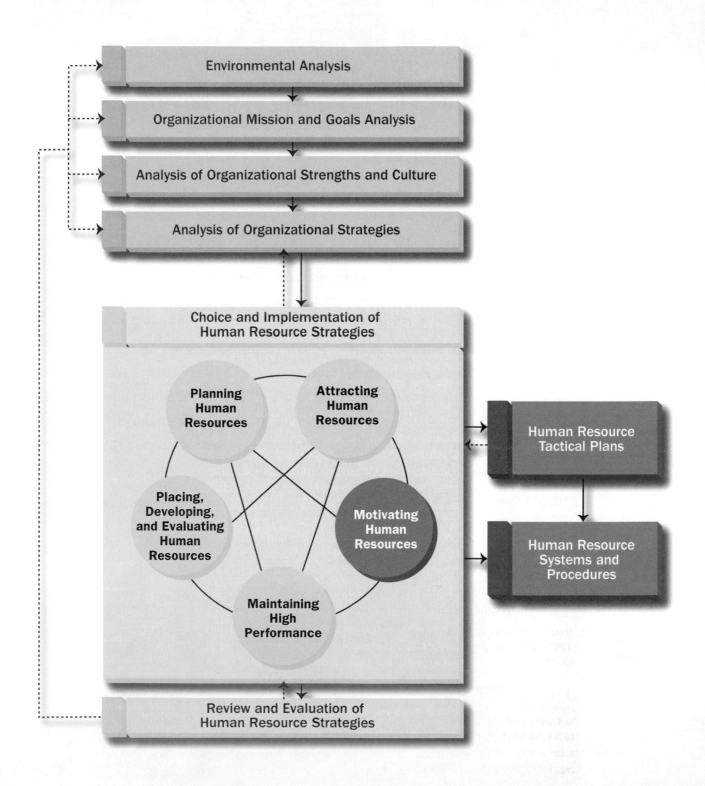

Chapter 10

Compensation Management

Management's challenge is to create an environment that stimulates people in their jobs and fosters company growth, and a key aspect of the environment is compensation.

—Milton L. Rock[1]

"If you give employees a piece, they'll bake you a much bigger pie."

—Australian Employee Ownership Association Online[2]

CHAPTER OBJECTIVES

After studying this chapter, you should be able to:

- *Explain* the objectives of effective compensation management.
- *Discuss* the consequences of mismanaged compensation programs.
- *Describe* how wages and salaries are determined.
- *Identify* the major issues that influence compensation management.
- *Explain* the differences between "equal pay for equal work" and "equal pay for work of equal value."
- *Evaluate* the advantages and disadvantages of incentive systems.
- *Explain* the major approaches to group incentive plans.

One way the human resource department improves employee performance, motivation, and satisfaction is through the development, implementation, and administration of compensation systems, which tie rewards to the achievement of company objectives. Compensation is the cash and non–cash rewards employees receive in exchange for their work. When the system is properly administered, employees are more likely to be satisfied and motivated to contribute to the achievement of organizational objectives. But when employees perceive their compensation to be inappropriate, performance, motivation, and satisfaction may decline dramatically. The following dialogue is an example of how not to administer pay policy:

> Joan Swensen walked into Al Jorgeson's office, slammed down her clipboard, and said, "I quit!"
>
> "What's the matter, Joan?" Al questioned. "You've been here two years, and I've never seen you so mad."
>
> "That's just the problem. I've been here two years, and this morning I found out that the new man you hired last week, Kurt, is making the same pay that I am," Joan said.
>
> "Well, he does the same work, he works the same hours, and he has the same responsibilities. Would it be fair to pay him less?" Al asked.
>
> "Doesn't experience count for anything around here? When you brought him into the shop, you told me to show him the ropes. So not only did I have more experience, but I am also responsible for training him," Joan responded.
>
> "Okay, okay, I'll talk with Human Resources this afternoon and see if I can get you a raise," Al conceded.
>
> "Don't bother. I'm quitting," Joan asserted. "If this company doesn't want to do what is right voluntarily, I'd rather work someplace else."

Compensation programs help to maintain an organization's human resources. When wages and salaries are not administered properly, the firm may lose employees and the money spent to recruit, select, train, and develop them. Even if workers do not quit, as Joan did in the opening illustration, they may become dissatisfied with the company.

Dissatisfaction arises because employee needs are affected by absolute and relative levels of pay, as shown in Figure 10-1. When the total, or *absolute*, amount of pay is too low, employees cannot meet their physiological or security needs. In industrial societies, the absolute level of pay usually is high enough to meet these basic needs, at least minimally. A more common source of dissatisfaction centres on *relative* pay, which is an employee's pay compared with that of other workers. For example, Joan's concern was over the relative amount of her salary in comparison with the new, less experienced employee, Kurt. Her additional experience and training responsibilities were not reflected in her pay as compared with Kurt's pay. She felt that her esteem needs were affected because she did not receive the recognition she thought she deserved.

FIGURE 10-1

Absolute and Relative Pay Levels in Relation to Employee Needs

Pay Levels	Employee Needs Primarily Served
Absolute	Physiological and security needs
Relative	Social and esteem needs

Since compensation affects the organization and its employees, this chapter examines the requirements for an effective compensation system. The chapter also discusses the objectives and procedures used to administer compensation. Then it concludes with a review of financial incentives.

OBJECTIVES OF COMPENSATION ADMINISTRATION

THE ADMINISTRATION of compensation must meet numerous objectives. Sometimes the ones listed in Figure 10-2 conflict with each other and trade-offs must be made.[3] For example, to retain employees and ensure equity, wage and salary analysts pay similar amounts for jobs of similar value. But a recruiter may want to offer an unusually high salary to attract a qualified recruit. At this point, the hiring manager (the manager of the line department) must make a trade-off between the recruiting and the internal equity objectives with the guidance of the human resource department.

Other objectives of compensation are to reward desired behaviour and to control costs. These objectives can conflict, too. For example, a department manager may

FIGURE 10-2

Objectives Sought Through Effective Compensation Administration

- *Acquire qualified personnel.* Compensation needs to be high enough to attract applicants. Since companies compete in the labour market, pay levels must respond to the supply and demand of workers. But sometimes a premium wage rate is needed to attract applicants who are already employed in other firms.

- *Retain present employees.* When compensation levels are not competitive, some employees quit. To prevent employee turnover, pay must be kept competitive with that of other employers.

- *Ensure equity.* The administration of wages and salaries strives for internal and external equity. Internal equity requires that pay be related to the relative worth of jobs. That is, jobs of similar value get similar pay. External equity involves paying workers at a rate perceived to be fair compared to what the market pays. Internal equity, also called internal consistency, refers to comparisons among jobs or skills levels inside a single organization. The focus is on comparing jobs and skills in terms of their relative contributions to the organization's objectives.

- *Reward desired behaviour.* Pay should reinforce desired behaviours. Good performance, experience, loyalty, new responsibilities, and other behaviours can be rewarded through an effective compensation plan.

- *Control costs.* A rational compensation program helps an organization to obtain and retain its work force at a reasonable cost. Without a systematic wage and salary structure the organization could overpay or underpay its employees.

- *Comply with legal regulations.* As with other aspects of human resource management, wage and salary administration faces legal constraints. A sound pay program considers these constraints and ensures compliance with all government regulations that affect employee compensation.

- *Further administrative efficiency.* In pursuing the other objectives of effective compensation management, wage and salary specialists try to design the program so that it can be efficiently administered. Administrative efficiency, however, should be a secondary consideration compared with other objectives.

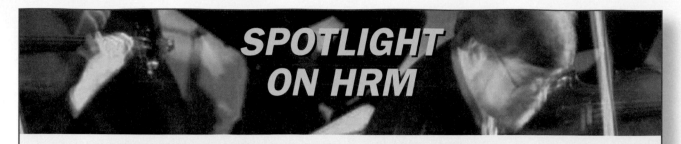

SPOTLIGHT ON HRM

PROFIT SHARING PLANS HELP KEEP GREAT WORKERS

The Owner-Manager, Larry Ginsberg

Successful entrepreneurs understand that their prosperity depends upon hiring and retaining great employees. One of the key concerns for workers is their compensation package. Compensation will usually include a base salary, commissions (if the position is related to sales or marketing), benefits, employee profit sharing plans and, if appropriate, stock option plans. To build and keep a winning team, you must determine an appropriate compensation package. Here's what to consider.

Base salary and benefits.

Your industry association will have information regarding the common base salary and benefits for your business. Confirm this information by talking to your peers. Another significant source is executive search consultants that specialize in your industry. The main advantages of using these consultants from time to time are they are professionally obliged not to steal your employees to fill other positions and they have a great deal of information about your industry.

As a general rule, you should pay somewhere in the third quartile (about 75 per cent) of the range for a particular position. For example, if the range is $28 000 to $40 000, your starting salary should be about $37 000. If you pay in the low part of the range, it is easy for new employees to move on to a competitor for much more money—after you have invested the time and effort to train them. Similarly, your benefits package should be at least comparable to the norm for the industry.

If a commission is paid to an employee, as opposed to salary, the employee may be able to claim certain tax deductible expenses that are allowed as an employee.

Employee profit sharing plans.

There are basically two types of employee profit sharing plans. The first is an annual bonus that is generally based upon overall company profit and/or tied to specific items, such as sales, that an employee can influence. A bonus can be set up as a liability in your company books at your fiscal year-end. For the bonus to be tax deductible to the firm in the fiscal year, Revenue Canada requires you to pay it within 180 days from your year-end.

The second type of plan is a trust that is set up to allow an employer to share profit from the business with some or all employees. This trust is called an Employees Profit Sharing Plan or EPSP. An EPSP allows an employer to deduct in the current fiscal year all monies paid to the trust within 120 days of the fiscal year-end. Employer contributions are determined using a formula that is tied to the company's profit.

Funds contributed are allocated among employees who are members of the plan. In addition, money earned by the trust and any capital gains or losses of the trust are allocated to the employees, who are taxed on these amounts.

The plan can be established to vest the benefits over time. This helps guarantee employee loyalty, as the funds are not available until they have been vested by the terms of the plan. For example, if the current-year profit allocation is set up to vest 50 per cent in the second year and 50 per cent in the third year from the date of the contribution, an employee who chooses to leave after one year receives no money. They only get a credit on their personal tax return for the tax paid on amounts not received. This plan is ideal to help knowledge-based companies retain their vital assets: employees.

The major advantages of an EPSP are that a company receives a current-year deduction but only needs to make the payment within 120 days, that employees who leave voluntarily lose the opportunity to participate in the plan, that funds in the plan are invested by the trustees and earn interest and that this plan does not affect any other employee compensation or retirement arrangement. But any company should consult with an accountant before setting up a plan.

Smart entrepreneurs are careful to structure their employee compensation packages to ensure they maintain the benefit from the training and experience they give their employees. Hiring a new employee is expensive and the related training is time-consuming; protecting this investment is critical to the long-term success of any venture.

Larry Ginsberg is co-author of Small Business, Big Money, *and can be reached by E-mail at ginsberg@ginsorg.com*

want to reward outstanding performance with a raise, but every raise adds to costs. Here again, the human resource manager must decide between two conflicting goals.

Regardless of the trade-offs, an overriding objective is to maintain legal compliance. For example, the Canada Labour Code requires employers to pay minimum wages and time and a half for overtime. Periodically, federal and provincial governments raise minimum wages, and employers must comply regardless of other objectives being sought.

Compensation objectives are not rules—they are guidelines. But the less these guidelines are violated, the more effective wage and salary administration can be. To meet these objectives, compensation specialists evaluate every job, conduct wage and salary surveys, and price each job. Through these steps, the appropriate pay level for each job is determined. Figure 10-3 depicts the three major phases of compensation management that take place after the initial job analysis phase. Each phase is discussed in the following sections.

www.hrdc-drhc.gc.ca

JOB EVALUATION

Job evaluation
Systematic process of assessing job content and ranking jobs according to a consistent set of job characteristics and worker traits.

Job evaluations are systematic procedures to determine the relative worth or value of jobs. Although there are several different approaches, each one considers the duties, responsibilities, and working conditions of the job. The purpose of job evaluation is to identify which jobs should be paid more than others. Since evaluation is subjective, it is conducted by a group of subject-matter experts. This job evaluation committee is usually made up of compensation specialists and representatives of line management responsible for the job(s) being evaluated.[4] They begin with a review of job analysis information to learn about the duties, responsibilities, and working conditions that shape their evaluation. With this knowledge, the relative worth of jobs is determined by selecting a job evaluation method. Before the enactment of pay

FIGURE 10-3

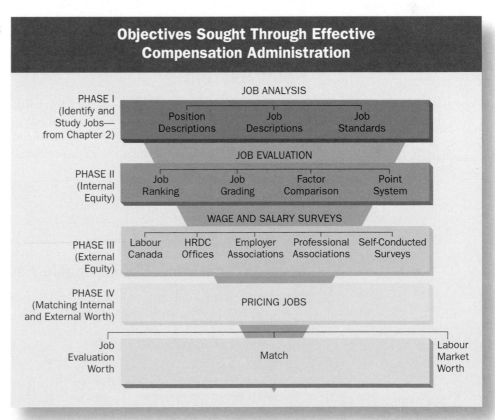

equity legislation there were a number of job evaluation methods, such as job ranking, job grading, and the point system. Now the point system is, by far, the most commonly used evaluation method since it provides, relatively, the best information regarding job values.[5] For comparison purposes we will provide brief descriptions of some of the other methods, but focus on the point system.

Job Ranking

Job ranking
One form of job evaluation whereby jobs are ranked subjectively according to their overall worth to the organization.

The simplest and least precise method of job evaluation is *job ranking*. Specialists review the job analysis information for each job. Then each job is ranked subjectively according to its importance in comparison with other jobs. These are overall rankings, although raters may consider the responsibility, skill, effort, and working conditions of each job. It is quite possible that important elements of some jobs may be overlooked while unimportant items are weighted too heavily. What is even more damaging, these rankings do not differentiate the relative importance of jobs. For example, the job of janitor may be ranked as 1, the secretary's job may get a 2, and the office manager is ranked as a 3. But the secretarial position may be three times as important as the janitorial job and half as important as the job of office manager. The job ranking approach does not allow for these relative differences between jobs. Pay scales based on these broad rankings ensure that more important jobs are paid more. But since the rankings lack precision, the resulting pay levels may be inaccurate.

Job Grading

Job grading
A form of job evaluation that assigns jobs to predetermined job classifications according to their relative worth to the organization.

Job grading, or job classification, is a slightly more sophisticated method than job ranking, but it, too, is not very precise. It works by having each job assigned a grade, as explained in Figure 10-4. The standard description in the figure that most nearly matches the job description determines the grade of the job. Once again, more important jobs are paid more. But the lack of precision can lead to inaccurate pay levels. The largest user of this approach has been the Canadian Public Service Commission, which is gradually replacing this approach with more sophisticated methods.

Point System

Point system
A form of job evaluation that assesses the relative importance of the job's key factors in order to arrive at the relative worth of jobs.

As mentioned before, research shows that the *point system* is used more than any other method. It evaluates the critical—also called compensable—factors of each job, determines different levels or degrees for each factor, and allocated points to each level. Although it is more difficult to develop initially, it is more precise than other methods because it can handle critical factors in more detail. This system requires six steps to implement. It is usually done by a job evaluation committee or an individual analyst. In most cases, organizations use a system that has predetermined job factors and assigned points to each factor. It is very rare that a company develops a system from scratch.

Step 1: Determine Compensable Factors

Figure 10-5 shows how the factor of responsibility can be broken down into:

a. safety of others;

b. equipment and materials;

c. assisting trainees;

d. product/service quality.

FIGURE 10-4

A Job Classification Schedule for Use With the Job Grading Method

Empire Machine Shop
Job Classification Schedule

Directions: To determine appropriate job grade, match standard description with job description.

Job Grade	Standard Description
I	Work is simple and highly repetitive, done under close supervision, requiring minimal training and little responsibility or initiative. *Examples:* Janitor, file clerk
II	Work is simple and repetitive, done under close supervision, requiring some training or skill. Employee is expected to assume responsibility or exhibit initiative only rarely. *Examples:* Administrative assistant I, machine cleaner
III	Work is simple, with little variation, done under general supervision. Training or skill required. Employee has minimum responsibilities and must take some initiative to perform satisfactorily. *Examples:* Parts expediter, machine oiler, administrative assistant II
IV	Work is moderately complex, with some variation, done under general supervision. High level of skill required. Employee is responsible for equipment or safety; regularly exhibits initiative. *Examples:* Machine operator I, tool and die apprentice
V	Work is complex, varied, done under general supervision. Advanced skill level required. Employee is responsible for equipment and safety; shows high degree of initiative. "Examples": Machine operator II, tool and die specialist

Step 2: Determine Levels (or Degrees) of Factors

Since the extent of responsibility, or other factors, may vary from job to job, the point system creates several levels (or degrees) associated with each factor. Figure 10-5 shows four levels, although more or fewer may be used. These levels help analysts to reward different degrees of responsibility, skills, and other critical factors.

Step 3: Allocate Points to Subfactors

With the factors listed down one side and the levels placed across the top of Figure 10-5, the result is a point system matrix. Points are then assigned to each subfactor to reflect the relative importance of different subfactors. Analysts start with level IV and weight each subfactor with the number of points they think it deserves. This allocation allows them to give very precise weights to each element of the job. For example, if safety is twice as important as assisting trainees, it is assigned twice as many points (100) as assisting trainees (50).

Step 4: Allocate Points to Levels (Degrees)

Once the points for each job element are satisfactory under column IV, analysts allocate points across each row to reflect the importance of the different levels.

For simplicity, equal point differences are usually assigned between levels, as was done for "safety of others" in Figure 10-5. Or point differences between levels can be variable, as shown for "assisting trainees." Both approaches are used depending on how important each level of each subfactor is.

Step 5: Develop the Point Manual

Analysts then develop a point manual. It contains a written explanation of each job element, as shown in Figure 10-6 for responsibility of equipment and materials. It also defines what is expected for the four levels (degrees) of each subfactor. This information is needed to assign jobs to their appropriate level.

Step 6: Apply the Point System

When the point matrix and manual are ready, the relative value of each job can be determined. This process is subjective. It requires specialists to compare job descriptions with the point manual for each subfactor. The match between the job description and the point manual statement reveals the level and points for each subfactor of every job. Once completed, the points for each subfactor are added to find the total number of points for the job. An example of this matching process for Machine Operator I appears below:

> The job description of Machine Operator I states "... operator is responsible for performing preventive maintenance (such as cleaning, oiling, and adjusting belts) and minor repairs." The sample point manual excerpt in Figure 10-6 states: "Level III: ... performs preventive maintenance and minor repairs...." Since the job description and the point manual match at Level III, the points for the equipment subfactor are 60. Repeating this matching process for each subfactor yields the total points for the job of Machine Operator I.

After the total points for each job are known, the jobs are ranked. As with the job ranking, and job grading systems, this relative ranking should be reviewed by department managers to ensure that it is appropriate.

FIGURE 10-5

Point System Matrix

Critical Factors	Minimum I	Low II	Moderate III	High IV
1. Responsibility				
a. Safety of others	25	50	75	100
b. Equipment and materials	20	40	60	80
c. Assisting trainees	5	20	35	50
d. Product/service quality	20	40	60	80
2. Skill				
a. Experience	45	90	135	180
b. Education/training	25	50	75	100
3. Effort				
a. Physical	25	50	75	100
b. Mental	35	70	105	150
4. Working conditions				
a. Unpleasant conditions	20	40	60	80
b. Hazards	20	40	60	80
			Total points	**1000**

Levels or Degrees

FIGURE 10-6

Point Manual Description of "Responsibility: Equipment and Materials"

1. *Responsibility*

   b. *Equipment and Materials.* Each employee is responsible for conserving the company's equipment and materials. This includes reporting malfunctioning equipment or defective materials, keeping equipment and materials cleaned or in proper order, and maintaining, repairing, or modifying equipment and materials according to individual job duties. The company recognizes that the degree of responsibility for equipment and materials varies widely throughout the organization.

   Level I.   Employee reports malfunctioning equipment or defective materials to immediate superior.

   Level II.   Employee maintains the appearance of equipment or order of materials and has responsibility for the security of such equipment or materials.

   Level III. Employee performs preventive maintenance and minor repairs on equipment or corrects minor defects in materials.

   Level IV.   Employee performs major maintenance or overhauls of equipment or is responsible for deciding type, quantity, and quality of materials to be used.

Beyond the four job evaluation methods discussed in this section, many other variations exist. Large organizations often modify standard approaches to create unique in-house variations. The "Hay Plan," for example, is one variation widely used by Canadian and U.S. firms. This proprietary method is marketed by a large consulting firm, Hay and Associates, and relies on a committee evaluation of critical job factors to determine each job's relative worth. Although other job evaluation approaches exist, all effective job evaluation schemes attempt to determine a job's relative worth to ensure internal equity.

WAGE AND SALARY SURVEYS

Internal equity
Perceived equity of a pay system in an organization.

External equity
Perceived fairness in pay relative to what other employers are paying for the same type of work.

Wage and salary surveys
Studies made of wages and salaries paid by other organizations within the employer's labour market.

ALL JOB EVALUATION techniques result in a ranking of jobs based upon their perceived relative worth. This assures *internal equity*; that is, jobs that are worth more will be paid more. But how much should be paid? What constitutes *external equity*?

To determine a fair rate of compensation, most firms rely on *wage and salary surveys*. These surveys discover what other employers in the same labour market are paying for specific key jobs. The labour market is the area from which the employer recruits. Generally, it is the local community in which the employer is located. However, the firms may have to compete for some workers in a labour market that extends beyond the local community. Consider how the president of one large university viewed the market:

> Our labour market depends on the type of position we are trying to fill. For the hourly paid jobs such as janitor, data entry clerk, and secretary, the labour market is the surrounding metropolitan community. When we hire professors, our labour market is Canada. We must compete with universities in other provinces to get the type of faculty member we seek. When we have the funds to hire a distinguished professor, our labour market is the whole world.

CP PHOTO ARCHIVE (Toronto Star)

A university professor may be recruited from a worldwide labour market. Such a person will be compensated according to his or her reputation in the academic community.

www.hrdc-drhc.gc.ca/

www.statcan.ca/
start.html

www.eoa-hrdc.com/
3519/menu/occnoc.stm

Sources of Compensation Data

Wage and salary data are benchmarks against which analysts compare compensation levels. This survey information can be obtained in several ways. One source is Human Resource Development Canada. It conducts surveys in major metropolitan labour markets periodically. Sometimes, these surveys are out of date in a fast-changing labour market, and so other sources may be needed. Many consultants provide this service for their clientele. Canada Human Resource Centres also compile wage and salary information for distribution to employers. When compiled frequently by the centre consulted, this information may be current enough for use by compensation analysts. A fourth source of compensation data may be an employer association, which surveys member firms. Employer associations—or a fifth source, professional associations—may be the only source of compensation data for highly specialized jobs.

The major problem with all these published surveys is their varying comparability. Analysts cannot always be sure that their jobs match those reported in the survey. Matching just job titles may be misleading. Federal, provincial, and association job descriptions may be considerably different, even when the jobs have the same title. Since most government published surveys rely on the National Occupational Classification (NOC), any job description should be compared with descriptions in the NOC.

Survey Procedure

www.salaries
review.com/Surveys/
methodology1.htm

www.erieri.com

Key jobs
Jobs that are similar and common in the organization and its labour market, e.g., accountant, tool-and-die maker.

To overcome the limitations of published surveys, some human resource departments conduct their own wage and salary survey. Since surveying all jobs is cumbersome and expensive, usually only **key jobs** are used. Then a sample of firms from the labour market is selected. Finally, these organizations are contacted by phone or mail to learn what they are paying for the key jobs. Most companies are willing to cooperate since they, too, need this information. Contacts through professional associations, such as the Canadian Manufacturers' Association and its local affiliates or provincial human resource associations, can further aid this process. Again, it is important to ensure that the comparisons are between similar jobs and not just similar titles.

At this point, all jobs are ranked according to their relative worth, as a result of the job evaluation process. Through wage and salary surveys, the rate for key jobs in the labour market is also known. This leaves the last phase of wage and salary administration, pricing the jobs.

PRICING JOBS

PRICING JOBS includes two activities: establishing the appropriate pay level for each job and grouping the different pay levels into a structure that can be managed effectively.

Pay Levels

The appropriate pay level for any job reflects its relative and absolute worth. A job's relative worth is determined by its ranking through the job evaluation process. The absolute worth of a job is influenced by what the labour market pays similar jobs. To set the right pay level means combining the job evaluation rankings and the survey wage rates. Of course, many other considerations will determine the final pay level, e.g., the organization's pay policy.

This information is combined through the use of a graph called a scattergram. As Figure 10-7 illustrates, its vertical axis shows the pay rates. If the point system is used to determine the ranking of jobs, the horizontal axis is in points. The scattergram is created by plotting the total points and wage level for each key job. Thus, each dot represents the intersection of the point value and the wage rate for a particular key job. For example, Key Job A in Figure 10-7 is worth 500 points and is paid $8 an hour.

Through the dots that represent key jobs, a *wage-trend line* is drawn as close to as many points as possible. (This line can be done freehand, or more accurately by a statistical technique called the *least squares method*.)[6] The wage-trend line helps to determine the wage rates for non-key jobs. There are two steps. First, the point value for the non-key job is located on the horizontal axis. Second, a line is traced vertically to the wage-trend line, then horizontally to the dollar scale. The amount on the vertical scale is the appropriate wage rate for the non-key job. For example, Non-key Job B is worth 700 points. By tracing a vertical line up to the wage-trend line and then horizontally to the vertical (dollar) scale, it can be seen in Figure 10-7 that the appropriate wage rate for job B is $10 per hour.

FIGURE 10-7

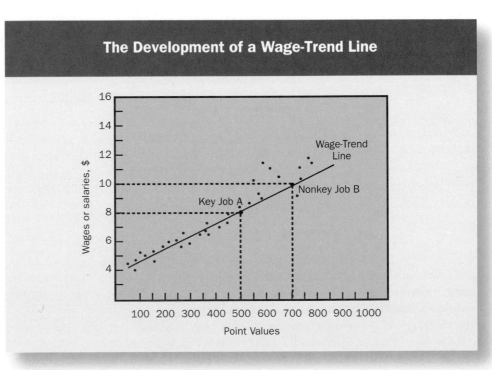

The Development of a Wage-Trend Line

The Compensation Structure

A medium-sized organization with 2000 workers and 325 separately identifiable jobs would present the wage and salary analyst with complex problems. The existence of 325 separate wage rates would be meaningless because the differences in wages between each job might be no more than a few cents.

Compensation analysts find it more convenient to lump jobs together into *job classes*. In the job grade approach, jobs are already grouped into predetermined categories. With other methods, the grouping is done by creating job grades based on the previous ranking, pay, or points. In the point system, for example, classifications are based on point ranges: 0 to 100, 101 to 150, 151 to 200, and so forth. This grouping causes the wage-trend line to be replaced with a series of ascending dashes, as shown in Figure 10-8. Thus, all jobs in the same class receive the same wage rate. A job valued at 105 points, for example, receives the same pay as a job with 145 points. Too many grades defeat the purpose of grouping; too few groupings result in workers with jobs of widely varying importance receiving the same pay.

The problem with flat rates for each job class is that exceptional performance cannot be rewarded. To give a worker a merit increase requires moving the employee into a higher job class. This upsets the entire balance of internal equity developed through job evaluations. To solve these problems, most firms use rate ranges for each class.

Rate ranges simply mean a pay range for each job class. For example, suppose the wage-trend line indicates that $10 is the average hourly rate for a particular job class. Every employee in that class receives $10 if a flat rate is paid. With a rate range of $2 for each class, a marginal performer can be paid $9 at the bottom of the range, as indicated in Figure 10-9. Then an average performer is placed at midpoint in the rate range, $10. When performance appraisals indicate above-average performance, the employee may be given a **merit raise** of, say, $0.50 per hour for the exceptional performance. If this performance continues, another merit raise of $0.50 can be granted. Once the employee reaches the top of the rate range, no more wage increases will be forthcoming. Either a promotion or a general across-the-board pay raise needs

Rate ranges
A pay range for each job class.

Merit raise
Pay increase given to individual workers according to an evaluation of their performance.

FIGURE 10-8

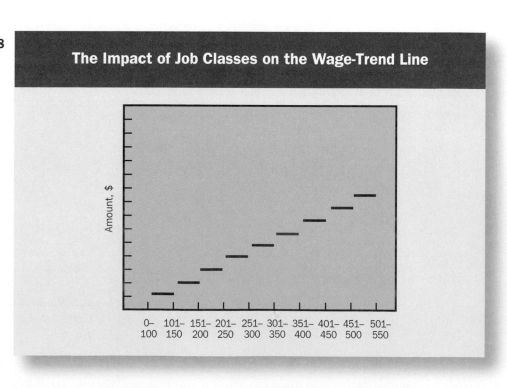

The Impact of Job Classes on the Wage-Trend Line

FIGURE 10-9

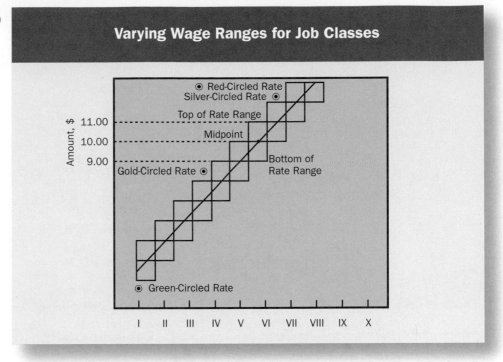

Varying Wage Ranges for Job Classes

to occur for this worker's wages to exceed $11. An across-the-board increase moves the entire wage-trend line upward.

As new jobs are created, the wage and salary section performs a job evaluation. From this evaluation, the new job is assigned to an appropriate job class. If the rate ranges are used, the new employee will start at the bottom of the range and receive raises, where appropriate, to the top of the rate range.

CHALLENGES AFFECTING COMPENSATION

EVEN THE MOST rational methods of determining pay must be tempered by several challenges. The implications of these contingencies may cause wage and salary analysts to make further adjustments to employee compensation.

Prevailing Wage Rates

Some jobs must be paid more than is indicated by their relative worth because of market forces. In the early 1990s, there was a scarcity of software specialists. Fitting these jobs onto a wage-trend line often resulted in a wage rate below their prevailing wage rate. Since demand outstripped supply, market forces caused wage rates for these specialists to rise above their relative worth when compared with other jobs. Firms that needed these talents were forced to pay a premium. Diagrammatically, these rates appear on a wage chart as a ***red-circled rate***, as seen in Figure 10-9. The term arises from the practice of marking out-of-line rates with a red circle on the chart. In the early 2000s the shortage of information technology professionals was so serious that firms first offered huge hiring bonuses, but were then eventually forced to raise salaries for these jobs, even at the entry level.[6] Some companies pay more than the maximum salary level to employees with long job tenure. This salary level appears then as *silver-circled*. *Gold-circled* salaries indicate payments beyond the maximum level if an employee receives a special merit pay that does not fit into the established range.

Red-circled rate
A rate of pay higher than the contractual, or formerly established, rate for the job.

Some jobs may be paid less than the established minimum. This happens when an organization uses salary caps (limits). For example, a company may pay newly hired employees with no experience rates 10 to 20 per cent below the pay minimum until they have "learned the ropes." This level is *green-circled*.

Union Power

When unions represent a portion of the workforce, they may be able to use their power to obtain wage rates out of proportion to their relative worth. For example, wage and salary studies may determine that $14 an hour is appropriate for a truck driver. But if the union insists on $18, the human resource department may believe paying the higher rate is less expensive than a strike. Sometimes the union controls most or all of a particular skill, such as carpentry or plumbing. This enables the union actually to raise the prevailing rate for those jobs.

Productivity

Companies must make a profit to survive. Without profits, the company cannot attract the investors necessary to remain competitive. Therefore, a company cannot pay workers more than they contribute back to the firm through their productivity. When this happens (because of scarcity or union power), companies usually redesign those jobs, train new workers to increase their supply, or automate.

Wage and Salary Policies

Most organizations have policies that cause wages and salaries to be adjusted. One common policy is to give nonunion workers the same raise as that received by unionized workers. Some companies have a policy of paying a premium above the prevailing wages to minimize turnover or to recruit the best workers. Also, some companies have automatic cost-of-living clauses that give employees automatic raises when the Statistics Canada cost-of-living index increases. Raises or policies that increase employee compensation move the wage-trend line upward.

Electricians belong to a dominant union, which is why their wage rates are so high.

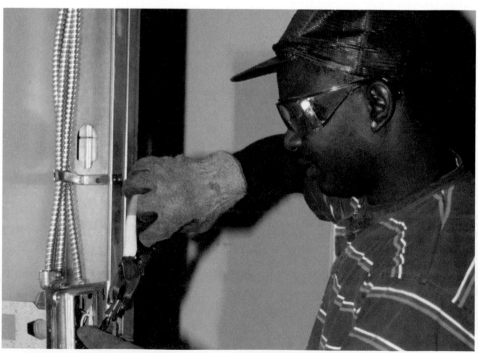

Digital Imagery © Photo Disc Inc. Photo by Hisham F. Ibrahim

Compa-ratio
Index that indicates how an individual's or a group's salary relates to the midpoint of their relevant pay grades.

A useful index for salary administrators is the *compa-ratio*. It is an indicator of how the salary of an employee relates to the midpoint of the relevant pay grade. A compa-ratio above or below 1 shows that the individual's salary is above or below the midpoint of the pay grade. The pay grade midpoint can be viewed as a benchmark for salary decision criteria such as performance, tenure, and experience. The formula for the individual compa-ratio is:

$$\text{Compa-ratio} = \frac{\text{Salary of the employee}}{\text{Midpoint of the pay grade}}$$

Also of interest to salary administrators is the compa-ratio for groups. A ratio above 1 indicates that a large number of employees are bunched at the top of the pay grade (top-heavy). A ratio below 1 may be caused by many new employees or may be an indication of high turnover. The formula for the group compa-ratio is:

$$\text{Compa-ratio} = \frac{\text{Average of salaries paid}}{\text{Midpoint of the pay grade}}$$

Government Constraints

Canada is a nation of wage-earners. What people earn bears a direct relationship to the economy and general welfare of the population. Since the 1930s, the federal government has regulated some aspects of compensation.

Canada Labour Code
Federal law regulating labour relations under federal jurisdiction.

The **Canada Labour Code** in its revised version of 1971 is the most comprehensive law affecting compensation rights for organizations under federal jurisdiction. It sets requirements for minimum wage, overtime pay, equal pay, child labour, and record-keeping. The minimum wage (see below) and overtime provisions require employers to pay at least a minimum hourly rate of pay regardless of the worth of the job. (When the minimum is increased by law, it may mean adjusting upward the wages of those who already earn above the minimum. If those just above minimum wage do not also receive raises, wage differentials will be squeezed together.[8] This is called wage compression.) For every covered job, the organization must pay one and a half times the employee's regular pay rate for all hours over 40 per week. Executive, administrative, professional, and other employees are exempt from the overtime provisions. Laws involving similar regulations have been enacted by each province for organizations under their jurisdiction.

Minimum Wages

www.fraserinstitute.ca/
media/media_releases/1999/
19990209.html

All provinces have minimum wage legislation that applies to most classes of workers, other than farm labourers and domestic servants. The legislation provides for a board to set minimum wage rates, and these rates are imposed by means of minimum wage orders that are periodically issued.[9] Wide discretion is given to all provincial boards for determination of the classes of employees for which minimum wages are to be established. The general minimum wage rates at the provincial and federal levels are given in Figure 10-10. The rates shown are typical for persons 18 years of age and over. For employees under 18, the rates are somewhat lower.

The federal government passed the Minimum Wages Act in 1935, in compliance with one of the three conventions adopted by the International Labour Organization. However, under the Constitution Act, 1867 (formerly the British North America Act), minimum wage legislation comes under provincial jurisdiction. The federal Minimum Wages Act currently applies to all government agencies, Crown corporations, and some selected industries as mentioned in Chapter Four.

FIGURE 10-10

Minimum Wage Rates Across Canada
(As of June 1, 2000)

Province		Current Minimum Wage
Alberta		$5.90
British Columbia		$7.60*
Manitoba		$6.00
New Brunswick		$5.75
Newfoundland		$5.50
N.W.T.	(age 16 and over, with road access)	$6.50
	(age 16 and over, without road access)	$7.00
	(under age 16, with road access)	$6.00
	(under age 16, without road access)	$6.50
Nunavut	(age 16 years)	$7.00
	(age 16 and under)	$6.50
Nova Scotia	(all persons)	$5.60**
	(unskilled persons)	$5.15
	(all persons)	$5.70
	(unskilled persons)	$5.25
	(all persons)	$5.80
	(unskilled persons)	$5.35
Ontario	(all persons)	$6.85
	(for students under 18 whose weekly hours are not in excess of 28 hours or where a student is employed during a school holiday)	$6.40
	Liquor servers	$5.95
P.E.I.	Will increase in increments to $6/hr Jan 1, 2002	$5.60
Quebec	(general minimum wage)	$6.90
	(those receiving gratuities)	$6.15
Saskatchewan		$6.00
Yukon	(all persons 17 and older)	$7.20

The federal minimum wage rate is adjusted with the adult general minimum wage rate established from time to time in each province and territory. The rate paid to any particular employee is based on the employee's province or territory of employment.

Source: Minimum Wage Rates Across Canada and Nearby U.S. States. Copyright © 2000 Province of British Columbia. All Rights Reserved. Reprinted with permission of the Province of British Columbia. * $8.00 effective Nov. 1, 2001. ** $5.70 effective Oct. 1, 2001.

Contracts with the Government

www.hrdc-drhc.gc.ca/con/news/labour/99-71.shtml

The Fair Wages and Hours of Labour Act applies to contracts made with the Government of Canada for all types of work. It is mandatory on the part of contractors dealing with the Government of Canada to pay fair wages and establish an eight-hour workday during all such work.[10]

Staff Records

The Canada Labour Code requires every employer in those industries falling under federal jurisdiction to provide information relating to wages of employees, their hours of work, general holidays, annual vacation, and conditions of employment whenever the Ministry of Labour demands it. Similar provisions exist in the provincial legislation. Accurate records are also to be kept, for example, on parental leave

www.fraserinstitute.ca/
media/media_releases/1999/
19990209.html

http://hradio.cbc.ca/programs/
checkup/archive/equity
chronology.html

www.psac.com/
home-e.htm

www.msp-sys.com/
en/legis.htm

www.fraserinstitute.ca/
publications/csr/1998/
september/payequity.html

www.uwo.ca/
aboutuwo/fequity/

www.msp-sys.com/
en/legis.htm

and severance pay relating to all affected employees. This is to ensure that all pro-visions of the legislation relating to such things as minimum wages, maximum weekly hours, and overtime payments are strictly adhered to by each employer.

Criticisms of Minimum Wage Regulations

It has been pointed out by some that minimum wage regulations increase the cost of production in Canada. This may eventually work against the workers rather than for them:

> In recent years, minimum wages across Canada have risen more than the average increase in manufacturing wages. And some economists are suggesting ... [that] ... it could lead to an intolerable increase [in unemployment] and cause the major burdens to fall precisely on the workers it was designed to help.[11]

Increases in minimum wages are usually accompanied by increases in unemployment figures of low-skilled and young persons in the workforce. It is also pointed out by some that continual increases in minimum wage rates may actually contribute to the inflationary trends in the economy.[12] There is, however, no conclusive evidence on the matter one way or the other at this time. Figure 10-11 shows the average hourly wages paid in different Canadian industries for the years 1981, 1988, 1991, 1997, and 2000. As can be seen, there has been a steadily increasing trend in most industries.

PAY EQUITY

Equal pay for work of equal value
The principle of equal pay for men and women in jobs with comparable content; based on criteria of skill, effort, responsibility, and working conditions; part of the Human Rights Act.

Pay equity
Policy to eliminate the gap between income of men and women, ensuring salary ranges correspond to value of work performed.

Equal pay for equal work
The principle or policy of equal rates of pay for all employees in an establishment performing the same kind and amount of work, regardless of sex, race, or other characteristics of individual workers not related to ability or performance.

IN 1977, the Canada Labour Code, Part I, was repealed and replaced by the Canadian Human Rights Act. Since this act prohibits, among other things, discrimination because of sex, it is illegal for companies to pay women less than men if their jobs involve equal skills, effort, responsibilities, and conditions. The government enforces these provisions by requiring wrongdoers to equalize pay and make up past discrepancies.

As first discussed in Chapter Four, an important issue in compensation management and equal opportunity is *equal pay for work of equal value*. Equal pay for work of equal value is the concept that jobs of comparable worth to the organization should be equally paid (referred to as *pay equity*). The idea goes beyond *equal pay for equal work* (referred to as equal pay). The latter concept has been part of the Canada Labour Code since 1971. It requires an employer to pay men and women the same wage or salary when they do the same work. Exceptions to equal pay are allowed when a valid seniority or merit system exists. Employers can pay more for seniority or to workers who perform better and merit higher pay. Exceptions are also allowed when pay is determined by the employee's production, such as sales commissions.

The pay equity concept, however, takes a different perspective. It became law in an amendment to the Canadian Human Rights Act in 1978. It makes it illegal to discriminate on the basis of job value (or content). For example, if a nurse and an electrician both received approximately the same number of job evaluation points under the point system, they would have to be paid the same wage or salary, regardless of market conditions. This approach to compensation is sought by governments as a means of eliminating the historical gap between the income of men and women, which results in women in Canada earning about 80 per cent as much as men.[13] This gap exists in part because women have traditionally found work in lower-paying occupations—teaching, retailing, nursing, secretarial work, and in such positions as receptionist and telephone operator.

FIGURE 10-11

Average Hourly Wage, by Industry, 1991–2000

Manufacturing	1991	1997	2000
Food	$13.89	$21.17	$24.78
Textile Products	11.80	15.52	17.80
Clothing	8.47	16.54	17.05
Wood Products	14.46	22.32	24.32
Furniture, Fixtures	10.42	18.33	21.37
Paper and Products	18.58	28.14	27.68
Printing, Publishing	16.04	21.93	23.22
Primary Metals	18.53	28.95	23.46
Metal Fabricating	14.55	21.78	24.83
Machinery	14.80	25.34	30.32
Transportation Equipment	17.06	26.33	31.24
Electrical Products	13.76	24.58	27.52
Nonmetallic Mineral Products	15.36	25.64	25.34
Petroleum Products	19.09	32.73	38.64
Chemicals and Chemical Products	15.71	26.32	28.27
All Manufacturing	14.94	20.30	25.45
Other Industries:			
• Mining	20.57	30.86	30.28
• Construction	17.56	20.04	19.62
• Engineering	18.54	19.72	22.30
Urban Transport	17.62	21.28	22.39
Highway, Bridge Maintenance	15.16	22.13	22.18
Restaurants, Caterers, and Taverns	9.72	12.35	13.12

Source: Average Hourly Wage, by Industry, 1981–2000, reproduced from the Statistics Canada Web site www.statcan.ca.

It should be emphasized, however, that the above-mentioned figure of 80 per cent as the earning gap between men and women is misleading, although it is widely used by proponents of equal pay to point to the "discrimination" in pay against women. This figure emerges if one compares all men and women wage-earners regardless of job tenure and skill level. But this is not an appropriate comparison. If a woman chooses to leave the labour force to have children and to bring them up and then returns to continue her career, she will have missed many training and advancement opportunities in her organization as compared to her male colleague who presumably continued to grow and advance in his career.

By using comparable groups, the pay gap decreases to between 5 per cent and 25 per cent, depending on the group studied.[13] For example, the income of single women age 35 to 44 was 94.5 per cent of that earned by men of the same age. (If one looks only at the most educated members of that age group—single females with a university degree—women actually made six per cent more than their male counterparts.) These differences are most likely "genuine" discrimination, because they cannot be

CP PHOTO ARCHIVE (Jeff Mcintosh)

Pay equity ensures equal pay for work of equal value. Rosemary Kaline, a worker for the Toronto Board of Education, received a pay raise because of the pay equity law.

www.statcan.ca/
Daily/English/991220/
d991220a.htm

www.tom.quack.net/
wagegap.html

www.canoe.ca/
MoneyColumnsUllrich/
mar3_ullrich.html

accounted for by differences in education, tenure, or skill level. There is no evidence, however, that there is a conspiracy among entrepreneurs and managers to keep the wages of female-dominated jobs down.*

Then what keeps women's wages below comparable men's wages? Society's expectations about the role of women in our culture determined to a large degree women's job choices. Traditionally, it was the son who, after high school, would go on to study for a profession and pursue a career, while the daughter had to be content to learn household skills, such as cooking and sewing, or at the most secretarial skills, such as typing and shorthand. This attitude has changed, as enrolments in our business, engineering, law, and medical schools demonstrate. But even today a woman's job choice is often influenced by her role as a homemaker and mother, as evidenced in the following study:

> Two researchers were asked to examine a manufacturing company whose management wanted to find out why in some jobs there were so few women despite the company's sincere employment equity program. They found that some of the higher-paying jobs were not attractive to women because of overtime requirements, shift work, and heavy lifting. Women felt that they had a stronger responsibility toward the family and could not afford to work overtime or do shift work. This—and other studies—shows that some contextual factors such as family considerations, which do not enter the job evaluation process, have a strong impact on job choices.[15]

What makes the issue of equal pay for work of equal value very tricky is the lack of any generally acceptable definition of "equal value" and how it can be measured. The definition offered in the guidelines issued by the Canadian Human Rights Commission is not of much help:

> Value of work is the value that the work performed by an employee in a given establishment represents in relation to the value of work of another employee, or group of employees, the value being determined on the basis of approved criteria, without the wage market or negotiated wage rates being taken into account.[16]

The approved criteria referred to above are skill, effort, responsibility, and working conditions. These criteria will be considered together, that is, they will form a composite measure. This does not mean that employees must be paid the same salary, even if their jobs are considered equal. The equal wage guidelines define seven "reasonable factors" that can justify differences in wages:

*A job is gender-dominated if, depending on jurisdiction, 60 to 70 per cent of the job occupants are from one sex.

1. Different performance ratings (ratings must be based on a formal appraisal system and be brought to the attention of each employee).

2. Seniority (based on length of service).

3. Red-circling (because of job re-evaluation).

4. Rehabilitation assignment (e.g., after lengthy absence because of sickness).

5. Demotion pay procedures (because of unsatisfactory work performance, or reassignment because of labour force surplus).

6. Procedure of phased-in wage reductions.

7. Temporary training positions.[17]

These factors justify a difference in wages only if they are applied consistently and equitably. It must be clearly demonstrable that existing wage differences are not based on sex.

Where does this leave the human resource manager? The Canadian Human Rights Act applies only to organizations under federal jurisdiction, such as federal government departments and Crown agencies, the RCMP, the Canadian Armed Forces, banks, airlines, most railway companies, and communication firms. In addition, all provinces have now enacted pay equity legislation, which means all organizations under their jurisdiction must comply with these laws. Fortunately, these pay equity laws are modelled after the federal law and use similar criteria.

A human resource manager has to ensure that the company's pay system is in line with the province's or the federal government's legislation. The following measures are suggested:

- Review the organization's human resource policies, procedures, and practices with the objective of determining relevance and consistency of application.

- Review recruiting and promotional decisions and track career trends, particularly with respect to compensation levels; examine how the organization has "treated" employees in the past.

- Review human resource planning techniques and procedures to determine consistency of application throughout the organization.

- Review the underlying philosophy and rationale of the job evaluation plan(s) currently used (e.g., are they appropriate for the organization today; has the evaluation process been as objective as possible; what "groups" fall under which plan, and is this appropriate?).

- By specific positions, examine the differential between earnings of men and women in the organization.

- By salary grade, examine the differential between earnings of men and women.

- For groups of positions performing work of "relative importance," examine the differential between earnings of men and women.

- Examine all employee benefits practices across the organization, including those in place for plant and hourly rated employees, to determine whether inequalities exist (e.g., to determine if overtime, vacation, and other benefit levels are consistently applied).[18]

Should inequalities be found, it would be advisable to eliminate them, or if the organization is large, it may be useful to implement an employment equity program. The initiation of such a program does not imply any past wrongdoing on the part of the organization, but it is encouraged by federal and provincial human rights commissions.

Provincial Legislation

As mentioned, all provinces have enacted pay equity legislation. The Manitoba and Ontario legislators took a new approach to pay equity legislation by creating Pay Equity Bureaus that are responsible for the administration and implementation of the laws. Both also take a proactive approach by requiring employers to evaluate all jobs in an organization under a single, gender-neutral job evaluation scheme, and to apply the scheme to classes of work where one sex predominates. In contrast, the laws of the remaining provinces are reactive, since they deal with inequities only if the latter are brought to the attention of the appropriate human rights commissions. Since the Ontario pay equity legislation seems to be the most comprehensive, a synopsis is shown in Appendix A to this chapter.

The Pay-for-Performance Model

www.paypeopleright
.com/rewardprin.html

www.careerjournal.com/
?content=cwc-jobstar-
salaries.htm

www.careerjournal.com/
?content=cwc-jobstar-
salaries.htm

www.callidussoftware
.com/defaultpm.asp

www.gov.on.ca/mczcr/owd/
english/guide/equity.htm

http://gateway.ontla.on.ca/
documents/Statusof
LegOUT/b/83_e.htm

Incentive systems provide the clearest link between pay and performance or productivity (performance = accomplishment of assigned tasks; productivity = measure of output). Incentive pay is directly linked to an employee's performance or productivity. Employees who work under a financial incentive system find that their performance (productivity) determines, in whole or part, their income. A typical example of an incentive pay is a salesperson's commission. The more the salesperson sells, the more he or she earns.

One of the most significant benefits of financial incentives is that better performance is reinforced on a regular basis. Unlike raises and promotions, the reinforcement is generally quick and frequent—usually with each paycheque. Since the worker sees the results of the desired behaviour quickly, that behaviour is more likely to continue. The employer benefits because wages are given in proportion to performance, not for the indirect measure of time worked. And if employees are motivated by the system to expand their output, recruiting expenses for additional employees and capital outlays for new work stations are minimized. As one economist observed:

> With fixed wages individual workers also have little incentive to cooperate with management or to take the initiative in suggesting new ideas for raising productivity. At the level of the individual worker, higher productivity has no immediate payoff—wages are fixed for the length of the contract. The immediate effect of higher productivity is, in fact, negative. Less labour is needed, and the probability of layoffs rises.

> The higher productivity growth rates of the Japanese may also be due to their bonus system that encourages labour to take a direct interest in raising productivity.[19]

Offsetting these advantages are significant problems. The administration of an incentive system can be complex. As with any control system, standards must be established and results measured. For many jobs, the standards and measures are too imprecise or too costly to develop. This means that the incentive system may result in inequities. Some incentive systems require less effort than other systems that pay the same. Sometimes workers make more than their supervisors, who are on salary. Another problem is that the employee may not achieve the standard because of uncontrollable forces, such as work delays or machine breakdowns.

Unions often resist incentive systems because they fear management will change the standard and workers will have to work harder for the same pay. This fear of a speed-up often leads to peer pressure against anyone who exceeds the group's output norms. The advantages of the incentive system are essentially lost when group pressures restrict output. And incentives tend to focus efforts on only one aspect (output, sales, or stock prices), sometimes to the exclusion of other dimensions (quality, service, and long-term objectives). Some of the more common incentive systems are outlined below.

Individual Incentive Plans

Piecework

Piecework

A type of incentive system that compensates workers for each unit of output.

Piecework is an incentive system that compensates the worker for each unit of output. Daily or weekly pay is determined by multiplying the output in units times the piece-rate per unit. For example, in agricultural labour, workers are often paid a specific amount per bushel of produce picked. Piecework does not always mean higher productivity, however. Group norms may have a more significant impact if peer pressure works against higher productivity. And in many jobs, it may be difficult to measure the person's productive contribution (for example, a receptionist), or the employee may be unable to control the rate of output (for example, an assembly-line worker).

Production Bonuses

Production bonuses

A type of incentive system that provides employees with additional compensation when they surpass stated production goals.

Production bonuses are incentives paid to workers for exceeding a specified level of output. They are used in conjunction with a base wage rate or salary. Under one approach, the employee receives a predetermined salary or wage. Through extra effort that results in output above the standard, the base compensation is supplemented by a bonus, usually figured at a given rate for each unit of production over the standard. Another variation rewards the employee for saving time. For example, if the standard time for replacing an automobile transmission is four hours and the mechanic does it in three, the mechanic may be paid for four hours. A third method combines production bonuses with piecework by compensating workers on an hourly basis, plus an incentive payment for each unit produced. In some cases, the employee may receive a higher piece-rate once a minimum number of units are produced. For example, the employee may be paid $10 an hour plus $0.30 per unit for the first 30 units each day. Beginning with the thirty-first unit, the bonus may become $0.40.

Commissions

In sales jobs, the salesperson may be paid a percentage of the selling price or a flat amount for each unit sold. When no base compensation is paid, the salesperson's total earnings come from commissions. Real-estate agents and car salespeople are often paid this form of straight commission. Figure 10-12 shows examples of different types of sales commission and bonus plans.

Maturity Curves

Maturity curves

A statistical device used to calculate compensation for workers based on their seniority and performance. Normally, such compensation plans are limited to professional and technical workers.

What happens when technical or scientific employees reach the top of their rate range? Generally, still higher increases can be achieved only by promotion into a management position. To provide an incentive for technical people, some companies have developed *maturity curves*. Employees are rated on productivity and experience. Outstanding contributors are assigned to the top curve as shown in Figure 10-13. Good but less outstanding performers are placed on the next-to-top curve. Through this technique, high-performing professionals continue to be rewarded for their efforts without being forced into a management position to keep increasing their earnings.

FIGURE 10-12

Examples of Sales Commission and Bonus Plans

Sales Plan Type	Content
Base salary only	No other compensation is offered.
Commission only	Total compensation is based on established commission schedule.
Base salary plus commission	The commission is over and above the guaranteed base salary. The salary commission mix varies with the type of product, territory, and sales support.
Base salary plus bonus	The bonus is over and above the guaranteed base salary. The bonus is usually based on task achievement; it is earned only when the established sales quota is met.

Source: J. A. Colleti and D. Cichelly, "Increasing Sales-Force Effectiveness Through the Compensation Plan," in Milton L. Rock and Lance A. Berger, (eds.), *The Compensation Handbook*, New York, NY: McGraw-Hill, 1991, pp.290-303. Used with permission.

Executive Incentives

www.aflcio.org/
paywatch/w_sampshar.htm

www.forbes.com/forbes
global/00/0515/0310104a
.htm

www.xpay.net/

Executive incentives vary widely. Young and middle-aged executives are likely to want cash bonuses to meet the needs of a growing or maturing family. As they get older, the need for present income is offset by retirement considerations. Here, bonuses may be deferred until the executive reaches the lower tax rates of retirement.

Executives are sometimes granted stock options—the right to purchase the company's stock at a predetermined price. This price may be set at, below, or above the market value of the stock. Thus, the executive has an incentive to improve the company's performance in order to enhance the value of the stock options. Generally, it is considered appropriate to give stock options only to those executives who can have a significant effect on company profits.

FIGURE 10-13

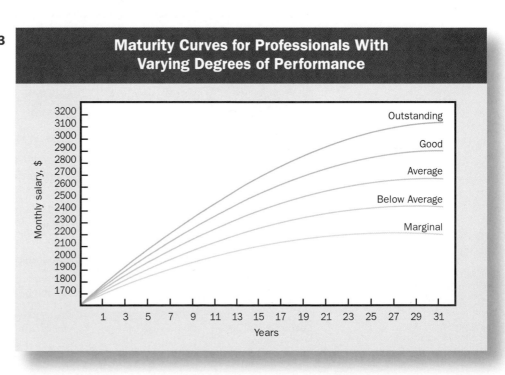

Maturity Curves for Professionals With Varying Degrees of Performance

Other forms of executive incentives exist, including incentive systems that allow executives to design their own compensation package. The common element in most executive incentive plans, however, is their relation to the performance of the organization. When these systems do not relate the incentive to performance, no matter what they are called, they are not incentive plans. Besides, executive incentives are increasingly being geared to promote long-term performance.[20]

Team-based Pay

www.ced.com

When students graduate and join an organization there is a high probability that they will be part of a team instead of working alone, and their performance will then be measured by how much they contribute to the team results. According to one study, 87 per cent of Fortune 1000 companies have created project teams and 47 per cent have permanent teams.[21] The team concept seems to work best in high-tech companies, where groups of engineers collaborate on solving problems or designing software. Bashker Biswas, director of human relations for Coopers & Lybrand, has an interesting view: "When I try to build a team environment, I say: individuals win trophies, teams win championships."[22] Figure 10-14 compares characteristics of team-based merit pay and individual merit pay.

There can be a number of advantages in a team-based pay system. For example, in project teams many jobs are interrelated, i.e., they depend on each other for making progress. A team approach tends to foster group cohesion and organizational commitment. Communication in cohesive teams tends to be more open and decision making can be more effective if a consensus approach is in the team's interest. Team-based pay often includes rewards for developing better interpersonal skills to improve cooperation and incentives for cross-training.

There are some potential disadvantages to team-based pay systems. If team cohesiveness is not strong, a free-loader effect may take place. As in any group, individual contributions to team goals vary. Some put in more effort, others less. If these differences are significant and the high performers do not receive satisfaction for their input, they may reduce their contributions. Usually, however, high-input members receive their satisfaction from being recognized as team leaders or higher-status members, e.g., as an expert or specialist. Another potential drawback may be social pressure on high performers to lower their input to avoid drawing management's

FIGURE 10-14

Contrasting Approaches

Team-based Merit Pay	Individual Merit Pay
Rewards teamwork and cooperation	Creates internal competition
Encourages group to improve work systems	Encourages withholding of information
Increases flexibility and ability to respond to changing needs	Individuals try to improve system—results in failure
Not incorporated in base pay	Decreases flexibility
Encourages information sharing and communication	Incorporated into base pay
Focus on wider organization	No focus on wider organization

Source: M. Thompson, "Team Working and Pay," Report 281, London, UK: The Institute for Employment Studies, 1995.

attention to low performers. This issue will most likely occur in a hostile management-union environment. It is also possible that the team approach is too effective, resulting in competition between teams and undesirable consequences, such as hoarding of resources or withholding of important information.

Team-based Incentive Plans

Several plans have been developed to provide incentives for teamwork. Most fall into one of the following categories: team results, production incentives, profit sharing, stock ownership, or cost-reduction plans.

Team Results

Under team-based pay plans, employee bonuses and salary increases are based on a team's overall results and are often shared equally. However, a team can also vote shares of a bonus pool to its various members, much like a Stanley Cup or Grey Cup winner votes its members full or partial shares of its championship reward, depending on individual contributions.

Production Incentive Plans

These plans allow groups of workers to receive bonuses for exceeding predetermined levels of output. They tend to be short-range and related to very specific production goals. A work team may be offered a bonus for exceeding predetermined production levels. Or it may receive a per-unit incentive that results in a group piece-rate.

Profit-Sharing Plans

Profit-sharing plans
A system whereby an employer pays compensation or benefits to employees in addition to their regular wage based upon the profits of the company. This is usually done on an annual basis.

www.psca.org

www.compensation
canada.com

www.compensation
canada.com/survey.html

www.dofasco.ca

Profit-sharing plans share company profits with the workers. The effectiveness of these plans may suffer because profitability is not always related to employee performance; a recession or new competitors may have a more significant impact. Even when outside sources do not seriously affect results, it is often difficult for employees to perceive their efforts as making much difference. Some companies further reduce the effectiveness of the incentive by diverting the employees' share of profits into retirement plans. Thus, the immediate reinforcement value of the incentive is reduced because the incentive is delayed. However, when these plans work well they can have a dramatic impact on the organization, because profit-sharing plans can create a sense of trust and a feeling of common fate among workers and management. One example comes from a leading Canadian producer of steel, Dofasco:

> Located in Hamilton, Ontario, Dofasco is one of the largest manufacturers of steel in Canada. Within a very competitive and technologically fast-changing industry, Dofasco has become a model of economic efficiency and effectiveness through the development of a "people-oriented" organization.
>
> The company has experienced great success through the mechanisms of a profit-sharing plan (on top of high wages relative to the industry average) and open, sincere, personal communications based on a healthy and cooperative management-employee relationship. Founded in 1912, the company has never been unionized, despite several efforts by the United Steelworkers of America, and since the introduction of its profit-sharing plan in 1938 it has had only three unprofitable years.
>
> Employees contribute a maximum of $300 a year to the Employees Savings and Profit-Sharing Fund. The company contributes 14 per cent of its pretax profits for distribution to employees as follows:
>
> An amount equal to 14 per cent of pre-tax profits is divided equally among all employees who have been with the company for more than two years.

Each employee's share is split into two, with one-half being deposited in the Fund (along with the employee's $300 contribution), to be saved for retirement. The company guarantees a payment of $900 each year. Employees can take the remaining one-half as cash or have it deposited into a deferred profit-sharing plan to postpone paying tax and to provide additional savings for retirement.

Over the nine-year period from 1988 to 1997, the average payout has been $3446. Some long-service workers who let the savings accumulate over their 40-year career have collected over $700 000 upon retirement.

Joan Weppler, vice president, corporate administration, puts the profit-sharing concept into perspective. She observes, "A profit-sharing plan that generates the same distribution to an hourly worker as to the president makes a powerful statement. It is just one manifestation of a culture which values and rewards the contribution of all employees.[23]

www.pension
consultant.com/profit
sharingplan/basics.htm

www.smartbiz.com/
sbs/arts/swp16.htm

www.trademarkpage
.com/epsp.htm

www.theautochannel
.com/content/news/date/
19970130/news03066
.html

www.nceo.org/
library/index.html

www.westwardpay
.com/articles/darkside.htm

www.fed.org/online
mag/sep97/booth.html

www.nceo.org/
training/index.html

In Canada the number of profit-sharing plans increased from approximately 2000 registered plans in the mid-1950s to more than 32 000 by 1982. Since a recent study found that more than 50 per cent of all profit-sharing plans are cash plans that do not require registration, the number of profit-sharing plans in Canada is probably well beyond 60 000. Three types of plans exist in Canada:

1. Current distribution plans distribute a share of a company's profits to all employees in direct cash payments or company stock.

2. Deferred payout plans are of two kinds: (a) employee profit-sharing plans (EPSP) and (b) deferred profit-sharing plans (DPSP), as defined in Sections 144 and 147 of the Income Tax Act. Both plans allow for deferred tax payments until the profits are actually paid out.

3. Combination plans are those wherein plans 1 and 2 may be combined.

How effective are profit-sharing plans in motivating employees? The evidence is not that clear-cut. Although companies with profit-sharing plans tend to be more profitable, it is by no means certain that the plan is the cause of increased profitability.[24] As usual, many factors play a role.

Studies show that the profitable companies with profit-sharing plans tend to have also open and two-way communication between management and employees. In addition, in these companies management tends to practise a participative management style, resulting in a supportive and satisfying work environment.[25] In summary, it can be said that profit sharing tends to contribute to higher motivation and productivity, but it does it in conjunction with other factors.[26]

Employee Stock Ownership Plans (ESOPs)

Employee Stock Ownership Plans (ESOPs) have become very popular in North America. One study indicates that the percentage of U.S. companies granting ESOPs has grown from 47 per cent in 1994 to 54 per cent in 1996. Because of a lack of tax incentives, only 25 per cent of Canadian companies offer an ESOP.[27] Unlike the more traditional profit-sharing plans, ESOPs give employees genuine ownership and voting power when it comes to major decisions relating to the company's future.

In 1994, General Printers was an operation chronically in the red, with absentee owners, employees who didn't care about their work, and the need for round-the-clock supervision.

Today the value of the Oshawa, Ontario, company has grown by 80 per cent and employees do a first-rate job with no managers on-site for two-thirds of the 24-hour workday. The icing on the cake was being named 1997 Business of the Year by the local chamber of commerce.

www.nceo.org/library/
retire.html

www.nceo.org/library/
esops.html

www.fed.org/resrclib/
articles/create-ownership-
culture.html

www.fed.org/onlinemag/
April96/2C-Destroy.html

www.isogroup.iserv
.net/board/messages/
4782.html

www.netnz.com/
gainsharing/Gainshare
chapter.html

www.silverstone
group.com

www.netnz.com/
gainsharing/Gainshare
chapter.html

www.scanlon
associates.org/

www.hr.com

The dramatic turnaround can be traced to one key change: the workers became co-owners of the commercial print shop. An employee share ownership plan (ESOP) was established that made them not just workers earning a wage, but investors in the firm with a stake in its success.

Christina Kobi, a Toronto lawyer, suggests that ESOPs can be modelled to fit the special needs of a company. This may include the need to:

- attract and retain employees, especially in high-tech, knowledge-based industries;

- motivate employees and improve their productivity;

- rescue a failing firm;

- provide a source of additional financing; or

- create something for firms to offer in lieu of wage and salary increases.[28]

Cost-Reduction Plans

Some critics of group incentive plans argue that profit-sharing schemes, such as those found at Dofasco, do not always reward employees' efforts if profits fall for reasons beyond the employees' control. For example, the average bonus received by workers at Lincoln Electric, a company with a cost-reduction plan, fell from $22 690 one year to $15 460 the next because of a slowdown in the economy during the early 1980s. Although $15 460 is a considerable bonus, the bonus is influenced by forces outside the employees' control.

Scanlon Plan
An incentive plan developed by Joseph Scanlon, which has as its general objective the reduction of labour costs through increased efficiency and the sharing of resultant savings among workers.

Another approach is to reward employees for something they can control: labour costs. Most cost-reduction plans seek to tap employee effort and ideas for ways to reduce costs. Often a committee of employees is formed to open new lines of communications that allow employee ideas to be heard, while the plan allows greater psychological and financial participation in the firm's day-to-day operations. Perhaps the best known of these approaches is the *Scanlon Plan*, which bases bonuses on improvements in labour costs, as compared with historical norms.[29] Under a Scanlon Plan group incentive, employees aim to reduce costs, and then they share in those savings. If, for example, employee productivity increases at the Canadian Valve and Hydrant Manufacturing Company, the ratio of payroll costs to net sales revenue improves. These savings are then shared with employees in the form of a bonus. Rucker and Improshare plans are similar to the Scanlon approach, but they differ in how bonuses are calculated and in other administrative matters. All three of these approaches differ from profit sharing in that they focus on something the employee can influence (costs), and not on something that employees may control only indirectly (profitability).

Pay Secrecy

Pay secrecy
Management policy not to discuss or publish individual salaries.

Pay secrecy is a touchy topic. Many employers prefer not to publish salary levels to avoid having to defend their pay decisions. If a pay policy is indefensible, disclosure may cause significant dissatisfaction among employees. Research has shown that employees generally prefer secrecy about individual salaries, but favour disclosure of pay ranges and pay policies.[30] Figure 10-15 shows the advantages and disadvantages of insisting on secrecy.

According to Lawler, pay secrecy has two major effects: a) it lowers the pay satisfaction of employees, and b) it reduces the employees' motivation to perform.[31] It is practically unavoidable that employees discuss and compare salaries. On the basis of rumours and speculations employees tend to overestimate the salaries of

FIGURE 10-15

Advantages and Disadvantages of Pay Secrecy

Advantages	Disadvantages
Most employees prefer to have their pay kept secret	May generate distrust in the pay system
Gives managers greater freedom	Employees may perceive that there is no relationship between pay and performance
Covers up inequities in the internal pay structure	

www.markels.com/
pay.htm

their colleagues, causing feelings of unfairness, inequity, and resentment. Pay secrecy also prevents employees from perceiving the connection between their performance and their pay. This relationship is discussed in more detail in Chapter Twelve under the topic of Expectancy Theory.

NEW APPROACHES TO PAY

SO FAR, this chapter has dealt with the traditional approach to compensation, paying for the job done. It means that once employees are hired, they are paid for doing what their job descriptions list as job responsibilities or tasks. The amount paid is determined through the process of job evaluation.

A new way of thinking about paying employees is based on the skills or knowledge they have. ***Skill or knowledge-based pay*** requires, first, the identification of the tasks that have to be performed in the organization. Second, the skills required to complete the tasks have to be identified. Third, skills must be priced so that pay rates can be determined. Typically, employees are paid only for those skills they are able to perform, but there is always an incentive to broaden one's skill level:

Skill or knowledge-based pay
Pay system based on the skills or knowledge that an employee has (in contrast to the more common job-based pay).

> NCR Canada's Engineering and Manufacturing Facility in Waterloo, Ontario, employs a staff of 600 to develop and manufacture products and systems for the document processing market. In 1988 management introduced the concept of work teams. Every employee learns all the seven basic functions in the production process. Staff members rotate across the functions every six weeks to first learn and later hone other skills. Wages are based on learning and performing all of the functions in a cell on a regular rotational basis. Individual and team performance is measured and rewarded.[32]

www.bizcenter.com/
skillpay.htm

http://garnet.berkeley.edu/
~iir/ncw/wpapers/mk1/

Many companies, especially in the manufacturing industry, provide incentives for the horizontal learning of skills, similar to the job enlargement principle. Workers learn a greater variety of skills so that they are able to perform different jobs. Volvo in Sweden has taken another approach; workers are encouraged to learn vertical skills. Volvo gives every member of a work group a pay increase if the group is able to function without a supervisor, a powerful motivation for the development of ***self-directed*** or ***leaderless work groups***.[33] A similar approach has been taken by Shell Canada in its Brockville, Ontario plant, as described below:

Self-directed work groups
Any of a variety of arrangements that allow employees to decide democratically how they will meet their group's work objectives.

> Fewer than 100 people are employed in this ultra-modern plant that produces lubricants. Information technology is the key for the design of this plant, putting a computer at the fingertips of every worker. This has drastically changed the working relationships in this plant. Missing are the traditional forepersons and supervisors

who tell people what to do and how to do it. Every worker, or team operator, is a supervisor of sorts. Operators must master all the jobs within his or her team, plus at least one skill in two other groups. Pay is based on a number of defined skills. The impact on pay was significant. The average salary increased by 22 per cent and some employees almost doubled their income.[34]

The greatest advantage of skill-based pay is the flexibility of the work force. This includes filling in after turnovers and covering for absenteeism, for employees who are being trained, and for those who are in meetings. Also, if a company's production or service process is changing frequently, it is extremely desirable to have a highly trained workforce that can adapt smoothly to changes. This advantage is likely to become increasingly important in the future because of the shorter life cycles of products, the increasing demand for product customization, and the need to respond quickly to market changes.[35] Lawler cites an example where a highly skilled workforce made a major difference:

> As part of some work I did with Johnson & Johnson, I designed a skill-based pay system for a plant that makes Tylenol. As a result of the Tylenol poisoning tragedy, J&J decided to completely redo its packaging of Tylenol to add greater safety. The skill-based plant quickly installed the new technology needed and got back into production. Not so with its sister plant, which was a traditional, job-based seniority-driven plant. Seniority rights and traditional pay grades got in the way of people's flexibility in adapting to the new technology.[36]

Other advantages come from the fact that skill-based pay may lead to leaner organizations. If multiskilled employees are able to fill in, the organization does not need to have as many extra employees to cover for absenteeism.

Disadvantages lie in the higher pay rates skill-based pay systems tend to generate. However, it does not mean that total wage costs must be higher. If the organization can make better use of its people, total costs can be significantly lower.[37]

Variable Pay

www.conferenceboard.ca

Variable pay
A performance-linked employee compensation approach that combines short-term and long-term variable compensation vehicles.

There is strong evidence that Canadian companies are shifting toward a more performance-linked compensation approach. A recent survey of the Conference Board of Canada found that 122 large companies use *variable pay* as part of their compensation system. Figure 10-16 shows the type of changes compensation systems are undergoing.[38]

The objectives of variable pay are (1) to improve business performance through changed employee behaviour, (2) to keep compensation competitive, and (3) to control labour costs. The advantage of the variable compensation approach is that it is performance-linked. Unlike merit pay, it is able to incorporate the performance of

FIGURE 10-16

Characteristics of Changing Compensation Systems

Traditional	Modern
Pay = 100% base salary	Variable component added
Entitlement-base increases	Performance-driven gains
Few incentive/bonus plans, restricted to executives	Many kinds of plans, extended throughout the organization

Source: Patricia L. Booth: "Strategic Rewards Management: The Variable Approach to Pay," Report 52–90; Ottawa. The Conference Board of Canada, 1990, p. 2. The Conference Board of Canada is a membership based, not-for-profit, independent applied research organization.

individuals, groups, business units, and corporate financial and stock price performances.[39] In the Conference Board of Canada survey, respondents believed that any variable portion of executive compensation should represent approximately 40 per cent of base salary, with a 20 per cent variable component for management and professionals and 10 per cent for other employees.[40]

The apparent objective of the participating companies is to develop a compensation system that combines both short- and long-term components (see Figure 10-17).

Survey respondents were asked to indicate the ideal and the actual balance between short- and long-term variable compensation vehicles for the three major employee groups in their organization. Survey participants felt that the current variable compensation reflects too much short-term emphasis. The existing forms of variable compensation for nonexecutives are predominantly short-term (nearly 100 per cent) in nature. That figure drops to 75 per cent for executives. As Figure 10-17 shows, companies would prefer a 50/50 split for executives, which they felt would encourage more executives to focus on the longer term. They also felt a 75/25 short-long balance would be optimal for management and professionals who, they believed, should be encouraged to take a longer-term orientation. Finally, the respondents felt that any variable compensation directed toward nonmanagement employees should be mainly of the short-term variety.

Broadbanding

www.auxillium.com

www.thetraining
tree.com/broadbanding.htm

Traditionally, salaries were grouped into a large number of pay grades. It was a system well suited for narrow and specialized jobs. In some organizations the grade number has become a status symbol. Any additional responsibility usually resulted in a new job evaluation and a move up in the pay grades. With the increased focus on knowledge workers and skill-based pay, broadbanding has become a popular alternative. It is defined as a strategy for salary structures that consolidate a large number of pay grades into a few "broad bands." The advantages are several:

- assists in flattening large, hierarchical organizations;
- encourages employees to broaden their skills and abilities;
- allows for a more flexible workforce and organization;
- de-emphasizes promotion;
- eases internal transfers;
- upports a new organizational climate; and
- simplifies paperwork.

FIGURE 10-17

Short-Term and Long-Term Balance of Variable Component (Percentage)

	Short-Term* Optimal	Short-Term* Actual	Long-Term* Optimal	Long-Term* Actual
Executives	50	75	50	25
Management & Professionals	75	100	25	0
Other Employees	100	95	0	5

*Short-term plus long-term equals 100 per cent.

Source: Patricia L. Booth: "Strategic Rewards Management: The Variable Approach to Pay," Report 52–90; Ottawa. The Conference Board of Canada, 1990, p. 6. The Conference Board of Canada is a membership based, not-for-profit, independent applied research organization.

Broadbanding
Consolidation of large number of pay grades into a few "broad bands."

Broadbanding is not a cure-all. With its high salary range maximums it does not have the salary control features of the traditional salary structure. Maintaining pay equity may also be more difficult. If two employees are in the same broad salary band doing similar work, and one is paid near the bottom of the range—because of lack of broader skills—and the other is paid near the top, how does one justify the salary differential to employees?[41]

International Pay

"Think globally, act locally!" has become a popular part of business strategies of international companies. For HR managers this policy has become quite a challenge. Traditionally, when companies went international, they imposed the "home-country system" on their overseas operations, which often led to serious discrepancies in HR policies. For example, it was possible that a Canadian middle manager in a Canadian subsidiary in Japan could be earning $100 000 (with generous "overseas benefits") while the Japanese counterpart, having the same job title and responsibilities, may be paid a quarter of the expatriate's salary, surely a cause for frictions.

The next generation of international enterprises were the multinational corporation (MNCs). For most of these, the strategy was to have each country's operation choose HR policies based on local customs and values. However, this approach made it impossible to integrate transnational organizational objectives. An integrated "global" strategy requires a common framework, but not a one-size-fits-all solution—quite a challenge when it comes to pay.

A good example is the differences in pay policies in the United States and Japan. US base pay levels and merit increases are highly individualized and based on performance. Contrast this to Japan, where salary differences among those in the same job or level are more reflective of family size (number of dependants), age, and experience (job tenure) more than performance differences. Also, in the United States individual contributions (e.g., as indicated by performance appraisal ratings) tend to play a significant role in an employee's remuneration. In contrast, Japan's semiannual bonuses, measured in months of salary, tend to be far less affected by individual differences.[42]

The third generation of international companies, the truly global enterprises, will preserve national cultural differences while maintaining organizational values that allow the application of a global strategy. For example, these companies hire employees based on their expertise, not nationality. A Japanese may work for a Canadian company in Germany. The Japanese employee would be expected to adapt to the German culture, while also maintaining his Japanese values. The company, in turn, would have developed a corporate culture, policies, and strategies that will allow it to conduct business in any country.[43] Pay policies will play a crucial role in the effectiveness of the organization.

The challenge for global HR managers is clear: develop HR policies that take into account global needs, national cultures, and individual differences, a difficult task. There is more discussion on these issues in Chapter Fourteen on Diversity Management.

PAY AND ORGANIZATIONAL STRATEGY

IN THE PAST, internal equity has been the major concern of organizations. Because of increased competitiveness, nationally and internationally, the focus is shifting now to maintaining a competitive advantage. The prerequisite for developing a strategic pay plan is a clear corporate strategic agenda.[44] Only then is it possible to identify the behaviours and skills needed for the organization to be successful.

Lawler suggests a concentration on seven areas that affect pay systems:

1. *Motivating Performance.* Money is still a strong motivator. Studies show that effective incentive systems can improve the motivation of individuals to perform by as much as 40 per cent.[45] A key determinant of the effectiveness of a pay system is the way performance is measured. Top management must be able to define the organizational behaviour it wants in accordance with its strategic plan.

2. *Identifying Valued Rewards.* As mentioned, pay is an important motivator, partially because it leads to other rewards, such as status and prestige. Because pay means different things to different people, management has to understand how and why it is important to individuals. Only then is it possible to develop an effective reward system for all employees in the organization.

3. *Relating Rewards to Performance.* It is essential for employees to perceive a connection between their pay and their performance.[46] This relationship is more effective the closer the tie is between the reward and the performance. The common year-end bonus does little to make individuals aware of any performance-reward connection.

4. *Setting Performance Goals.* Reward systems often fail because the goals are simply set too high. Effective goals must be acceptable and attainable. Employee participation in setting goals tends to increase goal acceptance and in many cases leads to increased productivity.[47]

5. *Motivation and Punishment.* An individual's motivation to perform is strongly influenced by the consequences of missing set objectives. If the consequences are particularly negative, an individual may not even attempt to succeed. This point is especially relevant in organizations that encourage risk taking in managerial decision making.[48] Organizations must ensure that their reward system allows for occasional failures. A good example is the 3M company, which has a reward system that encourages its managers to take risks. They are rewarded based on their long-term track record rather than on the immediate success or failure of a venture.

6. *Motivating Skill and Knowledge Development.* A crucial issue for an organization is to develop the right mix of skills for its business objectives.

7. A company in a knowledge work field needs different skills than a company in a service business. The pay system chosen must reinforce the development of the skills needed, and it has to work for all levels of the organization. The appropriate kinds of skills are determined to a large degree by the management style used in the organization as well as its type of business. An organization that is managed in a participative way needs very different skills than one that is managed in a top-down, autocratic way.

8. *Fostering Attraction and Retention.* The pay and reward system of an organization has a major impact on the attraction of individuals to work for it and on the retention of those individuals. Simply stated, companies that offer the most valued rewards tend to have the best attraction and retention rates.[49]

How these broad compensation strategies translate into more specific pay objectives is shown in Figure 10-18. It illustrates the pay philosophy of Honeywell Canada, which consists of four basic pay objectives and four basic pay principles.

Compensation principles originate from two sources: the overall strategy of the organization and its corporate values. If a company has as part of its strategy a strong emphasis on quality of customer service, the core principles must focus on rewards that reinforce such behaviour. If, on the other hand, top management

FIGURE 10-18

www.honeywell.com/

Honeywell Canada's Pay Philosophy

Pay Objectives

- To attract the best person available for each Honeywell job.
- To encourage growth both on an individual basis and as a participant on a work team.
- To recognize the importance of high-quality work performance and to reward it accordingly.
- To encourage a career-long commitment to Honeywell.

Pay Principles

- Pay must be fully competitive in the market, as defined by each business.
- Each individual's pay must be fair in relationship to the pay other employees receive within the same Honeywell business.
- Pay must be communicated. That communication must explain general pay principles, the specific pay system applicable, and the process used to determine individual levels under that system.
- Each Honeywell business has the basic responsibility for establishing and maintaining its own pay system.

Source: Courtesy of Honeywell Canada.

wants its managers to behave like entrepreneurs, the reward system must promote risk-taking behaviour, without punishment for failure.

Compensation consists of more than wages, salaries, and bonuses. Remuneration includes an ever-growing list of fringe benefits and services. Although these benefits are referred to as noncash compensation, they are a significant part of the total labour cost of most employees. The next chapter describes the range of benefits and services offered by employers.

SUMMARY

Employee compensation, if properly administered, can be an effective tool to improve employee performance, motivation, and satisfaction. Pay programs that are mismanaged may lead to high turnover, high absenteeism, more grievances, poor performance, and job dissatisfaction.

For compensation to be appropriate, it must be internally and externally equitable. Through job evaluation techniques, the relative worth of jobs is determined. This assures internal equity. Wage and salary surveys are used to determine external equity. With knowledge of the relative worth of jobs and external pay levels, each job can be properly priced.

The process of wage and salary administration is influenced by several challenges, including union power, the productivity of workers, the company's compensation policies, and government constraints on pay. The Canada Labour Code is the major federal law affecting compensation management. It regulates minimum wages, overtime, and child labour. The Canadian Human Rights Act seeks to eliminate sex-based pay differentials. All provinces have similar laws—labour codes and human rights legislation—for their jurisdictions. (A good example of government constraints on pay is wage and price controls. In 1975 the federal government introduced such a program in order to fight inflation. Pay and price increases were limited to a certain percentage and were controlled by an anti-inflation board. The program was abolished in 1978.[50])

Pay equity has become a major issue during the last few years. When the Canadian Human Rights Act was passed in 1977, it introduced the new concept of "equal pay for work of equal value," which requires employers to compare the content of jobs when determining pay scales and to pay equal wages for jobs of comparable value. The Canadian Human Rights Commission specifies four criteria by which jobs can be evaluated: skill, effort, responsibility, and working conditions. Provincial equal pay legislation is usually modelled after the federal law.

Financial incentives are another dimension of compensation management. Individual incentives attempt to relate pay to productivity. Group plans have the same objectives, but the relationship is often not as direct or obvious to workers. Some approaches pay a bonus for reaching a production target, others share the company's profits with workers, and still others share savings in labour costs.

TERMS FOR REVIEW

Visit the Web site at www.mcgrawhill.ca/college/schwind6 for a full glossary.

www.callidus
software.com/ans/
glossary/vcgindex.asp

REVIEW AND DISCUSSION QUESTIONS

1. What is the difference between absolute and relative pay with respect to motivation?

2. Why is job analysis information, discussed in Chapter Two, necessary before job evaluations can be performed?

3. Suppose that when you interview new employees, you ask them what they think is a fair wage or salary. If you hire them, you pay them that amount as long as it is reasonable and not below minimum wage laws. What problems would you expect?

4. Assume your company has a properly conducted compensation program. If a group of employees asks you why they receive different hourly pay rates even though they perform the same job, how would you respond?

5. Why is the point system superior to all other systems? Discuss the advantages and disadvantages of the system.

6. If you are told to find out what competitors in your area are paying their employees, how would you get this information without conducting a wage and salary survey?

7. Even after jobs are first priced using a wage-trend line, what other challenges might cause you to adjust some rates upward?

8. Since financial incentives give employees feedback for good performance and they relate pay to performance, why do most companies pay wages and salaries rather than financial incentives?

9. Explain the difference between "equal pay for equal work" and "equal pay for work of equal value" and the implications of the difference for a human resource manager.

10. Under what circumstances are pay differentials justified?

CRITICAL THINKING QUESTIONS

1. Suppose you manage a small business with 30 employees. You discover that some people are much more motivated by money and others by security. Is it possible to satisfy the needs of both groups? What difficulties may arise?

2. "Money is a strong motivator" and "In surveys on what employees want from their job, money ranks 5 or lower." How can you reconcile these two statements?

3. Obviously, profit-sharing plans are not an option as an incentive plan in non-profit and government organizations. Can you think of incentive plans that will fulfill a similar function?

4. "Minimum wages increase unemployment." Please comment on this statement often made by many economists. Do you agree?

WEB RESEARCH

The National Center for Employee Ownership
www.nceo.org/library/index.html

(a) What are the characteristics of an effective employee ownership plan? What steps should be followed in its development?

(b) Research seems to indicate that employee ownership plans have a different effectiveness depending on the size of the company. Try to determine what the relationship of the effect is to size and why there may be a difference in effectiveness.

An Interactive Net on Employee Ownership
www.nceo.org/training/index.html

Play the interactive game.

The Conference Board of Canada
www.conferenceboard.ca

(a) What different types of information are available to Canadian managers regarding incentive plans?

Gainsharing Difference Types of Plans
www.silverstonegroup.com/consult/projecon/compsys/gainshar.htm

(a) What type of gainsharing plans are available? What are their advantages and disadvantages?

INCIDENT 10-1

Compensation Administration at Reynolds Plastic Products

The Reynolds Plastic Products Corporation was recently purchased by a much larger organization, International Plastics Ltd. The human resource director of International Plastics is concerned that the wage and salary policies are irrational and in some cases actually violate the law. To evaluate the compensation system of the Reynolds Plastic subsidiary, a recent human resource management graduate, Thea Silverstein, was assigned to make an investigation. The key points of her report are summarized below:

- The wage range for hourly employees is $8.70 to $16.96 per hour.

- The amount of overtime paid by Reynolds is very modest; overtime is paid for all hours over 180 per month.

- The wage rates for different workers vary widely even on the same job; those employees who are heads of households receive approximately 18 per cent more than those workers who are not heads of households. Most of the heads of households are men.

- On highly technical jobs, the firm pays a rate that is 20 per cent above the prevailing wage rate for these jobs. All other jobs are paid an average of 15 per cent below the prevailing rate.

- Turnover averages a modest 12 per cent. However, in technical jobs turnover is less than two per cent; in nontechnical jobs turnover is nearly 20 per cent.

Absenteeism follows the same pattern.

1. What laws are probably being violated?

2. Develop a step-by-step plan of actions you would take and the order in which you would undertake them if you were made human resource director of the Reynolds subsidiary.

INCIDENT 10-2

Incentives at Karma Records

Joe Karma has owned and operated Karma Records since its founding in 1979. Joe was often heard to say, "I believe in paying people for what they do, not for how many hours they work." This management philosophy was expressed through a variety of incentive plans that Joe designed himself. Although he was firmly committed to the use of incentives, he hired a management consulting team to make recommendations about his compensation programs. To help the consultants, Joe wrote down the major features of each incentive program. His notes were as follows:

- Executives do not own any stock, but they each receive $1500 for each dollar the stock price goes up from the previous year.

- Every time sales go up 10 per cent, all the hourly employees receive a day off with pay or can work one day at double-time rates.

- Production workers get paid $0.25 for each record they press and $0.05 for each record they package.

- Sales personnel receive a $50 savings bond each time a new record store or department store starts stocking Karma Records.

1. What problems do you see with the incentives for (a) executives, (b) hourly workers, (c) production workers, (d) salespeople?

2. If you were a member of the consulting team, what incentives would you recommend for each group?

EXERCISE 10-1

A Realistic Job Evaluation Simulation

Form groups of three to five students. (Three students may need approximately 20 minutes, five students about 45 minutes for the exercise.)

Use the following rules:

1. Each student chooses a job that he or she is familiar with (ideally, a job description would be available, but is not essential). The jobs should be different, but from one organization (e.g., hospital, school, manufacturing plant).

2. Use the table below to record numbers.

Critical Factors	Job 1	Job 2	Job 3	Job 4	Job 5

1. Responsibility
   a. Safety of others
   b. Equipment and materials
   c. Assisting trainees
   d. Product/service quality

2. Skill
   a. Experience
   b. Education/training

3. Effort
   a. Physical
   b. Mental

4. Working conditions
   a. Unpleasant conditions
   b. Hazards

3. Using Figure 10-8, find consensus in your group in choosing the most appropriate point level for each job.

4. Example: For the job of a janitor, what level of responsibility for the safety of others (Critical Factor) is appropriate? Probably not a high one, so a good choice may be Level I, 25 points. For a bus driver or an emergency room nurse, the appropriate choice may be Level IV, or 100 points.

5. Choose one of the above jobs, called a key job. A key job is a well-known job, ideally common in many organizations (e.g., secretary, accountant, tool-and-die maker in the manufacturing industry, and so on.) Conduct a simulated wage survey. In this exercise it is sufficient to take an educated guess on what the key job is paid in the job market.

It does not matter whether you choose an hourly wage or a monthly or annual salary, but it must be the same for each job.

6. Calculate the pay coefficient by dividing the estimated wage by the point total of the key job, according to the formula

$$\text{Pay coefficient (pc)} = \frac{\text{wage of key job}}{\text{point total for key job}} = \frac{\$}{\text{point}}$$

7. Multiply all job point totals by the pay coefficient. The results are the wages/salaries for all the above jobs. In reality, this procedure would have to be done by the job evaluation committee for all jobs in the organization, often in the hundreds.

Comment

This exercise is a fairly realistic simulation of what is going on in a job evaluation committee. In all probability, the opinions in your group were very diverse when it came to determining the level for each job. The results, of course, are not realistic since the point table has been created artificially and not by a job evaluation committee, and the pay level of the key job has been estimated by you. Nevertheless, this exercise should have given you a good feel for the job evaluation process, using the point method. It also demonstrates the need to choose members of the committee who are knowledgeable about the jobs in the organization and are trained in the application of the point method. One more point: up to the wage survey, money was not part of the discussion, only points.

CASE STUDY

Maple Leaf Shoes Ltd., Compensation Policy

Maple Leaf Shoes Ltd. is a medium-sized manufacturer of leather and vinyl shoes located in Wilmington, Ontario. It was started in 1969 and currently employs about 400 persons in its Ontario plant and some 380 more in offices and warehouses throughout Canada.

Recently, the company has faced a number of issues and challenges that require immediate attention by management. First, the cost of production at Maple Leaf Shoes has been rising slowly but steadily. Labour costs currently account for over 53 per cent of manufacturing costs and have been increasing rapidly. Worker productivity levels have not shown any increase in the last three years. If the present trend continues, the firm is likely to lose its price advantage over its competitors. Already, in two out of six popular brands sold by Maple Leaf Shoes, the prices for the firm's products were equal to or higher than its competition.

Second, over 70 per cent of the company's staff are unionized. There are indications that remaining nonmanagerial staff are also about to be unionized. Management believes that this will reduce the already limited autonomy it possesses in hiring, terminating, and managing employees.

Robert Clark, president and majority shareholder of Maple Leaf Shoes, has recently begun reading about profit-sharing plans. Some time ago, in an airport VIP lounge, he met a CEO of a company that had a profit-sharing plan. The CEO had marvelled at the productivity of his employees, their commitment, quality consciousness, concern for customers, low absenteeism, and low turnover. That really got Clark's attention. The more he learned about this incentive system, the more he liked it, and the more he talked to his managers about it. Since the idea came from him, they tended to support it and even showed some enthusiasm. Among themselves, however, most were only lukewarm to the idea of letting workers have part of the company's profits. They could understand why managers would be part of the system since they made the company profitable, but blue-collar workers?

So far, Maple Leaf Shoes' workers were paid the straight union wages negotiated two years ago, when the old contract had expired. At that time management had tried to introduce a piece-rate incentive system, but no agreement could be reached on how the base rate would be set, which was something industrial engineers had to do. The unions did not trust Maple Leaf Shoes' engineers, whom they thought were on management's side.

Clark asked Jane Reynolds, his special assistant in the personnel department, whether she knew much about profit-sharing plans. She had taken some human resource management courses and remembered that profit-sharing plans had been discussed, but she could not remember whether such plans were more effective than other incentive plans. Clark then decided to call Tim Lance, the HR consultant, to look into the pros and cons of having a PS plan at Maple Leaf Shoes. He wanted to have the plan ready as soon as possible, since two of Maple Leaf Shoe's unions were about to start contract negotiations and he thought it would be a good bargaining tool. He hoped that union representatives would embrace the idea of sharing profit and perhaps moderate their wage demands.

However, he was in for a rude awakening. Once, he casually mentioned the concept of profit sharing to one of the union presidents, without revealing his ideas of introducing such a plan at Maple Leaf Shoes. He received the following response: "Profit sharing? Forget it. That is a management gimmick. Its only purpose is to make workers work harder and make the company more profitable. And the risk is too great that there are no or low profits. What do we have then? Nothing. We want our negotiated wages and nothing more."

Clark wondered whether it would still be possible to introduce a profit-sharing plan. The other CEO had mentioned that his union was a strong supporter of the plan. How could he sell his unions on this concept? Would Tim Lance know a solution?

Discussion Questions

1. You are the consultant. Clark has asked you to submit a proposal for a PS plan for Maple Leaf Shoes. You wonder about the appropriateness of such an incentive system for Maple Leaf Shoes, but you promised to look into it. What will you tell Robert Clark?

2. Do you see a possibility of convincing Maple Leaf Shoes' unions to buy in on a profit-sharing plan?

3. What other incentive plans are suitable for Maple Leaf Shoes?

CASE STUDY

Canadian Pacific and International Bank

All employees of the Canadian Pacific and International Bank (CPIB) were on a salary scale—even janitors and maintenance personnel. Several years ago management had decided to introduce the Hay System as its job evaluation method when it became apparent that the old internally developed ranking system was unsuitable for a modern organization. The Hay System had received mixed support from employees. Higher-level managers were more satisfied with it because they felt the system rewarded their higher responsibilities. Lower-level employees preferred the new system to the old one, because they believed they had more input into the evaluation process since they were represented on the Salary System Maintenance Committee, which was responsible for any requested or recommended changes to the value of a job. On the other hand, lower-level employees felt that the system was too complex to be easily understood and applied. The Salary Committee had to rely heavily on its Hay representative when adjustments were necessary.

Mary Keddy, senior vice president—human resources, was aware of the problem, which, she felt, was more perceived than real. She had more serious issues to deal with regarding the bank's salary system. CPIB was currently negotiating the takeover of International Investors Inc. (III), a well-known stock exchange brokerage firm in New York. International Investors Inc. had quite a different salary system, based on individually negotiated contracts. It also had a strict pay-secrecy policy, just the opposite of the CPIB policy. Keddy knew that it would be a challenge to integrate the III system with

that of the parent company's. Since it probably meant a major adjustment, perhaps it was time to consider something new. Keddy had read extensively about the new approach of skill-based pay and broadbanding and decided to look at these ideas more closely to determine whether they would fit the bank's needs.

The other issue she faced was how to deal with the bank's overseas branches. Until now the bank's HR policy had been to use a local approach, i.e., hire a host country HR manager, who would introduce policies and procedures based on the local culture. However, it turned out that this approach created difficulties when the bank tried to transfer local managers to the head office in Vancouver or to a branch in another country. These transferees did not fit into any of the existing systems. Something had to be done to overcome these obstacles.

Discussion Questions

a) Write a brief proposal to the board of directors, outlining the advantages and disadvantages of skill (or knowledge)-based pay and broadbanding. (Hint: Use the margin WebPages as resources for your arguments). Address also the issue of whether both approaches are suitable for banks and investment brokers.

b) Regarding the international pay issue, what aspects must be taken into account when developing a suitable system? List the aspects and give a brief explanation on why each must be considered.

SUGGESTED READINGS

Berger, Lance A., and Dorothy R. Berger, *The Compensation Handbook*, McGraw-Hill, 1999.

Collins, Denis, *Gainsharing and Power: Lessons from Six Scanlon Plans*, Cornell University Press, 1998.

Fay, Charles H., (editor), *The Executive Handbook on Compensation : Linking Strategic Rewards to Business Performance*, Simon & Schuster, 2000.

Frost, Carl F., John H. Wakeley, and Robert A. Ruh, *The Scanlon Plan for Organizational Development, Identity, Participation, and Equity*, MSU Press, 2000

Ghorpade, Jai, and Jerry T. Edge, *Understanding Skill-Based Pay An Approach to Designing and Implementing an Effective Program*, WorldatWork Publication (previously American Compensation Association), 1997 www.acaonline.org/bookstore/generic/html/pub1579630499.html

Gilbert, Dan, and Kenan S. Abosch, *Improving Organizational Effectiveness Through Broadbanding*, WorldatWork Publication (previously American Compensation Association), 1996 www.acaonline.org/bookstore/generic/html/pub1579630022.html

Jacobs, Carl D., "Creating a Viable Pay Plan for a Sales Staff," *ACA News*, a publication of the American Compensation Association, Nov/Dec. 1997, pp.39-41.

Kanungo, Rabindra N., and Manuel Mendonca, *Compensation—Effective Reward Management,* Second Edition, Toronto; John Wiley & Sons, 1997.

Long, Richard J., *Compensation in Canada: Strategy, Practice and Issues*, Toronto: ITP International Thomson Publishing, 1998.

McKay, Robert (editor), *Canadian Handbook of Flexible Benefits* John Wiley & Son Ltd, 1996).

Nelson, Bob, *1001 Ways To Reward Employees*, New York: Workman Publishing, 1994.

Quaid, Maeve, *Job Evaluation—The Myth of Equitable Assessment*, Toronto: The University of Toronto Press, 1993.

Rodrick, Scott, 2000 Employee Stock Ownership Plans : A Practical Guide to ESOPs and Other Broad Ownership Plans, Harcourt Brace Professional Publisher, 1999; www.net-storeusa.com/bfbooks/015/015606975X.shtml

Rosenbloom, Jerry S. (ed.), *The Handbook of Employee Benefits : Design, Funding and Administration (Handbook of Employee Benefits, Fourth Edition,* Richard Irwin, 1997.

Sierra, Lorenzo, "Growth Strategies—Finding Ways to Create Value," *ACA News*, a Publication of the American Compensation Association, November/December 1997, pp. 15-17.

Tyson, David E., *Profit Sharing in Canada*, Toronto: John Wiley & Sons Canada, Ltd. 1996. www.compensationcanada.com/book.html

Other Sources:

The ESOP Reader, a publication of the National Center for Employee Ownership, 1999. www.nceo.org/index.html

Employee Ownership Q&A Disk
Gives Microsoft Windows users point-and-click access to 500 questions and answers on all aspects of ESOPs in a fully searchable hypertext format. The keyword search allows users to search the entire file in seconds and see all the search "hits" in context. Distributed on a 1.44 MB 3.5-inch diskette with a printed manual. You can download a working demo (with most of the answers omitted). www.nceo.org/pubs/index.html

"Incentive Compensation and Employee Ownership," Third Edition, a publication of The National Center for Employee Ownership, 1999; www.nceo.org/pubs/ incentive.html

"Equity-Based Compensation for Multinational Corporations," Third Edition, a publication of The National Center for Employee Ownership, 2000, www.nceo.org/pubs/multinational.html

APPENDIX A

Synopsis of Bill 154 Ontario Pay Equity Act

The Pay Equity Act, which was passed by the Ontario legislature on June 15, 1987, and became effective January 1, 1988, provides for: "the redressing of systemic gender discrimination in compensation for work performed by employees in female job classes, in the establishments of all employers in the broader public sector and those in the private sector who employ 10 or more employees."

This act will require a thorough review of compensation practices to ensure that there are no compensation differences between men in male-dominated job classes and women in female-dominated job classes who have work that is judged to be equivalent through a systematic evaluation process.

The act is far-reaching. It will require:

- formulating a pay equity plan for each "establishment";
- formulating and negotiating a pay equity plan with unions;
- posting the pay equity plan (or plans) for employees to examine and approve; and
- cost up to one per cent per year of total Ontario employee payroll (pay and benefits).

It is important to note that all public-sector organizations and all private-sector organizations with over 100 employees in Ontario must prepare a pay equity plan and post this plan for employees to examine.

Broad Concepts

The broad concepts of the act include the following:

- Employers must equalize compensation for females in jobs or female-dominated job classes that are deemed of equivalent value to male-dominated job classes.
- Employees' compensation will be compared within one establishment.
- Establishment is defined as geographic area, such as Metropolitan Toronto, a county, or a regional municipality.
- Employees may be in full-time and part-time jobs, but seasonal jobs or work under one-third of the normal work period are not included unless regular and continuing.
- Jobs or classes will be composed of positions with similar duties and responsibilities, qualifications, recruiting procedures, and pay schedules.
- Comparisons will be done only when job classes of 60 per cent female incumbents and 70 per cent male incumbents are deemed to be of equal or comparable value.
- Comparisons will be made across an establishment (nonunion), within a bargaining unit, between bargaining units and nonunion positions if there are no male job class comparisons within a bargaining unit.
- Comparisons will be made of the job rates. Job rate is the highest rate of compensation for a job class.
- Comparable value is determined by a job evaluation process. The method must include skill, effort, responsibility, and working conditions and be free of any bias based on gender.

- Employers must adjust for inequities in compensation (pay and benefits) between female-dominated job classes and male-dominated job classes if they are found to be comparable, unless one of these allowed exclusions applies: seniority, temporary training, merit pay, red-circling, skills shortage.

- A pay equity plan will be negotiated with unions as part of the collective bargaining process, but not necessarily at the same time as contract renegotiation.

- Where a pay equity plan is not mandatory, the employer and union may choose to negotiate a plan.

- A Pay Equity Commission will be established. The Pay Equity Hearings Tribunal will hear cases where agreement cannot be reached. The Pay Equity Office will provide information, and resolve complaints.

What You Must Do to Comply with Legislation

- Conduct a pay equity audit, following the guidelines in Bill 154 and the steps outlined in this article.

- Develop a pay equity plan for each establishment.

- Adjust pay to achieve pay equity over time.

Contents of a Pay Equity Plan

- A pay equity plan must:

- describe the evaluation system;

- provide the results of evaluations and comparisons;

- set out dates when pay adjustments are to begin and when pay equity is to be achieved.

Timetable for a Pay Equity Plan

A plan must be developed and posted for each establishment by these dates:

Establishment	Employees in Ontario	Years After Proclamation
Broader public sector		2
Private sector	500+	2
	100–499	3
	50–99	4 (voluntary posting)
	10–49	5 (voluntary posting)

The plan must provide for greater adjustments for lower job classes needing increases to achieve pay equity.

Timetable for Pay Adjustments

Pay equity adjustments must begin according to these dates:

Establishment	Employees in Ontario	Years After Proclamation
Broader public sector		2
Private sector	500+	3
	100–499	4
	50–99	5
	10–49	6

A private-sector organization must make pay adjustments up to the maximum cost allowed each year. For public-sector employers, inequities must be adjusted within five years.

Implementation Conclusions

- Every broader public-sector organization must have a pay equity plan two years after proclamation.

- Eventually, every private-sector organization over 100 employees must have a pay equity plan.

- Smaller private-sector organizations (10-99) should have pay equity plans. Complaints can be made by employees to the commission whether or not a plan has been developed.

- Pay increases start for the private sector one year after the plan is required to be posted. For the public sector, pay increases start at the same time as the plan is required to be posted, i.e., two years after proclamation.

Reproduced by permission.

Chapter 11

Employee Benefits and Services

In many respects Canada's position in the area of fringe benefits is unique, striking a balance between the situation prevailing in the U.S. and that in Europe.

—Bill Megalli[1]

CHAPTER OBJECTIVES

After studying this chapter, you should be able to:

- *Describe* the objectives of indirect compensation.

- *Explain* how government furthers employee security and which major Canadian laws relate to it.

- *Identify* policies that minimize benefit costs.

- *Explain* the key issues in designing pension plans.

- *Identify* the administrative problems of employee benefits and services and suggest improvements.

- *Cite* benefits and services that are likely to become more common in the future.

EMPLOYEE BENEFITS

TO MANY PEOPLE, compensation means pay. Anything else an employer might provide is often considered so minor that it is called a "fringe benefit." As a matter of fact, most employers now make benefits an important part of the total compensation package and use them increasingly as a tool to attract, motivate, and retain key personnel. Some employers even go so far as to tailor-make benefit packages for individual employees to satisfy their special needs.

"Did you receive another job offer?" Carla asked her brother.

"Yes. I received a letter yesterday from a bank in Vancouver. That's my problem; I don't know which to accept," Ed responded. "The pay, working conditions, and job duties are almost identical. The people I met at both banks seem equally pleasant."

"What about fringe benefits?" Carla asked.

"What about them? They're only the extras. They don't make much difference," Ed answered.

"They don't make much difference? Are you kidding?" Carla questioned. "Some companies spend half as much on benefits as they do on wages."

"Now who's kidding? They're just fringes," Ed asserted.

"I'm not kidding. Let me give you an example. Suppose one bank pays all your supplementary health and life insurance and the other pays half. At a cost of $1000 a year, you would be $600 better off with the bank that pays all of your benefits," Carla said confidently.

Ed interrupted, "You mean $500."

"Don't forget taxes," Carla added. "To pay your half of the $1000 you would have to come up with $500, true. But to have $500, you would probably have to earn $600 before taxes. And that is $50 a month."

"Maybe I should find out more about their benefits before I decide," Ed pondered.

When employees such as Ed ignore benefits and services, they exclude from consideration all other forms of compensation except pay. Admittedly, pay is a major concern to employees. But since the typical organization spends a considerable share of its labour costs on benefits and services, ignorance such as Ed's raises questions about the role of pay and benefits. Simply put, what is the difference between pay and benefits?

Pay is called *direct compensation* because it is based on critical job factors or performance. Benefits and services are *indirect compensation* because they are usually extended as a condition of employment and are not directly related to performance. They include insurance, income security, time off, and scheduling benefits, in addition to educational, financial, and social services.

To explain the broad scope of benefits and services, this chapter discusses the objectives of indirect compensation. We follow this with an examination of legally required benefits. The chapter concludes with a description of voluntary benefit programs.

THE ROLE OF INDIRECT COMPENSATION

EMPLOYEE BENEFITS and services seek to satisfy several objectives. These include societal, organizational, and employee objectives.

Societal Objectives

Industrial societies have changed from rural nations of independent farmers and small businesses to urban nations of interdependent wage earners. This interdependence was illustrated forcefully by the mass unemployment of the Great

benefits.org

www.ifebp.org

Depression of the 1930s. Since that time, industrial societies have sought group solutions to societal problems.

To solve social problems and provide security for interdependent wage earners, governments rely on the support of employers. Through favourable tax treatment, employees can receive most benefits tax-free, while employers can deduct the cost of benefits as a regular business expense. The result has been a rapid growth in indirect compensation since the Second World War.

Today, benefits and services give many employees financial security against illness, disability, and retirement. In fact, the growth of benefits since the Second World War means that the average employer spends more than one-third of its payroll costs on benefits and services. No longer are benefits those "little extras" or "fringes." These outlays are a major and growing cost of doing business. As seen in Figure 11-1, the importance of such outlays has grown dramatically during the last 20 years. If this trend continues, benefits and services could amount to over one-half of most firms' payroll costs in the 1990s.

Organizational Objectives

From these large outlays for benefits, what do employers gain? Companies must offer some benefits if they are to be able to recruit successfully in the labour market. If a company did not offer retirement plans and paid vacations, recruits and present employees would work for competitors that did offer these "fringes." Similarly, many employees will stay with a company because they do not want to give up benefits, so employee turnover is lowered. For example, employees may stay to save pension credits or their rights to the extended vacations that typically come with greater seniority.

Vacations, along with holidays and rest breaks, help employees reduce fatigue and may enhance productivity during the hours the employees do work. Similarly, retirement, health-care, and disability benefits may allow workers to be more productive by freeing them from concern about medical and retirement costs. Likewise, if these benefits were not available to employees, they might elect to form a union and collectively bargain with the employer. (Although collective action is legal, many

FIGURE 11-1

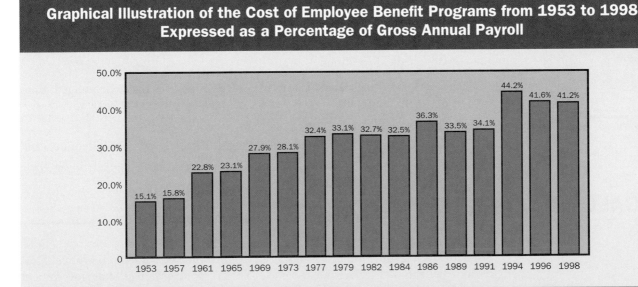

Source: Watson Wyatt Consulting, "32nd Annual Canadian Salary Survey," used with permission.

nonunion employers prefer to remain nonunion.) Therefore, it is accurate to state that indirect compensation may:

- reduce fatigue;
- discourage labour unrest;
- satisfy employee objectives;
- aid recruitment;
- reduce turnover; and
- minimize overtime costs.

Employee Objectives

Employees usually seek employer-provided benefits and services because of lower costs and availability. For example, company insurance benefits usually are less expensive because the employer may pay some or all of the costs. Even when the workers must pay the entire premium, rates are often lower because group plans save the insurer the administrative and selling costs of many individual policies. With group plans, the insurer also can reduce the adverse selection of insuring just those who need the insurance. Actuaries—the specialists who compute insurance rates— can pass these savings on to policyholders in the form of lower premiums.

Lower income taxes are another employee objective. For example, an employee in a 20 per cent tax bracket must earn $1000 to buy an $800 policy. But for $1000, the employer can buy the same insurance policy and give the worker a $200 raise. After taxes, the employee can keep $160 and the policy, while the employer is no worse off. And in many cases, the "buying power" of the company can allow it to negotiate a lower cost for the insurance policy. So the policy might cost only $600 instead of $800. Added to the $200 raise, the employer's outlays are only $800. By paying the employee to buy his or her own policy, the cost would have been $1000.

When the employer pays for a benefit, the employee achieves the benefit of partially being protected from inflation. For example, a two-week paid vacation is not reduced in value by inflation. The employee still receives two weeks off with pay. Or if a completely employer-paid insurance premium rises from $800 to $900, the worker is protected (although pay raises may be smaller since the employer has less money available for pay).

For some employees, the primary objective may be to obtain benefits and services—especially supplementary health and life insurance. Without employer-provided insurance, these policies may not be obtainable if the employee has a pre-existing medical condition.

The objectives of society, organizations, and employees have encouraged rapid growth of benefits and services. This growth has affected all areas of benefits and services, including insurance, income security, and time-off benefits.

www.ifebp.org/
pbbengen.html

There are two types of benefits and services: those that are legally required and those that employers voluntarily give. This chapter will focus first on the required type.

LEGALLY REQUIRED BENEFITS

LEGALLY REQUIRED benefits and services are imposed upon organizations by the government. As a result, employers must comply with the law and its procedures. Most of these benefits and services are designed to help employees. In general, government seeks to ensure minimum levels of financial security for the nation's work force. Figure 11-2 shows that the objective of providing financial security is to ease the monetary

FIGURE 11-2

Sources of Financial Protection for Workers		
Protection for Workers	**Sources of Protection**	**Legislating Government**
	Financial Security	
Fair remuneration	Minimum wage acts	Federal and provincial
Retirement	Canada Pension Plan	Federal (except in Quebec)
Involuntary unemployment	Employment Insurance	Federal
Industrial accidents	Workers' compensation acts	Federal and provincial
Medical care	Health insurance plans	Provincial
Child sustenance	Family Allowances	Federal

burdens of retirement, death, long-term disability, and unemployment. The loss of income from these causes is cushioned by the security provisions. The financial problems of *involuntary unemployment* are lessened by unemployment compensation. And job-related injuries and death are compensated under workers' compensation laws. None of these programs fully reimburses the affected workers; nevertheless, each worker does get a financial base to which additional protection can be added.

Legally required benefits and services are important to the human resource department for two reasons. First, top management holds the human resource department responsible for meeting these legal obligations. If the department is to meet this responsibility, it must ensure that the firm is in compliance with the law. Second, if the obligations are improperly handled, the result can be severe fines and more taxes. None of these outcomes contributes to the organization's objectives.

FINANCIAL SECURITY

Canada Pension Plan (CPP)
A mandatory, contributory, and portable pension plan applicable to all self-employed persons and employees in Canada, except those working for the federal government.

Contributory plans
Benefits that require the employer to contribute to the cost of the benefit.

Portability clauses
Allow accumulated pension rights to be transferred to another employer when an employee changes employers.

A LARGE MAJORITY of Canadians are financially dependent on their monthly pay-cheques. Only a small percentage of the population is self-employed; most others work for another person or organization. To protect the well-being of society, governmental regulations on retirement plans, employment insurance, disability compensation, and health care are imperative. The major legal provisions concerning the above matters will be discussed below. It should be emphasized that in Canada (unlike in the United States or in some other western countries), many of these regulations are provincially administered. To suit the specific work environments, many of these statutes and provisions vary from province to province.

The Canada Pension Plan (CPP) and the Quebec Pension Plan (QPP)

The *Canada Pension Plan (CPP)* (Quebec Pension Plan in the province of Quebec), which came into effect on January 1, 1966, is a mandatory plan for all self-employed persons and employees in Canada. Both CPP and QPP are *contributory plans*; that is, both the employer and the employee pay part of the costs. *Portability clauses* are applicable to the plans in Canada, meaning that pension rights are not affected by changes of job or residence. The plans are also tied to cost-of-living changes.

www.cbsc.org/english/
search/display.cfm?
Code=1468&Coll=
FE_FEDSBIS_E

www.drhc.gc.ca/isp/
cpp/soc/soc_e.shtml

CPP and QPP pay retirement pensions, disability pensions, and pensions for surviving spouses. They also pay lump-sum death benefits to eligible applicants, benefits to children of disabled contributors, and orphans' benefits where applicable. The tax-deductible contributions to both plans in 2000 were 7.8 per cent (to increase to 9.9 by 2003) of the total employee earnings, shared equally by employer and employee, up to a yearly maximum pensionable earning that is approximately the average industrial earning ($37 600 in 2000). Self-employed persons must pay the full contribution. The requirement for receiving a pension in Canada is being 65 years old (or 60 if not working) and having made contributions for at least one year. The retirement pension is approximately 25 per cent of the employee's average pensionable earnings. Recent changes include the flexibility to draw the CPP pension between age 60 and 70 with appropriate adjustments, and the possible splitting of the CPP pension following separation of legal or common-law spouses.

Since CPP and QPP provide retirees with only 25 per cent of their average pensionable earnings as pension benefits, supplementary payments are available from the federal government through Old Age Security (OAS) and Guaranteed Income Supplements (GIS). OAS is a monthly benefit paid to all persons 65 years of age and over; it is not necessary to be retired to be eligible for OAS. GIS was set up mainly for those who retired prior to the enactment of the CPP and were therefore ineligible for CPP. It is a basic supplement to other over-65 income. GIS and OAS are tied to the cost of living and will increase with the consumer price index. These additional benefits are designed to provide retirees with a guaranteed minimum income. To increase their pension benefits further, employees must turn to private pension plans.

On July 1, 1996, a clawback law was enacted that reduces OAS payments proportionally from 15 to 100 per cent if a pensioner has a net income exceeding $53 215 (in 2000). Since then OAS benefits have been reduced at the time of payment to reflect the clawback. The implications are that pensioners with supplementary income from private pension plans may lose the full amount of OAS.[2]

As of late 1999 and early 2000, the federal government and the provinces of British Columbia, Ontario, and Quebec include same-sex partners in the definition of spouse. The other provinces are expected to follow.[3]

Evaluation

Whether the government or private industry should plan and administer pensions is a question that has been debated for some time. However, any welfare society has to take care of its old, disadvantaged, and poor. It should also be noted that CPP is much greater in scope than an old-age pension plan and provides for other contingencies not usually covered by common pension plans. On these dimensions CPP and QPP have indeed played a crucial role in the past.[4]

Employment Insurance (EI)

Employment Insurance (EI)
A program to help alleviate the monetary problems of workers in Canada during the transition from one job to another.

In 1940, Canada started a program of Unemployment Insurance (UI), renamed *Employment Insurance* (EI) in 1995, to help alleviate people's monetary problems during the transition from one job to another. The Unemployment Insurance Act of 1971 significantly changed and added to the program. Since 1971 there have been several modifications to eligibility criteria and payment schedules. Currently, approximately 11 million Canadians are covered by the scheme. Most salaried and hourly workers who are employed for a minimum number of hours, depending on regional unemployment rates, are covered by EI. Self-employed persons are not eligible for benefits under the present regulations.

www.cbsc.org/english/
search/display.cfm?Code=2
769&Coll=FE_FEDS
BIS_E

www.hrdc-drhc.gc.ca/
ei/common/home.shtml

www.hrdc-drhc.gc.ca/
dept/guide/ei2.shtml

www.hrdc-drhc.gc.ca/
ei/legis/tcbepe.htm

www.nationalpost.com/

The new Employment Insurance Act will be implemented in two stages over six years, to be fully implemented in 2001-02. It has been fundamentally restructured. Key features are:

- benefits based on hours rather than on weeks worked;
- collection of premiums based on first dollar earned;
- reduction in the maximum benefit entitlement period;
- increased eligibility requirements for people entering the labour market;
- reduction in benefit rate based on an individual's claim history
- a family income supplement top-up for claimants in low-income families, and
- a lower income threshold for the clawback of benefits

To qualify for the benefits, an employee needs 420 to 700 hours of work, depending on the unemployment rate in a specific area. There are a few exceptions to these rules: if one entered the workforce the first time or is re-entering after an absence of two years, one needs a maximum of 910 hours of work; if one applies for sickness, maternity, or parental benefits, 700 hours of work are needed. (See homepage in margin for details.)

Benefits and Premiums

The benefit rate is 55 per cent of the average insured earnings of an employee up to a maximum of $750 (2000) per week. Low-income families (income less than $25 921) with children may receive up to 80 per cent. If EI has been claimed before, then a lower rate applies. Benefits can be received between 14 and 45 weeks, depending on number of hours worked in last 52 weeks and regional unemployment rate. Employees who quit their job without just cause, or are dismissed for misconduct, are ineligible.

http://www.hrdc-
drhc.gc.ca/dept/guide/ei2.
shtml

Electronic copies of the Employment Insurance system are available on the Internet.

Evaluation

Many believe that EI rules should be tightened. Some suggestions have been made to extend the minimum work period before a person can collect EI payments and to reduce the benefits as well as the benefit period (currently, in 2001, a maximum of 45 weeks). It is also contended by some that EI eliminates all incentive to work. The Macdonald Commission in 1985 and the Forget Commission in 1986 investigated the present system and made suggestions for significant changes regarding financing and eligibility.[5] It took the government nine years to make some significant changes. It is interesting to note that research indicates increased benefits result in higher unemployment levels.[6]

More information on Canadian benefits is available on the Internet.

Workers' Compensation Acts

Workers' compensation
Compensation payable by employers collectively for injuries sustained by workers in the course of their employment.

All 10 provinces and two territories (Nunavut is still under federal jurisdiction) have some act or other (usually called "Workers' Compensation Act" or "Ordinance") that entitles workers to **workers' compensation** in the event of personal injury by accident during their regular work (in Ontario, on January 1, 1998, the Workers' Compensation Act was replaced by the Workplace Safety and Insurance Act, with reductions in benefits and limits to entitlement). The administration is done provincially, and all the provincial acts are of the "collective liability" type: that is, compensation is payable by employers collectively. The industries covered by the act are classified into groups according to their special hazards, and all employers in each group are collectively liable for payment of compensation to all workers employed in that group. The annual contribution rate (a percentage of payroll) is determined on the basis of an employer's total annual payroll figures. However, an employer can also be charged a higher rate of contribution if there are many workers' compensation claims.

Benefits

http://benefits.org/

www.gov.on.ca/LAB/leg/
bill99e.pdf

http://info.load-otea
.hrdc-drhc.gc.ca/~fwcsweb/
homeen.shtml

Various types of benefits are available under the workers' compensation legislation: protection against accidents as a result of accident-prevention activities of the Workers' Compensation Board or employers' associations; first-aid and all necessary medical aid, including hospitalization; cash benefits during the period of disablement (typically 75 per cent of wages subject to an annual wage ceiling); rehabilitation (physical and vocational); and a pension available for life for any resulting permanent disability. When disablement is slight, a lump-sum payment is made.[7] In the case of a fatal accident, cash benefits are provided for the spouse and dependent children of the deceased employee.

The right of an employee to compensation is not affected by the employer's neglect or refusal to furnish information or to pay its assessment, or by its insolvency.[8] Also, the employee's right to compensation may not be assigned without board approval, and it cannot be waived or attached. All claims for compensation are received and adjudicated by the Workers' Compensation Board, whose decision is final (except in the four Atlantic provinces, where appeals are allowed).

Employer's Liability

As noted, all the provincial acts, and that of the Yukon Territory, are of the "collective liability" type—compensation is payable by employers collectively. However, an individual liability act is still in force in the Northwest Territories. In addition to the collective liability laws, there are laws of individual liability that provide for payment of compensation by particular employers. For all types of employment in the shipping industry, for example, the Merchant Seamen Compensation Act assigns

Workers' compensation covers a wide variety of benefits including rehabilitation treatments, cash benefits during disablement, and life-long pensions for permanent disabilities.

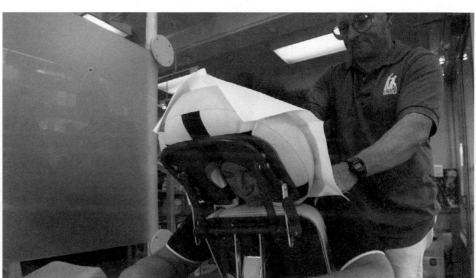

CP PHOTO ARCHIVE (Emile Wamsteker)

responsibility to individual employers. Similarly, while most industries in Ontario and Quebec are under the collective liability system, certain large corporations are individually liable to pay compensation. Part II of the acts in British Columbia, Manitoba, New Brunswick, Nova Scotia, Ontario, and Prince Edward Island specify industries wherein individual employer liability exists. Finally, compensation for federal government employees is covered under a separate enactment, the Government Employees Compensation Act.*

There is a trend in most provinces to remove health and safety provisions from the Workers' Compensation Board and place them under a separate industrial safety or occupational health and safety division. British Columbia, Prince Edward Island, and the Yukon, however, continue to place occupational health and safety under the compensation board. In almost all cases the occupational health and safety jurisdiction of the board comes under the heading "accident prevention." In Nova Scotia, Newfoundland, and the Northwest Territories, concurrent powers are shared between the board and the occupational health and safety authorities.

Health Insurance Plans

Canada's health and medical insurance is provided by provincial governments with assistance from the federal government. In April 1972, the scope of the Medical Care Act of 1966 was widened to include all of Canada. Since then, a major part of the cost of medical care has been paid for by taxes collected at the federal level.

Health insurance
Health and medical insurance provided by provincial governments with assistance from the federal government.

In addition to the provincial health insurance, group life and disability insurance is widely provided as an employee benefit in Canada. *Health insurance* takes care of the cost of hospitalization (room and board and hospital service charges), surgery, and other major medical goods and services. Some firms still offer major medical insurance for their employees whenever they travel outside the province or country. Increasingly, many organizations have also been providing dental insurance to their employees. In many cases, the cost of health and dental premiums is shared between the employer and the employee.

Managing Health Benefits

To keep ballooning health costs under control, William M. Mercer, a benefit consulting company, recommends that employers take the following measures:

www.benefitscanada
.com/health.html

www.wmmercer.com/

- Instead of having a set employee-paid deductible, ask staff to pay 20 per cent of any treatment.

- Stop out-of-country medical coverage for personal travel, or set a 30-day limit or a dollar maximum.

- Remember that many dental plans were designed in pre-fluoride days. Six-month checkups may not be necessary anymore.

- Where they are available, pay only for generic drugs, thus saving an average of six per cent on drug plans.

- With "maintenance drugs," such as birth control pills, ask employees to get larger amounts to save on dispensing fees.

An employer who builds a series of these alternatives into its benefit plans could probably save 15 per cent of costs.[9]

---

*It should be noted that in the fall of 1997, Ontario replaced the Workers' Compensation Act with the Workplace Safety and Insurance Act, with most provisions effective January 1, 1998, including reductions in benefits (to 85 per cent of net earnings) and limits to entitlement.

VOLUNTARY BENEFITS

Insurance Benefits

Insurance benefits spread the financial risks encountered by employees and their families. These risks are shared by pooling funds in the form of insurance premiums. Then, when an insured risk occurs, the covered employees or their families are compensated.

Life Insurance

Life insurance was the first form of insurance offered to workers by employers. As a result, group life insurance has become a practically universal element in corporate employee benefit programs. Several surveys show that 99 per cent of Canadian companies provide a group life insurance program for all of their employees.[10] There are two types of plans. Under the first, the deceased's family receives a lump-sum payment. Under the second, the family receives a generally lower lump sum than in the first case, plus a survivor's pension payable to the deceased's spouse for life. This amount is supplemented by family allowance benefits, CCP benefits, workers' compensation if the death is caused by a work-related accident or illness, and, in certain provinces, automobile insurance act benefits if death is the result of a traffic accident.

Employers generally pay the cost of these life-insurance plans. Coverage is commonly based on the employee's pay, often 100 per cent or 200 per cent of annual pay. Optional expanded coverage is usually available.

www.dentalplans.com/
frequentlyaskedquestions
.htm

Health-Related Insurance

In Canada, all citizens are covered by provincial health-care programs that pay for basic hospital care and offer comprehensive coverage for medically required services of physicians, surgeons, and other qualified health professionals. For this reason, employers in Canada offer only supplementary health insurance plans. This is in contrast to the United States, where health insurance is the most common form of coverage.[11]

Five years ago dental insurance plans were one of the fastest-growing additions to the total benefit package. The demand has levelled off. According to the latest survey, 86 per cent of the employers who responded offered dental plans.[12] Such plans, most of which are custom-designed, are usually provided at three levels: (1) simple fillings, X-rays, and extractions; (2) major restorative work such as bridgework, dentures, and crowns; (3) orthodontic work. Provincial dental plans cover emergency dental services required as a result of accidents. In addition, many provinces provide a limited dental-care program for children.

Salary Continuation Plans

If an employee misses a few days because of illness, it is usually not crucial from a financial point of view, since most employers grant paid sick leave for a limited time. It becomes more of a problem when an employee becomes disabled for a longer period of time or even permanently. Canadian companies offer short-term disability and long-term disability plans.

Short-term disability plan
Crediting a number of days to be used as sick leave.

A *short-term disability* plan typically involves crediting or allocating a certain number of days to an employee, to be used as sick leave for nonoccupational accidents or illnesses. Sick-leave credits may be cumulative or noncumulative. A plan is cumulative if insured credits earned during one year may be transferred to the

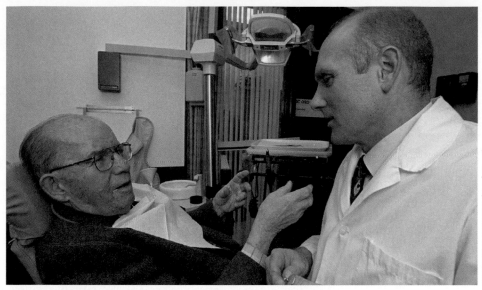

CP PHOTO ARCHIVE (Frank Gunn)

Dental insurance is a common benefit offered by many companies to their employees.

following year; it is noncumulative when the employee's entitlement is reviewed on a yearly basis or after each illness.

For workers who are disabled for a prolonged time, employers offer some form of **long-term disability insurance**. Such plans generally have a long waiting period (six months is very common), and they pay the employee a smaller amount (usually 50 or 60 per cent) of the income that working would have earned. Under most plans these payments, if necessary, are made until the normal retirement age is reached.

Long-term disability insurance
A benefit plan providing the employee with an income, in the case of long-term illness or injury.

EMPLOYEE SECURITY BENEFITS

IN ADDITION TO insurance, there are noninsurance benefits that enhance employee security. These benefits seek to ensure an income before and after retirement.

Employment Income Security

Discharges or layoffs may entail severe economic consequences for an employee; the impact, however, can be cushioned by employer-provided benefits. If employees have not been given at least two weeks' notice and if the dismissal was not for just cause, then according to the Canada Labour Code they are entitled to severance pay equal to two weeks' regular wages. For executives, who usually work on a contract basis, *severance pay* can reach six or twelve months' compensation.

Severance pay
Payment to a worker upon permanent separation from the company.

Layoffs may be eased by accrued vacation pay. A few companies go so far as to provide a **guaranteed annual wage (GAW)**. These plans assure the worker of receiving some minimum amount of work or pay. For example, employees may be promised a minimum of 1500 hours of work or pay a year (compare this with the "normal" 52, 40-hour weeks for a total of 2080 hours). Some employers guarantee 30 hours per week. Even on layoff, the employees draw some income.

Guaranteed annual wage (GAW)
An employer assures employees that they will receive a minimum annual income regardless of layoffs or a lack of work.

The auto industry is a leader in another method, *supplemental unemployment benefits (SUB)*. When employees are out of work, employment insurance benefits are supplemented by the employer from monies previously paid to the SUB fund. This assures covered employees an income almost equal to their previous earnings for as long as the SUB fund remains solvent.

Supplemental unemployment benefits (SUB)
Private plans providing compensation for wage loss to laid-off workers.

Retirement Security

Retirement plans were originally designed to reward long-service employees. Through employer generosity and union pressure, retirement plans have grown in scope and coverage, so that in Canada the average firm spends 6.3 per cent of its total payroll costs on government and private pension plans alone.[13]

Registered Pension Plans (RPP)

www.cbsc.org/english/
search/display.cfm?Code=1
524&Coll=FE_FEDSBIS_E

Defined benefit plans
Benefits defined by formula based on age and length of service, with employer assuming responsibility for funding.

Defined contribution plans
Based on amounts contributed by employer and employee, final pension depending on amounts contributed, investment income, and economic conditions at retirement.

Vesting
A provision in employer-provided retirement plans that give workers the right to a pension after a specified number of years of service.

Pension Benefits Standards Act
Federal act regulating pension plans in industries under the jurisdiction of the Government of Canada.

As of January 1999, 41 per cent of all Canadian employees are covered by RPPs, so called because they must be registered with Revenue Canada for preferential tax considerations.[14] Most employers contribute to such plans. Integrated RPPs—which make up approximately two-thirds of all RPPs—take into account benefits received from the Canada Pension Plan.[15]

Defined benefits plans. With a defined benefit pension plan, the employee receives a fixed dollar amount as a pension, depending on age and length of service. Many employees and unions prefer defined plans because of their predictable outcomes. These type of plans are also strictly regulated by the Employee Retirement Income Security Act.

Defined contribution plans. When employer and employee contribute to a pension plan, it is called a defined contribution plan; if only the employer makes the contributions, it is called a contributory plan. The employee makes a commitment to make regular payments into the plan, which are matched by the employer. A typical arrangement would be that the employee allows monthly or weekly deductions from his or her salary, say 5 per cent, and the employer either matches this amount or makes a higher contribution, up to a specific level. These amounts are usually invested in secure funds. After retirement the money is used to purchase an annuity or may be invested in other approved financial arrangements that pay a regular income to the retiree.

Two significant problems have developed in the administration of pension plans. First, some employers go out of business, leaving the pension plan unfunded or only partially funded. Second, some companies minimize their pension costs by having very long vesting periods. *Vesting* gives workers the right to pension benefits even if they leave the company. Thus, an employee who quits or is fired before the vesting period has passed often has no pension rights. Since both of these problems may impose hardships on employees and on the nation's welfare programs, Parliament has passed the *Pension Benefits Standards Act*.

Pension Benefits Standards Act

This act regulates pension plans in industries under the jurisdiction of the Government of Canada, such as banks, railways, shipping companies, and radio and other communication companies. In addition, eight provinces (Alberta, Saskatchewan, Manitoba, New Brunswick, Ontario, Quebec, Nova Scotia, and Newfoundland) have enacted their own pension benefits acts that in content are similar to the federal act. Pension plans in the remaining provinces, to qualify for tax deductions, must conform to certain standards set forth in the federal legislation. The Pension Benefits Standards Act requires that pension funds be held in trust for members, and that the funds not be held under the complete custody and control of either the employer or the employees. To accomplish this, the funding of a private pension plan must be carried out by one or more of the following means:

www.osfi-bsif.gc.ca/eng/
pensions/pensionregulations/
index.asp

- an insurance contract with a company authorized to conduct a life insurance business in Canada;

- a trust in Canada whose trustees are either a trust company or a group of individuals, at least three of whom live in Canada and one of whom must be independent of the employer and employees;

- a corporate pension society; and

- an arrangement administered by the Government of Canada or a provincial government.

PAID TIME-OFF BENEFITS

TIME PERIODS during which the employee is not working, but is getting paid, are the result of time-off benefits. Although time-off benefits may seem minor, according to one survey they were the costliest major category, comprising 11.2 per cent of gross annual payroll.[16]

On-the-Job Breaks

Some of the most common forms of time-off benefits are those found on the job. Examples include rest breaks, meal breaks, and wash-up time. Through a break in the physical and mental effort of a job, productivity may be increased. The major problem for human resource and line managers is the tendency of employees to stretch these time-off periods:

> When one human resource manager was confronted by a supervisor with the problem of stretched breaks, she suggested a simple solution. Each employee was assigned a specific break time—from 9:15 to 9:30 a.m., or 9:30 to 9:45 a.m., for example—but could not leave for break until the preceding employee returned. Since each clerk was anxious to go on break, the peer group policed the length of breaks and the stretched breaks ended.

Paid Sick Leave

Absences from work are unavoidable. Today, most companies pay workers when they are absent for medical reasons by granting a limited number of days of sick leave per year. Unfortunately, this is one of the most abused benefits; many workers take the attitude that these are simply extra days off. If the human resource policies prohibit employees from crediting unused sick leave to next year's account, absences increase near the end of the year. To minimize abuses, some companies require medical verifications of illness or pay employees for unused sick leave.

A few firms avoid the abuse question by granting "personal leave days." This approach allows an employee to skip work for any reason and get paid, up to a specified number of days per year. *Sick leave banks* allow employees to "borrow" extra days above the specified number when they use up their individual allocation. Then when they earn additional days, the days are repaid to the sick leave bank.

Holidays and Vacations

http://labour-travail.hrdc-drhc.gc.ca/policy/leg/e/stanf5-e2.html

Vacations are usually based on the employee's length of service, but federal and provincial laws specify a two-week (in Saskatchewan a three-week) minimum vacation entitlement. In some regions this increases to three weeks (in Saskatchewan four) after five, six, or ten years of service. Holidays are also federally and provincially regulated.[17] Like sick leave, however, this benefit is subject to abuse. Employees sometimes try to stretch the holiday by missing the workday before or after the holiday.

Policies that require attendance the day before and after a holiday as a condition of holiday pay lessen this problem. Figure 11-3 shows the federally regulated paid holidays in Canada.

Policies for vacations vary widely. Some companies allow employees to use vacation days a few at a time. Other companies insist that the worker take the vacation all at once. A few employers actually close down during designated periods and require vacations to be taken during this period. Still other companies negate the reason for vacations completely by allowing employees to work and then receive vacation pay as a bonus.

EMPLOYEE SERVICES

SOME COMPANIES go beyond pay and traditional benefits. They also provide educational, financial, and social services for their employees.

Educational Assistance

Tuition refund programs are among the more common employer services. These programs partially or completely reimburse employees for furthering their education. They may be limited only to courses that are related to the employee's job, or the employer may reimburse workers for any educational expenditure. In the future,

FIGURE 11-3

Federally Regulated Paid Holidays

Jurisdiction	Holidays	Pay for Holidays Not Worked	Exceptions	Pay for Holidays Worked
Federal Canada Labour Code and Labour Standards Regulations	New Year's Day, Good Friday, Victoria Day, Canada Day, Labour Day, Thanksgiving Day, Remembrance Day, Christmas Day, Boxing Day	An employee who is not entitled to wages for at least 15 days during the 30 days immediately preceding the holiday is entitled to 1/20th of the wages he has earned during those 30 days.	No pay for holiday not worked if: 1) holiday occurs during first 30 days of employment; or 2) employee is working by virtue of a permit establishing hours of work in excess of eight in a day or 40 in a week under the Code. Continuous operations: 1) same as 1) above; 2) employee did not report for work after having been called to work on that holiday; or 3) is unavailable to work on that holiday in contravention to his contract of employment.	Regular pay + $1\frac{1}{2}$ times regular rate. Continuous operations: regular pay + a) $1\frac{1}{2}$ times regular rate; or b) another day off with pay; or c) pay for next non-working day.

more companies may follow the lead of Kimberly-Clark Corporation in the United States:

> Kimberly-Clark created an educational savings account for employees and their dependants. The company gives employees credits for each year of service. Then when an employee or dependant wants to go to college, he or she can be reimbursed partially from the educational savings account established by the company.

www.princeton.edu
/hr/ben/staffed.htm

www.uoguelph.ca/
HR/CUPE1334.htm#Article
%20XV

www.kimberly-clark.com/

Financial Services

Probably the oldest service is employee discount plans. These programs—common among retail stores and consumer goods manufacturers—allow workers to buy products from the company at a discount.

Credit unions are another well-established employee service. The interest collected by the credit union on loans and investments is distributed to members in the form of dividends. The dividends (interest payments) are allocated in proportion to the amount employees have in their share (savings) account. The lower interest rate on loans, the higher interest on deposits, and payroll deductions for savings or loan repayments are the major employee advantages.

Stock purchase programs are another financial service. These plans enable employees to buy company stock—usually through payroll deductions. In some stock purchase programs, employee outlays may be matched by company contributions.

Social Services

Employers provide a wide range of social services. At one extreme are simple interest groups such as bowling leagues and softball teams. At the other extreme are comprehensive *employee assistance programs* designed to assist employees with personal problems:

Employee assistance programs
Comprehensive company program that seeks to help employees overcome their personal and work-related problems.

> A large bank had a high turnover rate among its entry-level workers. After study, it appeared that many new workers had problems with transportation, housing, child care, and so on. These difficulties were sometimes insurmountable for employees, and they would quit. To combat this situation, the bank created its "Contact" program. Each employee was informed of the program and given the telephone number to call whenever a work- or nonwork-related problem occurred. Then, when employees had child-care or transportation difficulties, they would call the Contact number. The Contact staff provided individual counselling or a referral service by informing employees of groups in the community that could help them. The program was not limited to just new employees, however. To help build better employee relations, the Contact staff tried to assist with all types of employee problems. This involved the staff in resolving employee quarrels, advising managers of employee complaints, and even helping workers solve family disputes.

Employee assistance programs like the one at this bank are becoming more common. Human resource managers realize that employee problems affect company performance.[18] Employer services that can lessen these problems offer potential dividends in employee performance, loyalty, and reduced turnover.

One employer service with a growing record of success is alcohol and drug rehabilitation. For example, human resource experts formerly recommended the discharge of alcoholic workers. During the last 10 years, however, an increasing number of human resource departments have implemented *alcohol and drug rehabilitation programs*. This service has saved many otherwise good employees in companies such as Canadian National Railways and General Motors of Canada. When rehabilitation has been effected, the company usually gains a hardworking, loyal employee:

www.benefits.org/ (search
for cap)

www.fgiworld.com/
eap.htm

www.relocatecanada
.com/

www.kenevacorp.mb.ca/
relocate.htm

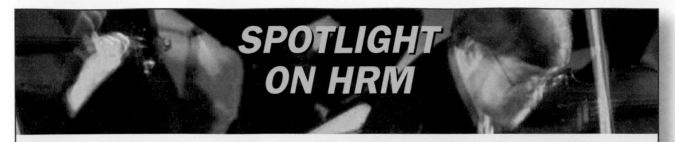

SPOTLIGHT ON HRM

WOMEN'S WORK

By Kathryn Dorrell

Juggling the roles of mom, daughter, wife and employee are taking their toll as women's absenteeism outpaces men's. Plan sponsors can implement strategies that acknowledge this reality.

A recent profile of Barbara Stymiest, president and chief executive officer of the Toronto Stock Exchange, in a prominent business magazine discussed the executive's demanding hours in the context of the fact that she has a young daughter. As the mom of an 18-month-old, I was interested in how Stymiest juggled a career and family. But at the same time, I couldn't help bristle at the realization that discussions of businessmen who also happen to be dads seldomly delve into this territory.

Balancing work and family life isn't the juggling act for most working men that it is for women. This seemingly sexist statement is a reality in many organizations, and it's backed up by a new Statistics Canada report, Women in Canada 2000.

In 1999, three times as many working women took time off to deal with personal and family issues than men. Female workers missed an average of seven days because of such commitments—up from two days in the mid-'70s—whereas working men missed one day, about the same as two decades ago. Meanwhile, 28% of women worked fewer than 30 hours a week compared to 10% of men, and 20% of these women say they did so because of personal and family responsibilities.

Putting some hard numbers behind the old adage that a woman's work is never done isn't about male bashing or even trying to change what are obviously still ingrained societal trends. (No, I'm not about to suggest that plan sponsors offer lunch-and-learn sessions teaching dads how to take their sick babies to the doctor.) With a growing number of women dominating the workforce—46% in 1999, up from 37% in 1976—and in increasingly senior positions, it simply makes good business sense for plan sponsors to acknowledge and confront this issue.

The Royal Bank has done just that. Three-quarters of its employees are women and it has implemented the kind of progressive benefits strategies that not only keep talented female employees in the working world but help them climb the proverbial ladder, even if it's with a baby or two and an aging parent in tow.

The bank offers leaves, that have ranged from one day to a year and are sometimes paid, for employees to deal with family matters. In addition, 30% of all employees are currently enjoying some sort of flexible working arrangement—be it flex hours or job sharing. And if a supervisor doesn't appear to be supportive of these initiatives, workers can take up the issue using an employee ombudsman phone service

Norma Tombari, manager of workforce solutions at the Royal Bank, believes that if the company didn't offer these programs it would lose many of its best workers to the competition. "I would love to see more men using these options," she adds. "But right now it's mostly women."

Another beacon of progress is the arrival of Catalyst on the Canadian consulting scene. The New York-based firm, which opened a Toronto office recently and has worked with Bell Canada, specializes in identifying barriers and opportunities for women in the workplace.

However, the best benefit for working women may actually be as simple as creating a work environment and communications strategy that conveys the message that organizations recognize men have personal and family commitments too.

"There is still such a stigma around men taking time off for family matters. It's a huge cultural shift that men are trying to fight. They don't want to say they can't stay for the 5 p.m. meeting because they have to pick up the kids for fear of how they will be viewed," says Judy Hauserman, senior vice-president at Aon Consulting. "If we approach this issue from only a gender perspective, we miss the point."

Kathryn Dorrell is associate editor with BENEFITS CANADA. kdorrell@rmpublishing.com.

CN spends over $1 million annually on employee assistance programs (EAPs), which includes an alcohol and drug rehabilitation program. The latter had been initially an internally managed project, but was outsourced in 1996 to a national rehabilitation service provider. The program is controlled by 20 committees across Canada, made up of CN managers, employees, and a representative of the service provider, to ensure a high standard of quality service to CN employees. Although an exact figure is not available, an evaluation study is in progress. Sheila Hagen-Bloxham, the western region coordinator of CN EAPs, states the benefits of the program far outweigh its expenses.[19]

Relocation programs
A company-sponsored benefit that assists employees who must move in connection with their job.

Relocation programs are the support in dollars or services a company provides to its transferred or new employees. At a minimum, this benefit includes payment for moving expenses. Some employees receive fully paid house-hunting trips with their spouse to the new location before the move, subsidized home mortgages, placement assistance for working spouses, and even family counselling to reduce the stress of the move. A transferred employee also may be able to sell his or her home to the employer for the appraised value in order to avoid having to sell it on the market.[20]

Employee assistance programs have traditionally involved personal interaction, especially if they were concerned with counselling services, and face-to-face communication was important. However, with the advancement of technology, especially the Internet, and the ease of access, employers have developed new ways to respond to their employees' needs faster and more effectively and efficiently. The most prominent of the recent developments in this field is the *online service delivery*. The scope of possibilities is vast: opportunities for live chat rooms, one-on-one video counselling, group-help bulletin boards, and online self-help applications are the tip of the technological iceberg for employee assistance programs. The goal of online assistance programs is not to replace counselling. Rather, for most people the move toward online services is viewed as an enhancement to services already offered.[21]

Onkine service delivery
EAP services available to employees through the Internet and intranet.

www.bnefits.org/interface
/benfit.eap.thm

Additional employee assistance activities are discussed in Chapter Thirteen in connection with counselling.

MANAGEMENT OF VOLUNTARY BENEFIT AND SERVICE PROGRAMS

A SERIOUS shortcoming of human resource management has been poor management of indirect compensation. Even in otherwise well-managed human resource departments, benefits and services have grown in a haphazard manner. Those costly supplements were introduced in response to social trends, union demands, employee pressures, and management wishes, and so human resource departments seldom established objectives, systematic plans, and standards to determine the appropriateness of benefits and services. This patchwork of benefits and services has caused several problems.

Problems in Administration

The central problem in supplementary compensation is a lack of employee involvement. Once a benefit program is designed by the human resource department and the labour union (if there is one), employees have little discretion. For example, pension and maternity benefits usually are granted to all workers equally. Younger employees view pensions as distant and largely irrelevant; older workers find maternity benefits are not needed. This uniformity fails to recognize individual differences and wishes. Admittedly, uniformity leads to administrative and actuarial economies; but when employees receive benefits they neither want nor need, these economies are questionable.

Since employees have little choice in their individual benefit package, most workers are unaware of all the benefits to which they are entitled:

> Two researchers designed a study to learn how knowledgeable selected workers were about their benefits. In two different plants—one with a union and one without—they asked employees to list all the benefits that they could recall. The average worker could not recall 15 per cent of the employer-provided benefits.[22]

Ignorance and the inability to influence the mix of benefits often lead to pressure from employees for more benefits to meet their needs. For example, older workers may request improved retirement plans, while younger workers seek improved insurance coverage of dependants. Often the result is a proliferation of benefits and increased employer costs. These costs, which represented 15.1 per cent of an employer's gross annual payroll in 1953, escalated to 41.2 per cent in 1998, an increase of 173 per cent.[23] Still, employee ignorance and confusion can lead to complaints and dissatisfaction about their benefit package.

Traditional Remedies

www.benefitscanada.com/C
ontent/2000/0600/01.html

www.wmmercer.com/

The traditional remedy to benefit problems has been to increase employee awareness, usually through publicizing employee benefits. This publicity starts with orientation sessions that explain the benefit programs and provide employee handbooks. Company newspapers, special mailings, employee meetings, bulletin-board announcements, and responses to employee questions are also used to further publicize the organization's benefit package:

> William M. Mercer Ltd., a large consulting firm specializing in compensation and benefit issues, with branches in 12 cities in Canada, offers seminars to recipients of benefits and training courses to compensation officers. However, publicizing the benefits and services attacks only the symptoms of the problem: lack of employee interest. Moreover, this reactive approach further adds to the costs of administration through increased "advertising" expenses.

A Proactive Solution: Cafeteria Benefits

Cafeteria benefit programs
Programs that allow employees to select the mix of benefits and services that will answer their individual needs.

www.benefits.org

Cafeteria benefit programs, or flexible benefit programs, allow employees to select benefits and services that match their individual needs. Workers are provided a benefit and services account with a specified number of dollars in the account. Through deductions from this account, employees "shop" for specific benefits from among those offered by the employer. The types and prices of benefits are provided to each employee in the form of a computer printout. This cost sheet also describes each benefit. Then, as illustrated in Figure 11-4, employees select their package of benefits and services for the coming year.

Figure 11-4 indicates how two different workers might spend the $3845 the company grants each worker. Workers A and B select two different sets of benefits because their personal situations differ dramatically. Worker A is a young parent who is supporting a family and her husband. A dental plan will assist in defraying the high expenses for dental work, especially if they plan to have another child. Worker B allocated fewer dollars for weekly income benefits. Instead, he put a large portion of his

FIGURE 11-4

Hypothetical Benefit Selection of Two Different Workers

Worker A

Age 27, female, married with one child. Husband in graduate school.

Worker B

Age 56, male, married with two grown and and married children. Wife does not work outside the home.

Worker A		Worker B
$345	Supplemental dental insurance	$0
	Supplemental health insurance:	
245	Maternity	0
935	$100 deductible	0
0	Prescription drug coverage	625
	Life insurance:	
100	$20 000 for worker	100
150	$10 000 for spouse	0
600	Vacations	900
300	Holidays	300
200	Pension plan	1615
0	Jury duty pay	0
100	Disability insurance	100
870	Weekly income benefit	205
$3845	Total	$3845

benefit monies into the company pension plan. Although this approach creates additional administrative costs and an obligation for the human resource department to advise employees, there are several advantages. The main advantage is employee participation. Through participation, employees come to understand exactly what benefits the employer is offering and employees can better match their benefits with their needs.[24] See also the Web page for flexible benefit programs.

Flexible benefits, until recently, have offered the usual choices of better long-term disability insurance, dental or vision care, prescription drug coverage, life insurance, group legal services, and so on, but it has become now more common that employers offer the opportunity to "purchase" more vacation. Not only this, but it is even possible to sell vacation time.[25] In the past, cafeteria plans often had different choices for single and married employees. The trend now is to offer the choices independent of marital status.

Technology is changing the way companies handle flexible benefits enrollment and communication. In the early days, paper enrollment forms and written communication pieces were the norm. While paper still plays a role in the process, in many companies interactive voice response systems (IVRs) and Web-based technologies are becoming the norm for the administration of flexible benefit plans, making the communication process more effective.[26]

Canadian Blue Cross offers now Health Spending Account administration services for companies with flexible benefit plans. It saves these companies the headaches of administering the plans and claims to be cheaper than if the company managed the plan on its own.[27]

www.benefits.org

www.flexaccounts.com/

www.padmin.com/benefit.html

www.bluecross.ca

Implications for Human Resource Management

The amount of change experienced in the field of employee benefits has been dramatic over the last decade. Retirement plans have been and are under constant legal review, tax reforms have added complexity, health-care policies have changed and their expenses gone up, all adding to the responsibilities of the human resource professional. Advances in computer hardware technology and the tremendous growth in the range of "friendly" software have resulted in human resource practitioners being able to develop their own applications.

To find the right approach for the administration of benefit plans, a needs analysis is an essential first step. The analysis should deal with five basic questions:

- What tasks need to be performed, how often, and how quickly?

- Who currently performs these tasks, and what does it cost now to perform them (including internal as well as external costs)?

- What alternative ways of performing these tasks are possible and practical?

- What will each alternative cost both to install and to maintain?

- How long will it take to implement each option, and can the implementation ever be truly completed?

The objective of the needs analysis is to identify the best administrative methodology to meet both the short- and long-term needs of the employer. The result of the analysis should be a report that can be used by decision-makers as a reference document against which a detailed implementation process can be tested.

The implications of financial security plans for human resource departments are several. First, human resource managers should make sure that the firm adheres to all provisions relating to minimum wages and pension deductions. For example, the Canada Labour Code requires every employer to furnish, from time to time, information relating to employee wages, hours of work, general holidays, annual vacations, and conditions of employment. As well, the Canada Labour Standards regulations require that each employee's social insurance number, sex, and occupational classification be recorded and kept ready for inspection. Accurate records of maternity leave, overtime, and termination should also be maintained.

Second, to avoid duplication, human resource managers need to consider CPP and other benefits available to employees when designing their firm's own benefit and service plans. In many provinces, some of the items included in private group insurance plans are already covered under the workers' compensation and health insurance plans.

Often, workers are only vaguely aware of these compensation laws and even less aware of their rights. Consider the comments one employee made to a human resource specialist:

> It really came as a surprise to me to learn that the province would pay me only 75 per cent of my wage while I was unable to work. On top of that the province paid nothing for the first seven days I was out. I guess I'm lucky that the disability wasn't permanent or my weekly benefit would have been even lower.

As this example illustrates, employees are sometimes unaware that workers' compensation pays only part of the regular paycheque. For example, every province pays disabled claimants only part of their regular pay to discourage self-inflicted accidents or malingering. Another common provincial rule provides for waiting periods to lessen claims for trivial accidents. Payments are eventually reduced—or even discontinued—to encourage persons with permanent disabilities to seek rehabilitation.

The limitations of workers' compensation coverage have two related implications for human resource departments. First, workers must be informed by the human resource department of the limited financial security provided by these laws. Second, gaps in the employee's financial security need to be closed with supplementary disability and health insurance. By responding to these needs, human resource departments can show a genuine concern for employee welfare.

Human resource specialists also need to be concerned about reducing accidents in order to lower the cost of workers' compensation. These costs are directly related to the claims made against the company by employees. The more that must be paid to these employees, the greater the cost. Yet even aside from cost considerations, many managers feel a moral obligation to provide a safe working environment:

> George Fitzgerald, the new human resource manager in a machine shop, was appalled when he learned that in the past two years one employee was totally blinded and another lost an eye while operating a grinding machine. Mr. Fitzgerald posted a sign that said, "Any employee who runs the grinding machine without safety goggles will be fired!" After 15 years (and several new signs) not one eye injury (or safety-related discharge) has occurred in the shop. A by-product of Mr. Fitzgerald's concern was that his workers' compensation premiums declined by 42 per cent.

Unfortunately, too few human resource departments achieve such a dramatic success. As a result, government interest in the physical security of workers has increased and safety laws have been enacted (see Chapter Fifteen).

Employment insurance payments have been increasing rapidly in the past few years. There are several things that human resource managers can do to improve the situation. First, they can institute human resource planning, which minimizes over-hiring and subsequent layoffs. With such planning, shortages and surpluses of personnel are anticipated. Then retraining or attrition can lead to proper staffing levels without layoffs. Second, they can educate other decision-makers—particularly production planners and schedulers. Production specialists may not realize that "hire, then lay off" policies increase payroll costs, which in turn raise production costs and selling prices. Third, human resource departments can review all discharges to make sure that they are justified. Unjustified dismissals by supervisors can be reversed or changed into intracompany transfers to prevent the higher payroll taxes that can result from dismissals or layoffs.

A fourth approach is to challenge all unjustified claims for employment compensation made against employers. Those claims that are successfully challenged may reduce costs in the future:

> Kevin Hirtsman was fired for stealing from the company, since the employee manual stated that stealing was grounds for immediate dismissal. When his claim for employment insurance was sent to the company for its comments, the human resource manager wrote back that Kevin was terminated for cause. Kevin's claim for employment compensation was denied.

Retention

Retention
A company's ability to keep employees.

The question has been raised what role benefits play in retaining employees. *Retention* of key employees has become a major issue, especially in high-tech companies.[28] Several studies have shown that innovative and flexible benefit plans are highly effective tools in attracting and retaining highly skilled staff.[29] "My sense is that benefits become increasingly important as a competitive advantage if you can't negotiate around the total compensation package," said Ann O'Neill, director of the Certified Employee Benefits Specialist program at Dalhousie University in Halifax.[30] This view is confirmed by an opinion survey on 307 CEOs of large Canadian companies.[31]

Noranda Mine's Director of Pensions and Benefits, Claude Gaudreau, offers these tips for success for designing a benefit plan:

- involve your employees;
- don't underestimate the amount of time required. The more people involved, the longer it will take;
- don't rush. It takes time to develop a good product;
- spend money on getting expertise.[32]

Benefit Audit

Benefit audit
System to control the efficiency of a benefit program.

Often, the administration of benefit plans still leaves room for improvement. One approach that readily identifies inefficiencies is a *benefit audit*. It usually consists of two components: a *claims audit*, which examines claims and claim trends, and an *organization audit*, which examines the efficiency and effectiveness of handling employee benefits within the employer organization, including dealings with an insurer or third-party administrator.

Studies by William M. Mercer, a benefit consulting company, have shown that many employers can save 0.5 to 1 per cent of their payroll costs through improved management of their benefit plans:[33]

One employer placed older, redundant factory workers on long-term disability instead of laying them off, which would have meant giving them termination packages of potentially up to one year's pay. The long-term disability plan was insured and the financial statements were charged with a disabled life reserve of around $40 000, or approximately one year's salary at this company. The employer never realized what his benefit staff was doing and never had the opportunity to make a business decision about long-term benefits.[34]

A benefit audit enables employers to:

- identify opportunities for financial and human resource savings;
- ensure that insurers or third-party administrators are doing a good job;
- exert effective control over their benefits area;
- identify who is in control of the benefits budget; and
- check how their employee claiming habits compare against other Canadian employers.

Goods and Services Tax Application to Benefits

Since 1991, the GST applies to some benefits, but not to others. Generally, GST must be paid on the following benefits:

- company cars (if also used for private purposes);
- car operating costs;
- tax-return preparation;
- short-term residential accommodation;
- holiday trips within continental North America;
- frequent flyer points;
- financial counselling; and
- parking.

Not affected are awards, health benefits, stock options, low-interest or no-interest loans, tuition fees, child care, a Christmas turkey, and gifts under $100.

EMERGING SERVICES AND TRENDS

www.benefitscanada
.com/electric/health/
healthindex.html

www.benefits.org/

www.benefitscanada.com/
sunlife/contents.html

www.benefitscanada
.com/Content/1999/
11-99/ben119903.html

SEVERAL STUDIES have attempted to predict the types of benefits that will be in demand over the next 10 years.[35] The more popular options for employees seem to be:

1. Increased medical coverage, with dental plans and optometrist services being the favourites; also greater assumption of costs of medical coverage by employers.

2. More and longer vacations, coupled with reduced length of service requirements; more holidays.

3. Increased pension coverage, with greater contributions by employers.

4. Cost-of-living adjustments of pension plans.

5. Improved portability of pension rights and earlier vesting.

6. Sabbatical leaves for managers, and paid educational leave for rank-and-file employees.

7. Child care, with the employer providing either fully or partially subsidized care facilities and staff.

8. Elder care, offering employees time off to take care of aging and dependent relatives, often coupled with counselling and special assistance.

9. As the federal government has already done, provinces will follow with legislation granting all benefits to same-sex couples.

10. More and more companies will grant benefits to part-time employees and even to retirees.

Some companies go to extremes when it comes to retaining key employees, offering such nontraditional benefits as free laundry, back-up child care, or dog walking services.[36]

> KPMG's 26 000 employees in its 125 US offices were recently given convenience services through LesConcierge. One call to an 800 number and employees may ask for "anything that's legal, ethical, and doesn't harm anyone else," says Kathie Linge, work/life director for KPMG. She used the service to find an electrician on the day after Thanksgiving and to hire an excavator to align the front of her house. She says that studies show that employees who use this program are more productive, more loyal, and more likely to recommend the company to other job applicants.[37]

Current trends indicate that indirect compensation will form a greater proportion of total compensation offered. Perhaps the employer share of contributions to the various current benefit plans will rise without any new types of benefits being added. Employees may also be able to make choices among benefits, and it may well become easier for employees to enroll in benefit plans through liberalized eligibility requirements.

Given the trends outlined above, it will be critical for top management in general and the human resource manager in particular to adopt a total compensation approach when decisions have to be made relating to pay. Organizations cannot afford to treat employee benefits and services independent of direct compensation, especially since they are growing at twice the pace of wages and salaries. For all practical purposes, it can be said that benefits have lost much of their importance as an attraction for new employees since most organizations offer relatively similar benefit packages. Employees see benefits more and more as rights, not as privileges.[38]

CP PHOTO ARCHIVE (Darnell Jean)

Child care, with the employer providing either fully or partially subsidized care facilities and staff, is emerging as an extended benefit for employees.

This change in employees' attitudes can be used by management in a positive way. If benefits are perceived as a normal part of a compensation package, they will arouse an employee's interest only if they fulfill a need (i.e., have a perceived value). It is then management's responsibility to maximize this perceived value. This is not a difficult objective, given that certain preconditions are met. One is a willingness on the side of management to listen to its employees and to allow them to have input into the development of a benefits and services program. Second, a greater familiarity with trends in the area of benefits is required on the side of management. It probably is not enough to leave the human resource or compensation manager with the responsibility to monitor trends and to make recommendations, usually limited to collective bargaining demands by unions. Employee benefits and services programs must be part of the overall organizational policy and strategy decisions that influence long-range planning.

Finally, management must take into account the changes in the labour force that will take place over the next 10 to 20 years. The average age of the labour force will increase, which will result in greater emphasis on pensions as part of the benefit package. More women will be working, and more will do so longer, making their job a career. What impact will this have on benefits and services (paid maternity leave, day-care centres, nurseries, and so on)? Part-time work also will become more common, with still unforeseeable consequences, since traditionally part-timers received few or no benefits. There can be little doubt that the issue of employee benefits and services will require more attention and occupy more of management's time than ever before.

Some companies have already taken the first step to extending benefits to part-time workers. In 1966 the Toronto-Dominion Bank included its 1500 casual part-time workers in its regular benefit plans. Later in the same year the Royal Bank of Canada followed suit, but went even further by making its 7500 part-time employees eligible for cash performance bonuses normally reserved for full-time staff.[39] This is a significant change in dealing with part-time employees who, for decades, have fought for the right to receive benefits.

Benefits and Strategy Implications

Benefits make up, on the average, 41 per cent of employees' salaries in Canada, or approximately $20 000 for each employee.[40] For an organization with 1000 or 10 000 employees, a very significant amount of money is committed, $20 or $200 million respectively. It would be expected that management be very interested in knowing how effectively such an amount is spent.

As outlined in Chapter One, management must look at the long-term objectives of the organization and match these with organizational conditions to create the necessary environment for reaching the objectives. Specifically, the following steps have to be taken:

- Define the objectives of the organization.

- Link objectives of the human resource department with the objectives of the organization.

- Assess the needs of the employees.

- Assess the legal requirements to ensure that laws are followed.

- Compare the company's benefits with those of the competition.

- Make sure the benefits are valued by the employees.

- Conduct an annual benefit audit.

It is important for human resource managers to integrate benefits into the wage and salary package. This compensation package has to fulfill short- and long-term goals. The short-term goals—for example, high motivation and productivity—are usually satisfied with merit pay and incentive systems that reward high performers. A common long-term goal is to retain good employees, an objective that can be achieved by a valued pension or a profit-sharing plan. Another strategy may address the need for downsizing by using an appropriate severance package. These are just a few items of a comprehensive pay strategy.

Listed in Appendix A to this chapter are the more common benefits and services, not all of which were mentioned in this chapter.

SUMMARY

Employee benefits and services are the fastest-growing component of compensation. The Canadian government has instituted compulsory programs that provide citizens with certain benefits and services. Financial security is achieved partially through such benefits as the Canada Pension Plan, employment insurance, and workers' compensation. The Canada Pension Plan provides income at retirement or upon disability. It also provides the family members of a deceased worker with a death benefit and a survivor's annuity, under certain conditions.

Employment insurance pays the worker a modest income to reduce the hardships of losing a job. These payments go to employees who are involuntarily separated from their jobs. Payments last until the worker finds suitable employment or until the worker receives the maximum number of payments permitted by the government.

Workers' compensation pays employees who are injured in the course of their employment. The payments are made to prevent the employee from having to sue to be compensated for injuries. If an employee dies, benefits are paid to the employee's survivors.

Health and medical insurance is provided by provincial governments with assistance from the federal government. In addition to the provincial health insurance, group life and disability insurance is widely provided as an employee benefit. More and more companies are also providing dental insurance for their employees

Voluntary benefits include insurance, security, and time-off benefits. Employee services encompass educational, financial, and social programs. This diversity contributes to several serious administrative problems. The most significant problem is the orientation of managers and human resource specialists toward cost savings. In pursuit of administrative and actuarial economies, most companies and unions do not allow individualized benefit packages in indirect compensation programs.

A major issue is ballooning health-care costs. Management must pay more attention to the efficient administration of such plans and to the control of their costs. Some studies have shown that savings of up to 15 per cent can be achieved if management pays attention to health benefit costs.

A significant development in the field of benefit administration is the benefit audit, consisting of a claims and an organization audit. The audit examines the efficiency and effectiveness of handling employee benefits, including insurers and third-party administrators.

If management wants to be up-to-date in benefits, it must be aware of the trends in the field. Changing demographics make changing demands on benefit systems: extra medical coverage, company pension plans with better portability and earlier vesting, child care, and elder care are some of the new developments in this field. In all probability, increased part-time work will necessitate offering benefits even to these employees. These developments will make it necessary for top management to adopt a total compensation package as part of a pay strategy.

TERMS FOR REVIEW

Visit the Web site at www.mcgrawhill.ca/college/schwind6 for a full glossary.

REVIEW AND DISCUSSION QUESTIONS

1.   Why has government been interested in providing financial security to workers through laws? What areas do you think are likely to receive government attention in the future to ensure employee financial security?

2. Some people believe that employment insurance has over a period of time worked against workers rather than for them. What is your opinion of employment insurance? Why?

3. Suppose a friend of yours contracted lead poisoning on the job. What sources of income could this person rely on while recovering during the next two months? What if it took two years for your friend to recover? Are other sources of income available?

4. Besides retirement income, what other benefits are provided through the Canada Pension Plan?

5. What changes should be made to the employment insurance system to eliminate its present weaknesses?

6. What factors have contributed to the rapid growth of benefits since the Second World War?

7. Briefly describe the benefits that an organization might give employees to provide them with greater financial security.

8. Why was the Pension Benefits Standards Act needed? What are its major provisions?

9. What are the common problems you would expect to find with the benefits and services program of a large company?

10. If you were asked to increase employee awareness of benefits, what actions would you take without changing the way the company provides benefits? If you could change the entire benefits program, what other methods would you use to increase employee awareness?

CRITICAL THINKING QUESTIONS

1. Suppose you are asked to explain why employees are better off receiving pay and benefits rather than just getting larger pay cheques that include the monetary value of benefits. What arguments will you use?

2. For each of the following groups of employees, what types of problems are likely to occur if a company goes from a five-day, 40-hour week to a four-day, 40-hour week: (a) working mothers, (b) labourers, (c) assembly-line workers?

3. Should companies pay educational assistance? Assume that it was for a degree in information technology. What if a competitor offers a higher salary to the successful graduate? How could you ensure the company's investment remains in the organization?

WEB RESEARCH

1. What are the characteristics of an effective Retirement Savings Program? Look at the following homepage: www.benefits.org/interface/benefit/ retire.htm

2. What are the advantages of a flexible benefit plan? Have a look at: www. benefits.org/interface/benefit/flex.htm

3. Employee Assistance Programs have become very popular with small and large companies. Give some good reasons for the introduction of an EAP: See: www.benefits.org/interface/benefit/ (search for "eap")

4. What are the eligibility criteria for the new Employment Insurance program? Give details.
www.cbsc.org/english/search/display.cfm?Code=1517&Coll=FE_FED SBIS_E

INCIDENT 11-1

Soap Producers and Distributors Ltd.

Soap Producers and Distributors Ltd. faced a severe employee turnover problem. The company's annual turnover rate was nearly 40 per cent among technical and white-collar workers. Among hourly paid employees, the rate was nearly 75 per cent.

Wage and salary surveys repeatedly showed that the company's pay levels were 10 to 11 per cent above comparable jobs in the labour market. The benefit program was not as impressive, but management thought it was competitive. Employees received supplementary health and life insurance, paid vacations and holidays, and a Christmas bonus of $500. Although some employees complained about the company's benefits, complaints varied widely and no one benefit or lack of benefit seemed to be the key issue.

To make Soap Producers and Distributors' problems worse, they operated in a tight labour market, which meant jobs sometimes took weeks to fill. To hire specialized workers almost always meant recruiting them from other cities and paying their moving expenses.

1. What additions do you think should be made to the company's benefit program?

2. What problems in the incident might be solved by a cafeteria approach?

3. To overcome the company's recruitment problems, what other changes do you suggest?

INCIDENT 11-2

International Sea Products' Pension Plan

In 1962, International Sea Products Ltd. established a private, noncontributory pension plan for all workers who had 20 years of service with the company. After the 20 years, workers were eligible for a pension beginning at the age of 65. The pension plan was funded by putting 2.5 per cent of each year's payroll into a trust fund administered by the company's vice-president of finance. Although employees were informed that there was an employer-paid pension fund, little explanation of the plan was offered. Whenever questioned, the president of the company would only state: "This company takes care of loyal employees."

1. What changes should be made in this company's pension plan to comply with the Pension Benefits Standards Act?

2. What other changes would you recommend to increase the effectiveness of the pension plan in improving employee morale?

CASE STUDY

Maple Leaf Shoes Ltd., Flexible Benefit Program

Maple Leaf Shoes Ltd. is a medium-sized manufacturer of leather and vinyl shoes located in Wilmington, Ontario. It was started in 1969 and currently employs about 400 persons in its Hamilton plant and some 380 more in offices and warehouses throughout Canada and abroad.

Sam Polanyi, president of Maple Leaf Shoes' Leather Workers Union, was working on a draft of his plan for the upcoming negotiations with management. He knew that he had to be prepared for some tough bargaining because Robert Clark, the company's president and chief negotiator, was no pushover. Almost all negotiations in the past had gone to the wire, sometimes just hours away from a strike, but so far there had always been a last-minute settlement.

Some of Sam's members had approached him to discuss the advantages of a flexible benefit plan. Apparently, some of the workers' spouses worked in companies that had such a plan, and the workers seemed to like it. It meant they could choose the kind of benefits most useful to them, which was not possible under the rigid "same for all" system the company was using now. Could he convince Bob Clark that it would be to the company's advantage? A flexible or cafeteria plan would certainly be more expensive, and that was the rub. Sam was willing to compromise on other issues to get the plan, but how could he sell Clark on it?

Discussion Question

Can you assist Sam Polanyi in his attempt to sell Robert Clark on a flexible benefit plan? What are the advantages and disadvantages of such plans?

CASE STUDY

Canadian Pacific and International Bank

Mary Keddy, senior vice president—human resources, was facing Michael Bennett, the bank's CEO, in his office. He had called her to an urgent meeting regarding the bank's benefit expenses. He showed her some figures he had received from the internal auditor. The data indicated that the bank's benefit expenses had reached almost 40 per cent of the bank's payroll. He also produced benchmark data from a survey, which showed that the industry average was close to 30 per cent. "Why is it that our benefit expenses are so much higher than those of our competitors?" he asked.

Mary pointed out that the data had assessed the financial services industry, not just banks, and that the industry included some trust companies with much lower benefit levels than banks which, by and large, had benefit expenses similar to those of the CPIB, although the CPIB certainly occupied the high end of the scale.

Mr. Bennett wondered whether these expenses were really justified. "Where is the pay-off?" he asked. Mary had no problems defending the bank's benefit outlays. She pointed out that the CPIB had the lowest turnover rate among banks, two per cent lower than any other, and that every employee attitude survey showed that the CPIB staff believed that the bank was a very good place to work and that job satisfaction was high. She also mentioned that the bank had no difficulties attracting top-flight applicants. She was convinced that the bank's generous benefit package contributed significantly to this level of satisfaction. She concluded her explanation by saying: "Mike, look at the level of customer satisfaction. We beat out every other bank on this measure. I am sure the reason is that happy employees mean happy customers. And there is the main pay-off."

Bennett appreciated Mary's explanation. He had always been proud when he had seen the results of internal surveys. No doubt, people liked to work for the CPIB. "Still," he wondered, "are there ways to cut the expenses without doing too much damage to employee satisfaction?" Mary agreed to look into that matter and to make suggestions regarding more efficient methods of delivering benefit services. She had heard and read about the use of the intranet and the Internet as more effective ways to administer benefit plans, but felt that she did not know enough about it to come up with convincing recommendations. It was obvious that she needed some expert advice.

Additional Information

The last time a benefit audit had been done was seven years ago—a year before Mary joined the bank. Ever since her arrival, Mary has been too busy introducing strategic changes in areas such as selection, diversity management, and training. In the last five years, the bank had also acquired several other financial institutions and expanded into other countries. But the need for a benefit audit had been on her mind for some time.

The bank's flexible benefit package includes, besides the usual supplementary health and life insurances, child care, elder care, a drug payment plan, wellness programs (the bank had its own exercise centre), personal counselling service (drugs, alcohol, smoking cessation), educational support, and financial advising. It was also possible to purchase more vacation time. Three full-time employees were responsible for administering the flexible benefit package. The administration expenses, including communication, were close to $300 000 annually. The bank uses a quite effective intranet mainly for training and public announcements.

Discussion Questions

1. Use Web research to find arguments for and against using the Internet and the bank's intranet for the administration and delivery of its benefit services

2. Is outsourcing benefit administration advisable? Why? What criteria should be used in making the decision?

3. If Mary asks for a benefit audit, what would the auditor look at?

SUGGESTED READINGS

Beam Jr., Burton T. and John J. McFadden, *Employee Benefits*, Fourth Edition, Dearborn Financial Publishing, 1997.

Beatty, Carol A. and Mary Lu Coates, *Employee Ownership: How Do You Spell Success?* Kingston, ON: IRC Press, Industrial Relations Centre, Queen's University, 1997.

Beam, T. Burton, and John J. McFadden, *Employee Benefits*, Real Estate Education Company, 1998.

Black, Ann, *New Era of Benefits Communication*, International Foundation of Employee Benefit Plans, 1997.

E-Merging Trends: Benefit Administration Moves to Net-based Management, an HR.com publication (electronic), August 2000, shop.hr.com/acb/showdetl .cfm?&DID =6&Product_ID=399&CATID=17

Employee Benefit Plans: A Glossary of Terms, Ninth Edition, International Foundation of Employee Benefit Plans, 1997.

Frantzreb, Richard B, ed., *The 1998 Compensation & Benefit Software Census*, International Foundation of Employee Benefit Plans, 1998.

Fundamentals of Employee Benefit Programs, Fifth Edition, Benefit Research Institute, 1997.

Johnson, Richard E., *Flexible Benefits: A How-To Guide*, Fifth Edition, International Foundation of Employee Benefit Plans, 1997.

Khemani, Ashim, and John W. Jackson, *Canadian Group Insurance Benefits: A Practitioner's Guide & Reference Manual*, Canadian Association of Insurance and Financial Advisors, 1997; includes 1998 supplement. www.ifebp.org/pbcangrp.html

Koskie Raymond, Mark Zigler, Murray Gold and Roberto Tomassini, editors and principal contributors, *Employee Benefits in Canada*, third edition, International Foundation of Employee Benefit Plans, 2000; www.ifebp.org/pbcanben.html

McKay, Robert J., *Canadian Handbook of Flexible Benefits*, International Foundation of Employee Benefit Plans, 1997.

McMahon, Fred, *Looking the Gift Horse in the Mouth The Impact of Federal Transfers on Atlantic Canada*, Atlantic Institute for Marketing Studies, 1998; http://aims.ca/

Nielson, Norma L., *Taxes and Employee Benefits in Canada,* International Foundation of Employee Benefit Plans, 1998; www.ifebp.org/pbtaxcan.html

Rosenbloom, Jerry S., *The Handbook of Employee Benefits: Design, Funding and Administration,* Fourth Edition, Irwin Professional Publishing, 1997.

"Taking stock: Extending Employee Ownership Through Options," A Special Edition of the *ACA Journal* (publication of the American Compensation Association), Spring 1998, Vol. 7, No. 1.

Walsh, Michael G., *Reforming the Canada Pension Plan*, IRC Press, Kingston, ON: Industrial Relations Centre, Queen's University, 1997.

Special Reports from Benefits Canada (www.benefitscanada.com):

Bowyer, Susan, and Margaret French, *Saving the Drug Plan*, April 2000.

Gratzer, David, *What Future Healthcare?* February 2000.

Davis, Andrea, *The Managed Care Solution,* October 1999.

Norton, Jim, and Sandra Pellegrini, *The Future of Flex*, September 1999.

APPENDIX A

Potential Benefits and Services

accidental death, dismemberment insurance
anniversary awards
annual reports to employees
athletic teams
attendance bonus
automobile lease plan
beauty parlours
bereavement leave
birthdays off
bonuses
business and professional memberships
cafeteria and canteen services
call-back and call-in pay
Christmas bonus
Christmas party
clean-up time
club membership
commissions
company medical assistance
company newspaper
company-provided automobile
company-provided housing
company-provided or subsidized travel
company stores
credit union
dances
day-care centres
deferred bonus
deferred compensation plan
deferred profit sharing
dental and eye care insurance
dietetic advice
discount on company products
educational activities (time off)
education costs
executive dining room
family allowances
financial counselling
free chequing account
free or subsidized lunches
group automobile insurance
group homeowners' insurance
group life insurance
health maintenance organization fees
holidays (extra)
home financing
home health care

income tax service
interest-free loans
jury duty time
layoff pay (SUB)
legal, estate planning, and other professional assistance
library and reading room facilities
loans of company equipment
long-term disability benefits
low-interest company loans
lunch-period entertainment and music at work
magazine subscription payments
nursery
nursing home care
paid attendance at business, professional, and other outside meetings
paid sick leave
parking facilities
parties and picnics
payment of optical expenses

personal counselling
personal credit cards
personal expense accounts
political activities (time off)
private pension plan
profit sharing
purchasing service
quality bonus
recreational facilities
religious holidays
relocation expense plan
resort facilities
rest periods
retirement gratuity
room and board allowances
sabbatical leaves
safety awards
salary continuation
savings plan
scholarship for dependants
service bonus
severance pay

shorter or flexible workweek
social service sabbaticals
stock appreciation rights
stock bonus plan
stock options plan
stock purchase plan
suggestion awards
supplementary hospital-surgical medical insurance
survivors' benefits
time spent on collective bargaining
time spent on grievances
training programs
vacation pay
vacations
voting time
waste-elimination bonus
weekly indemnity insurance
witness time
year-end bonus

Chapter 12

Work Options and Employee Motivation

Giving the worker a voice in managing his job by letting him share the overseer's role pays handsome dividends to him and his company.

—William J. Roche and Neil L. MacKinnon[1]

Genuine and lasting employee motivation is not something management does, but rather a process that management fosters and allows to happen.

—Michael Kavanagh[2]

CHAPTER OBJECTIVES

After studying this chapter, you should be able to:

- ■ *List* the advantages and disadvantages of shorter workweeks, flextime, and job sharing.

- ■ *Specify* the difference between part-time work and job sharing.

- ■ *Discuss* the implications of flexible staffing on strategic human resource planning.

- ■ *Define* the relationship between performance and job satisfaction.

- ■ *Explain* how the human resource function is able to assist managers in motivating their employees.

- ■ *Operationalize* the expectancy theory model of motivation.

WORK OPTIONS

Work options
Various and flexible alternatives to the traditional workplace or the traditional 40-hour workweek.

www.reflection.gc.ca/
report/report_e.txt

THE 40-HOUR workweek was designed for a workforce consisting largely of men with stay-at-home wives. Today, however, two-fifths of Canada's workforce are women, and 40 per cent of full-time workers have a spouse who also works full-time. As a result, men and women both are finding flexible ***work options*** an attractive and, in some cases, necessary alternative to the traditional 40-hour workweek.

"In the early 1990s, there was probably more resistance to the concept of flexibility from the Canadian population and business in general," says Norma Tombari, manager of workforce solutions in the human resources department of the Royal Bank Financing Group. "What I have found in terms of what's happening in the Canadian workplace is a growing interest in flexibility," she said, referring to extensive studies carried out for the bank in 1994 and 1997.

Among the findings of the 1997 survey, 63 per cent of the financial group's managers say they would highly recommend flexible work arrangements—a 29 per cent increase from 1994—and 37 per cent of managers reported greater employment efficiency, up 12 per cent.[3]

It is interesting to note that only one in three Canadian workers was holding a "typical" job in 1996 (Census datum). See Figure 12-1.

FIGURE 12-1

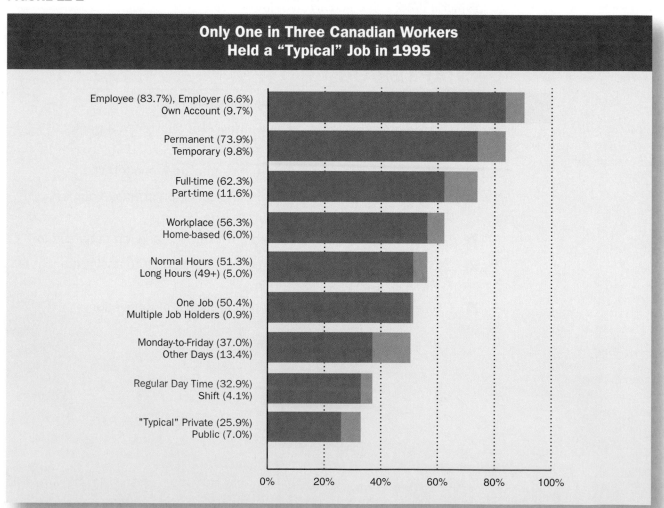

Source: Flexible Work Arrangements—Gaining Ground. HRDC. Reproduced with the permission of the Minister of Public Works and the Government Services Canada, 2001.

www.aarp.org/
confacts/money/
flexwork/html

When full-time work conflicts with family responsibilities and other personal needs, employees may want to change their work schedules to create more time for themselves or their families. Sometimes, older workers prefer to work less than full-time in the last years before retirement. In some cases, the choice to work less is based on health considerations. For people in high-stress jobs, overload and "burnout" can increase the risk of serious illness. People who want to change their work schedules without giving up their present jobs often find the answer in voluntary work options.

Well-designed work option programs can benefit both employees and employers. For employees, reduced or restructured work schedules can provide a better balance between work and personal life. Consequently, increasing numbers of employees are asking for more flexible work options. Unions are also discovering that voluntary work options can meet some members' desire for part-time work without loss of benefits or job security. As a result, many unions are now including work options in their negotiations.

For society as a whole, work options can help reduce the economic and social costs of unemployment. Because work options have the effect of spreading the available work among more people, they can be useful tools for creating new employment opportunities.

As can be expected, work options have also their negative aspects. Some employers use part-time jobs to save on wages and benefits. A number of part-time employees and those working for temporary staff agencies are choosing such jobs involuntarily because they may not have other options. The advantages and disadvantages of each option are discussed below.

FLEXIBLE WORK ARRANGEMENTS

www.at-home-
mothers.com/infoguides/
36a3.htm

www.work
options.com

www.aarp.org/
working_options/change
jobs/home.html

Shorter workweek
Employee scheduling variations that allow full-time employees to complete a week's work in less than the traditional five days.

THE LENGTH of the typical workweek has declined significantly since the early days of the Industrial Revolution, as illustrated in Figure 12-2. The norm of a five-day, 40-hour workweek remained relatively unchanged from the 1930s to the early 1970s. During the 1970s, however, several new approaches to scheduling work gained popularity: shorter workweeks, flextime, and job sharing. In the early 1990s, some more work options emerged: regular or "permanent" part-time work, home-based work or telecommuting, and phased retirement. Now, in 2001, the virtual office, employee leasing, and employee sharing have been added.

Shorter Workweeks

A *shorter workweek* compresses 40 hours of work into fewer than five full days. Some plans even shorten the workweek to fewer than 40 hours. The most popular version has been 40 hours of work compressed into four days. Fire departments and staff at some hospitals use a three-day, 36-hour schedule. Another option is the "weekender," where employees work 12-hour shifts on Saturdays and Sundays, but are paid 40 hours instead of the 24 hours actually worked. This arrangement was agreed upon by management and the union of the 3M Canada plant in London, Ontario.

The advantages include less time wasted due to start-up, wash-up, breaks, and clean-up. In addition, absenteeism and turnover tend to be lower and employee morale higher, and it seems to stimulate employee motivation and productivity. The disadvantages are that customers may be inconvenienced, there could be some scheduling problems, and the long hours could be boring and monotonous.[4] The longer working day may also result in more fatigue, which could pose a safety risk.

FIGURE 12-2

A Typical Work Schedule 148 Years Ago

Time Table of the Holyoke Mills,

To take effect on and after Jan. 3d, 1853.

The standard being that of the Western Rail Road, which is the Meridian time at Cambridge.

───◄●►───

MORNING BELLS.

First Bell ring at 4.40, A.M.   Second Bell ring in at 5, A.M.

YARD GATES

Will be opened at ringing of Morning Bells, of Meal Bells, and of Evening Bells, and kept open ten minutes.

WORK COMMENCES

At ten minutes after last Morning Bell, and ten minutes after Bell which "rings in" from Meals.

BREAKFAST BELLS

October 1st, to March 31st, inclusive, ring out at 7, A.M.; ring in at 7.30, A.M.

April 1st, to Sept. 30th, inclusive, ring out at 6.30, A.M.; ring in at 7, A.M.

DINNER BELLS.

Ring out at 12.30, P.M.; ring in at 1, P.M.

EVENING BELLS.

Ring Out At 6.30.* P.M.

Source: Labor's Long, Hard Road, Air Line Employees Association, International, p. 4. Air Line Employees Association—Talks Given by National Airlines Employee Mrs. Constance LaPare.

Another potential drawback is that some employers must pay overtime to nonmanagerial employees who have to work more than eight hours in a given day due to overlapping work requirements with those employees who are on a different schedule. Still, some companies report success with the shorter workweek:

> The Bank of Montreal's Oakville branches operate from 9:30 a.m. to 8:30 p.m. Monday to Friday, and 9:30 a.m. to 5:30 p.m. Saturday. Instead of staggering hours, the manager worked out a scheme for a compressed workweek. There are two teams at each branch, a Monday-Wednesday team and a Thursday-Saturday team. Each team works three days a week, 12.5 hours per day.

> The bank's initial concern that long days would mean more administrative errors has not been confirmed. On the contrary, according to management, accuracy has improved.[5]

Pros and Cons of the Compressed Work Week Approach

Pros	Cons
More flexibility in balancing work and family	Physically and mentally draining
One extra day off at full-time income	Extra child care may be needed
Commuting outside rush hours	

Some employers also use the shorter workweek as a means of avoiding layoffs. In 1997, British Columbia's InterFor, one of Canada's largest sawmills, minimized lay-offs from a major restructuring by changing shift arrangements.[6]

Flextime

Flextime
A scheduling innovation that abolishes rigid starting and ending times for each day's work.

A 1996 survey showed that 24 per cent of Canadian companies have introduced flexible time schedules, up from 17 per cent in 1991.[7] **Flextime** abolishes rigid starting and ending times for the workday. Instead, employees are allowed to report to work at any time during a range of hours. The day is usually divided into two periods, core time and flexible time. During the core time, the employee must be on the job, while during the flexible time the employee has the choice when to complete the required time. For example, starting time may be from 7 a.m. to 9 a.m., with all employees expected to work the core hours of 9 a.m. to 3 p.m. The workday usually remains unchanged at eight hours. Therefore, the end of the workday is variable also. Flextime is best suited for customer-independent units.

There are some variations in the flextime approach:

- flexitour, where employees choose their working time and have to stick to it for a period of time (e.g., a week or a month);

- gliding time, permitting flexible starting and quitting time;

- variable day, or flexible workdays (e.g., 12 hours one day and four hours the next);

- maniflex, with flexible workday, but core time on certain days (e.g., Monday and Friday); and

Flexiplace
A flexible work arrangement in which employees are allowed or encouraged to work at home or in a satellite office closer to home.

- *flexiplace*, allowing flexibility in working time and place (e.g., office and home).[8]

The examples below indicate how some of these options work:

Ontario Hydro has used a flextime arrangement for many years. Staff may start any time before 9 a.m. and leave any time after 3 p.m. as long as they work a full day. They also may adjust the length of their lunch hour. The schedule allows employees to avoid the worst of Toronto's traffic with an early start.

Glen MacLeod of the Bank of Montreal has been taking every Wednesday off for the past five years. As a senior manager of commercial banking in Toronto, he uses the arrangement to gain more time to pursue personal interests. By working two days in a row and then having a break he also feels more productive during his time in the office.[9]

The outcome of a flextime program, however, is contingent upon the nature of the firm's operations. For example, the major disadvantage of flextime is the difficulty in meeting minimum staffing needs early and late in the day. Assembly-line and customer service operations find this problem to be especially significant. But in many operations, users have reported noteworthy successes.[10]

A group of researchers conducted two field experiments, one on the shorter workweek and one on the introduction of flextime.[11] The studies reported improved organizational effectiveness (e.g., customer service), but a more interesting finding was that the reaction of the affected employees could be predicted before the introduction of the new schedule. The researchers had conducted a pre-test, asking the employees how they would react to the new schedules, and these anticipated reactions were confirmed in the follow-up study six months later. The lesson from these studies for human resource managers is that employees should have input into the development of a new schedule.

Pros and Cons of Flextime

PROS	CONS
Flexibility to schedule errands, take care of family illness	More difficult to coordinate group activities
Avoid rush hour traffic	Staff supervision may be more difficult
May assist in child care requirements	Potential customer dissatisfaction
Reduced absenteeism because of family commitments	

Job Sharing

Job sharing
A plan whereby available work is spread among the workers.

A third approach to employee scheduling that gained popularity during the 1970s is job sharing, also called job splitting. *Job sharing* involves one or more employees doing the same job, but working different hours, days, or even weeks. Most commonly, two people handle the duties of one full-time job:

> "It makes good business sense for us to offer work sharing," says Norma Tombari, manager of the Royal Bank of Canada's work and family program. "We get to recruit and keep good employees, and our customers benefit because employees who feel the company is supporting them provide better service."

> At the Royal Bank, work sharing seems to appeal primarily to working mothers trying to balance the demands of home and the office. Of the bank's 58 000 employees, 78 per cent are women. Tombari says the bank just had to look at its demographics to decide the program was worth implementing.[12]

The major advantage claimed for job sharing is increased productivity from workers who are not fatigued. Problems arise from the increased paperwork and administrative burden associated with two employees doing the job of one. Another problem is that of benefits. Human resource specialists are forced to decide whether job sharers should be given benefits equal with other employees or benefits that are scaled down in proportion to the employee's hours.[13]

www.shrm.org/
hrmagazine/articles/0196
share.html

www.pioneerplanet
.com/reprints/0105amy.htm

www.shrm.org/
hrmagazine/articles/
0196case.html

http://members.home.net/
ushipley/jobs.html

Regular or "Permanent" Part-time Work

The significantly increased benefit costs, especially health care and pensions, provide a great incentive for employers to make more use of *regular part-time work*, defined

---

Pros and Cons of Job Sharing

PROS	CONS
Individuals maintain work experience while devoting time to raising children, caring for elders, upgrading education	Salary and benefits lower than full-time job
Reduced absenteeism for personal appointments	Advancement possibilities limited
Potentially higher productivity	Higher administration costs
Training for two necessary	

www.usnews.com/
usnews/issue/971027/
27nont.htm

www.ilo.org/public/
english/support/publ/
revue/persp/97-4.htm

www.ccsd.ca/
xs_pt.htm

as "less than full-time work by employees on a company's regular payroll."[14] Statistics Canada officially defines part-time workers as those employees who work less than thirty hours per week. It is said that part-time workers are the fastest growing type of employees in Canada. In 1953 they made up only 3.8 per cent of the labour force. By 1990 they had increased their share to 15 per cent, and by 1996 to 18.9 per cent. It had been predicted that by 2000 this share would grow to 20 per cent, but there was actually a small decline, down to 18 per cent.[15] Statistics also indicate that the surge in part-time jobs had driven unemployment below seven per cent.[16]

Figure 12-3 shows the proportion of employees who work part-time in a number of countries. Figure 12-4 specifies part-time workers, male and female, in Canada as a percentage of all workers in 1987 and 1999.

One advantage of part-time work is that it increases flexibility so that employers can match the workforce with peak demands. Another advantage, from an employer's point of view, is that very often these part-time employees are paid no benefits. One 1997 study found that among 87 Canadian companies only 20 per cent paid benefits to their part-time employees.[17] Employers that do pay benefits tend to be in the public sector, such as health-care facilities and municipal governments.

In all probability, part-time employment will increase for the following reasons:

- the growing number of women in the labour force, with a preference for part-time positions;

- the higher demand in the service industries, which employ more than 40 per cent of all part-timers; and[18]

- the need for cost-cutting.[19]

Part-time work should not be confused with job sharing. Employees sharing jobs share a full-time job equally, including responsibilities and even the benefits. Part-time employees may be assigned any range of job responsibility, frequently without being paid benefits, or the benefits are prorated. Some part-timers are hired on an on-call or intermittent basis.

FIGURE 12-3

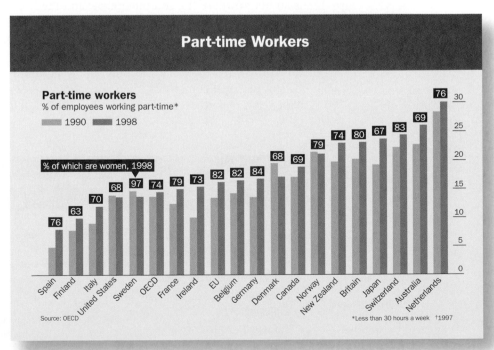

Source: © 1999 The Economist Newspaper Group Inc. Reprinted with permission. Further reproduction prohibited. www.economist.com.

FIGURE 12-4

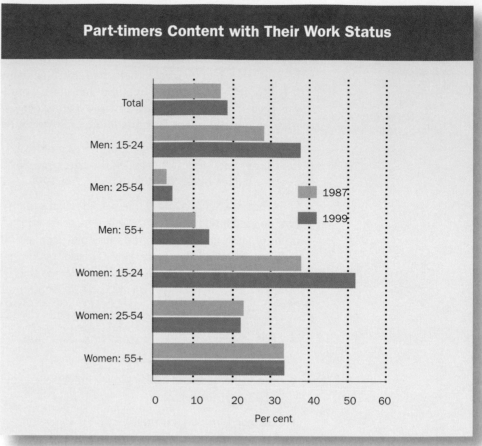

Source: Reprinted with permission from *The Globe and Mail.*

Telecommuting

Telecommuting
Paid labour performed at
the employee's home.

As an outgrowth of the computer age—and fuelled in part by futurist Alvin Toffler's image of the "electronic cottage" in his book *The Third Wave*—*telecommuting* is becoming increasingly popular.[20] Working at home suits the work habits and lifestyles of some personalities, particularly those self-disciplined self-starters who can work with a high degree of autonomy. Aiding in this trend are the decreasing costs of personal computers, modems, photocopiers, and fax machines. More than 50 per cent of these "telecommuters" have children in their home or office.[21]

Pros and Cons of Part-time Work

PROS	CONS
Individuals can maintain work experience while devoting time to raising children, elder care, upgrading education	Salary and benefits lower than full-time job
Reduced absenteeism for personal appointments	More difficult to coordinate group activities
May reduce staffing costs	Commitment and productivity may not be recognized by other employees

Digital Imagery © 2001 Photo Disc Inc. Photo by Patagonik Works

For a telecommuter, the home becomes the office. Working from home suits the work habits and life style of certain personalities very well.

www.ivc.ca/part3.html

www.youcanwork
fromanywhere.com/

www.gilgordon.com/

http://telecommute.org

www.telecommuting.org

www.nytac.org/

A 1997 survey by KPMG, involving more than 400 Canadian companies, found that six per cent of the latter's employees were telecommuters. Sixty-two per cent of firms said they have more telecommuters than three years ago and 52 per cent predicted an increase over the next three years.[22]

Telecommuting is ideal for employees who do independent jobs, such as insurance claim officers, catalogue sales agents, computer software writers, telephone solicitors, and so on. The "information highway" will probably increase the number of people working in the "electronic cottage industry." However, not everybody is positive about this new approach. Unions especially raise some objections. They fear that this trend will lead to new forms of exploitation.[23]

Telecommuting seems to have positive results on the bottom line for employers. When Bell Canada asked its 100 largest customers about the benefits of telecommuting, all reported productivity increases between 15 to 35 per cent. One of its subsidiaries experienced a reduction in absenteeism from eight to three days per employee due to telecommuting. The cost of setting up a telecommuting employee is also lower than office expenses. Pacific Bell pays $1700 per employee, far less than the cost of a work station. J.C. Penney sets up employees for half the cost of an office.[24] In the KPMG survey mentioned above, firms reported more effective use of time (71 per cent), improved employee lifestyle (57 per cent), retention of staff who would otherwise have left, and quality of work (34 per cent) as the top benefits of telecommuting.[25]

The following are some examples of telecommuters or home-based workers in Canada:

Dee McCrae no longer has to drive from her home in Mississauga to Nortel Networks Corporation's office in Brampton, Ontario. Instead, she simply hikes up the stairs to her ergonomically correct desk that Nortel set up as a home office. "The soft and the hard benefits are multifold," said Ms. McCrae, who acts as the liaison for Nortel's telecommuters in the greater Toronto region. It saves wear and tear on my car... the insurance, I save money on dry cleaning, save money on my wardrobe." Nortel, which has about 70 000 employees worldwide, boasts more than 7000 telecommuters, more than double the number it had in 1997.[26]

Pros and Cons of Telecommuting

PROS	CONS
Less commuting time	Isolation of employees from supervisors and coworkers
Better integration of work and family life	Lack of visibility (overlooked for promotion decision making)
Freedom to work independently and at own pace	Supervision more difficult
Less overhead cost for employers	Distractions at home (TV, kids, tradespeople)

http://telecommuting
.about.com/smallbusiness
.telecommuting/

www.telecommute.org/

www.publicworks.com

Thousands of kilometres away, reporter Terry Glavin sits on his houseboat in the Fraser River delta, gazing at passing gill-netters as he crafts stories about fishing and native affairs for the *Vancouver Sun.* "I'd be a sinner to complain," he says of an arrangement with the newspaper that lets him work at home. "I'm perfectly plugged into the kinds of stories I write about. All my neighbours are fishermen."

Elsewhere in Greater Vancouver, veteran Royal Bank of Canada employee Jan McNeill works at home while her four-year-old daughter plays nearby with a Dictaphone and calculator. In Ottawa, federal public servant Pierre Rondeau researches trademarks from a battery of home computers, and figures he saves $300 to $350 a month by not going into the office.[27]

As Joyce Everhart, managing editor of Public Works Online, comments: "Telecommuting, or teleworking, is a business solution that is here to stay."[28]

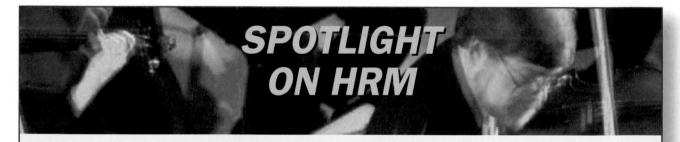

SPOTLIGHT ON HRM

WHEN HOME IS WHERE THE WORK IS

Michael Hepworth's "virtual company" is becoming less virtual these days.

He's discovered that sometimes situations are better managed by full-time staff that works within four old-fashioned office walls.

His company, Hepworth & Co. Ltd., turned its first $1 million in annual revenue with just three full-time employees, using part-time workers and home-based contractors for the rest.

But after six years of rapid growth, the firm, which specializes in customer satisfaction measurement and call centre management, has 10 full-time staff and is becoming less virtual and more traditional.

"The big challenge is getting the balance and deciding what competencies you need in-house and which contract people you need on certain projects," he says.

Mr. Hepworth is not alone. Many firms are discovering that as they gain more experience with home workers, virtual offices and telecommuting, they need to step back and assess the success of the extremely popular programs. And many are concluding the systems are not for everyone in every situation.

The emerging key to success is careful management, which mitigates the potential downfalls before they appear.

Mr. Hepworth, for example, says he's discovered that it is a lot easier for employees of his consulting firm to work from home when they have more experience with the company and understand the culture well.

"Our business is very sophisticated and I think it takes people a while to really understand it," he says.

Kris Sharma, a senior consultant at Ernst & Young, advises companies not to start telecommuting programs on an ad-hoc basic for a few employees. "You have to think about how to manage it and what the selection criteria should be to get the most suitable candidates," he says.

Companies end up failing to decide what they are trying to accomplish with the system, do not strategically target who makes the best home worker and do not define terms and conditions in advance.

If poorly selected, employees do not succeed as home workers and that leaves the company contending with ruffled feathers—at the very least—when it asks someone to return to the office.

Mr. Sharma recommends that firms start small, with a pilot project targeted at the best potential job categories, such as sales or telemarketing, where employees work independently and may often be out of the office anyway.

Companies also have to think about how they will manage a work force that does not "show up" at the office every day.

Janet Salaff, a professor of sociology at the University of Toronto, who is currently involved in a project to assess a large workforce's telecommuting system, points out that while many employees are more productive working from home, some are not.

To avoid problems, companies have to consider more systems of monitoring, interim deadlines, breaking longer projects into smaller components, or regularized routines.

"Guidelines are needed," she says. "You can't send people home without having these guidelines in place. You can't manage people the same way when they work at home."

Prof. Salaff says employees, whose jobs are complex, but not necessarily novel, do well working at home. Other people, however, who are constantly doing new things that require great creativity, who work extensively in teams and who have a lot of client contact often work best in the office.

"The risk of doing something wrong is greater when the employee deals with people outside [the company]," she says. "In those cases, the supervisors get quite anxious."

She says there is also a common complaint from workers who feel shut out of the lines of internal communication and worry about missing career advancement opportunities if they are out of sight.

Prof. Salaff says employees who are electronically linked not only to their bosses but also to their colleagues, say they have an easier time working from home. In one study she worked on, employees in a unit who were telecommuting had all worked together previously, often for years, so they had developed their own networks of communication.

Like Mr. Hepworth, she suggests new employees may not be as suited for homework. "There are a lot of ambiguous work conditions and office work can tell you what you should really be doing, rather than what's written down," Prof. Salaff says.

To keep their profiles high, employees are also becoming more strategic about making their accomplishments known to their supervisors, Prof. Salaff says.

She has discovered that many send monthly updates about their work and activities, even though they are not required and are not provided by workers at the office. Employees have also found ways to demonstrate they are working long hours, even when the boss can't wander by their offices and spot them during the evenings.

"They're quite creative about being present even if they're not specifically present," Prof. Salaff says.

"They will answer E-mail or voice-mail after dinner because they say it's a relaxing way to get a head start on the next day. But it also will be time stamped, so their bosses will see the time it's sent. They don't say they do it to get Brownie points but it's something their bosses will notice."

Source: Janet McFarland, "When Home Is Where the Work Is," *The Globe and Mail*, March 19, 1996, p. B14. Reprinted with permission from *The Globe and Mail*.

Virtual organization
An operational domain of any organization whose workforce includes a significant portion of remote workers.

The Virtual Organization

Is it possible to have a company with 1700 employees and no formal headquarters? Golder Associates, a Calgary company specializing in engineering and environmental consulting, is one of the Canadian companies with employees spread around the

Pros and Cons of the Virtual Organization

PROS	CONS
Working independently and at own pace	Communication tends to be more difficult
No commuting	Supervision difficult
Avoidance of rush hours	Isolation of employees from supervisor and colleagues
Lower overhead costs	Lack of role clarity

www.ascusc.org/
jcmc/vol3/issue4/
desanctis.html

www.hrdc-drhc.gc.ca/
stratpol/arb/publications/
bulletin/vol2n2/v2n2a7
e.shtml

globe, with nine managers in eight cities in Canada, the United States, Italy, and Australia. Communication is electronic most of the time, via e-mail and conference calls, with only four annual face-to-face meetings for strategic decisions. It seems to work very well for the company, which has had annual growth of more than 10 per cent since its creation in 1960, with revenues of $173 million in 1997.

> Having people all over the world ensures a better range of perspectives, says Hal Hamilton, president of Golder Associates. The bad part is that it puts extra stress on communication, coordination, and decision-making. Where we get into trouble is when the management teams around the world get disconnected from the needs and wants of our people," he says. But then "the phones start ringing and the e-mails start flying, and they get your attention very quickly."[29]

Phased Retirement

Phased retirement
Gradual phase into retirement with loss or reduction of pension benefits.

Some companies are allowing older employees to reduce their work activity and gradually phase into retirement without loss or reduction of pension benefits. The most typical pattern in *phased retirement* is to allow gradually shortened workweeks, a preferred schedule among older workers according to some surveys.[30] Most companies in the survey required that an employee first work a minimum of five years in the firm and be at least 55 years old in order to participate in a phased retirement program, and over half allowed employees to change their minds. An example of phased retirement is provided by McGill University:

> McGill University in Montreal offers its faculty members a preretirement package that allows a faculty member to choose to teach only half of his or her normal teaching load for 65 per cent of the salary. This assumes that the faculty member will still carry on with his or her normal administrative work (e.g., attending department and other committee meetings and being available for student counselling, and so on).[31]

Pros and Cons of Phased Retirement

PROS	CONS
More time for retiree to develop other interests	Loss of income before retirement
Chance to "try out" retirement	Not compatible with some pension benefit packages
Loss of key personnel is cushioned	

Pros and Cons of Employee Leasing

PROS	**CONS**
Staffing flexibility	Potential loss of trade secrets
Fast availability of professionals	Lack of employee commitment to the organization
No recruitment, hiring, benefits, or training costs	Expensive, at least short-term
No long-term commitments	Dual authority relationship

In 1997, The Quebec government adopted legislation to facilitate phased retirement and early retirement.[32]

Employee Leasing

www.napeo.org/
indinfo.htm

www.roughnotes
.com/rnmag/june97/
06p30.htm

www.bbb.org/
alerts/employee.asp

Employee leasing
The practice of outsourcing job functions, such as payroll, to organizations specializing in the field.

According to a report in the September 1997 issue of *HRMagazine*, a new type of organization has emerged and is already booming: the Professional Employer Organization (PEO), reaching revenues close to $500 million in 1998. A PEO is a new type of leasing company, providing a wide range of outsourced HR services, from payroll and taxes to hiring and discipline, depending on a client's needs. Clients tend to be small and mid-size employers with fewer than 100 employees, who cannot afford to hire top-flight HR experts.

"If you run a restaurant, chances are you're good at that, not at payroll," says Carl Kleimann, Senior Vice President of 1st Odyssey Group, a Houston PEO that manages 12 000 employees. "The growth of our industry is coming from businesses that are tired of the headaches of dealing with government regulations. They fear they didn't complete something correctly. They don't understand or don't want to hassle with wage and hour laws and employment laws. Fear of lawsuits is another concern."[33]

Sharing Employees (or Flexforce)

Some innovative companies came up with a new way to use their employees for mutual benefit, for employee and employer alike. Seasonal companies, like soft-drink bottlers or ice-cream manufacturers, experience a slowdown when their products are in lower demand. Rather than laying off employees, these companies found it useful to "loan" their employees to companies who tend to hire temporary workers during certain times of the year.

While not yet popular in Canada, two U.S. companies pioneered the sharing idea. Brooks Beverage Management Inc. (BBMI), a soft-drink bottler based in the city of Holland, Michigan, tried to find ways to avoid laying off its permanent staff during the annual production slowdown in September and October. Its partner was Haworth Inc., a neighbouring furniture manufacturer. Haworth was a fast-growing company and had a difficult time recruiting enough qualified workers. After some intense negotiations, both companies came to a satisfying solution for both sides.

Haworth had its own cyclical trend: Corporate America buys more office furniture at the end of the year, creating a peak demand that lasts through the beginning of the next year. Both companies tended to staff for the low periods and then supplement for the high-demand periods. With the involvement of employees, the

Pros and Cons of Employee Sharing

PROS	CONS
Keeping jobs permanent	Extra training required
No need for lay-offs during economic downturns	
Lower compensation expenses	
Task variety	

agreement called for the transfer, on a loan basis, of 31 employees from BBMI to Haworth, to cover the peak production period. The BBMI employees were put into assembly-line positions, requiring a minimum of training. In March, when production at Haworth slowed down and production at BBMI increased, the BBMI employees returned to their previous jobs. Both sides were very happy with this novel idea.[34]

FLEXIBLE STAFFING

Flexible staffing
Nonpermanent employment, allowing short-term assignments.

ALTERNATIVE arrangements in staffing an organization can also provide management with greater flexibility and increased work options. *Flexible staffing* (or a contingent staffing arrangement) describes a system where employees typically have nonpermanent ties to an employer, allowing short-term assignments with no guarantee of future employment. These arrangements are often closely linked to particular tasks—for example, a market analysis, overseeing or arranging a merger, assisting a small business to get off the ground, and so on.[35]

Temporary agency hires are persons hired through a temporary service firm who are employees of that agency, not of the company contracting for the service. It appears to be the most commonly used staffing alternative. From a management perspective, temporary agency hires provide considerable staffing flexibility during periods when companies are experiencing either a staffing shortage (e.g., during holiday seasons or unexpected high turnover), or a seasonal market demand for special services (e.g., income-tax filing assistance). Problems with the temporary agency staffing arrangement are high costs and uneven quality of work.[36]

An *internal temporary pool* consists of persons who are on call as needed. The pool is managed internally by the company. Because of the high costs of temporary agency hires mentioned above, many human resource managers rely more on internal temporary pools, consisting typically of people between jobs, retirees, homemakers returning to the work force, former employees, and students. Such pools tend to be small and consist mainly of individuals who perform clerical and administrative work. Retirees are perceived to be a good source of internal temporary pools, because they tend to know the requirements of the company and there seems to be a preference for coming back for a short period of time.[37]

Independent contractors are self-employed workers hired for a finite period of time, for example, as freelancers or consultants.[38] Employers tend to make use of this type of staffing very selectively, especially for skills not available in the organization. In many cases, former executives, who either left voluntarily or were "invited to leave," or employees who were laid off, took early retirement, or left the company to start their own businesses are hired back as consultants.[39]

Independent contractors whose skills are in high demand can take advantage of management's interest in flexible staffing. Contractors in professional or technical areas, for example, often like the autonomy and the financial advantages of being self-employed. Many such contractors can command higher compensation than they would as employees. Contracting out, however, can also be exploitative. For example, some "self-employed" women, hired to do routine clerical work for one employer, are given daily quotas to meet and are paid on a piece-rate basis. In effect, they perform as employees, but receive less compensation because they have no benefit protection.[40]

Sometimes questions arise about whether the individual is, in fact, an employee or a contractor. In doubtful cases, Canada Customs and Revenue Agency (CCRA) can be asked to make a ruling. To establish an employee's status, CCRA reviews certain activities that generally indicate whether individuals are employees:

- Did they have a set number of working hours each day?

- Did they have to account for their time?

- Were they given specific job instructions?

- Were they members of the company's benefit plans?

- Did they have use of the company's computer equipment and office supplies?

- Did the company supply them with offices?

- Were they given specific titles and business cards on the company's letterhead?

To summarize, to be considered independent contractors, workers must agree to do specific jobs with no commitment for numbers of hours. They also must work on their own without supervision. They have to bill the employer directly and receive cheques for the completed work. They must keep their own financial books and records of accounting. In addition, they must not receive any company benefits. Independent contractors operate from their own offices with their own equipment; they should go to employers only for meetings. They also must provide services to more than one organization.

In addition to the above rules, CCRA developed four tests, which assist human resource managers in deciding whether a person working for the organization should be considered to be an employee or an independent contractor:

www.bcarter.com/
tip073.htm

1. *Control Test.* This test determines whether the employee is restricted under a "master-servant" relationship. Usually, an employer has more control over an employee than over an independent contractor. For example, in a master-servant relationship, not only can the "master" order what is to be done, but also how and when. Independent contractors are usually free to choose how their services are to be performed.

2. *Ownership of Tools Test.* What tools or materials are needed for the work done? Who owns them? If the business owns them it looks more like an employer-employee relationship.

3. *Risk of Loss and Chance of Profit Test.* Who bears the financial risk that will provide an opportunity for profit? Who controls the pricing of the work done? If there is little financial risk, then again it looks more like a dependency relationship

4. *Integration Test.* This test answers the question of whether the work performed by an employee under an employment contract is done as an integral part of the business. If a worker were under contract for services, his or her work

Pros and Cons of Flexible Staffing	
PROS	**CONS**
Flexibility in staffing for short-term projects	Expensive
Fast availability of professionals	Uneven quality of work
No permanent commitment to employee	No loyalty to temporary employer

would be classified as only "necessary" to the business, and not an integral part of the company. The more "critical" the work is for the business, the less likely it is done by an independent contractor.[41]

The latest development in the area of flexible staffing seems to be the *just-in-time employee*, a term coined by *Business Week* in its special issue, The 21st Century Corporation.[42] *Business Week* describes a Human Capital Exchange (HCE) model, which works much like NASDAQ and the New York Stock Exchange, with the value of employees—free agents—determined by the open market... "lawyers down $2, engineers up a buck." *Business Week* quotes Christopher Meyer, director of the Center for Business Innovation, as saying that these free agents "are much more likely to get what they are worth—they will participate in the downside and the upside."

EMPLOYEE MOTIVATION

www.cba.uri.edu/
Scholl/Notes/Sources
Inducement_Matrix.htm

www.accel-
team.com/motivation/
theory_01.html

http://choo.fis.utoronto.ca/
fis/courses/lis1230/
lis1230sharma/motive1.htm

ONE OF THE MOST challenging skills of a manager is the ability to motivate employees. Management expects employees to be productive and show commitment to the organization. However, to be committed and productive employees must be motivated appropriately, which is not an easy task. Managers are able to offer incentives, but it is up to the employee to make use of them. It is like the proverbial horse that is led to the water; one cannot make it drink. What a manager can do is to increase the probability that an employee is motivated by creating the proper job environment in the organization. The second part of this chapter will use the expectancy theory model to explain how managers can create a motivating job environment. There are many other motivation models, but we feel that for the human resource manager the expectancy approach is the most practical one. This model is also useful for any other manager interested in motivating employees.

An organization's productivity is influenced by many factors. Employee motivation and satisfaction are just two of these, but they are important in all organizations. Human resource departments affect employee motivation and satisfaction through almost every activity they perform: training and development; performance and compensation; benefits and services; security, safety, and health.

Motivation and satisfaction are also affected by virtually every aspect of the organization—many of which the human resource department cannot directly control, such as supervisory treatment of employees, promotions, merit raises, and other human resource actions normally reserved for line managers. Human resource specialists can contribute to employee motivation and satisfaction, however, by assisting these decision-makers.[43]

Digital Imagery © 2001 Photo Disc Inc. Photo by Photolink

What motivates a mountain climber to endure one of the most difficult tasks? The answer: to satisfy a need, an inner drive.

Motivation
A person's drive to take action because that person wants to do so.

Employee Motivation and Job Satisfaction

Motivation can be defined as goal-directed behaviour. The behaviour results from a felt need that a person wants to satisfy. A more comprehensive definition emphasizes three distinct aspects of motivation that are important. First, motivation represents an energetic force that drives people to behave in particular ways. Second, this drive is directed toward something. In other words, motivation has strong goal orientation. Third, the idea of motivation is best understood within a systems perspective. That is, to understand human motivation, it is necessary to examine the forces within individuals and their environments that provide them with feedback and reinforce their intensity and direction.[44]

Job satisfaction
The favourableness or unfavourableness with which employees view their work.

Job satisfaction is a person's emotional reaction toward various aspects of work, usually the nature of work itself, pay, promotion, supervision, and peers. As with any attitude, satisfaction cannot be observed, it must be inferred from an employee's behaviour or verbal statements. Job satisfaction can best be understood in terms of discrepancy. Discrepancy is the result of how much a person wants or expects from the job compared to how much he or she actually receives.[45]

www.sbs.eku.edu/PSY/
FALKENBE/motive.htm

For many years, managers believed that "a happy worker is a productive worker," and considerable energies were invested in finding ways to make employees "happy" at work. However, more recent research has shown that the causal relationship may, in fact, be just the opposite, if certain conditions are met. It has been found that *only if performance is fairly and equitably rewarded do employees experience job satisfaction.*[46] Figure 12-5 shows the historical belief and the more recent insight. This new insight has significant implications for managers. For example, it is necessary for managers to make the *performance-reward connection* clear to every employee if they want to motivate them. And the manager must make sure that high performance is actually rewarded and not just taken for granted. It is also important for the manager to know that it is the *perceived* equity on the part of the employee that causes job satisfaction (equity, or fairness, is in the eyes of the beholder).

Expectancy theory model
Expectancy theory states that motivation is the result of the outcome one seeks and one's estimate that action will lead to the desired outcome.

The Expectancy Theory Model of Motivation

The *expectancy theory model* of motivation is probably the most practical and powerful tool for human resource managers to demonstrate to other managers the importance of all human resource functions in creating a motivating environment. If the expectancy theory model is operationalized and followed in an organization, there is a strong probability that its employees will be highly motivated. The theory even

www.cba.uri.edu/
Scholl/Notes/Motivational_
Diagnostic_Framework.html

www.mindef.gov.sg/
dag/scc/Counselink/
0199-01.htm

allows managers to use numbers to determine the strength of the motivation of their employees, although this is rarely done.[47] The expectancy model discussed here was developed by Porter and Lawler (1973).

Before we discuss the theoretical model, necessary to comprehend the practical application, let's discuss the practical application by operationalizing the theory in a step-by-step approach:

1. Recruitment and selection: Hire employees with the proper abilities and skills.
2. Orientation and training: Clarify employees' roles by setting goals, providing job descriptions, and honing skills.
3. Pay and incentives: Offer valued rewards for high performance. Make sure employees understand performance-reward connection.
4. Performance appraisal (communication and trust): Be a coach and counsellor, give feedback, and improve employees' self-esteem and confidence.
5. Motivation: Create the proper job environment through team building, job design, and employee participation (buy-in, empowerment).

At the heart of the model are three components: the effort-performance probability (EP), the performance-outcome probability (PO), and the value of an outcome (V). Expectancy suggests that an employee's productivity ultimately depends on his or her answers to the three questions shown in Figure 12-6 and listed below:

1. Given your abilities, experiences, self-confidence, and your understanding of your supervisor's expectations, on a scale of zero to one, what is the probability—your gut feeling—that your effort will result in a superior performance? (Can I do it?)
2. On a scale from zero to one, how sure are you that when you do a good job your boss will reward you? (What is in it for me?)
3. Of what value is the outcome to you? (How much do I want it?)

The complete Porter/Lawler model is shown in Figure 12-7. *Effort-performance probability* (EP) is the likelihood that an employee's effort results in high performance. If the employee is not prepared, has not understood the explanations regarding expectations, and has low self-confidence, his or her estimation of the probability to perform well will be low (e.g., .1 or .2). A more experienced

FIGURE 12-5

The Relationship Between Performance and Job Satisfaction

FIGURE 12-6

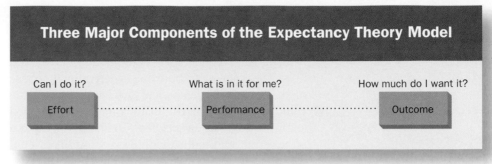

employee may feel a probability of .5 or .6 in succeeding, and a highly skilled, experienced, self-confident employee will be quite optimistic in succeeding, say .8 or .9, or will be absolutely sure: 1.0.

Performance-outcome probability (PO) is the likelihood—as perceived by the employee—that a high performance will be rewarded. The linkage between performance and outcome (rewards) has to be made clear to the employee. This is the responsibility of the manager.

FIGURE 12-7

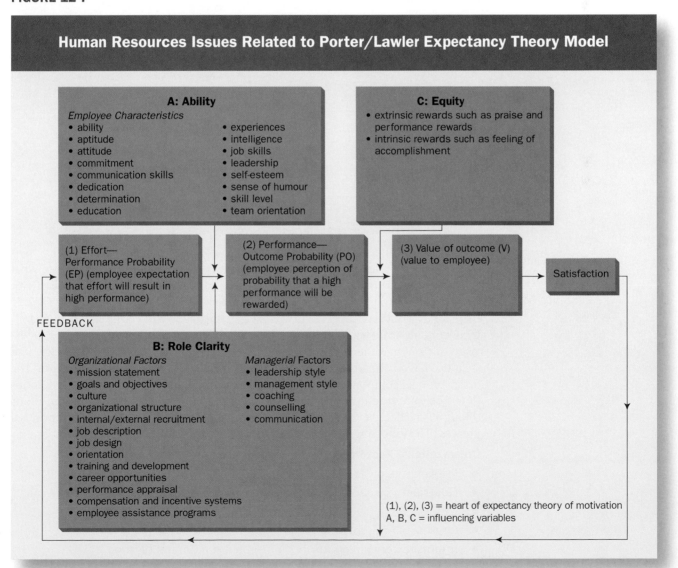

The *value* of an outcome or reward (V) is more difficult to measure. It would be easy if only money were involved—for example, bonuses or pay raises—but many outcomes are intangibles, such as praise, recognition, and intrinsic rewards, or have value beyond money, such as promotion, more vacation time, or a dinner with the boss. The value of an outcome is determined on a scale from −1 to +1 and is based on the personal preferences of each employee. A younger employee, for example, may value money (.9), may not care as much about a pension plan (.2), and may dislike a transfer to headquarters (-.6) (the minus sign is a reminder that job outcomes can be negative, that is, be demotivators). An older employee may have quite different preferences: .4 for money, .8 for a pension plan, and .7 for a transfer.

Of more practical importance to managers are the three other components of the expectancy model: ability, role clarity, and equity (boxes A, B, and C in Figure 12-7). Ability refers to the personal characteristics the employee brings to the job. *It also symbolizes one of the most crucial decisions a manager must make: hiring the right person for the job.* If something goes wrong here, it usually will haunt the manager and the organization for a long time. For the human resource manager, it is therefore necessary to ensure that the organization's selection system is working, that the recruitment process is done properly, and that employment planning is adequate. Moreover, it should be pointed out that all these functions cannot be done properly without having carried out a thorough job analysis, a good illustration of the systems concept in human resource management.

A listing of typical characteristics that recruiters look for in employees would contain:

- Ability
- Aptitude
- Attitude
- Commitment
- Communication skills
- Dedication
- Determination
- Education
- Experiences
- Intelligence
- Job skills
- Leadership
- Self-esteem
- Sense of humour
- Skill level
- Team orientation

This list is by no means complete. Recruiters must develop their own list of selection criteria, based on the specific job requirements in their organization.

Role clarity refers to the ability of a manager to explain to each employee what is expected regarding performance levels and standards. It is useful to look at two components of role clarity separately: the supervisor and the organization. Clearly, the leadership style of supervisors will have an impact on role clarity, as will their ability to communicate with employees and to build employee trust—both in the supervisor and among other employees, thereby creating a true team spirit. Management style also has an impact, but this is more influenced by the organizational culture. The organizational component also includes the orientation program, a valid job description, relevant training, and the clarity of the performance-reward connections through an effective wage and salary administration and performance appraisal process. The following is a listing of individual parts of the role clarity variable:

Organizational Factors
- Mission statement
- Goals and objectives
- Culture
- Organizational structure
- Internal/external recruitment

Managerial Factors
- Leadership style
- Management style
- Coaching
- Counselling
- Communication

- Job description
- Job design
- Orientation
- Training and development
- Career opportunities
- Performance appraisal
- Compensation and incentive systems
- Employee assistance programs

All of these factors are under the control of management in general or the specific supervisor. If many or most of these factors are in place in an organization and are used properly, management will have created an organizational environment that is highly conducive to motivating employees.

Some readers will have noticed that the above list is practically the contents listing of a human resource textbook. In other words: *the expectancy model shows the application of all human resource functions.* No other motivation model offers such a complete utilization of the field of human resource management.

The third variable, *equity*, was discussed earlier in the context of performance and job satisfaction. *Only if performance is fairly and equitably rewarded will employees experience job satisfaction.* Some of the characteristics of the equity variable include:

- extrinsic outcome/reward;
- intrinsic outcome/reward; and
- value of the outcome/reward.

Extrinsic rewards are given by the organization (pay, bonuses, time off) or the manager (praise, recognition). They are either tangible or intangible, for example, pay versus praise. *Intrinsic rewards* are related to performing the job. Examples of intrinsic rewards are feelings of task accomplishment, autonomy, and personal growth and development that come from the job. They are often described as "self-administered" rewards because engaging in the task itself leads to their receipt. Intrinsic outcomes should be of special interest to management because their only costs are some planning efforts on the side of the manager. A well-designed job, a valid job description with realistic performance standards, and achievable and agreed-upon goals should allow employees to experience task accomplishment and personal growth and development because of job success. When properly applied, extrinsic rewards (praise, recognition) tend to result in intrinsic rewards (pride, satisfaction, feeling of accomplishment). In other words, managers are able to give employees two rewards, which are free.

The (perceived) value of a reward is one of the more important motivating factors in the expectancy model. If managers want to motivate their employees, they must offer something of value to the employees—something that fulfills a need or needs. Organizations use mainly money as a reward, because it is much easier to administer than an individualized reward program. Still, managers can find out what their employees value and can take this into account when they want to reward deserving staff members.

The following story demonstrates how the expectancy model can be operationalized:

A bank manager needs to hire a teller. She interviews many applicants and decides on one who has the necessary abilities, skills, and traits. She gives the teller a thorough briefing on what will be expected of him, and explains how his performance will

Extrinsic rewards
Given reward, e.g., money, praise.

Intrinsic rewards
Felt reward, e.g., accomplishment, satisfaction.

www.mentalhelp.net/
psyhelp/chap4/chap4q.htm

www.p-management.com/
articles/9902.htm

be measured. The teller also receives a job description that explains all the tasks he is expected to fulfill, complete with performance standards, priorities, and accountabilities (role clarity).

The manager makes sure that for the first few days the trainee is working with an experienced teller who guides him through the routines. The manager also does some role-playing with the trainee to make sure that he knows how to react when he encounters an angry customer (thereby developing self-confidence, which translates into higher EP). She also makes it very clear to him that she is always available if he needs any help and that he can also rely on the support of his colleagues in the branch (supervisory and peer support raises self-confidence, resulting again in higher EP).

The manager explains to the new teller how the bank's pay system works, and she describes the performance appraisal system and the criteria that are used to assess a teller's performance. She also discusses the performance objectives with the teller and agrees with him on some realistic goals and sets deadlines for their accomplishment. During the discussion, she tries to find out what rewards are valued by the teller. If, for example, it turns out that the teller is more interested in time off than in bonuses, the manager will keep this in mind for reward purposes.*

With this approach, the manager has created the appropriate environment and preconditions for motivating the employee. It should be emphasized again that the hiring decision is the most crucial decision the manager has to make. If candidates are hired with the wrong attitudes or inadequate skills, or if they lack the necessary experience to do a job properly, their effort-performance probability will likely be low, a situation that is often difficult to remedy. However, a good hiring decision will not always ensure a motivated employee. *It is a necessary, but not sufficient, condition.* The motivating job environment must be created too. Conversely, a bungled hiring decision will probably not be remedied by a highly motivating environment. An employee with the wrong attitude, aptitude, or lack of skill or experience will gain little from a better job description or mission statement.

The expectancy model is valuable for managers because of its practicality. It explains the factors that influence or determine motivation, which in turn allows managers to influence some of these factors.

Figure 12-8 offers an indication of what keeps employees motivated and on their jobs. It is interesting to note, that *people issues* come first and second, *job-related topics* third and fourth, and *money* fifth.

Tailor-made Perks

The latest trend in reward plans is to allow employees to choose their rewards. Nortel Networks Corporation came up with the idea to thank employees by allowing supervisors and peers to recommend employees for special points that can be converted into money. The recommendations must be approved by two managers to avoid "back-scratching" between friends. For example, 5000 points would be a modest thank-you, worth about $100. Points can be cashed in or exchanged for merchandise or saved for higher-value prizes, such as a trip to the National Basketball Association all-star game, valued at 160 000 points.

Martin Cozyn, the compensation vice-president, says the beauty is that the rewards are immediate and concrete. Judy Zwickl, an associate director at the Conference Board of Canada's Centre for Management Effectiveness, says Nortel's reward scheme is in keeping with a general trend by companies to offer employees more choice. Choosing your own rewards, she says, can be viewed as an extension of such developments as flexible work arrangements and benefit plans.[48]

This is actually a true story, told by a bank branch manager during a management seminar given by the first author for the Institute of Canadian Bankers. She had used the expectancy model without knowing it.

FIGURE 12-8

http://goalmanager.com/i101
internal30.asp

What do you like about your current job? What are the things that keep you there?

People and work environment	66%
The management cares about me/Good relationship with management	33%
Challenging and exciting job	33%
Flexibility	24%
Salary	19%
Autonomy and creative freedom with job	16%
Training and learning opportunities	13%
Stock options	9%
I like the product/technology	9%
Teamwork	8%

Source: GoalManager Employee Motivation Survey 2000. Percentages are based on multiple responses to each question and thus will not add up to 100%. *Full Survey Results.* Courtesy of www.goalmanager.com.

STRATEGIC IMPLICATIONS OF WORK OPTIONS AND MOTIVATION

IF WE LOOK AT the major components of HR activities, they comprise recruitment and selection, development and evaluation, compensation and protection, and employee and labour relations. Alternative scheduling, flexible staffing, and motivation will influence all of them.

Recruitment and Selection

As noted, the recruitment and selection process is a critical part of the human resource management function. Managers must ensure that the most suitable person is chosen for the job as a precondition for high motivation. But human resource managers also have to consider that if flexible staffing is part of the human resource strategy, then attention must be paid to the type of applicants who fit into such positions. Employees with family responsibilities are more likely to be interested in job sharing, part-time schemes, homework, or flexible schedules than others. These options should be made clear during the hiring process.

Development and Evaluation

The expectancy model shows that training, development, and performance appraisals are important factors in increasing the motivation level of employees, but so are flexible work schedules and staffing options, at least for a number of employees. Flexible schedules and staffing tend to reduce employee absenteeism and turnover, resulting in substantial savings in the hiring and training of new employees. This allows employers to invest these savings into the training and development of their stable staff, a much more valuable investment than recurrent training of new employees.

Compensation and Protection

The motivating aspect of valued outcomes has been clearly demonstrated in the expectancy model. Managers must be trained to make the performance-reward connection clear to their employees. Flexible staffing options often have a significant impact on the compensation expenses of a company. For enterprises with low profit margins, such as supermarkets, or companies with peak service periods, such as airlines, substantial savings can be made by relying more on part-time employees who are often not paid benefits. Savings are also possible by allowing work options such as telecommuting or industrial cottages, where employees are willing to accept lower salaries for the convenience of working at home and at their own schedule.

Employee and Labour Relations

As a number of studies have shown, a motivating work environment tends to result in higher job satisfaction, with a number of other positive consequences, some of which already have been mentioned. There is some evidence that more satisfied employees tend to provide higher-quality customer service.

There is also the perception of managers that offering a flexible work environment—scheduling, staffing, work options—tends to make unions less attractive. There are few hard data on this aspect, but studies have shown a positive relationship between certain benefits (e.g., profit sharing), flexible work schedules, and company climates.[49]

Unions tend to look at work options, part-time work, and shorter workweeks as management strategies to save money at the expense of workers. But it has also been shown that a number of unions accept such strategies to gain job security for their members. Human resource strategies using alternative scheduling, flexible staffing, work options, and other motivational approaches as strategic tools seem to pay off in the long run.

SUMMARY

Alternative work scheduling and flexible staffing contribute to greater organizational flexibility and efficiency. They allow employers to optimize their human resources and, at the same time, accommodate special needs of employees.

The human resource function is directly and indirectly involved with employee motivation and job satisfaction. Human resource policies and programs have a major effect on organizational motivation.

The application of the expectancy theory model allows managers to create a motivating work environment. It shows that the hiring decision is one of the most crucial decisions a manager must make. It also emphasizes the need to provide role clarification, and to establish a clear performance-reward linkage. Furthermore, it stresses that the rewards offered have to be valued by the employees, and that the employees must perceive the rewards for their performance to be fair and equitable.

TERMS FOR REVIEW

Visit the Web site at www.mcgrawhill.ca/college/schwind6 for a full glossary.

REVIEW AND DISCUSSION QUESTIONS

1. Work options seem to be beneficial to some employees. Give examples of work options that are desirable to certain types of employees.

2. Discuss the attitudes of unions toward work options. Are the attitudes positive or negative? Why?

3. Some fire departments and hospital staff are using the three-day, 36-hour schedule. Do you see any negative aspects with this schedule?

4. The "weekender" option of the shorter workweek is now used by some companies. What is it, and why is it financially interesting to employees?

5. Discuss the advantages and disadvantages of the shorter workweek.

6. Some companies view the shorter workweek as an alternative to layoffs. Discuss this option from an employee's point of view.

7. Discuss the variations in the flextime approach.

8. "Flextime is a useful approach for both the employer and the employee." Discuss.

9. What are the positive aspects of job sharing for an employee? Are there negative aspects as well?

10. Comment on the statement: "Happy workers are productive workers."

11. Explain the relationship between job satisfaction and performance.

12. Discuss the practicality of the expectancy theory model from a manager's point of view.

CRITICAL THINKING QUESTIONS

1. In what ways are well-designed work option programs beneficial for both employers and employees?

2. Contract work has become very popular in recent years. Discuss some of the legal issues associated with this type of work arrangement.

3. Some companies maintain a virtual organization. What control mechanisms are available to the organization to make sure employees are doing what they are supposed to do? Do the usual HR tools (i.e., job description, performance appraisal, incentive systems) work? If not, why not?

4. Why is the hiring decision so crucial for managers with regard to the motivation of employees? Use the expectancy theory model for your explanation.

5. How should a HR manager find out what employees value as rewards? Is it acceptable to ask employees directly? Discuss. Are other methods preferable? Which? Why?

WEB RESEARCH

1. Using the Gil Gordon Web site, research the trends in telecommuting. www.gilgordon.com

2. How much support is there for the assertion that telecommuting results in higher productivity? If true, what accounts for this result?

3. If a telecommuter works for a company with high security needs (e.g., bank), how serious a problem will that be?

4. Compare the PRIDE System with the Expectancy Theory model. How do they differ? Which model seems to be more accurate, i.e., provides more useful information for managers? Which model do you prefer? Why? www.chartcourse.com/articlepride.htm

INCIDENT 12-1

The Bank Teller

Joanna Poulet was angry. She had been a teller in the bank for two years and always had acceptable performance evaluations. She had just heard from another teller that Mary, who had been hired only six months ago, had received a pay raise based on her quarterly performance assessment, while Joanna had received only the usual inflation increase. Joanna was sure that her own performance was superior to Mary's. She had fewer customer complaints and her cash always balanced, while Mary had several imbalances over the months. Admittedly, Mary had sold a few more of the bank's services, for example, VISA cards and deposits, but the manager had always stressed that he wanted satisfied customers, and he emphasized a balanced cash count in the evening.

Mary also had been sent to a training program that Joanna had expected to go to as well, but the manager had told Joanna that she was not "ready" for it, without explaining what he meant. Joanna suspected that the manager had some prejudice against her because of her native Indian origin, but that was difficult to prove. She wondered whether she should complain, ask for a transfer to another branch, or quit and go to another bank.

1. Identify the factors that seem to be the cause of the perceived inequity in this situation. How real are they?

2. What measures could reduce or avoid the perceived inequity?

INCIDENT 12-2

Health-More Foods Corporation

Health-More Foods Corporation of Vancouver has been growing at a compounded rate of 30 per cent for the last seven years. It entered the vitamin and health-food business at a time when many people were becoming increasingly concerned about natural foods and vitamins, and it sells high-quality products. It has captured a dominant position in its regional market and now has about 150 employees.

Because of its growth, it has had difficulty maintaining trained clerical employees. Billing errors have been at the rate of nine per cent, and accounts payable errors have been eight per cent. The new human resource director was asked to recommend corrective action, and he proposed and installed a simple two-step program. First, supervisors and employees in each work unit met to discuss and set goals for improvement. Then supervisors regularly praised employees who had fewer errors than standard, and results for each work unit were charted daily. Within one month the error rates for both billing and accounts payable declined to less than one per cent and remained there.

1. Discuss the two-step program and its results in terms of each component of the expectancy theory model of motivation presented in this chapter.

2. How many of the components of the model apply? Does one component apply better than the others? Discuss.

CASE STUDY

Maple Leaf Shoes Ltd., Alternate Work Arrangements

Maple Leaf Shoes Ltd. is a medium-sized manufacturer of leather and vinyl shoes located in Wilmington, Ontario. It was started in 1969 and currently employs about 400 persons in its Hamilton plant and some 380 more in offices and warehouses throughout Canada and abroad.

Robert Clark, the company's president and key shareholder, had invited Jane Reynolds, special assistant in the personnel department, to his office to discuss some urgent matters relating to the upcoming negotiations with the company's four unions. Clark was not sure whether Jane Reynolds was ready to assume the leadership in negotiating with the unions, since she had been with Maple Leaf Shoes for only two years. On the other hand, he had been impressed with the way she handled the human resource issues of the company since John McAllister, the human resource manager, had recently left the company for a similar job in Toronto. Clark had delayed a decision to fill the human resource manager's position because of his restructuring plans, and now the delay seemed to backfire. Would Reynolds be able to stand up against the experienced union negotiators?

Jane Reynolds assured Clark that she felt confident in her ability to negotiate with the unions. She had established good working relationships with the union executives when she dealt with some of the outstanding grievances. The union representatives felt that she had a good "business sense" and the grievance settlements had been win-win solutions for both sides.

She told Clark, however, that if she were to do the collective bargaining negotiations, she would be unable to take care of the routine human resource management issues of the company. Someone else would have to be appointed or hired to relieve her until the negotiations were over.

Clark was in a quandary. He did not have the time to negotiate with the unions himself since he was too busy with international trade negotiations, which were crucial for the survival of the company. If he delegated the negotiations with the unions to Reynolds, how could the human resource situation be handled best?

Or should he insist that she continue managing human resources and let the labour negotiations be handled by a professional, who would know little about Maple Leaf Shoes?

Discussion Question

1. Based on the discussions on work options in this chapter, what type of solution(s) are you suggesting to Robert Clark?

CASE STUDY

Canadian Pacific and International Bank

Ernie Kemball, an instructor in CPIB's training and development division, specialized in training managers and supervisors in developing human resource skills. One of his favourite topics was "How to motivate employees," an interesting, but, as he well knew, difficult topic to teach, because everyone is motivated by different needs.

To get managers involved immediately and to arouse their interest Ernie preferred to use the case-study approach. His opening remark to every motivation seminar was to quote Professor Kavanagh: "Genuine and lasting employee motivation is not something management does, but rather a process that management fosters and allows to happen." He would then proceed to introduce the first case:

"Let's begin by looking at what not to do in terms of creating a motivating work environment. Here is an excellent case and, let me add, a real one. It was written by Dr. Craig Pinder, a professor at the Faculty of Business Administration, University of Victoria. It is based on an interview with "Pamela Jones," a bank employee in Vancouver. Use the expectancy model and answer the following questions:

- Did management make the "right" hiring decision?

- How did management fare with respect to providing a motivating work environment?

- To what degree did management fulfill the expectations of Pamela?

- Was the performance-reward connection clear to her?

- What should management have done to create a truly motivating work environment?

PAMELA JONES

Pamela Jones enjoyed banking. She had taken a battery of personal aptitude and interest tests that suggested she might like and do well in either banking or librarianship. She applied for employment with a large chartered bank, the Bank of Winnipeg, and was quickly accepted.

Her early experiences in banking were almost always challenging and rewarding. She was enrolled in the bank's management development program because of her education (a B.A. in languages and some postgraduate training in business administration), her previous job experience, and her obvious intelligence and drive.

During her first year in the training program, Pamela attended classes on banking procedures and policies and worked her way through a series of low-level positions in her branch. She was repeatedly told by her manager that her work was above average. Similarly, the training officer who worked out of the main office and coordinated the development of junior officers in the program frequently told Pamela that she was "among the best three" of her cohort of 20 trainees. She was proud to be a banker and proud to be a member of the Bank of Winnipeg.

After one year in the management development program, however, Pamela found she was not learning anything new about banking or the bank itself. She was shuffled from one job to another at her own branch, cycling back over many positions several times to help meet temporary problems caused by absences, overloads, and turnover. Turnover—a rampant problem in banking—amazed Pamela. She could not understand for many months why so many people started careers "in the service" of banking, only to leave after one or two years.

After her first year, the repeated promises of moving into her own position at another branch started to sound hollow to Pamela. The training officer claimed that there were no openings at other branches suitable for her. On two occasions when openings did occur, the manager of each of the branches in question rejected Pamela, sight unseen, presumably because she had not been in banking long enough.

Pamela was not the only unhappy person at her branch. Her immediate supervisor, George Burns, complained that because of the bank's economy drive, vacated customer service positions were left unfilled. As branch accountant, Burns was responsible for day-to-day customer service. Eventually, George Burns left the bank to work for a trust company, earning $90 a month more for work similar to that he had been performing at the Bank of Winnipeg. This left Pamela in the position of having to supervise the same tellers who had trained her only a few months earlier. Pamela was amazed at all the mistakes the tellers made, but found it difficult to do much to correct their poor work habits. All disciplinary procedures had to be administered with the approval of head office.

After several calls to her training officer, Pamela was finally transferred to her first "real" position in her own branch. Still keen and dedicated, Pamela was soon to lose her enthusiasm.

At her new branch, Pamela was made assistant accountant. Her duties included the supervision of the seven tellers, some customer service, and a great deal of paperwork. The same economy drive that she had witnessed at her training branch resulted in the failure to replace customer service personnel. Pamela was expected to "pick up the slack" at the front desk, neglecting her own work. Her tellers seldom balanced their own cash, so Pamela stayed late almost every night to find their errors. To save on overtime, the manager sent the tellers home while Pamela stayed late, first to correct the tellers' imbalances, and then to finish her own paperwork. He told Pamela that as an officer of the bank, she was expected to stay until the work of her subordinates, and her own

work, was satisfactorily completed. Pamela realized that most of her counterparts in other branches were willing to give this sort of dedication; therefore, so should she. This situation lasted six months, with little sign of change in sight.

One day, Pamela learned from a phone conversation with a friend at another branch that she would be transferred to Hope, British Columbia, to fill an opening that had arisen. Pamela's husband was a professional, employed by a large corporation headquartered in Vancouver. His company did not have an office in Hope; moreover, his training was very specialized so that he could probably find employment only in large cities anyway.

Accepting transfers was expected of junior officers who wanted to get ahead in the bank. Pamela inquired at head office and learned that the rumour was true. Her training officer told her, however, that she could decline the transfer if she wished, but he could not say how soon her next promotion opportunity would come about.

Depressed, annoyed, disappointed, and frustrated, Pamela quit the bank.

This case was reproduced, with permission, from C.C. Pinder, *Work Motivation,* Glenview, Ill.: Scott, Foresman, 1984. All rights reserved by the author.

SUGGESTED READINGS

Bernadino, Adriana, Telecommuting: *Modeling the Employer's and the Employee's Decision-making Process*, NY: Garland Publications, 1996.

Booth, Pat, *Contingent Work: Trends, Issues and Challenges for Employers*, The Conference Board of Canada, 1997.

Cochrane, Peter, *Tips for Time Travelers: Visionary Insights into New Technology*, London: Orion Business, 1997.

Lawler, Edward E., *Rewarding Excellence: Pay Strategies for the New Economy*, San Francisco: Jossey-Bass, 2000.

McKie, W. Gilmore, and Laurence Lipset, *The Contingent Worker: A Human Resource Perspective*, SHRM Foundation, 2000.

Nollen, Stanley, and Helen Axel, *Managing Contingent Workers: How to Reap the Benefits and Reduce the Risks*, AMACOM, 1996.

Olmsted, Barney, and Suzanne Smith, *The Job Sharing Handbook, NWW Publications*, 1996.

Olmsted, Barney, and Suzanne Smith, *Managing in a Flexible Workplace: How to Select and Manage Alternative Work Options*, AMACOM, 1997.

Rogers, Jackie Krasas, *Temps: The Many Faces of the Changing Workplace*, Cornell University Press, 2000.

Smith, Ann, and Gordon Culp, "Motivation: What Works, What Doesn't," www.coxegroup.com/articles/motivation.html, undated.

Young, Lesley, "How Can I Ever Thank You?" *Canadian HR Reporter*, January 31, 2000, pp. 7-9.

Part Six 6

Maintaining High Performance

An organization's culture and working environment has an effect on the motivation and job satisfaction of its employees. To maintain good relationships, an effective communication process is essential. Good interpersonal relations also require appropriate and fair discipline procedures. Other important issues for human resource professionals include workplace safety and work force diversity. In unionized firms, effectively managing the labour–management process is also very important. Managing in a union environment requires familiarity with the legal requirements in dealing with unions, the collective bargaining process, and administration of the collective agreement.

The four chapters in Part Six discuss ways to create a positive work environment, maintain proper discipline, ensure a safe work force, manage workplace diversity, and deal with union–management issues.

Maintaining High Performance

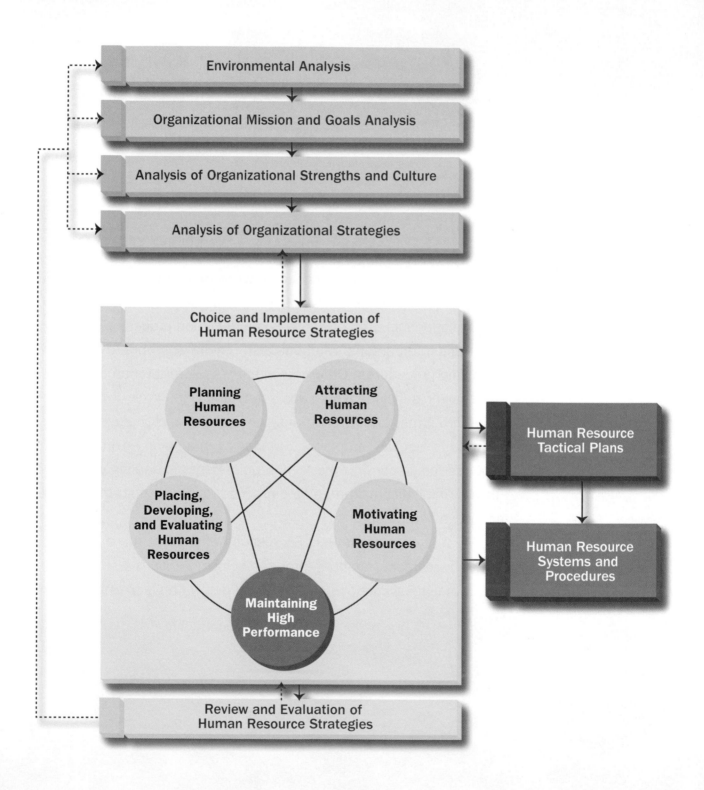

Chapter 13

Managing Employee Relations

The fundamental premise of high performance management systems is that organizations perform at a higher level when they are able to tap the ideas, skill, and effort of all their people.

Jeffrey Pfeffer and John Veiga[1]

CHAPTER OBJECTIVES

After studying this chapter, you should be able to:

- *Discuss* the importance of downward and upward communication in organizational settings.

- *Define* employee counselling and the major types of counselling.

- *Describe* how progressive discipline and wrongful dismissal work.

- *Explain* the different techniques available to improve quality of work life.

- *Outline* the major issues relating to downsizing the workforce and their implications for strategic human resource management.

www.statcan.ca

http://hrdc-drhc.gc.ca

www.reedassoc.com

www.amanet.org

www.cprn.com

In many ways, this entire book is about employee relations. How well the human resource department handles human resource planning, placement, training and development, evaluation, and compensation largely determines the state of employee relations. A mistake in any one of these areas can harm the employer-employee relationship. Even when these activities are performed properly, solid employee relations demand careful attention to organizational communication, employee counselling, discipline, and management of work groups. In addition, a number of organizations are becoming high involvement workplaces that emphasize human resource management. Consider the case of IBM:

> IBM operates in an industry that is characterized by fierce competition and rapid technological changes. IBM recognizes the fact that the quality of its human resources and effective utilization of these resources are critical to the strategic success of the firm. Human resource activities such as appraisal or training lose their effectiveness if they occur in isolation and are not related to other aspects of employee development. To tie the various employee development activities together and to facilitate motivation and satisfaction, IBM relies heavily on communication. Some of its approaches to employee communication include extensive career planning information and assistance, attitude surveys, suggestion systems, open-door policies, daily newspapers at some sites, and near-daily bulletins on educational opportunities and promotions.

> Beyond these formal methods, human resource specialists and line managers informally communicate with employees. This "management by walking around" is known at IBM as "trolling for open doors." IBM has an open-door policy whereby employees are free to walk into any manager's office with their problems. However, IBM management realizes that most workers are reluctant to take a problem to their boss's boss. Therefore, human resource specialists and line managers leave their offices and go out among the employees to learn what problems exist. As one IBM executive explained, "The only open-door policy that works is one where the manager gets up from the desk and goes through the door to talk to employees."

Open-door policy
A policy of encouraging employees to come to higher management with any concerns.

IBM's employee relations practices go beyond its extensive communication efforts. An ***open-door policy***, for example, allows employees to address their problems to higher levels of management, even executives. This "open" approach to communication demands that managers have skills in counselling and disciplining employees. Counselling skills are needed to draw out employee concerns before they become full-blown problems, requiring assistance from others. And when an employee performs improperly, effective disciplinary tools are necessary to resolve the problem while maintaining the employee's commitment to high levels of performance.

A number of employees express frustration with their employer. Almost 30 per cent of employees believe that their job offers little opportunity for them to use their abilities, and approximately 40 per cent report that employers made minimal effort to obtain employee opinions on work-related issues. According to John Stanek of International Survey Research, "Employees can't understand why they, the most important resource companies have, are not regularly tapped into. And they are getting angry."[2]

A study by Watson Wyatt Worldwide identified the following seven factors that were important in building employee commitment: trust in senior leadership, a chance to use skills on the job, job security, competitiveness of rewards, the quality of the organization's products/services, the absence of work-related stress, and the honesty and integrity of the employer's business conduct.[3]

www.watsonwyatt.com/
homepage/us/res/
work_usa5.htm

Although the focus of this chapter is on employee relations, an effective organization also pays considerable attention to relationships among workers. For example, employees should treat co-workers with dignity and respect. Several human resource initiatives, such as policies on workplace and sexual harassment, conflict resolution procedures, and employee involvement programs, play an important role in enhancing human relations.

STRATEGIC IMPORTANCE OF EMPLOYEE RELATIONS PRACTICES

"EMPLOYEE RELATIONS" is a complex blend of corporate culture, human resource practices, and individual perceptions. Virtually everything the human resource department does affects employee relations, directly or indirectly. But many human resource activities are largely unnoticed by employees, including, for example, recruitment, selection, and benefits administration. Other important human resource functions affect employees only periodically, as in the case of performance appraisal and salary review sessions. This necessitates ongoing activities to foster good employer-employee relations.

Why are employee relations practices important? At least four major reasons can be offered:

1. *Good employee relations practices improve productivity.* Employee productivity is significantly affected by two factors: ability and attitude. Ability is simply whether the employee is able to perform the job. Ability is influenced by such things as training, education, innate aptitude, tools, and work environments. Attitude, on the other hand, refers to an individual's willingness to perform the job. Attitude is affected by a myriad of factors, such as level of motivation, job satisfaction, and commitment to work. Good employee relations practices help improve both the ability and attitude of the employee. Through continuous monitoring of employee skills, attitudes, and quality of work environments, the organization is able to initiate timely corrective actions. The result is an improvement in employee productivity:

    Canada Heating and Ventilation (CHV) spends approximately 10 per cent of its gross revenue on training and educational programs for its employees. It is not unusual to see employees rise through the ranks in CHV and attribute their success to CHV's educational programs. Such practices have led to high employee morale and productivity. Several employees have been with the firm for over 20 years and believe that they still have a future in the company.

2. *Good employee relations ensure implementation of organizational strategies.* In Chapter One, the importance of the role that human resource activities play in achieving organizational goals was discussed. Goals and strategies, however well formulated, will not be attained unless they are well executed. This means that employees should be committed to the achievement of these goals. Unless employees understand their roles and are rewarded for exhibiting desired behaviours, it is unlikely that the organization will be able to generate grass-roots support for its plans. Good employee relations practices ensure that these goals and strategies are properly communicated to the employees and receive their commitment.

3. *Good employee relations practices reduce employment costs.* Good employee relations practices show concern for and interest in the employees. When this becomes part of the overall organizational culture, significant cost savings in terms of reduced absenteeism and turnover can emerge. Good employee relations practices also give the firm a recruiting advantage as most job applicants would like to work for an organization that treats them fairly and offers them a challenging job with potential for career growth:

    Nursing has a high burnout rate; further, technological advances occur continuously, necessitating retraining for nurses who have been away from work even for a short period. Because most of the workforce is largely female, many nurses leave the workforce for a few years for child-care considerations. To reverse the trend, several years ago Children's Hospital began a program wherein employees were treated as partners in identifying the larger organizational mission and became involved in making hospital policies. The result was astonishing. The turnover rate dropped significantly within a very short period. Several nurses who work for the hospital have been there for 15 to 20 years. As the vice-president of human resources comments, "Employees need to be treated fairly and be allowed to develop and participate.... If I work for a company that knows where it is going and can share that with me, then I am going to be more committed to that as a direction."[4]

4.   *Good employee relations help employees grow and develop.* As discussed in Chapter One, an important goal of human resource departments today is to help employees achieve their personal goals. A keen interest in the employee's work-related and career goals not only brings benefits to the organization (in terms of improved employee morale, loyalty, improved productivity, ready availability of skilled personnel within), but also helps it to meet its social objectives:

For instance, in industries such as electronics that face turbulent environments, future careers may less and less resemble the traditional bureaucratic patterns in which employees move to higher and more remunerative jobs over time. Instead, careers may consist of moves from one project to another or advances within a knowledge-based pay structure in which an employee remains in the same work team. Creativity, entrepreneurship, and teamwork often spell success or failure in such industries. This also means that employers have to prepare employees for new challenges by continuous training, feedback sessions, and career counselling.[5]

As Figure 13-1 shows, there are five major components of effective employee relations: communication, counselling, discipline, rights, and involvement. Each of these will be discussed in some detail below. In addition, a section of the chapter will address the issues of employee retention, job security and organizational downsizing.

EFFECTIVE EMPLOYEE COMMUNICATION

INFORMATION ABOUT the organization, its environment, its products and services, and its people is essential to management and workers. Without information, managers cannot make effective decisions about markets or resources, particularly human resources. Likewise, insufficient information may cause stress and dissatisfaction

FIGURE 13-1

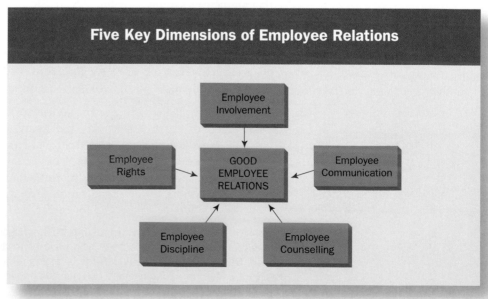

Five Key Dimensions of Employee Relations

among workers. This universal need for information is met through an organization's communication system. In small or unsophisticated firms, communication may be informal and subject to infrequent management intervention. In large multibillion-dollar enterprises, specialists may serve as employee communications directors or, in some instances, as chief information officers. The costs of poor employee communication can be substantial:

> Is one of your senior managers a "jerk"? If so, he or she may be costing your company millions of dollars. In today's economy, many people decide life is too short to work for a jerk. Losing top talent can be crushingly expensive. No company can afford to have a jerk as a manager. A lot of companies are beginning to penalize managers based on loss of talent.[6]

Most organizations use a blend of formal, systematically designed communication efforts and informal ad hoc arrangements. For convenience, most of these approaches can be divided into downward communication systems, which exist to get information to employees, and upward communication systems, which exist to obtain information from employees.

Downward Communication Systems

Downward communication
Information that begins at some point in the organization and feeds down the organization hierarchy to inform or influence others.

Human resource departments operate large communication systems to keep people informed. They try to facilitate an open, two-way flow of information, although often messages are of the top-down variety. *Downward communication* is information that begins at some point in the organization and proceeds down the organizational hierarchy to inform or influence others. Top-down methods are necessary for decision-makers to have their decisions carried out. These communications also help give employees knowledge about the organization and feedback on how their efforts are perceived.

Organizations use a variety of downward communication methods. The reason for this diversity is that multiple channels are more likely to overcome barriers and reach the intended receivers. For example, limiting messages to an electronic-mail format will be ineffective in organizations in which few employees use e-mail. Some common examples of downward communication approaches include in-house publications, information booklets, employee bulletins, prerecorded messages, electronic mail, and jobholder reports and meetings.

In-House Publications

Many organizations publish company magazines, newspapers, or bulletins for employees. Their purpose is to inform employees about current developments and to foster a long-term understanding about objectives and mission. The growth of desktop publishing and the ability to communicate using the resources of the Internet make the creation of professional-looking newsletters within the capabilities of both large and small firms. In-house publications frequently contain articles about company sports activities, community entertainment, and employee profiles that are designed to appeal to family members as well as employees:

> Saint Mary's University in Halifax publishes a monthly paper called *The Saint Mary's Times*, where details of the activities of the university faculty, staff, and students, as well as regional and national educational trends, are recorded. For instance, details of faculty research, publications, and community involvement, staff and student activities, and information about government announcements are listed in each issue, thus enabling every member of the university and its alumni to know what is going on in and around the university. The paper is available in hard copy and on the University's web page.

www.stmarys.ca/

Information Booklets

Human resource departments often distribute information booklets on various subjects to their employees. A well-known booklet is the employee handbook given to new employees to inform them about regulations and benefits. It is important that the information in employee handbooks is updated regularly and carefully reviewed—in some instances, information contained in employee handbooks has been used by former employees in litigation against the organization.

Other booklets are distributed on specialized subjects relating to human resource work, such as suggestion programs, employee assistance programs, wage incentives, retirement, and fringe benefits. When benefits such as life and medical insurance are purchased through an insurance company, that firm usually supplies the booklets. Similarly, a firm's pension carrier will provide information to members of the plan.

Employee Bulletins

Human resource departments publish a number of bulletins that concern their day-to-day operations. Historically, these were placed on employee bulletin boards and copies were sent to each manager, but now a growing number of organizations are using electronic media to communicate with employees. For example, job openings are posted so that all employees have an equal opportunity to apply for them. Holidays are announced, along with the regulations that govern payment and absences before and after holidays. Announcements are made about awards, retirements, and similar events. In their service role, it is the human resource department's responsibility to keep employees informed about events relevant to their employment.

Prerecorded Messages

Some organizations develop their own television programs for later replay to employees. These programs are viewed on television screens in company lunch-rooms and other locations. Large firms with branch operations especially use this approach to keep their branch employees informed about corporate developments or assist with orientation and training. Other firms prepare information films for the same kind of use.

> Cirque du Soleil, a Quebec-based entertainment company that tours many cities annually, has each of its divisions around the world make a 10-minute videotape of their workplace. Employees find that this allows them to have a much better sense of what is happening in locations other than their own.[7]

Some organizations use recorded telephone messages and automated voice mail to present the latest information. Employees can dial a certain number from any telephone, and a recorded message is played to them. In a typical program, the message takes about a minute and new information can be easily prepared. Employers are also beginning to utilize *interactive voice response (IVR)* systems as a tool to improving service and allowing HR staff to focus on strategic activities.[8]

Electronic Communication

A growing number of organizations are using *electronic mail* (or e-mail) as a means of communicating with employees. With network-linked computer terminals, managers can quickly and easily send a message to everyone in the organization (or select individuals or groups to receive the message). One study of e-mail users reported that 70 per cent of employees believe e-mail has increased or improved communications with their supervisor.[9] In addition, e-mail can be a vehicle for employee surveys. However, it is important to realize that not everyone uses e-mail regularly.

A fairly recent development in electronic communication involves the use of *intranets* (internal communications systems that function like a smaller version of the World Wide Web). A recent study of medium and large Canadian employers indicated that about 34 per cent have an HR intranet; the major reasons for firms not having intranets include limited access by employees to computers, HR concerns that employees are not ready for using intranets, and concerns over security.[10]

The most popular uses of Web technology are reported in Figure 13-2. However, firms are using intranets for a variety of purposes ranging from tracking benefit enrolments to providing copies of employee handbooks, policy manuals, and company newsletters.[11] Human resource departments have found intranet communication to be particularly effective as a means of updating handbooks and manuals and in eliminating some of the administrative burden associated with forms management. Examples of human resource departments using intranets include creating an electronic employee directory, setting up training registration information, using electronic pay stubs, updating of employee accounts, mapping performance achievements, managing succession planning, and creating discussion groups:[12]

> At Unisys, an intranet service and Internet site are being used to inform employees about current needs and potential jobs. There are plans to open an internet career centre listing job profiles and identifying the "hot career trends" for the next two to five years.[13]

> Intel, the large computer-chip company, has established an HR call centre. The centre is staffed with employees who can respond to employee queries regarding human resource management issues.[14]

> In trying to manage the flow of data, Inco worked with an outside firm to implement an electronic payroll system over a five-month period. The core modules of payroll included HR management, payroll, benefits, compensation, and time and attendance. Future modules may include health and safety, labour relations, and training.[15]

However, with intranet communication, the traditional top-down communication system becomes altered with communication opportunities extended to a much larger group of employees:

> In one manufacturing organization, the human resource management department knew that intranet communication would be meaningless for employees on the shop floor who did not have access to computers. They remedied the situation by installing a number of computer terminals in the lunch room and at selected work stations.

Intranets
Organization-specific internal computer network (mini-versions of the World Wide Web).

http://intrack.com/intranet/

http://intranetjournal.earth web.com/dlink.index-jhtml.72.982.-.0.jhtml

www.innergy.com/

www.cio.com/forums/intranet/

http://idm.internet.com/ix/

FIGURE 13-2

Most Popular Uses of Web Technology

- Corporate communications.
- Job postings.
- Benefits and retirement plan information.
- Recruitment.
- Employee opinion surveys.

Source: Frank Andree, "A How to Primer on Virtual HR," *Canadian HR Reporter*, January 11, 1999, pp. 18-19. Courtesy of *Canadian HR Reporter* published by Thomson Professional Publishing.

www.extranets.cc/

www.cadinfo.net/editorial/extranet.htm

www.intrack.com/intranet/extra.shtml

www.bigbear.ca/

www.state.sd.us/bit/document/internet.htm

A smaller number of companies have set up *extranets* (which are really intranets linked with vendors). For example, some firms have extranets with benefit providers such as insurance companies and pension managers—this allows employees to contact the benefit provider directly and inquire about the status of benefits or other features of the plan. In a recent hostile takeover, an organization used its Web site to communicate with employees from the rival firm:

> Big Bear Explorations Ltd., a Calgary-based oil and gas company, used its Web site to communicate with employees of the target firm (Blue Range Resource Corporation). Big Bear's Web site had a confidential e-mail question-and-answer feature that allowed employees, investors and shareholders to ask questions about the takeover.[16]

As a growing number of employees use the Internet, firms have begun developing policies on internet usage. Among the issues to be considered are the restriction of the Internet to business purposes, the right of employers to monitor employee usage of the internet, and specific prohibitions (relating to such concerns as copyright, distribution of viruses, or the posting or downloading of material that is threatening, abusive, defamatory, or obscene).[17] In addition, firms must be concerned with hackers obtaining confidential company and employee data.

A seven-step plan to protect the organization from the misuse of electronic communications includes: (1) developing and implementing a policy addressing electronic communications; (2) being aware of legal issues and limitations associated with monitoring electronic communications; (3) training employees and managers concerning the policy; (4) encouraging prompt reporting of policy violations and immediately addressing all complaints; (5) understanding your system; (6) examining the available tools for controlling Internet access; and (7) developing a policy for telecommuting.[18]

Information Sharing and Open Book Management

Some employers give reports to employees about the organization's economic performance. The reasoning is that economic information is just as important to employees as it is to shareholders. The report is presented in the same style as the annual report, except that it shows how the annual economic results affect workers.

Some organizations follow the reports with meetings that are organized and conducted in the same way as shareholder meetings. Top management attends the meetings, and all employees are invited. Management presents its reports, and employees

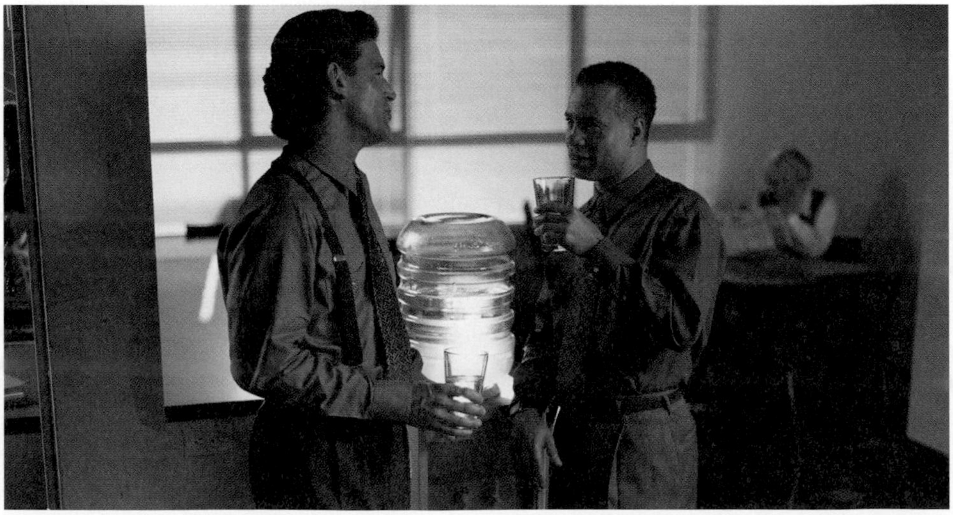

An informal gathering around the water cooler or coffee station is one method by which employees exchange information.

Digital Imagery © Photo Disc Inc. Photo by Keith Brofsky

are invited to question management and make proposals in the same way that owners do in stockholder meetings. These meetings improve communication and give jobholders a stronger feeling of belonging.

While many companies believe that the financial performance and budget goals of the firm are not the business of employees, some firms have adopted an approach of sharing such information with employees. Using *open book management*, some firms are making employees assume more responsibility for the success of the firm. The basic concepts involve educating employees about how the firm earns profits, giving workers a stake in the performance of the business, and providing feedback on how the company is doing.

> Eagle's Flight, a private company in Guelph, Ontario, has had open book management for about eight years. Co-owner Dave Loney indicates that the greatest benefit is the high level of trust among employees. Each Wednesday, all employees meet at head office to discuss issues and problems confronting the firm. As well, financial results are reviewed on a regular basis.[19]

Upward Communication Systems

Perhaps no area of communication is more in need of improvement in most organizations than upward communication. *Upward communication* consists of information initiated by people who seek to inform or influence those higher up in the organization's hierarchy. The cornerstone of all such messages is the employee and the supervisor. When a free flow of information travels between an employee and the supervisor, informal day-to-day communication is often sufficient for most situations. When open communication does not exist, or exists only for a limited range of issues, other approaches are needed.

How do organizations create open, upward communication? No universal formula exists. Each organization's human resource department must take an approach that is contingent upon the situation. However, one common element in most organizations is a genuine concern for employee well-being combined with meaningful opportunities for ideas to flow up the organization's hierarchy. Some of the more common upward communication channels include the grapevine, in-house complaint procedures, manager-employee meetings, suggestion systems, and attitude survey feedback.

Grapevine

Grapevine communication is an informal system that arises spontaneously from the social interaction of people in the organization.[20] It is the people-to-people system that arises naturally from human desires to make friends and share ideas. When two employees chat at the water cooler about their problems with a supervisor, that is a grapevine communication.

The grapevine provides a large amount of useful off-the-record feedback from employees. There are many opportunities for feedback because human resource specialists are in regular contact with employees as they discuss benefits, counsel employees, and perform other functions. Employees feel somewhat free to talk with human resource specialists since the occupation of human resource management is oriented toward human needs and resources. In addition, employees feel safe to express their feelings because human resource specialists do not directly supervise employees in other departments. Information from grapevine communications may also be revealed in employee attitude surveys. Some of the types of grapevine feedback that come to the human resource department are shown in Figure 13-3.

Upward communication
Communication that begins in the organization and proceeds up the hierarchy to inform or influence others.

Grapevine communication
An informal communication system that arises spontaneously from the social interaction of people in the organization.

FIGURE 13-3

Types of Grapevine Feedback to the Human Resource Department

- Information about the problems and anxieties that employees have.
- Incorrect feedback that is evidence of breakdowns in communication.
- Insights into goals and motivations of employees.
- Identification of job problems that have high emotional content, because intense feelings encourage grapevine communication.
- Information about the quality of labour relations, including grievance settlements.
- Information about the quality of supervision. Complaints about supervision are often brought informally to the attention of human resource specialists with the hope that they will do something.
- Information about areas of job dissatisfaction.
- Feedback about acceptance of new policies and procedures.

If the human resource department shows that it is responsive and can handle off-the-record information in confidence without putting the communicator in jeopardy, then open communication is further encouraged.

In an effort to enhance communications, some organizations use *management by walking around (MBWA)*. MBWA opens up the channels of communication by encouraging daily face-to-face contact by managers with employees. This approach helps develop a positive rapport between managers and employees and allows supervisors to keep informed about employee concerns.

Electronic Communication

Although the issue of electronic communication has been discussed in detail earlier in the chapter, it is important to recognize that e-mail, intranets, and discussion groups are also very useful in facilitating upward communication. Again, the importance of issues such as security of use, monitoring of employee messages, rules of conduct, and the need for a policy on the use of e-mail and internet usage needs to be emphasized.

In-House Complaint Procedures

How does an employee solve a problem if the supervisor is not receptive? In some organizations, the employee has no other option except to talk with the supervisor's superior. Although that may seem reasonable, most people in organizations are very reluctant to do that because they do not want to create negative feelings between themselves and their supervisor. To lessen the burden of "going over the boss's head," some organizations have installed in-house complaint procedures.

In-house complaint procedures
Organizationally developed methods for employees to register their complaints.

In-house complaint procedures are formal methods through which an employee can register a complaint. Normally these procedures are operated by the human resource department and require the employee to submit the complaint in writing. Then, an employee relations specialist investigates the complaint and advises the employee of the results. In some companies, the employee's name is known only by the employee relations investigator. However, if a supervisor is questioned about the issue, it may be obvious who filed the complaint so the person's anonymity is lost.

In recent years, there has been growing interest in *alternative dispute resolution* (ADR) programs. The goal of ADR is to resolve disputes in a timely, cost-effective manner. Some types of ADR programs include:

1. An *open door policy* in which an employee is encouraged to meet with his or her supervisor or another member of management to resolve workplace conflict.

2. A *peer review panel or ombudsperson* who hears an employee's presentation of the problem and makes recommendations. While the composition of the peer review panel may vary, a typical structure involves two individuals from a similar job classification as the employee and one management representative. It is estimated that about 90 per cent of disputes getting to peer review are settled at this level.

3. *Mediation* in which a neutral third party meets with the parties and tries to resolve the issue. Although the mediator cannot impose a settlement, his or her involvement is often instrumental in resolving the conflict.

4. *Arbitration* in which a neutral third party hears both parties' views of the case and makes a binding decision. While arbitration is common in unionized environments, it is also becoming more popular as a means of resolving disputes in nonunion settings.[21]

The last decade or so has seen considerable growth in the presence of a grievance system for nonunion employees. A *nonunion grievance procedure* can be defined as one that is in writing, guarantees employees the right to present complaints to management, and is communicated to employees.[22]

For example, a study of Canadian firms revealed that about 31 per cent had a grievance procedure for nonunion employees, with the typical procedure consisting of a three- or four-step process.[23] In setting up a nonunion grievance procedure, several issues exist. Some questions to consider include:

1. What subjects may be grieved? For example, can disciplinary actions be grieved?

2. Are all nonunion employees eligible to participate in the procedure?

3. Are employees protected from retaliation if they use the procedure?

4. Must the grievance be filed in writing? Are there time limits for employee filing and management response?

5. How many steps will the grievance procedure contain? Can an employee bypass his or her supervisor? What are the specific steps in the procedure?

6. Does the employee have the right to be present throughout the procedure? Can the employee have someone else (such as another employee, human resource staff member, lawyer) present the case? Can the employee call witnesses?

7. What is the final step in the procedure? For instance, who ultimately resolves the issue. (Some options include a senior line manager, HR professional, a panel (which can be comprised of just managers, managers and employees, or just employees), or outside arbitration.[24]

Manager-Employee Meetings

Closely related to in-house complaint procedures are meetings between managers and groups of employees to discuss complaints, suggestions, opinions, or questions. These meetings may begin with some information sharing by management to inform the group about developments in the company. However, the primary purpose of these meetings is to encourage upward communication, often with several levels of employees and lower-level management in attendance at the same time. Attendance at such meetings varies according to how the meetings are planned. In small facilities, it may be possible to get all the employees together annually or semi-annually; however, this does not reduce the need to keep in touch with employees on a regular basis. In large business units, different formats may be needed:

> One major bank's Open Meeting Program arranges meetings of about a dozen employees at a time. Meetings are held with different groups until at least one in five employees from each department attends. Employees are selected randomly and may decline to participate if they wish. A human resource specialist coordinates each meeting and develops the group report on a newsprint sheet in open discussions with the group. No employee names are used on the report, which becomes the basis of action plans with management. The program is repeated annually, and it has significantly improved upward communication.

Suggestion Systems

Suggestion systems are a formal method for generating, evaluating, and implementing employee ideas. If even one of these three elements—generating, evaluating, or implementing—is missing, the suggestion plan fails. All three are crucial to a successful suggestion system.

A successful suggestion system begins with the employee's idea and a discussion with the supervisor. Once the suggestion form is completed, the supervisor reviews and signs the form, indicating awareness of the suggestion, but not necessarily approval. The suggestion system office or committee receives the idea and acknowledges it to the employee through company mail. The idea is then evaluated, and the decision is communicated to the employee. If it is a good idea, implementation follows, with the employee receiving recognition and usually some award (often awards are equal to about 10 per cent of the first year's savings).

For suggestion systems to work, management must provide prompt and fair assessment of the ideas, supervisors must be trained to encourage employee suggestions, and top management must actively support the program. Unfortunately, this source of upward communication is ineffective in many companies because evaluations often take months or supervisors see suggestions as more work for them with few personal benefits.

Organizations placing a higher focus on teamwork may need to revamp their suggestion system program to reflect a group contribution. If rewards for suggestions are provided on an individual basis, employees within a work group may compete against one another to receive the reward.

Although most suggestion systems pay employees a percentage of the first-year savings, some companies pay a flat dollar amount in order to minimize the need for precision in evaluating the suggestion's exact dollar savings. This approach means that employees receive feedback about their suggestions much faster:

> In a large, multinational electronics corporation, the performances of supervisors is evaluated in part by the effectiveness of the suggestion system among their employees. Obviously, this approach causes supervisors to encourage employee suggestions. Another organization gives $25 to the supervisors for each employee suggestion that has been found viable.

A recent survey indicated that at least once a month, one-third of employees comes up with a suggestion that they believe will increase organizational performance. However, workers often perceive that they are not rewarded for coming up with suggestions.[25]

Suggestion systems
Specific procedures designed to encourage employees to recommend work improvements.

www.ideasmanagement
.com/help.htm

www.suggestionsystem
.com/consulting.htm

www.uncc.edu/policystate/
ps-72.html

Attitude Survey Feedback

What do employees think about the organization? Do they have problems or concerns? Do they understand the human resource department's benefit plan? Compensation program? Career planning efforts? Answers to these and many other questions can make a useful addition to the human resource department's information system.

Attitude surveys
Method to determine employees' thoughts about their organization using a broad survey.

Attitude surveys are systematic methods of determining what employees think about their organization. While surveys may be conducted through face-to-face interviews, they are usually done through questionnaires that employees complete anonymously. A number of organizations are now using web technology to conduct employee surveys.

An attitude survey typically seeks to learn what employees think about working conditions, supervision, human resource policies, and other organizational issues. New programs or special concerns to management also may be a source of questions. The resulting information can be used to evaluate specific concerns, such as how individual managers are perceived by their employees.

Attitude survey feedback
Results when the information collected is reported back to the participants who initially provided the information.

Attitude surveys can be a frustrating experience for employees if they do not see any results. It is only natural that people would like to know what the survey questionnaire uncovered. Otherwise the survey has little meaning to them, especially if it is re-administered in the future. Therefore, a summary of the survey results should be provided to employees for their reaction. However, feedback is not enough. Action is needed. Employees need to see that the survey results cause problems to be solved. Feedback of the results and action on the problem areas make *attitude survey feedback* a powerful communication tool:

> Maple Leaf Automotive Products has for several years relied on employee surveys as a method of facilitating organizational communication. Supervisors in the company are given a workbook to analyze survey results. Trained internal facilitators help the supervisors to interpret the survey results. Then the facilitators conduct a role-playing exercise with the supervisors to prepare them for the questions that employees are likely to ask.

> After the role-playing, the supervisor meets with the employees and presents the results. Together, problems are identified and solutions sought. From this meeting a prioritized list of action items emerges with dates for their completion. The result of all these efforts is not only that employees know what others in the organization feel, but it also helps the organization to develop an action plan to resolve its immediate and potential problems.

EMPLOYEE COUNSELLING

Counselling
Discussion of a problem with an employee, to help the employee cope with it better.

COMMUNICATIONS OFTEN involve one person talking with another. The purpose may be to give an order, share information, or solve a problem. *Counselling* is the discussion of a problem with an employee, with the general objective of helping the worker cope with it. The purpose is to help employees either resolve or cope with the situation so that they can become more effective both at work and away from the workplace:

> One company has a program available to employees and their families that covers both personal and work-related problems. The company maintains a 24-hour hotline and uses both company counsellors and community agencies. The service is strictly confidential.

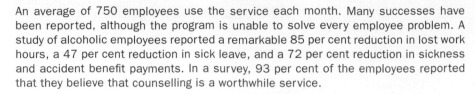

http://adtimes.nstp.com.
my/jobstory/may22a.htm

www.empcs.org.uk/

www.hurstplace.com/
employee.htm

admin.acadiau.ca/counsel/
Edisorder/index.html

www.canadausemployment
.com/article10.htm

www.eap-association.com/

www.eap-sap.com/eap/

www.eapinc.com/

www.reedassoc.com/
why.htm

An average of 750 employees use the service each month. Many successes have been reported, although the program is unable to solve every employee problem. A study of alcoholic employees reported a remarkable 85 per cent reduction in lost work hours, a 47 per cent reduction in sick leave, and a 72 per cent reduction in sickness and accident benefit payments. In a survey, 93 per cent of the employees reported that they believe that counselling is a worthwhile service.

Some firms advise managers to avoid giving personal advice to employees that is not related to the job because the managers are not professionally qualified to do so. There is a chance that they will give inappropriate or wrong advice that aggravates an employee's problem. A growing number of organizations have formal arrangements with outside professional counselling agencies to help their employees.

Counselling Functions

Counselling functions are the activities performed by counselling. Major counselling functions are as follows:

- *Advice.* Counsellors often give advice to those being counselled in order to guide them toward desired courses of action.

- *Reassurance.* The counselling experience often provides employees with reassurance, which is the confidence that they are following a suitable course of action and have the courage to try it.

- *Communication.* Counselling is a communication experience. It initiates upward communication to management, and also gives the counsellor an opportunity to provide insights to employees.

- *Release of emotional tension.* People tend to get emotional release when they have an opportunity to discuss their problems with someone else.

- *Clarified thinking.* Serious discussion of problems with someone else helps a person to think more clearly about these problems.

- *Reorientation.* Reorientation involves a change in an employee's basic self through a change in goals and values. Deeper counselling of the type practised by psychologists and psychiatrists often helps employees reorient values. For example, it helps them recognize their own limitations.

Employee Assistance Programs

Employee assistance program (EAP)
Comprehensive company program that seeks to help employees overcome their personal and work-related problems.

Organizations may establish an *employee assistance program (EAP)* to assist employees with personal problems (such as family or marital difficulties, substance abuse, or stress) that may be affecting their performance at work. While more discussion of EAPs is found in Chapter Eleven, it should be noted that a new initiative (the Canadian EAP Database Project) is being undertaken to provide a picture of what is happening across Canada, to establish a set of standardized practices, and to seek consistency in the business practices of EAP providers.[26]

An interesting development in providing EAP services involves the use of online communications. While online services are not a substitute for face-to-face employee contact, they may supplement existing EAP structures. Use of computer technology in providing EAP services may involve video counselling, chat rooms, bulletin boards, and self-help applications. However, it should be recognized that online services are not appropriate for every case; rather, they represent one of a number of alternative approaches to providing EAP services.[27]

EMPLOYEE DISCIPLINE

Discipline
Management action to encourage compliance with the organization's standards.

Counselling does not always work. Sometimes the employee's behaviour is inappropriately disruptive or performance is unacceptable. Under these circumstances, discipline is needed. **Discipline** is management action to encourage compliance with organization standards. It is a type of training that seeks to correct and mould employee knowledge, attitudes, and behaviour so that the worker strives willingly for better cooperation and performance. There are two types of discipline: preventive and corrective.

Preventive Discipline

Preventive discipline is action taken to encourage employees to follow standards and rules so that infractions are prevented. The basic objective is to encourage self-discipline among employees. In this way employees maintain their own discipline, rather than having management impose it.

Management has the responsibility for building a climate of preventive discipline. In doing so, it makes its standards known and understood. If employees do not know what standards are expected, their conduct is likely to be erratic or misdirected. Employees will better support standards that they have helped to create. They will also give more support to standards stated positively instead of negatively, such as "Safety first!" rather than "Don't be careless!" They usually want to know the reasons behind a standard so that it will make sense to them.

The human resource department has the major responsibility for preventive discipline. For example, it develops programs to control absences and grievances. It communicates standards to employees and encourages employees to follow them. It also gives training programs to explain the reasons behind standards and to build a positive spirit of self-discipline. On other occasions, it develops employee participation in setting standards in order to build commitment to them.

Preventive discipline
Action taken prior to any infraction, to encourage employees to follow the rules so infractions are prevented.

www.p-management
.com/articles/2008.htm

www.emporia.edu/ibed/
jour/jour22hr/peggyd.htm

www-personal.k-state
.edu/~ssteve/discnote.html

www.howtolaw.co.nz/
html/ml011.htm

www.fwlaw.com/
progressive.html

www.indiana.edu/~hrm/ca/
progdisc.html
http://fcn.state.fl.us/dms/hr
m/guides/disc/part1.html

www.bizmove.com/
personnel/m4i4.htm

Corrective discipline
Action that follows a rule infraction and seeks to discourage further infractions.

Corrective Discipline

Corrective discipline is an action that follows a rule infraction and seeks to discourage further infractions so that future acts are in compliance with standards. Typically the corrective action is a penalty of some type and is called a *disciplinary action*. Examples are a warning or suspension without pay. The objectives of disciplinary action are as follows:

● To reform the offender.

● To deter others from similar actions.

● To maintain consistent, effective group standards.

The objectives of disciplinary action are positive, educational, and corrective. The goal is to improve the future rather than punish the past. The corrective disciplinary interview often follows a "sandwich model," which means that a corrective comment is sandwiched between two positive comments in order to make the corrective comment more acceptable. An example is: "Your attendance is excellent, Roy (a positive comment), but your late return from coffee breaks disrupts our repair operations (negative). Otherwise, your work is among the best in our department (positive)." The supervisor then focuses on ways in which the two of them can work together to correct the problem.

Restrictions on Corrective Discipline

In general, discipline is substantially restricted by unions and government and the rules, laws, and regulations that have grown up around them. Corrective discipline is an especially sensitive subject with unions. They see it as an area where employees need protection from unreasonable management authority and to show employees that the union leadership cares for their interests.

Government is increasing its regulation of discipline, making it more difficult to administer unwarranted discipline. For example, an employee cannot be disciplined or dismissed for union activities (as defined by labour relations statutes), conditions controlled by human rights legislation (such as race, sex, religion), or refusing to perform hazardous or unsafe or unlawful activities. Other employment restrictions may also apply, depending on the circumstances and the laws of the provinces concerned.

Due process
Established rules and procedures for disciplinary action are followed and employees have an opportunity to respond to the charges.

Due process for discipline may be required of the employer by courts of law, arbitrators, and labour unions. Due process means that established rules and procedures for disciplinary action need to be followed and that employees are provided an opportunity to respond to charges made against them.[28] It is the human resource department's responsibility to ensure that all parties in a disciplinary action follow the proper rules and procedures so that due process will be used.

If a disciplinary action is challenged, the human resource department also must have sufficient documentation to support the action; therefore, human resource policy should require proper documentation for all employer disciplinary actions. Proper documentation should be specific, beginning with the date, time, and location of an incident. It also describes the nature of the undesirable performance or behaviour and how it relates to job and organizational performance. Specific rules and regulations that relate to the incident are identified. Documentation also includes what the manager said to the employee and how the employee responded, including specific words and actions. If there were witnesses, they should be identified. All documentation needs to be recorded promptly, while the supervisor's memory is still fresh. It should be objective, based on observations and not impressions.

Hot-stove rule
The principle that disciplinary action should be like touching a hot stove; with warning, immediate, consistent, and impersonal.

A useful guide for corrective discipline is the ***hot-stove rule***. The hot-stove rule states that disciplinary action should have the same characteristics as the penalty a person receives from touching a hot stove. These characteristics are that discipline should be with warning, immediate, consistent, and impersonal.

Progressive Discipline

Progressive discipline
A type of discipline whereby there are stronger penalties for repeated offences.

Most employers apply a policy of ***progressive discipline***, which means that there are stronger penalties for repeated offences. The purpose of this is to give an employee an opportunity to take corrective action before more serious penalties are applied. Progressive discipline also gives management time to work with an employee to help correct infractions:

> When Margaret Stoner had two unauthorized absences, the human resource department provided counselling. It also arranged for her to join a ride pool that allowed her to leave home 30 minutes later than with public transportation. Eventually her unauthorized absences stopped.

A typical progressive discipline system is shown in Figure 13-4. The first infraction leads to a verbal reprimand by the supervisor. The next infraction leads to a written reprimand, with a record placed in the file. Further infractions build up to stronger discipline, leading finally to discharge. Usually the human resource department becomes involved at the third step or sooner in order to assure that company policy is applied consistently in all departments.

FIGURE 13-4

A Progressive Discipline System

1. Verbal reprimand by supervisor.
2. Written reprimand, with a record in file.
3. One- to three-day suspension from work.
4. Suspension for one week or longer.
5. Discharge for cause.

It is essential that employers document efforts made to help employees. One possible program involves four steps:

1. Clearly indicate in writing the nature of the problem and the impact of the employee's performance or conduct on the organization;

2. Provide the employee with a clear and unequivocal warning that failure to improve behaviour will result in discipline (up to and including termination);

3. Establish through progressive discipline that the employee's performance was still unacceptable despite repeated warnings; and

4. Demonstrate that discipline was applied in a fair and consistent manner.[29]

Some progressive systems allow minor offences to be removed from the record after a period of time (typically between one to five years), allowing each employee to return to Step 1. But serious offences, such as fighting or theft, are usually not dealt with by means of progressive discipline. An employee who commits these offences may be discharged on the first offence.

Positive Discipline

Instead of using punishment to discipline employees, some organizations employ an approach called *positive discipline* which involves an acceptance on the part of the employee that a problem exists, an acknowledgement by the employee that he or she must assume responsibility for the behaviour, and the use of a problem-solving approach to resolving the problem. The key steps in using positive discipline are:

1. Focus on the specific problem rather than the employee's attitude or personality.

2. Gain agreement with the employee that a performance problem exists and that the employee is responsible for changing his or her behaviour.

3. Approach discipline as a problem-solving process.

4. Document suggested changes or commitments by the employee.

5. Follow up to ensure that the employee is living up to his or her commitments and to reduce the likelihood of having to take more severe action.[30]

DISMISSAL

Wrongful dismissal
Dismissal without just cause or reasonable notice of termination.

The ultimate disciplinary action is dismissal, which is separation from the employer (other terms used in this situation are fired, terminated, discharged, or separated). A nonunion employer who does not have just cause for dismissing an employee may be sued for *wrongful dismissal*.

The owner of a small business with 18 employees terminated a manager who had been with the firm for 22 years. Although there was no documented evidence to support his claim, the owner said that the manager's performance had been slipping over the past few years. Shortly after being released, the employee contacted an employment lawyer and the parties settled out of court for in excess of $100 000. The business owner had never heard of the law of wrongful dismissal and the settlement has put the business in jeopardy.

The law of wrongful dismissal is very complicated and human resource professionals without considerable expertise in this area are advised to seek prudent legal advice. Note that the dismissal of unionized employees (about 31 per cent of the non-agricultural workforce) is governed by the provisions of the collective agreement and the remedy exists with the grievance arbitration process (see Chapter Sixteen). Save for a few exceptions, an employer can terminate a nonunion employee at any time if just cause exists; however, in the absence of just cause, the employer is usually obligated to give the former employee "reasonable notice" or compensation in lieu of notice.

www.wwlia.org/ca-wd.htm

www.on.hrdc-
drhc.gc.ca/english/labour/
unjcom_e.shtml

http://info.load-otea.hrdc-
drhc.gc.ca/~legweb/clc3/
regs/r301tocen.htm

www.lawyers-
bc.com/wrongdis/default
.htm

www.lexum.umontreal.ca/
csc-scc/en/concept/
index.html

All provinces and the federal jurisdiction have employment standards legislation providing minimum periods of notice for employees terminated without cause. The amount of advance notice an employer is required to give an individual is dependent on the employee's length of service with the employer and some jurisdictions have specific notice periods that apply if the employer engages in a mass layoff or termination. However, it should be noted that the provisions under employment standards legislation are statutory *minimums* and the amount of reasonable notice awarded by the courts frequently exceeds such provisions.

One human resource management manager indicated that the company's practice was to provide the minimum notice provisions under employment standards legislation if terminating an employee. The reason for this approach was simply that the manager was uninformed about the law of wrongful dismissal.

Three jurisdictions (federal, Quebec, and Nova Scotia) provide an alternative forum for some wrongfully dismissed employees meeting specified period of service requirements (10 years in Nova Scotia, five years in Quebec, and one year for the federal jurisdiction). While the provisions of the statutes vary, the thrust of the legislation is to permit employees to bring their cases to an adjudication process in which the adjudicator may order reinstatement and damages if sufficient cause for dismissal does not exist. The specifics of the legislation are quite detailed and legal assistance is advised.

It has been said that every employee dismissal is evidence of management and human resource department failure, but this view is not realistic. Neither managers nor employees are perfect, so some problems cannot be solved regardless of how hard people try. Sometimes dismissal is better for both the worker and the organization. It gives the employee a chance to seek a new job where his or her abilities and temperament may be more appropriate. In addition, it sends a message to other employees that certain conduct will not be tolerated.

Determining Just Cause

Cause for dismissal under common law includes any act by the employee that could have serious negative effects on the operation or reputation of the organization. This typically includes incompetence and employee misconduct (such as fraud, drunkenness, dishonesty, insubordination, or refusal to obey reasonable orders). The onus for proving the existence of just cause is on the employer.[31]   Often there is a carefully planned termination interview to ensure that the separation is as positive and constructive as possible—the Supreme Court of Canada recently ruled that an employer must act in a way that demonstrates good faith and fair dealing in the dismissal of employees.[32]

While an employer may terminate an employee at any time if just cause exists, the courts' interpretation of what constitutes just cause for dismissal is often much different from managers' perceptions of cause. Although employers argued just cause for dismissal in 44 per cent of wrongful dismissal cases over a 15-year period beginning in 1980, the court found that just cause existed in only 37 per cent of the decisions—in other words, while employers often believe just cause was present, this belief is frequently not supported by the courts.[33]

Employers and the courts often differ in their assessment with respect to cause involving dismissal for incompetence. Employers were able to establish employee incompetence in less than 25 per cent of the cases in which they argued just cause for termination on the basis of incompetence—establishing cause on the grounds of incompetence is not easy (see Figure 13-5).

> A health care organization wanted to dismiss a problem employee in a secretarial position without having to provide reasonable notice or compensation. The secretary's supervisor asked the employee to learn some new computer software within a week. The employee was told that she would be tested on the new software at the end of the week and if she failed the test, her employment would cease. Not surprisingly, the employer's argument of incompetent work performance did not succeed.

With reference to employee misconduct cases, employers won about 40 per cent of cases involving dishonesty or theft, 41 per cent of cases in which the employer argued frailty of character (included in this category were cases of substance abuse; abuse of other employees, customers or the public; and off-duty conduct), 54 per cent of cases in which the employee was discharged for insubordination, and 67 per cent of cases in which the employee was discharged for conflict of interest or competing with the employer. Employees have a duty of fidelity to the employer and courts are more likely to find just cause if the employee fails to meet the duty of faithful service.

Contrary to the impressions of many managers, courts have consistently held that terminating an employee because of business or economic factors is not just cause for dismissal because such factors are not related to the employee's behaviour.

FIGURE 13-5

Requirements in Dismissing an Incompetent Employee

1. Have a reasonable and objective performance standard. It is the employer's responsibility to show that this standard has been effectively communicated to employees and that other employees have achieved the standard.

2. Document employee's performance indicating that he or she has failed to meet the standards (while other employees have been successful).

3. Have evidence of warnings given to the employee.

4. Show that appropriate training, support, time, and feedback has been provided to the employee to enable the employee to learn the tasks.

5. Demonstrate that the employee concerned had reasonable time to improve performance.

Source: Adapted from *Canadian Employment Law Today*, June 26, 1991, pp. 685-86, Toronto, ON: MPL Communications Inc. and Howard A. Levitt, *The Law of Dismissal in Canada*, Second Edition, Aurora, ON: Canada Law Book, 1992. Courtesy of Carswell, Thomson Professional Learning.

It is critical that employers seeking to dismiss employees due to declining demand or as a result of an organizational downsizing ensure that terminated employees are provided with reasonable notice or appropriate compensation. It is advisable to seek legal assistance to review the process and compensation or severance package offered to terminated employees.

Constructive Dismissal

www.emond-harnden.com/
farber.html

Constructive dismissal
Under common law, if an employer commits a major breach of a major term of the employment relationship, the employee may take the position that dismissal has taken place even though he or she has not received a formal termination notice.

Rather than terminate an employee, an employer may decide to change the individual's job in such a way that the employee decides to quit. A major change in the employment terms that results in an employee resigning may be considered as *constructive dismissal.* Some examples of constructive dismissal include a significant change in job function, a demotion, a demand for an employee's resignation, or a forced transfer.[34] The law relating to constructive dismissal is technical in nature and human resource professionals are advised to seek legal advice prior to changing a major term of an employment contract.

Reasonable Notice

An employer that does not have just cause for dismissal must provide a dismissed employee with "reasonable notice" or compensation (typically salary, benefits, and reasonable job search expenses) in lieu of notice. While several managers believe that the organization need only provide the minimum notice period outlined under employment standards legislation, it should be emphasized that these provisions are only minimums and courts may (and frequently do) award much greater notice periods.

The major factors used to predict notice include:

- the former employee's age, length of service, salary and occupational status—on average, older employees, long-service employees, more highly paid employees, and employees occupying more senior positions in the organization tend to receive higher periods of notice.

- an attempt to mitigate losses—employees who are terminated must make reasonable efforts to find similar alternative employment.

- a less favourable labour market—when alternative employment opportunities are limited, courts tend to award greater notice periods.

While each case is settled based on its own particular facts, some guidelines relating to wrongful dismissal have been developed. However, it should be underscored that these are only *guidelines* to provide some guidance to students relating to wrongful dismissal awards. Based on the guidelines, an employee in a clerical / blue-collar position will receive about two weeks' notice (or compensation in lieu of notice) for each year of service, an employee in a supervisory or lower-level management position will receive three weeks' notice (or compensation) for each year of service, and senior management and professional employees will receive one month notice (or compensation) for each year of service. In the past, it has been rare for notice periods to exceed 24 months.[35]

However, the 1997 decision of the Supreme Court of Canada in *Wallace v. United Grain Growers* has led to the awarding of extended periods of notice in a number of wrongful dismissal cases in which the employer was found to have terminated an employee in bad faith. In the *Wallace* case, the Court ruled that the employer had dismissed Wallace in "bad faith" and thus added an additional nine months onto a reasonable notice award of 15 months. Toronto employment lawyer Joe Conforti has concluded that "lower courts are awarding extended notice damages in levels that are wholly unpredictable and without discernible principle."[36]

www.soscanada2000.com/
severancepay.html

www.edmontonjournal.com/
news/alberta/
092598ab6.html

Employee Severance

In determining severance arrangements, companies should develop a basic severance formula and adapt it to specific cases in the organization. About 63 per cent of employers provide a dismissed employee with a lump sum payment, 28 per cent use a form of bridging pay (a series of regular payments), and 9 per cent do not follow a standard practice of payment. More than three-quarters of firms continue the individual's insurance benefits and most organizations offer some form of outplacement counselling.[37]

Managing the Dismissal

There are several guidelines to follow in dismissing an employee:

● prepare for the interview and conduct a rehearsal.

● consider the dismissal process from the employee's perspective and ask "how would I like to be treated in such a situation?"

● get to the point. Some experts suggest that you convey the message of termination within the first few sentences.

● select the time and place. Experts often suggest a meeting in the morning and during the middle of the week.

● have any necessary information ready (such as a severance package and outplacement counselling assistance).

● notify others in the organization and ensure that the individual's duties are covered.

● in some instances, special security arrangements may be necessary.

● discuss the process with other colleagues who have had to terminate employees.[38]

EMPLOYEE RIGHTS

www.careers.ubc.ca/
students/rights.html

www.carpentersunion.ca/
rights.html

EMPLOYEE RIGHTS refer to those rights desired by employees relating to job security and working conditions. Some of these rights are protected under law, others under the collective agreement with the union (if one exists), and yet others may be listed in the letter of appointment given to the employee at the time of hiring. Regardless of whether these rights are recorded in writing or currently protected by law and agreements, they have a significant impact on the human resource management activities of an organization. Progressive human resource managers recognize this and strive to provide fair and equitable working conditions that help the employee to maintain dignity on the job.

Right to Privacy

Ever since the early 1980s, Canadians have had the right of public access to government records. The same law (Access to Information Act) prohibits disclosure of any record that contains personal information unless the individual in question has consented to the disclosure or unless the information is publicly available. Privacy legislation generally does not cover private employer employee relationships. However, many proactive organizations attempt to establish policies and rules governing employee privacy and access rights. Today, a number of companies have written policies governing access to personal records. As well, a growing number of organizations are establishing policies with respect to Internet usage.

Employer concerns about employee privacy rights have prevented organizations from collecting unnecessary information at the point of hiring. Today many employers ensure that only job-related information is collected. There is an increasing realization among employers that collecting nonwork information is an unnecessary intrusion into the private lives of job applicants. Even when such additional information is not considered discriminatory (under human rights laws), many employers feel that such an action constitutes a moral violation of applicants' rights.

Privacy in the workplace is becoming an extremely sensitive issue and HR professionals must be aware of the legal and ethical concerns surrounding the issue. A recent survey by the American Management Association revealed that almost 75 per cent of U.S. companies reported monitoring employee communications and activities on the job, including e-mail, voice mail, telephone conversations, employee computer usage and using video cameras to observe employee performance, and one-quarter of the firms reported dismissing employees for misuse of telecommunications equipment.[39]

When considering employee monitoring, 11 per cent of employers recorded and reviewed telephone conversations, 30 per cent reviewed computer files, 38 per cent monitored the use of e-mail, 54 per cent monitored Internet communications, 15 per cent video-recorded employee job performance, 44 per cent recorded telephone use, and 19 per cent monitored computer use (such as time logged on, keystroke counts). Most of the monitoring was carried out as spot checks rather than ongoing surveillance. The major reasons for employee monitoring included legal compliance, limiting legal liability for employee actions, performance reviews, and obtaining productivity measures.[40]

Right to Fair Treatment

Earlier in this book we saw that an individual's age, race, gender, religion, physical disability, and so on, should not be considered when hiring unless it is a bona fide job requirement. As previously noted, an employer has an obligation to make reasonable accommodation to meet employee needs. The right of employees to fair treatment requires that these principles govern the actual work once the applicants are hired. Thus, employees have the right not to be discriminated against in all employment decisions (e.g., compensation, training) as well as the right to work in a safe and harassment-free environment. Proactive employers continuously monitor working conditions through employee surveys, open-door policies, presence of grievance committees, and so on. They also initiate new programs and policies to meet the changing needs of the workforce:

> Today, many organizations emphasize a pollution-free work environment. A number of organizations have banned smoking in any part of the workplace; others have rules governing the use of air sprays and perfumes. Several organizations respect the employees' right to be environmentally conscious by providing them with recycling bins and helping them cut down waste. Some other organizations have focused on reducing the noise level at the workplace.

Rights in Business Closings and Workplace Restructuring

The 1990s were characterized by businesses closing down or engaging in major workplace restructuring. In any business closure or downsizing, it is important to examine relevant provincial or federal legislation to ensure that notice requirements for mass layoffs are being observed. Many progressive employers try to provide employees with as much advance notice as possible and help the employees affected by job loss. Several organizations provide outplacement assistance by helping the terminated employee find alternative employment. In addition, the various governments have special departments to assist employees affected by a group reduction.

An organization's concern for employee rights not only prevents government intervention, but also results in higher employee satisfaction and good public relations. Many organizations are realizing that respecting employee rights is not only desirable from a humane and moral point of view, but often makes sound economic sense as well.

EMPLOYEE INVOLVEMENT

TO INCREASE employee productivity and satisfaction, human resource departments often attempt to improve the quality of work life. Most of the approaches to employee involvement focus on the increased participation of workers.

Quality of work life (QWL)
A generic term emphasizing the humanization of work.

Quality of work life (QWL) is affected by many factors: quality of supervision, working conditions, pay and benefits, and an interesting and rewarding job. While improvements in all these areas are critical for an overall improvement in the quality of work life, the emphasis in this chapter is on the job dimension. Several QWL efforts involve employees by giving them greater opportunities to affect both their own jobs and their contributions to the firm's overall effectiveness.[41]

www1.od.nih.gov/ohrm/qwl/

www.cprn.com/cprn.html

www.bmo.com/news/index.html

www.partnership-at-work.com/

www.eia.com/

www.hp.com/country/us/eng/companyinfo.htm

www.ibm.com/ibm/

www.tektronix.com/about/factsheet.html

www.gm.com/flash_home_page/

www.ford.com/servlet/ecmcs/ford/index.jsp?SECTION=ourCompany

> Bank of Montreal, a 1997 Optimas Award Winner, complements its human resource programs with a comprehensive work/life approach. The role of human resources is to create programs that ensure "committed, competent employees in a cost-effective manner." For example, the Institute of Learning was designed to help transform employees from order takers to innovative, energetic idea people who could work both for and with customers.[42]

A popular method used to improve quality of work life is employee involvement. *Employee involvement* (EI) consists of a variety of systematic methods that empower employees to participate in the decisions that affect them and their relationship with the organization. Through EI, employees feel a sense of responsibility, even "ownership" of decisions in which they participate. To be successful, however, EI must be more than just a systematic approach; it must become part of the organization's culture and management philosophy:[43]

> Organizations such as Hewlett Packard, IBM, and Tektronix have had such a philosophy ingrained in their corporate structure for decades. Others such as GM and Ford are trying to create a QWL corporate culture through employee empowerment approaches.

EI is based on two important principles. First, individuals tend to support systems or decisions that they helped to make. For example, if an employee was actively involved in developing a new credit collection procedure, then this individual is likely to ensure that the new procedure is carried out correctly. Second, employees who actually perform a task know more about it than anyone else, including their supervisor. Asking for information from employees who actually perform the job can provide insights not available from their supervisors or outside experts.

QWL and EI Interventions

A number of different interventions have been used to create employee involvement and improve the overall quality of work life. Some popular approaches are discussed below.

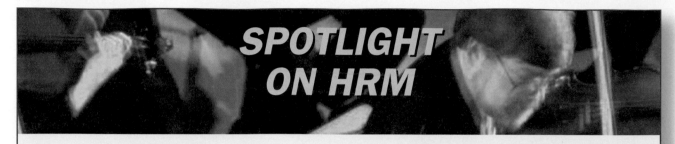

SPOTLIGHT ON HRM

WARM AND SNUGGLY

Forget lean and mean if you want to hold on to valued workers

One Friday evening last fall at 6 o'clock, Aris Kaplanis was packing his briefcase to go home for the weekend when one of his employees suddenly appeared at his door. Kaplanis, 45, is president and CEO of Teranet Land Information Services Inc., a high-tech, Toronto-based land registry company. The employee told Kaplanis that one of Teranet's IT people was on the verge of tears, overwhelmed by a combination of work and personal problems.

For the next three hours, Kaplanis consoled the despondent worker. As Kaplanis observes: "If an employee wants to discuss a personal problem, that's fine, let's have that kind of conversation, because we value our employees as people, not just as workers in our company."

While most high-tech companies claim they treat their IT staff extremely well, Teranet is one company that delivers. The proof? Teranet's annual turnover rate is less than 1%, compared with the IT industry's norm of between 10% and 20%. How does Teranet manage to hold onto IT people while everyone else seems to fail? It looks as if a family-like, humane corporate culture is a factor.

Teranet was once an organization owned by the Ontario government, whose purpose was to automate all documentation for four million parcels of land in the province. But in 1991, it was semi-privatized (50% is owned by the province, the rest by Miralta Capital Inc.). Back then, the company had 75 mostly unionized employees who were treated similarly to any other group of public servants.

Hired as Teranet's first president — having spent his career in the computer industry — Kaplanis recognized that the company's success depended on how capably he handled its workforce. "My perspective is that the company has two assets — one is the customers, the other is our employees," he explains. "Both of these assets have to be serviced."

First, Teranet brought in psychologists to help employees adjust to the shift from the public to private sector. It set up an employee assistance program for everyone, "so our employees or families can get on the phone if they are in a crisis situation and get help right away," says Kaplanis. The CEO began holding breakfast meetings with groups of employees once a month, where, over muffins and coffee, he polled them on how they were feeling and how Teranet's goals could be met. He also instituted a feedback system connected directly to his office, whereby employees can anonymously raise issues that bother them.

Teranet encourages an esprit de corps. Every month, there is a social event, such as a bowling or curling night. A summer picnic is held once a year, as is a one-day meeting in which every employee participates, from receptionists to senior managers. There, people are encouraged to air their opinions and aims. During last year's get-together, veteran employees were given free TV sets and those with less than a year's service, personal stereos. Teranet also prides itself on having a flat management structure and flex hours and allowing people to work out of their homes.

All of this seems to pay off. Teranet doubles in size every year and now boasts a staff of more than 500. Marilyn Barber, Teranet's vice-president of human resources, also believes that people stay with the company because, when they conduct job interviews, they consider whom a candidate might socialize with inside the company. "We think, 'Who is this person going to go to lunch with?' to make sure they are really a good fit," she explains. "[If] they develop friendship and loyalties, they'll want to stay with our company. It makes it very difficult to leave if it's very much like a family; it's easy to leave a job, but not so easy to leave a family."

Of course, having a president willing to give up a Friday evening to listen to an individual employee's litany of woes certainly doesn't hurt either.

Source: "Warm and Snuggly" by Bruce Livesay, *Report on Business Magazine*, March 1998, p.102. Courtesy of Bruce Livesay.

Quality Circles

A *quality circle* is a small group of employees with a common leader that meets regularly to identify and solve work-related problems.[44] When quality circles started in Japan, they were called "quality control circles," because their primary focus was to improve the overall quality of products manufactured in that country. They gained popularity in North America in the late 1970s and early 1980s.

Several characteristics differentiate quality circles (QC) from other EI programs:

1. Membership in the circle is voluntary for both the leader (usually the supervisor) and the members (usually hourly paid workers).[45]

2. The creation of quality circles is usually preceded by in-house training. Supervisors typically receive two or three days of training. Most of the time is devoted to discussions of small-group dynamics, leadership skills, and the QWL and QC philosophies. About a day of the training is spent on different approaches to problem-solving. Once the supervisor is trained, his or her employees are usually given one day of intensive training with a strong focus on problem-solving techniques.

3. The group is permitted to select the problems it wants to tackle. Management may suggest problems of concern to it, but the group decides which ones to select. Ideally, the selection process is made not by democratic vote, but by consensus, in which everyone agrees on the problem to be solved first:

At Solar Turbines International (a Caterpillar Tractor Company subsidiary), employees were frustrated by the lack of power hand tools. They studied the lost production time caused by waiting for tools and showed management how to save more than $30 000 dollars a year by making a $2200 investment in additional hand tools.

The employees at Solar Turbines did not select this problem to save management money; they did it because of the inconvenience that insufficient tools caused them. The fact that it saved more than a dozen times what it cost to fix is a typical by-product of successful quality circle efforts.

Socio-technical Systems

Another approach to QWL efforts are socio-technical systems. *Socio-technical systems* are interventions into the work situation that restructure the work, work groups, and the relationship between workers and the technologies they use to do their jobs.[46] There has also been considerable work in the area of ergonomics. *Ergonomics* is the study of the biotechnical relationships between the physical attributes of workers and the physical demands of the job, with the object of reducing physical and mental strain in order to increase productivity and QWL.

Codetermination

One of the first attempts at industrial democracy on a broad scale occurred in the former West Germany under the name "codetermination." *Codetermination* allows workers' representatives to discuss and vote on key management decisions that affect the workers through formal sessions with company management. This form of industrial democracy has since spread through most of Western Europe. As a result, decisions to close plants or lay off large numbers of workers meet with far more formal resistance in Europe than in North America. Since major Canadian corporations operate in Europe under codetermination, human resource management in multinational corporations is affected. For international human resource experts, codetermination is a consideration in the design of overseas jobs. Today, some North

---

Quality circle
A small group of employees with a common leader who meet together regularly to identify and solve work-related problems.

www.nw.com.au/~jingde/
homepa6.htm

http://sol.brunel.ac.uk/~jarvis/
bola/quality/circles.html

http://utl1.library.utoronto.ca/
www/aging/wp1_4_2.html

www.geocities.com/Heart
land/Acres/3257/
quality.html

http://ieiris.cc.boun.edu.tr/
faculty/kaylan/tqm/QC.html

www.lib.virginia.edu/etd/
theses/ArtsSci/English/
1998/Poliklas/cod.html

http://csf.colorado.edu/mai
l/pkt/jun98/0052.html

Socio-technical systems
Interventions into the work situation that restructure the work, work groups, and the relationship between workers and the technology they use to do their jobs.

Ergonomics
The study of biotechnical relationships between the physical attributes of workers and the physical demands of the job with the object of reducing physical and mental strain in order to increase productivity and quality of work life.

Codetermination
A form of industrial democracy, first popularized in West Germany, giving workers the right to have their representatives vote on management decisions.

Quality circles involve a small group of employee volunteers with a common leader that meet regularly to identify and solve work-related problems.

American organizations provide employees with considerable involvement in the decision-making process:

> At the General Motors Saturn plant, union members voted in favour of keeping their unique contract that rewards productivity and innovation. Under Saturn's "risk-and-reward" program, workers receive about 12 percent less in salary than other General Motors employees but can earn bonuses based on meeting efficiency and training targets. Moreover, Saturn employees have worker representation at every level of management and decisions are made by consensus.[47]

Self-Directed Work Teams or Groups

A more common approach to employee involvement is self-directed work teams or groups. *Self-directed work teams* are teams of workers without a formal, company-appointed supervisor who decide among themselves most matters traditionally handled by a supervisor. These groups of workers typically decide daily work assignments, the use of job rotation, orientation for new employees, training, and production schedules. Some groups even handle recruitment, selection, and discipline.

Self-directed work teams
Teams without formal supervision who direct their own work.

www.ganesha.org/sdwt/

http://users.ids.net/~brim/
sdwth.html

http://achievemax.com/
newsletter/previous/
harticle3.htm

www.mapnp.org/library/
grp_skll/slf_drct/slf_drct.htm

Although employee commitment has been declining, research indicates that 47 per cent of Fortune 1000 firms use teams to some extent and 60 per cent plan to increase the use of teams.[48] In some organizations, teams have been very successful:

> An apparel manufacturing plant placed employees responsible for sewing work in teams of 10 people. The use of teams was associated with increased productivity, better quality, and lower turnover and absenteeism. In improving team performance, attention was paid to team building exercises and training. In addition, special training programs for supervisors were also established.[49]

Some observers are critical of the increased focus on innovation and workplace teams. In a number of organizations, managers "stress the system" by speeding up the line, cutting the number of employees or machines, or having workers take on more tasks (at times through "multi-skilling"). Under such systems, workers may be required to act like machines. While management by stress may help in raising productivity (at least over the short term), workers often experience considerable personal stress and a sense of being "dehumanized."[50]

High Involvement Work Practices

There is growing evidence that human resource management practices do matter and are related to organizational performance. In one study, high work performance

www.eiro.eurofound.ie/
2000/02/Features/
uk0002156f.html

practices were related to lower turnover, higher productivity, and improved financial performance.[51] In another study, automobile assembly plants with team-based work systems and high commitment human resource management practices outperformed facilities without such characteristics.[52] The thrust of the work in this area has been away from focusing on any single human resource practice in favour of studying systems or bundles of practices and the strategic impact of human resource management on organizational performance.[53]

What does this mean for human resource management? The human resource function must focus on business level outcomes and problems, become a strategic core competency with the ability to understand the human capital dimension of the organization's major business priorities, and develop a systems perspective of human resource management.[54] Seven practices of successful organizations include (1) a focus on employment security, (2) selective hiring, (3) self-managed teams and decentralization of accountability and responsibility as basic elements of organizational design, (4) comparatively high compensation contingent on organizational performance, (5) extensive training, (6) the reduction of status differentials, and (7) the sharing of information with employees.[55]

High-involvement work practices
Work practices that allow employees to influence how their roles are performed.

To what extent are Canadian organizations pursuing high involvement workplace strategies? Results from two studies exploring *high-involvement work practices* are presented in Figure 13-6.[56] A 1996–97 survey of more than 600 Canadian organizations (excluding Atlantic Canada), found that 44 per cent of the responding firms had work teams and more than one-quarter reported having quality circles or quality of work life programs. Somewhat more popular were employee management joint programs (57 per cent) and problem-solving groups (66 per cent). The figure also shows the results of a similar study of more than 600 organizations located in Atlantic Canada. Note that the Atlantic Canada sample was made up of much smaller organizations and thus, it is not surprising that such firms had somewhat fewer programs.[57]

FIGURE 13-6

Employee Involvement Programs in Canadian Organizations

Type of Program	% of Organizations Located Across Canada (except four Atlantic Provinces)	% of Organizations in Four Atlantic Provinces
Quality circles	27	25
Quality of work life	33	29
Problem-solving groups	66	46
Work teams	44	28
Employee management joint programs	57	36
Total quality management	53	35
Job enlargement/enrichment	44	22

Source: Terry H. Wagar, *Employee Involvement, Strategic Management and Human Resources: Exploring the Linkages*, Wilfrid Laurier University, November 1997; and Terry H. Wagar, *Employee Involvement and Human Resource Management in Atlantic Canadian Organizations*, Saint Mary's University, May 1997.

JOB SECURITY, DOWNSIZING, AND EMPLOYEE RETENTION

No-Layoff Policies

In the past, loyal, hardworking employees could expect a secure job in return for dedicated work for the organization. However, this is no longer the case and the traditional *psychological contract* (the unwritten commitments between employers and employees) has been radically rewritten.[58] This new employment relationship has been described as follows:

> You're expendable. We don't want to fire you but we will if we have to. Competition is brutal, so we must redesign the way we work to do more with less. Sorry, that's just the way it is. And one more thing—you're invaluable ... We're depending on you to be innovative, risk-taking, and committed to our goals.[59]

Contrary to the downsizing trend of the 1990s, some organizations are developing no-layoff policies. These firms are using such policies as part of an integrated system of progressive HR practices—the idea is that employees who have job security are more receptive to change, more likely to be innovative and suggest changes that will improve the organization, and are more willing to "go the extra mile":

> According to Jon Slangerup, Vice President and General Manager at Federal Express, "the issue is not that employees are not getting their work done. It's a matter of discretionary effort—having employees do things above and beyond the call of duty every single day. To me, that is the difference between a great company and a good one."[60]

Organizational Downsizing

In many organizations, lifetime employment has been replaced by job insecurity. When we talk about downsizing, we are not dealing with a small number of firms. A national study completed in 1997 found that 49 per cent of Canadian organizations permanently reduced the workforce over a two-year period, with an average reduction of almost 13 per cent of the workforce. The majority of employers reported engaging in workplace restructuring and about half indicated a change in organization strategy. The most common benefit provided to displaced workers was severance pay (provided by 88 per cent of employers) while just over two-thirds of firms indicated that they provided outplacement counselling and an extended period of notice relating to termination.[61]

www.ewin.com/articles/
payper.htm

www.theoccupancybusiness
.com/care_05.asp

www.organisational-
solutions.co.uk/PCS.htm

Major corporations around the world continue to downsize. For example, Xerox announced plans to slash 5200 jobs in 2000, consumer products giant Unilever revealed that it will cut 25 000 jobs as part of a worldwide reorganization, and Coca-Cola said that 6000 employees will lose their jobs. According to Coca-Cola chairman and CEO Douglas Daft:

> "The world has changed. 2000 is a year of recovery." Although surprised by the scale and scope of the reorganization, analysts said Mr. Daft had effectively wiped the slate clean and begun a new era at Coca-Cola."[62]

Downsizing
Reducing employment to improve efficiency, productivity, and competitiveness.

Downsizing may be defined as "a deliberate organizational decision to reduce the workforce that is intended to improve organizational performance."[63] It has also been described a set of activities undertaken on the part of management and designed to improve organizational efficiency, productivity, and / or competitiveness."[64] It is possible to identify three types of downsizing strategies:

1. *workforce reduction*—a short-term strategy focused on cutting the number of employees through programs such as attrition, early retirement or voluntary severance incentive packages, or layoffs.

2. *work redesign*—this strategy takes somewhat longer to implement and requires that organizations critically examine the work processes and evaluate whether specific functions, products and / or services should be changed or eliminated.

3. *systematic change*—this is a long-term strategy requiring a change in the culture and attitudes and values of employees with the ongoing goal of reducing costs and improving quality. This strategy takes a long time to implement and thus the benefits only accrue over time.[65]

While firms frequently believe that downsizing will enhance organizational performance, study after study shows that "following a downsizing, surviving employees become narrow-minded, self-absorbed, and risk averse. Morale sinks, productivity drops, and survivors distrust management."[66]

It appears that the word "downsizing" is perceived differently in the new economy. According to Colleen Clarke, a career consultant, "the guilt factor is no longer there. Downsizing is no longer an anomaly, it's a rite of passage for companies. There is no shame in it at all anymore and often companies use downsizing to get rid of the deadwood."[67]

In addition, there is growing evidence that firms engaging in downsizing do not perform better financially—the bulk of the research indicates that the stock price of downsized firms often declines after a layoff announcement is made.[68]

Downsizing efforts often fail to meet organizational objectives. This is not surprising considering that many workforce reductions are carried out with little strategic planning or consideration of the costs to the individuals and employer. Frequently, cutting jobs is but a short-term response to a much more serious problem. In several instances, little attention is given to carefully examining and resolving critical human resource issues.

One organization had planned to contract out the maintenance of vehicles to local garages. While huge savings were projected, several of the local garages did not have repair bays big enough to accommodate the vehicles and the hoists were not strong enough to support the trucks.

Still, downsizing may be an appropriate strategic response for some organizations. However, downsizing is not a "quick fix" remedy—before implementing such a program, it is critical to carefully consider the decision, plan the process, and assess the consequences from the perspectives of the organization, the customer, the "survivors" (those employees that remain), and the victims (those that lose their jobs).

www.pamij.com/hickok.html

www.ncs.com/ncscorp/research/95-9.htm

http://advance.byu.edu/bym/1997/97spring/downsizing.html

www.csaf.org/downsize.htm

www.henrygeorge.org/intdown.htm

www.govexec.com/reinvent/downsize/0896s3.htm

www.transformation-mgt.com/downsize.html

www.foxperformance.com/consulting4.html

www.princetoninfo.com/sgdown.html

http://choo.fis.utoronto.ca/FIS/Courses/LIS1230/LIS1230.downsize.html

Downsizing and layoffs do not always produce financial benefits for the company, and for the employees, a drop in morale and productivity often results.

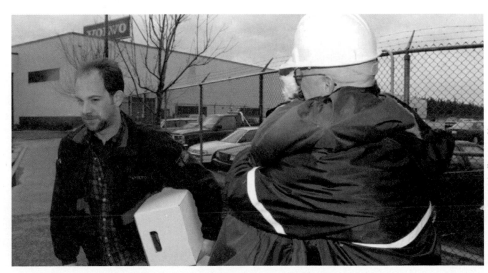

CP PHOTO ARCHIVE (Jeff McIntosh)

Although most organizations engage in the workforce-reduction stage of down-sizing, many ignore the critical elements of redesigning the organization and implementing cultural change.[69] From a best practices perspective, six key principles deserve attention:

1. Change should be initiated from the top but requires hands-on involvement from all employees.

2. Workforce reduction must be selective in application and long-term in emphasis.

3. There is a need to pay special attention both to those who lose their jobs and to the survivors who remain with the organization.

4. It is critical that decision-makers identify precisely where redundancies, excess costs, and inefficiencies exist and attack those specific areas.

5. Downsizing should result in the formation of small semi-autonomous organizations within the broader organization.

6. Downsizing must be a proactive strategy focused on increasing performance.[70]

Retaining key employees is often a major challenge during downsizing:

> During a major restructuring, Loewen Group developed a new program to keep employees from jumping ship. In addition to retention and performance incentives, Loewen's Key Employee Retention Program (KERP) focused on providing additional incentives to key executives who were essential to the successful implementation of the restructuring plan. The other component of the program was effective two-way communication of the restructuring process. The company also set up a 1-800 number to address employee concerns and questions.[71]

Human resource professionals have an important role to play in downsizing efforts and should be involved in the strategic process. HR people are often in a good position to advise on the impact of restructuring an organization (from a variety of perspectives including work groups, teams, departments, and individuals) to maximize productivity and retain quality performers. Similarly, HR can develop skill inventories and planning charts to evaluate the effects on human resource needs and projected capabilities.

Moreover, in light of the compelling evidence that most downsizings have dramatically negative impacts on those who survive, human resource experts can assist in coordinating and communicating the downsizing decision. There is growing evidence that effective communication can reduce some of the negative consequences associated with downsizing.[72] Finally, HR can assist in evaluating the downsizing program. Issues include monitoring who left the organization and who remains, job design and redesign, worker adjustment to change, the need for employee counselling, organizational communication, and a comprehensive review of the appropriateness of existing HRM policies and programs (such as training, compensation and benefits, and orientation of employees into the "new" organization).[73] However, recent research has shown that downsizing employees is professionally demanding and the "downsizers" may experience social and organizational isolation, a decrease in personal well-being, and poorer family functioning.[74]

Keeping Good Employees

While some employers continue to cut back on employees, keeping the good people is often a challenge for both growing and downsized organizations. Many companies lose half of their employees in three to four years and half their customers in five years—keeping employees is as critical as retaining customers because without loyal employees, you won't have loyal customers.[75]

Ernst & Young was losing 22 per cent of its female professionals each year and spending about $150 000 per job to hire and train replacements. In addition to mentoring, networking, and flexibility schemes, it established a women retention effort with a particular focus on the intense work environment—some of the initiatives include call-free holidays in which professionals do not check e-mail or voice-mail messages on holidays, flexible schedules, and reduced weekend travel.[76]

The American Management Association found that turnover was especially high among employees under 30 years of age and among information technology (IT) specialists. Almost 50 per cent of respondent organizations were most concerned with the loss of information systems and technology employees, followed by the loss of general management personnel (identified by about 17 per cent of employers as the group where retention was their greatest concern):[77]

A recent Sibson Canada study using exit interview data indicated that while pay was an issue, the primary reason for IT professionals leaving their employer was related to "psychic income factors." The key considerations were poor project management, low-quality internal IT leadership, lack of career direction, uncompetitive pay, outdated technology, job restructuring, low morale among IT employees, and a desire for a more dynamic work environment.[78]

Moreover, the problem is not unique to the private sector. Almost three-quarters of the knowledge workers in the public sector indicated that they had thought of quitting their job and about 20 per cent plan to quit within a one-year period:

The main reason for knowledge workers thinking of leaving the public sector is not getting a sense of accomplishment. While 50 per cent of workers define career success in terms of a sense of accomplishment, many find it difficult to feel they are making a contribution because of the work culture and government bureaucracy. Some workers receive no feedback on why a particular idea is not accepted and have no idea what happens to reports they produce.[79]

Among the factors in retaining key employees are:

1. Developing a planned approach to employee retention (which examines the usual company benefits, addresses individual needs, focuses on the long-term, is part of the vision of the organization, and is based on investment in employees);

2. Becoming an employer of choice with a goal of retaining employees from the day they join the organization;

3. Communicating the organizational vision and values frequently and in a clear and consistent manner;

4. Rewarding supervisors and managers for keeping good people; and

5. Using exit interviews to obtain information as to why people are leaving the organization.[80]

A recent global study by Towers Perrin indicated that benefits often fail to entice employees to remain with an organization:

A changing workforce that considers concepts of loyalty and tenure as old-fashioned places more importance on performance rewards and professional development than on benefit offerings. "The real motivators now are focused on the work environment and providing good training and development programs," according to Jim Murta, principal at Towers Perrin.[81]

www.keepemployees.com/
whitepapers.htm

www.worldatwork.org/
research/generic/html/
retention-survey-q1-6.html

www.sibson.com/solution/
retention/index.htm

www.thomas-staffing.com/
survey99/retention.htm

SUMMARY

The human resource department's role in organizational communication is to create an open two-way flow of information. Part of the foundation of any organizational communication effort is the view held by management of employees. If that view is one that sincerely strives to provide an effective downward and upward flow of information, then the human resource department can help develop and maintain appropriate communication systems.

Downward communication approaches include in-house publications, information booklets, employee bulletins, prerecorded messages, electronic mail, jobholder reports, and open book management. Multiple channels are used to help ensure that each message reaches the intended receivers. Perhaps the greatest difficulty in organizational communication is to provide an effective upward flow of information. In-house complaint procedures, manager-employee meetings, suggestion systems, and attitude survey feedback are commonly used tools.

Counselling is the discussion of a problem with an employee to help the worker cope with the situation. It is performed by human resource department professionals as well as supervisors. Counselling programs provide a support service for both job and personal problems, and there is extensive cooperation with community counselling agencies.

Discipline is management action to enforce organizational standards, and it is both preventive and corrective. The hot-stove rule is a useful general guide for corrective discipline. Most disciplinary action is progressive, with stronger penalties for repeated offences. Some disciplinary programs primarily emphasize a counselling approach.

Quality of work life efforts are systematic attempts by organizations to give workers a greater opportunity to take part in decisions that affect the way they do their job and the contribution they make to their organization's overall effectiveness. They are not a substitute for good, sound human resource practices and policies. However, effective QWL efforts can supplement other human resource actions and lead to improved employee motivation, satisfaction, and productivity. QWL is most commonly improved through employee involvement. Whether that involvement is in solving workplace problems or participating in the design of jobs, employees want to know that their contribution makes a difference.

In this era of downsizing and restructuring, it is important to understand the basic principles relating to wrongful dismissal law. Also, there is evidence that many downsizing efforts fail to meet organizational objectives. Human resource professionals have an important role to play in both growing and downsized workplaces.

TERMS FOR REVIEW

Visit the Web site at www.mcgrawhill.ca/college/schwind6 for a full glossary.

REVIEW AND DISCUSSION QUESTIONS

1. Think of a situation in which you learned some new information from the grapevine and took action on the basis of that information. Discuss.

2. List and describe the different types of programs that can be used by the human resource department to improve communication.

3. Discuss differences between preventive and corrective discipline. What examples of either one were applied to you on the last job you had?

4. What is progressive discipline? How does it work? Is its basic approach realistic in work situations? Explain your answer.

CRITICAL THINKING QUESTIONS

1. What are quality circles? As a manager, what steps would you take to create and maintain effective quality circles in your division?

2. Suppose you are a plant or division manager and you want to improve the quality of work life in your division. What steps would you take?

3. Think of an organization that you have worked in. What employee relations practices could be implemented to improve performance.

4. Assume you have been asked to terminate an employee. How would you conduct the termination interview?

WEB RESEARCH

1. Visit the Web sites of three Employee Assistance Program (EAP) providers. Compare the programs and approaches of the three providers. What similarities and differences do you observe?

2. Laws relating to dismissal vary in different countries. Using the Internet, examine dismissal law Web sites in Canada, the United States, and one other country. Compare the laws regarding dismissal among the three countries.

INCIDENT 13-1

The Machinist's Abusive Comments to the Supervisor

William Lee, a machine operator, worked as a machinist for Horace Gray, a supervisor. Horace told William to pick up some garbage that had fallen from William's work area, and William replied, "I won't do the janitor's work." Horace replied: "When you drop it, you pick it up." William became angry and abusive, calling Horace a number of uncomplimentary names in a loud voice and refusing to pick up the garbage. All employees in the department heard William's comments.

The situation was as follows. Horace had been trying for two weeks to get his employees to pick up garbage in order to have a cleaner workplace and prevent accidents. He talked with all employees in a weekly department meeting and to each employee individually at least once. He stated that he was following the instructions of the superintendent. Only William objected with the comment, "I'm not here to do the janitor's work. I'm a machinist."

William had been in the department for six months and with the company for three years. Horace had spoken to him twice about excessive horseplay, but otherwise his record was good. He was known to have a quick temper.

After William finished his abusive outburst, Horace told him to come to the office and suspended him for one day for insubordination and abusive language to a supervisor. The discipline was within company policy, and similar acts had been disciplined in other departments.

When William walked out of Horace's office, Horace called the human resource director, reported what he had done, and said that he was sending a copy of his action for William's file.

1.   As human resource director, what comments would you make?

2.   What follow-up actions should the human resource director take or recommend that Horace take? For example, do you recommend counselling for William? Would you reconsider disciplinary procedures and policies?

INCIDENT 13-2

The Alta Gas Plant

Utilizing a socio-technical system design, the Alta Gas Plant near Calgary created production teams so as to minimize turnover, improve the quality of production, maximize flexibility by having workers trained on various tasks, and reduce shutdown times by regularizing plant maintenance.

Under this new design, operation of the plant during a shift is handled by a five-member production team consisting of a coordinator and four technicians. Each technician rotates throughout the various jobs and progresses through the salary range by successfully completing a series of examinations. The team is centred in the control room and laboratory, and when their assignments scatter them throughout the plant, they maintain contact with portable radios. As the senior member of the team, the coordinator is not a supervisor in the usual sense. The coordinator rotates assignments with other members, but maintains an overview of the plant's operations and serves as a linking pin between the team and upper levels.

Team members not only operate the plant, but they assist in quality control and rotate through a maintenance cycle every fifth week. As part of their skill development, they select a trade in which they are interested, and during their main maintenance assignment they work with the journeymen (male/female) on projects and participate in planning.

To minimize the number of night shifts a person works, a complicated schedule has been developed involving five teams. There are two 12-hour production shifts and an eight-hour shift for maintenance. Teams rotate shifts on production and every fifth week are on maintenance work. Teams decide on their holiday schedules, with only one person gone at a time so the remaining members can cover the operations.

Recruitment of team member replacements is a joint process involving members in the reviewing of applications and in the on-site interviews. The team's choice is based on the following selection criteria: good skill levels, potential, and acceptability as a team associate.

Observers report that the team operation has resulted in high morale, excellent operating performances, improved plant maintenance because teams spot and correct problems earlier, better problem-solving in general, better individual skill utilization, and full interchangeability and flexibility in job assignments.

1. Speculate on the reactions the Alta employees might be having toward their system. Why?

2. Analyze the Alta design from a management perspective. Under what type of organizational characteristics would this design work or not work? Be sure and distinguish senior, middle, and lower management perspectives.

3. Discuss the applicability of the Alta Gas Plant model to organizations you are familiar with and list the potential advantages and disadvantages of the model to your situation.

CASE STUDY

Maple Leaf Shoes, Addressing Employee Relations

As she sat in her office in Winnipeg, Britney MacPherson thumbed through a 1975 textbook on personnel management. As manager of the Winnipeg location of Maple Leaf Shoes, she was responsible for the day-to-day operations of the facility. However, Britney was finding her job particularly challenging—although she had a B.Comm, which she received in 1976 from a well-known Ontario university, her university training had been focused on accounting and finance and she had only one course in human resource management (which was called personnel management when Britney completed the course). Things were unravelling in Winnipeg and Britney knew that she needed help. Unfortunately, her phone calls and e-mails to head office in Wilmington, Ontario, brought little assistance.

The company policy regarding employee communications was quite simple: "What goes on at the company stays at the company." This policy was communicated regularly to all employees. However, Joan Jorgenson, a clerk in the office, had violated this policy. A couple of weeks ago, Joan had struck up a conversation with a co-worker, Natalie King. During their talk, Natalie had mentioned that she had recently moved from Wilmington to Winnipeg because, according to Natalie, a senior member of management in the Wilmington office had become enraged when Natalie refused his sexual advances. He had threatened Natalie with dismissal but after a short discussion, an agreement was reached that Natalie would move to the Winnipeg location. Joan became enraged when she heard Natalie's story and immediately notified not only employees of the human rights commission in Ontario but also the media in both Winnipeg and Wilmington. Britney is now trying to decide how she should handle the situation.

Max MacSweeney is a 31-year-old accountant who has been employed by Maple Leaf Shoes for seven years (three years in Wilmington and the last four years in Winnipeg). Although Max is based in Winnipeg, he travels throughout Western Canada as part of his job. Max is considered to be a very good employee. He is well known in the business community, is very involved in the local association of management accountants, and is a highly visible member of a number of charitable organizations in the Winnipeg area. Max is married and has two children.

About three weeks ago, head office started monitoring the Internet usage of employees. Much to their surprise, they found that Max had visited several "pornographic" Web sites on four different evenings (while on business at the Wilmington office). The records revealed that he had spent an average of about three hours on each of the four evenings visiting such Web sites. While Max used company property (the computer he accessed the sites from was in an office assigned to him while in Wilmington) when visiting the "undesirable" sites, such visits were made outside of regular working hours. Just over one month ago, the company began providing Internet access to employees but has not developed a policy on Internet usage. Head office personnel in Wilmington have asked Britney to deal with the issue.

As they say, "problems often come in threes." Britney's head was aching as the phone rang. On the other line was Rob McEwen from head office in Wilmington. He wanted to find out what Britney was going to do about Paul Bertuzzi. Paul is a 44-year-old warehouse supervisor at the Winnipeg facility. He supervises eight employees, has been with Maple Leaf Shoes for just over 11 years, and earns $36 000 a year. Paul's performance evaluations are among the highest at the Winnipeg office, he attends night school and is two credits away from receiving his B.A., and is well liked by his co-workers.

One month ago, Paul went to Toronto to attend a two-day training program for warehouse supervisors. After the first day of sessions, Paul and two other warehouse supervisors (from the Montreal and Toronto facilities) went out for dinner. During the meal, the other two supervisors revealed to Paul that

they had developed a scheme in which they wrote off a small portion of the shoe inventory as wastage but actually kept the shoes and sold them to a friend at a discount. As one of the individuals said: "We're not talking about big money, Paul. However, I'm sure you could use an extra $100 to $150 a week. After all, we're all underpaid and our salaries are not keeping pace with inflation." In addition, they told Paul of a new money-making scheme and asked if he was interested in joining their "team." It appears that a shoe manufacturer overseas was interested in mass-producing Maple Leaf Shoes products—however, the new company needed more information on the latest shoe designs and production techniques. Under the scheme, the warehouse supervisors were going to get information for the overseas company in return for part-ownership in the business.

One week ago, an auditor uncovered the scheme. The two warehouse supervisors from Montreal and Toronto were fired. While the audit confirmed that no other Maple Leaf Shoes employees were involved in the scheme, Paul (and one other Maple Leaf Shoes employee) admitted knowing of the fraud. In discussions with top management, the point was raised as to whether Paul had a duty to report the fraud. Again, Britney has been asked to deal with the matter.

Discussion Questions

1. Consider the three issues Britney needs to address. Which one should be addressed first? Last? Explain your reasoning.

2. How should Britney deal with the Joan Jorgenson incident? What suggestions would you make to improve the policy on employee communications?

3. What disciplinary action (if any) would you recommend that Britney take with respect to the case involving Max MacSweeney?

4. Develop a company policy on Internet usage.

5. Do you recommend that Paul Bertuzzi be dismissed? Is there just cause for dismissal?

6. Regardless of your answer to Question 1, what would be "reasonable notice" in the event that a court ruled that your organization did not have just cause to terminate Paul? Explain your answer.

7. If you were in Paul Bertuzzi's position, would you have reported the scheme to senior management?

CASE STUDY

A Matter of Security at Canadian Pacific and International Bank

Brenda Reid joined Canadian Pacific and International Bank (CPIB) in 1990 and has been employed with CPIB since that time. Brenda, who is 38 years old, is a single mom with two young children (Norris, age seven, and Morris, age five). Brenda graduated from Mount Allison University in 1983 with a B.Comm., worked almost five years with another bank (from 1983 to 1988), and returned to school in 1988. She earned a Master of Business Administration degree from University of Saskatoon in 1990, specializing in finance and information systems. Upon graduation, she joined CPIB as an assistant manager and is now the manager of the main branch in Halifax (a position she assumed three years ago).

Brenda is considered a very strong performer and senior bank officials believe that she has senior upper-management potential. Brenda has participated in several management training programs and within the next year, the bank had planned to send her to the Advanced Management Seminar provided by the London University Business School. The Advanced Management Seminar is a prestigious program for international bankers with at least 10 years' experience.

Brenda earns just under $100 000 a year and her performance is very solid (she has consistently ranked within the top 20 per cent of bank managers). The only disciplinary incident in her file involved a written warning two years ago for misplacing her security pass card to the main Halifax branch. The card was ultimately found in a CPIB policy and procedures manual that she had borrowed.

On a Friday afternoon three weeks ago, Brenda decided to take home two files, each of which contained detailed financial and corporate information on a major CPIB corporate client in the Atlantic region. Brenda was scheduled to meet with representatives from each of the two companies the following Monday and removed the files from the bank in order to review them over the weekend. According to Brenda, taking files home to review was not unusual—several managers did it on a regular basis.

After leaving work on the Friday afternoon, Brenda met a few friends and went out for dinner in downtown Halifax. Later, the group attended a play at Neptune Theatre. When the play was over, Brenda returned to her minivan to find that her briefcase containing the two files had been stolen from the van (which she had locked). Brenda had put the briefcase under the front seat of the van. While Brenda's empty briefcase was found in the parking garage, its contents have not been recovered.

Although CPIB does not have a detailed policy relating to the removal of property from the bank offices, the CPIB handbook contains a provision informing all personnel to exercise extreme caution and care when removing CPIB property from the office. Interviews with loans officers and managers indicate that the typical procedure is to either keep the property on their person or secure the property in the trunk of a vehicle.

Brenda was devastated by the theft and reported it immediately to her supervisor. She broke into tears when discussing the incident with CPIB management, apologized profusely for her mistake, and promised that it would never happen again.

Discussion Questions

1. Would you recommend disciplinary action in this case? Why or why not?

2. Are there long-term implications for the human resource function as a result of this incident?

3. Assume head office has demanded a new policy addressing the security of bank property. Discuss the merits and drawbacks of having such a policy.

4. Develop a policy for CPIB.

SUGGESTED READINGS

Bamberger, Peter and Ilan Meshoulam, *Human Resource Strategy: Formulation, Implementation and Impact*, Thousand Oaks, CA: Sage, 2000.

Echlin, Randall Scott and Matthew L.O. Certosimo, *Just Cause: The Law of Summary Dismissal in Canada*, Aurora, ON: Canada Law Book, 1998.

Fitz-Enz, Jac, *The 8 Practices of Exceptional Companies: How Great Organizations Make the Most of Their Human Assets*, New York: American Management Association, 1997.

Handy, Charles, *Beyond Certainty: The Changing Worlds of Organizations*, New York: McGraw-Hill, 1996.

Heckscher, Charles, *White Collar Blues: Management Loyalties in an Age of Corporate Restructuring*, New York: Basic Books, 1995.

Levitt, Howard A., *The Law of Dismissal in Canada*, Aurora, ON: Canada Law Book, 1992.

Pfeffer, Jeffrey, *The Human Equation: Building Profits by Putting People First*, Boston, MA: Harvard Business School Press, 1998.

Reichheld, Frederick F., *The Loyalty Effect*, Boston, MA: Harvard Business School Press, 1996.

Wellins, Richard, William Byham, and Jeanne Wilson, *Empowered Teams*, San Francisco, CA: Jossey-Bass, 1991.

Chapter 14

Diversity Management

"While ... diversity brings stimulation, challenge and energy, it does not always lead to harmony. The mix of cultures, genders, life styles, and values often becomes a source of misunderstanding and conflict. Many enlightened managers, from CEOs in the executive suite to supervisors on the shop floor, want to create an environment where differences are valued and where people who look, talk and think differently can work productively together. However, the knowledge and skills to do so are not part of most managers' experience. Like explorers in a new land, they are entering uncharted areas."

—Lee Gardenswartz and Anita Rowe[1]

CHAPTER OBJECTIVES

After studying this chapter, you should be able to:

■ *Define* diversity management

■ *Discuss* the strategic importance of diversity management today

■ *List* the stages of diversity management

■ *Discuss* the various steps in managing diversity

■ *List* current industry practices in this field

■ *Discuss* the various barriers to diversity management, and

■ *Discuss* the special challenges facing global firms in the context of diversity management

www.gov.ns.ca/humr/dhr/ dmu/divers.htm

Before he delivers a lecture on gender identity to his philosophy class, Professor Michael Gilbert must decide what to wear. Most likely, he will put on a knee-length skirt, a long-sleeved blouse, and low pumps. Standing before a mirror at home, he'll fix his wig and apply make-up before heading out the door.

Professor Gilbert is a cross-dresser who teaches philosophy at a major Ontario university. He is among a growing cadre of "trans" people on campuses who are going public. Organizations for gay, lesbian, and bisexual students have already begun tacking a "T" on the end of their names to embrace "transgendered" or "transsexual" students. In the recent past, students and professors have also pushed universities to extend protection to transgendered people under policies to prevent discrimination against minorities.[2]

Welcome to the workforce of the new millennium! The emergence of "trans" persons and the demand for recognition of persons with non-traditional sexual orientation is but one dimension of the emerging workforce diversity. Consider some of these statistics:

- Approximately 50 per cent of the people living in some major Canadian cities such as Toronto and Vancouver are not of British, French, or other European origin. Over 3.1 million Canadians or approximately 11.2 per cent of the total population (as per 1996 census) were visible minorities such as Chinese, South East Asian, Black, Latin American, and Japanese.[3]

- Over a quarter of Canadians claim to be of more than one ethnic origin.

- In the near future, nearly 85 per cent of women in the age group 18-64 will be in the labour force. But only a tiny proportion of them will be in senior managerial positions or on the board of directors of major organizations. In the foreseeable future, women will continue to earn less than 80 cents for each dollar that men earn unless corrective actions are taken.

- Over six per cent of working Canadians have some disability.

- Canadians of Asian and African origins are more educated when compared to other ethnic groups, yet less than one percent of top executives in this country belong to these groups.[4]

A combination of factors including governmental policies, demographic and labour force changes, increasing global operations, technological revolution, and radical changes in social values have fundamentally changed the way Canadian organizations work and whom they employ. The traditional "one size fits all" managerial policies of the past will no longer suffice.[5] A diverse workforce requires managers with new leadership styles who understand their varying needs and creatively respond by offering flexible management policies and practices.

A number of research studies have indicated that men emerge in leadership positions in North America because they are more likely to exhibit traits that are associated with the behaviour of powerful authority figures in the past. These traits include: aggressiveness, initiating more verbal interactions, focusing on output issues rather than process issues, and less willingness to reveal information and expose vulnerability.[6]

Old boys' network
Set of informal relationships among male managers providing increased career advancement opportunities for men and reinforcing a male culture.

Many women are also hindered by lack of access to the ***old boys' network***, the set of informal relationships that develop among male managers and executives.[7] This results in exclusive fraternizing of men with men that reinforces a "culture" of men without women's perspective and condones behaviour that devalues women. The friendships and contacts built through the network become the basis for assignments and promotions and the network becomes the informal communication link that provides vital information about business from which women are excluded. This means that many women never reach positions of power.

In 2000, women filled 12 per cent of corporate officer jobs in Canada's 560 largest companies. They occupied 6.4 per cent of the strategically important line officer positions where their leadership is directly linked to profit and loss. They held less than five per cent of top posts in corporate Canada—executive vice president and above or what are referred to as "clout titles."[8] Only 7.5 per cent of directors at Canada's largest companies were women.[9]

Even in unconventional work settings, women often find themselves powerless as in the case of Canadian space researcher Judith Lapierre:

> Judith Lapierre, a Canadian space researcher who spent 110 days with a group of male scientists in an isolation chamber (a replica of a spaceship) in a Russian institute, withdrew from further tests citing sexual harassment by a Russian crew commander. Dr. Lapierre, a 32-year-old social medical expert from Quebec, complained that she was dragged away from television monitoring cameras in the chamber and kissed aggressively by the commander.[10]

The existing values, norms, and patterns of interactions among managers may also act as a *glass ceiling* that stunts the growth of women and minority persons beyond a certain level. Promotional opportunities are visible, but invisible obstructions seem to block the way. The perception of the existence of a glass ceiling results in frustration, reduced job and career satisfaction, alienation from the workplace, and ultimately higher employee turnover.

The situation of other minorities such as African Canadians and First Nations people is no better. As Professor Trigger of McGill University pointed out, until recently, "native people were treated as part of a vanishing past. They were seen as more akin to the forests in which they lived and the animals they hunted ... Canadian historical studies as a whole have suffered from the chronic failure... to regard native peoples as an integral part of Canadian society."[11] Despite the transformation of Canadian cities and towns into multi-cultural mosaics, prejudices against visible minorities continue to exist at the workplace.

This chapter introduces you to the concept of workforce diversity and helps you plan to meet the new workplace challenges. Some of the human resource management strategies and processes that recognize, foster, and capitalize on the diversity will be discussed in the following sections. We will also look at the special challenges facing global organizations where the challenge of diversity is felt to an even greater extent.

MEANING OF DIVERSITY MANAGEMENT

CANADA HAS ALWAYS been a diverse nation composed of a wide variety of different peoples. Beginning with the 50 distinct aboriginal nations who originally inhabited this country, Canada later became the home of the French, the English, other Europeans, the Chinese, Black Loyalists, the Russians, the Japanese, and the East Indians. In fact, Canada was a racially and ethnically diverse society even by Confederation in 1867.

Like trees in a vast forest, humans come in a variety of sizes, shapes, hues, and life-stages. This variety helps to differentiate us. While all of us share the important dimension of humanness, there are biological, cultural and other environmental differences that separate and distinguish us as individuals and groups.[12] It is these differences that provide the spectrum of human diversity and enrich our lives.

Given such myriad differences among humans, it is very difficult to arrive at a broad and universally acceptable definition that is inclusive yet does not overwhelm us in the process. Broadly, *workplace diversity* may be defined to *include important*

www.theglassceiling.com/about.htm

www.womenswire.com/glass/

www.international.ubc.ca/careers/students/career insight/31-03-99/equity.htm

Glass ceiling
Invisible, but real obstructions to career advancement of women and visible minorities, resulting in frustration, career dissatisfaction, and increased turnover.

Workplace diversity
Includes important human characteristics that influence values, perceptions of self and others, behaviours, and interpretations of events.

Canada's cultural mosaic raises several challenges for the manager who must successfully manage a diverse workforce.

Core dimensions of diversity
Age, ethnicity, and culture, gender, race, religion, sexual orientation, and capabilities.

Secondary dimensions
Education, status, language and income levels.

Managing diversity
Ability to manage teams made up of members with different cultural values.

human characteristics that influence an employee's values, perceptions of self and others, behaviours, and interpretation of events around him or her. Diversity, at a minimum, includes age, ethnicity and culture, gender, race, religion, sexual orientation, and mental and physical capabilities. (See Figure 14-1.) Several writers consider the above seven areas to be the ***core dimensions of diversity*** since they exert considerable impact on our early socialization and a powerful, sustained impact throughout our lives.

> For example, regardless of whether a particular employee is currently 20, 30, 40, 50 or 60 years old, his or her age has a bearing on how (s)he is perceived by others as well as the individual's ability to learn, perform (several tasks), and relate to the environment. Age, thus, is a core dimension that affects an individual's workplace perceptions and behaviours.

Several other ***secondary dimensions*** such as education, family status, language, and even income levels play important roles in shaping our values, expectations, behaviours, and experiences. Hence, their impact on employee behaviours at the workplace should not be belittled. They are, however, less visible, more mutable, and more variable in their impact on individual behaviours.

Managing diversity *recognizes that an organization is a mosaic where employees with varying beliefs, cultures, values, and behaviour patters come together to create a whole organization and where these differences are acknowledged and accepted.* Managing diversity has three major dimensions[13]: First, it assumes that effective management of diversity and differences among employees can add value to an organization; second, diversity includes all types of differences and not simply obvious ones such as gender, race, and so on; and third, organization culture and working environments are key items to focus on in managing diversity.

Another metaphor for diversity is the salad bowl[14]: like a mosaic, each employee makes a unique contribution to the larger bowl (or organization) while maintaining his or her own individuality and cultural or other identity. When diverse backgrounds and talents combine, they make a more effective and creative organization.

FIGURE 14-1

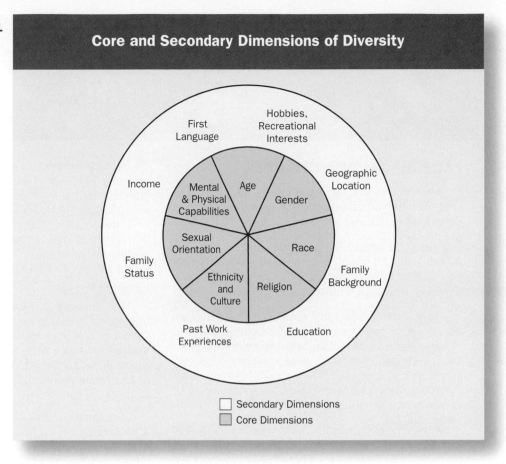

Core and Secondary Dimensions of Diversity

Secondary Dimensions
Core Dimensions

www.gov.ab.ca/mcd/
citizen/hr/pubs/stereotp.htm

Stereotyping
The process of using a few observable characteristics to assign someone to a preconceived social category.

Managing diversity requires an organization to treat its employees as individuals rather than as numbers or categories.[15] Most of us tend to group people using dimensions such as race, gender, and age. However, it is important to recognize that the same person may belong to multiple categorical groups:

> Thus, the same individual's identity can be composed of various facets: One can be an African-Canadian (race) woman (gender) who is older (age), married (marital status), and from a low-income family (income status).

This raises the important question: on which one or more of these identities should a human resource manager focus? Grouping people often results in *stereotyping*; yet, a grouping that gives added insights into the person's unique background, capabilities and individuality is likely to generate better workplace outcomes. Further, the differences between groups need not be intrinsic or innate; they can be differences attributed to history or prevailing culture and subject to change.

> For example, the way a typical Canadian views homosexual couples today is very different from the way he or she did 50 years ago.

Such attributed differences play a key role in human interaction. Cultural conventions and values set "rules" when interacting with others and reduce uncertainty for individuals in a society. These largely unwritten rules themselves have been changing. For several persons, many of these "rule changes" are welcome since they reduce inequity and injustice. For others, the pattern and pace of change heightens anxiety and discomfort because long-standing ideals are being eroded. How to change workplace rules that enhance productivity, growth, and commitment and at the same time minimize anxiety and uncertainty? Herein lies the challenge of managing diversity.

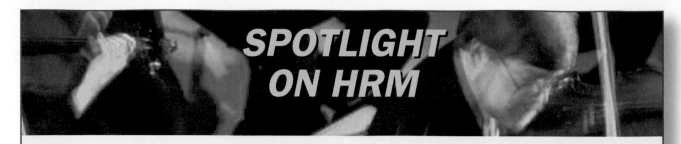

SPOTLIGHT ON HRM

FACE OF CANADA CHANGES

For the first time in history, the census has found that less than half of Canada's stock of immigrants have come from European countries.

The 1996 census figures on immigration found that 47 per cent of the total population of immigrants who now live in Canada were born in Britain and other European countries, Statistics Canada said yesterday.

And while it has been obvious for perhaps two decades that more and more of Canada's quota in immigrants are coming from Asia and the Middle East, the flow of newcomers from those areas and other non-European countries has been so swift in recent years that they have overtaken the older generations of European immigrants as the majority.

"The snapshot from the 1996 census tells us that a remarkable experiment is taking place in this country," said Myer Siemiatycki, a research associate of the Centre of Excellence in Immigration and Settlement. "It's really redefining for us our image of who is a Canadian."

Not only that, but because Canada's quota of immigrants has risen sharply since the 1980s and because the country's birth rate is so low, the proportion of the Canadian population that was foreign-born has risen to its highest level in more than 50 years.

In 1996, it was 17.4 per cent, up from 16.1 per cent in 1991. This is the highest proportion of immigrants in the Canadian population since 1941, when it was 17.5 per cent, senior Statistics Canada analyst Jane Badets said. The highest levels on record were through the 1910s, 1920s, and 1930s when the proportion rested at about 22 per cent after the massive waves of newcomers who settled the country early in the century.

The new statistics confirm that Canada is one of the world's magnets for immigrants. Australia, where 22 per cent of the population is foreign-born, is one of the few countries with a greater proportion of immigrants than Canada. The United States had 7.9 per cent at last count, France 6.3, and Britain 3.4, Ms. Badets said.

The rapid population change is happening against a backdrop of much fear among Canadians over how their society will adapt to so many people from such different cultures, said anthropologist Frances Henry of York University in Toronto.

The two concerns are that Canada accepts too many immigrants and that they are not white-skinned, she said, pointing to recent opinion polls. "We're in a state of enormous transition," Prof. Henry said.

Source: Alanna Mitchell, "Face of Canada Changes," *The Globe and Mail*, November 5, 1997, p. A1. Reprinted with permission from *The Globe and Mail*.

STRATEGIC IMPORTANCE OF DIVERSITY MANAGEMENT

SEVERAL FACTORS make diversity management strategically important.

1. Changing Workforce

As detailed in Chapters One and Three, the Canadian labour market is undergoing rapid and continuous transformation. The average member of the workforce of the past was male, white, approximately 30 years old, and usually held a high school diploma or lower. These men also worked within the region of their birth, were married, and had children. Typically, their wives stayed home to take care of their family. Today's work force, in contrast, includes women, ethnic minorities, native

www.gov.ns.ca/humr/dhr/
dmu/dmu.html

Canadians, people with physical disabilities, and people with alternative life styles (for example, people with same sex partners). If one includes other forms of heterogeneity (such as age and language differences), the workforce diversity is even more striking. Given this state of affairs, diversity management is not merely desirable, but mandatory if an organization is to effectively attract, utilize, and develop human resources.

2. Importance of Human Capital

Changes in production technology have dramatically increased the importance of human capital. In the past, the entrepreneur raised capital, invested in fixed assets (like a factory), hired others to work, and kept all emerging profits for himself or herself. In today's world of "intellectual capitalism," the situation is quite different. In knowledge-intensive firms, it is not clear who owns the company, its tools, and its products. Often, today's organization may not even have a factory (and may be getting products manufactured by a subcontractor in Taiwan or Mexico). The only tools seen may be computers, cellular telephones, and fax machines. The knowledge-worker may be the key to the success or failure of the firm. Often the departure of even a few workers can spell disaster for the firm. The most valuable parts of the firm's operation may be reflected in human tasks of sensing, judging, and making decisions. In today's information age, no one can afford to use human capital inefficiently.

> As General Electric's Chairman Jack Welch pointed out, with competition fierce, "the only ideas that count are the A ideas. There is no second place. That means that we have to get everybody in the organization involved. If you do that right, the best ideas will rise to the top."[16]

3. Diversity as a Competitive Advantage

www.businessweek.com

Proactive organizations recognize that competitive strength often lies in focusing on their employees and their clients. In a Canadian survey, 25 per cent of senior executives viewed the increasing diversity of the workforce as a competitive opportunity and a sustainable source of competitive advantage.[17] Globalization and changing domestic markets (because of demographic changes, immigration, etc.) mean that a firm's customers are no longer a homogeneous group of persons.

> One writer estimates the spending power of minorities in Canada at about $76 billion. A diverse workforce enables an organization to develop a greater understanding of the needs of diverse customers.[18]

For Canada, this is particularly important since our biggest trading partner, the United States, itself is undergoing rapid transformation in its population resulting in greater work force diversity.

Further, many of the growing export markets for Canadian firms are located in East Asia, South Asia, Latin America, and Africa. It is imperative that we understand the needs of a diverse population and respond effectively and in a timely fashion to maintain our competitive advantage.

> Royal Bank, through its Leveraging Diversity strategy, makes the employee differences increase the competitive advantage of the firm. The bank looks at leveraging diversity as a proactive process to gain a business advantage from the differences and similarities of employees and the marketplace. It recognized that "hammering a wealth of diverse pegs into one-size-fits-all holes can stifle creativity, and give business too narrow a focus." By actively focusing on the needs of women, aboriginal people, and ethnic, racial, or other employee groups, the bank's Diversity Business Council could recognize definite business advantages. Consider these:

Women on a product development team give male team members perspective on how female customers may respond to new product ideas.

Partnerships with aboriginal people result in increased economic and business opportunity to the aboriginal community and improved success for service providers.

Employees who grew up on the East Coast give the marketing team in central Canada some first-hand insights into regional tastes and expectations.

Customers in a predominantly Chinese neighbourhood are served by employees who speak the language and relate to the customer needs.

Older or retired employees of the bank understand and serve the needs of the seniors' market.[19]

Managers learn to achieve productivity gains by leveraging the strengths of all employees. The bank recognizes that there is a world of opportunity to be gained from tapping people's differences and pooling their insights and experiences.[20]

A study of men and women in first-line sales-management positions at a British firm found that on a wide range of measures, the women in the group consistently showed superior results. The women-led teams showed higher levels of effectiveness in business to business selling, job satisfaction, lower levels of burnout, and less conflict.[21]

www.taketheleap.com/
define.html

Paradigm shift
Fundamental change in a paradigm, e.g., shift from paper filing systems to computer filing systems.

4. Paradigm Shift

There has been a revolutionary change in organizational assumptions about people and their work. A paradigm is a shared mindset that reflects a fundamental way of thinking and understanding the world around us. Since our beliefs and understanding direct our behaviour, a *paradigm shift* can have a profound effect on the behaviour of organizations. Figure 14-2 shows the old paradigm and the new paradigm (in the context of diversity) that has replaced it in recent years. Such dramatic changes necessitate fundamental alterations in the way we think, operate, and manage people.

FIGURE 14-2

A Comparison of Traditional and New Paradigms

Traditional

- Organizational success is linked to standardization
- Diversity is a cost
- Rules and policies are to be shaped by senior executives
- Emphasis on "masculine" values of competitiveness, aggressiveness and individuality
- Change employee behaviours and attitudes to suit the organization's culture

New

- Success is linked to individual's contribution
- Diversity is a competitive advantage
- Rules and policies are to be shaped to satisfy the customer and the employee
- Recognition that "feminine" values of openness, flexibility, and relationship orientation are equally important for organizational success
- Modify organizational culture to suit the needs of the employees

Reprinted with permission by Pearson Education Canada Inc.

5. Increasing role of work teams

Teams play a dominant role in modern organizations. Work teams are charged with task accomplishment to enable firms to distance themselves from the competitors and ensure survival.[22] While teams always reflected some degree of diversity, today the differences among members are even greater. Race, gender, ethnicity, age, education levels, sexual orientation, and so on, are among key factors that separate team members. The differences must be considered as "value added" rather than as "problematic" and the team leader today must have the skills to facilitate and inspire (rather than coach and control as in the past). Assimilation into a homogeneous culture may result in loss of synergy. Valuing differences, on the other hand, can result in improved creativity and innovative problem solving.

Past writings indicate that employee morale and satisfaction are related to the way in which employee and group identities are defined and respected.[23] Indeed, the overall organizational effectiveness measures such as work quality, productivity, absenteeism, and turnover may be significantly influenced by the way individuals and groups are treated. Effective handling of workforce diversity can lead to added creativity, problem solving, and intra-organizational communication.[24]

STAGES OF DIVERSITY MANAGEMENT

Developmental stages
Five stages through which the concept of diversity has evolved over time.

THE CONCEPT OF managing diversity itself has evolved over a period of time, often undergoing fundamental transformation along the way. A careful analysis of an organization's culture and practices may place it in one of the following *developmental stages*.

Stage 1: Diversity under Duress

Many organizations engage in diversity management practices simply because they have no other choice. Faced with a situation demanding the use of a diverse workforce, they do the minimal to accommodate different employees. The case of women and Japanese Americans in the U.S. military is a good example in this instance:

> Women and Japanese-Americans were "tolerated" in the U.S. military during the second world war. African-American soldiers were required to remain separate and could not get closer than 50 feet to their white counterparts. After World War II, women were discouraged from participating in the workforce.

Here, diversity is, typically, looked at as a necessary and temporary deviation. It is as if the decision makers within a firm do not see the essential merit of a diverse workforce,[25] but are prepared to accept it as a "necessary evil." There are no changes planned in systems or organizational culture to accommodate these differences.

> A typical response of these organizations is: "We just received a notification from the government about a possible audit of our equity program. We could lose our contract. What do we have to do to meet the governmental quotas?"[26]

Stage 2: Levelling the Playing Field

Next comes the notion of providing equal opportunity for all groups and subgroups. Firms actively pursue policies that avoid any form of discrimination at an individual level: the assumption being that once equal opportunities for entry were provided, the disadvantaged groups would work through the organizational chain and would soon be represented in higher levels of organizational hierarchy.

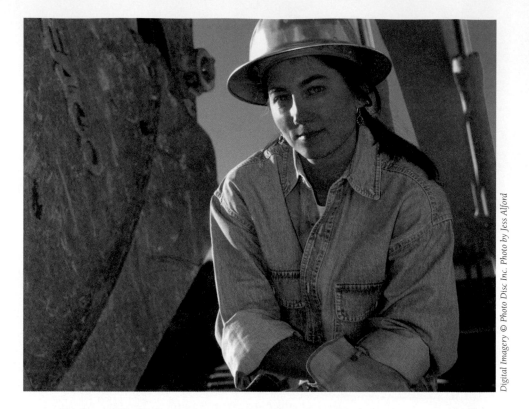

Today's workforce includes more women participating in careers that were typically exclusive to men.

Digital Imagery © Photo Disc Inc. Photo by Jess Alford

The Charter of Rights and Freedoms of the Canadian Constitution Act of 1982 and the human rights legislation in various provinces aimed to remove obstacles from the path of individuals (who were different) from joining and thriving in organizations. For instance, a policy that required a high school diploma and a specified intelligence test score for recruitment to unskilled jobs may violate the equal treatment policy since it has an adverse impact on persons who belong to certain racial or socio-economic backgrounds. Requiring employers to establish bona-fide occupational qualifications for various jobs ensures that all individuals get fair treatment at their workplace.

Some firms claim to have "open doors to all":

Several employers claim they have diversity by citing they "hire women and minorities" or "treat all employees equally irrespective of whether they are women, blacks, disabled, or old." The typical response of some of these employers is: "Look, ... we don't have a problem. We like women here. And women like us. We like minorities here.. there's no problem here."[27]

Needless to say, these organizations do not understand or value differences or hope to benefit from diversity in a meaningful way.

Stage 3: Tilting the Playing Field

When efforts to provide equal entry opportunities do not produce desired representation levels in upper organizational hierarchies, the emphasis may have to change to giving preferential treatment to protected (or disadvantaged) work groups who were hitherto shut out from employment in several professions or jobs. This approach emphasizes more than just treating persons in the same way, it also requires special measures and accommodation of differences.

A five-year (1987-1992) review of statistical reports submitted by 345 Canadian employers revealed that although the number of employees belonging to disadvantaged groups increased slightly, their representativeness in some professions or in higher levels of hierarchy was not equitable. In 1992, women constituted only 44.7 per cent of the workforce (in 1987 it was 40.9 per cent). The proportion of other groups in the work force were (1987 figures in brackets) found to be: visible minorities 7.9 per cent (5 per cent); persons with disabilities 2.5 per cent (1.6 per cent); and aboriginal people 1.0 per cent (0.7 per cent). Women in general were concentrated in clerical, sales, or service occupations (for example, 76.4 per cent of all clerks were women), while their representation in managerial positions or in skilled crafts was very limited (e.g., only 9.3 per cent of managerial positions or 2.6 per cent of skilled job categories were occupied by women).[28]

This meant that four disadvantaged groups—women, aboriginal people, persons with disabilities, and persons who because of their race or colour were a visible minority in Canada—required special help. Employers, hence, needed to analyze the workforce and establish firm policies to correct imbalances or injustice. (See Chapter Four for a discussion of the concepts of underutilization and concentration in jobs.) The emphasis now shifts to organizational policies that go beyond hiring (e.g., promotion, compensation).

Stage 4: Valuing Diversity

Preferential actions in hiring, promotion or training often lead to polarization at the workplace. Advancement for some can be seen as resulting in losses for others. Also, for sustained progress of the disadvantaged groups, a simple one-time action by a firm may not be adequate. These factors often result in the fostering of diversity-friendly attitudes and relationships at work place. Diversity training programs, which focused on exploring personal attitudes and values on diversity-related matters and eliminating employee stereotypes and biases against "outgroups," are popular in firms that value diversity.

Stage 5: Managing Diversity

While understanding and appreciating diversity is essential for fostering good relationships at the workplace, understanding alone does not result in effective management of diversity issues. Also, valuing diversity had its focus primarily at the personal level (e.g., changing people's attitudes and cognitions) which does not, by itself, empower the workforce or help employees achieve their full potential. The emphasis at this stage is on changing organizational systems and their core culture.

Diverse employees are represented in all levels and stages of human resource management within organizations, and employee empowerment is recognized as critical for improving performance, morale and decision quality.

Organizations that genuinely practise diversity recognize that diversity is more than a human resource management issue and affects all strategies and processes of the organization. Diversity management is tied to the strategic plan, and every employee from senior executives to the lowest-level employee contributes to fostering a diverse workforce.

Bank of Montreal is a good example of an organization that took the notion of diversity management seriously. Finding that women held 91 per cent of the bank's non-management jobs but only 9 per cent of the executive positions, the bank made an early attempt to tap the vast potential of its female workforce. The bank established a Task Force on the Advancement of Women to identify the constraints facing women who wanted career progress in the bank. Clear goals and action plans were established to eliminate these hurdles. Surveys, focus groups, intensive interviews, and so on were carried out to find solutions for faster advancement of women to executive careers.

Apart from the financial benefits it received by tapping a hitherto forgotten resource, the bank also received numerous awards for its success in improving the work climates of women, aboriginals, and people with disabilities. The Catalyst Award from a New York think tank, the Distinction Award from YWCA, and Catalyst: Mercury Awards from the International Communications Academy of Arts and Sciences in New York are particularly noteworthy in this context.[29]

Several factors such as an organization's size, culture, management professionalism, and concern with societal concerns affect its diversity management posture. Below we discuss steps in introducing diversity at the workplace.

STEPS IN DIVERSITY MANAGEMENT

TRANSFORMING AN organization's culture is a time-consuming process. Effective, system-wide changes require both attitudinal and behavioural changes. To bring an organization to Stage 5 discussed above may, at times, take several years of commitment. In almost all instances, diversity management efforts require four key steps (see Figure 14-3). These are discussed below:

1. Identify Ideal Future State

Implementing a diversity management program begins with an accurate portrayal of its current workforce composition and a forecast of its future workforce.[30] Organizational members have to be identified accurately using demographic categories such as age, gender, ethnicity, education, and disability. Some organizations also expand this to identify the number of employees belonging to other distinct groups on the basis of their language, race, sexual orientation, income level, social class, parental status, and marital status. Practical considerations that vary among firms determine which aspects of diversity can be accommodated. Once the firm has an accurate picture of its workforce composition (and likely future needs), it is critical to assess the values and needs of the work force. Surveys, focus groups, and interviews with individual employees and work groups are employed to identify present and ideal future states at work.

> For example, through surveys and focus groups, American Express Travel-Related Services found its employees were experiencing significant difficulties in balancing work and family responsibilities. Through follow-up focus groups, the firm identified fourteen possible solutions including part-time work, job sharing, child-care centres and compressed work weeks.[31]

FIGURE 14-3

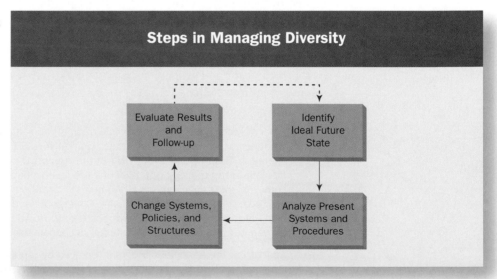

Steps in Managing Diversity

Source: Adapted from Hari Das, *Strategic Organizational Design: For Canadian Firms in a Global Economy*, Scarborough, Ontario: Prentice Hall, 1998, p. 340. Reprinted with permission by Pearson Education Canada Inc.

2. Analyze Present Systems and Procedures

The next step is to examine how the present systems are operating. Current policies, systems, practices, rules, and procedures have to be examined for their appropriateness for a diverse work force. Included here are work assignments, recruitment and hiring, orientation, training, compensation, employee communication, human resource development, and performance appraisal. The validity and fairness of the various systems and rules for different cultures and their compatibility with different cultural norms are assessed at this stage.

3. Change Systems, Procedures, and Practices

All existing systems and practices have to be reviewed for their continued relevance to the organizational mission, strategy, and environmental demands. Those that are found lacking should be modified or even discontinued. Five factors are particularly critical in this context:

1. Senior Management Commitment

In most organizations, changing systems and internal practices is no simple task. Senior management commitment to diversity is one of the most important elements of ensuring the success of diversity efforts; so is whole-hearted support from the unions. While they may be started with considerable enthusiasm, diversity efforts will fail unless all managers and employees see them as an integral part of the firm's business philosophy. This means that particular attention should be paid to communication, hiring, and reward structures to promote diversity.

In the past, several organizations have confused diversity with hiring women, minorities, and the physically challenged. However, simply hiring more women or other minorities in the absence of a genuine commitment to diversity does not achieve any beneficial outcomes. Indeed, some recent research studies indicate that women often leave organizations and start their own companies to avoid "glass ceilings" at work.

> A study of 650 female entrepreneurs showed that many started their own businesses to avoid discrimination at work. Sixty per cent of respondents who had come out of private corporations were frustrated with their past work environments, with many saying their employers did not take them seriously or did not value them.[32]

Sometimes, changes in the way an organization operates can result in simultaneous achievement of organizational goals and diversity targets. Royal Bank's selection system for hiring telephone sales agents is a good example of this:

> When Royal Bank recruited telephone sales agents for its Royal Direct Call Centre in Moncton, applicants competed on a level playing field: the bank used interactive voice response (IVR) and multimedia computers to screen job seekers. All applicants were asked to dial a 1-800 number. An automated voice gathered information about skills such as sales and computer experience. The top candidates progressed to multi-media computer assessments that presented them with confused or irate clients and gave them a chance to respond. Only after the computer screening did the applicants with the highest scores have their first face-to-face interview. The result is that many applicants (and hires) felt that they were being judged on their merits and basic skills without outside factors such as race, gender, or an unconventional employment history biasing the decision. This also helped the bank to attract men to a position that hitherto was concentrated with women. Typically, call centres have a ratio of 80 to 90 per cent women. The new system resulted in a ratio of 73 per cent women and 27 per cent men.[33]

Simply changing a few human resource procedures (such as selection process) without necessary changes in internal culture and processes, however, may not be enough. Consider the experience of Ann States in Western Paper and Pulp Corporation:

> When Ann entered Western Paper and Pulp Corporation as the junior work supervisor, she was the only black woman in her unit. During the job interview, the human resource manager had communicated to Ann the company's strong commitment to diversity management. However, what she experienced at the workplace was very much at odds with the firm's avowed policy. She found that her boss rarely gave her any challenging job assignments; her co-workers often hinted that she would not have been hired but for her skin colour. At some office parties, she was not given a chair at the head-table although other supervisors of her rank were seen there. Frustrated and doubting her career growth potential within the firm, Ann left her job after six months.

Figure 14-4 shows the areas where a firm must make changes if diversity initiatives are to succeed. Mere verbal support of system and policy changes is unlikely to produce tangible results. Linking diversity initiatives to business goals and incorporating diversity goals into performance criteria (reflected in salaries) ensures the accountability of managers for diversity.

2. Establishment of a Diversity Committee

Diversity committee
A committee entrusted to oversee diversity efforts, implement processes, and serve as a communication link.

One approach to increase employee involvement is through the establishment of a *diversity committee*. This committee will oversee diversity efforts, implement portions of the process, and serve as a communication link among employees, managers, and union officials. The number of members in the committee shows variation across organizations. Thus, small organizations may have only two or three members, while larger organizations typically employ six to eight members. What is perhaps even more important than size of the committee is its composition and power. Committee members should not be limited to the traditional "disadvantaged" groups (e.g., women, visible minority), but should represent all employee groups broadly (e.g., occupational groups, geographic location, age groups). The committee should have power not only to identify budgets necessary for diversity efforts but also to hire outside experts, where necessary, to further diversify initiatives and oversee internal communication and education strategies.

FIGURE 14-4

Systems and Practices Requiring Modification During a Diversity Effort

- Recruitment and selection processes and criteria
- Orientation
- Work assignments
- Performance management
- Reward systems
- Employee communication systems
- Training
- Career and management development policies and programs
- Employee Counselling practices
- Benefits policy
- Group and team practices
- Leadership skills and practices
- Job descriptions and specifications

Royal Bank has a Diversity Business Council that is entrusted, among other things, with the following responsibilities:

- To identify the opportunity 'gaps' and the problems of omission that stand in the way of making the differences work.

- To develop a transition plan to achieve gender gap objectives by a predetermined date.

- To formulate action plans to close the gaps observed.

- To get buy-in, and accountability from, unit heads and all senior management to implement the action plans.

- To build in a process to measure results.[34]

3. Education and Retraining

Training in the importance of diversity must be provided to all employees from the CEO to the lowest level employee. Different types of training and training methodologies are used to meet the unique needs of different work group segments.

> For example, a training approach to familiarize work supervisors with new appraisal procedures may employ role plays and case studies. To train the same firm's assembly workers in communication with members of other cultures, these methods are likely to be less successful.

A diverse workforce, while adding to the strategic advantage of the firm, also provides a major managerial challenge. Many Canadians in the workforce today may have origins in cultures or ethnic groups that have vastly different assumptions about work, relationships, and group norms. Thus, a large number of Asians, Africans, Middle Eastern, Latin American, and Canadian aboriginal persons who originate in rural-based societies have traditional ways of organizing reality and dealing with problems and events.[35] Figure 14-5 shows a comparison of the values and assumptions held by mainstream, urban-industrialized Canadians and persons originating from other cultures. Similar value and behaviour differences can be seen between mainstream employees and other work force segments as well (e.g., persons of different sexual orientation; persons who belong to different religious groups). Only a deep commitment to understanding the cultural and work-related values held by different work groups will prepare the organization to manage the challenges of diversity.[36]

To sensitize the workers to the cultural values and norms held by other groups, a variety of training and employee development techniques may have to be employed. Alternate training approaches, learning principles, and evaluation criteria were discussed in Chapter Seven. Transference of learning to workplace must be given particular importance when evaluating the effectiveness of alternate delivery mechanisms. Giving managers and employees new tools and information without permitting them to put them to use only creates frustration. Hence it is critical that key issues learned during training are incorporated into day-to-day work.

4. Wide Communication of Changes

Changes in internal systems and procedures must be communicated to all members. Information should be provided on what changes will occur, what the likely results will be, how important these changes are for the success of the organization, accomplishments until this point, and responses to questions related to diversity initiatives. Some of the communication methods in the context of diversity management are listed in Figure 14-6. More on employee communication strategies was discussed in Chapter Thirteen.

FIGURE 14-5

A Comparison of Values and Assumptions of Mainstream Canadians and Members of Some Other Cultures

	Mainstream Canadians	Members of Some Other Cultures
1. Assumptions about time	Time is critical; it is scarce and linear in its transition.	Clock-time is not important; time is measured by events; time is cyclical.
2. Decision making practices	Rational procedures are important; logic is the essence of decision making.	Intuitive, holistic problem solving is as (and sometimes even more) important.
3. Focus at work	Achieving organizational outcomes is critical.	Human relations and affiliation with others is as (and sometimes more) important.
4. Verbal communication	"Small talk" is preferable to silence. Use "direct" style (e.g., "No" or "I can't do that"). "Elaborate" style where quantity of talk is high; description includes great detail and often there is repetition. Communication emphasizes an individual's "personhood."	Silence during conversation is normal. Use "indirect" style (e.g., rather than a "no," say, "it might be possible" or "it is interesting in principle"). "Succinct" style with low quantity of talk; under-statements and silence used to convey meaning. Communication is related to an individual's role and hence is "contextual."
5. Non-verbal gestures in communication	Eye contact is perceived as a sign of attention or even trustworthiness. A smile usually signifies happiness or pleasure. A "V" with fingers connotes victory. An "O" with fingers means Okay in the U.S. and in some parts of Canada.	Looking directly into another's eyes signifies disrespect and rudeness. A smile may connote embarrassment or discomfort in some instances. This gesture has an offensive connotation in some settings. It means zero or worthless in France.
6. Other general assumptions	Individualism and competition are good; conflicts at work are natural.	The group is the key; cooperation and harmony are critical for success.
7. Values underlying dual employee behaviours	Individuals can and should display own abilities and achievement in the best possible light; self-selling acceptable; can interrupt, criticize, or confront others and offer unsolicited suggestions. Prefer fight to flight in situations of conflict. Can show anger, frustration, and disappointment.	Individuals should be humble and modest by not presenting themselves too favourably; should downplay own accomplishments; interruptions and questionings are disrespectful to others; avoiding loss of personal or group honour and "face" is a top priority. Prefer flight to fight in situations of conflict. Should exert and expect self-control and restraint in emotional expression.
8. Dress and appearance	"Dress for success" ideal; dress seen as an indication of commitment to the firm and the profession; formal, conforming dress valued.	Dress is often an indication of cultural and religious beliefs, position, and prestige.

Source: Adapted, updated and summarized from a variety of sources including the following: W.B. Gudykunst and S. Ting-Toomey, *Culture and Interpersonal Communication*, Newbury Park, CA: Sage Publications, 1998; Lee Gardienswartz and Anita Rowe, *Managing Diversity*, New York: Irwin Professional Publishing, 1993, p. 37; G. Hofstede, *Culture's Consequence: International Differences in Work Related Values*, Beverly Hills, CA: Sage Publications, 1980; L.H. Chaney and J.S Martin, *Communication and Conflict: Readings in Intercultural Relations*, Needham Heights, MA: Ginn Press, 1994.

At Warner-Lambert Canada, education and communication of diversity initiatives are ongoing. To ensure inclusion of all employees, early communication focusing on increasing awareness of human rights is attempted.[37]

5. Evaluate Results and Follow-up

www.nadm.org

www.shrm.org/hrmagazine/
articles/

Diversity audits
Audit to uncover underlying dimensions, causes, interdependencies, and progress-to-date on diversity management matters.

Unless the firm monitors the progress of the diversity effort on a systematic basis, corrective actions may not follow. Monitoring will also ensure that quantitative and qualitative indices of change are available to the management, the union, and the workforce. These results should be widely communicated and the gaps between targets and accomplishments publicized along with the proposed corrective actions. The various data collection techniques discussed in Chapter Seventeen are relevant for this purpose. Indices such as number of hires, promotions, absenteeism, turnover, salary levels, grievances, harassment complaints, and so on, are useful for gauging progress, but should not be used in exclusion since qualitative responses from employees may convey other dimensions of work climate and the intensity of employee feelings. More progressive organizations employ *diversity audits* on a regular basis to uncover the underlying dimensions, causes, and progress-to-date on diversity management related matters. Prompt follow-up actions to accelerate accomplishments are necessary and should be planned in consultation with the senior managers and the unions to ensure success.

CURRENT INDUSTRY PRACTICES

IN THE PREVIOUS section, we discussed the need for changing key systems and procedures within organizations to implement diversity management. This section provides an overview of popular industry practices to achieve this objective. As will be seen, the approaches are as varied as organizations. The choice of specific mechanisms should be made after a careful consideration of the unique challenges and constraints facing an organization.

FIGURE 14-6

Communication Methods in Diversity Initiatives

- Employee newsletters
- Company magazine
- Electronic mail messages
- Special diversity bulletins, brochures, and pamphlets
- Special promotional events (e.g., "Diversity awareness day")
- Material available on company intranets and Web sites
- Diversity information sessions
- "Questions and Answers" booklets
- Notices and memos in employee cafeteria and lounges
- Formation of informal networks or committees representing different groups (e.g., women, physically challenged)
- Posters at workplace

Diversity Training Programs

Diversity training programs
Training programs aimed at importing new skills to motivate and manage a diverse workforce.

Managers and lower-level supervisors need to learn new skills that will enable them to manage and motivate a diverse workforce. Often, outside experts are invited to mount *diversity training programs* in organizations. Indeed, in many firms this is one of the first actions taken to implement diversity management. Such training programs help to create awareness of the bottom-line impact of diversity management and the role of managers, supervisors, and co-workers in creating a work climate that is found comfortable by all employees, irrespective of their gender, age, sexual orientation, racial or ethnic identity, and physical or mental capabilities.

> Petro-Canada, Du Pont Canada, and Levi Strauss & Co. (Canada) are examples of firms that have pursued diversity training programs in the past.[38] The Toronto Transit Commission has used a four-day, residential simulation of a fictitious transit organization to convey the challenges of bringing an equitable pay system into a firm that employs a diverse workforce.[39]

Awareness training
Training to create understanding of the need to manage and value diversity.

Skill-building training
Training employees to correctly respond to cultural differences at the workplace.

Experts suggest two types of training: *awareness training* and *skill-building training*. Awareness training focuses on creating an understanding of the need for managing and valuing diversity. It is also meant to increase participants' self-awareness of diversity-related issues such as stereotyping and cross-cultural insensitivity.

Once individuals develop an awareness, they can then monitor their feelings, reactions, etc., and make conscious decisions about their behaviour, often resulting in improved interpersonal communication. Skill-building training educates employees on specific cultural differences and how to respond to differences in the workplace. Often awareness and skill-building training are combined.

www.gendertraining.com/
www.diversitymatters.ca/

Another issue to be resolved by a trainer in managing diversity is content versus process training. Content training relates to the question: "Should a training program focus solely on the knowledge and skills related to a single culture?" This would be appropriate for a manager working with a work force consisting mainly of members of one culture. However, as mentioned before, statistics show that the Canadian work force is becoming more culturally diverse; more likely the manager will need to deal effectively with employees from several different cultures in an organization.

In the long run it is therefore more practical, although more difficult, to focus on process training; that is, supervisors and employees have to learn about diversity. Participants in a process-oriented diversity training program develop an understanding of how management style, the interpersonal communication process, teamwork, and other managerial issues are affected by diversity. After such a training program participants may not have all the answers, but they will have plenty of questions.

Ideally the trainers themselves will reflect diversity. A team of male and female, white and black (or Asian) trainers could work together to cover different topics in a diversity training program. It probably would make participants from different minorities and racial and cultural backgrounds feel more comfortable.

Useful training methods for diversity training are metaphors, stories, and parables. A metaphor is a figure of speech that makes an implied comparison between things that are not literally alike. Consider these examples:

> A popular saying among the group-oriented Japanese managers is: "Nails that protrude will be hammered in," implying that a nonconforming group member will be put under pressure to conform.

Parables (or fables) are stories with a moral:

> Two men had a disagreement. To have it resolved they went to a wise man. The first man explained the problem as he saw it. The wise man listened carefully, thought about it for quite some time, and said: "You are right."

Then the second man explained the problem as he saw it. The wise man listened carefully, thought about it for quite some time, and said: "You are right."

A third man, who had listened to the stories, spoke up: "Master," he said, "but both cannot be right." The wise man listened carefully, thought about it for quite some time, and said: "You are right."

The moral of the story is that for all of us perception is reality.

Stories can also be used as tools to get a message across. Here is a story told by a manager with Caterpillar Tractor Company:

When we opened a joint venture with Mitsubishi Heavy Industries in Japan we had to familiarize our Japanese counterparts with Caterpillar production processes. After having given an explanation we would ask: Everything clear?" and our Japanese colleagues would respond with: "Hai." Since we had learned that "hai" meant "yes" we assumed that everything had been understood, and we would say: "OK, let's do it." We found out too late that to the Japanese "hai" really means "I heard you." As a result of the misinterpretation we discovered that the Japanese managers had often not understood what we had told them, but they could not admit it because to them that meant to lose face. After several such experiences we installed blackboards in each office and established the following rules:

1. Talk slowly and look for signs of confusion.

2. Each explanation has to be repeated by the receiver.

3. Oral explanations have to be given also in writing.

4. Whenever possible drawings have to be used.

We found that with these rules we dramatically improved communication with our Japanese counterparts.[40]

These tools for diversity training can be used in many different ways. Stories can be told live, on audio- or videotape, or be given as handouts. Parables can be shared in a classroom exercise or included as a special feature in an in-house publication, and metaphors can be presented by the trainer or developed by participants. Experienced trainers will have such tools in their own libraries.

www.aimd.org

www.diversityhotwire.com

www.gradschools.com/
diversity/

Mentoring Programs

Mentoring programs
Programs encouraging members of disadvantaged groups (e.g., women) to work with a senior manager who acts like a friend and guide in achieving career success.

Some firms encourage *mentoring programs* where women, visible minorities, or members of other disadvantaged groups are encouraged to work with a senior manager who acts like a friend, philosopher, and guide in achieving career success within the firm.

In the past, Canadian National initiated a program where a woman employee moving toward a managerial position learns the job under a senior manager. At the end of a two-year period, if found effective in carrying out her responsibilities, the woman will be given a permanent job.[41]

To assist with internal and external mentoring and networking, Deloitte & Touche set up a series of Executive Women Breakfast Forums in partnership with AT&T.[42]

Mentors may be identified formally or informally. Organizations can bring greater predictability into diversity outcomes by establishing formal mentoring systems since they result in greater tangible results and accountability on the part of both mentors and protegés.

One large Canadian bank lists all relevant details of its senior managers on its Web site. All new hires are encouraged to select someone from the list and contact him or her on a regular basis for receiving helpful hints for day-to-day performance and long-term career advice. Both the mentor and the protege are encouraged to submit reports of their deliberations to the bank.

Mentoring, to be most effective, should be used in conjunction with a complete diversity initiative and not as a stand-alone ritual. Mentors also have to be carefully selected since not everyone can be an effective mentor. Past writings indicate that mentors should hold high rank within the organizational hierarchy, be confident and active, possess counselling skills, understand the power structure within the firm, and be respected by other managers.[43] The results of discussions between the mentor and protegé should be recorded and kept in the files for later use. In some organizations, a manager's performance evaluation reflects the person's contributions as mentor.

Alternate Work Arrangements

Alternate work arrangements
Non-traditional work arrangements (e.g., flextime, telecommuting) that provide more flexibility to employees, while meeting organizational goals.

Often, removal of negative factors can enhance employee performance and career growth. This is especially so in the case of women who have multiple and conflicting role demands from work and family or older workers who find the traditional work arrangements difficult. Several **alternate work arrangements** such as flexible work hours, telecommuting, extended leave, job sharing, etc., have been used in the past to accommodate the unique needs of employee groups. These arrangements are discussed in more detail in Chapter Twelve on alternate work arrangements.

> Some of these alternate work arrangements (e.g., extended leave) have been particularly aimed at women who, because of their child-bearing role, face conflicts between work and family demands. These alternate career paths and work patterns (collectively labelled mommy track by some) recognize the fact that men and women face differing challenges in bringing up children. Of late, daddy track has also been gaining in popularity to recognize the needs of men who opt to spend some time raising children but want to pursue their old career once the children are older.

> To address the balancing of work and family issues, Deloitte & Touche offered adoption assistance, elder-care consultation and referral, child-care resource and referral, back-up child-care, and flexible work arrangements—including reduced work hours, flextime, and parental leave.[44]

Apprenticeships

Apprenticeships
A form of on-the-job training in which young people learn a trade from an experienced person.

Apprenticeships are similar to mentoring except that they relate to junior-level or technical jobs and often involve working with prospective employees before they formally join the organization. Such programs are particularly useful to attract visible minorities, women, the physically challenged, and other disadvantaged groups to non-traditional jobs within the firm.

> In the past, Warner-Lambert worked with the Scarborough Board of Education to offer training for students with disabilities within the organization. Hewlett-Packard worked with high schools to provide cooperative tracks to employment especially focusing on disadvantaged groups.[45]

Support Groups

Support groups
Groups of employees who provide emotional support to a new employee who shares a common attribute with the group (e.g., racial or ethnic membership).

Employees belonging to racial or other groups that are underrepresented in the organization may often feel lonely and uncomfortable at the workplace. Sometimes, this might be simply a feeling of loneliness and distance from mainstream workers. In other instances, the new employee may even face hostility from other members of the work group, especially when others perceive that the employee's minority status resulted in preferential treatment during hiring. Co-worker hostility is more likely to happen when a visible minority employee (or woman) is hired for a job that is nontraditional for that group. Often the result is employee alienation, which in turn results in high turnover. To overcome this problem, some firms organize **support groups** that are designed to provide a nurturing climate for employees who may otherwise feel unwanted or shut out. Socialization in such groups not only enables the newcomer to share concerns and problems but also to assimilate the organization's culture faster.

Communication Standards

Communication standards
Formal protocols for internal communications within an organization to eliminate gender, racial, age, or other biases in communications.

Words, language, signs, jokes, and even gestures that may be neutral or even "fun" to some employees may be offensive to many others. Indeed, the use of some language or words can amount to harassment since they create a "hostile environment" (see Chapter Four). Realizing this factor, several organizations have established formal protocols for internal messages and communication to avoid offending members of different gender, racial, ethnic, age, or other groups.

> The use of "he" when referring to managers in policy manuals has the result of perpetuating the "male" image of a manager. There is no reason why a "chairman" of a meeting is a man; the more progressive organizations recognize this and use the term "chairperson." Similarly, there is no reason why automobiles, yachts, or some other equipment should be referred to as "she" rather than "it."

www.aphis.usda.gov/
mb/wfd/

BARRIERS TO DIVERSITY MANAGEMENT

WHILE CONSIDERABLE interest in diversity management exists, few organizations are prepared for the resistance that invariably follows the introduction of this concept at the workplace. Resistance to diversity management may emerge from employee groups, unions, work supervisors, and managers. Employee groups and unions fear the emergence of new systems that may bring in hiring quotas, employment and promotion criteria that result in reverse discrimination policies, and lowering of power, status, and rewards. Managers and supervisors share several of the same concerns and may also fear that the new procedures will alter internal systems and performance standards and reduce autonomy. On several occasions, the resistance may originate from misperceptions, lack of understanding of the need for change, prevailing stereotypes, and even rumours about negative outcomes associated with diversity implementation elsewhere. As one writer summed it up, "while the list of opposing rationales runs the gamut from the seemingly reasonable to the ridiculous, all these explanations share a common trait. Each one is a fearful response to change....Regardless of which particular reasons are offered, the common emotion that fuels the fire of backlash is fear. When individuals perceive diversity as a threat, they often react with denial, dread, hostility, cynicism and/or contempt."[46]

While the reason for resistance may show some variation across employees and groups, its impact is almost always to slow down or stop the change program. To counter resistance, it is very important that the organization anticipates it and uses proactive strategies. *The presence of a qualified trainer* and consultant who conveys the importance of diversity to the various organizational groups and members is a must for success. *Clear articulation of the rationale* behind the change and the likely consequences of change (or lack of change now) may result in an attitude change in the context of diversity management. *Involvement* of managers, workteams, and other powerful members in the change process and identification of strategies for successful diversity initiative may reduce their fears about the change. It can also result in teams and employees taking ownership for successful change in their settings.

> At Warner-Lambert Canada, a Diversity Task Force was established to increase the success of employee buy-in and to eliminate barriers. The Task Force is composed of people from all functional areas of the organization. To reduce resistance, individuals from the senior levels of the organization provide leadership and are the diversity champions.[47]

Targeting managers and employees most ready to embrace the value of diversity and providing them with the knowledge and skills required to make diversity management work has been found to be useful in several settings. Such a strategy of *positive momentum building* enables the creation of role models and success stories that others can see and emulate. Whatever the approach used, one important principle to bear in mind is never to exclude *mainstream workers* (usually, the white males or whites in many organizations) from the changes. When "diversity" is perceived to mean only women, visible minorities, or other disadvantaged groups or when "diversity management" is seen to benefit only some groups, employee commitment to it may disappear fast. If the credibility is lost once, it may be very difficult to regenerate interest in the concept.

Changing the culture of an organization is a complex and time-consuming task. Introduction of diversity management into traditional cultures requires questioning of established assumptions and systems and sustenance of new values and behaviours through systematic and continuous efforts. A mere change in organizational chart or job description or a simple proclamation committing the firm to diversity is unlikely to result in desired changes.

DIVERSITY CHALLENGE FOR GLOBAL FIRMS

www.shrm.org

THE CHALLENGE of managing a diverse workforce assumes even greater importance in global firms. The impact on human resource management practices varies depending on the extent of internationalization of a firm's operation as well as the strategy it employs to reach foreign markets.

Several firms simply extend their operations into other countries by adapting their products, services, and processes to foreign markets. They are essentially domestic firms that build on their existing capabilities to penetrate international markets.

Bombardier and Magna are examples of Canadian companies that have adapted their existing capabilities to penetrate European markets. They have not changed much else about their normal operations to expand their operations globally.

On the other end of the spectrum are organizations that provide considerable autonomy to their foreign operations. They use flexible structures and procedures to suit the customs and preferences of people in each country or region where they operate. The foreign operations have a wide latitude to set goals, policies, systems, and procedures that are appropriate to the local conditions.

Organizations such as Phillips, Unilever, and Shell have given considerable autonomy to their foreign operations to set their own goals and systems and identify practices that fit local operations.

Indeed, as foreign operations grow in size and complexity, most organizations provide greater autonomy and flexibility to their foreign units to respond to local needs and demands. Naturally, the degree of internationalization plays a key role in determining the challenges to human resource managers.

International human resource management requires addition, deletion, and modification of traditional human resource functions. Employee-related activities that need to be added include relocation services, orientation to new cultures and customs, home rental/sale while on foreign assignments, and translation services to help employees communicate and adapt to foreign settings. Several procedures currently used in the context of benefit planning, tax planning and counselling, investment management, health services, and so on may have to be modified significantly to make them suitable for foreign locations. Several human resource and employee policies related to minimum wages, incentives, employee involvement in decision making, and so on may have to be altogether deleted if they do not match the governmental policies and culture of the host country. Below we discuss five key areas that require a close look in the context of international human resource management.

1. Recruitment and Selection of Personnel

Expatriates
Home country nationals sent to foreign locations on temporary or extended stay.

Host country nationals
Local citizens employed by a foreign-owned firm (in the host country).

Third country nationals
Natives of a country other than the home or host country of the firm that has hired them.

The employees working in foreign locations of the company may be expatriates, host country nationals, or third country nationals. *Expatriates* are home country nationals who are sent to foreign locations on temporary or extended stay. *Host country nationals* are local citizens of the host country while *third country nationals* are natives of a country other than the home or host countries who are currently residing in the host country. Each recruiting source has its own unique advantages (see Figure 14-7); however, increasingly, there has been a trend away from use of expatriates to local (or host country) nationals to minimize culture shock, reduce costs, and meet the demands of local governments. The laws in most countries require the employment of local personnel if adequate numbers of skilled employees are available. This means that expatriates and third country nationals, in most instances, will require work permits and visas from local government. This can delay movement of expatriates and third country nationals into new locations. Hence, planning ahead becomes critical in global operations.

The two sources of potential applicants for openings are present employees and new hires. The reassignment of present employees offers an opportunity for career development of the employee in addition to filling a job opening.

Several large companies such as Dow Chemicals, Gillette, and Procter and Gamble move executives around the world.

FIGURE 14-7

Benefits of Alternate Recruiting Sources for Global Operations

Expatriates
- Familiarity with company culture and practices
- Greater control over human resource movements and planning
- Provide valuable overseas experience to company employees
- Can become an integral part of career development of employees
- The firm can reuse newly learned skills and overseas experiences on future occasions

Host Country Nationals
- Fluent in local language
- Knowledge of local customs and culture
- Typically less expensive than expatriates
- Host country governments favour this
- Avoids problems associated with transfer of company personnel
- The firm does not have to get work permits or visas for employees, speeding up the hiring process

Third Country Nationals
- May know several languages
- Most likely to have an international outlook
- Their experience is likely to be broader and may facilitate firm's entry into other foreign locations

Although an international assignment often looks attractive to first-time applicants, career, family, language, and cultural considerations may cause more experienced candidates not to apply. Dual-career families, children, and assignments to less developed areas are often significant barriers to recruitment.

A lack of knowledge about internal openings can also be a barrier. Some employees are reluctant to apply for international jobs because they fear they will lose touch with developments at headquarters, harming their opportunities for career advancement. As a result, many employees are forced to rely on an informal network when the HR department does not create systematic linkages among people to address these concerns. To overcome these barriers, the organization may consider other sources of recruits as illustrated by Colgate-Palmolive's example:

> In the past, Colgate-Palmolive's senior management noted that the company was having difficulties securing top executive talent for its international operations. Since Colgate's international business is crucial to the company's overall success, management decided to re-examine its recruitment and development practices in this area. As a result, Colgate developed a new strategy recruiting students from reputed undergraduate and MBA programs whose experience, education, and language skills demonstrated their commitment to an international career.[48]

Several of the recruiting devices discussed in Chapter Five can, after appropriate modifications, be used for recruiting employees abroad. Naturally, the local cultural values and customs should be borne in mind in all instances. In the case of developing countries, recruiting skilled employees can pose a major challenge because of economic and social conditions.

> The high rate of illiteracy in several less developed countries make print ads irrelevant for several lower-level job positions. In small towns, recruiting may have to be done by word of mouth.

The selection of a person to fill an international opening requires the firm to consider more than just technical or managerial ability. The person's ability to manage a diverse workforce and adapt to the company and country culture are also critical here. This means that the person selected should be mature and emotionally stable while possessing all relevant managerial and technical competencies. Some past writings indicate that one in four (and in some instances, one in two) expatriate managers fail in their new job assignments costing their employers anywhere from US$40 000 to $250 000.[49] The manager's inability to adapt to new settings, the spouse's inability to adapt to the new surroundings, family-related problems, and mismatch between manager personality and new work culture, etc. have been found to be key factors causing expatriate manager failure.[50]

For women managers, working in some foreign settings that have given historically low status to women may pose special problems although host country nationals often view women first as foreigners and only secondly as women. This means that cultural barriers that typically constrain women in male-dominated societies may not totally apply in the case of female expatriates. Indeed, the success rate for female expatriates has been estimated to be about 97 per cent—a rate far superior to that of men.[51] Part of this may be attributable to the fact that many firms do not send women abroad unless they are the very best in their group. The increased visibility of women expatriates and the novelty factor (since senior women managers are rare in several foreign settings) may also account for their higher success rate.[52] Some of the characteristics associated with expatriate manager success are listed in Figure 14-8.

Transnational teams
Teams composed of members of multiple nationalities working on projects that span several countries.

Increasingly, many firms use *transnational teams* composed of members from multiple nationalities working on projects that span several countries. Such teams are vital for carrying out assignments that no single manager may be able to do alone. They are also very important when the firm is not yet fully organized (with a clear organizational structure, systems, and processes) to meet the unknown challenges facing it in foreign locations. These teams of experts can transcend existing organizational structure, transfer technology and other resources from one region or country to another, respond to new challenges, and make faster decisions. When forming such teams care should be taken to represent all critical functions and skills and include persons who also have the interpersonal skills to work as a team.

When one large European beer manufacturer formed a transnational team to consolidate production facilities abroad, it made sure that team members were drawn from

FIGURE 14-8

Core competencies (of expatriate managers) Core attributes such as cultural adaptability, multidimensional perspective, and resourcefulness needed by managers to successfully work abroad.

Core Competencies of an Expatriate Manager

Past writings indicate that successful expatriate managers possess several core competencies. Here are the key ones:

Multidimensional Perspective

Ability to consider multiple dimensions of a problem and their interrelationships and ability to integrate them. Ability to conceptualize and resolve a problem at multi-functional, multi-product, multi-industry, and multi-country levels.

Cultural Adaptability

Ability to understand and adapt to local cultural norms and practices without losing track of one's objectives.

Decision-Making Ability

Strategic thinking ability, ability to process information and identify creative alternatives to problems, evaluate and test alternatives for their feasibility, and ability to modify own decision process to suit the needs of the situation.

Team-Building and Leadership Ability

Ability to understand the motivations of a culturally diverse work force, bring them together as a high-performing team to accomplish organizational objectives.

Resourcefulness

Ability to adapt own actions and practices to the needs of the situation. Ability to accurately gauge the various political, cultural, technological, and other constraints surrounding own firm and find creative solutions to meet them.

Negotiation Skills

Ability to conduct successful strategic business negotiations in a multicultural and political environment. An understanding of the motivations of the "other side" at the bargaining table and ability to identify solutions that result in win-win solutions.

Change-agent Skills

Ability to bring about changes in a foreign setting and influence others into newer ways of thinking and acting. Ability to understand the cultural parameters surrounding oneself and adapt one's change strategy to meet these cultural requirements.

Source: Summarized and adapted from a number of sources including the following: C.G Howard, "Profile of the 21st Century Expatriate Manager," *HR Magazine*, 1992, June pp 93-100. Reprinted with the permission of *HR Magazine* published by the Society for Human Resource Management, Alexandria, VA; Gary Hogan and Jane Goodson, "The Key to Expatriate Success", *Training and Development Journal*, 1990, Vol.44, No.1, Jan, pp 50-52 Copyright © January 1990, Volume 44 No. 1 Training and Development, American Society of Training & Development. Reprinted with permission. All rights reserved; Raymond Stone, "Expatriate Selection and Failure: HR Planning, 1991, Vol. 14, No.1, pp 9-18; Allan Bird and Roger Dunbar, "Getting the Job Done over There: Improving Expatriate Productivity," *National Productivity Review*, 1991, Vol. 10, No. 2, Spring pp 145-156. Copyright © 1991. Reprinted by permission of John Wiley & Sons, Inc.; Rosalie Tung, "Selection and Training of Personnel for Overseas Assignments," *Columbia Journal of World Business*, 1981, Vol. 16, No. 1, Spring, pp 68-78.

all major regions in Europe. The team members were also selected on the basis of their unique expertise in an area like marketing, finance, or production management.

Whether selecting managers or teams, firms can adapt and use the various methods discussed in Chapter Six. Many firms use interviews, tests, and assessment centres for selecting managers for foreign locations. Tests measuring attitudes and characteristics necessary for working in foreign settings and ability to learn foreign languages are currently available. Prior track record within the firm and the industry and prior experience in foreign settings is usually given considerable weight by many employers when selecting personnel for foreign locations. Some firms not only focus on a person's ability to work in a foreign culture but also the spouse's adjustment to the new setting.

While most firms only interview the candidate, there are firms that interview both the candidate and the spouse. This is a recognition of the importance of spousal adjustment to foreign locations. However, this also raises questions of validity and fairness in selection procedures and may be valid grounds for discrimination complaints by rejected candidates.

2. Orientation, Training, and Development

Global managers have to be more versatile, aware of global issues, sensitive to challenges provided by cultural diversity, capable of managing decentralized operations, and making in-roads into the new social milieu.[53] Recognizing this, many firms focus on providing additional orientation, training, and development activities for their international staff.

The orientation should touch on the policies, place, procedures, and people whom the new job incumbent will encounter in the near future. Unlike new employee orientations, which in many firms may last only a few hours, international orientations may begin weeks or even months before and last for weeks after an assignment is made. Although pre-departure orientation is common and important, an on-site orientation after arrival in an international post is often necessary to help the new job incumbent to settle well into the role. Details of culture, language, local customs, social attitudes toward time and punctuality, power, teamwork, use of titles, social taboos, and degree of formality in interaction with the local population, etc. are integral components of such an orientation. The employee's spouse may also be invited to participate in such an orientation.

One large firm with global operations invites the spouse of the newly hired employee to all orientation events. An integral part of the orientation in this firm is a two-week language and culture orientation course, which both the husband and wife attend. The orientation often includes a visit from an employer or spouse who has served in the location. Apart from the personal touch, repatriated families are likely to have keen insights about a particular locale.[54]

Departing employees need to be trained in the local language, cultural norms of the host country, and managing personal and family life in the new location.[55]

Language. While English is almost universally accepted as the primary language for international business, Canadian managers will significantly enhance communication by being familiar with other foreign languages. Many Canadian managers are also already familiar with French, which should facilitate international travel and communication. However, English and French usage abroad may show systematic variations.

In England, to "table" a topic at a meeting means to discuss it now; in Canada, it means to postpone discussion of a subject. The "elevator" is a "lift" in several countries, just as "gum" is "glue." The trunk of a car is a "dickey" in India, a word that denotes a male organ in New Zealand.

Cultural norms
Values and norms that
determine behaviours of
individuals and groups in
different cultures.

Cultural Norms. Learning the language is only one part of communicating with another culture. The expatriate employee must also learn about how the locals think and behave in a specific setting.

Different societies show consistent and marked differences on several cultural dimensions. For example, countries like Canada and the U.S. score high on individualism, or preference for a social framework in which individuals are supposed to take care of themselves and their immediate families only. In contrast to this, many Asian and South American countries value collectivism, or a preference for a tightly knit social framework in which individuals can expect their relatives, clan, or other ingroup to look after them in exchange for unquestioning loyalty. Canadians and Americans score high on masculinity, or a preference for achievement, heroism, assertiveness, and material success; while Nordic countries such as Sweden or Finland value femininity or a preference for relationships, modesty, caring for the weak, and quality of life.

> In Japan, the decision-making process most frequently used in organizations is **ringisei**, decision making by consensus. Most widely used by lower and middle level managers, ringisei requires the circulation of documents to organizational members to gain their approval before implementation. This enables the subordinates to voice their views and influence the final decision.

This means that when dealing with members of other cultures, Canadian managers need to make a basic attitudinal shift away from monocultural assumptions that value conformity to organizational rules. Such a shift necessitates different behaviours even in casual meetings. The basic nuts and bolts of social interaction vary widely and need to be learned for each specific culture.

Managing Personal and Family Life. *Culture shock*, a cultural disorientation that causes physical and emotional stress and inability to respond to situations appropriately, is experienced by many expatriates. Hundreds of day-to-day events and factors are involved—such as inability to communicate to local citizens (because of language differences), differences in technology that have an impact on everyday events (e.g., making telephone calls, cooking, shopping), and a myriad of other everyday matters. This means that a firm's pre-departure training should prepare the expatriate employee for all major aspects of life abroad. Even minor frustrations can, if unanticipated and unprepared for, become catastrophic events that drain the new employee emotionally and physically.

Culture shock
Cultural disorientation causing expatriates stress and the inability to respond appropriately.

Ringi-sei
Japanese, literally "bottom-up decision making."

The Japanese often use a decision-making process known as **ringi-sei**, *which is decision making by consensus.*

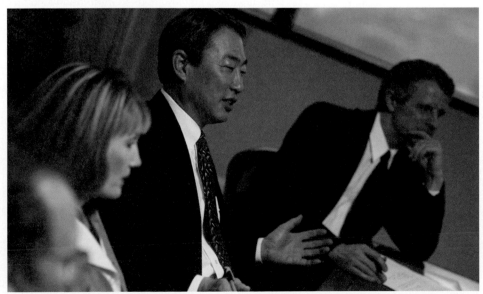

Digital Imagery © Photo Disc Inc. Photo by Keith Brofsky

Cross-Cultural Training Methods

A number of training methods aimed at preparing employees for a foreign work environment have been tried. Some of the more promising approaches are described below.

Sensitivity training. This has been successfully used by several organizations to prepare managers for overseas assignments. The objective of sensitivity training is to increase self-awareness and the ability to assess the impact of one's own behaviour on others. (This method was discussed in Chapter Seven.)

Culture assimilators. These consist of a series of episodes dealing with interpersonal issues in a cross-cultural situation. By responding to individual episodes and referring to explanations describing why their responses were appropriate or not, trainees have an opportunity to test their cross-cultural effectiveness and to learn about the appropriate responses in a specific culture. Studies have shown that assimilator-trained subjects performed better in another culture than subjects who did not receive such training. The following is an example of a culture assimilator episode:

> You offer a Japanese manager a generous gift if he would be helpful in getting your sales bid accepted by his boss. He reacts by sucking air through his teeth. You assume that:
>
> (a) he is pleasantly surprised;
>
> (b) he is deeply embarrassed;
>
> (c) he is unsure how to respond and would prefer more information and clarification; or
>
> (d) it is a sign that the value of the proposed gift is insufficient to obtain his support.
>
> The correct answer is (b). Japanese respond to embarrassing situations by sucking air through their clenched teeth. This reaction is often accompanied by the comment: "That will be difficult," which to the Japan expert means, "No, don't bother."

Critical incidents. These are brief descriptions of effective or ineffective behaviours that illustrate problems an expatriate employee may encounter in an organization abroad. Below are examples of an effective and an ineffective behaviour:

> When a newly appointed Canadian manager took over his job in Mexico he was complimented by his employees for his mastery of the Spanish language. He explained that he had studied the language for six months intensively before coming to Mexico.
>
> The Japanese employees of an international company suggested to the foreign chief executive officer that a new company building should be dedicated on *taian*, a day of good luck. The CEO rejected the idea because it would have meant waiting another three weeks.

Cases. Cases are more detailed and complex than critical incidents. They illustrate a variety of cross-cultural problems in management within a single setting. The Maple Leaf Shoes Limited Case at the end of this chapter provides a good example of the challenges of working in a multi-national, multi-racial team.

Role-play. Role-play is a semistructured activity. Participants are given a description of a situation with specific role instructions, but no script, forcing the participants to improvise their reactions to the setting. The results usually reveal personal values and biases that can be analyzed and discussed. A significant learning experience can be achieved if participants are asked to advocate a position that is contrary to their own beliefs. Studies indicate that this method is relatively effective in changing a person's attitudes.[56]

Simulation. Simulation is a common cross-cultural training method. A popular simulation game is *Ba Fa' Ba Fa'*.[57] Participants are divided into two cultures: Alpha and

Beta. After learning the "rules" of their own culture, participants have to interact with members of the other culture. Since the interaction rules for each culture are different, confusion and frustration, even hostility, result. These experiences are then discussed at a debriefing session.

It is unlikely that any single method will be sufficient to prepare an employee for the complex experiences that lie ahead when going abroad.[58] More likely, a combination of the methods described will be most effective, as people react differently to different methods. Whatever the method(s) chosen, effective diversity training aims to develop a *global mindset* for managers. Mindsets can be defined as the differing ways the subject at hand is perceived, understood, reasoned about, and acted upon by individuals. Persons with a global mindset are able to:

- look at events in the context of the bigger, broader picture;

- recognize the diversity and inherent contradictory forces that exist in any situation;

- appreciate and even welcome ambiguity and surprises; and

- understand the need for change and establish processes that facilitate change.

A global mindset, thus, indicates the capacity to scan the world with a broad view—always looking for unexpected trends and opportunities to achieve the firm's and the individual manager's objectives.[59] In today's global marketplace, this is, perhaps, what distinguishes a leader from other organizations.

Global mindset
Capacity to scan the world with a broad view, to value diversity, and to appreciate change.

3. Performance Appraisal

Employees in international operations need to be evaluated and require assistance in career planning. Performance appraisal is particularly difficult in *home country evaluations* because the evaluator may be thousands of kilometres away and may not fully understand the challenges faced by the person being evaluated.[60] Geographical and cultural distance pose severe communication problems for expatriates and home country managers. While improvements in information technology have significantly reduced the distance and time barriers, this has not always facilitated communication between an individual and his or her superior in the home office. A conscious effort to overcome this communication problem is often required as in the case of Dow Chemicals.

Home country evaluations
Performance appraisal carried out by an expatriate's home office.

> At Dow Chemicals, a senior manager in the same function is assigned to the role of godfather to an employee. The employee and his mentor (or "godfather") are expected to keep each other informed about performance and other matters that affect the person's career. The godfather then becomes involved with pay raises and locating a job in the home country when the employee is repatriated.[61]

When *host country evaluations* take place, the evaluator has a better awareness of the constraints under which an expatriate works. However, even here problems exist. Local cultural values may bias one's perception of the manager's effectiveness.

Host country evaluations
Performance appraisal carried out by an expatriate's local (or host) office.

> For example, a manager who uses a participative or consultative style of leadership may be considered as "weak" or ineffective by members of a culture that in the past have been under autocratic leaders and expect their leader to make all important decisions.

Further, local evaluators may not possess adequate information about the larger organizational priorities. Even actions that are not appropriate from the point of view of local operations may be desirable for the long-term growth and success of the parent organization in the region.

Given this, the appraisals should attempt to balance the two sources of appraisal information.[62] While the host country managers are in a good position to observe day-to-day behaviours of the employee concerned, the individual is still formally tied to the parent organization for his or her pay, career development, and other decisions. This factor should be kept in mind when designing an appraisal system.

4. Compensation Decisions

International compensation and protection go beyond pay and benefits. Pay is expanded to compensate for additional taxes, living expenses, and personal costs. Incentives may be added, especially for assignments to less desirable locations. Supplements may be given to cover extra costs of educating children, making return trips to the home country, and paying wages of servants. Benefits may include a company car, a driver, club memberships, housing, and other "perks" normally reserved for top management. Several firms also offer *relocation assistance*—which can range from buying the employee's home at its market value to shipping household goods, cars, and other possessions abroad.

> A few of the human resource department's concerns at a large international firm in the area of compensation management include the following: developing an overseas compensation and benefits plan, taking into account cost of living differences and any special needs; giving tax advice and financial counselling; supervising the sometimes extensive paperwork involved; assisting with housing and selection of good schools; and helping the employees set up bank accounts and make cash transfers. The firm also provides support in the following areas: transferring medical, dental, and school records and assisting with inoculations; helping with absentee ballots and international driving licences; helping the spouse get work permits, providing language training, and assisting with moves of household furniture and goods abroad.[63]

Relocation assistance
Financial or other assistance to help expatriates move to the new work destination.

Different countries and cultures value different rewards. HR managers should be sensitive to this fact when designing compensation systems. While nonfinancial incentives such as independence, prestige, and so on are powerful motivators, money may be a key driving force for many Canadians. Other cultures are more likely to emphasize security, family, respect, and social recognition over monetary compensation. The overall culture also plays a powerful role in determining the type of incentives appropriate in a setting:

> Thus, in individualistic cultures such as Canada, paying for individual achievement and performance is common and expected. However, in collectivistic cultures such as Japan or Taiwan, pay plans may have to pay greater attention to equity and personal needs of employees.[64]

A useful philosophy in this context may be "think globally and act locally." While the compensation plan should achieve the overall strategic intent of the organization, it should also be flexible enough to recognize the workforce diversity and differing needs of employees in different locations and cultures.[65]

5. Sensitizing Employees to Cultural Differences

Challenges to workforce diversity are amplified in international HR management. Diversity increases as foreign nationals are transferred to the home country; it also increases when home employees are transferred to other countries. Diversity is also increased with the immigration of other country nationals to home and host countries. Compounding this is a growing maze of international alliances among organizations, with the key determinant of their success often being how well human resource policies can be integrated and implemented.[66] Further, the developing countries, many of which have traditional cultures and were locations of ancient civilizations, may be the growing markets of the world:

> Over the next 20 years or so, the working-age population in developing countries will rise by roughly 70 million—which exceeds the combined population of North America and Europe. This can have profound implications for the markets for various products

as well as where and how the work is done. For example, immigration of large numbers of persons from developing economies can change the work force profile in North America and Europe just as the transfer of several low-skilled and semi-skilled jobs to these countries can affect the work practices and employee movements in the developed world.

The HR department can play an important role in this setting by initiating diversity training and impressing on top management the need for implementing diversity. It can act as a catalyst by initiating the various steps in diversity management discussed earlier in this chapter. The HR department can further its contribution to the organization by being abreast of cultural differences among the company's international operations and proactively working with operating managers and project leaders to identify solutions to cultural or national differences that may impede a company's strategy.

Indeed, effective diversity training enables the managers to develop a global mindset. Mindsets can be defined as the differing ways the subject at hand is perceived, understood, reasoned about, and acted upon by individuals. A global mindset indicates the capacity to scan the world with a broad view—always looking for unexpected trends and opportunities to achieve the firm's and the individual manager's objectives.[67] Persons with a global mindset are able to:

- look at events in the context of the bigger, broader picture;
- recognize the diversity and inherent contradictory forces that exist in any situation;
- appreciate and even welcome ambiguity and surprises; and
- understand the need for change and establish processes that facilitate change.

Finally, a successful HR manager may even be able to influence the values held by residents of a foreign country. Thus, a firm that is dedicated to employment equity through its actions may demonstrate to the host nationals the value of hiring disadvantaged groups. Such demonstration can, albeit slowly, mould public opinion in favour of providing more opportunities to persons who were hitherto shut out from specific job positions.

> For example, some developing countries, Moslem-dominated regions, and Japanese companies have not afforded women an equal employment opportunity. In some Moslem cultures, women are discouraged from working side by side with men; in others, tradition defines the jobs a woman can hold.

Opening up job positions to minority and disadvantaged groups can result in the improvement of the overall quality of life for employees and thus contribute to the achievement of the personal objectives of the HR department discussed in Chapter One.

SUMMARY

Managing a culturally diverse workforce is a major challenge facing Canadian managers in this decade and beyond. It means that Canadian managers must cope with employees who have different beliefs, customs, and values. This makes diversity management a vital issue today.

Workplace diversity includes important human characteristics that influence an employee's values, perceptions of self and others, behaviours, and interpretation of events around him or her. Diversity, at a minimum, includes age, ethnicity and culture, gender, race, religion, sexual orientation, and mental and physical capabilities. Several writers consider the above seven areas to be the core dimensions of diversity since they exert considerable impact on our early socialization and a powerful, sustained impact throughout our lives.

Organizations may have different postures in the context of diversity management and may fall into any one of the five stages. To implement effective diversity management an organization has to go through four steps: identifying the ideal future state; analyzing present systems and procedures; changing systems, policies, and structures where necessary; and evaluating results and follow-up. Implementing a diversity management program begins with an accurate portrayal of its current work force composition and a forecast of its future workforce. Organizational members have to be identified accurately using demographic categories such as age, gender, ethnicity, education, and disability. Some organizations also expand this to identify the number of employees belonging to other distinct groups on the basis of their language, race, sexual orientation, income level, social class, parental status, and marital status. The next step is to examine how the present systems are operating. Current policies, systems, practices, rules, and procedures have to be examined for their appropriateness for a diverse workforce. After this is done, all existing systems and practices have to be reviewed for their continued relevance to the organizational mission, strategy, and environmental demands. Those that are found lacking should be modified or even discontinued. Finally, the progress of the diversity effort has to be monitored on a systematic basis and corrective actions taken. Monitoring will also ensure that quantitative and qualitative indices of change are available to the management, the union, and the workforce. These results should be widely communicated and the gaps between targets and accomplishments publicized along with the proposed corrective actions.

Several popular industry practices to diversity management—such as diversity training programs, mentoring programs, alternate work arrangements, apprenticeships, and support groups—were discussed in this chapter.

For Canadian firms with global operations, diversity management offers a greater challenge. The challenges in international human resource management with a particular focus on cultural diversity issues were outlined in this chapter. Some issues in the areas of global workforce selection, training, management development, appraisal, and compensation were discussed along with possible solutions in some settings.

TERMS FOR REVIEW

Visit the Web site at www.mcgrawhill.ca/college/schwind6 for full glossary.

REVIEW AND DISCUSSION QUESTIONS

1. Why is management of diversity important for an organization today?

2. What are the steps in implementing a diversity management program?

3. What are some likely persons or groups who may resist introduction of diversity management in organizations? Why? What can you do to overcome their resistance?

4. What are some unique challenges in international human resource management?

5. Some persons believe that the best way to manage employees is to treat them equally irrespective of their sex, race, age, or other characteristics. Do you agree? Why?

6. What are the key training approaches to prepare expatriates for foreign assignments?

CRITICAL THINKING QUESTIONS

1. If you are a manager in a software manufacturing firm who is about to be transferred to China to work with a joint venture partner firm there for the next 18 months, what factors will you be concerned about? What actions will you take?

2. You are a senior executive in a consulting firm with its head office in Toronto. As part of your global expansion strategy, your firm recently started two new offices abroad: one in Jakarta and another in Mexico City. You have been placed in charge of the new project. You decide to hire consultants in Canada and send them to these offices on one- or two-year assignments initially. You feel that this strategy will help you to start operations immediately and give global experience to your newly hired consultants. What will be your considerations when you hire the consultants? What actions will you take to ensure their success abroad?

3. Choose an organization that you are familiar with. Are any of its rules, practices, or policies likely to be found undesirable by its female, minority, or older employees? Why?

4. If 40 per cent of your employees are women, but if women account for only two per cent of the executive cadre and six per cent of the managerial cadre, what steps will you take to improve the status of women in your organization?

5. You manage a work team of 14 persons, about eight of whom are over the age of 40. Three of these persons have elderly relatives to look after and frequently absent themselves from work to take care of their relatives' family or medical needs. What possible actions can you take to ensure that the needs of the employees are met, while at the same time maintaining high productivity at the workplace?

6. John and Ted are members of your work team and are gay. Both are good workers, but socialize with each other and go for lunch and coffee breaks together. While both John and Ted are very pleasant and do everything that is expected of them (including pitching in when needed), several others in the team find it hard to accept them as equals and pass sarcastic comments whenever John and Ted are not around. You know that four of the other nine employees hold very conservative values. Whenever John or Ted touch each other, others seem to mind it very much. Recently, one of the co-workers mentioned to you casually that he finds the situation "awful." What action would you take and why?

WEB RESEARCH

Select any two industries and calculate the percentage of women, minorities, and other disadvantaged groups who are employed in these sectors. What are the implications for diversity management practices in organizations in these sectors? *(Hint: You may begin your research with the Web sites of Statistics Canada, Human Resource Development Canada, and Industry Canada.)*

INCIDENT 14-1

Precision Softwares Ltd.[1]

Dave Bennett, the CEO of Precision Softwares Ltd., looked at the three men sitting around the table. He knew they had a difficult decision to make. The position of General Manager, Finance became vacant 10 days ago due to the sudden departure of Ken McDonald and they had to make a quick decision on who should occupy Ken's position. Dave had asked Keith Macdonald (General Manager, Marketing), Karen Miller (Human Resource Manager), and Mark Thompson (General Manager, Production) to make a recommendation on the matter. Given the expansion targets of the firm, the new job incumbent was likely to play an important role in the planning function within the firm.

Precision Softwares began operations 10 years ago and rapidly grew in size because of its user-friendly softwares and competitive prices. The company had several large customers in the private industry; however, over 40 per cent of the firm's business came from government contracts, especially large departments of the federal and Ontario governments, which were computerizing most of their routine operations.

Precision Softwares currently employs 240 persons and expects to hire 30 more in the next 18 months. Most of these new hires will be programmers. To get the federal government contracts, the firm had to comply with the Employment Equity Act of 1986. Currently, the firm has less than five per cent representation of women and other protected class workers in supervisory positions and less than one per cent in middle and senior management ranks.

Given the urgency for hiring a new finance manager, Dave and his management team had decided to fill the position internally. They had two strong internal candidates to choose from: Bill Wallace and Doug March. Both Bill and Doug had been with the firm for over 10 years (12 and 11 respectively) and were considered to be very good employees. Both had similar qualifications—Bill had his MBA from the University of British Columbia and had attended several professional development programs after his graduation from the university. Doug had an MBA from the University of Western Ontario and was currently working for the Certified

---

[1] *Incident written by Professor Mallika Das as a basis for class discussion. All rights reserved by the author Mallika Das © 2000.*

Management Accountant's designation. Both were considered to be hardworking and ambitious men. "No wonder they seem uncomfortable making a decision," thought Dave. Aloud, he said, "So, you really have no preference? Are you sure?"

Keith (Manager, Marketing), looked around at the other two and finally said: "We didn't say that, Dave. We were only pointing out that both are equally qualified. However, I personally would be more comfortable with Bill."

Karen and Mark both looked relieved that Keith had spoken for them. Dave sensed that something was bothering the three people. He looked at Keith and asked, "Why do you all prefer Bill? I don't see anything in his résumé or his files that indicates he's a stronger candidate. Or am I missing something?"

All three looked even more uncomfortable now. Mark finally asked: "Have you talked to Doug recently, Dave?"

"No," Dave replied. "Actually, because of my travel schedules, I haven't seen him for a while. The last time I saw him was at his presentation to the Board about our proposed acquisition of ProTech Softwares. I was very impressed with the way he handled that.... Why do you ask?"

Mark spoke softly: "Don't get me wrong, Dave. We do like Doug and we do think he is a great employee. However, Doug has changed a lot lately. He is more and more involved with the Native Indian Council now. He spends all his free time on the reserve. Actually, he has moved to a house just outside the reserve and commutes from there every day. It's an hour's drive from our head office."

"He has also changed in appearance, Dave," Keith added. "He has started growing his hair and has quite a nice pony tail now. He has more hair than Karen," he laughed.

"Do you know he fasts on some days to seek his spiritual self?" asked Mark with a twinkle in his eyes.

"What has all this got to do with our decision?" asked Dave.

"We feel that Doug is becoming more and more distant from us, Dave," Keith said. "I feel we don't know him any more. While I'm not saying everyone should be in a three-piece suit, I do believe a person's attire says a lot about him or her. After all, all of us adhere to some informal dress codes, don't we? I don't feel too comfortable with Doug any more, Dave. And I am worried about how our clients would react to a finance manager who sports a ponytail. It just doesn't go well with the post. Bill, on the other hand, is a steady, stable character. A family man, you know....I, rather we, feel that he will be better equipped to deal with bankers and others."

Mark said, "Doug doesn't come for any of the parties held on Saturday evenings. He spends Saturday evenings at the Native Council. Because he is the only Native Canadian in this company, I can understand his longing for his own people, but still...." He did not complete the sentence.

Dave looked at the other two. From their facial expressions, he could see that they were in broad agreement with Mark.

Dave knew he had the final say on the matter. He could see that the three managers were somewhat uncomfortable with the changes in Doug's behaviour. Since a good alternate candidate for the position existed, was there any reason to hire Doug? Yet, Dave felt he had to give Doug a fair chance. He rated both candidates to be more or less equally competent. He also knew that Doug was very well liked by most employees and could motivate his subordinates to put in extra work when needed.

There was also a strong likelihood that Doug may leave the organization if he does not get the promotion. And that could be disastrous!

"Maybe I should have a chat with Doug before I make a decision," thought Dave. Aloud, he said:

"Let me think this one through for a little while. I'll let you know what I think later today."

Discussion Questions

1.   Are Keith, Mark, and Karen justified in feeling the way they do?

2.   Should Dave speak with Doug about his appearance?

3.   If you were in Dave's position, whom would you promote? Why?

INCIDENT 14-2

Highland Tastes[2]

Steve McDonald, the manager of Highland Tastes, was at his wit's end. He had just finished talking to Michael, one of the waiters at Highland Tastes, the small restaurant that he managed. "It's always one thing or another with Michael. I wish I had never hired him!" thought Steve. "For now, I'll ask Cindy to take the birthday cake over to table 6." But he knew he had to find a solution to this problem.

Highland Tastes was a family-owned restaurant located in Sydney, Nova Scotia, and had been started by Steve's father Russell 20 years ago. It had taken a while for Russell to get his restaurant on a firm footing, but now it was a thriving business. Steve had taken over from his father just two years ago. Two months ago, he had hired Michael who, as a Jehovah's Witness, did not believe in celebrating birthdays. One of the customers at table 6 was celebrating his birthday and, as was the custom at Highland Tastes, a small complimentary birthday cake was to be served to the customer. Usually, the server would take over the cake with a candle, light the candle, and wish the customer "Happy Birthday." Some of the waiters and waitresses would even sing "Happy Birthday." This had been a tradition at Highland Tastes ever since it had opened and customers had come to expect it.

Today, when Steve learned of the customer's birthday, he handed a chocolate birthday cake to Michael. Michael had said very politely, "I can take the cake to the table, but I will not wish the customer "Happy Birthday." Steve, who was not familiar with the beliefs of the Jehovah's Witnesses, was shocked. Michael had told him that it was against his religious beliefs to celebrate or take part in the celebration of anyone's birthday, for birthdays were not recognized in the Bible. "I am not asking you to sing 'Happy Birthday'; I just want you to wish him a 'Happy Birthday'—that's just common courtesy, Michael," Steve had argued. But Michael had been adamant.

Steve now realized why Michael had not participated in his father's sixtieth birthday party, which had been attended by all the other employees. Steve's father was particularly fond of Michael and had asked about his absence. Now Steve realized that it was Michael's religious beliefs that prevented him from participating in the celebrations.

This was not the first time that Michael's religious beliefs had caused friction in the workplace. One month ago, at Christmas time, all the employees had gathered

[2] Incident written by Professor Mallika Das of Mount Saint Vincent University. All rights reserved by the author. Mallika Das © 2000.

together to put up a Christmas tree and decorate the dining room. Michael, who was on duty, had been asked to pitch in, but had refused because his religious beliefs did not permit him to celebrate Christmas. Some of the other employees had been really upset at his adamant refusal to join in. Thomas, one of the other waiters, had almost come to blows with Michael over the issue. Steve had stepped in and calmed Thomas down. While he had found it hard to accept Michael's behaviour, he had told Thomas and the other employees that no one should be forced to participate in a religious custom. "After all, Thomas," Steve had said, "you wouldn't like it if you were forced to participate in a Hindu or Muslim festival, would you?" Thomas had backed off, but Steve knew that there has been tension between Michael and the others ever since.

"Not participating in Christmas—I can understand that," thought Steve. "But this is different. It has nothing to do with any particular religion. It is just a friendly gesture. Why can't he be flexible? After all, he is from the area and should have known that we do this in this restaurant before joining us. He should have told me," thought Steve. He also knew that Michael was a good worker. He was pleasant and friendly and customers always seemed to like him. He was willing to work odd shifts and never complained when he had to work on a long weekend.

Steve decided to ask Cindy to take the cake over to the table. Cindy was quick to show her displeasure. "Why should we have to accommodate Michael every time? It is not even my table. Does Michael show such flexibility? OK, I'll do it this time, but I think you should talk to Michael. We can't cover for him all the time."

"I wonder what will come up next," thought Steve. "Maybe it was a mistake to hire him."

Discussion Questions

1. Would refusing to wish a customer "Happy Birthday" constitute valid grounds for disciplinary procedures?

2. What would you do if you were in Steve's position? Why?

3. Could this situation have been prevented? How?

EXERCISE 14-1

How Does it Feel to Be a Member of a Minority?[3]

Consider a work or social situation in the past when you were different from others present on the basis of your gender, race, age or generation, ethnicity, sexual orientation, or religious beliefs, and that you vividly remember (If you have not faced a situation yourself, interview an individual who has faced a situation such as this.) Briefly narrate the event below and then complete the three tables that follow:

The event:

How others treated me:	Yes	No	Comments
Others didn't treat me as an equal	____	____	_____
When I gave opinions, the others ignored me	____	____	_____
Followed my comments with "Yes, but..." statements	____	____	_____

[3] Exercise prepared by Professor Hari Das of Saint Mary's University, Halifax. All rights reserved by the author. Hari Das © 2000.

	Yes	No	Comments
Others ignored my presence	___	___	_____
Others tried to humour me	___	___	_____
Others treated me as "special"	___	___	_____
Others doubted my ability to do things	___	___	_____
Others took a special effort to ask for my opinions	___	___	_____
Other: (Please specify)	___	___	_____

What I felt:	Yes	No	Comments
Frustrated	___	___	_____
Angry	___	___	_____
Energized	___	___	_____
Lonely	___	___	_____
Determined to do better than others	___	___	_____
Different and strange	___	___	_____
Out of control	___	___	_____
Lost confidence in myself	___	___	_____
Other: (Please specify)	___	___	_____

What I did:	Yes	No	Comments
Kept quiet	___	___	_____
Interacted only with a few group members	___	___	_____
Went better prepared for future meetings	___	___	_____
Questioned the group's treatment of me	___	___	_____
Played a more active role than others	___	___	_____
Voiced my concerns politely but firmly	___	___	_____
Went through the motions but withdrew from the group mentally	___	___	_____
Stopped attending future group meetings	___	___	_____
Other: (Please specify)	___	___	_____

CASE STUDY

Maple Leaf Shoes Ltd.: Managing a Diverse Team[4]

Jane Reynolds looked at the man sitting in front of her. Wang looked quite upset. "Something is bothering him," thought Jane. Wang had called her a few minutes ago and requested a meeting. His manner had been polite but Jane could sense that he was agitated about something.

As soon as he sat down Wang had said very politely: "I want to be transferred to another location,

Ms. Reynolds." Jane was totally surprised because she hadn't expected this at all!

"We can talk about a transfer—that is a possibility. But you seem very upset, Wang. Is something the

[4] Case written by Professor Mallika Das of Mount Saint Vincent University, Halifax as a basis for class discussion. All rights reserved by the author. Mallika Das © 2000.

matter? Is there a specific reason for this request?" Jane asked.

"I cannot work with the team anymore, Ms. Reynolds. I feel I am not taken seriously. My ideas are not considered worthwhile. And...." Wang hesitated.

"Go on," Jane said encouragingly.

"I hate to say this Ms. Reynolds, but... but I think Rod and Jeff don't like me or Alfred. You know...." Wang said and looked away.

"Oh no, not a racial problem...," thought Jane. Aloud, she said: "But the Indonesian project is due in two weeks, Wang. Can't we wait until after it's finished? I can talk to Jeff and Rod if you want...."

Wang looked up. "No, Ms. Reynolds, it has to be now. If that is not possible, I may have to consider other alternatives...."

"Resign?" asked Jane. Wang just looked down and said nothing.

Jane was really getting worried now. "Please, let's talk about this a bit more. You are a valuable employee, and you can contribute a lot to this company, especially now that we are planning to expand to other countries. We want to keep you here, Wang. I'm sure things are not as bad as they seem. Please tell me, what's wrong?" Wang looked up and started talking in a soft voice.

* * *

Maple Leaf Shoes Limited. is a medium-sized manufacturer of leather and vinyl shoes located in Ontario (see end of Chapter One for details of the firm). To meet the demands of an increasingly competitive market, Maple Leaf was planning to expand its operations by starting a new plant in Indonesia.

It was to develop a plan for this joint venture with an Indonesian partner that the company had put together this project team. The four-member team was considered to be a well-balanced one. Jeff was a finance major and had been involved in new project teams before. In the organizational hierarchy, Jeff held the highest rank in the team and considered himself to be the team leader. Rod, an accountant, brought with him several years of experience in the company and was considered an expert in costing. Alfred and Wang were added to the team for their experience in production and international business. Alfred, whose parents had immigrated to Canada in the early 1990s from Hong Kong, had managed a

shoe company there. Wang, also a recent immigrant from Korea, was an expert in designing shoes and had several years of experience as a production supervisor in his native country. They were both considered excellent employees and had received extremely positive performance reviews during the last two years.

* * *

After Wang left, Jane thought over what he had just said. As far as she could see, Wang had three major complaints: (1) that Jeff disliked him because he was Korean and Jeff made racist jokes about Korean and Chinese people; (2) that Jeff and Rod were unwilling to listen to his (or Alfred's) ideas; and (3) they insulted him by ridiculing his ideas in front of others. She had asked Wang for some time to sort things out in her own mind. Wang seemed to have calmed down considerably by the end of the conversation and had agreed to wait for a couple of days for a decision from her about the transfer.

Jane wondered whether Wang was overreacting. She knew that Jeff was prone to slightly off-colour jokes. She remembered a few meetings she had sat in just to get a feel for the work the team was doing. Jeff, who was an outgoing person with a strong sense of humour, always seemed to get along with Wang and Alfred. He used to tease Alfred about how he (Jeff) could not afford some of the things "like you rich Chinese people from Hong Kong can." Alfred would just smile—Jane knew Alfred was not very rich—he had come in as a student and had received immigration later. Jeff was a little more serious when dealing with Wang who, at age 49, was more than 10 years older than him. But he would still joke with Wang about "Chinese" food—Jane remembered Jeff's joke about how Chinese ate anything—"cats, dogs, and what not." Wang did not seem to mind the jokes; even though he would gently remind Jeff that he was not Chinese, he never lost his temper. Anyway, Wang and Alfred ought to know that Jeff constantly cracked jokes about everyone—women, and racial or ethnic groups. His Scottish jokes were always popular at Christmas parties and he got along with everyone in the company.

Jane called Jeff and Rod and set up a lunch-time meeting with them. After they had ordered lunch, she briefed them quickly on Wang's visit and his comments. Both Rod and Jeff looked upset on hearing that Wang was considering leaving the team.

Jane: *So you had no idea this was coming?*

Jeff: *No, not at all. I thought I got along well with them. I know I crack jokes about the Koreans and Chinese, Jane. But you know me. Boy, I don't think there's anyone I haven't cracked jokes about! These guys are too sensitive.... why didn't he just tell me he didn't like my jokes? If I knew I was offending him, I'd have stopped. Honestly, Jane, I didn't know.*

Rod: *(intervening) To be frank, Jane, that's half the problem. We never know what is going on in their minds. They never speak up at meetings or tell us if they disagree with us or don't like our proposals. Half the time they don't even look at us directly.*

Jane: *But something must have happened recently. You know Wang has a lot of family here—he must have been really upset about something to want to leave Wilmington. Did anything happen yesterday?*

Jeff: *Well, Rod and I were having a meeting with Pat Lim in marketing about the Indonesian project. Alfred and Wang came into my office and said they would like to discuss the Indonesian project with me and Rod. I told them that that's exactly what we were talking to Pat about and they could join in. As usual, they kept muttering something about meeting separately, but frankly, Jane, I just didn't see the need for it. I insisted on hearing their ideas and guess what? They wanted us to redo our entire plans for the Indonesian expansion. Redo them totally! These are the plans we had worked on for the last month, Jane! We don't have that kind of time!*

Jane: *So what did you do?*

Jeff: *(looking embarrassed) I guess I blew up a little. I told Wang he needed to make up his mind on things and that it was too late to redo the plans. Pat and Rod agreed with me. I guess I made it clear that I was not happy with the way things were working between us.*

Rod: *I was taken aback too, Jane. You know we made that decision at our last meeting. Why didn't they raise their concerns earlier?*

Jeff: *That's exactly the way I feel about it too, Jane. Right at the beginning, I had suggested that we let them manufacture the Cariboo line as it was the most labour-intensive one. I thought it was the logical thing to do. Rod agreed with me too. Alfred did say that perhaps we should consider making the Fluffy*

Puppy line there because it is simpler to produce... But he didn't press the issue when I reiterated my case. And Wang had mumbled something about considering all options carefully without even looking at me directly. I thought they both finally had agreed—and now they want us to redo our entire plans!

Jane felt a little relieved. "If this is the only issue, I might be able to get them working together again," she thought to herself. Aloud, she said: "Perhaps they thought of something later on, Jeff. Also, you know Wang is a little shy and reserved by nature. He finds it hard to take an assertive stand on things."

Rod: *That's not all, Jane. I wonder if we will be able to work together at all. I've tried my best to get to know them, Jane. I've asked Wang and Alfred home for dinner but they refused. Two days ago when Jeff and I were going out to lunch, we asked them to join us, but they refused again. They do not seem to want to interact with us socially, Jane.*

Jane: *Can we change teams now, Jeff? Who else can be brought in at this stage?*

Jeff: *To be honest, Jane, I can't think of anyone. Besides, it would be difficult for someone new to come in at this stage—remember, we have only two weeks to go before the Indonesians come!*

Jane: *That's true. Let me think about it.... I'm sure we can work something out. I'll let you know what I think tomorrow.*

"I wish I knew how to handle this one!" Jane thought to herself as she reached her office. She knew something had to be done quickly—a new team couldn't be put together now. Besides, what kind of an impression would they be creating for their Indonesian partners if they dropped Wang and Alfred from the team? If Jeff and Rod couldn't work with Wang and Alfred, would they be able to work with their Indonesian partners? Jane knew she had to find a workable solution soon.

Discussion Questions

1. What cultural or other differences possibly account for the present situation?

2. Could such a situation have been avoided? Explain.

3. What should Jane do now? Why?

CASE STUDY

Canadian Pacific and International Bank: Planning for Diversity at HBI[5]

Rhonda Dickoff looked at the memo in front of her one more time. As the manager of human resources at HBI, she knew it was her responsibility to ensure that the organization followed the general guidelines set forth by the parent company, Canadian Pacific and International Bank. Further, as a medium-sized financial institution, HBI was also required to submit a report on its efforts to diversify its workforce. Since its acquisition of HBI, the top management of CPIB had made it clear that HBI had to increase the number of protected groups (women, visible minorities, aboriginals, and people with disabilities) and Mary Keddy, VP (Human Resources, CPIB), had asked for a report on HBI's plans to diversify its workforce. The memo from Ms. Keddy indicated that this would be a topic of discussion at her next meeting (two weeks from now) with Rhonda Dickoff.

Workforce Diversity at HBI

HBI is organized functionally into three major divisions: Operations, Marketing and Administration. Of the 155 top and senior middle-level managers in the firm, five were women. Ms. Dickoff was the highest-ranking female manager at HBI. The other four were Patricia Kimble (senior portfolio analyst), Sheila Allen (senior accountant), Wendy Goodwin (advertising manager) and Theresa Reitman (manager, customer relations—consumer accounts). Both Sheila Allen and Wendy Goodwin had been with HBI for

approximately five years while the other two were more recent entrants.

Dickoff knew that the overall picture at HBI (in terms of workforce diversity) was not very positive. While 90 per cent of the non-management employees were women, only 35 per cent of junior managers and 21 per cent of senior-middle level managers were female. Dickoff was aware that while some of the male managers were open to increasing the diversity in the management cadres of HBI, most were sceptical of such initiatives. One of the senior male managers had told her recently: "We should desist from having token women and minority managers. I don't think we are doing them or ourselves a favour by promoting them before they are good and ready...". Another had mentioned that women cannot expect to reach top levels without having the necessary experience. Ms. Dickoff knew that these opinions were shared by others in the organization. So she had prepared a table of the proportion of women and men at each level at HBI and some other relevant information about the workforce. These are provided in Table 1. She had also gathered information on the leadership ratings of the senior-middle level women managers (Table 2), but, given the short notice, had been

[5] Case prepared by Professor Mallika Das of Mount Saint Vincent University, Halifax as a basis for class discussion. All rights retained by the writer. Mallika Das © 2000.

TABLE 1

Workforce composition at HBI

Level	% Female	% with university education F	M	% with 5+ years experience F	M	Age F	M
Non-management	90	25	25	42	20	39	30
Supervisory	70	43	36	54	33	38	35
Junior	35	87	85	63	58	40	39
Senior middle	21	100	75	40	40	45	43
Top management[6]	0	–	67	–	67	–	57

[6] Excluding Mr. John Hopkins

TABLE 2

Profile of senior-middle level managers at HBI

Division	Experience (months)		Leadership Rating		% with univ. education	
	Male	Female	Male	Female	Male	Female
Administration	46.0	60.5	7.0	8.5	60	100
Marketing	43.7	44.5	7.7	8.0	50	100
Operations	45.5	11.0	7.2	9.0	92	100

unable to do so for the other female managers. However, she knew that the picture was similar at all levels of management.

HBI had been attempting to improve its workforce diversity for the past six years. In fact, it had started focusing on increasing the number of women and other protected group members being hired at management trainee level six years ago. At the management trainee level, nearly 20 per cent of the hires in the past five years had been female and over 80 per cent had remained with the firm. This was slightly higher than the proportion for male management trainees. While some of these women had made it into junior and middle management, most of the women at these levels had over 15 years' experience. It had also begun recruiting males at entry level (non-management cadre) before any other major financial institution. Several of these men had made it into supervisory and even junior management in the past few years.

Dickoff knew that she had to look into the numbers of other protected group members at HBI. HBI had hired some members of the other protected groups in the past six years, but only one—a visible minority person—had stayed with the firm. Mr. Johnson, in Marketing, had been with HBI for over five years and had a B.A. in Psychology. There were no other protected group members at HBI.

Dickoff looked at the memo again. *"Two weeks...that's not a long time. I have to get cracking..."* she said to herself.

Discussion Questions

1. Based on the data provided, what conclusions can you form about the status of male and female employees (managerial and other) at HBI?

2. What suggestions do you have for Dickoff to diversify the workforce (managerial and other) at HBI?

SUGGESTED READINGS

Brake, Terence, *The Global Leader: Critical Factors for Creating the World Class Organization*, Chicago, IL: Irwin Publishing, 1997.

Cox, Taylor, Jr. and Ruby Beale, *Developing Competency to Manage Diversity*, San Francisco, CA: Berrett-Koehler Publishers Inc., 1997.

Cross, Elsie and Margaret White, *The Diversity Factor*, Chicago, IL: Irwin Professional Publishing, 1996.

Poole, Phebe-Jane, *Diversity: A Business Advantage*, Ajax, ON: Poole Publishing Company, 1997.

Chapter 15

Ensuring Safety and Health at the Workplace

Health and safety plays a prominent part in the development of a strong corporate culture. The goal for HR practitioners should be to create, develop, and nurture a culture that is fully aware of the importance of safety and the advantages of a safety-oriented culture, and is willing to take the steps necessary to achieve it.

—Hugh Secord[1]

CHAPTER OBJECTIVES

After studying this chapter, you should be able to:

■ *Describe* the major Canadian laws relating to occupational health and safety.

■ *Assess* the traditional thinking with respect to occupational health and safety issues.

■ *Explain* the new thinking with respect to employee rights relating to occupational health and safety issues.

■ *Outline* the safety and health responsibilities of employers and employees.

■ *Discuss* the impact of stress on employees and the workplace.

■ *Summarize* the relationship between health and safety issues and human resource management.

Even today, there are too many employees injured at the workplace. Employers, supervisors and employees must work together to reduce on-the-job injuries and illness.

At the turn of the century, the thinking and attitudes of employers and employees toward accident prevention were quite different from today. Comments made during this period by employers illustrate this:

- "I don't have money for frills like safety."

- "Some people are just accident prone, and no matter what you do they'll hurt themselves some way."

- "Ninety per cent of all accidents are caused by just plain carelessness."

- "We are not in business for safety."

- "There's no place for sissies in dangerous work."[2]

Assumption of risk
An obsolete attitude toward accident prevention where the worker accepted all the customary risks and unsafe practices.

During this period, even the courts used a legal expression, "*assumption of risk*," meaning that the worker accepted all the customary risks associated with the occupation he or she accepted. Workers were also instructed to protect themselves from special hazards such as heat extremes or molten and sharp metal. Furthermore, the attitudes of employees paralleled those of the employers. Scars and stumps on fingers and hands were often proudly referred to as badges of honour. The thought that safety was a matter of "luck" was frequently reflected in such statements as, "I never thought he'd get it; he was always one of the lucky ones," or "When your number's up, there's not much you can do."

During a four-year period in the early 1900s, records of one steel company show that 1600 of its 2200 employees lost time from work because of injury. Statistically speaking, 75 per cent of this plant's entire workforce lost time from work because of accidents on the job.[3]

Careless worker model
An early approach to safety in the workplace assuming accidents were due to workers' carelessness.

Shared responsibility model
An approach to workplace safety that relies on the cooperation of employer and employees.

The early approach to safety in the workplace used the *careless worker model*. It assumed that most of the accidents were due to workers' failure to be careful or to protect themselves. Even if training was provided to make workers more aware of the dangers in the workplace, this approach still assumed that it was mainly the worker's fault if an accident happened. A new approach, the *shared responsibility model*, assumes that the best method to reduce accident rates relies on the cooperation of the two main partners: the employer and the employees (who may be represented by a union).[4] Accident rates are reduced if:

- management is committed to safety in the workplace;

- employees are informed about accident prevention;

- consultation between the employer and employees takes place on a regular basis (for example, the creation of a *health and safety committee*);

- there is a trusting relationship between the employer and staff; and

Health and safety committee
A committee to determine and assign responsibilities for effective workplace health and safety programs.

- employees have actual input into the decision-making process.

Over the last 20 years, along with the increased concern about the environment, there has been a growing emphasis on health and safety in the workplace. Strong union pressure, together with an increased public interest in greater corporate responsibility, has resulted in better and more comprehensive federal and provincial legislation and health and safety measures.

In Chapter Eleven, one of the topics was workers' compensation, which has as its aim the compensation of an employee for injuries suffered on the job. These programs have a serious defect: they are after-the-fact efforts. They attempt to compensate employees for accidents and illnesses that have already occurred. Many early supporters of these laws had hoped that costs would force employees to become more safety-conscious. Yet even with greater efforts by employers, accident rates continue to remain high. In addition, toxins and unhealthy work environments continue to create new health hazards.

> A 26-year-old man was working at a sawmill. He was trying to unjam an automatic pallet nailer when he became trapped in the unit. A nail fired from another machine hit him in the right side of his skull. He was freed from the machine by co-workers and taken to hospital.[5]

> A St. Catharines hospital was fined $85 000 after the death of an employee. The employee, a heating, air-conditioning and ventilation mechanic, was doing maintenance work in the hospital laundry room when he was electrocuted. The hospital pleaded guilty to a charge of failing to ensure that an employee was wearing safety gloves when working with high-voltage equipment.[6]

Workplace Injuries and Health Hazards

Human Resources Development Canada (HRCD) estimates that about three Canadian workers die every working day from an occupational injury or disease; every minute worked costs the Canadian economy about $77 500 in compensation payments to injured workers; the average number of days lost due to occupational injuries was more than six times greater than the number of days lost resulting from strikes or lockouts; and for every 100 employees, approximately five disabling injuries occur each year.[7] Workplace accidents and occupation-related illnesses cost more than $4.5 billion annually in compensation payments alone. The total cost is more than $9 billion a year when indirect expenses are taken into account, and this does not include the incalculable social toll associated with workplace-related accidents.[8] Nor are accidents a phenomenon unique to the manufacturing sector:

> Kate McDonald has been working in a dentist's office in Winnipeg for the last several years. About four years ago she found that she had continual spells of headaches, nausea, fainting, and overall lethargy. When repeated use of painkillers and symptomatic treatments did not improve the situation, she went to a specialist. Her illness was diagnosed as prolonged mercury poisoning.

By and large, work accidents are caused by a complex combination of unsafe employee behaviour and unsafe working conditions. Several factors contribute to the complexity of managing safety in the workplace: the effects of some industrial diseases do not show up for years; employers may "clean up" a health problem before a health inspector arrives; companies may fail to monitor or disclose health risks; or employees may fail to follow safe practices at the workplace or engage in dangerous behaviour (such as drinking alcohol or taking drugs while on the job). Consider what happened at a factory in Sarnia, Ontario:

> According to records from the Ontario Ministry of Labour, hundreds of former workers at a factory located in Sarnia, Holmes Insulations Ltd., were exposed to asbestos levels more than 8000 times higher than the level considered to be safe. Former workers at the factory have contracted cancer and other diseases at rates that experts call a huge "occupational health tragedy." The company, which ceased using asbestos in 1974, has new owners and now operates under a different name.[9]

Workplace Injuries

Data from Statistics Canada provide some perspective on the extent of workplace injury and illness in Canada. While the number of workplace injuries has declined in recent years, the direct cost of injuries (such as lost wages, first aid and medical treatment, rehabilitation, and disability compensation) has not. Moreover, workplace injuries result in several indirect costs (including lost production, recruiting, selecting and training of new employees, damage to facilities and equipment) which are incurred by the employer.

Research on the number of injuries and incidence rates are provided in Figure 15-1. In 1998, there were approximately 14.3 million workers in Canada and almost 800 000 injuries. Just over 47 per cent of the injuries required an employee to miss work time. When considering the injury incidence, there were 5.54 injuries for each 100 workers. When considering the gender of the worker, men were more than twice as likely as women to have a time-loss injury; when measured per 100 workers, 3.43 men and 1.55 women suffered a workplace injury. With reference to age, younger workers were most likely to be injured; the time-loss injury incidence rate per 100 workers was 2.93 for employees age 15 to 24, 2.59 for employees from age 25 to 54, and 1.91 for workers age 55 and over.[10]

Further information on workplace injuries and illnesses is provided in Figures 15-2, 15-3 and 15-4. Logging and forestry, construction, manufacturing, and transportation are among the most dangerous industries when considering time-loss injury rates. The most common type of injury involves strains and sprains, followed by contusions, crushing, or bruises. An employee is most likely to injure his or her back, while injuries to one's fingers or legs are the second and third most common body parts injured.

Health Hazards

It is possible to combine the various health hazards into four categories:[11]

1. *Physical agents*—exposure to physical elements such as noise, temperature, lighting, vibrations, and radiation.

2. *Biological agents/biohazards*—exposure to such natural organisms as parasites, bacteria, insects, viruses and so on.

3. *Chemical agents*—exposure to chemical compounds or other harmful toxic substances.

4. *Ergonomically related injuries*—caused by the work environment and including repetitive strain, stress, over-exertion/fatigue and back injuries. In simple

FIGURE 15-1

Injuries and Injury Incidence Rates in Canada

Year	Number of Injuries	Number of Time Loss Injuries	Number of Fatalities	Number of Work Days Lost
1994	818 687	430 756	725	17 639 363
1995	821 592	410 464	748	16 584 994
1996	778 492	377 855	703	15 851 878
1997	791 979	379 851	833	15 403 722
1998	793 666	375 360	798	15 539 606

Source: Work Safely for a Healthy Future, Statistical Analysis-Occupational Injuries and Fatalities Canada Occupational Safety and Health and Fire Prevention Division Operations Directorate, Labour. HRDC, Reproduced with the permission of the Minister of Public Works and the Government Services Canada, 2001.

FIGURE 15-2

Twelve Most Dangerous Industries in Canada

Industry	Time-Loss Injury Incidence Rates per 100 Workers
Logging and forestry	7.81
Construction	5,94
Manufacturing	5.82
Other services	5.49
Transportation	5.25
Health and social services	3.02
Wholesale trade	2.97
Mining	2.81
Retail trade	2.81
Government services	2.68
Accommodation, food and beverage services	2.62
Fishing and trapping	2.22

Source: Work Safely for a Healthy Future, Statistical Analysis-Occupational Injuries and Fatalities Canada Occupational Safety and Health and Fire Prevention Division Operations Directorate, Labour. HRDC, Reproduced with the permission of the Minister of Public Works and the Government Services Canada, 2001.

FIGURE 15-3

Twelve Most Common Time-Loss Injuries in Canada

Type of Injury	Number of Time-Loss Injuries
Sprains and strains	151 581
Contusion, crushing or bruise	50 303
Cut, laceration, puncture	34 325
Fracture	22 123
Inflammation or irritation	18 878
Multiple injuries	9 947
Scratches, abrasions	9 838
Burn or scald	7 183
Hernia, rupture	4 263
Dislocation	2 809
Concussion	1 878
Amputation	1 868

Source: Work Safely for a Healthy Future, Statistical Analysis-Occupational Injuries and Fatalities Canada Occupational Safety and Health and Fire Prevenion Division Operations Directorate, Labour. HRDC, Reproduced with the permission of the Minister of Public Works and the Government Services Canada, 2001.

FIGURE 15-4

Twelve Most Common Body Parts Injured

Body Part	Number of Time-Loss Injuries
Back	99 329
Finger	43 010
Leg	29 690
Shoulder	22 713
Multiple parts	22 084
Arm	18 564
Ankle	18 181
Hand	16 848
Eye	16 403
Wrist	14 957
Foot	12 508
Neck	9 277

Source: Work Safely for a Healthy Future, Statistical Analysis-Occupational Injuries and Fatalities Canada Occupational Safety and Health and Fire Prevention Division Operations Directorate, Labour. HRDC, Reproduced with the permission of the Minister of Public Works and the Government Services Canada, 2001.

terms, ergonomics involves the "study of the relationship between people and their jobs." More specifically, ergonomics uses scientific principles to examine the nature of the task that the employee is doing, the equipment or machinery needed to carry out the task, and the environment in which the task is carried out. Some examples in which ergonomics has been applied include preventing back injuries, developing proper work positions, organizing the work space, and managing the light at work.[12]

FEDERAL AND PROVINCIAL SAFETY REGULATIONS

www.hrdc-dhrc.gc.ca

www.ccohs.ca

www.webreference.com/rsi

THE CANADA LABOUR CODE (Part II) details the elements of an industrial safety program and provides for regulations to deal with various types of occupational safety problems. All provinces and the territories have similar legislation. A key element of these laws is the *Joint Occupational Health and Safety Committee*, which is usually required in every workplace with 20 or more employees. These committees have a broad range of responsibilities, such as those described here for the committee under federal jurisdiction:

● To meet at least once a month.

● To ensure adequate records are kept regarding accidents and health hazards.

● To deal with complaints by employees.

● To participate in investigations of health and safety-related injuries.

● To regularly monitor health and safety programs.

● To monitor records of injuries and illnesses.

- To cooperate with safety officers investigating a complaint or accident.

- To develop, establish, and promote health and safety programs and procedures.

- To obtain information from the employer and government agencies concerning existing or potential hazards in the workplace.[13]

Some other relevant federal laws are the Hazardous Products Act, the Transportation of Dangerous Goods Act, and the Canadian Centre for Occupational Health and Safety Act.

Hazardous Products Act
Federal act to protect consumers by regulating the sale of dangerous products.

Workplace Hazardous Material Information System (WHMIS)
Federal law requiring labels on all hazardous products and a Material Safety Data Sheet (MSDS) on each.

The *Hazardous Products Act*, which already had a broad industrial application, was substantially amended in 1985. Its primary objective was the protection of consumers by regulating the sale of dangerous products. It is now an important part of the *Workplace Hazardous Material Information System (WHMIS)*, which became law in 1988. It requires that suppliers label all hazardous products and provide a Material Safety Data Sheet (MSDS) on each one (see Figure 15-5 for class and division hazard symbols). In 1991, a WHMIS Enforcement Issues Subcommittee was formed to ensure that WHMIS is applied in all Canadian jurisdictions and there are ongoing discussions with other countries with the goal of having WHMIS become an international standard.[14]

www.hc-sc.gc.ca/eph/
ehd/psb/whmis.htm

The Hazardous Products Act also requires that an employer provide training to enable employees to recognize the WHMIS hazard symbols and understand the information in the MSDS. In addition to the symbol on it, the MSDS contains information on the properties and composition of the product or substance in question, the nature of the potential hazard that may result from misuse of the product (e.g., "Toxic Material—eye and skin irritant"), and suggested emergency treatment procedures.[15] Employees interested in learning more about particular hazards can obtain a great deal of information from the Internet.[16] Moreover, training will allow employees to take the necessary precautions to protect themselves:

> Ernest Meilleur, a construction worker in Ontario, was sprayed with a chemical called Uni-Crete XL, produced by Uni-Crete Canada under licence from Diamond Shamrock. As a result of the accident, he lost his eyesight. Although he was found to be 75 per cent responsible for his injury because he did not wear safety goggles, Uni-Crete Canada was found 20 per cent responsible and Diamond Shamrock 5 per cent, because of inadequate labelling of the product.[17]

The Transportation of Dangerous Goods Act makes Transport Canada, a federal government agency, responsible for handling and transporting dangerous materials by federally regulated shipping and transportation companies. It requires that such goods are identified, that a carrier is informed of them, and that they are classified according to a coding system.

In the Canadian Centre for Occupational Health and Safety Act, the Parliament of Canada established a public corporation with the following objectives:

(a)   to promote health and safety in the workplace in Canada and the physical and mental health of working people in Canada;

(b)   to facilitate

   (i)   consultation and cooperation among federal, provincial, and territorial jurisdictions, and

   (ii)   participation by labour and management in the establishment and maintenance of high standards of occupational health and safety appropriate to the Canadian situation;

FIGURE 15-5

WHMIS Class and Division Hazard Symbols

Class A — Compressed Gas

Class B — Flammable and Combustible Material

1 Flammable Gas   4 Flammable Solid
2 Flammable Liquid   5 Flammable Aerosol
3 Combustible Liquid   6 Reactive Flammable Material

Class C — Oxidizing Material

Class D — Poisonous and Infectious Material

1 Materials Causing Immediate and Serious Toxic Effects

2 Materials Causing Other Toxic Effects
3 Biohazardous Infectious Material

Class E — Corrosive Material

Class F — Dangerously Reactive Material

Source: From *Hazardous Products Act*, June 1987. Reproduced with the permission of the Minister of Public Works and the Government Services Canada, 2001.

(c)   to assist in the development and maintenance of policies and programs aimed at the reduction or elimination of occupational hazards; and

(d)   to serve as a national centre for statistics and other information relating to occupational health and safety.[18]

The centre is supervised by a board of governors made up of representatives of the federal government, labour, and employers. Several hundred organizations are now connected electronically with the centre and have access to information relating to health and safety generally and to hazardous materials specifically.

The administration of safety programs comes mainly under provincial jurisdiction. Each province has legislated specific programs for the various industries and occupations within it. Examples from Nova Scotia are the Occupational Health and Safety Act, the Industrial Safety Act, the Construction Safety Act, the Steam Boiler and Pressure Vessel Act, the Elevators and Lifts Act, the Engine Operators Act, and the Amusement Devices Safety Act.

Previously, the responsibility for enforcing these laws was divided between several agencies: the Occupational Safety Division of the Department of Labour, the Occupational Health Division of the Department of Health, the Mine Safety Division of the Department of Mines and Energy, and the Accident Prevention Division of the Workers' Compensation Board. This situation was similar in most provinces. Over the last several years, however, there has been a strong tendency to streamline the fragmented responsibilities by combining the different agencies into one body that (it was hoped) would be more efficient and effective—the Occupational Health and Safety Division under the umbrella of the Ministry of Labour. Almost all provinces have now consolidated their health and safety laws in a similar way.

www.awcbc.org

Safety Enforcement

All industrial units are inspected at least once a year to confirm their safe operation. Depending on the unit's accident record and its size, the safety inspectors may visit more or less frequently. For the purposes of such inspection, a safety officer may at any reasonable time enter any property or place used in connection with the operation of any business or undertaking. To carry out their duties effectively, safety inspectors are given a wide range of powers. Section 141 of the Canada Labour Code (Part II) details these powers:

(1) A safety officer may, in the performance of the officer's duties and at any reasonable time, enter any work place controlled by an employer and, in respect of any work place, may:

   (a) conduct examinations, tests, inquiries and inspections or direct the employer to conduct them;

   (b) take or remove for analysis, samples of any material or substance or any biological, chemical or physical agent;

   (c) be accompanied and assisted by such persons and bring with him such equipment as the safety officer deems necessary to carry out his duties;

   (d) take photographs and make sketches;

   (e) direct the employer to ensure that any place or thing specified by the safety officer not be disturbed for a reasonable period of time pending an examination, test, inquiry or inspection in relation thereto;

   (f) direct the employer to produce documents and information relating to the safety and health of employees or the safety of the workplace and to permit the safety officer to examine and make copies of, or extracts from, those documents and that information; and

   (g) direct the employer to make or provide statements, in such form and manner as the safety officer may specify, respecting working conditions and material and equipment that affect the safety or health of employees.

Provincial laws provide similar powers to the safety officers under their jurisdiction. However, there is evidence that some companies have been covering up accidents:

> A four-month investigation by the Ontario Workplace Safety and Insurance Board led to charging mining giant Placer Dome Ltd. with 31 counts of committing health and

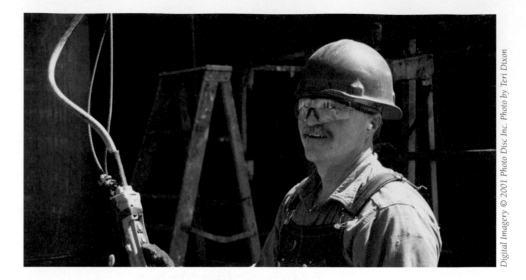

Digital Imagery © 2001 Photo Disc Inc. Photo by Teri Dixon

Safety gear, such as that worn by construction workers, is essential to reducing work injuries.

safety fraud. The 31 counts include failing to report accidents and filing misleading accident reports under the Workplace Safety and Insurance Act. The accidental injuries included fractures, lacerations, and finger amputations. According to Harry Hynd, Ontario director of the United Steelworkers of America, "We know that employers are convincing employees not to file injury reports. This is not an isolated incident of health and safety fraud; other companies are just better at covering up accidents."[19]

RESPONSIBILITY FOR HEALTH AND SAFETY

SO FAR THE FOCUS in this chapter has been on the legal requirements for maintaining a safe and healthy work environment. It should be emphasized, however, that these must be seen as the minimum requirements for employers. A major purpose of occupational health and safety laws is to stop injuries *before* they happen.

Although there is often a belief that the responsibility for health and safety rests primarily with the employer, this view is changing. A number of jurisdictions have legislation requiring the establishment of *joint* health and safety committees or health and safety representatives. The requirement of establishing a joint committee varies among the provinces; for example, a committee may be required if a workplace has a minimum number of employees (typically, 10 or 20 workers). The relevant legislation will outline the duties of the committee (such as maintaining records, conducting meetings, inspecting the workplace, and so on) and the makeup of the committee (number of members, employee representation on the committee, and so on).

There is also a focus on educating young employees about workplace safety. Several programs exist to make young workers aware of safety issues, to educate them about safety, and to provide information on rights and obligations under safety legislation.[20]

No law, by itself, can make a workplace safe. Only people can do this, and they can do it much better if they cooperate. It is far more effective—and less costly in the long run—if the responsibility for safety becomes a concern for everyone: top management, supervisors, and employees.

A study of 1500 workers by the Institute for Work and Health found that employees who are provided with modified work (for example, less intensive jobs, flexible schedules, or reduced hours) spent much less time on compensation (an average of 60.5

days) compared with workers who received no altered work arrangement (who spent an average of 102.6 days on compensation).[21]

Many organizations forget about safety issues when designing orientation programs. A comprehensive safety orientation program will address several issues such as fire safety, smoking at the workplace, accident procedures, personal clothing, protective equipment, material and chemical hazards, waste disposal, safety representatives and the safety committee, occupational health, and the safety policy or policies in existence. It is important that employees understand the various issues and know how to respond in a crisis situation.[22]

Top Management. Top management must set the policies and make concern for health and safety part of the organization's culture and strategy. Making it part of the culture and strategy ensures that health and safety aspects will be considered whenever business decisions are made and training programs developed.

Canadian National (CN) is one of the companies where top management sets safety policies and is actively involved in their enforcement. CN wants to be the "safest railroad in North America":[23]

> "AT CN, we are striving to render our [Health and Safety] Committees more proactive by providing them with training and information to facilitate that process," said Bill Hanson, District Safety and Loss Control Officer of the CN Maritime District. This attitude is confirmed by John LeBlanc, an electrician with CN and a member of an H&S committee: "Management has bent over backwards to make the commitment work. Any concerns we have brought up at the committee are written up and action is taken on them. The members also make sure safety rules are observed every day as they work at their jobs." Hanson again: "In the future, we see safety as being part of the way we do business."

Some organizations, recognizing that they lack the internal expertise to address safety issues, are now outsourcing some health and safety needs. Options for such firms include hiring a health and safety expert on a part-time or contract basis or seeking the assistance of a firm that specializes in health and safety. While the cost of a health and safety consultant generally ranges from $30 to $60 per hour, companies often save three to five times the cost of the consulting bill from lower experience ratings alone. According to safety consultant Geoff Wright:

> We get invited to a workplace that has just bought all new workstations and ergonomic chairs. And they would have ended up saving all that money, and prevented musculoskeletal injuries, if they had just asked for advice beforehand. The earlier an ergonomist is brought in, the cheaper it is. For every dollar you spend at the design stage, it will cost you a hundred times more to fix it at the implementation stage.[24]

Do members of the public believe that senior management should be held more responsible for safety in the workplace? A poll of Canadians indicated that 85 per cent would like to see corporate executives made criminally responsible for avoidable accidents that occur in the workplace.[25]

Supervisors. As part of their management training, supervisors must become proficient in managing safety, which means knowing about health and safety laws, safety regulations, training in observing safety violations, and learning communication skills to convey the necessary information to their employees. The ingredients of an effective safety training program include the following:

- accident investigation and analysis;
- communication skills and report writing;
- overview of legislative requirements;
- meeting with management and objective setting;

- organization and responsibility of joint health and safety committee;

- team problem-solving/problem-solving techniques;

- audits and inspections;

- principles of occupational health and safety; and

- ergonomics.[26]

Employees. While employers are responsible for providing a safe work environment, and supervisors are responsible for the safety of their people in the workplace, employees are responsible for working safely. Employees must be trained to understand safety rules and how to operate equipment safely. It is also important that a system of enforcement is in place, understood, and followed. If necessary, progressive discipline has to be applied for violation of safety rules in the same way as for other rule violations.

Good safety performance should be recognized and rewarded by managers. On the other side, unsatisfactory practices should be documented and corrected. Rewarding good performance is preferable. The objective of safety incentives should be to promote safety awareness and should therefore benefit as many workers as possible. Group awards may help to reinforce safety-consciousness through peer pressure.

www.iapa.on.ca

www.yworker.com

Quebecor Printing—Richmond Hill has received top honours from the Industrial Accident Prevention Association for cutting its accident rate by 75 per cent. Safety and Health spokesperson Jay Phillips said that planning and hard work by management, the union and employees helped win the award: "The workers bought in, and worker buy-in was very important. We also had union endorsement, which is very important."[27]

Implications for Human Resource Management

The human resource manager should ensure consistent enforcement of all safety and health rules. If human resource policies let one worker violate safety rules, others may follow. If an accident results, *it is the employer that is fined by the government.* By being firm—even if this means discharge of a valued employee—management sets the precedents and quickly convinces workers that safety is important.

The law also permits employees to refuse to work when working conditions are perceived to be unsafe. In such instances, the employee should report the circumstances of the matter to his or her supervisor or to the supervisor's manager and to the safety committee in the firm. In most jurisdictions, an employee with reasonable cause to believe that the work is unsafe will not receive any loss in pay for refusing to work.

When charged with a health and safety offence, a company's best defence is "due diligence," which means that the company took all reasonable steps to avoid the particular event. In examining the organization's behaviour, the court considers several factors including the magnitude of the risks involved and the nature of the potential harm, with a focus on the part of the safety program designed to prevent the accident in question. An effective safety program only helps establish due diligence—preparing a defence based on due diligence begins well before an accident ever happens.[28]

A study of 305 companies indicated that only 39 per cent had an integrated disability management program (which involves integrating the administration of short-term disability, long-term disability, and workers' compensation programs). While the direct costs of disability accounted for 5.6 per cent of payroll, firms with an integrated program reported a 16 per cent reduction in disability costs. Reasons for the lack of a

www.nidmar.ca

program included a lack of claims management or human resource information software, little coordination among departments, and a lack of formal accountability.[29]

Employees who are off the job due to sickness or injury represent a substantial cost to employers. For example, B.C. Hydro estimated the cost of sick leave, long-term disability, and workers' compensation absences at $15 million annually. A key element of the disability management program at B.C. Hydro involved the establishment of a joint labour-management program. Some of the important features of the program included:

- coordination of workers' rehabilitation and return to work;

- case management and support to workers; and

- development and maintenance of communication between the employee, employer, supervisors, physicians, fellow workers, and external agencies.

Benefits from the program included a 5.8 per cent reduction in sick days, a 14 per cent drop in days off for long-term disability, and a reduction of $700 000 in workers' compensation premiums.[30]

WORKPLACE STRESS

Stress management
Ways of dealing with the problem of stress.

www.stress.org

The term **"stress management"** is now part of the regular vocabulary of managers and employees, but what is *"workplace stress"*? Workplace stress is "the harmful physical and emotional responses that can happen when there is a conflict between job demands of the employee and the amount of control the employee has over meeting those demands."[31] However, it should be emphasized that not all stress is harmful. Moderate levels of stress may actually increase workplace performance.

The actual experience or the perceived threat of a corporate takeover, merger, downsizing, or plant closing, all of which could put large numbers of employees out of jobs, can lead to a variety of symptoms of stress that can harm employees' job performance. As shown in Figure 15-6, these symptoms involve both mental health and physical health. Persons who are stressed may become nervous and develop chronic worry. They are easily provoked to anger and are unable to relax. They may even develop stress-related physical ailments, such as stomach upsets. These conditions also occur from causes other than stress, but they are common symptoms of stress. Each individual's body has a pre-programmed response to stress called the *generalized stress response*. Figure 15-7 provides information on how the body responds to stress.

Whether stress will increase into something more serious depends on the severity and duration of the stress situation and the individual's ability to cope. What

FIGURE 15-6

Symptoms of Stress

- Nervousness and tension
- Chronic worry
- Digestive problems
- High blood pressure
- Inability to relax

- Excessive use of alcohol and/or tobacco
- Sleep problems
- Uncooperative attitudes
- Feelings of inability to cope
- Anger and aggression

FIGURE 15-7

Generalized Stress Response

- Increased blood pressure
- Increased metabolism
- Decrease in protein synthesis
- Decrease in immune system
- Decrease in allergic response system

- Increased cholesterol
- Localized inflammation
- Faster blood clotting
- Increase in blood sugar production
- Increase in stomach acids

Source: Workplace Safety and Insurance Board of Ontario, Basic Certification Training Program: Participant's Manual, 1999

seems to be most important is whether the person feels helpless and out of control. Severe stress can lead to depression; about 10 per cent of the workforce is suffering from depression, the cost of depression to the annual economy is about $16 billion a year, and depression is linked to higher suicide rates.[32]

Stress-related and other subjective conditions represent the greatest challenge to disability management within organizations.[33] A recent study indicated that workplace stress was more common than work-related illness or injury; while nine per cent of workers reported suffering from a workplace injury and nine per cent indicated that they suffered from work-related physical illnesses (such as headaches from noise or bad air), 25 per cent of employees stated that they had experienced stress, mental or emotional health problems arising from work. According to Rick Lush of the Hay Group:

> "Organizations have to deal with the culture they've created that's causing such a level of stress and anxiety for people on the job, right back to reassessing their strategy and looking at the impact of that strategy on workers. It's not necessarily change people have difficulty with, it's the uncertainty and loss associated with change. Today's unstable work environments are demanding from workers a flexibility many have not developed, coupled with increasing job expectations."[34]

There is a growing body of research indicating that stress may be associated with cardiovascular disease (in particular, among employees in psychologically demanding jobs that allow workers little control over the work process), musculoskeletal disorders (such as back injuries), psychological disorders (for example, depression and burnout), workplace injuries, suicide, cancer, ulcers and impaired immune functions.[35]

The Conference Board of Canada recently estimated the financial cost associated with stress in the Canadian workplace at more than $12 billion a year.[36] In addition, employer immunity from lawsuits as a result of contributing to the workers' compensation system is being eroded as more courts allow employees to sue their employers for stress resulting from a poisoned work environment. Howard Levitt, a well-known labour lawyer, notes:

> Courts are recognizing employees' stress claims and winning suits against employers. And theoretically, there's no limit to the award, unlike wrongful dismissal where there is a limit to the compensation. Most harassment occurs when a manager does not like the employee, when there is a personality conflict, or the employee is not doing a good job. And these types of harassment are not covered by human rights or workers' compensation legislation.[37]

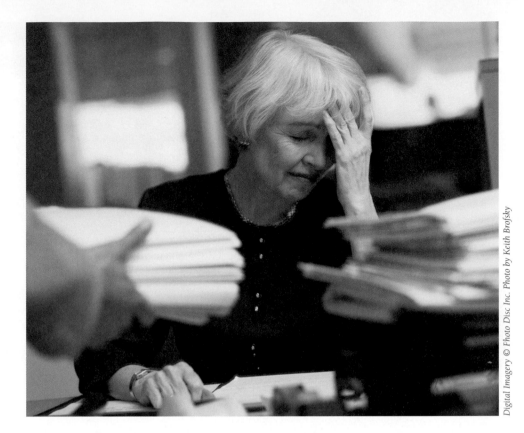

Too much stress on the job can lead to employee burnout.

Digital Imagery © Photo Disc Inc. Photo by Keith Brofsky

Causes of Stress

A model of job stress has been developed by the National Institute for Occupational Health and Safety.[38] According to the model, exposure to stressful working conditions (called "job *stressors*") can directly influence the health and safety of employees. However, the model also recognizes that individual and situational factors can intervene to strengthen or weaken the relationship between stressful job conditions and the risk of injury or illness. Examples of individual and situational factors include one's outlook or attitude, the presence of a support network of co-workers or friends, and the balance between work and family life. Although major distress can occur from only one stressor, usually stressors combine to affect an employee in a variety of ways until distress develops:

> Bill felt that he was doing well, but then he failed to get a promotion that he had sought. At about the same time, two of his key employees quit, and he had difficulty replacing them. Then his son got into trouble in high school, and the transmission failed on an automobile that he had planned to trade for a new one the next week. So many different problems were hitting Bill that he began to show signs of stress. He became easily upset, less considerate of employees, and less successful in meeting his deadlines.

Job Causes of Stress

Almost any job condition may cause stress, depending upon an employee's reaction to it. For example, one employee will accept a new work procedure, while another employee rejects it. There are, however, a number of job conditions that frequently cause stress for employees. Some of the major causes of workplace stress are outlined in Figure 15-8.

Stressors
Conditions that tend to cause stress.

FIGURE 15-8

Major Causes of Workplace Stress

Factors Unique to the Job
- workload
- work pace/variety/meaningfulness of work
- autonomy
- hours of work/shiftwork
- physical environment (noise, air quality, etc.)
- isolation (physical or emotional)

Role in the Organization
- role conflict/role ambiguity
- level of responsibility

Career Development
- under- or over-promotion
- job security
- career development opportunities
- overall job satisfaction

Relationships at Work
- supervisors/co-workers/subordinates
- threat of violence, harassment, and so on

Organizational Climate
- participation (or non-participation) in decision-making
- management style
- communication patters

Source: Adapted from L.R. Murphy, "Occupational Stress Management: Current Status and Future Direction," *Trends in Organizational Behavior*, 1995, pp. 1-14.

It is also possible to distinguish between *acute stressors,* which occur infrequently but are extremely stressful events (such as a major organizational change), and *chronic stressors,* which are the ongoing, daily problems and hassles that occur at work. While many wellness programs are aimed at chronic stress, organizations regularly ignore the impacts on employees associated with major organizational changes.

Psychological stress tends to be highest in jobs where employees have high demands but little latitude in making decisions, with 40 per cent of employees in such jobs scoring high on measures of psychological distress. In high-demand jobs that permitted greater employee involvement in decision making, 27 per cent of employees scored high on psychological-distress measures. Work-stress scores were highest in blue-collar and service occupations and lowest among employees in professional and administrative positions.[39]

Work overload and *time deadlines* put employees under pressure and lead to stress. Often some of these pressures arise from supervision and, therefore, a poor quality of supervision can cause stress. For example, the following stressful conditions are mostly created by poor supervision: an insecure workplace climate, lack of performance feedback, and inadequate authority to match one's responsibilities.

Workers frequently complain in private about "bad bosses." One Internet company believes it has a solution: it provides an on-line service that allows employees to anonymously rate their supervisor:

> It takes a worker about 15 minutes to complete a 60-item questionnaire about the boss. Co-workers can also complete their own evaluations. When the results are compiled, the boss is sent an e-mail inviting him or her to review the evaluation at a password-protected site. A service is also available to enable managers to find out what their workers think about them.[40]

Another cause of stress is *role ambiguity*.[41] In situations of this type, superiors and co-workers have different expectations of an employee's responsibilities in a job, so the employee does not know what to do and cannot meet all expectations. In addition, the job is often poorly defined, so the employee has no clear job description on which to depend. While team-based work has many virtues, it may also lead to increased stress:

> A change to empowerment may be a stressor in itself because it brings about substantial change. Also, work reorganizations break up work groups and destroy support systems that employees rely on at the workplace. Furthermore, there are instances of organizations using the team concept to extract more work from employees—according to clinical psychologist Patrick O'Laughlin, some organizations demand that employees work as a team, raise the productivity standard, and threaten the workers with dismissal if they don't meet the targets.[42]

A general and widely recognized cause of stress is *change of any type*, because it requires adaptation by employees. Change tends to be especially stressful when it is major, unusual, or frequent:

> A sales representative named Dorothy Wang developed job stress as a result of certain management changes. During the last 12 months she had three different sales managers, each with a different leadership style. As soon as Dorothy had adjusted to the style of one manager, she was forced to learn how to deal with another. She felt insecure and under constant pressure. She longed for the day when she would have only one sales manager for two or three years and a measure of stability would return to her world.

One particular type of change that has dominated the past decade is *organizational downsizing*. In many organizations, the "survivors" of workplace change are being asked to work longer hours and do more with limited resources. Working in such an environment may increase both employee stress and the probability of having an accident.[43] As well, downsizing may have an impact on an employee's family. Recent research suggests that the job loss of a parent affects their children. Perceptions of the job insecurity of a parent were associated with negative attitudes toward work and lower grades on exams.[44]

Closely associated with downsizing is the movement toward "lean production" practices aimed at increasing productivity through continuous improvement, better inventory management, and a focus on time and motion analyses. However, there is some evidence that lean production is also associated with higher injury rates and greater stress.

> At one truck manufacturer, the takeover of the firm by a multinational company was followed by the introduction of lean production techniques including a moving assembly line and the organizing of employees into work groups called "cells." Workers were asked to standardize and certify their procedures. Workers reported increased stress and depression and lower job satisfaction. There was also evidence of increased workplace accidents and reduced product quality.[45]

A recent study of stress in the Canadian workplace indicated that about 47 per cent of Canadian workers experience a great deal of stress at work and 41 per cent believe that their company does not do enough to help manage workplace stress.

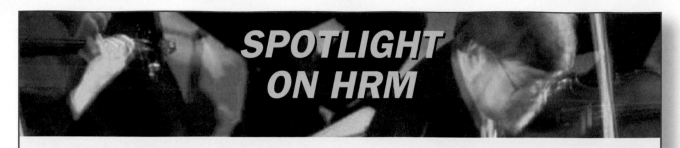

SPOTLIGHT ON HRM

PARENTS' JOB ANXIETY WREAKS HAVOC ON CHILDREN

A Queen's University researcher has documented a relationship that HR specialists have long recognized — children absorb the job anxieties of their parents. Business professor Dr. Julian Barling surveyed 154 commerce undergraduates and their parents and found that children's perceptions of their parents' job insecurities affects their attitudes about work and jobs and indirectly, their grades.

Barling, an expert in work and family relationships at the Kingston, Ont. university, said he undertook the study because "we need to be aware of how the next generation is being affected by current insecurity in the workplace." In his study, he found a close correlation between students' perceptions and their mid-term grades. Barling considers school performance to be a matter of great concern because "How children perform at school affects their self esteem and how they are perceived by peers, teachers and families. And, in the long term, grades obtained will influence the educational and occupational opportunities open to them."

In a companion study to be published this month in the *Journal of Applied Psychology*, Barling writes that children's perceptions of their parents' job insecurity also affect their beliefs and attitudes toward work. He notes that the waves of layoffs in both the public and private sectors in the last decade may produce a generation of young people with pre-existing negative work beliefs and attitudes which may not be amenable to change."

Parents anxious over more than security

Barling is not alone in his observations. "Professor Barling has quantified something I have been observing for well over a decade — children are sponges and readily absorb their parents' anxiety and ambivalence about work," said Barbara Moses, president of BBM Human Resource Consultants, Inc. and author of Career Intelligence. She added that parental anxieties extend beyond job insecurity to include dissatisfaction with promotions, wages, work load and perquisites.

"Is it any wonder that children are ambivalent? They see their parents tired and complaining, or more likely, they rarely see their parents. They grow to feel their parents are abused by work, and work denies them access to their parents. They see their parents as victims of their jobs and careers. And, despite these sacrifices, their employers treat them badly and let them go."

HR's role goes beyond EAPs

Moses said HR professionals have a role to play in reducing employee anxiety and the communication of this anxiety to sons and daughters. "At a minimum, HR should ensure that corporate communications do not unnecessarily incite job anxiety among employees," she said. "In addition, HR can promote career management among employees. Career support services reassure employees that they will be OK even if they lose their jobs. Encourage them to talk the language of employability rather than job security."

The assistance can be provided through support groups and Employee Assistance Programs, although Moses and others say EAPs are insufficient because they are reactive rather than proactive, and fail to address the needs of employees who do not identify themselves as anxious.

Sam Klarreich, president of the Berkeley Centre for Wellness, described the success of a support group he was involved with a few years ago at Imperial Oil. "We set up a group to help employees deal with on-the-job stress. We brought guest speakers, reprinted and shared articles on stress, held group discussions, published a newsletter. By working together the group members learned better ways to cope with stress. The program was such a success the group grew from an initial membership of 20 to over 200."

Source: Doug Burn, "Parents' Job Anxiety Wreaks Havoc on Children," *Canadian HR Reporter*, December 29, 1997, pp. 16, 20. Copyright © 1997 by MPL Communications Inc. Courtesy of *Canadian HR Reporter*. Published by Carswell, Thomson Professional Publishing.

About 64 per cent of workers reported feeling anxious or irritable, 42 per cent experienced insomnia, and 11 per cent reported booking off sick more often as a result of stress. When asked to indicate the most common factors contributing to stress, participants indicated that work load (43 per cent of respondents), personal financial responsibilities (35 per cent), balancing work with home or personal life (32 per cent), the work environment (26 per cent), and job security (23 per cent) were the major contributors.[46]

Other studies have reported that the most stressful personal problems are the death of a spouse or other close family member, divorce, marital separation, and major injury or illness.[47] At these times the human resource department needs to be especially supportive with its policies, counselling, and other programs.

Two psychiatrists at the University of Washington, Thomas Holmes and Richard Rahe, developed a stress factor measure that uses a 100-point scale to show what degree of stress different factors generate (see Figure 15-9). For example, the death of a spouse rates highest with 100 points, followed by divorce, marital separation, jail term, death of a close family member, personal injury or illness, marriage, and loss of a job. It is also important to note that even positive events can cause stress. Marriage, vacations, or receiving praise for an outstanding achievement can cause anxiety, irritation, and an increase in blood pressure.[48]

The stress scale is used in the following way:

1. Circle the number next to all events that have occurred to you during the last year.

2. If an event occurred more than once, increase the value by the number of times.

3. Add the circled numbers for your total stress score.

A score of 150 points or less indicates generally good health; a score of 150 to 300 points indicates a 35 to 50 per cent probability of stress-related illness; a score of 300 or more indicates an 80 per cent probability of stress-related illness.

Burnout

Burnout

A condition of mental, emotional, and sometimes physical exhaustion that results in substantial and prolonged stress.

Burnout is a condition of mental, emotional, and sometimes physical exhaustion that results from substantial and prolonged stress. It can occur for any type of employee, whether one is a professional employee, clerk, factory worker or human resource manager.[49] People with burnout may eventually become so emotionally exhausted that they go through the motions of work, but accomplish very little. As one employee described a burned-out associate, "His body is here today, but his mind stayed home."

With respect to burnout, the human resource department's role is a proactive one to help employees prevent burnout before it occurs. For example, the human resource department can train supervisors to recognize stress and rearrange work assignments to reduce it. Jobs may be redesigned, staff conflicts resolved, counselling provided, and temporary leaves arranged. Many other approaches to stress reduction are discussed throughout this book. The popular statement that "prevention is better than curing" definitely applies to burnout, because it has high human and economic costs. Weeks or months of rest, reassignment, and/or treatment may be required before recovery occurs. Some emotional or health damage can be permanent. Preventive strategies can yield impressive results:

> One large paper and forest products firm was faced with problems of employee absenteeism, a large number of accidents, and poor employee morale. After trying other methods that did not yield any great success, the company decided to make a counselling program available to all its employees. Most counselling problems related to the job, alcohol and drug abuse, marital relations, family problems, and personal finances. One year after the counselling program was started, there was a 43 per cent reduction in absences and a 70 per cent reduction in the number of accidents.

FIGURE 15-9

Stress Scale

Life Event	Mean Value
1. Death of spouse	100
2. Divorce	73
3. Marital separation	65
4. Jail term	63
5. Death of close family member	63
6. Personal injury or illness	53
7. Marriage	50
8. Fired at work	47
9. Marital reconciliation	45
10. Retirement	45
11. Change in health of family member	44
12. Pregnancy	40
13. Sexual difficulties	39
14. Gain of new family member	39
15. Business readjustment	39
16. Change in financial state	38
17. Death of close friend	37
18. Change to different line of work	36
19. Change in number of arguments with spouse	35
20. Mortgage over $10 000	31
21. Foreclosure of mortgage or loan	30
22. Change in responsibilities at work	29
23. Son or daughter leaving home	29
24. Trouble with in-laws	29
25. Outstanding personal achievement	28
26. Wife begins or stops work	26
27. Begin or end school	26
28. Change in living conditions	25
29. Revision of personal habits	24
30. Trouble with boss	23
31. Change in work hours or conditions	20
32. Change in residence	20
33. Change in schools	20
34. Change in recreation	19
35. Change in church activities	19
36. Change in social activities	18
37. Mortgage or loan less than $10 000	17
38. Change in sleeping habits	16
39. Change in number of family get-togethers	15
40. Change in eating habits	13
41. Vacation	13
42. Christmas	12
43. Minor violations of the law	11

Source: Reprinted with permission from *Journal of Psychosomatic Research*, Vol. II, T.H. Holmes and R.H. Rahe, "The Social Readjustment Rating Scale," 1967, pp. 213-18, Elsevier Science Ltd., Pergamon Imprint, Oxford, England.

Stress and Job Performance

Stress can be either helpful or harmful to job performance, depending upon the amount of it. Figure 15-10 presents a stress performance model that shows the relationship between stress and job performance. When there is no stress, job challenges are absent and performance tends to be low. As stress increases, performance tends to increase, because stress helps a person call up resources to meet job requirements. It is a healthy stimulus to encourage employees to respond to challenges. Eventually it reaches a plateau that represents approximately a person's top day-to-day performance capability. At this point, additional stress tends to produce no more improvement.

Finally, if stress becomes too great, performance begins to decline, because stress interferes with it. An employee loses the ability to cope, becomes unable to make decisions, and is erratic in behaviour. If stress increases to a breaking point, performance becomes zero, because the employee has a breakdown, becomes too ill to work, is fired, quits, or refuses to come to work to face the stress.

People have different tolerances of stressful situations. The level of stressors that one can tolerate before feelings of stress occur is one's *stress threshold*. Some persons are easily upset by the slightest change or emergency. Others are calm, cool, and collected, partly because they have confidence in their ability to cope. They feel very little stress unless a stressor is major or prolonged:

> Mabel Kelly worked at the driver's licence desk in a provincial government office. She faced a variety of problems, complaints, angry citizens, and red tape during the day, but it did not seem to trouble her. On the other hand, Malcolm Morgan, her associate at an adjoining desk, had difficulty with the complaints, anger, and abuse that he received. He began taking longer breaks and then extra breaks. He seemed nervous. Finally, he asked for a transfer to another office.

The two employees in the above example had different stress thresholds.

While several organizations have implemented programs to help employees deal with stress, such efforts are often met with resistance. The Royal Bank and its HRM group has worked hard at creating a culture that allows their wellness programs to succeed:

FIGURE 15-10

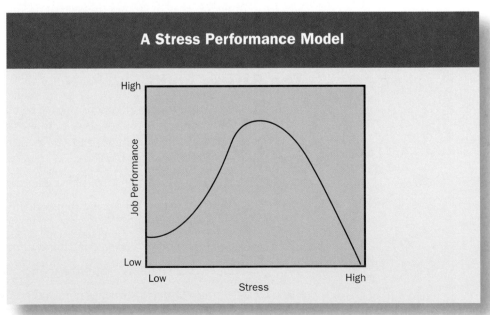

A Stress Performance Model

The Royal Bank introduced a flexible work arrangement program in the early 1990s. Now more than 10 000 employees take advantage of the program. According to Norma Tombari, manager for Workforce Solutions for the Royal Bank, "It's a slow process and we still meet with resistance. But you don't need someone at a desk nine-to-five all day long to be able to produce." More than 80 per cent of the program users indicated they had become more effective in managing work and family life and many also reported reduced stress, more energy, and fewer absences from work.[50]

Stress Management

There are several solutions to the problem of workplace stress. Curative solutions try to correct the outcome of stress, while preventive solutions attempt to change the cause of stress.

Curative Measures

It has become quite popular to offer employees the opportunity to relax through such activities as aerobic exercises, yoga, and meditation. Some companies have counselling professionals on staff or employ an external consulting service that provides assistance in diagnosing the causes of stress and developing ways to cope with it. For example, the Awareness, Attitude, Action (AAA) method to stress reduction focuses on developing awareness of stress-related problems, adjusting attitudes (accepting responsibility for your reactions and developing a positive outlook), and taking action (which usually revolves around time management and physical activity).[51]

Preventive Measures

There are different approaches to dealing with stress at the workplace. First, organizations can establish stress management training sessions and EAP assistance to help workers deal with stress. Second, some organizations are looking at improving working conditions in order to reduce stress at work—the employer needs to identify stressful situations and design strategies to reduce or eliminate the stressors. In managing stress, it may be necessary to bring in outside experts.[52]

Management should look at the structure of the organization and the design of jobs. Several Canadian organizations have developed programs that provide workers with more diversified tasks, greater control over decisions that affect their work, and a chance for wider participation in the overall production process. While some people recover from stressful situations easily, others allow stress to build up, and it is these individuals who are of special concern to the human resource department.

The Stress Audit

Human resource managers must be sensitive to the many possible sources and causes of stress at the workplace. It is possible to evaluate the extent of dysfunctional stress by performing a *stress audit*, which assists in identifying the causes of stress.[53] The stress audit asks the following questions:

1. Do any individuals demonstrate physiological symptoms?

2. Is job satisfaction low, or are job tension, turnover, absenteeism, strikes, or accident proneness high?

3. Does the organization's design contribute to the symptoms described?

4. Do interpersonal relations contribute to the symptoms described?

5. Do career-development variables contribute to the symptoms described?

6.   What effects do personality, sociocultural influences, and the nonwork environment have on the relationship between the stressors—individual careers, interpersonal relations, and organizational design—and stress?

Human Resource Actions to Reduce Stress

A desirable way to respond to stress is to try to remove or reduce its causes. For example, one option is to avoid the stress, and the human resource department can help by arranging a transfer to another job, a different supervisor, and different work associates.

The human resource department also helps employees improve their ability to cope with stress. Better communication improves an employee's understanding of stressful situations, and training courses can be provided on the subject of coping with stress. Counselling services may be an effective way to help employees deal with stress. Figure 15-11 shows some of the specific actions that the human resource department should take to reduce employee stress and burnout.

Managers and supervisors should be trained in stress management since they tend to have a considerable impact on the work environment and the working atmosphere or climate in an organization. Important skills and characteristics that will assist in creating a better organizational climate include interpersonal communication, an open leadership style, and willingness to delegate responsibilities and to accept input from employees into the management decision-making process.

> During a recent forum on "work rage," Canadian Auto Workers president Buzz Hargrove said that stress is not only the bosses' fault. He noted, "Employers are not solely to blame for the increase in workplace stress. We have a broader problem, in fairness to bosses. While the power imbalance between employers and employees is a constant source of attention, governments also have a real role to play in that they establish the legislative framework within which business and labour operate."[54]

Fitness and Employee Wellness Programs

Fitness programs, also called wellness or lifestyle programs, have become quite popular in organizations and have been shown to have a positive impact on reducing

FIGURE 15-11

Actions to Reduce Stress

- Ensure that an employee's workload is compatible with the individual's capabilities and resources.
- Design jobs to provide meaningful opportunities for employees to use their skills.
- Clearly define employee roles and responsibilities.
- Provide workers with the opportunity to participate in decision making.
- Improve the communications process.
- Increase opportunities for social interaction among employees.
- Develop appropriate work schedules.
- Train managers and employees to be sensitive to the symptoms of stress.
- Establish a stress management policy.

Source: National Institute for Occupational Health and Safety, *Stress at Work.*

stress and absenteeism and increasing productivity. Many employees want access to health promotion programs in the workplace and a recent Conference Board of Canada survey indicated that 52 per cent of organizations had some type of wellness program.[55] At one company, BCT.Telus, managers are held accountable if employees perform poorly on wellness initiatives; while the company spent $1.5 million on corporate health services activities over the past year, the savings from the program were $4.5 million (which translates to $3 of savings for each $1 spent in the program).[56]

How effective are fitness programs? While most evaluations have come from large American corporations with comprehensive programs, the evidence indicates that such programs:

- improve employee health;

- decrease health-care costs;

- improve employee satisfaction;

- decrease absenteeism and turnover; and

- improve corporate image.[57]

The findings from a 1996 health survey of employees of the City of Edmonton indicated that providing wellness information resulted in 16 per cent of employees changing their lifestyle behaviours. The average City employee who was active at least three times a week missed about six days a year, compared with a 9.5 days-a-year absenteeism rate for the City as a whole. In terms of cost savings, the 3.5-day difference resulted in an average cost avoidance of $552 per active employee (for a total savings of almost $230 000).[58]

To encourage wellness and a healthy lifestyle, a number of Canadian companies provide excellent fitness facilities and programs for their employees:

> Nortel operates a 4600-square-metre, fully equipped and staffed fitness facility at Bramalea, Ontario. The gym rivals the most luxurious private fitness clubs in its variety of high-tech equipment, fitness testing, professional staff, and in the 45 aerobic classes held each week. In cooperation with Fitness Canada and York University, Nortel is conducting a comprehensive study of the program's benefits to both the individual and to the company. The preliminary results have shown that the program has improved fitness, reduced absenteeism, and increased productivity.[59]

In the past, most fitness programs have been designed for white-collar staff. Yet research has shown that fitness levels of blue-collar workers are often lower than

More and more companies are promoting health by providing facilities and programs to benefit employee well-being.

Digital Imagery © Photo Disc Inc. Photo by Ryan McVay

those of white-collar employees, who tend to be more involved in physical activity on a regular basis than their blue-collar counterparts. A number of companies have recognized that creating company gyms only for white-collar workers will not achieve the goals of improving the health of all workers. Consider the extensive program at one manufacturing firm:

> At Husky Injection Molding Systems, employees have access to a 24-hour a day fitness centre (used by about 40 per cent of the employees), vegetarian meals in the cafeteria, and a $500 vitamin stipend. A doctor, massage therapist, and chiropractor visit the facility twice a week. Employee wellness is considered an important component in the company's strategy of attracting and keeping the best and brightest employees.[60]

Similarly, MDS Nordion, a leading firm in the health care sector, was a winner of the Healthy Workplace Award from the National Quality Institute. The wellness program at MDS Nordion is paying dividends: a turnover rate of just six per cent (much lower than the industry average of 10 per cent), sick-day usage has dropped from 5.5 days per year six years ago to just over three days a year now, and lost-time injuries reached an all-time low of 0.25 injuries per 100 person-years. Obviously, employee well-being is an important issue at MDS Nordion.

> In addition to carrying out health tests on its employees, MDS Nordion also regularly monitors its workforce through the use of its "Climate Metre," which measures 18 aspects of employee satisfaction with their work and their well-being. The wellness program has several components, including a broad range of fitness options (the fitness facility, known as the Well Cell, is used by about 35 per cent of employees) and the leadership fundamentals and dynamics program, a mandatory program designed to improve communication, conflict-resolution, and team-building skills.[61]

An interesting application of employee wellness using the Internet is a program called "Health Manager." The program, which was developed by medical specialists at the University of Montreal and McGill University, allows workers to ask questions about health problems and receive immediate responses. Other aspects of Health Manager include health education, health promotion, health referrals, and a health library.[62]

OTHER CONTEMPORARY SAFETY ISSUES

Sick Building Syndrome (SBS)

People spend up to 90 per cent of their lives indoors and a growing number report becoming sick while working in a particular building. Symptoms range from headaches to dizziness to nausea to eye, ear and/or throat irritation, to allergic reactions. Sick building syndrome may be caused by major combustion pollutants (caused, for instance, from malfunctioning heating systems), biological air pollutants (such as mites, mould, and dander), volatile organic compounds (including pesticides, solvents, and cleaners), and heavy metals (such as lead). Human resource professionals should take proactive steps to prevent sick building syndrome—it is estimated that SBS will cost about $1 billion annually in health costs and considerably more in lost productivity and employee stress.[63] The impact of sick building syndrome on an employee's life can be devastating:

> Jim Crane was the general manager of a well-known hotel chain. One day, he received a call about a leak in one of the hotel rooms. He and the hotel's engineer started ripping out the wall and discovered that the Aspergillus strain of mould was growing in a number of other rooms and had made its way into the ventilation and vending-machine areas. For a year, Crane worked on removing the mould, unaware that he was

inhaling the mould's toxic fungal spores. He developed chronic inflammation of his lungs and now must take 17 drugs every day. A lawsuit against his former employer is under way.[64]

Workplace Violence

One area of safety management that has been neglected to some extent concerns workplace violence. However, a scan of newspapers and television reports indicates that workplace violence is not always a rare event. In this era of restructuring and productivity improvement, there have been a number of accounts of terminated employees returning to the workplace and injuring or killing other employees. Recent evidence from the United States indicates that violence is the third-highest cause of all workplace deaths and the leading cause of workplace death for women. In terms of deaths per 100 000 workers, U.S. evidence indicates that the highest-risk industries include taxicab services, liquor stores, detective or protective services, gas service stations, and jewellery stores.[65] Some employers are developing extensive programs to address safety concerns and workplace violence:

> In an effort to increase workplace safety at their convenience stores, 7-Eleven (Southland Corporation) developed a crime-prevention plan. In addition to high-tech solutions such as personal alarms worn by clerks and high-resolution video-monitors, all employees must complete a comprehensive robbery and violence prevention training program that includes instructional videos and role plays.[66]

> At McDonald's Restaurants of Canada, personal safety is a major part of the management and staff training program, with the use of role-plays so that employees can anticipate and respond to potentially dangerous situations. In addition, the layout of restaurants and unobstructed and well-lit parking lots also contribute to increasing safety.[67]

Measures aimed at preventing or reducing the incidence of workplace violence include an anti-violence/zero tolerance policy, self-defence training, and safety and security measures.

Research suggests that workplace conflict is increasing, with employees dealing with the public (such as sales clerks and teachers) at greatest risk. In addition, many managers have less time to meet with employees and observe warning signs that the employee is having difficulty coping.[68]

What are the most common incidents of violence at the workplace? Research from the United States indicates that verbal threats are most common (accounting for 41 per cent of the incidents), followed by pushing or shoving (19 per cent), robbery (9 per cent), fist-fighting (9 per cent), and stalking (9 per cent).[69] Moreover, about 58 per cent of organizations report that their employees have expressed fear that violence may occur at work and 62 per cent of U.S. firms indicate that they have a written policy addressing workplace violence.[70] With the growth of the Internet, one of the most recent threats at the workplace involves "cyber-stalking," which is the use of electronic communications to harass or threaten another individual. Some organizations now use software that is designed to assist in "profiling" potentially violent employees or potential new hires, but opinion is divided as to the effectiveness of this technique.[71]

In light of the fatal shooting of four employees at OC Transpo in 1999, a coroner's inquest has called for legislation on workplace violence, including a zero-tolerance policy on harassment and violence. Violence should also include "psychological violence" such as bullying, teasing, or ridiculing.[72] In Nova Scotia, teachers are seeking to have violent students classified as workplace hazards under the Occupational Health and Safety Act:

According to one Nova Scotia teacher, the impact of a violent student's behaviour on a teacher and other students is not unlike the health risks and hazards of an environmentally unsound building. Another teacher commented that teachers aren't trained to deal with violent students, and that teachers are required to be counsellors and psychologists, but without receiving the necessary training.[73]

Ergonomics

Ergonomics
The study of relationships between the physical attributes of workers and their work environment to reduce physical and mental strain and increase productivity and quality of work life.

www.iea.cc

An area of health and safety that is attracting more attention is *ergonomics* (also known as human factors engineering). Ergonomics focuses on the interaction between employees and their total working environment.[74] An ergonomics program seeks to ensure that the physical and behavioural characteristics of the employee are compatible with the work system (including methods of work, machines and equipment, the work environment, and the workplace or workstation layout).[75]

While a number of organizations wait until employees complain about the work system or sustain an injury, proactive employers aim to ensure that the work system is compatible with employees. Consultants specializing in ergonomics can assist organizations in the design and implementation of the work system.

Two common types of injuries that may be reduced by the application of ergonomic principles are (1) overexertion and lower-back injury and (2) repetitive-strain injuries (RSI), which may include cumulative trauma disorder (CTD), overuse syndrome (OS), and musculoskeletal injury (MSI). Repetitive strain injuries are caused by repeated actions resulting in muscle or skeletal strain.

> A University of Waterloo professor of computer science who uses computers about six hours a day suddenly developed considerable pain in his wrists, elbows and shoulders. To combat the repetitive strain injury associated with using the computer, the professor made several changes including switching to another keyboard, adjusting the height and position of the monitor, learning to operate the mouse with his left hand, using a more comfortable chair, doing regular exercises, and taking breaks—in fact, the software on his computer has a feature reminding him when it is break time![76]

Recent data suggest that the most rapidly growing category of workplace illnesses involves ergonomic disorders. In 1981, when the IBM PC was introduced, 18 per cent of all illnesses reported to the Occupational Health and Safety Administration in the United States involved repetitive strain injuries. Three years later, that figure had grown to 28 per cent and to 52 per cent by 1992. Now it is estimated that about 70 per cent of all occupational illnesses will be repetitive strain injuries.[77]

The treatment of repetitive strain injuries is complex and varied. Some of the approaches used include physical treatments (such as physiotherapy or chiropractic treatments), postural treatments (often aimed at correcting bad habits relating to posture), relaxation (such as meditation), exercise and stretching, acupuncture and cognitive behavioural therapy (with a focus on coping with pain).[78]

A properly designed workstation can play a major role in reducing workplace injuries. The key factors in designing an ergonomically sound workstation relate to the layout of the workstation, the characteristics of control and display panels, seating arrangements at the workstation, and lighting quality and quantity.[79] While a number of organizations have moved to an open-office concept, workers complain about such things as reduced privacy and noise spillover:

> One woman at a public relations firm could not concentrate while a co-worker in an adjoining cubicle completed the ritual of clipping his nails. Another employee complained about the lack of privacy when she spoke on the phone to a former boyfriend while a different employee lamented hearing a co-worker blurt out a crude phrase to tell a client he had to use the washroom.[80]

AIDS

Acquired Immune Deficiency Syndrome (AIDS)

The disruption of the body's immune system caused by a virus called the Human Immunodeficiency Virus (HIV).

www.ohrc.on.ca

www.cdnaids.ca

A CHAPTER ON occupational health and safety would be incomplete if no reference were made to the *Acquired Immune Deficiency Syndrome (AIDS)* or the Human Immunodeficiency Virus (HIV) that causes AIDS. By the end of 1999, 49 000 individuals in Canada were living with AIDS, with approximately 400 people dying from AIDS during the year.[81] Both HIV and AIDS have a potentially immense impact on the human resource function.[82]

AIDS and Human Resource Management

Consider the following case that occurred more than a decade ago:

> Ron Lentz was hired January 4, 1988, by the Toronto Western Hospital as a nurse and fired on January 23. He complained to the Ontario Human Rights Commission that he was discriminated against because he was HIV-positive. The commission agreed and negotiated with the hospital a settlement that included reinstatement, about $14 000 in back pay, $1400 in benefits, $5000 in legal fees, restoration of seniority, and a clean employment record.[83]

This case points to problems that human resource managers have to face if one of their employees is HIV-positive, develops AIDS, or if a job applicant happens to mention that he or she has an HIV-related infection. It is a breach of human rights laws to discriminate against that person. But what if colleagues refuse to work with that person? What if a supervisor expressed concern about the employee's contact with customers? To be prepared for such questions, each employer should establish a policy and have an action plan in place before a case arises among employees or their dependants. Some recommendations on how to set up a successful AIDS program are outlined below.

1. *Policy*. A policy regarding HIV-infected employees should:
    *   protect an employee's right to privacy;
    *   guarantee the employee will not be isolated from other workers; and
    *   keep those diagnosed with AIDS productive as long as they are able.

2. *Mandatory Training*. Training for managers, supervisors, and union leaders should:
    *   present facts on HIV;
    *   address personal concerns about AIDS in the workplace;
    *   reiterate the company's policy;
    *   help with job restructuring; and
    *   discuss how to manage co-worker concerns.

    Education programs for all employees should:
    *   explain policy;
    *   present facts on transmission and prevention;
    *   encourage empathy for those with AIDS; and
    *   provide workshops or forums for frank, open discussion.

3. *Counselling and Support*. Companies should provide counselling to:
    *   help employees with AIDS cope with their disease;

- assist others in coming to terms with an HIV-infected co-worker; and

- explore with supervisors the issues involved in managing AIDS.[84]

Despite the considerable amount of information on HIV and AIDS, many individuals are not well informed about the disease. One of the problems human resource managers must deal with is the lack of knowledge on the part of employees. There are still questions asked such as "Can I get AIDS from germs in the air? From touching an infected worker? From a toilet seat? From infected water in a swimming pool? From insect bites?" It has been found that a comprehensive education program for co-workers can halt the hysteria that often results when a colleague is diagnosed with HIV or AIDS.[85]

OCCUPATIONAL HEALTH AND SAFETY STRATEGY

www.ccohs.ca

www.ctsplace.com

IT MUST BE REPEATEDLY stressed that top management's involvement in setting health and safety policies is essential. If it does not assume a leadership role, it sets an example by its inaction, and middle managers, first-line supervisors, and employees will behave accordingly. Part of an effective occupational health and safety strategy is to clearly assign responsibilities for plant safety and health programs to ensure that the company's policies are carried out. An occupational health and safety committee with enforcement authority is a very helpful tool to implement health and safety policies. Such a committee should be made up of representatives of management and employees, ideally with balanced representation. This increases the probability that the committee's decisions are accepted as fair by the employees.

It is important to have a control process in place. Causes of accidents should be identified and either eliminated or controlled to prevent recurrence. The human resource department should use its information system to monitor for patterns of accidents or health problems that may be otherwise overlooked. An effective training program is another critical part of a good occupational health and safety program. Moreover, a number of organizations are hiring occupational health and safety specialists to design and administer comprehensive workplace health and safety programs. Finally, management should continually encourage safety awareness on the part of supervisors and employees.

SUMMARY

Occupational health and safety has become an important aspect in organizations and will have an even higher priority for human resource managers in the future. The federal and provincial governments have created a variety of laws that require the attention of human resource professionals. Most occupational health and safety acts now require the establishment of safety committees in companies with twenty or more employees.

The Workplace Hazardous Material Information System (WHMIS) is a law that requires suppliers to provide detailed information on any danger their material may pose, but it also asks the user to make sure that the information is available and that employees are trained to understand it.

Accident prevention is a major concern, but human resource managers should not forget to look at the psychological aspect of the work environment. Stress-related losses—absenteeism, turnover, low productivity, accidents—cost Canada billions of dollars. Preventive programs such as employee assistance programs, professional counselling, time management, and fitness programs can go a long way to reduce stress-related costs.

AIDS and the workplace is an important issue facing human resource managers. Some organizations will experience individual cases of AIDS or HIV that, given present experiences, can lead to severe friction among work groups and irrational actions from some frightened employees. Human resource managers should be prepared for this by appropriate training and communication programs.

TERMS FOR REVIEW

Visit the Web site at www.mcgrawhill.ca/college/schwind6 for a full glossary.

REVIEW AND DISCUSSION QUESTIONS

1. Explain the legal term "assumption of risk."

2. What factors affect occupational accidents?

3. What responsibilities do Joint Occupational Health and Safety Committees have?

4. Explain the requirements of the Workplace Hazardous Material Information System (WHMIS).

CRITICAL THINKING QUESTIONS

1. Develop a strategy and identify the implementation steps you would follow to lower the incident rate of workplace accidents in your organization.

2. Think about a time when you felt under considerable stress. What were the causes of that stress? What efforts (by you and/or others) were or could have been taken to reduce the stress?

3. What can be done to prepare an organization for an AIDS case?

4. Consider an organization that you have worked in. Critically review its safety procedures and training. Evaluate the organization in terms of the presence of physical, biological, and chemical hazards. Also be sure to address issues relating to ergonomics.

WEB RESEARCH

1. Visit the Human Resources Development Canada Web site (hrdc-dhrc.gc.ca) and examine the relevant sections of the Canada Labour Code that deal with occupational health and safety. Also, explore other Web sites that address health and safety law within your province.

2. Go to the Web site of the American Institute of Stress (www.stress.org). Check out three other Web sites that also have information on workplace stress. Compare the information from the various sites.

INCIDENT 15-1

Safety at Canada Chemicals Ltd.

Canada Chemicals Ltd. is a large wholesaler of industrial chemicals in Ontario. It handles swimming pool supplies, industrial solvents, fertilizers, and special lubricants. The sales and clerical operations caused few safety worries, but the warehouse facilities caused Sam Peterson sleepless nights. Sam's title was manager of safety and security. He had worked in the human resource department since his job was created in 1984.

His biggest problem was the warehouse manager, Garfield McKenney. Gar simply did not appreciate safety. Nearly every action Sam took to improve safety resulted in objections from Gar, especially if it meant warehouse workers were to be slowed or delayed in their jobs. Most of the workers liked Sam, but they paid more attention to Gar. The only time employees wore their safety goggles, shoes, and acid-resistant gloves was when Sam was around. They knew Gar did not care and would not discipline good workers for safety violations unless company property was damaged.

One day a case of sulphuric acid was dropped, badly burning a new employee. The employee recovered after four weeks and two plastic surgery operations. Immediately after the accident, Sam requested a meeting with Gar, the human resource manager, and the general manager.

1. If you were the general manager, what would you do to gain greater cooperation on safety from (a) Gar and (b) the workers under him?

2. Should Sam be given authority to discipline those who violate safety rules?

INCIDENT 15-2

Night Work in a Hospital

Ann LeBlanc is a laboratory technician in one of the city hospitals in Halifax. As a technician, she has to work two day and three night shifts every week. She has been working at the hospital for the last eight years.

"This job is beginning to get to me," says Ann. "Night work is getting really harder and harder. I don't sleep or eat well on the three days when I have to work at night. I feel groggy most of the time."

Ann is one of four employees in the laboratory, three of whom have to work at night on a rotating basis. "All three of us have the same kinds of problems," Ann adds. "We all feel that our mental balance is lost at times. Sleep during the daytime does not help at all. It doesn't have the same depth as sleep at night. We also don't get a chance to spend time with our family most of the week. I would have quit a long time ago, but with the kids going to school we need the money.

"We are so sleepy at night that on several occasions we have been close to making serious mistakes. One day I mistook water for glycerine.... And Jackie almost fell down the stairs one day."

1. Can night work be called a health hazard? Why?

2. What can be done to eliminate the problems of night work?

CASE STUDY

Maple Leaf Shoes, Safety at the Workplace

As he sat in his cubicle (what some would call an office) sipping what remained of a cold cup of coffee, Jon Atherton thought about his family back home in Vancouver. He missed his wife and two young daughters, and at times, he longed for his old job and his life back in British Columbia. On the other hand, his family would be joining him in Wilmington in a couple of months and the job that he had left six weeks ago in Vancouver had ceased to provide much challenge. Although his job as a supervisor on the shop floor of a small manufacturing firm gave him some experience in the area of health and safety, his new position in Wilmington was that of safety coordinator. Deep down, he knew that he loved the work—it was just that upon his arrival in Wilmington, everything seemed to be in turmoil. As soon as he solved one problem, another one would pop up.

THE FIRST ISSUE

A week ago, Jon met with Sam Johnson, a 42-year-old man who had been with Maple Leaf Shoes for eight years. Sam is one of two non-union employees who works at the snack bar—his job requires that he serve customers and prepare "snack" foods (such as toast, muffins, and cold sandwiches) for employees. The snack bar is located in the employee lounge, a common hangout for employees on break or having lunch. Fellow employees get along well with Sam— he is always cheerful and his laugh can be heard throughout the lounge on a regular basis. As well, Sam's supervisor says that Sam is a solid performer. Jon also recalled that Sam is taking computer courses on a part-time basis at a nearby community college.

Jon thought back to his talk with Sam a week ago. Sam appeared to be uneasy and reserved when he entered Jon's office and told Jon he had something very important to tell him. Jon recalled how they

struggled to get through the conversation—ultimately, Sam revealed to Jon that he had become infected with the AIDS virus and asked Jon for advice. Jon and Sam had arranged to meet in a week's time.

Catherine Reading, who is 56 years of age and has been with Maple Leaf Shoes for 12 years, is the other employee who works with Sam at the snack bar. Catherine is a dependable worker and while she and Sam are not close friends, they get along well together at work. Other than a warning for being 14 minutes late a few years ago, Catherine has a clean work record.

Shortly after meeting with Jon, Sam told Catherine that he had been infected with the AIDS virus (saying "since you work with me, I felt I had to tell you"). Catherine was very troubled by this information. The next day, she reported for work but refused to work with Sam. Her supervisor asked Catherine if she was refusing to obey his orders. Catherine replied "Yes, I am. I am scared and I'll never work with someone that has AIDS." The supervisor told Catherine that refusing to carry out his request amounted to insubordination. He sent Catherine home and went to see Jon for advice.

Discussion Questions

1. Does Maple Leaf Shoes have just cause to dismiss Sam? Catherine?

2. What should Jon do in this case?

3. Develop a policy on AIDS and describe how you would administer this new policy.

THE SECOND ISSUE

Alexandra (Alex) Dixon, a 26-year-old employee at Maple Leaf Shoes, has been employed in her current secretarial position for almost two years. Prior to receiving the promotion to this position, Alex worked with Maple Leaf Shoes for six years as an office assistant. She is a single mother with a five year old daughter. Note that the secretarial staff are unionized.

Alex's performance evaluations have been slightly above average. However, her personnel file indicates that 18 months ago she received a three-day suspension because she and another employee were caught drinking on the job during regular working hours ("just a couple of drinks on a boring Friday afternoon" according to Alex).

Over the past few years, Maple Leaf Shoes has had some problems with substance abuse at work (although the problems have been confined almost entirely to employees in the production and warehouse facilities). In one case, a fork-lift operator under the influence of cocaine dropped a wooden pallet loaded with shoes from about 15 feet in the air—luckily, no one was seriously hurt. Six months ago, Alex's supervisor called in all of her staff to let them know that the company was concerned about safety and would not tolerate the use of drugs at work. There had not been problems of drug use among the office staff and the topic of drug use was not mentioned again.

Two weeks ago, Alex's supervisor thought that she saw Alex take a puff on a marijuana cigarette on company property (actually on the far side of the company parking lot) at the end of the day. The next day, the supervisor confronted Alex at her work station and accused her of taking drugs while at work. This meeting was witnessed by six other office employees. Alex admitted smoking the marijuana cigarette (saying that she only had about three puffs while on company property), made it clear that she was on her own time ("it was well past quitting time"), said that she was very sorry, and promised never to do it again. The supervisor told Alex that the company was clamping down on drug use and terminated Alex.

The union is grieving Alex's discharge. The collective agreement gives Maple Leaf Shoes the right to discipline or discharge an employee for "just cause."

Discussion Questions

1. Does Maple Leaf Shoes have just cause to terminate Alex?

2. In discharge cases, the grievance procedure at Maple Leaf Shoes goes directly to step 3 (a meeting between senior union and management representatives). The management side is looking to Jon for advice on how to proceed. Help Jon formulate an appropriate strategy.

CASE STUDY

Stressful Times at a CPIB Branch

The downtown branch of the Canadian Pacific and International Bank in Brandon, Manitoba, is known for its friendly service and high levels of employee morale. Although the branch gets very busy at times, the employees regard it as a good place to work. There is a spirit of cooperation among the employees and the bank manager, Marsha Cobourg, is well liked by the staff.

Roselynn Barkhouse, a 26-year-old customer service representative, has been employed at the Brandon branch for just over nine months. In general, co-workers describe Roselynn as a good, solid worker but most also agree that she is somewhat shy.

Three weeks ago, Roselynn was working at the counter when Roy Romanowski came in to deposit money into his business account. Roy has operated his small convenience store, which is located about three blocks from the bank, for 31 years. He is a loyal CPIB client and visits the bank at least once a day. Everyone in the area knows Roy—while he is a very hard worker, he is also an impatient man and not overly friendly. Some area residents refuse to buy anything from Roy's store because, in the words of one woman who lives near the store, "He is just so unfriendly, cold and abrupt, I will never support his store." However, Roy's wife and children, who also work in the family store, are well liked in the community.

Roy approached Roselynn's counter and gave her his deposit bag. A careful count of the money revealed that Roy had $2314 to deposit. Roselynn filled out the deposit slip for Roy, had him initial it, and went to the computer to enter the transaction. However, Roselynn mistakenly pressed the withdrawal button (instead of the deposit button) so when Roy looked at his passbook, it showed a withdrawal from his account of $2314. He noticed the error immediately because he always keeps a close eye on his account.

Upon seeing the error, Roy started to scream at Roselynn. The following conversation ensued:

Roy: "What are you doing? Are you stupid or something? You trying to steal my money? I work real hard for my money."

Roselynn: "I am very sorry, Mr. Romanowski. I will fix up the mistake right away."

Roy: "How can I trust you? I have always gone to this bank and they always treated me right. Now, this happens. How many mistakes have you made before? I want to see the manager. I want to get you fired. There is no room in the bank for stupid people."

At this point, two other employees and the manager, Marsha Cobourg, arrived at Roselynn's counter. Roselynn was in tears and once again, apologized to Roy. Within seconds, the error was corrected, and Cobourg also offered her apologies to Roy and walked him to the door.

Since the incident, however, Roy has continued to come into the bank at least daily (and more often when his store is busier). Whenever he enters the store, he makes a rude comment to Roselynn if she is working. Often his comments are overheard by other customers. At times, he also tells other people to avoid going to Roselynn's counter. Both Marsha Cobourg and Roselynn's co-workers have reassured her that her work is fine and have advised her just to ignore Roy.

Two days ago, Roy entered the bank and, as luck would have it, Roselynn was the next available representative. Roy, however, refused to go to her work station and made his intentions known to all the customers around him. The bank was very busy at the time and Roselynn burst into tears, left her counter and went home. The next day, she called Cobourg and told Marsha: "I am totally stressed out and just can't take it any more. I'm quitting and am going to look for work somewhere else. The job is just not worth it." Marsha tried to comfort Roselynn

and after much discussion, was able to get Roselynn to come in for a meeting the next day.

Discussion Questions

1. The day of the meeting between Roselynn and Marsha has arrived. Was arranging such a meeting a good idea?

2. What should Marsha try and achieve during the meeting? Were there any steps that could have been taken to prevent this incident from occurring?

The meeting with Roselynn ended at 11:00 a.m. and Marsha Cobourg went back to her office. Forty minutes later, as she glanced out her office door, she saw a man wearing dark glasses and a baseball hat burst into the bank. At the time, there were six bank employees and seven customers in the bank.

The man was waving a shotgun and yelling, "Everyone on the floor. Don't look up and don't try and stop me. No one will get hurt". He swore several times and ran to the cash station. "Open the drawer and give me the money." The bank representative at the cash station complied with his request and in a matter of seconds, the bank robber ran out the door.

Within a few minutes, the police arrived as Marsha had pressed the silent alarm in her office. Everyone was told to remain calm and the bank doors were locked. No new customers were allowed into the bank and everyone present when the robbery occurred had to remain inside. Each customer was interviewed by the police. Marsha also asked each customer how they were. Three of the customers were very upset—one woman who was in the bank with her one-year-old son was particularly distraught.

A number of the bank employees were also visibly upset. Others seemed to take a deep breath and appeared ready to deal with the business at hand.

One customer commented on how the atmosphere in the branch changed so rapidly. Prior to the robbery, everyone was relaxed and people were chatting. During the robbery, there was extreme tension. Then, the aftermath of the robbery was very different—some people were in shock, some seemed emotionally drained, and others were trying to think through what had occurred. The customer also noted that while a number of the bank employees were terribly upset, they seemed in total control during the robbery: "It was like they knew what to do. I only caught a glimpse of what happened but there was no show of fear or panic on the employees' faces. It was almost like they were doing a drill, but in real life."

After about 45 minutes, the customers were permitted to leave the bank. As Marsha returned to her office, she received a phone call from the police notifying her that they had just arrested a suspect as he was preparing to rob another bank.

Discussion Questions

1. Develop a safety training program for bank employees. What are the basic components of the program? What requirements would you build into such a program?

2. As a result of the robbery, a number of employees and customers may feel traumatized. What should the bank do in such a situation. Be sure to consider both short- and long-term suggestions.

SUGGESTED READINGS

D'Andrea, James A., David J. Corry and Heather I. Forester, *Illness and Disability in the Workplace: How to Navigate Through the Legal Minefield*, Aurora, Ont.: Canada Law Book, 2000.

Denenberg, Richard and Mark Braverman, *The Violence-Prone Workplace: A New Approach to Dealing with Hostile, Threatening and Uncivil Behaviour*, Ithaca, N.Y.: Cornell University Press, 1999.

Human Resources Development Canada, *Work Safely for a Healthy Future*, Ottawa: Government of Canada, 2000.

Keith, Norman A., *Canadian Health and Safety Law: A Comprehensive Guide to the Statutes, Policies and Case Law*, Aurora, Ont.: Canada Law Book, 2000.

Keith, Norman A., *Human Resources Guide to Preventing Workplace Violence*, Aurora, Ont.: Canada Law Book, 1997.

Ministry of Labour (Ontario), *A Guide to the Occupational Health and Safety Act*, Toronto: Government of Ontario, 2000.

Montgomery, James, *Occupational Health and Safety*, Toronto: Nelson Canada, 1996.

National Institute of Disability Management, *Strategies for Success: Disability Management in the Workplace*, Port Alberni, B.C.: NIDM, 1997.

Robertson, Dilys, "The Scope of Occupational Health and Safety in Canada," *HRM in Canada*, Scarborough, Ont.: Carswell, 1996.

Schaufeli, W.B. et al. eds., *Professional Burnout: Recent Developments in Theory and Research*. Washington, D.C.: Taylor and Francis, 1993.

Society for Human Resource Management, *1999 Workplace Violence Survey*, Alexandria, Virginia: SHRM, 1999.

Chapter 16

The Union-Management Framework

HRM focuses on the shared interests of workers and managers in the success of their enterprise. Conflict is de-emphasized in favour of "win-win" scenarios where problems are solved or put aside to fulfil organizational objectives. By contrast, industrial relations assumes conflict is inherent in the employment relationship.

—Daphne Gottlieb Taras, Allen Ponak, and Morley Gunderson[1]

CHAPTER OBJECTIVES

After studying this chapter, you should be able to:

■ *Describe* the structure of Canadian unions.

■ *Discuss* the major reasons why workers join unions.

■ *Identify* conditions that indicate unionization may occur.

■ *Explain* how a union organizing campaign is carried out.

■ *Summarize* the core legal principles relating to collective bargaining.

■ *Outline* the key steps in negotiating a union contract.

■ *List* common techniques to resolve disputes.

■ *Describe* how unions affect the human resource management environment.

■ *Suggest* ways to build union-management cooperation.

Workers may join together and form a *union*. A union is an organization with the legal authority to represent workers, negotiate the terms and conditions of employment with the employer, and administer the collective agreement.

Many successful companies have one or more unions among their employees. While unionized organizations are often lumped together, there is growing evidence that the quality of the relationship between an employer and union is a major factor in predicting firm performance. Still, the use of collective action puts new limits on the role of human resource management. Many times, operating managers find these new limitations hard to accept. Consider the views of one plant manager:

> "As plant manager, I don't think we need to worry about unions. Our company pays good wages and has a sound benefit program," argued Dave Weldon.

> "Sure, our pay and benefits are fair. But a union could promise our employees even more. Besides, workers don't always join unions for higher pay or better benefits. They may want a union because they feel unfairly treated," Stan commented.

> "Well, if any supervisor is treating workers unfairly, they could tell me. I would take action quickly. Since management at this plant takes care of workers, I don't think workers should want to join a union. If they did, I would try to stop it before it got out of hand," Dave added with little thought.

> "When your supervisor does something you don't like, do you complain to the company president?" Stan questioned. "Most workers are probably reluctant to complain to you about their supervisors. And workers have a legally protected right to join a union!"

WHY EMPLOYEES SEEK UNION REPRESENTATION

Collective agreement
A contract negotiated between union and employer, outlining terms and conditions of employment.

UNIONS DO NOT JUST HAPPEN. They are frequently caused by some management action or inaction that workers perceive as unfair. If workers feel a need to join together, then a union can be organized successfully. Once it is created, the union and management are legally obligated to sit down and bargain a labour contract called a *collective agreement*. The collective agreement, which is known as the "rule book" by some managers and union officials, addresses a variety of issues such as wages and benefits, hours of work, working conditions, and related issues such as grievance procedures, safety standards, probationary periods, and work assignments. The collective agreement is usually negotiated between the local union's bargaining committee and the human resource or industrial relations department.

The collective agreement places restrictions on management's rights in managing the workplace. When a new collective agreement is negotiated, it is important that supervisors and managers dealing with unionized employees are made aware of the terms of the agreement and provided training with regard to the interpretation and application of the new agreement. All too often, a union grievance arises because the supervisor did not understand the terms of the collective agreement:

> Shane Warren was a supervisor for a local municipality. Under the terms of the collective agreement, the employer was required to provide overtime opportunities on the basis of seniority. One evening, Warren needed an employee to work overtime doing snow removal. Rather than take the time to contact employees based on their seniority, he asked an employee in the shop who agreed to the overtime assignment. The union was successful in their grievance because Warren had failed to follow the collective agreement.

Causes of Unions

Why do employees join unions? The reasons for joining a union vary from person to person. Even workers in the same organization may have different reasons for joining a union because of their different perceptions. For example, consider the views of two bank tellers at a recently organized branch bank:

> Maria Tomas: I decided to join the union for many reasons. I'm not even certain which one was the main reason. One thing for sure, the branch manager now must prepare work schedules fairly. Before the union, we never had any say about them. The manager told us what hours we worked, and it was final. Now we can appeal to the union. Sure, I could have complained to the human resource department at head office. But then the manager might have become angry. That sure would reduce my chances for a merit raise or promotion. I supported the union, and I am proud of it.

> Paul Anglin: I really don't know why so many people wanted a union at this branch. This is the best job I have ever had, and the supervisor is really nice. All the union means is dues, rules, and maybe even a strike. I simply can't afford to miss a paycheque over some strike. To me, we were better off without a union.

Although it is hard to believe, both tellers have the same supervisor, work in the same bank branch, receive the same pay, and have the same job. The big difference between Maria and Paul is their views of the bank and the union. Had someone at the bank realized Maria's dissatisfaction and reacted favourably, she might agree with Paul's feelings. But when employees like Maria think they are being treated unfairly and believe that the human resource department is unable to help, union membership may seem desirable.

Since individual perceptions vary, there is no single force that motivates people to join unions. Instead, perceptions are shaped by a variety of reasons. Some of the more important ones are shown in Figure 16-1. When considering union joining, it is important to distinguish between the desire for union representation and the opportunity to do so.[2] Three factors—job dissatisfaction, individual attitudes towards unions in general, and perceived union instrumentality (beliefs about what unions can do for an employee)—appear to be most important in the decision of an individual to join a union.[3]

FIGURE 16-1

Workers' Major Reasons for Joining or Not Joining Unions

Major Reasons for Joining	Major Reasons for Not Joining
Learn a trade	Dislike unions
Find employment through union	Possess steady employment
Receive union benefits	Receive fair treatment
Acquire collective power	Want a management position
Seek change in management practices	Afraid of strikes
Dislike supervision/supervisory practices	Dislike dues
Receive peer pressure	Reject as unprofessional
Required by union shop	Unions not needed for self-employed
Want benefits promised during organizing drive	Management deterrent (legal and illegal)
Seek professional contacts	
Resolve professional issues	
Want better pay	
Social reasons	
Socio-political reasons	
Job security and protection	

Reasons for not joining a union are equally diverse. Workers who want to become managers may believe union membership damages their chances for promotion. Other employees view unions as "just another boss" that leads to extra costs, such as union dues or lost wages from strikes. Likewise, past experiences or isolated stories of union wrongdoing may cause some people to form a negative opinion of collective action. Or, more simply, policies and supervisory treatment may be fair, so that employees lack motivation to join a union:

> In 2000, Dofasco, which is a nonunion company and Canada's second-largest steel-maker, announced the largest payout to employees in the firm's 62-year history of sharing the wealth with employees. More than 7000 employees shared $53.3 million, which translated into a bonus of almost $8000 per employee just for working for the company. The company contributes 14 per cent of its pretax profit from its Hamilton steel-making operations to profit sharing.[4]

Professionals and Unions

Many professionals do not belong to unions. Instead, they belong to professional associations that are designed to further their knowledge and improve the image of the profession. However, several groups of professionals (including nurses, teachers, and university professors) have joined unions. While the reasons why professionals join unions are varied, such "white-collar" unions often emerge as a response to poor treatment by management—frequently relating to unacceptable supervisory practices, human resource policies, or professional issues.

> In the fall of 1997, teachers in Ontario engaged in a two-week strike in response to the legislative changes to education proposed by the Conservative government of Mike Harris. Several teachers expressed the view that "we've got to stand up to the government and protect the educational system."

There are several reasons why professionals do not join unions. Those who are self-employed would receive few benefits from such membership. Even those who work for an employer have little to gain if their treatment is professionally favourable. Some professional employees view unions as inappropriate. Finally, labour legislation across the country restricts members of certain professions (such as lawyers and doctors) from joining a union.

The past two decades have seen considerable growth in white-collar unionization. Some of the reasons for this trend are outlined below:

The formation of unions means more management interaction with Human Resources. If the union's needs are not met, a strike or walkout can result.

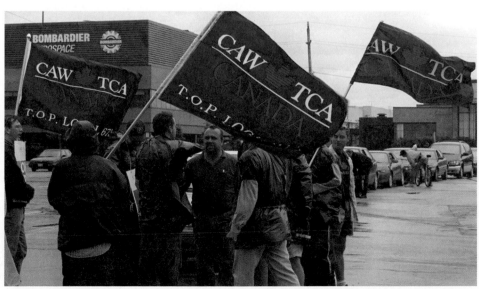

CP PHOTO ARCHIVE *(Tanis Toohey)*

- *Changes in Skill Level.* As skills become routinized because of technology (e.g., accounting tasks can be done effectively with a computer program, as can design work), professionals tend to seek protection of their domain by turning to unions and collective bargaining.

- *Inadequate Legislation.* Some professional employees are required to work long hours, but do not have to be paid time and a half for working more than eight hours a day or 40 hours a week as do other workers. As a result, such workers may look to union representation.

- *Changes in Union Image.* Unions have shed their image of representing mainly the interests of blue-collar workers and being militant in their dealing with employers (although some maintain this reputation).

Canadians' Views Toward Unions

A survey by the Angus Reid Group polled 1495 Canadian adults concerning their attitudes toward work, institutions, and social policy. While the survey provides important information, it should be emphasized that the results are aggregated and important differences may exist among workers based on demographic characteristics. Some of the major findings with regard to attitudes toward work and employers are reported below:

- 97 per cent of workers report taking a great deal of pride in their work;

- 86 per cent of workers are somewhat or very satisfied with their jobs;

- 83 per cent of workers indicate that they are treated fairly by their employer;

- 81 per cent of workers perceive that employers put profits ahead of employees;

- 73 per cent of workers think that they were paid fairly in the past year for their main employment;

- 57 per cent of workers state that they were very loyal to their employer;

- 55 per cent of workers believe that quite a few or most employers do not treat employees as fairly as they should;

- 37 per cent of workers are somewhat or very worried about losing their job; and

- 36 per cent of workers feel that employer/employee interests are opposed.[5]

Another section of the survey asked workers about their attitudes toward unions. The results for both the Canadian and American participants are reported in Figure 16-2. While about two-thirds of Canadian workers approve of unions, only one-third of nonunion employees would vote for union representation if an election were to be held tomorrow.

LABOUR UNIONS: GOALS AND STRUCTURE

LABOUR UNIONS alter the work environment. Their presence changes the relationship between employees and the organization, especially the role of supervisors and the human resource department. As seen through the eyes of one veteran supervisor, the human resource department's response to unions is not always well received by lower levels of management:

> When I started working here in the 1970s, supervisors had it made. We handled our own discipline, hiring, and firing. We had clout around here. Then we got a union. Immediately, the human resource department grew and got involved in everything we

FIGURE 16-2

Attitudes Towards Unions

Statement	Canada (%)	U.S. (%)
Workers who approve of union	67	70
Workers who believe that as a whole unions are good	52	57
Nonunion employees who, if an election were held tomorrow, would vote for unionization	33	47
Nonunion employees who would personally prefer to belong to a union	21	29
Nonunion employees who feel that unions are not needed since workers get fair treatment now	42	37

Source: Seymour Martin Lipset and Noah M. Meltz, "Canadian and American Attitudes Toward Work and Institutions," *Perspectives on Work*, December 1997, pp. 14-19.

did. We had training in how to deal with the union, training in the labour laws, training in what the contract meant, and training in all the new rules we had to follow.

Even worse, the human resource department started to have a bigger part in hiring, firing, and discipline. At the same time, I had to deal with the union representative. Of course, my manager still expected me to meet my department's objectives and its budget. Supervising sure is less satisfying than it used to be before the union and the human resource department made all these changes.

As this supervisor's comments indicate, unions have a major effect on the work environment, but in many other ways the environment remains unchanged. Supervisors and managers retain their primary responsibility for employee performance. Profit objectives and budgetary goals are not usually shared with the union (although this is changing in some organizations). Nor do unions reduce the need for effective human resource department policies and procedures. In short, management must still manage; and the union does not assume the responsibilities of the human resource department. To understand how and why unions influence human resource management, it is necessary to examine their goals and structure.

Union Goals and Philosophy

A union's objectives are influenced internally by the wishes of their members, aspirations of their leaders, and the financial and membership strength of the union. And like other organizations, unions are open social systems that are affected by their external environment. The financial condition of the employer, the gains of other unions, the inflation and unemployment rates, and government policies influence the union's objectives.

Yet among all these internal and external considerations, there exists a common core of widely agreed-upon objectives. Writing more than 80 years ago, one prominent labour leader stated that the mission for the labour movement was to protect workers, increase their pay, improve their working conditions, and help workers in general.[6] This approach has become known as *business unionism*, primarily because it recognizes that a union can survive only if it delivers a needed service to its members in a businesslike manner. But some unions have chosen to address broader social issues of politics and economics when such concerns are in the best interest of their

Business unionism
The practice of unions seeking to improve the wages, hours, and working conditions in a business-like manner.

Social (or reform) unionism
A characteristic of unions seeking to further members' interests by influencing the social, economic, and legal policies of governments. (See also *Business unionism.*)

members. This second kind of union, engaged in what is called *social (or reform) unionism*, tries to influence the economic and social policies of government at all levels—municipal, provincial, and federal.[7] In practice, union leaders pursue the objectives of social unionism by speaking out for or against government programs. For example, many union leaders rejected wage restraint legislation introduced by several governments in the 1990s because such controls removed the right of the union to engage in free collective bargaining with management over a variety of compensation issues.

Human resource management is influenced by both business and social unionism goals. The growth of benefits discussed in Chapter Eleven has resulted partly from union pressure. Even nonunionized employers have added many benefits in order to remain competitive in the labour market or to forestall unionization among their employees. Consider how one human resource department responded to the business and social goals of unions:

> Michelin Tire (Canada) Ltd. has three plants in Nova Scotia and is a major employer in the province. To prevent the employees from seeking unionization, management pays wages significantly above those provided by unionized companies in the region. In addition, the company provides several other benefits such as free dental insurance. To date, several attempts over the past two decades to unionize the company have failed—due, at least in part, to the human resource management practices of the company.

Union Structure and Functions

It has been argued that employees lost direct contact with the owners as employers grew larger, so unions emerged to help workers influence workplace decisions.[8] Through unions, workers were able to exert control over their jobs and their work environment.[9] Then when attempts were made by employers to cut wages or employment, the employees relied on their unions to resist these actions.[10] The most important levels of union structure are labour congresses, national and international unions, and local unions.

Canadian Labour Congress

Canadian Labour Congress (CLC)
A central labour congress formed in 1956 by the merger of the Trades and Labour Congress of Canada and the Canadian Congress of Labour.

The *Canadian Labour Congress (CLC)* represents many unions in Canada, and has a total membership of more than 2.5 million employees. The President, Ken Georgetti (a former past president of the British Columbia Federation of Labour), was elected in 2000. The CLC has five main functions: (1) representing Canada at the International Labour Organization, (2) influencing public policy at the federal level, (3) enforcing the code of ethics set out in its constitution, (4) providing services (such as research and education) for its member unions, and (5) resolving jurisdictional disputes among its member unions.

While the Canadian Labour Congress is the largest labour federation, it is not the only one. In addition to other federations at the national level, there are also federations operating at the provincial and municipal or regional level. For instance, the Quebec Federation of Labour is a provincial federation and the Waterloo (Ontario) Regional Labour Council is a regional federation.

Local Unions

Local union
The basic unit of union organization, formed in a particular plant or locality.

Craft union
A labour organization that limits membership to workers having a particular craft or skill or working in a closely related trade.

For most union members and industrial relations practitioners, the **local unions** are the most important part of the union structure.[11] They provide the members, the revenue, and the power of the entire union movement. Historically, the two major types of local unions were craft and industrial unions. *Craft unions* are composed of workers who possess the same skills or trades; these include, for example, all the

Industrial union
A union representing
primarily production,
maintenance, and related
workers, both skilled and
unskilled, in an industry.

carpenters who work in the same geographical area. *Industrial unions* include the unskilled and semiskilled workers at a particular location. When an employer has several locations that are unionized, employees at each location are usually represented by a different local union. Members of the Canadian Auto Workers are an example.

Figure 16-3 shows the structure of a typical local. The union *steward* is usually elected by the workers and helps them present their problems to management. If the steward of an industrial or mixed local cannot help the employee, the problem is given to the grievance committee, which takes the issue to higher levels of management or to the human resource department.[12] In craft unions, the steward, who is also called the representative, usually takes the issue directly to the business agent, who is often a full-time employee of the union.

National and International Unions

Many local unions are part of a larger union—which may be a *national union* (such as the Canadian Auto Workers or the Canadian Union of Public Employees) or an *international union* (such as the United Steelworkers of America or the International Brotherhood of Teamsters). National unions are based in Canada, while international unions have their headquarters outside of the country (typically in the United States).

National and international unions exist to organize and help local unions. They also pursue social objectives of interest to their members and frequently maintain a staff that assists the local unions with negotiations, grievance handling, and expert advice. Some national and international unions leave many key decisions (including bargaining a collective agreement) with their local unions. In other relationships, the national or international union plays a very active role in local union affairs. Figure 16-4 shows the membership of the largest unions in Canada. Note that of the 10 largest unions, five are from the public and quasi-public sector.

Secession

In 1960, about two-thirds of union members belonged to an international union. Over the past 40 years, that percentage has declined noticeably so that now only

FIGURE 16-3

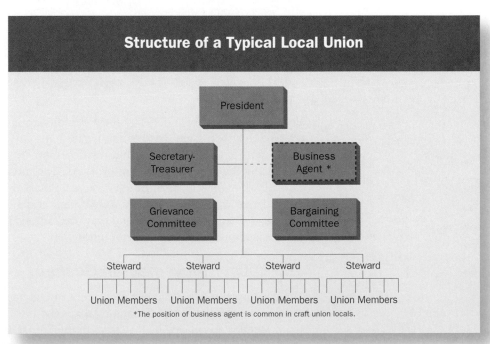

Source: Human Resources Development Canada. Structure of a Typical Union. Reproduced with the permission of the Minister of Public Works and the Government Services Canada, 2001.

FIGURE 16-4

Membership in Canada's Largest Unions (2000)

Union	Membership (000s)
Canadian Union of Public Employees (CLC)	461.8
National Union of Public and General Employees (CLC)	325.0
National Automobile, Aerospace, Transportation and General Workers Union of Canada	215.0
United Steelworkers of America (AFL-CIO/CLC)	200.0
United Food and Commercial Workers International Union (AFL-CIO/CLC)	200.0
Communications, Energy and Paperworkers Union of Canada (CLC)	144.3
Public Service Alliance of Canada (CLC)	142.3
Social Affairs Federation (CSN)	97.0
International Brotherhood of Teamsters (AFL-CIO/CLC)	93.0
Service Employees International Union (AFL-CIO/CLC)	81.5
Quebec Teaching Congress (CEQ)	81.5
Laborers' International Union of North America (AFL-CIO/CLC)	60.0
International Brotherhood of Electrical Workers (AFL-CIO/CLC)	57.0
United Brotherhood of Carpenters and Joiners of America (AFL-CIO/CLC)	56.0
Canadian Union of Postal Workers (CLC)	54.8
International Association of Machinists and Aerospace Workers (AFL-CIO/CLC)	50.0

Source: Human Resources Development Canada. HRDC, *Directory of Labour Organizations in Canada*, Ottawa, HRDC, 2000. http://labour-travail.hrdc-drhc.gc.ca/doc/wid-dimt/eng/dlo.cfm Reproduced with the permission of the Minister of Public Works and the Government Services Canada, 2001.

about 30 per cent of union members belong to international unions.[13] This trend, referred to as secession, has been motivated, in part, by a desire for more autonomy on the part of Canadian locals and the development of policies aimed at specifically addressing the needs of Canadian workers. The most dramatic breakaway occurred in 1985 when the Canadian Auto Workers union, led by former president Bob White, severed ties with the United Auto Workers and held its founding convention in Toronto. Canadian members of international unions have often complained that they receive a disproportionate share of union benefits.

The Labour Movement in Quebec

The development of the labour movement in Quebec is relatively independent of its development in the rest of Canada. Perhaps the most active role in organizing work-ers in Quebec was played by the clergy of the Roman Catholic Church. In 1921, there were enough unions to form the first national confederation, the Canadian and

Catholic Confederation of Labour (CCCL). Because of their religious nature, the unions in the CCCL strongly opposed the international unions, whom they perceived as antireligious and too materialistic. Only after the Second World War did the religious character of the CCCL change; the change became official by 1960, when the organization adopted its present name, the Confederation of National Trade Unions (CNTU). Although the CLC's Quebec arm, the Quebec Federation of Labour (QFL), with about 370 000 members, represents most of the province's unionized workers, the CNTU is the largest independent labour federation in Quebec, with about 240 000 members.

TRENDS IN UNION MEMBERSHIP

Union Growth and Decline

In 2000, about 3.7 million workers belonged to unions (about 30.5 per cent of the paid workforce). In terms of industry sector, education was the most highly unionized at 68.8 per cent, followed closely by utilities (67.6 per cent) and public administration (64.7 per cent). Agriculture, finance, and trade sectors had the lowest rate of unionization, with 3.5, 7.8, and 12.5 per cent respectively.

In recent years, the number of women members in Canadian unions has been increasing rapidly. In 1967, women made up only 20 per cent of total union membership; 33 years later, about 48 per cent of union members are female. While about one in six female employees belonged to a union in 1967, that ratio has doubled over 30 years and now about one in three women are union members. Thirty years ago, four out of ten male employees were union members; today that proportion has fallen to three in ten.

Historically, unions have been strong in the manufacturing and not-for-profit sectors. Smaller firms and employers in the service sector have been resilient to unionization. However, unions are placing greater emphasis on organizing service employers—recent successes include the Citizen's Bank of Canada in Vancouver (an on-line "virtual bank"), Starbuck's in a number of British Columbia locations, and Tim Horton's in London, Ontario. In Quebec, a McDonald's restaurant was closed just as its employees were to receive union accreditation; in response, the Quebec Labour Federation announced a Canada-wide union-organizing campaign aimed at McDonald's restaurants.[14] However, McDonald's has shown to be very persistent in remaining union-free. According to Bill Tieleman:

> Not a single worker at any of McDonald's more than 14,000 restaurants in North America has a union contract that would let him or her file a grievance over workplace terms and conditions. That means that close to a million workers negotiate for themselves against one of the most powerful corporations in the world. In 1997, McDonalds hired an unbelievable 15 lawyers in its efforts to defeat unionization at a single Quebec restaurant. Ultimately, the test of whether fast-food workers join unions is the same as in every other workplace: How fairly are they being treated by their employer?[15]

In comparing unionization across provinces, Newfoundland had the highest rate (39.2 per cent), followed closely by Quebec (36.1 per cent) while the lowest union density was in Alberta (21.1 percent).[16] Figure 16-5 provides further information on union membership in Canada. Of particular note is the lower probability that a part-time worker will be unionized and the difference in union density rates when comparing very small (less than 20 employees) and very large (more than 500 employees) employers.

FIGURE 16-5

Union Membership and Work Status, Occupation, and Firm Size

Characteristic	Union Membership Number of Members ('000)	Density (%)
Work Status:		
Full-time	3,113	31.6
Part-time	462	21.5
Occupation:		
Management	82	8.6
Administration	575	24.5
Natural and Applied Sciences	194	24.6
Health	409	62.2
Social and Public Services	560	62.0
Culture and Recreation	68	25.4
Sales and Service	611	19.7
Trades, Transport and Equipment	624	37.3
Primary Industry	40	16.9
Production Industry	433	37.9
Firm Size:		
Under 20 Employees	500	12.0
20 to 99 Employees	1,184	30.0
100 to 500 Employees	1,124	44.1
Over 500 Employees	786	55.4

Source: Reproduced from Statistics Canada, *Perspectives on Labour and Income*, Catalogue No. 75-001, Autumn 2000.

International Trends

On the global scene, a number of countries have experienced a decline in union density (that is, union members as a percentage of the paid non-agricultural workforce). Out of 92 countries providing union membership data, only 14 nations had a union density rate in excess of 50 per cent of the nonagricultural workforce, while 48 countries (52 percent of the sample) had a union density rate of less than 20 per cent. Explanations for the decline in union representation include (1) the decline in the manufacturing sector, (2) the constraints that globalization of financial markets have put on macroeconomic policies, and (3) competition from developing countries with low labour costs, resulting in the loss of low-skilled labour-intensive jobs in high-wage countries.[17] Union density rates for a selection of countries are provided in Figure 16-6.

THE IMPACT OF UNION REPRESENTATION

Strikes

Members of the public frequently associate unions with strikes. However, the reality is that most collective agreements are settled without the union resorting to strike action or the employer locking out the workers. Still, there are exceptions:

FIGURE 16-6

Union Membership in Selected Countries

Country	Union Density (%)
Argentina	38.7
Austria	41.2
Australia	35.2
Brazil	43.5
Canada	37.4
Denmark	80.1
Finland	79.3
Germany	28.9
Indonesia	3.4
Israel	23.0
Italy	44.1
Japan	24.0
Korea	12.7
Mexico	42.8
Netherlands	25.6
New Zealand	24.3
Poland	33.8
South Africa	40.9
Spain	18.6
Sweden	91.1
Switzerland	22.5
Thailand	4.2
United Kingdom	32.9
United States	14.2

Source: International Labour Organization, *World Labour Report: Industrial Relations, Democracy and Social Stability* (1997-98), Geneva: ILO, 1997. Copyright © International Labour Organization 1997.

In an effort to save 300 jobs set to be lost with the closure of a Molson's plant in Barrie, Ontario, 30 members of the Canadian Auto Workers union peacefully occupied the facility in an effort to draw attention to alternatives other than closure of the plant. In addition, a "boycott" van toured southern Ontario, encouraging the public and establishments serving alcohol to boycott Molson products.[18]

In studying why strikes occur, it is possible to classify strikes into one of two categories:

1. *Strikes as Mistakes/Misjudgment.* At least some strikes occur because the parties have uncertain and imperfect information when trying to negotiate an agreement or because one or both negotiation teams are inexperienced negotiators. For example, some negotiators become frustrated easily when bargaining and make their "final offer" too early or without carefully considering the implications of shutting down bargaining.

2. *Strikes as Collective Voice.* In a number of instances, the decision to go out on strike is not because of a mistake or misjudgment but because of a perception on the part of workers that they are not being treated fairly. A strike is considered a mechanism by which to voice discontent to management.[19]

What factors distinguish firms with lower strike activity? Strikes were less common in smaller firms and in organizations where:

- workers had more autonomy in the workplace;
- the employer introduced progressive human resource management practices;
- the union was in a strategically weak position; and
- employers have a large share of the market.[20]

The number of work days lost due to strikes and lockouts decreased marginally in the mid-1990s (see Figure 16-7). While the number of strikes has increased during the 1998-99 period, the number of workers involved and the number of person days not worked declined when compared with the 1996-97 data.

Wages and Benefits

What are the effects of unions on wages and benefits? The average hourly wage for full-time unionized employees in 1999 was $19.43 an hour (compared with $15.99 for nonunion workers). This difference was more dramatic when comparing part-time workers—$16.66 for unionized employees and $9.94 for nonunion workers. Moreover, as indicated in Figure 16-8, unionized employees tend to have more comprehensive benefit plan coverage.

FIGURE 16-7

Strikes and Lockouts in Canada

Year	Number of Strikes and Lockouts	Workers Involved ('000)	Person-days Not Worked ('000)
1987	668	582	3810
1988	548	207	4901
1989	627	445	3701
1990	579	270	5079
1991	463	253	2516
1992	404	150	2110
1993	381	102	1517
1994	374	81	1607
1995	328	149	1583
1996	330	282	3352
1997	284	258	3610
1998	381	244	2444
1999	413	159	2446

Source: Reproduced from Statistics Canada, *Perspectives on Labour and Income*, Catalogue No. 75-001, Autumn 2000.

FIGURE 16-8

Union Status and Work Conditions

Work Condition	Union Employees	Nonunion Employees
% of Employees with Pension Coverage	82.8	32.9
% of Employees with Supplemental Health Plan Coverage	83.7	44.4
% of Employees with Dental Plan Coverage	77.0	41.9
% of Employees with Paid Sick Leave	77.2	44.7
% of Employees with Paid Vacation Leave	84.1	65.3
% of Employees with Flexitime Option	16.7	27.1
% of Employees in Job Sharing Arrangement	12.1	6.8
Average Annual Paid Vacation Leave (days)	20.9	15.1

Source: Reproduced from Statistics Canada, *Perspectives on Labour and Income*, Catalogue No. 75-001, Winter 1997.

Unions and Productivity

One major issue of interest for human resource management and industrial relations practitioners is the relationship between unionization and productivity. On one hand, it can be argued that unions have a "monopoly" face that creates economic inefficiency by introducing restrictive and inflexible work rules, withdrawing labour in the form of a strike if an employer fails to meet union demands, and increasing compensation costs. On the other hand, it can also be asserted that unions have a "voice" face that increases productivity by reducing turnover, enhancing employee morale, improving communications with workers, and "shocking" management into employing more efficient workplace practices.[21] Studies have shown that unions:

- reduce employee turnover (fewer quits);

- increase tenure with the firm; and

- raise productivity or output per worker.[22]

However, the relationship between unionization and productivity is open to considerable debate and has not been universally agreed upon. In fact, management perceptions are opposite to some of the empirical work—while managers from both the union and nonunion sectors tend to believe that unions lower productivity, some studies indicate that in a number of industries, productivity is actually higher in unionized firms. There is also evidence that unions recognize the importance of increasing productivity:

> According to Prem Benimadhu, vice-president of the Conference Board of Canada, some unions are seeking out responsibility for productivity improvements, quality control and, in some instances, marketing of products and services. Unions can "take on productivity" by being involved in productivity programs. Unions, whose members do the work, are the ones who know where waste is in processes.[23]

THE LEGAL ENVIRONMENT

GOVERNMENT SHAPES the union management framework through both the enactment of laws and in their role as employer. Unlike the United States, where employers and unions across the country are regulated by the National Labour Relations Act, the federal government and each province has its own labour legislation. This division of responsibilities for trade union law is a result of the British North America Act (now the Constitution Act, 1867), which specifies the powers of the federal government and the provinces.

The issue of jurisdiction over labour relations is quite significant for human resource practitioners. The Canadian Parliament is restricted in its jurisdiction over labour relations matters to organizations involved in interprovincial trade and commerce (e.g., banks, airlines, railways, and federal government agencies). All other organizations fall under the jurisdiction of the provinces. It has been estimated that only about 10 per cent of the Canadian labour force comes under federal jurisdiction. Consequently, it is important that human resource practitioners are aware of the appropriate legislation.

The Common Core of Canadian Labour Legislation

The fact that each province and the federal jurisdiction all have their own labour relations statutes makes dealing with unions somewhat more difficult, particularly for employers operating in more that one province. Some of the key aspects of Canadian labour law (which will be discussed in more detail later) include:

* *right to join a union*—employees have the right to join a trade union of their choice and participate in the union's activities;

* *good faith bargaining*—in attempting to negotiate a *collective agreement*, both labour and management have a duty to "bargain in good faith";

* *no strikes or lockouts during the life of the collective agreement*—it is illegal for a union to strike or an employer to lockout employees during the life of the contract;

* *prohibition on unfair labour practices*—all jurisdictions have legislation prohibiting unfair labour practices by employers and unions; and

* *conciliation*—the right of a union to strike or an employer to lock out employees is (in most provinces) delayed until the conciliation process has been exhausted.

While each province and the federal jurisdiction have some unique features in their labour law, there is a "common core" of provisions contained in the various labour relations acts (refer to Figure 16-9).[24]

Labour Relations Boards

Labour relations boards (LRB)
Boards set up in the federal and all provincial jurisdictions to administer labour relations legislation.

To enforce labour legislation, the federal and all provincial governments have created their own **labour relations boards (LRB)**. At the federal level, the board is now called the Canada Industrial Relations Board. These agencies investigate violations of the law and have the power to determine: (1) whether a person is an employee for the purposes of the law; (2) whether an employee is a member of a trade union; (3) whether an organization is an appropriate bargaining agent for bargaining purposes; (4) whether a collective agreement is in force; and (5) whether any given party is bound by it. The enforcement procedures of an LRB are summarized in Figure 16-10.

FIGURE 16-9

Common Characteristics of Federal and Provincial Labour Legislation

1. All jurisdictions create labour relations boards to decide who has the right to participate in collective bargaining and what bargaining unit should be permitted to represent those who are organized.

2. Most jurisdictions (except Saskatchewan) prohibit strikes during the life of an agreement.

3. Most jurisdictions contain regulations that delay strike action until a conciliation effort has been made and has failed.

4. All jurisdictions require that a collective agreement be in force for at least one year.

5. All jurisdictions specify and prohibit certain "unfair labour practices" by management and unions.

In comparison to traditional courts of law, LRBs are more flexible in their procedures for solving a conflict. They may rely on expert testimony instead of looking for precedents, suggest a compromise, or even impose a solution upon the parties. In all jurisdictions, the boards' decisions are final and binding and cannot be appealed except on procedural matters. On the other hand, the boards may revise, rescind, or override any of their decisions.

When charges have been filed against an employer, the human resource department usually assists the organization's lawyer in preparing the case. The department compiles job descriptions, performance appraisals, attendance records, and other documents that help the company prove its case.

FIGURE 16-10

LRB Procedures for Redressing Unfair Labour Practices

1. The aggrieved individual or organization contacts the appropriate LRB office (federal or provincial) and explains the alleged violation.

2. If the case appears to have merit, the LRB informs the other party of the complaint and asks for a response.

3. The LRB gives the parties involved the opportunity to present evidence and to make representations. If the complaint cannot be solved informally, the LRB conducts an official hearing with the interested parties present and usually represented by legal counsel.

4. On the basis of the evidence, the board will either dismiss the case or, if one party is found guilty of a violation, issue a cease-and-desist order. In the event of noncompliance, this order is enforceable in a court of law.

5. It is up to the board to decide whether a verdict can be appealed or not. In any case, an appeal can be made in matters of jurisdiction, failure to pursue legitimate complaints, and procedural irregularities.

THE COLLECTIVE BARGAINING PROCESS

Union Organizing

It is worth remembering that a union begins only when workers create it.[25] While unions use professional organizers, the outcome of the organizing drive depends primarily upon the employees. As George Meany, the first president of the AFL-CIO in the United States, once commented:

> Despite the well-worn trade union phrase, an organizer does not organize a plant. Now, as in the beginning, the workers must organize themselves. The organizer can serve only as an educator; what he or she organizes is the thinking of the workers.[26]

Authorization cards
Cards that prospective union members sign to show support for a union.

In addition to professional organizers, employees interested in unionization often play an important role in convincing co-workers to join the union. During regular working hours, employees are not allowed to discuss unionization with co-workers. However, several other techniques are used to encourage workers to sign *authorization cards*—including handbills, speeches, conversations, and even home visits.

Depending on the jurisdiction, a union is typically certified either on the basis of card signatures or as a result of an election.

> In Ontario, the Conservative government changed the Ontario Labour Relations Act. Previously, a union could be certified automatically if at least 55 per cent of employees in the appropriate bargaining unit signed membership cards. Now, the union must win a certification vote (by obtaining a majority of the votes cast) in order to be certified.

Union organizers educate the workers by explaining how the union can reduce mistreatment. These professionals only assist workers; they do not cause workers to join a union. Even experienced organizers find it difficult to organize a truly well-managed and growing company with proactive human resource practices.[27]

Signs of Organizing Activity

Human resource departments can monitor the chances of union organizing by looking for the proper signs. One set of signs is found in the work environment. Figure 16-11 lists specific questions that can alert a human resource department to union activity. The higher the number of "yes" answers to the questions in the figure, the more likely it is that union activity will occur. The external factors shown in the figure are largely outside the human resource department's control. But external developments can cause the department to pay greater attention to the internal factors over which it has influence.

Another set of signs comes from changes in employee behaviour that suggest a union drive may be under way. Figure 16-12 indicates the type of behaviour to which supervisors and human resource specialists should be alert. It is important to remember that these are only indications of a possible union drive:

> One manager who observed some suspicious activities notified the human resource department. A few days later she was "pleasantly" surprised when the employees presented her with a gift certificate and a card as a Christmas present. What this manager saw was a group of employees passing around a card and collecting contributions for a gift. She thought they were signing up to join a union.

Once a union drive begins, management's choice of responses becomes limited in several important ways. A labour relations board (LRB) will protect workers from management reprisals. For example, the discipline of union supporters can result in legal

FIGURE 16-11

Environmental Factors that May Lead to Unionization

External Factors

- Have there been recent changes in the labour laws that affect your industry that might cause interest in your firm by union organizers?

- Has there been a sudden increase in unionization activity in your community or industry?

- Is your company planning a major increase in its work force that might stimulate union interest in organizing the firm before it becomes larger and more expensive to organize?

Internal Factors

- Has your organization failed to resolve systematically the union complaints made during previous, unsuccessful organizing attempts?

- Are employee turnover and absenteeism rates higher than the norms for your industry or community?

- Has the company failed to conduct job satisfaction surveys? Or, if they have been conducted, do they reveal a trend toward dissatisfaction?

- Are pay and benefits below average for the industry, community, or unionized firms?

- Is the company's procedure for resolving employee complaints largely not used by workers?

violations, unless the employer can prove the wrongdoer received the same punishment as other employees normally receive.

When unions are organizing, labour relations boards pay particularly close attention to the actions of employers. Unlike the United States, Canadian labour law provides employers with relatively little freedom to counter a union organizing drive.[28] Both the context and content of statements about unionization are carefully examined by labour relations boards. Consequently, employers are well advised to obtain prudent legal advice in the wake of a union organizing campaign.

FIGURE 16-12

Employee Behaviour that Suggests Union Activity

- Groups of employees in huddled conversations that end when a manager walks by
- More time in washrooms (where union cards are frequently signed)
- Problems being created or magnified by a few workers
- More militant employee behaviour
- An increase in questions about company policies and benefits
- Sources of gossip and information suddenly disappear

Source: Adapted from Howard Levitt, "Keep in Touch if You Want to Keep the Union at Bay," *Financial Post*, September 13, 1999, p. C11. Courtesy of *The Financial Post*.

Canadian labour relations boards are quite vigilant in enforcing unfair labour relations practices. Human resource administrators should stress to every member of management, from supervisor to chief executive officer, the following two cautions:

1. Can management actions be judged as unfair labour practices by the LRB?

2. Will management actions provide fuel for the organization drive?

When an unfair labour practice is committed by any member of management, it can lead to expensive, time-consuming lawsuits and (in some instances) automatic certification of the union. Moreover, union supporters can point to management violations as further justification for a union.

Unfair Labour Practices

Unfair labour practices
Those employer or union practices that are classed as unfair by labour relations acts.

To prevent employers from interfering with employee rights, the law prohibits specific *unfair labour practices* by management. These legal prohibitions are summarized in Figure 16-13. They require that management neither interfere with nor discriminate against employees who undertake collective action. These unfair labour practices also make dismissing these employees illegal and outlaw "blacklisting" and "yellow dog" contracts:

> Prior to the passing of progressive labour legislation, a common human resource policy was to require new employees to sign a "yellow dog" contract. This employment contract meant that if an employee assisted a union in any way, that person could be fired. Those who agreed to these contracts were often called "yellow dogs." And anyone who supported unions might be "blacklisted" by the previous employer giving a negative reference.[29]

Labour legislation also makes company-dominated unions illegal. In the past, some employers believed that if they could not prevent their employees from organizing, the next best thing would be to encourage a union they could dominate. Through threats, bribes, or infiltration, some companies tried to control union activities. For example:

> Robin Hood Multi-Foods Inc. in Ontario arranged for an employee to infiltrate the Service Employees International Union, take part in its deliberations, and report back

FIGURE 16-13

Unfair Labour Practices by Management

Each jurisdiction in Canada has specific provisions dealing with unfair labour practices by management. Some of the most common provisions addressing unfair labour practices are provided below. Activities that management may not engage in include:

1. Interfering in the formation of a union or contributing to it financially (although there have been allowances for the providing of an office for the union to conduct business and for paid leave for union officials conducting union business).

2. Discriminating against an employee because the individual is or is not a member of a trade union.

3. Discriminating against an employee because that individual chooses to exercise rights granted by labour relations statutes.

4. Intimidating or coercing an employee to become or not become a member of a union.

to general management about its activities. The Ontario Labour Relations Board issued a "cease and desist" order and required the company to post a notice in the plant explaining the board's order and making it clear that the company would not engage in any of a long, specified list of unfair labour practices.[30]

Unfair labour practices by unions are also prohibited. A summary of such practices is provided in Figure 16-14.

Obtaining Bargaining Rights

Legal recognition or bargaining rights may be obtained in three ways: (1) voluntary recognition, (2) through certification by a labour relations board, and (3) a prehearing vote or automatic certification resulting from unfair labour practice.

1. *Voluntary recognition* occurs if a union has organized a majority of employees and the employer is satisfied that the union did not apply undue pressure in the organization process. The employer then accepts the union as the legal bargaining agent without any involvement of a third party.

2. *Regular certification* may take different forms (depending on the jurisdiction):

   - In some provinces, if a substantial number of employees (usually between 50 and 60 per cent, depending on jurisdiction) sign union cards, the labour relations board may certify the unit without an election. If the union is unable to get enough employees to sign cards to qualify for automatic certification but still gets a significant number of card signatures (typically between 35 and 45 per cent of bargaining-unit members, again depending on the jurisdiction), an election is mandatory. A secret ballot is taken under the supervision of the labour relations board at the employer's place of business. If the union loses, another election among the same employees cannot be held for one year. If the union wins (that is, the majority of eligible employees who vote cast ballots in favour of the union), then the employer must prepare to negotiate with the union and attempt to reach a collective agreement.

   - Three provinces—Alberta, Nova Scotia, and Ontario—do not automatically certify unions based on card signatures. Rather, an election is held if there is sufficient support for the union in the form of signed cards. Again, the

FIGURE 16-14

Unfair Labour Practices by Unions

While each jurisdiction has laws regulating trade union conduct, some of the most important unfair labour practice provisions are presented below. Activities that a union is not permitted to engage in include:

1. Seeking to compel an employer to bargain collectively with the union if the union is not the certified bargaining agent.

2. Attempting, at the workplace and during working hours, to persuade an employee to become or not become a union member.

3. Intimidating, coercing, or penalizing an individual because he or she has filed a complaint or testified in any proceedings pursuant to the relevant labour relations statute.

4. Engaging in, encouraging, or threatening illegal strikes.

5. Failing to represent employees fairly.

union is certified if the majority of the ballots cast are in favour of the union. While employers generally favour a mandatory secret ballot vote for certification, the recent legislative change away from certification on the basis of card signatures was strongly opposed by unions in Ontario.

3. *Prehearing votes* are taken in cases when there are significant indications that an employer has committed unfair labour practices to prevent unionization. In such a case a union can ask an LRB to conduct a prehearing vote. In addition, most jurisdictions provide for automatic certification if employer actions (in the form of unfair labour practices) are such that the true wishes of employees may not be known.[31]

NEGOTIATING A COLLECTIVE AGREEMENT

ONCE A UNION is certified, the various labour relations statutes require both the union and management to *bargain in good faith*. This means that both sides are required to make a reasonable effort to negotiate a collective agreement. The failure of either party to do so can lead to unfair labour practice charges:

> The editor of a now-defunct newspaper found out by experience what "bargaining in good faith" means. He had decided to automate by installing computerized typesetting machines. When he told the president of the local typographical union, the president said, "Let's talk about it."
>
> "No! I've made up my mind and my decision is final. I own this newspaper, and I'll do with it what I want," the editor concluded.
>
> Upon reaching an impasse, the union charged the newspaper with refusal to bargain. Thirty months later a court of appeals upheld the LRB and ordered the owner to pay 30 months' back wages, with interest, to every striker. The total bill was $374 000.

The collective bargaining process has three overlapping phases. Preparation for negotiations is the first and often the most critical stage. The success of the second stage, face-to-face negotiations, largely depends on how well each side has prepared, the skill of the management and union negotiators, and the bargaining power of each side. The third phase involves the follow-up activities of contract administration. An organization may establish an industrial relations department or create a labour relations specialist position within the human resources department to administer the collective agreement and coordinate contract negotiations.

labour-travail.hrdc-drhc.gc.ca

Some collective agreements include a provision for final settlement of contract terms by arbitration. New Brunswick doctors sought this process in January 2001 after staging a three-day walkout to protest low wages and poor working conditions.

CP PHOTO ARCHIVE (Stephen McGillivray)

Preparing for Negotiations

The purpose of negotiations is to achieve a *collective agreement*. The agreement specifies the rights and responsibilities of management and the union. Detailed preparations are required if each party is to achieve its objectives.[32]

Collective bargaining does not occur in a vacuum. Labour relations specialists need to monitor the environment to obtain information about likely union demands. A number of strategies can be employed. First, the labour relations department must be sensitive to the rate of inflation and the settlements made by other unions. Information about potential union demands can also be found among union promises made during the organizing drive or among unmet demands from previous negotiations:

> During an organizing drive at an electronics company in the Maritimes the union promised to make day-care facilities for children of employees the key issue for the first negotiations. The majority of the employees were women who several times before had put forward similar requests to management, to no avail. The union won the election by a 155 to 28 margin, although the year before it had failed to get a majority.

> During the following negotiations, management again refused to consider day-care facilities, but relented when 95 per cent of the employees voted for strike action. A day-care centre was organized on a trial and cost-sharing basis. When the agreement expired and was renegotiated the following year, the union demanded that the company accept the full cost of the centre. Since management had just secured a lucrative supply contract and could not afford a strike, it agreed to the demand.

Management rights
As used in union–management relationships, those rights reserved for management that are within the collective agreement.

Another source of bargaining issues revolves around **management rights**. These rights provide management with the freedom to operate the business subject to any terms in the collective agreement.[33] They often include the right to reassign employees to different jobs, to make hiring decisions, and to decide other matters important to management.

Under what is known as the *residual rights theory* of management, employers argue that they have the authority over all issues not contained in the collective agreement. On the other hand, union leaders assert that residual rights do not exist and that they are free to bargain over any issue affecting workers. Most collective agreements have a management rights clause. A typical clause might be:

> Nothing in this agreement shall be deemed to restrict management in any way in the performance of all functions of management except those specifically abridged or modified by this agreement.[34]

In negotiating a collective agreement, management must be careful to include contract language that increases their flexibility at the workplace. For example, supervisors may want all job descriptions to include the phrase "and other duties assigned by management." This clause prevents workers from refusing work because it is not in their job description. The clause also gives supervisors greater freedom in assigning employees. Labour relations specialists in the human resource department may use a variety of sources (such as surveys, discussions, focus groups, provisions in other collective agreements, and information from grievance claims) to discover which rights are important.

Negotiating with the Union

After preparing for bargaining, the second phase of negotiations is face-to-face bargaining with the union. Discussions often start as much as 60 to 90 days before the end of the present contract. If the negotiations are for a first contract, they begin after the union is recognized by the employer or wins a certification election.

Negotiations cover a variety of issues relating to terms and conditions of employment including wages, hours of work, and working conditions. These areas are interpreted broadly. Wages mean all forms of compensation such as pay, insurance plans, retirement programs, and other benefits and services. *Hours of work* include the length of the workday, breaks, holidays, vacations, and any other component of the work schedule. *Working conditions* involve such issues as safety, supervisory treatment, and other elements of the work environment.[35] The techniques listed in Figure 16-15 provide some guidance in negotiating a collective agreement.

Successful bargaining usually begins with easy issues in order to build a pattern of give-and-take. Negotiations almost always take place in private, permitting more open discussion of the issues. When deadlocks occur, several tactics can keep negotiations moving toward a peaceful settlement. By settling easy issues first, bargainers often point to this progress and say, "We've come too far to give up on this impasse. Surely, we can find a solution." This sense of past progress may increase the resolve of both sides to find a compromise.

Compromises may be achieved by offering counterproposals that take into account the needs of the other party. Sometimes progress is made by simply dropping the issue temporarily and moving on to other items. Further progress on other issues may lead to compromises regarding earlier impasses. If no progress results, bargainers may request the assistance of federal or provincial mediators or conciliators.

Many management teams will exclude top executives. They are kept out of negotiations because top managers are often not experienced in collective bargaining. But their exclusion also gives management bargainers a reason to ask for a temporary adjournment when the union introduces demands that require a careful review. Rather than refusing the union's suggestion, management bargainers may ask for a recess to confer with top management (using the old adage "my hands are tied").

Experienced bargainers realize that the other side must achieve some of its objectives. If the employer is powerful enough to force an unacceptable contract on the union negotiating team, the union membership may refuse to ratify the contract or union officials and members may refuse to cooperate with management once the collective agreement goes into effect. They may encourage slowdowns and other uncooperative actions. Or when the agreement is being renegotiated, the desire to "get back" at management may lead to strike action.

FIGURE 16-15

Guidelines for Negotiations from "Getting to Yes"

- Don't bargain over positions—focus on solving the problem.
- Separate the people and the problem—attack the problem, not the people.
- Focus on interests—avoid thinking in terms of the bottom line.
- Develop options for mutual gain—consider alternatives that benefit both sides.
- Use objective criteria—yield to principle, not pressure.
- Develop your "Best Alternative to a Negotiated Agreement"—it is important to know your alternative position in the event that negotiations fail.

Source: Excerpt from *Getting to Yes 2/e* by Roger Fisher, William Ury and Bruce Patton. Copyright © 1981, 1991 by Roger Fisher and Willam Ury. Reprinted by permission of Houghton Mifflin Company. All rights reserved.

Ken Georgetti (left) celebrates with outgoing Canadian Labour Congress president Bob White after he was acclaimed president-elect at the CLC convention in Toronto, May 1999.

CP PHOTO ARCHIVE (Steve McKinley)

Mutual Gains Bargaining

Rather than go through the traditional adversarial approach to negotiating a collective agreement, some unions and employers are employing *mutual gains bargaining*. This approach moves away from the *us*-versus-*them* or win-lose attitude in favour of a win-win approach in which both parties work together to solve common problems. There is a feeling among some labour relations experts that the parties need to work together to compete and survive in the competitive economy of today.[36]

However, mutual gains bargaining does not mean "soft" bargaining or one side giving in. Rather, both parties sit down at the bargaining table as equals and engage in joint problem-solving activities. The process is usually preceded by training in conflict resolution for both employer and union representatives. In addition, mutual gains bargaining requires substantial commitment, trust, and respect, and a long-term focus on the part of both labour and management. Consider, for example, the experiences at Saskatchewan Power and Hercules Canada:

> According to Kevin Mahoney, former vice-president of Human Resources at Saskatchewan Power, "mutual gains bargaining encourages people to acknowledge their common ground and to focus attention on solving real problems. You throw the issue on the wall and hammer the issue instead of each other."
>
> To date, more than 200 employees (both union and management) have taken a training course on mutual gains bargaining. As Doug Morrison, education co-ordinator with the International Brotherhood of Electrical Workers, notes: "It doesn't take a rocket scientist to figure out that the old system of positional bargaining doesn't work well in today's business environment.
>
> At Hercules Canada, the employer and union (the United Steelworkers of America) have signed a collective agreement using the mutual gains approach. Joint accountability for several workplace issues (including job redesign, pension changes, and productivity improvements) was established. In addition, the parties also signed an "enabling agreement" that allows for decisions affecting union workers, including decisions to change the contract itself, to be made outside the bargaining process (if both union and management agree on the changes).[37]

What does a mutual gains enterprise need to succeed? At the workplace level, it is important to have high standards of employee selection, broad design of tasks and a focus on teamwork, employee involvement in problem solving, and a climate based on cooperation and trust. At the human resource policy level, key elements include a commitment to employment stabilization, investment in training and development, and a contingent compensation strategy that emphasizes participation, cooperation and contribution. Finally, at the strategic level, there must be a strong commitment from top management to the mutual gains concept, business strategies that support and are aligned with the mutual gains model, and an effective voice for human resource management in strategy making.[38]

Approving the Proposed Agreement

The bargaining stage of negotiations is completed when the agreement has been approved. Often final approval for the employer rests with top management, although the bargaining team may have the authority to commit the company.

Negotiations are not complete until the union also approves the proposed agreement. Typically, the union bargaining team submits the proposal to the membership for ratification. If a majority of the members vote for the proposal, it replaces the previous collective agreement. If members reject it, union and management bargainers reopen negotiations and seek a new compromise. Administration of the collective agreement begins when both sides sign it.

Conciliation and Mediation

Conciliation
A government-appointed third party attempts to bring together the parties to reconcile their differences.

What happens in the event that negotiations between labour and management break down? In their legislation, all jurisdictions provide for conciliation and mediation services. Actually, in most provinces, no strike action is permitted before a *conciliation* effort has been made and has failed.[39] A 10-year review of conciliation cases in Nova Scotia revealed that conciliation officers settled more than 90 per cent of the cases.[40] However, the results vary among provinces and some jurisdictions have not come close to matching the 90 per cent figure.

Conciliators are appointed by the federal or provincial minister of labour, at the request of either one or both of the parties involved or at the discretion of the ministers. A conciliator is requested to submit a report to the minister within a specified time period. If conciliation fails, strikes or lockouts can legally commence, usually two weeks after the submission of the conciliator's report. Although labour relations legislation may include an option to have a conciliation board meet with the parties, this is used infrequently.

Mediation
Process whereby disputing parties choose voluntarily to reconcile their differences through a third party.

With reference to *mediation*, often a mediator will meet separately with each bargaining team, especially when the negotiations take place in a hostile atmosphere. Effective mediation requires a high degree of sensitivity, patience, and expertise in the psychology of negotiation.

ADMINISTERING THE COLLECTIVE AGREEMENT

UPON RATIFICATION by union members and approval by management, the parties begin living with the collective agreement. What happens if the parties have a disagreement regarding the interpretation of a term of the agreement? As discussed below, alleged violations of the agreement typically go through the grievance procedure. A *grievance* is defined as a complaint by an employee or employer that alleges that some aspect of a collective agreement has been violated. Almost every collective agreement in Canada contains some type of formalized procedure for resolving disputes. Furthermore, all jurisdictions (except Saskatchewan) require that a grievance that cannot be resolved between the parties be submitted to an arbitrator or arbitration board whose decision is final and binding.

Grievance Procedures

While either management or the union may file a grievance when the collective agreement is violated, most decisions are made by management. There are considerably fewer opportunities for the union to break the agreement and cause a grievance to be initiated by management. Consequently, most grievances are filed by the union.

Grievance procedure
A formal procedure outlined in the collective agreement to resolve grievances.

The *grievance procedure* consists of an ordered series of steps. Figure 16-16 describes the steps through which an employee's grievance typically passes. An example further explains how grievances arise and are settled:

> Hanson Environment Services had an internal opening for the job of service representative. The job required making house calls to repair home air conditioners and heaters sold by the company. Only two employees applied for the job. The contract with the International Brotherhood of Electrical Workers stated: "Promotions are made on the basis of seniority, provided ability is equal." Mr. Hanson, the owner, selected the second most senior employee for the promotion.

> When Rick West found out he did not get the job even though he had more seniority, he talked with his supervisor. The supervisor said, "It is Mr. Hanson's decision. But you didn't get the job because you use profanity. We can't have you swearing in some customer's home. We would lose too much business."

> Together, Rick and the union representative wrote up a formal grievance and submitted it to the supervisor. Although the supervisor had two days to review the complaint before making a written decision, he handed it back to Rick immediately with "Denied" written across it. Then the union submitted the complaint to the shop manager, which was the next step in the procedure. The result was the same. Finally, the grievance was taken to Mr. Hanson. He, as owner of the business, explained his fear of losing business over Rick's profanity and denied the grievance.

> Finally, the union requested that the issue be submitted to arbitration and that a single arbitrator be chosen. Management agreed to that. The arbitrator ruled that management had no evidence that Mr. West ever used profanity in the presence of customers, and that the mere assumption he would do so was not sufficient grounds for denying his promotion.

FIGURE 16-16

Typical Steps in a Union–Management Grievance Procedure

- Preliminary discussion. The aggrieved employee discusses the complaint with the immediate supervisor with or without a union representative. At this stage, or at any other step in the process, management may resolve the grievance to the satisfaction of the union or the union may decide to drop the grievance. Otherwise, the grievance proceeds to the next step in the process.

- Step 1. The complaint is put in writing and formally presented by the shop steward to the first-level supervisor. Normally, the supervisor must respond in writing within a contractually specified time period, usually two to five days.

- Step 2. The chief steward takes the complaint to the department superintendent. A written response is required, usually within a week.

- Step 3. The complaint is submitted to the plant manager/chief administrative officer by the union plant or grievance committee. Again, a written response is typically required.

- Step 4. If Step 3 does not solve the dispute, arrangements are made for an arbitrator or an arbitration board to settle the matter.

The number of steps in the grievance procedure and the staff involved at each step will vary from organization to organization but most grievance procedures have between three and five steps. The purpose of a multistep grievance procedure is to allow higher-level managers and union representatives to look at the issue from different perspectives and to assess the consequences of pursing the matter further. This approach increases the chance that the dispute gets resolved without going to arbitration.

Handling Grievances

Once a grievance has been filed, management should seek to resolve it fairly and quickly. Failure to do so can be seen as a disregard for employee needs and is not conducive to building and maintaining effective labour relations and the day-to-day administration of the collective agreement. However, in resolving grievances, management should consider several issues. Most important, grievances should be settled on their merits. Political considerations by either party weaken the grievance system. Complaints need to be carefully investigated and decided on the facts. Second, the cause of each grievance should be recorded. Many grievances coming from one or two departments may indicate poor supervision, personality conflicts, or a lack of understanding of the contract. Third, the final solution to the grievance needs to be explained to those affected. Even though union leaders usually do this, management should not fail to explain its reasoning to the worker.[41]

Arbitration

All jurisdictions, with the exception of Saskatchewan, require that collective agreements include a provision for final settlement by arbitration, without stoppage of work, of all differences concerning the interpretation or administration of a contract. This means that as long as a collective agreement is in force, any strike or lockout is illegal. An arbitrator may be selected from a list provided by the appropriate ministry of labour or the parties may agree to the selection of an arbitrator. The arbitrator's decision is final and cannot be changed or revised, except in rare instances (such as corruption, fraud, or a breach of natural justice).[42] There is growing concern that the arbitration process is becoming too costly, too slow (some cases take two years or more to be resolved), and too legalistic.[43]

Arbitration
The resolution of a dispute relating to the interpretation of a clause in the collective agreement.

Arbitration holds two potential problems for labour relations practitioners: costs and unacceptable solutions. An arbitration case can cost both the union and employer several thousand dollars. There are also time commitment costs in terms of preparing for arbitration, attending the actual hearings, and case follow-up. From the perspective of management, a potential problem occurs when an arbitrator renders a decision that is against management's best interest. Since the ruling is binding, it may alter drastically management's rights and set a precedent for future cases. Suppose, for example, that management lays off several hundred workers, and the union convinces an arbitrator that management did not follow the contract's layoff procedure. The arbitrator may rule that all workers get their jobs back with back pay. Or if an arbitrator accepts the union's argument of extenuating circumstances in a disciplinary case, those extenuating circumstances may be cited in future cases. For example, consider what happened in a chain of convenience markets:

> The Quick Foods Market had a policy that stealing from the company was grounds for immediate discharge. Brandon Brown, a new employee, took a sandwich from the cooler and ate it without paying. He was discharged when caught by the store manager. The union argued that Brandon should get a second chance since he was a new employee. The arbitrator ruled in favour of management but added that discharge for such a minor theft might be too harsh a penalty if Brandon had not been a probationary employee.

This ruling implies that the judgment may have been different had a senior employee been caught stealing. The union may then use this argument to argue that discharge is an inappropriate penalty. There is a possibility that a different arbitrator may agree.

It is important for human resource specialists to seek a solution with the union before arbitration. In this manner, both parties avoid additional costs, delays, and the possibility of an unsatisfactory decision. When arbitration is unavoidable, human resource specialists should follow the guidelines in Figure 16-17. These suggestions offer the best chance of winning a favourable decision. If these guidelines reveal serious flaws with the party's case, settling the case before arbitration is usually advisable.

Contract Provisions

Every collective agreement contains specific terms and provisions. A number of the most common ones are listed in Figure 16-18. These clauses are important because they define the rights and obligations of the employer and the union. For instance,

FIGURE 16-17

Preparation Guidelines for Arbitration Hearings

1. Study the original grievance and review its history through every step of the grievance procedure.

2. Determine the arbitrator's role. It might be found, for instance, that while the original grievance contains many elements, the arbitrator is restricted by the contract to resolving only certain aspects.

3. Review the collective bargaining agreement from beginning to end. Often, other clauses may be related to the grievance.

4. Assemble all documents and papers you will need at the hearing. Where feasible, make copies for the arbitrator and the other party. If some of the documents you need are in the possession of the other party, ask in advance that they be brought to the arbitration.

5. Make plans in advance if you think it will be necessary for the arbitrator to visit the plant or job site for on-the-spot investigation. The arbitrator should be accompanied by representatives of both parties.

6. Interview all witnesses. Make certain that they understand the whole case, and the importance of their own testimony and the arbitration process.

7. Make a written summary of what each witness will say. This serves as a useful checklist at the hearing to make certain nothing is overlooked.

8. Study the case from the other side's point of view. Be prepared to answer the opposing evidence and arguments.

9. Discuss your outline of the case with others in your organization. A fresh viewpoint will often disclose weak spots or previously overlooked details.

10. Read as many articles and published awards as you can on the general subject matter in dispute. While awards by other arbitrators for other parties have no binding precedent value, they may help clarify the thinking of parties and arbitrators alike.

Source: *Labour Arbitrators Procedures and Techniques*, New York: American Arbitration Association, 1972, pp. 15–16. Courtesy of American Arbitration Association 2001.

FIGURE 16-18

Common Provisions in Union–Management Agreements

- Union recognition. Normally near the beginning of a contract, this clause states management's acceptance of the union as the sole representative of designated employees.

- Union security. To ensure that the union maintains members as new employees are hired and present employees quit, a union security clause is commonly demanded by the union. Common forms of union security include:

  a. Union shop. All new workers must join the union shortly after being hired.

  b. Agency shop/Dues check-off. All new workers must pay to the union an amount equal to dues, but are not required to join the union.

  c. Check-off. Upon authorization, management agrees to deduct the union dues from each union member's paycheque and transfer the monies to the union.

- Wage rates. The amount of wages to be paid to workers (or classes of workers) is specified in the wage clause.

- Cost of living. Unions may negotiate automatic wage increases for workers when price levels go up. For example, a common approach is for wages to go up based on an increase in the consumer price index above some specified amount.

- Insurance benefits. This section specifies which insurance benefits the employer provides and how much the employer contributes toward these benefits. Frequently included benefits are life and supplemental hospitalization insurance and dental plans.

- Pension benefits. The amount of retirement income, years of service required, penalties for early retirement, employer and employee contributions, and vesting provisions are described in this section if a pension plan exists.

- Income maintenance. To provide workers with economic security, some contracts give guarantees of minimum income or minimum work. Other income maintenance provisions include severance pay and supplements to employment insurance.

- Time-off benefits. Vacations, holidays, rest breaks, wash-up periods, and leave-of-absence provisions typically are specified in this clause.

- Seniority clause. Unions seek contract terms that cause human resource decisions to be made on the basis of seniority. Often senior workers are given preferential treatment in job assignments, promotions, layoffs, vacation scheduling, overtime, and shift preferences.

- Management rights. Management must retain certain rights to do an effective job. These may include the ability to require overtime work, decide on promotions into management, design jobs, and select employees. This clause reserves to management the right to make decisions that management thinks are necessary for the organization's success.

- Discipline. Prohibited employee actions, penalties, and disciplinary procedures are either stated in the contract or included in the agreement by reference to those documents that contain the information.

- Dispute resolution. Disagreements between the union and management are resolved through procedures specified in the contract.

- Duration of agreement. Union and management agree on a time period during which the collective agreement is in force.

union security is a very important issue from the union's perspective. In addition, some of the most frequent disputes concern seniority and discipline.

Union Security

Can an employee be required to join a union as a condition of employment? An employer and union can negotiate clauses dealing with union security and, in some jurisdictions, compulsory dues checkoff is required.

The highest form of union security is the *closed shop,* which requires an employee to be a union member prior to obtaining employment. The closed shop, which is frequently operated through a hiring hall, is common in construction and longshore industries.

Under a **union shop** security arrangement, the employer is free to hire an individual but as a condition of employment the new hire must join the union within a specified period of time after being hired. If the individual refuses to join the union, the employer is required to terminate the worker's employment.

Dues check-off, which is a very common provision in collective agreements, requires an employer to deduct union dues at source from the wages of an employee and remit the funds to the union. However, the employee is not required to join the union. In some jurisdictions, dues check-off clauses must be negotiated; in other jurisdictions, compulsory dues check-off is enshrined in law.

While the amount of dues varies, it is typically in the range of about one per cent of an employee's earnings. Almost 85 per cent of workers covered by a collective agreement are subject to a dues check-off requirement.[44] Some jurisdictions allow workers who object to joining a union on the basis of religious grounds to pay the equivalent amount to a registered charity.

Dues check-off clauses can take several forms. Of particular note is the *Rand Formula,* which had its origins in a historical arbitration case decided by Judge Rand, a former Chief Justice of the Supreme Court of Canada. Judge Rand recognized that union representation benefits all bargaining unit members and, therefore, all members should be obligated to pay union dues.

In an *open shop,* an individual does not have to join the union and is not required to pay dues.

Seniority

Unions typically prefer to have employee-related decisions determined by the length of the worker's employment, called *seniority*. Seniority assures that promotions, overtime, layoffs, and other employee concerns are handled without favouritism. As well, the influence of seniority is not restricted to the union environment; several nonunion organizations also place considerable weight on seniority in making human resource decisions.

Seniority is often very important in deciding layoff rights. For example, when a company plans a layoff, the most recently hired workers are the first to go. The remaining employees probably receive higher wages if there is a premium for longevity. Thus, the higher-paid employees are retained, even though the layoff was probably needed to reduce costs. And these layoffs may undermine a company's employment equity plan, since employees hired through the employment equity program may have low seniority.

Discipline

Unions often challenge the discipline of a union member. Due to the difficulty of trying to list employee behaviours that may warrant discipline, many collective

---

Union shop
A union security provision in which employers may hire anyone they want, but all workers must join the union within a specified period.

Seniority
Length of the worker's employment, which may be used for determining order of promotion, layoffs, vacation, etc.

agreements provide the employer with the right to discipline or discharge if "just cause" exists. In any disciplinary action, management must abide by the terms of the collective agreement. Arbitration cases are frequently lost because management failed to establish grounds for disciplinary action, neglected to document past disciplinary procedures, and failed to adhere to the provisions of the collective agreement.

> One Monday, Georgia Green was late for work. She explained to her supervisor that her son was sick and therefore child-care arrangements delayed her. Sally, Georgia's supervisor, said, "Okay, but get here on time from now on. You know how strict my boss is." The following three days Georgia was late. The contract stated, "Any employee late four days in one month is subject to a two-day suspension without pay." On Thursday morning, Sally told Georgia to go home, citing the contract clause.
>
> Georgia told the union what had happened. The union complained that Georgia's sick child should be grounds for an exception. The human resource manager disagreed. When the union representative asked to see Georgia's file, it was discovered that Sally did not give Georgia a written warning after the second tardiness. Again, the contract was specific: "No worker can be given a suspension for tardiness or absenteeism unless a written notice is given after the second occurrence." Not surprisingly, the company had to pay Georgia for the two days she was off because the contract's procedure was not followed.

In deciding discipline and discharge cases, the starting point is the collective agreement. However, many collective agreements have a provision indicating that the employer must have "just cause" to discipline or discharge an employee. In determining just cause, a number of factors may be important:

- nature and seriousness of the offence;
- due process and procedure;
- past record of the grievor;
- seniority and age of the grievor;
- knowledge of rules;
- previous warnings from management;
- lax enforcement/condonation by management in the past;
- unequal treatment of employees;
- provocation by management;
- isolated incident; and
- sincere apology/remorse on the part of the grievor[45]

Past Practice

The actions of managers and union officials sometimes change the meaning of the agreement. Consider again the incident involving Georgia Green. Suppose the supervisor had failed to discipline Georgia. Or suppose that human resource management had been sympathetic to Georgia's problem and decided against approving the suspension. The result might be seen to set a precedent.

Precedent
A new standard that arises from the past practices of either the company or the union.

A *precedent* is a new standard that arises from the past practices of either party. Once a precedent results from unequal enforcement of disciplinary rules, the new standard may affect similar cases in the future. Then any other tardy employee with child-care problems might demand special treatment too. In time, it may become difficult for management to control tardiness because precedents have created exceptions to the rules. If the human resource manager felt that an exception in Georgia's case was appropriate, the union and the company can sign a letter stating that this exception is not a binding precedent. Then other employees cannot rely on Georgia's case to win exceptions from the rule.

The fear of past practices usually causes two changes in human resource policies and procedures. First, employee-related decisions are often centralized in the human resource department. Supervisors are stripped of their authority to make decisions on layoffs, discipline, and other employee matters. Instead, supervisors are required to make recommendations to the human resource department to ensure uniformity and consistency of application and to prevent precedents.

The other change is to increase the training of supervisors in the administration of the contract. The training is needed to ensure that supervisors administer the remaining portions of the contract uniformly. For example, if each supervisor applies a different standard to tardiness, some employees may be disciplined while others with more lenient supervisors may escape discipline. In time, the union might argue that unequal treatment makes it unfair to discipline those who are late. The enforcement of the contract terms by supervisors then can lead to damaging precedents. Through centralization and training, human resource departments create a more uniform enforcement of the contract to avoid such damaging precedents and ensure consistency of application and effective administration of the collective agreement.

Public Sector Bargaining

Public Service Staff Relations Act (PSSRA)
This act provides federal public servants with the choice of either to opt for compulsory arbitration or the right to strike.

When Parliament passed the ***Public Service Staff Relations Act (PSSRA)*** in 1967, it essentially gave federal civil servants bargaining rights similar to those granted workers in the private sector—usually the right to bargain for wages, hours, and certain working conditions. More important, it also gave them the right to strike. This is in contrast to civil servants in the United States, who since 1962 have had the right to bargain collectively, but not to withhold their services. Under the PSSRA, the methods of conflict resolution are different from those in the private sector. Before a bargaining agent can give notice that it wishes to bargain, a decision must be made as to whether a conciliation-strike procedure or a binding-arbitration procedure will be used should a deadlock occur. The union has the right to choose different procedures for each subsequent collective agreement. If the strike route has been chosen, conciliation procedures must be followed before a strike can begin.

Another difference from the private sector is that the law allows the employer to designate certain employees as performing essential services, thus divesting them of the right to strike. The union, however, may challenge the list of "designated employees," in which case the Public Service Staff Relations Board makes the final decision.

Provincial Legislation

A comparison of the federal and provincial legislation for public service labour relations reveals little uniformity of treatment across Canada. In Saskatchewan, the public sector is treated the same as the private sector (meaning there is no special legislation), whereas in Alberta, Ontario, Nova Scotia, and Newfoundland, there are different legal frameworks for the public and private sectors, with severe restrictions on or even total prohibition of strikes. The remaining provinces are somewhere in between.

HUMAN RESOURCE PRACTICES IN THE UNION ENVIRONMENT

WHILE THERE IS A SIGNIFICANT and growing body of information about human resource management from the perspective of the employer, very little attention has been paid to examining what human resource management practices are found within unionized workgroups.

At the organization level, there is often a difference in the types of human resource management practices that union and nonunion firms introduce into the workplace. Relative to nonunion organizations, union firms are:

- more likely to use formal job postings to advertise a job opening;

- less likely to conduct performance appraisals;

- less likely to use performance appraisal information in salary, promotion, and layoff decisions;

- more likely to use seniority as the primary factor in pay progression; and

- less likely to use profit sharing.[46]

A key issue for human resource management practitioners involves obtaining union involvement in managing change. Bob White, former President of the Canadian Labour Congress, had this to say about unions and change:

> For workers, change will be judged to be positive if higher productivity is shared in the form of better wages and benefits; if change results in more rather than less security of employment; if change gives workers access to new skills and opportunities; and if change improves the overall quality of working life in terms of the ability of workers to make a productive contribution.[47]

Human Resource Management and Bargaining Unit Employees

A recent survey of Canadian union officials investigated a number of human resource issues in the unionized environment. Concerning human resource management policies, union officials were asked to indicate whether a number of specific HRM programs or practices applied to bargaining unit employees. As revealed in Figure 16-19, most employees (94 per cent) were covered by a pension plan, approximately three-quarters of respondents had a sexual harassment policy, 68 per cent had an orientation program for new hires, 67 per cent had an employee assistance plan (EAP), and 50 per cent had a formal performance appraisal system. However, only 37 per cent of respondents reported that the employer shared business information with union members.

Union officials were also asked to indicate whether bargaining unit employees were involved in a number of specific team-based and incentive programs (see Figure 16-20). As the figure reveals, 27 per cent of the union locals reported having autonomous work teams, 24 per cent had quality circles and 28 per cent had quality of worklife programs. Somewhat more popular were employee/management joint programs (61 per cent) and problem-solving groups (45 per cent). Unions have generally stayed away from contingency compensation plans such as profit sharing, productivity sharing, and employee stock ownership plans; overall, less than 10 per cent of respondents reported having such plans.

While some unions and employers are adopting more flexible work systems, others are waging large-scale battles over flexibility at work. The unions at Fletcher

FIGURE 16-19

HRM Program Coverage Among Canadian Unions

Type of Program	% of Unions Indicating Program Applies to Members
Formal Performance Appraisal System	50
Employee Attitude Survey	24
Sharing of Business Information	37
Employee Pension Plan	94
Employee Assistance Plan (EAP)	67
Orientation Program	68
Sexual Harassment Policy	78
Drug Testing Policy	8
Job Descriptions	75
HRM/IR Department	69

Source: Terry H. Wagar, *Labour Management Relations in Canada: A Longitudinal Survey of Union Officials*, Saint Mary's University, 1998.

FIGURE 16-20

Team-Based and Incentive Programs Among Canadian Unions

Type of Program	% of Unions Indicating Program Applies to Members
Quality Circles	24
Quality of Work Life (QWL)	28
Problem Solving Groups	45
Autonomous Work Teams	27
EE/MGT Joint Programs	61
Profit Sharing	8
Productivity Sharing Plan	10
Group/Team Incentives	23
Employee Stock Ownership Program	8
Job Sharing	31
Job Enlargement/Enrichment	22
Total Quality Management	37

Source: Terry H. Wagar, *Labour Management Relations in Canada: A Longitudinal Survey of Union Officials*, Saint Mary's University, 1998.

Challenge Canada Limited went out on strike in opposition to the company's desire to increase flexible work practices:

> Fletcher Challenge demanded an unprecedented eight-year contract, job flexibility, the right to outsource work, and a 365-day-a-year work schedule. Government-appointed mediators recommended a six-year contract, year-round operation, full flexibility in assigning work, and a wage increase of five per cent in the first year and two per cent in each subsequent year of the agreement. However, the company said it could not accept the wage costs unless they can be offset by gains from competitive labour practices. As well, the unions rejected the mediators' report as being too much in favour of the company.

STRATEGIC IMPLICATIONS FOR HUMAN RESOURCE MANAGEMENT

IN NONUNION facilities, an implicit objective of management is often to remain nonunion. Employers frequently adopt either a *union suppression* or a *union substitution* approach in order to avoid unionization. The union suppression approach involves fighting union representation. An employer may try to intimidate workers, threaten closing or moving the plant or facility, or discriminate against union supporters.

> An employer in the food services industry heard that four of the workers were discussing unionization as a means of improving wages and working conditions. Senior management learned about the issue and decided to terminate six employees—the four union activists and two other employees who were considered poor performers. The termination notices were issued under the guise of incompetent work performance.

The union substitution approach examines what unions bring to the employment relationship and then tries to introduce such features into the nonunion workplace. This approach requires that human resource specialists (within the constraints of organizational effectiveness and efficiency, law, technology, and other challenges) carefully do the following:

- *Design* jobs that are personally satisfying to workers.

- *Develop* plans that maximize individual opportunities while minimizing the possibility of layoffs.

- *Select* workers who are qualified.

- *Establish* fair, meaningful, and objective standards of individual performance.

- *Train* workers and managers to enable them to achieve expected levels of performance.

- *Evaluate* and reward behaviour on the basis of actual performance.

- *Provide* employees with a "voice" in the workplace.

- *Implement* a compensation plan in which wages/salary and benefits parallel those available in the union sector.

In other words, human resource managers need to actively apply the ideas discussed in earlier chapters of this book. Failure to implement sound human resource policies and practices provides the motivation and justification for workers to form unions.

Dealing with Unions

When unions are present, the human resource function is changed. Organizationally, the human resource department is expanded by the addition of specialists in labour relations. Such individuals deal with such critical areas as negotiations and contract administration, while human resource professionals attend to their more traditional roles. Although some organizations establish separate *industrial relations* departments to deal with labour relations issues, industrial relations is often considered a subset of human resource management.

Unionization may be associated with greater centralization of employee record-keeping and discipline to ensure uniformity of application. This change can mean that line managers lose some of their authority to the human resource department. They also find their jobs more difficult because of the new rules imposed by the contract—while management has the right to act, the union may have the right, under the contract, to react to management's actions. In other words, line managers may become dissatisfied because their authority diminishes while their responsibility increases. These added responsibilities are likely to be imposed at the request of human resource professionals, who may need to monitor the work environment more closely and need more information from the line managers. For example, the line manager may have to compile new reports on absenteeism, tardiness, productivity, and comments voluntarily made by workers about the union (and a growing number of organizations are using computer technology to collect such information). Often these demands on supervisors create a fertile ground for friction between line managers and human resource staff members.

Besides the high costs for record-keeping, additional staff, negotiations, and occasional strikes, unionized employers have less freedom to make unilateral changes. No longer can a manager simply decide what is desirable and then make the change. Instead, collective agreement provisions and labour laws must also be considered.

At Toronto-Hydro, a new absenteeism plan reduced absences by 30 per cent. Management believed that an average absenteeism rate of 10 sick days a year per employee was simply too high. Work was not getting done and training sessions had to be postponed. According to the company:

> The direct cost of work not getting done was almost $2.8 million a year, with the equivalent of about 100 employees not being at work on a given day. There was a need to change the view of "cultural absenteeism"—that sick days were only to be used when an employee was ill. The new attendance management program spelled out the new policy, provided each employee with an absenteeism profile comparing the individual with the new standard, and required any employee exceeding the standard to meet with his or her supervisor and set goals for improving absenteeism.

The union refused to participate in the attendance management program. It believed that all members were getting painted with the same brush regardless of whether they abused the benefit or not. As well, the union argued that the program was a violation of the collective agreement and decided to grieve the action by management.[48]

Are Canadian employers becoming more anti-union? Since the early 1980s, there have been claims that employers are adopting a tougher stand against unions and engaging in more "union-busting" techniques. A study of 161 unionized employers conducted during the 1992 to 1994 period indicated that 53 per cent of employers reported a tougher bargaining stand over the past decade. However, only 11 per cent of organizations attempted to reduce or eliminate the influence of unions and only 17 per cent actively avoided further unionization.[49]

Labour-Management Cooperation

Some unions and employers are moving toward greater cooperation and there is increasing acceptance that labour and management must cooperate and work together if they are to survive and prosper in the highly competitive global economy.[50]

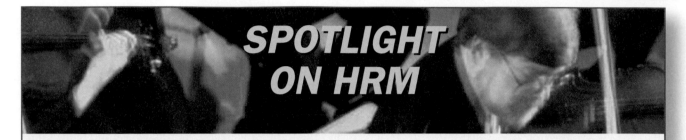

SPOTLIGHT ON HRM

FINDING COMMON INTERESTS: COMPANIES MOVE PAST LABOUR–MANAGEMENT SQUABBLES

When American Airlines bought into Canadian Airlines in 1993 to help Canadian through a severe cash flow problem, 700 mostly Vancouver-based management, clerical and service agent jobs were put on the chopping block.

To help staff adjust to job loss, a joint management-labour committee was struck to determine what services were needed and to find suppliers to provide them. The committee, made up of three management representatives as well as members from the Canadian Union of Autoworkers and the International Association of Machinists, developed an action plan that included a transition centre for displaced employees.

The corporation provided facilities, equipment and a computerized system to advertise job openings. Employees could use the centre for skills assessment, counselling services and advice on résumé writing. Both labour and management say the program has been a success, judging from numbers of employees using the centre and the volume of businesses seeking workers there.

This is one example of labour and company brass working together highlighted in a new Canadian Labour Market and Productivity Centre project. The national labour-business organization has produced a series of tools for unions and managers to assist them in tackling workplace change.

The package consists of two videos produced in partnership with TV Ontario that take a look at the lives of workers and managers in public and private sector organizations across Canada and offer training segments that lead viewers through the change process. Three booklets—one of which details 15 case studies—are also available to help workplace parties learn how to co-operate throughout the change process.

Some of the success stories from Canada's hospitals, provincial governments, blue-chip corporations and small businesses include:

- How a Lafarge Canada Inc. plant in Brookfield, N.S., introduced self-directed work teams and saved jobs at the cement production company;

- How LOF Glass of Collingwood, Ont., set up an Employee Initiative program aimed at getting workers' input on improving the automobile windshield and tail-light manufacturing outfit; and

- How the Westin Bayshore Hotel in Vancouver streamlined job classifications and duties to cross-train employees so they could provide better guest services.

"What's common to them is that both parties recognized that the best way to deal with a particular situation was a relatively collaborative approach versus an adversarial approach," said Derwyn Sangster, the project director at the CLMPC....

For many companies, the first step in bringing union and management together is to clear the air between the two. "In many cases their past relationship had not been a happy one," said Sangster. "Before they got into dealing with a particular change they had to get rid of some old baggage that if left untouched could erupt later and damage the process."

The major hurdle for many organizations profiled was creating trust, agreed Mary Porjes, a business representative on the CLMPC's workplace change task force.

"What we found when we looked at those workplaces that successfully implemented change was the trust that there was between management and labour," said Porjes, also a Toronto employment lawyer. "That to us seemed to be the prerequisite for the change process to happen successfully. That takes a lot of work and a lot of commitment by the stakeholders."

Source: Sharon Lebrun, "Finding Common Interests: Companies Move Past Labour–Management Squabbles," *Canadian HR Reporter*, May 19, 1997, p. 6. Copyright © 1997 by MPL Communications Inc. Reproduced by permission of , *Canadian HR Reporter* 133 Richmond St. W., Toronto, ON M5H 3M8.

There is growing evidence that organizational performance is enhanced when labour and management cooperate. For example, recent research using data from both employers and unions indicated that a more positive labour climate was associated with perceptions of higher productivity, enhanced product or service quality, and greater customer or client satisfaction.[51] However, cooperation is a very challenging process. As noted by David Haggard, national president of the Industrial Wood and Allied Workers of Canada:

> We realized that if we were going to survive as a trade union, we were going to have to get involved in the business of the organizations we work in. We have offered a market strategy to open up forestry market opportunities. And it's really for selfish reasons. If we don't do this, we will be downsized. It has not been easy. At one plant, the crew kicked out the entire union committee because they felt they were too close to management. A lot of our own people don't trust management.[52]

Obstacles to Cooperation

Industrial relations specialists often seek union cooperation to improve the organization's effectiveness. However, cooperation may not be politically attractive to union leaders who see little gain in cooperating with management. In fact, if leaders do cooperate, they may be accused by workers of forgetting the union's interests. These accusations can mean defeat by political opponents within the union. Thus, cooperation may not be in the union leader's best interest:

> In addition to political obstacles, union leaders may mistrust management. For example, bitter remarks during the organizing drive or arbitration case may convince union officials that human resource specialists are anti-union. Within this climate, cooperative gestures are often seen as tricks or gimmicks aimed at hurting the union. If cooperative proposals threaten the members or leaders, mistrust increases and cooperation usually fails.

While employers often have good reasons for seeking more cooperation with their unionized workforce, a number of cooperative programs have the underlying goal of increasing managerial domination in the workplace. As well, some employers use cooperation to "stress the system" by reducing employees or resources, giving workers more tasks, or speeding up the assembly line; such practices may dramatically increase the stress level of workers and dehumanize the workplace.[53]

Support for Cooperative Programs

In a recent study, employer and union participants were asked to indicate their perceptions of the degree of support for cooperative programs (using a six-point scale where 1 = no support and 6 = strong support for cooperative programs) for the five groups referred to in Figure 16-21. Although there was modest support for cooperative programs, one interesting finding was that employers perceived that the greatest opposition to cooperative programs came from national and international union leaders while union officials reported that management (supervisors and upper management) were most opposed to cooperative efforts.

Relationship-Restructuring Programs

A number of employers and unions are questioning whether the traditional approach to managing workplace conflict is too time-consuming and costly, results in lost productivity, and creates an environment of adversarial labour relations. As an alternative, some organizations and unions are using relationship-restructuring programs. Relationship-restructuring consists of three components:

FIGURE 16-21

Support for Cooperative Programs

Party of Interest	Average Response	
	Employers	Unions
Local Union Leaders	4.04	4.17
National/International Union Leaders	3.05	3.89
Local Union Members	4.09	3.67
Supervisors	4.00	3.17
Upper Management	4.40	3.26

Note: 6 point scale (1 = no support and 6 = strong support)

Source: Terry H. Wagar, *Employee Involvement, Strategic Management and Human Resources: Exploring the Linkages*, Wilfrid Laurier University, 1998; Terry H. Wagar, *Labour Management Relations in Canada: A Longitudinal Survey of Union Officials*, Saint Mary's University, 1998.

(1) Relationship Audit: the relationship audit involves collecting information about the organization, union and employees. Such information may include grievance complaints, absenteeism records, organization policies, and conflict resolution structures. It is also important to collect information from individuals (employer and union representatives) who can impact on the building of the relationship.

(2) Identification of Problems: once information is collected, it is necessary to identify problems and concerns. These may include communication deficiencies, inappropriate or ineffective policies or procedures, personal conflicts, unclear objectives or goals, and changes in corporate culture.

(3) Development of a Plan: the final step involves the implementation of a plan to address the problem areas. Getting "buy-in" from both labour and management is essential if the program is to succeed. Other important considerations include resource issues, sharing of information, developing priorities and a schedule for implementation, and on-going monitoring the success of the plan.[54]

Cooperative Methods

Cooperative methods
Techniques used to improve relations between the employer and the union and to facilitate cooperation.

Once human resource specialists realize the political concerns and suspicions of union leaders, several **cooperative methods** can be tried.[55] These techniques are summarized in Figure 16-22 and explained in the following paragraphs.

One of the most basic actions is *prior consultation* with the union. Not every management decision must be approved by the union. But actions that affect unionized employees may result in a grievance unless explained before the action is taken.

In one manufacturing organization, the employer introduced radically new production technology. However, before doing so, the employer met with the union, explained the reason for the change being made, indicated that the change would not result in the loss of any union jobs, and set up a joint committee to study how best to implement the new technology.

Human resource specialists can also build cooperation through a *sincere concern* for employees. This concern may be shown through the prompt settlement of

FIGURE 16-22

Methods of Building Labour–Management Cooperation

Managers and human resource specialists can build cooperation between the employer and the union through:

- *Prior consultation* with union leaders to defuse problems before they become formal grievances.

- *Sincere concern* for employee problems and welfare even when management is not obligated to do so by the collective agreement.

- *Training programs* that objectively communicate the intent of union and management bargainers and reduce biases and misunderstandings.

- *Joint study committees* that allow management and union officials to find solutions to common problems.

- *Third parties* who can provide guidance and programs that bring union leaders and managers closer together to pursue common objectives.

grievances, regardless of who wins. Or management can bargain sincerely with the union to reduce the need for a strike. As well, employers can establish programs (such as *employee assistance programs* and job counselling) that assist employees who are experiencing personal difficulties.

Training programs are another way to build cooperation. After a new contract is signed, the human resource department often trains just managers. The union does the same for its leaders. The result is that both sides continue their biases and misunderstandings. If human resource management sponsors training for both the union and management, a common understanding of the contract is more likely to be brought about. The training can be as simple as taking turns paraphrasing the contract. Or outside neutrals can be hired to do the training. Either way, supervisors and union officials end the training with a common understanding of the contract and a new basis for cooperation.

When a complex problem confronts the union and employer, *joint study committees* are sometimes formed. For example, one organization recently set up a joint committee with its union to establish a policy on sexual harassment. Other employers use joint study committees to address such issues as workplace rules, quality of work life, technological change, budget reduction strategies, and safety.

A final method of building cooperation is through the use of *third parties*, such as consultants or government agencies, who may act as change agents or catalysts to cooperation. For example, in Nova Scotia the provincial government has established and delivers a variety of joint union-management programs (including grievance mediation, joint supervisor-steward training, and labour-management committees) with the goal of increasing cooperation in the workplace.

There is no single best approach to building cooperation. Since each relationship is unique, the methods used will depend upon the situation. But if human resource and industrial relations professionals can build more cooperative relations with their unions, the employer gains higher productivity. In turn, there are more resources against which the union and its members can make demands. Improving union management relations, therefore, is a potentially significant role that can be played by human resource departments in unionized organizations.

SUMMARY

The labour management framework consists of unions, government, and management. Although each union is unique, unions share the common objectives of protecting and improving their members' wages, hours, and working conditions. To further these objectives, the union movement has created local, national, and international structures, plus federations at the provincial and federal levels.

In Canada, the federal government has jurisdiction in labour relations matters over Crown corporations, airlines, most railways, communication companies, and federal government agencies—or approximately 10 per cent of the labour force. All other organizations fall under the jurisdiction of the provinces, which have enacted separate but similar legislation.

Unionization often occurs when workers perceive the need for a union as a response to unsatisfactory treatment by management. During the organizing process, management's response is limited severely by laws and employee reactions. The employer's primary defence is sound policies implemented by competent supervisors before unionization begins.

If workers form a union, federal or provincial law requires management and the union to bargain in good faith. The success of the employer at the bargaining table is affected by its actions before negotiations begin. Negotiations with the union usually result in a "collective agreement" that must be approved by union members and top management. Once negotiated, the collective agreement is administered by the union and management.

In administering the agreement, human resource specialists face several challenges. For example, contract clauses place limits on management, day-to-day administration of the contract can lead to precedents, and limitations often result from the resolution of disputes through the grievance procedure or arbitration.

Although unions may represent the employees, management remains ultimately responsible for obtaining organizational performance and effectively utilizing the human resources. Through prior consultation, sincere concern for employees, training programs, joint study committees, or third parties, human resource specialists can lay the foundations of a cooperative union-management relationship.

TERMS FOR REVIEW

Visit the Web site at www.mcgrawhill.ca/college/schwind6 for a full glossary.

REVIEW AND DISCUSSION QUESTIONS

1. In your own words, summarize the primary objectives of unions.

2. What distinguishes craft, industrial, and mixed unions from each other?

3. What roles does the Labour Relations Board serve in labour management relations?

4. In preparing to negotiate an agreement with a union, what types of information would you gather before arriving at the bargaining table?

5. If you were asked to explain why various types of people are on the employer's bargaining team, what reasons would you give for (a) the company lawyer, (b) the director of industrial relations, (c) a wage and salary specialist, (d) a benefit specialist, and (e) the assistant plant manager?

6. Since grievance procedures are found in most contracts, both managers and unions must want them. Explain why both managers and unions want grievance procedures.

CRITICAL THINKING QUESTIONS

1. "Unions do not happen, they are caused by management." Do you agree or disagree with this statement? Why?

2. If you had to advise the manager of a small chain of bakeries how to prepare for a possible strike, what would you suggest?

3. Suppose an employee in your department is an active member of the union, but is performing improperly. After several sessions with the employee, performance is still unacceptable. What type of support would you want to gather before you terminated that employee? What legal complications might result from your action?

4. If you worked in the human resource department of a small company that is suddenly unionized, what changes would you expect to occur in the human resource department?

5. What role do you think federal and provincial governments will play in future labour management relations? What actions can unions and management take to reduce the probability of future government involvement?

6. Obtain a copy of two different collective agreements. Compare and contrast the contract items and the grievance procedure.

WEB RESEARCH

1. Visit the Web site of the International Labour Organization (www.ilo.org). What are the major objectives of the ILO? What are some of the major issues affecting workers around the world?

2. Go to the Web site for the Canadian Labour Congress (www.clc-cta.ca). Also visit the Web site for a provincial federation of labour (for instance, the Nova Scotia Federation of Labour). Compare and contrast the functions of the two federations. What similarities and differences exist? What assistance do the federations provide to organized labour?

INCIDENT 16-1

A Routine Discharge at ITC

Four months ago, Pete Ross was discharged from ITC. The supervisor requested that the human resource department discharge Pete because he was caught drinking alcohol in the employee locker room. Drinking on company property was prohibited, as it had been since publication of the ITC Employees' Handbook in 1971.

All employees of ITC were given a copy, and whenever new employees joined, as had Pete in 1984, they too were given one as part of the orientation program. The handbook stated in part: "The consumption of alcoholic beverages on company premises is grounds for immediate termination...."

The discharge appeared rather routine to the human resource manager and to the plant manager. Although drinking violations were uncommon, the plant manager believed clear-cut violations of company policy should be punished. Besides, he was frequently heard to say, "We must support our first-line managers."

Pete's fellow machinists did not see it as a "routine discharge." John Briggs, a fellow machinist, summed up the group's feelings: "Pete was a darn good machinist. He was seldom tardy, never absent, and always did a first-class job. If Pete did it, it was done right! That bugged George [the supervisor] because George would pressure Pete to get out the work and say, Don't worry about the quality; they only measure quantity.' But Pete wasn't slow. He'd turn out a quality product as fast as some people turned out junk. I don't think George liked Pete. I don't know if Pete took a drink before leaving the plant Wednesday evening, but I think George just wanted to can Pete."

The following Monday, John Briggs spent his rest breaks and lunch hour talking with the other machinists, telling them that "if we don't want to end up like Pete, we'd better get a union." He even had cards from the International Association of Machinists Union. By Monday evening, Briggs had thirty-two signed cards. There were 39 machinists in the shop.

On Tuesday morning, John Briggs was called into the supervisor's office. The plant manager and the supervisor grilled him. They asked him if he had been distributing authorization cards, who had signed them, and how many he had obtained. Briggs simply replied by saying, "That is none of your business." The plant manager adjourned the meeting without saying a word.

On Thursday (payday at ITC), Briggs received a termination notice with his paycheque. The notice was effective immediately. The notice said termination was for low productivity and excessive absences during the previous 12 months.

1. What unfair labour practices may have occurred?
2. Should management offer reinstatement to Pete Ross or John Briggs?
3. Was Briggs correct when he answered, "That is none of your business" to the questions about the authorization cards?

INCIDENT 16-2

The Reindeer Lake Paper Mill

The Reindeer Lake Paper Mill in Saskatchewan has been plagued with numerous problems since it began operations in 1992. Two years ago, the Canadian Paper Workers Union was successful in organizing the workers and negotiating a three-year collective agreement. After two years of operation under the agreement, human resource problems were growing worse; there were several illegal walkouts by small groups of workers to protest unresolved grievances. Management decided not to prosecute the employees although the wildcat strikes disrupted production.

Now, the human resource director expects a strike at the expiration of the collective agreement, because of low wages and unpleasant working conditions. The workers are claiming that inflation has exceeded the limited wage increases granted in the collective agreement. In addition, although working conditions meet federal and provincial health and safety regulations, the workers complain that heat, smell, and humidity in the plant make working very uncomfortable, especially during the summer months.

1. This case suggests several changes that should be made in the next collective agreement, given the company's past experiences. What changes do you think the human resource department should recommend?

2. What actions could the human resource department undertake immediately to reduce the problems that exist between workers and the company?

3. If management decided to implement the changes you suggest, what actions should be taken to win the support of union leaders?

CASE STUDY

Absenteeism at Maple Leaf Shoes

Another busy day for Jane Reynolds, Special Assistant to the Human Resource Manager. Pat Lim, the General Manager of Marketing (who has also assumed responsibility for the human resource function), had sent yet another memo to Jane.

First things first. Jane decided that resolving the Feltham grievance was her first priority. While she recognized the importance of developing a good attendance policy, that would take some time. At 11:00 a.m., Jane met with the employee, Glenda Feltham, and her union steward, Shaun Robberman. The facts of the Feltham grievance are reported below.

The Feltham Grievance

Ms. Glenda Feltham, who is 32 years of age, has worked at Maple Leaf Shoes for six years. During the past year, as a result of family and health problems, she was absent or late on a number of occasions. The collective agreement between Maple Leaf Shoes and the union does not specifically address the issue of absence from work; it merely states that "no employee may be given a written reprimand or written warning, or be suspended, demoted or dismissed unless the employer has just cause."

The absenteeism policy at Maple Leaf Shoes, which was developed several years ago as a joint effort between union and management, requires the application of progressive discipline for offences involving tardiness or absenteeism. The policy also provides for "wiping the slate clean" if an employee's attendance is satisfactory for a one-year period. Both union and management acknowledge that, at times over the years, the policy has not been strictly enforced. However, four months ago Maple Leaf management notified the union that it would strictly enforce the policy.

A review of Glenda Feltham's file showed that she has received the following disciplinary penalties:

Fourteen months ago—oral warning for being 22 minutes late.

Memorandum—Maple Leaf Shoes

To: Jane Reynolds

From: Pat Lim

Re: Absenteeism Case / Absenteeism Policy

Dear Jane:

As you are aware, we're having trouble with absenteeism at the plant. Could you look into the following grievance involving Glenda Feltham, discuss it with the union, and see if we can resolve it?

Also, the problem is much deeper than simply a single grievance. Please review the relevant part of the collective agreement and the absenteeism policy that we developed some years ago with the union. Meet with the union and see if we can put together a more proactive policy.

Don't hesitate to contact me if you need my assistance.

Regards,

Pat

Nine months ago—written warning for being absent for two days. Glenda failed to call in sick or provide any explanation for her absence upon returning to work.

Seven months ago—one-day suspension for being 1 hour and 14 minutes late.

Six months ago—five-day suspension for being absent for one day. Again, Glenda failed to call in sick or explain the reason for her absence.

It appeared that the five-day suspension alerted Glenda to the fact that unexplained absenteeism and lateness are not acceptable behaviours at Maple Leaf Shoes. After this suspension, Glenda was not late or absent for almost six months. However, one week ago, Glenda failed to show up at work or call in sick. When her supervisor called Glenda's home, no one answered. The next day, Glenda called in sick, but was reportedly seen that afternoon entering a local fitness club. The following day, Glenda showed up for work, met with her supervisor, and explained that her absence was due to the fact that her boyfriend of six years told her that he was moving out of their apartment and ending their relationship. She said that she was so upset she couldn't face coming to work or trying to explain her absence over the telephone.

Instructions:

Ask students to assume the role of management representatives (Jane Reynolds' perspective) or union repre-

sentatives (Shaun Robberman's perspective). The first objective is to ask the parties to meet and try to negotiate a resolution to the Glenda Feltham grievance.

The Policy on Absenteeism

Prior to meeting with the union to address the development of a new policy on absenteeism, Jane reviewed the absence records for the plant. She found that, on average, employees missed about 7.9 days a year. A recent consulting report for the industry indicated that the absence rate for the industry as a whole was 6.7 days a year. Jane realized that the number of absences varied among individuals, but still she was troubled by the high absenteeism rate at the Maple Leaf plant.

A review of the absenteeism policy indicated that the policy was very short and had not been updated in several years. The policy read as follows:

1. The need for managing absenteeism is recognized by both the employer and union. While some absence from work is unavoidable, management is concerned that an employee absence creates more work for other employees. Management also believes that it is important to acknowledge both healthy and sick employees.

2. In instances of absenteeism or lateness, the employer will apply principles of progressive discipline. If an employee is able to maintain a satisfactory attendance record for one year, all previous disciplinary infractions relating to attendance issues will be removed from the employee's file.

3. Management has the right to discipline employees for "excessive absenteeism." In the event that an employee will be late for work or absent from work, the employee is required to make a reasonable effort to contact the employer and indicate that he or she will be late or not present at work. Upon returning to work, the employee is required to provide an explanation for his or her lateness or absence. Depending on the circumstances, the employee may be asked to provide a doctor's note in support of the explanation.

Instructions:

The second objective of the case involves the joint meeting of union and management representatives in order to develop a new policy on absenteeism. Students should work in two groups—management and union—and work on developing a new policy. Several sources on the Internet are extremely helpful when developing an absenteeism policy.

CASE STUDY

Labour-Management Relations: CPIB and the Maple Leaf Trust Acquisition

The acquisition of Maple Leaf Trust has given Mary Keddy, senior vice president—human resources, some cause for concern. She has assigned two senior human resource management employees to review labour relations at Maple Leaf, with a particular focus on the Credit Card Centre, located in Mississauga, Ontario. The Credit Card Centre, which has been unionized for about four years, has had some labour turmoil since the certification of the Canadian Union of Bank Employees (CUBE). Negotiations for a first contract were very difficult but Maple Leaf Trust and CUBE were able to reach a two-year agreement without resorting to strike action. About 18 months ago, the parties negotiated a second contract (also two years in duration) that was settled after a short (two-day) strike. Approximately 285 unionized workers are employed at the Credit Card Centre, performing a variety of clerical and administrative tasks. Keddy believes that successful integration of the Credit Card Centre employees is very important but represents a major challenge to the human resources department.

A few weeks ago, Keddy met with the Pat Jameson, the human resource manager responsible for labour relations issues at the Credit Card Centre. In addition to discussing the adversarial relationship between labour and management, Keddy was able to obtain some data addressing labour relations issues at the Credit Card Centre. This information is summarized below.

Over the four years that the Credit Card Centre was unionized, employee grievances have increased by about 12 per cent a year. Jameson echoed the concern of the company with respect to the amount of time being spent by company officials, union representatives, and employees in contract negotiations and administering the collective agreement. According to Jameson, "During contract negotiations, we met with the union bargaining team on a weekly basis. Each meeting was a good six or seven hours, and it took us almost four months to ultimately hammer out a contract. Things were further complicated by the strike, and we also spent three days in conciliation. Furthermore, we seem to be spending way too much time dealing with grievances. While our wages are competitive, the morale at the Credit Card Centre is low and turnover is clearly a problem."

A review of company records revealed the following grievance pattern:

Total grievances filed:	398

Number settled at:

Step 1—First-level supervisor stage	55
Step 2—Second-level supervisor stage	232
Step 3—Senior HR manager stage	104
Arbitration	7

While some of the grievances involved more than one issue, most of them were single-issue matters. The breakdown of grievances based on the type of issue was also available:

Grievance issues:

Lateness or absenteeism	154
Overtime allocation	88
Other discipline or discharge	34
Job scheduling	67
Job posting	22
Multiple-issue disputes	33

Jameson also provided Keddy with the results of a recent survey of managers and employees at the Credit Card Centre. All of the managers and 266 of the 285 unionized employees completed the survey. The survey was conducted by a Toronto consultant and was supported by both the company and union (with the understanding that the completed survey forms would go directly to the consultant and the survey results would be provided in summary form to both the company and union). As Jameson noted, "We didn't think the union would cooperate, and we needed them on board in order to survey the unionized workers. I'm getting a sense that both management and the union are getting concerned about the impact of the negative labour relations climate on our ability to compete. And this is even more of an issue since we are now a part of CPIB." Some of the initial findings from the survey are provided below.

1. Assume that you are one of the two senior HRM employees assigned to examining labour relations at the Credit Card Centre. Review the above material for Mary Keddy and briefly summarize your major findings.

2. What specific recommendations would you give Mary? Are there any programs or initiatives that you would suggest?

Initial Results from the Labour-Management Survey

PART A:

Workplace Performance Measures	Average Management Response	Average Union Response
Workplace Productivity	3.66	3.54
Service Quality	3.78	3.45
Union Member Morale	3.64	2.43
Union Member Job Satisfaction	3.75	2.38
Quality of Union Member/ Supervisor Relations	3.98	2.93

Note: each of these questions was measured on a 5 point scale (1 = very low; 5 = very high).

PART B:

Labour Climate Measures	Average Management Response	Average Union Response
Grievances are settled promptly	4.01	2.87
The working conditions are fair	4.22	3.21
The parties cooperate to solve problems	3.88	2.63
The parties share information	3.66	2.44
The relationship is adversarial	2.94	4.09

Note: each of these questions was measured on a five-point scale (1 = strongly disagree; 5 = strongly agree).

SUGGESTED READINGS

Adams, George, *Canadian Labour Law* (2nd ed.), Aurora, ON: Canada Law Book, 2000.

Brown, Donald J.M. and David Beatty, *Canadian Labour Arbitration*, 3rd. ed., Aurora, ON.: Canada Law Book, 2000.

Craig, Alton W.J. and Norman A. Solomon, *The System of Industrial Relations in Canada*, 5th. ed., Scarborough, ON: Prentice Hall, 1996.

Fisher, Roger, William Ury and Bruce Patton, *Getting to Yes*, 2nd. ed., New York: Penguin, 1991.

Godard, John, *Industrial Relations*, Toronto, ON: McGraw-Hill Ryerson, 1994.

Gunderson, Morley, Allen Ponak and Daphne Gottlieb Taras, *Union-Management Relations in Canada*, 4th. ed., Toronto, ON: Addison Wesley Longman, 2001, p. 11.

Peirce, Jon, *Canadian Industrial Relations*, Scarborough, ON: Prentice Hall, 2000.

Swimmer, Gene, *Public Sector Labour Relations in an Era of Restraint and Restructuring*, Toronto, ON: Oxford University Press, 2000.

Walton, Richard E., Joel E. Cutcher-Gershenfeld, and Robert B. McKersie, *Strategic Negotiations: A Theory of Change in Labor Management Relations*, Boston, MA: Harvard Business School Press, 1994.

Part Seven 7

Strategy Evaluation

A human resource department must not become content with its performance. It must proactively search for new ways to help the organization and its people. One way is through an audit of its activities. The research findings from an audit point to opportunities for improvement. Another way to help the firm and its people is to anticipate future challenges. As a manager or human resource professional, audits give you feedback on how you perform, and so they may change the way you manage in the future.

Review and Evaluation of Human Resource Strategies

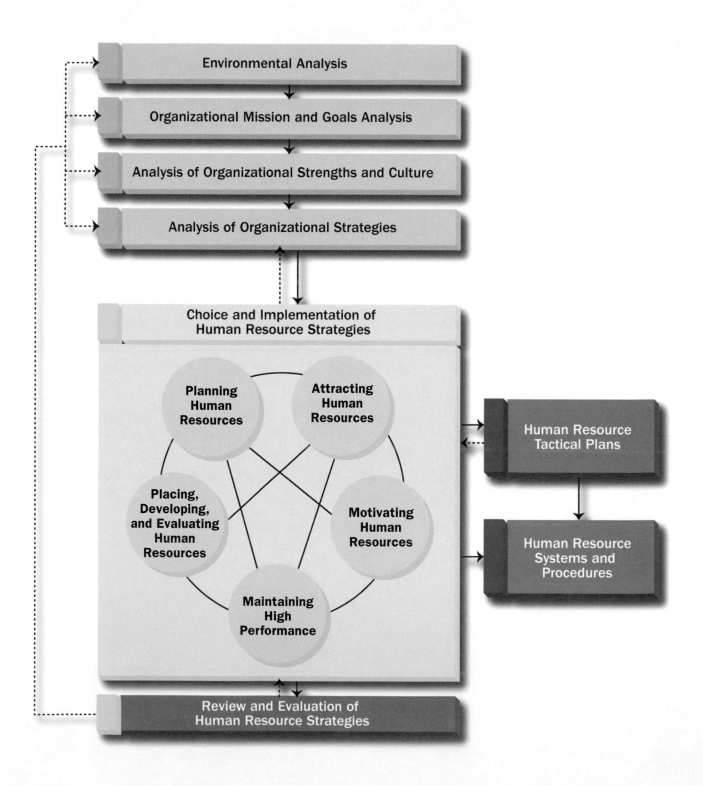

Chapter 17

Human Resource Auditing

"There is a new phenomenon sweeping the globe—a battle for the best in business talent. While some see it as a fight to attract high performers to their firms, the street smart know it is something entirely different: having the ability to hold onto the people you want to keep (and only those you want to keep) for longer than your competitors. To paraphrase Rudyard Kipling, 'If you can keep your heads when all around are losing theirs, then you are a manager, my son'."

—**Mike Johnson**[1]

CHAPTER OBJECTIVES

After studying this chapter, you should be able to:

- ■ *Discuss* the strategic importance of a human resource audit.

- ■ *Describe* the steps and research tools used in a human resource audit.

- ■ *Discuss* how a human resource department should prepare for the future.

How could Hudson's Bay have possibly let Wal-Mart steal a march on it? Why did Eaton's, which once dominated Canadian retail business, end up declaring bankruptcy? Why is Pan Am, which was one of the major world airlines 50 years ago, just a memory today?

No single answer can explain the failure of the once-successful organizations. Two writers suggested that all these failures share one underlying cause: a failure to reflect.[2] Organizations, particularly successful ones, are so caught up in carrying out their day-to-day work that they rarely, if ever, stop to think objectively about themselves and their businesses. Very few of them ask probing questions that might result in questioning their basic assumptions, refreshing their strategies, or re-engineering their systems.

Managerial expectations, global and domestic competition, and the growing diversity of the workforce, among other things, continuously pose challenges to an organization and question the continued relevance of its strategies. These, in turn, also challenge the role of human resource management within firms. More than ever, the HR department is expected to contribute to the firm's competitive advantage.[3] As a result, the importance of the human resource function and its impact have grown dramatically.

Besides furthering the organizational objective of competitive advantage, the department also must address the societal and employee goals discussed in Chapter One.[4] To do this, a human resource department today must perform several functions that were given only minor importance in the past (witness the increasing importance of employment equity, evaluation of training effectiveness, outplacement services, and so on).[5] However, a human resource department cannot assume that everything it does is correct. Unless there is a correct fit between the environments and the organization and its strategies and systems, the organization may become unsuccessful over time.[6] Errors happen. Policies become outdated. By evaluating itself, the human resource department finds problems before they become serious. Audits of past practices also reveal outdated assumptions that can be changed to help the department meet future challenges.

STRATEGIC IMPORTANCE OF HUMAN RESOURCE AUDITS

Human resource audit
An examination of the human resource policies, practices, and systems of a firm (or division) to eliminate deficiencies and improve ways to achieve goals.

A human resource audit evaluates the human resource activities used in an organization. The audit may include one division or an entire company. It gives feedback about the human resource function to operating managers and human resource specialists. It also provides feedback about how well managers are meeting their human resource duties. Research into HR practices may uncover better ways for the department to contribute to societal, organizational, and employee objectives. If the evaluation is done properly, it can also build support between the human resource department and operating managers. Consider the following example:

> **Linda Desmarais** (Manager, Underwriting Department): I know we make mistakes. Most errors are caught and corrected before any damage is done. But sometimes outside auditors catch our mistakes for us, so I'm glad that you are auditing the human resource department's procedures. I was beginning to wonder if your department thought it was above outside review."
>
> **Fred Nolin** (Human Resource Manager): "We realized that there is room for improvement. In fact, the reason we are doing this review is to check our methods and learn how we can better serve managers like yourself."
>
> **Linda Desmarais:** "What do you hope to discover?"

Fred Nolin: "First, we want to see if our present procedures are being followed. We need uniformity in our selection, career planning, compensation, and other activities. If there is a lack of consistency, we want to find out why. Maybe people don't understand our procedures. Or maybe our methods aren't practical and should be changed. Second, we are checking to ensure compliance with employee relations laws such as human rights, safety, and others. This audit is not a 'witch hunt.' We are simply trying to improve our performance."

As the above dialogue indicates, several benefits result from a human resource audit. Figure 17-1 lists the major ones. An audit reminds managers such as Linda of the department's contribution. It also creates a more professional image of the department among managers and human resource specialists.

Human resource research grows more important with each passing year for several reasons. First, human resource work carries with it many legal implications for the employer. Failure to comply with equal employment or safety laws, for example, subjects the organization to lawsuits. Second, "people costs" are significant. Pay and benefits often are a major operating expense for most employers. Improper compensation plans can be costly, even fatal, to the company's survival. Third, the department's activities help shape an organization's productivity and its employees' quality of work life. Fourth, the critical resource in many organizations today is not capital, but rather, information, knowledge, and expertise.[7] This means that audit of the calibre of a critical resource—namely, human resources—is necessary for the success of the organization. Finally, the growing complexity of human resource work makes research necessary. Today, more than ever before, human resource activities aimed at productivity improvement, succession planning, and cultural change are critical to competitive survival. More and more executives expect the department to make strategic contributions and place the function at a higher level in the organizational hierarchy.

> Over 50 per cent of 520 Canadian organizations surveyed in one study were found to have a vice-president in charge of human resources. Over 78 per cent of these organizations employed at least one trained professional to deal with human resource matters.[8]

Figure 17-2 summarizes the results of two large-scale research studies that aimed to identify indices of human resource management effectiveness in Canadian

FIGURE 17-1

Benefits of a Human Resource Management Audit

- *Helps* align human resource department goals with the goals and strategies of the larger organization
- *Provides* specific, verifiable data on human resource department's contributions
- *Improves* the professional image of the human resource department
- *Encourages* greater professionalism among members of the human resource department
- *Clarifies* human resource department's duties and responsibilities
- *Stimulates* uniformity of human resource policies and practices.
- *Finds* critical human resource problems
- *Ensures* timely compliance with legal requirements.
- *Reduces* human resource costs through more effective procedures
- *Helps* review and improve human resource department's information system.

FIGURE 17-2

Indices of Human Resource Management Effectiveness in Canadian Organizations

Index	Organizations Across Canada (Except Atlantic Canada) (n = 650)	Organizations in Four Atlantic Provinces (n = 1,277)
Overall productivity	4.38	4.38
Employee satisfaction	4.02	4.21
Employee commitment to organization	4.33	4.38
Grievance rate	2.02	1.90
Absenteeism	2.68	2.28
Turnover	1.99	2.11
Conflicts within organization	2.75	2.46
Employee quality of life	4.15	4.16

Note: All items are measured on a scale of 1 = very low; 6 = very high.

Source: Courtesy of *Canadian HR Reporter* published by Carswell, Thomson Professional Publishing.

organizations. Data such as these provide approximate benchmarks for individual firms to compare their own performance. Indices such as these also initiate new programs such as literacy training, which can significantly improve employee productivity and morale (see boxed item).

STEPS IN CONDUCTING HUMAN RESOURCE AUDITS

HUMAN RESOURCE auditing involves four major steps:

1. defining the scope of the audit;

2. choosing the research approach;

3. selecting research design and data collection method; and

4. data analysis, evaluation and report preparation.

Figure 17-3 shows these steps that are discussed in detail below:

The Scope of Human Resource Audits

The scope of an audit extends beyond just the human resource department's actions. The department does not operate in isolation. Its success depends on how well it performs and how well its programs are carried out by others in the organization. Consider how supervisors in a firm reduced the effectiveness of the performance appraisal process:

> To appraise performance, Kanata Electronics used a critical-incident procedure, which means supervisors had to record both positive and negative incidents as they occurred. To become a section supervisor, an employee needed three years of good or superior performance evaluations. However, in practice, supervisors stressed

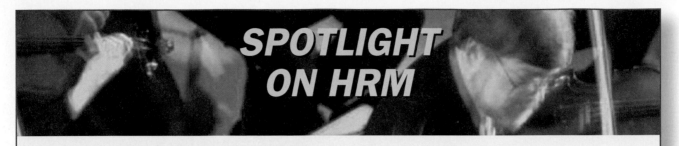

SPOTLIGHT ON HRM

LITERACY SKILLS TRAINING KEY TO WORKPLACE PRODUCTIVITY

Companies offer literacy skills training to their employees because enhanced reading, writing, and numeracy skills will ultimately contribute to a stronger bottom line through time savings, lower costs, and improvements in the quality of work. The Conference Board, in a recent survey of 41 companies that offer literacy skills training to their employees, found that these direct benefits are just the tip of the iceberg as to how companies will benefit from enhancing the literacy skills of their workforce. Other benefits included unleashing the potential of individual employees, cementing stronger labour-management relations, and moving the entire organization towards corporate goals set to ensure success in a highly competitive, often changing marketplace. All of these benefits from literacy skills training contribute to the company's bottom-line performance.

At the very core of these benefits is the significant impact that literacy training has on the self-esteem and self-confidence of the participating individuals. Employers noted that workers suffering from literacy deficits are very conscious of this fact and often try to hide this skills deficit from their co-workers. Their employees recognize that this skills deficit has cut them off from many opportunities to advance. Enhanced literacy training offers them the skills they want and need the most. Once obtained, ideas are better understood by employees as words and language take on more meaning. They have greater confidence in their ability to communicate, feel empowered, take ownership of their responsibilities, become more effective and active decision makers, and assume a more engaging and participative role in their organization...

How can we bring about the changes in behaviour and support that are needed to increase the strength and effectiveness of literacy skills training and developments in the workplace?

First, we can take action to raise awareness of the importance and value of improving literacy in the workplace. Many individuals and organizations can play a role here if they choose.

Employers who already run literacy training programs or who know their potential value can help by spreading the message, especially to their fellow employers.....

Employees can play an active role. By spreading the word among their co-workers that they personally enjoy real benefits from participating in literacy training they will encourage more employees to get involved themselves....

Second, we can establish more literacy training programs. Employers can play a leading role by establishing more programs in their workplace and provide more places in those programs for employees who wish to take part. Employers can work with their employees and, in some environments, with unions to determine what type of training is most needed and to create programs to meet the need. Some of these training programs may be supported in part by governments.

Third, we can enhance the literacy component of jobs and seek to create more literacy-rich jobs. Employers can work with employees to enhance the literacy dimensions of jobs to maintain literacy skills developed through training and apply them to create more value-added products and services.

Fourth, we can develop additional public policies that support literacy skills development. Governments already provide support and encouragement for literacy skills development. For example, the federal government's National Literacy Secretariat funds research into effective practices and supports pilot projects and other initiatives to enhance skills. In addition, governments might help to build broad support for workplace literacy by implementing labour market policies aimed at improving the ability of workers to acquire and enhance literacy skills.

Source: From the *Canadian HR Reporter*, May 19, 1997, p. 4. Copyright @ 1997 by MPL Communications Inc. Courtesy of *Canadian HR Reporter*. Published by Carswell, Thomson Professional Learning.

employee mistakes when they recorded incidents; as a result, few employees received the three years of good ratings needed to qualify for a promotion. Many of them blamed the human resource department's appraisal process for their lack of promotions.

FIGURE 17-3

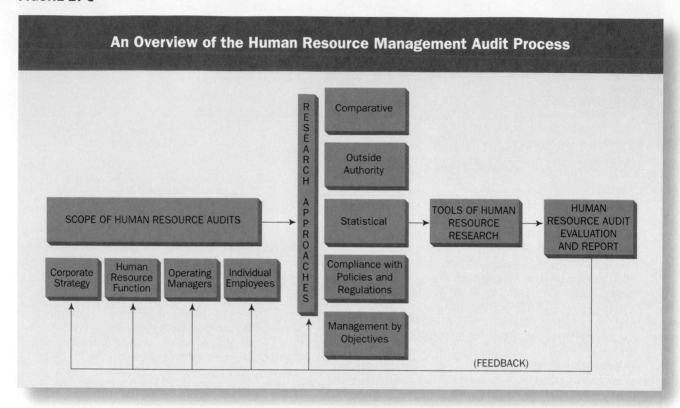

An Overview of the Human Resource Management Audit Process

An audit uncovered this misuse of the program and led to additional training for supervisors in the use of the critical-incident method. If the audit had not uncovered this problem, employee dissatisfaction might have worsened.

As the above example illustrates, "people problems" are seldom confined to just the human resource department. Indeed, in recent years, human resource professionals have found that the scope of the audit must transcend even the concerns of the department and operating managers. In practice, the modern type of audit typically focuses on corporate strategy, human resource systems, managerial compliance and employee satisfaction.

Audit of the Corporate Strategy

Audit of the corporate strategy
Assessment of a firm's strategy and fit with its mission and environments, with particular focus on HR policies and practices.

Human resource professionals do not set corporate strategy, but as discussed in Chapter One, they strongly determine its success. Corporate strategy is concerned with how the organization is going to gain a competitive advantage. Based upon such things as an assessment of the firm's environment, weaknesses, opportunities, and strengths, senior management devises ways of gaining an advantage. Whether the company stresses superior marketing (McCain Foods), service (IBM), innovation (Nortel), low-cost operations (Canadian Tire), or some other approach, human resource management is affected. Although not all human resource audits review corporate strategy and its fit with the external environment, these broader concerns merit mentioning here since understanding the strategy has strong implications for human resource planning, staffing, compensation, employee relations, and other human resource activities.

Although the department may lack both the expertise and resources to audit the corporate strategy and its fit with the external environment, the strategy/environ-

With 423 stores, 27 000 employees and revenues of $3.8 billion, Canadian Tire's low-cost operations put the chain among the country's largest retailers.

mental fit cannot be ignored. Human resource professionals must audit human resource policies and practices against the firm's strategic plans.

> Thus, employee turnover in a large accounting firm was a low-cost way to keep the firm's overall labour costs competitive since high turnover in entry-level jobs kept wages near the bottom of the rate range. An audit, however, revealed considerable dissatisfaction among recent accounting graduates about the number of billable hours required of them each week. Knowledge that the firm's strategy (to hire excess entry-level accountants) adversely affected employee satisfaction enabled the human resource department to take timely corrective actions.

Audit of the Human Resource System

Audit of the human resource system
Assessment of HR functions, systems, and activities to learn the extent to which they contribute to organizational, societal, and employee goals.

Audits should logically begin with a review of the human resource department's work. Figure 17-4 lists the major areas they cover. As shown in the figure, an audit should focus on the human resource management information system, staffing and development, and organizational control and evaluation. These three areas of the audit supplement one another and integrate with one another. As such, no single area should be overemphasized in the audit. As may be seen, an audit touches on virtually every topic discussed in this book.

For each item chosen for audit, the audit team of human resource specialists should:

- Identify who is responsible for each activity.
- Determine the objectives sought by each activity.
- Evaluate how these objectives reflect and support organizational strategies.
- Review the policies and procedures used to achieve these objectives.
- Sample the records in the human resource information system to learn if policies and procedures are being following correctly.
- Prepare a report recommending proper objectives, policies, and procedures.
- Develop a plan of action to correct errors in objectives, policies, and procedures.
- Follow up on the plan of action to see if it has solved the problems found through the audit.

FIGURE 17-4

Major Areas Covered in a Human Resource Audit

Human Resource Management Information System

Human rights legislation
- Information on compliance

Human resource plans
- Supply and demand estimates
- Skills inventories
- Replacement charts and summaries

Job analysis information
- Job standards
- Job descriptions
- Job specifications

Compensation administration
- Wage and salary levels
- Benefit package
- Employer-provided services

Staffing and Development

Recruiting
- Source of recruits
- Availability of recruits
- Employment applications

Selection
- Selection ratios
- Selection procedures
- Human rights legislation compliance

Training and orientation
- Orientation program
- Training objectives and procedures
- Learning rate

Career development
- Internal placement success
- Career planning program
- Human resource development effort

Organization Control and Evaluation

Performance appraisals
- Standards and measures of performance
- Performance appraisal techniques
- Evaluation interviews

Labour–management relations
- Legal compliance
- Management rights
- Dispute resolution problems

Human resource controls
- Employee communications
- Discipline procedures
- Change and development procedures

Human resource audits
- Human resource function
- Operating managers
- Employee feedback on human resource department

Audit teams
Teams responsible for assessing the effectiveness of the human resource function.

Admittedly, an audit of every human resource activity is time-consuming. As a result, very large organizations have full-time **audit teams** similar to those who conduct financial audits. These teams are especially useful when the human resource department is decentralized into regional or field offices. Through the use of audits, the organization can maintain consistency in its practices even though there are several human resource offices in different locations. Moreover, the mere existence of an audit team encourages compliance and self-audits between visits by the audit team:

Cliff Robertson, a regional human resource manager based in Winnipeg, realized that his chances for promotion to the corporate headquarters in Toronto depended on how well his region's human resource offices performed. The company's human resource audit team reviewed his region's performance every June. So in preparation for the audit, Cliff had each human resource office in the region conduct a self-audit in April. Then, in early May, the human resource administrators from the three branches met in Winnipeg to review the results of the audit, and during May, errors uncovered through the audit were corrected, if possible. Thus, when the corporate audit team completed its own review in June, it always gave Cliff's region high marks for compliance with company policies and with laws.

Audit of Managerial Compliance

Audit of managerial compliance
An audit to review how well managers comply with HR policies and procedures and labour laws.

An audit also reviews how well managers comply with human resource policies and procedures. If managers ignore these policies or violate employee relations laws, the audit should uncover these errors so that timely corrective action can be taken.

> The manager of a fast-food restaurant in British Columbia hired two high-school students to do janitorial work on a part-time basis. The two boys were glad to earn $5 an hour. But one boy's father complained to the government that the restaurant was paying below minimum wage. Not only was the parent company found guilty of violating the minimum wage laws, but the complaint triggered an investigation of the pay and overtime practices of the firm's other restaurants. Had this company used an internal human resource audit, the error could have been corrected before formal government action was taken.

Besides assuring compliance, the audit can improve the human resource department's image and contribution to the company. Operating managers may gain a higher respect for the department when an audit seeks their views. If the comments of managers are acted upon, the department will be seen as more responsive to their needs, and effective in achieving organizational objectives. Consider how one human resource manager improved her department's effectiveness:

> After several interviews with claims office managers, the audit team discovered a pattern to their comments. Most managers believed that although the human resource department filled job vacancies quickly, it did not train recruits before assigning them to a claims office. Day-to-day pressures in the claims office caused training to be superficial and led to many errors by new adjusters. The managers felt that the training should be done at the regional office by the human resource department. The regional human resource manager was pleased to learn that the selection process was satisfactory, and to solve the problem of field training, she created a one-week training program for claims adjusters with her next budget increase. Later feedback indicated that claims managers appreciated the department's responsiveness.

Audit of Employee Satisfaction

Audit of employee satisfaction
Assessment of employee satisfaction with a variety of work-related matters and the implications for HR practices and systems.

As mentioned in Chapter One, effective human resource departments meet both company and employee objectives. When employee needs are not met, turnover, absenteeism, and union activity are more likely. To learn how well employee needs are met, the audit team gathers data from workers. The team collects information about wages, benefits, supervisory practices, career planning assistance, and the feedback employees receive about their performance:

> The audit team of an automobile parts distributor received one common complaint from employees: they felt isolated because they worked in retail stores or warehouses located all over Canada. They had little sense of belonging to the large company of which they were a part. To bolster sagging morale and to help employees feel that they were members of a fast-growing and dynamic company, the human resource department started a biweekly "Employee Newsletter." The two-page letter was stuffed in every pay envelope each payday. It gave tips on new developments at headquarters and different field locations. The firm also hired a consultant to explore the introduction of a corporate intranet to which all employees could sign in for the latest

developments in the company. In this way, the department used the audit to make the firm more responsive to its employees' needs.

In many progressive organizations, employee attitude surveys are done regularly. This enables the organization to solve problems before they evolve into larger and more complex issues.

www.compensationlink.com

Research Approaches to Audits

Human resource audit may be done using a variety of research approaches. Sometimes the "research" is little more than an informal investigation or fact-finding effort. At other times, the approach may be advanced and rely on sophisticated research designs and statistics.[9] Whether informal or rigorous, this research seeks to improve the human resource activities of the organization. These applications-oriented efforts are called *applied research*. The most common forms of applied human resource research are summarized in Figure 17-5 and are explained below.[10]

Applied research
Applications-oriented research activities that aim to improve HRM practices and systems.

Comparative approach
HR audit approach comparing one firm's (or division's) HR practices with another firm (or division) to uncover areas of poor performance.

Comparative Approach

Perhaps the simplest form of research is the *comparative approach*. It uses another division or company as a model. The audit team then compares its results or procedures with those of the other organization. This approach commonly is used to compare the results of specific human resource activities or programs and their relation to absence, turnover, and salary data. This approach also makes sense when a new procedure is being tried for the first time.

> When B.C. Lumber installed an alcohol rehabilitation program, it copied salient features of a long-running similar program at another local firm. Later the results of the two programs were compared, which helped B.C. Lumber to remove "bugs" in its program.

Outside authority approach
HR audit approach relying on a consultant or published research as a standard against which HR programs are evaluated.

Outside Authority Approach

Alternatively, the human resource department may rely on an *outside authority approach*. Standards set by a consultant or from published research findings serve as benchmarks for the audit team.

FIGURE 17-5

Research Approaches of Human Resource Audits

Approach	Typically Focused on	Typical Benchmarks used
Comparative	Firm, division or activities	Comparable firm or industry standard
Outside Authority	HR programs and activities	Judgements of the expert or consultant involved
Statistical Approach	HR programs, activities, or outcomes	Company historical data along with industry and legal standards
Compliance Approach	HR programs, activities; manager and employee behaviours	Legal requirements and company rules
MBO Approach	Results of program or function activities	Objectives

A consulting firm specializing in human resource management indicated to Saskatoon Drugs that its orientation program was inadequate, resulting in high turnover of newly hired employees. After a detailed review, a new orientation plan was introduced in the firm. A comparison of employee turnover before and after the change and comparison to industry standards showed that the firm had benefitted by the new program.

At present, external comparison is one of the most popular approaches to evaluating human resource activities and services.

Statistical Approach

Statistical approach
Use of existing company records to generate statistical standards against which HR programs are evaluated.

Another approach is to develop statistical measures of performance based on the company's existing information system. For example, research into the company's records reveals its absenteeism and turnover rates. These data indicate how well human resource activities and operating managers control these problem areas. This *statistical approach* is usually supplemented with comparisons against external information, which may be gathered from other firms and often expressed as ratios:

Metro Groceries, which has an approximate workforce of 200 employees, had 32 quit during a year. The firm recognized that its turnover rate of 16 per cent was significantly higher than the industry average and decided to investigate the matter in detail.

Compliance Approach

Compliance approach
Review of past human resource practices to determine if they conform to formally stated policies and legally defensible standards.

The *compliance approach* is another human resource audit strategy. This method reviews past practices to determine if those actions followed company policies and procedures. Often the audit team reviews a sample of employment, compensation, discipline, and employee appraisal forms. The purpose of the review is to ensure that field offices and operating managers comply with internal rules and legal regulations:

An internal audit of the selection process used at Bio-Genetics Ltd. revealed that the employment manager followed the correct procedures. But the audit team noticed that many applications had comments written in the margins. These comments were added by operating managers who also interviewed applicants. Most of their notes referred to personal data that were not asked on the form, such as sex, age, marital status, ages of dependants, and race. Managers did this to help them remember individual candidates. But if some applicant was not hired, these comments could lead to charges of discrimination on the basis of age, sex, or race.

For global organizations, the existence of uniform human resource policies and practices throughout their world operations may be desirable, but hard to achieve. Several HR challenges facing global organizations were discussed in Chapter Fourteen. Different countries and cultures value different rewards; geographical and cultural distance pose severe communication problems for expatriate managers in performance appraisal, job design and employee relations; and the legal frameworks across various countries show marked differences making the same practice acceptable and unacceptable in different cultural settings. Given these differences, how does a HR department ensure common global standards? Yet, to ensure equity and improve predictability, some degree of uniformity in HR practices may be necessary. Compliance audits may provide an important tool in the context of "think globally, act locally" philosophy referred to in the earlier chapter.

Management-by-Objectives Approach

Management-by-objectives approach (MBO)
Assessment of HR functions and systems by comparing actual results with stated HR objectives.

A final approach is for human resource specialists and operating managers to set objectives in their area of responsibility. This *management-by-objectives approach (MBO)* creates specific objectives against which performance can be measured.[11] Then the audit team researches actual performance and compares it with the previously set objectives.

Operating managers may set a goal of resolving a higher percentage of grievances before they reach arbitration. Then the audit evaluates the trends in this area.

This is also a popular approach to evaluating the human resource department's function.

No single audit approach works for all situations. More commonly, audit teams use several of the strategies, depending on the specific human resource activities under evaluation. Whatever the approach used, it is desirable to involve managers in developing relevant criteria for evaluating the HR function. An Australian company's past experience provides a good example of how HR performance measurement indicators can be developed in a manner that enhances overall utility of the audit exercise:

> The HR staff at Australian Global Insurance (AGI), as part of its audit process, interviewed senior managers to identify appropriate HR performance indicators useful for strategic decision making. Fifty-two indicators were identified and were grouped into seven categories: organizational effectiveness, compensation, absenteeism and turnover, staffing, training and development, occupational health and safety, and other miscellaneous areas. Managers were also asked to rank the measures in order of importance for strategic decision making. HR performance indicators for each category and various items were next identified. (For example, a measure of internal recruitment was the time taken to fill vacancies from internal sources.) Such indicators allowed the HR function not only to indicate its contribution to bottom-line performance but also to benchmark practices of highly successful firms. The active involvement of senior management in determining these performance indicators also enhanced the overall usefulness of the audit.[12]

Research Design and Data Collection Method

Regardless of the audit team's approach, it must collect data about the organization's human resource activities. In practice, this is a very difficult task. Part of the reason lies in the fact that it is very difficult to define its effectiveness. Many of the indices available are subjective in nature and organization-dependent. Further, human resource management effectiveness at the organizational level may be quite different from the effectiveness and efficiency of the human resource department itself. In addition, one must also consider issues related to research efficiency. Most research requires a considerable investment in time and resources and some designs are more expensive than others.[13]

Typically, a number of tools may be needed to gauge human resource management effectiveness even approximately. Each research tool provides partial insights into the firm's human resource activities. If these tools are used skillfully, the team can weave these insights into a clear picture of the organization's human resource activities. These tools include:

- interviews;
- questionnaires and surveys;
- record analysis;
- external information;
- human resource experiments;
- focus groups.

Interviews

Interviews
Face-to-face meetings with employees and managers to collect information about the effectiveness of human resource programs, systems, and activities.

Interviews with employees and managers are one source of information about human resource activities. Their comments help the audit team identify areas that need improvement. Criticisms by employees may pinpoint those actions that the department should take to meet their needs. Likewise, suggestions by managers may reveal ways to provide them with better service. When their criticisms are valid, changes should be made. But when it is the human resource department who is right, it may have to educate others in the firm by explaining the procedures being questioned:

> Bob Gordon served as a member of the audit team at Canadian Furniture Company. He interviewed various managers, who complained that the frequent transfer of managerial staff was a problem. Bob understood their concerns. He explained that the unique type of furniture the company dealt with led to too many fluctuations in market demand for the company's products. Unless senior managers were frequently transferred to faraway branches, the sales of these branches could not be pulled up. Although many managers still disliked the situation, the audit interview helped them understand the need for the frequent transfers of managers.

Exit interview
Interviews with departing employees to gauge their impressions of a firm's strengths and weaknesses, especially relating to HR systems and policies.

Another useful source of information is the ***exit interview***.[14] Exit interviews are conducted with departing employees to learn their views of the organization. Figure 17-6 shows the typical questions asked during the interview. It is done separately from the human resource audit, and employee comments are recorded. Then during the audit these answers are reviewed to find the causes of employee dissatisfaction and other human resource management problems.

Cultural audits
Assessment of an organization's culture and subcultures and how they are revealed to members.

Interviews are also helpful in assessing a firm's internal culture. Such ***cultural audits*** aim to gauge the prevailing organizational culture and how it is revealed to

FIGURE 17-6

An Exit Interview Form

Saskatoon Kitchen Appliances Ltd.
Exit Interview Form

Employee's name _____   Date hired _____

Interviewed by _____   Interviewed on_____

Supervisor's name _____   Department _____

1. Were your job duties and responsibilities what you expected? _____

    If not, why? _____

2. What is your frank and honest opinion of:

    a. Your job? _____

    b. Your working conditions?_____

    c. Your orientation to your job?_____

    d. Your training provided by the company? _____

    e. Your pay?_____

    f. Your company-provided benefits and services?_____

    g. Your treatment by your manager? _____

3. What is your major reason for leaving the company?_____

4. What could we have done to keep you from leaving?_____

5. What could be done to make Saskatoon Kitchen Appliances a better place to work? _____

    _____

    _____

members. Given today's diverse workforce, audits should also focus on determining the existence of subcultures that have different views about the nature of work and how it should be done. While in-depth interviews can provide useful information, it should be emphasized that culture is often invisible even to close observers; and hence it must be assessed using a variety of tools including observation, focus groups, surveys, and content analysis of the prevailing stories, myths, language, and artifacts. Some of these were discussed earlier in Chapter Fourteen.

Questionnaires and Surveys

Questionnaires and surveys
Use of preprinted questionnaires (or e-mail) to gauge employee attitudes on a variety of work and company-related matters.

Many human resource departments supplement interviews with *questionnaires and surveys.* These tools are used because interviews are time-consuming, costly, and usually limited to only a few people. Through surveys of employees, a more accurate picture of employee treatment can be developed. Also, questionnaires may lead to more candid answers than face-to-face interviews.

Attitude survey
Systematic assessment of employees' opinions about various work-related factors, typically using a questionnaire.

One popular approach is an *employee attitude survey*. These multipage paper-and-pencil tests are used to learn how employees view their manager, their job, and the human resource department. Sometimes several hundred questions are asked. These questions seek answers to the critical issues listed in Figure 17-7. Then the answers are grouped into areas of analysis to find out where employee attitudes are high and where low. The survey results may also be compared across departments, to other similar firms, to past survey findings, or to corporate objectives. Further analysis may identify problems with specific supervisors, employee subgroups, jobs, or benefits:

FIGURE 17-7

Critical Concerns to Be Answered by Attitude Surveys

Employee Attitudes About Supervisors
- Are employees working in specific departments or under specific supervisors exceptionally satisfied or dissatisfied?
- Do specific supervisors need training in supervisory and human relations skills?
- Have attitudes improved since the last survey?

Employee Attitudes About Their Jobs
- What are common elements of jobs that cause negative attitudes? Positive attitudes?
- Can jobs that cause poor attitudes be redesigned to improve satisfaction?
- Can jobs that cause poor attitudes be given alternative work schedules (such as shorter workweeks or flextime)?

Perceived Effectiveness of the Human Resource Department
- Do employees think they work for a good or bad employer?
- Do employees think they have a career or merely a job?
- Do employees feel they have some place to turn in order to solve their problems, besides to their immediate supervisor?
- Do employees feel informed about company developments?
- Do employees know what is expected of them in their jobs?
- Are employees satisfied by the amount and type of feedback they get about their performance?
- Are employees satisfied with their pay? Benefits?

For many of its job positions, a large fast-food chain routinely employed students in the 18–24 age category. However, this age group is expected to decline in number in the next decade. Making matters worse, company audits revealed annualized turnover rates of 70 to 80 per cent, which cost the firm at least $1.5 million in recruitment and training costs.

The fast-food company conducted a survey of field managers in the restaurant industry. It revealed that over 50 per cent of the turnover was beyond management's control. However, the remainder of the turnover was accounted for by poor human resource and supervisory practices. Armed with this knowledge, the human resource department was able to take timely corrective actions to prevent further shrinkage of its workforce. The audit also revealed another increasing segment of the labour market—newly retired persons who are looking for part-time work. The fast-food chain began to target this group in its recruitment ads.

Attitude surveys give valuable feedback about required changes in jobs or supervision. The human resource department learns how its efforts are viewed by employees. Of particular importance are trends revealed through repeated, periodic administration of questionnaires. The discovery of research-based trends suggests whether specific challenges are becoming more or less important to those surveyed.

Attitude surveys using established survey instruments may also help a firm to compare its employee satisfaction with that of the general labour force. This enables a firm to establish benchmarks or clear human resource goals for the future.

Record Analysis

Not all problems are revealed through employee attitudes. Sometimes problems can be found only by studying records. This is particularly important while investigating compliance with company procedures and laws. The records normally reviewed by an audit team are listed in Figure 17-8 and discussed in the following paragraphs.

Safety and Health Audits. An analysis of safety and health records may reveal violations of provisions of the Canada Labour Code or other provincial safety and health regulations. Under the record-keeping requirements of the Canada Labour Code, Part IV, accurate records of all matters coming under the jurisdiction of the safety and health committee should be kept by every organization. A human resource audit can help to document the firm's compliance with safety and health requirements in each province. Number of employees who have made claims on workmen's compensation plans classified by job, employee category and time periods, number of safety violations observed, and number of complaints from employees about workplace safety are among popular indices looked at in this context.[15]

Record analysis
Review of past company records as part of an HR audit.

Safety and health audits
Audit of safety and health records to find past or potential violations and ways to eliminate them.

An audit can reveal that a certain segment of the population, such as retirees, is looking for part-time work.

CP PHOTO ARCHIVE (Todd Korol)

FIGURE 17-8

Records Commonly Reviewed as Part of a Human Resource Audit

Safety and Health Records

- Statistics on accidents before and after safety training programs.
- Number of employees who have made claims on workmen's compensation plans classified by job, employee category, and time periods.
- Number of safety violations observed in past audits.
- Number of complaints from employees about working conditions and workplace safety.

Productivity Records

- Cost of production of different components and products.
- Wastage, scrap rates (especially focusing on impact of training, bonuses, or other human resource programs on wastage).
- Absenteeism records.
- Employee turnover records.

Grievance Records

- Patterns in grievances (e.g., arising from specific contract clauses or supervisors).
- Clarity of clauses in union management agreements.

Compensation Records

- Statistics examining external and internal wage equity.
- Statistics on benefits offered along with trends in the firm; comparisons with industry data on file.

Human Rights Compliance Records

- Firm's compliance with all human rights laws as evidenced by its application form, job specifications, and so on.
- Number and patterns of sexual or other harassment charges.
- Workforce statistics on concentration, underutilization, and so on.
- Employment equity goals of the firm versus actual achievements.

Human Resource Implementation Records

- Comparisons of targets and achievements of HR department in various areas.
- Number of employee complaints on various HR related matters.
- Past feedback from managers on file on HR department's effectiveness or needed improvements.

Employee Files and Records

- Turnover and absenteeism records classified by age, gender, department, and so on.
- Comparison of the above across time, departments and industry data on file.
- Performance of employees before and after specific training programs.
- Career progression patterns of specific groups of employees (e.g., visible minorities, women).
- Accuracy, completeness and currency of information contained in random inspections.
- Number, type and patterns in disciplinary and interpersonal problems.

Special Programming Reports

- Results (planned versus actual) of special programs.

Job Placement/Selection Records

- Percentage of jobs filled internally.
- Performance evaluation of internally promoted candidates by their supervisors.
- Usefulness of existing replacement charts/summaries.
- Performance of recruits classified by source of recruits.
- Recruitment and selection costs (actual against plans and those of other firms).

Productivity audits
An analysis of production records, absenteeism, wastage records, and labour costs to identify and improve productivity levels.

Grievance audits
Audits to detect patterns in employee grievances.

Productivity Audits. An analysis of production records, absenteeism patterns, scrap rates and wastage, and so on, provides clues to the human resource department about prevailing productivity levels and trends. Statistics on absenteeism patterns and turnover figures may provide the human resource department with important clues about underlying, more serious problems.[16]

Grievance Audits. The audit team may also be able to uncover a pattern in employee grievances. Patterns may emerge by jobs, supervisors, union representatives, age groups, or contract provisions. If patterns are detected, human resource specialists seek out the underlying causes and take corrective action to reduce the causes of these complaints. Interviews with supervisors and union officials may reveal the underlying causes of grievances. And if union officials participate in finding patterns of grievances, they may support management's suggested changes:

> A grievance audit at the Kelowna Logging Company indicated that supervisors and managers were spending too much of their time dealing with grievances. In fact, the lost production time by workers and costs of arbitration were seriously reducing the company's profitability. Low profitability meant that the union had to accept the smallest wage increases in the area. The audit team asked the two top union officials to help review the causes of grievances. The union leaders thought the problem was a poor understanding of the contract by both supervisors and union representatives. The audit team's analysis fit the union leaders' comments. As a result, the company asked the town's part-time mayor to help train both sides. The training led to a noticeable drop in grievances.

Compensation audits
Study of wages, benefits, and services to see if they are fair and competitive.

Compensation Audits. Audit teams carefully review the human resource department's compensation practices. Primarily, they study the level of wages, benefits, and services that are provided. If jobs have been priced properly through job evaluations and salary surveys, pay levels will be fair. Benefits and services are also studied to learn if they are competitive with those of other employers and in compliance with government regulations.

Human rights compliance audits
Audits of hiring, placement, and compensation practices, to ensure compliance with human rights legislation.

Human Rights Compliance Audits. Although several large companies employ one or more persons to monitor the company's compliance with Canadian human rights legislation, the audit team serves as a further check on compliance. The team usually focuses on the hiring, placement, and compensation of all minority groups; if discriminating practices exist, it informs management of the need for corrective action.

Program and policy audits
Audit aimed at determining whether human resource policies and programs achieve their intended objectives and their impact on work procedures and employee behaviour and attitudes.

Program and Policy Audits. Besides safety, grievance, compensation, and human rights corrective action programs, audits evaluate many other human resource programs and policies. The purpose of these audits is to determine whether other programs and policies are doing what was intended:

> Two years after Seafood Canners Ltd. adopted a "promotion from within" policy, most supervisors were still recruited from outside the firm. Few workers applied for supervisory openings, even though these jobs were posted throughout the plant and employees were encouraged to apply. The audit team learned that during peak seasons, production workers earned more money than supervisors because of overtime pay and the incentive system. Many employees viewed supervisory jobs as entailing more responsibility and less pay. To remedy the problem, supervisors were given a percentage of their department's production bonus. A year later, 90 per cent of the supervisory openings were being filled internally.

As the Seafood Canners example illustrates, policies ("promotion from within") may conflict with other programs (the incentive system). And legal requirements (overtime pay) may conflict with the department's goals. Virtually every human resource policy and program affects at least one other. Thus, a thorough audit needs to include all the major human resource policies and programs and how they relate to each other.

Figure 17-8 also identifies other typical records reviewed by audit teams. These records are evaluated to find areas of poor performance and conflicts between policies, programs, and employee relations laws.

External Information

www.statcan.ca

www.hrdc-drhc.gc.ca

External information
Use of labour market-related and economic information and competitor and industry performance benchmarks to improve HR practices and systems in a firm.

Research into internal attitudes and records may uncover unfavourable trends. But outside comparisons also give the audit team a perspective against which the firm's activities can be judged. Some needed information is available readily, while other data may be difficult to find.

Most of the *external information* is available from the publications of Statistics Canada, Industry Canada and Human Resource Development Canada.

> For example, benchmarking workplace absenteeism is possible with Statistics Canada figures (available since 1977). Two types of absenteeism are particularly important to track: those due to illnesses or disability and those resulting from personal or family responsibilities. It is possible to compare past figures and compare them to industry, occupational, provincial, and demographic patterns (e.g., age, gender).

These agencies regularly publish information about future employment opportunities, employee turnover rates, workforce projections, area wage and salary surveys, severity and frequency rates of accidents, and other data that can serve as benchmarks for comparing internal information.[17]

Industry associations and boards of trade usually make available to members specialized data related to the industry. Of most use to audit teams are statistics on industry norms—such as turnover rates, absenteeism rates, standard wage rates, growth rates, standardized job descriptions, accident rates, benefit costs, and sample union-management agreements.

Professional associations often provide similar information to members of the profession. Studies conducted by the association may include salary and benefit surveys, demographic profiles, and other data that can serve as standards against which the human resource department's efforts are measured. Consultants and university research bureaus may be able to provide other needed information through research. Published reports of surveys on topics such as absenteeism can often provide important insights to the audit team.[18]

Human Resource Experiments

Field experiment
Comparison of impact of a treatment on experimental and control groups in real-life settings, while controlling for effects of extraneous factors.

Research experiments are yet another powerful tool available to an audit team. The ideal research design is a *field experiment* that allows the human resource department to compare an experimental and a control group under realistic conditions.

> For example, the human resource department may implement a safety training program for half of the department supervisors. This half is the experimental group. The control group is the other half of the department supervisors who are not given training. Then the subsequent safety records of both groups are compared several months after the training is completed. If the experimental group has significantly lower accident rates, this is evidence that the safety training program was effective.

Experimentation does have some drawbacks. Many managers are reluctant to experiment with only some workers because of morale problems and potential dissatisfaction among those who were not selected. Those involved may feel manipulated. And the experiment may be confounded by changes in the work environment or simply by the two groups talking with each other about the experiment. Several of these problems are lessened by using a research design that involves two organizations, as did one school board:

www.shrm.org

www.hr.mcmaster.ca

The human resource department of a rural school district gave all the elementary school teachers of one school a special two-day training program. The teachers at another school located 30 kilometres away did not receive the training. At the end of the year, the school board's audit team compared the teacher evaluations and pupil scores on province-wide tests to assess the success of the development program.

This design reduced the likelihood that the experimental and control groups would discuss the training with each other. For the school principals, it also prevented the problem of having half of their faculty in each group. Of course, the difficulty with this design is that it assumes the two organizations, their teachers, and their students were comparable before the experiment began.

Focus Groups

Focus group
An in-depth interview of a panel of eight to twelve persons on a given topic by a skilled discussion leader.

A *focus group* is a panel of eight to twelve employees or users of the human resource department's services that is used for an in-depth interview and audit of the human resource department. It involves an unbiased discussion leader who introduces a topic to the panel and directs the group discussion of it in an unstructured and natural fashion. After the initial warm-up period when members introduce themselves, the moderator (or discussion leader) sets the ground rules for the discussion and introduces the topic. Usually, focus groups last one to two hours.

A typical approach is to have the group discuss human resource practices in the company and the specific strategies or methods used by the department in achieving organizational goals. From this discussion, the moderator may direct the group to talk about how they feel about the human resource practices and then move on to a discussion of what changes and improvements they would like to see in the organization and its human resource policies.

The moderator attempts to let the group carry the conversation by itself, intervening only to introduce topics of importance that may not come up spontaneously, to move on when a topic has been exhausted, or to bring the discussion back to the area of interest when it has wandered into irrelevant areas. The interviews are usually taped so that the moderator can concentrate on keeping the discussion on track without fear of losing or missing information. To be effective, moderators must blend into the group so that they are accepted as a member rather than as a director who

Safety audits at Ontario Power Generation stations continuously monitor safety at the workplace. An ongoing safety audit not only reduces costs, it can save lives.

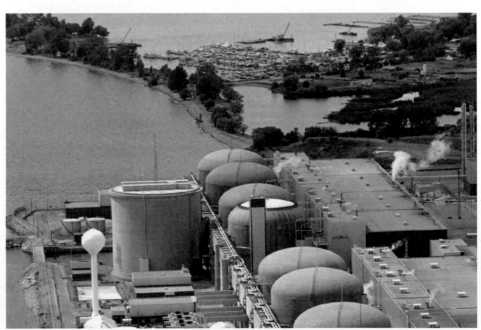

CP PHOTO ARCHIVE (Norm Betts)

asks questions that others are expected to answer. The results of a focus group are normally used for further research and testing. Focus groups are hence best thought of as an exploratory research tool that gives the human resource department some idea about how other units and managers perceive its role.

The Audit Report

Audit report
A comprehensive description of HR activities, containing commendation for effective practices and recommendations for improving ineffective practices.

For making the audit information useful and directive, it is compiled into an audit report. The *audit report* is a comprehensive description of human resource activities, which includes both recommendations for effective practices and recommendations for improving practices that are ineffective. A recognition of both good and bad practices is more balanced and encourages acceptance of the report.

Audit reports often contain several sections. One part is for line managers, another is for managers of specific human resource functions, and the final part is for the human resource manager. For line managers, the report summarizes their human resource objectives, responsibilities, and duties. Examples of duties include interviewing applicants, training employees, evaluating performance, motivating workers, and satisfying employee needs. The report also identifies "people problems." Violations of policies and employee relations laws are highlighted. Poor management practices are revealed in the report along with recommendations.

Those specialists who handle employment, training, compensation, and other human resource activities also need feedback. The audit report they receive isolates specific areas of good and poor performance.

> For example, one audit team observed that many job incumbents lacked qualified replacements. This information was given to the manager of training and development along with the recommendation for more programs to develop promising supervisors and managers.

The human resource manager's report contains all the information given to line managers and specialists within the human resource department. In addition, the human resource manager gets feedback about the following:

- attitudes of operating managers and employees toward the human resource department services;

- a review of the department's objectives and its organization to achieve them;

- human resource problems and their implications; and

- recommendations for needed changes, which may be stated in priority as determined by the audit team.

With the information contained in the audit report, the human resource manager can take a broad view of the human resource function. Instead of solving problems in a random manner, the manager now can focus on those areas that have the greatest potential for improving the department's contribution to the firm. Emerging trends can be studied and corrective action taken while the problems are still minor. Prompt response to the problems of operating managers may earn added support among them.

Perhaps most important, the audit serves as a map for future efforts and a reference point for future audits. With knowledge of the department's present performance, the manager can make long-range plans to upgrade crucial activities. These plans identify new goals for the department.[19] And these goals serve as standards—standards that future audit teams will use to evaluate the firm's human resource management activities.

PREPARING FOR THE FUTURE

AUDITS ARE NECESSARY, but they are backward-looking. They uncover only the results of past decisions. Although past performance should be evaluated, human resource departments also should look to the future in order to be more proactive. A proactive approach requires human resource managers and their staff to develop a future orientation. They must constantly scan their professional and social environment for clues about the future. New developments may mean new challenges.

> For example, high divorce rates may lead to more employer-provided child-care facilities and flexible work schedules so that working parents can fulfil their parental duties.

Without a future orientation, the human resource department becomes reactive, not proactive. And reactive approaches allow minor problems to become major ones. The area of planning provides an appropriate example:

> Several top managers of West Coast Paper Products Ltd. seldom took more than a one-week vacation. They felt that no one else was qualified to take their place for longer than a week. When one mill manager quit, the replacement problem became a crisis for several weeks until a new manager was found. Even then, the mill had problems for months until the new manager had learned the company's policies.

Had the human resource office used human resource planning, replacement procedures could have been developed ahead of time. Even without human resource planning, a future-oriented human resource manager would have questioned the lack of replacements.

Major environmental, governmental, technological, and professional challenges facing human resource departments were discussed in Chapters One and Four of this text. These and a few others are summarized in Figure 17-9. Some of these challenges have changed the basic orientation of the human resource function. Three of these are discussed below.

Globalization and Turbulence in Environments

Profound changes are altering the competitive environment. The Free Trade Agreement, the emergence of a closely integrated European Economic Community, the opening up of the former Communist Bloc, and the emergence of Asian Tigers such as Korea, Singapore, and Taiwan have qualitatively changed the nature of business, especially for an export-oriented nation such as Canada. The deregulation of communication, transportation, and financial institutions in many erstwhile "closed economies" add to the turbulence and intensity of competition in these industries. The combination of these and other trends has placed growing pressures on organizations to perform better in terms of productivity, quality, time, and service. Although technology, capital, material, and energy are vital inputs to any organization, improved performance ultimately rests with the people who use these resources. This means that the human resource function in the next decade should be particularly sensitive to the environmental turbulence and proactively deal with the emerging challenges.

> To survive and prosper in the new global economy, AT&T management mandated its HR department to focus on creating "learning forums" that not only engaged in the continuous training of the workforce but also fostered a new organizational culture.[20]

Improving Employee Productivity

Real wages cannot rise faster than productivity. The wealth and well-being of society depends on the productivity of its workforce. While productivity levels in Canadian

FIGURE 17-9

Selected Challenges Facing Human Resource Managers in the Early 2000s

- *Demographic changes.* The birthrate decline that started in the 1950s means the average age in the workforce will rise. Employee productivity may go up as workers gain experience. But those same people are likely to seek more job security and improved pensions affecting compensation costs.

- *Changing values.* Changing cultural and work values affecting workforce attitudes toward work, retirement, loyalty, attendance and tardiness shape the demands placed on human resource management.

- *Innovation.* To cope and survive in the new economy, human resource specialists will require continued innovation in own practices and facilitate organizational change and innovation.

- *Portable pensions.* Increased mobility of Canadian workers is likely to make it necessary to offer portable pension plans which in turn necessitate changes in HR systems.

- *Technological changes.* Revolutionary changes in technology necessitate fundamental changes in how, where and when work is done, which in turn require more frequent job redesign and improved systems for human resource planning, selection and training

- *Constitutional changes.* The political uncertainty about Quebec's role in the federation is likely to continue for the immediate future. The interprovincial migration patterns and supply of human resources to firms operating in Quebec will depend on these outcomes.

- *Employee rewards.* Strong demand for skilled workers have caused "wage compression" where the gap between the pay of new and senior workers has narrowed, offering limited rewards for experience and loyalty. If these trends continue, reward systems may focus more and more on noncash compensation and lean towards knowledge based pay.

- *Immigration.* Because of their different social and cultural backgrounds, the effective integration of new immigrants into the workforce will be a challenge for human resource specialists.

- *Global competition.* The removal of tariffs and opening up of markets in various parts of the world not only offers new opportunities for Canadian businesses, but also makes them more vulnerable to foreign competition, thus making productivity improvements mandatory.

- *Women and minority workers.* The higher participation rates of women in the workforce will create demands for greater equality in pay or career advancement opportunities. The entry of more visible minority workers into the labour market will necessitate better diversity management tools on the part of work supervisors and managers.

- *Dual-career families.* With the emergence of more dual career families, child care, elder care, spousal transfer, and so on will demand much greater attention from HR practitioners.

- *Protecting employee privacy.* With the growth of computerized information systems, companies maintain ever-growing databanks on employees. The need to ensure privacy to employees against abuse of this information may cause greater attention to be paid to the privacy of employee records.

industries have improved in recent years, they need to be constantly monitored and further improved if Canada is to remain competitive in the new world economic order. Increasingly, the competitive advantage is to be found in the creativity of employees. Tapping that wellspring may be the best hope for both emerging and mature industries.[21] Through pay and incentive systems geared to increased productivity, the human resource department can help align labour costs with performance.

Strategic Contribution

This entire text has emphasized a strategic approach to human resource management. This is because, increasingly, human resource managers are expected to contribute to the organization's strategic thinking. Marketing, production, and financial strategies depend upon the abilities of the firm's human resources to execute these plans. To assist with the "people side" of implementation, human resource directors will be forced to uncover, through audits and research, the causes and solutions to people-related problems. Their diagnostic abilities to assess present and potential human resource issues will be needed as they and their staff increasingly serve as internal consultants to others who are facing human resource related challenges.[22] They then will be called on to facilitate changes in the organization that maximize the human contribution. In short, the traditional administrative skills associated with human resource management must grow to accommodate diagnostic, assessment, consulting, and facilitative skills.

SUMMARY

A human resource audit evaluates the human resource activities used in an organization. Its purpose is to ensure that operating managers and human resource specialists are following human resource policies and maintaining an effective workforce.

The scope of the audit involves human resource specialists, operating managers, employees, and the external environment. Inputs are sought from all four sources because each has a unique perspective. To be truly effective, human resource activities cannot meet just the wishes of experts in the field. They must also meet the needs of employees and operating managers and the challenges from the environment.

The audit team uses a variety of research approaches and tools to evaluate human resource activities. Along with internal comparisons, audit teams need to compare their firm's efforts against those of other companies or against standards developed by external authorities and internal statistics. Or their approach may evaluate compliance with laws or with objectives set by management.

Data are gathered through interviews, questionnaire surveys, internal records, external sources, experimentation, or focus groups. Through these tools, the audit team is able to compile an audit report. The audit report provides feedback to top management, operating managers, human resource specialists, and the human resource manager. Armed with this information, the human resource manager then can develop plans to ensure that human resource activities better contribute to the objectives of the organization. If human resource management is to be responsible, it must review its past performance through audits and research. At the same time, it needs a future orientation to anticipate upcoming challenges. Finally, a proactive view encourages human resource management to contribute to both people and company goals. To be proactive requires modern information systems, increased professionalism, and a future orientation to meet the major environmental, governmental, and technological challenges facing human resource departments. These evolving challenges will cause human resource managers to find new approaches.

With all the challenges facing human resource management, its role is sure to grow in scope and importance. The key to this growth is unlocking the contribution that people make to organizations. It is through this contribution that organizations prosper. In turn, it is through our life-sustaining organizations that we prosper as individuals and as a society.

TERMS FOR REVIEW

Visit the Web site at www.mcgrawhill.ca/college/schwind6 for a full glossary.

Human resource audit . . . . (p.664)
Audit of the corporate strategy . . . . (p.668)
Audit of the human resource system . . . . (p.669)

REVIEW AND DISCUSSION QUESTIONS

1. What are the benefits of a human resource audit to an organization?

2. Why does a human resource audit go beyond just the actions of human resource specialists?

3. If you were asked to conduct an audit of a human resource function (e.g., compensation) what steps would you follow?

4. If you had to conduct an audit of employee job satisfaction, what tools would you use?

5. Explain why a human resource department should be proactive in its approach.

CRITICAL THINKING QUESTIONS

1. What research approach do you think should be followed for each of the following areas of concern to the human resource audit team: (a) evaluation of a new company-sponsored drug rehabilitation program, (b) an analysis of employee tardiness patterns, (c) the appropriateness of present recruiting costs?

2. Today, in cities such as Toronto and Vancouver, about a third of the citizens are visible minorities. What impact will such a heterogeneous workforce have on organizations? What changes in human resource practices may be necessary to meet this new reality?

3. Today, there is less and less government involvement in several sectors. Many former public sectors have been privatized; a "pay-as-you-go" mentality has become popular in several other sectors. What impact does this shift have for

human resource practices, especially in the areas of employee training, compensation, and development?

4. In the last two decades, many cultural values have changed—some rather drastically. Briefly describe how human resource management might be affected by (a) acceptance of same-sex families, (b) increased participation of women in the workforce especially in non-traditional sectors, (c) increased acceptability by society of divorce.

WEB RESEARCH

Search the Web sites of professional human resource associations and publishers in this country and internationally and gather information on the latest trends in auditing human resources. Write a brief report about the emerging trends and present it to your class.

INCIDENT 17-1

Maritime Coal Industries Ltd.

Maritime Coal Industries ran two underground coal mines and a coke oven for converting coal into industrial coke. The locations were about 60 kilometres apart, and so each operation had a branch human resource office. The branch offices did their own hiring, administration of employee benefits, safety programs, and labour relations with the local union. After reading an article about the merit of a human resource management audit, the human resource director at Maritime, Gabe Robertson, discussed the need for an audit with the three branch human resource officers. Their individual reactions are summarized below:

Tony Masone: We don't need an audit. It will take weeks to conduct, and it won't change a thing. Each of us branch human resource managers does the best job we know how. Besides, most of our actions are audited daily by the union. If we make a mistake in employee treatment, pay, benefits, safety, or most of the traditional audit areas, the union lets us know promptly. When you have a union, an audit is not needed.

Joyce McDonald: I disagree with Tony. The union would complain if we made an error against their members. But if our errors were detrimental to the best interests of Maritime, I doubt the union would say anything. Besides, in the matter of recruiting, selection, orientation, and training, the union has little say or interest. An audit might even reveal areas where each branch might improve. I for one welcome an audit and a chance to see how my office compares with the other two.

Sylvie Gagnon: Joyce makes a good case for an audit, but if we were having problems in training, selection, or the other areas she mentions, we'd know it. We have gotten along for years without an audit; I see no need to put in a lot of overtime and disrupt everything else just to compile a report that will tell us what we already know.

1. Assuming you agree with Joyce, what other arguments would you add to justify the overtime and disruption that worry Sylvie?

2. Even though the union contract specifies many areas in detail, briefly describe the possible benefits from an audit of Maritime's (a) compensation program, (b) safety program, (c) grievance process, and (d) labour relations training for supervisors.

3. Do you think Tony and Sylvie would have a different attitude if they and Joyce were assigned to the audit team? Why?

INCIDENT 17-2

Employee Attitudes at Anko Ltd.

Anko Ltd. rents sports equipment. Its main business is renting out ski equipment and snowmobiles. During the winter, the number of employees ranges between fifty and sixty at five locations in various winter resort areas. Al Anko, the owner, hired a management consultant to evaluate employee satisfaction and attitudes. After interviewing nearly 20 employees and supervisors, the consultant developed an attitude survey that was mailed to all employees. From the interviews and attitude surveys, the consultant made the following observations:

- Nearly two-thirds of the employees felt little loyalty to the firm because they considered their jobs temporary.

- Many employees applied to work at Anko because they were interested in skiing.

- Although the firm gave few benefits, many employees commented about the reduced rental rates on equipment as an important "extra" of their jobs.

- Every supervisor mentioned that the most important selection criterion was whether an applicant knows how to fit and adjust ski bindings.

- Over half of the employees worked split shifts from 7 to 10 a.m. and from 4 to 7 p.m., which were the hours most skis were rented and returned. Some employees liked those hours because they could ski during the day. However, employees who lived in the resort area all year long generally disliked the hours.

- Employee turnover was very low. But many employees indicated that they would quit if they could find a better-paying job.

- Several employees who had worked for Anko in previous years thought it was unfair that they received the same hourly wage as new employees.

1. If you were the consultant, what recommendations would you make to the owner about (a) the use of split shifts, (b) the types of people recruited, and (c) the treatment of employees who have worked for Anko more than one season?

2. Should Anko treat employees who permanently live in the resort areas differently from those who move there just for the ski season? If so, what differences in treatment would you recommend?

EXERCISE 17-1

An Audit of The Human Resource Management Course

Conduct an audit of this human resource management course following these steps:

1. Look at the course outline and list the objectives as stated there (or elsewhere by the instructor). Now evaluate to what extent each of these objectives was accomplished. [If there were several objectives, you may use a five-point scale to quantitatively summarize your evaluation. (5= completely; 1= not at all).]

2. Indicate the extent to which you gained mastery over the various topics:

   (5= very much; 3=moderate; 1=very little)

   - Role of human resource manager
   - Challenges facing HR managers

- Job analysis
- Human resource planning
- Legal challenges and human rights laws
- Recruitment
- Selection
- Orientation and training
- Management/career development
- Performance appraisal
- Compensation
- Employee relations
- Managing diversity
- Occupational safety and health
- Union-management relations
- Human resource audit

3. Now, evaluate the various teaching aids and class procedures using the following 5-point scale (5= excellent; 1=poor; N/A= not applicable).

- Lectures by the instructor
- Guest lectures
- Films and audio-visual material
- Field trips
- Class discussions
- Case discussions
- Cases used in the course
- Textbook
- Readings
- Overall classroom climate
- Assignments and exercises

4. Compared to other courses you have taken in a similar area, how would you rate this course? (5= much above them; 4= above them; 3= same as them; 2= below them; 1=much below them.)

5. What suggestions would you make to improve the overall quality and usefulness of this course?

CASE STUDY

Maple Leaf Shoes Ltd.

An Exercise in Human Resource Audit[1]

Jane Reynolds, senior assistant in the human resource department in Maple Leaf Shoes, was bewildered by the findings of the employee survey she had just completed. True, she had expected the results to show some of these trends; however, their magnitude and underlying patterns were quite puzzling.

Reynolds keyed a set of new codes into the computer. The screen flickered momentarily and a new set of figures and tables appeared on her computer screen. "This is going to be a very long day," she murmured to herself as she looked at the data on the screen.

_____

[1] Case written by Professor Hari Das of Department of Management, Saint Mary's University, Halifax, N.S. All rights retained by the author © Das, 2000.

She got up from her chair, stretched, and walked to the coffee machine to pour herself her seventh cup of coffee.

As she sat down at her desk, Reynolds took a sip of the warm coffee. Then she patiently began to key more numbers into the computer.

Maple Leaf Shoes Ltd., a medium-sized manufacturer of leather and vinyl shoes located in Ontario, has been going through some challenging times (see end of Chapter One for more details of the company and its operations). On the instruction of Robert Clark, Jane Reynolds had conducted an employee survey last week. She had wanted to survey the entire workforce, but this would have been too time-consuming. Instead, she selected the Lady's Shoes Division as the candidate for her survey. This was one of the larger divisions of the company and employed 202 persons. (Exhibit 1 shows the number of employees in the division and the profile of survey respondents.)

Reynolds had developed a short questionnaire in consultation with her friend (a business student in a local university). Reynolds wanted the questionnaire to be a short and easy one to understand and respond to. Her final questionnaire had 15 items anchored on a five-point scale (see Exhibit 2).

Reynolds received 80 responses for the survey, but did not expect to receive any more. She had reminded the staff twice about the importance of the survey and the need for getting their input to help make changes. But, by and large, she had received a lukewarm response to her requests, especially from plant employees. Three or four employees openly confronted her, asking, "Why should we waste our time, when nothing will change anyway." One male plant employee, muttering curses, had thrown the questionnaire into a nearby garbage can in her presence.

Exhibit 3 shows the results Reynolds received from her preliminary analysis of the data. She is aware of the need for further analysis of the data for each subgroup and each category.

Discussion Questions

1. What is your evaluation of the various steps taken by Reynolds to collect information from employees?

2. Based on the survey results, what conclusions would you form?

3. What actions would you recommend that the company take now? In the long term?

EXHIBIT 1

	Managerial		Supervisory		Clerical		Manufacturing	
Profiles of Survey Respondents								
	Male	Female	Male	Female	Male	Female	Male	Female
Number of employees	5	0	15	2	8	22	95	55
Number who responded to the survey	2	0	2	1	3	12	20	40

EXHIBIT 2

A Sample of Questionnaire Used

Maple Leaf Shoes

Employee Opinion Survey

Please take a few minutes to complete this brief questionnaire. The information you supply will help us make changes in the company in the near future. You can check (or circle) any number corresponding to an item. You don't have to disclose your name or employee number anywhere on this form. Please return all completed forms to Jane Reynolds in the Human Resource Department (Office 102A). Please call Local 5678 if you need clarification on any item below or have a question.

A. Work

1.	Satisfying	5	4	3	2	1	Frustrating
2.	Challenging	5	4	3	2	1	Boring
3.	Non-routine	5	4	3	2	1	Routine
4.	Has lot of potential for career growth	5	4	3	2	1	Has no potential for career growth

B. Pay

5.	Fair	5	4	3	2	1	Unfair
6.	Equitable	5	4	3	2	1	Not equitable
7.	Competitive with other firms	5	4	3	2	1	Not competitive with other firms

C. Supervisor

8.	Very professional in approach	5	4	3	2	1	Not at all professional in approach
9.	Has high leadership skills	5	4	3	2	1	Has no leadership skills
10.	Caring	5	4	3	2	1	Uncaring
11.	Controlling	5	4	3	2	1	Delegating

D. Working Conditions

12.	Safe	5	4	3	2	1	Unsafe
13.	Pleasant	5	4	3	2	1	Unpleasant
14.	Helpful co-workers	5	4	3	2	1	Unhelpful co-workers
15.	Receive all instructions on time	5	4	3	2	1	Do not receive most instructions on time

E. Information About You

Male _____   Female _____

Managerial _____   Supervisory _____   Clerical _____   Manufacturing _____

Age: 20-29 _____   30-39 _____   40-49 _____   50+ _____

Thank you for participating in the survey.

EXHIBIT 3

Preliminary Results Emerging From the Survey

Average scores for the various items in the survey are shown below.

		Managerial		Supervisory		Clerical		Manufacturing	
		Male	Female	Male	Female	Male	Female	Male	Female
A.	**Work**								
	1. Satisfying	3.8		3.6	3.2	3.5	3.6	3.1	3.0
	2. Challenging	4.1		3.9	3.8	3.3	3.2	3.0	3.1
	3. Non-routine	3.9		2.8	2.9	3.1	3.2	2.9	3.0
	4. Has potential for career growth	3.6		3.1	2.8	3.8	2.9	3.0	3.0
B.	**Pay**								
	5. Fair	4.0		3.9	3.6	3.6	3.4	3.6	3.1
	6. Equitable	4.2		4.2	3.4	3.9	3.3	3.8	3.0
	7. Competitive	3.9		3.8	3.6	3.7	3.5	3.6	3.4
C.	**Supervisor**								
	8. Professional	3.5		3.7	3.5	3.9	3.4	3.7	3.3
	9. Has leadership skills	3.6		3.8	3.2	3.9	3.2	3.7	2.9
	10. Caring	4.3		3.8	3.5	3.6	3.3	3.6	3.3
	11. Controlling	3.7		4.0	4.3	4.1	4.3	4.2	4.4
D.	**Working Conditions**								
	12. Safe	4.4		3.9	3.7	4.2	3.8	3.6	3.2
	13. Pleasant	4.2		4.0	3.8	4.0	3.9	3.5	3.1
	14. Helpful co-workers	4.4		4.3	3.7	4.1	3.8	4.0	3.4
	15. Timely receipt of instructions	4.3		3.6	3.6	4.0	3.9	3.4	3.3

CASE STUDY

Canadian Pacific and International Bank
Preparing for the Future[2]

Canadian Pacific and International Bank (CPIB) is one of Canada's premier financial institutions with assets over $150 billion. CPIB, which began as a "western" bank in the early 1950s in British Columbia, today employs over 25 000 persons and provides personal, commercial, corporate and investment banking services to individuals and businesses in 33 countries. More details of the bank are given at the end of Chapter One.

[2] Case written by Professor Hari Das of Department of Management, Saint Mary's University, Halifax, Canada. All rights retained by the author. Das © 2000.

Mary Keddy, senior vice president—human resources, is currently looking at the bank's plans for the immediate future and identifying their human resource implications. She identified the following as some of the more immediate challenges facing the human resource function:

1. Globally, CPIB serves more than six million customers in three key areas: personal and commercial banking, wealth management, and wholesale and corporate banking. This figure is expected to reach 10 million in the next three years. Most of the growth will come through foreign expansion and achieving a higher percentage of the wealth management market. With an aging North American and European market, this market is likely to grow much faster than commercial or wholesale banking.

2. Most of the routine banking will be done in the future through automated tellers and Internet banking. Compared to the 22 per cent of customers who use Web-based brokerage, CPIB expects over 65 per cent to be using this technology within five years.

3. CPIB primarily used a growth through acquisition strategy. In the last three years, it acquired three major investment brokerages and trusts. In the next five years, this number is likely to become even greater. While all the acquisitions have proved to be economically viable, they had also provided some challenges. The organizational culture of the brokerages and trust companies differed from that at CPIB, presenting a host of difficulties during the transition period.

4. As CPIB extends its operations to foreign countries, it has become increasingly difficult to institute similar HR practices across all its world branches. The compensation and performance appraisal systems must recognize cultural and economic differences across countries; yet, some degree of uniformity across all its operations is necessary to facilitate planning and human resource transfer and development. How to achieve uniformity without losing flexibility? There seems to be no simple answer. Also what is considered as unethical in Canada may be very acceptable in some of the Asian or African countries. For example, several manufacturers in developing economies employ seven- to eight-year-old children and pay low wages. These manufacturers are important customers of the bank—often accounting for 25 per cent or more of its loans in some regions. How can the Bank be ethical without placing too many constraints on the managers in foreign branches?

5. While the bank has been a progressive employer, the number of female senior managers in its ranks continues to be low. At the junior levels of management, the ratio between male and female managers is currently 65:35; however, as one goes up the hierarchy, the ratio changes drastically in favour of the males. Further, even at the supervisory and junior managerial level, the percentage of visible minorities has been insignificant (often amounting to less than one-tenth of one per cent). The bank would like to encourage more women, minorities, and people with physical disabilities to reach middle and senior managerial levels.

Discussion Questions

Assume Keddy has decided to conduct an audit of the human resource function of CPIB. How should she proceed further on the matter? What research approach should she take? What tools of research should she use? What additional external information should she collect?

SUGGESTED READINGS

Hamel, Gary, *Leading the Revolution*, Boston: Harvard Business School Press, 2000.

Johnson, Mike, *Winning the People Wars*, London: Pearson Education, 2000.

Orr, Brian, "The Challenge of Bench-marking HR Performance," *Canadian HR Reporter*, April 21, 1997, p.6.

Saks, Alan, Schmitt, Neal and Klimoski, Richard, *Research, Measurement and Evaluation of Human Resources*, Scarborough, Ontario: ITP Nelson, 2000.

REFERENCES

Chapter 1

1. Subhir Chowdhury, *Management 21C*, London: Pearson Education Limited, 2000, p. 12.

2. "The New Age of Discovery," *Time* (special issue), Winter 1997-98, pp. 11-66.

3. Robert Granford Wright, "Managing Management Resources through Corporate Constitutionalism," *Human Resource Management*, Summer 1973, p. 15.

4. Bruce Little, "We're Less Dependent But More Entangled," *The Globe and Mail*, May 15, 2000, p. A-2.

5. "Canada: A Special Report" *Time*, June 28, 1999, p. 41.

6. Andrew Purvis, "Super Exporter," *Time*, April 28, 1997, p. 37.

7. "Innovation in Industry," *The Economist*, February 20, 1999, pp. 5-28

8. "Canada's Ranking Slips in Ability to Innovate," *The Globe and Mail*, March 12, 1999, p. B-3.

9. *The World Competitiveness Year Book*, IMD International, Lausanne, Switzerland, 2000.

10. John McCallum, "Will Canada Matter in 2020?" *Royal Bank Current Analysis*, Royal Bank of Canada Economics Department, May 2000, p. 5.

11. CBC Television, *Venture*, undated.

12. Randall Litchfield, "The Sunrise Economy," *Canadian Business*, June 1992, pp. 85-86.

13. "Is Your Job Safe?" *Maclean's*, September 30, 1996, p. 48.

14. Ibid., pp. 48-49.

15. Simon Tuck, "Internet Milestone Set as 50% Connected in Canada," *The Globe and Mail*, May 1, 1999, p. B-1.

16. "Working from Home Cuts Employee Stress, Study Finds," *The Globe and Mail*, November 16, 1994, p. B-19.

17. Shari Caudron, "Working at Home Pays Off," *Personnel Journal*, Vol. 71, No. 11, November 1992, pp. 40-49.

18. See Lynne McGee, "Setting Up Work at Home," *Personnel Administrator*, Vol. 33, No. 12, December 1988, pp. 58-62.

19. "McCarthy's Reinvents the Practice," *The Globe and Mail*, December 6, 1999, p. M-1.

20. Gordon Arnaut, "Just What Does an Intranet Do?" *Report on Business Magazine*, May 1997, pp. 15-19.

21. Ross Laver, "Kids, Bosses and Work," *Maclean's*, February 24, 1997, p. 38.

22. Statistics Canada, *Gross Domestic Product at Factor Cost*, March 2000, www.statcan.ca.

23. "The Path to Unlocking Employee Knowledge," *The Globe and Mail*, October 25, 1999, p. M-1.

24. Employment Trends in the Information Economy," *Applied Research Bulletin*, Vol. 3, No. 2, 1997; HRDC Web site: www.hrdc-drhc.gc.ca.

25. "The Industries That Will Define the Decade," *The Globe and Mail*, April 21, 1997, p. A-6.

26. Statistics Canada, *Population 15 Years and Over by Highest Degree, Certificate or Diploma*, www.statcan.ca, June 2000.

27. Results of International Adult Literacy Survey reported on the Web site: http://www.nald.ca/nts/ials/ialsreps/high2.htm, February 10, 1998. Also see: Morton Ritts, "What if Johnny Still Can't Read," *Canadian Business*, May 1986, pp. 54-57, 124.

28. Results of Second International Assessment of Educational Progress quoted by Tom Fennell, "What's Wrong at School?" *Maclean's*, January 11, 1993, pp. 28-32.

29. Statistics Canada, *Population 15 years and Over by Highest Degree*, Ibid.

30. *Employability Skills Profile* prepared by Corporate Council on Education, a program of the National Business and Education Centre, The Conference Board of Canada, 255 Smyth Road, Ottawa, Ont. K1H 8M7, Undated.

31. *Workplace Education-PEI: Creating Partnerships with Business and Industry*, April 2000, Charlottetown, PEI, C1A 8W5.

32. "Our Coming Old Age Crisis," *Maclean's*, January 17, 1983, p. 24.

33. "Part-timers Being Shut Out, Study Says," *The Globe and Mail*, November 17, 1997, p. A-3.

34. John Porter, *The Vertical Mosaic: An Analysis of Social Class and Power in Canada*, Toronto: University of Toronto Press, 1965. See also V.V. Murray, "Canadian Cultural Values and Personnel Administration," in Harish Jain, ed., *Contemporary Issues in Canadian Personnel Administration,* Scarborough, Ont.: Prentice-Hall, 1974.

35. "Face of Canada Changes," *The Globe and Mail*, November 5, 1997, p. A-1.

36. "No Longer a Two-language Nation," *The Mail Star*, December 3, 1997, p. A-19.

37. Rae Corelli, "How Very Different We Are," *Maclean's*, November 4, 1996, pp. 36-39

38. Professor Richard Woodward of University of Calgary quoted by McMurdy, "Falling Expectations," *Maclean's*, January 4, 1993 p. 36.

39. Frank Vallee and Donald Whyte, "Canadian Society: Trends and Perspectives," in Harish Jain (ed). *Contemporary Issues in Canadian Personnel Administration*, p. 31.

40. Ibid., pp. 29-42.

41. Joe Chidley and Andrew Wahl, "The New Worker's Paradise," *Canadian Business*, March 12, 1999, pp. 37-38.

42. Andrew Campbell, "Turning Workers into Risk Takers," *Canadian Business*, February, 1985, p.109.

43. Hari Das, *Strategic Organizational Design*, Scarborough, Ontario: Prentice-Hall, 1998, pp. 324-329.

44. Ibid., p. 204.

45. Adapted and summarized from Randall Schuler and Susan Jackson, "Linking competitive strategies with Human Resource Management Practices," *Academy of Management Executive*, 1987, Vol. 1, No. 3, pp. 207-219; also see, Susan Jackson and Randall Schuler, "Understanding Human Resource Management in the context of organizations and their environments," *Annual Review of Psychology*, 1995, Vol. 46, pp. 237-264; Randall Schuler, Steven Galante, and Susan Jackson, "Matching Effective HR Practices with Competitive Strategy," *Personnel*, September, 1987.

46. "HRM Measurement Projects Issues First Report," *Resource*, December 1985, p. 2.

47. "Personnel People," *The New York Times*, May 11, 1986, p. 3-1.

48. Miles, R.E. and Snow, C.C., "Designing Strategic Human Resource Systems," *Organizational Dynamics*, Vol. 13, No. 1, 1984, pp. 36-52.

49. Schwenker, Kevin, Das, Hari, Mealiea, Laird, Schwind, Hermann, Thorne, Allister and Walsh, Gerald, *CCHRA National Standards Project- Phase III, The Nova Scotia Pilot Assessment Project*, National Capabilities Committee, Canadian Council of Human Resource Associations, December 1999.

50. Deloitte & Touche Human Resource Consulting Services, *The State of the Human Resources Management Function in Canada*, 1994, p. ii.

51. Arthur Young, Wayne Brockbank, and Dave Ulrich, "Lower Cost, Higher Value: Human Resource Function in Transformation" *Human Resource Planning*, Vol. 17, No. 3, 1994, pp. 10-12.

52. Schwenker, Kevin et al., 1999, op. cit., p. 44.

53. Schwenker, Kevin et al., 1999, op. cit., p. 44.

54. Peter Drucker, "The Coming of the New Organization," *Harvard Business Review*, January-February, 1988, p. 45.

55. "The End of Money?" *The Globe and Mail*, May 13, 2000, p. A-16.

56. "'Love Bug' Hits World's E-mail," *The Globe and Mail*, May 5, 2000, p. A-1.

57. Richard Blackwell, "Banks Give Shareholders a Voice" *The Globe and Mail*, March 3, 2000, page B-10.

58. "Finance Minister to Have Wide Bank Powers," *The Globe and Mail*, June 1, 2000, p. B-1.

59. Mary Janigan, "Feud Without End," *Maclean's*, April 24, 2000, p. 60.

60. "Scotiabank Warns of 'Intrusive' Consumer Regulation," *The Globe and Mail*, March 1, 2000, p. B-3.

61. Keith McArthur and Dawn Walton, "Protecting What Is Right," *The Globe and Mail*, February 15, 2000, p. B-16.

Chapter 2

1. Philip C. Grant, "What Use Is a Job Description?" *Personnel Journal*, Vol. 67, No. 2, February 1988, p. 50.

2. For example, see Susan Greenberg and Raymond Bello, "Re-Write Job Descriptions: Focus on Functions," *HR Focus*, Vol. 69, July 1992, p. 10; Michael Brannick, Joan Brannick, and Edward Levine, "Job Analysis, Personnel Selection and the ADA," *Human Resource Management Review*, Vol. 2, No. 3, 1992, pp. 171-182.

3. William Wooten, "Using Knowledge, Skill and Ability (KSA) Data to Identify Career Planning Opportunities: An Application of Job Analysis to Internal Manpower Planning," *Public Personnel Administrator*, Vol. 22, No. 4, 1993, pp. 551-563.

4. *Canadian Human Rights Reporter*, Vol. 6, 1985, p. 6.

5. Sidney Fine, *Functional Job Analysis Scales: A Desk Aid*, Kalamazoo, MI: Upjohn Institute for Employment Research, 1973.

6. Purdue Research Foundation, *Position Analysis Questionnaire*, West Lafayette, Indiana 47907, 1989.

7. Wayne Cascio, *Applied Psychology in Personnel Management*, Fourth edition, Englewood Cliffs, NJ: Prentice-Hall, 1991; p. 207.

8. Paul Sparks, "Job Analysis," in K. Rowland and G. Ferris, eds., *Personnel Management*, Boston: Allyn and Bacon, 1982; Edward L. Levine, Ronald A. Ash, H. Hall, and Frank Sistrunk, "Evaluation of Job Analysis Methods by Experienced Job Analysts," *Academy of Management Journal*, Vol. 26, No. 2, 1983, pp. 339-48; E.J. McCormick, *Job Analysis: Methods and Applications*, New York: AMACOM, 1979; Luis R. Gomez-Mejia, Ronald C. Page, and Walter W. Tormow, "A Comparison of the Practical Utility of Traditional, Statistical and Hybrid Job Evaluation Approaches," *Academy of Management Journal*, Vol. 25, No. 4, 1982, pp. 790-809; Ronald A. Ash and Edward Levine, "A Framework for Evaluating Job Analysis Methods," *Personnel*, November-December 1980, pp. 53-59.

9. E.L. Levine, R.A. Ash, and N. Bennett. "Explorative Comparative Study of Four Job Analysis Methods." *Journal of Applied Psychology*, Vol. 65, 1980, pp. 524-35 and E.L. Levine, R.A. Ash, H. Hall, and F. Sistrunk, "Evaluation of Job Analysis Methods by Experienced Job Analysts," *Academy of Management Journal*, Vol. 26, No. 2, 1983, pp. 339-48.

10. Employment and Immigration Canada, *National Occupational Classification*, 1993, Ottawa: Information Canada. See also Employment and Immigration Canada, Updates on CCDO, Ottawa: Information Canada (published for major groups annually); CCDO: Occupations in Major Groups, Employment and Immigration Canada, 1986.

11. Brian Orr, "Position Management Has Its Rewards," *Canadian HR Reporter*, March 24, 1997, p. 15.

12. Hari Das, Peter J. Frost, and J. Thad Barnowe, "Behaviourally Anchored Scales for Assessing Behavioural Science Teaching,"

Canadian Journal of Behavioural Science, Vol. 11, No. 1, January 1979, pp. 79-88; Tom Janz, "Estimating the Standard Deviation of Job Performance: A Behavioural Approach," *Administrative Sciences Association of Canada (Organizational Behaviour Division) Meeting Proceedings*, Vol. 2, Part 5, 1981, pp. 70-78.

13. Richard Mirabile, "Everything You Wanted to Know About Competency Modeling," *Training and Development*, August 1997, pp. 73-77.

14. Patricia A. McLagan, "Competencies: The Next Generation," *Training and Development*, May 1997, p. 41.

15. Jean-Pascal Souque, *Focus on Competencies*, Report No. 177-96, The Conference Board of Canada, 1996, p. 18.

16. Brian Orr, "The Challenge of Benchmarking HR Performance," *Canadian HR Reporter*, April 21, 1997, p. 6.

17. William H. Glick, G. Douglas Jenkins, Jr., and Nina Gupta, "Method Versus Substance: How Strong Are Underlying Relationships Between Job Characteristics and Attitudinal Outcomes?" *Academy of Management Journal*, Vol. 29, No. 3, 1985, pp. 441-64. See also Daniel A. Ondrack and Martin Evans, "Job Enrichment and Job Satisfaction of Quality of Working Life and Nonquality of Working Life Work Sites," *Human Relations*, Vol. 39, No. 9, 1986, pp. 871-89; D.R. Ilgen and J.R. Hollenbeck, "The Structure of Work: Job Design and Roles," in M.D. Dunnette and L.M. Hough, eds., *Handbook of Industrial and Organizational Psychology*, Vol. 2, Palo Alto: Consulting Psychologists Press, 1991, pp. 165-207.

18. Michael Losey, "HR Comes of Age," *HR Magazine*, 50th Anniversary Issue, 1998, pp. 40-53.

19. Robert Inman, "Workflow," *Transactions*, Vol. 28, No. 7, July 1996, pp. 555-56.

20. E. Joy Mighty and Judy Ann Roy, "Re-designing Job Design," *Global Business Trends: Contemporary Readings*, Cumberland, Maryland 21501: Academy of Business Administration, 1997, pp. 261-269.

21. E. Grandjean, *Fitting the Task to the Man*, Fourth Edition, Bristol, Pa.: Taylor and Francis, 1990; also see, Chris Knight, "Office Workers Frustrated with Their Workspace," *Canadian HR Reporter*, December 1, 1997, p. 21.

22. Monica Belcourt, Arthur Sherman, George Bohlander, and Scott Snell, *Managing Human Resources*, Second Edition, Toronto: Nelson Canada, 1999, pp. 112-113.

23. Glenn Harrington, "Ergonomics Preaches Prevention as Alternative to High Cost Injuries," *Canadian HR Reporter*, September 9, 1996, p. 22.

24. Ibid., p. 22.

25. Glenn Harrington, "Older Workers Need Ergonomic Aid," *Canadian HR Reporter*, November 17, 1997, p. 20.

26. Frederick Herzberg, Bernard Mausner, and Barbara Snyderman, *The Motivation to Work*, New York: Wiley, 1959. See also E.F. Stone and L.W. Porter, "Job Characteristics and Job Attitudes: A Multivariate Study," *Journal of Applied Psychology*, Vol. 59, 1975, pp. 57-64; Kae H. Chung and Monica F. Ross, "Differences in Motivational Properties Between Job Enlargement and Job Enrichment," *Academy of Management Review*, January 1977, pp. 113-21; J. Richard Hackman, June L. Pearce, and Jane Caminis Wolfe, "Effects of Changes in Job Characteristics on Work Attitudes and Behaviours: A Naturally Occurring Quasi-Experiment," *Organizational Behaviour and Human Performance*, Vol. 21, No. 2, 1978, pp. 289-304.

27. Ian Gellatly and Gregory Irving, "The Moderating Role of Perceived Autonomy on Personality-performance Relations within a Public Sector Organization," *ASAC 1999 Proceedings (Human Resources)*, Vol. 20, No. 9, 1999, University of New Brunswick, Saint John, NB.

28. Richard W. Woodward and John J. Sherwood, "A Comprehensive Look at Job Design," *Personnel Journal*, August 1977, p. 386.

29. M. Scott Myers, *Every Employee a Manager*, New York: McGraw-Hill, 1970.

30. P. Booth, *Challenge and Change: Embracing the Team Concept*, Ottawa: Conference Board of Canada, 1994.

31. For example, see: Donna Deeprose, *The Team Coach: Vital New Skills for Supervisors and Managers in a Team Environment*, New York: American Management Association, 1995.

32. Ageeth Balkema and Eric Molleman, "Barriers to the Development of Self-organizing Teams," *Journal of Managerial Psychology*, Vol. 14, No. 2, 1999, pp. 134-150.

33. For instance, see: Sparrow, Paul "New Employee Behaviours, Work Designs and Forms of Work Organization: What Is in Store for Future of Work?" *Journal of Managerial Psychology*, Vol. 15, No. 3, 2000, pp. 202-218.

34. William Bridges, "The End of the Job," *Fortune*, September 19, 1994, p. 64.

35. Peter Coy, "The 21st Century Organization," *Business Week*, August 28, 2000.

36. Karen May, "Work in the 21st Century: Implications for Job Analysis," The Society for Industrial and Organizational Psychology, www.siop.org/tip/backissues/tipapr96/may.htm, December 18, 2000.

Chapter 3

1. Abdul Rahman bin Idris and Derek Eldridge, "Reconceptualising Human Resource Planning in Response to Institutional Change," *International Journal of Manpower*, Vol. 19, No. 5, 1998, p. 346

2. Matt Hennecke, "The 'People' Side of Strategic Planning," *Training*, November 1984, pp. 25-32; Anil Gupta, "Matching Managers to Strategies: Points and Counterpoints," *Human Resource Management*, Vol. 25, No. 2, Summer 1986, pp. 215-34.

3. "Minority Lawyers Get Boost," *The Mail Star*, September 7, 2000, p. A-1.

4. For an example, see, Judith Cooksey, "Workforce Challenges for Dentists and Pharmacists," www.hrsa.dhhs.gov/newsroom/features/workforcechallenges.htm January 2000.

5. "Good Jobs, No Jobs," *The Globe and Mail*, January 15, 1997, p. B-3.

6. News From Canada Newswire quoted by www.globeinvestor.com, June 29, 2000.

7. A.L. Delbecq, A.H. Van de Ven, and D.H. Gustafson, *Group Techniques for Progress Planning: A Guide to Nominal and Delphi Process*, Glenview, Ill.: Scott, Foresman, 1975; J.M. Bartwrek and J.K. Muringhan, "The Nominal Group Technique: Expanding the Basic Procedure and Underlying Assumptions," *Group and Organizational Studies*, Vol. 9, 1984, pp. 417-32.

8. James W. Walker, "Human Resource Planning: Managerial Concerns and Practices," *Business Horizons*, June 1976, pp. 56-57. See also George S. Odiorne, "The Crystal Ball of HR Strategy," *Personnel Administrator*, December 1986, pp. 103-6; John A. Byrne and Alison L. Cowan, "Should Companies Groom New Leaders Or Buy Them?" *Business Week*, September 22, 1986, pp. 94-96.

9. John Hooper and R.F. Catalanello, "Markov Analysis Applied to Forecasting Technical Personnel," *Human Resource Planning*, 1981, Vol. 4, pp. 41-47.

10. Richard J. Niehaus, "Human Resource Planning Flow Models," *Human Resource Planning*, Vol. 3, 1980, pp.177-187.

11. P.F. Buller and W.R. Maki, "A Case History of a Manpower Planning Model," *Human Resource Planning*, Vol. 4, No. 3, 1981, pp. 129-37.

12. Brian Parker and David Caine, "Holonic Modelling: Human Resource Planning and the Two Faces of Janus," *International Journal of Manpower*, Vol. 17, No. 8, 1996, pp. 30-45.

13. www.statcan.ca

14. www.statcan.ca

15. Wayne Roth, "COPS: A Presentation of Results Using a Revised Framework" Research Paper Series T-95-3, HRDC, http://www.hrdc-drhc.gc.ca, 1995.

16. www.11.hrdc-drhc.gc.ca/doc/jf/trends/trends.shtml

17. "Notions and Numbers—The Canadian Occupational Projection System," Ottawa: Employment and Immigration Canada, WH-3-418 undated. See also these publications by Employment and Immigration Canada: "The Canadian Occupational Projection System—Supply Issues and Approaches," WH-3-335E, January 1983 and "Demand Methodology," WH-3-341, January 1983.

18. www.11-hrdc-drhc.gc.ca/jobfutures/noc/1111.html

19. R.J.Q. Castley, "The Sectoral Approach to the Assessment of Skill Needs and Training Requirements," *International Journal of Manpower*, Vol. 17, No. 1, 1996, pp. 56-68.

20. "Tools for Identifying Skill Shortages: A Cross-country Comparison," Research Paper Series No. T-96-3E, HRDC, http://www.hrdc-drhc.gc.ca, 1996.

21. Peggy Stuart, "New Internal Jobs Found for Displaced Employees," *Personnel Journal*, Vol. 71, No. 8, August 1992, pp. 50-56.

22. "Silver Parachute Protects Work Force," *Resource*, January 1987, p. 3. Later figures received through personal communication with the HR office of the company.

23. Massimo Commanducci, "The Shorter Workweek: Panacea or HR Headache?" *Canadian HR Reporter*, July 13, 1998, p. 1.

24. Ibid., p. 8.

25. Craig C. Pinder and Hari Das, "The Hidden Costs and Benefits of Employee Transfers," *Human Resource Planning*, Vol. 2, No. 3, 1979. See also Craig C. Pinder, "Employee Transfer Studies—Summary," Vancouver: Faculty of Commerce and Business Administration, University of British Columbia, November 1985; Jeanne M. Brett, "Job Transfer and Well Being," *Journal of Applied Psychology*, Vol. 67, No. 4, 1982, pp. 450-63; Jeanne M. Brett and James Werbel, The Effect of Job Transfer on Employees and Their Families, Washington, D.C.: Employer Relocation Council, 1980.

26. Ronald W. Clement, George E. Stevens, and Daniel Brenenstuhl, "Promotion Practices in American Business Colleges: A Comprehensive Investigation," *Manhattan College Journal of Business*, Spring 1986, pp. 9-15.

27. Laurence J. Peter and Raymond Hull, *The Peter Principle*, New York: William Morrow, 1969.

28. Jay F. Straight, Jr., "Introducing CHRIS: Chevron's Human Resource Information System," *Personnel Administrator*, May 1987, pp. 24-28.

29. For assessing HRIS needs, see, Gijs Houtzagers, "Implementation of a Human Resource Management Information System" www.hronline.com/lib/hris.html July 21, 2000.

30. Sandra E. O'Connell, "System Redesign Makes FedEx a Technology Leader," *HRMagazine*, April, 1994, pp. 33-37.

31. Ibid.

32. Sharon Lebrun, "Wired Workers Threaten Data," *Canadian HR Reporter*, January 27, 1997, pp.1-2.

33. Wayne Blackburn, a senior white-collar crime investigator quoted in Sharon Lebrun, 1997, op. cit. p.2.

34. Robert Bickel, "Building Intranets," *Internet World*, March 1996, http://www.internetworld.com

35. Guy Huntington, "Intranet Benefits," *Canadian HR Reporter*, September 9, 1996, p.6.

36. Sharon Lebrun, "Royal Bank Using Intranet to Drive Continuous Learning," *Canadian HR Reporter*, December 1, 1997, p. 9.

37. Gijs Houtzagers, "Electronic Services for HR," www.hronline.com/lib/hris.html , December 1, 1999.

38. HRIS 2000: Internet and Enterprise-wide Systems Seen as the Next Big Things in HRIS," *Canadian HR Reporter: Guide to HR Technology*, April 7, 1997, p. G-3.

39. Hari Das and Mallika Das, "One More Time: How Do We Place a Value Tag on Our Employees? Some Issues in Human Resource Accounting," *Human Resource Planning*, Vol. 2, No. 2, 1979, pp. 91-101.

40. For a discussion of the various models, see Das and Das, "One More Time."

Chapter 4

1. Canadian Charter of Rights and Freedoms, as part of the Constitution Act of 1982.

2. Ibid.

3. H.W. Arthurs, The Right to Golf: Reflection on the Future of Workers, Unions, and the Rest of Us Under the Charter, paper presented at the Conference on Labour Law Under the Charter, Industrial Relations Centre, Queen's University, September 1987. For a more detailed discussion of the impact of the Charter on Canadian labour relations, see S.D. Carter, "Canadian Labour Relations Under the Charter," *Relations Industrielles*, Vol. 43, No. 2, 1988, pp. 305-21.

4. "Human Rights and the Canadian Human Rights Commission," brochure published by the Canadian Human Rights Commission, Catalogue Number H21-35/1999.

5. Canadian Human Rights Act, Paragraph 2, Subsection (a).

6. Doreen Pitkeathly, "Phoenix Rising," *Human Resource Professional*, February 1990, pp. 16-18.

7. Annual Report of the Canadian Human Rights Commission, 1991, p. 59. See also Harvey Goldberg, "Accessibility: Measuring the Results of a Decade," *Human Rights Forum*, a publication of the Canadian Human Rights Commission, Vol. 2, Issue 2, Winter 1992, pp. 8-11; Joseph Wong, "Overcoming Systemic Racial Discrimination in Canada's Volunteer Sector," *Human Rights Forum*, Vol. 2, Issue 1, Fall 1991, pp. 2-4. See also *Human Rights Forum*, Vol. 1, Issue 3, Spring/Summer 1991, p. 12.

8. This case and the following cases have been taken from either Canadian Human Rights Commission, Legal Reports , Ottawa: Government of Canada, from 1979 to present, or from the Annual Reports of the Canadian Human Rights Commission, Ottawa: Government of Canada, 1980 to 1999.

9. "Accommodating Employees' Religious Beliefs," *The Worklife Report*, IR Research Services, Kingston, Ontario, Vol. 7, No. 5, 1990, p. 8. See also Annual Report of the Canadian Human Rights Commission, 1991, p. 63.

10. Annual Report of the CHRC, 1996, p. 56.

11. Annual Report of the CHRC, 1999, pp. 6-7.

12. *Human Rights Forum*, Vol. 2, Issue 2, Winter 1992, p.12.

13. Annual Report of the CHRC, 1996, p. 83.

14. "Correctional Service Agrees to Hire Ex-Convict," Release, a publication of the Canadian Human Rights Commission, Ottawa: Government of Canada, undated.

15. Annual Report of the CHRC, 1996, p. 85.

16. Annual Report of the CHRC, 1996, p. 86.

17. Annual Report of the CHRC, 1991, p. 31. See also "Canadian Human Rights Commission Policy on HIV/AIDS," June 1996.

18. Harassment and the Canadian Human Rights Act, a pamphlet published by the Canadian Human Rights Commission, November 1998.

19. Canadian Human Rights Act, Paragraph 46, Section 2(a), (b).

20. Personal communication with the director of the program, June 2000.

21. Tove Helland Hanner, "Affirmative Action Programs: Have We Forgotten the First Line Supervisor?" *Personnel Journal*, June 1979, pp. 384-89.

22. Ibid.

Chapter 5

1. Dave Ulrich, *Human Resource Champions*, Boston, Mass.: Harvard Business School Press, 1997, p.13.

2. For example, see, Bellizzi, J.A., and Hasty, R.W., "The Effects of Hiring Decisions on the Level of Discipline Used in Response to Poor Performance" *Management Decision*, Vol. 38, No. 3, 2000, pp.154-159.

3. Lisa Butler, "Corporate Culture Can Be Your Key to Success on the Hiring Front," *Canadian HR Reporter*, May 3, 1999, p. 22.

4. Lesley Young, "Canadian Workers Want to be Loyal" *Canadian HR Reporter*, June 14, 1999, p.1.

5. "Disabled at Pizza Hut," *Business Month*, September 1989, p. 16.

6. C.S. Manegold, Bill Powell, and Yuriko Hoshiai, "Hanging the Help-Wanted Sign," *Newsweek*, July 16, 1990, p. 39.

7. "What Benefits are Companies Offering Now?" *HR Focus*, Vol. 77, No. 6, June 2000, p. 5.

8. *Discussion Paper No. 156*, Ottawa: Economic Council of Canada, 1980.

9. "E-mail Is Now the Preferred Way to Receive Resumes," *HR Focus*, Vol. 77, Issue 7, July 2000, p. 8.

10. Larry Stevens, "Resume Scanning Simplifies Tracking," *Personnel Journal*, Vol. 72, No. 4, April 1993, pp. 77-79.

11. Alan Halcrow, "Employees Are Your Best Recruiters," *Personnel Journal*, November 1988, pp. 42-48.

12. James Breaugh, *Recruitment: Science and Practice*, Boston: PWS-Kent Publishing Company, 1992, p. 294.

13. S.L. Bem, *Bem Sex Role Inventory: manual*, Palo Alto, California: Consulting Psychologists Press, 1981.

14. James Breaugh, Recruitment: Science and Practice, op. cit., p. 294.

15. *Government of Canada Services for You*, Catalogue No. PF4-2/2000, Minister of Public Works and Government Services, 2000,

16. Al Doran, "Popularity of Recruiting on the Internet Up," *Canadian HR Reporter*, January 13, 1997, p. 8.

17. Ben V. Luden, "HR vs. Executive Search," *Personnel Journal*, May 1992, pp.104-110.

18. Al Doran, "Popularity of Recruiting on the Internet Up," *Canadian HR Reporter*, January 13, 1997, p. 8.

19. John J. Wypich, "The Head Hunters Are Coming," *Canada Commerce*, Fall 1986, pp. 27-28.

20. Pamela d'Eon Scott and Hari Das, "Searching for a Search Firm," *Journal of Academy of Business Administration*, July 2000, pp. 25-31.

21. Catano, V., Cronshaw, S., Wiesner, W., Hackett, R., and Methot, L. *Recruitment and Selection in Canada,* Toronto: ITP Nelson, 1997, p. 263.

22. Madalyn Freund and Patricia Somers, "Ethics in College Recruiting: Views from the Front Lines," *Personnel Administrator*, April 1979, pp. 30-33. Joe Thomas, "College Recruitment: How to Use Student Perceptions of Business," *Personnel Journal*, January 1980, pp. 44-46. Donald P. Rogers and Michael Z. Sincoff, "Favorable Impression Characteristics of the Recruitment Interviewer," *Personnel Psychology*, Autumn 1978, pp. 495-504.

23. Stephen Jackson, "Performance Based Selection Nets Top Performers" *Canadian HR Reporter*, January 25, 1999, p. 6.

24. Nathan Laurie and Mark Laurie, "No Holds Barred in Fight for Students to Fill Internship Programs," *Canadian HR Reporter*, January 17, 2000, p.15.

25. S. Drake, "Temporaries Are Here to Stay," *Human Resource Executive*, 1992, Vol. 6, No. 2, pp. 27-30.

26. Joey Goodings, "Job Fairs: It's a Jungle Out There," *Canadian HR Reporter*, February 22, 1999, p. G-11.

27. Al Doran, "Popularity of Recruiting....," *Canadian HR Reporter*, January 13, 1997, op. cit.

28. Yves Lermusiaux, "Recruiting Effectively over the Internet," *Canadian HR Reporter*, April 5, 1999, p. 2.

29. Mark Swartz, "Jobs Are Online: What About Job Seekers?" *Canadian HR Reporter*, June 2, 1997, p. 21.

30. Al Doran, "Paper Resumes Out, Electronic Resume Creation In," *Canadian HR Reporter*, February 8, 1999, p. 9.

31. Peg Anthony, "Track Applicants, Track Costs," *Personnel Journal*, April 1990, pp. 75-81. Also see William C. Delone, "Telephone Job Posting Cuts Costs," *Personnel Journal*, Vol. 72, No. 4, April 1993, pp. 115-18.

32. J.Ross, "Effective Ways to Hire Contingent Personnel," *HR Magazine*, February 1991, pp. 52-54.

33. Chris Knight, "Contractors Become Fixture in Workplace," *Canadian HR Reporter*, October 21, 1996, p.14.

34. Roger Smithies and Leslie Steeves, "Define Contractor Relationships with Care," *Canadian HR Reporter*, January 12, 1998, p.12.

35. T. Lee, "Alumni Go Back to Schools to Hunt Jobs," *Wall Street Journal*, June 11, 1991, p. B-1.

36. C.D. Fyock, "Ways to Recruit Top Talent," *HR Magazine*, 1991, Vol. 36, No. 7, pp. 33-35.

37. Al Doran, "The site Is Up: Now How Do You Attract Job-seekers?" *Canadian HR Reporter*, September 8, 1997, p. 9.

38. Al Doran, "The Site Is Up..." op. cit.

39. Richard Nelson Bolles, *Job Hunting on the Internet*, Berkeley, Calif.: Ten Speed Press, 1997.

40. Gabriel Bouchard, "A Panoply of Web Recruiting Ideas," *Canadian HR Reporter*, January 12, 1998, p. 4.

41. Debbie McGrath, "Is Your Internet Recruiting Strategy Sending Qualified Candidates to Your Competitors?" *Canadian HR Reporter* (Guide to HR Technology). October 6, 1997, pp. G22-G23.

42. Seyed-Mahmoud Aghazadeh, "Human Resource Management: Issues and Challenges in the New Millennium," *Management Research News*, 1999, Vol. 22, No.12, pp.19-32.

43. Ian Clark, "Corporate Human Resources and "Bottom-line" Financial Performance," *Personnel Review,* 1999, Vol. 28, No. 4, pp. 290-306.

44. Robert Sibson, "The High Cost of Hiring," *Nation's Business*, February 14, 1975, pp. 85-88; Magnus, "Is Your Recruitment All It Can Be?" pp. 54-63.J. Scott Lord, "How Recruitment Efforts Can Elevate Credibility," *Personnel Journal*, April 1987, Vol. 66, No. 4.

Chapter 6

1. Jeffrey Pfeffer, *Human Equation*, Boston: Harvard Business School Press, 1998, pp. 70-71.

2. Lawrence Rout, "Going for Broker: Our Man Takes Part in Stock-Selling Test," *The Wall Street Journal*, April 4, 1979, p. 1.

3. Merrill Lynch Web site, February 8, 1998

4. Ben Lupton, "Pouring the Coffee at Interviews?" *Personnel Review*, 2000, Vol. 29, No.1, pp. 48-68.

5. James Braham, "Hiring Mr. Wrong," *Industry Week*, March 7, 1988, pp. 31-34.

6. Stephen Jackson, "All of HR Reaps Benefits from Performance Based Job Descriptions," *Canadian HR Reporter*, September 7, 1998, p.12.

7. Sharon Lebrun, "Retailers Lose $3 Million a Day to Employees," *Canadian HR Reporter*, May 5, 1997, pp. 1-2.

8. J.W. Thacker and R.J. Cattaneo, *Survey of Personnel Practices in Canadian Organizations*, Working Paper No. W-87-03, University of Windsor, Faculty of Business Administration, April 1987.

9. H.C. Jain, "Human Rights: Issues in Employment," in H.C. Jain and P.C. Wright (editors), *Trends and Challenges in Human Resource Management*, Scarborough, ON: Nelson, 1994, p. 69.

10. Stephen Jackson, "Resumes: The Good, The Bad and The Maybe," *Canadian HR Reporter*, January 27, 1997, p. 9.

11. G.W. England, *Development and Use of Weighted Application Blanks*, Minneapolis: University of Minnesota Industrial Relations Center, 1971.

12. See for example, W.A. Sands, "A Method for Evaluating Alternative Recruiting-selection Strategies: The CAPER Model," *Journal of Applied Psychology*, 1973, Vol. 57, pp. 222-227; W.A. Owens, "Background Data" in M.D. Dunnette (ed.) *Handbook of Industrial and Organizational Psychology*, Chicago, IL: Rand McNally, 1976.

13. R.R. Reilly and G.T. Chao, "Validity and Fairness of Some Alternative Employee Selection Procedures," *Personnel Psychology*, 1982, Vol. 35, pp. 1-62.

14. J.E. Hunter and R.F. Hunter "Validity and Utility of Alternative Predictors of Job Performance," *Psychological Bulletin*, 1984, Vol. 96, pp. 72-98.

15. Al Doran, "Paper Resumes Out, Electronic Resume Creation In," *Canadian HR Reporter*, February 8, 1999, p. 9.

16. J.W. Thacker and R.J. Cattaneo, *Survey of Personnel Practices in Canadian Organizations*, 1987, op cit.

17. Norman Trainor, "Using Measurement to Predict Performance," *Canadian HR Reporter*, November 16, 1998, p. 7.

18. Martin Dewey, "Employers Take a Hard Look at the Validity and Value of Psychological Screening," *The Globe and Mail*, February 7, 1981, p. B1.

19. James Leduinka and Lyle F. Schoenfeldt, "Legal Development in Employment Testing: Albermarle and Beyond," *Personnel Psychology*, Spring 1978, pp. 1-13.

20. For an example of this, see, William G. Doerner and Terry Nowell, "The Reliability of the Behavioural-personnel Assessment Device (B-PAD) in Selecting Police Recruits," *Policing: An International Journal of Police Strategies and Management,* Vol. 22, No. 3, 1999, pp. 343-352.

21. Julie McCarthy and Richard Goffin, "Test Taking Anxiety in a Selection Context: The Moderating Role of Applicant Gender," Joanne D.Leck (ed.) ASAC-IFSAM 2000 Conference Human Resource Division Proceedings, 2000, Vol. 21, No. 9, pp. 69-77.

22. Costa, P.T. Jr., "Work and Personality: Using the NEO-PI-R in Industrial/Organizational Psychology" *Applied Psychology: An International Review*, Vol. 45, 1996, pp. 225-41.

23. Ian Gellatly and P. Gregory Irving, "The Moderating Role of Perceived Autonomy on Personality-performance Relations within a Public Sector Organization," in Gerard Seijts (ed.) ASAC 1999 (Human Resource Division) Proceedings, Vol. 20, No. 9, 1999, pp. 49-58.

24. For example, see, S. Adler, "Personality and Work Behaviour: Exploring the Linkages," *Applied Psychology: An International Review*, 1996, pp. 207-224.

25. Simon Taggar, "Personality, Cognitive Ability and Behaviour: The Antecedents of Effective Autonomous Work Teams," in Joanne Dick (ed.) ASAC-IFSAM 2000 Conference Human Resource Division Proceedings, 2000, Vol. 21, No. 9, pp. 59-66.

26. Robert Wood and Tim Payne, *Competency Based Recruitment and Selection*, Chichester, England: Wiley, 1998, pp.153-169.

27. S. Sillup, "Applicant Screening Cuts Turnover Costs," *Personnel Journal*, May 1992, pp. 115-16.

28. Electronic Selection Systems Corporation, AccuVision: Assessment Technology for Today, Tomorrow and Beyond, Maitland, Fla.: Electronic Selection Systems, Inc., 1992.

29. For example, see, R.C. Overton, H.J. Harms, L.R. Taylor, and M.J. Zickar, "Adapting to Adaptive Testing," *Personnel Psychology*, 1997, Vol. 50, pp.171-185.

30. Jeff Weekley and Casey Jones, "Video-based Situational Testing," *Personnel Psychology*, 1997, Vol. 50, pp. 25-49.

31. "Should You Tell All?" *Parade Magazine*, May 27, 1990, p. 5.

32. D.T. Lykken, "The Case Against the Polygraph in Employment Screening," *Personnel Administrator*, September 1985, pp. 59-65.

33. "Workplace Privacy," Ontario Commissioner's Report, *Worklife Report*, 1994, Vol. 9, No. 3, pp. 8-9.

34. Www.bsgcorp.com/journal/journal.html; December 25, 2000.

35. P.R. Sackett and M.M. Harris, "Honesty Testing for Personnel Selection: A Review and a Critique," *Personnel Psychology*, 1984, Vol. 37, pp. 221-45.

36. D.S. Ones, C. Visweswaran, and F.L. Schmidt, "Comprehensive Meta Analysis of Integrity Test Validities: Findings and Implications for Personnel Selection and Theories of Job Performance," *Journal of Applied Psychology*, August 1993, Vol. 78, pp. 679-703; see also: P.R. Sackett, L.R. Burris, and C. Callahan, "Integrity Testing for Personal Selection: An Update," *Personnel Psychology*, Autumn 1989, Vol. 42, pp. 491-529.

37. Dennis S. Joy, "Basic Psychometric Properties of a Pre-employment Honesty Test: Reliability, Validity and Fairness," in John W. Jones, ed., *Pre-employment Honesty Testing*, N.Y.: Quorum Books, 1991, pp. 65-88.

38. Bean, "More Firms Use 'Attitude Tests' to Keep Thieves Off the Payroll"; see also Robert M. Madigan, K. Dow Scott, Diana L. Deadrick, and J.A. Stoddard, "Employment Testing: The U.S. Job Service is Spearheading a Revolution," *Personnel Administrator*, September 1986, pp. 102-12.

39. Adelheid Nicol and Sampo Paunonen, "Workplace Honesty: The Development of a New Measure," in Caroline Weber (ed.) *ASAC 1998 (Human Resources Divison) Proceedings*, Vol. 19, No. 9, 1998, pp. 31-42.

40. Charles D. Johnson, Lawrence A. Messe, and William D. Crano, "Predicting Job Performance of Low Income Workers: The Work Opinion Questionnaire," *Personnel Psychology*, Summer 1984, Vol. 37, No. 2, pp. 291-99.

41. Lesley Young, "Reference Checking Skills Sorely Lacking," *Canadian HR Reporter*, January 25, 1999, p.1.

42. Hari Das and Mallika Das, "But He Had Excellent References: Refining the Reference Letter," *The Human Resource*, June-July 1988, pp. 15-16.

43. Stephen Jackson, "Objective Descriptions - Not Opinions - Should Be Aim of Reference Checks," *Canadian HR Reporter*, April 21, 1997, p.10.

44. Bob Smith, "The Evolution of Pinkerton" *Management Review*, September 1993, Volume 82, p. 56.

45. Stephen Jackson, "Give Job Applicants the Whole Truth," *Canadian HR Reporter*, March 24, 1997, p. 9.

46. Paula Popovich and John P. Wanous, "The Realistic Job Preview as a Persuasive Communication," *Academy of Management Review*, October 1982, p. 571.

47. Jane Easter Bahls, "Drugs in the Workplace," *HR Magazine*, February 1998, http://www.shrm.org/hrmagazine

48. Ted Thaler, "Substance Abuse Costing Employers Estimated $2.6-B," *Canadian HR Reporter*, October 24, 1990, p. 1.

49. B.L. Thompson, "A Surprising Ally in the Drug Wars," *Training*, November 1990.

50. C. Languedoc, "Battle Lines Forming over Worker Drug Test," *The Financial Post*, April 13, 1987, pp. 1, 4.

51. "Imperial Oil to Test Staff for Drugs," *The Globe and Mail*, October 5, 1991, p. B1. See also "Mandatory Drug Testing Attracts Controversy," *Canadian Employment Law Today*, April 9, 1991, pp. 635-46.

52. Jeffrey Miller, "Drug Testing Dealt a Blow by Federal Court" *Canadian HR Reporter*, September 21, 1998, p. 5.

53. Virginia Galt, "Total Ban Sought on Drug Testing by Employers," *The Globe and Mail*, February 22, 1992.

54. Canadian Human Rights Commission Annual Report 1993, Minister of Supply and Services Canada, 1994, Ottawa, pp. 35-36

55. Editorial: "The Case Against Drug Testing," *The Globe and Mail*, August 19, 1994, p. A18.

56. Jeffrey Miller, 1998, op cit, p. 5.

57. "Catch-22: Under Imperial Oil's Revamped Drug Policy" *Journal of the Addiction Research Foundation,* Vol. 22, No. 6, November-December, 1994, p.12.

58. Marc Belaiche, "Put Your Company's Best Foot Forward with New Hires," *Canadian HR Reporter*, September 21, 1998, p. 66.

59. See Hermann F. Schwind, "How Well Do Interviews Predict Future Performance?" The Human Resource, June-July 1987, pp. 19-20; G.P. Latham, L.M. Saari, E.D. Pursell, and M.A. Champion, "The Situational Interview," *Journal of Applied Psychology*, 1989, Vol. 65, No. 4, pp. 422-27.

60. Helen Gardiner and Rick Hackett, "Employment Interviewing: A Review and Analysis of Canadian Human Rights cases," Jacques Barrette (ed.): *ASAC 1997 (Human Resource Division) Proceedings,* 1997, Vol. 18, No. 9, pp. 46-55.

61. James G. Hollandsworth, Jr. et al., "Relative Contributions of Verbal Articulative and Nonverbal Communication to Employment Decisions in the Job Interview Setting," *Personnel Psychology*, Summer 1979, pp. 359-67. See also Angelo Kimicki and Chris A. Lockwood, "The Interview Process: An Examination of Factors Recruiters Use in Evaluating Job Applicants," *Journal of Vocational Behaviour*, 1985, Vol. 26, p. 117.

62. Stephen Maurer, "The Potential of Situational Interview: Existing Research and Unresolved Issues," *Human Resource Management Review*, 1997, Vol. 7, No.2, pp.185-201.

63. Tom Janz, "The Patterned Behavioural Description Interview: The Best Prophet of the Future is the Past," in Eder and Ferris, The Employment Interview, pp. 158-68; Janz, "The Selection Interview," p. 160; C. Orpen, "Patterned Behavioural Description Interview Versus Unstructured Interviews: A Comparative Validity Study," *Journal of Applied Psychology*, 1985, Vol. 70, pp. 774-76; J. Tom Janz, "Comparing the Use and Validity of Opinions Versus Behavioural Descriptions in the Employment Interview," unpub-lished manuscript, University of Calgary, 1988; Latham, "The Reliability, Validity and Practicality of Selection Interviews."

64. Michael Harris, "Reconsidering the Employment Interview: A Review of Recent Literature and Suggestions for Future Research," *Personnel Psychology*, 1989, Vol. 42, pp. 691-726.

65. M.A. McDaniel, D.L. Whetzel, F.L. Schmidt, and S.D. Maurer, "The Validity of Employment Interviews: A Comprehensive Review and Meta Analysis," *Journal of Applied Psychology*, 1994, Vol. 79, pp. 599-616.

66. McDaniel, Whetzel, Schmidt and Maurer, 1994, op. cit. A.I. Huffcutt and W. Arthur, Jr., "Hunter and Hunter Revisited: Interview Validity for Entry Level Jobs," *Journal of Applied Psychology*, 1994, Vol. 22, pp. 184-190.

67. Ibid.

68. Linda Thornburg, "Computer Assisted Interviewing Shortens Hiring Cycle," *HR Magazine*, February 1998, pp. 1-5.

69. William L. Tullar, Terry W. Mullins, and Sharon A. Caldwell, "Effects on Interview Length and Applicant Quality on Interview Decision Time," *Journal of Applied Psychology*, 1979, Vol. 64, No. 6, pp. 669-74.

70. D.H. Tucker and P.M. Rowe, "Consulting the Application Form Prior to the Interview: An Essential Step in the Selection Process," *Journal of Applied Psychology*, 1977, Vol. 62.

71. Stephen Jackson, "Interviewers Need to Be Taught, Not Told, How to Hire the Best," *Canadian HR Reporter*, June 16, 1997, p. 8.

72. Wayne Cascio, *Applied Psychology in Human Resource Management*, Fifth Edition, Upper Saddle River, NJ: Prentice-Hall, 1998, p. 199.

73. Michael H. Frisch, *Coaching and Counselling Handbook*, New York: Resource Dynamics, 1981.

74. Anthropologist Jennifer James quoted by Bob Rosner, "Coming of Age in HR" *Workforce,* August 2000, p. 61.

75. Stephen Jackson, "If Low Performers Outnumber High Performers, It's Time to Review Your Selection Process," *Canadian HR Reporter*, March 8, 1999, p. 8.

76. Sharon Ifill and Neil Moreland, "Auditing Recruitment and Selection Using Generic Benchmarking: A Case Study," *The TQM Magazine*, 1999, Vol. 11, No. 5, pp. 333-340.

Chapter 7

1. Bill Pomfret, "Sound Employee Orientation Program Boosts Productivity and Safety," *Canadian HR Reporter*, January 25, 1999, p. 17.

2. John Thomas Howe, "What's Right for You?" *Canadian HR Reporter*, May 17, 1999, pp. G3/G6.

3. Royal Bank of Canada, Annual Report, 1999.

4. William H. Mobley, "Some Unanswered Questions in Turnover and Withdrawal Research," *Academy of Management Review*, January 1982, pp. 111-16.

5. John T. Howe, "What's Right for You?" *Canadian HR Reporter*, Supplement to the May 17, 1999 issue, pp. G3-G6.

6. Steven L. McShane, *Canadian Organizational Behaviour,* Third Edition, McGraw-Hill Ryerson, 1998, p. 430.

7. Industry Report, in *Training*, Vol. 36, No. 11, October 1999, p. 58.

8. Steven L. McShane and Trudy Baal, "Employee Socialization Practices on Canada's West Coast: A Management Report," Faculty of Business Administration, Simon Fraser University, Burnaby, British Columbia, December 1984.

9. John P. Wanous, *Organizational Entry: Recruitment, Selection and Socialization of Newcomers*, Second Edition. Reading, Mass: Addison-Wesley, 1992, p. 185.

10. McShane and Baal, "Employee Socialization Practices."

11. Kenneth Oldfield and Nancy Ayers, "Avoid the New Job Blues," *Personnel Journal*, August 1986, pp. 49-56.

12. John P. Wanous, *Organizational Entry.*

13. Wayne F. Cascio and James W. Thacker, *Managing Human Resources*, Toronto: McGraw-Hill Ryerson Ltd., 1994, p. 265.

14. McShane and Baal, "Employee Socialization Practices."

15. Ronald E. Smith, "Employee Orientation: 10 Steps to Success," *Personnel Journal*, December 1984, pp. 46-48.

16. Cary Thorp, Jr., quoted in George T. Milkovich, William F. Glueck, Richard T. Barth, and Steven L. McShane, *Canadian Personnel/Human Resource Management*, Plano, Tex.: Business Publications, 1988, p. 439.

17. McShane and Baal, "Employee Socialization Practices."

18. M. Lubliner, "Employee Orientation," *Personnel Journal*, April 1978, pp. 207-8.

19. McShane, *Canadian Organizational Behaviour*.

20. Howard J. Klein and Natasha A. Weaver, "The Effectiveness of an Organizational-Level Orientation Training Program in the Socialization of New Hires," *Personnel Psychology*, Vol. 53, No. 1, Spring 2000, pp. 44-62.

21. Monica Belcourt, Philip C. Wright, and Alan M. Saks, *Managing Performance through Training & Development,* Second Edition, Scarborough: Nelson Canada, 2000, pp. 4-7.

22. Ann MacAulay, "The Long and Winding Road," Canadian HR Reporter, November 16, 1998, pp. G1/G10. See also http://recruit-ment.hsbc.com/commercial_banking/profiles/menu.htm and http://hsbc.co.uk/diversity/train.htm.

23. David McIntyre, "Training and Development 1993: Policies, Practices and Expenditures," Report 128-94, Ottawa: The Conference Board of Canada, 1994; Jean-Pascal Souque, "Focus on Competencies: Training and Development Practices, Expenditures, and Trends," Report 177-96, Ottawa, The Conference Board of Canada, 1996; Andrew Sharpe. "Training the Work Force: A Challenge Facing Canada in the 90s," Statistics Canada, Catalogue 75-001E, Perspectives on Labour and Income.

24. Kenneth N. Wexley and Gary P. Latham, *Developing and Training Human Resources in Organizations,* New York: HarperCollins Publishers Inc., 1991, pp. 35 and on.

25. Hideo Inohara, *Human Resource Development in Japanese Companies,* Tokyo: Asian Productivity Organization, 1990, p. 79.

26. Allan Pescurie and William C. Byham, "The New Look of Behavior Modeling," *Training & Development* , July 1996, pp. 24-30; see also Henry P. Sims, Jr. and Charles C. Manz, "Modeling Influences on Employee Behavior," *Personnel Journal*, January 1982, p. 58.

27. Ibid.

28. Irwin, Goldstein, *Training in Organizations*, Third Edition, Pacific Grove, CA: Brooks/Cole Publishing Co, 1993, pp. 242-243.

29. T.G. Cummings and C.G. Worley, *Organizational Development and Change*, Fifth Edition, Minneapolis/St. Paul: West Publishing, 1993, p. 198.

30. Personal communication with William Mosar of the Learning Resources Unit. EPD, July 2000.

31. Amir Bem, "Computer-based Training and Classroom Learning Go Hand-in-hand," Supplement to *Canadian HR Reporter*, May 17, 1999, p. G5.

32. Belcourt, Wright, and Saks, *Managing Performance through Training and Development*, pp. 138-140.

33. T. Middleton, "The Potential of Virtual Reality Technology for Training," *The Journal of Interactive Instructional Development*, Spring 1992, pp. 8-12. See also Ken Mark, "Virtual Training—At Your Pace, in Your Space," *Human Resource Professional*, February/March 1998, pp. 15-17.

34. Jacques Surveyer, "Net-based Learning Goes Mainstream," **The Computer Paper**, Eastern Edition (www.canadacomputes.com), July 2000, p. 68; Eugene Sadler-Smith, Simon Down, and Jonathan Lean, "'Modern' Learning Methods: Rhetoric and Reality," *Personnel Review*, April 29, 2000, pp. 474-490; "Web-based Training (WBT)", www.cybernetic-learning.com/multimediaweb. htm, June 27, 2000; "What is Web-based Training?" www.filename.com/ wbt/pages/whatiswbt.htm, July 27, 2000 ; "Internet-based Classes Get Better Results, Study Says," www.trainingreport. ca/articles/story.cfm?storyid=114, June 26, 2000; Kevin Dobbs, "Who's in Charge of e-Learning?", www.trainingsupersite.com/publica-tions/magazines/training/006cv1.htm , June 26, 2000; "Virtual Education—Is Canada Losing Its Place?", www.trainingreport.ca/articles/story.cfm?storyid=81

35. Donald L. Kirkpatrick, "Techniques for Evaluating Training Programs," *Journal of the American Society of Training Directors*, Vol. 13, 1959, pp. 3-9, 21 26; Vol. 14, 1960, pp. 13-18, 28-32. See also Hermann F. Schwind, "Issues in Training Evaluation: The Criterion," *Canadian Training Methods*, Vol. 7, No. 4, October 1975.

36. D.T. Campbell and J.C. Stanley, *Experimental and Quasi-Experimental Design,* Chicago: Rand McNally, 1963.

37. Thomas A. Steward, *Intellectual Capital: The New Wealth of Organizations*, Currency: Double day, 1997. See also: Gordon Pitts, "The Next Hot Market Commodity? Human Capital," *The Globe and Mail,* June 20, 2000; Lester Thurow, "Cheque-mate!" *The Globe and Mail,* June 5, 2000.

38. T.A. Kochan, "The Human Side of Technology," *ICL Technical Journal,* November 1988, pp. 391-400.

39. Lawrence Surtees, "Managing Technology: Nortel's New Vision Calls on the Web," *The Globe and Mail*, February 25, 1998, p. B29.

Chapter 8

1. World Competitiveness Report, IMD (International Institute for Management Development—Switzerland), 2000. http://www.imd.ch/wcy/ranking/ranking.cfm

2. Nikolina Menalo, "The 360 Degrees of Career Development," *ComputerWorld Canada*, July 28, 2000, p. 37.

3. Robert C. Camp, "Xerox Benchmarks the Spot," *Journal of Business Strategy*, 1992. See also Laurie J. Bassi and Scott Cheney, "Changes in Benchmarked Training," *Training and Development*, December 1996, pp. 29-30.

4. Ford Motor Company Annual Report 1999.

5. Kenneth N. Wexley and Gary P. Latham, *Developing and Training Human Resources in Organizations*, Second Edition, New York: HarperCollins, 1991.

6. Alexander Ross, "BMO's Big Man," *Canadian Business*, January 1994, pp. 58-63. See also John Partridge, "B of M Posts Record Profit," *The Globe and Mail*, November 24, 1993, p. B11.

7. A.P. Goldstein and M. Sorcher, *Changing Supervisor Behavior*, New York: Pergamon Press, 1974, p. 37.

8. Robert R. Blake and Jane Srygley Mouton, *The Managerial Grid III: The Key to Leadership Excellence*, Houston, Tex.: Gulf Publishing, 1985.

9. J.P. Campbell and M.D. Dunnette, "Effectiveness of T-Group Experiences in Managerial Training and Development," *Psychological Bulletin*, Vol. 70, 1968, pp. 73-104.

10. Rob McKenzie, "Benefits of Wilderness Training More Subtle than Substantial," *The Financial Post*, July 13, 1992.

11. T.G. Cummings and C.G. Worley, *Organization Development and Change*, Fifth Edition, Minneapolis/St. Paul: West Publishing, 1993, p. 168.

12. Ibid.

13. Gayle MacDonald, "An Open-book Approach to Motivation," *The Globe and Mail*, March 31, 1997, p. B9.

14. Dan MacLeod and Eric Kennedy, "Job Rotation System", a consulting report, 1993, dan@danmacleod.com

15. Cummings and Worley, *Organization Development and Change*, p. 691.

16. Peter M. Senge, *The Fifth Discipline: The Art and Practices of the Learning Organization*, New York: Doubleday/Currency, 1990.

17. Steven L. McShane, *Canadian Organizational Behaviour*, Homewood, Ill.: Irwin, 1999, p. 471.

18. Vijay K. Verma and Hans J. Thamhain, *Human Resource Skills for the Project Manager: The Human Aspects of Project Management*, Newton Square, PA: Project Management Institute, 1996.

19. See Senge, *The Fifth Discipline.*

20. Interview with Peter Senge by Patricia A. Galagan, *Training and Development Journal*, October 1991, pp. 37-44.

21. Jamie Harrison, "Molson Opens Learning Centre," *Canadian HR Reporter*, January 26, 1998, pp. 1-2. See also Norman L. Trainor, "Defining the Learning Organization," in the same issue, p. 9.

22. See Senge, *The Fifth Discipline*; see also M.A. Gephart, V.J. Marsick, M.F. Van Buren, and M.S. Spiro, "Learning Organizations Come Alive," *Training and Development*, December 1996, pp. 35-37. David A. Ganin, *Learning in Action: A Guide to Putting the Learning Organization to Work*, Cambridge, Mass: Harvard University Press, 2000.

23. Peter F. Drucker, *Innovation and Entrepreneurship*, New York, Harper and Row, 1985.

24. "Knowledge Workers and the New Economy," *Worklife*, 1997, Vol. 11, No. 1, 1997, p. 5.

25. "'Knowledge Management' Gaining Ground," *Newsline*, Fall 1997, Vol. 28, No. 1, pp. 14-17; a publication of the International Association for Management Education.

26. R.L. Williams and W.R. Bukowitz, "Knowledge Managers Guide Information Seekers," *HR Magazine*, January 1997, pp. 77-81.

27. Jean-Pascal Souque, "Focus on Competencies: Training and Development Practices, Expenditures and Trends," Report 177-96, Conference Board of Canada, 1996. See also Richard J. Mirabile, "Everything You Wanted to Know About Competency Modeling," *Training & Development*, August 1997, pp. 73-77; Patricia A. McLegan, "Competencies: The Next Generation," *Training & Development*, May 1997, pp. 40-47.

28. Ibid.

29. Ibid.

30. Ibid.

31. "Corporate and Campus-Based B-Schools Take Strategic Approach to Alliances," *Newsline*, Fall 1997, Vol. 2, No. 1, pp. 1-7; a publication of AACSB—The International Association For Management Education; see also Philip R. Theibert, "Train and Degree Them—Anywhere," *Personnel Journal*, February 1996, pp. 28-30.

32. "Retail Giants Support Ryerson," *Campus News*, Summer 2000, http://www.ryerson.ca/news/

33. Verna Alle, "12 Principles of Knowledge Management," *Training & Development*, November 1997, pp. 71-74.

34. Sharon Lebrun, "Royal Bank Using Intranet to Drive Continuous Learning," *Canadian HR Reporter*, December 1, 1997, p. 9.

35. Jen Ross, "Virtual University Education," *The Gazette*, student newspaper at Dalhousie University, December 3, 1997, p. 16.

36. Hermann F. Schwind, "Training for Managing Cultural Diversity," *Personnel Innovations*, a publication of the Canadian Public Personnel Association, Summer 1993, pp. 44-46.

37. Taylor H. Cox and Stacy Blake, "Managing Cultural Diversity: Implications for Organizational Competitiveness," *The Executive, Academy of Management*, Vol. 5, No. 3, 1991, pp. 45-56.

38. Douglas T. Hall, "Human Resource Development and Organizational Effectiveness," in Charles Fombrun, Noel M. Tichy, and Mary A. Devanna, eds., *Strategic Human Resource Management*, New York: John Wiley, 1984, pp. 159-81.

39. Barbara Moses, "Career Planning Mirrors Social Change," *Canadian HR Reporter*, May 17, 1999, p. G10.

40. Douglas T. Hall, "Managing Yourself: Building a Career," in A.R. Cohen (Ed.), *The Portable MBA in Management*, New York: Wiley, 1993, pp. 190-206.

41. "Job Futures—A Two-Volume Reference Set For Career Planning," Human Resources Development Canada, 1996. Catalogue Number MP43-181/1996E; see also William F. Rothenbach, "Career Development: Ask Your Employees for Their Opinions," *Personnel Administration*, November 1982, pp. 43-46, 51; Nigel Nicholson, "Career Systems in Crisis: Change and Opportunity in the Information Age," *The Academy of Management Executive*, November 1996, Vol. X, No.4, pp. 40-52.

42. Manuel London, "Redeployment and Continuous Learning in the 21st Century: Hard Lessons and Positive Examples from the Downsizing Era," *The Academy of Management Executive*, November 1996, Vol. X, No.4, pp. 67-79.

43. Ronald J. Burke and Tamara Weir, "Career Success and Personal Failure, Part I," *The Canadian Personnel and Industrial Relations Journal*, October 1980, pp. 7-17. See also Laird W. Mealiea and Swee C. Goh, "An Empirical Evaluation of the Fear of Success Construct for Women Working in a Sex Stereotyped Job," ASAC (Organizational Behaviour Division) Meeting Proceedings, Vol. 2, Part 5, 1981, pp. 112-23.

44. Speaking Notes for the Honourable Jane Stewart, Minister of Human Resources Development Canada, speech to the Annual National Child Day Luncheon, Ottawa, November 18, 1999.

45. Suzanne Spiker-Miller and Nathalie Kees, "Making Career Development a Reality for Dual-career Couples," *Journal of Employment Counseling*, March 1, 1995.

46. Eugene E. Jennings, *The Mobile Manager*, New York: McGraw-Hill, 1967.

47. "Working Issues, How to Make Your Career a Success in a New Workplace," *The Globe and Mail*, March 21, 1997, p. C3.

48. L.J. Bassi, G. Benson, and S. Cheney, "The Top Ten Trends," *Training & Development*, August 1997, pp. 27-42.

49. See *The Globe & Mail*, "How to Make Your Career a Success in a New Workplace."

50. Ibid.

51. Lesley Young, "Potential of Mentoring Programs Untapped," *Canadian HR Reporter*, April 10, 2000, pp. 1-2.

52. Personal communication with a Ford Motor Company HR Executive by the first author.

53. Adrian Gostick, "Recognition, Retention and Keeping Your Socks Up," *Canadian HR Reporter*, March 13, 2000, p. 15.

54. George Sallay, "Bank of Montreal's Virtual Career Centre," *Canadian HR Reporter*, November 16, 1998, p. G14.

55. Richard Koonce, "Using the Internet as a Career Planning Tool," *Training & Development*, September 1997, p. 15.

56. Nikolina Menalo, "The 360 Degrees of Career Development," *ComputerWorld Canada*, July 28, 2000, p. 37.

Chapter 9

1. Harry Levinson, "Appraisal of What Performance?" *Harvard Business Review*, July-August 1976, pp. 30-32, 34, 36, 40, 44, 46, 160.

2. Richard C. Grote, "Performance Appraisal Reappraised," *Harvard Business Review*, January 1, 2000.

3. Terry H. Wagar, "Union Status, Organization Size and Progressive Decision-Making Ideology as Predictors of Human Resource Management Practices," *International Journal of Employment Studies*, April 1996, pp. 79-93.

4. James M. McFillen and Patrick G. Decker, "Building Meaning into Appraisal," *Personnel Administrator*, June 1978, pp. 78-79.

5. Hermann F. Schwind, "Developing and Evaluating a New Performance Appraisal and Training Evaluation Instrument: The Behaviour Description Index," unpublished Ph.D. dissertation, University of British Columbia, 1978.

6. Testimony from several members of the Canadian Armed Forces, mostly officers, in classes of the first author.

7. J.S. Kane and E.E. Lawler, "Performance Appraisal Effectiveness: Its Assessment and Determinants," *Research in Organizational Behavior*, Vol. 1, 1980, pp. 425-78.

8. Kane and Lawler, "Performance Appraisal Effectiveness."

9. http://skepdic.com/cranial.html; http://skepdic.com/phren.html; http://landow.stg.brown.edu/victorian/race/rc3.html

10. G.R. Ferris, T.A. Judge, K.M. Rowland, and D.E. Fitzgibbons, "Subordinate Influence and the Performance Evaluation Process: Test of a Model," *Organizational Behavior and Human Decision Process*, 1995, Vol. 58, pp. 223-238.

11. Hermann F. Schwind, "Performance Appraisal: The State of the Art," in S.L. Dolan and R.S. Schuler, eds., *Personnel and Human Resources Management in Canada*, Minneapolis/St. Paul: West Publishing, 1987, pp. 197-210.

12. E.A. Locke and G.P. Latham, *A Theory of Goal Setting and Task Performance*, Englewood Cliffs, NJ: Prentice-Hall, 1990.

13. A.M. Mohrman, S.M. Resnick-West, E.E. Lawler, *Designing Performance Appraisal Systems*, San Francisco: Jossey-Bass, 1989.

14. R.L. Cary, and T.J. Keefe, "Observational Purpose and Valuative Articulation in Frame-of-reference Training: The Effects of Alternative Processing Models on Rating accuracy," *Organizational Behavior and Human Decision Processes*, Vol. 57, 1994, pp. 338-357. See also D.J. Schleicher and D.V. Day, "A Cognitive Evaluation of Frame-of-Reference Rater Training: Content and Process Issues," *Organizational Behavior and Human Decision Processes*, Vol. 73, No. 1, January 1998, pp. 76-101.

15. L.L. Cummings and D.P. Schwab, *Performance in Organizations: Determinants and Appraisal,* Glenview, Ill.: Scott, Foresman, 1973. See also M.M. Greller, "Subordinate Participation and Reaction to the Appraisal Interview," *Journal of Applied Psychology*, Vol. 60, 1975, pp. 544-49; W.F. Nemeroff and K.N. Wexley, "Relationships Between Performance Appraisal Interview Outcomes by Supervisors and Subordinates," paper presented at the annual meeting of the Academy of Management, Orlando, Florida, 1977; Daniel R. Ilgen, Janet L. Barnes-Farrell, David B. McKellin, "Performance Appraisal Process Research in the 1980s: What Has It Contributed to Appraisals in Use?", *Organizational Behavior and Human Decision Processes*, Vol. 54, No. 3, April 1993, pp. 321-368.

16. Mohrman et al., *Designing Performance Appraisal Systems.*

17. George Milkovich and Jerry Newman, *Compensation*, Sixth Edition, McGraw-Hill Irwin, 1999.

18. J.F. Hazucha, S.A. Gentile, and R.J. Schneider, "The Impact of 360-Degree Feedback on Management Skills Development," *Human Resource Management Review*, 1993, Vol. 3, No. 2, pp. 32-45.

19. Nat J. Salvemini, Richard R. Reilly, James W. Smither, "The Influence of Rater Motivation on Assimilation Effects and Accuracy in Performance Ratings," *Organizational Behavior and Human Decision Processes*, Vol. 55, No. 1, June 1993, pp. 41-60.

20. D.L. DeVries, "Viewing Performance Appraisal with a Wide-Angle Lens," *Issues and Observation*, 1984, pp. 6-9.

21. James D. Grant and Terry H. Wagar, "Dismissal for Incompetence: An Analysis of the Factors Used by Canadian Courts in Determining Just Cause of Termination," Proceedings of the Administrative Science Association of Canada, Personnel and Human Resource Division, edited by Natalie Lam, 1991, pp. 1-10.

22. John Meyer and Laryssa Topolnytsky, *Best Practices: Employee Retention*, Carswell Publishing, 2000.

23. K.R. Murphy and J.I. Constans, "Behavioral Anchors as a Source of Bias in Rating," *Journal of Applied Psychology*, November 1987, Vol. 72, pp. 573-586.

24. J. Peter Graves, "Let's Put Appraisal Back in Performance Appraisal: II," *Personnel Journal*, December 1982, p. 918.

25. Milan Moravec, "How Performance Appraisal Can Tie Communication to Productivity," *Personnel Administrator*, January 1981, pp. 51-52.

26. R. Rodgers and J.E. Hunter, "Impact of Management by Objectives on Organizational Productivity," *Journal of Applied Psychology*, 1991, Vol. 77, No. 2, pp. 322-336.

27. Richard J. Campbell, "Use of an Assessment Center as an Aid in Management Selection," *Personnel Psychology*, Vol. 46, 1993, pp. 691-699; see also: J.R. Kauffman et al., "The Construct Validity of Assessment Centre Performance Dimensions," *International Journal of Selection and Assessment*, Vol. 1, 1993, pp. 213-223; Lisa Donohue, Donna Denning, Richard J. Klimoski, Kenneth N. Wexley & Deborah L. Whetzel: Chipping Away at the Monument: A Critical Look at the Assessment Center Method http://www.ipmaac.org/conf00/index.html, June 3-7, 2000, Washington D.C.

28. G.C. Thornton, *Assessment Centers in Human Resource Management*, Reading, MA: Addison-Wesley, 1992; S.B. Parry, "How to Validate an Assessment Tool," *Training*, April 1993, pp. 37-42.

29. John P. Bucalo, Jr., "The Assessment Center—A More Specified Approach," *Human Resource Management*, Fall 1974, pp. 2-13. See also William C. Byham, "Starting an Assessment Center," *Personnel Administrator*, February 1980, pp. 27-32.

30. J.F. Hazucha, S.A. Gentile, and R.J. Schneider, "The Impact of 360-Degree Feedback on Management Skills Development," *Human Resource Management Review*, 1993, Vol. 3, No. 2, pp. 32-45.

31. R.J. Klimoski and R.G. Jones, "Staffing for Effective Group Decision Making: Key Issues in Matching People and Teams." In Klimoski & Jones (eds.) *Team Effectiveness and Decision Making in Organizations*, San Francisco: Jossey-Bass, 1995.

32. Robert Kent, "Why You Should Think Twice About 360 Degree Performance Appraisal," http://www.zigonperf.com/PMNews/think_twice_360.html, August 2000.

33. Bob Nelson and Peter Economy, "Can Software Improve Performance Appraisals?," *HR Reporter*, June 16, 1997, pp. 21-22.

34. Ian Turnbull, "Enterprise-wide Software Gaining Popularity," *Canadian HR Reporter*, June 16, 1997, pp. 10-11.

35. Michael Hammer and James Champy, *Reengineering the Corporation: A Manifesto for Business Revolution*, (New York: HarperCollins, 1993).

36. See Turnbull, "Enterprise-wide Software Gaining Popularity."

37. Ibid.

38. Robert S. Kaplan and David P. Norton, *The Balanced Scorecard: Translating Strategy into Action*, Harvard Business School Press, 1992. Robert S. Kaplan and David P. Norton, *The Strategy-Focused Organization: How Balanced Scorecard Companies Thrive in the New Business Environment*, Harvard Business School Press, 2000.

39. Peter C. Barnes, "Employee Surveys and the "Balanced Scorecard,"

ACCA Students' Newsletter, July 1999, a publication of the Association of Certified Chartered Accountants, UK, http://www.acca.org.uk/resources/publications/students_newsletter/1999/7-99p44.html

40. William J. Birch, "Performance Appraisal: One Company's Experience," *Personnel Journal*, June 1981, pp. 456-60.

41. Comment made by a human resource manager during a guest lecture in one of the authors' classes. He had worked for 15 years with a number of U.S. and Canadian department stores.

42. Schwind, "Performance Appraisal."

43. D.C. Smith, L.M. Kendall, and C.L. Hulin, *The Job Descriptive Index*, rev. ed., Bowling Green, Ohio: Department Psychology, Bowling Green University, 1985.

Chapter 10

1. Milton L. Rock and Lance Berger, eds., *Handbook of Wage and Salary Administration*, Third Edition, New York: McGraw-Hill, 1991, p. xiii.

2. Australian Employee Ownership Association Online http://www.aeoa.org.au/, September 2000.

3. Robert J. Greene, *Improving Merit Pay Plan Effectiveness*, ACA News, April 1998, pp. 26-29.

4. Rabindra Kanungo and Manuel Mendonca, *Compensation—Effective Reward Management*, Toronto: John Wiley and Sons, Canada Ltd. 1997, pp. 264-265.

5. Ibid.

6. Reuters: "Odd Perks Becoming the Norm," *The Globe and Mail*, June 22, 2000, p. B13. See also Madelaine Drohan, "Manitoba Finds Solutions for Job Crisis," *The Globe and Mail*, July 12, 2000, p. B12.

7. Issue Alert: State Minimum Wage Increase, http://chamber.cny.com/alert.letters/20000605th.html June 5, 2000

8. *Canadian Labour Law Reports*, Toronto: CCH, 1988, p. 771.

9. Ibid.

10. Marc Law, *The Economics of Minimum Wage Laws*, The Fraser Institute February 9, 1999.

11. Ibid. But see also Michael Goldberg and David Green, "Raising the Floor: The Economic and Social Benefits of Minimum Wages in Canada," Canadian Centre for Policy Alternatives, September 2, 1999. http://www.policyalternatives.ca/bc/nr9.html

12. Survey of Labour and Income Dynamics: The Wage Gap Between Men and Women, *The Daily (a Statistics Canada publication)* December 20, 1999 http://www.statcan.ca/Daily/English/991220/d991220a.htm

13. M. Gunderson, "The Female-Male Earnings Gap in Ontario: A Summary," Ontario Ministry of Labour, Toronto, February 1982. See also the editorial of *The Globe and Mail*, January 21, 1993, p. A16, and the letter to the editor by Nancy Riche, executive vice-president of the Canadian Labour Congress, February 17, 1993; Dawn McCoy-Ullrich, "Women's Career Selection, Not Legislation, the Answer to Solving Wage Gap Problem," *MoneyColumns*, December 21, 1999, http://www.canoe.ca/MoneyColumnsUllrich/mar3_ullrich.html; Luiza Chwialkowska, "StatsCan Study Casts Doubt on Male-Female Wage Gap," (Differences ascribed to experience, family commitments) *National Post*, Tuesday, December 21, 1999, http://www.tom.quack.net/wagegap.html

14. Ibid.

15. C.C. Hoffmann and K.P. Hoffmann, "Does Comparable Worth Obscure the Real Issues?" *Personnel Journal*, Vol. 66, No. 1, January 1987, pp. 82-95. See also "The Family in America," in *Public Opinion*, Washington, D.C.: American Enterprise Institute, January 1986, pp. 25-32, and B. Berger, "At Odds with America's Reality," in *Society*, Rutger's State University, July/August 1985, pp. 77-78.

16. "Equal Pay for Male and Female Employees Who Are Performing Work of Equal Value," interpretation guide for Section 11 of the Canadian Human Rights Act, Canadian Human Rights Commission, Ottawa, undated.

17. Ibid.

18. Hermann F. Schwind, "Equal Pay for Work of Equal Value," *Commercial News*, a publication of the Halifax Board of Trade, July 1981, pp. 28-31.

19. Lester Thurow, "Productivity Pay," *Newsweek*, May 3, 1982, p. 69.

20. Cathy Gedvilas, "Keys to Retaining Top Executive Talent," ACA News, January 1998, pp. 31-32; see also: Pearl Meyer, "A Picture of Executive Compensation Trends," *ACA News*, June 1997, pp. 21-23; "Did They Earn It?" *Forbes Magazine*, May 18, 1998.

21. Steve Ginsberg, "Team Pay Rewards the Players Behind the Superstars," *San Francisco Business Times*, August 15, 1997.

22. Ibid.

23. Personal communication.

24. David E. Tyson, *Profit Sharing in Canada*, Toronto: John Wiley and Sons, 1996. See also H.F. Schwind, S. Pendse, and A. Mukhopadhyay, "Characteristics of Profit Sharing Plans in Canada," *Journal of Small Business and Entrepreneurship*, Spring 1987, pp. 32-37. Richard J. Long, "Consequences and Moderators of Employee Profit Sharing: An Empirical Study," Proceedings of the Administrative Science Association (Human Resource Division), May 30-June 2, 1998, pp. 10-22.

25. Douglas L. Kruse, "Profit Sharing: Does It Make A Difference?" Washington, DC: W.E. Upjohn Institute for Employment Research, 1996; http://www.smartabiz.com/sbs/arts/swp16.htm; see also Hermann F. Schwind, "Do Profit Sharing Plans Motivate Employees?," in *Profit Sharing in Canada*, Toronto: Tyson & Associates Ltd., Vol. 1, No. 1, Autumn 1996, pp. 6-7. Richard J. Long, "Motives for Profit Sharing: A Study of Canadian Chief Executive Officers", Proceedings of the annual meeting of the Administrative Science Association HR Division, Vol. 17, No. 9, 1996, pp. 12-22. Larry Ginsbert, "Profit Sharing Plans Help Keep Great Workers," *The Globe and Mail*, November 2, 1998, p. B11.

26. Hermann F. Schwind, "Do Profit Sharing Plans Motivate Employees?"

27. Sandra L. Sussman, "Taking Stock in Employees," ACA News, a publication of the American Compensation Association, July/August 1997, pp.29-28. See also Richard J. Long, "Profit Sharing and Employee Ownership Schemes," in Malcolm Warner, ed., *The International Encyclopedia of Business and Management*, London: Thompson Business Press, 1996, Vol. 5, pp. 4151-4161. More information can be found in Michael A. Bennett, "Making the Case for Ownership: Employing Workers' Hearts, Not Just Their Hands," *ACA News*, a publication of the American Compensation Association, November/December 1997,pp. 19-21. Margot Gibb-Clark, "Share Plans Can Benefit More Than Employees," *The Globe and Mail*, February 14, 2000, p. B6.

28. Sharon Lebrun, "ESOP Saves the Day," *Canadian HR Reporter*, November 1997, pp. 1-2.

29. Carl F. Frost, John H. Wakeley, and Robert A. Ruh, *The Scanlon Plan for Organizational Development*, Michigan University Press, 2000. See also Anita Hagianati, Economist, Testimony before the

Congressional Subcommittee on Employee Protection, July 16, 1998; http://www.epfnet.org/t980716.htm

30. K. Tracy, M. Renard, and M. Ostrow, "Impact of Pay Policies on Motivation Reflected in the Looking Glass Simulation." Proceedings, Southwest Division of Academy of Management, March 1993, pp. 141-145.

31. Edward. E. Lawler, "Secrecy and the Need to Know," in *Readings in Managerial Motivation and Compensation*, edited by Marvin Dunnette, Robert House, and Henry Tosi; East Lansing: Michigan State University Press, 1972.

32. Anil Verma and Deborah Irvine, "Investing in People," a report by the Information Technology Association of Canada, Willowdale, Ontario, March 1992.

33. Edward E. Lawler III, *Strategic Pay*, San Francisco, Calif.: Jossey-Bass, 1990. See also Gerald E. Leford, Jr., "The Design of Skill-Based Pay Plans," in Rock and Berger, eds., *Handbook of Wage and Salary Administration*.

34. Bruce Little, "How to Make a Small, Smart Factory," *The Globe and Mail*, February 2, 1993, p. B24.

35. Lawler, *Strategic Pay*.

36. Ibid.

37. Ibid.

38. Patricia L. Booth, "Strategic Rewards Management: The Variable Approach to Pay," Report 52-90 of the Conference Board of Canada, April 1990.

39. Ibid.

40. Ibid.

41. Barbara Paus, "Broadbanding Highly Effective, Survey Shows," *ACA News*, July/August 1998, pp. 40-42.

42. Hideo Inohara, *Human Resource Development in Japanese Companies*, Second Edition, Tokyo: Asian Productivity Organization, 1998.

43. Nancy Adler, *International Dimensions of Organizational Behavior*, South-Western College Publishing, 1997.

44. Lawler, *Strategic Pay*.

45. A.S. Binder, *Paying for Productivity*, Washington, D.C.: Brookings Institution, 1990.

46. Edward E. Lawler, *Motivation in Work Organizations*, Jossey-Bass, May 1994.

47. A.A. Shikdar and B. Das, "A Field Study of Worker Productivity Improvements," *Applied Ergonomics* Vol. 26, Feb. 1995, pp. 21-27.

48. Edward E. Lawler, *Rewarding Excellence: Pay Strategies for the New Economy*, Jossey-Bass, 2000.

49. Ibid.

50. Allan M. Maslow and Gene Swimmer, *Wage Controls in Canada, 1975-78: A Study of Public Decision Making*, Toronto: Institute for Research on Public Policy, 1982.

Chapter 11

1. Bill Megalli, "The Fringe Benefit Debate," *The Labour Gazette*, July 1978, p. 313.

2. William M. Mercer, "Benefit Legislation in Canada," December 17, 1999.

3. Andrea Davis, "Ruling Solidifies Same Sex Benefits," *Benefits Canada*, July 1999, p. 41.

4. Kimberly K. Wedell, "Covering New Grounds in Benefits—Looking Ahead to 2000 and Beyond," *Employee Benefits Journal*, December 1999, pp. 3-9.

5. Report of the Royal Commission on the Economic Union and Development Prospects for Canada (Macdonald Commission), Minister of Supply and Services Canada, 1985, Vol. II; Commission of Inquiry into Unemployment Insurance (Forget Commission), Minister of Supply and Services Canada, 1986.

6. National Post (editorial), "EI: Not Working," July 11, 2000.

7. Mercer, "Benefit Legislation in Canada."

8. http://info.load-otea.hrdc-drhc.gc.ca/~fwcsweb/homeen.shtml

9. David Gratzer, "What Future Healthcare?" Health Benefits Special Reports, February 2000, http://www.benefitscanda.com/health.html

10. William M. Mercer, 1999 Director Compensation Study: Trends and Issues of the TSE 100, November 1999. See also 32nd Annual Canadian Salary Survey, Watson Wyatt Consulting, Toronto, 2000.

11. Chamber of Commerce of the United States, Washington D.C., Health Care Benefits, 2000. http://www.chamberbiz.com/bizcenter/P05_4428.cfm

12. Janet White, "The Dental Business," Benefits Canada, March 1999. http://www.assure.ca/library/periodic/bcmar99a.htm

13. 32nd Annual Canadian Salary Survey, Watson Wyatt Consulting, Toronto, 2000. http://www.watsonwyatt.com/homepage/index.html

14. The Daily, Tuesday, October 31, 2000, at Statistics Canada, http://www.statcan.ca/Daily/English/001031/d001031b.htm

15. Mercer, 1999 Director Compensation Study.

16. 32nd Annual Canadian Salary Survey.

17. http://labour-travail.hrdc-drhc.gc.ca/policy/leg/e/stand8-e2.html

18. Sharon Lebrun, "One Size Doesn't Fit All: EAPs Bend to Changes in Employee Demographics," *Canadian HR Reporter*, November 4, 1996, pp. 13-14.

19. Personal communication with Sheila Hagen-Bloxham, Western Regional Coordinator of CN EAPs.

20. Craig C. Pinder, "Comparative Reactions of Managers and Their Spouses to Corporate Transfer Policy Provisions," *Relations Industrielles*, Vol. 37, 1978, pp. 654-65. See also Craig C. Pinder and H. Das, "Hidden Costs and Benefits of Employee Transfers," *Human Resource Planning*, Vol. 2, No. 3, 1979, pp. 135-45.

21. Scott Ion, "Are You Ready for Online EAP Services?" *Canadian HR Reporter*, May 3, 1999, pp. 17-19. Jean-Guy Sauriol, "The Cyber-connection," *Benefits Canada*, October 1999.

22. William H. Holley, Jr. and Earl Ingram II, "Communicating Fringe Benefits," *Personnel Administrator*, March-April 1973, pp. 21-22. See also "3rd Annual Communications Awards", *Benefits Canada magazine*, June 2000; Charles Benayon, "Lack of EAP Awareness—What's It Costing You?" *Canadian HR Reporter*, December 14, 1998, pp. 25-27; Jim Browning, "The EAP Conundrum: It Doesn't Pay to Cut Costs in Employee Communication," *Canadian HR Reporter*, May 3, 1999, pp. 18-19.

23. 32nd Annual Canadian Salary Survey.

24. Roland Theriault, *Mercer Compensation Manual—Theory and Practice*, Boucherville, QU: G. Morin Publisher Ltd., 1992, p. 459.

25. Jon J. Meyer, "The Future of Flexible Benefit Plans," *Employee Benefits Journal*, June 2000, pp. 3-7.

26. Ibid.

27. http://www.bluecross.ca

28. Don Faller, "Sink-or-Swim Benefits Packages Offer Lifeline in Tight Labor Market," Employee Benefit News, September 15, 2000. http://www.benefitnews.com/subscriber/00_09_15/feature4.html

29. Craig Gunsauley, "Benefits Are Key to Successful Retention Strategies," Employee Benefit News, August 2000. http://www.benefitnews.com/subscriber/00_08/quality1.html

30. "Benefits: Evolving for the Future," report from the Health Alliance, http://www.benefitscanada.com/electric/health/part1.html

31. Dorenda McNeil, Mercer Canada Resource Centre, "Beyond the Bottom Line—What CEOs Are Thinking," News Release, February 26, 1999. http://www.wmmercer.com/canada/english/resource/resource_news_topic12.html

32. "Staking a Claim in Flex," Benefits Canada, undated. http://www.benefitscanada.com/sunlife/staking.html

33. Fred Holmes, "Benefit Audit Could Yield Treasure Trove of Savings," The Bottom Line, January 1990, p. 19.

34. Ibid.

35. Meyer: The Future of Flexible Benefit Plans; Wedell: Covering New Ground in Benefits—Looking Ahead to 2000 and Beyond; Gaelyn Mitchell, "E-Benefits: Taking It Online," Employee Benefits Journal, June 2000, pp. 42-44; David Gratzer, "What Future Healthcare?" February 2000, http://www.benefitscanada.com/health.html. Jim Norton and Sandra Pellegrini, "The Future of Flex," September 1999, http://www.benefitscanada.com/health.html

36. Jill Elswick, "Never Enough Fluff," Employee Benefit News, May 2000,_http://www.benefitnews.com/subscriber/00-05/feature2.html

37. Ibid.

38. Sonya Felix, "Gimme Gimme," Benefits Canada Magazine, July 2000, http://www.benefitscanada.com/content/2000/07-00/01.html

39. "Royal Bank Gives Benefits to Part-Timers," The Globe and Mail, September 4, 1996.

40. Watson Wyatt, 32nd Annual Canadian Salary Survey.

Chapter 12

1. W.J. Roche and N.L. MacKinnon, "Motivating People with Meaningful Work," Harvard Business Review, September/October 1968, pp. 42-56.

2. M. Kavanagh, "In Search of Motivation," in T.T. Herbert, Organizational Behavior: Readings and Cases, New York: Macmillan, 1976.

3. Paula Kulig, "Flextime Increasing in Popularity with Employers," Canadian HR Reporter, September 7, 1998, pp. 1-3.

4. Leslie A. Perlow, "Finding Time: How Corporations, Individuals, and Families Can Benefit from New Work Practices," Ithaca, NY: Industrial Labor Relations Press, Cornell University, 1997.

5. Kulig, "Flextime Increasing in Popularity with Employers."

6. Sharon Lebrun, "New Work Styles Gain Converts," Canadian HR Reporter, June 2, 1997, p. 16.

7. Bredan Lipsett and Mark Reesor, "Flexible Work Arrangements," Applied Research Bulletin, Human Resource Development Canada, 1997.

8. Ibid.

9. Rosemary Collins, "Flex Appeal," Canadian Banker, May/June 1997, pp. 12-16.

10. Canadian Labour Market and Productivity Centre, "Changing Times, New Ways of Working," Toronto, 1997.

11. R.B. Dunham, J.L. Pierce, and M.B. Castaneda, "Alternative Work Schedules: Two Field Quasi-Experiments," Personnel Psychology, Vol. 40, 1987, pp. 215-42.

12. See Kulig, "Flextime Increasing in Popularity with Employers," See also Rosemary Collins, "Flex Appeal," Canadian Banker, May/June 1997, pp. 12-16.

13. Elizabeth Sheley, "Job Sharing Offers Unique Challenges," HRMagazine, January 1996; see also Catherine Roseberry, "Flex Options—Advantages & Disadvantages," http://telecommuting.about.com/smallbusiness/telecommuting/lbrary/blflexoptions.htm, October 2000.

14. Bettina Lankard Brown, "Part-Time Work and Other Flexible Options," ERIC Digest #192, 1998.

15. Sharon Lebrun, "New Work Styles Gain Converts," Canadian HR Reporter, June 2, 1997, p. 16; Bruce Little, "Part-timers content with Their Work Status," The Globe and Mail, November 27, 2000, p. B9.

16. Bruce Little, "Canada Sees Spurt of New Jobs," The Globe and Mail, October 7, 2000, p. B1.

17. Pat Booth, "Contingent Work: Trends, Issues and Challenges for Employers," The Conference Board of Canada, 1997.

18. Brown, "Part-Time Work and Other Flexible Options."

19. Grant Schellenberg, "The Changing Nature of Part-time Work," The Canadian Council on Social Development, November 17, 1997.

20. David Quigley, "Plugged in! Computers Let Millions of Canadians Punch a Clock at Home," Edmonton Sun, Dec. 12, 1999.

21. "Work and Family" (cover story), Business Week, June 28, 1993, pp. 80-88.

22. Chris Knight, "Lifestyle Issues Push Telecommuting," Canadian HR Reporter, April 21, 1997, p. 12.

23. Virginia Galt, "Oh, Give Me a Home ...," The Globe and Mail, September 19, 1992, pp. A1-A4.

24. Joseph A. Gibbons, "Telecommuting—The Experiment that Works," Canadian HR Reporter, September 9, 1996, pp. 16-17.

25. See Chris Night, "Lifestyle Issues Push Telecommuting."

26. Galt, "Oh, Give Me a Home...."

27. Business Focus: "Telecommuting Causing Work Condition Worries," The Globe and Mail, Friday, January 7, 2000, p. B8.

28. Joyce Everhart, "Telecommuting: A Business Solution That Is Here to Stay," http://www.publicworks.com, November 21, 2000.

29. David North, "Is Your Head Office a Useless Frill?," Canadian Business, November 14, 1997, pp. 78-80. See also: Sacha Cohen, "On Becoming Virtual," Training & Development, May 1997, pp. 30-38; Sandra O'Connell, "The Virtual Workplace Moves at Warp Speed," HRMagazine, March 1996, pp. 51-57.

30. Survey by Watson Wyatt Consultants, "Employers Turn To Phased Retirement As Workers Age and Labor Shortages Increase," September 8, 1999.

31. http://www.mcgill.ca/academic/5_1.htm

32. Mercer Communique, June 6, 1997

33. Carolyn Hirschman, "All Aboard," *HRMagazine*, September 1997, pp.80-85. See also Laura Beller, "Employee Leasing What Are The Opportunities for Agents?" http://www.roughnotes.com/rnmag/june97/06p30.htm

34. Valerie Frazee, "Share Thy Neighbor's Workers," *Personnel Journal*, June 1996, pp. 81-84.

35. Susan N. Houseman, "Flexible Staffing Arrangements," A Report on Temporary Help, futurework, August 1999 http://www.dol.gov/dol/asp/public/futurework/conference/staffing/exec_s.htm

36. David Nye, "Not Made in Heaven," *Across the Board*, October 1996, Vol. 33, No. 9, pp. 41-46. See also Anthony V. Martin, "Outsourcing: Is Contingent HR For You?" *HR Focus*, November 1997, Vol. 74, No. 11, pp. 13-14.

37. H. Axel, "Job Banks for Retirees," The Conference Board, Report No. 929, 1989.

38. "Hiring Employees and Independent Contractors," Western Economic Diversification Canada, http://www.wd.gc.ca/eng/search/default.htm

39. K. Gay, "Contracts Taking the Place of Loyalty for Many," *The Financial Post*, November 20, 1993, p. 26.

40. Sharon Lebrun, "Growing Contract Workforce Hindered by Lack of Rules," *Canadian HR Reporter*, May 1997, pp. 1-2; Chris Night, "Contractors Become Fixture in Workplace," *Canadian HR Reporter*, October 21, 1996, pp. 14-15.

41. Tim Cestnick, "How to Check If You're Really Self-employed," *The Globe and Mail*, October 7, 2000, p. N5. See also: Daphne Kelgard, "Beware of the Legal Pitfalls of Contract Workers," *Canadian HR Reporter*, September 8, 1997, pp. 18-19. A more comprehensive discussion of the legal and tax issues involved can be found in: Joanne Magee, "Whose Business Is It? Employees Versus Independent Contractors," *Canadian Tax Journal*, 1997, Vol. 45, No. 3.

42. Michelle Conlin, "And Now, the Just-in-time Employee," *Business Week*, August 28, 2000, pp. 169-170.

43. Edward E. Lawler, *Rewarding Excellence: Pay Strategies for the New Economy*, San Francisco: Jossey-Bass, 2000.

44. Donald J. Campbell, Kathleen M. Campbell, Ho-Beng Chia, "Merit Pay, Performance Appraisal, and Individual Motivation: An Analysis and Alternative," *Human Resource Management*, 1998, Vol. 37, No. 2, pp. 131-146.

45. P.C. Smith, L.M. Kendall, and C.L. Hulin, *The Job Descriptive Index*, rev. ed., Bowling Green, Ohio: Department of Psychology, Bowling Green State University, 1999.

46. Steven L. McShane, *Canadian Organizational Behaviour*, Third edition, McGraw-Hill Ryerson Limited, 1998, p. 182.

47. L.W. Porter and E.E. Lawler, *Managerial Attitudes and Performance*, Homewood, Ill.: Irwin, 1968.

48. Elizabeth Church, "Nortel Workers Pick Tailor-made Perks," *The Globe and Mail*, December 8, 2000, p. B11.

49. H.F. Schwind, S. Pendse, and A. Mukhopadhyay, "Characteristics of Profit-Sharing Plans in Canada," *Journal of Small Business and Entrepreneurship*, Spring 1987, pp. 32-37.

Chapter 13

1. Jeffrey Pfeffer and John Veiga, "Putting People First for Organizational Success," *Academy of Management Executive*, May 1999, p. 43.

2. "Workers Frustrated With Employers, *Canadian HR Reporter*, March 8, 1999, pp. 9, 12.

3. "What Drives Employee Commitment (and the Higher Productivity That Follows)," *HRFocus*, April 2000, p. 9.

4. Charlene M. Solomon, "The Loyalty Factor," *Personnel Journal*, September 1992, pp. 52-62.

5. For example, see Rosabeth M. Kanter, *When Giants Learn to Dance*, New York: Simon and Shuster, 1989; Charles Handy, *Beyond Certainty: The Changing Worlds of Organizations*, New York: McGraw-Hill, 1996; Jac Fitz-Enz, *The 8 Practices of Exceptional Companies: How Great Organizations Make the Most of Their Human Assets*, New York: American Management Association, 1997.

6. "Companies Are Waking Up to the Huge Costs of Harbouring a Jerk in Their Ranks," *Financial Post*, January 15, 2000, p. D6.

7. Gillian Flynn, "Acrobats, Aerialists and HR: The Big Top Needs Big HR," *Workforce*, August 1997, pp. 38-45.

8. "The Truth About Leveraging HR Information Services," *HRFocus*, June 2000, pp. 11-12.

9. "How E-mail Has Become Integral to the Workplace," *HRFocus*, July 2000, p. 8. More details of the survey can be found at www.vault.com.

10. Muriel Draaisma, "Few Companies Use HR Intranets," *Workplace News Online*, September 2000.

11. Martha I. Finney, "Harness the Power Within," *HR Magazine*, January 1997, pp. 66-74.

12. Samuel Greengard, "12 Ways to Use an Intranet," *Workforce*, March 1997, p. 94.

13. Dominic Bencivenga, "Employers and Workers Come to Terms," *HR Magazine*, June 1997, pp. 91-97.

14. Brenda P. Sunoo, "HR Managers Unplug," *Workforce*, April 1997, pp. 37-42.

15. Lesley Young, "Managing the Flow of Data at Inco," *Canadian HR Professional*, October 18, 1999, pp. G1, G12.

16. Lesley Young, "Web Used to Target Rival's Employees During Hostile Takeover," *Canadian HR Reporter*, February 8, 1999, pp. 1, 3.

17. See "Sample Clauses for Internet Policy," *Canadian HR Reporter*, November 3, 1997, p. 19.

18. "How to Protect Your Company from Misuse of Electronic Communications," *HRFocus*, April 2000, p.7.

19. Pam Robertson and Sue Matthews, "Open (Book) Sesame!" *Canadian HR Reporter*, December 1, 1997, pp. 29-30.

20. F. Rice, "Champions of Communication," *Fortune*, June 3, 1991, pp. 111-20.

21. Shari Caudron, "Blow the Whistle on Employment Disputes," *Workforce*, May 1997, pp. 50-57.

22. See Peter Feuille and Denise R. Chachere, "Looking Fair or Being Fair: Remedial Voice Procedures in Nonunion Workplaces," *Journal of Management*, 1995, Vol. 21, pp. 27-42.

23. Terry H. Wagar, "Grievance Procedures in the Non-Union Environment," *Labour Arbitration Yearbook*, 2000 (in press).

24. These are just some of the issues discussed in Peter Feuille and Denise R. Chachere, "Looking Fair or Being Fair: Remedial Voice Procedures in Nonunion Workplaces."

25. Survey by Angus Reid Group completed for the Royal Bank. See *Canadian HR Reporter*, November 3, 1997, pp. 1, 3.

26. Lesley Young, "National EAP Database Will Standardize Delivery," *Canadian HR Reporter*, December 13, 1999, p. 3.

27. Scott Ion, "Are You Ready for Online EAP Services?" *Canadian HR Reporter*, May 3, 1999, pp. 17, 19.

28. Howard A. Levitt, *The Law of Dismissal in Canada*, Second Edition, Aurora, ON: Canada Law Book, 1992.

29. Paul Falcone, "The Fundamentals of Progressive Discipline," *HR Magazine*, February 1997, 90-94.

30. This material is based largely on the video *Discipline Without Punishment (Revised)* which was released in 1996 by Owen Stewart Performance Resources.

31. Howard A. Levitt, *The Law of Dismissal in Canada*, Second Edition.

32. *Wallace v. United Grain Growers Ltd.*, Supreme Court of Canada, October 30, 1997.

33. Terry H. Wagar, "Wrongful Dismissal: Perception vs. Reality," *Human Resources Professional*, June 1996, pp. 8, 10.

34. Howard A. Levitt, *The Law of Dismissal in Canada*, Second Edition.

35. An excellent source of information on reasonable notice awards is Ellen Mole, *The Wrongful Dismissal Handbook*, Second Edition, Toronto: Butterworths, 1997.

36. Jeffrey Miller, "Lower Courts Raise Employers' Costs With Higher Extended-Notice Damages," *Canadian HR Reporter*, May 31, 1999, p. 5.

37. This information is based on a report prepared by Murray Axmith and Associates entitled the *1997 Canadian Hiring and Dismissal Practices Survey*.

38. More detail on these points is provided in Jeffrey Connor, "Disarming Terminated Employees," *HR Magazine*, January 2000, pp. 113-116.

39. See American Management Association, "American Companies Increase Use of Electronic Monitoring," April 12, 2000 (www.amanet.org).

40. American Management Association, *Workplace Testing: Monitoring and Surveillance*, AMA, 2000.

41. Lisa Copenhaver and Robert H. Gust, "Quality of Worklife: The Anatomy of Two Successes," *National Productivity Review*, Winter 1982/83, p. 5. Also see Edward E. Lawler, Susan A. Mohrman and Gerald E. Ledford, *Employee Involvement and Total Quality Management*, San Francisco, Jossey-Bass, 1992; J.L. Cotton, *Employee Involvement*, Newbury Park, CA: Sage, 1993.

42. Gillian Flynn, "Bank of Montreal Invests in Its Workers," *Workforce*, December 1997, pp. 30-38.

43. Brian E. Becker, Mark A. Huselid, Peter S. Pickus and Michael F. Spratt, "HR as a Source of Shareholder Value: Research and Recommendations," *Human Resource Management*, Spring 1997, pp. 39-47.

44. William B. Werther, Jr., "Quality Circles: Key Executive Issues," *Journal of Contemporary Business*, Vol. 11, No. 2, n.d., pp. 17-26; Edward E. Lawler and Susan A. Mohrman, "Quality Circles After the Fad," *Harvard Business Review*, January-February 1985, pp. 65-71.

45. Kathleen D. Ryan and Daniel K. Oestreich, *Driving Fear Out of the Workplace: How to Overcome Barriers to Quality, Productivity and Innovation*, San Francisco, CA: Jossey-Bass, 1991.

46. William A. Pasmore, *Designing Effective Organizations: A Sociotechnical Systems Perspective*, New York: Wiley, 1988.

47. "Saturn Workers Like Unique Pact," *Hamilton Spectator*, March 12, 1998.

48. James W. Bishop and K. Dow Scott, "How Commitment Affects Team Performance," *HR Magazine*, February 1997, pp. 107-111.

49. Ibid.

50. A good review of this perspective is presented in Mike Parker and Jane Slaughter, "Management by Stress," *Technology Review*, October 1988, pp. 37-44.

51. Mark Huselid, "The Impact of Human Resource Management Practices on Turnover, Productivity, and Corporate Financial Performance," *Academy of Management Journal*, June 1995, pp. 635-672.

52. John Paul MacDuffie, "Human Resource Bundles and Manufacturing Performance: Organizational Logic and Flexible Production Systems in the World Auto Industry," *Industrial and Labor Relations Review*, January 1995, pp. 197-221.

53. For an extensive review of the current literature, see Steven Wood, "Human Resource Management and Performance," *International Journal of Management Reviews*, Vol. 1, pp. 367-413.

54. Brian E. Becker, Mark A. Huselid, Peter S. Pickus and Michael F. Spratt, "HR as a Source of Shareholder Value: Research and Recommendations."

55. Jeffrey Pfeffer and John Veiga, "Putting People First for Organizational Success."

56. The samples are not random as all participants in both surveys had responded to an earlier study three years previously. For further discussion of some of the findings see Terry H. Wagar, "Managing Human Resources and Change: What's Happening in Canadian Organizations?," *Human Resources Professional*, February/March 1998, pp. 27-30.

57. There are several excellent references on this topic. See, for instance, Gordon Betcherman, Kathryn McMullen, Norm Leckie, and Christina Caron, *The Canadian Workplace in Transition*. Kingston: IRC Press, 1994; Report of the Advisory Committee on the Changing Workplace, *Collective Reflections on the Changing Workplace*, Ottawa: HRDC, 1997; and *Changing Workplace Strategies: Achieving Better Outcomes for Enterprises, Workers, and Society*, Ottawa: HRDC, 1997. In addition, the July 1996 issue of *Industrial Relations*, the August 1996 issue of the *Academy of Management Journal*, and the Fall 1997 issue of *Human Resource Management* were specifically devoted to this topic.

58. Denise Rousseau, "Changing the Deal While Keeping the People," *Academy of Management Executive*, 1996, Vol. 10, pp. 50-59.

59. B. O'Reilly, "The New Deal: What Companies and Employees Owe One Another," *Fortune*, June 13, 1994, p. 44.

60. Ken Mark, "No More Pink Slips," *Human Resources Professional*, November 1996, pp. 21-23.

61. Terry H. Wagar, "Factors Affecting Permanent Workforce Reduction: Evidence From Large Canadian Organizations," *Canadian Journal of Administrative Sciences*, September 1997, pp. 303-314; Terry H. Wagar, "The Death of Downsizing—Not Yet!" *Human Resource Professional*, March 1999, pp. 41-43. Also see, "Workers Still Face Downsizing Woes," *The Globe and Mail*, April 18, 2000, p. W1.

62. See "Xerox to Slash 5,200 Jobs," *The Globe and Mail*, April 1, 2000, p. B7; "Unilever to Slash 25,000 jobs in Worldwide Reorganization," *The Globe and Mail*, February 23, 2000, p. B9; "World Has Changed at Cola-Cola as 6,000 Lose Jobs," *Financial Post*, January 27, 2000, p. C10.

63. Steve W.J. Kozlowski, Georgia T. Chao, Eleanor M. Smith and Jennifer Hedlund, "Organizational Downsizing: Strategies, Interventions, and Research Implications," in C.L. Cooper and I.T. Robertson, eds., *International Review of Industrial and Organizational Psychology*, 1993, Vol. 8, pp. 263-332.

64. Kim Cameron, "Strategies for Successful Organizational Downsizing," *Human Resource Management*, Summer 1994, p. 192.

65. Ibid.

66. Wayne Cascio, "Downsizing? What Do We Know? What Have We Learned?," *Academy of Management Executive*, 1993, Vol. 7, pp. 95-104. Also see Terry H. Wagar, "Exploring the Consequences of Workforce Reduction," *Canadian Journal of Administrative Sciences*, December 1998, pp. 300-309.

67. Lesley Young, "Employees Shaken by Downsizing Tremors," *Canadian HR Reporter*, June 5, 2000, p. 3.

68. See, for instance, Nancy Ursel and Marjorie Armstrong-Stassen, "The Impact of Layoff Announcements on Shareholders," *Relations Industrielles*, 1995, Vol. 50, pp. 636-649.

69. Kim Cameron, "Strategies for Successful Organizational Downsizing."

70. Kim Cameron, Sarah Freeman, and Anil Mishra, "Best Practices in White Collar Downsizing: Managing Contradictions," *Academy of Management Executive*, 1991, Vol. 5, pp. 57-73.

71. David Brown, "Hanging On to Nervous Employees," *Canadian HR Professional*, October 19, 1999, pp. 1, 19.

72. See, for instance, Terry H. Wagar, "What Do We Know About Downsizing?" *Benefits and Pensions Monitor*, June 1996, pp. 19-20, 69.

73. These issues are discussed in more detail in Mark Mone, "Relationships Between Self-Concepts, Aspirations, Emotional Responses, and Intent to Leave a Downsizing Organization," *Human Resource Management*, Summer 1994, pp. 281-298.

74. Barry Wright and Julian Barling, "The Executioners' Song: Listening to Downsizers Reflect on their Experiences," *Canadian Journal of Administrative Sciences*, December 1998, pp. 339-355.

75. This is discussed in more detail in Frederick F. Reichheld, *The Loyalty Effect*, Boston: Harvard Business School Press, 1996.

76. Keith H. Hammonds, "Accountants Have Lives, Too, You Know," *Business Week*, February 23, 1998, pp. 88, 90.

77. See American Management Association, *1999 AMA Human Resources Conference Onsite Survey*, at www.amanet.org.

78. Laura Dunne, "Exit Price Key to Retaining IT Talent," *Canadian HR Reporter*, January 26, 1998, p. 6.

79. Joey Goodings, "Most Federal Knowledge Workers Think About Quitting," *Canadian HR Reporter*, February 22, 1999, pp. 3, 6.

80. Charlene M. Solomon, "Keep Them! Don't Let Your Best People Get Away," *Workforce*, August 1997, pp. 46-51.

81. Lesley Young, "Benefits Won't Bait Workers, Study Shows," *Canadian HR Reporter*, February 8, 1999, pp. 1, 8.

Chapter 14

1. Lee Gardenswartz and Anita Rowe, *Managing Diversity: A Complete Desk Reference and Planning Guide*, Burr Ridge, Illinois: Irwin Professional Publishing Co., 1993, p. 4.

2. Robin Wilson, "To Sir-uh, Madam-With Love," *The Globe and Mail*, February 21, 1998, p. D-9.

3. "Visible Minorities Cluster in Canada's Largest Cities," *The Globe and Mail*, February 18, 1998, p. A-3.

4. Mallika Das, "Workforce 2000: Diversity in the Workplace" in *Managing Diversity: Gender and Other Issues*, Third Edition, Open Learning Program, Halifax: Mount Saint Vincent University, 1997, p. 4. Also see, A.V. Subbarao, *Managing Workforce Diversity in Canada: Problems and Prospects*, Working Paper 94-25, University of Ottawa, 1994.

5. Mallika Das, 1997, op. cit.

6. J.E. Baird Jr. and P.H. Bradley, "Styles of Management and Communications: A Comparative Study of Men and Women," *Communication Monographs*, June 1979, Vol. 46, pp. 101-110; Susan LeBlanc, "The Feminine Factor: Do Women Do Business Differently than Men?" *The Mail Star*, September 26, 1995, p. C-1; S.H Applebaum and B.T. Shapiro, "Why Can't Men Lead Like Women?" *Leadership and Organization Development Journal*, 1993, Vol.14, pp. 28-34; J.B. Rosener, "Ways Women Lead," *Harvard Business Review*, Nov.-Dec. 1990, Vol. 68, pp. 119-125.

7. A. DePalma, "Women Can Be Hindered by Lack of 'Boys' Network." *Boulder Daily Camera*, November 12, 1991, p. B-9.

8. Elizabeth Church, "Women Still Shut Out of Many Top Posts," *The Globe and Mail*, February 10, 2000, p. B-15.

9. Keith McArthur, "Group Calls for Equal Numbers on Boards," *The Globe and Mail*, January 20, 2000, p. B-15.

10. Geogrey York, "Space Researcher Quits over Sexual Harassment," *The Globe and Mail*, March 27, 2000, pp. A1, A8.

11. Bruce G. Trigger, *Natives and Newcomers*, Montreal: McGill University Press, 1985, p. 3-4.

12. Marilyn Loden, *Implementing Diversity*, Chicago, IL: Irwin, 1996, p.14.

13. Kandola, R., "Managing Diversity: New Broom or Old Hat?" *International Review of Industrial and Organizational Psychology,* 1995, Vol. 10, pp. 131-167.

14. Anne Marie Francesco and Barry Allen Gold, *International Organizational Behaviour*, New Jersey: Prentice Hall, 1998, p. 225.

15. Mallika Das, 1997, op. cit., p. 13.

16. GE's Chairman, Jack Welch, quoted by Thomas Stewart, 1997, op. cit., p. 106.

17. Christine Taylor, "Building a Business Case for Diversity," *Canadian Business Review*, Spring, 1995, pp.12-14; also see, Christine Taylor, *Building a Business Case for Valuing Ethnocultural Diversity*, Ottawa: The Conference Board of Canada, 1995.

18. Professor Belcourt quoted by Cleta Moyer in "Diversity Management: The Bottom Line Impact of an Equitable Employment System," *Human Resources Professional*, 1995, pp. 21-22.

19. "Making the Differences Work," a progress report on closing the gender-gap and leveraging diversity at Royal Bank Financial Group, October, 1996, p.1.

20. Ibid.

21. Elizabeth Church, "Female Led Sales Teams Have Superior Morale, Performance, Study Finds," *The Globe and Mail*, February 17, 2000, p. B-14.

22. Lee Gardenswartz and Anita Rowe, *Diverse Teams at Work*, Chicago, IL: Irwin, 1994, p. 17.

23. Taylor Cox, Jr. and Ruby Beale, *Developing Competency to Manage Diversity*, San Francisco, CA: Berrett-Koehler Publishers Inc, 1997, p. 31.

24. Cox and Beale, 1997, op. cit., p. 32.

25. Phebe-Jane Poole, *Diversity: A Business Advantage*, Ajax, ON: Poole Publishing Company, 1997, pp. 21-25.

26. See Phebe-Jane Poole, 1997, op. cit., p. 23.

27. Trevor Wilson, *Diversity at Work*, New York: John Wiley and Sons, 1996, p. 43.

28. Subbarao, A.V. "Managing Workforce Diversity in Canada: Problems and Prospects," Working paper no. 94-25, University of Ottawa, April 1994, p. 2.

29. Michelle Martinez, "Equality Effort Sharpens Bank's Edge," *HR Magazine*, January, 1995, pp. 38-43.

30. Hari Das, *Strategic Organization Design: For Canadian Firms in a Global Economy*, Scarborough, Ontario: Prentice-Hall, 1998, p. 340.

31. Susan Jackson and Associates, *Diversity in the Workplace*, New York: Guildford Press, 1992, pp. 203-226.

32. "Women Flee Jobs to Start Firms: Study," *The Globe and Mail*, February 26, 1998, p. B-17.

33. Making the differences work, Royal Bank report, October 1996, op. cit., p. 4.

34. Making the differences work, a progress report on closing the gender gap & leveraging diversity at Royal Bank Financial Group, October, 1996, p. 6.

35. *Managing Diversity: A Guide to Effective Staff Management*, The McDonald Series, Cross Cultural Communications International Inc., Winnipeg, undated, p. 24.

36. Lee Gardenswartz and Anita Rowe, *Managing Diversity*, New York: Irwin Professional Publishing, 1993, p. 37.

37. Christine Taylor, *Building a Business Case for Valuing Ethnocultural Diversity*, Ottawa, ON: The Conference Board of Canada, 1995.

38. C. Moyer, "Diversity Management: The Bottom-line Impact of an Equitable Employment System," *Human Resources Professional*, November 1995, pp. 21-22.

39. D. Davies, "Equity Equations: Scrapping Equity Programs When Profits Are Down Does Not Add Up," *Human Resources Professional*, April 1993, p. 15.

40. Personal communication by the first author with a U.S. Caterpillar-Mitsubishi executive in the CM joint venture plant in Sagamihara, Japan, 1991.

41. D. Davies, 1993, op. cit.

42. Gillian Flynn, "Deloitte & Touche Changes Women's Minds. Cultural Audit Boosts Retention," *Personnel Journal,* April 1996, pp. 56-68.

43. For example, see, Susan Vinnicombe and Nina Colwill, *The Essence of Women in Management*, London: Prentice-Hall, 1995.

44. Gillian Flynn, 1996, op. cit.

45. D. Davies, 1993, op. cit., p. 17.

46. Marilyn Loden, 1996, op. cit., p. 79.

47. Christine Taylor, 1995, op. cit.

48. Paul Brocklyn, "Developing the International Executive," *Personnel*, March 1989, p. 44.

49. For example, see Gary Hogan and Jane Goodson, "The Key to Expatriate Success," *Training and Development Journal*, January 1990, Vol. 44, No.1, pp. 50-52; Raymond Stone, "Expatriate Selection and Failure," *Human Resource Planning*, 1991, Vol.14, No.1, pp. 9-18; Allan Bird and Roger Dunbar, "Getting the Job Done over There: Improving Expatriate Productivity," *National Productivity Review*, Spring 1991, Vol.10, No. 2, pp.145-156.

50. Raymond Stone, "Expatriate Selection and Failure," *Human Resource Planning*, 1991, Vol.14, No.1, pp. 9-18; Rosalie Tung, "Selection and Training of Personnel for Overseas Assignments," *Columbia Journal of World Business*, Spring 1981, Vol.16, No.1, pp. 68-78.

51. C.G. Howard, "Profile of the 21st-Century Expatriate Manager," *HR Magazine*, June 1992, pp. 93-100.

52. Nancy Adler, "Women Managers in a Global Economy," *HR Magazine*, 1993, Vol. 38, No. 9, September, pp. 52-55; Hilary Harris, "Women in International Management: Opportunity or Threat?" *Women in Management Review*, 1993, Vol. 8, No. 5, pp. 9-14.

53. Peter Blunt, "Recent Developments in Human Resource Management: The Good, the Bad and the Ugly," *International Journal of Human Resource Management*, June 1990, pp. 45-59; Sheila Rothwell, "Leadership development and International HRM," *Manager Update*, 1993, No. 4, Summer, pp. 20-32.

54. See Brocklyn, op. cit., p.46; also see, Nancy Napier and Richard Peterson, "Expatriate Re-entry: What do Repatriates Have to Say?" *Human Resource Planning*, March 1991, pp.19-28.

55. Edward Dunbar and Allan Katcher, "Preparing Managers for Foreign Assignments," *Training and Development Journal*, September 1990, Vol. 44, No. 9, pp. 45-47; Paul Sullivan, "Training's Role in Global Business," *Executive Excellence*, September 1991, No. 9, pp. 9-10.

56. B.T. King and I.L. Janis, "Comparison of the Effectiveness of Improvised versus Non-Improvised Role-Playing in Producing Opinion Change," *Human Relations*, May 1956, pp. 177-86; see also W.A. Scott, "Attitude Change through Reward of Verbal Behaviour," *Journal of Abnormal and Social Psychology*, July 1957, Vol. 55, pp. 72-75.

57. R.G. Shirts, Ba Fa' Ba Fa', A Cross-Cultural Simulation, Del Mar, CA: Sirrile, 1977.

58. H.F. Schwind, "The State of the Art in Cross-Cultural Management Training," *International HRD Annual*, Vol. 1, R. Doktor, ed., American Society for Training and Development, Washington, D.C., 1985.

59. Stephen Rhinesmith, "Global Mindsets for Global Managers," *Training and Development*, October 1992, pp. 63-68.

60. R.S. Schuler, J.R. Fulkerson and P.J. Bowling, "Strategic Performance Measurement and Management in Multinational Corporations," *Human Resource Management*, Fall 1991, Vol. 30, No. 3, pp. 365-392.

61. See Brocklyn, op. cit.; also see Werther and Davis, op. cit., p. 79.

62. Stewart Black and Hal Gregersen, "Serving Two Masters: Managing the Dual Allegiance of Expatriate Employees," *Sloan Management Review*, Summer 1992, Vol. 33, No. 4, pp. 61-71.

63. Ellen Brandt, "Global HR," *Personnel Journal*, March, 1991, p. 41.

64. L. Gomez-Mejia and T. Welbourne, "Compensation Strategies in a Global Context," *Human Resources Planning*, 1991, Vol.14, No.1, pp. 29-41; Richard Hodgetts and Fred Luthans, "U.S. Multinationals' Compensation Strategies for Local Management: Cross Cultural Implications," *Compensation and Benefits Review*, March-April 1993, Vol. 25, No. 2, pp. 42-48.

65. Douglas Carey and Paul Hows, "Developing a Global Pay Program," *Journal of International Compensation and Benefits*, July-August, 1992, pp. 26-33; Mariah De Forest, "Thinking of a Plant in Mexico?" *Academy of Management Executive*, February 1994, pp. 33-40.

66. Wayne Cascio and Manuel Serapio, Jr., "Human Resource Systems in an International Alliance: The Undoing of a Done Deal?" *Organizational Dynamics*, Winter 1991, pp. 63–74.

67. Stephen Rhinesmith, "Global Mindsets for Global Managers," *Training and Development*, October 1992, pp. 63–68.

Chapter 15

1. See Leslie Ebbs, "The Safety Culture," *HR Professional*, October-November 1998, p. 23.

2. F.E. Bird, Jr., *Management Guide to Loss Control*, Atlanta, GA: Institute Press, 1974.

3. Ibid.

4. R.D. Clarke, "Worker Participation in Health and Safety in Canada," *International Labour Review*, March/April 1982, pp. 199-206.

5. "Man Gets Nail in Head," *The Globe and Mail*, February 28, 1998, p. A6.

6. "Hospital Fined After Electrocution," *Canadian HR Reporter*, February 23, 1998, p. 3.

7. Human Resources Development Canada, *Work Safely for a Healthy Future*, Ottawa, ON: Government of Canada, 2000.

8. Human Resources Development Canada, *Occupational Injuries and Their Cost in Canada: 1993-1997*, Ottawa, ON: Government of Canada, 1999.

9. Martin Mittelstaedt, "Factory's Staff Faced Massive Asbestos Levels, Records Show," *The Globe and Mail*, February 11, 1999, pp. A1, A14.

10. HRDC, *Work Safely for a Healthy Future*.

11. This information is taken from Dilys Robertson, "The Scope of Occupational Health and Safety in Canada," *HRM in Canada*, Scarborough, ON: Carswell, 1996.

12. Also see James Montgomery, *Occupational Health and Safety*, Toronto, ON: Nelson Canada, 1996.

13. Part II of the Canada Labour Canada was recently amended. For more information, see Human Resources Development Canada, "An Overview to Part II of the Canada Labour Code," which is available at the HRDC web site (hrdc-drhc.gc.ca).

14. James Montgomery, *Occupational Health and Safety*.

15. Commerce Clearing House, *Canadian Master Labour Guide*, North York, ON: CCH, 2000.

16. The Health Canada web site is particularly informative. See www.hc-sc.gc.ca/hpb/lcdc/biosafety/msds.

17. *At the Centre*, the newsletter of the Canadian Centre for Occupational Health and Safety, July 1985, p. 13.

18. More information on the Canadian Centre for Occupational Health and Safety is available from the Centre's web page (www.ccohs.ca) and from their annual reports.

19. Lesley Young, "Employers Caught in Accident Coverups," *Canadian HR Reporter*, August 9, 1999, pp. 1 ,10.

20. See, for example, Ontario's Young Worker Awareness Program. More information about the program is available at www.yworker.com.

21. "Back to Work with Back Injuries," *Canadian HR Reporter*, February 9, 1998, p. 11.

22. Bill Pomfret, "Sound Employee Orientation Program Boosts Productivity and Safety," *Canadian HR Reporter*, January 25, 1999, pp. 17, 19.

23. Wayne Pardy, "How CN Keeps Safety on Track," *Canadian Occupational Safety*, March/April 1993, pp. 19-21.

24. Lesley Young, "Are You Sure You've Got Health and Safety Covered?," *Canadian HR Reporter*, May 17, 1999, pp.18-19.

25. Mark MacKinnon, "Canadians Want Executives to Pay for Fatal Mistakes in Workplace," *The Globe and Mail*, June 6, 2000, p. A2.

26. Ibid.

27. Jamie Harrison, "Injury Reduction Earns Quebecor Top Honours," *Canadian HR Reporter*, January 26, 1998, pp. 1, 6.

28. Daniel Black, "Due Diligence: Your Company's Best Defence Against an Occupational Health and Safety Offence," *Canadian HR Reporter*, May 31, 1999, pp. 17, 19.

29. Sharon Lebrun, "Disability Management Underused," *Canadian HR Reporter*, December 29, 1997, p. 7. See also, Doug Burn, "Disability Management," *Human Resources Professional*, October 1996, pp. 33-35.

30. For more details see *Strategies for Success: Disability Management in the Workplace*, Port Alberni, B.C.: National Institute of Disability Management, 1997.

31. Canadian Centre for Occupational Health and Safety, *Workplace Stress*, www.ccohs.ca.

32. Michael Petrou, "Action Demanded on Workplace Despair," *Financial Post*, July 31, 2000, p. C3.

33. Sharon Lebrun, "Disability Management Underused."

34. See, "Workplace Stress More Prevalent Than Illness, Injury," *The Globe and Mail*, April 8, 1998, p. A2.

35. International Labour Organization, *Encyclopaedia of Occupational Health and Safety*, 4th ed., Waldorf, MA: ILO.

36. Jack Santa-Barbara, "Preventing the Stress Epidemic," *Canadian HR Reporter*, March 8, 1999, p. 19.

37. Lesley Young, "Stressed Workers Are Suing Employers," *Canadian HR Reporter*, May 3, 1999, pp. 1, 6.

38. National Institute for Occupational Health and Safety, *Stress at Work*, Washington, DC: U.S. Department of Health and Human Services, 1999.

39. Statistics Canada, *Work Stress and Health*, 1999.

40. Simon Avery, "On-line Service to Rate the Boss," *Financial Post*, May 18, 2000, p. C9.

41. John R. Schermerhorn, Julian Cattaneo and Andrew Templer, *Management: The Competitive Advantage*, 2nd ed., Toronto, ON: Wiley, 1995, p. 613.

42. Paul Froiland, "What Cures Job Stress?" *Training*, December 1993, pp. 32-36.

43. Jennifer Laabs, "Cashing in on Safety," *Workforce*, August 1997, pp. 53-58.

44. Doug Burn, "Parents' Job Anxiety Wreaks Havoc on Children," *Canadian HR Reporter*, December 29, 1997, pp. 16, 20.

45. Patrick McGuire, "Worker Stress, Health Reaching Critical Point," *APA Monitor Online*, May 1999, www.apa.org/monitor/may99.

46. Krista Foss, "The Truth About Sex, Work and Stress," *The Globe and Mail*, May 17, 2000, pp. A1, A6.

47. T.H. Holmes and R.H. Rahe, "The Social Readjustment Rating Scale," *Journal of Psychosomatic Research*, 1967, Vol. 11, pp. 213-18.

48. Holmes and Rahe, "The Social Readjustment Rating Scale." Various applications of this scale are available on the Internet.

49. W.B. Schaufeli et al. eds., *Professional Burnout: Recent Developments in Theory and Research*, Washington, D.C.: Taylor and Francis, 1993.

50. "Flex-time Solutions in Practice," *Canadian HR Reporter*, October 4, 1999, p. 2.

51. John M. Kelly, "Get a Grip on Stress," *HRMagazine*, February 1997, pp. 51-54.

52. National Institute for Occupational Health and Safety, *Stress at Work*.

53. National Institute for Occupational Health and Safety, *Stress at Work*.

54. Virginia Galt, "Stress Not Just the Boss's Fault," *The Globe and Mail*, October 5, 2000, p. B15.

55. David Brown, "Wellness Programs No Magic Cure," *Canadian HR Reporter*, October 4, 1999, p. 2.

56. Lesley Young, "Managers At BCT Telus Held Accountable for Wellness," *Canadian HR Reporter*, February 28, 2000, p. 9.

57. Raymond and Wales, "Healthy Staff Convey Positive Image."

58. Judy Sefton, "The Case for Preventive Health Programs," *Canadian HR Reporter*, September 8, 1997, p. 6.

59. W. List, "Fitness Plans Include Blue-Collar Workers," *The Globe and Mail*, April 21, 1991, p. A16.

60. Sharon Lebrun, "Wellness Jackpot," *Canadian HR Reporter*, October 20, 1997, pp. 13,1 9.

61. Lesley Young, "Healthy Workplace Keeps in Touch With Employees," *Canadian HR Reporter*, February 28, 2000, p. 9.

62. Sharon Lebrun, "Is There a Doctor on the Home Page?" *Canadian HR Reporter*, November 3, 1997, p. 11.

63. This information is based on an article by Kat Morgan, "Sick Building Syndrome," *Human Resources Professional*, February-March 1998, pp. 39-40.

64. Michelle Conlin, "Is Your Office Killing You," *Business Week*, June 5, 2000, pp. 114-130.

65. Linda Micco, "Night Retailers Take Stock of Workers' Safety," *HR Magazine*, June 1997, pp. 79-85.

66. Ibid.

67. Doug Burn, "Preventing Violence in the Workplace," *Human Resources Professional*, October-November 1998, pp. 15-20.

68. Dana Flavelle, "Rising Stress Blamed for Workplace Rage," *Halifax Mail Star*, April 11, 2000, p. C3.

69. Society for Human Resource Management, *1999 Workplace Violence Survey*, Alexandria, VI: SHRM, 1999.

70. Risk and Insurance Management Society, *1999 Workplace Violence Survey and White Paper*, www.rims.org.

71. "Two Prescriptions for Preventing Violence," *HRFocus*, April 2000, p. S2, S3.

72. Lesley Young, "On-the-job Harassment Precipitates Co-worker Violence: Inquest," *Canadian HR Reporter*, March 27, 2000, pp. 1, 3.

73. Rebecca MacEachern, "It's Like the Sick Building Syndrome," *The Daily News*, May 21, 2000, p. 5.

74. James Montgomery, *Occupational Health and Safety*.

75. P. Laing, *Accident Prevention Manual for Business and Industry: Engineering and Technology*, Washington, D.C.: National Safety Council, 1992.

76. Rose Simone, "Long Hours at Computer Can Result in Pain," *Kitchener Record*, February 5, 1998, pp. C1-C2.

77. See www.webreference.com/rsi.html.

78. For further information, see http://home.clara.net/ruegg/info.html.

79. Ergonomic issues are discussed in much more detail in James Montgomery, *Occupational Health and Safety*.

80. Nancy Stuart, "Open Offices Drive Workers Up The Wall," *The Globe and Mail*, October 6, 2000, p. B11.

81. Data on Canada and other countries around the world are available from the UNAIDS: The Joint United Nations Programme on HIV/AIDS at www.unaids.org.

82. Information on AIDS can be obtained from the Canadian Aids Society's various publications available at www.cdnaids.ca.

83. J.J. Breckenridge, "Nurse with AIDS Gets Job Back, But Row Over Dismissal Goes On," *The Globe and Mail*, June 29, 1988, p. A10.

84. *Business Week*, February 1, 1993, p. 53.

85. The Canadian Human Rights Commission has considerable information about AIDS on its Web site (www.chrc-ccdp.ca). Similarly, information is readily available from provincial human rights commissions. For example, see the Ontario Human Rights Commission's "Policy on HIV/Aids-Related Discrimination" at www.ohrc.on.ca.

Chapter 16

1. Morley Gunderson, Allen Ponak and Daphne Gottlieb Taras, *Union-Management Relations in Canada*, 4th. ed., Toronto, ON: Addison Wesley Longman, 2001, p. 11.

2. Gregor Murray, "Unions: Membership, Structure and Actions," in Morley Gunderson and Allen Ponak, eds., *Union-Management Relations in Canada*, 3rd ed., Don Mills, ON: Addison-Wesley, 1995.

3. Julian Barling, Clive Fullagar and Kevin Kelloway, *The Union and its Members: A Psychological Approach*, New York: Oxford University Press, 1992.

4. "What a Joy to Work for Dofasco," *The Globe and Mail*, February 23, 2000, pp. B1, B8.

5. Seymour Martin Lipset and Noah M. Meltz, "Canadian and American Attitudes Toward Work and Institutions," *Perspectives on Work*, December 1997, pp. 14-19.

6. Samuel Gompers, *Labor and the Common Welfare*, Freeport, NY: Books for Libraries Press, 1919, p. 20.

7. An editorial in *Canadian Labour*, June 1968, p. 5.

8. Frank Tannenbaum, *The Labour Movement, Its Conservative Functions and Consequences*, New York: Alfred A. Knopf, 1921.

9. Selig Perlman, *A Theory of the Labour Movement*, New York: Macmillan, 1928.

10. Charles Lipton, *The Trade Union Movement in Canada, 1827-1959*, Montreal, QC: Canadian Social Publications, 1967, p. 4.

11. Leonard Sayles and George Strauss, *The Local Union*, New York: Harcourt, Brace and World, 1967.

12. Gerald E. Phillips, *The Practice of Labour Relations and Collective Bargaining in Canada*, Toronto, ON: Butterworths, 1977.

13. Human Resources Development Canada, *Directory of Labour Organizations in Canada*, Ottawa, ON: HRDC, 2000.

14. "Teamsters Going After McDonald's," *The Globe and Mail*, March 19, 1998, p. A11.

15. Bill Tieleman, "Did Somebody Say McUnion?: Not if They Want to Keep Their McJob," *The Financial Post*, March 29, 1999, p. C5.

16. Ernest B. Akyeampong, "Unionization—an update: Special 2000 Labour Day Release."

17. International Labour Organization, *World Labour Report: Industrial Relations, Democracy and Social Stability (1997-98)*, Geneva: ILO, 1997.

18. Tim O'Shea, "Making Sense of the CAW Molson Brewery Occupation and Boycott," *Canadian HR Reporter*, January 17, 2000, pp. 1, 16.

19. John Godard, "Strikes as Collective Voice: A Behavioral Analysis of Strike Activity," *Industrial and Labor Relations Review*, October 1992, pp. 161-175.

20. Ibid.

21. Richard B. Freeman and James L. Medoff, *What Do Unions Do?* New York: Basic Books, 1984.

22. Morley Gunderson and Douglas Hyatt, "Union Impact on Compensation, Productivity, and Management of the Organization," in Morley Gunderson, Allen Ponak and Daphne Gottlieb Taras, eds., *Union-Management Relations in Canada*, 4th ed., Toronto, ON: Addison Wesley Longman, 2001.

23. Lesley Young, "Canada's Organized Labour Ready to Ally With Business," *Canadian HR Reporter*, March 13, 2000, pp. 1, 18.

24. George W. Adams, *Canadian Labour Law*, 2nd ed., Aurora, ON: Canada Law Book, 1997.

25. George Meany, "Organizing: A Continuing Effort," *The American Federationist*, July 1976, p. 1.

26. Ibid.

27. For an interesting view of union organizing in the United States, see William E. Fulmer, "Step by Step Through an Organizing Campaign," *Harvard Business Review*, 1991, Vol. 59, pp. 94-102.

28. Donald D. Carter, "Collective Bargaining Legislation," in Morley Gunderson and Allen Ponak, eds., *Union-Management Relations in Canada*, 3rd ed., Don Mills, ON: Addison-Wesley, 1995.

29. Jack Williams, *The Story of Unions in Canada*, Toronto, ON: J.M. Dent and Sons, 1975.

30. Wilfred List, "Food Processing Firm Used Employee as Spy, Board Certifies Union," *The Globe and Mail*, July 30, 1981, p. 2.

31. George Adams, *Canadian Labour Law* (2nd ed.).

32. Richard E. Walton, Joel E. Cutcher-Gershenfeld, and Robert B. McKersie, *Strategic Negotiations: A Theory of Change in Labor-Management Relations*, Boston: Harvard Business School Press, 1994.

33. Jon Peirce, *Canadian Industrial Relations*, Scarborough: Prentice Hall, 2000.

34. Ibid.

35. D.A. Peach and P. Bergman, *The Practice of Industrial Relations*, 3rd ed., Toronto: McGraw-Hill Ryerson, 1991, pp. 136-38.

36. Dan Cameron, "The Interest Based Approach to Union-Management Negotiation," *Human Resources Professional*, February-March 1999, pp. 37-39.

37. Claudine Kapel, "The Feeling's Mutual," *Human Resources Professional*, April 1995, pp. 9-13.

38. Thomas A. Kochan and Paul Osterman, *The Mutual Gains Enterprise*, Boston, Mass.: Harvard Business School Press, 1994.

39. Each jurisdiction has defined procedures relating to conciliation and mediation. As well, the distinction between these terms has been blurred. Consequently, human resource professionals need to consult the relevant legislation for their jurisdiction.

40. See the *Nova Scotia Department of Labour Annual Reports* for the 1989 to 1999 period.

41. James C. McBrearty, *Handling Grievances: A Positive Approach for Management and Labor Representatives*, Tucson, AZ.: Division of Economics and Business Research, University of Arizona, 1972, pp. 3-6. See also George W. Bohlander, "Fair Representation: Not Just a Union Problem," *Personnel Administrator*, March 1980, pp. 36-40, 82.

42. The judicial review of labour board and arbitration decisions is a very technical area of labour law. For an in-depth treatment, see Richard L. Charney and Thomas E.F. Brady, *Judicial Review in Labour Law*, Aurora, ON: Canada Law Book, 1997.

43. These issues are discussed in more detail in Terry H. Wagar, "The Arbitration Process: Employer and Union Views," in W. Kaplan, J. Sack and M. Gunderson, eds., *Labour Arbitration Yearbook 1996-1997*, Toronto, ON: Lancaster House, 1995, pp. 3-11.

44. Anthony Giles and Akivah Starkman, "The Collective Agreement," in Morley Gunderson, Allen Ponak and Daphne Gottlieb Taras, *Union-Management Relations in Canada*, 4th ed., Toronto, ON: Addison Wesley Longman, 2001, p. 285.

45. For a comprehensive review of the arbitration process, see Donald J.M Brown and David M. Beatty, *Canadian Labour Arbitration*, 3rd. ed., Aurora, ON: Canada Law Book, 2000.

46. These findings are based largely on Ignace Ng and Dennis Maki, "Human Resource Management in the Canadian Manufacturing Sector," *International Journal of Human Resource Management*, December 1993, pp. 897-916.

47. This quote is taken from Human Resources Development Canada and the Organisation for Economic Co-operation and Development, *Changing Workplace Strategies: Achieving Better Outcomes for Enterprises, Workers and Society*, Hull: HRDC, 1997.

48. This example is taken from Sharon Lebrun, "Toronto Hydro Absenteeism Plan Raises Union Ire," *Canadian HR Reporter*, April 21, 1997, pp. 1-2.

49. John Godard, "Managerial Strategies, Labour and Employment Relations and the State: the Canadian Case and Beyond," *British Journal of Industrial Relations*, September 1997, pp. 399-426.

50. See, for instance, William N. Cooke, *Labor-Management Cooperation*, Kalamazoo, Mich.: W.E. Upjohn Institute, 1990; Thomas A. Kochan and Paul Osterman, *The Mutual Gains Enterprise*.

51. See, for instance, Terry H. Wagar, "Is Labor-Management Climate Important? Some Canadian Evidence," *Journal of Labor Research*, Winter 1997, pp. 101-112 and Terry H. Wagar, "The Labour-Management Relationship and Organization Outcomes: Some Initial Findings," *Relations Industrielles*, 1997, Vol. 52, pp. 430-447.

52. Lesley Young, "Canada's Organized Labour Ready to Ally with Business."

53. Guillermo Grenier and Raymond Hogler, "Labor Law and Managerial Ideology: Employee Participation as a Social Control System," *Work and Occupations*, August 1991, pp. 313-333. For an excellent discussion of management by stress, see Mike Parker and Jane Slaughter, "Management by Stress," *Technology Review*, October 1988, pp. 37-44.

54. John Sanderson and Colin Taylor, "Using a Relationship-Restructuring Program to Allay Poisonous Disputes," *Canadian HR Reporter*, April 6, 1999, pp. 18-19.

55. For a review of the U.S. approach, see Warner Woodward and Christopher Meek, *Creating Labor-Management Partnerships*.

Chapter 17

1. Mike Johnson, *Winning the People Wars*, London: Pearson Education Limited, 2000, p. xv.

2. Michael Hammer and Steven Stanton, "The Power of Reflection," *Fortune*, November 24, 1997, pp. 291-296.

3. Ian Clark, "Corporate Human Resources and 'Bottom Line' Financial Performance" *Personnel Review,* 1999, Vol. 28, No. 4, pp. 290-306.

4. Ann Svendsen, "Social Audits Good for the Bottom Line," *The Globe and Mail*, February 12, 1998, p. B-2.

5. Terry Wagar, *Human Resource Management and Labour Relations: A Study of Canadian Organizations and Human Resource Management and Labour Relations: Preliminary Results from Atlantic Canada,* Department of Management, Saint Mary's University, Halifax, October 1993.

6. Andrew Templer and Julian Cattaneo, "A Model of Human Resources Management Effectiveness," *Canadian Journal of Administrative Sciences*, 1995, Vol.12, No.1, pp. 77-88.

7. Christopher Bartlett, "Companies Must Gear Up for a Management Revolution," *The Globe and Mail,* January 16, 1998, p. B-23.

8. James W. Thacker and R. Julian Cattaneo, Survey of Personnel Practices in Canadian Organizations, unpublished manuscript, University of Windsor, Faculty of Business Administration, March 1993.

9. Fred Luthans and Terry L. Maris, "Evaluating Personnel Programs through the Reversal Technique," *Personnel Journal*, October 1979, pp. 692-97.

10. George Odiorne, "Evaluating the Personnel Program," in Joseph Famularo, ed., *Handbook of Modern Personnel Administration* (New York: McGraw-Hill, 1972), chapter 8. See also Mahler, "Auditing PAIR," Vytenis P. Kuraitis, "The Personnel Audit," *Personnel Administrator*, November 1981, pp. 29-34.

11. Odiorne, "Evaluating the Personnel Program."

12. Peter Howes and Pat Foley, "Strategic Human Resource Management: An Australian Case Study," Human Resource Planning, 1993, Vol.16, No. 3, p. 64.

13. Alan Saks, Neal Schmitt and Richard Klimoski, *Research, Measurement, and Evaluation of Human Resources*, Scarborough, ON: ITP Nelson, 2000, pp. 38-39.

14. Robert Wolfe, "Most Employers Offer Exit Interviews," *HR News*, June 1991, p. A2.

15. For example see, Russ Kisby, "The ROI of Healthy Workplaces," *Canadian HR Reporter*, October 20, 1997, p. 31.

16. Spinks, Nora, "The Absence of Absence in the Changing Workplace," *Canadian HR Reporter*, March 24, 1997, pp.19-20.

17. Brian Orr, "The Challenge of Benchmarking HR Performance," *Canadian HR Reporter*, April 21, 1997, p. 6.

18. For example, see, Ian Cunningham and Philip James, "Absence and Return to Work: Towards a Research Agenda," *Personnel Review*, 2000, Vol. 29, No.1, pp. 33-47.

19. For example, see, Linda Alker and David McHugh, "Human Resource Maintenance?" *Journal of Managerial Psychology*, 2000, Vol. 15, No. 4, pp. 303-323.

20. Martin Plevel, Sandy Nellis, Fred Lane and Randall Schuler, "AT& T Global Business Communication Systems: Linking HR with Business Strategy," *Organizational Dynamics*, Winter, 1994, p.62-66.

21. For example, see, W.A. Oechsler, "Workforce and Workforce 2000+: The Future of Work Environment," *International Archives of Occupational and Environmental Health*, 2000, Vol. 73, No. 9, pp. 28-32.

22. For a good discussion on HR's emerging role, see Seyed-Mahmoud Aghazadeh, "Human Resource Management: Issues and Challenges in the New Millennium" *Management Research News*, 1999, Vol. 22, No. 12, pp. 19-32.

INDEX